Investments: Theory and Applications

Investments: Theory and Applications

Mark Hirschey
University of Kansas

Harcourt College Publishers
Fort Worth Philadelphia San Diego New York Orlando Austin San Antonio
Toronto Montreal London Sydney Tokyo

Publisher Mike Roche
Executive Editor Mike Reynolds
Market Strategist Charlie Stutesman
Developmental Editor Kim Bartman
Project Editor Christy Goldfinch
Art Director Vicki Whistler
Production Manager Lois West

Cover by Bill Brammer

ISBN: 0-03-026887-7 (*Wall Street Journal* edition 0-03-033166-8)
Library of Congress Catalog Card Number: 00-107184

Copyrights and Acknowledgments appear on page 844, which constitutes a continuation of the copyright page.

Address for Domestic Orders
Harcourt, Inc., 6277 Sea Harbor Drive, Orlando, FL 32887-6777
800-782-4479

Address for International Orders
International Customer Service
Harcourt, Inc., 6277 Sea Harbor Drive, Orlando, FL 32887-6777
407-345-3800
(fax) 407-345-4060
(e-mail) hbintl@harcourt.com

Address for Editorial Correspondence
Harcourt College Publishers, 301 Commerce Street, Suite 3700, Fort Worth, TX 76102

Web Site Address
http://www.harcourtcollege.com

Printed in the United States of America

0 1 2 3 4 5 6 7 8 9 048 9 8 7 6 5 4 3 2 1

Harcourt College Publishers

Dedication

For Christine—I still do.

The Dryden Press Series in Finance

Amling and Droms
Investment Fundamentals

Berry and Young
Managing Investments: A Case Approach

Besley and Brigham
Essentials of Managerial Finance
Twelfth Edition

Besley and Brigham
Principles of Finance

Boone, Kurtz, and Hearth
Planning Your Financial Future
Second Edition

Brigham and Houston
Fundamentals of Financial Management
Eighth Edition

Brigham, Gapenski, and Klein
2000 Cases in Financial Management: Dryden Request

Brigham, Gapenski, and Ehrhardt
Financial Management: Theory and Practice
Ninth Edition

Conroy
Finance Interactive

Brigham, Gapenski, and Daves
Intermediate Financial Management
Sixth Edition

Brigham and Houston
Fundamentals of Financial Management
Concise Second Edition

Chance
An Introduction to Derivatives
Fourth Edition

Clark, Gerlach, and Olson
Restructuring Corporate America

Cooley
Advances in Business Financial Management: A Collection of Readings
Second Edition

Dickerson, Campsey, and Brigham
Introduction to Financial Management
Fourth Edition

Eaker, Fabozzi, and Grant
International Corporate Finance

Gardner, Mills, and Cooperman
Managing Financial Institutions: An Asset/Liability Approach
Fourth Edition

Gitman and Joehnk
Personal Financial Planning
Eighth Edition

Greenbaum and Thakor
Contemporary Financial Intermediation

Hall
Effective Use of a Financial Calculator

Harrington and Eades
Case Studies in Financial Decision Making
Third Edition

Hayes and Meerschwam
Financial Institutions: Contemporary Cases in the Financial Services Industry

Hearth and Zaima
Contemporary Investments: Security and Portfolio Analysis
Second Edition

Johnson
Issues and Readings in Managerial Finance
Fourth Edition

Kidwell, Peterson, and Blackwell
Financial Institutions, Markets, and Money
Seventh Edition

Koch and MacDonald
Bank Management
Fourth Edition

Leahigh
Pocket Guide to Finance

Maness and Zietlow
Short-Term Financial Management

Mayes and Shank
Financial Analysis with Lotus 1-2-3 for Windows

Mayes and Shank
Financial Analysis with Microsoft Excel

Mayo
Financial Institutions, Investments, and Management: An Introduction
Sixth Edition

Mayo
Investments: An Introduction
Sixth Edition

Osteryoung, Newman, and Davies
Small Firm Finance: An Entrepreneurial Analysis

Reilly and Brown
Investment Analysis and Portfolio Management
Sixth Edition

Reilly and Norton
Investments
Fifth Edition

Sandburg
Discovering Your Finance Career

Seitz and Ellison
Capital Budgeting and Long-Term Financing Decisions
Third Edition

Siegel and Siegel
Futures Markets

Smith and Spudeck
Interest Rates: Principles and Applications

Stickney and Brown
Financial Reporting and Statement Analysis: A Strategic Perspective
Fourth Edition

Preface

It is fascinating to note that much of what is "short and snappy" in the investments literature tends to be wrong. For example, many popular books on investing spotlight hard-to-explain breakdowns of financial theory, such as the overwhelming success of "investment superstars," and seem to argue that anyone can easily take advantage of obviously inefficient financial markets. This "10 easy lessons" approach is plainly incorrect. It is the type of get-rich-quick scheme that leaves students and investors poorer for the experience. It is similarly unfortunate that some popular textbooks in the investment field focus on the theory of financial markets and refuse to acknowledge real-world behavior that is inconsistent with that theory. The "blind allegiance to existent theory" approach ignores valuable signposts that may point to better ways of understanding financial markets. This approach also overlooks much of what is fascinating about the world of investments. Compounding the problem is the fact that much of the correct and useful literature on investing tends to be long and boring. As a result, many students and individual investors come away with the mistaken impression that the theory of finance has little if anything to say about the way Wall Street actually works.

To remedy the situation, this text adopts a new and unique approach. Both theory *and* practice are studied as useful guides to our "random walk down Wall Street." Throughout the text, financial theory is used as a practical guide to understanding the workings of real-world financial markets. Financial theory is a framework that gives context and meaning to much of what occurs on Wall Street every day. No theory can hope to explain all real-world behavior at all times. Financial theory is no exception. Sometimes, some stock and bond prices "seem out of whack" with the underlying economic fundamentals. They might be, or perhaps it is simply our understanding of the economic fundamentals that is "out of whack." In any event, you do not disregard financial theory that correctly describes real-world behavior 99-plus% of the time just because it fails miserably less than 1% of the time. To be sure, it is fun to investigate the less than 1% failure rate and seek better and more complete understanding of so-called pricing anomalies. Detective work on such outliers is not only fun and interesting, it often leads to better theory.

To help students see the practical usefulness of financial theory, material from traditional financial publications, such as *Barron's* and Wall Street's bible, *The Wall Street Journal,* is carefully integrated throughout the text. Much of what is curious and interesting about investments is played out on the pages of these publications. Also fascinating is the ongoing explosion of financial analysis and stock market information found on the Internet. The birth of the Internet dovetails perfectly with the desire of Generation Xers to take personal control of their own financial futures. The explosion of online interest in stock investing also reflects the need of now-aging Baby Boomers to find productive means of paying for retirement, and college tuition for some of those same Generation Xers. The Internet is simply an awesome tool for information gathering and analysis. Several examples are used throughout the text to illustrate the practical value of the Internet as an information-gathering device.

As one who sometimes wonders if he spends too much time "surfing the Web," it is important to recognize that information gathering on the Internet and elsewhere is different from acquiring wisdom about how to use it. To simply collect and collate information is not the same thing as to make sense out of it. The useful backdrop provided by financial theory together with the efficient information-gathering potential of the Internet can be a wicked and highly profitable combination. Information without context is as useless as knowing the situation but being unable to do anything about it. Both information and understanding are essential.

In its writing, I have strived to impart two important characteristics to this text. First, I focus on the many useful and practical implications of financial theory. The usefulness of financial theory lies in the logical framework it provides for characterizing and *predicting* stock and bond returns. The old saw, "That may be okay in theory, but it doesn't work in practice," is plainly incorrect. Useful financial theory describes and predicts asset return patterns. If a given theory does not describe and predict actual practice, it should be rejected in favor of models that successfully describe and predict real-world behavior. The reason why financial theory forms the basis for the study of investment decision making is simple—it works. Financial theory works not just in the classroom, but more importantly, it works in the everyday "lab" on Wall Street. There is no conflict between useful theory and practice. The study of financial theory is helpful because the task of successful investment management is made easier through the careful combination of this theory and practical business experience. To be sure, some financial theories that were once popular and generally accepted have failed the test of time. They have been discarded, as they should be. It is important to focus on that which is correct and useful.

Second, you may note that this text uses a conversational tone that is sometimes missing in "serious" books on investing. This approach reflects a personal bias. This text is about *money*. Every business student wants to ask the *big* question: "How do people get rich?" or more importantly, "How do people *get* rich and *stay* rich?" No one ever asks. Today, such a question is just not "politically correct." In the good old days, it simply was not cool. However, the *big* question is an important one from both a practical and philosophical standpoint. How do people earn a significant amount of money in the market, and how do they make it grow? Why do some businesses and investors earn above-normal returns while many others languish? These are appropriate issues for an investments class, and this text meets them head on. In so doing, this text breaks the taboo against talking about money and wealth. Even in business schools, students and their professors seldom seem to talk about money in their classes. This is a big mistake. Money is an interesting subject; it is a serious subject. It is *seriously interesting.*

Just as textbooks on human sexuality must cover details of the human reproductive system, this text studies the anatomy of Wall Street. Wall Street is a real place with customs, history, and traditions that are fascinating. However, to focus on such institutional detail without any framework for analysis would be to lose the broader message for all the details. To avoid this trap, the text provides both a practical and theoretical framework that describes the nature and functioning of securities markets. Every knowledgeable financial manager and investor must understand financial theory to appreciate its value and limitations.

The focus of this text is on stocks, bonds, and financial derivatives, such as options, futures, and futures options. This study provides the necessary backdrop for understanding the dynamic process of return generation for all types of investments, including real estate, art, and antiquities. By studying both the theory and practice of successful portfolio management, students can come to appreciate the methods and techniques of the effective security analyst and portfolio manager. This is not only helpful to those students considering a career in the investments field, but to all students in terms of their personal financial planning.

Learning Aids

The text features a number of valuable learning aids. Among the most important of these are:

- Each chapter incorporates a wide variety of simple numerical examples and detailed practical illustrations of chapter concepts. These features portray the valuable use and real-world implications of covered material.
- Each chapter makes use of a wide variety of information resources available on the Internet. Each Internet address ("uniform resource locator," or URL), which can be consulted for further information, is given in blue.
- Each chapter features three vignettes of "Wall Street Wisdom" to show current examples of how the concepts introduced in *Investments: Theory & Applications* can be applied in real-world situations. These features are based on information discussed in articles from *The Wall Street Journal, Barron's,* or a variety of resources on the Internet. This feature stimulates student interest in the material and offers a popular basis for classroom discussion.
- Each chapter contains an end-of-chapter "Investment Application" case study to show a detailed current example of how to apply the concepts introduced in *Investments: Theory & Applications.* Like the "Wall Street Wisdom" features, "Investment Applications" are based on information from the Internet and the traditional business press. This feature stimulates student interest and offers a popular basis for classroom discussion and student projects.
- The text also incorporates several regression-based illustrations of chapter concepts using actual company data, or data adapted from real-world situations. Like all aspects of the text, this material is self-contained and intuitive.
- Effective investors and investment managers in the new millennium must be sensitive to the special challenges posed by an increasingly global marketplace. To increase student awareness of such issues, the text also features a number of examples that relate to global business topics.
- More than 350 end-of-chapter questions are also provided, after having been subject to necessary revision and class testing. Questions are designed to give students the opportunity to grasp basic concepts on an intuitive level and express their understanding in a nonquantitative fashion.
- Students considering a career in the securities business will find *Investments: Theory & Applications* to be a valuable tool for gaining understanding and expertise about federal securities laws, industry rules and regulations, the operation of financial markets, and the uses, features, and tax treatment of securities products. Indeed, the layout of the text is intended to help students prepare for professional exams administered by the National Association of Securities Dealers, Inc. Several end-of-chapter questions are also modeled after Chartered Financial Analyst exam questions to show students the problem-solving process used on professional examinations for people in the money-management business.

- Last but definitely not least, a course home page on the Internet is maintained and constantly updated as a valuable information resource for both students and instructors alike. Several links to information resources on the Internet give users a leg up in their use of this vital information-gathering resource.

Instructor's Resources

Investments: Theory & Applications is designed to make teaching and learning the material both simple and enjoyable. The *PowerPoint Lecture Presentation* provides an easy and effective way to highlight the most important chapter elements. The *Instructor's Manual & Test Bank* offers learning suggestions and answers for all chapter questions. Up-to-date and class-tested sample exams are also available on the instructor's Web site.

Acknowledgments

Several individuals have aided in the preparation of *Investments: Theory & Applications.* Helpful suggestions and constructive comments have been received from a great number of instructors and students. Numerous reviewers have also provided insights and assistance in clarifying difficult material. Among those who have been especially helpful in the development of the text are Indudeep Chhachhi, Western Kentucky University; James P. D'Mello, Western Michigan University; Stevenson Hawkey, Golden Gate University; Eric M. Haye, Ramapo College of New Jersey; Reinhold P. Lamb, University of North Carolina at Charlotte; Steven Mann, University of South Carolina; Brian Maris, Northern Arizona University; Joseph Vu, DePaul University; and Dennis Zocco, University of San Diego.

The University of Kansas, students, and colleagues have together provided a stimulating environment and general intellectual support. I am grateful for their efforts. I am also indebted to Harcourt College Publishers staff and would like to thank executive editor Mike Reynolds, marketing strategist Charlie Stutesman, developmental editor Kim Bartman, editorial assistant Amy Holmes, project editor Christy Goldfinch, art director Vicki Whistler, and production manager Lois West for their special efforts. Finally, I want to thank my wife, Christine, for her encouragement, support, and assistance.

Every effort has been made to minimize errors in the text. However, errors do occasionally slip through despite diligent efforts to provide an error-free product. Readers are invited to correspond with me directly concerning any corrections or other suggestions.

Finally, in the writing of the text, I have attempted to be brief and to the point. In the interest of brevity, many interesting but nonessential topics are avoided. In some ways, any text on investing is intended as a jumping-off point in a lifetime of learning and discovery. My lifelong fascination with stocks began at the tender age of 15. Ever since then I have wondered what took me so long to get started! For more than 30 years, I have thought about common stock investing almost every waking moment. I sincerely hope this text will help you appreciate the vagaries of Wall Street and help you come to share my fascination with The Market!

Mark Hirschey
e-mail: mhirschey@ukans.edu
October 2000

About the Author

Mark Hirschey, Ph.D. (University of Wisconsin–Madison), is Professor and Stockton Research Fellow in the School of Business at the University of Kansas, where he teaches undergraduate and graduate courses in investment theory and analysis. Professor Hirschey is president of the Association of Financial Economists and member of several professional organizations. He has published articles in the *Journal of Finance, Journal of Financial Economics, American Economic Review, Journal of Business, Financial Analysts Journal, Financial Management, Journal of Accounting Research, Review of Economics and Statistics,* and other leading academic journals. He is co-editor of *Advances in Financial Economics* (with Kose John and Anil Makhija) and author of *Managerial Economics,* Revised Edition.

Contents in Brief

Table of Contents

PART 1

Introduction to Investments

CHAPTER 1

Importance of Studying Investments

Bond ghouls, speculators, and top government officials like the venerable chairman of the Federal Reserve System sometimes seem to have it in for stock and bond investors. Bond prices and interest rates are extremely sensitive to changes in investor expectations. Even a whiff of inflation can send bond prices tumbling and bond yields soaring. As a result, bond investors are always on the lookout for "good" economic news because they fear that economic strength will produce inflation, higher interest rates, and lower bond prices. On the other hand, if news reaches the bond market that hoped-for budget surpluses might allow the government to pay down the national debt and reduce the issuance of long-term bonds, bond yields plummet as investors bid up the price of 30-year Treasury bonds.

When bond prices first plunge and then turn around and soar, bond investors are left shaking their heads. Stock market investors can also get whipsawed. When inflation is muted, interest rates are tame and the economy surges ahead. In a good economic environment, corporate profits rise and share prices tend to advance. However, even in a banner economic environment, lots of stocks turn in losing performances. To be successful, investors must continually monitor domestic and foreign competition, material costs, new product innovations, changes in regulation, and so on.

The purpose of this book is to help students make sense of financial markets for stocks, bonds, and financial derivatives. Investment theory is enormously helpful in this regard. It provides a guidepost to help investors understand asset pricing and investment institutions and helps them avoid the many pitfalls on Wall Street.[1]

Nature of Investing

Future Value

Investing is an important subject. Whether you realize it or not, you make important investment decisions every day. For example, if you decide to buy rather than lease a car, you are making a significant investment decision. Your purchase deci-

---

[1]See Gregory Zuckerman and E. S. Browning, "Market Plunges, Then Comes Up for Air," *The Wall Street Journal,* April 5, 2000, C1, C20.

sion involves a substantial cash outlay prior to the enjoyment of the many benefits bestowed by automobile ownership. In return for your initial cash outlay, you receive a "flow" of automobile services that lasts as long as you own your car. Financially speaking, automobile owners receive an implicit return on their investment because ownership precludes the necessity of making regular lease payments. By comparing the amount of an initial cash outlay to buy a car with the amount of lease payments that would be required in lieu of a purchase decision, a buyer can calculate the "investment" rate of return on a car purchase. This annual rate of return often falls in the range of 8–10% per year when the value of dealer rebates and cash discounts are considered.

If you buy a house instead of rent an apartment, you are also making an investment decision. Whenever goods are purchased that yield benefits that extend beyond one year, an investment is made. Consumer goods that provide nonmonetary benefits that extend beyond one year are called consumer durables. Examples include cars, personal computers, and furniture. Nondurable goods such as food, clothing, and personal services are typically "consumed" within a one-year period. Most of the time, when one thinks of the word *investment,* images of buying stocks, bonds, or real estate come quickly to mind. However, an investment is made whenever an item is purchased on the reasonable expectation of a flow of monetary or nonmonetary benefits over time. So when thinking about investing, think about the concept in its most general sense. An investment is simply postponed consumption.

Of course, the reason for postponing consumption today is the hope for an increased level of consumption tomorrow. The amount of an allowed increase in future consumption is called the return on investment. This return is often expressed on a per-dollar basis as an interest rate.

A simple way of thinking about the investment process is to think about the difference between present sums and future values. Investing is simply the means of converting present sums into future values. Whenever you calculate the **future value** of a present sum, you must consider the dollar amount of the investment, the rate of interest, the number of time periods, and the method of compounding.

future value
A fair equivalent of money in some prospective period.

The future value of a present sum using once-a-year, or annual, compounding is

$$\text{Future value} = \text{Present sum} \times (1 + \text{Interest rate})^t \quad \textbf{1.1}$$

where t is the number of years (or time periods) involved.

For example, the future value of a \$5,000 investment earning 8% interest over a period of 15 years is roughly \$15,860 because

$$\begin{aligned} \text{Future value} &= \text{Present sum} \times (1 + \text{Interest rate})^t \quad \textbf{1.2} \\ &= \$5{,}000 \times (1 + 0.08)^{15} \\ &= \$15{,}860 \end{aligned}$$

Present Value

An alternative way of looking at the process of investment is to look at present-day dollars rather than future dollars. Notice that in the equation above, the future value of a present sum is expressed. If instead one wishes to express the present value of a future sum, an analogous technique called present-value analysis is used.

present value Present-day worth.

Using **present value** analysis, the time value of money concept is used to discount the value of future dollars back to their present-day equivalent. Instead of growing current dollars into future dollars, present-value analysis is the process of shrinking future dollars into their present-day equivalent. The present value of a future sum is given by the expression

$$\text{Present value} = \frac{\text{Future sum}}{(1 + \text{Interest rate})^{t}} \tag{1.3}$$

where t is again the number of years (or time periods) involved.

For example, the present value of \$15,860 to be received in 15 years when an 8% rate of return can be earned on investment is, as before, \$5,000 because

$$\begin{aligned} \text{Present value} &= \frac{\text{Future sum}}{(1 + \text{Interest rate})^{t}} \\ &= \frac{\$15{,}860}{(1 + 0.08)^{15}} \\ &= \$5{,}000 \end{aligned} \tag{1.4}$$

Notice the similarity of the present-value equation with the prior future-value equation. Calculating the future value of a present sum is the other side of the coin from calculating the present value of a future sum. Both approaches can be used to evaluate investment opportunities. When looking at the future value of a present sum, one considers the amount that a given dollar amount of investment will accumulate to over time. When looking at the present value of a future sum, one is simply calculating the value in present-day dollars of an amount to be received at some point in the future.

Compound Interest

Annual versus Continuous Compounding

compound interest Rate of cumulative increase.

continuous compounding Constant accrual of interest.

annual compounding Once-a-year interest.

In the preceding example, \$5,000 grew into \$15,860 over a period of 15 years with once-a-year, or annual, compounding. This is one of the two most popular methods of allowing for **compound interest.** The other is called continuous compounding. With **continuous compounding,** more "interest on interest" is earned than under the alternative assumption of once-a-year or **annual compounding.**

A simple expression for the continuous compounding method of showing interest is

$$\text{Future value} = \text{Present sum} \times e^{rt} \tag{1.5}$$

where e is the so-called Napierian constant (and equal to 2.7182818 . . .), r is the interest rate, and t is the number of years (or time periods) involved. Although the continuous compound method of accounting for interest may at first appear complex, calculating the future value of a present sum is quick and easy using an inexpensive hand-held calculator or a computer spreadsheet.

With continuous compounding, more "interest on interest" is earned. This means, for example, that with continuous compounding at 8% over a 15-year period, $5,000 grows to $16,600 because

$$\begin{aligned}\text{Future value} &= \text{Present sum} \times e^{rt} \\ &= \$5{,}000 \times e^{0.08 \times 15} \\ &= \$16{,}600\end{aligned} \tag{1.6}$$

where t is the number of years (or time periods) involved.

In the event of continuous compounding, $16,600 to be received in 15 years has a present value of $5,000 because

$$\begin{aligned}\text{Present value} &= \frac{\text{Future sum}}{e^{rt}} \\ &= \frac{\$16{,}600}{e^{0.08 \times 15}} \\ &= \$5{,}000\end{aligned} \tag{1.7}$$

where, once again, e is the Napierian constant, r is the interest rate, and t is the number of years (or time periods) involved. Using continuous compounding at 8% interest, $5,000 is the present-value equivalent of $16,600 to be received in 15 years. The annual versus continuous methods of compounding interest are merely two different ways of characterizing the growth in investment value over time. Both are used successfully to distinguish between superior and inferior investment alternatives. Although it matters little which approach is used to rank investment choices, it is essential to focus on only one method of compounding interest when making an "apples to apples" comparison of investment alternatives. For example, using annual compounding at 10% over a 10-year period, $10,000 grows to $25,937. Using continuous compounding at 9.53% over a 10-year period, $10,000 grows to that same amount, $25,937. This means that over a 10-year period, annual compounding at 10% results in the same future value as a continuously compounded 9.53%, because continuous compounding results in more "interest on interest." Such an investment is superior to any similar investment that yields less than a 10% annual rate of return when using annual compounding or less than a 9.53% rate of return when using continuous compounding. In this case, it is a mistake to turn down an investment alternative that promises to yield a continuously compounded 9.75% per year. Similarly, it is wrong to prefer an investment alternative that promises 9.75% per year when interest is compounded on an annual basis.

Rule of 72

One of the most useful simple rules that any investor uses to evaluate investment is the so-called **Rule of 72.** Look at Table 1.1. The Rule of 72 is a rule of thumb. Any rule of thumb is a simple technique used to make a complex subject easier to apply in real-life situations. The Rule of 72 says to simply divide the number 72 by any interest rate percentage, and the resulting number is the number of years it will take to double your investment. For example, the number 9 divided into 72 equals 8, and it takes eight years at a 9% rate of return to double your investment.

rule of 72
Divide the number 72 by any interest rate percentage. The result is the number of years it takes to double your investment.

TABLE 1.1 **Rule of 72**

Divide the number 72 by any interest rate percentage. The result is the number of years it takes to double your investment (e.g., at 9%, an investment doubles in eight years).

How Many Years Will It Take?	What Interest Rate (%) Is Required to Double Your Money?		
	Continuous Compounding	**Annual Compounding**	**Rule of 72**
1	69.3	100.0	72.0
2	34.7	41.4	36.0
3	23.1	26.0	24.0
4	17.3	18.9	18.0
5	13.9	14.9	14.4
6	11.6	12.2	12.0
7	9.9	10.4	10.3
8	8.7	9.1	9.0
9	7.7	8.0	8.0
10	6.9	7.2	7.2
11	6.3	6.5	6.5
12	5.8	5.9	6.0
13	5.3	5.5	5.5
14	5.0	5.1	5.1
15	4.6	4.7	4.8
20	3.5	3.5	3.6
25	2.8	2.8	2.9
30	2.3	2.3	2.4

Similarly, if you invest and earn 6%, the number 6 divided into 72 yields 12. This means at 6% interest, or when realizing a 6% rate of return on investment, money will double in a period of 12 years.

Table 1.1 shows both common methods of accounting for interest, the annual method of compounding and continuous compounding. Remember that with continuous compounding, interest is earned on a continual basis; with annual compounding, interest is earned on a once-a-year basis. The difference is the amount of "interest on interest" earned. As shown in Table 1.1, money growing at 9.9% will double in seven years if interest is compounded continuously. Ten years of continuous compounding at a 6.9% growth rate will lead to a doubling of the initial investment. With annual compounding of interest, money growing at 12.2% will double over six years. With continuous compounding, money growing at 7.2% will double in just 10 years. What is illustrated in Table 1.1 is the similarity between continuous and annual compounding when very long investment horizons are considered. Also illustrated is the fact that the Rule of 72 gives a good rule-of-thumb approximation for estimating the length of time it will take for an investment to double. From the third column in Table 1.1, it is clear that the interest rate derived using the Rule of 72 closely approximates the annual rate of interest when using annual compounding.

WALL STREET WISDOM 1.1

Wall Street Ethics

Pick up *The Wall Street Journal* or a leading financial magazine like *Forbes,* and it's not hard to find evidence of unscrupulous behavior. Indeed, it can be discouraging to note the amount of press coverage devoted to companies or top management cited for fraud or waste of shareholder assets. Intense media coverage sometimes gives the mistaken impression that base, immoral, or unscrupulous behavior is common in business. Sometimes it's far too easy to gain the mistaken impression that "dirty" business is standard operating procedure in corporate America.

Unethical conduct is consistent neither with the long-run interests of stockholders nor with the enlightened self-interest of management and other employees. Although famous examples of unscrupulous behavior are unfortunate, it is important to recognize that such scandals occur only infrequently. Every business day on Wall Street and on Main Street, thousands of business transactions, some involving billions of dollars in cash and securities, are made on the basis of simple phone conversations.

Without honesty and trust, the business of investing would more than simply slow down; it would stop dead in its tracks. Fraud and scandal are the stark exception to standard operating procedure on Main Street *and* Wall Street. Management guru Peter Drucker has written that the purpose of business is to create a customer—someone who will want to do business with you and your company on a regular basis. The only way this can be done is to make sure that you continually take the customer's perspective. For example, a financial advisor must continuously ask how investor needs can be met better, cheaper, or faster. Don't wait for customers to complain or seek alternate advice; seek out ways of helping before they become obvious. When customers benefit, so do you and your company. In almost all circumstances, it's best to see every business transaction from the standpoint of those you are dealing with.

In analyzing an investment opportunity, for example, strive to see how it creates an opportunity for both the buyer *and* the seller. Only when there are benefits for both parties will there be an incentive for a lasting business relationship. It's natural to see things from one's own viewpoint; it is typically much more beneficial to see things from the perspective of the person sitting on the other side of the table.

To become successful in investments, everyone must adopt a set of principles. For better or worse, we are known by the standards we adopt. Some ethical rules to keep in mind when conducting business might include the following:

- Above all else, keep your word. Say what you mean, and mean what you say.
- Do the right thing. A handshake with an honorable person is worth more than a ton of legal documents from an unscrupulous individual.
- Accept responsibility for your mistakes, and fix them. Be quick to share credit for success.
- Leave something on the table. Profit *with* your customer, not *off* your customer.
- Stick by your principles. Principles are not for sale at any price.

To gain some perspective on the conduct of notorious "corporate losers," consider the experience of one of America's most famous "winners"—Omaha billionaire Warren E. Buffett, chairman of Berkshire Hathaway, Inc. Buffett and Charlie Munger, the number two man at Berkshire, are famous for doing multimillion dollar deals on the basis of a simple handshake. At Berkshire, management relies on the character of the individuals who they are dealing with rather than expensive accounting audits, detailed legal opinions, or liability insurance coverage. Buffett says that after some early mistakes he learned to go into business only with people he likes, trusts, and admires. Although a company won't necessarily prosper because its managers display admirable qualities, Buffett says he has never made a good deal with a bad person.

Doing the right thing makes sense from an ethical perspective. It makes business sense as well. When it comes to investing, nice guys, such as Warren Buffett, often finish first.

See: Todd Goren, "Warren Buffett Posts 6.05% Stake in Aegis Realty," *Wall Street Journal, Interactive Edition,* <http://www.wsj.com>, April 4, 2000.

"Miracle" of Compound Interest

In Table 1.2, notice how similar the amounts are resulting from a $10,000 investment at 6%, 9%, and 12% when only one year of investment returns are considered. Starting from $10,000, a 6% rate of return in one year will result in a final investment value of $10,600. Similarly starting from $10,000, 9% and 12% rates of return generate ultimate investment values of $10,900 and $11,200, respectively. Over a single year, there is no large difference among 6%, 9%, and 12% rates of return. Over a single year, 9% is simply one-half again as good as a 6% return. Over a single year, a 12% rate of return leads to simply twice the total investment return that would be earned with 6%. What is intriguing is how different rates of interest compound to widely differing amounts over extended periods.

For example, remember that the Rule of 72 states that over a 12-year period, 6% interest leads to a doubled amount of investment. If you look in Table 1.2 under the 6% column, you can see that over 12 years a $10,000 investment grows to $20,122, or roughly doubles. Over 24 years at 6% interest, an investment of $10,000 grows to $40,489, or roughly quadruples. Over 36 years, an investment of $10,000 at 6% interest grows to $81,473, or doubles roughly three times. This is very similar to that predicted by the Rule of 72. According to the Rule of 72, money growing at 6% roughly doubles in 12 years, it doubles twice in 24 years, and doubles three times in 36 years.

These returns are starkly different from those achieved with a 9% rate of return on investment. Remember from the Rule of 72 that an investment yielding 9% will roughly double every eight years. Notice from Table 1.2 that in eight years at 9% interest, money grows from $10,000 to $19,926. In an additional eight years, that money will grow from $10,000 to $19,926 to $39,703, or roughly quadruples. In just

TABLE 1.2 **Compound Interest Leads to Amazing Growth**

Over a 24-year period, a 9% return leads to twice the wealth of 6% returns, and 12% returns almost quadruple the wealth generated by a 6% return.

Number of Years	Look What $10,000 Turns into with an Investment Return of:		
	6%	9%	12%
1	$10,600	$10,900	$11,200
2	11,236	11,881	12,544
3	11,910	12,950	14,049
4	12,625	14,116	15,735
6	14,185	16,771	19,738
8	15,938	19,926	24,760
12	20,122	28,127	38,960
16	25,404	39,703	61,304
20	32,071	56,044	96,463
24	40,489	79,111	151,786
28	51,117	111,671	238,839
32	64,534	157,633	375,817
36	81,473	222,512	591,356
40	102,857	314,094	930,510

(Note: Annual compounding is assumed.)

another eight years, such an investment will double once more to $79,111, or roughly $80,000. What is interesting to note is that a 9% rate of return over 24 years is much better than one-half again as profitable as one that yields a 6% rate of return. Notice from Table 1.2 that over 24 years, a $10,000 investment growing at 9% leads to $79,111, whereas a similar investment growing at 6% grows to only $40,489. This means that over a 24-year investment horizon, a 9% rate of return results in twice the wealth being generated as that created by a 6% rate of return. With compound interest, the divergence between a 6% and a 9% rate of return grows exponentially as the length of the investment horizon increases. If you go 40 years, for example, $10,000 growing at 9% becomes $314,094. Over 40 years at 6%, $10,000 grows to $102,857. This means that over a 40-year investment horizon, 9% growth more than triples the amount earned at 6%.

The effect of differences in the rate of compound interest on the amount earned from investment becomes even clearer when one considers a 12% rate of return. Remember that over a one-year period, 12% returns simply twice the total amount earned on a 6% investment. According to the Rule of 72, money growing at 12% doubles over six years; over 12 years it would double again, or quadruple. Over 18 years it will double a third time; over 24 years it would double a fourth time, and so on. Table 1.2 shows that over a period of six years, a $10,000 investment growing at 12% accumulates to $19,738, or roughly doubles. Over a period of 12 years at 12% interest, $10,000 grows to $38,960, or doubles roughly twice (roughly quadruples). It doubles twice more, or quadruples again, over an additional 12 years. Over 24 years, $10,000 grows by almost 16-fold to $151,786. It is impressive to recognize that over 24 years, 12% interest results in much more than simply twice the rate of return earned on 6%. Over 24 years, a $10,000 investment growing at 12% will mature to nearly four times the amount generated by a 6% rate of return. This means that over a 24-year period, 12% interest is much more than twice as much as 6%. In fact, it is almost four times as much.

Table 1.2 illustrates that over an extended period, compound interest results in amazing growth. Over extended periods, 9% growth generates far more total return than does 6%. The amount earned with 12% growth can become stunning over an extended period.

Practical Implications of Compound Interest

Numbers shown in Table 1.2 represent more than simple illustrations of the amazing growth created by compound interest. The actual numbers fairly reflect investment returns that have been earned over time on stock and bond investments in the United States (see Figure 1.1). For example, a 12% rate of return is commensurate with the rate of return earned on broadly diversified portfolios of stock market investments since World War II. In other words, a broadly diversified portfolio of common stocks could be expected over the long term to return to the investor a 12% rate of growth. At the other end of the spectrum, a 6% rate of return is a typical average for long-term bond investors. This means that over an extended period of time a broadly diversified portfolio of high-grade bonds could be expected to yield investors a rate of interest on the order of 6%. Between these two extremes of 6% and 12% is the 9% rate of return typically earned by mutual fund investors. Mutual funds typically own a blend of stocks and bonds and must pay

FIGURE 1.1 **Building Wealth by Investing in Stocks, Bonds, and Treasury Bills**

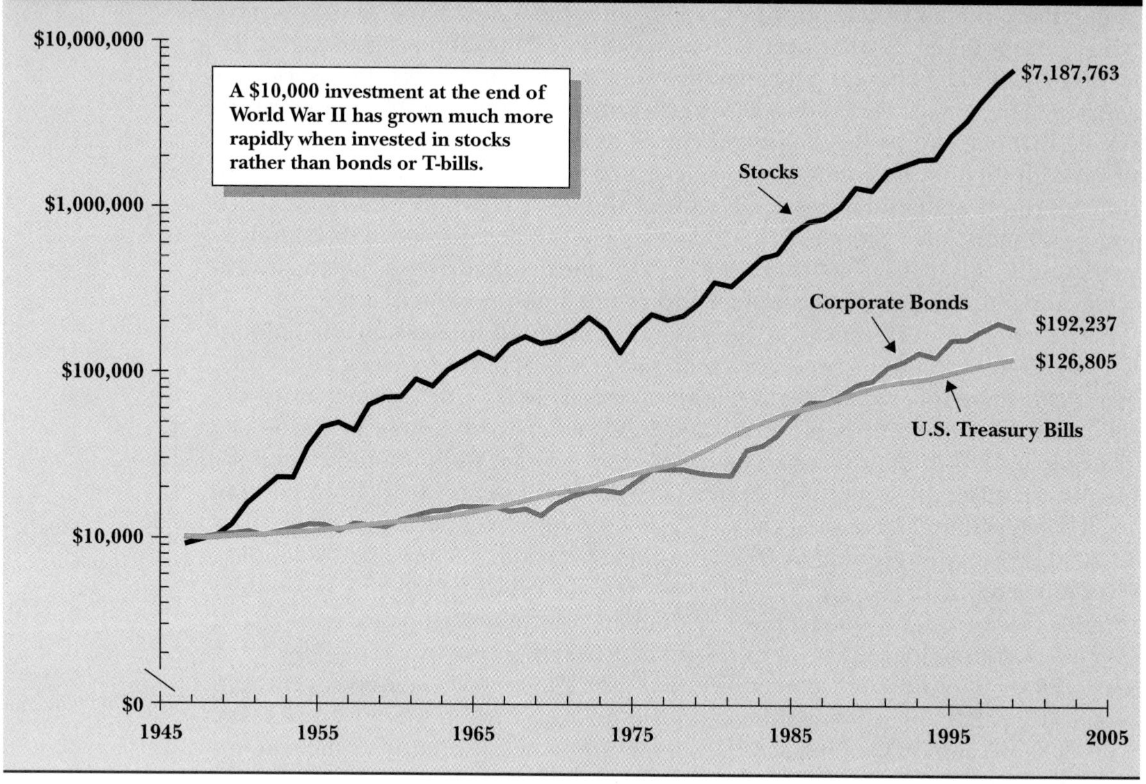

the trading and management costs involved with running a mutual fund. As a result, they return investors about 9%, on average, or roughly 3% below the return earned on broadly diversified portfolios of common stocks.

For today's investor, the 12% rate of return described in Table 1.2 is more than just a theoretical rate of return. On a theoretical level, it is the rate of interest earned on broad market indexes, such as the Standard & Poor's (S&P) 500. However, The Vanguard Group of Investment Companies in Valley Forge, Pennsylvania, also has a mutual fund called the Vanguard 500 Index Trust. This mutual fund owns all 500 stocks in the S&P 500 Index and provides investors with a return very near the rate of return on the S&P 500. Investors today have the opportunity to invest in a broadly diversified portfolio of common stocks in which the expected rate of return is nearly 12%. Alternatively, investors today have the opportunity to invest in broadly diversified bond index funds that might be expected to yield over time a 6% rate of return. Alternatively, investors today might choose to invest in a combination of both stock and bond index funds that can be expected to return 9% per year.

Now, let's say that the sole benefit gained through studying investments is to learn about and become comfortable with the superior rate of return on stocks versus bonds over extended time frames. If a young investor, say a 25-year-old, were to invest in stocks versus bonds in his or her retirement account, the wealth advantage over time could be substantial. As shown in Table 1.2, if a 25-year-old were to invest $10,000 in a broadly diversified portfolio of common stocks, by the time that investor reached the age of 65, he or she would have the potential to earn a compounded rate of return of 12% per year and a cumulative investment amount of $930,510. This is a significant difference from the 6% return expected on a broadly diversified portfolio of bonds. Note that $10,000 invested in a broadly diversified bond portfolio returning 6% per year would grow into only $102,857 over a 40-year time frame. The long-term stock market investor has a tremendous advantage over the bond market investor when it comes to extended time periods for investment. If the only thing that you get out of studying investments is to learn how to better manage your individual retirement account or how to better manage other long-term investments, this will have been a most profitable exercise.

Simple illustrations of the amazing growth resulting from compound interest provide a helpful introduction to the nature of investing. It's not the whole story, but it is a useful beginning. Investing is about money. It is not just about accumulating money and helping it grow. It is about how people feel about money. Therefore, the theory of investing involves economics and psychology. Wall Street is a real place. It's an interesting place. It's a place well-worth studying.

Investment Objectives

Investing for Retirement

Investing is important because everyone must invest to provide for vital future needs such as cars, homes, education, and retirement income. By studying investment theory and analysis, it becomes possible to improve investment results. Saving money for a down payment on a home is a perfect example. Using high-yield money market instruments, individual savers can often increase the interest earned over certificates of deposit offered by commercial banks or savings and loan institutions. Effective selection of stock and bond investments is an important consideration for all investors seeking to improve their chances for a satisfactory retirement income.

Thirty years ago, it was common for individual companies to offer employees **defined-benefit retirement plans.** Under a defined-benefit retirement plan, employees are promised a fixed retirement income of, say, 1% times the number of years served times the last year's salary. For example, suppose in your last year of employment you earned a salary of $50,000 per year. Furthermore, assume that you had worked for your employer for 30 years. This means that you might be entitled to a company pension of 30 times 1% times $50,000, or $15,000 a year. Such a substantial pension would provide a meaningful supplement to social security payments and any other retirement income from investments.

defined-benefit retirement plan Employer promises to pay a fixed retirement income.

Over time, defined benefit plans in the United States have been abandoned in favor of what are called **defined-contribution** plans. Under a defined-contribution retirement plan, individual employees are paid a retirement income based on the total value accumulated in their retirement portfolio.

defined-contribution retirement plan Employees are paid a retirement income based on the total value accumulated in their retirement portfolio.

For example, consider the data provided in Table 1.3. Assume that an individual investor contributes $6,000 per year, or $500 per month, into her retirement plan with a major employer. If those funds are invested to earn a return of 6% per year, such an employee would accumulate $220,714 over a 20-year period. Instead

TABLE 1.3 **Returns (%) on Stocks, Corporate Bonds, and Treasury Bills, 1946–present**

Since the end of World War II, common stocks have greatly outperformed corporate bonds and U.S. Treasury bills.

Year	Large Company Stocks (S&P 500)	Long-Term Corporate Bonds	U.S.Treasury Bills
1946	−8.1	1.7	0.4
1947	5.7	−2.3	0.5
1948	5.5	4.1	0.8
1949	18.8	3.3	1.1
1950	31.7	2.1	1.2
1951	24.0	−2.7	1.5
1952	18.4	3.5	1.7
1953	−1.0	3.4	1.8
1954	52.6	5.4	0.9
1955	31.6	0.5	1.6
1956	6.6	−6.8	2.5
1957	−10.8	8.7	3.1
1958	43.4	−2.2	1.5
1959	12.0	−1.0	3.0
1960	0.5	9.1	2.7
1961	26.9	4.8	2.1
1962	−8.7	8.0	2.7
1963	22.8	2.2	3.1
1964	16.5	4.8	3.5
1965	12.5	−0.5	3.9
1966	−10.1	0.2	4.8
1967	24.0	−5.0	4.2
1968	11.1	2.6	5.2
1969	−8.5	−8.1	6.6
1970	4.0	18.4	6.5
1971	14.3	11.0	4.4
1972	19.0	7.3	3.8
1973	−14.7	1.1	6.4
1974	−26.5	−3.1	8.0
1975	37.2	14.6	5.8
1976	23.8	18.7	5.1
1977	−7.2	1.7	5.1
1978	6.6	−0.1	7.2
1979	18.4	−4.2	10.4
1980	32.4	−2.8	11.2
1981	−4.9	−1.2	14.7
1982	21.4	42.6	10.5
1983	22.5	6.3	8.8
1984	6.3	16.9	9.9
1985	32.2	30.1	7.7
1986	18.5	19.9	6.2
1987	5.2	−0.3	5.5
1988	16.8	10.7	6.4
1989	31.5	15.5	8.4
1990	−3.2	6.9	7.8
1991	30.6	20.2	5.6
1992	7.7	8.7	3.5
1993	10.0	13.0	2.9
1994	1.3	−5.8	3.9
1995	37.4	26.7	5.6
1996	23.1	1.4	5.2
1997	33.4	13.5	5.3
1998	28.6	10.5	5.3
1999	21.0	−7.0	4.9
Mean Return	13.0	5.6	4.8

of investing in a broadly diversified bond portfolio earning 6% per year, consider the possibility of investing in common stocks yielding 12%. In common stocks returning 12% per year over a period of 20 years, a total retirement portfolio of $432,315 would accumulate. Having chosen common stocks rather than bonds, such an employee would be able to fund a much higher level of retirement income than that afforded by the bond investor.

This example makes clear that when employees have defined-contribution retirement plans, it is necessary that they themselves accept responsibility for the management of their retirement assets. Under a defined-contribution retirement plan, the employer accepts no responsibility for the amount accumulated in an individual employee's retirement account. The freedom to match individual retirement strategies with individual risk attitudes is a compelling advantage of defined-contribution retirement plans. At the same time, this greater flexibility brings along with it a greater level of employee responsibility. If the individual employee fails to understand the fundamental relationships between risk and expected return and the pluses and minuses of stock and bond investing in the long run, such an individual is apt to pay a startling cost in terms of reduced retirement income.

Investing to Meet Other Financial Goals

Of course, the importance of learning about investing extends beyond the need for intelligent retirement planning. Funding an adequate retirement income is a prime concern to many investors, but it is not their sole concern. Many parents also wish to help children afford a quality college education. Carefully selected stock and bond investments can make an important contribution toward paying the costs of college education, especially when an extended investment horizon is possible.

For example, Table 1.2 shows that if parents of a newly born baby were to invest $10,000 in a common stock portfolio returning 12% over a 20-year period, this would accumulate to $96,463. This is an amount sufficient to carry a large share of the expected costs of a private college education in America today. However, Table 1.3 shows that if parents of a newborn child were to contribute $100 per month, or $1,200 per year, over a 20-year period into a common stock portfolio returning 12% per year, such a portfolio would grow to $86,463. Again, this is an amount sufficient to pay a large share of the cost of an undergraduate education.

These simple examples illustrate how anytime an investor has a long-term financial goal, stock and bond investing can play a significant role in achieving those objectives. From this standpoint, it is fair to say that all students have an important interest in learning as much as they can about investment theory and practice. Even small improvements in one's ability to manage a retirement portfolio, a college tuition portfolio, or any long-term investment can lead to significant rewards.

Suppose that as a result of reading this text you were able to earn a 12% rate of return on your retirement portfolio, rather than a more conventional 9% annual rate of return. Over a 20-year investment horizon, Table 1.3 shows that $12,000 per year, or $1,000 per month, contributed into a retirement program would yield $864,629 when invested in a broadly diversified portfolio of common stocks. This is a startling improvement over the $613,921 earned on a stock and bond portfolio yielding 9% per year. It is almost twice the $441,427 accumulated in a bond portfolio yielding 6% per year. The difference between earning 12% and 9% or 6% over an extended time frame is huge. It would be an extremely satisfactory payoff from learning about investments.

Essence of Time

Finally, it is important to emphasize the role that the length of investment horizon, or time itself, plays in building a significant and successful investment portfolio. Again, consider the data shown in Table 1.3. This table shows that a young investor investing only $100 per month, or $1,200 per year, over a 40-year time horizon would accumulate $920,510 in a common stock portfolio yielding 12%. Because of the advantage of time, this is a much lower investment requirement than that required by a middle-aged investor seeking to accumulate a similar amount. Consider the middle-aged investor contributing $12,000 per year toward retirement, or 10 times as much as that contributed by the young investor. A middle-aged investor contributing $12,000 per year toward retirement in a common stock portfolio yielding 12% would accumulate $864,629. This means that the advantage of a longer investment horizon gives the young investor more than 10 times the benefit from investing for retirement as that earned by the middle-aged investor.

There is an old saying that rich people have three things in common: Rich people tend to be smart, lucky, and *old.*

As a student or novice investor, perhaps you don't have the advantage of a substantial amount to invest. You also need to increase your understanding of securities markets to take full advantage of available opportunities. Despite these limitations, the undeniable advantage enjoyed by all young investors is an extremely long investment horizon. The advantage of a long investment horizon can overcome the temporary disadvantage of not having a significant sum to invest. With a sufficiently long investment horizon, the amount that any young investor is able to accumulate through a careful investment program can be significant.

As shown in Table 1.4, an investment of as much as $1,000 per month over 40 years results in $9,205,097 in retirement wealth. This is a level of wealth seldom

TABLE 1.4 Long-Term Payoff to Regular Investing Can Be Huge

Young investors can accumulate significant wealth through regular investing of modest amounts. The longer you wait to start investing, however, the greater the cost to building significant wealth.

Amount Invested per Year	Number of Years	Wealth Created with an Investment Return of: 6%	9%	12%
Young Investor				
$300	40	$46,429	$101,365	$230,127
$1,200	40	185,714	405,459	920,510
$2,000	40	309,524	675,765	1,534,183
$6,000	40	928,572	2,027,295	4,602,549
$12,000	40	1,857,144	4,054,589	9,205,097
Middle-Age Investor				
$300	20	11,036	15,348	21,616
$1,200	20	44,143	61,392	86,463
$2,000	20	73,571	102,320	144,105
$6,000	20	220,714	306,961	432,315
$12,000	20	441,427	613,921	864,629

WALL STREET WISDOM 1.2

Can You Bank on the Stock Market?

During a typical year since the end of World War II, major stock market averages like the Dow Jones Industrial Average have risen on the order of 10–12% per year. More recently, investor rates of return on common stocks have averaged more than 15% per year. With inflation tamed, interest rates have plummeted, and the stock market has soared. For investors, the 1980s and the 1990s have been the best of times.

On average, common stocks have returned roughly 6% more than the rate of inflation in the United States this century. This means that long-term stock investors have enjoyed a "real" increase of 6% per year in the amount of goods and services that they can buy with the proceeds from money set aside for investment in common stocks. A real return of 6% per year might seem modest, especially in light of the stupendous returns earned by stock market investors in the late 1990s. In fact, 6% real returns compound to a significant amount over sustained periods. At 6% interest, money doubles every 12 years, doubles twice in 24 years, and doubles a third time in 36 years. Thus, over only 36 years, an investment of $10,000 grows to a real value of $81,473. An investment of only $2,000 per year compounding at a real return of 6% grows to a real value of $238,242 over 36 years.

In fact, to many it may seem surprising that common stocks might grow as fast as 6% per year in real terms given that the overall economy as measured by Gross Domestic Product tends to grow at only 3% per year in real terms. For more than a century, real economic growth of 3% per year has been fueled by population growth of roughly 1% per year plus technical change (productivity growth) of 2% per year. How can stocks grow at 6% in a world that's growing at 3%?

The answer is deceptively simple. Major corporations tend to be financed on almost a 50/50 basis with debt and equity. Although common stocks have earned a real return of 6% per year for investors, bond holders have earned no net real return. In other words, the real return to bond holders has just been enough, on average, to offset the effects of inflation. Another way of looking at it is to think of the 6% real rate of return earned by stockholders as the entire real return earned on investments financed by both debt and equity.

Looking ahead, is it likely that common stocks will continue to outperform bonds for long-term investors? The answer again is yes. Whenever a corporation issues debt, it must invest in projects with an expected return that is greater than the amount of interest paid or risk the possibility of default. A company would never issue debt at, say, 8% to invest in projects with an expected rate of return of 8%. If it did so, there would be a 50/50 chance that a given project would prove unprofitable. If enough such projects were undertaken, there would be a 50/50 chance of the corporation going broke. To have a satisfactory margin of safety, corporations must expect to obtain a rate of return on investment that significantly exceeds the cost of debt financing. This profit margin is the return for risk taking. It is also the source of the real rate of return earned by stockholders.

Mortgage rates at your local bank always exceed the rate of interest paid on savings deposits. The difference, called interest margin, pays for the bank's cost of doing business (heat, lights, wages) and profits. In the long run, no bank can pay savings rates higher than the amount received on loans. In the long run, stocks also must pay a higher return than the rate of interest paid on bonds. Of course, savings balances don't fluctuate every day like stock prices, but a broadly diversified portfolio of common stocks resembles a savings account that pays 10–12% annual "interest" to long-term investors.

See: Gregory Zuckerman and E. S. Browning, "Market Plunges, Then Comes Up for Air," *The Wall Street Journal,* April 5, 2000, C1, C20.

achieved in our economy. It is seldom achieved because it is difficult. As is always the case, any worthwhile objective requires sacrifice. Building significant retirement wealth requires a significant sacrifice in terms of postponed consumption. To achieve significant retirement income objectives also typically requires a substantial investment horizon.

Theory of Finance

Theory Provides a Road Map

Today, many novice investors are primarily concerned with two simple questions. First, how do you access investment information? The answer is often simple and direct: "on the Net!" The Internet and traditional financial publications offer today's investors a wealth of valuable investment information and analysis, often for free. A second common and important question: How does an investor efficiently organize financial information? Many novice investors today are seasoned in the use of personal computers and financial software. In many instances, even novice investors are adept at organizing a wealth of financial information available on individual companies. To be sure, answers to these two questions are important for all investors. Both are addressed in detail in Chapter 2.

However, before addressing these two important questions, a third and perhaps more basic question must be asked: How do you process, or make sense of, investment information? This is where the theory of finance comes into play. Just as the effective practices of successful investors give clues about how to proceed, so too does investment theory provide a useful road map or context for analyzing investments problems. The road map provided by the theory of finance explains that economic forces determine the prices for stocks, bonds, and other assets such as real estate, art, and collectibles. As demonstrated throughout this chapter, the first and most fundamental concept of investments is the idea of compound interest. Money grows over time according to the economic fundamentals. Compound interest can create an astounding increase in the value of a company or investment over time.

The powerful effect of compound interest can be further illustrated by a famous historical example. It is well known that Peter Minuit, governor of the Netherlands, bought the island of Manhattan in 1626. Manhattan Island is the home of famous New York landmarks and tourist attractions such as Broadway, Central Park, Rockefeller Center, and Wall Street. Minuit bought the island in 1626 from Indians who may have been passing through the area. He paid for the island with beads, cloth, and trinkets worth a mere $24. In the year 2000, 374 years had passed since the year 1626. An interesting example of compound interest can be seen by calculating the hypothetical value of $24 invested over this time frame at a modest rate of interest, say 6%.

To calculate the value of $24 invested for 374 years at 6%, simply take 1.06 to the 374th power times $24. That amount equals $70 billion. In other words, Peter Minuit's purchase of Manhattan Island was at a present-day equivalent price of $70 billion. Of course, this is merely a hypothetical example. Over that 374-year period, there was no safe, secure investment that yielded 6% per year. Treasury bills and Treasury bonds didn't exist in the 17th century. They are a relatively recent invention. Present-day investors simply have far more reliable investment opportunities to consider than were available in the era of Peter Minuit. Nevertheless, as this simple example illustrates, even a very modest amount of $24 invested for an extended period of time can yield a tremendous fortune.

portfolio Diversified collection of stocks, bonds, and other assets.

Key Investment Concepts

In addition to the compound interest concept, another key idea in investments theory is the concept of a **portfolio.** A portfolio is a diversified collection of stocks and bonds or other assets. An investor's intent in creating a portfolio of assets is to provide the basis for a stable rate of return. Portfolio theory tells us that diversification has the potential to reduce anticipated risk for a given expected return. Each individual firm has various influences that affect its risk. Firm-specific risk is tied to the chance that a key executive might leave the firm or die, important products might lose out to new competitors, or vital brand names would be lost. By forming an investment portfolio, firm-specific risks tend to cancel out.

A further fundamental investment theory is the idea that **risk** and **expected return** are related. The price of higher expected return is greater anticipated risk. This means that if a low-risk U.S. Treasury bill yields 6% interest, bonds that yield more than 6% per year are, by definition, not Treasury bills. If you want to earn higher than risk-free rates of return, you must be willing to assume higher levels of risk. The importance of recognizing the relationship between risk and expected return is that, holding the length of the investment horizon constant, higher expected return is typically accompanied by greater volatility.

risk
Chance of economic loss.

expected return
Anticipated gain.

A fourth key investments concept is the **efficient market hypothesis.** The efficient market hypothesis states that every security at every point in time is fairly priced. Prices are neither too low (undervalued) nor too high (overvalued). It is true, but nevertheless astounding, that the average professional investor cannot beat the market. On the one hand, it is natural to assume that the average professional would perform in line with market averages. For example, if the average annual rate of return on a widely diversified portfolio of stocks is 12%, over any significant period of time it is natural to expect roughly one-half of all professional investors to earn more than 12% per year and one-half to earn less than 12%. After all, the stock market is largely an institutional market, and you would expect one-half of the institutions to do better than average and one-half of the institutions to earn less than average. However, this is only true *before* expenses are considered. The average investment professional is highly trained, extremely diligent, and *expensive.* With 3% per year in management fees, brokerage expenses, promotional expenditures, and other costs, the net rate of return on an investment portfolio yielding a 12% gross rate of return is only 9%. Given average expenses of 3% per year, the typical institutional investor would earn only 9% per year for their customers; one-half of the institutional investors would earn more than 9% per year, and one-half would earn less than 9% per year.

efficient market hypothesis
Idea that every security at every point in time is fairly priced.

In fact, this is what mutual fund performance data show. Over extended periods of time and after expenses have been accounted for, only a small percentage of the institutional investors are able to outperform the market averages. Studies show that as many as 90% of professionally managed mutual funds and pension funds underperform the broad market averages over periods of time as short as 10 years. These findings are consistent with the notion that the stock market is very efficient at ferreting out underpriced bargains.

Lessons from Investment Practice

Investment Superstars

The typical investor cannot expect to beat the market averages. To consistently outperform, it takes a superstar. In the investment management business, it takes a superstar such as Warren Buffett, Peter Lynch, or Sir John Templeton. In major league baseball, it takes a superstar like Mark McGwire. Mark McGwire earns extraordinary compensation derived from his ability to hit home runs. The fact that Mark McGuire makes millions of dollars per year does not mean that it is easy to make millions playing baseball. His extraordinary returns reflect his extraordinary ability as a power hitter. Similarly, extraordinary returns for investment superstars, such as Warren Buffett, reflect superior ability to hit the ball out of the investment park.

Omaha-based Warren Buffett, chairman and chief executive officer of Berkshire Hathaway, looks for wonderful businesses selling at reasonable prices. A wonderful business is one that generates a high rate of profit for the amount of money committed to the enterprise. In terms of accounting information, the **return-on-equity** measure is the best available indicator of the firm's ability to profitably use operating and financial leverage. The return on equity is simply the ratio of net income divided by **stockholders' equity,** or book value per share. On average, return on equity falls in the range from 10% to 12% per year for the broad cross-section of businesses in the United States. Firms that consistently earn less than 10–12% find that it becomes difficult to raise new funds for expansion and improvement. As a result, low-profit firms are forced to either improve their operations or shrink and retrench. To attract additional funds for expansion, firms must offer above-average rates of return. Over the long run, investing larger amounts of capital tends to drive down the rate of profit per dollar invested. Thus, high-profit firms tend to earn lower rates of return over time as more and more capital is committed to the enterprise. At the same time, low-profit firms see their profit rate rise over time as investors redeploy funds to other, more profitable uses. This recurring pattern, or tendency, of profit rates to return toward long-term industry and economy-wide averages is called **regression to the mean.**

return on equity Accounting net income divided by **stockholders' equity,** or book value per share.

regression to the mean Tendency of profit rates to return toward long-term industry and economy-wide averages.

When Buffett looks for wonderful businesses that are highly profitable, he is looking for companies that consistently earn 20–25% rates of return on stockholders' equity, or more. When Buffett says he is looking for stocks selling at reasonable prices, he is looking for companies whose price does not already reflect the company's superior profitability. A reasonable price is usually defined in terms of the **price-earnings ratio** (P/E) paid, where P/E is defined as the market value of the firm divided by net income. On a per-share basis, P/E is the company's stock price divided by earnings per share. A P/E of 20 means that the stock price is 20 times higher than each dollar of earnings per share. However, a P/E of 20 implies that the firm has five cents in earnings for each dollar of market value.

price/earnings ratio Stock price divided by earnings per share.

Another legendary investor is Fidelity Investment's Peter Lynch. Peter Lynch is credited with taking the Magellan Mutual Fund from a few million dollars in assets to $14 billion before his retirement in 1993. Peter Lynch enjoyed fantastic success as the most successful mutual fund manager of our era by focusing on stocks that had rapid growth at a modest price, as measured by the firm's P/E ratio. When Peter Lynch looked for outstanding growth, he was looking for firms that had the ability to grow earnings per share by 10%, 15%, or even 20% per year. Like Buffett, Lynch prefers bargains. He prefers high-growth companies that sell for no more than the market average P/E.

A third legendary investor of recent years has been Sir John Templeton of the Franklin-Templeton group of mutual funds. Sir John is known as the father of global investing. He promotes searching far and wide for the best bargains available. In Sir John's opinion, the best stock market bargains are companies selling at low prices relative to their book value of tangible assets. This means that Templeton looks for companies that sell at a cheap price relative to the company's book value, per share. Templeton's reasoning is that firms tend to grow earnings when book values grow, and as book value grows higher share prices will follow.

In all three cases, Warren Buffett, Peter Lynch, and Sir John Templeton, a successful investor has profited by considering stocks as part ownership in the company's underlying businesses. Notice that none of them thinks of stocks as a simple piece of paper; none uses trading rules that favor stocks that are going up or stocks that are going down. Instead, they seek to develop an independent judgment of what a company is worth based on its economic prospects compared with those of companies in general. In considering the development of their own stock selection techniques, individual investors would be well advised to consider the underpinnings of the historical success enjoyed by these legendary investors.

Asset Valuation

How do investment superstars value stocks? Although individual techniques vary slightly, a recurring theme is that investment superstars value stocks on an economic basis in terms of the prorated value of the underlying business.

To illustrate, consider the example shown in Table 1.5. This example illustrates the economic rate of return and economic value of one acre of Iowa farmland. For simplicity, assume that such a parcel would be able to generate 150 bushels of corn per acre. Furthermore, assume that the price of a bushel of corn is $2.50. This means that $375 in revenue would be generated from corn raised on this one acre of Iowa farmland. Furthermore, assume that planting and tillage costs, seed, fertilizer costs, harvesting costs, taxes, and so on total $225 per acre. This means that gross profit per acre is $150. To yield an 8% rate of return, an investor would pay no more than $1,875 per acre. This means that the economic value per acre of such land is $1,875. Of course, $1,875 is a very high price for farmland. It reflects the fact that Iowa farmland is among the most productive of all agricultural land in the world. If the land were less productive, it would sell at a much lower price.

Because cropland in Iowa, southern Minnesota, Illinois, and South Dakota is so productive, investors that demand an 8% rate of return can pay up to $1,875 per acre, or $150 of net profit per acre divided by 0.08. It's as simple as that. This assumes, of course, that fertilizer is putting back into the soil necessary nutrients. If an investor could buy such farmland for $1,000 per acre, he or she would scoop

TABLE 1.5 Illustration of the Economic Value of Iowa Farmland

Bushels of corn produced per acre	150
Price of corn per bushel	× $2.50
Total revenue per acre	$375
Planting, tillage costs	−75
Seed and fertilizer costs	−40
Harvesting costs	−90
Taxes, insurance, etc.	−20
Gross profit per acre	$150
Interest rate	8%
Economic value per acre	$1,875

it up because it would then produce a 15% return. It would be a heck of a deal. If someone came along, borrowed a bunch of cash, and bid up the price to $4,000 per acre, they would go broke. Such farmland wouldn't support a price of $4,000 an acre for agricultural use. When you have a situation in which energy costs skyrocket, a poor crop comes in, or the price of corn collapses, investors who borrowed to buy farmland at $4,000 per acre go broke. It is not usually the first bad year but it is the second bad year that knocks out marginal farmers. The simple fact is that there is an economic value underpinning that farmland.

It's the same way with stocks. Sometimes, inexperienced investors bid up the price of some Internet stock, figuring that revenues, earnings, and book values don't matter. For brief periods of time, sometimes they don't. This is especially true when there is a lot of uncertainty. However, in the long run, revenues, earnings, and book values matter a great deal. If earnings for America Online, Yahoo!, and Amazon.com absolutely explode to the upside over the next few years, their current stock prices will be justified. They may even rise. If earnings of those companies do not explode, those stocks are going to get crushed. In the long run, an investor can do no better than the company invested in. If the company prospers, so too do its investors. If the company fails to generate above-average profits, its investors won't be able to earn above-average rates of return.

The fundamental point made by the data in Table 1.5 is that the value of an asset like farm real estate is determined by economic considerations. This is the same for the value of stocks, bonds, and investments of all types. The value of any asset depends on how much profit is generated and the rate of interest demanded by the investor. The most successful investors of our time look at stocks and bonds much like a farmer would look at investing in real estate.

Psychology and the Stock Market

According to the efficient market hypothesis, current stock prices reflect all relevant risk and return information. This implies that near-term stock price changes are random and independent. In a rational pricing environment, investing in the stock market is a **fair game** in which the expected excess return for each security is zero. Taken literally, this means that every stock at every point in time is an equally good buy or sell.

fair game
When the expected excess return for each security is zero.

At the same time, a large and growing literature on stock market anomalies suggests that unexplained systematic abnormal returns may reflect market inefficiency and/or more elusive errors in expected return calculation (model misspecification). Several recent studies show that average returns on common stocks are related to firm characteristics such as size, earnings/price, high cash flow/price, book-to-market equity, past sales growth, long-term past return, and short-term past return. Some academic scholars in the field of finance argue that perceived mispricing of fundamental factors disappears in a three-factor model and argue that asset pricing appears rational within this framework.

However, George Soros, among others, suggests that subtle psychological influences can help explain certain anomalous pricing situations. In the words of George Soros, "Classical economic theory assumes that market participants act on the basis of perfect knowledge. That assumption is false. The participants' perceptions influence the market in which they participate, but the market action also influences the participants' perceptions. They cannot obtain perfect knowledge of the market because their thinking is always affecting the market and the market is affecting their thinking."

Within this context, it becomes reasonable to regard the efficient market hypothesis as a "working hypothesis" regarding *primarily* rational investors who *typically* price securities in a rational fashion. However, history seems to suggest that outbreaks of crowd behavior, typified by "extraordinary popular delusions and madness," are occasionally observed in various markets.

WALL STREET WISDOM 1.3

Buying Stocks Like Pigs

Classics: An Investor's Anthology is a marvelous compilation of short essays on investments by investing luminaries such as Warren E. Buffett, Benjamin Graham, John Maynard Keynes, and T. Rowe Price, Jr., among others. It is stock-market advice "right from the horse's mouth." It is the actual opinion of investing heavyweights in their own words.

One of my favorite selections from *Classics* is a short story by John Train, a former Wall Street broker and columnist from *Forbes*. The title of Train's story is "How Mr. Womack Made a Killing." Train tells the tale of a reader from Houston, Texas, who was in the drill rig business and an avid stock trader. Unfortunately, at the end of each year, he always had a net loss. He tried every technical and fundamental approach but somehow always ended up with a loss. It may sound impossible that someone could lose money in the rip-roaring stock market of the 1950s, but he did.

Discouraged and frustrated, Train's reader went into a Merrill Lynch office in Houston. A senior account executive sitting at the front desk observed the long-familiar frown on his face and motioned for him to come over to his desk. "Would you like to see a man who had *never* lost money in the stock market?" the broker asked. "This investor has never had a loss, and I've handled his account for nearly 40 years." Then, the broker gestured to Mr. Womack, a powerful man dressed in overalls, who was looking at the stock quotes. "If you want to meet him, you had better hurry," the broker advised. "He only comes in here once every few years, except when he is buying. He is a rice farmer and a hog raiser from Baytown."

Train's reader was surprised to learn that this stranger was happy to talk about stocks. He pulled a sheet of paper from his pocket with a list of stocks that he had just finished selling. The man had just sold more than 50 stocks with significant long-term capital gains. Many had gone up 100%, 200%, and even 500%. His investing technique was the ultimate in simplicity. During a bear market, Womack would read in the paper that the market was down and that the experts were predicting further declines. Then, Womack would pick 30 solid, profit-making companies that had fallen in price below $10. He would come to Houston and buy a $25,000 "package" of them to hold for a few years. When the market was bubbling again and the experts were talking about new highs, Womack would come to town and sell the whole package.

Womack equated buying stocks with buying a truckload of pigs. The cheaper he could buy the pigs, the more profit he would make when the next seller's market came along. In fact, Womack would rather buy stocks than pigs. Pigs do not pay a dividend. And you have to feed pigs.

Now, I realize that in the Internet era, a hog farmer like Mr. Womack doesn't sound all that sophisticated. In fact, he might be. In December 1998, I went to Iowa to visit a friend on the weekend before Christmas. I also saw something I had never seen before. Hog farmers were giving away sow pigs! Pork prices had plummeted to a 50-year low of 10¢ a pound, a price so cheap that it wouldn't pay for the butchering of the hogs. Hog farmers were calling friends and relatives in the city and asking them to come out and pick up a hog and take it to a packing plant. Needless to say, my family started to enjoy pork roast, bacon, and ham like never before.

I remembered John Train's story about Mr. Womack. With hog prices down, tractor sales had plummeted, and farm equipment stocks had gotten crushed. Following the now long-departed Mr. Womack's advice, I bought John Deere & Co. (DE) at $31.38.

Check it out on Yahoo! How am I doing?

See: Charles D. Ellis and James R. Vertin, eds., *Classics: An Investor's Anthology* (Homewood, IL: Business One Irwin, 1989).

Structure of This Text

Objectives

This text should help you accomplish the following objectives:

- Develop a clear understanding of the many useful and practical implications of financial theory.
- Acquire a framework for understanding the returns on all financial assets, including stocks, bonds, and financial derivatives.
- Gain familiarity with the institutions and language of Wall Street so as to facilitate the development of an effective personal investment strategy.

For students seeking preparation for a career on Wall Street, this text gives essential background in financial theory and practice. For all students, this text shows how financial theory and analysis can be used to gain understanding of financial markets and point toward the solution to crucial investment decision problems.

Throughout the text, the emphasis is on the *practical* application of financial theory to help understand the field of investments and the methods used by successful investors. It is vitally important to avoid the all-too-common trap of focusing on knowable but unimportant facts. For example, a student might learn with precision the hours of operation, number of securities offered for sale on the New York Stock Exchange (NYSE), and intricate details of the NYSE specialist system but have no facility whatsoever about how to value individual securities. The knowledgeable student of investments is one who comes to appreciate *how* investments perform and *why* they perform as they do.

A unique feature of this text is its consideration of the real investment success of superstar investors such as Warren Buffett, Peter Lynch, and Sir John Templeton. Warren Buffett's professor in the MBA program at Columbia University, Benjamin Graham, said that in the short run the market is a voting machine run by fear and greed. In the long run, the stock market is a weighing machine in which economic fundamentals dictate. A very important characteristic of this text is its focus on the economic underpinnings of market values for stocks, bonds, and financial derivatives. Economic theory, along with a little bit of psychology, helps investors organize and efficiently process investments information.

Topic Development

Financial theory offers a useful framework for characterizing the pattern of returns observed for stocks and bonds and is a practical guide to successful investments practice. The basic test of financial theory, or any theory in business, is its ability to explain real-world behavior. This text highlights the complementary relation between financial theory and investments practice. Financial theory is used to understand the experience of seasoned and novice investors. Practical experience leads to the development of better theory. The old saw "that might be good in theory, but doesn't work in practice" is plainly incorrect. Good theory explains and predicts successful practice. Theory that doesn't explain and predict successful practice is bad and must be discarded. Indeed, some incorrect financial theories have arisen from time to time and have been rejected. Those that remain are extraordinarily beneficial to the serious investor. Concepts such as compound interest, the efficient market hypothesis, and diversification have endured because they are useful.

Chapter 2, "Sources of Investment Information," completes our introduction to investments by showing how information and investment analysis found on the Internet can be of immense value to both experienced and novice investors. Such information is a wonderful complement to traditional sources of investment information from the popular press, financial press, and Wall Street research. Employment opportunities in the booming financial services industry are also discussed as an aid to students considering a career in investments. Chapter 3, "Overview of Equities Markets," begins an interesting introduction to equity securities by explaining various institutional aspects of Wall Street, including the organization of securities markets and financial regulation. More specific information on the products and process of Wall Street is given in Chapter 4, "Buying and Selling Equities." Types of investor accounts, procedures for buying and selling securities, and taxes, among other such issues, are discussed. Chapter 5, "Risk and Return," focuses on one of the most fundamental concepts in investments, the idea that there is no free lunch on Wall Street. The price of higher expected return is an increase in return volatility. Market values for stocks, bonds, and all financial instruments depend on their essential economic characteristics. Understanding the economic underpinnings of financial markets helps investors form reasonable investment expectations and effective investment strategies.

Fixed income securities are the subject of Chapter 6, "Bond Market," and Chapter 7, "Bond Valuation and Management." Too many investors know too little about fixed-income securities. The bond market rivals the stock market in size and economic importance and merits careful investor attention. Bond types, risk characteristics, and bond-trading dynamics are important considerations for the knowledgeable investor. Informed investors are also familiar with bond-trading dynamics, interest-rate risk considerations, and important fixed-income concepts such as duration and convexity. The value of bonds is determined by the risk-adjusted present value of future interest and principal payments. Similarly, the value of common stocks is determined by the risk-adjusted present value of future cash flows. Therefore, this analysis of bond concepts and pricing is important as a guide to understanding the fixed-income securities market and lays the groundwork necessary for understanding equity pricing.

With the groundwork provided by fixed-income analysis, the foundation has been laid for common stock analysis and selection. In Chapter 8, "Common Stock Basics," financial statement analysis is seen as the starting point for common stock valuation and selection. Key measures of profitability, firm size, and growth are considered as useful indicators of economic value. Advantages and limitations of traditional accounting information are also explored. Chapter 9, "Investment Environment," considers the macroeconomic setting, competitive circumstances, and legal environment as important investment considerations. In Chapter 10, "Growth Stock Investing," firm valuation is seen to depend on fundamental economic trends, earnings and dividend growth opportunities, and interest rates. In Chapter 11, "Value Investing," the vital role played by intrinsic economic value in common stock valuation is explored. This chapter also examines the concept of "growth at a reasonable price" and how both growth and value are essential characteristics of desirable common stock investments.

Efficient markets, and the efficient market hypothesis, is perhaps the most talked-about concept in the field of investments. It should be. The efficient market hypothesis is the cornerstone of modern financial theory and gives investors a framework within which all investment decisions can be evaluated. Chapter 12, "Efficient Market Hypothesis," explores this fundamental concept. The idea that stocks are priced in a market environment in which buyers and sellers rationally value the firm's future earnings prospects is a bedrock consideration for all investors. In Chapter 13, "Capital Asset Pricing Theory," the conceptual framework provided by the academic finance literature is seen as a fundamentally useful contribution to investment practice. Chapter 14, "Stock Market Anomalies," highlights several interesting exceptions to the predictions of conventional financial theory. This sharpens investors' focus on both the strengths and limitations of traditional theory and points the way toward better theory.

Investment management is a growing and lucrative field. Chapter 15, "Mutual Funds," covers basics of mutual fund investing. Mutual funds offer an attractive method for participating in stock and bond markets. The mutual fund industry is also one of many possibilities for those interested in pursuing careers in the blossoming financial services sector. Chapter 16, "Global Investing," discusses investment opportunities and investor strategies in the global economic environment. At first, it may seem anomalous to have a specific chapter devoted to "global investing." After all, isn't all successful investing global in orientation? Of course it is, and global topics are carefully integrated throughout this text. At the same time, the growing importance of global risks and returns and the explosion of investor interest in global investment opportunities merit special attention. Established and emerging global markets, global investing risks, multinational investment opportunities, and global mutual fund strategies are all examined.

Finally, this text turns its attention to the fascinating world of financial derivatives and their markets. In Chapter 17, "Options Markets and Strategies," the development of options markets, options concepts, and trading methods are explored. Theoretical foundations of options pricing, notably the Black-Scholes Option Pricing Model, are also investigated as useful means for options pricing. Chapter 18, "Futures Markets," traces the development of financial derivative markets for agricultural commodities, natural resources, and financial instruments. Common economic features of financial derivatives, the law of one price, and the notions of hedging and speculation are also carefully evaluated. Again, the usefulness of theory as a guide to successful investment practice is emphasized.

Summary

- Whenever you calculate the **future value** of a present sum, you must consider the dollar amount of the investment, the rate of interest, the number of time periods, and the method of compounding. Using **present-value** analysis, the time-value-of-money concept is used to discount the value of future dollars back to their present-day equivalent.
- There are two popular methods of accounting for future growth, or **compound interest.** The most popular is once-a-year or **annual compounding.** The other is **continuous compounding.** With continuous compounding, more "interest on interest" is earned. The **Rule of 72** says to simply divide the number 72 by any

interest rate percentage. The result is the number of years that it takes to double your investment. For example, the number 9 divided into 72 equals 8, and it takes eight years at a 9% rate of return to double your investment.

- Under a **defined-benefit retirement plan,** employers promise employees a fixed retirement income of, say, 1% times the number of years served times the last year's salary. Under **defined-contribution retirement plans,** individual employees are paid a retirement income based on the total value accumulated in their retirement portfolio. When employees have defined-contribution retirement plans, they must accept responsibility for the management of their retirement assets.
- A **portfolio** is a diversified collection of stocks and bonds or other assets. Portfolio theory tells us that diversification has the potential to reduce anticipated risk for a given expected return.
- **Risk** and **expected return** are related. The price of higher expected return is greater anticipated risk. This means that if a low-risk U.S. Treasury bill yields 6% interest, bonds that yield more than 6% per year are, by definition, not Treasury bills.
- The **efficient market hypothesis** states that every security at every point in time is fairly priced. Prices are neither too low (undervalued) nor too high (overvalued).
- In terms of accounting information, the **return-on-equity** measure is the best available indicator of the firm's ability to profitably use operating and financial leverage. The return on equity is simply the ratio of net income divided by **stockholders' equity,** or book value per share.
- High-profit firms tend to earn lower rates of return over time as more and more capital is committed to the enterprise. At the same time, low-profit firms see their profit rate rise over time as investors redeploy funds to other more profitable uses. This recurring pattern, or tendency, of profit rates to return toward long-term industry and economy-wide averages is called **regression to the mean.**
- On a per-share basis, the **price/earnings ratio** is the company's stock price divided by earnings per share. A P/E of 20 means that the stock price is 20 times higher than each dollar of earnings per share. However, a P/E of 20 implies that the firm has five cents in earnings for each dollar of market value.
- In a rational pricing environment, investing in the stock market is a **fair game** in which the expected excess return for each security is zero. Taken literally, this means that every stock at every point in time is an equally good buy or sell.

Questions

1. Financial theory is useful because it is
   a. able to predict stock and bond prices.
   b. logical.
   c. mathematically rigorous.
   d. derived from economic principles.

2. A P/E of 20 implies that the firm has five cents in earnings for each dollar of
   a. stockholders' equity.
   b. book value.
   c. market value.
   d. sales.
3. Using annual compounding, the present value of $39,703 to be received in 16 years when a 9% rate of return can be earned on investment is
   a. $9,406.
   b. $10,000.
   c. $5,000.
   d. $157,633.
4. According to the efficient market hypothesis, outstanding stock market returns earned by an investment superstar cannot be due to
   a. luck.
   b. conventional wisdom.
   c. superior stock-picking skill.
   d. superior stock market timing ability.
5. Which among the following is *not* consistent with the regression to the mean concept?
   a. persistent rates of return on stockholders' equity that average 20% per year
   b. Over the long run, investing larger amounts of capital tends to drive down the rate of profit per dollar invested.
   c. Low-profit firms see their profit rate rise over time as investors redeploy funds to other more profitable uses.
   d. the normal rate of return concept
6. According to the "Rule of 72," a 9% rate of return will double your money in
   a. eight years.
   b. nine years.
   c. 27 years.
   d. 72 years.
7. At a 6% annual rate of return, an annuity of $10,000 per month has an investment cost of
   a. $120,000.
   b. $1 million.
   c. $2 million.
   d. $16.7 million.
8. Present value falls with
   a. an increase in the future sum.
   b. a decrease in the discount rate.

c. a decrease in the time horizon.

d. an increase in the interest rate.

9. When compared with a continuously compounded rate of return, an equivalent dollar profit can be earned with an annual compounded rate of return that is

a. higher.

b. lower.

c. the same.

d. none of these.

10. Over a 36-year period, an investment growing at 12% compounds to a final value that is

a. twice that of an investment growing at 6%.

b. four times that of an investment growing at 6%.

c. six times that of an investment growing at 6%.

d. 16 times that of an investment growing at 4%.

11. The annual rate of return earned on broad market measures of common stocks since World War II is roughly

a. 4%.

b. 12%.

c. 20%

d. 24%.

12. Over an extended investment horizon, a broadly diversified portfolio of high-grade bonds could be expected to yield an annual rate of interest on the order of

a. 3%.

b. 6%.

c. 9%.

d. 12%.

13. The annual difference between returns on broad measures of common stock returns and the average annual rate of return earned by mutual fund investors is roughly

a. 1%.

b. 3%.

c. 5%.

d. 9%.

14. Under a defined-benefit retirement plan, employees are promised

a. a fixed lump sum amount at retirement.

b. employer matching of employee retirement plan contributions.

c. a variable amount at retirement, depending on retirement plan performance.

d. a fixed retirement income.

15. Under a defined-contribution retirement plan, individual employees are paid a retirement income based on the
    a. number of years of service.
    b. employee's final year's salary and years of service.
    c. employee's retirement plan contributions.
    d. total value accumulated in their retirement portfolio.
16. Portfolio theory tells us that diversification has the potential to
    a. increase anticipated risk for a given expected return.
    b. reduce expected return for a given anticipated risk.
    c. reduce anticipated risk for a given expected return.
    d. reduce transaction costs.
17. A decline in the value of the firm caused by firm-specific risk might be caused by a
    a. decline in interest rates.
    b. rise in interest rates.
    c. drop in the overall market.
    d. failed new-product introduction.
18. Higher expected return is typically accompanied by
    a. lower volatility.
    b. leverage.
    c. greater volatility.
    d. drop in interest rates.
19. The efficient market hypothesis is consistent with the notion that
    a. every security is *always* fairly priced.
    b. the average professional investor will underperform the market before expenses.
    c. some securities are overvalued.
    d. some securities are undervalued.
20. The return on equity
    a. measures long-term stock market rates of return.
    b. falls with a rise in financial leverage.
    c. is the ratio of net income divided by book value per share.
    d. rises with a decline in operating leverage.

Investment Application

How Much Does a Million Dollars Cost?

Have you ever watched a state-run lottery commercial on television and thought about winning? I'll bet you have. Most of us do. If you have daydreamed about winning the lottery or inheriting a fortune, how much did you have in mind? How much money would you have to win or inherit to qualify as rich? Take a minute. Write down in the margin on the left the minimum amount that you would have to win in the lottery to consider yourself rich. Also write down the minimum annual income you would need to consider yourself rich. Then, let's look at some numbers.

According to the most recent (1997) data available from *The Statistical Abstract of the United States,* per-capita income in the United States is $25,598. Income before taxes for the median (or the "middle") household is $35,492, and $29,312 after taxes. There are presently about 101 million households in the United States. Roughly 16.4% earn household income before taxes of $75,000 per year. Of these, 8.2 million report household income in excess of $100,000 per year. Incomes run highest in family households with a married couple. Among 70.2 million family households, median income is $43,082, 20.7% report family income greater than $75,000 per year, and 10.4% report family income in excess of $100,000 per year. The cutoff point for the top 5% of U.S. families according to income before taxes is $128,000 per year.

All these numbers relate to income, not to wealth. What does the distribution of wealth look like? The numbers may surprise you. For all families, the median level of wealth is only $55,600. This includes financial and nonfinancial assets, like homes and cars, and adjusts for debt, like mortgages. Among families earning between $50,000 and $100,000 per year, median net worth is $121,100. Among the few families earning in excess of $100,000 per year, median net worth is $482,000, or less than five times annual gross income. It is perhaps surprising that high-income families accumulate relatively modest amounts of wealth. When a politician cries out that the time has come to tax the rich, she or he is describing a family that often includes two wage earners with a combined income of roughly $100,000, and a net worth of less than one-half of a million dollars.

Now, let's get back to the minimum amount of wealth you consider necessary to qualify as rich. Is it more than $500,000? If so, fewer than one in 20 families in the United States command such a level of wealth. Similarly, if an income in excess of $128,000 per year is required before you would consider yourself rich, then only one in 20 families would enjoy a similar level of income in the United States. If the amount of wealth required exceeds $1 million or the amount of income necessary exceeds $250,000, then you are well into the very narrow end of the wealth and income distribution in the overall population. For argument's sake, let's assume that $1 million is the amount of money required to become rich. Although some might have a higher number in mind, none of us would have much sympathy for a "poor millionaire."

Within the field of investments, there are some difficult issues that must be dealt with. However, there are a number of interesting simple issues as well. One of the easiest questions one might ask is, How much does a million dollars cost? However, the answer is not as simple as one might suspect.

As shown in Table 1.6, the "cost" of $1 million depends on two factors: what type of investment is chosen and the length of the investment horizon. In this table, conservative assumptions are made regarding the expected rates of return on common stocks, bonds, and money market securities. Although equities have jumped sharply during the past few years, the century-long average rate of return on common stocks is near 10% per year, with a 50/50 split between capital gains and dividend income. Similarly, long-term investors have long been able to earn roughly 5% per year on bonds and 4% per year on money market securities. Against an inflation rate of 4% per year, the after-inflation or real return on stocks can be expected to average 6% per year. The real return on long-term bonds is liable to

TABLE 1.6 After Taxes, How Much Does $1 Million Cost?

	Common Stocks (10%, 6% real)	
How Long Is My Investment Horizon (in Years)?	**Future Dollars Growing @ 7.5%**	**Current Dollars Growing @ 3.5%**
1	$930,233	$966,184
2	865,333	933,511
3	804,961	901,943
4	748,801	871,442
5	696,559	841,973
6	647,962	813,501
7	602,755	785,991
8	560,702	759,412
9	521,583	733,731
10	485,194	708,919
11	451,343	684,946
12	419,854	661,783
13	390,562	639,404
14	363,313	617,782
15	337,966	596,891
20	235,413	502,566
25	163,979	423,147
30	114,221	356,278
35	79,562	299,977
40	55,419	252,572
45	38,603	212,659
50	26,889	179,053
55	18,730	150,758
60	13,046	126,934
65	9,088	106,875

Based on the assumption of a 50/50 split between capital gains and dividends, with one-half of capital gains realized per year. Also assume an income tax rate of 40% plus a capital gains tax rate of 20%. Given these assumptions, for example, the expected net after-tax rate of return on common stock is 7.5% [= 2.5% + 0.8(2.5%) + 0.6(5%)].

average on the order of 1%, and money market returns are apt to offer no more than a recovery of the cost of inflation. It seems safe to assume a state plus federal income tax rate of 40% and a state plus federal capital gains tax rate of 20%. Remember, any capital gains or interest income comes on top of salary and wages income and will be taxed at the investor's highest marginal tax rate. Of course, all bond and money market interest income is fully taxable, but there is some potential for deferred taxes in the case of common stock investments. Based on the assumption of a 50/50 split between capital gains and dividends, with one-half of capital gains realized per year, the expected net after-tax rate of return on common stock is 7.5% [= 2.5% + 0.8(2.5%) + 0.6(5%)].

As shown in Table 1.6, an investment of $9,088 in a broadly diversified portfolio of common stocks has the ready potential to grow to $1 million over a 65-year period. In real terms, an investment of $106,875 in a broadly diversified portfolio of common stocks has the ready potential to accumulate to $1 million over a 65-year period. Although this is a relevant investment period for a new baby, the rest of us need to plan for a somewhat earlier retirement. Over 30 years, $114,221 should do the trick in nominal terms, and $356,278 is required to produce $1 million in real terms.

TABLE 1.6 ***(continued)***

30-Year Government Bonds (5%, 1% real)		T-Bills and Money Market Funds (4%, 0% real)	
Future Dollars Growing @ 3%	**Current Dollars Decaying @ −1%**	**Future Dollars Growing @ 2.4%**	**Current Dollars Decaying @ −1.6%**
$970,874	$1,010,101	$976,563	$1,016,260
942,596	1,020,304	953,674	1,032,785
915,142	1,030,610	931,323	1,049,578
888,487	1,041,020	909,495	1,066,644
862,609	1,051,536	888,178	1,083,988
837,484	1,062,157	867,362	1,101,614
813,092	1,072,886	847,033	1,119,526
789,409	1,083,723	827,181	1,137,730
766,417	1,094,670	807,794	1,156,230
744,094	1,105,727	788,861	1,175,030
722,421	1,116,896	770,372	1,194,136
701,380	1,128,178	752,316	1,213,553
680,951	1,139,574	734,684	1,233,286
661,118	1,151,085	717,465	1,253,339
641,862	1,162,712	700,649	1,273,719
553,676	1,222,633	622,302	1,380,696
477,606	1,285,642	552,715	1,496,658
411,987	1,351,899	490,909	1,622,359
355,383	1,421,570	436,015	1,758,618
306,557	1,494,831	387,259	1,906,321
264,439	1,571,869	343,955	2,066,429
228,107	1,652,876	305,494	2,239,985
196,767	1,738,058	271,333	2,428,117
169,733	1,827,630	240,992	2,632,050
146,413	1,921,818	214,044	2,853,111

To see the problem with investing in bonds or money market funds for retirement, notice the devastating effects of taxation and inflation on the long-term value of bond and money market portfolios. With 65 years to go, an investor needs to invest in excess of $1.9 million to generate a $1-million bond portfolio. With 65 years to invest, a $1-million money market portfolio has a "cost" of more than $2.8 million. Over extended periods of time, taxes and inflation simply devastate the value of fixed-income securities.

A. Use the data in Table 1.6 to show how much income per year could be generated after taxes and after inflation from a $1-million portfolio invested in common stocks. In other words, what is the income equivalent to a net worth of $1 million?

B. Why do so few individuals accumulate a significant amount of retirement wealth? Will you? If so, use the data in Table 1.6 to show how.

Selected References

Bernardo, Antonio E., and Kenneth L. Judd. "Asset Market Equilibrium with General Tastes, Returns, and Informational Asymmetries." *Journal of Financial Markets* 3 (February 2000): 17–43.

Bessembinder, Hendrik. "Trade Execution Costs on NASDAQ and the NYSE: A Post-Reform Comparison." *Journal of Financial and Quantitative Analysis* 34 (September 1999): 387–407.

Chakravarty, Sugato, and John J. McConnell. "Does Insider Trading Really Move Stock Prices?" *Journal of Financial and Quantitative Analysis* 34 (June 1999): 191–209.

Davis, James L., Eugene F. Fama, and Kenneth R. French. "Characteristics, Covariances, and Average Returns: 1929 to 1997." *Journal of Finance* 55 (February 2000): 389–406.

Dobson, John. "Is Shareholder Wealth Maximization Immoral?" *Financial Analysts Journal* 55 (September/October 1999): 69–75.

Docking, Diane Scott, Mark Hirschey, and Elaine Jones. "Information and Contagion Effects of Bank Loan-Loss Reserve Announcements." *Journal of Financial Economics* 43 (February 1997): 219–239.

Fama, Eugene F., and Kenneth R. French. "The Corporate Cost of Capital and the Return on Corporate Investment." *Journal of Finance* 54 (December 1999): 1939–1967.

Freund, Steven, and Gwendolyn P. Webb. "Recent Growth in Nasdaq Trading Volume and its Relation to Market Volatility." *Journal of Financial Research* 22 (Winter 1999): 489–501.

Gillan, Stuart L., John W. Kensinger, and John D. Martin. "Value Creation and Corporate Diversification: The Case of Sears, Roebuck & Co." *Journal of Financial Economics* 55 (January 2000): 103–137.

Guay, Wayne R. "The Sensitivity of CEO Wealth to Equity Risk: An Analysis of the Magnitude and Determinants." *Journal of Financial Economics* 53 (July 1999): 43–71.

Himmelberg, Charles P., R. Glenn Hubbard, and Darius Palia. "Understanding the Determinants of Managerial Ownership and the Link between Ownership and Performance." *Journal of Financial Economics* 53 (September 1999): 353–384

Hirschey, Mark, Vernon J. Richardson, and Susan Scholz. "How 'Foolish' Are Internet Investors?" *Financial Analysts Journal* 56 (January/February 2000): 62–69.

Morris, Victor F. "A Traitor to His Class: Robert A. G. Monks and the Battle to Change Corporate America." *Financial Analysts Journal* 55 (September/October 1999): 90–91

Song, Moon H., and Ralph A. Walking. "Abnormal Returns to Rivals of Acquisition Targets: A Test of the Acquisition Probability Hypothesis." *Journal of Financial Economics* 55 (February 2000): 143–171.

Spirrison, Bradley. "VC-Backed IPOs Soar in Late Summer." *Venture Capital Journal* (November 1, 1999): 5, 14.

CHAPTER 2

Sources of Investment Information

The "Investment Dartboard" is one of The Wall Street Journal's *most popular features. Each "contest" pits the best stock tips from a handful of Wall Street pros against the market averages, and a handful of stocks randomly selected by dart-throwing journal staffers. Results are measured for capital gains or losses only, thus omitting dividends, from the market close on the day before publication of the story announcing the contest through the end of the sixth month. Participants pick only one stock to buy or sell (short). To rule out thinly traded and highly volatile "penny stocks" selling for less than $1, the minimum market price is $2, both at time of selection and when the contest begins. Minimum market capitalization is $50 million, and average daily trading volume must be $100,000 or more. Each stock must be listed on the New York Stock Exchange, the American Stock Exchange, or the Nasdaq Stock Market.*

There is no prize—just the glory, or the embarrassment, of publicly pitting your stock-picking skills against the investment professionals and the forces of chance. Still, stock-picking notoriety in the dartboard contest might lead to future business, and giant Wall Street egos always like a challenge. Unfortunately, contest results, reported on a regular basis, tend to bruise those giant egos. Wall Street pros often underperform the market averages and a handful of randomly selected stocks.

The fact that Wall Street professionals fail to consistently beat the market serves as a warning to novice and experienced investors alike. Be aware that the best and most well intentioned Wall Street information and advice offers no guarantee of market-beating results![1]

Ways of Wall Street

Caveat Emptor!

More than 50 years ago, a man by the name of Fred Schwed wrote a fascinating little book about Wall Street, titled *Where Are the Customers' Yachts?* The book took its title from a sinister old gag that said, "Once in the dear dead days beyond recall,

[1]See Georgette Jansen, "Darts Get Smart, Picking Tech and Trouncing Professionals," *The Wall Street Journal,* March 9, 2000, C1, C14.

an out-of-town visitor was being shown the wonders of the New York financial district. When the party arrived at the Battery, one of his guides indicated some handsome ships anchored in the harbor. He said, 'Look, those are the bankers' and brokers' yachts.' 'Where are the customers' yachts?' asked the naive visitor."[2]

Where Are the Customers' Yachts? has a playful way of making a serious point. When it comes to money, it is best to remember the age-old axiom: *Caveat emptor!* Buyer beware. Whenever an investor reads a table-pounding buy recommendation, it is best to assume that the author has some stocks or bonds to sell. Similarly, whenever an investor hears a frantic sell recommendation, it is best to assume that the commentator is looking to buy at a lower price. Neither the advice nor the wisdom on Wall Street is free.

When today's investor thinks about the stock market, the context is apt to be the recent market experience of the 1980s and 1990s. Recent experience gives investors a useful context with which to form return expectations for stocks and bonds in the 21st century. However, it's useful to keep in mind that the most bullish U.S. stock market environment of this century did not occur during the 1980s and 1990s. It was during the 1950s. Schwed's book, first written in 1940 and revised in 1955, had relevance then as it does today. The late 1940s and 1950s saw an amazing boom in the stock market, as the peacetime economy geared up to satisfy pent-up consumer demand for new cars, homes, household goods, and other consumer products.

Wall Street is a real place with real people. At the corner of Wall Street and Broad Street in New York City, in the borough of Manhattan, lies a building that houses the New York Stock Exchange (NYSE). It is the heart of the financial district for the United States and for the world. Wall Street, as pundits are often happy to note, is a street with a river at one end and a graveyard at the other. In fact, this is true. Wall Street is bounded at one end by the Hudson River and at the other extreme by Trinity Church, which has a courtyard graveyard. However, Schwed describes the typical description of Wall Street as incomplete: He says it omits the kindergarten in the middle.

When one considers recent investor enthusiasm for Internet stocks and anything "dot.com," it's easy to guess what Schwed might have to say about the sophistication of present-day investors. In the eyes of many knowledgeable investors, the vast potential of the Internet is for real. In 1999, however, Internet stock prices were out of this world.

Wall Street Has a Language of Its Own

Just as consumers need to become Internet savvy to become efficient in the 21st century, so too do investors need to become Internet savvy to gain the full advantage of the information potential of this new and exciting medium. A good place to start is to simply get up to speed on Internet terms and terminology with any one of a number of glossaries of Internet terms. For example, you might want to consult one offered by Matisse Enzer (<http://www.matisse.net/files/glossary.html>).

Do you know what ADSL is? ADSL is an acronym. It stands for asymmetric digital subscriber line. This is a method for moving data over regular phone lines. An ADSL circuit is much faster than a regular phone connection, and the wires

---

[2] Fred Schwed, Jr., *Where Are the Customers' Yachts?* (Simon & Schuster, New York, 1940), 7.

coming into the subscriber's premises, either an office or a home, are the same copper wires used for regular phone service. An ADSL circuit must be configured to connect two specific locations. It's similar to a leased line. ADSL is a term that we are apt to hear much more about in the years ahead. It is one of the hundreds of Internet terms that can be better understood by consulting Matisse's glossary.

In a similar way, it's important not to get stumped by investments jargon. Table 2.1 gives addresses for a number of top financial and investing glossaries available on the Internet. The financial glossary provided by SiliconInvestor is a top choice (see <http://www.siliconinvestor.com/misc/glossary/alist.html>), but all such glossaries can help investors get over the language barrier that separates newcomers from experienced pros on Wall Street. For example, when you think of *Head & Shoulders,* do you think of a leading dandruff shampoo produced by Cincinnati-based and Dow Jones Industrial Average–component Procter & Gamble Company? If so, you are just not up to speed with one of the most famous terms used by **chartists,** or **technicians.** Chartists, or technicians, are Wall Street analysts who use price and volume graphs to study historical changes in the demand and supply conditions for stocks in the hope that they might develop successful trading rules to capitalize on expected changes. In technical analysis, a chart formation is called a **head and shoulders** when a stock price reaches a peak and declines, rises above its former peak and again declines, rises again but not to the second peak, and then again declines. The first and third peaks are shoulders, while the second peak is the formation's head. Technical analysts generally consider a head and shoulders formation to be a very bearish indication. Head and shoulders and other "classic" trading patterns are institutional aspects of what makes Wall Street interesting.

chartist
Analyst who picks stocks based on the pattern of past price and volume data.

technician
Chartist.

head and shoulders
Chart formation that resembles an upper torso.

TABLE 2.1 Top Financial and Investing Glossaries on the Internet

Stumped by investments jargon? Check out these financial and investing glossaries on the Internet.

Web Site	Internet Address[a]
CBS MarketWatch Financial Glossary	cbs.marketwatch.com/data/glossary.htx
CNNfn Glossary of Business Terms	www.cnnfn.com/resources/glossary
Equity Analytics, Ltd., Directory of Financial Glossaries	www.e-analytics.com/glossdir.htm
Glossary of Technical Analysis Terms	centrex.com/indicate.html
Glossary of Financial and Trading Terms	centrex.com/terms.html
Homeowners Finance Real Estate Dictionary	www.homeowners.com/dictionary.html
SiliconInvestor Glossary	www.siliconinvestor.com/misc/glossary/alist.html
Wall Street Directory Glossary	www.wsdinc.com/pgs_idx/w_indi.shtml
The washingtonpost.com Business Glossary	www.washingtonpost.com/wp-srv/business/longterm/glossary/glossary.htm
Web Investors' Dictionary	www.webinvestors.com/dict.html

[a]Internet addresses are sometimes referred to as the URL, or uniform resource locator, address. Be sure to use the http:// prefix for each URL.

WALL STREET WISDOM 2.1

Why Does Campbell's Soup Have a Web Site?

Relationship marketing is one of the most important concepts in business. The idea is to develop a long-term relationship with the consumer. Firms want to capture a customer, more than just snare a single sales transaction.

How do you attract and retain customers? Better still, how do you attract and retain the most profitable customers? Successful companies know they must get close to the customer to better serve and anticipate product and service needs. Attracting and retaining valued customers is more than just delivering high-quality products. It involves developing a long-term relationship with customers. In some ways, it's like running your business the way the old-fashioned grocer did in the 19th century. To know them is to serve them better.

A good example of relationship marketing is provided by General Motor's (GM) Saturn Division. Over the years, Saturn has prided itself on the notion that it not only manufactures a superior automotive product, it provides superior service after the sale as well. Part of this superior service involves better listening to its customers and responding to their suggestions. During early summer, for example, thousands of Saturn owners typically respond to the company's invitation to attend a three-day picnic at company headquarters in Spring Hill, Tennessee. Not only is it a way to thank owners for their business, it is a proven means of building customer loyalty.

With the powers of the Internet, the potential for relationship marketing has never been better. Mail-order merchants Cabela's, L. L. Bean, and Lands' End, among others, have spent millions of dollars developing computer capabilities to better track and anticipate customer needs. In the past, Cabela's customers who ordered camping equipment and hiking boots were good candidates for the company's camping and outdoor gear catalog. Lands' End customers who ordered chinos also received specialized catalogs featuring discounts on casual attire.

In the not-too-distant future, all this is about to change by virtue of the Internet. Suppose you are a real fan of the styles and prices offered by Eddie Bauer. If you buy your goods at <http://www.eddiebauer.com>, you are doing Spiegel, Inc., owners of Eddie Bauer, a multitude of favors. Obviously, customers cut the company's catalog printing, mailing, and labor costs by shopping online rather than using one of their catalogs or mall stores. By keying in order information, online customers also create an electronic database that identifies relevant price points, style, and seasonal preferences. This makes it possible for Spiegel to send low-cost e-mail messages to regular customers when new styles are introduced or when items bought some time ago are apt to have worn out. Online commerce makes it possible for Spiegel to offer its products at "special" prices that might vary from one customer to another. Style-conscious customers can be set up to receive individualized notices of new full-price products, while cost-conscious bargain hunters might be among the first to hear about discounts on overstocked items.

Internet-based relationship marketing has much more potential for some products than with others, obviously. Clothing is an example of the high-margin, repeat-customer product that is ideally suited for this type of product promotion. Niche markets, like high-quality wine or distinctive "microbrew" beer, are also obvious possibilities. Another obvious choice includes financial services, such as mutual funds, checking accounts, and life, car, and home insurance. At parcel delivery giant FedEx, *customers* track package locations using the Internet, thus improving customer satisfaction and cutting costs.

All this leads to a simple question: Why in the world does Campbell's Soup have a Web site (<http://www.campbellssoup.com>)? While a "soup club" seems like a stretch, the "Creative Kitchen" gives simple homemade dinner ideas, recipes, and nutrition information. Then there is the "Online Shop," where you can buy distinctive gifts and Campbell "collectibles." Both help Campbell's connect with customers. Just as important, Campbell's uses the Internet to effectively communicate with suppliers about order plans, inventory stockouts, and so on.

In all kinds of businesses, the Internet is cutting costs and boosting revenues.

See: <http://www.campbellsoup.com>.

It is important to note, however, that there is no significant historical evidence to suggest that technical analysis like that implied by head and shoulders trading patterns can lead to above-average profits over time. It is interesting, sometimes extremely interesting, to look at the day-to-day movement of stock prices. What is unfortunate is that many investors realize only too late that you can't count on past patterns of price and volume data to indicate the future. No one drives down the freeway by focusing on the rearview mirror. At 70 miles per hour, you'd better look through the windshield.

Internet Revolution

The Internet Is for Real

The potential of the Internet as an information resource and mode of communication is undeniable. Some analysts argue the Internet has the potential to become more important than the printing press, arguably the most important invention in communications technology prior to the Internet. While the printing press made widespread dissemination of information easy and inexpensive, it is a one-way method of communicating from the printer to the general public. The Internet is a two-way method of communication that is even cheaper than the printed form. It is the potential for feedback from one investor to another, or from one consumer to another, that makes the Internet a unique communications tool.

For the first time, the Internet gives investors and consumers in New York City, in Jackson, Wyoming, and in the wilds of Africa, the same timely access to widely publicized company financial news and information. With the Internet, up-to-the-minute global news and analysis are just mouse clicks away from large and small investors on a worldwide basis. The Internet also gives global consumers and investors the opportunity to communicate with one another and thereby *create* fresh news and information. Over the Internet, customers can communicate with investors about pricing or product quality concerns. Similarly, investors can communicate with customers about the threat posed by potential competitors. In a sense, the Internet makes the production of financial news and information somewhat more democratic by reducing the information-gathering advantages of traditional print and broadcast media.

With the Internet, large and small investors are also able to give and receive up-to-the-minute commentary and analysis concerning the investment implications of company news and information. Message boards and "chat rooms" give investors the opportunity to trade anonymous tips and information about specific companies. Unfortunately, too many tech-savvy investors have too little experience with calculating expected rates of return or determining economic factors that shape a firm's ability to generate sustainable profits and attractive long-term rates of return. As a result, the Internet has proved a fertile space for stock price manipulation and securities fraud.

The Internet Is Revolutionary

Years ago, the personal computer was introduced as a marvelously effective computing device and document processor. It still is. Investors who want to create spreadsheets to manipulate operating data can do so easily and quickly. Similarly, anyone who wants to create eye-catching documents can do so with inexpensive and easy-to-use PC software.

To appreciate the awesome potential of the Internet, consider what has already been accomplished by the "old-fashioned" medium of television. Just after the Berlin Wall came tumbling down in November 1989, I traveled to Berlin to participate in an academic conference. At every opportunity, I asked local residents what had changed at that particular point in history to cause the Berlin Wall to come down. Like millions, I was fascinated by the fact that the Berlin Wall had indeed been demolished, thus reuniting Germany. But why had these momentous changes occurred in 1989? Why did the Berlin Wall come down during November of 1989 instead of, say, during 1961 and the Berlin blockade? Why didn't the Soviet Bloc crack in the 1950s when Hungary and Yugoslavia were in ferment?

That the communistic system was flawed as an economic and political model is now obvious to everyone. It placed an extraordinary burden on the citizens of the former Soviet Union and Eastern Bloc countries. The economic inefficiency of communism resulted in an extremely low standard of living for millions of hard-working and talented people. The fact that communism was grossly inefficient explains its downfall. However, long-apparent economic inefficiency doesn't explain why the downfall of communism, punctuated by the fall of the Berlin Wall in November 1989, took place at that point in history.

In dozens of instances, I heard a startling answer to a simple but important question: "Why did the Berlin Wall come down in November 1989? "It was CNN," was the common refrain. "CNN?" I asked. "You mean the news on CNN couldn't be kept from the people anymore?" "Oh no, it wasn't the news on CNN, it was the commercials." Apparently, before CNN became widely popular around the globe, millions of people under Communist rule had no idea of the level of consumption and the quality of life enjoyed by people in the Western world. Once CNN broadcast advertisements showing the wonderful variety of consumer goods and services available in the West, the secret was out and communism was doomed.

Of course, CNN was not the sole cause of the fall of communism. The important role played by political and religious leaders and other factors should not be minimized. Still, it is worth noting the important role played by communications technology in the downfall of communism.

What does this have to do with the Internet? Everything. With the Internet, not just consumer news and information is a mouse click away, but the ability to communicate attitudes, impressions, and ideas has been spread around the globe. The Internet is truly the enemy of despots and dictators. Not just consumer news and information are a mouse click away. The ability to communicate attitudes, impressions, and ideas has been spread around the globe.

Internet Commerce

From a business perspective, the Internet is the enemy of high prices and high profit margins. For example, in the pre-Internet era, anyone looking for a good deal on a high-quality vacuum cleaner might go to Wal-Mart to look for the best bargain available. Alternatively, a shopper might have gone to a specialty shop that has a variety of high-quality vacuums and seek out the best value for the money. Those options still exist. With the Internet, a third alternative is now available. In large and small towns everywhere, if you want to buy a vacuum cleaner you can jump on the Internet, do a search on vacuum cleaners, and get information on hundreds of different wholesalers that are willing to sell high-quality vacuums at extremely attractive prices. Even with a few dollars for Federal Express or UPS delivery, it's possible to have vacuums delivered in Lawrence, Kansas, from <http://www.vacdepot.com/> in Houston, Texas, for example, at prices far below those offered by the local vacuum cleaner shop. Of course, specialty shops that offer vacuum cleaners, wine and spirits, or designer clothing will not stand idly by as Internet-based retailers drive them out of business.

Catalog retailers, like Lands' End, Spiegel, or Eddie Bauer, are obvious near-term beneficiaries of the Internet, as they sell their goods on the Web rather than by printing expensive catalogs that need to be mailed out to widely dispersed consumers. It is important to keep in mind when considering the investment potential of Internet-based commerce that successful firms must maintain significant competitive advantages. The Internet, by itself, is a tool for the consumer to improve his or her access to information about product quality, prices, and performance. In the same way, the Internet is a tool that companies can use to reduce prices, to get closer to the customer, and to find out how to better meet and exceed customer needs and aspirations.

Investment Information on the Internet

Stock Quotes and Financial Information

Why do you log onto the Internet? Studies show that national and international news, information gathering on specific topics, and entertainment are prime attractions that bring people to the Internet. Information about the weather is big on the Internet. A second big interest is financial news and information. **Stock quotes,** for example, in **real time** are often sought by investors several times during the trading day. When it comes to financial news and information, the Internet is an awesome tool.

stock quotes
Share prices.

real time
Up to the minute, current.

Table 2.2 shows a number of leading Web sites for investment information. <http://cbs.marketwatch.com>, for example, is among the best at focused financial news and information. This Web site has excellent stock price and volume information and pertinent financial data on individual companies, industries, and the overall economy. Late-breaking news tied to individual companies is offered on a real-time basis. This gives today's individual investors more detailed and more timely information than Wall Street professionals enjoyed until recently. Another terrific financial information Web site on the Internet is <http://www.dailystocks.com>. This is a super Web site for quotes, charts, news, Securities and Exchange Commission (SEC) filings, stock research reports, earnings estimates, magazine articles, and fundamentals. Shown in Figure 2.1, dailystocks.com is a big favorite for up-to-the-minute news and analysis of individual firms.

EDGAR
Electronic retrieval analysis system for SEC filings.

The best free Web site for government reports filed by individual companies is called **EDGAR** (<http://www.edgar-online.com>). Experienced investors know

ticker symbol Unique one-, two-, three-, or four-letter code for any company.

10Q Quarterly accounting information filed with the SEC.

10K Annual accounting information filed with the SEC.

proxy statement Annual meeting announcement and shareholder voting information.

that if you want complete details about SEC reports for an individual company, all you have to do is ask EDGAR. EDGAR is an acronym for Electronic Retrieval Analysis System for SEC filings. It is a for-profit company that specializes in providing investor access to SEC reports and filings. For example if you want the latest quarterly report on Microsoft Corporation, go to the EDGAR Web site and key in MSFT, which is the four-letter **ticker symbol** for Microsoft. EDGAR will provide a plain text report of Microsoft's most recent quarterly accounting earnings information, or the Schedule **10Q report.** Other important bits of information available on EDGAR include the firm's Schedule **10K report,** or annual financial report, and the company's Schedule 14A or **proxy statement,** or annual meeting announcement. The annual meeting announcement is a very interesting document because it includes information about who are members of top management, the boards of directors, and other large investors in the firm. The proxy statement also tells how much company stock is owned by management and the board of directors.

TABLE 2.2 Where to Look for Investments Information on the Internet

Widespread uses of the Internet are for e-mail and messaging, information search, online commerce (shopping), and chat. Check out these Internet sites to see why perhaps the most popular use of the medium is investments analysis.

Web Site	Internet Address[a]	Description
Briefing.com	www.briefing.com	Concise analysis of important events affecting stocks and bonds.
CBS MarketWatch	cbs.marketwatch.com	Among the best at focused financial news and information, excellent stock charting.
CNNfn	www.cnnfn.com	Exhaustive coverage of top stories, markets, small business, world business, industry trends, etc.
DailyStocks	www.dailystocks.net	A super Web site for quotes, charts, news, SEC filings, research reports, earnings estimates, magazine articles, fundamentals, and more. Check it out!
EDGAR Online	www.edgar-online.com	Electronic retrieval and analysis of company SEC filings.
freerealtime.com	www.freerealtime.com	Real-time stock quotes, news, and information at the right price—free!
Investorama	www.investorama.com	Full-featured versions of some of today's best investing and personal finance software—free!
MSN MoneyCentral	www.moneycentral.com	Investing highlights for customized portfolios, market reports, mutual fund directory, retirement and wills, taxes, real estate, smart buying, insurance, etc.
Morningstar.com	www.morningstar.com	Comprehensive mutual fund commentary and analysis.
Yahoo!	quote.yahoo.com	A terrific Web site with U.S. markets, world markets, quotes, financial news, message boards, chat, etc. Organize your news (life) with my.yahoo.com.

[a]Be sure to use the http:// prefix for each URL.

FIGURE 2.1 **DailyStocks.com Gives Investors a Wealth of Market and Financial Information**

DailyStocks.com! - The web's first and biggest stock research site! Press Ctrl-D & Bookmark Now!
Home-Markets-Today's EPS-Screening-Quotes-StockSheet-Directory-Funds-Canada-Options-Compare-Top 20

What is Stock Gigablast Research?
Fund or Stock Symbol: [ ] Quotes ?
Go Lookup

NEW! To be notified of future updates, Enter your email
Your email Add

You can enter multiple symbols for Gigablast research. Choose 'Classic Research' for classic layout.
Click Here for old homepage.

FREE! DailyStocks Recommend s 2 Weeks of Investor's Business Daily, and find out how some people make 200% a year!

Navigation Bar: Calendars | Columns | Earnings | EDGAR Filings | Filters | Futures | Insiders | IPOs | Market Commentary | Market Numbers | Miscellaneous | Mutual Funds | News Headlines | SEC Filings | Stock Screens | Stock Splits | Tech Stocks | Upgrades/Downgrades | U.S. Economy |

Market Numbers

RealTm Indices
Major Indices
Active/Winners/Losers(NYSE)
Active/Winners/Losers(AMEX)
Active/Winners/Losers(NASDAQ)
Active/Winners/Losers(also!)
New Hi/Lows
New Hi/Lows(closing) new
Volume Alerts
Price Gap Alerts NEW!
Breadth Indicators
Winners and Losers NEW!
Widely Held NEW!
Dow Jones Indu. Avg.™
S&P 500
S&P's Market Snapshot new
Mutual Funds
Industry Groups
Industry Indices
Options
Short Interest NEW!
BigCharts
1-m Chart D | N | SP
S&P's World Equity Watch new
World Indices(current)
Global Indices(DBC)
Global Stocks(DBC)
SE Asia Currencies(DBC)
Digest Graphs
S&P's Commodities new
More Details...

Market Commentary

S&P's Daily Commentary new
Market Commentary Links NEW!
Bloomberg Movers NEW!
Bloomberg Movers
WallStreetCity
ABCNews/TheStreet
ABS Live
TheStreet
DBC Snapshot
DBC Stock Movers
Stock Watch
Fool News
Briefing Comments
Briefing Story Stocks
Indiv. Investor
Before the Bell NEW!
Prudential Sec.
MSN
MoneyBR
MoneyDaily
S&P's Equity Insight new
S&P Snapshot new
S&P's Stock of the Week new

S&P'sStock Picks and Pans new
S&P MarketMovers new
S&P's MarketViews new
S&P's Word on the Street new
Stocks to Watch NEW!
Bloomberg Preview
SmartMoney
S&P's Credit Week Focus new
S&P's Economic Insight new
S&P's Sector Scorecard new
S&P's Global Market Focus new
S&P's Treasury Mkt Watch new
S&P Technical Market Insight new
S&P's Wealth for Women new
NBR
WSJ Highlight
AmExpress (RelStrength,Lo-Hi P/E)
After the Bell NEW!
dljpreopening
dlj afterhours
dlj mergers/acquistions
More Details...

News Headlines

Biz Headlines
Financial News Links NEW!
Bloomberg's Top News
Business Wire
CBS MarketWatch
CNNfn
Excite's Investment News
Federal Filings News
Industry News
International News
IPO News
PR Newswire
Securites Firms News
Standard & Poor's
StockSmart Internet News
Today's SEC Filings
Yahoo! US Markets

Calendar

S&P's Econ. Calendar new
DailyStocks Today
Economic Calendar Links NEW!
Earnings Calendars NEW!
Investment Net Events
Earnings(rolling 6 days)
Earnings(this Week)
Tech Earnings(1 mo)
Stock Splits Calendars
Upcoming Stock Splits
Recent Stock Splits
Stock Buybacks
Econ. data this week
Econ. data this month

Earnings

CBS EarningsWire
CBS Surprises
DailyStocks Surprises
FirstCall DJIA's EPS
FirstCall S&P Scoreboard
FirstCall EPS Surprises
FirstCall Upcoming EPS
FirstCall Revisions
I/B/E/S
MSN Investor
Yahoo
Zacks EPS Surprises
BigCharts EPS(N)
BigCharts EPS(A)
BigCharts EPS(Q)
MF Conference Calls
MF Falling Margins
MF Rising Margins
MF Beat Estimates
MF Missed Estimates

(continued)

FIGURE 2.1 ***(continued)***

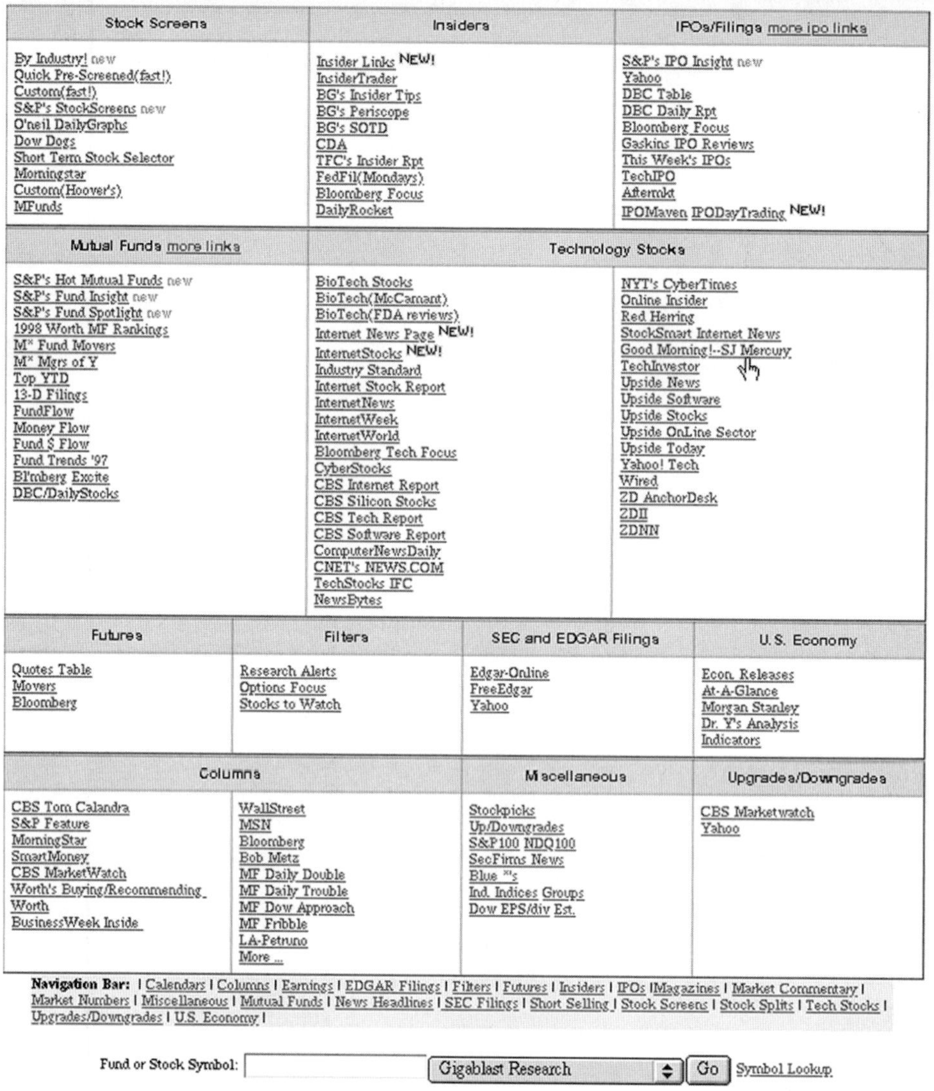

Stock Screens	Insiders	IPOs/Filings more ipo links
By Industry! new Quick Pre-Screened(fast!) Custom(fast!) S&P's StockScreens new O'neil DailyGraphs Dow Dogs Short Term Stock Selector Morningstar Custom(Hoover's) MFunds	Insider Links NEW! InsiderTrader BG's Insider Tips BG's Periscope BG's SOTD CDA TFC's Insider Rpt FedFil(Mondays) Bloomberg Focus DailyRocket	S&P's IPO Insight new Yahoo DBC Table DBC Daily Rpt Bloomberg Focus Gaskins IPO Reviews This Week's IPOs TechIPO Aftermkt IPOMaven IPODayTrading NEW!

Mutual Funds more links	Technology Stocks	
S&P's Hot Mutual Funds new S&P's Fund Insight new S&P's Fund Spotlight new 1998 Worth MF Rankings M* Fund Movers M* Mgrs of Y Top YTD 13-D Filings FundFlow Money Flow Fund $ Flow Fund Trends '97 Bl'mberg Excite DBC/DailyStocks	BioTech Stocks BioTech(McCamant) BioTech(FDA reviews) Internet News Page NEW! InternetStocks NEW! Industry Standard Internet Stock Report InternetNews InternetWeek InternetWorld Bloomberg Tech Focus CyberStocks CBS Internet Report CBS Silicon Stocks CBS Tech Report CBS Software Report ComputerNewsDaily CNET's NEWS.COM TechStocks IFC NewsBytes	NYT's CyberTimes Online Insider Red Herring StockSmart Internet News Good Morning!--SJ Mercury TechInvestor Upside News Upside Software Upside Stocks Upside OnLine Sector Upside Today Yahoo! Tech Wired ZD AnchorDesk ZDII ZDNN

Futures	Filters	SEC and EDGAR Filings	U.S. Economy
Quotes Table Movers Bloomberg	Research Alerts Options Focus Stocks to Watch	Edgar-Online FreeEdgar Yahoo	Econ. Releases At-A-Glance Morgan Stanley Dr. Y's Analysis Indicators

Columns		Miscellaneous	Upgrades/Downgrades
CBS Tom Calandra S&P Feature MorningStar SmartMoney CBS MarketWatch Worth's Buying/Recommending Worth BusinessWeek Inside	WallStreet MSN Bloomberg Bob Metz MF Daily Double MF Daily Trouble MF Dow Approach MF Fribble LA-Petruno More ...	Stockpicks Up/Downgrades S&P100 NDQ100 SecFirms News Blue **'s Ind. Indices Groups Dow EPS/div Est.	CBS Marketwatch Yahoo

Navigation Bar: | Calendars | Columns | Earnings | EDGAR Filings | Filters | Futures | Insiders | IPOs |Magazines | Market Commentary | Market Numbers | Miscellaneous | Mutual Funds | News Headlines | SEC Filings | Short Selling | Stock Screens | Stock Splits | Tech Stocks | Upgrades/Downgrades | U.S. Economy |

Fund or Stock Symbol: [ ] Gigablast Research Go Symbol Lookup

Source: <http://dailystocks.com>.

13D
Filings made to the SEC within 10 days of an entity attaining a 5% or more position in any class of a company's securities.

Form 144
Filings submitted to the SEC by holders of restricted stock who intend to sell shares.

Schedule **13D** filings are made to the SEC within 10 days of an entity attaining a 5% or more position in any class of a company's securities. Any subsequent change in holdings or intentions must be reported on an amended filing (see Figure 2.2). SEC **Form 144** filings must be submitted by holders of restricted securities, sometimes called letter stock, who intend to sell shares. Note that 144 filings are only notices of intentions to sell shares. Sometimes, these shares aren't sold even though the owner has filed a Form 144 (see Figure 2.3). Small investors have easy access to this information on edgar.com and in leading financial publications such as *Barron's*.

FIGURE 2.2 **Schedule 13D Filings to the SEC Track Changes in Large Ownership Positions**

January 24, 2000 — BARRON'S • MARKET WEEK — MW11

13D FILINGS

INVESTORS REPORT TO THE SEC

13Ds are filed with the Securities and Exchange Commission within 10 days of an entity's attaining a 5% or more position in any class of a company's securities. Any subsequent change in holdings or intentions must be reported on an amended filing. This material has been extracted from filings released by the SEC between January 13 and 19.

Source: Federal Filings Business News, Washington

Activists

Lodgian (LOD)
▶ A group that includes **Casuarina Cayman Holdings** is requesting that Lodgian reconsider granting it access to customary due diligence information. The Casuarina group expressed dismay regarding Lodgian's "ongoing refusal" to cooperate with its request for internal documents and is no longer willing to offer $6.50 a share for the stock. The Casuarina group currently holds 3,091,800 shares (11.1% of the total outstanding).

Baldwin Piano & Organ (BPAO)
▶ **Bolero Investment Group** delivered a January 12 letter to Baldwin Piano, urging the sale of the company. The investment group contends that "Baldwin lacks the requisite sense of urgency in dealing with the challenges that have plagued the company," and the group proposes the company "immediately take the necessary steps to achieve [its] sale as promptly as possible on terms which will maximize shareholder value." The Bolero group currently holds 403,569 shares (11.7%).

Alterra Healthcare (ALI)
▶ A group that includes **AR Investments** has requested a meeting with an officer of Alterra to discuss areas of "potential mutual interest." The group currently holds 1,765,100 shares (8%).

New Filings

Amresco Capital Trust (AMCT)
▶ A group that includes **Farallon Capital** holds 542,100 shares (5.4%) after buying 257,100 shares from November 11, 1999, to January 7 at $8.23-$9.16 each. The group has no current plans or proposals but, consistent with its investment intent, might engage in talks with one or more Amresco shareholders.

Cylink (CYLK)
▶ Investors led by **LeRoy C. Kopp** own 6,013,570 shares (20.2%) after buying them from November 16, 1999, to January 14 at $9.69-$14.70 each.

Increases in Holdings

Larscom (LARS)
▶ A group led by **Kopp Investment Advisers** raised its stake to 2,297,000 shares (27.5%) when it purchased 150,000 shares January 13 and 14 at $10.51-$11.04 each.

Chart House Enterprises (CHT)
▶ A group that includes investor **Samuel Zell** increased its position to 3,517,629 shares (29.9%) after buying 110,300 shares from January 11 to 14 at $4.13-$4.98 apiece.

First Financial Fund (FF)
▶ A group led by investor **Stewart R. Horejsi** raised its stake to 3,742,200 shares (15.2%) after acquiring 417,100 shares from January 3 to 14 at $7.81-$8 a share.

Barringer Technologies (BARR)
▶ A group led by **Lionheart Group** increased its stake to 605,500 shares (8.8%) by buying 120,000 from December 9, 1999, to January 12 at $5.74-$6.44 per share.

CB Richard Ellis Services (CBG)
▶ A group headed by investor **Richard C. Blum** owns 3,275,810 shares (15.8%) after purchasing 1,677,800 shares January 4 and 5 at $11.38-$12 each.

Decreases in Holdings

Henley Healthcare (HENL)
▶ **Maxxim** reduced its ownership stake to 2,400,000 shares (32.8%) after selling 125,000 shares from December 12, 1999, to January 4 at $2-$3.06 a share.

Bell Industries (BI)
▶ **First Carolina Investors** (FCAR) lowered its stake to 468,900 shares (4.9%) by selling 286,900 from December 30, 1999, to January 14 at $5.88-$8.38 each.

VisionAamerica (VSNA)
▶ Investor **Harmeet Singh Chawla** reduced his ownership to 486,806 shares (5.3%) when he sold 112,800 from January 7 to 19 at $3.97-$5 apiece.

Millbrook Press (MILB)
▶ A group including **Applewood Capital** lowered its ownership to 1,466,035 shares (45%) after selling 595,113 on December 16, 1999, at $1.63 per share.

Brio Technology (BRYO)
▶ **General Atlantic Partners** cut its stake to 3,308,258 shares (12.3%) when it sold 324,900 shares from January 7 to 18 at $46.44-$51.19 a share.

For SEC FORM 144 FILINGS *by holders of restricted securities, see page MW71.*

Source: *Barron's*, January 24, 2000, MW11.

FIGURE 2.3 **SEC Form 144 Filings Show Insider Intentions to Sell Shares**

144 FILINGS

SEC Form 144 must be filed by holders of restricted securities (also called letter stock) who intend to sell shares. Shares Indicated: the number to be sold. Sales Date: the approximate date of the sale. (Sometimes, shares aren't sold, even though their owner has filed a Form 144.) Title: AF: affiliated person; AI: affiliate of investment adviser; B: beneficial owner of at least 10% of a security; BC: beneficial owner as custodian; BT: beneficial owner as trustee; CB: chairman of the board; CP: controlling person; D: director; DO: director and beneficial owner; DS: indirect shareholder; GP: general partner; H: officer, director and beneficial owner; IA: investment adviser; LP: limited partner; MC: member of committee or advisory board; O: officer; B: officer and beneficial owner; OD: officer and director; OS: officer of subsidiary; OX: divisional officer; P: president; R: retired, resigned, deceased, no longer with the company; SH: shareholder; T: trustee; UN: unknown; VP: vice president and VT: voting trustee.

Company	Shares Indicated	$ Value	Sale Date	Seller	Title
American Software	50,000	400,000	1/4/00	Newberry, Thomas L	CB
Applied Power	28,150	985,250	1/4/00	Burkart, Philip T	VP
Cell Genesys	50,000	678,125	12/30/99	Carter, David W	D
Celsion Corp	44,117	132,351	1/4/00	Grohs, Dawn	O
Cognos Inc	35,000	2,110,000	1/4/00	Ashe, Robert G	VP
Commerce One	2,661	545,505	1/3/00	Sippi, Roger J	D
Computer Sciences	3,200	90,650	1/4/00	Arnold, Kirk	OX
Cooper Cameron	7,601	334,725	1/4/00	Myers, Franklin	VP
Costar Group	10,000	300,000	12/30/99	Heitzman, Fred A	VP
Costco Cos	44,000	3,955,499	1/3/00	Maron, Edward B	VP
Dell Computer	109,000	5,179,996	1/4/00	Hirschbiel, Paul O	D
Dell Computer	345,600	154,828,800	1/4/00	Luft, Klaus	D
Dell Computer	6,600	317,200	1/4/00	Saunders, Charles H	VP
Gannett Inc	14,240	1,161,450	1/3/00	Chapple, Thomas L	VP
Globalstar Telecomm	3,808	171,360	1/3/00	Targoff, Michael B	D
GT Interactive Software	200,000	450,000	1/6/00	Bond, Charles F	P
Hertz Corp	25,000	1,237,500	1/3-5/00	Nothwang, Joseph R	VP
Hertz Corp	75,138	3,719,331	1/3/00	Olson, Frank A	CB
Hertz Corp	19,793	979,753	1/3-4/00	Steele, Donald F	VP
International Paper	4,000	228,500	1/7/00	Faraci, John V	VP
International Paper	12,300	702,638	1/7/00	Melican, James P	VP
International Paper	3,200	182,800	1/7/00	Parrs, Marianne M	VP
International Paper	8,600	479,450	1/7/00	Smith, Wesley C	VP
Jabil Circuit	2,040	145,350	1/3/00	Krajcirovic, Frank	VP
Johnson Controls	7,550	420,472	1/4/00	Fox, Stacy L	O
Leapnet Inc	75,000	407,813	12/30/99	Smith, Frederick	CB
Meade Instruments	13,000	352,924	12/30/99	Christensen, Brent W	O
Medix Resources	25,000	62,500	1/6/00	Newman, Joel C	D
Morgan Stanley D W	10,000	1,300,000	1/4/00	DeMartini. Richard M	OS
National Mfg Technologies	40,000	30,000	12/29/99	Gayhart, Roy L	O
Public Storage Inc	11,000	261,938	1/7/00	Gerich, Obren B	VP
Public Storage Inc	10,000	238,125	1/7/00	Gerich, Obren B	VP
Retail Entertainment Group	25,167	31,459	1/5/00	Vanderkelen, Kevin M	D
Sandy Creek Corp	50,000	7,500	12/21/99	Lerner, Leslie M	P
Technical Communications	30,000	195,000	1/6/00	Awan, M M	D
Titan Motorcycle of America	170,000	425,000	1/5/00	Keery, Patrick	D
Unify Corp	8,550	256,500	12/30/99	Kopp, Walter	VP
Wells Fargo	3,350	135,884	12/30/99	Young, John A	D
Willamette Industries	5,000	230,000	1/3/00	Wheeler, Samuel C	D
Yankee Energy System Inc	3,200	140,400	1/5/00	Fink, J K	OS
Yellow Corp	327,500	5,403,750	1/6/00	Myers, A M	CB

Source: *Barron's,* January 24, 2000, MW71.

Would you buy stock in a company in which top management did not have a substantial ownership interest? Many investors wouldn't invest in a company unless management owns a meaningful number of shares. It's only natural to be suspicious of someone who would recommend that you purchase stock in a company that they themselves would not buy. When top management does not have sufficient confidence in the company's future to have a substantial ownership interest, that's usually a bad sign. In the same way, it's often regarded as beneficial when management has a large portion of its current income, in terms of salary and bonus payments, dependent on the company's stock price performance.

Another Web site that is a super source of up-to-the-minute information about individual companies is <http://freerealtime.com>. On many different Web sites, it is possible to get stock quote information that is delayed by 15 or 20 minutes. Usually that's okay. In some fast-moving markets, however, delayed quotes can be different from up-to-the-minute information. Freerealtime.com offers up-to-the-minute, or real-time, stock quotes, news, and information. As its name suggests, a prime attraction of freerealtime.com is that quote information is provided without charge.

Mutual fund investors will enjoy <http://www.morningstar.net>. Morningstar is a watchdog for the mutual fund industry. It offers comprehensive mutual fund commentary and analysis on a timely basis. If you are interested in top-performing growth and income funds, the best-performing international fund, or efficient ways to gain exposure to emerging Asian markets, Morningstar is a top source for information. Similarly, if you want to find out about top-yielding money market accounts, go to Morningstar.

Message Boards

Yahoo! is another terrific Web site for information about global currency and securities markets, financial news, delayed stock quotes, and so on (see Figure 2.4). Like many super Web sites, it offers a wealth of timely information. Also making <http://quote.yahoo.com> interesting is the fact that it offers one of the broadest and most active free stock message boards on the web. A **stock message board** is a Web site where anonymous individuals post information about individual companies or investment styles. If you have an investment interest in Microsoft, for example, you can go to the Yahoo Web site and see what other investors are thinking.

stock message board
Web site where anonymous individuals post information about individual companies or investment styles.

The Microsoft message board on quote.yahoo.com may have as many as 25, 50, or even 100 posts per day. These posts give timely views of other investors on late-breaking news, the company's investment potential, and the many risks facing Microsoft investors on a daily basis.

In many instances, message boards are the free-for-alls that one might expect when buyers and sellers sort out the reasons behind their purchases. At their best, message boards are a free source of informative data on company prospects. At their worst, "the boards" are forums that can be easily manipulated by the childish display of misinformation, rumor, and gossip.

Investment Web sites indicated in Table 2.2 are useful starting points for investors seeking to take advantage of information available on the Internet. By no means should this be considered an exhaustive list. There are literally hundreds of

FIGURE 2.4 **Yahoo! Is a Top Web Site for Stock Quotes and News Headlines Tailored to Fit Investor Interests**

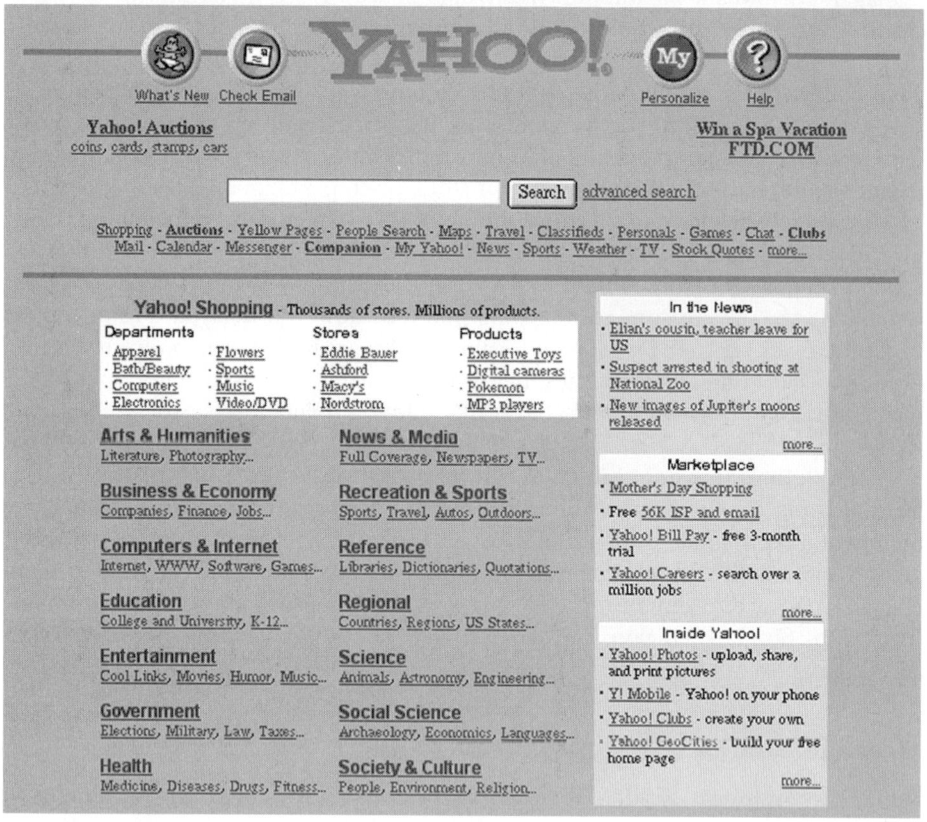

Source: <http://www.yahoo.com>.

stock information Web sites on the Internet. "Surfing the Web" for investment information can be both enjoyable and productive. If you have an investment question, perhaps the best advice is simply to go to the Internet, log onto Yahoo or the portal of your choice, sit back, and be amazed. There is a terrific amount of useful free information available on the Internet. That's why they call it the "World Wide Web."

Financial Press

Financial Newspapers

Another important source of financial news and information is the traditional financial press. Like many businesses, the financial press is quickly migrating to the Internet. In fact, the financial press is probably ahead of the curve, because magazine and newspaper publishers have witnessed first-hand the rapid growth of Internet portals such as Yahoo. Table 2.3 shows a number of important print media outlets for investment information.

WALL STREET WISDOM 2.2

Ask EDGAR!

Most investors start their detailed analysis of individual companies with the company annual report. Annual reports can be obtained for free from any publicly traded company by calling or writing the company's investor information office. Most companies today also have corporate Web sites that allow browsers to view their annual report online. If you want a print version, an e-mail request to the Investor Relations Department should do the trick.

The most compelling advantage of reading the corporate annual report is that it gives investors and prospective investors a detailed look at the company's current financial income statement, cash flow, and balance sheet information. It also provides a detailed perspective on the company's plans for future growth. Usually printed in bold color, the annual report is an effective means of promoting an optimistic view of the company's investment potential.

If the corporate annual report can be viewed as a "marketing" document, then required regular filings with the U.S. Securities and Exchange Commission (SEC) must certainly be thought of as "legal" documents. The fluid prose, bold color, and hyperbole of corporate annual reports are clearly absent from SEC filings. Filed in plain black and white, SEC reports are in dry prose that emphasize the many risks and compelling challenges facing the firm. The company's annual report often seems to tell investors "buy this stock." The annual 10-K report to the SEC, which gives annual income, cash flow, and balance sheet information, emphasizes the firm's investment risks, legal challenges, major competitors, and so on. The 10-K annual report provides a comprehensive overview of the company for the past year. The filing is due 90 days after the close of the company's fiscal year and contains information about the company's history, corporate structure, competitive environment, income statement, cash flow data, and balance sheet information. The 10-K reads almost like a "please don't sue us" document.

Another important report that is filed with the SEC on a regular basis is the firm's 14A form. This report provides official notification to designated classes of shareholders of matters to be brought to a vote at the annual shareholders meeting. The 14A form is commonly referred to as the company's "proxy statement." Among the various bits of useful information contained in the proxy statement are data on the level of pay for managers and the board of directors, the structure of management compensation, and details on the company's use of stock option incentives for top management and other employees. Importantly, the proxy statement details the amount of common stock held by top managers, the board of directors, and other large unaffiliated owners, such as mutual funds and pension funds. Because share ownership represents hard evidence of management's affinity for owning a "piece of the action," it tells shareholders and prospective shareholders if management truly believes the rosy view of company prospects given in the annual report. Significant insider stock ownership suggests that management has a positive view of company prospects and strong incentives to maximize shareholder value. When insider stock ownership is immaterial, it seems difficult to argue that management has a positive view of company prospects and/or strong incentives to maximize the stock's price.

Individual investors can obtain important SEC reports without charge by calling or writing any public company. Such reports are also freely available on the Internet at the EDGAR Web site. EDGAR is an acronym for Electronic Data Gathering, Analysis, and Retrieval, the system used by publicly traded companies to transmit filings to the SEC. EDGAR is a federally registered trademark of the SEC, but EDGAR Online, Inc., is neither approved by nor affiliated with the SEC.

Literally hundreds of SEC filings for an individual company may be available on EDGAR. Noteworthy examples include the 10-Q quarterly report, which provides a continuing view of a company's financial position, and 13D filings made by persons reporting beneficially owned shares of common stock in a public company or changes in ownership.

If you want facts and nothing but the facts, just ask EDGAR!

See: The EDGAR-Online Web site at <http://www.edgar-online.com>.

TABLE 2.3 Traditional Print Media for Investments Information

Traditional print media offer a wealth of investments information at a modest price. Many also offer free information on the Internet.

Financial Publication	Internet Address[a]	Description
Barron's	www.barrons.com	Biting market commentary once a week, portfolio analysis, and databank.
Business Week	www.businessweek.com	Timely business news and analysis, techcenter; useful business school, career, and small business information.
Forbes	www.forbes.com	Terrific commentary on economics and financial markets from an all-star stable of regular columnists. Stimulating reviews of companies and mutual funds.
Fortune	www.fortune.com	Famous for *Fortune 500* company list. Interesting advice on career development.
Inc.	www.inc.com	"The publication (and Web site) for growing companies."
Investor's Business Daily	www.investors.com	Founder William O'Neal dispenses stock picking, charting, and momentum strategies. Big on investor education.
Money	www.money.com	Interesting market commentary, company and mutual fund analysis aimed at novice investors. Lots of personal finance advice.
USA Today	www.usatoday.com	Don't underestimate "McPaper's" Money section when it comes to business, economic, and financial news. It's terrific!
The Wall Street Journal	www.wsj.com	*The* daily paper when it comes to financial news and information. Print subscribers get interactive access at a bargain price.
Worth	www.worth.com	The best in consumer and personal finance. Listen to what Peter Lynch has to say about mutual funds.

[a]Be sure to use the http:// prefix for each URL.

Of course, the first and most important source of daily Wall Street information is *The Wall Street Journal,* published by Dow Jones, Inc. *The Wall Street Journal* is the stock and bond investor's daily newspaper when it comes to financial news and information. Some do not realize that subscribers can get interactive access to *The Wall Street Journal* at a bargain price. On the Internet Web site for *The Interactive Wall Street Journal,* for example, you can read tomorrow's headlines for the print version of *The Wall Street Journal. The Interactive Wall Street Journal* is an extremely useful tool for news and information searches on individual companies. As you may already know, in each day's print version of *The Wall Street Journal,* typically on page B-2, there is a company index that lists all firms mentioned in news stories. If you want to find information about Intel, for example, readers can quickly turn to those specific pages that show news, articles, or other information pertinent to Intel investors.

Using *The Interactive Wall Street Journal* information search for individual companies is much simpler. By simply entering in the name of the company, Intel, or its ticker symbol, INTC, readers can search both the print and electronic versions of *The Wall Street Journal, Barron's* financial weekly, and all other sources compiled by the Dow Jones news service. Information can be viewed from current is-

FIGURE 2.5 **Tomorrow's Headlines Are Available on the Internet Edition of *The Wall Street Journal***

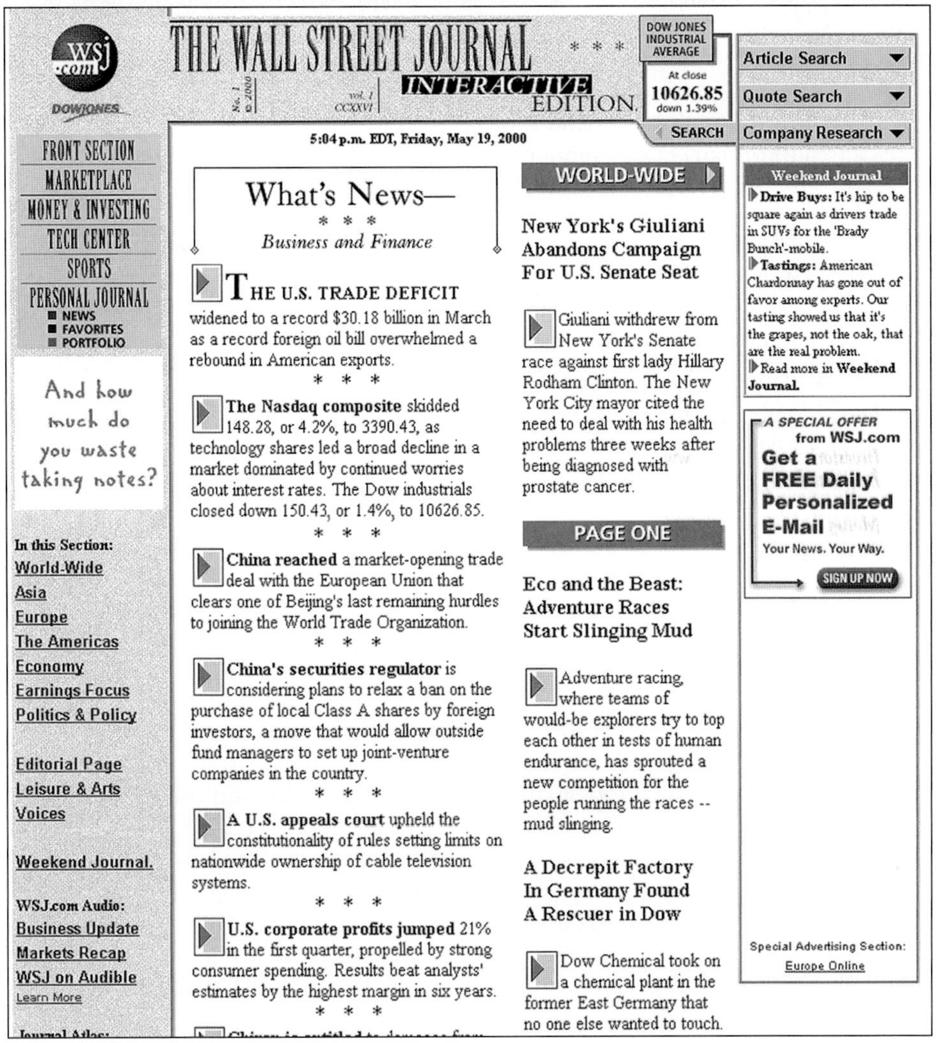

THE WALL STREET JOURNAL INTERACTIVE EDITION

WSJ.com DOWJONES

DOW JONES INDUSTRIAL AVERAGE
At close
10626.85
down 1.39%

SEARCH

Article Search
Quote Search
Company Research

5:04 p.m. EDT, Friday, May 19, 2000

FRONT SECTION
MARKETPLACE
MONEY & INVESTING
TECH CENTER
SPORTS
PERSONAL JOURNAL
NEWS
FAVORITES
PORTFOLIO

And how much do you waste taking notes?

In this Section:
World-Wide
Asia
Europe
The Americas
Economy
Earnings Focus
Politics & Policy

Editorial Page
Leisure & Arts
Voices

Weekend Journal

WSJ.com Audio:
Business Update
Markets Recap
WSJ on Audible
Learn More

What's News—
* * *
Business and Finance

THE U.S. TRADE DEFICIT widened to a record $30.18 billion in March as a record foreign oil bill overwhelmed a rebound in American exports.
* * *

The Nasdaq composite skidded 148.28, or 4.2%, to 3390.43, as technology shares led a broad decline in a market dominated by continued worries about interest rates. The Dow industrials closed down 150.43, or 1.4%, to 10626.85.
* * *

China reached a market-opening trade deal with the European Union that clears one of Beijing's last remaining hurdles to joining the World Trade Organization.
* * *

China's securities regulator is considering plans to relax a ban on the purchase of local Class A shares by foreign investors, a move that would allow outside fund managers to set up joint-venture companies in the country.
* * *

A U.S. appeals court upheld the constitutionality of rules setting limits on nationwide ownership of cable television systems.
* * *

U.S. corporate profits jumped 21% in the first quarter, propelled by strong consumer spending. Results beat analysts' estimates by the highest margin in six years.
* * *

WORLD-WIDE

New York's Giuliani Abandons Campaign For U.S. Senate Seat

Giuliani withdrew from New York's Senate race against first lady Hillary Rodham Clinton. The New York City mayor cited the need to deal with his health problems three weeks after being diagnosed with prostate cancer.

PAGE ONE

Eco and the Beast: Adventure Races Start Slinging Mud

Adventure racing, where teams of would-be explorers try to top each other in tests of human endurance, has sprouted a new competition for the people running the races -- mud slinging.

A Decrepit Factory In Germany Found A Rescuer in Dow

Dow Chemical took on a chemical plant in the former East Germany that no one else wanted to touch.

Weekend Journal
Drive Buys: It's hip to be square again as drivers trade in SUVs for the 'Brady Bunch'-mobile.
Tastings: American Chardonnay has gone out of favor among experts. Our tasting showed us that it's the grapes, not the oak, that are the real problem.
Read more in **Weekend Journal**.

A SPECIAL OFFER from WSJ.com
Get a FREE Daily Personalized E-Mail
Your News. Your Way.
SIGN UP NOW

Special Advertising Section:
Europe Online

Source: <http://www.wsj.com>.

sues and from all information published during the past 30 days. More detailed searches and the text for older articles can also be obtained, although sometimes a modest additional charge is required. If an investor had just a single source of printed and electronic information about stock and bond investing, *The Wall Street Journal* and *The Interactive Wall Street Journal* would be hard to beat.

Financial Periodicals

Another fascinating source of investment information is *Barron's* financial weekly, also published by Dow Jones, Inc. It is a sister publication to *The Wall Street Journal.*

The most obvious difference between *Barron's* and *The Wall Street Journal* is, of course, the fact that *Barron's* is a financial weekly published on Saturdays, whereas *The Wall Street Journal* comes out on a daily basis. Because of its once-a-week appearance, *Barron's* focuses on market commentary and portfolio analysis, rather than company-specific news.

Barron's is a top source for information about trends in technology stocks, for example, the mutual fund industry, or investing in general. Each week's issue features a wealth of market commentary about movements in interest rates and stock prices in the United States and in foreign markets, such as Asia, as well as industry-specific news and information. One of the most useful features of *Barron's* is that it provides a weekly "market laboratory" of investment statistics. This laboratory gives a host of financial statistics, data, and valuation ratios on stocks, bonds, credit conditions, and the economy. In addition to its wealth of information on stocks and the economy, *Barron's* is well known for its witty and engaging commentary. Check out Al Ableson's column "Up and Down Wall Street." You'll probably find his acerbic style amusing and enjoy the way he pokes holes in the typical "bull roar" surrounding Wall Street favorites.

Business Week, published by McGraw-Hill, Inc., is another top source for financial news and information. *Business Week* is a good source for timely business news and analysis and technical information on individual sectors of the economy. It even has information about top business schools. For example, its once-a-year survey of business schools gives readers timely information about admission standards and quality and strengths of various business schools around the country. *Business Week* is also a top source of information about careers and small business opportunities.

Another favorite for financial news, analysis, and commentary is *Forbes* magazine. *Forbes* gives biweekly commentary on economics and the financial markets from an all-star stable of regular columnists. It also offers a stimulating review of individual companies, big and small businesses, and mutual funds. Portfolio strategy is a focus of financial columnists found in every issue. Many who subscribe to *Forbes* for its financial news and information begin reading each issue in the back few pages where financial columnists, such as portfolio manager David Dreman, give on-the-spot analysis of market trends.

Fortune magazine, published by media giant Time-Warner, Inc., is another timely source of financial news and information. This biweekly publication is most famous for its *Fortune* 500 list of the 500 largest companies in the United States. The original list of 500 top industrials (according to sales) has been expanded. Today, *Fortune* covers the top 500 companies in America, along with the second 500, the so-called *Fortune* 1000. It also covers global corporations. *Fortune* is an interesting source for information about career opportunities, as well as trends and strategies followed by the management of top corporations.

If you are interested in corporate strategy but more focused on smaller as opposed to larger organizations, *Inc.* is a top choice. *Inc.* bills itself as the publication and Web site for growing companies. If you're thinking of starting a company, want to know how companies go public, sell stock to the public for the first time, or other important challenges facing smaller companies, consult *Inc.*

Investors interested in consumer news and personal financial planning often enjoy *Money* magazine, also published by Time-Warner, Inc. *Money* offers interesting market commentary and company and mutual fund analysis aimed at the novice investor on a monthly basis. It has lots of personal financial advice and planning information. If you're just getting started in investments, *Money* is a good place to start. *Worth* is another magazine on personal finance but is aimed at both the novice and the experienced investor. *Worth* magazine offers the best in consumer and personal finance. In particular, if you are interested in mutual funds, selection, analysis, and strategy, read what Peter Lynch has to say in his monthly column. *Worth* magazine is a natural place to look for detailed information in the mutual fund industry.

Other Popular Sources

Of course, this is far from a complete list of publications from the financial press that focus on investments and the economy. *The Wall Street Journal* isn't the only newspaper that features financial news and information. *Investor's Business Daily*, or *IBD* for short, was founded by William O'Neal and dispenses a wealth of information about stock picking, charting, and momentum strategies. *IBD* is also big on investor education. If you want to see a graphic approach to stock analysis and selection, *IBD* is a good place to start.

Other prominent national publications with an interest in finance include the *New York Times* and the *San Francisco Chronicle*. The *San Francisco Chronicle* is especially well known for its coverage of technology stocks and the Internet, which is not surprising given its close proximity to Silicon Valley.

Finally, investors sometimes underestimate the value of *USA Today*. The *USA Today* Money section is a top selection for information about financial news and information. Don't underestimate what some call "McPaper." When it comes to *USA Today's* money section, there is a wealth of economic and financial news provided. In fact, it is terrific. Give the money section of *USA Today* a chance. I think you will be surprised at the quality of the information provided and the insightful nature of the analysis.

Wall Street Research

Analyst Opinion Summaries

Another important source of investment information is the Wall Street community. Wall Street firms provide detailed information about individual companies, industries, the overall economy, and global stock and bond markets. Investors tend to closely follow such research and quickly act on analyst recommendations. Thus, there is a great deal of investor interest in the changing opinions of Wall Street analysts. Information about Wall Street research on Intel Corporation can be found by going to the Yahoo Web site, for example, and searching under the Intel ticker symbol (INTC) for news items related to the company. News items often include upgrade or downgrade information from Wall Street buy/sell analysts. For detailed information about the Wall Street research community's opinion about Intel, go to the research link on quote.yahoo.com.

Figure 2.6 shows that the average analyst recommendation for Intel in early 2000 was a positive 1.58 on a 1-to-5 scale, where 1 is a strong buy and 5 is a strong sell. This means that on a 1-to-5 scale, the average analyst regarded Intel as a strong-to-moderate buy. Notice that of the 39 analysts covering Intel at that point in time, 19 rated Intel a strong buy, 14 regarded Intel as moderately attractive, and six regarded Intel as a hold. At that point in time, no Wall Street analysts were so concerned about the future stock market potential of Intel as to rate the stock either a moderate sell or strong sell.

FIGURE 2.6 Detailed Summaries of Wall Street Research Are Available on the Internet

Research Summary

Number of brokers recommending as:		Average Recommendation (Strong Buy) 1.00 – 5.00 (Strong Sell)		Earnings Per Share		
Strong Buy	23	This Week	**1.39**	Last Quarter	(Mar 2000)	0.71
Moderate Buy	11	Last Week	1.51	Surprise		2.90%
Hold	3	Change	0.1			
Moderate Sell	0			**Consensus Estimates**		
Strong Sell	0	**Covering Brokers**		This Quarter	(Jun 00)	0.70
				This Year	(Dec 00)	3.01
				Next Year		3.50

For more in-depth analysis covering over 6,000 equities, a free trial to Zacks premium services is available. Current subscribers can login to Zacks.

Earnings Estimates & Recommendations

	This Quarter (Jun 00)	Next Quarter (Sep 00)	This Year (Dec 00)	Next Year (Dec 01)
Earnings Estimates				
Avg Estimate	0.70	0.76	3.01	3.50
# of Analysts	26	23	33	29
Low Estimate	0.58	0.60	2.44	2.62
High Estimate	0.74	0.82	3.25	4.00
Year Ago EPS	0.51	0.55	2.33	3.01
EPS Growth	37.50%	37.75%	29.02%	16.45%
Consensus EPS Trend				
Current	0.70	0.76	3.01	3.50
7 Days Ago	0.69	0.74	2.93	3.43
30 Days Ago	0.68	0.73	2.88	3.36
60 Days Ago	0.68	0.73	2.85	3.34
90 Days Ago	0.66	0.72	2.81	3.31

Number of brokers recommending as:	Months Ago 0	1	2	3
Strong Buy	23	22	19	19
Moderate Buy	11	12	14	13
Hold	3	6	6	6
Moderate Sell	0	0	0	0
Strong Sell	0	0	0	0
Mean*	1.39	1.51	1.58	1.57

*(strong buy) 1.00 – 5.00 (strong sell)

Industry: ELEC COMP-SEMIC
Ranked 22 of 91

Earnings Date (Approx.): 18-Apr-00

(continued)

In terms of earnings per share, the consensus earnings per share estimate among the 37 analysts then covering Intel was 69¢ for the first quarter of 2000. Actual earnings for Intel were 71¢, or 2.90% higher. This is regarded as a positive surprise and bullish for Intel stock. For the second quarter of 2000, meaning the quarter ending on June 30, 2000, Intel was expected to earn 70¢ per share. For the entire calendar year 2000, expected earnings per share for Intel were $3.01 and $3.50 for the year 2001. Figure 2.6 also shows a history of how those estimates have

FIGURE 2.6 ***(continued)***

Earnings Growth

	Last 5 Years	This Year (Dec 00)	Next Year (Dec 01)	Next 5 Years	Price/Earn (Dec 00)	PEG Ratio (Dec 00)
Intel Corp	16.5%	29.5%	16.5%	19.9%	38.6	1.31
ELEC COMP-SEMIC	11.6%	28.1%	35.5%	30.7%	53.9	1.92
S&P 500	9.2%	10.4%	8.1%	15.2%	25.4	2.44

Earnings History

	Mar 1999	Jun 1999	Sep 1999	Dec 1999	Mar 2000
Estimate	0.54	0.54	0.57	0.63	0.69
Actual	0.57	0.51	0.55	0.69	0.71
Difference	0.03	−0.03	−0.02	0.06	0.02
% Surprise	5.56%	−5.56%	−3.51%	9.52%	2.90%

Research Abstracts - Intel Corp **(NasdaqNM:INTC)**

18-Apr-2000 - Intel Corp. - Robertson Stephens on 18-Apr-00 - *Zacks*
21-Mar-2000 - Intel Corp. - Hambrecht & Quist on 21-Mar-00 - *Zacks*
21-Mar-2000 - Intel Corp. - Robertson Stephens on 21-Mar-00 - *Zacks*
21-Mar-2000 - Intel Corp. - Hambrecht & Quist on 21-Mar-00 - *Zacks*
20-Mar-2000 - Intel Corp. - Robertson Stephens on 20-Mar-00 - *Zacks*
14-Mar-2000 - Intel Corp. - Robertson Stephens on 14-Mar-00 - *Zacks*
13-Mar-2000 - Intel Corp. - Robertson Stephens on 13-Mar-00 - *Zacks*
13-Mar-2000 - Intel Corp. - Robertson Stephens on 13-Mar-00 - *Zacks*
13-Mar-2000 - Intel Corp. - Robertson Stephens on 13-Mar-00 - *Zacks*
1-Mar-2000 - Intel Corp. - Securities Corporation of Iowa on 1-Mar-00 - *Zacks*
29-Feb-2000 - Intel Corp. - Hambrecht & Quist on 29-Feb-00 - *Zacks*
24-Feb-2000 - Intel Corp. - Robertson Stephens on 24-Feb-00 - *Zacks*
24-Feb-2000 - Intel Corp. - Robertson Stephens on 24-Feb-00 - *Zacks*
24-Feb-2000 - Intel Corp. - Robertson Stephens on 24-Feb-00 - *Zacks*
23-Feb-2000 - Intel Corp. - Robertson Stephens on 23-Feb-00 - *Zacks*
24-Jan-2000 - Intel Corp. - Robertson Stephens on 24-Jan-00 - *Zacks*
14-Jan-2000 - Intel Corp. - Robertson Stephens on 14-Jan-00 - *Zacks*

changed over time. The number of brokers recommending Intel as a strong buy, moderate buy, and so on, is also given, as is information about how those opinions have changed over the past few months. As you can see from Figure 2.6, the number of analysts recommending Intel as a strong buy grew from 19 to 23 over the period in question. This means that Wall Street in general had become more bullish about Intel. Remember, however, even though Wall Street is bullish about Intel, it may not be as bullish about Intel as it is about some other companies in the electronic component and semiconductor industry.

Also notice from Figure 2.6 that in the electronic component semiconductor industry, Intel was ranked 22nd out of 91 firms. To see how Intel's Wall Street rating compares with other firms in its industry, investors can simply click on the Yahoo site to see a comparative ranking. This list provides an investment opinion for all 91 companies in Intel's industry. Listed are companies from International Rectifier (rated 1.0) through Standard Microsystems Corporation (rated 3.0). This means that industry competitors are ranked from a table-pounding buy of 1.0, all the way down to a moderate hold (3.0) recommendation. Within this context, it is important to remember that in Wall Street terminology a hold recommendation is actually negative.

bullish Optimistic prospect of rising prices.

bearish Pessimistic prospect of falling prices.

On Wall Street, a cheery consensus is regarded as **bullish.** The bull metaphor is used to describe a stock that is thought to be ready to charge ahead like a raging bull. Therefore, if a Wall Street analyst is bullish about a stock, he or she expects the stock to charge ahead during the coming period. On the other hand, if an analyst regards a stock as having poor prospects for the future, the analyst is said to be **bearish** regarding the company's prospects. A bearish consensus means that Wall Street analysts in general expect a stock price to go down. In the metaphor of a bear, analysts expect the stock to "go into hibernation." At a minimum, a bearish outlook for a stock means that the stock is expected to underperform the market. In the extreme, a bearish consensus means that a stock is so risky that it has the potential to go down, rather than up, in price.

For a more detailed look at the earnings prospects for Intel or any company, one can consult the detailed research information available on Yahoo. In the case of Intel, for example, one can note that the consensus regarding Intel has become increasingly bullish over time. Notice how the average recommendation over the past quarter has gone from a bullish 1.62 to an even more bullish 1.58. This means that the consensus with respect to Intel is becoming more and more positive over time. It is worth pointing out that although many investors regard a bullish consensus on Wall Street as favorable for a stock, this is not always the case. If all of Wall Street is already positive on the prospects for Intel, who is going to buy it at the higher price? If the consensus is already positive, doesn't that mean that all the bulls already own Intel?

Company Reports

Of course, research-consensus earnings information from Yahoo or more detailed research information from Yahoo or alternate Web sites is only a starting point. More elaborated Wall Street wisdom on individual stocks can be obtained from the detailed earnings reports provided for individual companies. Merrill Lynch, for example, is the largest Wall Street stock investment banker, stock brokerage, and research house. Merrill Lynch has been long recognized for its excellence in analyzing individual companies, industry trends, and the future course of U.S. and global markets. Merrill Lynch research teams are rated number 1 in the United States, Europe, Asia, and Latin America. As the biggest and the best when it comes to Wall Street research, Merrill Lynch analyst opinions demand attention from investors.

For example, Figure 2.7 shows the cover page from a detailed earnings report from Merrill Lynch on technology leader Hewlett-Packard. With quarterly earnings per share (EPS) of 87¢, Hewlett-Packard reported slightly above Merrill Lynch's bullish operating EPS estimate of 82¢. (Operating earnings reflect Hewlett-Packard's business operations before adjustment for extraordinary or unusual items.) Therefore, in reporting its robust EPS performance, Hewlett-Packard had slightly surprised Wall Street, or "beaten the Street estimates." No wonder Hewlett-Packard stock continues to delight stockholders. It has a history of beating the optimistic estimates provided by Wall Street analysts, such as those employed by Merrill Lynch.

Figure 2.7 shows only the first page of a detailed two-page report on Hewlett-Packard provided by Merrill Lynch. Such reports can be obtained by Merrill Lynch customers from its Web site on the Internet (<http://askmerrill.com>). Alternatively, customers can find copies of printed reports at Merrill Lynch offices around the country. Merrill Lynch's more detailed analysis of Hewlett-Packard goes into great detail concerning expense controls exercised by Hewlett-Packard during the quar-

FIGURE 2.7 **Wall Street Firms Such as Merrill Lynch Provide In-Depth Research on Hundreds of Leading Companies**

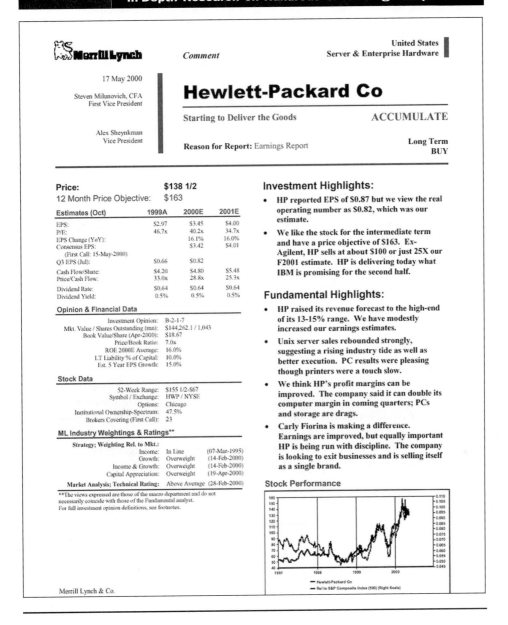

Merrill Lynch | *Comment* | United States
Server & Enterprise Hardware

17 May 2000

Steven Milunovich, CFA
First Vice President

Alex Sheynkman
Vice President

Hewlett-Packard Co

Starting to Deliver the Goods — ACCUMULATE

Reason for Report: Earnings Report — Long Term BUY

Price: **$138 1/2**
12 Month Price Objective: $163

Estimates (Oct)	1999A	2000E	2001E
EPS:	$2.97	$3.45	$4.00
P/E:	46.7x	40.2x	34.7x
EPS Change (YoY):		16.1%	16.0%
Consensus EPS: (First Call: 15-May-2000)		$3.42	$4.01
Q3 EPS (Jul):	$0.66	$0.82	
Cash Flow/Share:	$4.20	$4.80	$5.48
Price/Cash Flow:	33.0x	28.8x	25.3x
Dividend Rate:	$0.64	$0.64	$0.64
Dividend Yield:	0.5%	0.5%	0.5%

Opinion & Financial Data

Investment Opinion:	B-2-1-7
Mkt. Value / Shares Outstanding (mn):	$144,262.1 / 1,043
Book Value/Share (Apr-2000):	$18.67
Price/Book Ratio:	7.0x
ROE 2000E Average:	16.0%
LT Liability % of Capital:	10.0%
Est. 5 Year EPS Growth:	15.0%

Stock Data

52-Week Range:	$155 1/2-$67
Symbol / Exchange:	HWP / NYSE
Options:	Chicago
Institutional Ownership-Spectrum:	47.5%
Brokers Covering (First Call):	23

ML Industry Weightings & Ratings**

Strategy; Weighting Rel. to Mkt.:		
Income:	In Line	(07-Mar-1995)
Growth:	Overweight	(14-Feb-2000)
Income & Growth:	Overweight	(14-Feb-2000)
Capital Appreciation:	Overweight	(19-Apr-2000)
Market Analysis; Technical Rating:	Above Average	(28-Feb-2000)

**The views expressed are those of the macro department and do not necessarily coincide with those of the Fundamental analyst.
For full investment opinion definitions, see footnotes.

Investment Highlights:

- **HP reported EPS of $0.87 but we view the real operating number as $0.82, which was our estimate.**
- **We like the stock for the intermediate term and have a price objective of $163. Ex-Agilent, HP sells at about $100 or just 25X our F2001 estimate. HP is delivering today what IBM is promising for the second half.**

Fundamental Highlights:

- **HP raised its revenue forecast to the high-end of its 13-15% range. We have modestly increased our earnings estimates.**
- **Unix server sales rebounded strongly, suggesting a rising industry tide as well as better execution. PC results were pleasing though printers were a touch slow.**
- **We think HP's profit margins can be improved. The company said it can double its computer margin in coming quarters; PCs and storage are drags.**
- **Carly Fiorina is making a difference. Earnings are improved, but equally important HP is being run with discipline. The company is looking to exit businesses and is selling itself as a single brand.**

Stock Performance

Merrill Lynch & Co.

ter, Unix server sales, and the revenue outlook for future periods by product group and distribution channel. For example, a more detailed company report on Merrill Lynch shows how revenues are growing when Hewlett-Packard sells its computer products to individual customers on the Internet, in retail outlets, and to companies and other larger organizations such as universities. In addition to "hard" news, Merrill Lynch security analysts also consider harder to quantify "soft" news and nonquantitative information. For example, what is the ultimate outcome for Hewlett-Packard from the antitrust lawsuit brought against Microsoft Corp.? In January 2000, Merrill Lynch, like all investors, could only speculate. Although we now know how this suit turned out and its short-term ramifications for computer hardware vendors like Hewlett-Packard, back in mid-2000 the outcome of this suit was still anybody's guess.

Industry Reports

In addition to detailed reports about individual companies like Hewlett-Packard, Merrill Lynch also produces a variety of in-depth reports on important industries and economic sectors. In Figure 2.8, for example, the cover page of a Merrill Lynch report titled "Internet Appliances: Appliances Are in Full Bloom" is provided. In this report, Merrill Lynch analyzes trends in the market for hand-held communications devices that are soon expected to offer consumers cost-effective and convenient wireless access to the Internet. This rapidly evolving sector is witnessing a convergence of once-popular hand-held calendar (or schedule) organizers with cellular telephone technology.

Palm, Inc., was an early pioneer in this field, and still is a global provider of handheld computing devices. As such, Palm is a potent competitor to Hewlett-Packard in the emerging hand-held device market. In early 2000, many analysts continued to describe the worldwide personal companion hand-held device market as including small, pocket-sized devices that feature pen-based input and allow users to automatically copy and conform, or synchronize, information between the device and a personal computer. As such hand-held devices become more powerful and ubiquitous, they are sure to become popular means for collecting and organizing information, sending and receiving e-mail, trading online, and so on. In other words, the personal computers of the very near future will increasingly resemble the hand-held organizers of the recent past.

This is the type of information that individual investors might consider in choosing to buy or sell a stock such as Hewlett-Packard. Again, it is important to keep in mind that shortly after publication such information is often quickly reflected in the stock prices of companies like Hewlet-Packard, Intel, and others. When Merrill Lynch publishes an analyst report, it is fair to assume that its largest customers have already carefully analyzed the information and used it in their investment decisions.

U.S. Market Outlook

In addition to buy/sell recommendations on individual companies and detailed surveys of performance in individual industries, Merrill Lynch and other Wall Street research houses provide painstaking research on expected trends in the U.S. economy and on how those trends are likely to affect stock markets both here and abroad. In December 1999, an example of overall market research done by Merrill Lynch titled "2000—The Year Ahead, Meeting the Millennium" was produced.

Of course, the objective of such analysis is to identify stock and bond investment strategies that will help Merrill Lynch customers outperform overall market averages. As a focal point of this effort, Merrill Lynch identifies what it refers to as "The 2000 Collective Wisdom Portfolios" (see Table 2.4). The primary objective of the U.S. Collective Wisdom Portfolio is to maximize capital gains over a one-year time frame. This portfolio represents the best investment ideas from Merrill Lynch research in the United States. The stock selection process begins with "The Year Ahead" publication from the Global Securities Research and Economics Group. Each fundamental equity analyst writes a summary report on his or her industry

FIGURE 2.8 **Timely Wall Street Coverage Helps Investors Follow Industry Trends**

Merrill Lynch

Comment

United States

3 May 2000

William G. Crawford
Vice President

Steven Milunovich, CFA
First Vice President

Internet Appliances

Appliances Are In Full Bloom

Reason for Report: Hardware Heaven Conference

Industry

Fundamental Highlights:

- **Palm said it will introduce a sub-$99 device with instant messaging and always-on notification.**
- **Sony likely will soon come out with its handheld based on the PalmOS. Sony's deal with Symbian for the EPOC operating system is for Sony's smartphone unit, which is separate from the handheld division.**
- **Both Palm and RIM described demand as strong, with RIM's CEO admitting that distribution was a limiting factor on sales. Palm's sales continue to ramp even as Handspring's Visor shows strong results.**
- **Research In Motion is addressing the contention in its channel, which should have the added benefit of uniting its partners behind the Blackberry wireless messaging platform. RIM has a early but dominant lead in wireless messaging infrastructure.**
- **Our Internet appliance panel concluded that most people would continue to use multiple devices in the future despite the likely introduction of all-in-one devices. Localized information was a strong theme for applications, with examples given from NeoPoint, Vindigo, Kozmo.com, and Scout Electromedia.**

Merrill Lynch & Co.
Global Securities Research & Economics Group
Global Fundamental Equity Research Department

and includes a focus recommendation for the coming year. From the focus recommendations in the United States, a Merrill Lynch committee, composed of research, economic, and market analysts, select stocks to form the U.S. Collective Wisdom Portfolio. All such selections enjoy Merrill Lynch's intermediate and long-term buy or accumulate ratings. Stocks are automatically removed from this model portfolio when Merrill Lynch's opinion is downgraded, restricted, or placed under

TABLE 2.4 Merrill Lynch's Collective Wisdom Portfolios

Company	Ticker	Industry
A. US Collective Wisdom Portfolio		
Alcoa	AA	Nonferrous Metal
Citigroup Inc.	C	Banks—Multinational
Coca Cola Co.	KO	Beverages
Cox Communications	COX	Media—Cable
El Paso Energy	EPG	Natural Gas
Exxon Mobil Corp.	XOM	International Oil
Guidant Corp.	GDT	Health and Medical Tech
Lowe's Corp.	LOW	Retailing—Hardline
Motorola	MOT	Telecommunications Equipment
Oracle Systems	ORCL	Server and Enterprise Hardware
Proctor & Gamble	PG	Consumer Products
Solectron Corp.	SLR	Technology—Electronics
Sprint PCS	PCS	Wireless Communication Services
Texas Instruments	TXN	Technology—Semiconductors
B. International Collective Wisdom Portfolio		
CRH Plc.	CRHCY	Building Materials (Ireland)
Deutsche Telekom	DT	Telecommunications (Germany)
Grupo Televisa	TV	Media Broadcasting (Mexico)
Hutchison Whampoa	HUWHY	Conglomerate (Hong Kong)
Kyocera	KYO	Elecronics and Semiconductors (Japan)
Mettler-Toledo	MTD	Process Controls (Switzerland)
News Corp.	NWS	Media and Entertainment (Australia)
Nippon Telephone & Telegraph	NTT	Telecommunication (Japan)
Nokia	NOK	Wireless Communication Equipment (Finland)
SAP Aktiengesellschaft	SAP	Technology—Software (Germany)
Sony	SNE	Electronics (Japan)
Total Fina	TOT	International Oil (France)

Data source: <http://www.askmerrill.com>.

extended review. Existing stocks can also be replaced when Merrill Lynch believes another selection offers better prospects. When evaluating these picks for the year 2000 and beyond, remember that the investment selections presented may not be suitable for all investors. It is crucial that investors consider such selections within the context of personal risk tolerances and investment goals.

In its analysis of "2000—The Year Ahead, United States," Merrill Lynch described the U.S. stock market as having a two-tiered or bifurcated characteristic. On the one hand, large capitalization stocks represented by those in the Dow Jones Industrial Average and in the Standard & Poor's (S&P) 500 Index appeared strong. Large-cap stocks in technology and a flood of new market entries tied to the Internet were expected to extend their already strong bull market cycle. However, in Merrill Lynch's view, the increased volatility of this group of stocks suggested that a distribution phase or gradual topping in the overall market was developing. If the Merrill Lynch research department's assessment of the overall market is indeed correct, small-caps and low-priced basic industry stocks are apt to outperform the overall market over the next few years. Such a change in market sentiment would be dramatic, given the fact that the small- and mid-cap sectors of the U.S. market have been in a bear market cycle since at least the second half of 1999. Nevertheless, as seen in Table 2.4, Merrill Lynch is sticking with technology and other recent stock market winners, at least for the moment.

Merrill Lynch also provides extensive ongoing coverage of fixed-income markets. Its *Fixed Income Digest* is a monthly strategy guide for individual investors. It provides a monthly review of the taxable and tax-exempt securities markets with a focus on market opportunities for the individual investor. Merrill Lynch also includes a monthly recommended list by product, asset allocation models, and market performance data. Reports like "Managing Your Bond Portfolio through Market Volatility" highlight attractive bond market investments and discuss how investors can position their portfolios for volatile markets, introduce current tax-minimization strategies, and so on.

Global Outlook

In addition to their market assessment for the United States, Merrill Lynch research also expresses its opinion regarding the United Kingdom, continental Europe, and the emerging markets in the Middle East, Latin America, and Asia. Merrill Lynch corporate and governmental clients here and abroad use these market assessments to time the sale of new stocks and new bonds to individual and institutional customers. Similarly, pension funds and other institutional investors use Merrill Lynch's market assessments to guide their investment strategy during coming periods.

Like its U.S. market analysis, Merrill Lynch's global market analysis aims toward identifying stocks and bonds that will help Merrill Lynch clients outperform the market averages. Like the U.S. Collective Wisdom Portfolio, Merrill Lynch's International Collective Wisdom Portfolio seeks to help clients maximize capital gains over a one-year time frame. This portfolio represents the best investment ideas from Merrill Lynch research around the globe. Equities from the following regions may be represented: Europe, Asia, Pacific (except Japan), Latin America, Australia/New Zealand, Japan, and Canada. International Collective Wisdom stocks enjoy Merrill Lynch's top buy or accumulate ratings, are not from countries or industry groups that are out of favor, and tend to be well capitalized, liquid, and actively traded in the United States. As seen in Table 2.4, Merrill Lynch's global selections tend to reflect the firm's confidence in technology, telecommunication, and restructuring opportunities.

It is interesting to note that Merrill Lynch's diverse research staff sometimes comes out with conflicting market analysis. For example, during the late 1990s as the overall market soared skyward, Merrill Lynch's quantitative analysis group said, "We are perplexed that the consensus is now extremely bullish." The quantitative research group communicated a multitude of investor concerns regarding the health of the equity market. They also expressed surprise that in the light of deteriorating economic fundamentals for large-cap companies, investors had apparently decided to ignore those concerns and turn decidedly bullish. It is fascinating that the quantitative strategy group at Merrill Lynch uses a contrarian argument as a sell-side indicator. Excess bullishness was seen as portending a rough market during 2000. This is the same period for which the Merrill Lynch market analysis group argued that "companies are well girded to meet the challenge."

The fact that a highly respected Wall Street research house such as Merrill Lynch has conflicting opinions between its various analysts and employees is not surprising. However, conflicting opinions may be confusing to individual and institutional investors who look to Merrill Lynch for clear guidance concerning expected market performance in the year ahead. Conflicting opinions issued by different departments of the same Wall Street research house are not as unusual as one might expect. This makes it difficult for investors to judge the quality and predictability of Wall Street research. Similarly, such conflicting opinions make it difficult for outside commentators to judge the effectiveness of investment strategies recommended by Wall Street analysts. Nevertheless, and despite obvious difficulties with assessing its effectiveness, Wall Street research remains an interesting source of company information and analysis. At a minimum, stock and bond market commentary gives investors an opportunity to test their own judgments against those of Wall Street's best analysts.

Investments as a Profession

Financial Job Market Overview

It is clear that all students have a practical interest in compiling a self-sufficient amount of retirement wealth. As a result, investment is a subject of practical interest to everyone. The economics of investing is also a compelling and interesting academic subject. How do successful investors create and grow wealth? Why do some firms grow and prosper while others wither and die? The psychology of money is similarly fascinating. How much is enough? Is gaining wealth productive? Therefore, from a variety of perspectives the study of money and investing is a fascinating subject and well worth studying.

In addition, some students may seek to earn a productive living in the investments field. For this reason, studying investments is also an important practical field of study. Employment opportunities in financial services are expected to grow rapidly in the years ahead. In addition, the amount of financial sophistication demanded of finance specialists and nonspecialists is also expected to rise. For example, corporate treasurers and chief financial officers must understand financial theory and practice if they are to efficiently finance firm growth and financial needs. Personnel and human resource heads also need to understand investment theory and practice in order to help employees with an increasingly complex array of deferred benefit retirement plans, such as 401K plans and 403(b)-7 plans. In addition to such opportunities for improved job market prospects in financial and nonfinancial occupations, there is a growing number of career opportunities in the investments field.

Table 2.5 shows a variety of employment opportunities in the financial services industry. Employment opportunities are most numerous with commercial banks, savings institutions, insurance carriers, and real estate companies. With respect to banks and savings institutions, many career opportunities in the investments field involve simple information processing. Nevertheless, many banks and savings institutions are moving toward offering financial planning and investment advice. This means that financial account executives in many banks and savings institutions offer savers a wide variety of investment products, including certificates of deposit, bonds, mutual funds, and individual stocks. Insurance companies offer a wide variety of career opportunities for executives interested in designing variable and fixed-annuity products for sale to individual and institutional investors. Many people with a background in financial theory and practice work for insurance

WALL STREET WISDOM 2.3

The Wall Street Journal

For millions of global investors, the newspaper has arrived when *The Wall Street Journal* plops on their desk. Never mind that today many investors get their *Journal* information using desktop computers and *The Wall Street Journal, Interactive Edition*. In either case, the *Journal* is commonly regarded as the definitive daily source for market-moving news and in-depth coverage of company, industry, and global market information.

Of course, the *Journal* is a timely source of stock quotes, bond prices, and mutual fund information. The *Journal*'s "Data Bank" and "Markets Data Center" features offer daily information for companies listed on the New York Stock Exchange, the American Stock Exchange, and the Nasdaq over-the-counter market. Detailed coverage is also provided for other stock markets in the Americas, such as Argentina, Brazil, Canada, and Mexico. Asian stock markets are also given extensive coverage given investor interest in the emerging markets of China, Hong Kong, India, Indonesia, and South Korea and in the developed markets of Australia and Japan. European stocks also get extensive coverage, especially markets in Britain and Germany. The *Journal* also provides extensive coverage of credit markets, including analysis of trends in interest rates and bond prices, foreign exchange, commodities, mutual funds, and personal finance.

The *Journal*'s "Money & Investing" section gives investors high-quality, timely coverage of the global financial marketplace. For example, on Monday, April 26, 1999, the *Journal* started with the story that Comcast Corp. spent the prior weekend huddling with its bankers to come up with a counteroffer to AT&T Corp.'s unsolicited bid for MediaOne Group, paving the way for what could turn into a spirited battle between the two cable television giants. Even as Comcast continued to search for ways to stave off AT&T, MediaOne negotiated a confidentiality agreement with the phone company, the first step in proceeding with formal merger talks, said people familiar with the matter. Comcast and AT&T stocks prices were down while MediaOne rose on this news, as investors prepared for a bidding war.

Other examples of the *Journal*'s market-moving news on that day included First Union Corp.'s announcement that it had agreed to acquire Everen Capital Corp. for $1.1 billion in stock, a deal that will help give the big bank a presence on the West Coast and help it market its Evergreen mutual funds. Harvey Golub also announced his plans to retire in two years as chief executive of the American Express Co. President and Chief Operating Officer Kenneth Chenault will be named to succeed him at the helm of the financial-services company.

The *Journal* also features a wealth of in-depth market coverage. Whether an investor's focus is on U.S. stocks, European stocks, bonds, or currencies, the *Journal* gives valuable daily information.

Pages of coverage are also dedicated to providing insight and perspective on investing or specific market segments, like tech stocks. The "Getting Going" and "Intrinsic Value" columns give new and experienced investors useful investment primers.

One of the most popular *Journal* features is the daily "Heard on the Street" column. For example, in mid-1999, the *Journal*'s Susan Warren reported that investors betting on strong gains in chemical stocks, a bellwether for economically sensitive companies, might have to wait a year or more for a payoff. While bulls are heartened by signs that Asia and Latin America could be on the brink of recovery, chemical companies could face several more quarters of weak earnings, analysts said. Until the fundamentals change, buying chemical stocks indiscriminately "is just dead money," said Sergey Vasnetsov, an analyst at BT Alex Brown. "Heard in Europe" and "Heard in Asia" give similarly interesting analysis of stocks in foreign markets. A companion column on the Interactive *Journal*, called "Heard on the Net," uncovers stories from the world of online investment forums.

To get comprehensive coverage of the investments field, it's easy to see why so many investors start with *The Wall Street Journal*, or better yet, The *Wall Street Journal, Interactive Edition*.

See: *The Wall Street Journal, Interactive Edition* at <http://www.wsj.com>.

TABLE 2.5 Career Opportunities in Investments[a]

Employment and career opportunities in the financial services industries are expected to grow rapidly in the years ahead. In addition, the amount of financial sophistication demanded of nonspecialists is also expected to rise. For example, personnel in human resource departments increasingly need to understand investment theory and practice to help employees with an increasingly complex array of deferred benefits, such as 401K plans, and retirement investment opportunities.

Type of Employer	Number of Establishments	Number of Jobs
Banks and Savings Institutions	104,505	2,100,089
Business Credit Institutions	39,439	445,590
Federal and Federally Sponsored Credit Agencies	1,349	21,298
Holding Companies, Trust Management	10,381	108,235
Insurance Agents, Brokers, and Services	121,662	635,536
Insurance Companies	38,977	1,516,643
Mortgage Bankers and Brokers	16,152	178,976
Mutual Fund Management	829	16,572
Personal Credit Institutions	16,900	158,790
Real Estate	229,493	1,231,471
Security and Commodity Brokers	19,237	312,846
Security and Commodity Exchanges and Services	11,940	93,598

[a]For additional information, see U.S. Department of Commerce, *Census of Financial, Insurance, and Real Estate Industries, 1992, Subject Series: Establishment and Firm Size* (U.S. Government Printing Office, Washington, D.C., 1995).

companies that need to assess risks for various types of life insurance products and policies for smokers versus nonsmokers, for example. Financial risk analysts are also often called on by property and casualty insurance companies that need to assess the risks of theft or weather damage, for example.

Of course, many job opportunities are available in the insurance industry for agents, brokers, and financial managers in the information services area. Such employees are close to insurance company clients and need to be fully aware of customer risk attitudes, retirement objectives, and investment resources.

The real estate industry is also a prime employer of personnel with an investments background. Of course, most of the people employed in the real estate industry are directly involved with customers in terms of buying and selling homes or commercial properties. There are additional job opportunities for others involved in the administration end of the business.

Brokerage Business

stock broker Financial agent who acts as go-between for stock buyers and sellers.

One of the most interesting areas in the financial services sector is the stock brokerage business. A **stock broker,** sometimes referred to as an account executive, usually works with individual investors and institutions in advising and executing orders for individual common stocks or bonds. Although the broker may receive a base salary, it is common for the main part of a broker's compensation to come in the form of commission income. In a typical arrangement, an individual broker might receive 35–50% of the total commissions generated. This means, for example, that if an individual broker were to generate gross commissions of $200,000 per year, he or she would receive a gross income of between $70,000 and $100,000.

At Merrill Lynch, for example, a typical broker earns in excess of $100,000 a year. This means that the typical Merrill Lynch broker generates $200,000–$285,000 in gross commissions per year. In an era when commission rates average 0.5% to 1% of the amount invested, this implies a tremendous amount of investment activity being administered by such an account executive.

To illustrate, consider an account executive who has a net income of $100,000 per year based on a 50% share of the total amount of commissions generated. Such an executive would generate gross commissions of $200,000 per year. If the gross commission generated per dollar invested is 1%, such an executive would have customers generating $20 million per year in buy or sell orders. This is a significant amount of investment activity and a very high standard of performance for an individual financial executive. Identifying a large number of high net-worth individuals, gaining their confidence, and turning them into productive customers is difficult. Generating and maintaining the customer base necessary to provide $20 million per year in transactions is a daunting task indeed.

You can be sure that the typical account executive at Merrill Lynch, for example, is not only highly educated, bright, and talented, he or she is also extremely hardworking. In fact, the long-term odds against success as an account executive at a top brokerage firm like Merrill Lynch are high. It is usual for top brokers at Merrill Lynch and other firms to have career spans as short as only two to five years. At top firms such as American Express Financial Advisors, Merrill Lynch, or Salomon, Smith Barney, it is common for only 3–5% of successful management trainee candidates to be with the firm after three years. The dropout or failure rate is extremely high when compared with most other professions. It is easy to understand why. All top financial firms devote significant resources toward making individual account executives successful. If any individual account executive is unable to generate significant commissions, she or he is quickly replaced in the search for high-production account executives.

Investment Management

Job opportunities at the glory end of the securities business include **security analysts** and **portfolio managers.** Unfortunately, few persons are actively employed in these positions. For example, Table 2.4 shows that the total number of security and commodity brokers in the United States is in a range near 300,000. At the same time, the total number of employees at mutual fund management companies is as few as 20,000. Moreover, most of the employees at mutual fund companies answer the phone. The number of mutual fund employees engaged in security analysis or portfolio management can be a veritable handful.

security analyst Financial specialist who seeks to identify investment opportunities.

portfolio manager Financial specialist engaged in managing investments for others.

In Kansas City, home of the American Century Mutual Funds, several hundred employees help mutual fund investors identify appropriate mutual fund investment opportunities, establish individual retirement accounts, and help with other safekeeping services. Of the several hundred employees with American Century Funds, there are perhaps only 25–30 who are security analysts. Even these lucky few face stiff competition. All security analysts, of course, hope one day to become portfolio managers. At American Century Funds, the number of active portfolio managers at any point in time typically measures less than a dozen. Only a very small fraction of the number of employees at a typical mutual fund colossus such as the American Century Family of Funds is employed in security analysis or portfolio management. The reason is simple.

Computer technology makes it possible for an individual security analyst to cover a broad array of firms in a number of different industries. With the use of powerful desktop computers, it is relatively easy to engage in fundamental analysis of company operations, assets, and prospects. It is also fairly simple to gain a wide array of timely information by consulting investment Web sites on the Internet, along with proprietary data networks. Portfolio managers with high-powered investment tools are able to manage an extremely large amount of money with very little human assistance.

In some ways, mutual funds can be compared with hospitals. Most hospitals have lots of employees but very few brain surgeons. Mutual funds, banks, and pension funds have lots of employees, but very few actually analyze securities or make portfolio investment decisions.

Financial Planning

A relatively new field for students with backgrounds in financial theory and analysis is the financial planning business. This is a service business in which the planner gets to know the individual client and tries to match client risk and return preferences with a broad array of appropriate investment opportunities. Financial planners may include specially trained representatives of insurance companies, accounting firms, banks, or mutual fund organizations. Some financial planners are independent.

certified financial planner Financial professional who helps individuals identify and meet financial needs.

The **certified financial planner** (CFP) designation is earned by thousands of individuals who pass a series of exams offered by the College of Financial Planning, which is a division of the National Endowment for Financial Education. To qualify as a CFP, the applicant must demonstrate proficiency in five areas through extensive training and testing: financial plan processing and insurance, investment planning, income tax planning, retirement planning and employee benefits, and estate planning.

For information about the CFP program, write directly to the CFP Board, 4695 South Monaco Street, Denver, Colorado 80237-3403 (phone: 303-220-4800). Information can also be obtained from colleges and universities that sponsor CFP classes and programs. The CFP designation in financial planning compares with the certified professional accountant, or CPA, designation in the field of accounting.

Investment Banking

investment banker Financial professional who helps companies meet financial needs (e.g., issue stock).

At the other end of the investments business from the stock broker and the financial planner, who deal mainly with individual investors, is the **investment banker,** who deals mainly with institutional clients. Investment bankers are primarily involved in the distribution of securities from issuing corporations to the general public.

The investment banker goes to companies in need of debt or equity financing, arranges to sell those securities to the general public, and acts as an intermediary between individual investors and the issuing corporations. Investment bankers also advise corporate clients on financial strategies and often help arrange mergers and acquisitions. To be sure, the investment banker's job is not passive. Investment bankers aggressively seek out corporate clients who need financial advice. Investment bankers tend to be talented, hardworking, and extremely aggressive. It is a "pressure cooker" occupation with enormous risk and staggering potential rewards. Individual investment bankers have been known to make in the tens of millions of dollars per year in total compensation. On the other hand, the penalty for failure can be extreme. Widespread layoffs during industry downturns are common. It is not rare for an individual investment banker to go from making millions of dollars of compensation one year to getting fired the next year.

This review of career opportunities in investments and the financial services industry is not meant to be exhaustive. Certainly, it is not meant to be discouraging. This is definitely a growth industry. Still, students are well advised to remember that compensation in the field of investments is performance based. Rewards for success are substantial. Penalties for underperformance are swift.

Summary

- **Chartists** or **technicians** are Wall Street analysts who use price and volume graphs to study historical changes in the demand and supply conditions for stocks in the hope that they might develop successful trading rules to capitalize on expected changes. In technical analysis, a chart formation is called a **head and shoulders** when a stock price reaches a peak and declines, rises above its former peak and again declines, rises again but not to the second peak, and then again declines.
- A wealth of stock market information is available on the Internet. **Stock quotes,** or share prices, in **real time** are often sought by investors several times during the trading day. **EDGAR** is an acronym for Electronic Retrieval Analysis System for SEC filings. Go to the EDGAR Web site and key in the one-, two-, three-, or four-letter **ticker symbol** for any company, and EDGAR will provide a plain text report of that company's most recent quarterly accounting earnings information, or the **10Q report.** Other important bits of information available on EDGAR include the firm's **10K report,** or annual financial report, and the company's **proxy statement,** or annual meeting announcement. Schedule **13D** filings are made to the SEC within 10 days of an entity attaining a 5% or more position in any class of a company's securities. SEC **Form 144** filings must be submitted by holders of restricted securities, sometimes called letter stock, who intend to sell shares.
- A **stock message board** is a Web site where anonymous individuals post information about individual companies or investment styles. If you have an investment interest in Microsoft, for example, you can go to the Yahoo Web site and see what other investors are thinking.
- On Wall Street, a cheery consensus is regarded as **bullish.** The bull metaphor is used to describe a stock that is thought to be ready to charge ahead like a raging bull. On the other hand, if an analyst regards a stock as having poor prospects for the future, the analyst is said to be **bearish.** A bearish consensus means that Wall Street analysts in general expect a stock price to fall.
- One of the most interesting areas in the financial services sector is the stock brokerage business. A **stock broker,** sometimes referred to as an account executive, usually works with individual investors and institutions in advising and executing orders for individual common stocks or bonds. Job opportunities at the glory end of the securities business include **security analysts** and **portfolio managers.** Unfortunately, the number of persons actively employed in these positions is small.
- The **certified financial planner** (CFP) designation is earned by thousands of individuals who pass a series of exams offered by the College of Financial Planning,

which is a division of the National Endowment for Financial Education. To qualify as a CFP, the applicant must demonstrate proficiency in five areas through extensive training and testing: financial plan processing and insurance, investment planning, income tax planning, retirement planning and employee benefits, and estate planning.

- At the other end of the investments business from the stockbroker and the financial planner, who deal mainly with individual investors, is the **investment banker,** who deals mainly with institutional clients. Investment bankers are primarily involved with the distribution of securities from issuing corporations to the general public.

Questions

1. Wall Street analysts who study trading volume to develop successful trading strategies are called
   a. chartists.
   b. momentum-based investors.
   c. value investors.
   d. growth-stock investors.
2. Technicians consider a head and shoulders stock price formation to be
   a. bullish.
   b. bearish.
   c. neutral.
   d. none of the above.
3. Significant historical evidence suggests that technical analysis can lead to
   a. significantly above-average profits over time.
   b. slightly above-average profits over time.
   c. significantly below-average profits over time.
   d. none of the above.
4. The Internet is apt to make information-related barriers to entry
   a. lower.
   b. higher.
   c. obsolete.
   d. none of the above.
5. By expanding the level of competition among sellers, the Internet is apt to decrease industry
   a. profits.
   b. profit margins.
   c. sales.
   d. cash flows.
6. By expanding the level of product quality and price information among consumers, the Internet is apt to decrease industry
   a. profits.

   b. profit margins.
   c. sales.
   d. cash flows.
7. The Internet makes the production of financial news and information more
   a. diffuse.
   b. concentrated.
   c. costly.
   d. difficult.
8. Stock trading on the Internet is likely to
   a. reduce stock market volatility.
   b. increase market returns.
   c. increase stock market volatility.
   d. reduce market returns.
9. Anonymous tips communicated on Internet message boards are prone to
   a. reduce stock market volatility.
   b. increase market returns.
   c. increase stock market volatility.
   d. reduce market returns.
10. As an information device, the Internet is analogous to
    a. television.
    b. radio.
    c. a computer spreadsheet.
    d. the telephone.
11. EDGAR is
    a. a nonprofit news organization.
    b. a government agency.
    c. an arm of the Securities and Exchange Commission.
    d. a for-profit corporation.
12. Annual accounting information is filed with the SEC on the
    a. 10K report.
    b. 10Q report.
    c. 13D report.
    d. Form 144.
13. Reports submitted to the SEC by holders of restricted stock who intend to sell shares are called
    a. Form 144 filings.
    b. 10K reports.
    c. proxy statements.
    d. 13D reports.

14. Letter stock is
    a. preferred stock.
    b. common stock.
    c. restricted with respect to sale.
    d. none of the above.
15. It is difficult for investors to profit from Wall Street research because such research opinions
    a. seldom influence stock prices.
    b. are quickly reflected in stock prices.
    c. are seldom reputable.
    d. tend to be ignored by investors.
16. Bullish analyst recommendations tend to
    a. drive stock prices down.
    b. drive stock prices up.
    c. hurt investment banking opportunities.
    d. cause trading volume to decline.
17. The most common analyst recommendation is
    a. a strong sell.
    b. a weak sell.
    c. to hold.
    d. to buy.
18. Finance professionals who work with individual investors and institutions in advising and executing orders for individual common stocks or bonds are called
    a. brokers.
    b. portfolio managers.
    c. analysts.
    d. certified financial planners.
19. Finance professionals primarily involved with the distribution of securities from issuing corporations to the general public are called
    a. security analysts.
    b. technicians.
    c. investment bankers.
    d. chief financial officers.
20. An initial 13D filing would typically be regarded as
    a. bearish.
    b. evidence of illegal corporate activity.
    c. bullish.
    d. none of these.

Investment Application

Internet Chat: How Much Is Free Stock Advice Worth?

Nowhere is the exploding interest in Internet investing more evident than on the Internet itself. "Dot.com daffiness" or "Tilt-a-whirl Technology" is how Barron's describes it.[3] When it comes to Internet investing, poring over earnings reports and balance sheets does no good because the biggest winners among Internet stocks seldom have any earnings, book values, meaningful revenues, or fundamental value — at least when measured using conventional criteria. In the upside-down world of Internet investing, Internet stock analysts sometimes describe a lack of earnings as an *advantage* because most Internet stocks are fairly *immune* from earnings disappointments. How can they have disappointing growth in earnings when they have no earnings?

Table 2.6 shows the cyberhome for a handful of Internet stock chat and stock advice Web sites. Because all of them are new, there is little basis on which to judge their potential for success or the usefulness of the advice offered. Being free, however, has its advantages. All are wildly popular with "newbie" investors who tend to be comfortable using sophisticated technology but fairly naive when it comes to the world of investing. Of all the sites mentioned, one of the most popular is *The Motley Fool,* run by brothers David and Tom Gardner. These irreverent but Internet-savvy investors have built an online following that celebrates the virtues of interactive investment analysis. To appreciate the impact of online chat and Internet stock advice, a little history about *The Motley Fool* may prove instructive.

In July 1993, David Gardner, Tom Gardner, and Erik Rydholm launched *The Motley Fool* as an offline investment newsletter designed to "educate, enlighten, and entertain investors." *The Motley Fool* name comes from Shakespeare's "As You Like It." According to David Gardner, Fools were the happy fellows paid to entertain the king and queen with self-effacing humor that instructed as it amused. In fact, Fools were really the only members of their societies who could tell the truth to the King or Queen without having their heads lopped off. After all, as David and Tom Gardner write, "The Wise would have you believe that 'A Fool and his money are soon parted.' But in a world where three-quarters of all *professional* money managers lose to the market averages, year in and year out, how Wise should one aspire to be?"[4]

Unfortunately for the Gardners, the offline newsletter version of *The Motley Fool* was a commercial failure. After attracting only 38 subscribers during its first month of operation, the Gardners made the momentous decision to take their "conversation" about stocks to cyberspace. *The Motley Fool* originally appeared on America Online on August 4, 1994.[5] The rest, as they say, is cyberhistory. Today,

---

[3]See Randall W. Forsyth, "The Best Place to Look for Info on 'Net Stocks Is the 'Net," *Barron's,* January 4, 1999, 49.

[4]See David Gardner and Tom Gardner, *The Motley Fool Investment Guide* (New York, NY: Simon & Schuster, 1996), 14.

[5]See David Gardner, "Welcome to the Motley Fool Online!" <http://www.fool.com/School/StepOne.htm>; also see David Gardner and Tom Gardner, *The Motley Fool Investment Guide* (New York, NY: Simon & Schuster, 1996).

TABLE 2.6 Leading Internet Stock Advice and Message Board Web Sites

Increasingly, the best place to look for Internet stock advice is the Internet itself. Many sites offer investors a plethora of free information and advice. Unfortunately, the speed with which false and misleading information can be communicated on the Internet has raised the concern of the Securities and Exchange Commission.

Web Site	Internet Address[a]	Description
The Bull Market Report	www.bull-market.com	E-mail financial newsletter with (bullish) market and stock commentary.
Internetstocks.com	www.internetstocks.com	Insight from leading Internet stock analysts at BancBoston Robertson Stephens.
IPO.com	www.ipo.com	The latest initial public offering news and information.
The Motley Fool	www.fool.com	An online forum designed to "educate, amuse, and enrich investors." A constant stream of witty investment advice spills over to hyperactive message boards.
Silicon Investor	www.techstocks.com	Billed as the largest financial discussion site on the Web.
Softwarestocks.com	www.softwarestocks.com	The latest news on key companies and advice on how to analyze software stocks.
TheStreet.com	www.thestreet.com	A full menu of stock analysis, market commentary, and biting satire.
Upside Magazine	www.upside.com	Lively, if not irreverent, coverage about high-tech companies and their managements.
Wired Magazine	www.wired.com	Provocative commentary, technology, and business news.
Yahoo! Finance	messages.yahoo.com	Hyperactive stock message boards.

[a]Be sure to use the http:// prefix for each URL.

America Online is the most popular online service, advertising a worldwide membership of 20 million members, and *The Motley Fool* is its most popular Web site. *The Motley Fool* also attracts a large and growing audience on the Internet.[6] *The Motley Fool* features a daily portfolio update that provides market commentary and tracks the day-to-day performance of 8 to 12 stocks held in *The Rule Breakers Portfolio* and a host of linked Web sites such as the *Lunchtime News, Nightly News,* and *The Fool School.* Perhaps *The Motley Fool's* most popular feature is a series of message boards where *Motley Fool* employees and individual investors "chat" about investment prospects, hard news, and rumors surrounding individual companies.

At the present time, *The Rule Breakers Portfolio* comprises a mix of high-flying Internet stocks (like AOL, Amazon.com, and @Home), small high-tech stocks (like Iomega Corp. and 3Dfx), larger high-tech companies (like Amgen and Lucent

[6]*The Motley Fool* is on the Internet at <http://www.fool.com>; and *The Daily Dow,* a Web site devoted exclusively to promoting the Dogs of the Dow and various other investment strategies tied to the DJIA, is featured at <http://www.fool.com/DDow/DD>.

Technologies), and beaten-down Dow stocks (like DuPont and Exxon). Interestingly, the largest holding in *The Rule Breakers Portfolio* is AOL itself, and *The Motley Fool* is quick to extol the virtues of AOL.

For example, following the AOL/CompuServe/WorldCom merger agreement on September 8, 1997, AOL got what The Motley Fool Jeff Fischer called the "full Foolish coverage," including posts titled "CSRV Divvied Up,"[7] and "CompuServe Divided,"[8] along with links to the "AOL/CSRV Analyst Call," AOL message boards, and so on.[9] Not known for tempered enthusiasm, *The Motley Fool* employees jumped into action on a number of fronts following the AOL/CompuServe/WorldCom announcement. For example, Alex Schay (The Motley Fool Nexus) cheered the AOL/CompuServe/WorldCom agreement with the words "AOL has managed to purchase just the pieces that fit into its scheme for world online domination."[10] Just as quickly, in a post on the AOL message board, The Motley Fool Jeanie chortled, "AOL will now be able to tout that magic 10 million+ subscriber number."[11] Similarly, The Motley Fool Nico enthused, "I know it's far too early to even speculate before all the official announcements, but given the rather close new relationship between WorldCom and AOL, does anyone foresee an eventual merger of the two?"[12]

Of course, the unbridled enthusiasm expressed for AOL by *The Motley Fool* makes interesting copy. Perhaps equally fascinating to note is a post made with little fanfare on a corner of Fooldom called "Foolishly Answered Questions" (or FAQ, for short). On September 11, 1997, The Motley Fool AnnC wrote: "*The Motley Fool* currently has three main revenue sources: *The Motley Fool* is paid a *fixed percentage of the usage fees* generated by [America Online for] users such as yourself coming and spending time in our area, *The Motley Fool* is paid by *advertisers,* [and] *The Motley Fool* generates money from its retail operations."

Apparently, *The Motley Fool* didn't regard this as a material conflict of interest because "usage is the only revenue source which comes directly from America Online and [usage represents] less than half the total revenues *The Motley Fool* takes in."[13] More recently, Jean Macaulay (The Motley Fool Jeanie) wrote that AOL now "has the right to buy almost 20% of our [*The Motley Fool*] stock at a set price, but they haven't exercised that right. They are a means of distribution for us, but they

---

[7]See Alex Schay, "CSRV Divvied Up," September 8, 1997, <http://www.fool.com/Features/1997/sp970908AOLCompuuServe.htm>.

[8]See Randy Befumo (The Motley Fool Templr), "CompuServe Divided," <http://www.fool.com/Features/1997/sp970908AOLCompuuServe001.htm>.

[9]See Jeff Fischer, "Fool Portfolio Report," September 12, 1997, <http://www.fool.com/FoolPort/1997/FoolPort970912.htm>.

[10]See Alex Schay, "CSRV Divvied Up," September 8, 1997, <http://www.fool.com/Features/1997/sp970908AOLCompuuServe.htm>.

[11]See The Motley Fool Jeanie, "Re:ANS??" no. 257 in America Online, September 8, 1997, <http://208.206.41.243/scripts/news/FOOLNEWS.exe>.

[12]See The Motley Fool Nico, "AOL-WorldCom Deal," no. 258 in America Online, September 8, 1997, <http://208.206.41.243/scripts/news/FOOLNEWS.exe>.

[13]See The Motley Fool AnnC, "How Does the Motley Fool Make Money?" Foolishly Answered Questions, September 11, 1997; and The Motley Fool AnnC, "Is There a Conflict of Interest in Owning America Online?" Foolishly Answered Questions, September 11, 1997.

[14]See Jean Macaulay (The Motley Fool Jeanie) "For Prof. Hirschey," no. 687 in America Online, March 6, 1998, <http://boards.fool.com/Registered/Message.asp?id=1060151000398004&sort=postdate>.

don't pay us anything, including usage payments, any more. [This change supercedes the former usage payments as described by The Motley Fool AnnC back in Sept 1997] Our revenue now comes primarily from advertising, publishing, and retail activities."[14]

A. Is it possible that *The Motley Fool's* objectivity regarding the investment merits of AOL was and is affected by its business relationship with them? Is it likely?

B. Describe some simple means for dealing with any material conflict of interest between *The Motley Fool* and any of the companies featured on its Web site.

C. Going back to the question posed at the beginning of this Investment Application, how much is free stock advice worth?

Selected References

Barber, Brad M., and Terrance Odean. "Trading Is Hazardous to Your Wealth: The Common Stock Investment Performance of Individual Investors." *Journal of Finance* 55 (April 2000): 773–806.

Booth, G. Geoffrey, Raymond W. So, and Yiuman Tse. "Price Discovery in the German Equity Index Derivatives Market." *Journal of Futures Markets* 19 (September 1999): 619–643.

Brockman, Paul, and Dennis Y. Chung. "An Analysis of Depth Behavior in an Electronic, Order-Driven Environment." *Journal of Banking and Finance* 23 (December 1999): 1861–1886.

Butler, Kirt C., and Hakan Saraoglu. "Improving Analysts' Negative Earnings Forecasts." *Financial Analysts Journal* 55 (May/June 1999): 48–56.

Chung, Kee H., Bonnie F. Van Ness, and Robert A. Van Ness. "Limit Orders and the Bid–Ask Spread." *Journal of Financial Economics* 53 (August 1999): 255–287.

Gombola, Michael J., and Feng-Ying Liu. "The Signaling Power of Specially Designated Dividends." *Journal of Financial and Quantitative Analysis* 34 (September 1999): 409–424.

Grinblatt, Mark, and Matti Keloharju. "The Investment Behavior and Performance of Various Investor Types: A Study of Finland's Unique Data Set." *Journal of Financial Economics* 55 (January 2000): 43–67.

Harford, Jarrad. "Corporate Cash Reserves and Acquisitions." *Journal of Finance* 54 (December 1999): 1969–1997.

Hirschey, Mark, Vernon J. Richardson, and Susan Scholz. "How 'Foolish' Are Internet Investors?" *Financial Analysts Journal* 56 (January/February 2000): 62–69.

Jaffe, Jeffrey F., and James M. Mahoney. "The Performance of Investment Newsletters." *Journal of Financial Economics* 53 (August 1999): 289–307.

Noe, Christopher F. "Voluntary Disclosures and Insider Transactions." *Journal of Accounting and Economics* 27 (June 1999): 305–326.

Prentice, Robert A., Vernon J, Richardson, and Susan Scholz. "Corporate Web Site Disclosure and Rule 10b-5: An Empirical Evaluation." *American Business Law Journal* 36 (Summer 1999): 531–578.

Vafeas, Nikos. "Board Meeting Frequency and Firm Performance." *Journal of Financial Economics* 53 (July 1999): 113–142.

Veronesi, Pietro. "How Does Information Quality Affect Stock Returns?" *Journal of Finance* 55 (April 2000): 807–838.

[14]See Jean Macaulay (The Motley Fool Jeanie) "For Prof. Hirschey," no. 687 in America Online, March 6, 1998, <http://boards.fool.com/Registered/Message.asp?id=1060151000398004&sort=postdate>.

PART 2

Equity Securities

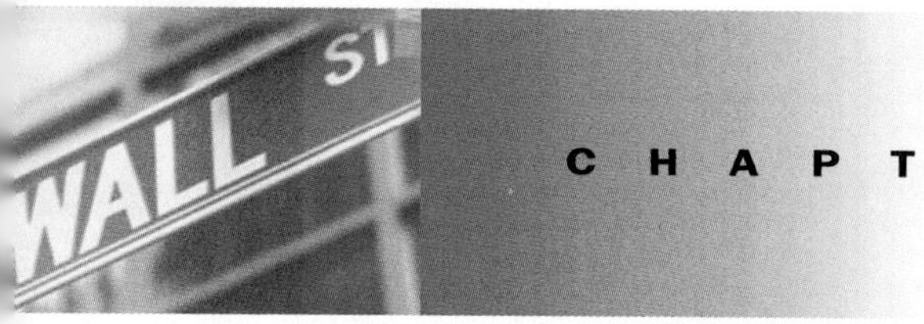

CHAPTER 3

Overview of Equities Markets

Stock and bond investors laughed in the face of danger during early 2000 and bid up stock and long-term bond prices as the Federal Reserve engineered a continuing series of quarter-point increases in short-term interest rates. Usually, stock and bond investors fear higher interest rates. Holding all else equal, higher interest rates reduce the present value of future earnings and typically result in lower stock prices. Similarly, when interest rates rise, the present value of future interest and principal payments falls, and the value of long-term bonds diminishes.

In early 2000, investors bet heavily that this time would be different. Both equity and fixed-income investors believed that the Fed's long-term impact on stock and bond markets would continue to be constructive. Rather than spark a giant sell-off, the Fed's decision to gradually tighten short-term interest rate guidelines in a series of one-quarter of a percentage point moves caused investors to bid up equity prices. Fixed-income investors also bid up long-term bond prices, and yields fell. In so doing, investors were betting that the Fed had inflation under control and that stocks and long-term bonds would continue to do well in a world of strong earnings, steady growth, and moderate inflation.

It will be a couple of years or more before investors know with certainty whether the Fed indeed engineered the much anticipated "soft landing" for the economy and kept stock and bond markets on their steady upward course. Both stock and bond markets are discounting mechanisms, and it is what happens to future interest rates that matters most. If the Fed's series of increases in short-term interest rates portends a period of rising long-term interest rates, it is possible that stock and bond market bulls will have been ill advised to laugh in the face of danger.[1]

Major U.S. Securities Exchanges

New York Stock Exchange

New York Stock Exchange Largest stock market in terms of market capitalization.

Located in New York City on the corner of Wall Street and Broad Street, the **New York Stock Exchange (NYSE)** is a private partnership founded for the purpose of providing an auction market for common and preferred stocks. Since 1817, New

[1]See Gregory Zuckerman, "Dow Industrials and Nasdaq Post Surges of More Than 200 Points," *The Wall Street Journal*, April 26, 2000, C1, C13.

York Stock Exchange specialists have maintained an orderly stock market. Today, roughly 3,700 issues from more than 3,000 companies are listed on the NYSE. The NYSE is open for business daily from 9:30 AM to 4:00 PM EST, except on weekends and holidays, or about 252–254 days per year. The NYSE is what is called an **agency auction market.** Trading on the NYSE takes place in the form of bids and offers by exchange members, acting as agents for institutions or individual investors. Buy and sell orders meet directly on the trading floor, and prices are determined by the interplay of supply and demand. By way of contrast, in the over-the-counter (OTC) market stock prices are determined by a network of dealers who buy and sell out of inventory.

agency auction market
Market in which brokers represent buyers and sellers and prices are determined by supply and demand.

At the NYSE, each listed stock is assigned to a single post, where the **specialist** manages the auction process. NYSE members bring all orders for NYSE-listed stocks to the exchange floor electronically or by a floor broker. As a result, the flow of buy and sell orders for each stock is directed to a single location. This stream of diverse orders is one of the great strengths of the exchange. It provides liquidity—the ease with which securities can be bought and sold without wide price fluctuations. When an investor's transaction is completed, the best price will have been exposed to a wide range of would-be buyers and sellers. The NYSE is the largest U.S. securities market in terms of the value of companies listed and the dollar value of trading activity. The NYSE is the largest equities marketplace in the world and is home to 3,025 companies. As of year-end 1999, the NYSE had 280.9 billion shares listed and available for trading worth approximately $12.3 trillion (see Table 3.1). The NYSE accounts for about 80% of the more than one billion shares per day total trading volume. Eight regional exchanges generate 10% of composite volume. The largest regional exchanges are the Midwest Stock Exchange in Chicago and

specialist
Employee of a NYSE firm who manages the market for an individual stock.

TABLE 3.1 The NYSE Is the Largest Equities Market in the World

	January 2000	1999
NYSE Average Daily Stock Volume (millions)	1074.2	809.2
NYSE Annual Turnover Rate (%)	96%	78%
NYSE Average Price per Share Traded	$44.28	$43.88
NYSE ADRs in Non-U.S. Stocks (millions)	91.1	65.3
NYSE Dollar Value of Trading Activity (billions of dollars)	$47.6	$35.5
Average Daily Program Volume on NYSE (millions)	205.4	157.5
Programs as % of Total NYSE	19.1%	19.4%
Dow Jones Industrial Average	10,940.53	11497.12
S&P 500 Index	1,394.46	1469.25
NYSE Composite Index	621.73	650.30
NYSE Bond Volume (millions)	$206.5	$3,220.3
NYSE Average Daily Bond Volume (millions)	$10.2	$12.8
Total Equity IPOs (domestic) (billions of dollars)	$3.1	$58.6
NYSE Total Equity IPOs (domestic)	$2.4	$28.7
Total Industrial IPOs (domestic)	$3.1	$55.7
NYSE Industrial IPOs (domestic)	$2.4	$26.1
Total Closed-End IPOs	$0.0	$2.9
NYSE Closed-End IPOs	$0.0	$2.6
Seat Prices	$2,300,000	$2,300,000
Number of Firms	413	414
Number of Firms Dealing with Public	282	281

Data source: <http://www.nyse.com>.

TABLE 3.2 NYSE Listing Standards

Standards for U.S. Corporations

A. Minimum Quantitative Standards:	
Distribution and Size Criteria	2,000 U.S.
Round Lot Holders (number of holders of a unit of trading—generally 100 shares)	
or:	2,200
Total Shareholders	
. . . together with:	100,000 shares
Average Monthly Trading Volume (for the most recent six months)	
or:	500
Total Shareholders	
. . . together with:	1,000,000 shares
Average Monthly Trading Volume (for the most recent 12 months)	1,100,000
Public Shares	outstanding
Market Value of Public Shares:	$100,000,000
Public Companies	$60,000,000
IPOs, Spin-offs, Carve-outs	
B. Minimum Quantitative Standards: Financial Criteria Earnings	
Aggregate pretax earnings over the past 3 years of $6,500,000 achievable as:	$2,500,000
Most Recent Year	$2,000,000
Each of Two Preceding Years	
or:	
Most Recent Year	$4,500,000
(All 3 years must be profitable)	
or:	
For companies with not less than $500 million in global market capitalization and $200 million in revenues in the past 12 months:	
C. Operating Cash Flow	
Aggregate for the 3 Years Operating Cash Flow (each year must report a positive amount)	$25,000,000
or:	
D. Global Market Capitalization	$250,000,000
Revenues for the Past Fiscal Year	$1,000,000,000
Average Global Market Capitalization	$60,000,000
REITs (less than 3 years operating history)	$60,000,000
Stockholders' Equity Funds (less than 3 years operating history)	
Net assets	

Standards for Non-U.S. Corporations

Round Lot Holders (number of holders of a unit of trading—generally 100 shares)	5,000 worldwide
Public Shares	2.5 million worldwide
Public Market Value	$100 million worldwide
Pretax Income Aggregate for the past 3 years	$100 million
. . . together with	
Minimum in each of the 2 most recent years	$25 million
or:	
For companies with not less than $500 million in global market capitalization and $200 million in revenues in the past 12 months:	
Aggregate "Cash Flow" for past 3 years	$100 million
. . . together with	
Minimum in each of the 2 most recent years	$25 million
or:	
Market Capitalization	$1 billion
and	
Revenue (most recent fiscal year)	$250 million

Data source: <http://www.nyse.com>.

the Pacific Stock Exchange in San Francisco and Los Angeles. Electronic trading on Instinet and other systems and in the OTC market accounts for 5–10% of composite trading in NYSE-listed securities.

To be listed on the NYSE, both domestic and foreign-based firms are expected to meet certain qualifications and to be willing to keep the investing public fully informed. At a minimum, the company must be a going concern or be the successor to a going concern. In determining eligibility for listing, particular atten-

TABLE 3.3 NYSE Listing Fee Schedule

Listing Fees for U.S. Corporations		Listing Fees for Non-U.S. Corporations	
A. Original Listing Fees			
Original Fee (one-time charge)	$36,800	Original Fee	$36,800
plus		plus	
Initial Fee (paid on listing of shares)			
Shares Issued:	Per Million	Shares or ADRs Issued:	Per Million
1st and 2nd million	$14,750	1st and 2nd million	$14,750
3rd and 4th million	7,400	3rd and 4th million	7,400
5th and up to 300 million	3,500	5th and up to 300 million	3,500
In excess of 300 million	1,900	In excess of 300 million	1,900
		Minimum Fee	$100,000
B. Continuing Annual Fees			
Per Share Rates:	Per Million	Per Share or ADR Rates:	Per Million
1st and 2nd million	$1,650	1st and 2nd million	$1,650
In excess of 2 million	830	In excess of 2 million	830
Minimum Fees for Shares or ADRs Listed:	Per Million	Minimum Fees for Shares or ADRs Listed:	Per Million
Up to 10	$16,170	Up to 10	$16,170
10+ to 20	24,260	10+ to 20	24,260
20+ to 50	32,340	20+ to 50	32,340
50+ to 100	48,410	50+ to 100	48,410
100+ to 200	64,580	100+ to 200	64,580
200+	80,440	200+	80,440
Maximum Annual Fee	$500,000	Maximum Annual Fee	$500,000

Data source: <http://www.nyse.com>.

tion is given to such qualifications as the degree of national interest in the company, its relative position and stability in the industry, and whether it has good prospects and is engaged in an expanding industry.

NYSE listing requirements for domestic companies call for a minimum firm size and distribution of the company's shares within the United States. This distribution of shares can be accomplished through domestic public offerings, acquisitions made in the United States, or by other similar means. As shown in Table 3.2, minimum quantitative listing standards for the NYSE start with a minimum total number of **round lot** holders, shareholders who own at least 100 shares, and minimal trade volume. Listed companies must meet minimum earnings, operating cash flow, or global market capitalization standards. Listing standards for foreign-based corporations are designed to enable major foreign corporations to list their shares on the NYSE. The principal criteria for foreign companies focus on worldwide rather than U.S. distribution of a foreign company's shares and apply where there is a broad liquid market for a company's shares in its country of origin. Non-U.S. corporations may elect to qualify for listing under either the listing standards for non-U.S. corporations or the NYSE's domestic listing criteria. However, an applicant company must meet all the criteria within the standards under which it seeks to qualify for listing.

round lot 100 shares.

There are initial and continuing fees associated with an NYSE listing. Domestic corporations must pay an initial listing fee that includes a fixed charge and a sliding-scale amount tied to the number of outstanding shares. As shown in Table 3.3, the minimum initial listing fee is $36,800 plus $14,750 per million shares for the first and second million shares, plus $7,400 for the third and fourth million shares, $3,500 for the fifth through the 300th million shares, and $1,900 for each million shares in excess of 300 million. For example, the initial listing fee for a company with five million shares of common stock would consist of a one-time charge of \$36,800, plus \$29,500 for the first and second million shares, plus \$14,800 for the third and fourth million shares, plus \$3,500 for the fifth million shares, or a total of \$84,600 (= \$36,800 + \$29,500 + \$14,800 + \$3,500). Listed domestic companies also must pay a continuing annual fee of \$1,650 per million shares outstanding on the first and second million and \$830 per million on those shares outstanding in excess of two million. For example, the continuing annual fee for a company with 40 million shares of issued common stock is \$34,840 per year (+ \$1,650 × 2 + \$830 × 38), figured as the sum of \$3,300 for the first and second million shares, plus \$31,540 for the third through the 40th million shares. To maintain the desirability of NYSE membership for their largest and most valued companies, a maximum continuing annual fee of \$500,000 has been established. NYSE listing fees for non-U.S. corporations are determined in a similar manner.

As shown in Figure 3.1, the NYSE sponsors an extraordinarily informative Web site. Investors can use the NYSE Web site to obtain stock quotes, get the latest information about listed companies, and learn more about how the NYSE and the investment community work. It also has a wealth of valuable price and volume data for the overall market.

FIGURE 3.1 **The NYSE Web Site Is a Valuable Resource for Investor Information**

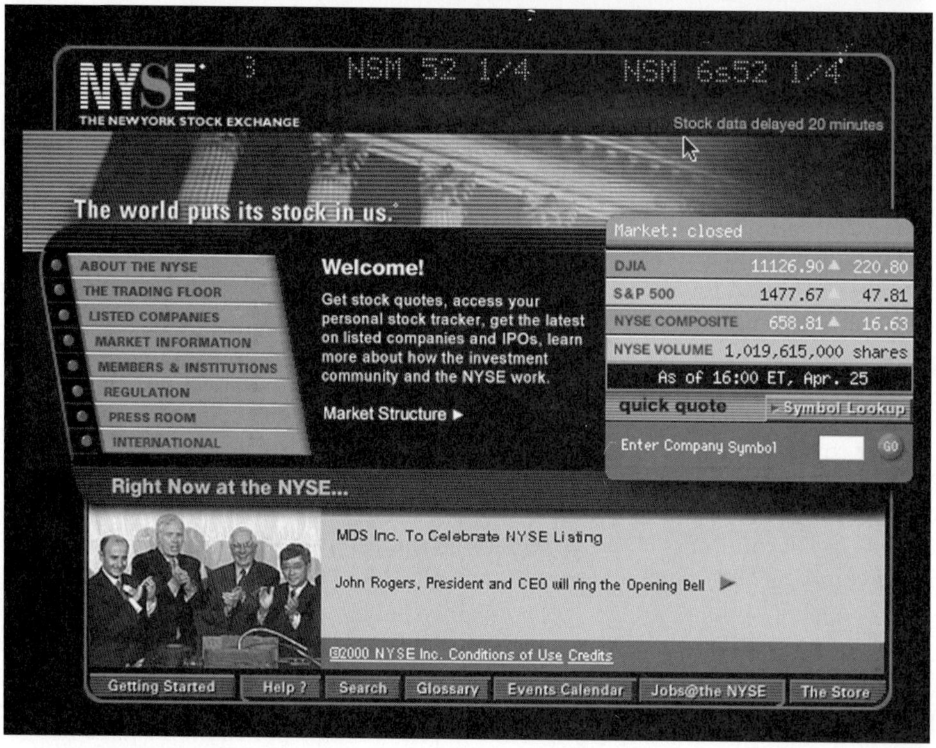

Source: <http://www.nyse.com>.

American Stock Exchange

On October 30, 1998, the **National Association of Securities Dealers, Inc. (NASD)** and the **American Stock Exchange (AMEX)** officially joined forces. The NASD is a self-regulatory organization of the securities industry, with particular responsibility for the regulation of the Nasdaq Stock Market and the OTC markets. With the Nasdaq-AMEX Market Group, companies and their shareholders enjoy the benefits of two distinctive market structures under one corporate roof. AMEX remains a specialist central auction market. With plans underway to revolutionize its trading technology, the NASD will ensure that the AMEX is the state-of-the-art auction marketplace. Nasdaq, a multiple dealer market system, will continue to evolve. Enhancements planned for the Nasdaq trading system will maximize use of its technology, providing a more efficient screen-based process for exchanging stocks.

National Association of Securities Dealers, Inc. (NASD) A self-regulatory organization of the securities industry.

American Stock Exchange (AMEX) Nation's second largest stock exchange.

As the nation's second largest floor-based stock auction exchange, the AMEX has a significant presence in both listed equities and equity derivative securities. Today, AMEX is on the leading edge of exchanges worldwide in developing successful new investment products and innovative services for companies and investors. The market capitalization of stocks listed on the AMEX more than quadrupled over the 1994–98 period, to a level that now stands in excess of $100 billion.

Regular financial guidelines for listing on the AMEX include minimum pretax income of $750,000 in the latest fiscal year, or two of the most recent three years, **public float** of $3 million, stock price of $3, and stockholders' equity of $4 million. Public float includes shares not held by any officer or director of the issuer or by any person who is the beneficial owner of more than 10% of the total outstanding shares. In other words, public float is the market value of common stock held by unaffiliated institutional and individual investors. Less strenuous alternate financial guidelines include a public float of $15 million, share price of $3, a three-year operating history, and stockholders' equity of $4 million. In all cases, companies listed on the AMEX must have 500,000 to one million shares available to the public and 400–800 public shareholders.

public float Common stock held by unaffiliated institutional and individual investors.

Options Exchanges

The **Chicago Board Options Exchange (CBOE)** revolutionized options trading by creating standardized listed stock options. Prior to that time, options were traded on an unregulated basis and did not have to adhere to the principle of "fair and orderly markets." The quick acceptance of listed options propelled CBOE to become the second largest securities exchange in the country and the world's largest options exchange. Today, CBOE accounts for more than one-half of all U.S. options trading and more than 90% of all index options trading.

Chicago Board Options Exchange (CBOE) Primary exchange for standardized, listed stock options.

The CBOE was originally created by the **Chicago Board of Trade (CBOT)** but has always been managed and regulated as an independent entity. After four years of planning, the CBOE opened on April 26, 1973, trading call options on 16 underlying stocks. Put options were introduced in 1977. By 1975, options had become so popular that other securities exchanges began entering the business. Today, options are traded on five U.S. exchanges, including the CBOE, NYSE, AMEX, Pacific Stock Exchange, and Philadelphia Stock Exchange. The CBOE now lists options on more than 1,200 widely traded stocks.

Chicago Board of Trade (CBOT) Primary place where buyers and sellers exchange commodities.

Ten years after stock options first traded on the CBOE, options on broad-based stock indexes were introduced. The first such index option, the Standard & Poor's

(S&P) 100 Index (ticker symbol OEX), was introduced on March 11, 1983. OEX has become the most active index product in the options market. The CBOE also trades options on the S&P 500 Index (SPX), the index that many U.S. money managers use as a benchmark for portfolio performance.

WALL STREET WISDOM 3.1

The NYSE

In 1790, the federal government refinanced all federal and state Revolutionary War debt by issuing $80 million in bonds. These government bonds became the first major issues of publicly traded securities and marked the birth of the U.S. investment markets. Just two years later, in 1792, 24 prominent brokers and merchants gathered on Wall Street to sign the now-famous Buttonwood Agreement, agreeing to trade securities on a common commission basis. The New York Stock Exchange traces its beginnings to this historic pact. The Bank of New York was the first corporate stock traded under the Buttonwood tree, and the first company listed on the NYSE.

It was not until 25 years later, in 1817, that the New York brokers established a formal organization, the New York Stock and Exchange Board and rented rooms for their trading activities at 40 Wall Street. At that time, they also adopted a constitution. In 1863, the New York Stock and Exchange Board adopted its present name. Two years later, the NYSE moved into its first permanent home, at 10–12 Broad Street, just south of Wall Street. This move established Wall and Broad as the center of securities trading in America. In 1868, membership in the NYSE became a "property right," enabling members to sell their seats. On April 22, 1903, the NYSE moved to 18 Broad Street, a facility that is still in use today.

Over its more than 200-year history, the NYSE has participated in signal events in our nation's history. When armed conflict engulfed Europe, securities exchanges around the world suspended operations to arrest plunging prices. The NYSE closed its doors on July 31, 1914, and did not fully reopen for four months, the longest shutdown in exchange history. Stock prices fell sharply on October 24, 1929, "Black Thursday," with record volume of nearly 13 million shares. Five days later, the market crashed on volume of more than 16 million shares, a level not surpassed for 39 years, and ushered in the Great Depression. In 1945, victorious American troops were welcomed home with a ticker tape parade as the exchange closed for business from August 15 through the 16 for V-J Day.

On October 19, 1987, the Dow Jones Industrial Average experienced a one-day drop of 508 points, the first drop of more than 500 points in the DJIA's history. Volume surged to a then unprecedented 604 million shares. Next-day volume reached 608 million shares. On October 27, 1997, the DJIA plunged a record 554 points and triggered NYSE "circuit breaker" rules for the first time. Trading was halted for the day at 3:30 PM, one-half hour before the regular close.

As of December 31, 1999, the estimated market capitalization of all publicly traded equities on all exchanges throughout the world was $32.7 trillion, up from only $22.8 trillion only two years earlier. Of this amount, the NYSE accounts for $10.8 trillion of market capitalization for companies domiciled in the United States. The global market capitalization for NYSE-listed U.S. companies is $16.8 trillion, up from $11.8 trillion only two years earlier, but a significant portion of this trading activity takes place in foreign markets. (The NYSE also accounts for more than $1.5 trillion in non-U.S.-domiciled companies.) Nasdaq has jumped from $1.7 trillion in total market cap in 1997 to $4.2 at year-end 1999. Tokyo now accounts for $4.2 trillion in world market capitalization, about the same as Nasdaq. The London market represents about $2.8 of global market capitalization, and Germany has $1.2 trillion.

In total, major world equities markets account for more than 70% of the total value of equities traded throughout the world. The NYSE is the undisputed world leader and accounts for more than one-third of the total value of world equities. The AMEX, once an important equity exchange, is now only responsible for roughly $100 billion of equity market capitalization, or 0.3% of the global total. Other developed and emerging markets around the world account for the rest.

Without a doubt, the NYSE provides the most liquid and visible forum for the trading of securities worldwide.

See: NYSE Web site at <http://www.nyse.com>.

Futures Exchanges

Futures exchanges are associations of members organized to provide competitive markets for the trading of futures and options on futures for commodities, natural resources, and financial instruments. U.S. futures and futures option trading is concentrated on seven major exchanges. Among these seven futures exchanges, the CBOT, Chicago Mercantile Exchange, and the New York Mercantile Exchange are commonly regarded as the "big three." They account for more than 90% of U.S. futures and futures options trading activity. While futures and futures options on some popular contracts are listed on more than one U.S. futures exchange, trading on the exchange that first introduced a given product tends to be dominant. As a result, the various U.S. futures exchanges tend to be known by their relative size and by the types of futures contracts with which they are associated. For example, the Chicago Merc is widely known for its market leadership in developing and trading financial instruments that multinationals and global investors can use to hedge foreign currency risk.

Other important U.S. futures exchanges include the New York Cotton Exchange, Coffee, Sugar & Cocoa Exchange, MidAmerica Commodity Exchange, Kansas City Board of Trade, and the Minneapolis Grain Exchange.

Over-the-Counter Markets

Nasdaq National Market Securities

Trading on the **Nasdaq Stock Market,** the world's first electronic stock market, began in 1971. Today, Nasdaq is the fastest growing stock market in the United States and features many of the fast-growing high-tech companies investors have come to crave. Just behind the NYSE, Nasdaq ranks second among the world's securities markets in terms of total dollar volume. Nasdaq lists more than 5,400 domestic and foreign companies, more than any other stock market in the world. The market capitalization of Nasdaq-listed companies exceeds $4 trillion. Nasdaq's share volume exceeds 200 billion shares per year, and the dollar volume of trading exceeds $6 trillion per year. During recent years, share trading volume on Nasdaq has rivaled that on the NYSE, but the value of shares traded is still much greater on the NYSE.

Nasdaq Stock Market
Largest organized equities market by trading volume and number of listed companies.

What distinguishes Nasdaq is its use of computers and a vast telecommunications network to create an electronic trading system that allows market participants to meet over the computer rather than face to face. Since making its debut as the world's first electronic stock market, Nasdaq has been at the forefront of innovation, using technology to bring millions of investors together with the world's leading companies.

On Nasdaq, trading is executed through an advanced computer and telecommunications network that serves as a model for stock markets worldwide. The Nasdaq Stock Market trades more shares per day than any other major U.S. market. Another major distinguishing feature is Nasdaq's use of multiple financial intermediaries. Nasdaq is a **negotiated market** in which investors deal directly with **market makers.** Market makers are NASD member firms that use their own capital, research, retail, and/or systems resources to represent a stock and compete with each other to buy and sell the stocks they represent. There are more than 500 member firms that act as Nasdaq market makers.

negotiated market
Price determination through bargaining.

market makers
Member firms that use their own capital to trade and hold an inventory of NASD stocks.

customer order flow Customer buy/sell activity.

market maker spread Difference between bid and ask prices.

inside market Highest bid and lowest offer prices.

One of the major differences between the Nasdaq Stock Market and the NYSE is Nasdaq's structure of competing market makers. Each market maker competes for **customer order flow** through displaying buy and sell quotations for a guaranteed number of shares. Once an order is received, the market maker will immediately purchase for or sell from its own inventory or seek the other side of the trade until it is executed. All this typically occurs in a matter of seconds. The difference between the price at which a market maker is willing to buy a security and the price at which the firm is willing to sell is called the **market maker spread.** At any point in time, this difference between a market maker's bid and ask depends on market supply and demand conditions and the level of the market maker's own inventory. Because each market maker positions itself to either buy or sell inventory at any given time, each individual market maker spread is not fully reflective of the market as a whole. The **inside market** is the highest bid and the lowest offer prices among all competing market makers in a Nasdaq security. On Nasdaq, the typical stock has 10 market makers actively competing with one another for investor order flow.

When a company submits an application for inclusion of any class of its securities in the Nasdaq national market, it pays the Nasdaq Stock Market, Inc., a one-time company listing fee of $5,000 plus a fee calculated on the basis of the total outstanding shares. For example, for companies with up to one million outstanding shares, the minimum Nasdaq listing fee is $34,525. For companies with more than 19 million outstanding shares, the Nasdaq listing fee is $90,000. Companies must also pay the Nasdaq Stock Market, Inc., an annual fee calculated on the basis of the total shares outstanding for each issue. For up to one million outstanding shares, the minimum Nasdaq's annual fee is $10,710. For companies with more than 100 million outstanding shares, Nasdaq's annual fee is $50,000. However, it is important to keep in mind that Nasdaq is in keen competition with the NYSE for company listings. To get or keep desired listings, the board of directors of the Nasdaq Stock Market may choose to defer or waive all or any part of the prescribed annual fees. As initial requirements, companies must have significant net tangible assets or operating income, a minimum public float of 500,000 shares, at least 400 shareholders, and a bid price of at least $5. The Nasdaq national market operates from 9:30 AM to 4:00 PM EST, with extended trading in SelectNet from 8:00 AM to 9:30 AM EST and from 4:00 PM and 5:15 PM EST. The Nasdaq International Service is an extension to the Nasdaq Stock Market's trading systems that allows early morning trading from 3:30 AM to 9:00 AM EST on each U.S. trading day. This Nasdaq service enables participants to monitor trades during London market hours. NASD members are eligible to participate in this session through their U.S. trading facilities or through those of an approved U.K. affiliate.

Nasdaq SmallCap Market Market for smaller companies that trade prior to full listing on the Nasdaq national market.

penny stocks Equities priced below $1.

Nasdaq SmallCap Market Securities

The **Nasdaq SmallCap Market** comprises more than 1,400 companies that seek the sponsorship of Nasdaq market makers, have applied for listing, and meet specific and financial requirements. Minimum criteria for listing on the Nasdaq SmallCap Market are far less strenuous than for any other national market. The minimum bid price required for common and preferred stock is only $1. This $1 bid price requirement is meant to provide a safeguard against certain unscrupulous market activity associated with low-priced **penny stocks** and enhances the credibility of the market. For initial listing, companies must have $4 million in net tangible assets, or $50 million in market capitalization or $750,000 in net income in two of the past three fiscal years. Public float of at least one million shares worth at least $5 million, a $4 minimum bid price, three market makers, and 300 round lot holders are also required. For continued listing, companies must have $2 million in net tangible assets, or $35 million in market capitalization, or $500,000 in net income in two of the past three fiscal years. Public float of at least 500,000 shares worth at least $1 million, a $1 minimum bid price, two market makers, and 300 round lot holders are also required. Listed companies are also required to meet minimum **corporate governance** requirements such as distribution of annual and interim reports, a minimum of two independent directors, and an accounting audit committee in which independent directors are a majority.

Once a company is approved and listed on this market, market makers are able to quote and trade the company's securities through a sophisticated electronic trading and surveillance system. The Nasdaq SmallCap Market operates from 9:30 AM to 4:00 PM EST, with extended trading in SelectNet from 8:00 AM to 9:30 AM EST and from between 4:00 PM and 5:15 PM EST.

Over-the-Counter Bulletin Board

The **OTC Bulletin Board (OTCBB)** is a regulated quotation service that displays real-time quotes, last-sale prices, and volume information in OTC equity securities. An OTC equity security generally is any publicly traded equity that is not listed on Nasdaq or a national securities exchange. OTCBB securities include national, regional, and foreign equity issues, warrants, units, and **American Depositary Receipts (ADR)**. In June 1990, the OTCBB began operation on a pilot basis, as part of important market structure reforms to improve efficiency in the OTC equity's market. The Penny Stock Reform Act of 1990 mandated the Securities and Exchange Commission (SEC) to establish an electronic system that met the requirements of section 17B of the Exchange Act. The system was designed to facilitate the widespread publication of quotation and last-sale information. Since December 1993, firms have been required to report trades in all domestic OTC equity securities through the Automated Confirmation Transaction Service within 90 seconds of the transaction.

OTC Bulletin Board (OTCBB) Regulated quotation service for very small over-the-counter equity securities.

American Depositary Receipts (ADR) Coupons that signify ownership of foreign stocks.

As of January 4, 1999, companies represented on the OTCBB were required to report their current financial information to the SEC, banking, or insurance regulators to meet eligibility requirements. Nonreporting companies whose securities were already quoted on the OTCBB were granted a grace period to comply with the new requirements. Those companies were phased in beginning July 1999. By June 2000, current financial information about all domestic companies that are quoted on the OTCBB became publicly available.

The OTCBB provides investors with access to more than 6,500 securities offered through more than 400 participating market makers. The OTCBB electronically transmits real-time quote and volume information and displays indications of interest and prior-day trading activity. The OTCBB is a quotation medium for subscribing members, not an issuer listing service. It should not be confused with the Nasdaq Stock Market. OTCBB securities are traded by a community of market makers that enters quotes and trade reports through a highly sophisticated computer network. The OTCBB is unlike the Nasdaq Stock Market in that it does not impose listing standards, provide automated trade executions, maintain relationships with quoted issuers, or have the same obligations for market makers.

The OTCBB is monitored by an online market surveillance system to help ensure compliance with the existing rules of the SEC and NASD. Nasdaq has no business relationship with the issuers quoted in the OTCBB. These companies do not have any filing or reporting requirements with the Nasdaq Stock Market, Inc., or NASD. However, issuers of securities are subject to periodic filing requirements with the SEC or other regulatory authorities.

For more detailed information about the OTCBB, see Nasdaq's excellent Web site at <http://www.nasdaq-amex.com>.

U.S. Large Company Indexes

Dow Jones Industrial Average

In 1882, Charles H. Dow and Edward Davis Jones started Dow Jones & Co. From an unpainted basement office next to the NYSE, they published a tip sheet called the *Customer's Afternoon Letter*, a precursor to *The Wall Street Journal*. At that time, people on Wall Street found it difficult to discern whether stocks generally were rising, falling, or treading water. To remedy the problem, Dow invented the first stock average in 1884. He began with 11 stocks. Most of them were railroads. The mechanics of the first stock average were simple. Computing with paper and pencil, Dow simply added up 11 stock prices and divided by the number 11. The idea of using an index to differentiate short-term changes in individual stock prices from the market's long-term trends was unique. At the time, Dow compared his average with placing sticks in the sand to determine, wave after wave, whether the tide was coming in or going out. If the average's peaks and troughs rose progressively higher, then a bull market prevailed. If peaks and troughs dropped lower and lower, a bear market was present.

After introducing his 11-stock average, Dow decided to create separate indexes to track industrial and railroad stocks. On May 26, 1896, Dow began tracking a 12-stock industrial average. In the autumn of 1896, Dow expanded his original index to track 20 railroad stocks. Remember, at the turn of the century, railroads were the first major corporations. It is easy to see why investors were more interested in the progress of railroad stocks than in advancement of a fledgling industrial sector.

At first, the Dow Jones & Co. stock averages were published irregularly, but daily publication in *The Wall Street Journal* began on October 7, 1896. In 1916, the industrial average was expanded to 20 stocks. That number was raised again to 30 on October 1, 1928, where it remains today (see Figure 3.2). Also in 1928, *Journal* editors began calculating index averages with special divisors, instead of the number of stocks, to avoid distortions caused by stock splits or company substitutions. The Dow Jones utility average came along in 1929, more than a quarter-century after Dow's death at age 51 in 1902. The railroad average was renamed the transportation average in 1970. Through habit, Dow Jones & Co. indexes are commonly referred to as "averages" even though that description is technically incorrect.

Dow Jones Industrial Average (DJIA) Price-weighted index of 30 large industrial stocks.

Dow's simple invention has been an enduring hit. It provides a convenient benchmark for comparing individual stocks to the course of the market. It also gives a basis for comparing the market with other economic indicators. What is now referred to as the **Dow Jones Industrial Average (DJIA)** also gives investors a common focal point. Investors often ask, "How did the market do today?" The answers always seem to revolve around the DJIA.

FIGURE 3.2 **The Dow Jones Industrial Average Is the Most Popular Stock Market Index**

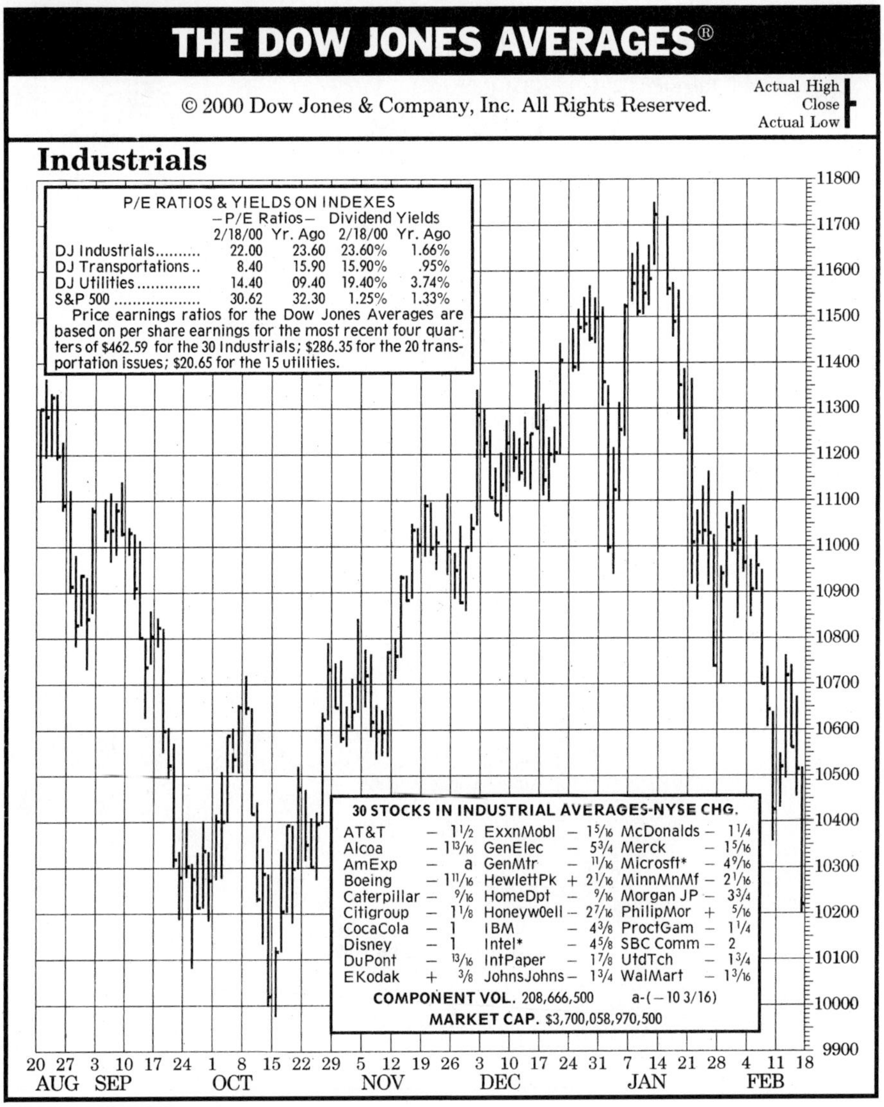
THE DOW JONES AVERAGES®
© 2000 Dow Jones & Company, Inc. All Rights Reserved.
Actual High
Close
Actual Low
Industrials
P/E RATIOS & YIELDS ON INDEXES
–P/E Ratios– Dividend Yields
2/18/00 Yr. Ago 2/18/00 Yr. Ago
DJ Industrials.......... 22.00 23.60 23.60% 1.66%
DJ Transportations.. 8.40 15.90 15.90% .95%
DJ Utilities............. 14.40 09.40 19.40% 3.74%
S&P 500 .... 30.62 32.30 1.25% 1.33%
Price earnings ratios for the Dow Jones Averages are based on per share earnings for the most recent four quarters of $462.59 for the 30 Industrials; $286.35 for the 20 transportation issues; $20.65 for the 15 utilities.
30 STOCKS IN INDUSTRIAL AVERAGES-NYSE CHG.
AT&T – 1 1/2 ExxnMobl – 1 5/16 McDonalds – 1 1/4
Alcoa – 1 13/16 GenElec – 5 3/4 Merck – 1 5/16
AmExp – a GenMtr – 11/16 Microsft* – 4 9/16
Boeing – 1 11/16 HewlettPk + 2 1/16 MinnMnMf – 2 1/16
Caterpillar – 9/16 HomeDpt – 9/16 Morgan JP – 3 3/4
Citigroup – 1 1/8 Honeyw0ell – 2 7/16 PhilipMor + 5/16
CocaCola – 1 IBM – 4 3/8 ProctGam – 1 1/4
Disney – 1 Intel* – 4 5/8 SBC Comm – 2
DuPont – 13/16 IntPaper – 1 7/8 UtdTch – 1 3/4
EKodak + 3/8 JohnsJohns – 1 3/4 WalMart – 1 3/16
COMPONENT VOL. 208,666,500 a-(–10 3/16)
MARKET CAP. $3,700,058,970,500
11800
11700
11600
11500
11400
11300
11200
11100
11000
10900
10800
10700
10600
10500
10400
10300
10200
10100
10000
9900
20 27 3 10 17 24 1 8 15 22 29 5 12 19 26 3 10 17 24 31 7 14 21 28 4 11 18
AUG SEP OCT NOV DEC JAN FEB

Source: *The Wall Street Journal,* February 14, 2000, C3.

Table 3.4 illustrates how the 30 stocks in the DJIA have changed since October 1, 1928. Changes in the composition of the DJIA, or any Dow Jones & Co. indexes, are made solely at the discretion of the editors of *The Wall Street Journal.* Neither the companies, the respective stock exchanges, nor any official agencies are consulted. Additions or deletions can be made at any time to achieve better representation of the broad market and of American industry. Each of the 30 stocks in the DJIA are major factors in their industries, listed on the NYSE or Nasdaq, and widely held by individuals and institutional investors. In an effort to better reflect the growing importance of

TABLE 3.4 How the 30 Stocks in the Dow Jones Industrial Average Have Changed since October 1, 1928

Original DJIA Members 10/1/28	1929	1930s	1950s
Victor Talking Machine	Natl Cash Register ('29)	IBM ('32)	
		AT&T ('39)	
Wright Aeronautical	Curtiss-Wright ('29)	Hudson Motor ('30)	Aluminum Co. of
		Coca-Cola ('32)	America ('59)
		National Steel ('35)	
North American		Johns-Manville ('30)	
International Nickel			
International Harvester			
Westinghouse Electric			
Texas Gulf Sulphur		Intl Shoe ('32)	Owens-Illinois ('59)
		United Aircraft ('33)	
		National Distillers ('34)	
U.S. Steel			
American Sugar		Borden ('30)	
		Du Pont ('35)	
American Tobacco		Eastman Kodak ('30)	
Standard Oil (N.J.)			
General Electric			
General Motors			
Texas Corp.			Texaco*('59)
Goodrich		Standard Oil (Calif) ('30)	
Allied Chemical & Dye			
Chrysler			
Atlantic Refining		Goodyear ('30)	
Paramount Publix		Loew's ('32)	Intl. Paper ('56)
American Can			
Bethlehem Steel			
General Railway Signal		Liggett & Myers ('30)	
		Amer. Tobacco ('32)	
Mack Trucks		Drug Inc. ('32)	Swift & Co. ('59)
		Corn Products ('33)	
Sears Roebuck			
American Smelting			Anaconda ('59)
Postum Inc.	General Foods*('29)		
Nash Motors		United Air Trans. ('30)	
		Procter & Gamble ('32)	
Union Carbide			
Radio Corp.		Nash Motors ('32)	
		United Aircraft ('39)	
Woolworth			

Note: Year of change shown in ( ); * indicates name change, sometimes following a takeover or merger.
Data sources: *The Wall Street Journal,* March 13, 1997, C32; and October 27, 1999, C.I.

technology, several substantive changes were made during the 1990s. Most recently, on November 1, 1999, high-tech giants Microsoft Corp., Intel Corp., and SBC Communications were added to the DJIA, along with home-improvement retailer Home Depot Inc. Microsoft, the largest U.S. equity in terms of market capitalization, and Intel, the sixth largest U.S. equity, were the first Nasdaq-listed stocks added to the DJIA. All members of the DJIA are also components of the S&P 500 Index.

Today, the 30 stocks in the DJIA represent roughly 30% of the roughly $15 trillion market capitalization of all U.S. equities. Because it is based on such large, frequently traded stocks, the DJIA can be measured with precision on a minute-by-

TABLE 3.4 ***(continued)***

1970s	1980s	1990s	Current DJIA Members
			AT&T
			Aluminium Co. of America
	American Express ('82)		American Express
Inco Ltd.*('76)	Boeing ('87)		Boeing
	Navistar*('86)	Caterpillar ('91)	Caterpillar
		Travelers Group ('97)	Citigroup
		Citigroup*('98)	
	Coca-Cola ('87)		Coca-Cola
	USX Corp.*('86)	Disney (Walt) ('91)	Disney (Walt)
			Du Pont
			Eastman Kodak
Exxon*('72)			Exxon
			General Electric
			General Motors
		Hewlett-Packard ('97)	Hewlett-Packard
	Chevron*('84)	Home Depot ('99)	Home Depot
	Allied-Signal*('85)	Honeywell*('99)	Honeywell
IBM ('79)			IBM
		Intel ('99)	Intel
			International Paper
	Primerica*('87)	J.P. Morgan ('91)	J.P. Morgan
		Johnson & Johnson ('97)	Johnson & Johnson
	McDonald's ('85)		McDonald's
Esmark*('73)			Merck
Merck ('79)			
		Microsoft ('99)	Microsoft
Minn. Mining ('76)			Minn. Mining
	Philip Morris ('85)		Philip Morris
			Procter & Gamble
		SBC Communications ('99)	SBC Communications
United Tech.*('75)			United Technologies
		Wal-Mart Stores ('97)	Wal-Mart Stores

minute basis during the trading day. This is not always true with indexes that contain less frequently traded stocks. The DJIA is the oldest continuous barometer of the U.S. stock market and far and away the most widely quoted indicator of U.S. stock market activity.

The DJIA remains a price-weighted stock index. This means that the component stocks are accorded their relative weights based on share prices. Originally, the DJIA was calculated by adding up stock prices of all 30 component stocks and then dividing by 30. Although that concept remains active today, the sum total of prices for all 30 stocks is now divided by a number called the **DJIA divisor.** The divisor has been decreased over the years to eliminate distortions caused by stock splits and company substitutions. Otherwise, following stock splits, for example, the

DJIA divisor Adjustment factor used to account for stock splits.

DJIA would decline even though there has been no negative effect on the performance of the DJIA "basket" of stocks.

The formula used to determine the DJIA is simply:

$$\text{DJIA}_t = \frac{\sum_{i=1}^{30} P_{it}}{\text{DJIA divisor}} \tag{3.1}$$

where P is the stock price for the ith DJIA component company at any given point in time t.

The current value of the DJIA divisor is published daily on page C3 of *The Wall Street Journal* and on a weekly basis in *Barron's*. On February 14, 2000, for example, the divisor equaled 0.20145268. Because the DJIA divisor is less than one, the DJIA rises or falls by more than one point with every $1 change in the value of any component stock. As of February 14, 2000, for example, a $1 rise in any component stock would cause the DJIA to rise by 4.96 points (= 1/DJIA divisor = 1/0.20145268). Because the DJIA is a price-weighted index, a 10% change in the value of a high-priced DJIA stock would have a much larger impact on the index than a similar percentage change in the value of a low-priced component. For example, a 10% rise in a DJIA stock selling for $100 (e.g., Microsoft) is a $10 change in the stock price and results in a 49.6-point rise in the DJIA. A 10% rise in a DJIA stock selling for $20 (e.g., Philip Morris) is a $2 change in the stock and results in a 9.92-point rise in the DJIA.

Table 3.5 shows the percentage change in share prices for the 10 DJIA components that were the largest contributors to the change in the DJIA on Wednesday, February 16, 2000. Notice how a relatively modest –1.96% change in high-priced General Electric had a greater effect on the DJIA than larger percentage changes in the lower-priced DJIA components, such as SBC Communications. Of course, big percentage changes in high-priced DJIA stocks such as Intel lead to big changes in the index.

It is also interesting to note that when the DJIA = 11,000, one share of all 30 component companies costs roughly $2,215 (= 11,000 × DJIA divisor = 11,000 × 0.20145268). As of February 14, 2000, the market capitalization of all 30 DJIA stocks combined was roughly $3.8 trillion. Dow Jones & Co. also publishes transport (20 stocks), utility (15 stocks), and composite averages (65 stocks). The DJ Equity Market Index includes 709 stocks and was introduced in 1988. Up-to-date information on all Dow Jones & Co. stock indexes and publications can be obtained on the Internet at <http://www.dowjones.com>.

Standard & Poor's 500 Index

S&P 500 Index Popular value-weighted market index.

The Standard & Poor's Corp. introduced a 90-stock average in 1928, but it was not until 1957 that it offered an expanded index of 500 stocks. Today, the **S&P 500 Index** is the most popular value-weighted market index. Companies included in the S&P 500 are chosen according to industry representation, liquidity, and stability criteria. Initially, the S&P 500 included 400 industrials, 40 utilities, 40 financial, and 20 transportation stocks. In recent years, the composition of the S&P 500 has changed periodically to maintain its reflection of the overall market. In early 2000, for example, the S&P 500 included 378 industrials, 40 utilities, 71 financial, and 11 transportation stocks. Of these S&P 500 companies, 448 (89.6%) were listed on the NYSE, and 52 (10.4%) were traded on Nasdaq.

TABLE 3.5 Index Movers for the DJIA and the S&P 500 on February 16, 2000

Dow Jones Indus. Avg. Company Name	10,561.41 Last	−156.68 pts. Change (%)	−1.46% Index pt
AMER EXPRESS (AXP)	152.38	−4.24	−33.51
INTEL CORP (INTC)	107.19	−4.30	−23.89
WAL-MART STO (WMT)	52.88	−6.93	−19.55
HOME DEPOT I (HD)	56.44	−5.25	−15.51
J.P. MORGAN (JPM)	112.81	−2.43	−13.96
GEN ELECTRIC (GE)	134.56	−1.96	−13.34
PROCTER & GA (PG)	93.38	−2.42	−11.48
COCA-COLA CO (KO)	53.75	−3.48	−9.62
SBC COMMUNIC (SBC)	38.81	−4.02	−8.07
BOEING CO (BA)	37.31	−3.40	−6.52
S&P 500 Index Company Name	**1,387.67 Last**	**−14.38 pts. Change (%)**	**−1.03% Index pt**
WAL-MART STO (WMT)	52.88	−6.93	−2.08
INTEL CORP (INTC)	107.19	−4.30	−1.91
GEN ELECTRIC (GE)	134.56	−1.96	−1.05
HOME DEPOT I (HD)	56.44	−5.25	−0.85
SBC COMMUNIC (SBC)	38.81	−4.02	−0.66
PFIZER INC (PFE)	34.19	−3.87	−0.63
MICROSOFT CO (MSFT)	97.63	−0.95	−0.57
COCA-COLA CO (KO)	53.75	−3.48	−0.57
AMERICA ONLI (AOL)	51.63	−3.84	−0.55
YAHOO INC (YHOO)	161.56	−4.96	−0.53

Data source: <http://www.bloomberg.com>.

Despite the fact that the S&P 500 is a large-cap index, it is important to recognize that stocks in the S&P 500 are not the 500 largest companies but an index designed to capture the returns of stocks from across the broad spectrum of the U.S. economy. In early 2000, the market capitalization of the entire S&P 500 totaled $11.8 trillion. Each stock's weight in the S&P 500 Index is proportionate to its market capitalization, computed as stock price times the number of outstanding shares. The average capitalization was $23.5 billion for S&P 500 firms, but the median (or middle) firm size was $7.6 billion. This means that the average firm size is skewed upward by the truly enormous size of the giants found at the top the S&P 500 firm size distribution. At the high end, the market capitalizations of Microsoft Corp., Cisco Systems, and General Electric Co. sum to more than $1.25 trillion and together comprise more than 10% of the overall index (see Table 3.6). The top 25 S&P 500 stocks account for roughly one-quarter of the market cap of the overall index. At the low end, the market capitalization of small S&P 500 stocks typically runs in the range from $300 million to $400 million, or less than 1% of the size of S&P 500 leaders.

The formula used to determine the S&P 500 is written:

$$\text{Value-weighted index value} = \frac{\Sigma P_t Q_t}{\Sigma P_0 Q_0} \times \text{Index base value} \qquad \textbf{(3.2)}$$

where P is price and Q is number of outstanding shares. (Note: 1941–43 index base of 10 was established.)

TABLE 3.6 The S&P 500 Is the Most Popular Value-Weighted Large-Cap Index

A. S&P 500 Statistics

Total Market Value ($ Billion)	11,740
Mean Market Value ($ Million)	23,479
Median Market Value ($ Million)	7,608
Weighted Avg. Market Value ($ Million)	130,041
Largest Cos. Market Value ($ Million)	505,037
Smallest Cos. Market Value ($ Million)	382
Median Share Price ($)	38.437
P/E Ratio	31.72
Dividend Yield (%)	1.20

B. Top 10 S&P 500 Companies

Company	Rank	Market Value $ Millions	% of Index	Cum % of Index
Microsoft Corp	1	507,719	4.34	4.34
Genl Electric	2	438,406	3.75	8.09
Cisco Systems	3	374,624	3.20	11.29
Intel Corp	4	330,525	2.83	14.12
Exxon Mobil	5	288,130	2.46	16.58
Wal-Mart Stores	6	243,842	2.08	18.66
Intl Bus. Machines	7	202,242	1.73	20.39
Citigroup Inc	8	192,185	1.64	22.04
Merck & Co	9	184,212	1.57	23.61
Lucent Tech	10	173,887	1.49	25.10

Note: All data as of January 31, 2000.
Data source: <http://www.spglobal.com>.

Companies selected for the S&P 500 represent a broad cross-section from across the spectrum of the U.S. economy. Ownership of a company's outstanding common shares is also scrutinized to screen out closely held companies. Trading volume of a company's stock is also measured on a daily, monthly, and annual basis to ensure ample liquidity and efficient share pricing. Companies in emerging industries and/or industry groups not fully represented in the index are obvious candidates for addition. From time to time, stocks are also removed from the index following mergers, bankruptcies, or other liquidations. Stocks are removed from the S&P 500 as close as possible to the actual transaction date following mergers or acquisitions. In the event of bankruptcy, a company is removed from the index immediately after filing Chapter 11 or as soon as an alternative recapitalization plan that radically changes the company's debt/equity mix is approved by shareholders. In other instances, a company can be removed from the index because it no longer meets current criteria for inclusion or is no longer representative of its industry group.

equity benchmark Performance standard.

As shown in Figure 3.3, despite obvious differences in the method of construction, the DJIA and the S&P 500 closely track each other over time. Both are attractive measures of short- and long-term trends in the prices of large company stocks. Although the DJIA is a long-time favorite with individual investors, the S&P 500 is preferred as an investment **equity benchmark** by many institutional investors. The S&P 500 is used as a standard against which performance is measured by 97%

FIGURE 3.3 **DJIA and S&P 500 Closely Track Performance of Large-Company Stocks**

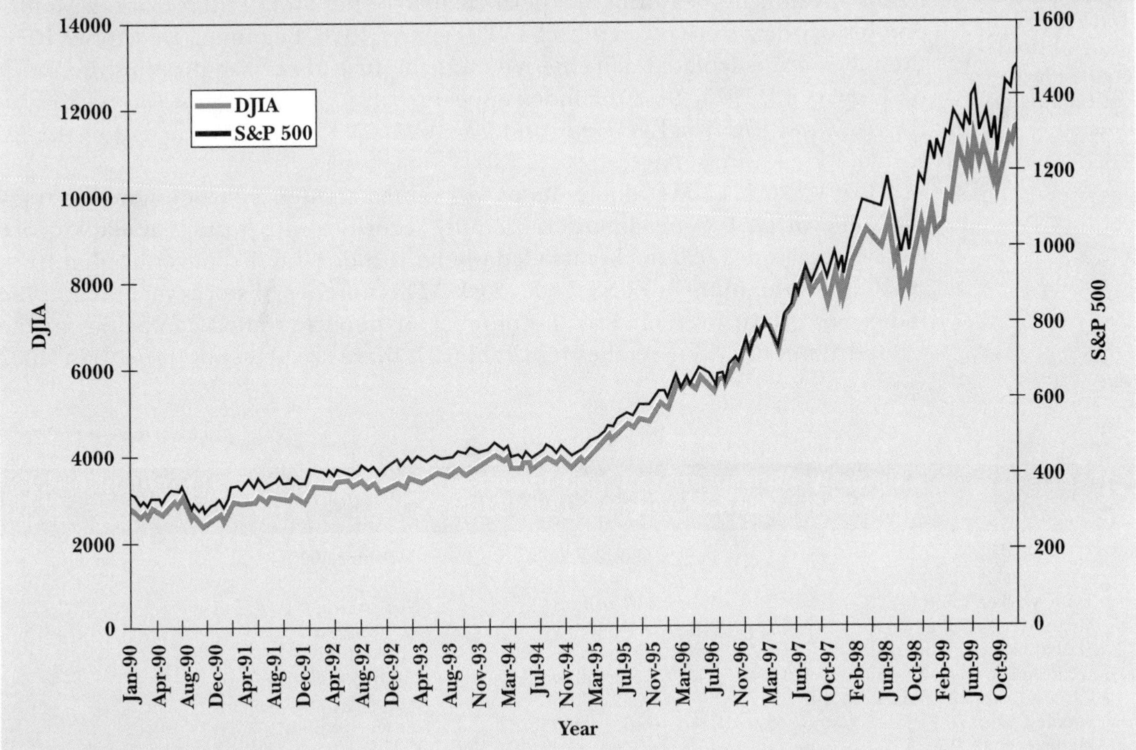

of U.S. money managers and pension plan sponsors. In addition, more than $1 trillion in investment funds is indexed to the S&P 500.

Current information on the S&P 500 can be obtained on the Internet at the company's Web site at <http://www.spglobal.com>.

Russell Indexes

The **Russell 3000 Index** measures the performance of the 3,000 largest U.S. companies based on total market capitalization, which represents approximately 98% of the investable U.S. equity market. Today, the average market capitalization of Russell 3000 companies is approximately $5 billion. The median market capitalization is approximately $800 million. The index has a market capitalization range from a high-end value in excess of $500 billion (for Microsoft) to roughly $180 million.

Russell 3000 Index Market capitalization index for the 3,000 largest U.S. companies (98% of U.S. market cap).

The **Russell 1000 Index** measures the performance of the 1,000 largest companies in the Russell 3000 Index. The Russell 1000 captures approximately 92% of the total market capitalization of the Russell 3000 Index and roughly 90% of the total market capitalization of publicly traded stocks in the United States. The average market capitalization of Russell 1000 companies is roughly $15 billion. The median market capitalization of Russell 1000 companies is approximately $5 billion. The smallest company in the index has an approximate market capitalization of $1.5 billion.

Russell 1000 Index Market capitalization index for the 1,000 largest U.S. companies (90% of U.S. market cap).

Wilshire (5000) Equity Index

Wilshire (5000) Equity Index Total dollar value of the U.S. equity market (in billions of dollars).

Wilshire Associates, Incorporated, created the **Wilshire (5000) Equity Index** in 1974 to aid investors in measuring the performance of the overall stock market. Month-end history data were created back to December 1970. Beginning December 1979, the index was calculated daily. *Barron's* was the first to publish the Wilshire index on January 13, 1975. Now, the index appears daily in *The Wall Street Journal,* the *Los Angeles Times, The New York Times,* and *The Washington Post* and is carried by the Associated Press wire service.

The Wilshire (5000) Equity Index is a value-weighted index designed to track the value of all U.S.-headquartered equity securities with readily available price data. There were 5,000 stocks included when the index was first introduced in 1974, or 10 times the number of S&P 500 stocks. The number of stocks included in the index has grown over time as the number of publicly traded companies in the United States has risen. As shown in Table 3.7, there are presently more than 7,000

TABLE 3.7 Company Characteristics and Industry Diversification for the Wilshire Total Stock Market Indexes (12/31/99)

	Wilshire 4500	Wilshire 5000
Total Market Value ($)	3.97 trillion	15.8 trillion
Mean Market Value ($)	601 million	2,230 million
Median Market Value ($)	105 million	129 million
Weighted Average Market Value ($)	7,598 million	110,678 million
Largest Company's Market Value ($)	84.49 billion	602.43 billion
Smallest Company's Market Value ($)	under 1 million	under 1 million
Median Share Price	$10.00	$11.25
P/E Ratio	57.7	35.0
Price/Book	37.3	22.8
Current Yield	0.83%	1.07%

	Number of Companies	Company Number as % of Wilshire 4500	Market Cap as % of Wilshire 4500	Number of Companies	Company Number as % of Wilshire 5000	Market Cap as % of Wilshire 5000
NYSE	1,345	20.36%	33.26%	1,759	24.80%	62.83%
AMEX	492	7.45%	2.22%	494	6.96%	0.85%
Nasdaq	4,768	72.19%	64.52%	4,840	68.24%	36.32%
Capital Goods	311	4.71%	2.89%	333	4.69%	4.65%
Consumer Durables	225	3.41%	2.01%	240	3.38%	1.62%
Consumer Nondurables	1,372	20.77%	17.36%	1,507	21.25%	24.67%
Energy	230	3.48%	2.54%	259	3.65%	4.44%
Finance	1,298	19.65%	15.53%	1,369	19.30%	14.09%
Materials and Services	1,643	24.88%	25.62%	1,724	24.30%	10.60%
Technology	1,137	17.21%	23.50%	1,214	17.12%	29.60%
Transportation	142	2.15%	1.29%	153	2.16%	0.87%
Utilities	247	3.74%	9.26%	294	4.14%	9.46%
Totals	**6,605**	**100.0%**	**100.0%**	**7,093**	**100.0%**	**100.0%**

Data source: Wilshire Associates, Inc., <http://www.wilshire.com>.

WALL STREET WISDOM 3.2

Global Financial Data on the Web

When it comes to the quantity and quality of available financial information, it is a whole new world on the World Wide Web. If you have any doubts about the quantity and quality of free financial information available on the Internet, check out Global Financial Data's Web site.

Global Financial Data offers the most extensive, long-term historical indexes on stock markets, interest rates, exchange rates, and inflation rates available anywhere. Included in their database are more than 5,000 data files covering more than 150 different countries. Data are recorded on a daily, weekly, monthly, and annual basis.

Of particular interest may be a wealth of free annual data series. From the Global Financial Data Web site, students and other researchers can download annual information about

- stock markets since 1693
- inflation rates since 1264
- interest rates since 1700
- commodity prices since 1257
- exchange rates since 1800
- Global Financial Data's world stock market indexes
- total returns since 1800

These free annual series are only a small representation of the data that are available. More comprehensive data series, on a monthly, weekly or daily basis, are available for purchase at competitive prices.

Global Financial Data's long-term financial database includes information about consumer price indexes, wholesale price indexes, futures and commodity prices, and historical exchange rates. The long-term stock market database is made up of world dollar stock market indexes, stock market yields, P/E (price/earnings) ratios, and total return indexes. The foreign interest rate database includes discount rates, Euro currency rates, interbank offer rates, private discount rates, government bond yields, and industrial bond yield files, to mention just a few of the many important data series offered.

The U.S. interest rate database incorporates U.S. money market and bond market yields, Moody's and Standard & Poor's interest rate indices and yields, and daily U.S. interest rates. The U.S. daily stock market database covers the Dow Jones & Co. Averages, Standard & Poor's Indexes, New York Stock Exchange Indexes, American Stock Exchange Indexes, and the NASDAQ/Over-the-Counter Indexes. The U.S. stock market sector database includes sector stock price indexes from Moody's and Standard & Poor's.

Global Financial Data's foreign daily stock market database encompasses a Canadian daily stock market database, major foreign stock market indexes, and detailed descriptions of index construction methodology. Extensive stock market data from both developed and emerging foreign markets are available. If you want to learn the ABCs of foreign stock market performance, where A is Austria, B is Bahrain, and C is the Czech Republic, the Global Financial database is a good place to look.

As is always the case when it comes to long-term financial data, some caveats are in order. Users of the Global Financial database, or any such information, must keep firmly in mind that the quality of financial data has improved greatly through the years. This means that very old data are not apt to be as precise as recent data. Moreover, financial markets are very different today than they were 10 or 25 years ago, let alone 50 or 100 years ago. The concept of publicly traded common stock is a fairly recent phenomenon. In the United States, a liquid and actively followed stock market has a history that began during the post–World War II period. It is also hard to know what to make of consumer price information that stretches back 50 or 100 years. For example, how much have PC prices fallen over the past 10 years? How much did cable TV cost in 1900?

Still, much of what you find on the Global Financial Data Web site is very useful. All of it is interesting.

See: Global Financial Data is on the Internet at <www.globalfindata.com>.

stocks in the Wilshire Equity Index. The index offers an excellent approximation of dollar changes in the U.S. equity market. On December 31, 1999, the market capitalization of the Wilshire Equity Index was $15.8 trillion. This number measures the market capitalization of all 7,000-plus stocks included in the index. Therefore, the market capitalization of the overwhelming bulk of liquid listed and unlisted equities in the United States was then roughly $15.8 trillion. The capitalization of the index can be accounted for with 62.8% NYSE, 0.8% AMEX, and 36.3% Nasdaq stocks.

U.S. Medium-Sized Company Indexes

Nasdaq Composite Index

Nasdaq Composite Index Market value–weighted index of all 5,000-plus stocks listed on the Nasdaq Stock Market.

The **Nasdaq Composite Index** measures all common stocks listed on the Nasdaq Stock Market. The index is market-value weighted. This means that each company affects the index in proportion to its market capitalization. Market capitalization is measured by the last sale price multiplied by total outstanding shares. It is calculated throughout the trading day.

Today, the Nasdaq index incorporates 5,000-plus companies, more than most other stock market indexes. Because it is so broad based, the Nasdaq Composite Index is one of the most widely followed and quoted major market indexes. The Nasdaq Composite Index has been actively followed since 1971.

The rapid rate of price appreciation for the Nasdaq Composite Index during the 1990s is unprecedented for such a large and widely followed market index. As shown in Figure 3.4, the Nasdaq Composite rocketed from 457.90 to 4069.31, or 888.69%, during the 1990s. This represents a decade-long 24.4% annual rate of share-price appreciation for Nasdaq stocks. During the most favorable market environment in history, capital gains on the Nasdaq far outstripped stellar capital gains of 411.24% for the DJIA (15.2% per year) and 410.28% for the S&P 500 (15.2% per year). At the start of the new millennium, it is no wonder that some investors are concerned that such gains are unsustainable.

Nasdaq 100 Index

Nasdaq 100 Index Market capitalization–weighted index of Nasdaq's largest companies.

The **Nasdaq 100 Index** reflects Nasdaq's largest companies across major industry groups, including computer hardware and software, telecommunications, retail/wholesale trade, and biotechnology. As shown in Table 3.8, many Nasdaq 100 stocks are often in the news or have become household names, such as Microsoft, Intel, and Dell Computer.

Launched in January 1985, the Nasdaq 100 Index represents the largest and most active nonfinancial domestic and international issues listed on the Nasdaq national market based on market capitalization. As of December 21, 1998, however, the Nasdaq 100 Index was rebalanced to a modified market capitalization–weighted index. Such rebalancing is expected to retain the general economic attributes of capitalization weighting while providing enhanced diversification. To accomplish this, Nasdaq will review the composition of the Nasdaq 100 Index on a quarterly basis and will adjust component weights if certain pre-established distribution requirements are not met. Eligibility criteria for the Nasdaq 100 Index includes a

FIGURE 3.4 **The Nasdaq Index Greatly Outperformed the Large-Cap DJIA and S&P 500 during the 1990s**

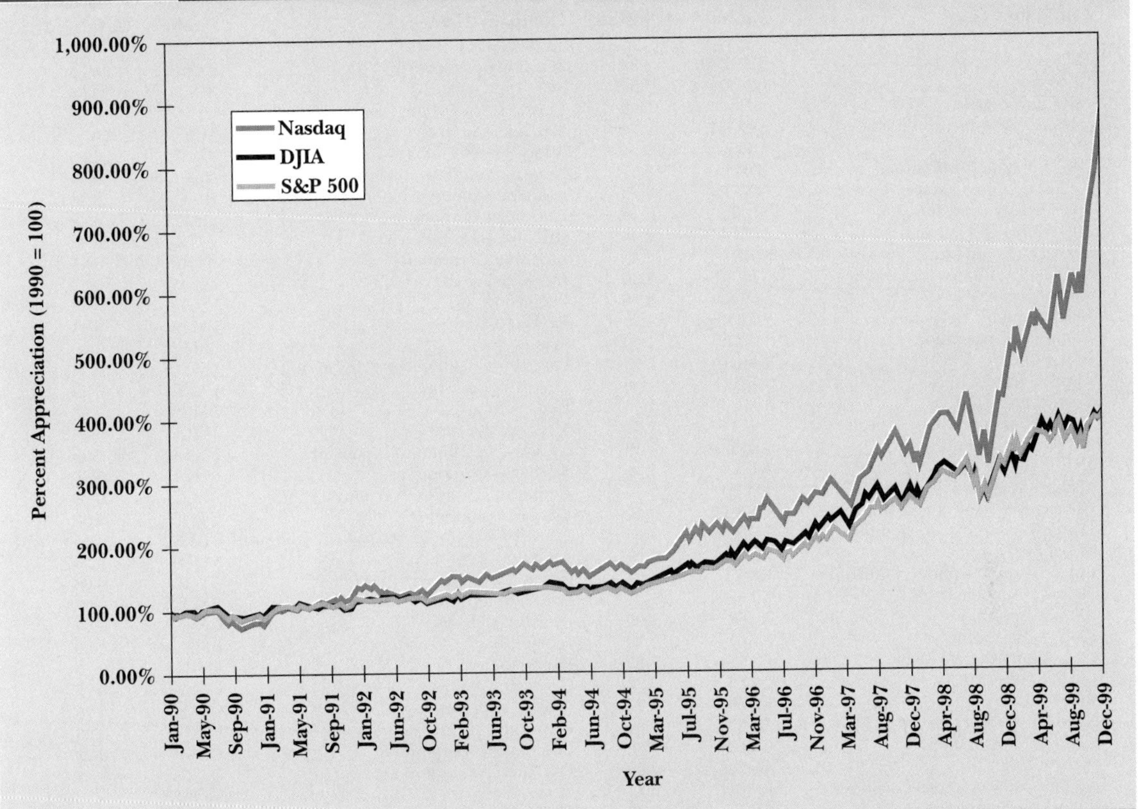

minimum average daily trading volume of 100,000 shares. Companies also must have been listed for a minimum of two years. If a security would otherwise qualify to be among the top 25% of issuers included in the index by market capitalization, then a one-year seasoning criteria would apply. If the security represents a foreign entity, the company must have a world-wide market value of at least $10 billion, a U.S. market value of at least $4 billion, and an average trading volume of at least 200,000 shares per day. In addition, foreign securities must be eligible for listed-options trading. Component stocks are adjusted annually to reflect changes in market capitalization. Every 15 seconds during the trading day, the Nasdaq Stock Market calculates and disseminates the value of the Nasdaq 100 Index.

The large number of securities in the Nasdaq 100 Index makes it an effective vehicle for securities traders. In October 1993, the Nasdaq 100 Index began trading on the CBOE. On April 10, 1996, the Chicago Mercantile Exchange began trading futures and futures options on the Nasdaq 100 Index. As seen in Table 3.8, the Nasdaq 100 Index is dominated by large technology stocks such as Microsoft Corp., Cisco Systems, Inc., Intel Corp., MCI-WorldCom, Inc., and Dell Computer Corp.

TABLE 3.8 The Nasdaq 100 Index Is Dominated by High-Tech Stocks

Company Name	Symbol	% Of Index (Adjusted)	Company Name	Symbol	% Of Index (Adjusted)
Microsoft Corporation	MSFT	8.82	3Com Corporation	COMS	0.53
Cisco Systems, Inc.	CSCO	7.50	SDL, Inc.	SDLI	0.53
Intel Corporation	INTC	5.90	Chiron Corporation	CHIR	0.52
QUALCOMM Incorporated	QCOM	5.39	MedImmune, Inc.	MEDI	0.52
Oracle Corporation	ORCL	3.46	Adobe Systems Inc.	ADBE	0.50
JDS Uniphase Corporation	JDSU	2.85	Network Solutions, Inc.	NSOL	0.49
Nextel Communications, Inc.	NXTL	2.73	EchoStar Communications Corporation	DISH	0.48
Sun Microsystems, Inc.	SUNW	2.72	PanAmSat Corporation	SPOT	0.48
MCI WORLDCOM, Inc.	WCOM	2.38	Paychex, Inc.	PAYX	0.48
Global Crossing Ltd.	GBLX	2.23	At Home Corporation	ATHM	0.45
VERITAS Software Corporation	VRTS	2.20	Lycos, Inc.	LCOS	0.43
Yahoo! Inc.	YHOO	2.16	PeopleSoft, Inc.	PSFT	0.42
Dell Computer Corporation	DELL	1.70	RF Micro Devices, Inc.	RFMD	0.41
Immunex Corporation	IMNX	1.69	Staples, Inc.	SPLS	0.40
CMGI, Inc.	CMGI	1.63	Parametric Technology Corporation	PMTC	0.39
Applied Materials, Inc.	AMAT	1.60	USA Networks, Inc.	USAI	0.39
Amgen Inc.	AMGN	1.45	BMC Software, Inc.	BMCS	0.38
Level 3 Communications, Inc.	LVLT	1.31	McLeodUSA Inc.	MCLD	0.38
Apple Computer, Inc.	AAPL	1.19	NEXTLINK Communications, Inc.	NXLK	0.38
Xilinx, Inc.	XLNX	1.16	Starbucks Corporation	SBUX	0.37
Maxim Integrated Products, Inc.	MXIM	1.14	American Power Conversion Corporation	APCC	0.36
Conexant Systems, Inc.	CNXT	1.12	QLogic Corporation	QLGC	0.36
Linear Technology Corporation	LLTC	1.06	Adelphia Communications Corporation	ADLAC	0.35
Siebel Systems, Inc.	SEBL	1.05	Sanmina Corporation	SANM	0.35
LM Ericsson Telephone Company	ERICY	1.04	Atmel Corporation	ATML	0.28
Network Appliance, Inc.	NTAP	1.01	Bed Bath & Beyond Inc.	BBBY	0.27
Altera Corporation	ALTR	1.00	Concord EFS, Inc.	CEFT	0.27
PMC — Sierra, Inc.	PMCS	0.99	Biomet, Inc.	BMET	0.26
i2 Technologies, Inc.	ITWO	0.95	Fiserv, Inc.	FISV	0.26
Citrix Systems, Inc.	CTXS	0.90	Genzyme General	GENZ	0.26
Biogen, Inc.	BGEN	0.86	Cintas Corporation	CTAS	0.25
Metromedia Fiber Network, Inc.	MFNX	0.84	Eletronic Arts Inc.	ERTS	0.25
Comcast Corporation	CMCSK	0.82	Compuware Corporation	CPWR	0.21
Amazon.com, Inc.	AMZN	0.80	Quintiles Transnational Corp.	QTRN	0.21
Applied Micro Circuits Corporation	AMCC	0.75	Molex Inc.	MOLX	0.20
CIENA Corporation	CIEN	0.75	CNET, Inc.	CNET	0.19
Intuit Inc.	INTU	0.74	Synopsys, Inc.	SNPS	0.19
eBay Inc.	EBAY	0.73	Adaptec, Inc.	ADPT	0.18
Novell, Inc.	NOVL	0.72	Network Associates, Inc.	NETA	0.18
VoiceStream Wireless Corporation	VSTR	0.72	Smurfit-Stone Container Corporation	SSCC	0.18
KLA-Tencor Corporation	KLAC	0.71	PACCAR Inc.	PCAR	0.17
BroadVision, Inc.	BVSN	0.70	Legoto Systems, Inc.	LGTO	0.16
Comverse Technology, Inc.	CMVT	0.69	Sigma-Aldrich Corporation	SIAL	0.16
Tellabs, Inc.	TLAB	0.65	Microchip Technology Inc.	MCHP	0.14
ADC Telecommunications, Inc.	ADCT	0.64	Dollar Tree Stores, Inc.	DLTR	0.11
Gemstar International Group, Ltd.	GMST	0.64	VISX, Inc.	VISX	0.09
NTL Incorporated	NTLI	0.62	PacifiCare Health Systems, Inc.	PHSY	0.08
RealNetworks, Inc.	RNWK	0.61	Apollo Group, Inc.	APOL	0.07
Costco Wholesale Corporation	COST	0.57	Herman Miller, Inc.	MLHR	0.06
Vitesse Semiconductor Corporation	VTSS	0.55	Northwest Airlines Corporations	NWAC	0.05

Note: All data as of February 11, 2000.
Data source: <http://www.nasdaq.com>.

Although the Nasdaq 100 Index reflects Nasdaq's largest companies across major industry groups, it is clearly focused on the high-tech sector. Major industry groups represented in the Nasdaq 100 include computer hardware and software, telecommunications, retail/wholesale trade, and biotechnology. Many investors take the performance of the Nasdaq 100 as a proxy for high-tech issues in general.

Standard & Poor's MidCap 400 Index

For a company to be considered a large-capitalization, or large-cap, stock, it generally must have a total market capitalization in excess of $10 billion. The stock price performance of the large-cap segment of the market is captured by the DJIA and the S&P 500. Performance of the mid-cap market segment is captured by a number of indexes, including the **S&P MidCap 400 Index.**

S&P MidCap 400 Index Market cap index for 400 medium-sized domestic stocks.

Middle-capitalization, or mid-cap, stocks generally feature a total market capitalization between $1.5 and $10 billion. The average size of S&P 400 MidCap Index firms is roughly $2 billion, and the median market cap is $1.5 billion. The smallest firms in the index have a market capitalization of roughly $125–$150 million. This index is used by more than 95% of U.S. managers and pension plan sponsors, but a relatively minor $25 billion in investable funds is indexed to the S&P MidCap 400 Index.

The S&P MidCap 400 Index consists of 400 domestic stocks chosen for market size, liquidity, and industry group representation. Like the S&P 500, the S&P MidCap 400 Index is a market value–weighted index and was the first benchmark of mid-cap stock price movement. Because of its relatively recent introduction, S&P MidCap 400 Index is relatively unknown among many individual investors. It is, however, an increasingly popular measure for the performance of the mid-sized company segment of the U.S. market.

Wilshire 4500 Index

The **Wilshire 4500 Index** is the Wilshire 5000 minus the companies from the S&P 500 Index. As is the case with the Wilshire 5000, this fund is misnamed. There are approximately 6,700 stocks represented in the Wilshire 4500, and about two-thirds of those stocks are mid-sized companies. The Wilshire 4500 was created December 31, 1983. Its current capitalization can be accounted for by 60% NYSE, 3% AMEX, and 37% Nasdaq stocks.

Wilshire 4500 Index Mid-cap index of Wilshire (5000) Index companies minus the S&P 500.

As shown in Table 3.7, the market capitalization of the Wilshire 4500 is roughly $4 trillion, or one-quarter that of the Wilshire 5000 index. Because the Wilshire 4500 is the Wilshire 5000 minus the S&P 500, this means that the S&P 500 accounts for roughly 75% of the market capitalization of the Wilshire Equity Index and one-quarter of the market capitalization of publicly traded equities in the United States. Clearly, the total market capitalization of U.S. equities is dominated by a relatively small number of truly enormous companies.

U.S. Small Company Indexes

Russell 2000 Index

Small-capitalization, or small-cap, stocks are generally described as those publicly traded corporations with less than $1.5 billion in total market capitalization. The **Russell 2000 Index** measures the performance of the 2,000 smallest companies in the Russell 3000 Index, which represents approximately 8% of the total market capitalization of the Russell 3000 Index. At the present time, the average market capitalization of Russell 2000 stocks is somewhat greater than $600 million. The median market capitalization is approximately $500 million. The largest company in the index has a market capitalization of roughly $1.5 billion.

Russell 2000 Index Small company stock price index for the 2,000 smallest companies in the Russell 3000 Index.

Unlike most other indexes, the companies in the Russell 2000 change once a year and once a year only, and if a company gets taken over or delisted, it is not replaced. Changes are announced on April 1 each year and implemented on May 1.

S&P SmallCap 600 Index

S&P SmallCap 600 Index Market cap–weighted index of 600 small domestic stocks.

The **S&P SmallCap 600 Index** consists of 600 domestic stocks chosen for market size, liquidity (bid-asked spread, ownership, share turnover, and number of no trade days), and industry group representation. Like all major S&P indexes, the S&P SmallCap 600 Index is a market value–weighted index (stock price times the number of outstanding shares), with each stock's weight in the index proportionate to its market value.

The average market capitalization of S&P SmallCap 600 Index stocks is roughly $600 million, and the median market capitalization is $444 million. The S&P SmallCap 600 Index is gaining acceptance as the preferred benchmark for both active and passive management due to its low turnover and fairly good liquidity. Approximately $8 billion is indexed to the S&P SmallCap 600 Index.

Global Stock Indexes

Major Global Stock Market Indexes

Nikkei 225 Index Leading measure of Japanese stock market.

FTSE-100 Capitalization-weighted index of the 100 top companies on the London Stock Exchange.

TSE-35 Market basket of 35 blue-chip Canadian companies.

Hang Seng Index Market cap–weighted measure of Hong Kong stocks.

The second largest national stock market in terms of market capitalization is the Japanese stock market. Japanese market performance is measured by the **Nikkei 225 Index** (see Figure 3.5). The Nikkei is a price-weighted average of 225 stocks from the first (most liquid) section of the Tokyo Stock Exchange. It was started on May 16, 1949. The world's third largest equity market is in London. The U.K. market is widely followed by using the **FTSE-100.** The FTSE-100 is a market capitalization–weighted index published by the *Financial Times* of the 100 top market cap companies, from 27 industries, on the London Stock Exchange (LSE). FTSE-100 companies comprise roughly 70% of the market cap of all LSE companies. The "footsie" is the London stock market equivalent of the DJIA, just like the Nikkei is the Japanese market equivalent of the DJIA.

Canada features the second largest national stock market in North America. Trading activity on the Toronto Stock Exchange is captured by the **TSE-35,** a market basket of 35 blue-chip Canadian companies. The TSE-35 accounts for roughly 45% of the total market cap of Canadian stocks.

The Hong Kong market is one of the most dynamic major stock markets in the world. This market is measured by the **Hang Seng Index.** Hang Seng companies must be among the top 90% of all Hong Kong stocks in terms of market cap and trading activity. Only the largest 33 companies from 10 industries are included, but the Hang Seng captures more than 80% of the market cap of all Hong Kong companies.

Morgan Stanley Capital International Indexes

Morgan Stanley Capital International (MSCI) is a subsidiary of Morgan Stanley Dean Witter & Co., a global financial services firm and a market leader in securities, asset management, and credit services. MSCI has been an industry leader in providing global equity benchmark indexes for more than 30 years. MSCI indexes are the most widely used benchmarks for international portfolio managers. More

FIGURE 3.5 **Bloomberg.com Is a Top Choice for Market News and Information**

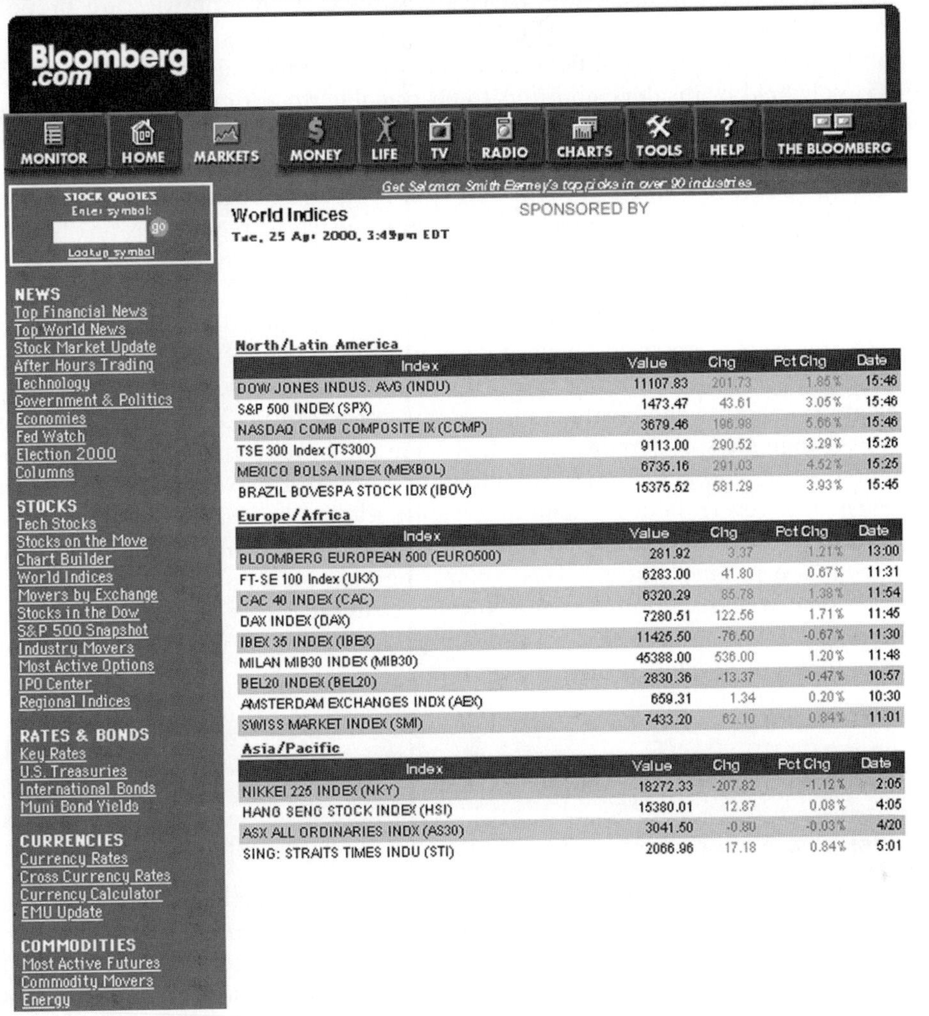
Bloomberg.com

MONITOR | HOME | MARKETS | MONEY | LIFE | TV | RADIO | CHARTS | TOOLS | HELP | THE BLOOMBERG

Get Salomon Smith Barney's top picks in over 90 industries

STOCK QUOTES
Enter symbol:
Lookup symbol

NEWS
Top Financial News
Top World News
Stock Market Update
After Hours Trading
Technology
Government & Politics
Economies
Fed Watch
Election 2000
Columns

STOCKS
Tech Stocks
Stocks on the Move
Chart Builder
World Indices
Movers by Exchange
Stocks in the Dow
S&P 500 Snapshot
Industry Movers
Most Active Options
IPO Center
Regional Indices

RATES & BONDS
Key Rates
U.S. Treasuries
International Bonds
Muni Bond Yields

CURRENCIES
Currency Rates
Cross Currency Rates
Currency Calculator
EMU Update

COMMODITIES
Most Active Futures
Commodity Movers
Energy

World Indices
SPONSORED BY
Tue, 25 Apr 2000, 3:49pm EDT

North/Latin America

Index	Value	Chg	Pct Chg	Date
DOW JONES INDUS. AVG (INDU)	11107.83	201.73	1.85%	15:46
S&P 500 INDEX (SPX)	1473.47	43.61	3.05%	15:46
NASDAQ COMB COMPOSITE IX (CCMP)	3679.46	196.98	5.66%	15:46
TSE 300 Index (TS300)	9113.00	290.52	3.29%	15:26
MEXICO BOLSA INDEX (MEXBOL)	6735.16	291.03	4.52%	15:25
BRAZIL BOVESPA STOCK IDX (IBOV)	15375.52	581.29	3.93%	15:45

Europe/Africa

Index	Value	Chg	Pct Chg	Date
BLOOMBERG EUROPEAN 500 (EURO500)	281.92	3.37	1.21%	13:00
FT-SE 100 Index (UKX)	6283.00	41.80	0.67%	11:31
CAC 40 INDEX (CAC)	6320.29	85.78	1.38%	11:54
DAX INDEX (DAX)	7280.51	122.56	1.71%	11:45
IBEX 35 INDEX (IBEX)	11425.50	-76.50	-0.67%	11:30
MILAN MIB30 INDEX (MIB30)	45388.00	536.00	1.20%	11:48
BEL20 INDEX (BEL20)	2830.36	-13.37	-0.47%	10:57
AMSTERDAM EXCHANGES INDX (AEX)	659.31	1.34	0.20%	10:30
SWISS MARKET INDEX (SMI)	7433.20	62.10	0.84%	11:01

Asia/Pacific

Index	Value	Chg	Pct Chg	Date
NIKKEI 225 INDEX (NKY)	18272.33	-207.82	-1.12%	2:05
HANG SENG STOCK INDEX (HSI)	15380.01	12.87	0.08%	4:05
ASX ALL ORDINARIES INDX (AS30)	3041.50	-0.80	-0.03%	4/20
SING: STRAITS TIMES INDU (STI)	2066.96	17.18	0.84%	5:01

Source: <http://www.bloomberg.com>.

than 1,200 institutional clients worldwide currently use MSCI benchmarks. In North America and Asia, more than 90% of institutional international equity assets are benchmarked to MSCI indexes. In Europe, more than one-half of continental fund managers currently use MSCI indexes as their benchmark according to a recent Merrill Lynch/Gallup survey.

Europe, Australasia, Far East (EAFE) Index
Leading global stock index of stocks from 21 countries.

The **Europe, Australasia, Far East (EAFE) Index** is perhaps MSCI's most famous index. The EAFE stock index is designed to measure the investment returns of developed countries outside of North America. When the index was first constructed in 1969, 14 countries were included. The index now includes stocks from 21 countries. The most recent addition was Portugal in 1997.

The process used to select stocks for the EAFE index is extensive. Stocks from each country are divided into industry groups, and then representative stocks are selected from each industry group. This ensures that all industries are proportionally weighted in the index. The MSCI EAFE also ensures that the stocks have good liquidity and high free float, meaning a large percentage of shares that are not closely held by insiders, and thus freely tradable. In addition, cross-ownership is tracked to ensure that the market weight given each company is accurate.

emerging markets Stock markets in developing nations.

There is no clear-cut set of characteristics to define an **emerging market.** Markets develop as economic growth accelerates, companies begin to raise capital in the public markets, trading mechanisms are set in place, regulations are liberalized, and investor interest grows. As markets have evolved, MSCI has expanded its emerging market's universe. These markets display Gross Domestic Product (GDP) per capita that is substantially below the average for developed economies. For example, the average emerging market covered by MSCI has a GDP per capita that is roughly 15% of the GDP per capita for developed markets. As always, GDP figures must be approached with caution because they can be distorted by inflation and exchange rates. Emerging markets also tend to have substantially greater government regulation. Sometimes, rules limit or ban foreign ownership in emerging markets. Lax government regulation, irregular trading hours, and/or less sophisticated back office operations, including clearing and settlement capabilities, are also common in emerging markets. Some emerging markets also feature restrictions on repatriation of initial capital, dividends, interest, and/or capital gains. All emerging markets involve companies with greater perceived investment risk than leading firms in **developed markets.**

developed markets Stock markets in mature countries.

Securities Market Regulation

Legislative Foundation

The securities markets in the United States operate according to laws passed by the Congress and the state legislatures. In the Congress, the Committee on Banking, Housing, and Urban Affairs of the Senate and the Committee on Commerce of the House of Representatives monitor the securities industry. Both committees measure the effectiveness of current laws and seek to determine the need for additional legislation. The Securities Act of 1933 and the Securities Exchange Act of 1934 are the most significant laws for investors, issuers of securities, and brokers/dealers. The 1933 act is primarily concerned with the issuance of new securities. It requires companies going public to register and supply financial and other material information concerning their securities offerings. The purpose is, of course, to enable investors to make informed decisions. At the same time, the 1933 act exempts private placements and transactions that involve a limited number of investors, strictly limited dollar amounts, or are offered only on an intrastate basis.

The Securities Exchange Act of 1934 focuses on securities trading. It authorized the creation of the SEC as the primary agency responsible for administering federal securities laws. The 1934 act also stipulated that the registration of securities offerings required by the 1933 act was to be done with the SEC. The 1934 act also authorizes the SEC to enforce federal securities statutes, rules, and regulations. SEC

WALL STREET WISDOM 3.3

Everybody Wants to Regulate Securities

Investors and savers are well aware of the growing competition for investment dollars. Anyone with money to invest is on a first-name basis with bankers, insurance agents, and stockbrokers. Financial professionals from each of these industries are going head-to-head for investor dollars. What may be surprising is that state and federal regulators are also going head to head for control of an increasingly competitive financial marketplace.

This "regulator's brawl" involves heavyweight contenders such as the Federal Reserve, Comptroller of the Currency, and the Federal Deposit Insurance Corp. Each of these traditional bank regulators wants to maintain its role as a primary authority over bank borrowing and lending practices as banks and other financial institutions expand into the securities business. In fact, traditional bank regulators have managed to get a number of limits on the Securities and Exchange Commission's authority over banks' securities operations. However, SEC officials apparently do not trust bank regulators to do a good job regulating the securities business of banks. The SEC favors a public display of securities law enforcement actions, including stiff fines when warranted. SEC officials have gone on record as stating that market integrity and investor protection are not principal concerns of banking regulation and that banking regulation is not an adequate substitute for vigorous SEC supervision.

Of course, bank regulators resent the insinuation that they are soft on the industry. The frequency and intensity of bank examinations are far greater than the SEC's examination of brokers/dealers. Sometimes, regulators can get into a snit about a single issue involving an individual financial institution. In 1998, for example, the SEC accused SunTrust Bank, Inc., of manipulating loan-loss reserves to smooth out year-to-year fluctuations in reported earnings. When the SEC pressed SunTrust to restate earnings, they enraged bank regulators who had been warning banks to increase reserves in anticipation of an economic slowdown. Representatives of the Office of the Comptroller, the Fed, and the Federal Deposit Insurance Corporation all urged the SEC to take "extreme caution" on the reserve issue.

Clashes between the SEC and traditional bank regulators appear to be based on deep-rooted philosophical differences. For the most part, banking regulators tend to be mainly concerned with keeping banks in business. This stems from the fact that taxpayers end up footing the bill when loans made by insured banks and savings and loans go sour. On the other hand, the SEC is specifically focused on protecting stock and bond investors from issuer fraud and from market manipulation.

To be sure, antiquated financial services laws adopted in the 1930s are bound to be fundamentally altered, and soon. Proponents of new financial services sector regulation say that such legislation will pave the way for one-stop financial service shops that offer everything from basic checking accounts, to auto and life insurance, to annuities, to mutual funds, to stock and bond brokerage services. Until new comprehensive legislation is enacted, it remains unclear how federally insured deposits can be protected from imprudent lending practices. In a proposal backed by the Federal Reserve, financial institutions that offer insured deposits could be forced to form bank holding companies with affiliates that offer new nonbank activities. In a proposal backed by the Treasury Department, banks would have a choice between a bank holding company structure and one that uses operating subsidiaries for nonbank services.

In the insurance industry, many are concerned that new federal laws allowing broader competition in the industry will preempt state insurance laws that tend to protect insurers from vigorous price competition. As a result, the insurance industry has largely lined up behind state and local government officials that want to maintain state regulation of insurance practices.

Such turf battles among regulators add to the level of confusion facing both individual investors and reporting companies. Until Congress settles the matter and finally passes a comprehensive regulatory reform bill for the securities industry, everyone will keep asking, "Who's in charge and what are the rules?"

See: Jathon Sapsford, "Banks and Securities Regulators Unveil Panel to Recommend Disclosure Rules," *The Wall Street Journal*, April 28, 2000, A2.

rules governing brokers/dealers include mandatory registration with the SEC, financial responsibility requirements, restrictions on borrowing, and the prohibition of security price manipulation or deceptive sales or purchase practices. SEC rules governing issuers include ongoing disclosure requirements and regulation of the proxy solicitation and tender offer processes—both of which relate to shareholder voting.

State securities laws actually predate the federal securities laws. The first state securities laws were passed by Kansas in 1911. Within 20 years, virtually all states had enacted parallel regulations. In an effort to make securities laws uniform, since the mid-1950s about 40 state legislatures have passed their own versions of the Uniform Securities Act. Like the federal laws, state securities laws focus on registration of securities, registration of brokers/dealers and agents, and antifraud provisions.

Self-Regulatory Organizations

self-regulatory organizations (SRO) Industry group with oversight authority granted by the SEC.

The SEC delegates significant regulatory authority to a number of securities industry member-owned and member-operated organizations. Known as **self-regulatory organizations (SRO),** these organizations oversee securities markets and participating member firms. Noteworthy SROs include the NASD, NYSE, AMEX, CBOE, a number of the regional stock and options exchanges, and the Municipal Securities Rulemaking Board.[2]

When originally adopted, the 1934 act only empowered the SEC to regulate the exchange markets. The Maloney Act of 1938 expanded the scope of the 1934 act by authorizing the registration of national securities associations to regulate the business of broker/dealer members in the OTC markets, subject to SEC supervision and authority. Although the NYSE, AMEX, and regional stock and option markets are registered exchanges, the NASD is the only national securities association registered under the amended 1934 act. Any broker or dealer required to register with the SEC under the 1934 act must also become a member of the NASD unless its business is conducted only on a national exchange of which it is a member, such as the specialists on NYSE and AMEX. Thus, all brokers/dealers registered in the United States that do business with the public are required to be members of the NASD and are regulated by it.

Responsibilities of the SROs include the formulation of rules governing business practices and markets. SROs must periodically review business practices to ensure fair dealing by members with their customers. Securities firms are examined for compliance with net capital and other financial and operational requirements. Markets surveillance is carried out to ensure fair dealing and an absence of market manipulation. SROs also take enforcement actions when members or industry professionals violate the securities laws or SRO rules and are responsible for the imposition of disciplinary sanctions. Finally, SROs arbitrate disputes between investors and firms, as well as disputes between firms.

The SEC oversees SROs by using the authority granted by Congress. All SRO rules and regulations must be approved by the SEC before they can take effect. Because the SROs are self-regulatory in nature, they are fully funded by member and listed company fees. No taxpayer money is used.

---

[2]For an excellent review of securities regulation, see *Securities Regulation in the United States, Third Edition.* Copies can be obtained from the National Association of Securities Dealers, Inc. 1735 K Street, NW Washington, DC 20006-1500.

Allocation of Responsibility

The NASD regulates the Nasdaq Stock Market and the vast OTC securities markets. The NASD has self-regulatory jurisdiction over not only Nasdaq and the OTC equity markets but also over members' sales practices for corporate debt, mutual funds, municipal securities, government securities, limited partnerships, and variable annuities. For its more than 5,500 broker/dealer members, the NASD has authority to monitor sales practices, which it carries out through field inspection programs. The NASD also regulates the financial soundness and operating condition of broker/dealer members who are not members of the NYSE or the AMEX and members of regional exchanges that are not exchange specialists or floor brokers.

The NASD also has regulatory responsibilities in many other areas, including testing, registration, and licensing of securities industry professionals. The NASD conducts fairness reviews of the level of underwriter compensation in new offerings. The NASD also ensures that member advertising and sales literature is accurate and not misleading.

Subject to SEC approval, the Municipal Securities Rulemaking Board formulates rules governing the origination, sale, and trading of municipal securities. The NASD, as the sole self-regulator for the securities industry in this area, enforces these rules for all brokers/dealers. Commercial bank activity is monitored by traditional bank regulators: the Federal Reserve System, the Office of the Comptroller of the Currency, and the Federal Deposit Insurance Corporation (FDIC).

Market Surveillance

Stock Watch is a key NYSE tool for protecting the integrity of the market in NYSE-listed securities. It is a computerized system that automatically flags unusual volume or price changes in any listed stock, helping the exchange guard against manipulation and insider trading.

Stock Watch Computerized system to flag unusual volume or price changes.

Most large volume or price changes can be explained by company news, trends in the industry, or national economic factors. However, when no legitimate explanation is evident, the NYSE launches an investigation. The investigation begins by contacting the company to find out whether there are any pending announcements. At the same time, surveillance personnel draw on an electronic audit trail to reconstruct the details of every trade that takes place. Rebuilding the "time of execution" enables NYSE investigators to see whether any member firm stands out in the trading.

The next step is to contact the firm and obtain the names of the customers involved in questionable trades. These names are automatically matched against the names of officers, directors, and other corporate and noncorporate insiders to detect any possible connection or illicit flow of information. This task is performed by using the Automated Search and Match (ASAM) system, which contains the names of 800,000 executives, lawyers, bankers, and accountants, plus public profile data on officers and directors of approximately 80,000 public corporations and 30,000 corporate subsidiaries. Customer trading information is also analyzed for geographic concentrations and compared with names and chronological events provided by NYSE-listed companies and member firms.

No single regulator has complete oversight over all trading activity because stocks may be traded in multiple markets. With the advent of derivatives such as futures and options, trading activity in one market can also be used to manipulate

Intermarket Surveillance Group Coordinated effort to detect cross-market manipulative trading.

the price of the underlying security in another market. For this reason, the SROs formed the **Intermarket Surveillance Group** to share surveillance information and coordinate efforts to detect cross-market manipulative trading. Advanced computer-based surveillance systems are operated by NASD regulation to oversee activity in the Nasdaq Stock Market and other markets run by Nasdaq with StockWatch Automated Tracking (SWAT) and Research and Data Analysis Repository (RADAR). Through these systems, every bid and offer quotation and trade in every security on the Nasdaq market is subject to computerized scrutiny.

If, after an investigation is completed, any suspicious trading practices are uncovered, an individual SRO can take disciplinary action and/or turn the information over to the SEC for further consideration.

Securities Arbitration

securities arbitration Private form of dispute resolution.

An interesting aspect of securities trading regulation is the extensive use of a unique private form of dispute resolution called **securities arbitration**.

Each day on the NYSE, more than 900 million shares of stock worth more than $30 billion change hands. Disputes sometimes arise. For more than 100 years, NYSE arbitration has been used to resolve disputes between brokers and investors. Arbitration is often viewed as an attractive alternative to lengthy and expensive litigation. In June 1987, the Supreme Court of the United States upheld the arbitration process as a fair, equitable, and efficient method for settling disputes within the securities industry.

Arbitration enables a dispute to be resolved quickly and fairly by impartial persons—known as arbitrators—who are knowledgeable educators, lawyers, or other professionals. Claims involving the activities of stockbrokers may be arbitrated if the claim is filed within six years of the date of the event in dispute. A securities customer always has the right to require a stockbroker to submit to the arbitration process. In choosing arbitration as a means of resolution, all parties waive the right to pursue the matter through the courts.

The NYSE provides neutral arbitration panels to hear and decide disputes in more than 30 major cities throughout the United States. Typically, a panel for a case consists of one arbitrator with securities industry experience and two arbitrators who have no affiliation with the securities industry. At the hearing, parties present testimony and evidence to the arbitrators. Those who testify are subject to cross-examination by the opposing sides and to questions by the arbitrators. Both sides make opening statements, present their cases, and make concluding statements. Although legal representation is not required, it is advised. When the arbitrators reach their decision and have signed an award, copies are mailed to the parties involved. Generally, the arbitrators' decision is final and is only subject to review by the courts in rare circumstances.

Circuit Breakers

circuit breakers Rules to halt securities trading in volatile markets.

Circuit breakers are rules to halt securities trading under certain circumstances. They represent an interesting example of securities market regulation that exemplifies the high level of cooperation between the SEC and SROs. Under rules proposed by the various exchanges and approved by the SEC, all U.S. stock and futures exchanges halt trading to restore order when prices plummet. By calling a brief "timeout" during periods of panicky market turmoil, it is hoped that investors will refocus on investment opportunities and economic strengths and bring a halt to any tendency for contagious selling activity. This policy was first approved by the SEC for the NYSE following the October 1987 stock market crash. Circuit breakers subsequently were adopted by the other exchanges. This means that once trading is halted on the NYSE, trading is also halted on Nasdaq and all other U.S. stock, options, and futures exchanges.

Circuit breakers were tripped for the first time on October 27, 1997, when the Dow closed after a 554-droppoint. On that day, the NYSE and all other major securities markets stopped trading for 30 minutes after the Dow fell 350 points and closed early when the decline resumed. Whether the use of circuit breakers stemmed the market's decline on that day remains debatable. Some market participants complained that the speed and breadth of the market's decline actually worsened as panicked traders quickly exited the market. Others complained that the decline—which amounted to 7.2%—was too small to justify an early end to trading. These complaints led the investment community to propose changes that were approved by the SEC.

Under current rules, at the end of each calendar quarter, the NYSE figures the average daily closing value for the DJIA during the preceding month and multiplies that figure by 10%, 20%, and 30%. The resulting figures, rounded to the nearest 50, become the circuit breakers for the following quarter. A decline of 10% before 2:00 PM EST results in a one-hour trading halt. A decline of 10% at or after 2:00 PM EST but before 2:30 PM causes a 30-minute halt in trading. A two-hour trading interruption follows a 20% decline before 1:00 PM. If such a decline occurs after 1:00 PM but before 2:00 PM, trading is halted for one hour. After 2:30 PM, trading is halted if the market is off 20%. If at any time during the trading day the DJIA is off 30%, trading is suspended for the rest of the day. These circuit breakers apply not only to the trading of stocks but also to options on stocks and stock indexes, stock index futures, and options on stock index futures.

Trading halts are also important for mutual fund shareholders. On a typical day, mutual funds calculate net asset values after the market ceases trading for the day at 4:00 PM EST. Investors must place orders to buy or sell shares before the close of the NYSE to receive that day's prices. With trading halts, investors must be sure to place their buy or sell orders prior to the market close if they want to get that day's prices. The end-of-trading-day deadline applies no matter when—or why—the market closes.

Qualifying to Become a Securities Professional

Any securities professional associated with a broker/dealer firm—including partners, officers, directors, branch managers, department supervisors, and salespersons—must register with the NASD and other relevant SROs through their firm. The registration application requires information about the individual's prior employment and disciplinary history. Individuals must also provide fingerprints, which are then submitted to the Federal Bureau of Investigation for a criminal record check. The SROs have the authority to bar any person from working in the securities industry for, among other reasons, the violation of SEC requirements or conviction of a felony.

Securities professionals must also qualify through examinations administered by the NASD. The series of qualification examinations covers knowledge of the federal securities laws and SEC rules and regulations. Also covered on these exams are questions concerning the nature of various securities, the operation of financial markets, economic theory and risk, corporate finance, accounting, fair sales practices, types of customer accounts, and taxes. Prospective principals of securities firms must also pass examinations that test knowledge of laws, rules, and regulations governing supervision of investment banking, trading and market making, brokerage and sales activities, and compliance with financial responsibility. Financial and operational principals must also demonstrate knowledge of laws, rules, and regulations regarding keeping and preserving records, net capital requirements, customer protection, financial reporting, extension of credit, uniform practice, and fair practice.

Summary

- Since 1817, the **New York Stock Exchange** has maintained an **agency auction market.** Trading at the NYSE takes place by open bids and offers by exchange members acting as agents for institutions or individual investors. Each listed stock is assigned to a single post where the **specialist** manages the auction process. Minimum listing standards for the NYSE start with a minimal number of **round lot** holders, shareholders who own at least 100 shares.
- The **National Association of Securities Dealers, Inc., (NASD)** is a self-regulatory organization of the securities industry. Guidelines for listing on the nation's second largest stock exchange, the **American Stock Exchange (AMEX)**, include a **public float** of $3 million. Public float is the amount of common stock held by unaffiliated institutional and individual investors.
- The **Chicago Board Options Exchange (CBOE)** revolutionized options trading by creating standardized listed stock options. The CBOE was created by the **Chicago Board of Trade (CBOT)**, an institution formed in 1848 to facilitate the exchange of commodities.
- The **Nasdaq Stock Market** is a **negotiated market** in which investors deal directly with **market makers.** Market makers are NASD member firms that compete with each other to buy and sell the stocks they represent. Each market maker competes for **customer order flow,** or buy/sell business. The difference between the price at which a market maker is willing to buy a security and the price at which the firm is willing to sell is called the **market maker spread.** The **inside market** is the highest bid and the lowest offer prices among all competing market makers in a Nasdaq security.
- The **Nasdaq SmallCap Market** is a national market with minimal listing criteria. A $1 bid price requirement rules out low-priced **penny stocks** and enhances the credibility of the market. **The OTC Bulletin Board (OTCBB)** is a regulated quotation service that displays real-time quotes, last-sale prices, and volume information in over-the-counter (OTC) equity securities, which might include **American Depositary Receipts (ADR)** or trading certificates that represent ownership of shares of foreign companies.
- The **Dow Jones Industrial Average (DJIA)** is a price-weighted index calculated by adding the prices of 30 large industrial stocks and dividing by a number called the **DJIA divisor.** The DJIA divisor is an adjustment factor used to account for stock splits. The **S&P 500 Index** is the most popular value-weighted

market index. The DJIA is a long-time favorite with individual investors; the S&P 500 is preferred as an investment **equity benchmark** to judge institutional investor performance. The **Russell 3000 Index** measures the performance of the 3,000 largest U.S. companies based on total market capitalization. The **Russell 1000 Index** measures the performance of the 1,000 largest companies in the Russell 3000 Index. The Russell 3000 captures approximately 98% of the total market capitalization of publicly traded stocks. The Russell 1000 Index accounts for 90% of the total market capitalization of publicly traded stocks in the United States. The **Wilshire 5000 Equity Index** approximates the total dollar value of the U.S. equity market.

- In the United States, medium-sized company stock price performance is captured by the **Nasdaq Composite Index,** a market value–weighted index of all 5,000-plus stocks listed on The Nasdaq Stock Market. The **Nasdaq 100 Index** reflects Nasdaq's largest companies such as Microsoft, Intel, and Dell Computer. The **S&P MidCap 400 Index** consists of 400 domestic stocks chosen for market size, liquidity, and industry group representation. The **Wilshire 4500 Index** is the Wilshire 5000 minus the companies from the S&P 500.
- The most popular U.S. small-company stock-price index is the **Russell 2000 Index,** composed of the 2,000 smallest companies in the Russell 3000 Index. The **S&P SmallCap 600 Index** consists of 600 domestic stocks.
- Major global stock market indexes include the United Kingdom's **FTSE-100,** Japan's **Nikkei 225 Index,** the **TSE-35,** and Hong Kong's **Hang Seng Index.** Global stock market performance is also tracked by a variety of indexes compiled by Morgan Stanley Capital International, a subsidiary of Morgan Stanley Dean Witter & Co. The **Europe, Australasia, Far East (EAFE) Index** is a value-weighted index of stocks from 21 countries. All **emerging markets** involve companies with greater perceived investment risk than leading firms in **developed markets.**
- Industry **self-regulatory organizations (SRO)** oversee securities markets and participating member firms. Noteworthy SROs include the NASD, NYSE, AMEX, CBOE, a number of the regional stock and options exchanges, and the Municipal Securities Rulemaking Board. **Stock Watch** is a computerized system that automatically flags unusual volume or price changes in any listed stock, thus helping the NYSE guard against manipulation and insider trading. The **Intermarket Surveillance Group** shares surveillance information and coordinates efforts to detect cross-market manipulative trading. **Securities arbitration** enables a dispute to be resolved quickly and fairly by impartial persons. **Circuit breakers** halt securities trading under certain circumstances.

Questions

1. The market capitalization of all 30 DJIA stocks combined is roughly what share of the total market capitalization of U.S. equities?
   a. 10%
   b. 20%
   c. 30%
   d. 50%

2. The 500 stocks in the S&P 500
   a. include 400 industrials, 40 utilities, 40 financial, and 20 transportation stocks.
   b. are chosen based on industry representation, liquidity, and stability.
   c. are the 500 largest companies according to market capitalization.
   d. are the 500 largest listed companies according to market capitalization.
3. The Russell 2000 Index measures the performance of
   a. a subcomponent of the Russell 3000, after eliminating the largest 1,000 stocks.
   b. the 2,000 largest U.S. companies based on total capitalization.
   c. approximately 98% of the market value of the U.S. equity market.
   d. the 2,000 largest listed U.S. companies based on total capitalization.
4. The Nasdaq Composite Index
   a. represents all common stocks listed on the Nasdaq Stock Market and includes more than 7,500 companies.
   b. represents all common stocks listed on the Nasdaq Stock Market and includes more than 25,000 companies.
   c. measures the geometric rate of return on domestic and non-U.S.-based common stocks listed on the Nasdaq Stock Market.
   d. is market-value weighted.
5. Electronic trading on Instinet, Nasdaq, and other systems accounts for
   a. more than 500 million shares per day of trading in NYSE-listed securities.
   b. more than one billion shares per day of trading in NYSE-listed securities.
   c. 5–10% of composite trading in NYSE-listed securities.
   d. 50% of composite trading in NYSE-listed securities.
6. At the NYSE, the auction process for each listed stock is assigned to a
   a. specialist.
   b. broker.
   c. dealer.
   d. member.
7. The New York Stock Exchange maintains an orderly market in roughly
   a. 500 issues.
   b. 3,700 issues.
   c. 7,400 issues.
   d. 25,000 issues.
8. Nasdaq is
   a. an auction market.
   b. a negotiated market.
   c. an agent auction market.
   d. the largest stock exchange in the United States.

9. Which one of the following is *not* a self-regulatory organization:
   a. the National Association of Securities Dealers.
   b. the New York Stock Exchange.
   c. the Security and Exchange Commission.
   d. the Municipal Securities Rulemaking Board.
10. Before they can take effect, all self-regulatory organization rules and regulations must be approved by the
    a. National Association of Securities Dealers.
    b. Securities and Exchange Commission.
    c. various state regulatory bodies.
    d. U.S. Congress.
11. Securities professionals must qualify through examinations administered by the
    a. NASD.
    b. SEC.
    c. NYSE.
    d. Nasdaq.
12. Microsoft Corp. comprises roughly 4% of the market value of stocks included in the S&P 500 Index. On a day that Microsoft stock rises by 2%, it causes a rise in the S&P 500 of
    a. 2%.
    b. 0.08%.
    c. 4%.
    d. 2 points.
13. The S&P 500 is a
    a. price-weighted index.
    b. value-weighted index.
    c. equally weighted index.
    d. share-weighted index.
14. NYSE composite volume *does not* include trading on
    a. AMEX.
    b. the floor of the NYSE.
    c. regional exchanges.
    d. the NASD system.
15. On the London Stock Exchange, the *least* actively traded stocks are called
    a. alpha stocks.
    b. beta stocks.
    c. gamma stocks.
    d. omega stocks.

16. A Wilshire (5000) Index value of 13,500 signifies
    a. an increase of 1,350% from the index base of 10 in 1956–58.
    b. an increase of 13,500% from the index base of 100 in 1956–58.
    c. a total market capitalization for U.S. stocks of $13.5 trillion.
    d. a total market capitalization for U.S. stocks of $13.5 billion.
17. Assuming a divisor of 0.2, when the DJIA is at 11,000 a round lot of all 30 component stocks has an investment cost of
    a. $2,200.
    b. $11,000.
    c. $55,000.
    d. $220,000.
18. Assuming a divisor of 0.2, a 100-point rise in the DJIA reflects an average increase in the price of each component stock of
    a. $3.33.
    b. $16.67.
    c. $0.20.
    d. none of these.
19. The largest 1,000 stocks comprise roughly what percentage of the value of the Russell 3000?
    a. 50%
    b. 33%
    c. 10%
    d. 90%
20. A computerized system to flag unusual volume or price changes on the NYSE is called
    a. intermarket surveillance.
    b. an SRO.
    c. a circuit breaker.
    d. stock watch.

Investment Application

Buying Direct: Dividend Reinvestment Plans (DRIPs)

A dividend reinvestment plan (DRIP) is an investment program offered by corporations for their shareholders. DRIPs allow shareholders participating in the plan to easily and cheaply reinvest cash dividends in additional shares of the company. Basically, DRIPs allow shareholders to buy additional shares in their company at little or no commission cost in lieu of receiving cash dividends. Although there are some exceptions, fees associated with DRIPs are generally paid by the company offering the plan. Therefore, DRIPs allow shareholders to build on their investment in a company on a regular basis with little or no transactions costs. If there are shareholder fees to be paid, they are usually minimal and only a fraction of the cost of brokerage fees.

Many DRIPs also offer a feature known as optional cash payment plans. These plans are sometimes referred to as dividend reinvestment/share purchase plans. The optional cash payment feature gives investors the option to purchase additional shares of company stock by making additional voluntary cash contributions. The frequency of optional cash purchases permitted varies from plan to plan, but regular cash purchases are generally allowed on a monthly or quarterly basis. Such plans may have minimum and/or maximum permitted purchase amounts per transaction or per year. As with reinvested dividends, shares acquired with optional cash payments often result in little or no commission being charged to the individual investor.

A unique feature of DRIPs is that they typically allow plan participants to purchase and hold fractional shares. For example, suppose a shareholder enrolled in a DRIP owns 130 shares of stock in a company that pays a quarterly dividend of 30¢ per share. The total quarterly dividend income due such a shareholder would be \$39 (= \$0.30 × 130). Furthermore, assume that this company's common stock was selling for \$45 on the New York Stock Exchange (NYSE). On the **dividend payment date,** the administrator of the company's DRIP would purchase on behalf of the shareholder 0.867 (= \$39/\$45) shares of stock in the company. Of course, 0.867 is actually the prorated number of shares to be purchased on behalf of this individual shareholder. In practice, on or about the dividend payment date, the plan administrator purchases the total amount of common stock that can be bought with the combined sum of dividend income to be reinvested by all DRIP participants. By pooling individual purchases through a DRIP, participants can minimize transactions costs and brokerage expenses. In some instances, sponsoring corporations use DRIPs as a cost-efficient means for raising new equity capital. In such cases, the corporation simply issues new shares to DRIP participants on the dividend payment date.

Shares purchased through DRIPs are held in electronic or book entry–based form by the company or its DRIP administrator. The DRIP administrator is usually a large bank or trust company appointed by the company to keep a record of each registered shareholder's name and address and number of shares owned. The DRIP administrator receives fee income from plan participants or sponsoring corporations to compensate for necessary transaction costs and administrative expenses. In some instances, the DRIP administrator is also the corporation's transfer agent or bank responsible for transferring ownership of shares and ensuring that certificates are properly issued and canceled. This is the same manner in which mutual fund shares are issued and held. Any shares held in a DRIP retain all the rights and privileges of registered shares held and retained by the shareholder. DRIP statements showing a history of transactions and the number of shares currently held are typically issued on a monthly or quarterly basis. When desired, DRIP participants can request that plan holdings be liquidated or that a certificate be issued for any portion of the whole number of shares owned. However, fees are sometimes charged or other limits placed on plan withdrawals.

A very attractive feature of some DRIPs is that they offer a sizeable discount on purchases of additional shares with reinvested dividends. Such discounts can be as much as 3–5% of the amount of reinvested dividend income. In its simplest terms, this means that shares purchased with reinvested dividends can sometimes be acquired by plan participants at only 97% or 95% of their actual market price. As a result, the DRIP participants sometimes have the opportunity to acquire 3% or 5% more shares than could be purchased in the absence of such a discount. Discount DRIPs are especially popular with utilities and other companies that have the recurring need to raise additional equity capital. For such companies, offering a discount on reinvested dividends is a cost-effective means for raising additional equity because it obviates the need to pay investment banker fees, which can sometimes amount to 5–8% of the amount of new equity capital.

Companies often enhance DRIPs with a variety of additional features to make them more attractive to investors. In Canada, some companies offer their shares within what is called a registered retirement savings plan (RRSP). Contributions within such plans are tax deductible within specified limits, and earnings are tax-exempt until withdrawn. In the United States, some DRIPs have similar provisions that allow plan participants to accumulate shares within their individual retirement accounts. In both cases, DRIPs can offer participants the opportunity to tax-shelter their investments. Automatic investment choices are also sometimes available to give participants the option of making convenient automatic investments from their bank account on a monthly or quarterly basis. Keep in mind, however, that participation in a DRIP does not automatically shelter dividend income from regular income taxes. In the United States and Canada, dividend income is typically subject to tax as regular income. Only when a DRIP is featured within a RRSP or IRA does it become possible to avoid taxes on dividend income.

On a fundamental level, the investor benefits of any specific DRIP depend on the investment merits of the company itself. An investor should never purchase a company's stock simply because it has an attractive DRIP. The decision to buy or sell any security must be based on the investment merits or demerits of the company. However, if an investor has made the decision to buy a given security, DRIPs can make an excellent vehicle for those looking to build their investment over time in a cost-effective manner. DRIPs often provide for the purchase of shares at regular intervals for little or no commission. All DRIPs accommodate the small investor by allowing for small purchases that would not otherwise be cost-effective.

In most instances, the minimum requirement for joining most DRIPs is that you have to be a registered shareholder. This typically means that you have to own at least one share of the company's stock. In general, such shares must be held in your own name; they cannot be held in your behalf by a broker. This initial share of stock must be purchased and delivered to you through a traditional broker or transferred to you from another shareholder. Once share ownership has been established, investors should acquire the DRIP documentation of the company whose plan you are thinking of joining.

This can be done either by contacting the company itself or its stock transfer agent. In many DRIP plans, companies have begun offering so-called no-load stock purchase programs to first-time investors. Companies such as Enron Corp., General Electric Co., Home Depot, Inc., IBM, Lucent Technologies Inc., Motorola, Inc., Nokia Corporation, Pfizer Inc., SBC Communications Inc., and Wal-Mart Stores Inc. offer the most popular DRIP programs. Today, roughly one-half of the 1,000 companies with DRIPs allow open enrollment.

FIGURE 3.6 **Information about DRIP Investing Is Available on the Internet**

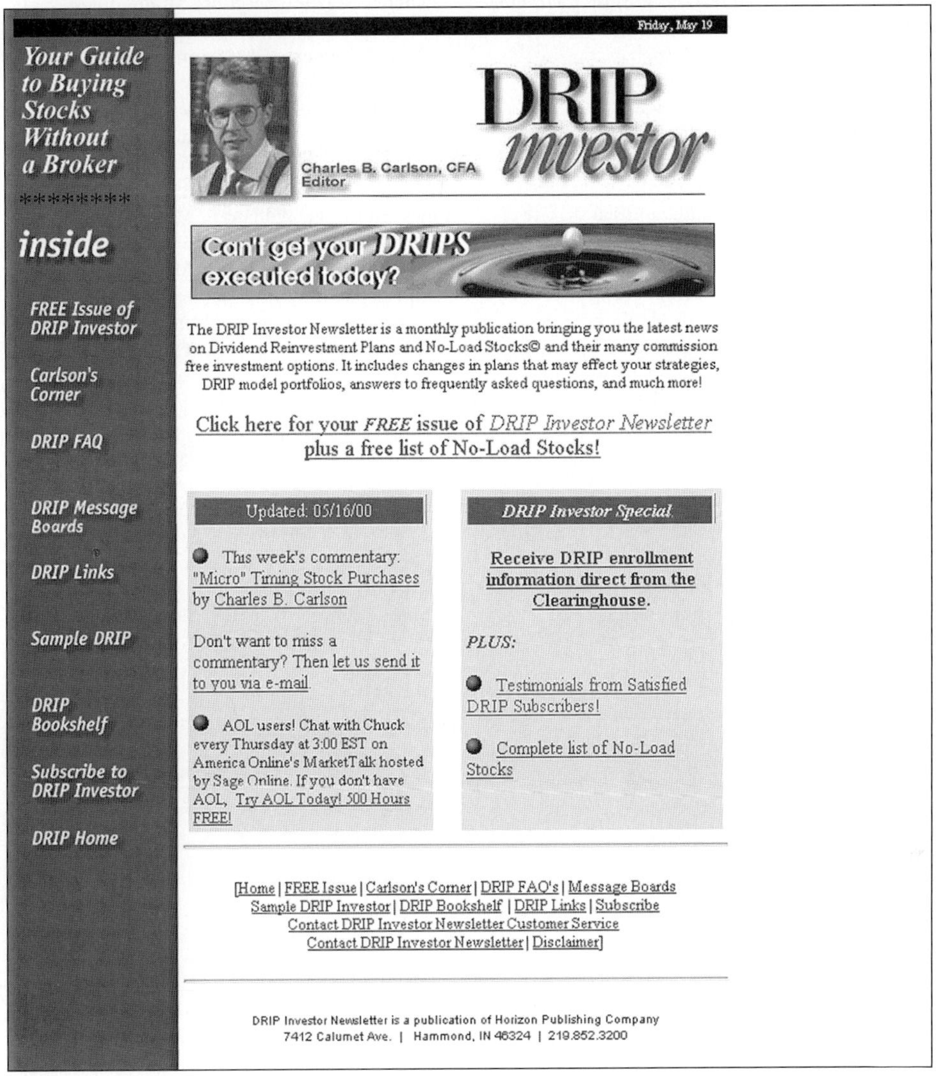

Source: <http://www.dripcentral.com>.

DRIP plan documentation, plus an enrollment/authorization form, can also be obtained from a number of Web sites on the Internet that specialize in DRIPs. One of the best of these Web sites is DRIP Central at <http://www.dripcentral.com> (see Figure 3.6).

A. Explain why company management that fears an unfriendly takeover bid from an unwanted corporate suitor might favor a DRIP.

B. Can you think of any disadvantages faced by a small investor wanting to participate in a DRIP?

Selected References

Bertsimas, Dimitris, Leonid Kogan, and Andrew W. Lo. "When is Time Continuous?" *Journal of Financial Economics* 55 (February 2000): 173–204.

Bhattacharyya, Sugato, Rajdeep Singh. "The Resolution of Bankruptcy by Auction: Allocating the Residual Right of Design." *Journal of Financial Economics* 53 (July 1999): 269–294.

Burkart, Mike, Denis Gromb, and Fausto Panunzi. "Agency Conflicts in Public and Negotiated Transfers of Corporate Control." *Journal of Finance* 55 (April 2000): 647–678.

Cushing, David, and Ananth Madhavan. "Stock Returns and Trading at the Close." *Journal of Financial Markets* 3 (February 2000): 45–67.

Ferguson, Robert. "Saving Social Security." *Financial Analysts Journal* 56 (January/February 2000): 13–16.

Fisher, Kenneth L., and Meir Statman. "Investor Sentiment and Stock Returns." *Financial Analysts Journal* 56 (March/April 2000): 16–23.

Forsythe, Robert, Thomas A. Rietz, and Thomas W. Ross. "Wishes, Expectations and Actions: A Survey on Price Formation in Election Stock Markets." *Journal of Economic Behavior & Organization* 39 (May 1999): 83–110.

Gande, Amar, Manju Puri, and Anthony Saunders. "Bank Entry, Competition, and the Market for Corporate Securities Underwriting." *Journal of Financial Economics* 54 (October 1999): 165–195.

Hong, Harrison, and Jeremy C. Stein. "A Unified Theory of Underreaction, Momentum Trading and Overreaction in Asset Markets." *Journal of Finance* 54 (December 1999): 2143–2183.

Hong, Harrison, and Jiang Wang. "Trading and Returns under Periodic Market Closures." *Journal of Finance* 55 (February 2000): 297–354.

Jones, Steven L., William L. Megginson, Robert C. Nash, and Jeffry M. Netter. "Share Issue Privatizations as Financial Means to Political and Economic Ends." *Journal of Financial Economics* 53 (August 1999): 217–253.

Lie, Erik, and Heidi J. Lie. "The Role of Personal Taxes in Corporate Decisions: An Empirical Analysis of Share Repurchases and Dividends." *Journal of Financial & Quantitative Analysis* 34 (December 1999): 533–552.

Narayanan, Ranga. "Insider Trading and the Voluntary Disclosure of Information By Firms." *Journal of Banking and Finance* 24 (March 2000): 395–425.

Okunev, John, and Patrick Wilson. "What is an Appropriate Value of the Equity Risk Premium?" *Journal of Investing* 8 (Fall 1999): 74–79.

Schooley, Diane K., and Debra Drecnik Worden. "Investors' Asset Allocations versus Life-Cycle Funds." *Financial Analysts Journal* 55 (September/October 1999): 37–43.

CHAPTER 4

Buying and Selling Equities

On May 17, 1792, 24 stock brokers signed an agreement to trade with one another beneath a buttonwood outside 68 Wall Street, and the business relationship that formed the basis for the New York Stock Exchange (NYSE) was born. At the same time, several treasured Wall Street traditions were established, some of which continue to this day.

One of the most cherished Wall Street traditions concerns the quoting of stock prices in "pieces of eight." A couple of hundred years ago, merchants used to make change by cutting dollar coins into half-dollars, quarters, and so on. At that time, the smallest consistently recognizable part of a dollar was one-eighth. As a result, the minimum unit for pricing goods and merchandise was one-eighth of a dollar. On Wall Street, setting bid and ask prices in terms of minimum $\frac{1}{8}$ *increments, or* $\frac{1}{16}$ *(or one "teeny"), remained common long after computers made it feasible to quote prices in increments of five cents or even a penny.*

All this changed in January 2000 when the Securities and Exchange Commission (SEC) mandated that the securities industry convert to the decimalization of equity prices. Although this might seem like a small matter, the minimum unit for securities pricing is important. The bid-ask spread for individual stocks and bonds represents the inventory markup for dealers, and industry insiders fear that decimalization will squeeze profit margins. In mandating change in the way equity prices are quoted, the SEC expressed hope that investor transaction costs would indeed fall and that stock prices would become easier to understand.

It remains to be seen whether decimalization will, in fact, make a "teeny" bit of difference.[1]

Simple Buy-Sell Decisions

Bid-Ask Spreads

The quoted **bid** is the highest price an investor is willing to pay to buy a security. Practically speaking, this is the highest currently available price at which an investor

bid
Highest price an investor is willing to pay.

[1]See Judith Burns, "SEC Drops Plans for Decimal Trading in July, Seeks Comments on Alternatives," *The Wall Street Journal, Interactive Edition,* April 14, 2000.

ask
Lowest price an investor will accept to sell.

bid-ask spread
Gap between the bid and ask prices.

can sell shares of stock or any other security. The quoted **ask** is the lowest price an investor will accept to sell a stock. Practically speaking, this is the quoted offer at which an investor can presently buy shares of stock. The **bid-ask spread** is the gap between the bid price and the ask price. It is the price markup faced by investors and the profit margin earned by the exchange specialist or Nasdaq market maker.

To illustrate, consider the data shown in Table 4.1. On the date shown, controversial tobacco and consumer products manufacturer Philip Morris, Inc., had traded 5,498,200 shares by 11:39 AM EST. The last trade for 200 shares occurred at a price of \$19.69($19\frac{11}{16}$). This trade took place a little more than two hours after the start of regular trading on the NYSE. This price was 19¢($\frac{3}{16}$) higher than the

TABLE 4.1 Up-to-the-Minute Free Stock Quotes and News Are Available on Freerealtime.com

A. NYSE-listed Philip Morris, Inc., enjoys a deep market with significant demand and supply near the last price.

PHILIP MORRIS COS-New York Stock Exchange: MO

Time	**Last**	**Change (%)**	**Bid (size)**	**Ask (size)**
11:39	19.69	▲ .19 (0.96)	19.63 (1,000)	19.69 (631)
Day Volume	**Day Open**	**Day High**	**Day Low**	**Last Size**
5,498,200	19.50	19.88	19.38	200
Latest Tics	**52 Wk High**	**52 Wk Low**	**Avg Trade Size**	**# of Trades**
−+−+	47.50	18.69	2,679	2,052

11:39:28 AM EST, Friday, February 18, 2000—data are real time.

B. Nasdaq's T. Rowe Price & Associates has a relatively thin market with limited demand and supply near the last price.

T. ROWE PRICE ASSOC-NASDAQ Stock Market: TROW

Time	**Last**	**Change (%)**	**Bid (size)**	**Ask (size)**
11:37	33.13	▼ .19 (0.56)	32.81 (5)	33.13 (1)
Day Volume	**Day Open**	**Day High**	**Day Low**	**Last Size**
132,700	33.13	33.50	32.38	300
Latest Tics	**52 Wk High**	**52 Wk Low**	**Avg Trade Size**	**# of Trades**
++−+	43.25	25.88	481	276

11:37:32 AM EST, Friday, February 18, 2000—data are real time.

Data source: <http://freerealtime.com>

close of \$19.50(19½), on the previous trading day. (All stocks used to be quoted in ⅛ or 1/16 increments of a dollar, following a long-standing tradition on Wall Street. This custom is going by the wayside, however, as electronic trading makes decimal quotation of stock prices feasible and practical.) Notice that Philip Morris has been assigned the **ticker symbol** "MO." Stocks listed on the NYSE are assigned unique one-, two-, or three-letter stock symbols to facilitate transaction speed and accuracy. Over-the-counter stocks are typically assigned unique four-letter symbols given the larger numbers of such companies.

ticker symbols Unique stock identifier.

Although much of the information contained in Table 4.1 is self-explanatory, **bid size** and **ask size** information may merit some explanation. Bid size is the number of round lots represented on the buy side of the market. A **round lot** is 100 shares of stock, so a bid size of 1,000 means that the bid of \$19.63 for Philip Morris is good for 100,000 shares worth \$1,963,000. Ask size is the number of round lots represented on the sell side of the market, so ask size of 631 means that the ask price of \$19.69 for Philip Morris is good for up to 63,100 shares worth \$1,243,439. The depth of the market for Philip Morris is obvious. Philip Morris stock enjoys significant **market depth.** Individual or institutional shareholders can buy or sell a significant amount of Philip Morris stock at prices near the last quote of \$19.69. Because the bid size is somewhat larger than ask size, demand is somewhat greater than supply at the current bid-ask spread. This tends to place some upward pressure on Philip Morris's stock price. If the ask size were somewhat larger than the bid size, supply would be somewhat greater than demand at the current bid-ask spread, and there would be some near-term downward pressure on Philip Morris's stock price.

bid size Number of shares sought by current buyers.

ask size Number of shares offered by current sellers.

round lot 100 shares of stock.

market depth Number of active buyers and sellers.

The contrast is striking between the market depth for NYSE-listed Philip Morris and Nasdaq's T. Rowe Price & Associates, a Baltimore-based mutual fund provider. As shown in Table 4.1, panel B, T. Rowe Price has a bid for only 500 shares at \$32.81, and the ask is \$33.13 for only 100 shares. Notice that the market for T. Rowe Price has nowhere near the depth of the market for Philip Morris. When the bid-ask spread is expressed in percentage terms, notice that the size of the bid-ask spread is larger for T. Rowe Price than in the case of Philip Morris stock. On a percentage basis, the bid-ask spread is only 0.32% of the bid price for Philip Morris but 0.95% of the bid for T. Rowe Price. This means that there is a relatively high level of uncertainty among investors concerning the correct valuation of T. Rowe Price versus the relatively low level of uncertainty among investors regarding the true value of Philip Morris. Given much larger bid-ask spreads for less-liquid Nasdaq stocks such as T. Rowe Price, investors face significantly higher transaction costs for buying or selling such securities. This explains why active traders tend to prefer large NYSE-listed stocks such as Philip Morris.

In Table 4.1, notice that the bid price is lower than the ask price for both Philip Morris and T. Rowe Price. This is almost always the case. The bid price is the highest amount that a potential buyer is willing to pay. The ask price is the lowest price the most eager seller is willing to accept. Thus, in normal circumstances, the bid-ask spread is positive. In some unusually volatile markets, an **inverted bid-ask spread** is observed. In such instances, the quoted bid price is actually higher, not lower, than the quoted ask price.

inverted bid-ask spread When the quoted bid price is higher than the ask price.

An example of an inverted bid-ask spread is shown for Amazon.com in Table 4.2. Prior to the market open, the indicated bid price was \$130, but the indicated

TABLE 4.2 The Bid-Ask Spread Becomes Inverted When the Bid Price Exceeds the Ask Price

A. Prior to the market open, an inverted bid-ask spread portends a weak opening for Amazon.com.

AMAZON.COM (NASDAQ: AMZN)

Time	**Last**	**Change (%)**	**Bid (size)**	**Ask (size)**
16:01	132.38	0 (0.0)	130 (1)	129.25 (1)
Day Volume	**Day High**	**Day Low**	**Day Open**	**Last Size**
43,800	0	0	0	100
Latest Tics	**52 Wk High**	**52 Wk Low**	**Avg Trade Size**	**# of Trades**
+−+−	221.25	13.38		0

Mon, May 17, 09:27:31 EDT, 1999—quotes are real time.

B. After the market open, a weak market pushed Amazon.com's stock price down sharply.

AMAZON.COM (NASDAQ: AMZN)

Time	**Last**	**Change (%)**	**Bid (size)**	**Ask (size)**
10:01	128	−4.38 (3.31)	128 (1)	128.06 (1)
Day Volume	**Day High**	**Day Low**	**Day Open**	**Last Size**
1,607,500	130.69	127	130	800
Latest Tics	**52 Wk High**	**52 Wk Low**	**Avg Trade Size**	**# of Trades**
−−−+	221.25	13.38	550	2,919

Mon, May 17, 10:01:13 EDT, 1999—quotes are real time.

Data source: <http://freerealtime.com>

market order Instruction to buy or sell at the current market price.

limit order Instruction to buy or sell at a specified price.

stop order Market order to buy or sell a certain quantity of a security if a specified price is reached or passed.

stopped out When a position is offset by the execution of a stop order.

ask price was only $129.25. This suggests that market makers for Amazon.com suspected that there would be substantial selling pressure after the market opened. Why would some potential buyer bid $130 for a stock that had willing sellers at $129.25? This is a very good question. Perhaps the $130 bid price was submitted by a potential buyer after the close of trading on the prior day. Such a bidder might not be aware of market conditions just prior to the market open on the following morning. However, the market for volatile stocks such as Amazon.com can change rapidly, and perhaps the bidder willing to pay $130 simply wanted to be sure of buying the stock. In most instances, an inverted bid-ask spread occurs when the bid size is very small compared with the ask size. If the bid size is only 100 shares, an eager seller of 10,000 shares might be willing to accept a lower price. During the crash of 1987, several inverted bids on the Nasdaq could be explained by the absence of ready buyers.

Types of Orders

A **market order** is an instruction to immediately buy a security at the current ask price or to sell a security at the current bid price. This contrasts with a **limit order,** whereby the customer specifies a price at which to execute a buy or sell decision. A limit order can be executed only if the market price reaches at least the specified price target. With a buy limit order, securities are bought at or below the specified price target. With a sell limit order, securities are sold at or above the specified price target. With a limit order, an investor might instruct a broker to "Buy 100 shares of Walt Disney at $35 or less." Alternatively, a limit order might instruct a broker to "Sell 100 shares of Walt Disney at $35 or better."

Wall Street investors use a wide variety of market and limit orders. A **stop order** is a market order to buy or sell a certain quantity of a security if a specified price (the stop price) is reached or passed. A position is said to be **stopped out** when the position is offset by the execution of a stop order. A **buy stop order** is a buy order that is to be held until the market price rises to a specified stop price, at which point it becomes a market order. Buy stop orders are often used by short sellers who wish to limit their risk exposure but are not permitted for over-the-counter trading. A **stop-loss order** is a stop order to sell a long position at a specified price that is below the current market price. A **stop-limit order** is an order to buy or sell a certain quantity of a security at a specified price or better but only after a specified price has been reached. A stop-limit order can be thought of as a simple combination of a stop order and a limit order.

A **day order** is an order to buy or sell that automatically expires if it cannot be executed during the trading session in which it is entered. An **open order** is created when an investor places an offer to buy or sell a security at a price that differs from the current market price. An open order stays active until it is executed (filled) or canceled by the investor. In some instances, brokers set a time limit of 30–60 days on open orders. After such time has passed, open orders are sometimes automatically canceled unless the investor instructs the broker to keep it active. Another expression for an open order is a **good 'til canceled order.**

In most instances, investors are willing to accept partial executions. For example, if a day order is placed to sell 500 shares of Walt Disney at $35, most investors would be willing to sell 100, 200, or any fraction of 500 shares at that price. If this is not the case, different instructions must be communicated to the executing broker. **All or none** is a stipulation to a buy or sell order that instructs the broker to either fill the entire order or do not fill it at all. With all-or-none orders, partial fulfillment of an order is not allowed. **Fill-or-kill** orders are a special type of all-or-none order. A fill-or-kill order must immediately be filled in its entirety or, if this is not possible, completely canceled. All-or-none and fill-or-kill orders are used when investors are concerned about the potential for paying higher brokerage commissions on orders that are executed in piecemeal fashion.

Dollar-Cost Averaging

Every investor would love to perfectly time buy and sell decisions. However, this simply isn't possible. The mythical investor who always "buys at the bottom and sells at the top" doesn't exist. No investor knows if an individual stock purchase will prove profitable. If the company is in a good business and the stock is held for a sufficiently long period of time, then chances are that a profit will be made

buy stop order Buy order that is to be held until the market price rises to a specified stop price.

stop-loss order Stop order to sell a long position at a specified price that is below the current market price.

stop-limit order Order to buy or sell a certain quantity of a security at a specified price or better but only after a specified price has been reached.

day order Instruction to buy or sell during the present trading session.

open order A limit order that has yet to be executed.

good 'til canceled order Open order.

all or none Buy or sell instruction that must be filled exactly or not at all.

fill-or-kill All-or-none order that must be immediately filled or canceled.

following a purchase decision. However, there are no guarantees offered on Wall Street.

In a similar vein, one of the most famous maxims on Wall Street is to "Buy low, and sell high." That sound and simple investment advice is as old as the market. Once again, however, such advice is much easier to give than to carry out. Over brief periods of time, financial markets are inherently unpredictable. It is simply not possible to consistently choose the best time to buy or sell.

dollar-cost averaging Strategy of investing a fixed amount in a security at regular intervals.

Fortunately, there is a simple mechanical means by which an individual investor can benefit from market volatility. This method is called **dollar-cost averaging.** Dollar-cost averaging is a simple investment strategy of investing a fixed amount in a particular security at regular intervals. Because the amount invested remains constant, the investor buys more shares when the price is low but fewer shares when the price is high. As a result, the average dollar amount paid, or the average cost per share, is always lower than the average price per share.

Table 4.3 offers a simple illustration of the dollar-cost averaging concept. The example depicts a simple strategy of investing $400 per month, or $4,800 per year. Three different market environments are shown. A rising market is illustrated, along with a falling market and a directionless but highly volatile market. In each case, the average share price is $18. This average is just the $216 total of all monthly share prices divided by 12, the number of months. What is different about each market is the amount of volatility.

TABLE 4.3 Illustration of Dollar-Cost Averaging

When a fixed dollar amount is invested at regular intervals, the investor buys more shares when prices are low, but fewer shares when prices are high. As a result, the average cost per share is always lower than the average price per share.

		Rising Market		Falling Market		Volatile Market	
	Monthly Investment	**Share Price**	**Shares Purchased**	**Share Price**	**Shares Purchased**	**Share Price**	**Shares Purchased**
	$400	$4.00	100	$50.00	8	$40.00	10
	400	8.00	50	25.00	16	25.00	16
	400	8.00	50	25.00	16	16.00	25
	400	10.00	40	20.00	20	10.00	40
	400	12.50	32	20.00	20	8.00	50
	400	12.50	32	20.00	20	4.00	100
	400	16.00	25	16.00	25	4.00	100
	400	20.00	20	16.00	25	8.00	50
	400	20.00	20	10.00	40	10.00	40
	400	25.00	16	5.00	80	16.00	25
	400	40.00	10	5.00	80	25.00	16
	400	40.00	10	4.00	100	50.00	8
Totals	$4,800	$216.00	405	216.00	450	$216.00	480
Average price		$18.00	$11.85	$18.00	$10.67	$18.00	$10.00
High price		$40.00		$50.00		$50.00	
Low price		$4.00		$4.00		$4.00	
Volatility (standard deviation)		$11.36		$12.04		$13.95	

In a rising market, the example shows that if an investor buys $400 per month worth of stock, relatively more shares will be purchased at low prices and relatively fewer shares will be bought at high prices. The attractiveness of dollar-cost averaging is evident in that the investor's average purchase price of $11.85 is less than the $18 average share price. Dollar-cost averaging also works to the investor's advantage in a falling market. In this falling market example, the investor's average cost is only $10.67 versus the average price of $18 per share. The relative advantage enjoyed in a falling market versus a rising market has nothing to do with the direction of change in the market. In this example, the falling market is slightly more volatile than the rising market. The benefit gained through dollar-cost averaging is in direct proportion to the level of price volatility. The more volatile prices are, the greater the benefit that will be gained through dollar-cost averaging. If prices are completely stable, there would be no benefit at all gained through dollar-cost averaging.

To see the impact of price volatility on the advantage gained through dollar-cost averaging, look at the volatile market illustration in Table 4.3. When share prices are most volatile, the investor is able to purchase 480 shares at an average price of only $10. When it comes to dollar-cost averaging, the more volatile the better. It doesn't matter whether stock prices are going up or down. Dollar-cost averaging will result in the greatest discount from the average share price in the most volatile market environments.

The example illustrated in Table 4.3 shows that dollar-cost averaging is an appropriate means for investing a stream of money over time. However, it is important to recognize that dollar-cost averaging does not guarantee an investment profit. Dollar-cost averaging is an attractive means for long-term investing because it allows regular long-term investors to reduce the effects of market risk by acquiring more shares when share prices are at their lowest. The average cost of shares purchased by regular investors will always be lower than the average share price. To be sure, dollar-cost averaging cannot be used to eliminate the risks of investing in financial markets. It does not ensure a profit or protect against a loss in declining markets. Neither will dollar-cost averaging prevent a loss if it is discontinued when the value of an account is less than its cost. On both economic and psychological grounds, it is often difficult to continue making periodic investment payments when stock prices are going down. Before starting a dollar-cost averaging investment strategy, the investor should establish his or her willingness and financial ability to continue making purchases through good and bad market periods. The success of dollar-cost averaging depends on the investor making regular purchases irrespective of market conditions.

It is also worth pointing out that there is no guarantee that dollar-cost averaging will always be the most efficient means for investing a large lump-sum amount. Share prices tend to rise over time with growth in aggregate economic activity. As a result, it may be best to invest large lump-sum amounts as early as possible and thereby take advantage of long-term compound interest, rather than wait and engage in a program of dollar-cost averaging over time. Sporadic investors can sometimes benefit more if all their money is invested in one lump sum at the earliest moment and lowest share price. However, even in the case of investing a lump sum, dollar-cost averaging can reduce the risk of buying at the worst absolute time. Some investors take a dollar-cost averaging approach to investing large lump-sum amounts, say, $50,000, to reduce risk.

Think of dollar-cost averaging as a type of "steady-as-you-go" investment strategy. Instead of trying to choose the right time to invest, dollar-cost averaging helps the investor reduce risk and build a significant investment portfolio over time.

Dollar-Cost Averaging for Retirement

defined contribution retirement plans Retirement plan in which the employer is responsible only for making specified payments into the plan.

Dollar-cost averaging is a good method for investing in company-sponsored **defined contribution retirement plans,** such as 401-k plans. Defined contribution plans are the most common pension plans offered by employers. Under a defined contribution pension plan, the employer is responsible only for making specified contributions into the plan on behalf of qualifying participants. Sometimes, employer contributions are used to match additional voluntary contributions made by employees. Most often, the employee simply directs the employer to deduct a specific amount from his or her paycheck on a weekly or monthly basis. At the time of retirement, the amount of retirement income generated by a defined contribution plan depends solely on the amount of income that can be generated from investments made possible by employer and employee contributions.

defined benefit retirement plan Pension plan in which the corporate sponsor agrees to make specified dollar payments.

Years ago, defined benefit plans were much more popular than defined contribution plans. A **defined benefit retirement plan** is a pension plan in which the corporate sponsor agrees to make specified dollar payments to qualifying employees, such as $1,000 per month. Sometimes, the amount of benefit paid depends on both the number of years of service and the salary income of the plan participant. For each year of service, employees might be entitled to an annual pension equal to 1.5% of their highest annual income. Thus, a 25-year employee making $40,000 per year might be entitled to a pension of $15,000 per year. Defined benefit pension plans work much like an annuity. There is no residual benefit for the employee's survivors. Defined benefit pension plans represent a type of debt obligation for the plan sponsor. By contrast, defined contribution retirement plans represent an employee asset.

Dollar-cost averaging makes a defined contribution retirement plan an effective tool for building significant retirement assets. In the same way, dollar-cost averaging is an appropriate means for investing in individual retirement accounts (IRA) or other long-term investments. The longer an investment strategy is maintained, the more likely it is to help the investor cope effectively with market volatility. Individual investors can also enjoy the benefits of dollar-cost averaging by having their financial institution electronically transfer a fixed amount of money to their investment account on a monthly, bimonthly, or quarterly basis. Typically, such services allow investors to choose the date, the frequency, and the amount to be invested on a regular basis.

Buying on Margin

Margin Accounts

margin account Account that holds securities purchased with a combination of cash and borrowed funds.

A **margin account** is an investor account that holds securities purchased with a combination of cash and borrowed funds. Brokerages earn a significant portion of their total profit by making such loans. The loan in the margin account is collateralized by stocks or bonds. If the value of these securities drops sufficiently, the owner will be asked to either put up more collateral or sell some of the securities held in the account.

WALL STREET WISDOM 4.1

Why Is Margin Debt Dangerous?

Humorist Will Rogers used to joke that making money in the stock market was easy. "Buy a stock," Rogers said, "and sell it when it goes up. If it doesn't go up, don't buy it." Such circular logic makes for good humor but is tough to implement in practice. In the real world, even strong companies with improving prospects can have discouragingly poor stock market performance in the short run. Sometimes, attractive equities can be purchased at bargain prices, only to sink in an overall market downturn. Even stock market billionaire Warren Buffett has argued that for him it is *easy* to figure out what will happen in the stock market, but it is *impossible* to tell when. Notice Buffett's use of the words *easy* and *impossible.* For someone with a crystal-clear grasp of the economics of the situation, such as Buffett, projecting stock market returns in the long run may indeed be easy. However, even then, projecting the timing of stock market returns is not easy. According to Buffett, flawless stock market timing is more than difficult; it is impossible.

The impossibility of flawless market timing is what makes buying stocks on margin dangerous. If a long-term investor buys an attractively priced equity and it immediately plummets 30%, the long-term investor can hold on and wait for better prices. Patience will ultimately be rewarded as market conditions improve and other investors recognize the company's long-term virtues. By avoiding the use of debt, the long-term investor can determine the timing of both purchase and sale decisions. This lets the long-term investor avoid being forced out of a stock at low prices, perhaps just before a favorable turn in the company's prospects. The holding period flexibility enjoyed by long-term investors contrasts sharply with the situation faced by short-term investors who use leverage.

All investors who use leverage are short-term investors, or traders. If a trader buys an attractively priced equity by using 50% margin and it plummets 25–30%, the customer's account equity will fall below the minimum maintenance margin requirement, and a margin call will be issued. If the margin account customer is unwilling or unable to add additional funds within a few days, the brokerage firm will sell sufficient equities to restore the required amount of equity. In a sharply correcting market, a series of unmet margin calls can result in rapid sales of attractive securities at ruinously low prices. Margin account customers can lose a significant portion of their account's equity within a matter of days. Margin account customers give up the flexibility of waiting for better prices following an unexpected downturn in the overall market.

Other, more subtle problems also can emerge for investors who use leverage. Easy access to margin credit sometimes causes investors to become less conscientious in making their buy and sell decisions. When paying cash, an investor's ultimate investment return depends solely on the carefulness with which securities with attractive economic fundamentals are identified and the prudence with which appropriate purchase prices or sell targets are identified.

When leverage enters into the equation, a third important determinant of investor returns is introduced. Even typical short-term fluctuations in the overall market can cause outsized changes in the value of the investor's portfolio when leverage is used. This can have the effect of lulling some investors into a false sense of confidence about their ability to pick stock market winners. When leverage is aggressively used, some traders find it difficult, if not impossible, to clearly determine if their short-term success in the market is due to superior stock-picking ability (skill) or instead due to their fortuitous use of leverage (luck). Lucky investors who use leverage often become overly aggressive and ultimate losers when their good luck runs out, as it eventually will.

Cautioning comments about the use of leverage are especially apropos in the current stock market environment. Anyone with an investment perspective dominated by the rollicking stock market of the 1990s has insufficient appreciation for the damage that can be inflicted by temporary but sharp downturns in the overall market.

See: Ruth Simon, "Margin Calls Rise, Adding Pressure to Selloff," *The Wall Street Journal,* April 17, 2000, A3, A17.

Minimum initial margin for stock purchases in the United States is 50%. This means that an investor can buy up to $10,000 worth of stock with only $5,000 worth of investment capital. The legal minimum maintenance margin for common stocks is 25%, but most brokerages require 30%. This means that a previously purchased stock position could fall to as little as $10,000 in value and be maintained with only $3,000 worth of investment capital. For investment-grade corporate bonds, minimum initial margin is 30% and maintenance margin is 25%. In the case of long-term Treasury bonds, minimum initial and maintenance margin is 10%. By using significant leverage, bond investors can transform these typically low-risk securities into very high-risk investments.

Margin rules are federally regulated by the Federal Reserve Board, but margin requirements and interest rates may vary above legal minimums between individual brokers and dealers. Many brokers require higher initial and maintenance margin for highly concentrated accounts that hold fewer than three securities and for accounts that hold especially volatile securities (e.g., Internet stocks).

margin debt Amount borrowed to buy or maintain a security investment.

margin call Broker demand for additional collateral.

In Wall Street terminology, **margin debt** is the amount borrowed to buy or maintain a security investment. A **margin call** is a formal notification by one's broker, usually by telephone or telegram, demanding additional collateral because of adverse price movements. For example, suppose that a margin account customer's equity falls to as little as 25% following a decline in the value of securities held. A phone call from the investor's broker will typically result, and the investor will be asked to increase the account's equity back to 50% within three business days. If the investor is unable or unwilling to provide additional cash or securities collateral, the broker will liquidate sufficient securities in the account to bring the account's equity back up to 50%. Thus, during adverse market conditions, margin calls can have the effect of forcing investors to liquidate positions following a sharp price decline.

Initial and maintenance margin requirements are similar to security deposits. They protect the lending broker from the loss of lent funds. Typically, the chance of a broker losing money on a margin loan is very modest. Brokers monitor the value of customer accounts on a daily, if not hour-by-hour, basis. Brokers are also quick to issue margin calls in the event of adverse price changes. Stocks and bonds can be readily liquidated, and there is a low probability of an immediate 30–50% loss in the value of a margin investor's total portfolio. Even if the worst happens and a broker suffers a loss on a margin loan, the brokerage customer remains legally responsible for the total amount borrowed.

broker call rate Interest rate charged to finance margin loans.

For lenders, margin loans represent a very low risk loan. The **broker call rate,** or broker loan rate, is the interest rate that banks and brokerage houses charge to finance margin loans to investors. The broker call rate is one of the least expensive interest rates available to borrowers. Brokers sometimes charge high-risk investors the broker call rate plus a modest markup or service charge.

Margin Call Risk

Although margin accounts are a low-risk proposition for lenders, they entail substantial risks for margin account customers. Buying stocks with borrowed funds, called buying on margin, is risky for investors because they implicitly agree to sell in the event of a sharp downturn in the value of their portfolio. Temporary market downturns do no lasting damage to the stock portfolios of patient buy-and-hold investors. However, even a temporary market downturn can cause a margin call and force the liquidation of margin account securities at ruinously low prices. The use of margin account debt can greatly amplify the typical risks of stock and bond investors.

Stock purchased with 50% initial margin triggers a 30% maintenance margin call following only a 28.6% decline in price. To see this is the case, note that the initial amount of margin debt is simply 50% of the initial purchase price, P_0, of a given stock. In equation form, this means that:

$$\text{Debt} = 0.5P_0 \tag{4.1}$$

To ensure 30% maintenance margin, total debt must be less than or equal to 70% of the current market price, P, of any stock purchased on margin. In equation form, this means that

$$\text{Debt} \leq 0.7P \tag{4.2}$$

After substitution from Equation 4.1 into Equation 4.2, it is clear that

$$0.5P_0 \leq 0.7P \tag{4.3}$$

In words, this means that 50% of the initial purchase price must be less than or equal to 70% of the current market price. Dividing each side of Equation 4.3 by P_0 and 0.7 gives

$$0.714 \leq P/P_0 \tag{4.4}$$

In words, this means that 0.714 must be less than or equal to the ratio of the current market price divided by the initial purchase price. Alternatively, a stock purchased with 50% initial margin could fall by as much as 28.6% in price before triggering a 30% maintenance margin call.

Table 4.4 illustrates how the use of margin debt increases the volatility of returns earned on investment. Panel A of Table 4.4 shows how the use of 50% initial margin debt increases the volatility of returns earned on the purchase of 1,000 shares of stock at $10. Notice that this implies initial investor equity of $5,000 and initial margin debt of $5,000. The investor's equity will double from $5,000 to $10,000 with a 50% rise in the stock's price from $10 to $15 but get wiped out by a 50% decline in the stock's price from $10 to $5. Also, notice that a margin call is triggered at a price between $7 and $8, specifically at $7.14. This means that the investor's broker will demand additional equity if the stock's price falls by 28.6%. If the investor is unable or unwilling to quickly provide additional equity, the broker will sell out the investor's position, and the investor will recognize a significant loss. In that event, the investor is unable to "weather the storm" of even a short-term decline in the stock's price. This makes stock purchases using margin debt risky. In making a margin purchase, the investor opens him- or herself to the possibility of being forced to sell if the stock falls substantially for even a brief period of time. Even temporary downturns in the stock's price can lead to permanent losses for margin buyers.

The biggest problem with using leverage to buy stocks is simple: Margin calls come at the worst possible time. Like bankers, brokers always want margin debt repaid at a time that is least convenient for the investor.

TABLE 4.4 Leverage Increases Potential Gains and Losses

An investment purchase using 50% initial margin will double with a 50% rise in price or get wiped out following a 50% fall in price. Such margin purchases trigger a margin call after a 28.6% price decline. A short sale using 50% initial margin will double with a 50% fall in price or get wiped out following a 50% rise in price. Such short sales trigger a margin call after only a 15.3% rise in price.

Panel A: Buying on Margin
Investment results with an initial purchase of 1,000 shares at $10 using 50% initial margin.

Stock Price	Investor Equity	Required Equity with 30% Maintenance Margin	Excess Equity (deficiency)
$5	$ 0	$1,500	($1,500)
6	1,000	1,800	(800)
7	2,000	2,100	(100)
8	3,000	2,400	600
9	4,000	2,700	1,300
10	5,000	3,000	2,000
11	6,000	3,300	2,700
12	7,000	3,600	3,400
13	8,000	3,900	4,100
14	9,000	4,200	4,800
15	10,000	4,500	5,500

Panel B: Selling Short on Margin
Investment results with an initial short sale of 1,000 shares at $10 using 50% initial margin.

Stock Price	Investor Equity	Required Equity with 30% Maintenance Margin	Excess Equity (deficiency)
$5	$10,000	$1,500	$8,500
6	9,000	1,800	7,200
7	8,000	2,100	5,900
8	7,000	2,400	4,600
9	6,000	2,700	3,300
10	5,000	3,000	2,000
11	4,000	3,300	700
12	3,000	3,600	(600)
13	2,000	3,900	(1,900)
14	1,000	4,200	(3,200)
15	0	4,500	(4,500)

Other Problems with Leverage

Table 4.4 makes clear that margin buyers face exaggerated losses from even mild downturns in stock prices. It turns out that this is only the most obvious of many problems faced by investors who use leverage. Most buyers of stock on margin are aware that they are exposed to an enormous risk of loss following even a temporary downturn in prices. This can have the effect of forcing investors who use margin debt to sell at the worst possible time. The use of margin debt can also tempt investors to sell too soon following even a modest price increase. Because margin debt amplifies the investor's profit from an appreciating stock price, large changes in the value of a margin account can occur on a daily basis. This can tempt margin buyers to prematurely sell stocks bought at a bargain purchase price. Use of margin debt greatly increases the volatility of an investor's holdings and results in excessive trading activity and unreasonable transactions costs.

Many investors also find that they make poorer investment selections when using borrowed money. Think of it as a type of "other people's money" problem. Government spending is the most famous example of the other people's money problem. Taxpayers often criticize government waste and argue that they get poor value out of tax dollars spent by the government. Many taxpayers believe that they get better value out of each dollar that they themselves get to spend at the grocery store, for example. Everybody knows best his or her own personal preferences. Nobody else knows as much about a consumer's preferences as that consumer does.

Buying stocks and bonds with borrowed funds can make investors careless when it comes to security selection. Because leverage amplifies the returns from rising prices, the advantage gained from leverage in a rising market can obscure the benefits of superior stock selection. Sometimes, investors can come to neglect the importance of careful security selection when using leverage. Such negligence increases the odds of making poor selections and exposes the margin account investor to a greater chance of loss.

The ability to borrow can also cause margin account customers to buy too much of an individual security or otherwise neglect the importance of prudent diversification. In this way, common stock investors behave much like home buyers. Realtors care most about how much adjusted monthly income the buyer has and how large a monthly payment the buyer can pay. Almost all home buyers take on a significant mortgage obligation to buy a much larger or nicer house than they could otherwise afford. This usually translates into a poor investment decision. Even a low-cost 7% mortgage results in a 4.2% after-tax cost of funds when the home buyer's marginal tax rate is 40%. In many communities, prices for existing homes are appreciating at a slower pace. Sometimes, the slow pace of price appreciation for existing homes is obscured by real estate professionals who quote the average rate of price change for all homes, both new and old. New homes tend to be larger and more plush than older homes. New homes also tend to be relatively expensive and boost the average price of all homes over time. Most home buyers also fail to count the high cost of maintenance when considering the rate of home price appreciation. As a result, the home owners' actual rate of price appreciation is often much less than popularly perceived and below the after-tax cost of mortgage interest. The reason to buy a house is that the kids need a place to park their bikes. Do not fool yourself into thinking that residential real estate is a great investment and made better by the ability of buyers to use enormous leverage.

As shown in Figure 4.1, the skyrocketing use of margin debt on Wall Street has long-term investors and regulators concerned about how such debt could magnify a typical downturn if speculators are forced to sell in a declining market. Exacerbating such risks is the fact that the use of margin debt seems highest among day traders and others who like to trade fast-moving tech stocks. In considering the advantages and disadvantages of margin accounts, investors should consider the fact that none of the most successful stock investors of our time use leverage. Neither Warren Buffett, Peter Lynch, nor John Templeton advocates the use of

FIGURE 4.1 **Use of Margin Debt Has Skyrocketed, Especially among High-Tech Investors**

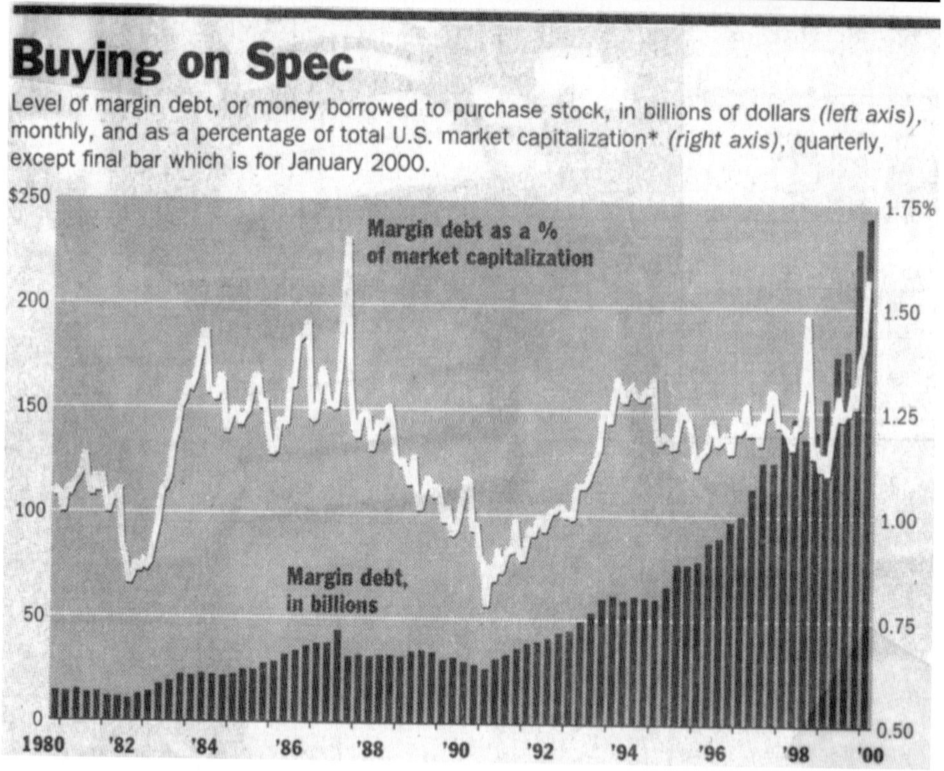

Source: Greg Ip, "Margin Debt Set a Record in January, Sparking Fresh Fears over Speculation," *The Wall Street Journal,* February 15, 2000, C2, C3.

margin accounts. Moreover, many of the most successful business managers of our time shun the use of corporate leverage in the operation of their own companies. Take giant Microsoft Corp., for example. With a market value of roughly $500 billion, Microsoft certainly represents a good credit risk to any lender. They could borrow billions of dollars at very competitive rates of interest. Why do you suppose that Microsoft has *zero* debt? Could it be that Bill Gates and company have concluded that it is a bad idea to use borrowed funds to make acquisitions or buy back its own stock? Has Microsoft concluded that it is best to focus on making excellent software?

For a bit of contrast with Microsoft's no-debt posture, take a look at the annual report for General Motors Corp. (GM). GM uses lots of leverage and has a balance sheet that features just about every modern form of financial obligation one can imagine. It also has some financial derivatives that are hard to imagine and extremely difficult to evaluate. GM's financial structure has all the modern "bells and whistles." GM also has a stock price that has appreciated little over the past 30 years. Meanwhile, Microsoft stock continues to forge ahead. It makes one wonder if GM stockholders would be better off if management were to forget about financial engineering and instead focus on engineering high-quality cars that are fun to drive.

Selling Short

How to Profit from Falling Prices

Sometimes, investors identify a company with poor and deteriorating fundamentals. The stocks of such companies are obvious candidates for a sell decision, providing the stock is held in the investor's portfolio. In some cases, an investor does not presently own companies with poor and deteriorating fundamentals but would still like to profit from the impending decline in the company's stock price. A **short sale** is one way to profit from the decline in a company's stock price. A short sale is the sale of borrowed stock. The borrower hopes to repurchase identical shares for return to the lender, or **cover the short,** at a lower price, thus making a profit. Lenders of stock sold short profit from interest and dividend income during the lending period.

short sale Sale of borrowed stock.

cover the short Return of borrowed shares.

Although the purchase of stock on margin is risky, the short sale of stock is an inherently riskier proposition. If a stock is bought, the potential loss is limited to the amount invested. The potential gain from a stock purchase is unlimited, or "the sky's the limit." It is important to keep in mind that all short sales are margin account transactions because they involve the use of borrowed stock. With a short sale, the potential gain is limited to the amount of proceeds obtained when the borrowed stock is sold short. If such a company went bankrupt and its stock price went to zero, all sale proceeds could be kept by the short seller. However, although the potential gain from a short-sale transaction is limited, the potential loss is unlimited. Short sellers can lose an enormous amount of money if they are on the wrong side of an overpriced stock that continues to gallop skyward.

Short interest data are reported by brokers to the SEC once a month. A summary of this information is published in leading financial publications such as *Barron's* and *The Wall Street Journal.* The *Wall Street Journal Interactive Edition* and Yahoo! also show detailed short interest data on the Internet for all companies on the NYSE, the American Stock Exchange (AMEX), and Nasdaq. Figure 4.2 shows short interest highlights for stocks traded on the NYSE. Details for companies listed on the AMEX and Nasdaq are published separately.

Notice that the amount of **short interest** in a particular stock is reported in two different ways. The number of shares sold short is presented as a useful overall indicator of the level of bearish sentiment on a stock. When short interest is high, the market consensus is negative. The number of shares sold short relative to the average daily trading volume in a stock, called the **short interest ratio,** is also provided as a useful indicator of the relative amount of short interest. When either measure of short interest is high, bearish sentiment is significant. Usually, this portends negative future performance for the company and its stock price. At times, however, aggressive speculators regard the amount of short interest as an indicator of the amount of latent buying interest in a stock. This is because short sellers may be forced to buy the stock and cover their shorts in the event of a sharp upward spike in the stock price. Such short covering can add dramatically to price volatility. When a volatile stock is pushed sharply higher by momentum players, the effect of frantic short covering can be a bit like throwing kerosene on a raging fire.

short interest Number of shares sold short.

short interest ratio Short interest expressed in terms of day's trading volume.

In making a margin purchase, the investor opens her- or himself to the possibility of being forced to sell if the stock price falls only modestly for even a brief

FIGURE 4.2 **Information about Short Interest Is Broadly Reported Once a Month**

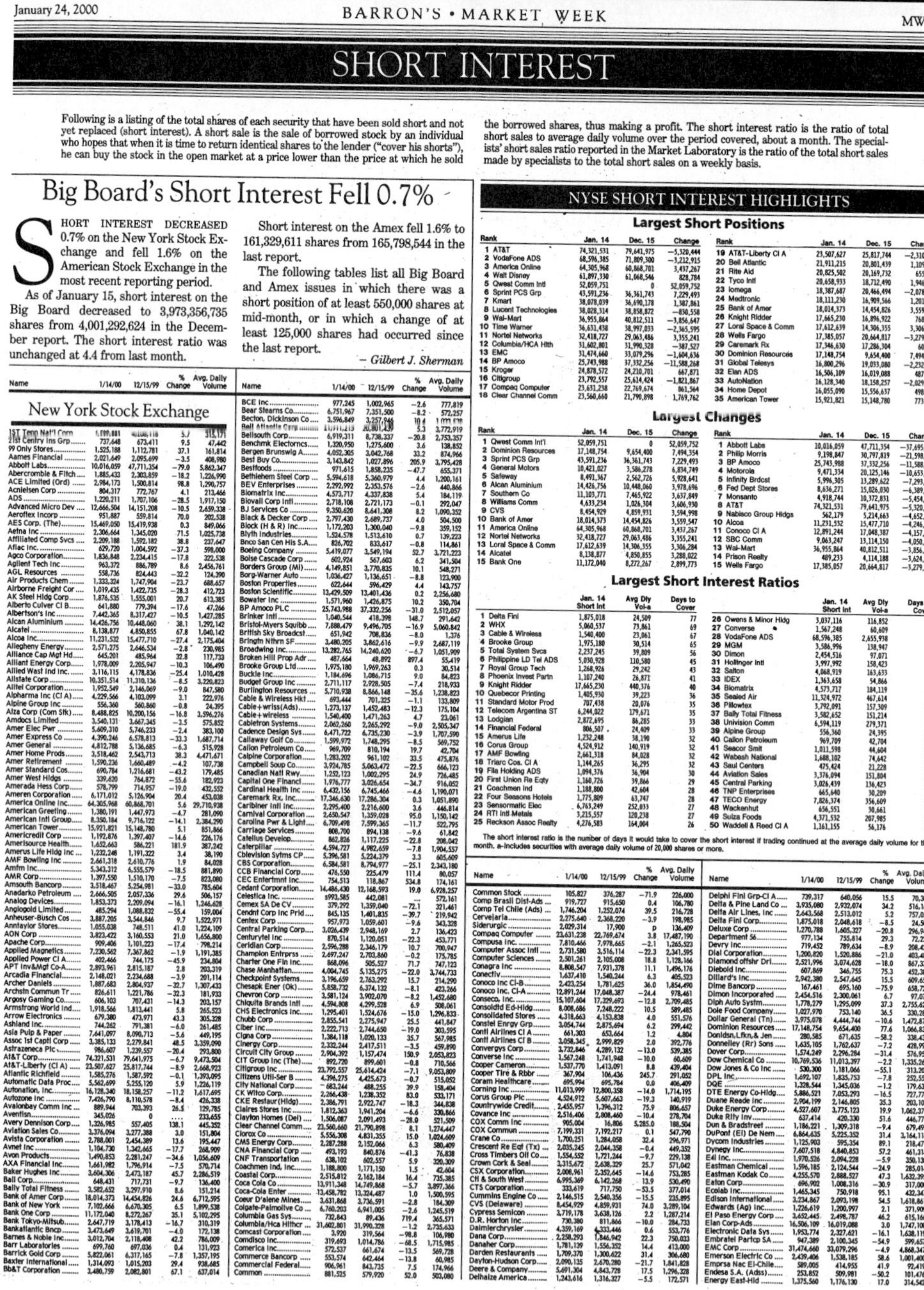

Source: *Barron's,* January 24, 2000, MW 53.

period of time. In making a short sale, the investor becomes open to the possibility of being forced to buy if the stock price rises for even a brief period of time by even smaller amounts. Even a small temporary price rise in an overpriced stock price can lead to permanent losses for short sellers. If momentum investors jump into an appreciating stock, a **short squeeze** can result as buyers "squeeze" short sellers to cover their short positions at truly wild prices. Making matters worse for short sellers is the fact that widely published short interest data identify prime short squeeze candidates. A successful short seller must master both the economics and the psychology of the situation.

short squeeze Pressure on short sellers caused by rapidly appreciating stock prices.

Margin Call Risk for Short Sellers

Selling short is even more risky than the purchase of a stock on margin because a rise in stock price both cuts the short seller's equity *and* increases the short seller's margin requirement. Short sales with 50% initial margin trigger a 30% maintenance margin call following only a 15.3% rise in price.

To see this is the case, remember that margin debt for a short seller consists of two parts, initial margin debt plus any debt incurred from a *rising* stock price:

$$\begin{aligned} \text{Debt} &= \text{Initial debt} + \Delta\text{Debt} \\ &= (P - 0.5P_0) + (P - P_0) \end{aligned} \tag{4.5}$$

In Equation 4.5, P_0 refers to the initial price, and P is the current price of any stock sold short. Margin debt rises for short sellers following an increase in stock prices because they are liable to pay a greater total amount to repurchase borrowed shares. After simplification, Equation 4.5 becomes

$$\text{Debt} = 2P - 1.5P_0 \tag{4.6}$$

At all times, margin debt must remain below 70% of the current market value of borrowed shares:

$$\text{Debt} \leq 0.7P \tag{4.7}$$

Then, when Equations 4.6 and 4.7 are combined,

$$2P - 1.5P_0 \leq 0.7P \tag{4.8}$$

After simplification, Equation 4.8 becomes

$$1.153 \geq P/P_0 \tag{4.9}$$

Following a short sale in a margin account, the number 1.153 must be greater than or equal to the ratio of the current market price divided by the initial price at which the short sale decision was made. The current market price of a stock sold short can be no more than 15.3% higher than its original price before a 30% maintenance margin call is triggered.

Notice how quickly a margin call is triggered when a stock price moves the wrong way for a short seller. In the case of a stock purchase with 50% margin debt, a 30% margin call occurs only when the stock price has fallen by at least 28.6%. In the case of a short-sale transaction with 50% margin debt, a similar margin call occurs when the stock price has risen by only 15.3%. Margin calls occur about twice as fast following adverse price moves for short sellers as they do for stock buyers.

The reason for this difference is simple. When a stock price falls, the margin buyer's equity and required margin both fall. When a stock price rises, the short seller's equity falls while the amount of required margin rises. This "squeezes" the short seller.

Panel B in Table 4.4 (page 124) illustrates how the use of 50% initial margin debt increases the volatility of returns earned on the short sale of 1,000 shares of stock at $10. Notice that this again implies initial equity of $5,000 and initial margin debt of $5,000. The investor's equity will double from $5,000 to $10,000 with a 50% fall in the stock's price from 10 to 5 but gets wiped out by a 50% rise in the stock's price from 10 to 15. Also notice that a margin call is triggered at a price between 11 and 12, specifically at $11.53, or roughly 11½. This means that the investor's broker will demand additional equity if the stock's price rises by only 15.3%. If the investor is unable or unwilling to quickly provide additional equity, the broker will buy the stock and cover the investor's short position. In that event, the investor will recognize a significant loss. With only a modest short-term uptick in the stock's price, the investor is "squeezed" into either providing more equity or buying the stock.

Anatomy of a Short Squeeze

In a rising market, short sellers become active momentum players. During recent years, for example, Internet and technology stocks such as Amazon.com, America Online, Lucent Technologies, and Yahoo! skyrocketed in price. These lofty prices attracted short sellers. However, as momentum buyers continued to favor Internet and technology stocks, prices continued to advance and short sellers became increasingly eager to end their private "nightmare" by buying them back and thereby covering their shorts. As Internet stock prices skyrocketed, short sellers got killed. Such episodes tend to end badly for buyers, too, because ridiculously high stock prices collapse when demand from short covering is exhausted. Over the next couple of years, it will be interesting to track the stock price performance of America Online, Qwest Communications, Lucent, Nortel Networks, and various other stocks highlighted in Figure 4.2.

For some insight in this regard, it is interesting to note the stock price performance of recent stock price bubbles. Figure 4.3 shows a classic bubble in the stock price of a small high-tech stock caused, at least in part, by massive short covering by scared bears as the stock's price rose to unbelievable heights. The example depicts the stock price performance of portable disk-drive maker Iomega Corp., which culminated in a sharp upward spike in May 1996, followed by a sharp sustained collapse in price. On May 22, 1996, Iomega's stock price surged to a peak of $27.56 (27 9/16) during a day of frenzied short-covering activity when trading volume in the stock surged to 17 million shares. This price was more than 126 times the split-adjusted price of 21.35¢ on January 1, 1994. Ten trading days later, Iomega had lost one-third of this value; within a month, it was down by one-half. By the end of 1998, Iomega's share price had fallen by more than 72% to only $7.31 (7 5/16). What the heck happened? Despite the unprecedented success of Iomega's Zip and Jaz drive and disk products and stunning revenue growth, a host of new competitors emerged to erode the company's profitability and long-term outlook. The shorts were right. Iomega was ridiculously overpriced in May of 1996. Unfortunately for them, many simply did not have the stomach and/or capital to withstand the price surge to $27.

FIGURE 4.3 **Classic Short-Squeeze Example: Iomega Corp. Stock 1996–98**

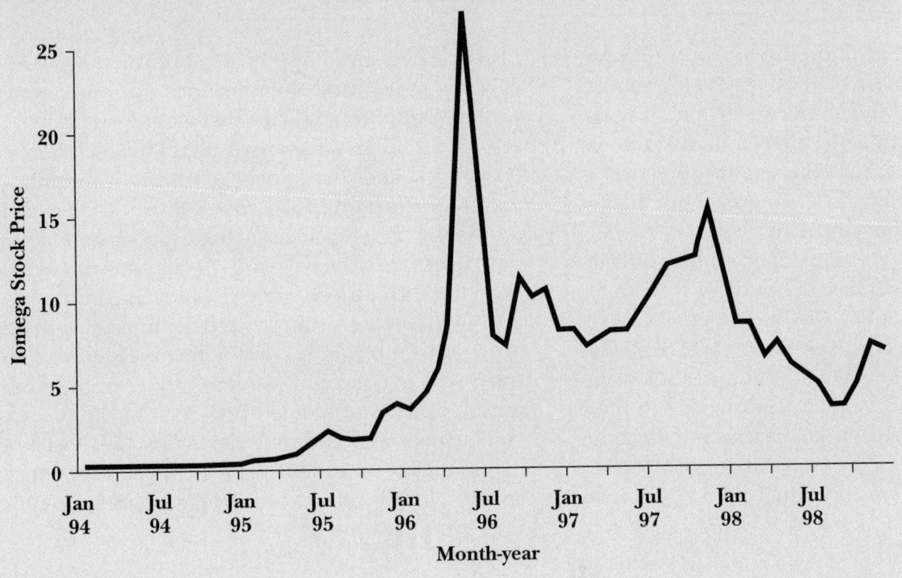

Ways to Limit Short-Selling Risk

Before profiting from a short-selling strategy, the investor must overcome a number of daunting practical problems with short selling. As a long-term strategy, short selling suffers from the "problem" that stocks usually go up. Therefore, a successful short seller is a good trader during generally adverse market conditions. Stock selection *and* timing are both vital to a profitable short sale.

If one remains undaunted by the formidable risks, prudence demands that some risk-controlling strategies be adopted by short sellers. A simple rule of thumb for risk control includes the admonition that short sellers should limit short positions to no more than 20% of their investment portfolio and limit losses to 20% price appreciation. Never lose more than 4% of the portfolio on one position. It is also prudent to avoid heavily shorted stocks. Finally, short stocks only when their prices are falling. Never get in the way of momentum buyers.

Initial Public Offerings

IPO Process

When a corporation needs new capital to expand production facilities, build inventories, and so on, it must issue debt or equity securities. Newly issued securities are sold in the **primary market.** All subsequent trading of those securities is done in the **secondary market.** Secondary markets involve the organized trading of outstanding securities on exchanges and over-the-counter markets. The NYSE, Nasdaq, the bond markets, and so on, are secondary markets.

primary market
Market for new securities.

secondary market
Market for seasoned securities.

WALL STREET WISDOM 4.2

IPO Means "It's Probably Overpriced"

Next time you find yourself on the lookout for a hot Initial Public Offering, or IPO, ask yourself a simple, basic question. Would this underwriter like to make me happy or curry favor with some giant institutional investor such as Fidelity Investments? If the answer is not obvious, a brief glimpse at how the IPO market actually works may prove instructive.

On Wall Street, it has been suspected that individual investors rarely get a piece of hot IPOs. Now, there is hard evidence. Recently, *The Wall Street Journal* reviewed a half-dozen secret Wall Street "pot lists" that show which investors get IPO allocations. Lists of institutional investors that regularly participate in IPOs are known as pot lists because underwriters collect the orders and fees for such investors in a shared "pot." By contrast, orders from individual investors are solicited and received by individual brokers who may or may not share these commissions with other underwriters. Evidence confirms that giant institutional investors get the lion's share of IPOs for which demand is strongest and that individual investors are only apt to get an allocation for IPOs with tepid demand. Interestingly, Fidelity Investments, the Boston mutual fund giant, routinely gets IPO allocations that are twice the size of those given to other large institutional investors. By threatening to reduce its trading activity with noncomplying securities firms, Fidelity is routinely able to coerce investment bankers into giving it outsized pieces of coveted IPOs.

Fidelity is also known as being less than forthcoming about its investment plans for shares obtained in an IPO. Ideally, investment bankers look to establish

FIGURE 4.A **A Peek at the "Pot"**

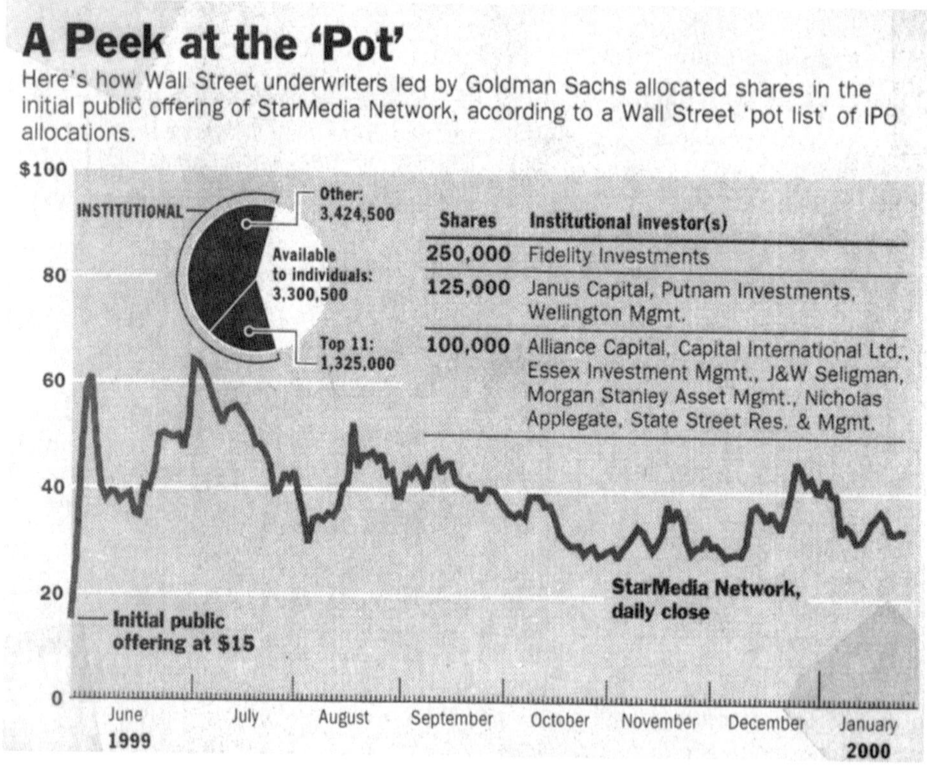

Source: *The Wall Street Journal,* January 27, 2000, C1.

a stable aftermarket for the shares they bring public by asking IPO buyers to maintain their investment for long-term capital appreciation. Get-rich-quick artists who immediately sell IPO shares on the first trading day in a fast-moving market can undermine desired price stability. As a result, speculators who quickly resell shares bought in an IPO are sometimes shut out from subsequent offerings. However, Fidelity is such a big and regular customer that investment bankers are reluctant to enforce traditional "gentleman's agreements" against reselling IPOs for a quick trading profit.

Of course, it should not be surprising that Wall Street favors its best customers with its most desirable IPOs. As would be true of most businesses, underwriters do their best to ably serve the needs of their best customers. What is perhaps surprising about the *Journal*'s pot list disclosures is the precision of the IPO allocation process and the amount of clout that Fidelity displays.

An interesting case in point is provided by the IPO of StarMedia Network, a New York online network targeting Spanish and Portuguese Web users. StarMedia went public in a $120 million IPO led by Goldman Sachs on May 25, 1999. In Wall Street terminology, the deal was "hot"; StarMedia stock price quadrupled in the first four trading days. A pot list of StarMedia's institutional investors shows that Fidelity got 250,000 shares, whereas other mutual fund groups, such as Janus, Putnam, and Wellington Management, got 125,000 shares apiece. Individual investors seeking shares in the company typically had to buy in the secondary market at much higher post-IPO prices (see Figure 4.A).

The bottom line on IPO investing for the small individual investor is simple. On Wall Street, individual investors rarely get a piece of hot IPOs. The really good stuff is reserved for the investment banker's very best customers. If demand is robust and a first-day pop in the IPO price seems likely, such shares are reserved for giant institutions who bring a recurring stream of revenue to the investment banker. If a small investor can get an IPO allotment, that is a strong signal of weak demand from the investment banker's best institutional customers.

The upshot: If an individual investor can get an IPO allocation, he or she probably does not want it. It is not apt to be a hot IPO. Too often for the individual investor, the IPO market is a "heads I lose, tails they win" proposition.

See: Terzah Ewing, "Average IPO since Beginning of 1999 Is Down 10%," *The Wall Street Journal*, April 26, 2000, C1, C20.

An **initial public offering (IPO)** is a corporation's first sale of stock or bonds to the public. Securities offered in an IPO are made by companies seeking outside equity capital and a public market for their stock. Notable recent IPOs include eBay, the person-to-person Internet trading community; Inktomi, a producer of large-scale network software; and Red Hat, an open software service provider. Investors purchasing stock in an IPO must be prepared to accept large risks for the possibility of large gains.

initial public offering (IPO)
Newly issued securities.

A **seasoned issue** is the issuance of a security for which there is already an existing public market. For example, when IBM sells additional stock or bonds to the general public, such securities are seasoned issued. Many IPOs during 1998–99 quickly returned to the market to raise additional funds through seasoned new issues. **Secondary offerings** are the public sale of previously issued securities held by large investors, corporations, or institutional investors. For example, corporate insiders are a typical source of secondary offerings when they sell large blocks of stock obtained through incentive compensation plans. The fundamental distinction between primary and secondary offerings is that the issuing corporation receives the proceeds of primary offerings, but the issuing corporation does not receive any sale proceeds in a secondary offering. Many secondary offerings are handled informally by securities firms and are usually offered at a fixed price related to the current market price of the stock.

seasoned issue
Issuance of a security for which there is already an existing public market.

secondary offerings
Public sale of previously issued securities held by large investors, corporations, or institutional investors.

private placement Sale to a small group of investors, generally under exemption of SEC and state securities registration requirements.

offering circular SEC filing that describes a private placement.

investment bank Investment backer who endorses and sponsors a company's new securities. Also called an **underwriter.**

road show Series of presentations to promote company securities.

firm commitment underwriting Security offering in which the underwriter purchases the entire issue from the corporation and reoffers it to the general public.

best-efforts underwriting Security offering in which the investment banker simply agrees to make its best effort at selling the agreed-on amount of securities.

Federal securities laws require U.S. companies with more than 500 investors and $10 million in net assets to register with the SEC and file annual reports containing audited financial statements. All companies that list their securities on the Nasdaq Stock Market or a major national stock exchange such as the NYSE also must file with the SEC. When investments or businesses are offered for sale to a small group of investors, generally under exemption of SEC and state securities registration requirements, this is referred to as **private placement** or a private offering.

Some smaller companies do not have to register their securities or file reports on EDGAR. For example, companies raising less than $5 million in a 12-month period may be exempt from registering the transaction under a rule known as Regulation A. Instead, these companies must file an **offering circular** with the SEC containing financial statements and other information. Smaller companies raising less than one million dollars do not have to register with the SEC, but they must file a Form D. Form D is a brief notice that includes the names and addresses of owners and stock promoters but little other information.

In most instances, corporations seeking additional investment capital hire an **investment bank,** or **underwriter,** to act in the role of advisor and distributor. Investment banking services include underwriting of debt and equity securities; advising on mergers, acquisitions, privatization, and restructuring; and participating in real estate, project finance, and leasing activities. Successful underwriters have a roster of regular customers, such as pension funds, mutual funds, and insurance companies, for new issues. Highly respected investment bankers must be sure to bring only high-quality IPOs to the attention of their regular institutional customers or risk the loss of potentially lucrative future business. At the same time, investment bankers are always on the prowl for more companies with securities to sell and more institutional customers. As a result, an important part of the IPO process is the **road show** before institutional investors and the general public, in which issuing companies and their investment bankers discuss the investment merits of the corporation's securities. This is a useful means of drumming up interest in the offering and determining investors' appetite for the firm's securities under different pricing scenarios. Throughout this process, the issuing corporation and the investment banker come to agreement on several things, including the amount of capital needed by the corporation, type of security to be issued, price of the security to be issued, and the amount of compensation (or commission) paid by the firm to the investment banker. Table 4.5 shows a roster of leading investment bankers.

There are two broad categories of agreements between investment bankers and issuing corporations. With a **firm-commitment underwriting,** the investment banker agrees to purchase the entire issue from the corporation and then reoffer such securities to the general public. Under this type of agreement, the investment banker guarantees to provide a certain sum of money to the corporation. Any risk associated with failing to resell securities to institutional investors and the general public falls entirely on the investment bank. If the investment banker fails in its bid to resell securities issued on a firm commitment, the corporation still receives the agreed-on amount, and the investment banker suffers a loss. In a second type of securities agreement, known as a **best-efforts underwriting,** the investment banker simply agrees to make its best effort at selling the agreed-on amount of debt and equity securities. If the investment banker fails in its bid to

TABLE 4.5 Merrill Lynch Leads the List of Top Global Investment Bankers

1999 Underwriting Rankings
Biggest Corporate Financings of 1999.

Top 10 Global Stock Issues

Issuer	Date	Amount (in millions)
Enel Societa Per Azioni	Nov. 1	$16,451.5
Nippon Telegraph & Teleph.	Nov. 8	14,969.0
Deutsche Telekom	June 26	11,350.6
Telstra (Australia)	Oct. 16	10,350.5
East Japan Railway	July 26	5,600.0
United Parcel Service	Nov. 9	5,470.0
Repsol	July 6	4,667.8
Tracker Fund of Hong Kong	Nov. 8	4,290.0
Deutsche Bank	April 27	4,253.2
Telecom Eireann	July 7	3,762.2

Top 10 Global Debt Issues

Issuer	Date	Amount (in millions)
Ford Motor Credit	July 9	$8,600.0
AT&T	March 23	8,000.0
Tecnost International	July 19	6,340.6
Wal-Mart Stores	Aug. 5	5,750.0
Ford Motor Credit	Oct. 21	5,000.0
DaimlerChrysler N. Amer.	Aug. 17	4,500.0
Conoco (El du Pont de Nem.)	April 15	4,000.0
Charter Comm. Intl	March 12	3,575.0
Sprint Capital	April 29	3,500.0
Repsol Intl Finance (Repsol)	May 19	3,458.0

Global Stocks and Bonds
U.S. public and Rule-144a issues and euro-market issue, ranked by 1999 proceeds.

	1999			1998	
Manager	Proceeds (in billions)	Issues	Market Share	Proceeds (in billions)	Rank
Merrill Lynch	$417.46	2,380	12.5%	$394.49	1
Salomon Smith Barney	324.64	1,751	9.8	285.00	4
Morgan Stanley Dean Witter	301.45	2,609	9.1	291.45	2
Goldman Sachs	268.11	1,313	8.1	287.90	3
Credit Suisse First Boston	239.99	1,415	7.2	215.11	5
Lehman Brothers	201.44	1,071	6.1	202.18	6
Deutsche Bank	140.58	901	4.2	84.80	12
J.P. Morgan	134.48	716	4.0	140.70	7
Chase Manhattan	131.02	1,158	3.9	93.09	9
ABN Amro	103.68	1,230	3.1	63.65	13
TOP 10 TOTALS	$2,262.86	14,544	68.0%	$2,058.37	-
INDUSTRY TOTALS	$3,326.68	21,844	100.0%	$2,925.88	-

Global Stocks
U.S. public and Rule-144a issues and euro-market issue, ranked by 1999 proceeds.

		Market Share	
Top Managers	1999 Proceeds (in billions)	1999	1998
Morgan Stanley Dean Witter	$580.7	16.9%	13.3%
Goldman Sachs	539.5	15.7	13.4
Merrill Lynch	423.9	12.4	13.8
Salomon Smith Barney	249.7	7.3	5.3
Credit Suisse First Boston	238.3	6.9	4.6
Deutsche Bank	165.7	4.8	5.3
Donaldson, Lufkin & Jenrette	139.5	4.1	4.9
Warbug Dillon Read	134.2	3.9	8.3
Lehman Brothers	129.7	3.8	3.5
J.P. Morgan	117.8	3.4	3.3
TOP 10	$2,719.11	79.2%	75.6%
INDUSTRY	$3,432.33	100.0%	100.0%

(continued)

TABLE 4.5 ***(continued)***

Global Debt
U.S. public and Rule-144a and euro-zone issues.

Top Managers	**1999 Proceeds (in billions)**	**Market Share 1999**	**1998**
Merrill Lynch	$375.3	1.9%	13.0%
Salomon Smith Barney	299.9	1.6	10.0
Morgan Stanley Dean Witter	250.6	1.3	9.7
Credit Suisse First Boston	219.0	1.1	7.7
Goldman Sachs	218.1	1.1	9.3
Lehman Brothers	187.6	1.0	7.2
Deutsche Bank	127.6	0.7	2.9
Chase Manhattan	127.5	0.7	3.4
J.P. Morgan	123.7	0.6	5.0
ABN Amro	98.4	0.5	2.2
TOP 10	**$13.04**	**10.5%**	**70.1%**
INDUSTRY	**$19.32**	**100.0%**	**100.0%**

Data source: *The Wall Street Journal,* January 3, 2000, R24.

sell securities issued under a best-efforts offering at agreed-on prices, the corporation receives only the amount sold, less necessary commissions. When a best-efforts underwriting fails to raise the anticipated amount for debt and equity securities, the investment banker loses out on potential commission income but suffers no necessary capital loss. Best-efforts underwritings are called **all-or-none offerings** when the underwriter agrees to do its best to sell an entire issue by a certain date, but if all securities are not sold by that time, all money is returned to purchasers and the issue is canceled.

all-or-none offerings Requirement for a complete sale.

In a firm-commitment underwriting, the investment banker commits both its reputation and its investment capital to the success of the underwriting. With a best-efforts underwriting, the investment banker only commits its reputation. Therefore, a firm-commitment underwriting entails a greater level of risk for the investment banker. When a large and highly respected corporation, such as IBM, seeks to offer debt or equity securities, it is almost always done on a firm-commitment basis. Investment bankers fight tooth-and-nail in the attempt to get a slice of such business. The result of such competition is very low commission rates of 1–1.5% of the amount raised. IPOs by lesser-known companies, especially risky startups in high-tech or Internet-related businesses, are much more likely to be made on a best-efforts basis and may entail commission rates of as much as 6–8% or more.

underwriting syndicate Group of underwriters who agree to participate in selling an issue.

syndicate manager Lead investment bank.

underwriter's allotment Investment banker's allocation.

dealers agreement Contractual obligation of syndicate members.

Many times, investment banks do not want to take on all the risk of an offering, so they form a **syndicate,** or group of underwriters who agree to participate in selling the issue. The lead investment bank, or **syndicate manager,** is responsible for determining the offering price, sets the timing of the issue, responds to any deficiency letters by the SEC, modifies selling commissions, and controls advertising and the amount of each **underwriter's allotment.** Finally, the syndicate manager has prime responsibility for the **dealers agreement,** which specifies how securities dealers who are not part of the syndicate may contract to purchase some of the securities from the issue.

Figure 4.4 shows a **tombstone ad** for a recent IPO. Essential bits of information included in a tombstone ad consist of the name of the new issue, number of shares offered, the offering price, and a list of the lead investment bankers and syndicate members. Lead investment bankers are usually identified by their prominent placement at the top of the list of participating firms. Syndicate members are usually arrayed from top to bottom according to the amount of participation in the offering.

tombstone ad Advertisement announcing security offering.

FIGURE 4.4 **IPO Announcements Give Basic Details about the Offering**

This advertisement is neither an offer to sell nor a solicitation of any offer to buy these securities.
The offer is made only by the Prospectus.
February 15, 2000
4,500,000 Shares
EMERGE INTERACTIVE
Class A Common Stock
Price $15 Per Share
Copies of the Prospectus may be obtained in any State in which this announcement is circulated only from such of the Underwriters as may lawfully offer these securities in such State.
Adams, Harkness & Hill, Inc.
First Union Securities, Inc.
FAC/Equities
Banc of America Securities LLC
Chase H&Q
Deutsche Banc Alex. Brown
Lehman Brothers
J.P. Morgan & Co.
Prudential Volpe Technology Group
a unit of Prudential Securities
Thomas Weisel Partners LLC
First Montauk Securities Corp.
Janney Montgomery Scott LLC
Legg Mason Wood Walker
Incorporated
Parker/Hunter
Incorporated
Pennsylvania Merchant Group
Wedbush Morgan Securities

Source: *The Wall Street Journal,* February 15, 2000, C21.

Regulatory Requirements

registration statement SEC document that describes an offering.

filing date Date that the investment bank submits a registration statement with the SEC.

cooling-off period Marketing period.

preliminary prospectus Preliminary statement of offering characteristics. Also called **red herring.**

effective date Date that securities are offered to institutional investors and the general public.

deficiency letter Disapproval notice issued by the SEC.

indication of interest Expression of intent to buy.

due diligence Required analysis.

final prospectus Final statement of offering.

Following the Securities Act of 1933, when a company makes a public offering it must file a **registration statement** with the SEC. The day the investment bank submits the registration statement with the SEC is known as the **filing date.** Contained in this registration statement is a description of the company's main line of business, biographical material on officers and directors, and the amount of shares held by officers, directors, and other large shareholders owning more than 10% of the company (so-called insiders). Complete financial statements must also be submitted, along with information about how proceeds of the offering are going to be used. After the registration statement has been filed, the SEC requires a **cooling-off period** during which the issuing company and the investment banker try to drum up interest in the issue. They do this through a **preliminary prospectus,** which is sometimes referred to as a **red herring** because it has red printing across the top and in the margins. Contained in the preliminary prospectus is much of the information from the registration statement. The public offering price and the effective date of the IPO are not contained in the red herring. The public offering price is determined on the effective date after investor interest in the issues has been determined. Assuming the IPO is, in fact, approved by the SEC, securities are offered to institutional investors and the general public on the **effective date.** If the SEC does not approve a given issue, a **deficiency letter** is issued and the effective date is postponed.

During the cooling-off period, the issuing company and its investment banker may not provide any other information to the investment bank's clients beyond that which is contained in the preliminary prospectus. When a given institutional investor or other client of the investment banker expresses an **indication of interest,** such information is dutifully recorded as a useful indication of potential demand for the issue under a given set of pricing assumptions. Although no firm orders can yet be taken, indications of interest are a critical guide to the investment banker in its final pricing of the issue. Just prior to the effective date, the issuing corporation and its investment banker have a **due diligence** meeting to ensure that material changes have taken place between the filing date and the effective date. Once the effective date arrives, a **final prospectus** is issued, the security can be sold, and money is collected.

Underwriters and dealers get paid out of the proceeds of the offering. The public offering price stated on the face of the prospectus is what the general public pays. However, the issuing corporation receives a lower price determined by the agreed-upon spread. Any dealer or broker participating in the underwriting is compensated out of the spread as specified in the underwriting agreement. The managing underwriter typically receives a manager's fee for each share sold. Each member of the underwriting syndicate is also entitled to an underwriting allowance to compensate for expenses and risks incurred. The selling group is also allocated a portion of the spread as a selling concession (or commission). A reallowance is also paid to securities firms that contact members of the syndicate to purchase part of the issue to fill its own customer orders after the effective date. Because this firm has incurred no risk and made little effort in the underwriting, reallowance fees tend to be minimal.

Table 4.6 shows the magnitude of the IPO and secondary offerings during the 1990s. Nasdaq has long been an important market for the initial listing of IPOs. During recent years, however, the NYSE has become much more aggressive in seek-

TABLE 4.6 Initial and Secondary Public Offering Increase the Supply of Publicly Traded Stocks and Bonds

Year	Nasdaq Offerings	Dollar Value of Nasdaq Offerings (Millions)	NYSE Offerings	Dollar Value of NYSE Offerings (Millions)	AMEX Offerings	Dollar Value of AMEX Offerings (Millions)	Total Offerings	Total Dollar Value of Offerings (Millions)*
A. Initial Public Offerings								
1990	134	$2,403.15	19	$2,074.17	5	$149.88	158	$4,627.20
1991	320	$7,730.16	49	$8,351.15	11	$268.98	380	$16,350.29
1992	442	$13,585.91	80	$15,661.62	6	$111.65	528	$29,359.18
1993	520	$16,069.65	97	$22,308.17	11	$146.85	628	$38,524.67
1994	444	$13,186.80	82	$18,163.61	13	$269.00	539	$31,619.41
1995	476	$16,733.92	72	$14,752.75	9	$283.08	557	$31,769.75
1996	680	$24,498.15	88	$11,947.60	18	$510.13	786	$36,955.88
1997	494	$19,367.03	87	$18,202.38	22	$880.47	603	$38,449.88
1998	273	$13,757.27	68	$35,848.15	21	$386.95	362	$49,992.37
1999	485	$50,425.22	49	$54,418.51	11	$138.00	545	$104,982.06
*B. Secondary Public Offerings**								
1991	241	$8,139.93	155	$19,635.24	40	$1,850.87	436	$29,626.04
1992	223	$7,019.45	172	$23,724.70	47	$1,458.57	442	$32,202.72
1993	343	$13,525.78	195	$32,737.70	45	$1,875.14	583	$48,138.62
1994	222	$8,851.20	140	$24,074.48	24	$721.36	386	$33,647.04
1995	372	$24,641.07	142	$29,862.17	21	$561.21	535	$55,064.45
1996	428	$27,751.01	169	$28,547.54	19	$713.67	616	$57,012.22
1997	355	$25,649.19	158	$31,711.87	31	$1,562.53	544	$58,923.59
1998	215	$19,651.72	257	$47,838.49	23	$1,332.65	495	$68,822.86
1999	281	$53,454.93	108	$47,230.24	11	$794.00	400	$101,479.59

Note: *1990 secondary public offering data not available.
Data source: <http://www.nasdaq.com>.

ing out IPOs, especially in the technology area. Until recently, the NYSE enjoyed a dominant share of the subsequent trading activity for more seasoned companies making secondary offerings. In recent years, many secondary offerings have been made by cash-starved high-tech companies on Nasdaq. Notice how the tremendous IPO boom of 1999 resulted in the total market value of IPOs exceeding the value of secondary offerings. Clearly, companies have rushed to satisfy the investor's appetite for exciting new issues, especially in high-tech and the Internet.

Figure 4.5 gives a useful long-term perspective on the current IPO boom. The strength of the late 1990s bull market in equities is perhaps most forcefully reflected in the market for IPOs. For example, although the number of IPOs reached a peak in 1996, the record $105 billion raised during 1999 was more than twice the previous record amount. More money was raised in 1999 than during the 1970s and 1980s *combined.* Looking forward, it is reasonable to expect a sharp slowdown in the pace of IPOs. IPO activity often tends to follow dramatic growth in the overall market averages, sometimes with a slight lag. Ominously, difficult market periods often tend to follow ebullient IPO markets, such as that experienced during 1998–99.

FIGURE 4.5 **Stock Market Surge of the Late 1990s Sparked an Unprecedented Boom in the IPO Market**

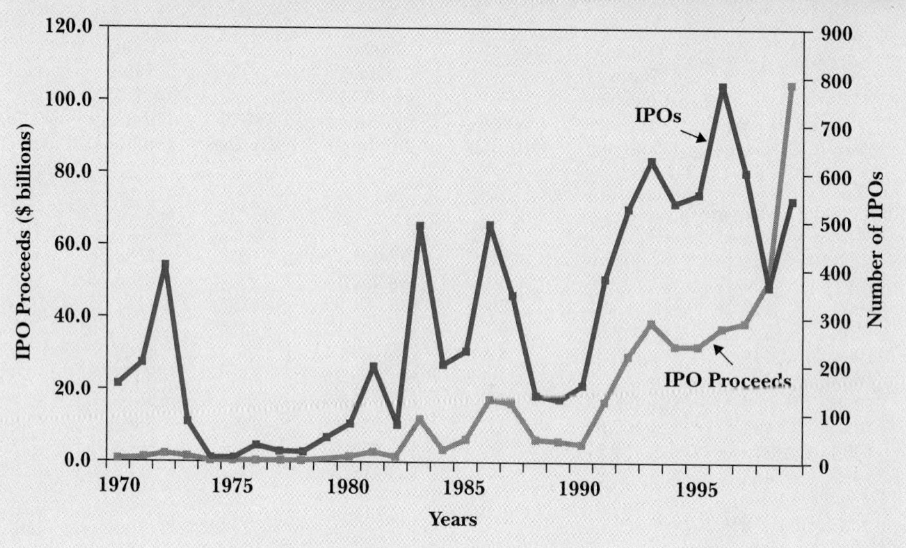

Postissue Performance of IPOs

hot IPO
IPO with limited shares and high demand.

A **hot IPO** is an IPO in which shares are limited and demand is very high. Virtually every recent Internet IPO qualifies as a hot IPO. Hot IPOs create an interesting dilemma for both issuing corporations and their investment bankers. Generally, investment bankers allocate shares of hot IPOs to their top-performing stockbrokers and most loyal clients. For both, the opportunity to participate in hot IPOs is a reward for past business and an expression of hope for more fruitful interactions in the future. For the investment banker, a hot IPO represents a delicate balancing act. On the one hand, the investment banker wants to offer securities for the issuing corporation at a high price to fairly compensate the company for giving up a significant ownership stake. On the other hand, the investment banker wants to price the IPO at an attractive level to offer its institutional clients a fair reward for the risk of investing in unseasoned securities. With too high an initial price, the offering fails, and the investment banker risks the loss of both customer goodwill and its own investment capital. With too low an initial price, the issuing corporation suffers a loss of potentially vital investment capital, investors reap exorbitant trading profits, and again, the investment banker risks the loss of customer goodwill.

In a delicate balancing of conflicting interests, most IPOs are priced so that initial buyers can expect to see near-term gains that appear substantial on a percentage basis. It is the issuing company's hope that investors will be sufficiently impressed with its favorable experience in buying the company's securities that they will become willing buyers of future secondary offerings. To mitigate the problem of short-term traders dumping their shares shortly after the IPO, many investment bankers closely monitor how long buyers maintain their holdings. Short-term traders who quickly **flip** their shares of a hot IPO seldom have the opportunity to participate in future IPOs.

flip
A purchase quickly followed by a sale.

When considering the postissue performance of IPOs, it is essential to keep in mind that the pricing of all IPOs is made within the context of ongoing business relationships among issuing corporations, investment bankers, institutional investors, and the general public. When one notices the first-day performance of especially "hot" Internet IPOs during recent years, for example, it is easy to conclude that the market for IPOs is hopelessly inefficient. The first-day performances of Phone.com, Commerce One, Broadcade Communications, and so on, lead even the novice investor to conclude that huge excess profits await anyone who participates in the IPO market. This simply is not true.

Table 4.7 shows the postissuance performance of recent attention-grabbing IPOs. Notice the spectacular one-day returns for top-performing IPOs. In an ebullient bull market, one-day IPO returns in excess of 100% can be common. However, such spectacular IPO profits are only possible if an investor is able to get a share allocation at the initial offering price. Most individual shareholders are shut out of this process. In the IPO market, small investors seldom are able to participate in those IPOs for which demand is greatest. Another problem is posed by the fact that the postissuance performance of IPOs varies in ways that are hard to predict. Investors should not expect to receive above-market risk-adjusted returns for a portfolio of IPOs. Fueling investor interest in IPOs are hot IPOs such as Phone.com, a software provider for patching wireless phones into the Internet, which came public in June 1999 at $16 a share and rose to $175 by November 1999. However, for every Phone.com success story, there are several disappointing stories about IPO performance. Studies suggest that the median IPO underperforms the Russell 3000 Index by roughly 30% in the three years after it comes public. The hottest new issues can be particularly disappointing for long-term investors. Studies show that IPOs with the biggest one-day price gains underperform the market by two to three percentage points per month during the following year.

In short, investor celebrations about the *IPO* success stories of 1998–99 may be a bit premature. Let's wait and see how such wunderkind fare in a bear market caused by even a mild recession. In the IPO market, the initials *IPO* are jokingly referred to as "It's Probably Overpriced." It is typically best to wait six months or more after an IPO to buy such shares at the then-discounted price.

Individual Retirement Accounts

Major Recent Changes

Individual retirement accounts (IRAs) provide a powerful way to save money for retirement. The 1998 law changed IRAs in important ways. Presently, the law

- Allows most taxpayers to make tax-deductible contributions to traditional IRAs.
- Provides exceptions for postsecondary educational expenses and for first-time home purchases to the IRS-imposed 10% penalty on withdrawals from IRAs before age 59½.
- Permits two nondeductible, tax-free IRAs—the Roth IRA and the Education IRA.

TABLE 4.7 Investors Focus on the Outstanding Performance of Hot IPOs but Many IPOs Perform Poorly

A. Leaders of the Pack
Networking and computer stocks delivered top performance during 1999.

Issuer	Offer Date	Offer Price	First Day's Close	Price 12/3	Change from Offer Price*	Return from 1st Day Close	Current Underwriter	Business Description
Phone.com	6/10	$16.00	$40.13	$168.75	2,009.4%	741.1%	Credit Suisse First Boston	Software for patching wireless phones into Internet
Commerce One	7/1	21.00	61.00	336.94	1,504.5	452.4	Credit Suisse First Boston	E-commerce service provider
Brocade Communications	5/24	19.00	45.25	143.75	1,413.2	535.4	Morgan Stanley Dean Witter	Fiber channel switching for storage area networks
Scient Corp.	5/13	20.00	32.63	148.09	1,380.9	807.9	Morgan Stanley Dean Witter	E-business and technology strategy consultant
Red Hat	8/11	14.00	52.06	201.00	1,335.7	286.1	Goldman Sachs	Open software service provider
Internet Capital Group	8/4	12.00	24.44	164.06	1,267.2	571.3	Merrill Lynch	Manager of business-to-business companies
Redback Network	5/17	23.00	84.13	153.00	1,230.4	263.7	Morgan Stanley Dean Witter	Equipment seller for high-speed broadband Internet access
Purchasepro.com	9/13	12.00	26.13	145.13	1,109.4	455.5	Prudential Securities	Provider of "e-marketplaces" for products and services
VerticalNet	2/11	16.00	45.38	96.00	1,100.0	323.1	Lehman Brothers	Operates business-to-business communities
F5 Networks	6/4	10.00	14.88	118.50	1,085.0	696.6	Hambrecht & Quist	Provider of traffic management solutions for Internet servers
Kana Communications	9/21	15.00	51.50	167.88	1,019.2	226.0	Goldman Sachs	Consultant specializing in online customer transactions
Vitria Technology	9/16	16.00	48.25	178.25	1,014.1	269.4	Credit Suisse First Boston	Software for real-time e-business
Vignette Corp.	2/18	19.00	42.69	105.00	1,005.3	391.9	Morgan Stanley Dean Witter	Internet relationship management software provider
Liberate Technologies	7/27	16.00	20.38	169.50	959.4	731.9	Credit Suisse First Boston	Software providing customers access to Internet applications and services
Ditech Communications	6/9	11.00	12.50	111.50	913.6	792.0	Deutsche Banc Alex. Brown	Equipment for expanding telecommunications networks
E.Piphany	9/21	16.00	45.19	159.50	896.9	253.0	Credit Suisse First Boston	Enabling companies to understand customer needs
Foundry Networks	9/28	25.00	156.25	237.00	848.0	51.7	Deutsche Banc Alex. Brown	Networking products for internet service providers
Juniper Networks	6/24	34.00	98.88	302.81	790.6	206.3	Goldman Sachs	Internet infrastructure solutions
Ariba	6/22	23.00	90.00	204.63	789.7	127.4	Morgan Stanley Dean Witter	Business-to-business solutions for Intranet and Internet businesses
Allaire Corp.	1/22	20.00	43.75	174.94	774.7	299.9	Credit Suisse First Boston	Software for Web development

TABLE 4.7 ***(continued)***

B. Also-Rans
Some of the more imitative Internet offerings are being rejected by the public.

Issuer	Offer Date	Offer Price	First Day's Close	Price 12/3	Change from Offer Price*	Return from 1st Day Close*	Current Underwriter	Business Description
Insurance Management Solutions	2/11	$11.00	$11.00	$2.75	−75.0%	−75.0%	Raymond James	Claims processing for insurance
Argosy Education Group	3/8	14.00	13.44	4.50	−67.9	−66.5	Salomon Smith Barney	Postgraduate education
Intelligent Life	5/13	13.00	13.00	4.56	−64.9	−64.9	ING Barings	Online research on consumer banking
MCM Capital Group	7/9	10.00	9.34	3.63	−63.8	−61.2	CIBC World Markets	Buyer and servicer of receivables
Skechers USA	6/9	11.00	10.63	4.00	−63.6	−62.4	Deutsche Banc Alex. Brown	Footwear manufacturer
Cyber Merchants Exchange	5/14	8.00	N/A	3.00	−62.5	N/A	Ace Diversified Capital	Business-to-business commerce for retail merchants
Seminis	6/29	15.00	15.06	5.94	−60.4	−60.6	Goldman Sachs	Producer of enhanced fruit and vegetable seeds
WESCO International	5/11	18.00	20.00	7.31	−59.4	−63.4	Lehman Brothers	Products and services for electrical industry
Comps.com	5/5	15.00	14.25	6.16	−59.0	−56.8	Volpe Brown Whelan	Commercial real estate sales on- and offline
Azurix Corp.	6/9	19.00	19.13	7.81	−58.0	−59.2	Merrill Lynch	Water management consultant
Packaged Ice	1/29	8.50	8.53	3.56	−58.1	−58.2	Banc of America Securities	Manufacturer of packaged ice
Boyds Collection	3/5	18.00	18.06	7.69	−57.3	−57.4	Donaldson Lufkin & Jenrette	Seller of handcrafted collectibles and gifts
Statia Terminals Group	4/22	20.00	18.38	9.13	54.4	−50.3	Bear Stearns; Morgan Stanley Dean Witter	Marine terminal company handling imported oil
National Medical Health Card Systems	7/28	7.50	7.31	3.49	54.2	−53.0	Ryan Beck	Prescription benefit services
Hi-Q Wason	9/21	7.00	7.00	3.38	51.8	−51.8	Nutmeg Securities	Provider of bottled water
Vialog Corp.	2/5	8.00	5.38	3.94	−50.8	−26.7	Bear Stearns	E-group communications services
Cybear	6/18	16.00	16.44	7.94	−50.4	−51.7	Warburg Dillon Read	Health care information and productivity applications
Trion Technology	6/4	7.00	6.50	3.50	−50.0	−46.2	New York Broker	Tracking instruments for transportation
CareerBuilder	5/11	13.00	16.00	6.50	−50.0	−59.4	Credit Suisse First Boston	Online recruitment
ProVantage Health Services	7/13	18.00	21.19	9.13	−49.3	−56.9	Merrill Lynch	Pharmacy benefit management, products, and services

*Through 12/3/99. Returns adjusted for stock splits.
Data source: *Barron's*, December 13, 1999, 38.

TABLE 4.8 Adjusted Gross Income Limitations for Deductible Contributions to Traditional IRAs

Tax Year	Single Filers	Married Filing Jointly
2000	$32,000 to $42,000	$52,000 to $62,000
2001	$33,000 to $43,000	$53,000 to $63,000
2002	$34,000 to $44,000	$54,000 to $64,000
2003	$40,000 to $50,000	$60,000 to $70,000
2004	$45,000 to $55,000	$65,000 to $75,000
2005	$50,000 to $60,000	$70,000 to $80,000
2006	$50,000 to $60,000	$75,000 to $85,000
2007+	$50,000 to $60,000	$80,000 to $100,000

Most taxpayers may contribute up to $2,000 per person each year to a traditional IRA, Roth IRA, or a combination of the two. Limits on contributions to the new Education IRAs are independent of this $2,000 limit.

Eligible taxpayers can deduct contributions to traditional IRAs from gross income. A person with earned income who is not covered by an employer-sponsored retirement plan may deduct IRA contributions of up to $2,000 per year regardless of income. For someone who is covered by a retirement plan at work (an active participant), contributions to an IRA may be totally deductible, partially deductible, or not deductible at all, depending on the taxpayer's adjusted gross income (AGI). In 2000, for example, married couples filing jointly can make deductible contributions of up to $2,000 each if their AGI is less than $52,000, even if both spouses are active participants in employer-sponsored plans. Deductible contributions in the year 2000 for single filers phase out at AGIs between $32,000 and $42,000 or $52,000–$62,000 for married couples filing jointly. As shown in Table 4.8, these thresholds for deductible contributions to IRAs increase over time. Note that taxpayers who cannot make deductible contributions to traditional IRAs or make contributions to the new Roth IRAs may still make nondeductible contributions of up to $2,000 per year to a traditional IRA. Doing so can be advantageous because the earnings grow tax deferred until the money is withdrawn.

Major tax-law provisions for IRA accounts are shown in Table 4.9.

Tax Deferral Benefits of IRAs

There is a close similarity between the tax deferral benefits that can be derived from a traditional tax-deductible IRA and a Roth IRA. In a traditional IRA, no tax is due on the income contributed to the retirement plan. Taxes on the initial contribution and on its investment income are both paid at the point of withdrawal during retirement. In a Roth IRA, tax is due on the income contributed to the retirement plan, but no tax on the initial contribution nor on its investment income is due at the point of withdrawal during retirement.

Assuming constant tax rates, money invested in a traditional IRA and in a Roth IRA will yield the same retirement nest egg. If tax rates are higher during the contribution period than during retirement, then the traditional IRA is often preferable to the Roth IRA. If tax rates are higher during retirement than

TABLE 4.9 Summary of IRA Provisions

	Traditional IRA	Roth IRA	Educational IRA
Annual contribution limit	■ Lesser of $2,000 or 100% of earned income (minus any Roth IRA contribution)	■ Lesser of $2,000 or 100% of earned income (minus any contribution to a traditional IRA)	■ $500 per beneficiary
Eligibility	■ Must be under age 70½ and have earned income ■ A spouse can make a deductible contribution of up to $2,000 (subject to AGI limits).	■ Any age with earned income (subject to AGI limits) ■ Spouse can make contributions of up to $2,000 (subject to AGI limitations).	■ Beneficiary must be younger than age 18. ■ Contributions must come from taxpayers who meet the AGI limits. ■ No contributions allowed if contributions to a qualified state prepaid tuition program are made
Deductibility	■ Full deduction allowed if taxpayer is not an active participant in an employer-sponsored plan ■ Deduction allowed for active participants who meet AGI limits	■ Nondeductible	Nondeductible
Taxation of qualified distributions	■ Distributions of deductible contributions and all earnings taxed as ordinary income ■ Distributions attributable to nondeductible contributions are nontaxable.	■ Tax-free distributions after age 59½ if the Roth IRA is held more than five years ■ Tax-free distributions before age 59½ if the Roth IRA is held more than five years and the owner dies, becomes disabled, or uses proceeds (up to a $10,000 lifetime maximum) for first-time home purchase	■ Tax-free distributions if used for qualified postsecondary educational expenses, such as tuition, fees, books, supplies, equipment, and certain room and board expenses
Taxation and penalties on early distributions	■ Ordinary income tax due on deductible contributions and earnings, plus a 10% penalty on distributions before age 59½	■ Ordinary income tax on earnings portion of distributions, possible 10% penalty ■ Withdrawals of converted Roth IRA assets that occur within the first five years after conversion typically subject to a 10% penalty	■ Entire balance must be distributed before the beneficiary reaches age 30 or transferred into another family member's Education IRA ■ Earnings portion of distributions taxable as ordinary income and possibly subject to penalty

during the contribution period, then the Roth IRA can be preferable to the traditional IRA. The traditional IRA and the Roth IRA options give retirement investors the opportunity to speculate on changes in income tax policy. In most instances, it is safe to presume that income and income tax rates will be higher during one's working years (the contribution period) than during retirement. This gives the nod to the traditional IRA over the Roth IRA. Also working in favor of the traditional IRA is the risk that future changes in tax policy might cause distributions from Roth IRAs to become taxable. However, a factor working in favor of the Roth IRA is that it provides an opportunity for investors to hedge against dramatic future increases in income tax rates. A Roth IRA lets investors "lock in" their current tax rate and hedges against a future tax rate increase. The Roth IRA is attractive for investors who fear that tax rates may be higher when they retire than the tax rates they pay now. For the Roth IRA to be the wrong choice, the tax rate applicable when an investor takes IRA distributions cannot be substantially higher than the investor's tax rate during the contribution period. Remember, if the tax rate is the same when money is contributed and withdrawn, there is no difference in the amount received from the Roth IRA versus a traditional tax-deductible IRA.

IRA versus Roth IRA

A simple illustration can be used to show the tax-deferral benefits of IRA investing. The basic message to be gained is that whenever legally possible, an investor should seek to shelter investment income from taxes. Table 4.10 shows the substantial tax deferral benefits of IRA investing. In panel A, the compound return from a conventional taxable investment is illustrated. The after-tax value is shown for a $2,000 investment per year earning 12%, when marginal annual tax rates of 30%, 40%, or 50% are paid. With a 30% marginal tax rate, for example, a 12% per year annual rate of return is reduced to 8.4% per year. An investment of $2,000 per year growing at an 8.4% annual rate of return compounds to $170,715 over a 30-year time horizon. Panel B also shows the after-tax value of an annual investment of $2,000 earning 12% when the marginal income tax rate is 30%. Unlike panel A, in panel B tax payments are deferred until retirement. If an investment of $2,000 per year is allowed to compound for 30 years at 12%, the before-tax value of the investment rises to $482,666. If 30% of the value of this investment is paid in taxes at the end of 30 years, the after-tax value realized is $337,866 (see Table 4.10).

The $167,151 advantage gained through tax deferral is stunning. It stems from the fact that, over an investment horizon of 30 years, an annual investment compounding at 12% per year results in far more interest-on-interest than an investment earning only 8.4% per year. Even after paying a 30% tax at the end of 30 years, the after-tax proceeds from an investment compounding at 12% are sufficiently large so as to exceed the total proceeds earned on an investment earning 8.4% per year after taxes. Remember, when an investment grows at a compound rate of interest, total investment value grows faster and faster in dollar terms over time. The advantage of tax deferral lies in the fact that it allows a larger sum to accumulate prior to the payment of taxes. By comparing the values in panel A with those in panel B in Table 4.10, the substantial tax benefits gained through tax deferral become obvious.

As it turns out, comparable tax deferral benefits can be gained through investing in either a traditional IRA or a Roth IRA. With a traditional IRA, taxes are paid going out. With a Roth IRA, taxes are paid going in. Therefore, a before-tax investment of $2,000 per year in a traditional IRA is equivalent to an after-tax investment of $1,200 per year when the marginal tax rate is 40%. If $2,000 per year is contributed to a traditional IRA earning 12% interest for 30 years and a 40% tax is paid at the end of that time, an after-tax distribution of $289,599 will result. This is the same amount as would be derived from an annual $1,200 investment in a Roth IRA growing at 12% per year for 30 years.

Assuming the same tax rate during the contribution and retirement periods, there is no difference in the tax deferral advantages of traditional IRAs and Roth IRAs. An investor would prefer a traditional IRA if the tax rate is expected to be higher during the accumulation years than during the payout years. If an investor expected tax rates to go down during retirement, that investor would prefer the traditional IRA. If tax rates were projected to rise sharply over time, the Roth IRA would be preferred to the traditional IRA.

On a practical level, investors might well want to be skeptical about promises that earnings on Roth IRA accumulations will never be taxed. Government at both

TABLE 4.10 Tax Deferral Benefits of IRAs Are Substantial

Tax deferral until the point of retirement results in a meaningful tax saving. When income taxes are paid on an annual basis, the return on investment and amount accumulated over time are cut dramatically.

A. Conventional Taxable Investment

	After-tax value of a $2,000 investment per year earning 12% with annual income taxes paid at a rate of:		
Number of Years	**30%**	**40%**	**50%**
1	$1,400	$1,200	$1,000
2	2,918	2,486	2,060
3	4,563	3,865	3,184
4	6,346	5,344	4,375
5	8,279	6,928	5,637
10	20,671	16,737	13,181
15	39,217	30,623	23,276
20	66,977	50,282	36,786
25	108,527	78,114	54,865
30	170,715	117,515	79,058

B. Tax-Deferred IRA or Roth IRA Investment

	After-tax value of a $2,000 investment per year earning 12% with deferred income taxes paid at a rate of:		
Number of Years	**30%**	**40%**	**50%**
1	$1,400	$1,200	$1,000
2	2,968	2,544	2,120
3	4,724	4,049	3,374
4	6,691	5,735	4,779
5	8,894	7,623	6,353
10	24,568	21,058	17,549
15	52,192	44,736	37,280
20	100,873	86,463	72,052
25	186,667	160,001	133,334
30	337,866	289,599	241,333

the state and federal level has been known to renege on such promises in the past and may do so in the future. Investors in traditional IRAs also have the potential to defer taxes during their retirement years. Taxes on undistributed IRA contributions can also be postponed at the time of death if IRAs are bequeathed to one's spouse or children. IRA taxes can be permanently avoided when the IRA is donated to charitable institutions. To sum up, many astute investors prefer the traditional IRA to the Roth IRA because tax rates traditionally fall during retirement, future tax rate changes are difficult to predict, and Roth IRA distributions may become taxable in the future.

Education IRAs

The new Education IRA is an educational savings account rather than a retirement account. Parents, grandparents, or anyone else who meets the AGI limitations may make a nondeductible contribution to an Education IRA on behalf of any child who is younger than the age of 18. Unlike contributions to a traditional or a Roth IRA, contributions to Education IRAs must be made by December 31 rather than by April 15. The aggregate of all contributions to all Education IRAs for each child is $500 per year, but contributions are phased out for higher AGIs, $95,000–$110,000 (single) and $150,000–$160,000 (married filing jointly). However, no contribution to an Education IRA can be made in any year in which contributions are made on behalf of the same beneficiary to a qualified state prepaid tuition program.

Withdrawals from Education IRAs are tax free if they are used for qualified postsecondary educational expenses such as room, board, and tuition. However, the earnings portion of distributions not used for educational expenses are treated as taxable income and subject to a 10% penalty unless the distribution is due to death or disability or unless the distribution occurs in a year in which the beneficiary receives a qualified scholarship. Any balance remaining in an Education IRA must be distributed within 30 days of when the beneficiary reaches the age of 30, or within 30 days of the beneficiary's death if earlier. At that point, the beneficiary must pay both tax and 10% penalty on earnings. However, the balance may be rolled over to an Education IRA for another family member who is younger than age 30 (and thus continues to grow on a tax-deferred basis).

Taxes

Capital Gains Tax Deferral

Conventional capital-gains taxes are levies on nominal returns earned by investors. These nominal returns include both real returns and compensation for persistent inflation. Relentless inflation of roughly 3.5% per year threatens the future well-being of all investors. To fund an adequate retirement income or to fund college costs, investors must focus on *real* investment returns, after due consideration for inflation and taxes. Nominal returns represent gross income, and you can only spend net income.

Capital gains tax deferral is a compelling virtue of long-term stock investing. In important respects, the capital gains tax is really a transaction tax; capital gains taxes can be postponed by the patient investor. By themselves, tax considerations should never dictate investment decisions. From an investor's perspective, paying an income or capital gains tax may only be the second worst thing that could happen following the sale of an investment. Of course, the worst outcome is the realization of a loss. Still, practical portfolio management demands that tax considerations be carefully considered when making portfolio changes. After all, taxes can take a large chunk out of investment returns, and it is the net return after taxes and inflation that is most important in terms of the amount of consumption that can be funded from investment income.

WALL STREET WISDOM 4.3

It's a 24-Hour Trading Day

The New York Stock Exchange (NYSE), American Stock Exchange, and the Nasdaq stock markets are open for business from 9:30 AM to 4:00 PM EST. This is a full business day on the East Coast, but regular trading ends at only 1:00 PM PST. On the West Coast, trading begins for early birds at 6:30 AM EST and ends before the work day is half over.

In response to investor demands and some gentle nudging from the Securities and Exchange Commission, both the NYSE and the Nasdaq Stock Market are formulating plans that would greatly extend stock and bond trading hours in the United States. Before too long, the trading day will be extended to 10 hours or more in the United States and proceed on an uninterrupted 24-hour basis around the globe.

The move is designed to let individual investors trade stocks and bonds after the market's traditional trading session just like big institutional investors. Insurance companies, pension funds, and mutual funds have long traded after hours through such venues as Instinet, owned by Reuters, and Tradebook, owned by Bloomberg. Big institutions, through far-flung brokers, also can trade stocks on various exchanges around the world. For example, DaimlerChrysler, the third largest auto company in the United States, is a truly global stock. It trades on 18 stock exchanges around the world on almost a 24-hour basis.

Many small investors find the idea appealing. Most major companies announce earnings and other important corporate news after the markets' close to give both small and large investors time to digest such news. At the present time, small investors are unable to trade on such market-moving information until the next morning and the start of Wall Street trading. By then, some large institutional investors have already made their moves in the after-hours electronic market. This is very frustrating for many small investors, and both Nasdaq and the NYSE are paying attention. They have heard a powerful demand for expanding trading hours, and they are putting plans in motion to offer big and small investors the opportunity to trade stocks on a 24-hour basis.

To get things started, Nasdaq is considering plans to trade stocks between 5:00 PM and 9:00 PM EST. Participation of market makers would be voluntary, but all Nasdaq rules governing executions would apply. It will likely start by offering trading in up to 500 stocks. The NYSE is studying a plan to extend hours, opening at 5:00 AM and trading until at least 9:00 PM EST. By beginning trading at such an early hour, NYSE trading activity would overlap with continental markets and the United Kingdom. This is especially important given the growing prevalence of foreign stocks on the NYSE and the popularity of U.S. stocks with foreign investors. If trading hours are extended as late as 9:00 PM EST, big and small investors on the West Coast would also have trading hours extended to 5:00 PM PST. For the first time, this would give West Coast investors a full working day within which to evaluate market activity. A later close would also extend NYSE trading beyond the open of the Japanese, thus affording Asian investors the opportunity to participate more broadly in the U.S. market.

Of course, there are many questions about extended NYSE and Nasdaq trading hours. Will there be enough volume to let investors execute trades without volatile price swings? Will there be enough volume to allow NYSE specialists and Nasdaq market makers to cover incremental costs and achieve a reasonable profit? Only time will tell.

Nasdaq market makers are being lined up to help ensure sufficient volume and liquidity. Some suggest that only limit orders be accepted when extended trading gets underway. With limit orders, investors specify the price at which they will buy or sell. This protects investors against receiving very low bids when markets are thin and many investors have gone home for the day. Although a number of important issues must be addressed, the move to extended trading hours is unmistakable.

See: Maitta V. David, "Late Trading: Compaq Slips, Nortel Soars on 1Q Earnings," *The Wall Street Journal, Interactive Edition,* April 25, 2000. (http://www.wsj.com).

Capital Gains Rates

Since January 1, 1998, gains on securities held for more than a year are considered long term in nature. Net long-term capital gains are taxed at a maximum rate of 20%. The rate for taxpayers in the lowest tax bracket is 10%. Gains on securities held one year or less are considered short-term capital gains, which are taxed as ordinary income. There has been no change in this basic rule for many years.

Qualified Five-Year Gain

The Taxpayer Relief Act of 1997 provided a new holding period with capital gains rates ranging from a maximum of 18% to a rock-bottom 8% for the lowest tax bracket. These rates will generally apply only to investments that are bought after 2000 and held more than five years, so benefits from this provision usually will not appear before 2006. However, there is an important exception to this rule: People in the lowest tax bracket will get to use the 8% capital gains rate for investments held more than five years but sold after 2000.

Tax laws as they pertain to investments have many nuances and ramifications that cannot be covered here. For more detailed information or to make financial decisions appropriate to your specific circumstances, consult your tax or financial adviser.

Gift and Estate Tax Provisions

Gift and estate tax provisions can also have important investment implications. The unified estate and gift tax credit is a transfer tax on lifetime gifts that a person makes, plus the value of any estate that the person leaves on death. Through 1997, the unified credit could be used to eliminate tax on a total of $600,000 of taxable gifts and estate. Estate taxes were assessed only if the value of the decedent's property exceeded $600,000.

Under the 1997 law, the threshold will increase gradually until it reaches $1 million in 2006. Up to $1.3 million of the value of qualified family-owned businesses may be excluded subject to rules that coordinate the deduction with the unified credit. Since 1999, various estate and gift tax limitations are indexed, including the $10,000 annual exclusion for gifts and the $1 million exemption from the generation-skipping transfer tax.

Exclusion for Gain on the Sale of a Principal Residence

An important advantage tied to investing in real estate is a relatively new tax provision that permits exclusion of up to $250,000 for single filers, or $500,000 for joint filers, of the gain on sale of a principal residence. Historically, any gain on the sale of a home could be deferred if the purchase price of the new principal residence was at least as high as the sales price of the old principal residence. Presently, the gain exclusion of the sale of a principal residence makes home ownership much more attractive than otherwise.

Summary

- The **bid** is the highest price that an investor is willing to pay. The **ask** is the lowest price that an investor will accept to sell. The **bid-ask spread** is simply the gap between the bid and ask prices. Stocks are assigned **ticker symbols** to facilitate transaction speed and accuracy. **Bid size** is the number of **round lots,** groups of 100 shares of stock, represented on the buy side of the market. Significant **market depth** exists when a large number of buyers and sellers are active in the market. In normal circumstances, the bid-ask spread is positive. In some unusually volatile markets, an **inverted bid-ask spread** is observed and the quoted bid price is higher than the ask price.

- A **market order** is an instruction to buy or sell at the current market price. In a **limit order,** the customer specifies a price at which to buy or sell. A **stop order** is a market order to buy or sell a certain quantity of a security if a specified price (the stop price) is reached or passed. A position is said to be **stopped out** when the position is offset by the execution of a stop order. A **buy stop order** is a buy order that is to be held until the market price rises to a specified stop price, at which point it becomes a market order. A **stop-loss order** is a stop order to sell a long position at a specified price that is below the current market price. A **stop-limit order** is an order to buy or sell a certain quantity of a security at a specified price or better but only after a specified price has been reached. A **day order** is an order to buy or sell during the present trading session. An **open order** stays active until it is executed or canceled by the investor. Another expression for an open order is a **good 'til canceled order. All or none** is a stipulation to a buy or sell order that instructs the broker to either fill the entire order or not fill it at all. **Fill-or-kill** orders must be filled immediately or canceled.
- **Dollar-cost averaging** is a simple investment strategy of investing a fixed amount in a particular security at regular intervals. Because the amount invested remains constant, the average dollar amount paid, or the average cost per share, is always lower than the average price per share. It is a good method for investing in company-sponsored **defined contribution retirement plans,** in which the employer is responsible only for making specified contributions into the plan on behalf of qualifying participants. A **defined benefit retirement plan** is a pension plan in which the corporate sponsor agrees to make specified dollar payments to qualifying employees, such as $1,000 per month.
- A **margin account** is an investor account that holds securities purchased with a combination of cash and borrowed funds. **Margin debt** is the amount borrowed to buy or maintain a security investment. A **margin call** is a broker's formal demand for additional collateral because of adverse price movements. The **broker call rate** is the interest rate that banks and brokerage houses charge to finance margin loans to investors.
- A **short sale** is the sale of borrowed stock. The borrower hopes to repurchase identical shares for return to the lender, or **cover the short,** at a lower price, thus making a profit. Notice that the amount of **short interest** in a particular stock is reported in two different ways. The number of shares sold short is presented as a useful overall indicator of the level of bearish sentiment on a stock. When short interest is high, the market consensus is negative. The number of shares sold short relative to the average daily trading volume in a stock, called the **short interest ratio,** is also provided as a useful indicator of the relative amount of short interest. If momentum investors jump into an appreciating stock, a **short squeeze** can result as buyers "squeeze" short sellers to cover their short positions at truly wild prices.

- The first buyer of a newly issued security buys that security in the **primary market.** All subsequent trading of those securities is done in the **secondary market.** Primary markets are where new issues, called **initial public offerings (IPO),** are sold by corporations to raise new capital. IPOs are a corporation's first sale of stock or bonds to the public. A **seasoned issue** is the issuance of a security for which there is already an existing public market. **Secondary offerings** are the public sale of previously issued securities held by large investors, corporations, or institutional investors. When investments or businesses are offered for sale to a small group of investors, generally under exemption of SEC and state securities registration requirements, this is referred to as **private placement,** or a private offering. Such companies must file a hard copy of the **offering circular** with the SEC containing financial statements and other information. Corporations seeking additional investment capital hire an **investment bank,** or **underwriter,** to act in the role of advisor and distributor. An important part of the IPO process is the so-called **road show** for institutional investors and the general public in which issuing companies and their investment bankers discuss the investment merits of the corporation's securities.
- With a **firm-commitment** offering, the investment banker agrees to underwrite or purchase the entire issue from the corporation and then reoffer such securities to the general public. In a **best-efforts** underwriting, the investment banker simply agrees to make its best effort at selling the agreed-on amount of debt and equity securities. A best-efforts underwriting is called an **all-or-none offering** when the underwriter agrees to do its best to sell an entire issue by a certain date, but if all securities are not sold by that time, all money is returned to purchasers and the issue is canceled.
- A **syndicate** is a group of underwriters who jointly agree to participate in selling the issue. The lead investment bank, or **syndicate manager,** determines the offering price, sets the timing of the issue, responds to any deficiency letters by the SEC, modifies selling commissions, and controls advertising and the amount of each **underwriter's allotment.** The syndicate manager has prime responsibility for the **dealers agreement,** which specifies how securities dealers who are not part of the syndicate may contract to purchase some of the securities from the issue. Essential bits of information included in a **tombstone ad** include the name of the new issue, number of shares offered, the offering price, and a list of the lead investment bankers and syndicate members.
- Following the Securities Act of 1933, when a company makes a public offering it must file a **registration statement** with the SEC. The day the investment bank submits the registration statement with the SEC is known as the **filing date.** The SEC requires a **cooling-off period** during which the issuing company and the investment banker try to drum up interest in the issue. They do this through a **preliminary prospectus,** which is sometimes referred to as a **red herring** because it has red printing across the top and in the margins.
- Assuming the IPO is, in fact, approved by the SEC, securities are offered to institutional investors and the general public on the **effective date.** If the SEC does not approve a given issue, a **deficiency letter** is issued and the effective date is postponed. Just prior to the effective date, the issuing corporation and its investment banker have a **due diligence** meeting to ensure that material changes have taken place between the filing date and the effective date. Once

the effective date arrives, a **final prospectus** is issued, the security can be sold, and money is collected.

- The public offering price stated on the face of the prospectus is the amount paid by institutional and individual investors who receive an allotment of the IPO. However, the issuing corporation receives a lower price determined by the agreed-upon spread. A **hot IPO** is an IPO in which shares are limited and demand is high. Short-term traders who quickly **flip** their shares of a hot IPO seldom have the opportunity to participate in future offerings.

Questions

1. The highest quoted price that an investor is willing to pay to buy a security is called the
   a. ask.
   b. market.
   c. bid.
   d. none of these.
2. Bid size is the number of
   a. round lots represented on the buy side of the market.
   b. shares represented on the buy side of the market.
   c. round lots represented on the sell side of the market.
   d. shares represented on the sell side of the market.
3. A trading order that is canceled unless executed within a designated time period is called a
   a. stop-loss order.
   b. limit order.
   c. market order.
   d. none of these.
4. Dollar-cost averaging is a simple investment strategy
   a. that ensures that the average price per share is always lower than the average cost per share.
   b. for buying a fixed number of shares in a particular investment at regular intervals.
   c. involving a changing dollar amount of investment at regular time intervals.
   d. none of these.
5. Defined benefit plans are
   a. the most common types of pension plans offered by employers.
   b. pension plans in which the employer is responsible only for making specified contributions into the plan on behalf of qualifying participants.
   c. typically funded by regular employee contributions.
   d. none of these.

6. Stocks can be purchased for a combination of cash and borrowed funds in a
   a. margin account.
   b. cash account.
   c. IRA account.
   d. none of these.
7. Initial and maintenance margin requirements are set by the
   a. Federal Reserve System.
   b. NYSE.
   c. NASD.
   d. SEC.
8. Stock purchases with 50% initial margin trigger a 30% maintenance margin call following a
   a. 15.3% rise in price.
   b. 24.3% decline in price.
   c. 28.6% decline in price.
   d. 20% decline in price.
9. Short sales with 50% initial margin trigger a 30% maintenance margin call following a
   a. 50% rise in price.
   b. 15.3% rise in price.
   c. 20% rise in price.
   d. 22.9% fall in price.
10. Organized trading of outstanding securities on exchanges and over-the-counter markets is called the
    a. primary market.
    b. secondary market.
    c. IPO market.
    d. bond market.
11. An IPO is an
    a. initial public offering.
    b. investment participation obligation.
    c. investment placement organization.
    d. investment partnership opportunity.
12. The New York Stock Exchange is a
    a. negotiated market.
    b. network of dealers.
    c. secondary market.
    d. regional exchange.

13. Limit orders
    a. specify a certain price at which a market order takes effect.
    b. specify a particular price to be met or bettered.
    c. are executed at the best price available.
    d. are orders entered for a particular day.
14. The market for equities is predominantly a
    a. primary market.
    b. market dominated by individual investors.
    c. secondary market.
    d. market dominated by foreign investors.
15. Primary markets
    a. involve the organized trading of outstanding securities on exchanges.
    b. involve the organized trading of outstanding securities in the over-the-counter market.
    c. involve the organized trading of outstanding securities on exchanges and over-the-counter markets.
    d. are where new issues (IPOs) are sold by corporations to raise new capital.
16. The role of investment banker does *not* include
    a. giving companies advice on the price, amount, and timing of an issue.
    b. a commitment to maintain a continuous primary market for listed issues.
    c. managing a syndicate for distribution on a firm-price (dealer) or best-efforts (broker) basis.
    d. helping maintain an after market for over-the-counter issues.
17. A stock is said to be under accumulation if volume expands on days when the price
    a. moves down.
    b. is unchanged.
    c. moves up.
    d. none of the above.
18. On the NYSE, firms that make a market in a given security are called
    a. brokers.
    b. specialists.
    c. members.
    d. arbitragers.
19. The short interest ratio is the ratio of total short sales to average
    a. monthly trading volume.
    b. annual trading volume.
    c. daily trading volume.
    d. shares outstanding.

20. In selling a stock short,
    a. dividends are ignored.
    b. the seller must complete the transaction within a specified period.
    c. the short seller must have a margin account.
    d. the seller immediately receives the net proceeds.

Investment Application

Web Brokers

Online stock trading is hot! Today, online trading accounts for more than 30% of the stock transactions made by individual investors. This was up from virtually nothing in 1996. More than 350,000 online trades are made every day, and that number is growing daily. In fact, online trading is so popular that scores of employers are restricting employee access to online brokers at the office. It seems that keeping track of personal portfolios is keeping some employees occupied at work.

Of course, what initially attracted brokerage customers to the Internet was the lure of bargain-basement commission rates. Over the past few years, however, the industry has begun to mature, and service quality has emerged as an equally important consideration. Apparently, the customers of online brokers are turning their attention away from demanding rock-bottom prices in favor of high-quality executions and up-to-the-minute financial information. Of course, customers are demanding that both be provided at very competitive prices. Commissions charged by online brokers appear to have hit bottom, at roughly $10 per trade. Instead of cutting prices further, online brokers have turned their attention to improving service reliability and greatly expanding the range of financial information offered on their Web sites. Many online broker Web sites now offer a full menu of financial news and information.

According to *Barron's,* DLJ Direct is first among the very best online brokers (see Table 4.11). DLJ Direct offers numerous research tools combined with informative and easy-to-use trading screens. DLJ Direct also gives customers a variety of ways to reach the firm. Other top online brokers include Discover Brokerage Direct, National Discount Brokers, and Web Street Securities. These firms are standout performers according to four criteria:

- Ease of Use: Does site layout make sense and minimize the number of mouse clicks it can take to get from one place to another?
- Reliability and Range of Offerings: How often is the site down? Can customers make phone trades when the Web is unavailable? "Range of offerings" describes what can be traded online. Almost all top sites offer equities, mutual funds, options, and bonds.
- Amenities: Can you get quotes, charts, news, and analysis quickly on a well-laid-out screen? Is it easy to see how your holdings or other issues that you are watching are performing?
- Commissions: Most discount brokers charge an extra $3–$5 for limit orders, but low-cost market orders expose investors to the possibility of paying higher prices during volatile markets. It is best to use an online broker that charges minimum rates for limit orders.

TABLE 4.11 How the Online Brokers Stack Up

(For full details, check their respective Web sites.)

Website/Phone	Stocks	Mutual Funds	Options	Bonds	*Barron's* Rating	Online Amenities	Limit Order Commissions	High Account Balance Benefits
	What can be traded online?							
Ameritrade www.ameritrade.com 1-800-454-9272	L, S	LO, NL	Yes	Yes	**	MarketGuide, news	$13	None
Brown & Company www.brownco.com 1-800-822-2021	L, S	No	Yes	No	***	Links to additional research No free research	$10	None
Datek www.datek.com 1-888-463-2835	L, S	LO, NL, NTF	Yes	Yes	***½	Free RT quotes, BigCharts, NewsAlert, Thomson	$9.99	None
Discover www.discoverbrokerage.com 1-800-688-6896	L, S	LO, NL, NTF, X	Yes	Yes	****	Blue Chip Basket, Equity Research (subscription), Quicken/Money data download	$19.95	
DLJDirect www.dljdirect.com 1-800-825-5723	L, S	LO, NL, NTF, X	Yes	Yes	****	StockCenter, FundCenter, S&P, Zacks, Thomson, Briefing.com, Market Monitor	$20	"Select Client" over $100K, commission reductions, IPOs, toll-free dedicated help, more powerful portfolio manager, RT quotes
E*Trade www.etrade.com 1-800-387-2331	L, S	LO, NL, NTF	Yes	Yes	***½	No fee IRA, extensive links to 3rd-party sites, limited RT quotes, E*Trade Internet funds	$19.95	30+ Trades: PowerTrade RT quotes, TraderDesk 75+ Trades: Platinum. Level 2RT quotes
National Discount Brokers www.ndb.com 1-800-888-3999	L, S	LO, NL, NTF, X	Yes	Yes	****	NDB University, Zacks, DBC Online, extensive mutual fund and stock screening	$19.75	IRA fee waived if balance over $10,000
SureTrade www.suretrade.com 1-401-642-6900	L, S	LO, NTF	Yes	Yes	***½	RT Quotes, links to Zacks, Briefing.com, iSyndicate, Reuters, others	$9.95	None
A. B. Watley, Ultimate Trader www.abwatley.com 1-888-229-2853	L, S	LO, NL	Yes	Yes	***	Connects direct to Watley via Internet. Fast and flexible, level II quotes, DJ news	$12.95–$23.95, depends on level of service and trade frequency	Frequent trader benefits: commissions waived, free level 2
Web Street Securities www.webstreetsecurities.com 1-800-932-8723	L, S	LO, NL	Yes	No	****	RT quotes, baseline reports, lots of Java scrolling tickers, RT portfolio valuation	$14.95, free if order is 1000+ shares	None

Legend: L, long; S, short; LO, load; NL, noload; NTF, no transaction fee; X, exchange; Y, yes; N, no.
Source: "How the Online Brokers Stack Up," *Barron's*, March 15, 1999, 32.

To be sure, the online trading industry is facing growing pains. *Barron's* reports that several online customers are fed up with recent service slowdowns and interruptions. Many fear the potential for complete breakdowns in online trading systems during periods of high market volatility. Some savvy online customers fear that a breakdown in online trading could itself contribute to panic buying and selling of stocks favored by Internet brokerage customers. It is perhaps unsurprising that the customers of Web brokers favor companies that have the potential to benefit directly or indirectly from the growth of the Internet. Still, it is intriguing that the stocks of Web brokers are big favorites among the stock-buying customers of those same Web-based brokers.

Barron's reports that roughly 40% of online customers maintain accounts with more than one online broker to protect themselves from being buffeted during volatile markets. Online trading is also drawing increased scrutiny from the SEC. The SEC is worried that inexperienced day traders are recklessly speculating with their IRAs. The speed and low cost of online executions are wonderful, but a lot of unsophisticated investors are going to get hurt in a severe market downturn.

To counter the perception that online trading is primarily for speculators and gamblers and head off increased SEC regulation, the online brokerage industry is tightening its standards. Although online brokers love customers who use hefty margin to buy and sell stocks on a daily basis, the industry has started to raise margin requirements for the most volatile stocks. Some firms are also forcing traders to use limit orders when bidding for IPOs. This is especially true for Internet IPOs in which first-day trading activity can plunge and soar wildly. Still, there is nothing to keep online investors from speculating wildly with their own money, and many are.

A. Explain how the use of limit orders can reduce risk for individual investors.

B. Explain how the widespread use of limit orders could increase the potential for a severe market correction.

Selected References

Asness, Clifford S. "Stocks versus Bonds: Explaining the Equity Risk Premium." *Financial Analysts Journal* 56 (March/April 2000): 96–113.

Barber, Brad M., and Terrance Odean. "Too Many Cooks Spoil the Profits: Investment Club Performance." *Financial Analysts Journal* 56 (January/February 2000): 17–25.

Datta, Sudip, Mai Iskandar-Datta, and Ajay Patel. "Some Evidence on the Uniqueness of Initial Public Debt Offerings." *Journal of Finance* 55 (April 2000): 715–744.

Doukas, John, and Lorne N. Switzer. "Common Stock Returns and International Listing Announcements: Conditional Tests of the Mild Segmentation Hypothesis." *Journal of Banking and Finance* 24 (March 2000): 471–501.

Dunbar, Craig G. "Factors Affecting Investment Bank Initial Public Offering Market Share." *Journal of Financial Economics* 55 (January 2000): 3–41.

Gerke, Wolfgang, Stefan Arneth, and Christine Syha. "The Impact of the Order Book Privilege on Traders' Behavior and the Market Process: An Experimental Study." *Journal of Economic Psychology* 21 (April 2000): 167–189.

Goldstein, Michael A., and Kenneth A. Kavajecz. "Eighths, Sixteenths, and Market Depth: Changes in Tick Size and Liquidity Provision on the NYSE." *Journal of Financial Economics* 56 (March 2000): 125–149.

Gomes, Armando. "Going Public without Governance: Managerial Reputation Effects." *Journal of Finance* 55 (April 2000): 615–646.

Guenther, David A., and Michael Willenborg. "Capital Gains Tax Rates and the Cost of Capital for Small Business: Evidence from the IPO Market." *Journal of Financial Economics* 53 (September 1999): 385–408.

Hasbrouck, Joel. "The Dynamics of Discrete Bid and Ask Quotes." *Journal of Finance* 54 (December 1999): 2109–2141.

Kim, Moonchul, and Jay R. Ritter. "Valuing IPOs." *Journal of Financial Economics* 53 (September 1999): 409–437.

LeClaire, John, and Kevin Dennis. "Going Private—Private Equity Investors Discover Public Market Orphans." *Venture Capital Journal* (November 1, 1999): 44–45.

Lee, Philip J., Stephen L. Taylor, and Terry S. Walter. "IPO Underpricing Explanations: Implications from Investor Application and Allocation Schedules." *Journal of Financial and Quantitative Analysis* 34 (December 1999): 425–444.

Morris, Victor F. "The New Financial Capitalists: Kohlberg Kravis Roberts & Co. and the Creation of Corporate Value." *Financial Analysts Journal* 55 (May/June 1999): 98–100.

Puri, Manju. "Commercial Banks as Underwriters: Implications for the Going Public Process." *Journal of Financial Economics* 54 (October 1999): 133–163.

CHAPTER 5

Risk and Return

At least once every few months, The Wall Street Journal *or* Barron's *runs a cover story describing how smart, talented, and sophisticated investors got swindled out of a substantial fortune because they forgot the simple fact that anticipated risk and expected return are related.*

In the fall of 1992, for example, David Mobley started a hedge fund to invest in stocks and financial derivatives. According to Mobley, his Maricopa Investment Fund has turned in results that eclipse even the best performances of Wall Street icons Warren Buffett, George Soros, and Julian Robertson. Mobley says that his operation has had steady annual gains exceeding 50% after fees that amount to 30% of the yearly total return. More astounding still, Maricopa reports no losing years and only five down months in its 88-month history through December 1999. Lofty investment returns with little or no risk? Gee, that sounds too good to be true. In fact, that is just what the Securities and Exchange Commission (SEC) alleges. In February 2000, the SEC charged that Mobley actually lost $59 million of the $149 million entrusted to him by investors. None of Maricopa's purported investment results were ever examined by independent auditors, and Mobley appears to have defrauded investors by forging trade and account information after steering client funds into a series of improper investments that turned out to be money-losing propositions.

Why do intelligent people fall victim to investment swindles? No one knows for sure, but it might be the "believing is seeing" problem. If investors want to believe that astronomical risk-free returns are possible, they sometimes close their eyes to economic reality. Unfortunately, such investors typically learn that when your eyes are closed, the crooks will rob you blind.[1]

saving
Accumulation of money to meet some short-term goal.

investing
Assuming measured risk in the pursuit of higher rates of return over an extended period.

Distinguishing Saving from Investing

Saving

The terms **saving** and **investing** are used interchangeably, but there are several important differences between them. Saving is the accumulation of money to meet some short-term goal. For example, one might save for a new car or for a down

[1]See: Charles Gasparino, "SEC Says Fund Carried Out Fraud of $59 Million," *The Wall Street Journal,* February 23, 2000, C8.

payment on a new house. Savings vehicles include bank money market accounts and certificates of deposit. Both pay a fixed rate of interest and enjoy government protection against loss. Money market mutual funds are another popular savings vehicle but carry no government guarantee against loss of principal and may have fluctuating yields.

Of course, any funds put into a savings account do not remain with the bank. They are funneled out into the economy to generate interest income to cover bank expenses, profit requirements, and the level of interest paid to savers. Bankers take on the credit risk associated with making loans and get paid in the form of net interest income for their loan processing and credit evaluation services. In a real sense, savers pay bankers and other financial intermediaries to take on the risk and effort involved with putting their savings dollars to work. As a result, the level of interest paid to savers is always less, and sometimes substantially less, than the amount of gross interest income generated by their savings.

Investing

Investing involves assuming a measured degree of risk in the pursuit of higher rates of return over an extended time period. Whereas money market instruments are prime savings vehicles, investors generally focus on a mix of stock and bond investments for long-term capital appreciation and growth of income. Long-term investment programs based on stocks and bonds typically offer higher rates of return than the interest generated on savings but entail the risk of substantial short-term loss.

Investing means putting money to work to directly capitalize on economic growth. Investors are more directly responsible than savers for funneling their investment dollars into the economy to generate interest income or investment profit. As such, investors take on some of the responsibility for assessing the investment risk and reward potential of various investment opportunities. Savers pay bankers and other financial intermediaries a significant amount to take on the effort involved with putting savings dollars to work. Investors do more of this work and claim a greater share of the amount of interest income or investment profit generated by their savings. To be sure, investing entails risk. Whereas savings offer no potential for capital gain and involve only a minimal risk of loss, investing offers the potential for capital gains while also exposing the investor to the risk of capital loss. Capital losses can sometimes be substantial.

Still, it is imperative to recognize that neither saving nor investing is without risk. Interest income derived from savings is typically subject to state, local, and federal income taxes. As a result, after-tax rates of return on savings often fail to keep pace with **inflation.** Long-term investing in stocks and bonds has typically resulted in rates of return that significantly outpace inflation, but short-term losses can sometimes be substantial.

inflation
Rising prices.

Types of Financial Assets

Cash Reserves

A first major class of financial assets is generally referred to as **cash reserves,** or short-term money market instruments. The primary attraction of cash reserves is that they offer modest income with stability of principal. Although investing in cash

cash reserves
Short-term money market instruments.

reserves allows one to protect the initial value of an investment, there is a cost in that only meager rates of return are typically offered on cash reserves. Cash reserves provide income that rises and falls with short-term interest rates.

Treasury bills U.S. Treasury obligations with maturities of one year or less.

Treasury notes Treasury obligations with maturities of more than one year but less than 10 years.

Treasury bonds Treasury obligations with maturities of 10 years or more.

One of the most common uses of cash reserves is to buy **Treasury bills.** Treasury bills are debt obligations of the U.S. Treasury that have maturities of one year or less. By contrast, **Treasury notes** are debt obligations of the U.S. Treasury that have maturities of more than one year but less than 10 years. **Treasury bonds** are Treasury obligations with maturities of 10 years or more. Another popular means for investing cash reserves is to buy bank savings deposits, which are accounts that pay interest, typically at very low levels, do not have any specific maturity, and usually can be withdrawn on demand. A bank certificate of deposit, or CD, is a bank savings deposit that has a specific time of maturity, cannot be withdrawn on demand, and therefore, pays a somewhat higher rate of interest.

Bonds

bonds Interest-bearing debt obligations.

Another important class of investment assets are **bonds,** or interest-bearing debt obligations issued by corporations, the federal government and its agencies, and state or local governments. Bonds represent a loan to the issuer and provide income during their lifetime, plus a promise to repay principal on maturity. Although bonds generally offer higher and steadier income than cash reserves, their principal value fluctuates as interest rates change. In general, when interest rates rise, bond prices decline. When interest rates decline, bond prices rise. One of the largest classes of outstanding bonds is the wide variety of debt securities issued by the U.S. Department of the Treasury. In addition to such Treasury securities, there exists a wide variety of U.S. government agency bonds. For example, the Federal Home Loan Mortgage Corporation, an affiliate of the Federal Home Loan Bank, creates a secondary money market in conventional residential loans and in Federal Housing Authority (FHA) and Veterans Administration (VA) loans by purchasing mortgage loans from members of the Federal Reserve System and the Federal Home Loan Bank systems.

Of course, corporate bonds are simply debt obligations issued by individual firms. Municipal bonds are interest-bearing securities issued by local governments that are typically free of federal income taxes.

Stocks

common stock A proportionate ownership stake in a corporation.

A third important type of investment asset is **common stock.** Equity securities represent ownership interest in a corporation. Figure 5.1 shows a common stock certificate for movie and entertainment giant Walt Disney Company. Stocks such as Disney offer the potential for current income from dividends and capital appreciation resulting from an increase in value over time. Although common stocks offer the long-term potential for superior rates of return to bonds, stocks are more susceptible to short-term price risks. Stock prices fluctuate over short time periods. At times, this volatility can be violent.

Investment in common stock represents the establishment of an ownership position in a company. Ownership of a share of a corporation's common stock gives the owner a proportionate interest in its profits and dividends or other distributions. In the event of a takeover, each individual shareholder is entitled to a proportionate share of the takeover bid or purchase price. Over time, as some real-

FIGURE 5.1 **Walt Disney Co. Stock Signifies Ownership in a Real "Mickey Mouse" Organization**

ized profits are reinvested in the business, the value of each shareholder's investment is allowed to build. At any point in time, the market value of a firm's common stock depends on many factors, including the company's current profitability, growth prospects, interest rates, and conditions in the overall stock market. Stocks appeal to long-term investors for their potential to provide competitive returns through dividends and capital growth. Over the long term, stocks have consistently offered investors the best opportunity to stay ahead of inflation and increase the value of their investment.

Measuring Historical Returns

Components of Required Return

Investors evaluate the attractiveness of investments based on a necessary trade-off between risk and expected return. The cost of higher expected return is the necessity of having to accept greater risk. In other words, there tends to be a positive relationship between risk and expected return. Required return consists of two main components.

The first component of required return can be thought of as the "reward for postponing consumption." Because investors must forego consumption to invest, they demand a monetary reward for waiting as part of their expected return. The reward for postponing consumption is the **nominal risk-free rate,** which consists of

nominal risk-free rate
Monetary reward for postponing consumption.

WALL STREET WISDOM 5.1

Day Trading

A long-term investor used to be described as someone who bought stocks on the basis of their investment merit and expected to hold them indefinitely. More recently, a long-term investor has tended to be described as someone who buys stocks on their investment merit and holds them for sufficiently long a period to qualify for favorable long-term capital gains tax treatment. Today, given that investors can trade stocks in tax-exempt individual retirement accounts, many revert to the quick-draw trading habits of professional investors. Large mutual funds, for example, have total portfolio turnover rates that average 75–80% per year. This means that their average portfolio holding period is less than 18 months.

When long-term investors hold their securities for as little as a few months, the concept of a trader rather than an investor takes on a whole new meaning. Traders used to be described as speculators who might turn over their portfolio two or three times per year. Jesse L. Livermore is one of the most famous of all Wall Street speculators. His book, *How to Trade Stocks: The Livermore Formula for Combining Time Element and Price,* remains an investment classic. Livermore argues that speculation is serious business. According to Livermore, a speculator cannot be successful trading every day. One should only trade big moves, no more than four or five times per year. According to Livermore, stocks have character and personality. Be fearful of abnormal movements. An uptick in volatility is cause for concern. In the face of danger, do not argue, get out. Livermore was not one to fight the tape. "The trend is your friend," he said. How did it all work out for Livermore? Apparently, it did not work well at all. Livermore made and lost four fortunes. He committed suicide in 1940 at age 63.

Still, the lure of quick and easy profits is a powerful elixir for present-day speculators. When commissions for Internet brokers are as low as $5 for up to 5,000 shares, active traders have taken to turning over their portfolio as often as once per day! By definition, a "day trader" is a speculator who likes to go home at the end of the trading day "flat." Flat means all in cash or with a portfolio that has zero risk. However, remember that a stock's price is a faithful reflection of the balance of short-term supply and demand at any point in time. This means that there is a 50% chance of an uptick and a 50% chance of a downtick. If short-term price moves are random—and all stock market evidence seems to agree on this point—then there is no profitable way to predict short-term market moves. Speculators who use their Internet-linked computers to make dozens of rapid stock trades each day are gambling, not investing. This has caused many to ask how a country that spends millions encouraging its poorest citizens to play state-run lotteries can object to speculation by the better heeled. Doesn't anyone who falls for day-trading firms' get-rich-quick pitches pretty much deserve the drubbing he or she will get? Some say yes, others say no.

Regulators contend that day trading abuses need to be controlled to maintain fair and efficient markets. State securities regulators are already cracking down on firms that use pie-in-the-sky claims and loans that exceed margin limits to recruit and keep day traders. The regulatory arm of the National Association of Securities Dealers, NASD Regulation, proposes stronger disclosure of the risks that day traders are running and wants dealers to determine whether day trading clients have the experience and staying power for rapid-fire trading.

The problem faced by day traders is a simple one. The minimum account size required for day trading is often as little as $50,000, but commissions, computer software, and other expenses can often run as high as $1,500 per month and more. In a market in which 10–12% annual returns are common, there simply is not room to profitably trade when costs run as high as 60% of capital per year. Rapid-fire trading is too often a rapid-fire ticket to enormous trading losses.

See: Ruth Simon, "Margin Investors Learn the Hard Way That Brokers Can Get Tough on Loans," *The Wall Street Journal,* April 27, 2000, C1, C19.

the **risk-free rate of return** plus an amount equal to the expected rate of inflation. A second important component of required return is the **required risk premium.** This amount varies with the amount of risk entailed. High-risk investments involve a higher-risk premium; low-risk investments involve a lower-risk premium. The expression for required return can be written:

risk-free rate of return Return without chance of default or volatility (T-bill return).

$$\begin{aligned}\text{Required return} &= \text{Nominal risk-free rate} + \text{Required risk premium}\\ &= \text{Risk-free rate} + \text{Expected inflation} + \text{Required risk premium}\end{aligned} \quad \textbf{(5.1)}$$

required risk premium Necessary compensation for risk taking.

Because long-term bonds tend to be more sensitive to change in interest rates, it is reasonable that the required return on long-term bonds is higher than on short-term money market instruments. Similarly, the greater volatility of common stocks implies a higher required return on equities than on either money market instruments or long-term bonds. However, before the investment merit of stocks, bonds, and other asset classes can be determined, it is necessary to clearly and accurately measure investment returns. Measurement is sometimes more difficult than one might imagine.

Arithmetic Average versus Geometric Mean

Many fundamental mistakes made by investors stem from the common inability to accurately measure investment returns. Investors often wrongly focus on **arithmetic average return** when judging portfolio performance. The arithmetic average return is upward biased and cannot be used to depict the return on investment over time.

arithmetic average returns Sum of investment returns divided by number of periods or securities.

To see that this is indeed the case, consider the formula for the arithmetic average return:

$$\text{Arithmetic average return} = \frac{\sum_{t=0}^{N} \text{Return}_t}{N} \quad \textbf{(5.2)}$$

where Σ indicates summation, t is time (over N time periods), and Return is the percentage return in any given period (e.g., +50% or −25%).

The problem lies in the way investors "see" annual rates of return. Most investors tend to be linear thinkers. They see simple arithmetic average returns. If a stock appreciates by 100% and then falls by 50%, the arithmetic average return for two periods is 25% per year (= [100% + (−50%)]/2).

In fact, no net profit is made. If a $10 stock jumps to $20 (up 100%) and then falls back to $10 (declines by 50%), it has fallen back to its initial price. The actual investment return is 0% per year over the two-year holding period.

Accurate measurement of annual investment returns requires calculation of the **geometric mean return.** The geometric mean return is the appropriate measure of the compound rate of return earned on investment over time. The formula for geometric mean is

geometric mean return Compound rate of return earned on investment.

$$\text{Geometric mean return} = \Pi\ \text{Return}_t^{1/N} - 1 \quad \textbf{(5.3)}$$

where Π indicates product, Return a holding-period return measured in ratio form (e.g., 1.50 for a 50% positive return), and all other variables are as before.

If a \$10 stock jumps to \$20 (up 100%) and then falls back to \$10 (declines by 50%), it has a geometric mean return of 0% = $(2 \times 0.5)^{1/2} - 1$. This is the same as the 0% actual investment return earned over the two-year holding period.

Given the importance of correctly calculating annual rates of return and in light of how often common mistakes are made, a more detailed example seems appropriate.

Jackrabbit Fund

Everyone likes a winner. Everybody loves a big winner. In investing, a big winner is a stock or a mutual fund that absolutely crushes the competition. Table 5.1 depicts a typical comparison.

The Jackrabbit High-Tech Fund promises to beat the competition by finding the latest winning investments in PC technology, desktop software, and Internet communications. Not for the faint of heart, Jackrabbit is only appropriate for investors who seek the significant return potential of high-tech stocks but also understand the high risks of technology stock investing. If this sounds familiar, good. It should. Literally hundreds of such high-risk/high-reward potential stock funds are commonly advertised in *The Wall Street Journal* and on the Internet.

Look at Jackrabbit Fund performance. In 1996, Jackrabbit turned in admirable performance, +33.3%. Any investor would be happy with this type of performance. If you kept it up, you would become very rich indeed. Did Jackrabbit keep it up? Unfortunately, it did not. In the 1997–99 period, Jackrabbit stumbled and turned in a money-losing performance. However, such down years are to be expected when seeking above-average returns. An investor only has to stay the course, right? Proof positive came in 2000 when Jackrabbit was up a stunning 211.9%. Now you're talking, right? If you take a simple arithmetic average of Jackrabbit's annual rates of return over the 1996–00 five-year period, it earned a stunning 31.1% per year. Boy, are they thumping the competition.

TABLE 5.1 Arithmetic Average versus Geometric Mean Return Calculation

Year	Jackrabbit High-Tech Fund	Low-Tech Express Fund	Category Killer Fund	Boring Portfolio Fund
1996	33.3%	−4.5%	23.9%	8.7%
1997	−18.3%	40.3%	6.6%	66.8%
1998	−34.5%	36.6%	28.1%	35.9%
1999	−37.1%	58.0%	28.9%	−8.1%
2000	211.9%	14.8%	−5.2%	−33.3%
Arithmetic average:	31.1%	29.0%	16.5%	14.0%
Geometric mean:	7.0%	27.1%	15.6%	8.6%
Total return:	40.0%	232.0%	106.7%	50.9%
Start:	\$29.25	\$30.88	\$22.25	\$21.63
Finish:	\$40.94	\$102.50	\$46.00	\$32.63
Initial investment:	\$10,000.00	\$10,000.00	\$10,000.00	\$10,000.00
Terminal value:	\$13,995.90	\$33,198.38	\$20,674.16	\$15,086.71

It sure looks that way. Compare Jackrabbit to three other popular mutual funds. Based on arithmetic average returns, the Low-Tech Express Fund appears to have done a bit worse than Jackrabbit over this five-year period. Low-Tech has had some good years, but "even a blind pig finds an acorn once in awhile." Surely Jackrabbit will shine next year. After all, Jackrabbit has momentum! Hands down, Jackrabbit is thumping the rest of the competition, isn't it? Surely, Jackrabbit is doing much better than stodgy old Category Killer and the Boring Portfolio.

In fact, Jackrabbit is not thumping the rest of the competition. When it comes to calculating investment rates of return, Jackrabbit's actual returns are not as good as the arithmetic average returns shown in Table 5.1. In this illustration, the Jackrabbit Fund appears to be the hot performer, and the Boring Portfolio seems the obvious loser. The Low-Tech Express and Category Killer funds seem to fall between these two extremes. When it comes to investment rates of return, looks can be deceiving. Jackrabbit actually *underperforms* all other funds shown in Table 5.1.

The arithmetic average rate of return for the Jackrabbit is 31.1% and higher than the arithmetic average return for the other three funds shown in Table 5.1. However, Jackrabbit's geometric mean return is only 7.0% [$= (1.33 \times 0.817 \times 0.655 \times 0.629 \times 3.119)^{1/5}$]. This is the lowest geometric mean return for the four funds shown in Table 5.1. The geometric mean return for Low-Tech is 27.1%, 15.6% for Category Killer, and 8.6% for the Boring Portfolio. Rather than hopelessly outclassed by Jackrabbit, each of these other investments provides superior returns. The total compounded return over this five-year holding period ranges between 232.0% for Low-Tech to only 40.0% for Jackrabbit.

The reason why Jackrabbit's overall performance is so anemic is simple. Tremendous upside rates of return are necessary to compensate for the harmful effects of portfolio losses. If you lose 50% of your portfolio, a 100% return is necessary to get back to even. In this case, even Jackrabbit's stunning one-year performance of +211.9% is insufficient to fully overcome the effects of prior devastating losses. By avoiding serious losses, the Low-Tech Fund is able to turn in stunning overall performance without any single year that approaches Jackrabbit's success in 2000.

Of course, there is no Jackrabbit Fund. The names of all four mutual funds illustrated in Table 5.1 are hypothetical, obviously. Still, as the reader might suspect, these are not purely hypothetical numbers. Over the 1994–98 period, shareholders in Apple Computer Inc. enjoyed the annual rates of return attributed to the Jackrabbit High-Tech Fund. The Low-Tech Express Fund depicts investor returns for the American Express Company over this same period. The Category Killer Fund is Caterpillar Inc., and who could be more boring than Boeing Co.? What Table 5.1 actually does is to compare the performance of three investment-grade securities with a risky high-tech stock that has had periods of euphoric outperformance, such as in 1998, and despondent underperformance, such as during 1995–97. Apple Computer stock sold for $29.50 in 1994. By 1998, Apple's stock price had improved to $40.94. Who could pick a stodgier investment alternative than American Express? Many of us could do worse. American Express stock jumped from $23.91 to $102.27 over the 1994–98 period. Even Caterpillar, which grew from $20.24 to $45.50, more than doubled over this time period. Also beating Apple was Boeing, which went up by more than 50% from $20.15 to $32.63.

The lesson to be learned from Table 5.1 is a very simple one. Building significant wealth requires that investors avoid significant financial losses. The key to building significant wealth is not necessarily to pick an outstanding performer that will double or triple in one year. The key to success is being able to identify companies that have the ability to grow at an above-average rate without the risk of a dramatic downturn in the companies' performance and their stock price performance.

Like the fable of the "Tortoise and the Hare," Table 5.1 shows that "slow and steady" wins the investment race. Investors are too often mesmerized by the "home run" potential of high-risk jackrabbitlike stocks. They focus on the alluring potential of the big hit and minimize the devastating effects of significant losses. By overlooking the long-term potential of tortoiselike performers, they turn their backs on high-quality companies that have a proven ability to deliver outstanding long-term results.

Over the long run, bet on the turtles.

Historical Returns

Stocks in the Long Run

As discussed in Chapter 3, Dow Jones & Co. began publishing the 30-stock component Dow Jones Industrial Average (DJIA) in 1928. Returns on the DJIA Index give investors the longest-running series of annual rates of return on common stocks that is consistently measured and systematically reported.

As seen in Table 5.2, the geometric mean price appreciation (capital gain) on the DJIA from 1928 to the present is 5.77%, compared with a mean dividend return of 4.37%. Over this period, the mean total rate of return on the DJIA was 10.42%, or roughly 10% per year. It is interesting to note that almost one-half of the total rate of return earned by stockholders over this period came in the form of dividend income. These figures are held down by the fact that 1929 marked the beginning of the Great Depression and a devastating crash in stock prices. From a high of 381.17 on September 9, 1929, to the low of 41.22 on July 8, 1932, stock prices collapsed a stunning 89.19%. To say the least, this was an unusually severe bear market.

median return "Middle" rate of return.

If one considers the **median return,** or "middle" rate of return, on the DJIA as a more appropriate measure of central tendency, then 11.37% is an appropriate expectation for capital gains during a typical year. Together with median dividend income of 4.06%, this suggests a median 14.68% total rate of return for common stock investors. Investors are realistic when they project total returns of 10–15% per year from a diversified portfolio of common stocks. Over this 72-year time frame, capital gains were positive in 49 years (68.1% of the time) and negative in 23 years (31.9% of the time). On a total return basis, returns were positive in 54 years (75% of the time) and negative in only 18 years (25% of the time).

Stocks usually go up.

Stocks versus Fixed-Income Securities

Which investment class, stocks, bonds, or cash reserves, has performed best over time? Historically, the answer has been common stock. Common stocks have offered the highest average annual returns of the primary classes of investment assets. Table 5.3 shows annual rates of return from 1950 to the present for the Standard & Poor's (S&P) 500 Index, a good proxy for large-company stocks. Also shown are rates of return for long-term Treasury bonds, U.S. Treasury bills, and the rate of inflation as measured by the annual rate of change in the Consumer Price Index. U.S. Treasury bills mature in less than one year and offer a good proxy for money market instruments.

As mentioned in Chapter 3, Standard & Poor's Corp. introduced a 90-stock average in 1928, but it was not until 1957 that it offered an expanded index of 500 stocks. To give a longer-term perspective on the performance of the S&P 500, return data have been extended backward in time to 1950 to show how such firms would have performed had the S&P 500 Index been established earlier. The S&P 500 is a common investment benchmark for institutional investors, and the post–World War II period is a conventional time frame for modern equity and debt markets. One must be cautious in interpreting such data, however, because selection bias can cloud these hypothetical returns. All S&P 500 firms are chosen on the basis of their significant market capitalization, so firms included in the S&P 500 in 1957 were corporate success stories at that time. For example, no railroads that went bankrupt during the Great Depression were included in the S&P 500 in 1957. It would paint an unrealistically rosy picture of common stock returns to consider hypothetical returns on S&P 500 component stocks from, say, 1900 to the present. Data on S&P 500 firms that stem from the 1950s are both realistic and reliable.

Total return is measured by the sum of dividends, interest income, and capital gains or capital losses. The time period covered is from 1950 to the present. Over this time frame, the before-tax geometric mean rate of return earned on the S&P 500 was 13.61%. Long-term government bonds had a total return of 5.57%, and U.S. Treasury bills paid an average interest income of 5.16%. These returns compare with an average annual rate of inflation of 4.00%.

total return
The sum of dividends, interest income, and capital gains or capital losses.

The three best years for stock returns since 1950 were 52.62% (in 1954), 43.36% (in 1958), and 37.43% (in 1995). These spectacular one-year returns were more than three times higher than typical rates of return earned by common stock investors during remaining years. It is interesting to note that each of these years of outstanding stock return performance followed years of subpar performance. This suggests that outstanding one-year performance often reflects earnings and book value growth achieved over longer periods of time.

Positive rates of return are enjoyed by common stockholders during most years. Common stock investors suffered losses during only 10 years. The three worst years for stock returns during this period were −26.47% (in 1974), −14.66% (1973), and −10.78% (in 1957). It is also interesting to note that unusually good or unusually bad stock return performance is typically followed by periods of above-normal performance. As noted earlier, stock prices rebounded smartly in 1958 from the deep bear market experienced in 1957. The devastating bear market of 1973–74 represented a severe correction from the euphoric "Nifty Fifty" market peak of 1972 and ushered in the longest and most impressive bull market in stock-market history.

Like common stock investors, investors in long-term Treasury bonds are prone to experience significant volatility. Since 1950, the three best years for long-term bond investors produced a total return of +40.36% (1982), +31.67% (1995), and +30.97% (1985). A dramatic downturn in interest rates leads to impressive capital gains for long-term bondholders. Similarly, any dramatic rise in interest rates can lead to significant capital losses. Since 1950, the three worst years for long-term bond investors produced total returns of −9.18% (1967), −8.74% (in 1999), and −7.77% (1994). The usual culprit behind rising interest rates is an increase in inflation. During the past half-century, the worst years for high rates of inflation were 13.31% (in 1979), 12.40% (in 1980), and 12.20% (in 1974). The best years for tame inflation were −0.50% (in 1954, when prices actually fell), 0.37% (in 1955), and 0.62% (in 1953). Notice how an upsurge in inflation proves to be

TABLE 5.2 The Dow Jones Industrial Average, 1928–99

Year	Dow at Start of Year	Year's High Close	Date	Year's Low Close	Date	Year's Close	Change Points	Change %
1928	203.35	300.00	31-Dec	191.33	20-Feb	300.00	97.60	48.22%
1929	307.01	381.17	03-Sep	198.69	13-Nov	248.48	−51.52	−17.17%
1930	244.30	294.07	17-Apr	157.51	16-Dec	164.58	−83.90	−33.77%
1931	169.84	194.36	24-Feb	73.79	17-Dec	77.90	−86.68	−52.67%
1932	74.62	88.78	08-Mar	41.22	08-Jul	59.93	−17.97	−23.07%
1933	59.29	108.67	18-Jul	50.16	27-Feb	99.90	39.97	66.69%
1934	100.36	110.74	05-Feb	85.51	26-Jul	104.04	4.14	4.14%
1935	104.51	148.44	19-Nov	96.71	14-Mar	144.13	40.09	38.53%
1936	144.13	184.90	17-Nov	143.11	06-Jan	179.90	35.77	24.82%
1937	178.52	194.40	10-Mar	113.64	24-Nov	120.85	−59.05	−32.82%
1938	120.57	158.41	12-Nov	98.95	31-Mar	154.76	33.91	28.06%
1939	153.64	155.92	12-Sep	121.44	08-Apr	150.24	−4.52	−2.92%
1940	151.43	152.80	03-Jan	111.84	10-Jun	131.13	−19.11	−12.72%
1941	130.57	133.59	10-Jan	106.34	23-Dec	110.96	−20.17	−15.38%
1942	112.77	119.71	26-Dec	92.92	28-Apr	119.40	8.44	7.61%
1943	119.93	145.82	14-Jul	119.26	08-Jan	135.89	16.49	13.81%
1944	135.92	152.53	16-Dec	134.22	07-Feb	152.32	16.43	12.09%
1945	152.58	195.82	11-Dec	151.35	24-Jan	192.91	40.59	26.65%
1946	191.33	212.50	29-May	163.12	09-Oct	177.20	−15.71	−8.14%
1947	176.39	186.85	24-Jul	163.21	17-May	181.16	3.96	2.23%
1948	181.04	193.16	15-Jun	165.39	16-Mar	177.30	−3.86	−2.13%
1949	175.03	200.52	30-Dec	161.60	13-Jun	200.13	22.83	12.88%
1950	198.89	235.47	24-Nov	196.81	13-Jan	235.41	35.28	17.63%
1951	239.92	276.37	13-Sep	238.99	03-Jan	269.23	33.82	14.37%
1952	269.86	292.00	30-Dec	256.35	01-May	291.90	22.67	8.42%
1953	292.14	293.79	05-Jan	255.49	14-Sep	280.90	−11.00	−3.77%
1954	282.89	404.39	31-Dec	279.87	11-Jan	404.39	123.49	43.96%
1955	408.89	488.40	30-Dec	388.20	17-Jan	488.40	84.01	20.77%
1956	485.78	521.05	06-Apr	462.35	23-Jan	499.47	11.07	2.27%
1957	496.03	520.77	12-Jul	419.79	22-Oct	435.69	−63.78	−12.77%
1958	439.27	583.65	31-Dec	436.89	25-Feb	583.65	147.96	33.96%
1959	587.59	679.36	31-Dec	574.46	09-Feb	679.36	95.71	16.40%
1960	679.06	685.47	05-Jan	566.05	25-Oct	615.89	−63.47	−9.34%
1961	610.25	734.91	13-Dec	610.25	03-Jan	731.14	115.25	18.71%
1962	724.71	726.01	03-Jan	535.76	26-Jun	652.10	−79.04	−10.81%
1963	646.79	767.21	18-Dec	646.79	02-Jan	762.95	110.85	17.00%
1964	766.08	891.71	18-Nov	766.08	02-Jan	874.13	111.18	14.57%
1965	869.78	969.26	31-Dec	840.59	28-Jun	969.26	95.13	10.88%
1966	968.54	995.15	09-Feb	744.32	07-Oct	785.69	−183.57	−18.94%
1967	786.41	943.08	25-Sep	786.41	03-Jan	905.11	119.42	15.20%
1968	906.84	985.21	03-Dec	825.13	21-Mar	943.75	38.64	4.27%
1969	947.73	968.85	14-May	769.93	17-Dec	800.36	−143.39	−15.19%
1970	809.20	842.00	29-Dec	631.16	26-May	838.92	38.56	4.82%
1971	830.57	950.82	28-Apr	797.97	23-Nov	890.20	51.28	6.11%
1972	889.30	1036.27	11-Dec	889.15	26-Jan	1020.02	129.82	14.58%
1973	1031.68	1051.70	11-Jan	788.31	05-Dec	850.86	−169.16	−16.58%
1974	855.32	891.66	13-Mar	577.60	06-Dec	616.24	−234.62	−27.57%
1975	632.04	881.81	15-Jul	632.04	02-Jan	852.41	236.17	38.32%
1976	858.71	1014.79	21-Sep	858.71	02-Jan	1004.65	152.24	17.86%
1977	999.75	999.75	03-Jan	800.85	02-Nov	831.17	−173.48	−17.27%
1978	817.74	907.74	08-Sep	742.12	28-Feb	805.01	−26.16	−3.15%
1979	811.42	897.61	05-Oct	796.67	07-Nov	838.74	33.73	4.19%
1980	824.57	1000.17	20-Nov	759.13	21-Apr	963.99	125.25	14.93%
1981	972.78	1024.05	27-Apr	824.01	25-Sep	875.00	−88.99	−9.23%
1982	882.52	1070.55	27-Dec	776.92	12-Aug	1046.54	171.54	19.60%
1983	1027.04	1287.20	29-Nov	1027.04	03-Jan	1258.64	212.10	20.27%
1984	1252.74	1286.64	06-Jan	1086.57	24-Jul	1211.57	−47.07	−3.74%
1985	1198.87	1553.10	16-Dec	1184.96	04-Jan	1546.67	335.10	27.66%
1986	1537.73	1955.57	02-Dec	1502.29	22-Jan	1895.95	349.28	22.58%
1987	1927.31	2722.42	25-Aug	1738.74	19-Oct	1938.83	42.88	2.26%
1988	2015.25	2183.50	21-Oct	1879.14	20-Jan	2168.57	229.74	11.85%
1989	2144.64	2791.41	09-Oct	2144.64	03-Jan	2753.20	584.63	26.96%
1990	2810.15	2999.75	16-Jul	2365.10	11-Oct	2633.66	−119.54	−4.34%
1991	2610.64	3168.83	31-Dec	2470.30	09-Jan	3168.83	535.17	20.32%
1992	3172.41	3413.21	01-Jun	3136.58	09-Oct	3301.11	132.28	4.17%
1993	3309.22	3794.33	29-Dec	3241.95	20-Jan	3754.09	452.98	13.72%
1994	3756.60	3978.36	31-Jan	3593.35	04-Apr	3834.44	80.35	2.14%
1995	3838.48	5216.47	13-Dec	3832.08	30-Jan	5117.12	1282.68	33.45%
1996	5177.45	6560.91	27-Dec	5032.94	10-Jan	6448.27	1331.15	26.01%
1997	6448.27	8259.31	06-Aug	6391.69	11-Apr	7908.25	1459.98	22.64%
1998	7965.04	9374.27	23-Nov	7539.07	31-Aug	9181.43	1273.18	16.10%
1999	9212.80	11497.10	31-Dec	9120.70	22-Jan	11497.10	2315.67	25.22%
Arithmetic average								**7.87%**
Geometric mean								**5.77%**
Median								**11.37%**

Data source: Dow Jones & Company.

TABLE 5.2 ***(continued)***

Book Value	P/Book	Earns	P/E	Divs	% Yield	Total Return
N.A.	N.A.	N.A.	N.A.	N.A.	N.A.	48.22%
N.A.	N.A.	19.94	12.5	12.75	5.13%	−12.04%
N.A.	N.A.	11.02	14.9	11.13	6.76%	−27.00%
N.A.	N.A.	4.09	19.0	8.40	10.78%	−41.88%
N.A.	N.A.	−0.51	N.A.	4.62	7.71%	−15.36%
N.A.	N.A.	2.11	47.3	3.40	3.40%	70.10%
N.A.	N.A.	3.91	26.6	3.66	3.52%	7.66%
N.A.	N.A.	6.34	22.7	4.55	3.16%	41.69%
85.55	2.10	10.07	17.9	7.05	3.92%	28.74%
88.30	1.37	11.49	10.5	8.78	7.27%	−25.56%
87.13	1.78	6.01	25.8	4.98	3.22%	31.28%
95.58	1.57	9.11	16.5	6.11	4.07%	1.15%
98.75	1.33	10.92	12.0	7.06	5.38%	−7.34%
102.33	1.08	11.64	9.5	7.59	6.84%	−8.54%
107.50	1.11	9.22	13.0	6.40	5.36%	12.97%
113.03	1.20	9.74	14.0	6.30	4.64%	18.45%
118.33	1.29	10.07	15.1	6.57	4.31%	16.40%
122.74	1.57	10.56	18.3	6.69	3.47%	30.12%
131.40	1.35	13.63	13.0	7.50	4.23%	−3.91%
149.08	1.22	18.80	9.6	9.21	5.08%	7.32%
159.67	1.11	23.07	7.7	11.50	6.49%	4.36%
170.12	1.18	23.54	8.5	12.79	6.39%	19.27%
194.19	1.21	30.70	7.7	16.13	6.85%	24.48%
202.60	1.33	26.59	10.1	16.34	6.07%	20.44%
213.39	1.37	24.78	11.8	15.43	5.29%	13.71%
244.26	1.15	27.23	10.3	16.11	5.74%	1.97%
248.96	1.62	28.18	14.4	17.47	4.32%	48.28%
271.77	1.80	35.78	13.7	21.58	4.42%	25.19%
284.78	1.75	33.34	15.0	22.99	4.60%	6.87%
298.69	1.46	36.08	12.1	21.61	4.96%	−7.81%
310.97	1.88	27.95	20.9	20.00	3.43%	37.39%
339.02	2.00	34.31	19.8	20.74	3.05%	19.45%
369.87	1.67	32.21	19.1	21.36	3.47%	−5.87%
385.82	1.90	31.91	22.9	22.71	3.11%	21.82%
400.97	1.63	36.43	17.9	23.30	3.57%	−7.24%
425.90	1.79	41.21	18.5	23.41	3.07%	20.07%
417.39	2.09	46.43	18.8	31.24	3.57%	18.15%
453.27	2.14	53.67	18.1	28.61	2.95%	113.83%
475.92	1.65	57.68	13.6	31.89	4.06%	−14.88%
476.50	1.90	53.87	16.8	30.19	3.34%	18.53%
521.08	1.81	57.89	16.3	31.34	3.32%	7.59%
542.25	1.48	57.02	14.0	33.90	4.24%	−10.96%
573.15	1.46	51.02	16.4	31.53	3.76%	8.58%
607.61	1.47	55.09	16.2	30.86	3.47%	9.58%
642.87	1.59	67.11	15.2	32.27	3.16%	17.75%
690.23	1.23	86.17	9.9	35.33	4.15%	−12.43%
746.95	0.83	99.04	6.2	37.72	6.12%	−21.45%
783.61	1.09	75.66	11.3	37.46	4.39%	42.72%
798.20	1.26	96.72	10.4	41.40	4.12%	21.98%
841.76	0.99	89.10	9.3	45.84	5.52%	−11.75%
890.69	0.90	112.79	7.1	48.52	6.03%	2.88%
859.41	0.98	124.46	6.7	50.98	6.08%	10.27%
928.50	1.04	121.86	7.9	54.36	5.64%	20.57%
975.59	0.90	113.71	7.7	56.22	6.43%	−2.81%
881.51	1.19	9.15	114.4	54.14	5.17%	24.78%
888.21	1.42	72.45	17.4	56.33	4.48%	24.74%
916.70	1.32	113.58	10.7	60.63	5.00%	1.26%
944.97	1.64	96.11	16.1	62.03	4.01%	31.67%
986.48	1.92	115.59	16.4	67.04	3.54%	26.12%
1008.95	1.92	133.05	14.6	71.20	3.67%	5.93%
1075.47	2.02	215.46	10.1	79.53	3.67%	15.52%
1276.14	2.16	221.48	12.4	103.00	3.74%	30.70%
1331.52	1.98	172.05	15.3	103.70	3.94%	−0.40%
1301.31	2.44	49.27	64.3	95.18	3.00%	23.32%
1146.03	2.88	108.25	30.5	100.72	3.05%	7.23%
1117.81	3.36	146.84	25.6	99.66	2.65%	16.38%
1305.32	2.94	256.13	15.0	105.66	2.76%	4.90%
1337.33	3.83	311.02	16.5	116.56	2.28%	35.73%
1414.04	4.56	353.88	18.2	131.14	2.03%	28.05%
1595.14	4.96	391.29	20.2	136.10	1.72%	24.36%
1691.68	5.43	389.24	23.6	153.69	1.67%	17.77%
1688.27	6.81	463.19	24.8	153.92	1.34%	26.56%
	1.8		**17.7**		**4.38%**	**12.19%**
					4.37%	**10.42%**
	1.5		**15.0**		**4.06%**	**14.68%**

TABLE 5.3 **Total Returns on Common Stocks and Government Bonds, 1950–99**

Year	Common Stocks	Long-Term Treasury Bonds	Short-Term Treasury Bills	Inflation Rate
1950	31.71%	0.06%	1.20%	5.79%
1951	24.02%	−3.93%	1.49%	5.87%
1952	18.37%	1.16%	1.66%	0.88%
1953	−0.99%	3.64%	1.82%	0.62%
1954	52.62%	7.19%	0.86%	−0.50%
1955	31.56%	−1.29%	1.57%	0.37%
1956	6.56%	−5.59%	2.46%	2.86%
1957	−10.78%	7.46%	3.14%	3.02%
1958	43.36%	−6.09%	1.54%	1.76%
1959	11.96%	−2.26%	2.95%	1.50%
1960	0.47%	13.78%	2.66%	1.48%
1961	26.89%	0.97%	2.13%	0.67%
1962	−8.73%	6.89%	2.73%	1.22%
1963	22.80%	1.21%	3.12%	1.65%
1964	16.48%	3.51%	3.54%	1.19%
1965	12.45%	0.71%	3.93%	1.92%
1966	−10.06%	3.65%	4.76%	3.35%
1967	23.98%	−9.18%	4.21%	3.04%
1968	11.06%	−0.26%	5.21%	4.72%
1969	−8.50%	−5.07%	6.58%	6.11%
1970	4.01%	12.11%	6.52%	5.49%
1971	14.31%	13.23%	4.39%	3.36%
1972	18.98%	5.69%	3.84%	3.41%
1973	−14.66%	−1.11%	6.93%	8.80%
1974	−26.47%	4.35%	8.00%	12.20%
1975	37.20%	9.20%	5.80%	7.01%
1976	23.84%	16.75%	5.08%	4.81%
1977	−7.18%	−0.69%	5.12%	6.77%
1978	6.56%	−1.18%	7.18%	9.03%
1979	18.44%	−1.23%	10.38%	13.31%
1980	32.42%	−3.95%	11.24%	12.40%
1981	−4.91%	1.86%	6.96%	8.94%
1982	21.41%	40.36%	11.59%	3.87%
1983	22.51%	0.65%	8.64%	3.80%
1984	6.27%	15.48%	10.20%	3.95%
1985	32.16%	30.97%	7.87%	3.77%
1986	18.47%	24.53%	6.41%	1.13%
1987	5.23%	−2.71%	6.37%	4.41%
1988	16.81%	9.67%	7.33%	4.42%
1989	31.49%	18.11%	9.15%	4.65%
1990	−3.17%	6.18%	8.07%	6.11%
1991	30.55%	19.30%	5.96%	3.06%
1992	7.67%	8.05%	3.68%	2.90%
1993	9.99%	18.24%	2.98%	2.75%
1994	1.31%	−7.77%	4.03%	2.67%
1995	37.43%	31.67%	5.77%	2.54%
1996	23.07%	−0.93%	5.24%	3.32%
1997	33.36%	15.08%	5.38%	1.70%
1998	28.58%	13.52%	5.31%	1.61%
1999	21.04%	−8.74%	4.94%	2.30%
Arithmetic average	**14.84%**	**6.07%**	**5.16%**	**4.04%**
Median	**17.59%**	**3.58%**	**5.10%**	**3.34%**
Geometric mean	**13.61%**	**5.57%**	**5.16%**	**4.00%**
Standard deviation	**16.45%**	**10.70%**	**2.69%**	**3.09%**
Coefficient of variation	**1.11**	**1.76**	**0.52**	**0.76**

Data source: Federal Reserve.

bad medicine for both stock and long-term bond investors, just as a fall in inflation proves to be a tonic for bull markets in both stocks and bonds. Also notice how interest rates on Treasury bills tend to track the rate of inflation. Investors in such money market instruments typically receive a rate of interest that is roughly equivalent to the rate of inflation.

Inflation Problem

Investors face the ever-present danger that inflation, or a general increase in the cost of living, will reduce the value of any investment. If a particular investment earns a **nominal return** of 6% but the rate of inflation is 4%, the return after inflation, or **real return,** is only 2%. What makes the rate of inflation a particularly serious threat to the value of even a well-diversified portfolio is the fact that income taxes are typically paid on nominal returns. Thus, if an investor must pay a 40% marginal tax rate on a bond paying 6% interest, the after-tax rate of interest is only 3.6%. If inflation is indeed averaging 4%, the bond investor is falling behind even if all after-tax interest is reinvested. This is why bond investors often find that the real value of their investment tends to erode over time given the dual threats posed by taxes and inflation. This is especially true in the case of investors in bonds and other fixed-income investments because taxable interest income constitutes all the return earned by buy-and-hold bond investors.

nominal return Gross investment profit expressed as a percentage.

real return Investment return after inflation.

Figures in Table 5.3 show that inflation has consumed almost all the before-tax interest earned on money market instruments. On an after-tax basis, therefore, money market instruments have proved to be a losing proposition. Inflation has also consumed a large portion of the mean total return earned by investors in long-term bonds and large-company common stocks. After accounting for inflation, investors in large-company common stocks earned an average annual real rate of return of 9.61% (= 13.61% − 4.00%) before taxes. Long-term Treasury bonds provided investors with a "real" long-term average annual return of only 1.57% (= 5.57% − 4.00%) before taxes, just a bit ahead of the 1.16% (= 5.16% − 4.00%) real rate of return on Treasury bills. After accounting for both inflation and income taxes (at 40%), the real after-tax rate of return has been 4.17% (= [13.61% × (1 − 0.4)] − 4.00%) on common stocks, −0.64% (= [5.57% × (1 − 0.4)] − 4.00%) on Treasury bonds, and −0.90% (= [5.16% × (1 − 0.4)] − 4.00%) on Treasury bills. Because income taxes are paid on nominal rates of return, the modest returns earned on fixed-income investments are generally insufficient to offset the dual effects of inflation and taxes. The numbers show that fixed-income investing is largely a losing proposition, once both taxes and the rate of inflation are considered. Over the long term, common stocks are the only investment class with a documented record of providing investors with meaningful real returns after taxes.

Cumulative Returns

The modest average annual return advantage of common stocks over fixed-income securities accumulates to a stunning total differential over an extended investment horizon. For example, Table 5.4 shows that a $1 investment in common stocks in 1950 compounded to a total value of $589.38 by the end of 1999. This is more than 47 times the $12.38 cumulative value of a similar $1 investment in Treasury bonds. This is despite the fact that long-term Treasury bonds are the second-best asset class and provided investors with a significant premium over the amount earned by investors

TABLE 5.4 Cumulative Total Returns on Common Stocks and Government Bonds, 1950–99

Year	Common Stocks	Long-Term Treasury Bonds	Short-Term Treasury Bills	Inflation Rate
1950	1.3171	1.0006	1.0120	1.0579
1951	1.6335	0.9613	1.0271	1.1200
1952	1.9335	0.9724	1.0441	1.1299
1953	1.9144	1.0078	1.0631	1.1369
1954	2.9217	1.0803	1.0723	1.1312
1955	3.8439	1.0664	1.0891	1.1354
1956	4.0960	1.0067	1.1159	1.1678
1957	3.6545	1.0818	1.1509	1.2031
1958	5.2390	1.0160	1.1687	1.2243
1959	5.8656	0.9930	1.2031	1.2426
1960	5.8932	1.1298	1.2351	1.2610
1961	7.4779	1.1408	1.2615	1.2695
1962	6.8250	1.2194	1.2959	1.2850
1963	8.3812	1.2341	1.3363	1.3062
1964	9.7624	1.2775	1.3836	1.3217
1965	10.9778	1.2865	1.4380	1.3471
1966	9.8734	1.3335	1.5065	1.3922
1967	12.2411	1.2111	1.5699	1.4345
1968	13.5949	1.2079	1.6517	1.5023
1969	12.4394	1.1467	1.7603	1.5940
1970	12.9382	1.2856	1.8751	1.6816
1971	14.7896	1.4556	1.9574	1.7381
1972	17.5967	1.5385	2.0326	1.7973
1973	15.0170	1.5214	2.1735	1.9555
1974	11.0420	1.5876	2.3473	2.1941
1975	15.1497	1.7336	2.4835	2.3479
1976	18.7613	2.0240	2.6096	2.4608
1977	17.4143	2.0100	2.7433	2.6274
1978	18.5566	1.9863	2.9402	2.8646
1979	21.9785	1.9619	3.2454	3.2459
1980	29.1039	1.8844	3.6102	3.6484
1981	27.6749	1.9194	4.1413	3.9746
1982	33.6001	2.6941	4.5778	4.1284
1983	41.1635	2.7116	4.9806	4.2853
1984	43.7444	3.1314	5.4712	4.4545
1985	57.8127	4.1012	5.8936	4.6225
1986	68.4907	5.1072	6.2566	4.6747
1987	72.0727	4.9688	6.5988	4.8809
1988	94.1882	5.4493	7.0179	5.0966
1989	110.6990	6.4362	7.6053	5.3336
1990	107.1898	6.8339	8.1992	5.6595
1991	139.9363	8.1529	8.6584	5.8327
1992	150.6695	8.8092	8.9623	6.0018
1993	165.7213	10.4160	9.2222	6.1669
1994	167.8923	9.6066	9.5819	6.3315
1995	230.7344	12.6491	10.1185	6.4923
1996	283.9648	12.5314	10.6456	6.7079
1997	378.6954	14.5177	11.2056	6.8219
1998	486.9266	16.4804	11.8006	6.9317
1999	589.3759	15.0400	12.3836	7.0912

Data source: Federal Reserve.

in short-term Treasury bills. On a before-tax basis, Treasury bond and Treasury bill investors were able to achieve a modest real rate of return on their investment over this period. Nevertheless, the advantage to common stock investors is stunning.

For further perspective on the long-term advantage enjoyed by common stock investors, Figure 5.2 shows the cumulative value resulting from a $10,000 investment in 1950 in each respective asset class. The common stock investor commanded a portfolio with a total value of $5.9 million in 50 years. By contrast, the Treasury bond investor's portfolio grew to only $150,400 over this period. The Treasury bill investor's wealth increased to only $123,836. In tax-sheltered accounts, such as individual retirement accounts, fixed-income investors were able to achieve only a modest gain over the rate of inflation. However, common stock investors were able to build a significant amount of wealth over this period.

In considering the practical relevance of the long-term advantage of investing in stocks versus bonds, investors might be expected to have two basic questions. First, is such a long investment horizon relevant for the typical investor? Second, is the long-term average-rate-of-return advantage of stocks over bonds apt to be replicated in the future? The answer to both questions is yes. Students who are 20–30 years old have an investment horizon of 30–40 years within which to finance a comfortable retirement income. For them, it is realistic to think in terms of very long investment horizons. Even for investors who are 40–50 years of age, significant time exists for them to benefit mightily through long-term investing. For all long-term investors, it pays to carefully consider the long-term advantages of common stock investing. Common stock investors benefit from rising earnings and dividend income made possible by economic growth. Common stock investors will benefit so long as economic growth is robust, and it has been robust in the United States and much of the world for generations.

FIGURE 5.2 **Cumulative Investment Value of $10,000 Investment in Stocks and Bonds, 1950–2000**

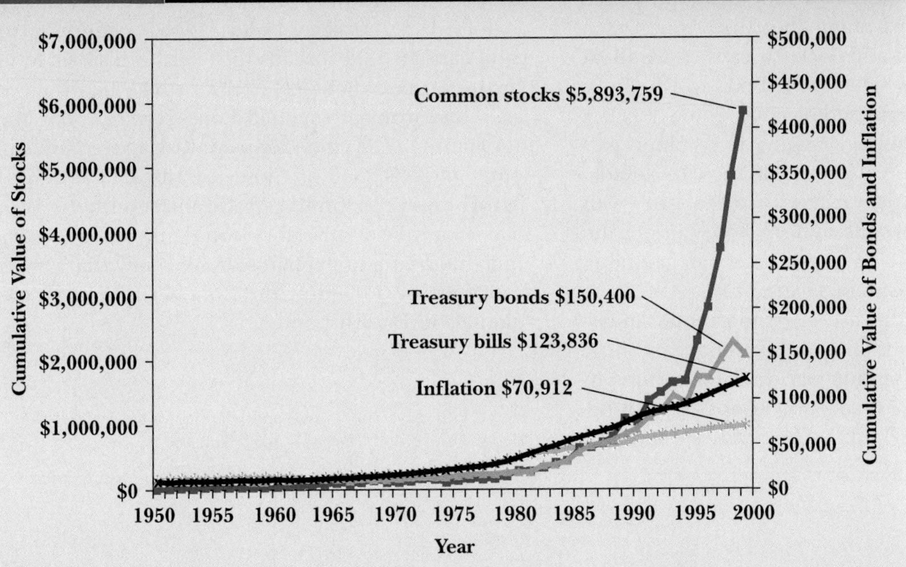

WALL STREET WISDOM 5.2

Risk Seekers Big and Small

The success of state-run lotteries is convincing evidence that many "little" people display risk-seeking behavior, especially when small sums of money are involved. The profitability of state-run lotteries stems from the fact that ticket buyers are willing to pay $1 for a bet that has an expected return of less than $1. When only 50% of lottery ticket revenues are paid out in the form of prizes, for example, each $1 ticket has an expected return of only 50¢. In such circumstances, the "price" of $1 in expected return is $2 in certain dollars. The willingness to pay such a premium for the unlikely chance at a lottery payoff that might reach into the millions of dollars stems from the fact that such opportunities are rare and lottery ticket buyers value them highly. Many have no opportunity for hitting the jackpot in their careers. The lottery is their only chance, however remote, at a substantial sum of money. The success of state-run lottery promotions is noteworthy because it is fairly unusual. Typically, consumers and investors display risk-averse behavior, especially when substantial sums of money are involved.

Gambling is one of America's great growth industries. Over the past decade, the gambling industry has enjoyed average yearly growth in per-capita spending and gross revenues of roughly 10% per year. With such impressive results, it is little wonder that several midwestern and southern states have licensed gambling on riverboats, many of them anchored in some of the nation's poorest towns along the Mississippi Delta. Roughly 100 riverboats and dockside casinos are afloat as more than a dozen states from Texas to Rhode Island search for more jobs and revenue. Some 20 states now have Indian gambling, ranging from bingo parlors to casinos as big and glamorous as those in Nevada. Interestingly, gambling fever has spread to states with long traditions of fiscal conservatism. For example, the state of Minnesota, with its Native American gambling halls, has more casinos than Atlantic City.

If legislative agendas are any indication, Americans can expect to see even more riverboat gambling, card clubs, off-track betting parlors, and casinos in their own backyards. Indian-run casinos are also becoming increasingly popular. Americans are so eager to gamble that they are shifting long-established leisure-time expenditures. Today, U.S. consumers spend more on legal games of chance than on movie theaters, books, amusement attractions, and recorded music combined!

Some of the recent popularity of gambling can be traced to demographics and broader spending trends. The population is aging, and an older population tends to favor participant amusements that are not strenuous. Pouring quarters into a slot machine is easy and apparently appealing to a growing number of Americans. The growth in gambling has also coincided with a glacial shift in social attitudes. Within a generation, gambling has gone from being a moral vice to mass-market entertainment. Analysts contend that it was church and charity "Las Vegas Nights" and "Bingo Nights" that laid the legal groundwork for Indian tribes to broaden their gambling operations.

Of course, not only "little" people are involved. Many high-rollers also have displayed an amazing appetite for risk during recent years. In 1998, for example, Myron S. Scholes and Robert C. Merton, who shared the 1997 Nobel prize in economics for their work on options-pricing theory, lost *billions of dollars* of their own and other investor's money in a high-risk bet on the difference in yield between different debt instruments. Although computer models showed that the yield on Danish bonds was attractive *vis-à-vis* U.S. Treasury bonds, global economic turmoil caused yield spreads to widen to historic levels. In the process, Scholes' and Merton's heavily leveraged and ironically named Long-Term Capital Management (LTCM) got slammed. Risk assessment computer models such as those used by LTCM tend to ignore low-probability catastrophic events. It is too bad that LTCM investors could not do the same. Imagine trying to explain to your family that you lost your fortune, including the Nobel Prize money, speculating on Danish bonds.

See: Erin E. Arvedlund, "Fear and Loathing in the Halls of the Hedge Fund Hotel," *Barron's*, April 24, 2000, 10.

Risk Concepts and Measurement

Valuation Risk

The total return earned on common stocks and the risks associated with owning them depend on when such investments are made. The time-honored maxim "buy low, sell high" is certainly an equation for stock market success, but near-term stock market performance is unpredictable. What is "low" and what is "high" are typically not known until it is too late to profit from the knowledge.

Long-term investors should be very skeptical about simpleminded projections of recent rates of return as useful projections of what might be expected in the future. This is especially true when recent rates of return are distinctly higher or sharply lower than long-term averages. In the short run of a few years, stock prices can and do race ahead of basic improvements in the firm's ability to increase earnings and dividends. This is clearly the case during the historic bull market of the late 1990s when the ratio of stock market prices relative to earnings, called the P/E ratio, reached historic highs. Over this period, the ratio of dividends paid relative to stock market prices, called the dividend yield, reached historic lows. Also as seen in Table 5.2, the protracted bear market of 1972–74 saw an historic decline in stock prices despite growing earnings and dividends. By the bottom in 1974, P/E ratios had reached historic lows, whereas dividend yields jumped sharply.

Annual rates of return earned by equity investors over the 20-year 1980–2000 period are the best on record for any similar period. During the 1980s and 1990s, the annualized return of the S&P 500 Index was 17.87%, compared with the long-term geometric mean of 13.61%. In retrospect, stock prices were clearly "low" as the 1980s began. By historical standards, the S&P 500 also offered generous dividend yields at that time of about 5.64%, compared with a historical average of about 3.50%. Measured by P/E ratios, the typical stock was then low compared with earnings, at 9.2 times earnings versus a more typical 14 times earnings. In 1980, the DJIA paid a dividend yield of 5.64% versus the long-term mean of 4.37% and featured a P/E ratio of only 7.9 times earnings versus the long-term average of 17.7. In retrospect, it is clear that stocks were relatively cheap in 1980 and offered a wonderful base for above-average performance during subsequent years. As inflation and interest rates dropped sharply throughout the 1980s and 1990s, stock prices skyrocketed, and stock market investors benefited enormously.

At the start of the new millennium and after having experienced one of the biggest bull markets in history, stock prices can no longer be considered "cheap" by historical standards. As of January 1, 2000, the S&P 500 yielded only 1.14%, the lowest on record by a significant margin, and traded at a stunning 33.4:1 times earnings per share. At the same time, the DJIA yielded only 1.32% and traded at a whopping 24.6:1 times earnings per share. Whether stocks will continue to move higher as we enter the new millennium or retreat from current levels is anyone's guess. Historically, following periods when stock prices have surged ahead of basic improvements in business, stock prices have often "rested" while earnings and dividends "catch up" and justify higher prices. However, stock prices sometimes correct sharply to lower levels, as they did during the 1987 correction, and then move upward when earnings growth resumes. In any event, it is highly unlikely that returns for equity investors over the next few years will approach the above-average returns earned during the 1980s and 1990s. Equity investors should have modest expectations about prospective returns going forward and should be prepared for the possibility of significant short-term downward volatility.

Risk Measurement Concepts

To an investor, risk is tied to the chance of loss. Chance of loss depends on return volatility. Therefore, the most popular measures of investment risk are tied to the volatility of investment returns. In practical terms, the amount of stock market volatility is measured by the amount of "bounce" in stock prices. If a stock had a price of 30 and never varied, it would have zero volatility. There would be no chance of loss for investors. That is the good news. The bad news is that a stock permanently stuck at 30 would also have zero profit potential. What investors seek are investment opportunities that have a desirable trade-off between risk and return.

standard deviation A common risk measure.

A common measure of return volatility is the **standard deviation** of investment returns. This number, measured in percentage terms, is calculated as the square root of the variance of the annual rate of return on investment. The formula for standard deviation is written

$$\text{Standard Deviation} = \sqrt{\frac{\sum_{t=0}^{N} (\text{Return}_t - \text{Average Return})^2}{N}} \tag{5.4}$$

The explanation for this somewhat complicated formula is actually simple. Volatility results from both upward and downward price movements. One avoids the problem of plus and minus deviations canceling each other out, and thus understating risk, by squaring the deviation from average returns and then taking the square root of that difference.

Students never have to go through the laborious process of calculating the standard deviation of annual returns by hand. Such calculations are easily made with statistical or spreadsheet software, such as Microsoft Excel. To illustrate, look at Table 5.3 once again. Notice that the standard deviation of annual returns on common stocks is 16.45%, higher than the standard deviation of 10.70% for long-term Treasury bonds. This means that stocks are riskier than bonds. Also, notice how the standard deviation for both common stocks and Treasury bonds is much higher than the 3.09% standard deviation for short-term Treasury bills. Both stocks and Treasury bonds are much riskier than Treasury bills.

coefficient of variation A common risk/reward measure.

Whereas the standard deviation is an absolute measure of risk, the **coefficient of variation** is a useful *relative* measure of the risk/reward relationship. The formula for the coefficient of variation is simply standard deviation divided by expected return:

$$\text{Coefficient of Variation} = \frac{\text{Standard Deviation}}{\text{Average Return}} \tag{5.5}$$

Think of the coefficient of variation as a risk/reward ratio. When using the coefficient of variation measure of relative risk, it is important to recognize that this measure depends on the arithmetic average.

As shown in Table 5.3, the coefficient of variation, or risk/reward ratio, for common stock is 1.11 (= 16.45%/14.84%). This means that when it comes to common stock investing, the "cost" of each percentage point of expected return is 1.11% in standard deviation (or risk). For Treasury bonds, the "cost" of each percentage point of expected return is 1.76% in standard deviation (or risk). Even though stocks are riskier than bonds because they have a higher standard deviation of annual returns, they involve a somewhat better risk/reward trade-off. Since 1950, stock investors have enjoyed a lower amount of risk for each percentage point of expected return than the risk/reward trade-off for Treasury bond investors.

Also notice from Table 5.3 that Treasury bills offer a very low risk/reward trade-off of only 0.76. This means that the "cost" of each percentage point of expected return is only 0.76% in standard deviation (or risk) for Treasury bill investors. However, it is worth pointing out that the very low risk associated with Treasury bill investing has a cost in terms of expected return. Before taxes, Treasury bill investors earn only a meager premium, at best, over the inflation rate.

Another risk concept is called return comovement. It measures the extent to which returns move up or down together. **Covariance** is an absolute measure of comovement that varies between plus and minus infinity, $-\infty$ and $+\infty$,

covariance An absolute measure of comovement that varies between plus and minus infinity, $-\infty$ and $+\infty$.

$$\text{Covariance}_{ij} = \frac{\sum_{t=0}^{N} (\text{Return}_{it} - \text{Avg. Ret.}_{i}) \times (\text{Return}_{jt} - \text{Avg. Ret.}_{j})}{N} \quad \textbf{(5.6)}$$

where i and j are different individual securities or indexes. Related to covariance is the statistical concept of correlation. **Correlation** is a relative measure of comovement that varies between -1 and $+1$:

correlation A relative measure of comovement that varies between -1 and $+1$.

$$\text{Correlation}_{ij} = \frac{\text{Covariance}_{ij}}{\text{Std. Dev.}_{i} \times \text{Std. Dev.}_{j}} \quad \textbf{(5.7)}$$

Again, i and j are different individual securities or indexes.

Table 5.5 illustrates the correlations in total returns for common stocks, Treasury bonds, Treasury bills, and inflation from 1950 to the present. In terms of correlation, a value of -1 means that returns from two asset classes are perfectly

TABLE 5.5 Correlations in Total Returns for Stocks, Bonds, Bills, and Inflation, 1950–2000

	Stocks	Bonds	Bills	Inflation
Stocks	100.00%			
Bonds	20.99%	100.00%		
Bills	−11.13%	33.50%	100.00%	
Inflation	−29.97%	−16.88%	63.12%	100.00%

Data source: Federal Reserve.

inversely correlated. In that case, a positive return of 10% in one asset class would correspond with a negative return of −10% in some other asset class. A correlation value of +1 means that returns from two different asset classes are perfectly in sync. They move in lock-step fashion up and down together. Investors seeking diversification look for investments that have high expected returns that tend to be inversely correlated.

Notice from Table 5.5 that the correlation in annual returns on common stocks and the inflation rate is −29.97%. This means that an uptick in inflation is accompanied by a downturn in stock prices. Of course, the reason behind this inverse relation between stock returns and the inflation rate is that an uptick in inflation causes short-term interest rates to rise. The positive association between inflation and short-term interest rates is reflected in the positive 63.12% correlation between the inflation rate and interest rates on short-term Treasury bills. In Table 5.5, it is also interesting to note that both stock and Treasury bond investors benefit from a downturn in the rate of inflation. This stems from the fact that when interest rates fall, the present value of future dividends and interest payments tends to rise.

Finally, some individual investors find it tedious to calculate conventional risk indicators. In practice, investors sometimes measure the risk of individual securities by contemplating the high/low range in stock prices over a 52-week period. For example, a stock priced at $40 with a 52-week high of $60 and a low of $30 is obviously more volatile than one priced at $40 with a high of $45 and a low of $35. In most circumstances, the ratio of 52-week high/low stock prices is both easy to calculate and a useful method of risk measurement.

Holding Period Returns

Although common stocks have consistently provided the highest average annual rate of return to long-term investors, it is important to keep in mind that this average involves a substantial amount of year-to-year variation. Similarly, the typically lower rates of return earned on bonds and money market instruments involve a meaningful amount of return volatility. Remember from Table 5.3, the standard deviation of annual returns on common stocks is 16.45%, 10.70% on long-term Treasury bonds, 2.69% on Treasury bills, and 3.11% for the rate of inflation. It is a simple fact that investing in common stocks and long-term bonds involves substantial variation in the year-to-year rate of return.

The simplest means available to long-term investors for "smoothing out" the effects of year-to-year volatility in the rates of return on common stocks and long-term bonds is for them to simply adopt an extended **investment horizon,** or holding period, as shown in Table 5.6.

investment horizon
Holding period.

You may have noticed in Tables 5.2 and 5.3 that rates of return on stocks and long-term Treasury bonds have been relatively high during recent years. Total returns on common stocks, in particular, have been at historic highs. This fact is demonstrated in Table 5.6, which shows compound annual rates of returns on stocks, bonds, and money market instruments for holding periods of five, 10, and 20 years in length. During the five-year period ended December 31, 1999, for example, the S&P 500 returned an average 28.55% per year. This is the best five-year period for common stock investing since 1950. During the 10-year period ended December 31, 1999, the S&P 500 returned an average 18.20% per year. This is the second-best decade for common stock investing since 1950. Stock investors earned 17.87% per year during the 20-year period ending in 1999. This is the best 20-year period since 1950—in fact, it's the best 20-year period this century!

During recent years, stocks have easily outperformed long-term Treasury bonds, money market instruments such as Treasury bills, and the rate of inflation. In interpreting this comparison, one must be aware that stock dividend yields have moved significantly lower during recent years than during prior periods. Recall from Table 5.2 that current dividend yields are now much lower than typical, and P/E ratios today are much higher than average. This means that stock prices have risen so swiftly during the 1980s and 1990s that the rate of stock price appreciation has outstripped both earnings and dividend growth. Future rates of return for stock market investors are apt to trend lower toward long-term averages.

As shown in Table 5.6, the best way of protecting against a sharp downward correction in stock prices is to maintain a broadly diversified portfolio of common stocks for an extended period of time. Since 1950, negative returns have been earned by common stock investors during only two of 44 rolling five-year periods. Over this same period, positive returns have been earned during each rolling 10-year and 20-year period. Just as important, it is worth noting that the coefficient of variation, or risk-reward ratio, for stock market and bond investors tends to improve the longer the investment horizon. There is no way to eliminate investment risk in any given period without also eliminating the potential for profits higher than the risk-free returns earned by Treasury bill investors. However, over the long run, investors in stock and long-term bonds can mitigate risk by sustaining their investments for an extended period of time.

The basic point made in Tables 5.4 and 5.6 is simple but important. All investments carry an element of risk. Notice that each line depicting cumulative investment returns has some variability and that the amount of year-to-year variability is greatest in the case of common stocks. However, over extended time horizons, year-to-year variability and the standard deviation of annual returns may be less than a fully satisfactory measure of risk. Over an extended time frame of 20 years, for example, it may become more relevant to compare the distribution of stock returns with the distribution of bond returns to infer the probability of outperforming bonds with stocks or the chance of overcoming the effects of inflation with a broadly diversified portfolio of common stocks. In Table 5.6, it is easy to see that over an extended time horizon, there is an extraordinarily high probability of outperforming bonds with stocks. Similarly, there is a very high probability that stocks will provide a more satisfactory hedge against inflation than that provided by bond investments.

Based on the evidence, it seems fair to conclude that over long investment horizons of five, 10, or 20 years, stocks offer the highest positive returns after taxes and after inflation. Next best are long-term bonds, but they break even (at best) after taxes and inflation. In the long run, short-term Treasury bills and money market instruments deplete capital. Over significant investment horizons, the probability is extremely small of beating stock returns with a portfolio that includes a meaningful proportion of long-term bonds. Over significant investment horizons, the probability of beating stock returns with money market instruments is nil. When planning for retirement, stocks beat bonds.

TABLE 5.6 Total Returns on Common Stocks and Government Bonds for Overlapping Holding Periods of Five, 10, and 20 Years, 1950–99

	Common Stocks			Long-Term Treasury Bonds		
Terminal Year	**5 Years**	**10 Years**	**20 Years**	**5 Years**	**10 Years**	**20 Years**
1950						
1951						
1952						
1953						
1954	23.92%			1.56%		
1955	23.89%			1.28%		
1956	20.18%			0.93%		
1957	13.58%			2.16%		
1958	22.30%			0.16%		
1959	14.96%	19.35%		−1.67%	−0.07%	
1960	8.92%	16.16%		1.16%	1.22%	
1961	12.79%	16.43%		2.53%	1.73%	
1962	13.31%	13.14%		2.42%	2.29%	
1963	9.85%	15.91%		3.97%	2.05%	
1964	10.73%	12.82%		5.17%	1.69%	
1965	13.25%	11.06%		2.63%	1.89%	
1966	5.72%	9.20%		3.17%	2.85%	
1967	12.39%	12.85%		−0.14%	1.13%	
1968	10.16%	10.01%		−0.43%	1.75%	
1969	4.97%	7.81%	13.43%	−2.14%	1.45%	0.69%
1970	3.34%	8.18%	12.10%	−0.02%	1.30%	1.26%
1971	8.42%	7.06%	11.65%	1.77%	2.47%	2.10%
1972	7.53%	9.93%	11.67%	4.90%	2.35%	2.32%
1973	2.01%	6.01%	10.85%	4.72%	2.11%	2.08%
1974	−2.35%	1.24%	6.87%	6.72%	2.20%	1.94%
1975	3.21%	3.27%	7.10%	6.16%	3.03%	2.46%
1976	4.87%	6.63%	7.91%	6.81%	4.26%	3.55%
1977	−0.21%	3.59%	8.12%	5.49%	5.20%	3.15%
1978	4.32%	3.16%	6.53%	5.48%	5.10%	3.41%
1979	14.76%	5.86%	6.83%	4.33%	5.52%	3.46%
1980	13.95%	8.44%	8.31%	1.68%	3.90%	2.59%
1981	8.08%	6.47%	6.76%	−1.06%	2.80%	2.64%
1982	14.05%	6.68%	8.30%	6.03%	5.76%	4.04%
1983	17.27%	10.61%	8.28%	6.42%	5.95%	4.01%
1984	14.76%	14.76%	7.79%	9.80%	7.03%	4.59%
1985	14.71%	14.33%	8.66%	16.83%	8.99%	5.97%
1986	19.87%	13.82%	10.17%	21.62%	9.70%	6.94%
1987	16.49%	15.26%	9.27%	13.02%	9.47%	7.31%
1988	15.38%	16.33%	9.55%	14.98%	10.62%	7.82%
1989	20.40%	17.55%	11.55%	15.50%	12.61%	9.01%
1990	13.14%	13.93%	11.15%	10.75%	13.75%	8.71%
1991	15.36%	17.59%	11.89%	9.81%	15.56%	9.00%
1992	15.89%	16.19%	11.33%	12.13%	12.58%	9.12%
1993	14.51%	14.94%	12.76%	13.83%	14.41%	10.10%
1994	8.69%	14.40%	14.58%	8.34%	11.86%	9.42%
1995	16.57%	14.84%	14.59%	13.10%	11.92%	10.45%
1996	15.20%	15.28%	14.55%	8.98%	9.39%	9.54%
1997	20.24%	18.05%	16.65%	10.51%	11.32%	10.39%
1998	24.06%	19.18%	17.75%	9.61%	11.70%	11.16%
1999	28.55%	18.20%	17.87%	9.38%	8.86%	10.72%
Arithmetic average	**12.91%**	**11.87%**	**10.80%**	**6.10%**	**6.09%**	**5.80%**
Median	**13.76%**	**13.44%**	**10.85%**	**5.32%**	**5.10%**	**4.59%**
Geometric mean	**12.71%**	**11.76%**	**10.75%**	**5.96%**	**6.00%**	**5.75%**
Standard deviation	**6.74%**	**4.91%**	**3.23%**	**5.45%**	**4.52%**	**3.37%**
Coefficient of variation	**0.52**	**0.41**	**0.30**	**0.89**	**0.74**	**0.58**

Data source: Federal Reserve.

TABLE 5.6 *(continued)*

Short-Term Treasury Bills			Inflation Rate		
5 Years	10 Years	20 Years	5 Years	10 Years	20 Years
1.41%			2.50%		
1.48%			1.42%		
1.67%			0.84%		
1.97%			1.26%		
1.91%			1.49%		
2.33%	1.87%		1.90%	2.20%	
2.55%	2.01%		2.12%	1.77%	
2.48%	2.08%		1.68%	1.26%	
2.40%	2.18%		1.33%	1.29%	
2.72%	2.31%		1.30%	1.40%	
2.83%	2.58%		1.24%	1.57%	
3.09%	2.82%		1.33%	1.72%	
3.61%	3.05%		1.86%	1.77%	
3.91%	3.15%		2.23%	1.77%	
4.33%	3.52%		2.84%	2.07%	
4.93%	3.88%	2.87%	3.82%	2.52%	2.36%
5.45%	4.26%	3.13%	4.54%	2.92%	2.34%
5.38%	4.49%	3.28%	4.54%	3.19%	2.22%
5.30%	4.60%	3.39%	4.61%	3.41%	2.35%
5.64%	4.98%	3.64%	5.41%	4.12%	2.75%
5.92%	5.43%	4.00%	6.60%	5.20%	3.37%
5.78%	5.62%	4.21%	6.90%	5.71%	3.70%
5.92%	5.65%	4.34%	7.20%	5.86%	3.80%
6.18%	5.74%	4.44%	7.89%	6.24%	3.98%
6.23%	5.94%	4.72%	7.94%	6.67%	4.34%
6.69%	6.31%	5.09%	8.15%	7.37%	4.92%
7.77%	6.77%	5.51%	9.22%	8.05%	5.46%
9.68%	7.78%	6.12%	10.06%	8.62%	5.87%
10.78%	8.46%	6.51%	9.46%	8.67%	6.01%
11.12%	8.65%	6.80%	8.39%	8.16%	6.12%
11.01%	8.83%	7.12%	6.54%	7.34%	6.26%
10.30%	9.03%	7.31%	4.85%	7.01%	6.36%
8.60%	9.14%	7.38%	3.30%	6.63%	6.24%
7.59%	9.17%	7.44%	3.41%	6.39%	6.31%
7.10%	9.09%	7.50%	3.53%	5.93%	6.30%
6.81%	8.89%	7.59%	3.67%	5.09%	6.22%
6.83%	8.55%	7.66%	4.13%	4.49%	6.26%
6.71%	7.65%	7.72%	4.53%	3.91%	6.24%
6.31%	6.95%	7.70%	4.22%	3.81%	6.21%
5.62%	6.35%	7.49%	3.89%	3.71%	5.91%
4.73%	5.76%	7.29%	3.49%	3.58%	5.44%
4.30%	5.55%	7.28%	2.78%	3.46%	5.22%
4.22%	5.46%	7.28%	2.84%	3.68%	5.14%
4.57%	5.44%	7.29%	2.59%	3.40%	4.89%
5.05%	5.33%	7.20%	2.37%	3.12%	4.52%
5.26%	5.00%	6.92%	2.29%	2.89%	3.98%
5.36%	5.62%	6.01%	4.10%	4.34%	4.87%
5.34%	5.55%	6.92%	3.51%	3.71%	5.22%
5.33%	5.59%	5.99%	4.07%	4.32%	4.89%
2.57%	2.28%	1.66%	2.52%	2.23%	1.41%
0.48	0.41	0.28	0.62	0.51	0.29

WALL STREET WISDOM 5.3

Excessive Risk Taking at Loews?

Bearish and stubborn can be painful traits when stock prices are rising fast in a bull market. Consider the case of Laurence A. Tisch, chairman and CEO of Loews Corp., who was stubbornly bearish about the stock market during its meteoric rise of the late 1990s. Tisch's failed bet that the market would fall cost Loews a whopping $917.7 million. The first quarter of 1998 was even worse, when trading losses of $533.4 million wiped out the company's quarterly earnings. After losing close to $1.5 billion betting against a raging bull market, you might think that Tisch would pull in his claws. No way. If anything, Loews's bets against the market kept getting bigger, not smaller. In a filing with the Securities and Exchange Commission dated March 31, 1998, Loews stated: "The company continues to maintain these positions and has experienced additional significant losses."

How things got so crazy is worth looking into, but first here is a little background. Bear is a Wall Street metaphor for someone who believes that stocks are ready to fall or go into hibernation like a bear does during winter. Bull is a Wall Street metaphor for someone who believes that stocks are ready to rise or charge ahead like a mad bull. If someone is bullish, they buy stocks in the hope of profiting from a rise in prices. If someone is bearish, it is a bit trickier, but there is a way of profiting from a decline in stock prices. It is called short selling. What you do is instruct your broker to go out and borrow (not buy) stock in a company that you regard as overpriced. Then, you sell the shares and deposit the cash in a money market account. If the stock price goes down, you can buy back the borrowed shares at a lower price, return the borrowed shares to the lender, and pocket the difference. Short sellers lose when stock prices rise, and the "sky is the limit" in terms of potential losses.

Why would Tisch make such an outlandish bet against the market? Is he a reckless risk taker? Maybe, maybe not. Loews is a holding company, or conglomerate. Its $20 billion in revenues comes from an 84% stake in CNA Insurance, 50% stake in Diamond Offshore Drilling, 98% of Bulova Watch, and 100% of Loews hotels and Lorillard Tobacco. Tisch is personally responsible for assembling this "portfolio" of operating companies; he has a well-deserved reputation as a street-smart buyer. In the case of Diamond Offshore, for example, Tisch started buying offshore drilling rigs and oil tankers during the late 1980s when they sold for little more than scrap value. Today, Loews' stake in Diamond Offshore is worth roughly $3.5 billion. Similarly, in 1994 Tisch bought bonds heavily for the CNA portfolio. When interest rates fell and bond prices rose, CNA and Loews cleaned up.

Tisch and his family own more than 36% of Loews, worth $1.8 billion. As such, no one can attribute Tisch's market bet to an "other people's money" problem at Loews. In all fairness to Tisch, it must also be pointed out that the market value of Loews's publicly traded equity investments rose smartly during the period in which Tisch lost more than a billion dollars shorting the overall market. Although Tisch's hedging strategy has not paid off yet, Loews is still far better off than it would have been had Tisch simply sold Loews's equity investments.

When asked about his bearish view of the market, Tisch argues that he is not trying to hit a home run, he simply wants to maintain Loews's sound financial footing. By early 2000, Loews stock had fallen to the mid-40s, off more than 50% from an all-time high of 110 in 1997. Check it out. Look up Loews (LTR) on the NYSE in today's edition of *The Wall Street Journal*. Is the stock price up or down from when Tisch dug in his heels, ignored the critics, and went into deep hibernation?

See: Andrew Bary, "Sector Rotation Turns Off Tech Types," *Barron's*, April 3, 2000, MW3.

Sources of Volatility

Company Risk

For a long-term investor seeking maximum potential rewards, stocks would seem to be the most attractive asset class. However, for most investors, investment return is only half of the equation that needs to be considered when creating an investment portfolio. Although stocks and bonds offer higher expected returns than money market instruments, they also involve greater volatility. Such volatility has the potential to undermine the potential of long-term investments, especially when investors are scared out of or forced out of equity investments during sometimes vicious bear markets. Finding an appropriate risk/reward trade-off is key.

By owning individual stocks and bonds, the investor is exposed to **firm-specific risk,** or the chance that problems with an individual company will reduce the value of investment dramatically. Such specific risk can be eliminated through diversification by using mutual funds. Broad diversification across several stocks and bonds greatly diminishes the adverse impact associated with an unfavorable outcome following investment in any single stock or bond. Diversified mutual funds are a convenient and low-cost way for investors to avoid firm-specific risk. Studies in financial economics show that firm-specific factors such as the quality of management, operating and financial leverage, and changes in product quality are responsible for slightly less than one-half of the total volatility in company stock returns. Slightly more than one-half of the volatility in common stock prices can be traced to factors beyond the immediate control of the firm.

firm-specific risk Chance that problems with an individual company will reduce the value of investment.

Changes in the overall economic environment cause roughly one-third of the volatility in common stock returns. Unanticipated changes in the growth in aggregate economic activity, as measured by Gross Domestic Product, changes in interest rates, or fluctuation in the value of the dollar all cause stock market volatility. Such changes affect companies in different ways. For example, highly leveraged companies are apt to be more affected by an unanticipated rise in interest rates than companies that do not use financial leverage. Nevertheless, such a rise in interest rates reduces the present value of future profits and typically reduces stock prices for both leveraged and unleveraged companies.

Sector-related factors that affect cyclical companies, so-called value or growth stocks, or emerging growth companies account for roughly 15% of stock price volatility. For example, a cut in the capital gains tax rate would tend to favor growth companies with stock prices that rise at above-average rates. By contrast, a cut in the amount of tax paid on dividend income would tend to favor value stocks that pay above-average dividends.

Industry-related factors are also important. Surprising variation in the level of competition provided by domestic and foreign competitors, changes in the method or scope of regulation, or fluctuations in the cost of inputs and raw materials are all important. Such factors cause roughly 10% of stock price volatility. It is crucial for investors to remember that although company fortunes rise or fall based on the success of management's efforts, such success is not fully within the control of company management.

Table 5.7 gives perspective on common stock risk. Panel A shows stock market winners over a given 52-week period. In a period of generally rising prices, it is typically easy to find several dozen of the roughly 25,000 publicly traded companies that have risen by truly astounding amounts. One-year returns of 200%, 300%, or 500% are sometimes observed. In retrospect, the reasons behind such outstanding returns seem obvious. In prospect, only a few companies with exciting stock market potential deliver as promised. At the same time, as shown in panel B, it is common to find dozens of individual high-quality or "blue-chip" companies that have fallen by 30%, 40%, 50%, or more. Among smaller companies, losses of 90% and

TABLE 5.7 **Risk and Return Characteristics of Individual Common Stocks**

In any given 52-week period, a handful of companies soar to impressive heights. At the same time, several high-quality blue-chip stocks suffer withering losses. Among smaller companies, devastating losses are routinely experienced.

A. Stock Market Winners			**retlyr (%)**	**Last**	**52-Wk Hi**	**52-Wk Lo**
XCELERA.COM INC	C	XLA	28385.80	190.00	215.00	0.67
CURAGEN CORP	C	CRGN	3260.00	231.00	232.13	5.00
NETOPTIX CORP	C	OPTX	2900.00	165.00	166.88	3.75
MEDAREX INC	C	MEDX	2855.60	99.75	115.38	2.88
HYSEO INC	C	HYSQ	2609.90	120.25	123.00	2.50
PUMA TECHNOLOGY INC	C	PUMA	2316.00	113.25	142.50	3.75
CALIFORNIA AMPLIFIER INC	C	CAMP	2306.90	43.63	45.00	1.69
ZI CORP	C	ZICA	2089.40	39.00	40.88	0.81
TRIQUINT SEMICONDUCTOR	C	TQNT	1956.00	227.13	261.00	10.34
ORTEL CORP	C	ORTL	1913.70	161.09	189.50	6.00
CLARUS CORP	C	CLRS	1788.90	85.00	98.00	3.50
INTERLEAF INC	C	LEAF	1705.60	60.94	63.50	2.75
ABGENIX INC	C	ABGX	1659.40	281.50	282.50	12.75
ION NETWORKS INC	C	IONN	1597.10	37.13	42.63	2.00
DIGITAL LIGHTWAVE INC	C	DIGL	1555.70	63.13	75.00	2.50
B. Blue Chip Laggards						
SEABOARD CORP	C	SEB	−56.40	158.00	380.06	155.00
PROGRESSIVE CORP	C	PGR	−54.90	57.69	152.13	51.75
NACCO INDUSTRIES INC A	C	NC	−45.10	47.69	93.50	44.50
AETNA INC	C	AET	−44.50	40.31	99.88	38.56
CINTAS CORP	C	CTAS	−42.30	40.56	73.50	38.25
PACIFICARE HLT SYS B NEW	C	PHSY	−40.40	43.06	100.38	31.13
CARDINAL HEALTH INC	C	CAH	−38.00	44.69	77.88	37.00
COMERICA INC	C	CMA	−37.80	39.75	70.00	39.44
CENTURA BANDS INC	C	CBC	−37.60	39.00	69.25	38.63
LOEWS CORP	C	LTR	−36.80	48.44	84.19	48.25
BRITISH AIRWAYS PLC ADR	C	BAB	−36.30	44.00	88.50	42.25
MARKETWATCH.COM INC	C	MKTW	−36.20	42.13	107.00	26.13
UNILEVER N.V.	C	UN	−35.90	45.19	79.38	40.56
HARTFORD LIFE INC	C	HLI	−35.70	37.00	59.00	31.00
LILLY, ELI & CO	C	LLY	−35.30	60.19	97.75	60.19
C. Small-Cap Laggards						
T&W FINANCIAL CORP	C	TWFC	−93.20	0.81	14.50	0.38
CAREMATRIX CORP	C	CMDC	−93.00	1.56	23.00	1.50
EXCELSIOR-HENDERSON MTR	C	BIGXQ	−92.40	0.72	10.00	0.66
JUST FOR FEET INC	C	FEETQ	−91.70	1.25	18.38	1.19
COYOTE SPORTS INC	C	COYT	−89.00	0.34	4.50	0.25
UNITED ROAD SERVICES INC	C	URSI	−88.60	1.88	18.88	1.00
DAY RUNNER INC	C	DAYR	−88.10	1.63	13.94	1.22
NCS HEALTHCARE INC CL A	C	NCSS	−87.40	1.78	15.50	1.44
FRUIT OF THE LOOM LTD	C	FTL	−86.20	1.75	13.88	0.56
AMRESCO INC	C	AMMB	−85.80	1.34	10.56	1.00
PHARMAPRINT INC	C	PPRT	−85.10	1.81	12.63	0.88
CHS ELECTRONICS INC	C	HS	−84.80	1.06	12.00	0.44
BELMONT BANCORP	C	BLMT	−84.30	2.94	19.50	2.63
PATHWAYS GROUP INC	C	PTHW	−84.20	2.34	15.25	0.88
CENTRAL EUROPEAN MEDIA	C	CETV	−84.10	11.75	114.00	5.38

Data source: <http://www.dailystocks.com>.
Note: All data are as of 2/17/00.

more, virtual wipeouts, are encountered with disturbing frequency. Remember, a loss of 50% is only offset by a subsequent 100% return. It is virtually impossible to recover from a loss of 90% and more. Individual investors should keep this in mind when tempted to invest a large part of their portfolio in the stock of new, small, or untested companies.

Stock Market Volatility

Although diversification reduces the risk of loss from a single investment, there remains **market risk** tied to the chance that the overall stock or bond markets will decline in value. The overall stock market is influenced by actual and anticipated changes in the economic growth, the pace of inflation, interest rates, and so on. The most severe bear market since World War II occurred in 1973–74. During those two years, it was common for even broadly diversified portfolios of common stocks to decline by as much as 35–50%. At such times, stock and bond investors must remember that time has a moderating effect on market risk. The longer an investor holds a broadly diversified portfolio of stock or bond investments, the lower is the chance of losing money and the greater are the odds of earning a return close to the long-term average.

market risk General fluctuation in stock and bond prices.

The overall stock market fluctuates from day to day and year to year with changes in the business climate and investor perceptions. In the short run, stock returns are volatile because they are driven by changing investor expectations manifested in hope and fear. Long-run returns on equity investments are determined by fundamental economic factors such as dividend yield and the rate of growth in dividends and earnings. Thus, although common stocks have considerable price volatility in the short term, the element of time tends to even out such price swings and make such volatility more tolerable for long-term investors. For investors thinking about truly long-term goals such as providing for a retirement income, bond and money-market investments have little day-to-day price volatility but little chance of keeping pace with inflation, especially after taxes are considered.

Most investors are aware that the widely followed stock market averages, such as the DJIA or the S&P 500, can routinely vary by 1%, 2%, or even 3% in a single day. For example, the percentage of trading days on which the DJIA rose or fell 1% rose above 30% in 1998. What makes this an ominous increase in volatility is that it takes place in a period when investors have very high expectations concerning the future.

The most popular measure of investor expectations and market valuation risk is given by P/E ratios. High P/E ratios usually signify high risk, and low P/E ratios typically signal low valuation risk. However, P/E ratios for the DJIA, as shown in Table 5.2, can be distorted during recessions when massive write-offs at even a single DJIA component can cause index earnings to collapse and the DJIA P/E ratio to soar. In 1981, for example, the DJIA P/E ratio soared to 114.4 because of a collapse in earnings caused by massive write-offs following a deep recession. Similar peaks of 64.3 times earnings in 1991 and 47.3 times earnings in 1933 were caused by significant earnings shortfalls at a few DJIA companies. To get a clear picture of conventional DJIA P/E ratios during typical operating conditions, it is necessary to control for periods of dramatic earnings shortfalls. Figure 5.3 illustrates the actual DJIA P/E ratio data from Table 5.2, after index earnings have

FIGURE 5.3 **The DJIA Is at All-Time Highs Compared with Earnings, Book Values, and Dividends**

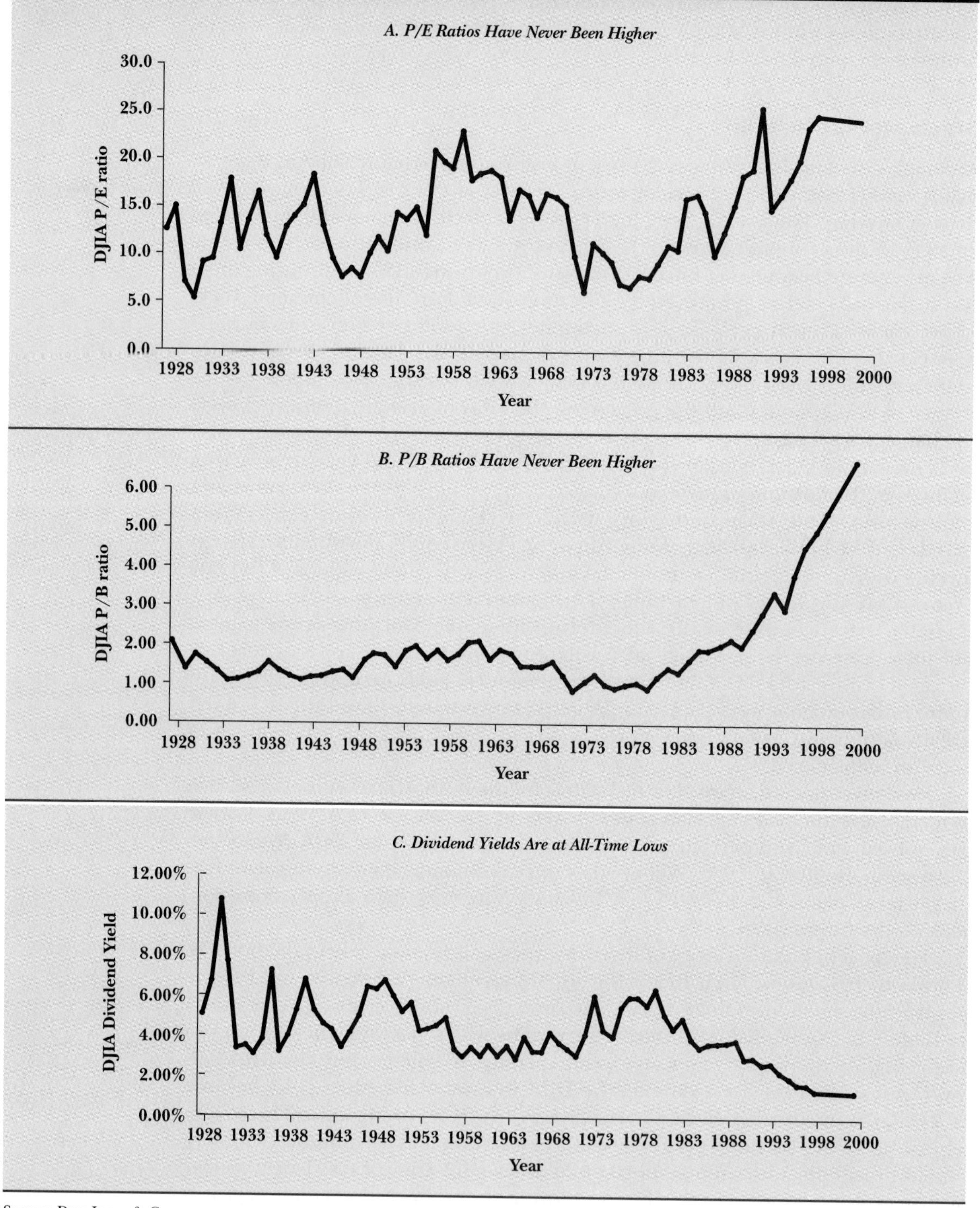

Source: Dow Jones & Company.

been normalized for three brief periods (1931–35, 1982–83, 1991–92) when index earnings plummeted by 50% or more in a single year. In those three instances, actual prior-year earnings were used instead of depressed current-year earnings.

After adjustment, it is easy to see in Figure 5.3, panel A, that P/E ratios for the DJIA almost always fall within a band from 10:1 and 20:1. At the start of 2000, a 24.8:1 P/E ratio for the DJIA is roughly twice the long-term median of 13.6:1 and among the highest on record. What makes an elevated P/E ratio for the DJIA at the start of the new millennium worrisome is that further rapid surges in earnings are unlikely. Corporate earnings performance was fantastic during the late 1990s, and further gains will be extremely difficult. Coming out of recession, a sharp rebound in earnings is typical. Coming on top of an already robust economic expansion, further earnings gains will be tough to come by.

Another popular measure of investor expectations and market valuation risk is given by price-book (P/B) ratios. High P/B ratios usually signify high risk, and low P/B ratios typically signal low valuation risk. Unlike P/E ratios, P/B ratios do not tend to be distorted by economic recessions. Until recently, P/B ratios for the DJIA almost always fell within a band from 1:1 and 2:1 (see Figure 5.3, panel B). At the start of 2000, a 6.8:1 P/B ratio for the DJIA is roughly four times the long-term median of 1.5:1, and the highest on record. As in the case of elevated P/E ratios, an elevated P/B ratio for the DJIA at the start of the new millennium is worrisome in that further rapid surges in earnings seem unlikely.

A similar picture of high investor expectations and high valuation risk in the market is given when one considers dividend yield information, as shown in Figure 5.3, panel C. High dividend yields reflect investor caution and concern about future business prospects. Low dividend yields reflect investor optimism and enthusiasm for future business prospects. Historically, investment returns have been best when investors have bought stocks during periods of high dividend yields and sold stocks during period of low dividend yields. Hence, the time-tested admonition to "buy fear, sell greed." As we begin the new millennium, dividend yields on common stocks are far below the long-term median of 4.37%, and the lowest on record.

Although some contend that dividends are unimportant for growth-stock investors, it is worth remembering that roughly 40% of the total return earned by common stock investors comes in the form of dividend income (see Table 5.2). Over the long run, dividends matter. Some may explain away the importance of the recent decline in dividend income by contending that because dividends are taxed as regular income, tax-savvy companies tend to announce share repurchases in lieu of dividend increases. To be sure, shareholder-friendly corporations are making increased use of share repurchases as an efficient means for returning excess cash flow to shareholders. At the same time, however, many companies are issuing a record number of shares tied to executive and employee stock-option incentive plans. Because the scope of share repurchases is roughly offset by the pace of new share issuance, the recent decline in dividend income represents a real decline in the amount of cash payments received by shareholders.

Given historically high P/E ratios and historic lows for dividend yields, common stock investors face a significant amount of **valuation risk** at the turn of the century. More than investor psychology and the "greed/fear" factor is at work. The economics of supply and demand also enters the picture. When companies are able to earn above-normal rates of return on investment, expansion occurs until the point when subsequent investment in plant and equipment is able to earn only

valuation risk
Chance of loss due to relatively high stock prices.

a risk-adjusted normal rate of return. In the stock market, investor returns fall when the rate of profit growth enjoyed by companies begins to falter. Additional supply-demand considerations are also at work. The veritable flood of initial public offerings for "anything.com" that occurred in 1998–99 points out how happy Wall Street is to supply the stock-buying demands of eager investors. A rising tide of new Internet companies creates competition for winning investment ideas. It also causes competition for Internet investor dollars.

Robust periods of economic expansion are typically accompanied by rising stock prices and growing investor enthusiasm. Such robust periods often give way to subsequent periods of more tepid economic growth (or recession) and relatively lackluster market environments. Conversely, periods of anemic economic growth are typically accompanied by stagnant or falling stock prices and deepening investor pessimism. Such lackluster periods often give way to subsequent periods of more rapid economic growth and typically bullish market environments. This process, often described as **reversion to the mean,** is an inherent characteristic of economic and stock market environments.

reversion to the mean
Tendency of stock and bond returns to return toward long-term averages.

Based on economic history, it is fair to project that stock market returns in the United States over the next decade are not apt to match those of the 1990s. Increasing volatility and high expectations are often a troubling mix, as investors learned in 1987. Some long-term investors recall that on October 19, 1987, the DJIA dropped a heart-stopping 508 points, or 23%. Similarly, the fact that the DJIA fell 512.61 points, or 6.4%, on August 31, 1998, still haunts some long-term investors. However, the long bear market of 1973–74 erased enormous amounts of shareholder wealth with a slow but steady decline. A similarly extended period of negative stock market performance would be devastating to U.S. investors. In fact, slow bear markets can be even more devastating to investors than crashes followed by quick recoveries. (If you are going to have your arm cut off, it is no favor to have it done one inch at a time.) Looking forward, U.S. investors may want to consider the advantage of international diversification, and the potential advantages of investing in Japan and Asian markets, which have vastly underperformed the U.S. market during the 1990s (see Chapter 16).

Bond Market Risk

Like the stock market, the bond market is also influenced by economic expectations. Credit problems tend to be more severe during economic downturns, whereas rapid economic growth boosts the demand for credit. During economic expansions, surges in the demand for credit to finance new plant and equipment cause higher interest rates and adversely affect the value of outstanding bonds.

Although the bond market is typically less scary than the stock market, there have been times when some bonds were just as risky as stocks. As seen in Table 5.3, bond market volatility can be significant. Bonds are linked to prevailing interest rates in the economy. As interest rates rise, bond prices fall. When rates fall, bond prices rise. The price volatility of a bond depends on its maturity. The longer the maturity of a bond, the greater its sensitivity to interest rates. Short-term bonds that mature in two to five years are the least risky. Intermediate-term bonds with maturities of five to 10 years experience somewhat greater price fluctuations. Long-term bonds with maturities of more than 10 years expose investors to the most substantial price swings.

TABLE 5.8 **An Illustration of Interest-Rate Risk for a 6% Bond Selling at Par of $1,000**

Bond Type	Term to Maturity (years)	Decline in bond value following an increase in rates			Rise in bond value following a decrease in rates		
		+1	+2%	+3%	−1%	−2%	−3%
Treasury bill (Money-market)	6 months	0%	0%	0%	0%	0%	0%
Treasury note	2	−1.84%	−3.63%	−5.38%	1.88%	3.81%	5.78%
Treasury note	5	−4.16%	−8.11%	−11.87%	4.38%	8.98%	13.83%
Treasury bond	10	−7.11%	−13.59%	−19.51%	7.79%	16.35%	25.75%
Treasury bond	20	−10.68%	−19.79%	−27.60%	12.55%	27.36%	44.87%
Treasury bond	30	−12.47%	−22.62%	−30.96%	15.45%	34.76%	59.07%

Table 5.8 shows an indication of the potential impact on bond investors in the event of an increase or decline in interest rates of between 1% and 3%. **Interest rate risk** is the chance of loss in the value of fixed-income investments following a rise in interest rates. Notice how rapid increases in prevailing interest rates can have a devastating effect on the value of long-term Treasury bonds. A steep 3% rise in long-term interest rates will cause a sharp −30.96% change in the value of a 30-year Treasury bond. Smaller, but meaningful, changes of −19.51% and −5.38% in principal value would be noted in the cases of 10-year Treasury bonds and 5-year Treasury notes, respectively. Similarly impressive changes in bond values follow declines in interest rates. A 3% plunge in long-term interest rates will cause a stunning 59.07% rise in the value of a 30-year Treasury bond. Smaller but meaningful jumps of 25.75% and 5.78% in principal value would be noted in the cases of 10-year Treasury bonds and 5-year Treasury notes, respectively. Of course, interest rate changes on the order of −3% are huge and not typically seen within a short period of time. However, as illustrated in Tables 5.3 and 5.6, such changes in interest rates have occurred since 1950 over periods of as short as one to three years. Long-term bonds are more risky than many investors realize.

interest rate risk Chance of loss in the value of fixed-income investments following a rise in interest rates.

In addition to interest rate risk, bond investors are also subject to **credit risk.** Credit risk is the chance that an individual issuer of a bond will fail to make timely payments of principal and interest. Low-quality bonds have a greater risk of these types of default and generally offer higher yields to help compensate investors. Government bonds offer the lowest yields but carry the highest credit ratings and have the lowest risk of default. Money market instruments generally provide a stable principal and, therefore, are subject to only minimal credit risk. The effect of credit risk on bond values is studied in detail in Chapter 6.

credit risk Chance of loss due to issuer default.

Summary

- **Saving** is the accumulation of money to meet some short-term goal. **Investing** involves assuming a measured degree of risk in the pursuit of higher rates of return over an extended time period. Neither is without risk. After-tax returns on savings often fail to keep pace with **inflation.** Long-term investing in stocks and bonds has typically resulted in rates of return that significantly outpace inflation, but short-term losses can sometimes be substantial.

- A major class of financial assets is **cash reserves,** or short-term money market instruments. The primary attraction of cash reserves is that they offer modest income with stability of principal. A common use of cash reserves is to buy **Treasury bills,** which are debt obligations of the U.S. Treasury that have maturities of one year or less. **Treasury notes** are debt obligations of the U.S. Treasury that have maturities of more than one year but less than 10 years. **Treasury bonds** are Treasury obligations with maturities of 10 years or more. **Bonds** are an important class of investment assets and include interest-bearing debt obligations issued by corporations, the federal government and its agencies, and state and local governments. A third important type of investment asset is **common stock.** Ownership of common stock gives the owner a proportionate interest in a corporation's profits and dividends or its other distributions.
- The reward for postponing consumption is the **nominal risk-free rate,** which consists of the **risk-free rate of return** plus an amount equal to the expected rate of **inflation.** A second important component of required return is the **required risk premium.** High-risk investments involve a higher-risk premium; low-risk investments involve a lower-risk premium.
- Investors often wrongly focus on **arithmetic average returns** when judging portfolio performance, and the arithmetic average is upward biased. It cannot be used to accurately depict the compound rate of return earned on investment over time. The **geometric mean return** is the appropriate measure of the compound rate of return earned on investment over time. When returns are highly volatile, the **median return,** or "middle" rate of return, is a useful measure of central tendency. **Total return** is measured by the sum of dividends, interest income, and capital gains or capital losses.
- Investors face the ever-present danger that inflation, or a general increase in the cost of living, will reduce the value of any investment. If a particular investment earns a **nominal return** of 6% but the rate of inflation is 4%, the return after inflation, or **real return,** is only 2%.
- A common measure of return volatility is the **standard deviation** of investment returns. This is the square root of the variance of the annual rate of return on investment. The standard deviation is an absolute measure of risk. The **coefficient of variation** is a useful *relative* measure of the risk/reward relationship. The formula for the coefficient of variation is simply the standard deviation divided by expected return. **Covariance** is an absolute measure of comovement that varies between plus and minus infinity, $-\infty$ and $+\infty$. **Correlation** is a relative measure of comovement that varies between -1 and $+1$. The simplest means available for "smoothing out" the effects of year-to-year volatility in rates of return is for investors to adopt an extended **investment horizon,** or holding period.
- By owning individual stocks and bonds, the investor is exposed to **firm-specific risk,** or the chance that problems with an individual company will reduce the value of investment dramatically. Firm-specific risk can be mitigated through diversification. Although diversification reduces the risk of loss from a single investment, there remains **market risk** tied to the chance that the overall stock or bond markets will decline in value. Given historically high P/E ratios and historic lows for dividend yields, common stock investors face a significant amount of **valuation risk** at the turn of the century. Economic expansion is typically ac-

companied by rising stock prices and growing investor enthusiasm. Anemic economic growth is typically accompanied by stagnant or falling stock prices and deepening investor pessimism. This process of fluctuating returns, described as **reversion to the mean,** is an inherent characteristic of economic and stock market environments.

- Like the stock market, the bond market is influenced by economic expectations. **Interest rate risk** is the chance of loss in the value of fixed-income investments following a rise in interest rates. In addition to interest rate risk, bond investors are also subject to **credit risk.** Credit risk is the chance that an individual issuer of a bond will fail to make timely payments of principal and interest.

Questions

1. A broadly diversified portfolio of high-grade (blue chip) stocks could be expected to yield long-term investors an annual rate of return on the order of
   a. 25–30%.
   b. 20–25%.
   c. 15–20%.
   d. 10–15%.
2. The arithmetic average return for a stock with a three-year performance history of +50%, −50%, and +30% is
   a. 30%.
   b. 10%.
   c. −1%.
   d. −10%.
3. The geometric mean return for a stock with a three-year performance history of +100%, −50%, and +95% is
   a. −1%.
   b. 25%.
   c. 30%.
   d. 48.3%.
4. Federal government issues with a 2- to 10-year maturity are called
   a. Treasury notes.
   b. Treasury bills.
   c. Treasury bonds.
   d. None of the above.
5. Since 1928, dividend income has represented roughly what share of the long-term total return on the DJIA?
   a. one-third
   b. one-quarter
   c. one-half
   d. none of these

6. The expected real (after inflation) annual rate of return on Treasury bills and money market funds is
   a. 5%.
   b. 4%.
   c. 1%.
   d. −1%.
7. Annual total returns on the DJIA are positive
   a. 90% of the time.
   b. 75% of the time.
   c. 50% of the time.
   d. 25% of the time.
8. No significant annual total return volatility is experienced by investors in
   a. common stocks.
   b. corporate bonds.
   c. Treasury bonds.
   d. money market instruments.
9. Since World War II, the annual rate of return on common stocks after inflation and taxes has been about
   a. 20%.
   b. 14%.
   c. 10%.
   d. 6%.
10. Since World War II, the annual real after-tax rate of return on Treasury bonds has been roughly
    a. 10%.
    b. 6%.
    c. −1%.
    d. −4%.
11. The probability of outperforming a broadly diversified portfolio of common stocks with a portfolio of long-term bonds over a 30-year holding period is roughly
    a. 100%.
    b. 80%.
    c. 67%.
    d. 0%.
12. The standard deviation of the annual rate of return on common stocks is approximately
    a. 16%.
    b. 10%.
    c. 6%.
    d. 3%.

13. The expected return on a security with possible outcomes of $X_1 = 10\%$; $X_2 = 20\%$; $X_3 = 25\%$ and associated probabilities of $P(X_1) = 0.2$; $P(X_2) = 0.5$; $P(X_3) = 0.3$ is

    a. 17.5%. c. 25%.

    b. 19.5%. d. 20%.

14. In general, the link between equity prices and interest rates is

    a. direct.

    b. exponential.

    c. not material.

    d. inverse.

15. The link between the nominal interest rate (i), the real interest rate (r), and the expected inflation rate (ei) is

    a. $i = r + ei$.

    b. $r = i + ei$.

    c. $i = r \times ei$.

    d. not material.

16. The present value of $200 to be received in eight years at a discount rate of 9% is about

    a. $50. c. $200.

    b. $100. d. $400.

17. The annual rate of return for common stocks in the post–World War II period is about

    a. 20%.

    b. 14%.

    c. 10%.

    d. 6%.

18. Holding all else equal, common stock investors benefit from a rise in

    a. inflation.

    b. interest rates.

    c. economic growth.

    d. correlation between stock and bond prices.

19. The arithmetic mean of annual stock returns is

    a. unbiased.

    b. downward biased.

    c. upward biased.

    d. the square root of geometric returns.

20. For a stock with a volatility of 10, the probability of a price move *outside* a band ± 20% of the current stock price is roughly

    a. 67%. c. 99%.

    b. 95%. d. none of these.

Investment Application

Do I Need to Save 10% for Retirement?

Most of us were not born into significant wealth. We do not have the opportunity to begin our investment careers with $100,000, $10,000, or even $1,000. Many investors start accumulating their retirement wealth with as little as $30 per month. If setting aside a portion of your monthly income is the only viable means for ac-

TABLE 5.9 Retirement Income Provided by a 10% Savings Plan

A. Cumulative Value of Savings as Last Year–Salary Percentage

Funding Percentage: 10.0%

Working Years	Retirement Fund Real Rate of Return					
	1.0%	2.0%	3.0%	4.0%	5.0%	6.0%
1	0.1000	0.1000	0.1000	0.1000	0.1000	0.1000
2	0.2010	0.2020	0.2030	0.2040	0.2050	0.2060
3	0.3030	0.3060	0.3091	0.3122	0.3152	0.3184
4	0.4060	0.4122	0.4184	0.4246	0.4310	0.4375
5	0.5101	0.5204	0.5309	0.5416	0.5526	0.5637
6	0.6152	0.6308	0.6468	0.6633	0.6802	0.6975
7	0.7214	0.7434	0.7662	0.7898	0.8142	0.8394
8	0.8286	0.8583	0.8892	0.9214	0.9549	0.9897
9	0.9369	0.9755	1.0159	1.0583	1.1027	1.1491
10	1.0462	1.0950	1.1464	1.2006	1.2578	1.3181
11	1.1567	1.2169	1.2808	1.3486	1.4207	1.4972
12	1.2683	1.3412	1.4192	1.5026	1.5917	1.6870
13	1.3809	1.4680	1.5618	1.6627	1.7713	1.8882
14	1.4947	1.5974	1.7086	1.8292	1.9599	2.1015
15	1.6097	1.7293	1.8599	2.0024	2.1579	2.3276
16	1.7258	1.8639	2.0157	2.1825	2.3657	2.5673
17	1.8430	2.0012	2.1762	2.3698	2.5840	2.8213
18	1.9615	2.1412	2.3414	2.5645	2.8132	3.0906
19	2.0811	2.2841	2.5117	2.7671	3.0539	3.3760
20	2.2019	2.4297	2.6870	2.9778	3.3066	3.6786
21	2.3239	2.5783	2.8676	3.1969	3.5719	3.9993
22	2.4472	2.7299	3.0537	3.4248	3.8505	4.3392
23	2.5716	2.8845	3.2453	3.6618	4.1430	4.6996
24	2.6973	3.0422	3.4426	3.9083	4.4502	5.0816
25	2.8243	3.2030	3.6459	4.1646	4.7727	5.4865
26	2.9526	3.3671	3.8553	4.4312	5.1113	5.9156
27	3.0821	3.5344	4.0710	4.7084	5.4669	6.3706
28	3.2129	3.7051	4.2931	4.9968	5.8403	6.8528
29	3.3450	3.8792	4.5219	5.2966	6.2323	7.3640
30	3.4785	4.0568	4.7575	5.6085	6.6439	7.9058
31	3.6133	4.2379	5.0003	5.9328	7.0761	8.4802
32	3.7494	4.4227	5.2503	6.2701	7.5299	9.0890
33	3.8869	4.6112	5.5078	6.6210	8.0064	9.7343
34	4.0258	4.8034	5.7730	6.9858	8.5067	10.4184
35	4.1660	4.9994	6.0462	7.3652	9.0320	11.1435
36	4.3077	5.1994	6.3276	7.7598	9.5836	11.9121
37	4.4508	5.4034	6.6174	8.1702	10.1628	12.7268
38	4.5953	5.6115	6.9159	8.5970	10.7710	13.5904
39	4.7412	5.8237	7.2234	9.0409	11.4095	14.5058
40	4.8886	6.0402	7.5401	9.5026	12.0800	15.4762

cumulating a retirement nest egg, a basic question must be addressed. How much must be set aside to build a satisfactory retirement income?

Table 5.9 provides information that can be used to help determine that amount. A first step in this process is to calculate the amount of investment wealth generated by various savings plans during one's working years. Then, it is necessary to calculate the amount of retirement income that can be provided by that wealth.

TABLE 5.9 ***(continued)***

B. Wealth Requirement Necessary to Fund 100% of Final Salary

Retirement Years	Retirement Fund Real Rate of Return 1.0%	2.0%	3.0%	4.0%	5.0%	6.0%
1	0.9901	0.9804	0.9709	0.9615	0.9524	0.9434
2	1.9704	1.9416	1.9135	1.8861	1.8594	1.8334
3	2.9410	2.8839	2.8286	2.7751	2.7232	2.6730
4	3.9020	3.8077	3.7171	3.6299	3.5460	3.4651
5	4.8534	4.7135	4.5797	4.4518	4.3295	4.2124
6	5.7955	5.6014	5.4172	5.2421	5.0757	4.9173
7	6.7282	6.4720	6.2303	6.0021	5.7864	5.5824
8	7.6517	7.3255	7.0197	6.7327	6.4632	6.2098
9	8.5660	8.1622	7.7861	7.4353	7.1078	6.8017
10	9.4713	8.9826	8.5302	8.1109	7.7217	7.3601
11	10.3676	9.7868	9.2526	8.7605	8.3064	7.8869
12	11.2551	10.5753	9.9540	9.3851	8.8633	8.3838
13	12.1337	11.3484	10.6350	9.9856	9.3936	8.8527
14	13.0037	12.1062	11.2961	10.5631	9.8986	9.2950
15	13.8651	12.8493	11.9379	11.1184	10.3797	9.7122
16	14.7179	13.5777	12.5611	11.6523	10.8378	10.1059
17	15.5623	14.2919	13.1661	12.1657	11.2741	10.4773
18	16.3983	14.9920	13.7535	12.6593	11.6896	10.8276
19	17.2260	15.6785	14.3238	13.1339	12.0853	11.1581
20	18.0456	16.3514	14.8775	13.5903	12.4622	11.4699
21	18.8570	17.0112	15.4150	14.0292	12.8212	11.7641
22	19.6604	17.6580	15.9369	14.4511	13.1630	12.0416
23	20.4558	18.2922	16.4436	14.8568	13.4886	12.3034
24	21.2434	18.9139	16.9355	15.2470	13.7986	12.5504
25	22.0232	19.5235	17.4131	15.6221	14.0939	12.7834
26	22.7952	20.1210	17.8768	15.9828	14.3752	13.0032
27	23.5596	20.7069	18.3270	16.3296	14.6430	13.2105
28	24.3164	21.2813	18.7641	16.6631	14.8981	13.4062
29	25.0658	21.8444	19.1885	16.9837	15.1411	13.5907
30	25.8077	22.3965	19.6004	17.2920	15.3725	13.7648
31	26.5423	22.9377	20.0004	17.5885	15.5928	13.9291
32	27.2696	23.4683	20.3888	17.8736	15.8027	14.0840
33	27.9897	23.9886	20.7658	18.1476	16.0025	14.2302
34	28.7027	24.4986	21.1318	18.4112	16.1929	14.3681
35	29.4086	24.9986	21.4872	18.6646	16.3742	14.4982
36	30.1075	25.4888	21.8323	18.9083	16.5469	14.6210
37	30.7995	25.9695	22.1672	19.1426	16.7113	14.7368
38	31.4847	26.4406	22.4925	19.3679	16.8679	14.8460
39	32.1630	26.9026	22.8082	19.5845	17.0170	14.9491
40	32.8347	27.3555	23.1148	19.7928	17.1591	15.0463

For simplicity, let's look at retirement wealth and retirement income in real terms, after accounting for the effects of inflation. Long-term bonds generate real returns for investors on the order of 1–2% per year. However, common stock investors have enjoyed real returns of as much as 5–6% per year during the post–World War II period. Although nominal rates of return on long-term bonds and common stock vary widely from year to year, these real returns have been stable. Thus, real returns of 1–2% for long-term bond investors and 5–6% for common stock investors represent a reasonable expectation of future returns.

For purposes of illustration, a 6% real return is a very conservative expectation for a broadly diversified portfolio of common stocks. If you look at the 6% column on the left-hand side of Table 5.9 and go to the 40th row, the number 15.4762 has a very practical interpretation. Suppose a young woman graduates from college at 25 years of age with a bachelor's degree in business administration. Furthermore, let's assume that she takes a job with a Big Six accounting firm at a starting salary of $50,000 a year. For simplicity, let's also assume that salary raises received during her working career are just sufficient to offset the rising cost of living. (This is a conservative assumption because most workers receive real increases in pay during their careers.) If she saves 10% of her income each year of her working life and invests the proceeds at a real return of 6%, the cumulative value of her wealth at retirement will be $773,810 (= $50,000 × 15.4762). To avoid taxes, such an accumulation of wealth must take place within a tax-sheltered retirement plan, such as an individual retirement account (IRA) or a 401-k plan. To be sure, the amount accumulated for retirement will actually be more than $773,810. The actual amount will be boosted in nominal terms by the effects of inflation. It is also important to recognize that the $773,810 amount has a simple interpretation in the light of a starting salary of $50,000 per year. This amount is 15.4762 times her starting salary of $50,000 per year.

The number 15.4762 is interesting because it has a very simple interpretation in terms of the amount of retirement income it can generate. The right-hand side of Table 5.9 illustrates the retirement wealth necessary to fund 100% of one's final salary at various interest rates. Whereas the left-hand side of Table 5.9 shows the amount of cumulative investment generated from a given investment per period, the right-hand side shows the stream of annuity payments that can be generated by various levels of wealth. At the time of retirement, the retiree switches to an annuity payment mode. Look at the 6% column, and the 40 years of retirement income row. Notice the number 15.0463. What this number means is, again, simple. If a retiree has wealth at the point of retirement equal to 15.0463 times her last year's salary and invests those funds at a real rate of interest of 6%, such wealth would be sufficient to fund a retirement income equal to her last year's pay for 40 years. In the present example, the manager has accumulated a retirement wealth of 15.4762 times her salary, which is more than enough to fund a full salary during a retirement of as long as 40 years. Even if she is healthy and makes it to retirement at 65, chances are not good that she will live past 105. As a result, a 40-year 10% savings plan generates more wealth than necessary to provide a retirement income equal to 100% of your last year's pay for the rest of your natural life.

This simple illustration explains why it has been a common rule of thumb in investing to advise employees to save at least 10% of their income for retirement. It is only one of many possible scenarios. If a comfortable retirement at less than

100% of one's final salary is feasible, a lower level of retirement savings or a shorter working career becomes possible. As illustrated in Table 5.9, there is an obvious trade-off involved between the amount saved for retirement, the real return on investment, the number of working years, and the number of retirement years. Notice the wonderful advantage gained by workers who begin saving for retirement early during their working careers. For example, 10% of income invested at 6% accumulates to only 3.6786 times final salary for a worker with only 20 years until retirement. Such a worker would have to set aside a whopping 42.1% (= 15.4762/3.6786 × 10%) of his salary to accumulate a retirement wealth equal to 15.4762 times his final salary over an investment horizon of 20 years.

A. Suppose you are 45 years old, have no retirement savings, and wish to retire at 70% of your final salary in 15 years. How much of your income needs to be set aside to fund a retirement income for 30 years?

B. Now assume that such a high level of savings simply is not feasible. How much saving is required if you extend your working career to 65 years of age?

C. Is the assumption of retiring at 100% of final salary necessary to fund an adequate retirement lifestyle?

Selected References

Barber, Brad M., and Terrance Odean. "Too Many Cooks Spoil the Profits: Investment Club Performance." *Financial Analysts Journal* 56 (January/February 2000): 17–25.

Chang, Eric C., Grant R. McQueen, and J. Michael Pinegar. "Cross-Autocorrelation in Asian Stock Markets." *Pacific-Basin Finance Journal* 7 (December 1999): 471–493.

Corgel, John B., and Chris Djoganopoulos. "Equity REIT Beta Estimation." *Financial Analysts Journal* 56 (January/February 2000): 70–79.

Crouhy, Michel, Dan Galai, and Robert Mark. "A Comparative Analysis of Current Credit Risk Models." *Journal of Banking and Finance* 24 (January 2000): 59–117.

Gompers, Paul, and Josh Lerner. "Money Chasing Deals? The Impact of Fund Inflows on Private Equity Valuation." *Journal of Financial Economics* 55 (February 2000): 281–325.

Hirschey, Mark. "How Much Is a Tulip Worth?" *Financial Analysts Journal* 54 (July/August 1998): 11–17.

Ibbotson, Roger G., and Paul D. Kaplan. "Does Asset Allocation Policy Explain 40, 90, or 100 Percent of Performance?" *Financial Analysts Journal* 56 (January/February 2000): 26–33.

Jackson, Patricia, and William Perraudin. "Regulatory Implications of Credit Risk Modeling." *Journal of Banking and Finance* 24 (January 2000): 1–14.

Jarrow, Robert A., and Stuart M. Turnbull. "The Intersection of Market and Credit Risk." *Journal of Banking and Finance* 24 (January 2000): 271–299.

Mingo, John J. "Policy Implications of the Federal Reserve Study of Credit Risk Models at Major U.S. Banking Institutions." *Journal of Banking and Finance* 24 (January 2000): 15–33.

Minton, Bernadette A., and Catherine Schrand. "The Impact of Cash Flow Volatility on Discretionary Investment and the Costs of Debt and Equity Financing." *Journal of Financial Economics* 53 (July 1999): 423–460.

Nofsinger, John R., and Richard W. Sias. "Herding and Feedback Trading by Institutional and Individual Investors." *Journal of Finance* 54 (December 1999): 2263–2295.

Rzepczynski, Mark S. "Seeing Tomorrow: Rewriting the Rules of Risk." *Financial Analysts Journal* 55 (September/October 1999): 88–89.

Solnik, Bruno, and Jacques Roulet. "Dispersion as Cross-Sectional Correlation." *Financial Analysts Journal* 56 (January/February 2000): 54–61.

Treacy, William F., and Mark Carey. "Credit Risk Rating Systems at Large U.S. Banks." *Journal of Banking and Finance* 24 (January 2000): 167–201.

PART 3

Fixed Income Securities

CHAPTER 6

Bond Market

The U.S. bond market, with a market value of roughly $14.1 trillion, is among the largest securities markets in the world. Bond prices quickly reflect changes in the credit quality of individual issuers and changes in aggregate economic conditions. For large buyers and sellers of debt instruments, the bond market is very efficient. Large bond mutual funds with significant operating expenses have a difficult time matching, let alone beating, market interest rates.

At the same time, the secondary market for outstanding bonds can be relatively liquid for buyers and sellers of less than a "round lot," a quantity of bonds worth $1 million in face amount or par value. For small buyers and sellers, transaction costs can average as much as 3 or 4% of the principal amount. A commission of as much as $300–$400 might be owed on the sale or purchase of 10 $1,000 bonds, or $10,000 worth. For small investors, the bond market is an expensive place to trade.

Against this backdrop, it becomes hard to understand the lack of popularity for bond index funds. Low-cost bond index funds that passively track the market routinely produce top returns and soundly beat almost all the competition.[1] Strangely, bond fund buyers are not buying. Although stock index funds that track the Standard & Poor's 500 Index have caught on with the public, bond index funds are largely ignored. Bond index funds are getting passed up by investors, even though they boast the same low-cost, broad-diversification qualities that have made stock index funds a rip-roaring success.

Bond Market Overview

Amount of Public and Private Debt

bond dealers
Securities firms and banks that act as financial intermediaries between bond issuers and investors.

The bond market is the organized trading mechanism through which corporations and government agencies that need to borrow money are matched to investors with funds to lend. **Bond dealers** are securities firms and banks that act as financial intermediaries between the **bond issuer** and **bond investors.** Bond issuers sell newly minted bonds in the **primary bond market** to dealers who then resell those bonds to investors in the **secondary bond market.** Once bonds have been issued and sold

[1]See: Sonoko Setaishi, "Treasury Yields Climb to Four-Week Highs on Strong Economic Data, Rebound in Stocks," *The Wall Street Journal,* April 26, 2000, C22.

to individual and institutional investors, bond dealers use their capital to maintain active secondary markets. Dealers bid for bonds that investors wish to sell and offer bonds from their own inventory when investors wish to buy.

As illustrated in Figure 6.1, at the start of 2000, the U.S. bond market represented roughly $14.1 trillion in outstanding debt obligations. By way of comparison, at the start of 2000, the market value of common and preferred stock in the United States was roughly $15.8 trillion, as captured by the Wilshire 5000 Equity Index. This makes the U.S. bond market one of the world's largest securities markets. Of the $14.1 trillion in U.S. debt obligations, the largest share is accounted for by U.S. Treasury bills, notes, and bonds. The total value of U.S. Treasury obligations is on the order of $3.2 trillion and represents roughly one-quarter (22.7%) of the U.S. bond market. Corporate bonds are the second largest debt category, with roughly $2.9 trillion, and represent 20.6% of the total. Other major debt categories include mortgage-backed securities ($2.2 trillion, or 15.6% of the total), money market securities ($2.1 trillion or 14.9%), municipal bonds ($1.5 trillion or 10.6%), federal agency obligations ($1.5 trillion or 10.6%), and asset-backed securities ($719.5 billion or 5.1%). As shown in Figure 6.2, comprehensive interest rate information for all major bond indices is reported on a daily basis in *The Wall Street Journal* and the financial press.

The U.S. bond market has grown rapidly during recent years. In the private sector, there is the pressing need to fund plant and equipment investment for an expanding economy. In the public sector, an increasing level of debt financing has been used to fund a growing number of public programs. On an overall basis, the U.S. bond market grew from only $4.5 trillion in 1985 to more than $14.1 trillion in 1999, a 7.9% compound annual rate of growth. Over this period, growth was especially rapid in the federal agency mortgage-backed securities market in which the total value of bonds outstanding rose at a 42.5% annual rate. Much government-guaranteed debt financing funds housing and includes mortgage-backed securities issued by Ginnie Mae (Government National Mortgage Association), Fannie Mae (Federal National

bond issuer
Entity that supplies new bonds (supply source).

bond investors
Individuals and institutions that purchase bonds for interest income and long-term capital gains.

primary bond market
Market for new bonds; the issuer-to-investor market.

secondary bond market
Market for previously issued bonds; an investor-to-investor market.

FIGURE 6.1 Outstanding Level of Public and Private Debt

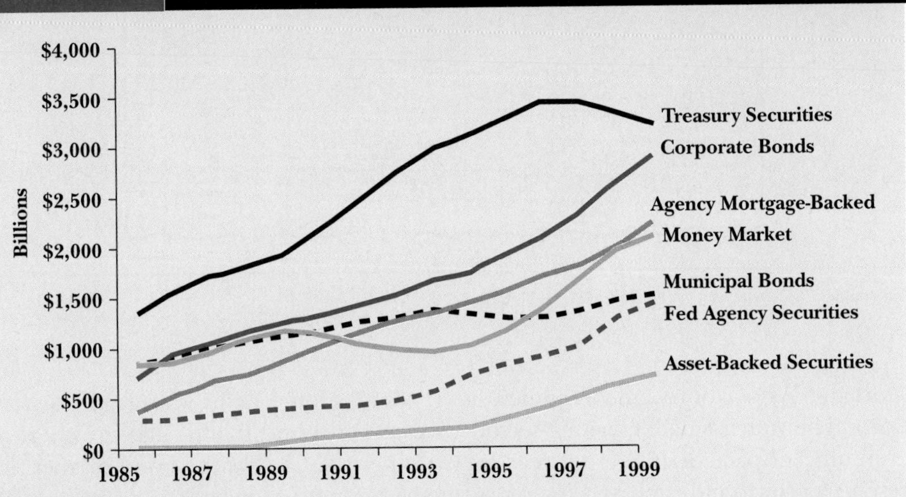

Data sources: U.S. Department of Treasury, Federal Reserve System, Federal National Mortgage Association, Government National Mortgage Association, and Federal Home Loan Mortgage Corporation.

FIGURE 6.2 **Bond Market Data Are Reported Daily in *The Wall Street Journal***

BOND MARKET DATA BANK 2/24/00

BOND YIELDS

TREASURY ISSUES*				MUNICIPAL ISSUES† (Comparable Maturities)				
MATURITY	COUPON	PRICE	YIELD	Aaa YIELD	TAX EQUIV.	MUNI/TREAS YIELD RATIO	52-WEEK RATIO HIGH	52-WEEK RATIO LOW
02/28/02	6.500	100.00	6.500	4.55	6.60	70.0	73.7	63.4
02/15/03	5.500	97.05	6.568	4.70	6.81	71.5	74.6	64.4
11/15/04	5.875	97.11	6.535	4.87	7.06	74.6	78.4	68.5
02/15/10	6.500	101.03	6.350	5.25	7.60	82.6	86.7	76.5
05/15/30	6.250	101.22	6.126	5.95	8.63	97.2	98.1	87.2

* Most recent auctions.

† From Delphis Hanover. Tax equiv. based on 31% bracket.

MAJOR INDEXES

HIGH	LOW (12 MOS)		CLOSE	NET CHG	% CHG	12-MO CHG	% CHG	FROM 12/31	% CHG
U.S. TREASURY SECURITIES (Lehman Brothers indexes)									
5680.14	5529.99	**Intermediate**	5669.03	+ 16.59	+ 0.29	+ 119.67	+ 2.16	+ 29.89	+ 0.53
8503.22	7817.09	**Long-term**	8307.91	+ 41.54	+ 0.50	+ 38.57	+ 0.47	+ 386.68	+ 4.88
1659.12	1446.80	**Long-term**(price)	1526.00	+ 7.38	+ 0.49	99.61	− 6.13	+ 55.76	+ 3.79
6251.84	6042.87	**Composite**	6236.60	+ 22.48	+ 0.36	+ 101.04	+ 1.65	+ 116.78	+ 1.91
U.S. CORPORATE DEBT ISSUES (Merrill Lynch)									
1023.88	976.88	**Corporate Master**	1010.30	+ 3.76	+ 0.37	+ 12.87	+ 1.29	+ 12.33	+ 1.24
733.62	710.98	**1-10 Yr Maturities**	732.11	+ 3.05	+ 0.42	+ 16.25	+ 2.27	+ 5.15	+ 0.71
816.60	754.03	**10+ Yr Maturities**	787.15	+ 2.16	+ 0.28	− 3.82	− 0.48	+ 18.40	+ 2.39
514.50	498.85	**High Yield**	507.40	+ 0.14	+ 0.03	+ 6.29	+ 1.26	− 0.71	− 0.14
737.36	707.08	**Yankee Bonds**	733.14	+ 2.67	+ 0.37	+ 16.26	+ 2.27	+ 7.33	+ 1.01
TAX-EXEMPT SECURITIES (Bond Buyer Muni Index, from Dec. 22, 1999)									
106-24	91-04	**Bond Buyer 6% Muni**	92-22	+ 0-06	+ 0.20	− 13-02	− 12.34	+ 0-14	+ 0.47
146.78	141.73	**7-12 yr G.O.**	144.36	+ 0.16	+ 0.11	− 1.95	− 1.33	+ 0.42	+ 0.29
153.73	143.11	**12-22 yr G.O.**	147.80	+ 0.49	+ 0.33	− 4.64	− 3.04	+ 2.30	+ 1.58
147.89	132.49	**22+ yr Revenue**	136.35	+ 0.54	+ 0.40	− 9.97	− 6.81	+ 1.99	+ 1.48
MORTGAGE-BACKED SECURITIES (current coupon; Merrill Lynch: Dec. 31, 1986 = 100)									
318.57	302.87	**Ginnie Mae**(GNMA)	318.15	+ 1.77	+ 0.56	+ 6.93	+ 2.23	+ 2.18	+ 0.69
314.29	299.59	**Fannie Mae**(FNMA)	312.07	+ 1.10	+ 0.35	+ 5.15	+ 1.68	+ 0.29	+ 0.09
191.17	181.90	**Freddie Mac**(FHLMC)	191.17	+ 0.68	+ 0.36	+ 4.58	+ 2.45	+ 1.64	+ 0.87
BROAD MARKET (Merrill Lynch)									
832.75	804.30	**Domestic Master**	830.90	+ 2.85	+ 0.34	+ 13.35	+ 1.63	+ 9.54	+ 1.16
930.00	896.97	**Corporate/Government**	924.40	+ 3.02	+ 0.33	+ 13.51	+ 1.48	+ 13.58	+ 1.49

TAX-EXEMPT BONDS

Representative prices for several active tax-exempt revenue and refunding bonds, based on institutional trades. Changes rounded to the nearest one-eighth. Yield is to maturity. n-New. Source: The Bond Buyer.

ISSUE	COUPON	MAT	PRICE	CHG	BID YLD
Atl Ga Wtr&Wstwtr 99A	5.000	11-01-38	82¼	+ ½	6.21
CA State genl oblig	5.750	12-01-29	97	+ ⅛	5.96
CAHlthFinAuth	6.125	12-01-30	94⅞	+ ⅛	6.51
ClarkCoNV arpt	6.000	07-01-29	98⅝	+ ⅛	6.10
Del River Prt Auth	5.750	01-01-26	97½	+ ⅛	5.94
Det MI sewage disp	6.000	07-01-29	98⅞	+ ⅛	6.08
EmpireStDevCpNY	6.000	01-01-29	99¼	+ ¼	6.06
FL Pts Fin Comm99	5.500	10-01-29	91¼	+ ⅛	6.15
FLStBdEd	5.750	06-01-29	96⅞	+ ⅛	5.98
Harris Co Hlth Fac Tex	5.375	07-01-29	87	+ ⅛	6.36
MA Wtr PollTr	5.750	08-01-29	95⅞	+ ⅛	6.05
MA Wtr Res Auth	5.750	08-01-39	94⅞	+ ¼	6.09
MA Wtr Res Auth	5.750	08-01-30	95¾	+ ¼	6.05
Mass Tpk Auth	5.000	01-01-39	81⅞	+ ⅛	6.25
MDHlth HigherEd	6.000	07-01-39	98⅝	+ ⅛	6.09
Mesa IndDev AZ	5.625	01-01-29	92⅞	+ ⅛	6.15
Metro TransAuth NY	6.000	04-01-30	99⅝	+ ⅛	6.03
Metro TransAuth NY	5.875	04-01-25	98⅜	+ ¼	6.00
MI StHosp	6.125	11-15-26	95⅞	+ ⅛	6.45
Miami-Dade Co Educ	5.750	04-01-29	97	+ ¼	5.97
Miami-Dade Expwy	6.375	07-01-29	103¾	+ ⅛	5.92
Miss Dev Bk Ser99A	5.000	07-01-24	85⅝	+ ⅝	6.13
Mmphs-Shlby Airpt	6.000	03-01-24	98⅜	+ ⅛	6.13
Monty BMC Spc Care	5.000	11-15-29	81⅞	+ ⅛	6.36
NJ Hlth Fac Fin Auth	4.750	07-01-28	79¾	+ ⅛	6.28
NYC Genl Obl Bds	5.000	03-15-29	81⅝	+ ¼	6.39
NYC Trans FinAuth	6.000	11-15-29	99⅛	+ ⅛	6.06
NYC Trans FinAuth	6.000	11-15-24	99⅜	+ ¼	6.05
NYC TSASC tobacco	6.250	07-15-34	96¾	+ ¼	6.48
NYC TSASC tobacco	6.375	07-15-39	98⅛	+ ⅛	6.50
Ohio Air Qty Dev	5.150	05-01-26	87⅛	+ ¾	6.13
Ore St DptAdmSvc	6.000	05-01-26	99⅝	+ ⅛	6.03
Phila Sch Dist PA	5.750	03-01-29	96	+ ⅜	6.04
San Diego Pub Fac Ca	5.000	05-15-29	84⅝	+ ⅛	6.13
Tampa FL Water	5.750	10-01-29	96⅞	+ ⅛	5.98
VirginIsl PubFinAuth	6.125	10-01-29	97¾	+ ¼	6.29
WA St var purp gen	6.000	01-01-25	99⅛	+ ⅛	6.07
Wash Co Auth PA	6.150	12-01-29	100	+ ⅛	6.15
Washoe NV ltd cnv	6.400	07-01-29	99¾	+ ⅛	6.42
Wichita KS hosp	6.250	11-15-24	95¾	....	6.60

Source: *The Wall Street Journal*, February 25, 2000, C20.

Mortgage Association), and Freddie Mac (Federal Home Loan Mortgage Corporation). The much smaller private-sector asset-backed bond market has grown at an even quicker pace of 46.3% per year over this period. Clearly, the bond market represents a growth industry, and the mortgage-backed and asset-backed securities parts of the business have enjoyed explosive development.

FIGURE 6.2 ***(continued)***

MORTGAGE-BACKED SECURITIES

Indicative, not guaranteed; from Bear Stearns Cos./Street Pricing Service

		PRICE (Mar) (Pts-32ds)	PRICE CHANGE (32ds)	AVG LIFE (years)	SPRD TO AVG LIFE (Bps)	SPREAD CHANGE	PSA (Prepay Speed)	YIELD TO MAT.*
30-YEAR								
FMAC GOLD	6.5%	93-20	+ 12	9.5	128	+ 2	135	7.65%
FMAC GOLD	7.0%	95-31	+ 12	9.4	139	+ 2	140	7.76
FMAC GOLD	7.5%	98-07	+ 11	9.3	151	+ 4	150	7.88
FNMA	6.5%	93-16	+ 12	9.5	127	+ 2	135	7.64
FNMA	7.0%	95-28	+ 11	9.5	137	+ 2	140	7.74
FNMA	7.5%	98-03	+ 10	9.3	149	+ 3	150	7.86
GNMA	6.5%	93-08	+ 12	11	127	+ 2	100	7.61
GNMA	7.0%	95-27	+ 12	10.3	140	+ 2	120	7.75
GNMA	7.5%	98-05	+ 11	9.7	153	+ 4	140	7.88
15-YEAR								
FMAC GOLD	7.0%	98-05	+ 07	5.7	97	+ 6	150	7.48%
FNMA	7.0%	98-12	+ 06	5.7	87	+ 7	150	7.37
GNMA	7.0%	98-08	+ 08	5.7	95	+ 5	145	7.45

*Extrapolated from benchmarks based on projections from Bear Stearns prepayment model, assuming interest rates remain unchanged.

COLLATERALIZED MORTGAGE OBLIGATIONS

Spread of CMO yields above U.S. Treasury securities of comparable maturity, in basis points (100 basis points = 1 percentage point of interest)

MAT	SPREAD	CHG FROM PREV DAY
SEQUENTIALS		
2-year	81	unch
5-year	103	unch
7-year	114	unch
10-year	138	unch
20-year	164	unch
PACS		
2-year	70	unch
5-year	84	unch
7-year	102	unch
10-year	120	unch
20-year	153	unch

GUARANTEED INVESTMENT CONTRACTS

Source: T. Rowe Price GIC Index

	1 YEAR		2 YEARS		3 YEARS		4 YEARS		5 YEARS	
	RATE	CHG	RATE	CHG	RATE	CHG	RATE	CHG	RATE	CHG
High	6.65%	unch	7.51%	−0.08	7.63%	−0.05	7.71%	−0.03	7.74%	−0.06
Low	6.23	unch	6.86	−0.06	7.18	−0.03	7.24	−0.04	7.31	−0.03
INDEX	6.44	−0.07	7.27	−0.06	7.46	−0.01	7.55	−0.01	7.60	−0.01
TOP QUARTILE RANGE	6.65%	6.65%	7.51%	7.50%	7.63%	7.63%	7.71%	7.66%	7.74%	7.70%
SPREAD vs. TREASURYS	+0.15		+0.79		+0.91		+1.03		+1.01	

GIC rates quoted prior to 10:30 am (Eastern) net of all expenses, no broker commissions. Rates represent best quote for a $2-$5 million immediate lump sum deposit with annual interest payments. Yield spreads based on U.S. Treasury yields, as of 10:30 am (Eastern), versus the index rate unadjusted for semi vs. annual interest payments. CHG reflects change in rate from previous day. INDEX is average of all rates quoted. Universe is investment grade.

INTERNATIONAL GOVERNMENT BONDS

COUPON	MATURITY (Mo. /yr.)	PRICE	CHANGE	YIELD*	COUPON	MATURITY (Mo. /yr.)	PRICE	CHANGE	YIELD*
JAPAN (3 p.m. Tokyo)					**GERMANY** (5 p.m. London)				
6.00%	12/01	110.27	− 0.06	0.29%	4.50%	08/02	99.33	+ 0.22	4.723%
4.10	12/03	112.15	− 0.13	0.82	3.25	02/04	94.29	+ 0.25	4.867
1.70	03/10	99.62	− 0.17	1.85	5.375	01/10	99.75	+ 0.39	5.400
2.40	03/20	100.27	− 0.34	2.38	6.25	01/30	106.93	+ 0.27	5.764
UNITED KINGDOM (5 p.m. London)					**CANADA** (3 p.m. Eastern Time)				
8.00%	12/00	101.26	+ 0.01	6.302%	4.50%	06/01	98.48	+ 0.23	5.769%
6.50	12/03	101.08	+ 0.22	6.172	5.50	09/02	98.83	+ 0.45	6.012
5.75	12/09	103.03	+ 0.89	5.347	6.00	06/08	99.31	+ 0.78	6.107
6.00	12/28	125.56	+ 1.72	4.421	8.00	06/27	129.66	+ 0.30	5.816

*Equivalent to semi-annual compounded yields to maturity

Total Rates of Return on International Bonds

In percent, based on J.P. Morgan Government Bond Index, Dec. 31, 1987=100

	— LOCAL CURRENCY TERMS —					— U.S. DOLLAR TERMS —				
	INDEX VALUE	1 DAY	1 MO	3 MOS	SINCE 12/31	INDEX VALUE	1 DAY	1 MO	3 MOS	SINCE 12/31
Japan	199.51	− 0.18	− 0.84	+ 0.59	− 0.64	217.51	− 0.12	− 5.68	− 5.28	− 8.41
Britain	343.23	+ 0.55	+ 3.00	+ 0.77	+ 1.59	291.44	+ 0.33	− 0.16	+ 0.05	+ 0.94
Germany	223.20	+ 0.28	+ 1.34	+ 0.45	+ 0.68	178.32	− 0.49	+ 0.71	− 1.87	+ 0.05
France	295.87	+ 0.29	+ 1.35	+ 0.22	+ 0.56	238.89	− 0.48	+ 0.71	− 2.10	− 0.07
Canada	314.44	+ 0.48	+ 2.98	+ 1.99	+ 2.45	280.09	+ 0.80	+ 1.75	+ 2.64	+ 1.90
Netherlands	236.83	+ 0.29	+ 1.45	+ 0.60	+ 0.75	188.92	− 0.48	+ 0.82	− 1.73	+ 0.12
Euro	269.16	+ 0.01	+ 0.37	+ 0.99	+ 0.60	225.49	− 0.76	− 0.25	− 1.35	− 0.03
Global-a	264.72	+ 0.21	+ 1.25	+ 0.75	+ 0.91	235.13	− 0.07	− 0.34	− 1.49	− 1.17
EMBI+-b	180.50	− 0.08	+ 3.79	+ 7.85	+ 3.39	180.50	− 0.08	+ 3.79	+ 7.85	+ 3.39

a-18 int'l gov. markets b-external-currency emerging mkt. debt, Dec. 31, 1993=100.

Tracking the Bond Market

Because the bond market includes a wide variety of debt securities with varying credit quality and other characteristics, no one price or yield index can be used to fully describe changes in the overall bond market. As shown in Figure 6.3, the trend in long-term interest rates is often summarized through reference to changes in the **current yield** for the 30-year Treasury bond. The 30-year Treasury bond is a benchmark

current yield
Bond's promised interest payment divided by its current purchase price.

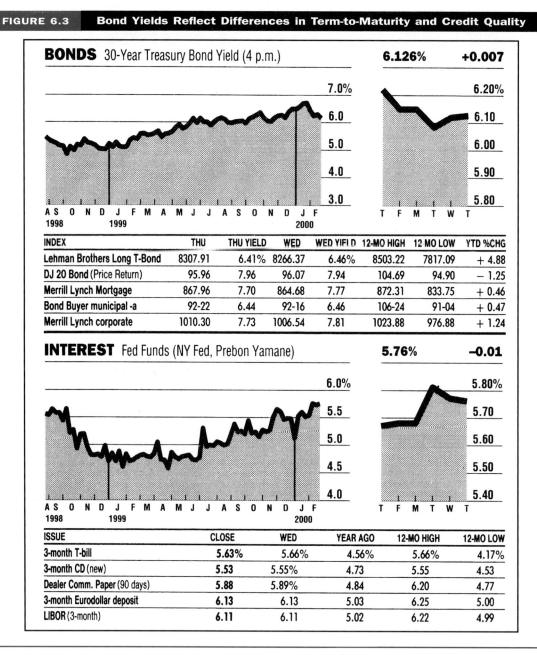

FIGURE 6.3 **Bond Yields Reflect Differences in Term-to-Maturity and Credit Quality**

BONDS 30-Year Treasury Bond Yield (4 p.m.) **6.126%** **+0.007**

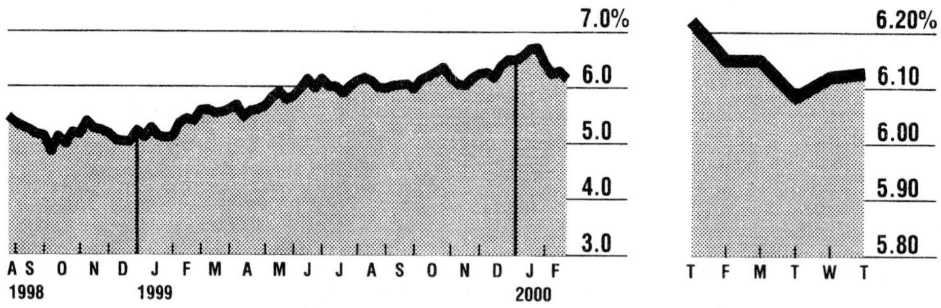

INDEX	THU	THU YIELD	WED	WED YIELD	12-MO HIGH	12 MO LOW	YTD %CHG
Lehman Brothers Long T-Bond	8307.91	6.41%	8266.37	6.46%	8503.22	7817.09	+ 4.88
DJ 20 Bond (Price Return)	95.96	7.96	96.07	7.94	104.69	94.90	− 1.25
Merrill Lynch Mortgage	867.96	7.70	864.68	7.77	872.31	833.75	+ 0.46
Bond Buyer municipal -a	92-22	6.44	92-16	6.46	106-24	91-04	+ 0.47
Merrill Lynch corporate	1010.30	7.73	1006.54	7.81	1023.88	976.88	+ 1.24

INTEREST Fed Funds (NY Fed, Prebon Yamane) **5.76%** **−0.01**

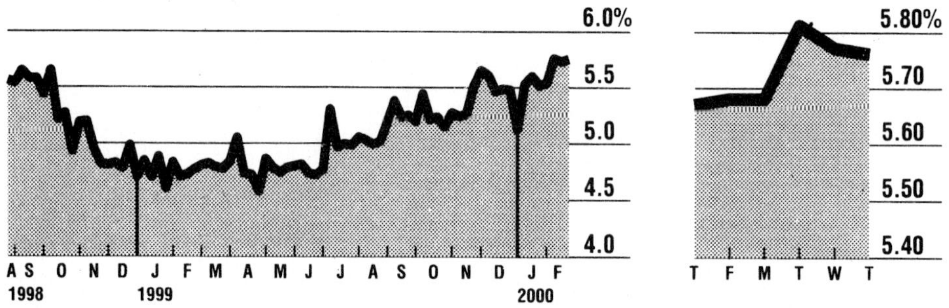

ISSUE	CLOSE	WED	YEAR AGO	12-MO HIGH	12-MO LOW
3-month T-bill	**5.63%**	5.66%	4.56%	5.66%	4.17%
3-month CD (new)	**5.53**	5.55%	4.73	5.55	4.53
Dealer Comm. Paper (90 days)	**5.88**	5.89%	4.84	6.20	4.77
3-month Eurodollar deposit	**6.13**	6.13	5.03	6.25	5.00
LIBOR (3-month)	**6.11**	6.11	5.02	6.22	4.99

Source: *The Wall Street Journal,* February 25, 2000, C1.

holding-period risk
Chance of loss during periods of adverse change in bond prices.

statistic for long-term bond yields and captures the **holding-period risk** typical of long-term bonds. Holding-period risk is the chance of loss incurred by bondholders that might be forced to liquidate bond holdings during periods of adverse change in bond prices. Because Treasury bonds are backed by the full faith and credit of the U.S. government, like all Treasury securities, they entail no **default risk.** As a result, 30-year Treasury bonds offer the lowest interest rates available on any long-term debt security. More adventuresome long-term bond investors can earn a slight risk premium, usually 1–2% per year, by investing in high-grade corporate bonds. Bond price and yield changes in such securities are captured by indexes maintained by Dow Jones & Co. and various brokerages such as Merrill Lynch. More than 5,000 taxable government, investment-grade corporate and mortgage-backed securities are included in the Lehman Brothers Aggregate Bond Index. Because of the vast number of securities in this index (many of which are fairly illiquid), index funds tracking this index do it by sampling the index. Merrill Lynch Taxable Bond Indexes are value-weighted total (coupon plus capital change) returns for a range of bond types. The Salomon Brothers Broad Investment-Grade Bond Index is a value-weighted total return for 3,800 government and corporate securities. Price and yield trends for long-term tax-free municipal bonds are tracked by the Bond Buyer Municipal Bond Index.

default risk Chance of nonpayment of interest or principal.

Figure 6.3 also illustrates how the trend in interest rates for short-term securities that involve no holding period or default risk is captured by changes in the yield on three-month Treasury bills and the overnight **federal funds rate.** The fed funds rate is the amount charged to member banks of the Federal Reserve System that need funds to maintain required balances with the Federal Reserve. Member banks are required to keep a certain percentage of their assets on deposit with the Federal Reserve Bank in their geographic region to provide collateral for savings and checking deposits. Although the fed funds rate is for bank-to-bank lending, the **discount rate** is the interest rate charged on loans made by the Federal Reserve itself. The discount rate changes infrequently according to Federal Reserve policy, but the fed funds rate changes on a daily basis according to credit market demand and supply conditions. Next to the 30-day Treasury bill rate, the federal funds rate is the lowest but most volatile of all money market rates. It is typically a bit lower than rates on bank certificates of deposit (CD) and short-term corporate loans (commercial paper). Modestly higher than the fed funds rate are short-term rates in Europe for dollar-denominated loans, the **Eurodollar** market, and **London Interbank Offered Rates (LIBOR).**

federal funds rate Overnight bank lending rate.

discount rate Interest rate charged by the Federal Reserve to member banks.

Eurodollar Dollar deposit in a European bank.

London Interbank Offered Rates (LIBOR) London fed funds rate.

Trading Activity

The stock market has large and active exchange markets, such as the New York Stock Exchange (NYSE) and American Stock Exchange (AMEX), plus active over-the-counter (OTC) markets such as Nasdaq. By contrast, the bond market functions largely as an OTC market. It has no primary physical location. This is despite the fact that a limited amount of bond trading takes place on the NYSE. In terms of relative market size, the NYSE is far more important for stock investors than for bond investors. The bond market largely functions as a sophisticated electronic information, communications, and processing network. It is through this network that debt securities are bought and sold from dealer to dealer and, in turn, are bought and sold by individual and institutional investors.

An interesting characteristic of the bond market is its relatively low average trading volume, at least when noninstitutional investors are considered. In the stock market, average trading volume measured in terms of the number and value of shares traded is substantial. On the NYSE, for example, average trading volume in stocks is roughly one billion shares per day, with an average value of trading volume of $45–$50 billion per day. Stock-related trading activity on the NYSE averages just short of $12 trillion per year, compared with a total market capitalization for NYSE stocks of roughly $12.3 trillion. There is an ownership turnover rate of 96% per year in the typical NYSE company. By way of contrast, NYSE trading activity in the $2.5 trillion corporate bond market is fairly anemic. The **par value** of corporate bonds

par value Face amount, usually $1,000.

traded on the NYSE averages a minuscule $10.2 *million* on a typical trading day, and NYSE bond-trading volume averages a tiny $2.5 billion per year.

As shown in Figure 6.4, total bond-trading volume on the NYSE and in the OTC market varies from extremely active in the highly liquid Treasury securities market to relatively dormant in other sectors of the bond market. In the $3.2 trillion Treasury security market, for example, trading volume averages an active $190.7 billion per day, or 6.0% of the total market capitalization of Treasury securities. In the similarly large $2.9 trillion corporate bond market, total trading activity averages only $10.0 billion per day, or only 0.3% of corporate bond market capitalization. In total, daily bond trading averages roughly $334.6 billion per day, or roughly 2.3% of the roughly $14.1 trillion in total par value of outstanding debt securities.

Historically, small investors have tended to buy and hold bond market investments for current income and long-term capital appreciation. Similarly, many pension funds and other long-term investors have turned to bonds as a durable component of a diversified portfolio. Much of the observed trading activity seen in the bond market, particularly in the Treasury securities market, is driven by hedge funds and other speculators seeking to profit from short-term movements

FIGURE 6.4 New Issues Volume, Daily Trading Volume, and the Market Value by Type of Debt Security

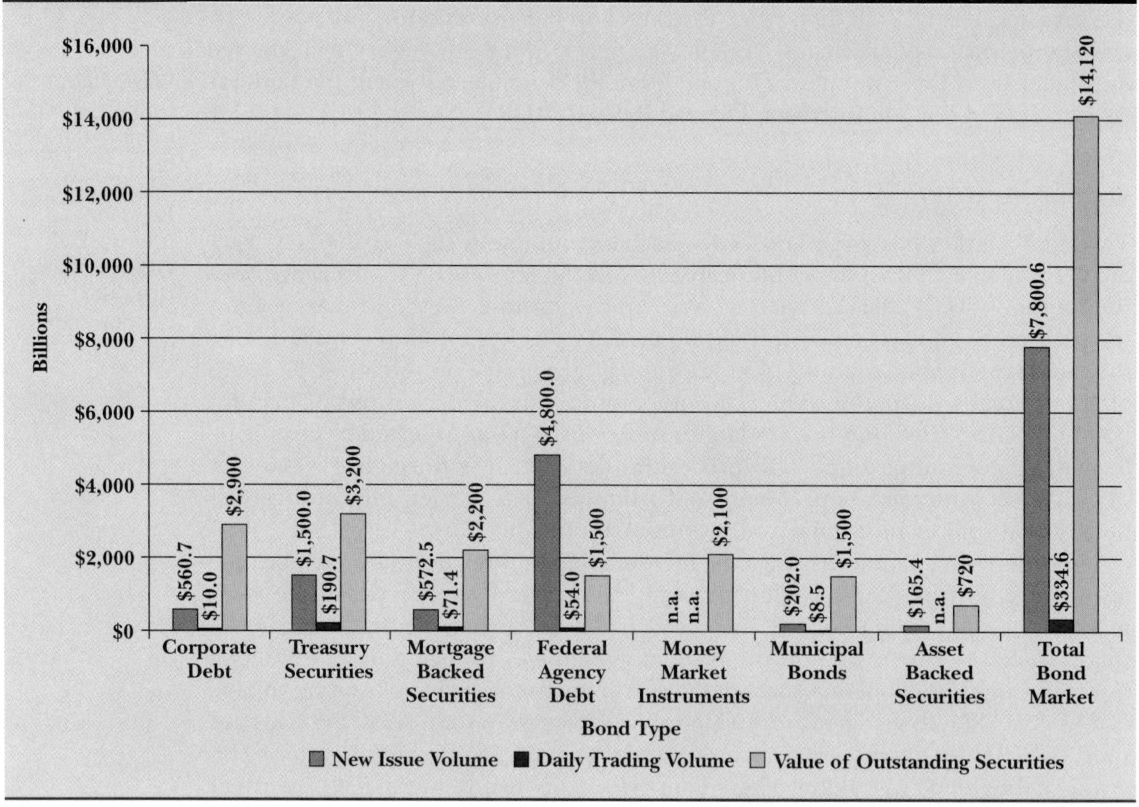

Data sources: Federal Home Loan Mortgage Corporation, Federal National Mortgage Association, Federal Reserve System, Government National Mortgage Association, Municipal Securities Rulemaking Board, Securities Data Company, and U.S. Treasury Department. All data are for 1999.

in interest rates and currency markets. For many small investors, the bond market has historically been relatively illiquid. Bid-ask spreads in the bond market, in which a **round lot** is equal to $1 million in par value, have simply been too wide to allow small investors to pursue short-term trading strategies. However, thanks to the Internet, bond market liquidity and efficiency are improving over time as standardized market practices and technology-based innovations improve the overall level of competition between both sellers and buyers.

round lot In the bond market, $1 million of par value.

Bond Ownership

Most bonds are bought by institutions such as pension funds, insurance companies, and mutual funds. Millions of individual investors also buy bonds directly or through pension plans, insurance companies, and mutual funds. In general, bonds appeal to investors looking for dependable income, relative safety of principle, and diversification. Investment strategies that combine bonds and stocks generally result in more stable investment performance over time than those limited to just bonds or equities. Municipal bonds and Treasury securities also offer significant tax advantages that can appeal to high-income individuals.

As shown in Figure 6.5, public ownership of Treasury securities is largely concentrated in the hands of institutional investors. Only 5.5% of the total is held by individuals. A whopping 42.8% of the total value of Treasury securities is held by foreign investors, largely foreign governments. Much of the rest is held by state

FIGURE 6.5 Estimated Ownership of U.S. Treasury Securities by Private Investors

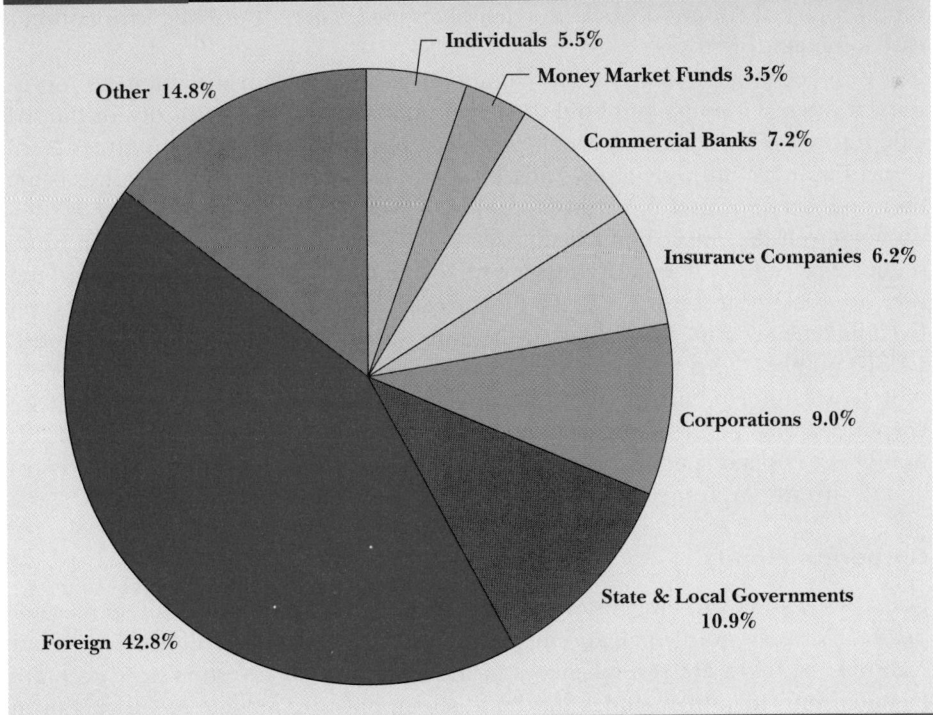

Data source: *Treasury Bulletin* (1998 data).

and local governments (10.9%), corporations (9%), commercial banks (7.2%), insurance companies (6.2%), and money market mutual funds (3.5%). Clearly, the bond market tends to be an institutional market rather than one dominated by small investors.

How to Read Bond Tables

Bond Listings

For investors accustomed to reading stock listings, bond-pricing tables look somewhat different and can be hard to understand, at least initially (see Figure 6.6). Once investors become familiar with bond-pricing terminology, bond tables become understandable and provide the information needed to make informed investment decisions.

In the stock tables published in *The Wall Street Journal,* investors can look up a specific company and see high, low, and last prices for the prior trading day. Online such information is readily provided for thousands of companies on a 15-minute delayed basis throughout the trading day. The reason that detailed stock price information is readily available is simple. Stock market investors tend to focus on the roughly 7,000 securities that are actively traded on the NYSE, AMEX, and Nasdaq. Although this is an impressive number, there are far fewer stocks listed on the three major stock markets than there are bond issues outstanding. With more than 1.5 million individual securities listed in the municipal bond market alone, it simply is not possible for newspapers to list every bond outstanding in the debt markets. Listing daily pricing information for the municipal bond market alone would take up to 100 pages in *The Wall Street Journal.* In addition, because widely followed common stocks are actively traded, current pricing information is easy to obtain for stocks.

maturity
Time when bond principal and all interest will be paid in full.

Most retail bond investors purchase their securities with the intent to receive regular interest income and hold their bond investments until **maturity,** or the specific future point in time at which promised principal and interest payments will be paid in full. With only tepid trading activity, listing daily prices for bonds is neither necessary nor useful. Because only a small fraction of outstanding bonds trade on any given day, most bond listing services only provide investors with a representative price or benchmark to gauge what a fair price would be for the bond that they are seeking to buy or sell. To find precise bid-ask information for any given fixed-income security, bond market investors supply their broker with the bond's **CUSIP** number. This unique code numbering system was developed by the Committee on Uniform Security Identification Procedures as a method for identifying corporate, U.S. government, and municipal securities. Investors can use CUSIP numbers to obtain specific bond-pricing information on the Bond Market Association's investor Web site on the Internet at <http://www.bondmarket.com>.

CUSIP
Unique code to identify financial securities.

Corporate Bonds

Bond tables show the basic information needed to compare prices for similar corporate, Treasury, municipal, and mortgage-backed bonds. When considering bond investments, there are several pieces of information that investors need to know. Essential information includes the bond's coupon rate, term-to-maturity, call in-

FIGURE 6.6 **Corporate Bond Trading Activity Is Muted Compared with Stock Trading Activity**

NEW YORK EXCHANGE BONDS

Quotations as of 4 p.m. Eastern Time
Thursday, February 24, 2000

Volume $8,752,000

	Domestic Thu.	Domestic Wed.	All Issues Thu.	All Issues Wed.
Issues Traded	177	180	186	191
Advances	64	69	65	73
Declines	72	80	77	87
Unchanged	41	31	44	31
New highs	3	1	3	2
New lows	13	15	15	17

SALES SINCE JANUARY 1
(000 omitted)

2000	1999	1998
$380,394	$515,543	$664,338

Dow Jones Bond Averages

1999 High	1999 Low	2000 High	2000 Low		2000 Close	2000 Chg.	2000 %Yld	1999 Close	1999 Chg.
106.88	96.80	96.48	94.90	20 Bonds	95.96	−0.11	7.96	104.13	−0.81
104.72	94.96	95.09	93.20	10 Utilities	93.78	+0.11	7.87	102.03	−1.11
109.44	98.31	98.50	96.47	10 Industrials	98.14	−0.32	8.05	106.23	−0.52

CORPORATION BONDS
Volume, $8,373,000

Bonds	Cur Yld.	Vol.	Close	Net Chg.
AES Cp 8s8	8.7	10	91 7/8	+ 7/8
ATT 5 1/8 01	5.2	55	97 7/8	− 1/8
ATT 7 1/8 02	7.1	30	100 3/8	+ 5/8
ATT 6 1/2 02	6.6	5	98 1/4	...
ATT 6 3/4 04	6.9	55	97 5/8	...
ATT 5 5/8 04	6.0	28	93 5/8	+ 1/8
ATT 7s05	7.1	25	98 7/8	− 1/8
ATT 7 3/4 07	7.6	179	102 3/8	+ 1/4
ATT 6s09	6.7	99	89 7/8	+ 1/4
ATT 8 1/8 22	8.1	20	100 7/8	...
ATT 8 1/8 24	8.0	42	101 1/2	+ 7/8
ATT 6 1/2 29	7.7	127	84 7/8	+ 1/2
ATT 8 5/8 31	8.3	45	103 3/4	+ 1/4
Aames 10 1/2 02	13.2	4	79 1/2	+ 1/4
Alza 5s06	cv	31	107 1/2	+ 3/4
Alza zr14	...	33	50	− 3
ARetire 5 3/4 02	cv	20	67 1/2	+ 1 1/4
Amresco 10s03	14.3	135	70	+ 2
Amresco 10s04	14.5	61	69 1/8	− 7/8
Argosy 13 1/4 04	12.4	55	106 1/2	− 1/2
BkrHgh zr08	...	1	68	− 2
BellPa 7 1/8 12	7.6	5	93 3/4	− 1 3/8
Bellso 6 3/8 28	7.6	25	83 1/2	...
BellsoT 6 1/4 03	6.5	20	96 3/4	− 1
BellsoT 6 3/8 04	6.7	5	95 3/8	− 1 7/8
BellsoT 7s05	7.0	55	99 1/4	− 3/8
BellsoT 5 7/8 09	6.6	90	89 3/8	+ 1 1/8
BellsoT 8 1/4 32	8.2	319	100 1/8	− 3/8
BellsoT 7 7/8 32	8.0	65	98 1/8	− 1/2
BellsoT 6 3/4 33	7.9	126	85 1/4	+ 3/8
BellsoT 7 5/8 35	8.0	40	95 7/8	+ 3/8
BethSt 8 3/8 01	8.4	17	100	+ 1/8
BethSt 8.45s05	9.0	31	93 1/2	+ 1/8
Bevrly 9s06	10.0	90	90	− 2
Bluegrn 8 1/4 12	cv	25	73 1/8	+ 1/8
Bordn 8 3/8 16	10.4	10	80 3/4	− 1 1/2
BosCelts 6s38	11.3	2	53	...
CaterpInc 6s07	6.7	4	89 1/4	− 1/4
CentrTrst 7 1/2 01	cv	88	93 1/32	− 1 15/32
ChaseM 6 1/2 05	6.9	7	94	− 1/8
ChaseM 6 3/4 08	7.2	2	94 1/4	+ 1/2
ChaseM 6 1/8 08	6.8	5	90 1/8	− 1/2
ChaseM 6 1/2 09	7.1	25	92 1/8	+ 1/4
ChespkE 9 5/8 05	10.1	40	95	+ 1/4
ChespkE 9 1/8 06	10.1	30	90 1/2	...
ChiqBr 10s09	11.9	10	84	+ 1/8
ClrkOil 9 1/2 04	13.2	61	72	+ 2 1/4
CoeurDA 7 1/4 05	cv	165	52	− 1
Coeur 6 3/8 04	cv	10	54	− 2 3/4
CmclFd 7.95s06	8.8	12	90 1/8	− 7/8
Consec 8 1/8 03	8.1	80	99 3/4	− 1/8
DelcoR 8 5/8 07	9.3	62	93	...
DevonE 4.9s08	cv	15	89	− 2
Dole 7s03	7.8	20	90 1/8	− 7/8
Dole 7 7/8 13	8.7	13	91	...
DukeEn 5 7/8 01	6.0	20	98 1/8	...
DukeEn 6 5/8 03	6.8	12	97 5/8	...
DukeEn 6 1/4 04	6.5	44	95 3/4	...
DukeEn 7 7/8 24	8.0	10	98 1/8	− 7/8
DukeEn 6 3/4 25	7.8	49	86 1/2	+ 3/4
EMC 6s04	cv	105	149	+ 4
FedDS 10s01	9.9	49	101 9/16	− 7/16
FedDS 8 1/8 02	8.1	10	100 7/8	− 1
FnclFed 4 1/2 05	cv	7	78 1/4	− 2 3/4
FordCr 6 3/8 08	6.9	20	92 3/4	+ 7/8
GBCB 8 3/8 07	9.6	4	87	...
GMA 9 3/8 00	9.4	5	100 3/16	...
GMA 7s00	7.0	4	99 25/32	− 5/32
GMA 5 1/2 01	5.7	22	96 1/8	...
GMA 7s01	7.1	10	99	− 1/2
GMA 7s02	7.1	10	99	− 1/2
GMA 6 5/8 02	6.8	24	97 5/8	...
GMA 5 7/8 03	6.2	2	95 1/8	...
GMA zr12	...	5	374 1/2	− 1 1/2
GMA zr15	...	14	299 3/8	− 5 5/8
GenesisH 9 3/4 05	61.9	811	15 3/4	+ 1/4
Hexcel 7s03	cv	10	67	+ 1
Hilton 5s06	cv	80	73 3/4	...
Hollgnr 9 1/4 07	9.7	125	95 1/4	− 3/4
Hollngr 9 1/4 06	9.7	91	95 5/8	+ 5/8
Honywll zr05	...	10	65	...
IllPwr 6 1/2 03	6.8	10	96	− 3 1/2
IBM 6 3/8 00	6.4	70	99 3/4	...
IBM 7 1/4 02	7.2	19	100 5/8	...
IBM 5 3/8 09	6.2	15	86 3/8	+ 1/8
IBM 7 1/2 13	7.5	10	99 3/4	+ 1/4
IBM 8 3/8 19	7.7	45	108 7/8	+ 7/8
IPap dc5 1/8 12	7.0	20	73 1/2	+ 1
IntShip 9s03	9.2	5	97 3/4	+ 1/8
KaufB 9 3/8 03	9.4	32	99 1/2	+ 1/2
KaufB 7 3/4 04	8.2	30	94	+ 1/2
KaufB 9 5/8 06	9.6	60	100 1/4	+ 3/8
KentE 4 1/2 04	cv	678	88 3/4	+ 1 1/4
KerrM 5 1/4 10	cv	25	97 1/8	− 1 7/8
KerrM 7 1/2 14	cv	67	93	− 1/2
Kolmrg 8 3/4 09	cv	3	95	− 3/4
Koppers 8 1/2 04	10.9	9	78	...
Leucadia 7 3/4 13	8.6	25	90 3/8	− 2 1/8
LibPrp 8s01	cv	55	113 1/2	+ 2
Loews 3 1/8 07	cv	12	77 1/2	− 1/2
LgIsLt 7.05s03	7.3	5	96	− 1/4
LgIsLt 9s22	8.6	17	104	− 1
LgIsLt 8.2s23	8.4	22	98 1/8	+ 3/8
Lucent 6.9s01	6.9	25	100 1/4	+ 3/8
Lucent 7 1/4 06	7.4	5	98 5/8	− 1
MBNA 8.28s26	9.1	15	90 1/2	+ 1/4
MSC Sf 7 7/8 04	cv	11	86 1/2	+ 1/2
MailWell 5s02	cv	15	84	− 5
Malan 9 1/2 04	cv	5	87 3/4	...
MarO 7s02	7.2	135	97 1/2	− 1/2
Mascotch 03	cv	25	74 1/2	+ 1/2
Medtrst 7 1/2 01	cv	35	88	− 1 3/8
MPac 5s45f	...	85	51	...
Motrla zr13	...	2	174	+ 9
NatData 5s03	cv	16	87 1/2	...
NYTel 7 3/8 11	7.8	23	94 1/2	− 1/4
NYTel 7s25	7.9	43	88 3/8	− 1 1/4
Noram 6s12	cv	10	84	− 2 1/2
OffDep zr07	...	21	70	+ 4
OreStl 11s03	11.0	19	100 1/8	− 3/8
ParkElc 5 1/2 06	cv	15	84	+ 1/4
ParkerD 5 1/2 04	cv	14	73 1/2	...
PhilIP 7 1/8 28	8.1	70	88	+ 3/4
Polaroid 11 1/2 06	11.2	10	103	− 1/2
PotEl 5s02	cv	5	93 7/8	− 1 1/8
PrmHsp 9 1/4 06	9.6	4	96	...
PSvEG 6 1/8 02	6.3	50	96 7/8	− 3/8
PSEG 6 1/2 04	6.8	2	96 1/8	...
PSvEG 7s24	7.7	10	91 1/8	− 1/8
Quanx 6.88s07	cv	15	92	− 1
Quest 10 3/4 06	10.3	15	104 3/4	− 5/8
Rallys 9 7/8 00	10.3	10	96	− 25/32
RalsP 9 1/4 09	8.6	28	107 7/8	...
RelGrp 9s00	9.7	30	93	...
RelGrp 9 3/4 03	12.2	40	80	+ 1/4
ReynTob 8s01	8.3	20	96 1/2	+ 1 3/4
ReynTob 8 5/8 02	9.1	10	88	+ 5/8
ReynTob 7 5/8 03	9.7	15	78 1/2	+ 1 5/8
ReynTob 8 3/4 05	11.7	28	75	+ 5 1/2
ReynTob 8 3/4 07	12.5	1	70	− 13 1/2
ReynTob 9 1/4 13	12.3	10	75	+ 8
RobMyr 63	cv	135	91 1/4	− 2 1/2
Safwy 10s01	9.7	30	103 1/4	...
Safwy 9.65s04	9.2	5	105 1/8	− 1/8
Shoney zr04	...	100	12	...
SilicnGr 5 1/4 04	cv	5	75	+ 1
Simula 8s04	cv	8	60	+ 7/8
SouBell 4 3/4 00	4.8	2	98 11/16	+ 3/32
SoCG 6 7/8 02	7.0	5	97 3/4	− 3 7/8
StdCmcl 07	cv	30	46 3/4	− 1/2
StoneC 9 7/8 01	9.9	71	99 29/32	− 7/32
StoneC 10 3/4 02A	10.7	17	100 1/4	...
StoneC 10 3/4 02O	10.5	25	102 1/8	− 5/8
StoneC 11 1/2 04	11.1	112	103 1/2	− 1/8
StoneCn 6 3/4 07	cv	100	83 3/8	− 5/8
StoneC 12 1/4 02	12.1	70	101	...
TVA 6 1/8 03	6.4	34	96 1/2	...
TVA 7 3/4 30	7.8	25	99	...
TVA 8 1/4 34	8.3	15	99 5/8	...
TVA 7 1/4 43	7.6	5	95 1/4	+ 1/4
TVA 6 7/8 43	7.5	34	91 3/8	+ 3/8
TVA 7.85s44	7.9	25	99 1/8	+ 1/8
Tenet 8s03	8.1	23	99	...
Tenet 8s05	8.3	75	96	...
Tenet 8 5/8 07	9.0	25	96	...
TerR 4s19	5.8	25	69	− 3
Texco 8 5/8 10	...	20	104	− 3 1/2
TmeWar 7 3/4 05	7.7	105	100 1/2	...
TmeWar 9 1/8 13	8.5	118	108	− 1
TmeWar 9.15s23	8.6	137	106 5/8	− 3 1/2
US Timb 9 5/8 07	10.4	18	93	...
WsteM 4s02	cv	23	89	− 1/4
Webb 9 3/4 03	10.4	10	94	− 5/8
Webb 9s06	10.4	75	86 3/8	+ 3/4
Webb 10 1/4 10	11.6	23	88	+ 1/4
WebbDel 9 3/8 09	11.1	19	84 1/2	...
Weirton 10 3/4 05	10.6	40	101 3/4	+ 1/4
WhlPit 9 3/8 03	9.0	10	104	+ 1/8

FOREIGN BONDS
Volume, $379,000

Bonds	Cur Yld.	Vol.	Close	Net Chg.
APP Fn zr12	...	50	16	...
AshanC 5s03	cv	35	68	...
EmpICA 5s04	cv	30	56	− 2
Inco cv04	cv	25	93	− 1
Inco 7 3/4 16	cv	46	86 3/8	+ 1/8
SeaCnt 12 1/2 04A	12.5	130	99 5/8	− 2
SeaCnt 12 1/2 04B	12.4	117	100 1/2	...
SeaCnt 9 1/2 03	9.8	96	96 3/4	− 1/8
TelArg 11 7/8 04	11.0	30	108	− 1/4

EXPLANATORY NOTES
(For New York and American Bonds)

Yield is Current yield.

cv-Convertible bond. cf-Certificates. cld-Called. dc-Deep discount. ec-European currency units. f-Dealt in flat. il-Italian lire. kd-Danish kroner. m-Matured bonds, negotiability impaired by maturity. na-No accrual. r-Registered. rp-Reduced principal. st, sd-Stamped. t-Floating rate. wd-When distributed. ww-With warrants. x-Ex interest. xw-Without warrants. zr-Zero coupon.

vj-In bankruptcy or receivership or being reorganized under the Bankruptcy Act, or securities assumed by such companies.

AMEX BONDS

Volume $119,000

SALES SINCE JANUARY 1

2000	1999	1998
$23,830,000	$25,010,000	$54,425,000

	Thu.	Wed	Tue.	Mon.
Issues Traded	9	8	9	8
Advances	4	5	3	4
Declines	4	3	5	3
Unchanged	1	0	1	1
New highs	0	0	1	0
New lows	1	0	1	0

Bonds	Cur Yld.	Vol.	Close	Net Chg.
AltLiv 5 1/4 02	cv	10	61 1/2	+ 1
ExcelLeg 9s04	cv	20	82	− 1 1/2
FriedeGld 4 1/2 04	cv	25	48	− 1
vjFruitL 7s11f	...	10	31 1/2	− 1/8
Impac 11s04	13.8	7	80	...
SwBell 6 7/8 11	7.4	20	92 1/2	+ 3/8
TWA 11 3/8 06	29.6	12	38 1/2	+ 1 1/2
Trump 13 7/8 05f	...	5	79	− 1
Viacom 7 3/4 05	7.8	10	100	+

NASDAQ

Convertible Debentures

Thursday, February 24, 2000

Issue	Vol.	Close	Net Chg.
AdaptB 5 1/4 03	35	360 1/2	+ 10 1/2
Agnico 3 1/2 04	40	70	+ 1
Avatar05	100	86 1/4	− 3/4
Baker 7s02	150	81	+ 1
DrgEmp 7 3/4 14	30	51	...
DuraPh 3 1/2 02	60	83 1/2	− 1/4
Jacobsn 6 3/4 11	30	71	+ 1
Kaman 6s12	14	88 1/8	+ 1/8
OHM 8s06	5	86	...
PhyCor 4 1/2 03	5	47	− 1/4
Telxon 7 1/2 12	10	98	− 1

Source: *The Wall Street Journal,* February 25, 2000, C15.

formation, recent price, and current yield. All bond tables provide this basic information. Because corporate bonds are sometimes actively traded by institutional investors, corporate bond listings often show both the current yield and the volume traded. Corporate bond listings would look like those shown in Figure 6.6 and Table 6.1, panel A.

TABLE 6.1 Sample Listings for Corporate, Treasury, and Municipal Bonds

Panel A: Corporate Bond Listings

Bonds	Cur. Yield.	Vol.	Close	Net Chg.
BosCelts 6s 38	11.3	2	53	—
IBM 8.38 19	7.7	45	108.88	$+\frac{7}{8}$

Panel B: Treasury Bond Listings

Rate	Maturity	Bid	Ask	Chg.	Ask Yield
5.88	Nov 04	97:09	97:10	+13	6.54
6.25	May 30	101:20	101:21	+3	6.13

Panel C: Municipal Bond Listings

Issue	Coupon	Maturity	Price	Yield-to-Maturity
Nevada GO Bds	5.00	5-15-28	$97\frac{1}{8}$	5.19
Nebraska Public Power District	5.00	1-1-28	97	5.20

Data sources: *The Wall Street Journal* and the Bond Market Association.

The bond-issuing companies are a professional basketball team, The Boston Celtics, and computer hardware, software, and services giant IBM. The interest rate paid is indicated as a percentage of $1,000, the bond's par value. The Celtic's bond pays 6% interest. The IBM bond pays 8.38%. The small "s" in the Celtic listing simply separates the interest rate from the year the bond matures, 2038. The IBM bond matures in 2019.

The basketball team's bond has a current yield of 11.3% based on its closing price of $530 per $1,000. The volume traded on the NYSE the prior day amounted to $2,000 in face value, or two bonds, and the bond price was unchanged. Similarly, the IBM bond had a volume of $45,000 and closed at $1,087.50, near its par value of $1,000, up $8.75 for the day.

Treasury Bonds

A typical listing for Treasury bonds is shown in Table 6.1, panel B. The first row shows that the Treasury bond indicated pays bondholders 5.88% interest income and is due to mature in November 2004. Numbers in the bid and ask columns are percentages of the bond's **face amount** of $1,000, sometimes referred to as the **principal amount.** In these quotations, the numbers after the colons represent 32nds, so 09, for example, equals $\frac{9}{32}$% of the $1000 face value, or $2.8125. Thus a bid of 97:09 means that a buyer was willing to pay $972.8125, compared with the seller's lowest asking price, 97:10, or $973.125, a difference of only 31.25¢ per thousand dollars of face amount.

face amount Stated bond principal obligation (also par value).

principal amount Face amount or par value.

By looking at the bid and ask prices, notice that an investor who bought such a bond at par value would suffer a principal loss of $27.1875 or of slightly more than 2.7% if it were sold at the present time. The reason for such a loss can be explained by the rate column. The Treasury note in question pays a lower interest rate than that paid on newly issued Treasury notes of similar maturity. It is less attractive than newly issued Treasury notes. As a result, current investors are only willing to buy the Nov. 04 5.88s if they can be purchased at a **discount to par.**

discount to par Mark down from par value.

The effect of falling interest rates on bond prices can also be illustrated in the case of long-term Treasury bonds. In the next row of Table 6.1, panel B, a long-term Treasury bond maturing in May 2030 is priced to yield 6.13%. Notice that in February 2000 an unusual situation persisted whereby long-term Treasury bonds had a yield-to-maturity that was somewhat below that of short-term and intermediate-term Treasury securities. This atypical situation existed because bond investors projected a decline in interest rates and rushed to lock in attractive long-term rates, and thereby drove up long-term bond prices. Because current investors would pay a **premium to par** to purchase the existing Treasury bond, they bid up its current market price, and its yield-to-maturity fell to 6.13%. Obviously, interest rates had fallen slightly from the 6.25% coupon rate paid when this Treasury bond was newly issued. Given this Treasury bond's relatively attractive coupon interest rate, it is presently selling in the secondary market for roughly 101:21, or $1,016.5625. This represents a slight premium of $16.5625 (or 1.66%) to the bond's initial par value or face amount.

premium to par Excess of market price over face amount.

Municipal Bond Market

The tax-exempt bond market is perhaps the most popular bond market sector for individual investors. About 30% of all outstanding municipal bonds are held by individuals. For that reason, it is particularly important that investors have an understanding of how to read municipal bond price information.

Table 6.1, panel C, shows two examples of 20-year municipal bonds paying 5% interest that would cost about $970 and provide roughly a 5.2% yield-to-maturity. The slight price difference observed may be attributable to slightly different credit ratings. In the first row, State of Nevada general obligation bonds are shown to offer a coupon rate of 5% with a maturity in May 2028. The most recent price of this bond, shown as a percentage of its face value, was $971.25, or $28.75 less than its initial offering value, or par value, of $1,000. If the buyer's bid was accepted, such a buyer would pay a lower price than when the bond was first issued because prevailing interest rates are now higher than 5% on similar tax-exempt bonds. Because a new buyer is able to buy at a discount to par, such buyers would earn a yield-to-maturity of 5.19%, or more than the stated interest rate.

The second issue, offered by the Nebraska Public Power District, has the same coupon, or interest rate, of 5% and matures in January of the same year, 2028. Just as in the Nevada bond example, sellers of the Nebraska bond would receive less than the amount paid for the bond when it was originally issued. The current price of $970 per bond represents a 3% loss in market value for buyers at the original issue price of $1,000.

Corporate Bonds

Uses of Corporate Debt

Corporations raise capital to finance investments in inventory, plant and equipment, research and development, and general business expansion. In deciding how to raise

WALL STREET WISDOM 6.1

Do Corporate Bonds Predict Stock Prices?

When business is good, companies borrow aggressively to build new plant and equipment, grow inventories, and finance new product introductions. Thus, business expansions tend to be accompanied by rising interest rates and falling bond prices. Eventually, as interest rates rise, companies are able to justify fewer and fewer new investment projects, and capital spending tends to taper off. Faced with higher borrowing costs, consumers also begin to cut back on borrowing and demand begins to level off. The combined effects of slowing business demand for new plant and equipment spending and slowing consumer demand for new goods and services cause robust economic expansions to slow down. Eventually, a general business slowdown ensues, and the economy enters a period of tepid growth, or flat-to-negative economic growth.

During economic downturns, business activity decelerates and corporate borrowing tends to taper off. With a reduction in the supply of new bonds, bond prices tend to rise and interest rates fall. The ensuing downturn in borrowing costs encourages businesses to fund new investment projects, and consumers begin to seek credit to fund purchases of new goods and services. As business confidence is restored, economic conditions improve and the overall economy begins a general economic recovery. About this time, the stock market also begins to advance as investors foresee favorable effects on business profits during the coming economic recovery.

The predictable link between interest rates, economic activity, and stock prices has led many stock market observers to use bond prices as a leading indicator of where the stock market is headed. As a result, stock market analysts study relative price patterns for corporate bonds and the Dow Jones Industrial Average (DJIA). Over the past several years, and throughout the rip-roaring bull market since 1982, corporate bonds have been a consistent early predictor of stock market problems. For example, corporate bond prices topped out six months before the stock market crash of 1987, 11 months before the start of the 1990 bear market, and nine months before an intermediate market top in 1994. More recently, corporate bond prices topped out in December 1998, and the DJIA hit its most recent high 13 months later, on January 14, 2000.

Based on experience, seasoned market observers suggest that the corporate bond market is predicting a tough time for the stock market in mid- to late 2000 and beyond. Given the lofty level of stock prices in 2000, even a moderate correction could take bullish investors by surprise. A typical correction would send the DJIA hurling toward 9500; a severe correction would send the DJIA down to 8000. Nasdaq corrections tend to be more intense than for the major market indexes. A moderate correction would send Nasdaq from its 2000 high near 5,000 to 3,500 or below. A severe correction could send the Nasdaq to 2,500 as tech stocks plummet and Nasdaq investors run for cover.

Stay tuned!

See: Sy Harding, "Dinosaur Thinking," *Barron's*, March 6, 2000, 22.

---

book-entry form Computer record of ownership for bonds with no certificate.

bridge financing Short-term loans to satisfy temporary borrowing needs.

capital for investment, corporations can issue debt, equity, or a mixture of both. The driving force behind a corporation's financing strategy is the desire to minimize its cost of capital. In doing so, corporations take advantage of a wide variety of debt instruments that can be used to match financing requirements with investor needs.

By taking advantage of changing market conditions, corporate bond issuers can also lower borrowing costs. Most corporate debt securities offer bond investors predictable cash flows and rates of return. They are generally secure investments because, as creditors to the issuing corporation, bondholders have a significant claim on corporate cash flow and assets. Most corporate bonds are not issued directly by corporations but are instead purchased by underwriters, who then make them available to investors. Following their issuance, many corporate bonds trade in an efficient OTC market maintained by national and regional bond dealers. The corporate bond market is now valued in excess of $2.9 trillion. Unlike common stock, which features a certificate that signifies ownership, corporate bonds are commonly issued in **book-entry form** only. This means that a brokerage statement is the bond investor's only proof of ownership.

Although corporations typically tap the securities markets for long-term funding needs, they also issue debt instruments for shorter periods to finance imports, to meet seasonal cash-flow needs, or to create **bridge financing** until conditions are right for longer-term debt issues.

Corporate Bond Characteristics

Bond certificates state the corporation's obligation to pay back a given amount of money at a specific time and rate of interest to the bondholder. The precise terms of the legal agreement between the corporation and the bondholder are called the **indenture.** Printed on the bond certificate, the indenture specifies the duties and obligations of the trustee (usually a bank or trust company hired by the corporation), how and when the principal will be repaid, the rate of interest, a description of any property to be pledged as collateral, callable features, and steps that the bondholder can take in the event of default. Interest on corporate bonds is usually paid twice a year.

Traditionally, many corporate bonds were sold as **bearer bonds,** or **coupon bonds.** Both feature coupons that are submitted twice a year to an authorized bank for the payment of interest. For example, a 30-year $1,000 bearer bond paying 8% interest would have 60 coupons for $40 each. Such bonds are highly negotiable and can be used like cash. Although there are still many bearer bonds in circulation, they make tracking interest income difficult for the Internal Revenue Service, and the Tax Reform Act of 1982 ended the practice of issuing bearer bonds. Today, all fixed-income securities are sold as **registered bonds.** They come with the name of the bondholder on them, and interest income comes twice a year in the form of a check. At maturity, the registered owner receives a check for the principal. Since 1986, all U.S. government bonds have been sold in book-entry form. The owner of book-entry bonds has no certificate. Instead, a Federal Reserve Board computer keeps track of bond ownership and required interest payments. A growing number of corporate bonds are also being sold in book-entry form.

Although many municipal bonds are sold in denominations of $5,000, the face value of a corporate bond is always $1,000 unless specified otherwise. An **unsecured corporate bond** is backed only by the reputation, credit record, and financial stability of the corporation. Unsecured bonds, sometimes referred to as **debentures,** are generally issued by the largest and most creditworthy corporations. A **senior bond** has prior claim to other junior securities in the event of default or bankruptcy. Every debt security has priority or senior claim to preferred stock, which, in turn, has priority to common stock. **Mortgage bonds** or **equipment trust certificates** are often referred to as senior bonds because they are senior to any other type of debt instrument. A debenture that is **subordinated** comes behind every other creditor but still ahead of preferred and common stock.

Corporations often issue mortgage bonds backed by real estate or other physical assets of the corporation. Pledged assets typically have a market value greater than the bond issue. If the company defaults on mortgage bonds, real assets are sold off to satisfy the mortgage bondholders. With a **closed-end mortgage bond,** pledged assets can

indenture
Legal terms of bond agreement.

bearer bonds
Bonds with ownership defined by possession.

coupon bonds
Bonds with physical interest vouchers.

registered bonds
Bonds sold in book-entry form.

unsecured corporate bond
Debt backed only by the reputation, credit record, and financial stability of the corporation.

debentures
Unsecured debt.

senior bond
Debt with prior claim to other securities in the event of default.

mortgage bonds
Debt backed by a property lien.

equipment trust certificates
Debt backed by an equipment lien.

subordinated
Less important.

closed-end mortgage bond
Debt secured by assets pledged to that specific bond issue.

open-end mortgage bond Debt with pledged assets that can be sold to pay off multiple bond issues.

only be sold to pay off a specific bond issue. With an **open-end mortgage bond,** proceeds from the sale of pledged assets can be used to pay off multiple bond issues.

Equipment trust certificates are the corporate equivalent of a personal automobile loan. When a consumer borrows money for a new car, a substantial down payment is followed by monthly installment payments. At no time throughout the life of the loan is the car worth less than the amount of the outstanding loan. Many transportation and computer leasing companies use this same type of financing. Usually, 20–50% of the purchase price is paid as a form of down payment, with the balance paid off over a term of three to 10 years. When the loan is fully paid, the company receives clear title from the trustee. If the company defaults on its loan, equipment is sold and the bondholders are paid off. Many equipment trust certificates are **serial bonds.** Each payment represents both interest and a repayment of principal.

serial bonds A series of bonds to be retired in sequence.

The most junior grade of corporate bonds is called an **income bond.** As their name implies, income bonds only pay interest to the extent that the issuing corporation has earned income. Income bonds are the only bond type in which failure to pay interest in a timely fashion does not lead to immediate default. Usually, income bonds are issued by the least creditworthy corporate borrowers or by companies already in bankruptcy.

income bond Bonds with interest that must be paid only in the event of positive earnings.

U.S. Treasury Securities

Treasury Securities Market

The federal government has three potential sources of funds to support various projects. A first obvious source is tax revenues. When funding additional federal spending through higher taxes proves unpopular, the federal government sometimes turns to a second alternative: simply printing money. Of course, if too much new money is introduced into circulation, inflation will rise, and economic confidence can be undermined. The federal government's third option for raising spendable funds is to issue public debt. When the federal government spends more than it receives in tax revenues or can be financed through an increase in the money supply, it must borrow in the bond market.

The Federal Reserve System, through its New York branch, uses the Treasury securities market to implement monetary policy. If the Fed wishes to increase the money supply, it simply buys Treasury securities, thereby injecting funds into the financial system, and reduces interest rates. If the Fed wishes to decrease the money supply, it simply sells Treasury securities, thereby withdrawing funds from the financial system, and increases interest rates. In this manner, the Fed tries to manage growth in the economy and tame the rate of inflation.

The Treasury securities market is also an efficient means for financing federal deficits at the lowest possible cost. Treasury securities carry the "full faith and credit" backing of the U.S. government and have long been considered among the safest fixed-income investments in the world. Maintaining this reputation for safety and ensuring market liquidity and efficiency are of prime importance to U.S. taxpayers. An increase of only one-hundredth of 1%, or one basis point, in the interest rate on new U.S. government bonds could cost taxpayers hundreds of millions of dollars per year.

Figure 6.7 shows interest rate quotes provided for the Treasury securities market on a daily basis in *The Wall Street Journal* and other leading financial publications. Notice the large number of Treasury securities and the very small bid-ask spreads typical of this market.

FIGURE 6.7 Trading in Treasury Bonds, Notes, and Bills Is Active

TREASURY BONDS, NOTES & BILLS

Thursday, February 24, 2000

Representative Over-the-Counter quotations based on transactions of $1 million or more.

Treasury bond, note and bill quotes are as of mid-afternoon. Colons in bid-and-asked quotes represent 32nds; 101:01 means 101 1/32. Net changes in 32nds. n-Treasury note. Treasury bill quotes in hundredths, quoted on terms of a rate of discount. Days to maturity calculated from settlement date. All yields are to maturity and based on the asked quote. Latest 13-week and 26-week bills are boldfaced. For bonds callable prior to maturity, yields are computed to the earliest call date for issues quoted above par and to the maturity date for issues below par. *-When issued.

Source: Telerate/Cantor Fitzgerald

U.S. Treasury strips as of 3 p.m. Eastern time, also based on transactions of $1 million or more. Colons in bid-and-asked quotes represent 32nds; 99:01 means 99 1/32. Net changes in 32nds. Yields calculated on the asked quotation. ci-stripped coupon interest. bp-Treasury bond, stripped principal. np-Treasury note, stripped principal. For bonds callable prior to maturity, yields are computed to the earliest call date for issues quoted above par and to the maturity date for issues below par.

Source: Bear, Stearns & Co. via Street Software Technology Inc.

GOVT. BONDS & NOTES

Rate	Maturity Mo/Yr	Bid	Asked	Chg.	Ask Yld.
$5\frac{1}{2}$	Feb 00n	99:30	100:00	....	5.36
$7\frac{1}{8}$	Feb 00n	99:31	100:01	....	4.14
$5\frac{1}{2}$	Mar 00n	99:30	100:00	....	5.38
$6\frac{7}{8}$	Mar 00n	100:02	100:04	....	5.41
$5\frac{1}{2}$	Apr 00n	99:29	99:31	....	5.62
$5\frac{5}{8}$	Apr 00n	99:29	99:31	....	5.70
$6\frac{3}{4}$	Apr 00n	100:03	100:05	....	5.74
$6\frac{3}{8}$	May 00n	100:02	100:04	....	5.70
$8\frac{7}{8}$	May 00n	100:20	100:22	....	5.57
$5\frac{1}{2}$	May 00n	99:27	99:29	....	5.79
$6\frac{1}{4}$	May 00n	100:01	100:03	....	5.80
$5\frac{3}{8}$	Jun 00n	99:25	99:27	....	5.79
$5\frac{7}{8}$	Jun 00n	99:30	100:00	....	5.82
$5\frac{3}{8}$	Jul 00n	99:23	99:25	+ 1	5.87
$6\frac{1}{8}$	Jul 00n	100:01	100:03	+ 1	5.88
6	Aug 00n	99:30	100:00	....	5.99
$8\frac{3}{4}$	Aug 00n	101:07	101:09	....	5.96
$5\frac{1}{8}$	Aug 00n	99:15	99:17	....	6.07
$6\frac{1}{4}$	Aug 00n	100:01	100:03	....	6.06
$4\frac{1}{2}$	Sep 00n	98:31	99:01	+ 1	6.17
$6\frac{1}{8}$	Sep 00n	99:30	100:00	....	6.11
4	Oct 00n	98:16	98:18	+ 1	6.19
$5\frac{3}{4}$	Oct 00n	99:21	99:23	+ 1	6.16
$5\frac{3}{4}$	Nov 00n	99:19	99:21	+ 1	6.23
$8\frac{1}{2}$	Nov 00n	101:17	101:19	+ 1	6.18
$4\frac{5}{8}$	Nov 00n	98:24	98:26	+ 1	6.23
$5\frac{5}{8}$	Nov 00n	99:15	99:17	....	6.25
$4\frac{5}{8}$	Dec 00n	98:18	98:20	+ 1	6.31
$5\frac{1}{2}$	Dec 00n	99:09	99:11	+ 1	6.30
$4\frac{1}{2}$	Jan 01n	98:09	98:11	+ 1	6.35
$5\frac{1}{4}$	Jan 01n	98:31	99:01	+ 1	6.33
$5\frac{3}{8}$	Feb 01n	99:01	99:03	+ 1	6.35
$7\frac{3}{4}$	Feb 01n	101:08	101:10	+ 1	6.34
$11\frac{3}{4}$	Feb 01	105:01	105:03	+ 1	6.28
5	Feb 01n	98:21	98:23	+ 2	6.33
$5\frac{5}{8}$	Feb 01n	99:08	99:10	+ 1	6.34
$4\frac{7}{8}$	Mar 01n	98:11	98:13	+ 2	6.40
$6\frac{3}{8}$	Mar 01n	99:29	99:31	+ 1	6.40
5	Apr 01n	98:12	98:14	+ 2	6.39
$6\frac{1}{4}$	Apr 01n	99:25	99:27	+ 2	6.38
$5\frac{5}{8}$	May 01n	99:00	99:02	+ 1	6.43
8	May 01n	101:24	101:26	+ 1	6.42
$13\frac{1}{8}$	May 01	107:23	107:25	+ 2	6.37
$5\frac{1}{4}$	May 01n	98:17	98:19	+ 2	6.42
$6\frac{1}{2}$	May 01n	100:01	100:03	+ 2	6.41
$5\frac{3}{4}$	Jun 01n	99:00	99:02	+ 2	6.48
$6\frac{5}{8}$	Jun 01n	100:04	100:06	+ 3	6.47
$5\frac{1}{2}$	Jul 01n	98:20	98:22	+ 2	6.47
$6\frac{5}{8}$	Jul 01n	100:04	100:06	+ 2	6.48
$7\frac{7}{8}$	Aug 01n	101:28	101:30	+ 3	6.47
$13\frac{3}{8}$	Aug 01	109:15	109:17	+ 2	6.49
$5\frac{1}{2}$	Aug 01n	98:17	98:19	+ 3	6.43
$6\frac{1}{2}$	Aug 01n	99:31	100:01	+ 3	6.48
$5\frac{5}{8}$	Sep 01n	98:20	98:22	+ 4	6.50
$6\frac{3}{8}$	Sep 01n	99:23	99:25	+ 3	6.52
$5\frac{7}{8}$	Oct 01n	98:29	98:31	+ 3	6.53
$6\frac{1}{4}$	Oct 01n	99:17	99:19	+ 4	6.50
$7\frac{1}{2}$	Nov 01n	101:15	101:17	+ 4	6.53
$15\frac{3}{4}$	Nov 01	114:21	114:25	+ 4	6.51
$5\frac{7}{8}$	Nov 01n	98:27	98:29	+ 4	6.53
$6\frac{1}{8}$	Dec 01n	99:09	99:10	+ 6	6.52
$6\frac{1}{4}$	Jan 02n	99:14	99:16	+ 5	6.53
$6\frac{3}{8}$	Jan 02n	99:22	99:23	+ 5	6.53
$14\frac{1}{4}$	Feb 02	113:31	114:03	+ 5	6.53
$6\frac{1}{4}$	Feb 02n	99:14	99:16	+ 5	6.52
$6\frac{1}{2}$	**Feb 02n**	**99:31**	**100:00**	....	**6.50**
$6\frac{5}{8}$	Mar 02n	100:03	100:05	+ 6	6.54
$6\frac{5}{8}$	Apr 02n	100:03	100:05	+ 6	6.54
$7\frac{1}{2}$	May 02n	101:28	101:30	+ 6	6.54
$6\frac{1}{2}$	May 02n	99:27	99:29	+ 6	6.54

Rate	Maturity Mo/Yr	Bid	Asked	Chg.	Ask Yld.
$6\frac{1}{2}$	**Feb 10n**	**100:31**	**101:00**	**+ 17**	**6.36**
$11\frac{3}{4}$	Feb 05-10	120:19	120:25	+ 11	6.76
10	May 05-10	113:27	113:31	+ 11	6.77
$12\frac{3}{4}$	Nov 05-10	127:25	127:31	+ 12	6.77
$13\frac{7}{8}$	May 06-11	135:14	135:20	+ 13	6.76
14	Nov 06-11	138:14	138:20	+ 14	6.75
$10\frac{3}{8}$	Nov 07-12	121:11	121:17	+ 13	6.75
12	Aug 08-13	133:10	133:16	+ 15	6.75
$13\frac{1}{4}$	May 09-14	143:31	144:05	+ 16	6.74
$12\frac{1}{2}$	Aug 09-14	139:25	139:31	+ 16	6.73
$11\frac{3}{4}$	Nov 09-14	135:21	135:27	+ 16	6.68
$11\frac{1}{4}$	Feb 15	144:27	145:01	+ 22	6.50
$10\frac{5}{8}$	Aug 15	139:25	139:31	+ 22	6.49
$9\frac{7}{8}$	Nov 15	132:31	133:05	+ 21	6.48
$9\frac{1}{4}$	Feb 16	127:08	127:14	+ 19	6.47
$7\frac{1}{4}$	May 16	108:03	108:05	+ 17	6.43
$7\frac{1}{2}$	Nov 16	110:24	110:28	+ 17	6.43
$8\frac{3}{4}$	May 17	123:19	123:25	+ 19	6.44
$8\frac{7}{8}$	Aug 17	125:04	125:10	+ 19	6.44
$9\frac{1}{8}$	May 18	128:15	128:21	+ 19	6.43
9	Nov 18	127:17	127:23	+ 18	6.43
$8\frac{7}{8}$	Feb 19	126:15	126:21	+ 18	6.42
$8\frac{1}{8}$	Aug 19	118:25	118:29	+ 17	6.41
$8\frac{1}{2}$	Feb 20	123:06	123:12	+ 17	6.41
$8\frac{3}{4}$	May 20	126:04	126:10	+ 17	6.41
$8\frac{3}{4}$	Aug 20	126:10	126:16	+ 17	6.41
$7\frac{7}{8}$	Feb 21	116:28	117:00	+ 15	6.39
$8\frac{1}{8}$	May 21	119:27	119:31	+ 14	6.39
$8\frac{1}{8}$	Aug 21	119:30	120:04	+ 15	6.39
8	Nov 21	118:23	118:27	+ 14	6.38
$7\frac{1}{4}$	Aug 22	110:12	110:16	+ 13	6.37
$7\frac{5}{8}$	Nov 22	114:27	114:31	+ 13	6.37
$7\frac{1}{8}$	Feb 23	109:01	109:03	+ 12	6.37
$6\frac{1}{4}$	Aug 23	98:25	98:27	+ 11	6.35
$7\frac{1}{2}$	Nov 24	114:11	114:15	+ 11	6.33
$7\frac{5}{8}$	Feb 25	116:01	116:05	+ 10	6.33
$6\frac{7}{8}$	Aug 25	106:27	106:29	+ 9	6.33
6	Feb 26	96:01	96:03	+ 8	6.31
$6\frac{3}{4}$	Aug 26	105:18	105:20	+ 8	6.31
$6\frac{1}{2}$	Nov 26	102:14	102:16	+ 8	6.30
$6\frac{5}{8}$	Feb 27	104:00	104:02	+ 7	6.31
$6\frac{3}{8}$	Aug 27	100:27	100:29	+ 6	6.31
$6\frac{1}{8}$	Nov 27	97:23	97:25	+ 6	6.29
$3\frac{5}{8}$	Apr 28i	91:16	91:17	+ 10	4.14
$5\frac{1}{2}$	Aug 28	89:21	89:23	+ 5	6.28
$5\frac{1}{4}$	Nov 28	86:14	86:16	+ 4	6.27
$5\frac{1}{4}$	Feb 29	86:16	86:18	+ 5	6.26
$3\frac{7}{8}$	Apr 29i	95:16	95:17	+ 8	4.14
$6\frac{1}{8}$	Aug 29	98:13	98:14	+ 2	6.24
$6\frac{1}{4}$	**May 30**	**101:20**	**101:21**	**+ 3**	**6.13**

U.S. TREASURY STRIPS

Mat.	Type	Bid	Asked	Chg.	Ask Yld.
May 00	ci	98:27	98:27	+ 2	5.57
May 00	np	98:27	98:27	+ 2	5.49
Aug 00	ci	97:12	97:12	+ 2	5.82
Aug 00	np	97:11	97:11	+ 2	5.89
Nov 00	ci	95:27	95:28	+ 3	6.03
Nov 00	np	95:26	95:26	+ 3	6.10
Feb 01	ci	94:11	94:12	+ 5	6.10
Feb 01	np	94:09	94:10	+ 5	6.17
May 01	ci	92:22	92:22	+ 5	6.35
May 01	np	92:20	92:21	+ 5	6.41
Aug 01	ci	91:04	91:05	+ 6	6.42
Aug 01	np	91:02	91:02	+ 6	6.49
Nov 01	ci	89:22	89:23	+ 7	6.45
Nov 01	np	89:17	89:18	+ 7	6.54
Feb 02	ci	88:07	88:08	+ 7	6.46
May 02	ci	86:27	86:28	+ 8	6.47

Mat.	Type	Bid	Asked	Chg.	Ask Yld.
Aug 13	ci	42:03	42:09	+ 6	6.50
Nov 13	ci	41:15	41:20	+ 6	6.49
Feb 14	ci	40:26	41:00	+ 5	6.49
May 14	ci	40:07	40:12	+ 5	6.48
Aug 14	ci	39:20	39:25	+ 5	6.47
Nov 14	ci	39:02	39:07	+ 5	6.46
Feb 15	ci	38:15	38:20	+ 3	6.46
Feb 15	bp	38:21	38:26	+ 2	6.42
May 15	ci	37:29	38:03	+ 3	6.45
Aug 15	ci	37:12	37:17	+ 3	6.44
Aug 15	bp	37:17	37:22	+ 2	6.41
Nov 15	ci	36:27	37:00	+ 3	6.43
Nov 15	bp	37:00	37:05	+ 2	6.40
Feb 16	ci	36:10	36:16	+ 3	6.42
Feb 16	bp	36:17	36:23	+ 2	6.38
May 16	ci	35:26	35:31	+ 3	6.41
May 16	bp	36:10	36:16	+ 3	6.32
Aug 16	ci	35:10	35:15	+ 4	6.40
Nov 16	ci	34:27	35:00	+ 3	6.38
Nov 16	bp	35:06	35:12	+ 3	6.32
Feb 17	ci	34:10	34:15	− 1	6.38
May 17	ci	33:25	33:30	− 1	6.38
May 17	bp	33:31	34:05		6.34
Aug 17	ci	33:09	33:14	− 2	6.37
Aug 17	bp	33:16	33:21	+ 1	6.33
Nov 17	ci	32:24	32:30	− 4	6.37
Feb 18	ci	32:10	32:16	− 3	6.36
May 18	ci	31:28	32:02	− 2	6.35
May 18	bp	32:01	32:07	+ 1	6.32
Aug 18	ci	31:13	31:19	− 2	6.34
Nov 18	ci	30:31	31:04	− 2	6.34
Nov 18	bp	31:02	31:08	+ 1	6.32
Feb 19	ci	30:17	30:22		6.33
Feb 19	bp	30:22	30:27		6.30
May 19	ci	30:02	30:07		6.33
Aug 19	ci	29:20	29:25		6.32
Aug 19	bp	29:27	30:01		6.28
Nov 19	ci	29:06	29:11		6.32
Feb 20	ci	28:26	29:00		6.30
Feb 20	bp	28:31	29:04		6.27
May 20	ci	28:13	28:19		6.29
May 20	bp	28:16	28:22		6.28
Aug 20	ci	28:00	28:05		6.29
Aug 20	bp	28:03	28:09		6.27
Nov 20	ci	27:25	27:31		6.25
Feb 21	ci	27:09	27:14	− 1	6.26
Feb 21	bp	27:13	27:19	− 1	6.24
May 21	ci	26:29	27:02	− 1	6.26
May 21	bp	26:30	27:04	− 1	6.25
Aug 21	ci	26:17	26:22	− 1	6.25
Aug 21	bp	26:19	26:24	− 1	6.24
Nov 21	ci	26:08	26:13	− 1	6.23
Nov 21	bp	26:08	26:14	− 1	6.22
Feb 22	ci	25:26	25:31	− 1	6.23
May 22	ci	25:13	25:18	− 1	6.23
Aug 22	ci	25:01	25:07	− 1	6.23
Aug 22	bp	25:08	25:13	− 1	6.19
Nov 22	ci	24:21	24:27	− 1	6.23
Nov 22	bp	24:26	24:31	− 1	6.20
Feb 23	ci	24:11	24:16	− 1	6.22
Feb 23	bp	24:15	24:20	− 1	6.20
May 23	ci	24:00	24:05	− 1	6.21
Aug 23	ci	23:22	23:27	− 1	6.21
Aug 23	bp	23:27	24:00	− 1	6.17
Nov 23	ci	23:12	23:17	− 1	6.20
Feb 24	ci	22:31	23:04	− 1	6.20
May 24	ci	22:21	22:26	− 1	6.20
Aug 24	ci	22:11	22:16	− 1	6.19
Nov 24	ci	22:03	22:08	− 1	6.17
Nov 24	bp	22:06	22:12	− 2	6.15
Feb 25	ci	21:28	22:02	− 1	6.15
Feb 25	bp	21:31	22:04	− 1	6.13
May 25	ci	21:20	21:25	− 1	6.14
Aug 25	ci	21:07	21:13	− 1	6.15
Aug 25	bp	21:10	21:15	− 1	6.13
Nov 25	ci	20:31	21:04	− 1	6.14
Feb 26	ci	20:19	20:24		6.15
Feb 26	bp	20:27	21:00		6.10
May 26	ci	20:09	20:14		6.15
Aug 26	ci	20:00	20:05		6.15
Aug 26	bp	20:06	20:11		6.11
Nov 26	ci	19:24	19:29		6.14
Nov 26	bp	19:30	20:03		6.10
Feb 27	ci	19:19	19:24	− 1	6.11
Feb 27	bp	19:21	19:26	− 1	6.09
May 27	ci	19:11	19:16	− 1	6.10
Aug 27	ci	19:01	19:06	− 1	6.10
Aug 27	bp	19:02	19:07	− 2	6.09
Nov 27	ci	18:26	18:31	− 1	6.09
Nov 27	bp	18:27	19:00	− 1	6.08
Feb 28	ci	18:17	18:22	− 1	6.09
May 28	ci	18:09	18:14	− 1	6.08

Source: *The Wall Street Journal,* February 25, 2000, C15.

primary dealers Investment bankers that buy new Treasury securities.

The Treasury issues securities through regularly scheduled public auctions. Key participants in these auctions are various investment bankers known as **primary dealers.** Primary dealers are obligated to bid at every auction for their own account and on behalf of customers and to make a continuous secondary market in Treasury securities. Once Treasury securities are issued, primary dealers provide bids and offers in the secondary market and maintain a working inventory of bonds. Primary dealers act in conjunction with bondbrokers, who act as intermediaries between dealers and institutional and individual customers. Trading volume in the Treasury securities market is enormous. It averages roughly $190.7 billion a day. It is the world's most liquid securities market. The liquidity and efficiency of this market help maintain the value of the U.S. dollar in world trade and allow the dollar to remain the world's preeminent exchange currency. The U.S. Treasury is the largest issuer of debt securities in the world. An estimated $3.2 trillion in marketable Treasury securities are presently outstanding. Principal buyers of Treasury securities include a wide range of institutional investors such as pension funds, mutual funds, insurance companies, and international investors. As shown in Figure 6.5, only 5.5% of outstanding Treasury securities are directly held by individual investors. However, many large institutional investors such as mutual funds hold Treasury securities on behalf of individuals.

T-Bills, T-Notes, and T-Bonds

Treasury securities are the safest of all bonds in circulation. They enjoy the full-faith-and-credit backing of the U.S. government and rely on the interest and principal paying might of the U.S. taxpayer. Seasoned Treasury securities trade in the secondary or capital market.

T-bills Treasury bills (mature in less than one year).

At the initial point of issue, most Treasury bills have maturities of three months and six months. They are sold by government auction on a once-a-week basis. Once-a-month, nine-month, and one-year Treasury bills are also auctioned. The face amount or par value of T-bills can vary from $10,000 to $1 million. All such **T-bills** are very actively traded, highly liquid, direct short-term obligations of the U.S. government. T-bills do not pay interest. Instead, they are issued by the government and purchased by investors at a discount. For example, an investor might buy at auction a $10,000 three-month T-bill for $9,877.28. The investor would then receive a full $10,000 when the T-bill reached maturity in three months. Of the $10,000 to be received in three months' time, $9,877.28 represents a repayment of principal and $122.72 represents a payment of taxable interest income. In this example, the compounded rate of return earned by the T-bill investor is approximately 5% per year.

T-bills are the only Treasury security issued at a discount without any stated interest rate. As illustrated above, T-bill interest rates are determined at auction through the simple forces of supply and demand. If government borrowing needs rise, the supply of T-bills will increase, T-bill prices will fall, and investor yields will rise. Conversely, if investor demand for T-bills rises, T-bill prices will rise and investor yields will fall. Finally, it is interesting to note that T-bills are only offered to investors in what is called book-entry form. This means that records of T-bill ownership are kept in computer databases maintained by the federal government. T-bill investors do not receive any type of bond certificate.

T-notes Treasury notes (mature in one to 10 years).

Treasury notes are direct obligations of the U.S. government that have maturities ranging from one year to 10 years. **T-notes** pay interest on a semiannual basis and always expire at par value, which may vary from $5,000 to $10,000 to $1 million. Different length T-notes are auctioned at various periods throughout the year. Treasury bonds are direct obligations of the U.S. government that pay interest on a semiannual basis and have very long-term maturities. **T-bonds** mature anywhere from 10 to 30 years. Thirty-year T-bonds are callable beginning five years prior to maturity.

T-bonds
Treasury bonds (mature in 10–30 years).

WALL STREET WISDOM 6.2

The Big Squeeze in T-Bills

The U.S. Treasury securities market is the largest and most liquid bond market in the world. Bid-ask spreads are typically no more than 1:32, or one-thirty-second of a dollar (or 3.125¢) on bonds with par value or face amount of $1,000. The market is so liquid that round lots are quoted in terms of $1 million in face amount, and even the very largest institutional buyers and sellers can trade freely without fear of moving the bid-ask spread.

However, even in this largest and most liquid of all bond markets, illicit trading activity by large bond dealers has resulted in significant market disruptions. In February 2000, for example, nearly nine years after Salomon Brothers' Treasury auction bidding scandal, the government began taking a look into another alleged manipulation of the Treasury securities market. According to *The Wall Street Journal,* the Securities and Exchange Commission led an inquiry into whether traders at two Wall Street dealers, Warburg Dillon Read and Aubrey Lanston & Co., attempted a short squeeze in the market for Treasury securities during early 1999.

Warburg Dillon Read and Aubrey Lanston are among a handful of Wall Street brokerages that enjoy primary dealer status in the Treasury securities market. Primary dealer status gives Wall Street firms the authority to deal in new issues of Treasury securities. They act as wholesale distributors of Treasury securities to their individual and institutional clients. To facilitate broad and ready access to the Treasury securities market, the U.S. Treasury does not want any single primary dealer to enjoy a monopoly as the sole distributor of any single issue of new government bonds. Thus, when the government regularly issues new Treasury securities, an auction is conducted and bids are solicited from a number of primary dealers. To ensure competition among a small number of active bidders, each primary dealer is limited in the amount of any individual issue that can be purchased. Therefore, in planning the amount and size of Treasury security bids, primary dealers must take into account the amount of demand from its individual and institutional investors, the size of the issue, and likely demand from other primary dealers. If demand is apt to be strong in the face of limited supply, chances are high that bond prices will be firm in the secondary market. In such cases, bullish primary dealers may become active bidders. If demand is prone to be weak in the face of abundant supply, bond prices are apt to be weak in the secondary market. In such instances, bearish primary dealers might short bonds in the effort to profit from falling bond prices (and rising yields).

Short squeezes occur when bond dealers snatch up much of the available supply of a given Treasury security, drive up its price, and "squeeze" short sellers into paying still higher prices to cover their short positions. Because bond dealers regularly trade hundreds of millions of dollars in Treasury securities, even a modest and temporary short squeeze can cost speculators millions of dollars in losses and generate millions of dollars in ill-gotten gains for the perpetrators of the short squeeze. Of course, short squeezes in the secondary market are not necessarily illegal and can occur as a natural by-product of quickly changing demand and supply conditions. Specific federal rules pertaining to primary dealers are only intended to guard against short squeezes in the primary, or new issue, bond market. Nevertheless, firms or individuals can be charged with a violation of federal security laws if they create a short squeeze through intentional manipulation of the market. To prove market manipulation, regulators must establish that a perpetrator intended to manipulate the market and show a significant market impact.

In the bond market, in which trading is frenetic and market conditions can change in a heartbeat, evidence of manipulation is hard to establish. Still, it is noteworthy that regulators must remain vigilant to prevent manipulation of even the largest and most liquid part of the bond market.

See: Charles Gasparino, John Connor, and Gregory Zuckerman, "SEC Probes Whether Two Firms Tried 'Squeeze' in Treasury Bills," *The Wall Street Journal,* February 25, 2000, C1, C5.

Agency and Asset-Backed Securities Markets

Agency Securities

government-sponsored enterprises Private corporations with a public purpose.

Certain U.S. government agencies and **government-sponsored enterprises** issue debt securities to help finance desirable private-sector activities such as home ownership, farming, and education. These bond issuers are able to borrow at favorable rates and funnel proceeds into sectors of the economy that would not otherwise enjoy such affordable financing. As shown in Figure 6.8, the federal agency market includes debt securities issued by Fannie Mae, Freddie Mac, the Federal Farm Credit System, Federal Home Loan Banks, the Student Loan Marketing Association (Sallie Mae), and the Small Business Administration, among others. Although most agency securities do not carry the government's full-faith-and-credit guarantee, their credit quality is enhanced by their government-sponsored status. The agency securities market is much smaller than the Treasury securities market, with roughly $900 billion versus $3.2 trillion in outstanding debt. Nevertheless, this market is highly efficient and liquid. Most agency securities are purchased by institutional investors such as pension funds and insurance companies. Many individual investors hold agency securities indirectly through mutual funds.

Mortgage-Backed Securities

Agency and government-sponsored asset-backed securities are issued to support important social priorities such as boosting the supply of funds for personal residential housing. For example, Fannie Mae and Freddie Mac are often described as private corporations with a public purpose. Both started out as government-owned enterprises but were converted into privately held corporations in 1968 (for Fannie Mae) and 1970 (for Freddie Mac). Both presently have common stock traded on the NYSE. The purpose of each company is to help create a continuous flow of funds to mortgage lenders such as commercial banks, mortgage bankers, savings institutions, and credit unions. Both Fannie Mae and Freddie Mac supply lenders with money by purchasing home mortgages in the secondary market. Fannie Mae and Freddie Mac assemble these mortgages into diversified packages or **pools** of such loans and then issue securities that represent a proportionate share in the interest and principal payments derived on that pool. This is sometimes referred to as the **mortgage securitization process.**

pools Diversified loan portfolios.

mortgage securitization process Process of creating diversified loan portfolios and selling proportionate shares to investors.

Mortgage-backed securities are bought by dealers and sold to investors around the world. As the underlying mortgage loans are paid off by homeowners, investors receive monthly payments of interest and principal. Before the invention of mortgage-backed securities, people in some parts of the country found it hard to get mortgages simply because of limited access to funding sources. Lenders can now sell the mortgage loans that they generate and use the proceeds to make new mortgage loans. This results in a constant replenishment of the supply of mortgage funds and makes mortgages more affordable.

Fannie Mae and Freddie Mac get their resources from equity investors and by borrowing from both private investors and the Treasury Department. Both earn a profit margin because the amount of interest paid on mortgage-backed securities tends to be about 1% per year less than the amount earned on the underlying pool of mortgages. Competition limits the size of this profit rate and ensures that the

FIGURE 6.8 **Over-the-Counter Trading Is Active in Government Agency Securities**

GOVERNMENT AGENCY & SIMILAR ISSUES

Thursday, February 24, 2000

Over-the-Counter mid-afternoon quotations based on large transactions, usually $1 million or more. Colons in bid-and-asked quotes represent 32nds; 101:01 means 101 1/32.

All yields are calculated to maturity, and based on the asked quote. *-Callable issue, maturity date shown. For issues callable prior to maturity, yields are computed to the earliest call date for issues quoted above par, or 100, and to the maturity date for issues below par.

Source: Bear, Stearns & Co. via Street Software Technology Inc.

Fannie Mae Issues

Rate	Mat.	Bid	Asked	Yld.
5.63	3-01	99:02	99:04	6.52
4.63	10-01	96:30	97:00	6.59
6.63	1-02	99:22	99:24	6.76
5.38	3-02	97:08	97:10	6.81
6.25	11-02	98:10	98:13	6.91
5.25	1-03	95:16	95:19	6.96
5.75	4-03	96:16	96:19	6.97
4.75	11-03	92:17	92:20	7.04
5.13	2-04	93:11	93:14	7.05
5.88	4-04*	95:06	95:09	7.21
5.63	5-04	94:21	94:24	7.09
6.50	8-04	97:24	97:27	7.07
7.10	10-04*	98:20	98:23	7.43
7.13	2-05	100:06	100:09	7.05
5.75	6-05	94:04	94:07	7.07
5.75	2-08	91:14	91:18	7.16
6.00	5-08	92:22	92:26	7.17
5.25	1-09	87:14	87:18	7.17
6.50	4-09*	92:24	92:28	7.59
6.40	5-09*	92:16	92:20	7.52
6.38	6-09	94:13	94:17	7.19
6.63	9-09	96:02	96:06	7.18
7.25	1-10	100:17	100:21	7.16
6.25	5-29	89:17	89:21	7.09
7.13	1-30	100:08	100:12	7.09

Freddie Mac

Rate	Mat.	Bid	Asked	Yld.
4.98	4-00	99:24	99:26	6.11
5.00	2-01	98:18	98:20	6.51
5.38	3-01*	99:14	99:16	5.89
5.75	6-01	98:30	99:00	6.57
4.75	12-01	96:21	96:23	6.72
5.50	5-02	97:06	97:08	6.86
5.75	7-03	96:09	96:12	6.97
5.58	12-03*	99:22	99:25	5.64
5.00	1-04	92:30	93:01	7.08
6.00	6-04*	94:20	94:23	7.45
6.25	7-04	96:26	96:29	7.08
7.09	11-06*	93:26	93:29	8.28
6.70	1-07	97:00	97:03	7.24
7.10	4-07	99:11	99:14	7.20
6.22	3-08*	99:26	99:30	6.23
5.75	4-08	91:06	91:10	7.18
5.13	10-08	86:28	87:00	7.17
5.75	3-09	90:14	90:18	7.19
0.00	11-14	35:12	35:16	7.15
0.00	11-19	26:04	26:08	6.89
0.00	12-25	17:24	17:28	6.79

Farm Credit Fin. Asst. Corp.

Rate	Mat.	Bid	Asked	Yld.
9.38	7-03	106:31	107:02	7.00
8.80	6-05	106:26	106:29	7.20
9.20	9-05*	101:16	101:19	6.37

Federal Farm Credit Bank

Rate	Mat.	Bid	Asked	Yld.
6.28	6-01	99:14	99:16	6.66
6.10	9-01	98:29	98:31	6.80
5.70	6-03	95:30	96:01	7.07
6.75	6-07	98:27	98:30	6.93
5.75	12-28	86:06	86:10	6.84

Federal Home Loan Bank

Rate	Mat.	Bid	Asked	Yld.
4.49	11-00	98:07	98:09	7.09
4.98	11-00	99:00	99:02	6.35
5.62	1-01	99:06	99:08	6.49
5.20	9-01	99:30	100:00	5.20
4.86	10-01	96:30	97:00	6.86
4.63	10-01	96:10	96:12	7.05
4.66	10-01	96:19	96:21	6.86
4.95	11-01	100:00	100:02	4.91
6.18	12-01	98:18	98:20	6.99
4.99	12-01	96:18	96:20	6.98
5.01	2-02	96:22	96:24	6.83
4.64	10-02	94:02	94:04	7.14
4.68	10-02	94:15	94:17	6.98
6.18	10-02	97:23	97:25	7.11
5.66	1-03	96:16	96:19	6.99
5.37	1-03	95:19	95:22	7.05
5.42	1-03	95:30	96:01	6.95
6.03	5-03*	96:22	96:25	7.17
5.76	6-03	96:10	96:13	6.99
5.57	9-03	95:01	95:04	7.17
5.63	9-03	95:22	95:25	7.01
5.13	9-03	94:03	94:06	7.00
4.78	10-03	92:06	92:09	7.22
5.06	10-03*	99:27	99:30	5.08
5.28	12-03*	93:22	93:25	7.18
9.50	2-04	109:20	109:23	6.68
7.00	7-07*	96:10	96:13	7.64
7.00	8-07*	97:00	97:03	7.52
5.80	9-08	91:10	91:14	7.16

Financing Corporation

Rate	Mat.	Bid	Asked	Yld.
10.70	10-17	133:24	133:28	7.26
9.80	11-17	132:27	132:31	6.61
9.40	2-18	121:10	121:14	7.24
9.80	4-18	129:07	129:11	6.93
10.00	5-18	130:27	130:31	6.97
10.35	8-18	134:08	134:12	7.00
9.65	11-18	128:00	128:04	6.94
9.90	12-18	130:05	130:09	6.98
9.60	12-18	127:02	127:06	6.98
9.65	3-19	127:28	128:00	6.97
9.70	4-19	128:07	128:11	6.99
9.00	6-19	120:08	120:12	7.05
8.60	9-19	116:13	116:17	7.03

GNMA Mtge. Issues

Rate	Mat.	Bid	Asked	Yld.
5.50	30Yr	87:02	87:04	7.47
6.00	30Yr	90:15	90:17	7.47
6.50	30Yr	93:12	93:14	7.59
7.00	30Yr	95:31	96:01	7.72
7.50	30Yr	98:10	98:12	7.86
8.00	30Yr	100:17	100:19	7.99
8.50	30Yr	102:16	102:18	8.07
9.00	30Yr	103:30	104:00	7.96
9.50	30Yr	105:05	105:07	8.10

Inter-Amer. Devel. Bank

Rate	Mat.	Bid	Asked	Yld.
6.13	3-06	96:10	96:13	6.87
6.63	3-07	98:07	98:10	6.93
12.25	12-08	131:12	131:16	7.33
8.88	6-09	110:11	110:15	7.30
8.40	9-09	107:24	107:28	7.24
8.50	3-11	108:05	108:09	7.39
7.13	3-23*	94:07	94:11	7.65
7.00	6-25	102:27	102:31	6.75
6.80	10-25	100:18	100:22	6.74

Resolution Funding Corp.

Rate	Mat.	Bid	Asked	Yld.
8.13	10-19	114:24	114:28	6.75
8.88	7-20	123:17	123:21	6.72
9.38	10-20	125:12	125:16	7.02
8.63	1-21	120:28	121:00	6.74
8.63	1-30	117:04	117:08	7.21
8.88	4-30	131:23	131:27	6.46

Student Loan Marketing

Rate	Mat.	Bid	Asked	Yld.
6.05	9-00	99:23	99:25	6.46
7.00	12-02	99:22	99:25	7.09
7.30	8-12	99:04	99:08	7.39
0.00	10-22	19:30	20:02	7.23

Tennessee Valley Authority

Rate	Mat.	Bid	Asked	Yld.
6.00	11-00	99:05	99:07	7.19
6.50	8-01	99:12	99:14	6.89
6.38	6-05	96:24	96:27	7.10
3.38	1-07	93:24	93:27	4.43
6.75	11-25	99:02	99:06	6.82
8.25	4-42*	107:08	107:12	7.61
7.25	7-43*	99:26	99:30	7.26
6.88	12-43*	96:13	96:17	7.14

World Bank Bonds

Rate	Mat.	Bid	Asked	Yld.
8.13	3-01	101:14	101:16	6.58
6.38	5-01	99:16	99:18	6.74
6.75	1-02	99:10	99:12	7.10
12.38	10-02	111:14	111:16	7.46
5.25	9-03	95:02	95:05	6.81
6.38	7-05	97:30	98:01	6.82
6.63	8-06	98:24	98:27	6.85
8.25	9-16	115:12	115:16	6.69
8.63	10-16	119:00	119:04	6.70
9.25	7-17	120:26	120:30	7.13
7.63	1-23	108:24	108:28	6.85
8.88	3-26	121:02	121:06	7.08

FEDERAL INTEREST RATES

The following tables, provided by the Internal Revenue Service, show the applicable federal interest rates, the adjusted applicable federal ranges, the adjusted federal long-term rate and the federal long-term tax exempt rate for March 1900.

Revenue ruling 2000–11, setting forth this information, will be published in Internal Revenue Bulletin 2000–10 dated March 6, 2000.

APPLICABLE FEDERAL INTEREST RATES

	Annual	Semi Annual	Quarter	Month
Short-Term				
AFR	6.45%	6.35%	6.30%	6.27%
110% of AFR	7.11	6.99	6.93	6.89
120% of AFR	7.77	7.62	7.55	7.50
Mid-Term				
AFR	6.80%	6.69%	6.63%	6.60%
110% of AFR	7.50	7.36	7.29	7.25
120% of AFR	8.19	8.03	7.95	7.90
150% of AFR	10.29	10.04	9.92	9.84
175% of AFR	12.05	11.71	11.54	11.43
Long-Term				
AFR	6.75%	6.64%	6.59%	6.55%
110% of AFR	7.43	7.30	7.23	7.19
120% of AFR	8.13	7.97	7.89	7.84

ADJUSTED APPLICABLE FEDERAL INTEREST RATES

	Annual	Semi Annual	Quarter	Month
Short-Term				
AFR	4.34%	4.29%	4.27%	4.25%
Mid-Term				
AFR	4.97%	4.91%	4.88%	4.86%
Long-Term				
AFR	5.84%	5.76%	5.72%	5.69%

ADJUSTED LONG TERM RATE 5.84%
LONG-TERM TAX-EXEMPT RATE 5.84%
ANNUITY RATE 8.2%

Source: *The Wall Street Journal,* February 25, 2000, C15.

benefits of an active secondary mortgage market are passed on to home buyers and renters in the form of lower housing costs. Fannie Mae and Freddie Mac have become so successful that together they purchase more than 50% of all residential loans originated during a given year.

When the government split off Fannie Mae into a private corporation, it split Fannie Mae into two parts. Ginnie Mae is the second part. Ginnie Mae is a government agency within HUD created by Congress to ensure adequate funds for government loans insured by the Federal Housing Administration (FHA) and guaranteed by the Department of Veterans Affairs (VA) and Veterans Administration. Ginnie Mae issues **modified pass-through certificates** that represent an interest in a given pool of FHA and VA mortgages. As homeowners make their mortgage payments, a proportionate share passes through to the investor on a monthly basis. Each payment the investor receives is part interest and part repayment of principal. The minimum denomination is $25,000. Ginnie Mae bonds are backed by the full faith and credit of the U.S. government, but interest payments are subject to state and local taxes.

modified pass-through certificates Ginnie Mae issues that represent interest in a pool of FHA and VA mortgages.

Today, most mortgage securities are issued and/or guaranteed by Ginnie Mae, Fannie Mae, and Freddie Mac. Mortgaged-backed bonds sold by Fannie Mae and Freddie Mac are regarded as safe and pay relatively low semiannual interest that is exempt from state and local income taxes. Other private institutions, such as subsidiaries of investment banks, financial institutions, and home builders, have also built a profitable business packaging mortgage pools. Such private-label mortgage securities carry double-A or triple-A credit ratings from nationally recognized rating agencies. Institutional investors in the roughly $1.75 trillion agency mortgage securities market include life insurance companies, pension funds, and trust funds. Primarily through mutual funds, individual investors have also become significant buyers of mortgage-backed securities.

Another prime beneficiary of agency and asset-backed securities is the agricultural lending market. For example, the Farm Credit Association supervises loans made to farmers and ranchers. They are secured by mortgages made by federal land banks through the Federal Land Banks Association. These are considered moral obligations of the U.S. government. Interest received by investors is free from state and local taxes but not federal income tax. The Federal Intermediate Credit Bank (FICB) is a group of 12 banks authorized to make loans to farmers. The money is to be used for expenses, machinery, and livestock. The loans may not run for more than 10 years. Similarly, the Bank for Cooperatives makes loans to farm cooperatives. Again, these loans are not direct obligations of the U.S. government but are considered moral obligations. Interest received by investors is free from state and local taxes but not federal income tax.

Table 6.2 shows a comparison of various mortgage-backed security characteristics in terms of their security, minimum investment, and payment characteristics. Notice important differences between mortgage-backed securities issued by government-sponsored enterprises and various private issuers.

Other Asset-Backed Securities

The concept of creating diversified pools of loans and then issuing asset-backed securities to share in interest and principal payments has become popular and highly profitable during recent years. Transforming individual loans into diversified pools of related securities has been extended from home mortgages to a broad range of consumer and commercial debt. Typical examples include credit card debt, auto loans, home equity loans, and equipment leases. The asset-backed securities market not only provides a ready source of funds for lending to consumers and other borrowers, but it also facilitates specialization among financial service providers as it frees manufacturers from financing requirements.

TABLE 6.2 Comparison of Mortgage Security Characteristics

Comparison of Pass-Through Mortgage Securities Characteristics

Security	Guarantee	Minimun Investment	Payment Date
Ginnie Mae I and II	Full and timely payment of principal and interest, backed by the full-faith-and-credit guarantee of the U.S. government	\$25,000 minimum; \$1 increments	15th or the 20th of the month for Ginnie Mae I and II pools, respectively, following the record date and every month thereafter
Ginnie Mae Platinum	Full and timely payment of principal and interest, backed by the full-faith-and-credit guarantee of the U.S. government	\$25,000 minimum; \$1 increments	15th or the 20th of the month for Ginnie Mae I and II pools, respectively, following the record date and every month thereafter
Fannie Mae MBS	Full and timely payment of principal and interest, guaranteed by Fannie Mae	\$1,000 minimum; \$1 increments	25th of the month following the record date and every month thereafter
Freddie Mac PC (75-day PC)	Full and timely payment of interest and ultimate payment of principal guaranteed by Freddie Mac	\$1,000 minimum; \$1 increments	15th of the second month following the record date and every month thereafter
Freddie Mac Gold PC	Full and timely payment of interest and scheduled principal guaranteed by Freddie Mac	\$1,000 minimum; \$1 increments	15th of the month following the record date and every month thereafter

Comparison of CMO/REMIC Mortgage Securities Characteristics

Security	Guarantee	Minimum Investment	Payment Date
Ginnie Mae REMIC	Full and timely payment of principal and interest, backed by the full-faith-and-credit guarantee of the U.S. government	\$1,000 minimum; \$1 increments	16th or the 20th of the month for Ginnie Mae I and II collateral, respectively, following the record date and every month thereafter
Freddie Mac Remic	Full and timely payment of interest and scheduled principal, guaranteed by Freddie Mac	\$1; \$1 increments (most dealers, however, require a minimum investment of \$1,000 or more)	15th of the month following the record date and every month thereafter
Fannie Mae REMIC	Full and timely payment of interest and scheduled principal, guaranteed by Fannie Mae (Collateral of Fannie Mae "G" series is also backed by the full faith and credit of the U.S. government.)	\$1,000 minimum; \$1 increments	18th or the 25th of the month following the record date and every month thereafter
Agency-Backed, Private-Label CMO/REMIC	Collateral guaranteed by Ginnie Mae, Fannie Mae, or Freddie Mac. Structure provides basis for AAA rating, but these securities carry no explicit government guarantee; they are the sole obligation of their issuer.	Varies	Varies; may be monthly, quarterly, or semiannually; with or without payment delay
Whole-Loan Backed, Private-Label CMO/REMIC	Credit support provided by some combination of issuer or third-party guarantee, letter of credit, overcollateralization, pool insurance, and/or subordination. Generally rated AA or AAA	Varies	Varies; may be monthly, quarterly, or semiannually; with or without payment delay

Data source: The Bond Market Association.

Like mortgage-backed securities, asset-backed securities are underwritten by dealers and sold to investors around the world. As the underlying loans are repaid by borrowers, interest income and principal repayments are passed on to investors. In some instances, insurance or letters of credit are used to enhance the creditworthiness of asset-backed securities and increase their appeal among investors.

The asset-backed securities market is one of the fastest-growing areas in the financial services sector. At this point, the total value of outstanding asset-backed securities approaches $1 trillion. Investors in asset-backed securities include pension funds, mutual funds, insurance companies, and other financial institutions.

The Repurchase (or Repo) Market

repo market Securities lending market.

The ability of securities firms to price securities effectively and to underwrite issues of government and corporate debt depends on their ability to finance their holdings. The repurchase market or securities lending markets are commonly referred to as the **repo market.** It is essential for the smooth functioning of all the fixed income markets. Highly liquid debt security markets require readily available funding to ensure continuous liquidity. Repurchase agreements (repos) are the most important source of liquidity in the Treasury and agency securities markets.

In a typical repo agreement, a securities dealer wishing to finance a bond position sells the bonds to a cash investor while simultaneously agreeing to repurchase them at a later date for an agreed-on price. The investor receives a return for providing the funds during the specified period. A "reverse repo" is just the opposite or reverse of a repo. In a reverse repo agreement, the seller agrees to repurchase them at a future point in time. The term of any repo or reverse repo agreement can be custom tailored for any debt instrument over any period, ranging from overnight to one year.

The repo market began as a means through which securities dealers could finance their bond "inventories" and still serves this vital purpose today. Large institutional investors have discovered that they can often earn better short-term yields by investing idle cash in the repo market than by investing in bank deposits or money market instruments. This is because the immense size of many repo agreements makes simple borrower-lender transactions more cost-effective than traditional lending agreements.

The outstanding volume of repos is enormous and growing rapidly. In excess of $2 trillion of repo agreements are recorded on a daily basis among primary dealers in U.S. government securities alone. Securities firms, pension funds, state and local governments, and mutual funds use the repo market as a relatively safe haven for cash investments. For large lenders and borrowers, it is often a safe and flexible alternative to bank deposits and money market instruments. This is because most repo agreements are typically executed in conjunction with U.S. Treasury bonds, mortgage securities, or other forms of highly liquid debt securities.

Money Market

money market Buying and selling short-term debt securities that can be quickly converted into cash.

Market Characteristics

The **money market** is the market used for buying and selling short-term debt securities that can be quickly converted into cash. The buyer of a money market instrument is the lender; the seller of a money market instrument is the borrower. By definition, money market instruments have a term-to-maturity of one year or less. Most have a maturity that is much shorter, on the order of six months or less. As in the case of T-bills, the majority of money market instruments are issued at a discount from par or face value. This means that the money market lenders do not receive explicit interest payments but earn interest income in the form of a short-term appreciation in the value of money market instruments. For the most part, $100,000 is the minimum face amount traded in the money market. Obviously, this market is dominated by institutional investors. Smaller investors participate via money market mutual funds that have minimum investment requirements as low as $1,000.

Money market instruments are generally regarded as safe. Of course, some money market instruments are safer than others. Given very short maturities, both corporate and government-issued market instruments are free from interest-rate risk. Despite the fact that only blue-chip private-sector issuers are able to participate in the money market, only government-issued money market instruments are also free from default risk.

Money Market Instruments

In terms of dollar volume, the money market is dominated by trading in Treasury securities. In addition to T-bills, Treasury notes, and Treasury bonds with one year or less to maturity are also traded. The outstanding volume of such securities gives great liquidity to the money market. Huge trading volume ensures low dealer bid-ask spreads and low customer trading costs. Dealer spreads in the T-bill market, for example, often range as low as six to eight **basis points,** or 0.06–0.08%. Dealer spreads in the market for privately issued money market instruments, called **commercial paper,** tend to be slightly higher.

Common forms of commercial paper include promissory notes issued by finance companies in denominations that range from $100,000 to $5,000,000. Issued by finance companies such as General Motors Acceptance Corp., finance dealer paper typically matures in 15 to 170 days. Although early buybacks can usually be negotiated with dealers, finance dealer paper often has only a limited secondary market. Industrial dealer paper includes the very short-term promissory notes of leading industrial firms. Generally used to finance inventories, industrial dealer paper is sold in denominations of $500,000 to $5,000,000. Such obligations typically have maturities from 30 to 180 days and enjoy only a limited secondary market.

Bankers' acceptances are time drafts drawn on and accepted by banking institutions that substitute their credit for that of an importer or other holder of merchandise. Bankers' acceptances range in denomination from $25,000 to $1,000,000 and have terms-to-maturity that run up to 270 days. They feature an active secondary market in which bid-ask spreads tend to be on the order of 50 basis points, or 0.5%, or less. **Negotiable certificates of deposit** are time deposits at commercial banks that range from $100,000 to $1,000,000 in denomination and feature an active secondary market.

State and local governments are also active in the money market. Local public housing agencies issue **project notes** secured by a contract with federal agencies and by the pledge of the full faith and credit of the U.S. government. These are sold in denominations of $1,000 to $1,000,000, mature in periods of up to one year, and enjoy an active secondary market. **Tax anticipation notes** are issued by municipalities that expect a near-term receipt of additional tax revenues. **Bond anticipation notes** are issued when revenue is anticipated from a bond issue.

basis points
1/100th of 1% (e.g., ½% is 50 basis points).

commercial paper
Money market instruments issued by private entities.

bankers' acceptances
Time drafts drawn on and accepted by banking institutions.

negotiable certificates of deposit
Time deposits at commercial banks.

project notes
Local public housing agency issues secured by the full faith and credit of the U.S. government.

tax anticipation notes
Municipal bonds issued on the expectation of the near-term receipt of additional tax revenues.

bond anticipation notes
Municipal bonds issued on the expectation of the near-term receipt of funds from a bond issue.

revenue anticipation notes Municipal bonds issued on the expectation of the near-term receipt of revenue from the state or federal government.

Revenue anticipation notes are sometimes issued in anticipation of revenue from the state or federal government. Municipal notes have an initial term-to-maturity of 60 days to one year and are typically available in denominations of about $25,000.

The generally short maturities of money market instruments permit borrowers great flexibility in funding short-term cash needs. Money market instruments also appeal to investors who seek protection from sometimes highly volatile interest rates. From the investor's perspective, money market instruments represent a liquid, low-risk investment that generally offers a higher yield than bank deposits. The rising popularity of money market mutual funds has been a major factor in the growth of demand for money market instruments. Now estimated at roughly $1.5 trillion dollars, the immense size and easy liquidity of the money market makes it an extraordinarily cost-effective source of corporate financing.

Municipal Bonds

Tax Advantages

municipal bonds Debt issued by state or local governments.

An estimated 50,000 state and local governments and their agencies borrow money by issuing **municipal bonds** to build, repair, or improve schools, streets, highways, hospitals, sewer systems, and so on. Municipal bond issuers repay their debts in two ways. Projects that benefit the entire community, such as schools, courthouses, and municipal office buildings, are typically funded by general obligation bonds repaid with tax revenues. Projects that benefit only certain users or user groups, such as utilities and toll roads, are typically funded by revenue bonds that are paid for with user fees.

When the federal income tax law was adopted in 1913, interest on municipal bonds was excluded from federal taxation. The underlying rationale is that it would be improper for the federal government to tax state and local operations. As a result, municipal bond investors are willing to accept lower yields than those they can obtain from taxable bonds. Generally speaking, after adjusting for risk, investors look to equate the after-tax interest income earned on taxable bonds with the after-tax return earned on municipal bonds. The appropriate tax rate consideration is the highest *marginal* federal tax rate paid by the typical municipal bond investor. As a result, state and local governments are able to borrow at interest rates that are, on average, 30–40% lower than would otherwise be possible. Given the taxing authority of state and local governments, the municipal securities market is generally regarded as having relatively high quality. Municipal bonds have a safety record that is second only to that of the U.S. Treasury bond market and appeal to a wide variety of bond investors.

Under present federal income tax law, the interest income received from investing in municipal bonds is free from federal income taxes. In most states, interest income received from securities issued by governmental units within the state is also exempt from state and local taxes. In all 50 states, interest income from securities issued by U.S. territories and possessions is exempt from federal, state, and local income taxes. If a resident of New York City buys a municipal bond issued by the City of New York, interest income is not subject to income taxes imposed by the federal government, New York State, or New York City. If the same investor bought a municipal bond from a city in Connecticut, state and local taxes would be payable on the accrued interest. Keep in mind that any capital gains realized from the sale of municipal bonds is not exempt from tax. Only accrued interest on municipal bonds enjoys favorable tax treatment.

One of the best ways to appreciate the tax-exempt advantages of municipal securities is to compare them with similar bond investments that produce taxable interest income. For example, suppose an investor files a joint return with $175,000 in taxable income and has interest income subject to the highest marginal federal income rate of 36%. Now, assume such an investor has $50,000 to invest in a tax-exempt municipal bond yielding 5% or a corporate bond yielding 7.5% in taxable interest income. Which investment is most advantageous on an after-tax basis? In this case, the municipal bond investment is preferable. A $50,000 municipal bond investment at 5% yields $2,500 per year in tax-free income. A $50,000 investment in a 7.5% bond yields $3,750 in taxable interest income per year. With a marginal tax rate of 36%, such an investment would yield only 4.8% after taxes and generate only $2,400 in after-tax income. In this example, the municipal bond provides the best after-tax yield. The tax-exempt security makes an even better investment if one also accounts for state and local income taxes. Table 6.3 shows the tax-equivalent yields for various tax-exempt interest rates, depending on the taxpayer's income tax bracket.

TABLE 6.3 Tax-Equivalent Yields

Taxable Income*						
Single Return	$0– $25,750	$25,751– $62,450	$62,451– $130,250	$130,251– $283,150	$283,151 & over	**Sample Effective Marginal Rate for Certain High-Income Taxpayers**
Joint Return	$0– $43,050	$43,051– $104,050	$104,051– $158,550	$158,551– $283,150	$283,151 & over	
Tax Bracket	15%	28%	31%	36%	39.6%	**41%****
Tax-Exempt Yields (%)			**Taxable Yield Equivalents (%)**			
2.0%	2.35%	2.78%	2.90%	3.12%	3.31%	**3.39%**
2.5	2.94	3.47	3.62	3.91	4.14	**4.24**
3.0	3.53	4.17	4.35	4.69	4.97	**5.08**
3.5	4.12	4.86	5.07	5.47	5.79	**5.93**
4.0	4.71	5.56	5.80	6.25	6.62	**6.78**
4.5	5.29	6.25	6.52	7.03	7.45	**7.63**
5.0	5.88	6.94	7.25	7.81	8.28	**8.47**
5.5	6.47	7.64	7.79	8.59	9.11	**9.32**
6.0	7.06	8.33	8.70	9.37	9.93	**10.17**
6.5	7.65	9.03	9.42	10.16	10.76	**11.02**
7.0	8.24	9.72	10.14	10.94	11.59	**11.86**
7.5	8.82	10.42	10.87	11.72	12.42	**12.71**
8.0	9.41	11.11	11.59	12.50	13.25	**13.56**

*The income brackets to which the tax rates apply are adjusted annually for inflation. Those listed above are estimated for 1999.

**The Internal Revenue Code phases out the personal exemption deduction for taxpayers with adjusted gross income in excess of $189,950 (married, filing jointly) and $126,600 (single taxpayers). In addition, certain itemized deductions are reduced for taxpayers with adjusted gross income in excess of $126,600. In general, the limit on itemized deductions will increase the effective marginal tax rate by 1%, and the personal exemption phaseout will increase the effective marginal tax rate by 0.8% for each exemption claimed.

Data source: The Bond Market Association.

clientele effect Ownership influence resulting when specific securities have special appeal to certain investors.

Notice that the favorable tax treatment of municipal bond interest income has a twofold effect. First, it allows local governments to issue bonds at interest rates that fall significantly below interest rates on taxable instruments. And second, the favorable tax treatment of municipal bond interest income creates a **clientele effect** whereby such securities are of primary appeal to those investors with the highest taxable income. As shown in Figure 6.9A, property and casualty insurance companies and commercial banks are major investors in municipal bonds, with each holding about 13.8% and 7.2% of the total value of all municipal bonds, respectively. As shown in Figure 6.9B, high-income individuals, investing directly or through mutual funds and bank personal trust accounts, hold about three-quarters of the roughly $1.5 trillion of municipal debt outstanding.

Municipal Bond Types

general obligation bonds Municipal bonds backed by the full faith and credit of the issuer.

A wide variety of municipal bonds are issued by state and local governments to support general and specific financing needs. **General obligation bonds** are backed by the full faith and credit of the issuer for prompt payment of principal and interest. Issued by cities, counties, and school districts, such bonds often enjoy added security because issuing authorities can raise property taxes to ensure payment.

FIGURE 6.9 Municipal Bond Holdings

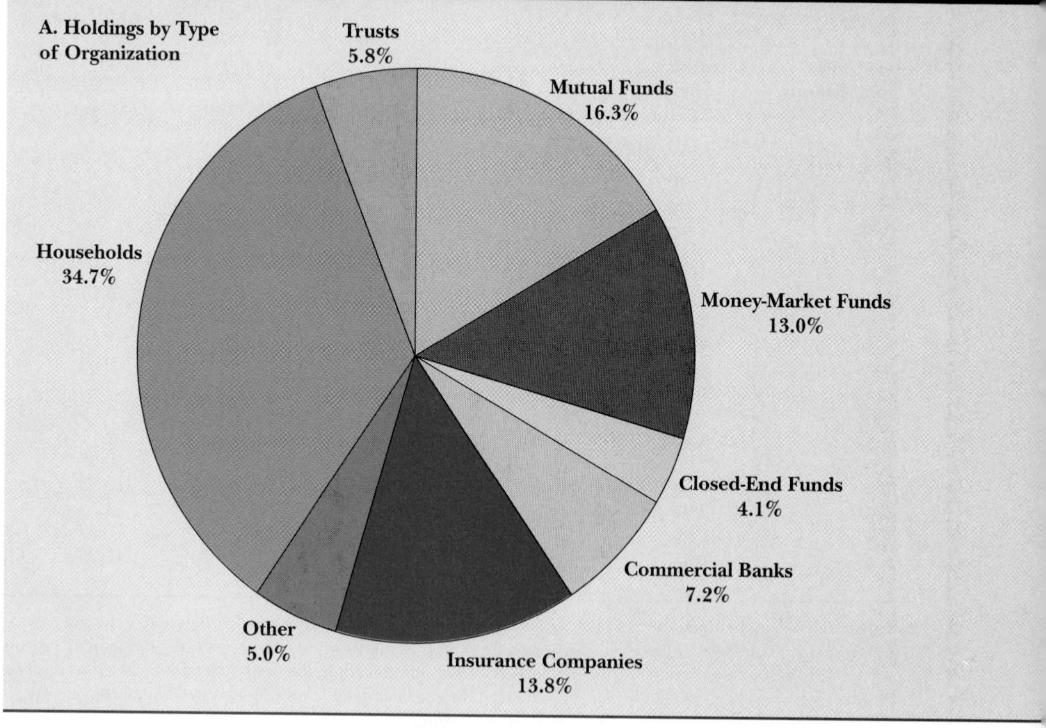

Data sources: Internal Revenue Service and the Bond Market Association <http://bondmarket.com>.

These guarantees are of an unlimited nature because issuers can raise taxes as high as necessary to ensure full repayment of bond principal and interest. If sufficient tax revenues are not forthcoming, property and other assets can be sold to satisfy legal claims. As a result, general obligation bonds are among the most creditworthy of all municipal bond instruments. **Limited tax bonds** and **special tax bonds** are payable from a pledge of the proceeds from a specific tax. Such taxes could be a gasoline tax, a special assessment levy, or an ad valorem tax.

Revenue bonds are payable from the earnings of revenue-producing government agencies or public enterprises. Examples include water and sewer utilities, school districts, and airport authorities. Many such agencies or enterprises have the ability to levy service charges or fees (e.g., landing fees at the local airport). The creditworthiness of government agencies and public enterprises is analyzed in terms of historical or potential earnings compared with financing requirements. Many communities also issue **industrial revenue bonds** to develop industrial and/or commercial property for the benefit of private users. Money raised from this type of municipal bond issue is used to pay for the construction of new facilities, which are then leased to a corporate guarantor. The safety of industrial revenue bonds depends on the creditworthiness of the issuing municipality and the corporate guarantor. The yield on revenue bonds is generally somewhat higher than on general

limited tax bonds Bonds payable from the proceeds of a specific tax.

special tax bonds Limited tax bonds.

revenue bonds Bonds payable from the earnings of revenue-producing government agencies or public enterprises.

industrial revenue bonds Bonds used to develop industrial and/or commercial property for the benefit of private users.

FIGURE 6.9 ***(continued)***

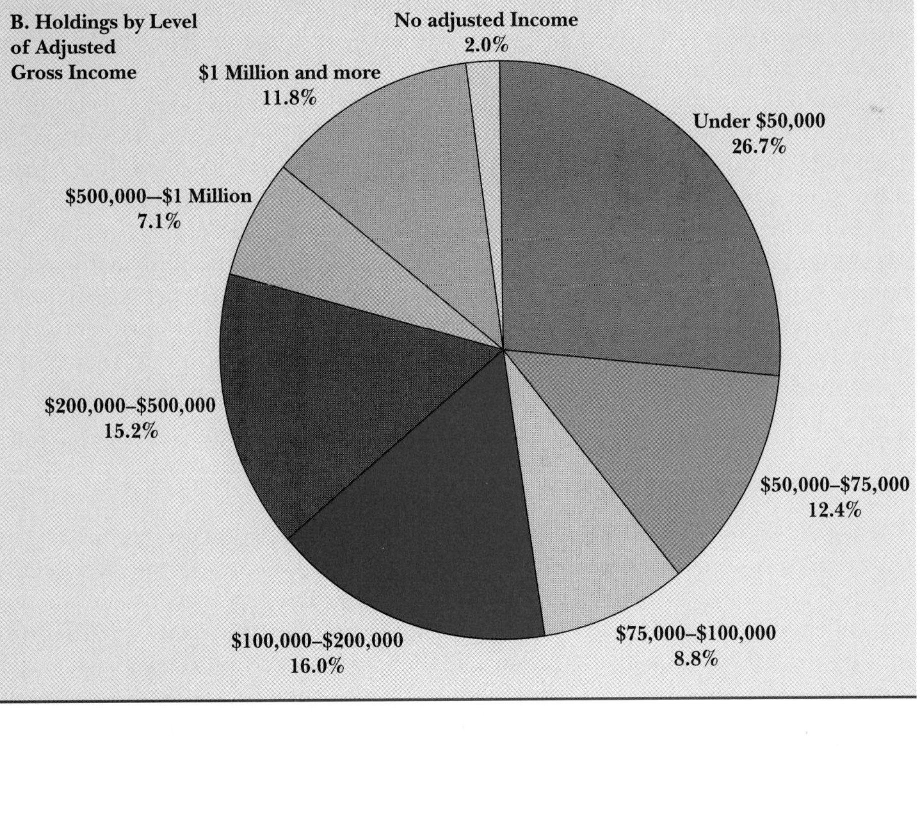

obligation bonds because tax receipts tend to be more predictable than fee-based revenue streams. Nevertheless, revenue bonds have compiled a good payment record over a long period of time.

A large number of other municipal bond types are also traded. Housing bonds, for example, are issued by both state and local governments. These bonds are typically secured by mortgages on single-family homes. Added bondholder protections come in the form of federal subsidies for low-income families, FHA insurance, VA guarantees, and private mortgage insurance. **Moral obligation bonds** are a type of special-purpose municipal bond. They were first introduced in the 1960s by New York State, which implied that in the event of a shortfall the state would make up the difference. **Double-barreled bonds** are tax-exempt municipal bonds backed by a pledge of two or more sources. Double-barreled bonds are similar to general obligation bonds that are backed by a second source of revenue to increase their safety.

moral obligation bonds
Bonds backed by the good name of the issuer.

double-barreled bonds
Tax-exempt municipal bonds backed by a pledge of two or more sources.

Sources of Bond Market Information

Print and Broadcast Media

If one is interested in buying or selling bonds, a good place to start is to compare prices among similar securities. An easy place to check bond prices is in the financial media, such as *The Wall Street Journal, Investor's Business Daily,* or *Barron's.* Each of these publications has extensive tables showing representative bond prices in recent trades. These publications also offer excellent running commentary about factors influencing the fixed-income securities market. Investors must recognize that bond prices and other information in printed financial publications represent historical snapshots. Current prices and trading information can and does vary based on current market conditions.

In addition, with the growth of business news channels on cable television, the broadcast media have become an important source of bond market information. On CNBC and CNNfn, investors can check on benchmark Treasury bond prices during the day and keep abreast of economic releases that effect bond yields.

The Internet has also become a rich source of bond market information, with many sites providing comprehensive market data and descriptive information about bonds. Perhaps the best of these is maintained by the Bond Market Association at <http://www.bondmarket.com>. In addition to being an excellent primary source for bond market information, this excellent Web site also provides a gateway to bond market information on the Internet with literally dozens of valuable bond market links.

Bond Market Association

The Bond Market Association, a nonprofit organization headquartered in New York City, represents securities firms and banks that underwrite, trade, and sell debt securities. The association stems from the Investment Bankers Association of America, which was founded in 1912. It became a separate organization in 1976, representing dealers in municipal, Treasury, federal agency, and mortgage-backed debt securities. The association's representation of mortgage-backed and government securities was enhanced in 1980 through a merger with the Government National

WALL STREET WISDOM 6.3

Barbells and Dumbbells

Every amateur weight lifter is familiar with barbells. Barbells are long iron bars with heavy weights attached at each end. Weight lifters use them to build stamina and strength. With a narrow handle, barbells are relatively easy to lift and maneuver, even when a substantial amount of weight is balanced at the end of the handle bar. Of course, lifting hundreds of pounds of iron is never truly easy.

In the bond market, a barbell strategy might result in a portfolio becoming evenly split between short-term Treasury bills that mature in 90 days or less and long-term Treasury bonds that might have a term-to-maturity of as long as 30 years. Therefore, a barbell bond investment strategy resembles a weight lifter's barbell in that the portfolio manager's fixed-income investments are equally balanced at both ends of the term-to-maturity spectrum. A barbell bond investment strategy sometimes becomes attractive when long-term interest rates offer a significant premium over the interest income earned on short-term and intermediate-term issues. Risk-averse bond investors often pursue a barbell strategy when they have significant short-term funding needs but also believe long-term rates are poised to decline. In February 2000, unprecedented volatility rocked the long-term bond market as bond investors pursued what some market observers referred to as a "dumbbell" bond investment strategy. In this case, the term *dumbbell* is not a term typically used to describe a bond investment strategy. When it comes to bond investing, the term *dumbbell* has the same meaning as it does in popular expression, as in "havc you lost your cotton-picking mind?"

Long-term bond investors were hit with unprecedented losses as interest rates on 30-year Treasury bonds rose from 4.88% in October 1998 to 6.598% in January 2000. Thus, it was with some trepidation that bond investors awaited the market effects stemming from long-anticipated short-term interest rate increases engineered by Federal Reserve Board Chairman Allan Greenspan in February 2000. On the one hand, it seemed like a safe bet that market interest rates would rise and long-term bond prices would fall in the wake of fed-engineered short-term rate increases. Long-term bond investors typically demand a significant interest rate risk premium over the amount earned on short-term bonds, and a decline in long-term bond prices would be a typical fallout from rising short-term rates. On the other hand, Greenspan had widely telegraphed the Fed's intention to raise short-term rates, and it might be reasonable to expect that the long-term bond market had already "priced in" the effects of a widely anticipated rate increase. Thus, as the long-anticipated fed announcement of an increase in interest rates was made in February 2000, the bond market was on pins and needles as investors and speculators waited to see if long bond prices would fall or remain stable in the face of rising short-term rates.

What few anticipated was that long-term rates would *fall* and long bond prices would *rise* in response to the Fed's action. William Gross is managing director and in charge of bond investment strategies for Pacific Investment Management Co. In the investments world, Gross is widely regarded as one of the most savvy bond investors. In mid-January, Gross realized that prices for long-term Treasury bonds would rise and yields would fall because falling federal deficits were shrinking the supply of long-term bonds, even as the Fed was engineering a series of increases in short-term interest rates. Gross bought large amounts of long-term Treasury bonds and dumbfounded Wall Street traders who had expected prices for Treasury securities to remain weak amid rising interest rates. The surprising strategy earned the nation's largest bond fund more than $200 million in trading profits and triggered panicked trading that roiled the market and left even seasoned bond professionals reeling.

Was this an example of shrewd bond trading or a simple example of dumb luck? Check Yahoo! and see what has happened to rates on long-term Treasury bonds. If they have fallen, Gross is a genius. If they have risen, maybe Gross is mortal after all.

See: Gregory Zuckerman, "Pimco Provided Spark for Turmoil in Bonds," *The Wall Street Journal*, February 25, 2000, C1, C2.

Mortgage Association Dealers Association and, in 1983, with the Primary Dealers Association. In 1984, the association formed a money market committee, and in 1994, the funding division was established to better represent repo and securities lending.

Membership in the association is open to any bona fide dealer in bonds and other debt securities. The association's objectives include endorsement of "open and free access to the public securities markets throughout the world." The Bond Market Association has approximately 264 member and associate-member firms and 21 affiliates. At least 20% of member firms are substantially owned by foreign institutions.

The Bond Market Association speaks for the bond industry and advocates its positions. In New York, Washington, D.C., London, and Tokyo and with issuer and investor groups nationwide, the association represents members' interests. It keeps members informed of relevant legislative, regulatory, and market practice developments and provides a forum through which the industry can review and respond to current issues. The association also strives to standardize market practices and commonly used documentation, both to promote efficiency and to reduce costs. It helps members solve common problems and develop more efficient management, operations, and communications methods, thereby benefiting not only the industry but the investing and taxpaying public as well. The association also strives to educate legislators, regulators, the press, and investors on the size and importance of the bond market. It publishes books, brochures, manuals, and other educational materials and sponsors seminars, conferences, and informational meetings on topics of current interest. The association also compiles and tracks various industry-related statistics on a historical basis and disseminates the information through published research reports and on the Internet at <http://www.bondmarket.com>.

Summary

- **Bond dealers** are securities firms and banks that act as financial intermediaries between the **bond issuer** and **bond investors.** Bond issuers sell newly minted bonds in the **primary bond market** to dealers who then resell those bonds to investors in the **secondary bond market.** Once bonds have been issued and sold to individual and institutional investors, bond dealers use their capital to maintain active secondary markets.
- The 30-year Treasury bond is a benchmark statistic for the **current yield** on long-term bonds and reflects the **holding-period risk** typical of long-term bonds, or the chance of loss during periods of adverse changes in bond prices. Because all Treasury securities are backed by the full faith and credit of the U.S. government, they entail no **default risk.** The trend in interest rates for short-term securities that involve no holding period or default risk is captured by changes in the yield on three-month Treasury bills and the overnight **federal funds** rate. The fed funds rate is the amount charged to member banks of the Federal Reserve System who need funds to maintain required balances with the Federal Reserve. Although the fed funds rate is for bank-to-bank lending, the **discount rate** is the interest rate charged on loans made by the Federal Reserve itself. Modestly higher than the fed funds rate are short-term rates in Europe for dollar-denominated loans, the **Eurodollar** market, and **London Interbank Offered Rates (LIBOR).**

- Bonds are debt securities that pay a rate of interest based on the initial or **par value** of the bond. In the bond market, a **round lot** is measured in terms of $1 million in par value. Most debt securities carry an interest rate that remains fixed until **maturity,** or the specific future point in time at which principal and interest will be paid in full. For specific price-yield information, investors supply their broker with the bond's **CUSIP** number. This unique code numbering system was developed by the Committee on Uniform Security Identification Procedures. Bond interest rates are commonly expressed as a percentage of the **face amount** of the bond, sometimes referred to as its **principal amount.** If a bond is trading for less than the face amount, it is trading at a **discount to par.** If a bond is trading for more than the face amount (usually $1,000), it is trading at a **premium to par.** Corporate bonds are commonly issued in **book entry form,** without any certificate.
- Corporations and other borrowers sometimes issue debt for short periods to finance imports, to meet seasonal cash-flow needs or to create **bridge financing** until conditions are right for longer-term debt issues. The precise terms of the legal agreement between the corporation and the bondholder are called the **indenture. Bearer bonds,** or **coupon bonds,** feature vouchers that are submitted twice a year to authorized banks for the payment of interest. Today, all fixed-income securities are sold as **registered bonds.** Since 1986, all U.S. government bonds have been sold in book-entry form. The owner of book-entry bonds has no certificate. An **unsecured corporate bond** is backed only by the reputation, credit record, and financial stability of the corporation. Unsecured bonds, sometimes referred to as **debentures,** are generally issued by the largest and most creditworthy corporations.
- A **senior bond** has prior claim to other junior securities in the event of default. **Mortgage bonds** or **equipment trust certificates** are often referred to as senior bonds because they are senior to any other type of debt instrument. A debenture that is **subordinated** comes behind every other creditor but still ahead of preferred and common stock. With a **closed-end mortgage bond,** pledged assets can only be sold to pay off a specific bond issue. With an **open-end mortgage bond,** proceeds from the sale of pledged assets can be used to pay off multiple bond issues. **Serial bonds** are a series of bonds to be retired in sequence. The most junior grade of corporate bonds is called an **income bond.**
- The Treasury issues its securities through regularly scheduled public auctions using **primary dealers.** Short-term (one year or less) **T-bills** are very actively traded, highly liquid, direct short-term obligations of the U.S. government. T-bills do not pay interest and are purchased by investors at a discount. Intermediate-term (one to 10 year) **T-notes** pay interest on a semiannual basis and always expire at par value, which may vary from $5,000 to $10,000 to $1 million. **T-bonds** mature anywhere from 10 to 30 years.
- Certain U.S. government agencies and **government-sponsored enterprises** issue debt to help finance desirable private-sector activities such as home ownership, farming, and education. Fannie Mae and Freddie Mac assemble these residential mortgages into diversified packages or **pools** of such loans and then issue securities that represent a proportionate share in the interest and principal payments derived on that pool. This is sometimes referred to as the **mortgage securitization process.** The Government National Mortgage Association (or Ginnie Mae) issues **modified pass-through certificates,** which represent an interest in a given pool of FHA and VA mortgages.

- The **repo market,** or security lending market, is an important complement to the **money market,** in which short-term debt securities are bought and sold. Bid-ask spreads in this market are tiny and measured in **basis points,** or 1/100th of 1%. Money market instruments issued by private entities are called **commercial paper. Bankers' acceptances** are time drafts drawn on and accepted by banking institutions that substitute their credit for that of an importer or other holder of merchandise. **Negotiable certificates of deposit** are time deposits at commercial banks that range from $100,000 to $1,000,000 in denomination and feature an active secondary market. Local public housing agencies issue **project notes** secured by a contract with federal agencies and by the pledge of the full faith and credit of the U.S. government. **Tax anticipation notes** are issued by municipalities that expect a near-term receipt of additional tax revenues. **Bond anticipation notes** are issued when revenue is anticipated from a bond issue. **Revenue anticipation notes** are sometimes issued in anticipation of revenue coming in from the federal government or, in the case of a local municipality, an anticipation of revenue from the state or federal government.
- An estimated 50,000 state and local governments and their agencies borrow money by issuing **municipal bonds.** Under present federal income tax law, the interest income received from investing in municipal bonds is free from federal income taxes. The favorable tax treatment of municipal bond interest income creates a **clientele effect** whereby such securities are of primary appeal only to those investors with the highest taxable income.
- A large number of municipal bond types are traded. **General obligation bonds** are backed by the full faith and credit of the issuer for prompt payment of principal and interest. **Limited tax bonds** and **special tax bonds** are payable from a pledge of the proceeds from a specific tax. Such taxes could be a gasoline tax, a special assessment levy, or an ad valorem tax. **Revenue bonds** are payable from the earnings of revenue-producing government agencies or public enterprises. Many communities also issue **industrial revenue bonds** to develop industrial and/or commercial property for the benefit of private users. **Moral obligation bonds** are a type of special-purpose municipal bond. **Double-barreled bonds** are tax-exempt municipal bonds backed by a pledge of two or more funding sources.

Questions

1. Compared with the market capitalization of domestic common stocks, the U.S. bond market is
   a. five times as large.
   b. three times as large.
   c. roughly the same.
   d. one-third as large.
2. Preferred stock
   a. has a specified life.
   b. has a price that does not fluctuate.
   c. is a debt security.
   d. has dividends that are not tax deductible for issuers.

3. Bond-trading volumes are highest for
    a. Treasury securities.
    b. corporate debt.
    c. municipal bonds.
    d. asset-backed securities.
4. Treasury bonds have initial maturities of
    a. less than 1 year.
    b. less than 5 years.
    c. less than 10 years.
    d. 10–30 years.
5. An example of a federal agency security is
    a. a Ginnie Mae pass-through certificate.
    b. The Washington Public Power Supply System's bonds.
    c. a Treasury note.
    d. Philadelphia Electric bonds.
6. Treasury bills do *not*
    a. have an initial maturity of one year or less.
    b. get sold on an auction basis.
    c. pay interest every six months.
    d. enjoy a federal guarantee of principal *and* interest.
7. Public ownership of Treasury securities is largely concentrated in the hands of
    a. insurance companies.
    b. corporations.
    c. state and local governments.
    d. institutions.
8. The rate of return on money market securities is
    a. slightly below the Treasury bill rate.
    b. slightly above the Treasury bill rate.
    c. set by regulation.
    d. slightly below the insured bank CD rate.
9. Select the *false* statement about Treasury bills:
    a. Typical maturities are 13 and 26 weeks.
    b. A good secondary market exists for T-bills.
    c. T-bills are sold at par and pay interest at maturity.
    d. T-bills are sold on an auction basis every week.
10. Select the *false* statement about money market securities:
    a. CDs are negotiable.
    b. Banker's acceptances are not negotiable instruments.
    c. The secondary market for commercial paper is weak.
    d. Eurodollars are dollar-denominated deposits held in foreign banks.

11. Select the *true* statement about federal agency securities:
    a. Federally sponsored credit agencies are nonprofit institutions.
    b. Fannie Mae securities are a direct obligation of the U.S. government.
    c. Federally sponsored credit agency securities are guaranteed by the Federal government.
    d. Ginnie Mae is a wholly owned government agency.
12. The quoted market price of a 10% coupon bond with semiannual discounting, three years to maturity, and a market return of 8% is
    a. $1,000.
    b. $105.25.
    c. $1,260.
    d. $125.88.
13. Treasury notes have an initial term-to-maturity of
    a. 2–10 years.
    b. 1 year or less maturity.
    c. more than 10 years.
    d. more than 30 years.
14. Current yield is the
    a. internal rate of return that equates the prevailing market price with future interest and principal payments.
    b. approximate yield-to-call for premium bonds.
    c. coupon interest divided by the average of market and call prices.
    d. coupon rate expressed as a percentage of the prevailing market price.
15. The present value of $1 million to be received in 36 years at a discount rate of 6% is roughly
    a. $125,000.
    b. $67,500.
    c. $500,000.
    d. $8 million.
16. The smallest measure used for quoting bond yields is
    a. a percentage point.
    b. the yield-to-maturity.
    c. an inflection point.
    d. a basis point.
17. The interest rate charged by the U.S. Federal Reserve, the nation's central bank, for loans to member banks is the
    a. federal funds rate.
    b. Treasury bill rate.
    c. prime rate.
    d. discount rate.

18. The interest rate charged on overnight loans from one U.S. commercial bank to another is called the
    a. federal funds rate.
    b. LIBOR rate.
    c. prime rate.
    d. discount rate.
19. Bonds sold in book-entry form are called
    a. indentures.
    b. coupon bonds.
    c. debentures.
    d. registered bonds.
20. Double-barreled bonds are tax-exempt municipal bonds
    a. payable from the earnings of revenue-producing government agencies or public enterprises.
    b. used to develop industrial and/or commercial property for the benefit of private users.
    c. backed by the good name of the issuer.
    d. backed by a pledge of multiple income sources.

Investment Application

Bills, Notes, Bonds, and Inflation

Treasury securities are considered the safest of all debt instruments because they are legally backed by the "full faith and credit" of the U.S. government. This designation is the highest level of backing given on a U.S. government security. It means that the federal government pledges to use its full taxing and borrowing authority to pay promised interest and to repay the full amount of borrowed principal or face amount of the security. The federal government can also avoid default by simply printing more money. Notice that the cash in your pocket, called a Federal Reserve Note, is simply a non-interest-bearing certificate that enables the holder to demand payment of "one dollar" from the U.S. Treasury. Of course, there is a bit of circular reasoning at work here because the U.S. Treasury defines "one dollar" as one Federal Reserve Note. A demand at the Treasury for the payment of "one dollar" in exchange for one Federal Reserve Note will be met by the issuance of one new, crisp Federal Reserve Note. The advantage of holding T-bills or other Treasury securities over cash is that Treasury securities pay interest income, but the cash held in your pocket earns a 0% rate of return. The advantage of cash over Treasury securities, of course, is that only cash is widely recognized as the currency of choice for the purchase of goods and services.

The price of Treasury securities at any point in time is simply set by the interplay of supply and demand. When bond investors project a market-wide decline in interest rates, they scramble to lock in current interest rates, bid up bond prices, and yields begin to fall. In such instances, bond investors are simply trading cash for Treasury securities. When bond investors project a rise in interest rates, they dump bond portfolios, causing bond prices to fall and yields begin to rise. This represents a simple trade of Treasury securities for cash. Remember, bond prices are just the terms of trade for bonds expressed in terms of cash. If the Treasury Department flooded the marketplace with an immense supply of new bonds, Treasury bond prices would plummet, and interest rates would soar. Conversely, if a budget surplus cut borrowing needs and allowed the federal government to begin to buy back Treasury securities, the supply of new bonds would fall, Treasury bond prices would rise, and interest rates would drop.

Although many investors feel comfortable with the notion that bond prices and interest rates are determined by the forces of supply and demand, they feel less comfortable with the concept that the "price" of money is set in a similar fashion. Indeed, what is the "price" of money? The answer is simple. When a consumer buys a blouse for $40, the terms of trade are simply one blouse: $40. Not only is the blouse price $40, the "worth" of that same $40 is one blouse. If importers flooded the marketplace with an immense supply of new blouses, blouse prices would plummet, and the value of cash would rise. Conversely, if an import embargo cut the supply of new blouses, blouse prices would rise, and the value of cash would fall. The market for all goods and services works the same way. If the money supply rises faster than the pace of growth in the overall economy, prices rise and **inflation** occurs. If the money supply rises slower than the pace at which the overall economy grows, prices fall and **deflation** occurs. When the money supply and the overall economy grow at the same rate, price stability ensues. During the 20th century, the U.S. economy has been marked by persistent inflation that averages on the order of 3–4% per year. Falling prices, or deflation, is seldom seen and has not been experienced in the United States since the 1930s and the Great Depression.

Given the enormous size of the Treasury securities market, a strong link is forged between bond prices, interest rates, and the rate of inflation. A rise in the rate of inflation causes a sharp decline in the value of future interest and principal payments and a downturn in bond prices. This is especially true in the case of T-bonds and other long-term debt securities. Because current market prices are determined on the basis of investor expectations, even the "whiff" of an uptick in inflation can throw a scare into bond investors and create bond-market turmoil. However, if investors expect a downturn in inflation, the worth of future interest and principal payments rises, and bond prices rise. Again, it is prices and interest rates on long-term bonds that are most sensitive to a downturn in inflationary expectations. Short-term bond prices and interest rates are less sensitive to changes in overall market conditions.

Thus, it is important to recognize that although all federal government debt obligations are free from default risk, the value of long-term government obligations is subject to changes in market interest rates. The market prices of long-term T-bonds are not guaranteed and will fluctuate daily—just like the prices of any other long-term bonds. Only T-bills that have a term-to-maturity of one year or less are free from the risk of bond market fluctuations triggered by changes in market interest rates. Although the amount of interest rate risk borne by short-term T-note holders is modest, the exposure to fluctuating interest rates and bond prices can be significant during rapidly changing markets.

As shown in Table 6.4, total rates of return earned by investors in Treasury securities can fluctuate widely. This is especially true in the case of long-term T-bonds. In 1999, for example, long-term T-bond investors suffered a loss of 8.74% in the

TABLE 6.4 Total Returns on Treasury Bonds, Treasury Notes, and Treasury Bills, 1950–Present

Year	Long-Term Treasury Bonds (> 10 y)	Intermediate-Term Treasury Notes (< 10 y)	Short-Term Treasury Bills (< 1 y)	Inflation Rate	T-Bill Real Return
1950	0.06%	0.70%	1.20%	5.79%	−4.59%
1951	−3.93%	0.36%	1.49%	5.87%	−4.38%
1952	1.16%	1.63%	1.66%	0.88%	0.78%
1953	3.64%	3.23%	1.82%	0.62%	1.20%
1954	7.19%	2.68%	0.86%	−0.50%	1.36%
1955	−1.29%	−0.65%	1.57%	0.37%	1.20%
1956	−5.59%	−0.42%	2.46%	2.86%	−0.40%
1957	7.46%	7.84%	3.14%	3.02%	0.12%
1958	−6.09%	−1.29%	1.54%	1.76%	−0.22%
1959	−2.26%	−0.39%	2.95%	1.50%	1.45%
1960	13.78%	11.76%	2.66%	1.48%	1.18%
1961	0.97%	1.85%	2.13%	0.67%	1.46%
1962	6.89%	5.56%	2.73%	1.22%	1.51%
1963	1.21%	1.64%	3.12%	1.65%	1.47%
1964	3.51%	4.04%	3.54%	1.19%	2.35%
1965	0.71%	1.02%	3.93%	1.92%	2.01%
1966	3.65%	4.69%	4.76%	3.35%	1.41%
1967	−9.18%	1.01%	4.21%	3.04%	1.17%
1968	−0.26%	4.54%	5.21%	4.72%	0.49%
1969	−5.07%	−0.74%	6.58%	6.11%	0.47%
1970	12.11%	16.86%	6.52%	5.49%	1.03%
1971	13.23%	8.72%	4.39%	3.36%	1.03%
1972	5.69%	5.16%	3.84%	3.41%	0.43%
1973	−1.11%	4.61%	6.93%	8.80%	−1.87%
1974	4.35%	5.69%	8.00%	12.20%	−4.20%
1975	9.20%	7.83%	5.80%	7.01%	−1.21%
1976	16.75%	12.87%	5.08%	4.81%	0.27%
1977	−0.69%	1.14%	5.12%	6.77%	−1.65%
1978	−1.18%	3.49%	7.18%	9.03%	−1.85%
1979	−1.23%	4.09%	10.38%	13.31%	−2.93%
1980	−3.95%	3.91%	11.24%	12.40%	−1.16%
1981	1.86%	9.45%	6.96%	8.94%	−1.98%
1982	40.36%	29.10%	11.59%	3.87%	7.72%
1983	0.65%	7.41%	8.64%	3.80%	4.84%
1984	15.48%	14.02%	10.20%	3.95%	6.25%
1985	30.97%	20.33%	7.87%	3.77%	4.10%
1986	24.53%	15.14%	6.41%	1.13%	5.28%
1987	−2.71%	2.90%	6.37%	4.41%	1.96%
1988	9.67%	6.10%	7.33%	4.42%	2.91%
1989	18.11%	13.29%	9.15%	4.65%	4.50%
1990	6.18%	9.73%	8.07%	6.11%	1.96%
1991	19.30%	15.46%	5.96%	3.06%	2.90%
1992	8.05%	7.19%	3.68%	2.90%	0.78%
1993	18.24%	11.24%	2.98%	2.75%	0.23%
1994	−7.77%	−5.14%	4.03%	2.67%	1.36%
1995	31.67%	16.80%	5.77%	2.54%	3.23%
1996	−0.93%	2.10%	5.24%	3.32%	1.92%
1997	15.08%	8.38%	5.38%	1.70%	3.68%
1998	13.52%	10.21%	5.31%	1.61%	3.70%
1999	−8.74%	−3.99%	4.94%	2.30%	2.64%
Arithmetic average	**6.07%**	**6.26%**	**5.16%**	**4.04%**	**1.12%**
Median	**3.58%**	**4.65%**	**5.10%**	**3.34%**	**1.20%**
Geometric mean	**5.56%**	**6.07%**	**5.12%**	**4.00%**	**1.09%**
Standard deviation	**10.70%**	**6.54%**	**2.69%**	**3.09%**	**2.51%**
Coefficent of variation	**1.76**	**1.04**	**0.52**	**0.76**	**2.24**

Data source: *Federal Reserve Bulletin.*

TABLE 6.5 Correlations in Total Returns for T-Bonds, T-Notes, T-Bills, and Inflation, 1950–Present

	Treasury Bonds	Treasury Notes	Treasury Bills	Inflation
Treasury Bonds	100.00%			
Treasury Notes	93.10%	100.00%		
Treasury Bills	33.50%	52.15%	100.00%	
Inflation	−16.88%	3.30%	63.12%	100.00%

Data source: *Federal Reserve Bulletin.*

value of their holdings during the course of a single year. Although such losses are rare for T-bond investors, such investors experienced negative total returns (before taxes) during 17 years since 1950, or during 34% of the past 50 years. Investor rates of return on intermediate-term T-notes can also show disturbing volatility. T-note investors suffered a negative total return of −3.99% during 1999 and losses during seven of the past 50 years. Although T-bill investors earned a positive rate of return before taxes during each year since 1950, these total returns are often meager.

Table 6.5 shows how rates of return earned on T-bonds and T-notes are highly correlated (closely related) over time and the common disparity between short-term and long-term rates. The correlation between investor total returns for T-bonds and T-notes is 93.10%. This means that common economic factors cause a rise or fall in long-term and intermediate-term interest rates. Notice how the low correlation between investor total returns on T-bonds and T-bills implies that a rise in money market interest often leads to a highly variable increase in long-term interest rates, and vice versa. Whereas T-bill interest rates closely track the rise and fall in the rate of inflation, the inflation rate is inversely related to investor total returns on T-bonds. A rise in the rate of inflation reduces the value of interest and principal payments to be received in the future and represents especially bad news for T-bond investors.

A. Notice from Table 6.4 that the rate of interest earned by T-bills was substantially in excess of the inflation rate during the early to mid-1980s. Why did investors demand such a high after-inflation or real return during this period?

B. Would T-bond holders prefer that a federal government surplus be used to reduce taxes or pay down the debt? Why?

Selected References

Aintablian, Sebouh, and Gordon S. Roberts. "A Note on Market Response to Corporate Loan Announcements in Canada." *Journal of Banking and Finance* 24 (March 2000): 381–393.

Anderson, Ronald, and Suresh Sundaresan. "A Comparative Study of Structural Models of Corporate Bond Yields: An Exploratory Investigation." *Journal of Banking and Finance* 24 (January 2000): 255–269.

Asness, Clifford S. "Stocks versus Bonds: Explaining the Equity Risk Premium." *Financial Analysts Journal* 56 (March/April 2000): 96–113.

Attari, Mukarram. "Discontinuous Interest Rate Processes: An Equilibrium Model for Bond Option Prices." *Journal of Financial and Quantitative Analysis* 34 (September 1999): 293–322.

Boot, Arnoud W. A., and Anjan V. Thakor. "Can Relationship Banking Survive Competition?" *Journal of Finance* 55 (April 2000): 679–714.

Fleming, Michael J., and Eli M. Remolona. "Price Formation and Liquidity in the U.S. Treasury Market: The Response to Public Information." *Journal of Finance* 54 (October 1999): 1901–1915.

Gordy, Michael B. "A Comparative Anatomy of Credit Risk Models." *Journal of Banking and Finance* 24 (January 2000): 119–149.

Hong, Gwangheon, and Arthur Warga. "An Empirical Study of Bond Market Transactions." *Financial Analysts Journal* 56 (March/April 2000): 32–46.

Jordan, Bradford D., Randy D. Jorgensen, and David R. Kuipers. "The Relative Pricing of U.S. Treasury STRIPS: Empirical Evidence." *Journal of Financial Economics* 56 (April 2000): 89–123.

Kahn, Charles, George Pennacchi, and Ben Sopranzetti. "Bank Deposit Rate Clustering: Theory and Empirical Evidence." *Journal of Finance* 54 (December 1999): 2185–2213.

Kang, Jun-Koo, and Rene M. Stulz. "Do Banking Shocks Affect Borrowing Firm Performance? An Analysis of the Japanese Experience." *Journal of Business* 73 (January 2000): 1–23.

Lopez, Jose A., and Marc R. Saidenberg. "Evaluating Credit Risk Models," *Journal of Banking and Finance* 24 (January 2000): 151–165.

Parrino, Robert, and Michael S. Weisbach. "Measuring Investment Distortions Arising from Stockholder-Bondholder Conflicts." *Journal of Financial Economics* 53 (July 1999): 3–42.

Perumpral, Shalini, Dan Davidson, and Nilanjin Sen. "Event Risk Covenants and Shareholder Wealth: Ethical Implications of the 'Poison Put' Provision in Bonds." *Journal of Business Ethics* 22 (Part 1) (November 1999): 119–132.

Wang, Hung-Jen. "Symmetrical Information and Credit Rationing: Graphical Demonstrations." *Financial Analysts Journal* 56 (March/April 2000): 85–95.

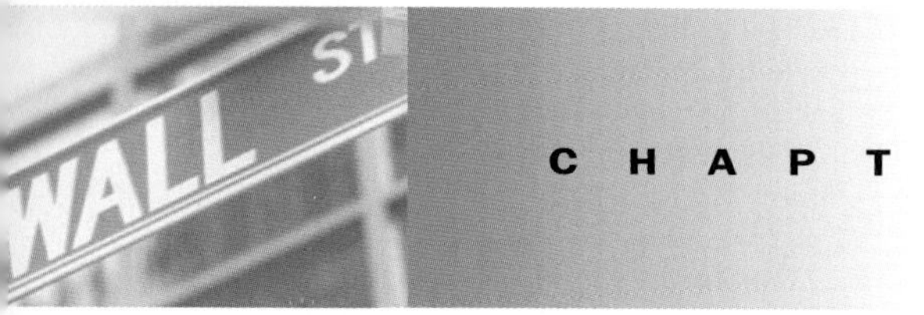

C H A P T E R 7

Bond Valuation and Management

During the fall of 1998, heads rolled when Wall Street firms suffered enormous losses on risky Asian, Russian, and other emerging-market bonds. Citigroup, Lehman Bros., Merrill Lynch, and other leading investment bankers saw their common stock prices tumble by 60–80% as rumors swept through the Street that one or more of them might fail as a result of the turmoil. Federal Reserve Board Chairman Alan Greenspan became so concerned about the potential financial meltdown that he moved quickly to trim interest rates and boost bond prices. Following three rapid-fire Fed moves to cut interest rates, bond prices stabilized and then recovered, and panic was averted.

After such a close call with financial disaster, one might think that investment bankers and institutional bond buyers might back off from making highly leveraged bets on the direction of interest rates and the interest-rate spread among bonds of various risk classes, right? Wrong. Within months, the lure of potential trading profits had Wall Street firms adding highly risky bonds to trading accounts.

It is ironic that the Fed's action to stem the harmful fallout from risky bond bets gone bad may, in fact, cause even bigger bets to be placed in the future. The Fed's string of three interest-rate cuts during the fall of 1998 may have created a false sense of security among bond traders that future trouble would also be contained. Indeed, by early 2000, Wall Street firms and their customers appeared willing to bet that the Fed will deftly manage the tricky task of engineering a "soft landing" in the economy with a series of gradual interest-rate increases.

Maybe it will. Maybe it won't.[1]

Bond Valuation

Economic Characteristics

When an investor purchases a bond, she or he is lending money to a corporation, municipality, federal agency, or some other issuer. In its simplest form, a bond is a debt security, similar to an IOU. In return for such a loan, the issuer promises to pay a specified rate of interest during the life of the bond and to repay the face

[1]See: Gregory Zuckerman, "Long-Term Capital Chief Acknowledges Flawed Tactics," *The Wall Street Journal*, August 21, 2000, C1, C2.

amount of the bond (the principal) when it comes due. As described in Chapter 6, bond types include corporate bonds, municipal bonds, U.S. government securities, mortgage and asset-backed securities, federal agency securities, and foreign government bonds. Several key variables determine the essential economic characteristics of any bond. These variables include the bond's interest payment obligation, price, yield, maturity, redemption features, and credit quality. In combination with the prevailing **market interest rate,** these factors determine the value of any bond and determine the degree to which it matches the financial objectives of any given investor.

market interest rate
Prevailing rate of interest on essentially identical securities.

Bonds are debt securities that pay a rate of interest based on the stated face amount or par value of the bond. This interest rate can be fixed or variable. Most debt securities carry a fixed rate of interest. It is also most common for bond investors to receive interest payments twice per year, or on a semiannual basis. For example, a $1,000 bond sold at par with a 7% interest rate pays interest of $70 per year, in $35 payments every six months. When the bond matures, typically in 10, 20, or 30 years, bond investors will also receive the full face amount of the bond.

Although fixed-rate bonds are most common, some sellers and buyers of debt securities prefer having an interest rate that is adjustable on a daily, monthly, or annual basis. This allows the interest rate paid on a given bond to closely track market interest rates. Interest rates on floating-rate bonds are reset periodically to keep in line with changes in an underlying **benchmark interest rate.** Rates on short-term Treasury bills or 30-year Treasury bonds are popular interest rate benchmarks.

benchmark interest rate
Interest rate standard.

Another popular bond type, called **zero coupon bonds (or zeros),** makes no periodic interest payments. Instead of regular interest payments, the bond investor receives a single payment at the time of maturity that equals a return of the original purchase price (or principal) plus the total interest earned. Zero coupon bonds are sold at an original price that is a substantial discount from their face amount. For example, a bond with a face amount of $1,000, maturing in 30 years, and priced to yield 7% might be purchased for about $131. At the end of 30 years, the bond investor will receive $1,000. The difference between $1,000 and $131 represents the interest income to be received, based on an interest rate of roughly 7%, which compounds until the zero coupon bond matures.

zero coupon bonds
Discount bonds that pay no coupon interest.

Zero coupon bonds were introduced in mid-1982. They have become popular among issuers because they avoid the need to make periodic interest and principal payments. Long-term bond investors have been attracted to zeros because they eliminate **interest reinvestment risk,** or the chance that a subsequent rise in interest rates will reduce the amount earned on reinvested interest income. Today, the three largest categories of zero coupon securities are offered by the U.S. Treasury, corporations, and state and local governments. As with all bond issues, zeros issued by the Treasury are generally considered the safest because they are backed by the full faith and credit of the U.S. government. Municipal zeros also offer a high degree of safety and, because the interest earned is usually tax free, can generate attractive returns when calculated on a taxable equivalent basis. Zero coupon bonds issued by a corporation or the U.S. Treasury generate taxable income even though bondholders receive no periodic cash payments. Each year, holders of zero coupon bonds must pay taxes on a prorated share of the bond's expected appreciation between the time of purchase and the time of maturity. For that reason, many bond investors prefer to hold zero coupon bonds within an individual retirement account (IRA) or other tax-sheltered retirement account, such as a 401-k plan.

interest reinvestment risk
Loss in reinvested interest income due to rising interest rates.

Present Value of a Bond

An interesting feature of bond-pricing tradition is that bond prices are conventionally quoted as a percentage of par, where par is typically \$1,000. This means that a bond price of 95 implies a bond market value of \$950 (= 95% × \$1,000), a bond price of 98½ implies a bond market value of \$985 (= 98.5% × \$1,000), and so on. Although the initial or par value of a bond is typically set by the issuer at \$1,000, from that point until the time of maturity its price is set by the forces of supply and demand in the marketplace. Whereas newly issued bonds normally sell at or close to their face value or principal amount, prices for **seasoned bonds** can fluctuate widely.

seasoned bonds Bonds traded from one investor to another.

Prices for seasoned bonds depend on a number of factors, including prevailing market interest rates, the supply and demand for similar types of bonds, credit quality, and the term-to-maturity and tax status of individual bonds. If a bond is trading for more than the face amount (usually \$1,000), it is trading at a premium. A bond trading for \$1,400 is trading at a premium of \$400, and a bond trading at \$700 is trading at a \$300 discount. If an investor buys a bond trading at a premium, the investor receives a yield-to-maturity less than the one stated on the face of the bond. If an investor buys a bond trading at a discount, the investor will earn a higher yield-to-maturity than the amount stated on the face of the bond. Remember, the face amount or par value of a bond is important because that amount represents the dollar repayment obligation on the part of the issuer.

In general economic terms, the economic value of a bond equals the present value of all expected interest and principal payments:

$$\text{Present Value}_{\text{Bond}} = \text{Present Value}_{\text{Interest}} + \text{Present Value}_{\text{Principal}} \quad \textbf{(7.1)}$$
$$= \sum_{t=1}^{N} \frac{\text{Cash Payment}}{(1 + \text{Yield})^t}$$

where N is the number of years until maturity, when all promised interest and principal payments have been made, and *Yield* is the market interest rate on securities with the same essential economic characteristics.

As shown in Equation 7.1, the value of a bond rises with an increase in the face amount of the security and the amount of promised interest.

Conversely, bond value falls with a decline in the face amount or the amount of promised interest. Holding all else equal, a rise in prevailing interest rates has the effect of increasing the denominator of the above expression, and thereby reducing bond value. In general, the value of a bond will fall with a rise in prevailing interest rates. The value of a bond will rise with a decline in prevailing market interest rates.

Bond Pricing

settlement date Date when buyer takes effective possession of a security.

maturity date Date when security expires or ceases to accrue interest.

To calculate the price for an individual bond, the investor needs information about the bond's settlement, maturity, coupon rate, yield, redemption value, frequency of interest payment, and day count basis. A bond's **settlement date** is the date on which the buyer takes effective possession of the security. For an initial public offering, the settlement date is the day after the issue date. In most instances, bond transactions are governed by a one-day settlement period, so the settlement date typically follows the transaction date by one day. The **maturity date** is the date when the security expires or ceases to accrue interest. The time remaining until maturity is the simple difference between the maturity date and the settlement date. Another important component of bond valuation is the **bond coupon rate,** expressed as a percentage of par value. This interest rate often differs from the security's yield-to-maturity, which is closely determined by prevailing market interest rates. **Bond redemption value** is the amount to be received from the issuer on the maturity date. This amount is usually equal to par value, which is typically $1,000. Most bonds pay **semiannual interest** in two equal installments. And finally, in the United States it is conventional to calculate bond interest rates on the **day count basis** of 30 days per month and 360 days per year.

bond coupon rate
Bond interest rate expressed as a percentage of par value.

bond redemption value
Amount to be received from issuer on maturity date.

semiannual interest
Interest paid in two equal installments per year.

day count basis
Method for calculating interest rates, usually 30 days per month and 360 days per year.

The specific formula that can be used to calculate the expected price for any individual bond is:

$$\text{Price} = \left[\frac{\text{Redemption Value}}{\left(1+\dfrac{\text{Yield}}{\text{Frequency}}\right)^{\left(N-1+\frac{DSC}{E}\right)}}\right] + \left[\sum_{k=1}^{N}\frac{100\times\dfrac{\text{Coupon Rate}}{\text{Frequency}}}{\left(1+\dfrac{\text{Yield}}{\text{Frequency}}\right)^{\left(k-1+\frac{DSC}{E}\right)}}\right] - \left[100\times\frac{\text{Coupon Rate}}{\text{Frequency}}\times\frac{A}{E}\right] \quad \textbf{(7.2)}$$

In Equation 7.2, *DSC* is the number of days from settlement to the next coupon date, *E* is the number of days in the coupon period within which the settlement date falls, *N* is the number of coupons payable between settlement date and redemption date, and *A* is the number of days from the beginning of the coupon period to the settlement date.

Although Equation 7.2 appears daunting, bond investors never need to make such calculations by hand. Powerful spreadsheet software programs such as Microsoft Excel use financial formulas that incorporate this information and can be used to quickly and easily calculate bond prices.

To illustrate, consider the variety of bond-pricing information given in Table 7.1. As usual, all bonds shown have a face amount, or par value, of $1,000, and pay semiannual interest. In the case of the bond shown in column (1), the coupon interest

TABLE 7.1 Bond Valuation Depends on Promised Cash Payments and the Prevailing Interest Rate

	Bond Type				
	(1)	(2)	(3)	(4)	(5)
Face amount	$1,000	$1,000	$1,000	$1,000	$1,000
Semiannual interest	$27.50	$37.50	$25.00	$45.00	$35.00
Coupon interest rate	5.50%	7.50%	5.00%	9.00%	7.00%
Yield (market interest rate)	5.75%	6.50%	7.00%	7.25%	7.25%
Issue date	1/26/72	2/16/85	4/9/93	11/6/82	10/12/01
Settlement date (purchase date)	1/26/01	2/16/01	1/14/01	7/16/01	10/13/01
Maturity date	1/26/02	2/16/06	4/9/14	11/6/23	10/13/31
Term-to-maturity (years)	1.0	5.0	13.2	22.3	30.0
Bond price (% of par)	99.76	104.21	82.91	119.19	96.96
Bond valuation	$997.60	$1,042.11	$829.11	$1,191.89	$969.59
Duration (years)	0.99	4.28	9.30	10.77	12.68
Modified duration (years)	0.96	4.14	8.99	10.39	12.24

rate is 5.5% of par, or $27.50 every six months. The yield-to-maturity, or market interest rate, for this security is 5.75%. This is also the market interest rate for securities of essentially the same payment terms and credit quality. It is a 30-year bond issued on January 26, 1972, that expires on January 26, 2002, and was last purchased for investment on January 26, 2001. As of that purchase or settlement date, the bond had a remaining term-to-maturity of one year and a price, expressed as a percentage of par value, of 99.76. This implies an economic valuation as of January 26, 2001, of $997.60.

Notice from the bond-pricing examples given in Table 7.1 that bond prices exceed the face amount of $1,000 when yield-to-maturity is less than the bond's coupon rate. Bond prices are less than par value when the market interest rate is higher than the bond's coupon yield.

Yield-to-Maturity

Common Maturities

Bond maturities generally range from one day for overnight loans up to 30 years for long-term obligations. In rare instances, both corporate and government bonds have been issued for terms of up to 100 years! Bonds are often classified according to time to maturity by using the following broad classifications:

- Short-term notes have initial maturities of up to five years.
- Medium-term notes or bonds have initial maturities of five to 12 years.
- Long-term bonds generally have initial maturities of 12 or more years.

average life Typical period before refunding.

Some bonds, especially mortgage-backed securities, are typically priced and traded on the basis of the bond's expected **average life** rather than on the basis of any stated term-to-maturity. When mortgage rates decline, homeowners often move quickly to prepay their mortgage. This may reduce the expected average life of the bondholder's investment. When mortgage rates rise, the reverse tends to be true. Homeowners tend to be slow to prepay their fixed-rate mortgages in the face of rising interest rates. Under such circumstances, bondholders often find that their principal remains committed for a longer-than-expected holding period.

The investor's choice of a preferred term-to-maturity depends on when principal repayment is required, the investment return sought, and the investor's risk tolerance. Many bond investors prefer short-term bonds for their comparative stability of principal and interest payments. In turn, such investors are willing to accept the typically lower rates of return offered on short-term bonds. Bond investors seeking greater overall returns tend to favor long-term securities despite the fact that such bonds are more vulnerable to interest rate fluctuations and other market risks.

call provisions Contractual authority that allows the issuer to redeem bonds prior to scheduled maturity.

Call Provisions

Although the time to maturity offers a useful guide as to how long an individual bond can be expected to remain outstanding, most bonds have contractual provisions that can substantially alter their expected life. Most bonds have **call provisions** that allow the issuer to repay the investors' principal at a specified date and price

WALL STREET WISDOM 7.1

The Ratings Game

When bond investors look for independent assessments of borrower creditworthiness, they typically turn to big bond-ratings houses, such as Moody's and Standard & Poor's. For decades, bond investors have trusted these firms to give impartial credit-quality information that they can use to avoid losses of principal payments or interest income. Bond buyers have the highest level of confidence in the creditworthiness of "investment grade" debt obligations and are willing to invest in such issues at the lowest possible rate. Often, the highest-rated corporate debt is offered to the bond market at interest rates that are only 50–75 basis points (0.5–0.75%) above the risk-free rate on Treasury securities of a similar term-to-maturity. Bonds judged to be of medium-grade investment quality often yield 100–150 basis points (1–1.5%) more than similar Treasury securities. High-yield corporate bonds, or bonds judged to be "below investment grade," can yield as much as 400–500 basis points (or 4–5%) more than risk-free Treasuries. As a result, corporations and other bond issuers are eager to achieve the highest possible bond ratings and thereby earn the ability to issue fixed-income obligations at the lowest possible interest expense.

Although the ultimate customer, or consumer, of bond-rating services is the investor who buys bonds, debt issuers such as municipalities and corporations actually pay for the service. This can be a source of conflict, because if a rating house puts out negative ratings, it risks alienating issuers, who can take their business elsewhere. At the same time, issuers must be careful not to offend the ratings houses out of fear that it will adversely affect their credit rating and interest costs. At times, issuers seem almost eager to pay the stiff fees demanded by the bond-rating houses. In some instances, the bond-rating houses send out bills for their bond-rating services even before they have been formally retained to by the issuing company to review the credit quality of a pending issue.

The trust of bondholders in the effectiveness and integrity of the bond-rating houses is so complete that large pension funds in several states are effectively prohibited from investing in below-investment-grade bonds. Based on the premise that a "prudent investor" would only purchase investment-grade bonds, losses from investing in more speculative below-investment-grade issues can expose the fixed-income portfolio manager to bondholder sanctions, costly litigation, and worse. With state laws restricting large pension funds from investing in below-investment-grade bonds, bond issuers have a ready-made market for their bond-rating services. Even large, well-known bond issuers of unquestioned credit quality, such as IBM, must seek the bond-rating houses' seal of approval before their bonds can be sold. At the same time, entry into the bond-rating business is difficult because bond investors demand evidence of issuer credit quality from bond-rating companies with a long-standing reputation for independence and integrity.

This has created a wonderful business situation for the major bond-rating houses. However, even in the best of businesses, problems are encountered. The bond-rating business is no exception and has recently experienced some turbulence. The major bond-rating houses have been roundly criticized for missing some large financial blowups, such as the New York City fiscal crisis, the Orange County municipal bond fiasco, and the financial meltdown in Asia. Following massive bondholder losses, bond-rating houses have been rocked by costly litigation. As a result, some of the major bond-rating houses, such as Standard & Poor's Ratings Services, now ask bond issuers to agree that bond ratings are nothing more than "opinions" protected under the First Amendment. They also want bond issuers to agree that any bond-rating house liability should be limited to the amount of fees paid.

In the future, it is fair to expect bond-rating houses to be even more circumspect about what they do and do not say about credit quality.

See: Erin White, "Dun & Bradstreet Selects Loren to Lead Credit-Report and Information Business," *The Wall Street Journal,* May 17, 2000, B12

and thereby redeem the bond prior to scheduled maturity. Bonds are commonly called by issuers following a significant drop in prevailing interest rates. Bonds also tend to be called when the issuer's credit quality rises substantially following an upturn in the company's business prospects or a rise in a government agency's tax receipts. If called, the call date is usually on one of the two dates when semiannual interest is due. The reasons behind early bond redemptions are obvious. When interest rates fall or credit quality improves, new bonds can be issued at lower interest rates. Call provisions represent an important advantage for issuers because they represent a refinancing opportunity or option. Call provisions entail no obligation to refinance on the part of the issuer. **Call protection** is the amount of time before a newly issued bond is callable.

call protection Amount of time before a newly issued bond is callable.

Call provisions represent something of a double-edged sword for bond investors. If interest rates fall or credit quality improves, bonds are apt to be called prior to scheduled maturity. This denies bond investors the upward revaluation in bond prices that would otherwise follow such favorable developments. However, if interest rates rise or credit quality deteriorates, bond prices tumble, and call provisions are not apt to be exercised. As a result, bond investors are likely to have the opportunity to keep bonds to scheduled maturity only in the event of adverse influences on bond prices. For unsophisticated bond investors, call provisions can have the effect of making bonds a "heads they win; tails you lose" proposition. Fortunately, the situation is not as bad as it might seem. Call provisions must be explicitly detailed in the bond offering circular. In an efficient bond market, call provisions are fully considered by bond investors and fully reflected in market prices. Bonds with limited call protection usually have a higher expected return to compensate for the risk that the bonds might be called for early redemption.

Call provisions facilitate debt refinancing on terms favorable to the issuing corporation or issuing entity. Other refinancing options also exist. For example, suppose a corporation has a series of bonds coming due in the year 2010 that are presently trading at $850. The company is free at any time to place an order with a bondbroker to buy however many it wishes. For lightly traded issues, the company might make a formal **bond tender offer** announcement in large financial newspapers, such as *The Wall Street Journal.* It might offer to repurchase part or all of the issue at a slight premium, say, $875, to the current market price. The company can offer to buy back all the issue or part of the issue. If they offer to buy back part of the issue, it will probably be on a first-come-first-served basis. The company would then probably sell a new bond issue to repay bondholders for the bonds the company was buying back. This type of transaction is called a **refunding** and is designed to reduce financing costs or improve financial flexibility.

bond tender offer Offer to buy an entire outstanding class of securities.

refunding Retirement of seasoned securities with proceeds from a new issue.

Expected Yield Calculation

Bond yield is the bond investor's expected rate of return based on the price paid plus the anticipated amount and timing of interest and principal payments. There are two different expected yield calculations that are of fundamental interest to bond buyers and sellers.

Yield-to-maturity or **yield-to-call** are often more economically meaningful than the simple current yield calculation. Yield-to-maturity or yield-to-call calculations tell a bond investor the total rate of return that might be expected if he or she were to buy and hold the bond until it matures or is called away by the issuer. These

yield-to-maturity Investor return from settlement day until security expiration.

yield-to-call Investor return from settlement day until repurchased by company.

calculations are informative also because they enable the bond investor to compare bonds with different maturity and coupon characteristics. Both yield-to-maturity and yield-to-call calculations involve computing the internal rate of return on a bond investment. This internal rate of return is the interest rate that equates the current purchase price of the bond with the economic value of all anticipated future interest and principal payments. Therefore, the yield-to-maturity equals all interest payments received from the time of purchase until the point of maturity plus any capital gain resulting from the purchase of a bond at a discount from par, or face, value. Alternatively, the yield-to-maturity equals all interest payments received prior to the point of maturity, minus any capital loss resulting from the purchase of a bond at a premium to par. Thus, yield-to-maturity will be more than the current yield for bonds purchased at a discount. Yield-to-maturity is less than the current yield for bonds purchased at a premium. It is important to remember that bond prices and bond yields are *inversely* related. As bond prices fall, yield-to-maturity increases. Rising bond prices portend falling yields.

For example, if a newly issued 30-year bond is bought for a purchase price of $1,000 (or par) and the promised interest rate is 7% ($70), then the current yield and the yield-to-maturity on the bond are both 7% (= $70 ÷ $1,000). If such a bond had a remaining term-to-maturity of 30 years and was purchased in the secondary market at a discount for $933 with interest payments of $70 per year the yield-to-maturity would equal roughly 7.57% (using a spreadsheet or handheld calculator). If such a bond were purchased at a premium for $1,077, given interest payments of $70 per year, the yield-to-maturity would equal roughly 6.42%. Notice that yield-to-maturity is higher than current yield for discount bonds, and that yield-to-maturity is lower than current yield for premium bonds.

The detailed formula that can be used to compute expected yield-to-maturity for any fixed-income security is

$$\text{Yield} = \left\{ \frac{\left(\frac{\text{Redemption Value}}{100} + \frac{\text{Coupon Rate}}{\text{Frequency}} \right) - \left[\frac{\text{Par}}{100} + \left(\frac{A}{E} \times \frac{\text{Coupon Rate}}{\text{Frequency}} \right) \right]}{\frac{\text{Par}}{100} + \left(\frac{A}{E} \times \frac{\text{Coupon Rate}}{\text{Frequency}} \right)} \right\} \times \frac{\text{Frequency} \times E}{DSR} \tag{7.3}$$

In Equation 7.3, A is the number of days from the beginning of the coupon period to the settlement date (accrued days), DSR is the number of days from the settlement date to the redemption date, and E is the number of days in the coupon period.

As in the case of the bond-pricing formula, the formula used to calculate yield-to-maturity appears complicated. Happily, bond investors need not make such calculations by hand. Powerful spreadsheet software programs like Microsoft Excel use financial formulas that can be used to quickly and easily calculate the expected yield-to-maturity.

To illustrate, consider the expected yield-to-maturity calculations shown in Table 7.2. As in Table 7.1, all such bonds have a face amount or par value of $1,000 and pay semiannual interest. For the bond example shown in column (1), the coupon interest rate is 4% of par, or $20 every six months. This is a 30-year bond issued on July 4, 1972, that expires on July 4, 2002, and was last purchased for

TABLE 7.2 Yield-to-Maturity Depends on Promised Cash Payments and the Bond's Current Market Price

	Bond Type				
	(1)	(2)	(3)	(4)	(5)
Face amount	$1,000	$1,000	$1,000	$1,000	$1,000
Semiannual interest	$20.00	$35.00	$27.50	$38.75	$36.25
Coupon interest rate	4.00%	7.00%	5.50%	7.75%	7.25%
Issue date	7/4/72	6/12/76	2/14/85	4/25/75	12/24/01
Settlement date (purchase date)	7/4/01	6/12/01	1/26/01	1/1/01	12/25/01
Maturity date	7/4/02	6/12/06	2/14/15	4/25/25	12/25/31
Term-to-maturity (years)	1.0	5.0	14.1	24.3	30.0
Bond price (% of par)	98.21	104.65	88.92	106.54	100.00
Bond valuation	$982.10	$1,046.50	$889.20	$1,065.40	$1,000.00
Yield-to-maturity	5.87%	5.91%	6.73%	7.18%	7.25%

investment on July 4, 2001. As of that purchase or settlement date, the bond had a remaining term-to-maturity of one year and a price of 98.21, in which price is expressed as a percentage of par value. This implies an economic valuation as of July 4, 1976, of $982.10.

Notice from the bond-pricing examples given in Table 7.2 that yield-to-maturity exceeds the coupon rate when bond prices are less than the par value of $1,000. The yield-to-maturity is less than the bond's coupon rate when the current market price of the bond exceeds par value.

The yield-to-call is calculated the same way as yield-to-maturity but assumes that a bond purchased at a premium will be called and that the bond investor will receive the face value of the bond at the call date. Call provisions are especially important for bonds trading in the secondary market at a significant premium, because such bonds have a significant chance of being called. Call provisions are much less important for bonds trading in the secondary market at a significant discount, because such bonds are not apt to be called by issuers. If an issuing company wanted to retire or refinance outstanding debt trading at a significant discount to par, open-market purchases at a discount would be much more attractive than redemption at par.

Put Provisions

bond put provisions Investor option to sell bond back to issuer.

Whereas many bonds have call provisions that give bond issuers the option to refinance at favorable interest rates, **bond put provisions** give investors the option to require issuers to repurchase bonds at a specified time and price prior to scheduled maturity. Bond investors typically exercise put options when interest rates have risen, when the credit quality of the issuer has deteriorated, or when a serious threat of credit quality deterioration is present.

For example, bondholders might exercise a put option in the event of an important divestiture, merger, or takeover that requires the issuance of a significant amount of new debt financing. Issuers will sometimes attempt to appease such bondholders through a change in bond covenant provisions or an increase in interest rates. In the event bondholders do indeed exercise their put option, proceeds received by bondholders from the bond repurchase can often be reinvested at a higher rate of interest.

Interest Rate Risk

Changing Market Conditions

From the time that a bond is originally issued until the time it matures, its price in the secondary market fluctuates according to changes in general credit market conditions or issuer-specific changes in credit quality. Constant fluctuation of bond prices in the secondary market reflects evolving investor expectations as investors process information about likely changes in the overall economy and economic policy. Because all long-term bonds are priced, at least in part, within the context of aggregate credit market conditions, all long-term bonds are sensitive to market-wide changes in interest rates. This is called **interest-rate risk.**

interest-rate risk Chance of bondholder loss due to market-wide fluctuation in interest rates.

When prevailing interest rates rise, newly issued bonds offer a promise to pay interest that is higher than that offered on older seasoned bonds. As a result, when market interest rates rise, market prices for outstanding bonds fall to bring the yield-to-maturity for new buyers of such seasoned bonds into line with higher-yield new issues. Similarly, when the prevailing rate of interest falls, market prices for outstanding bonds rise to bring the yield-to-maturity for new buyers of such seasoned bonds into line with higher-yield new issues.

Bond investors must be aware that bond prices fluctuate on a day-to-day basis. If a bond investor wishes to sell a previously purchased bond, either capital gains or losses can be incurred. If market interest rates have risen, the sale of previously purchased bonds typically leads to a capital loss. If market interest rates have fallen, the sale of previously purchased bonds typically leads to a capital gain. During periods of volatile change in interest rates, the gains and losses experienced by bond investors can be substantial. Although very short-term bonds issued by highly creditworthy institutions involve little or no risk, long-term bonds issued by even the highest-quality issuers involve substantial risk.

Table 7.3 illustrates the interest rate risk for various Treasury securities that all feature a 6% coupon and sold at an initial par of $1,000. These data illustrate how sensitive the value of various Treasury securities can be to rising and falling interest rates. Consider a hypothetical two-year Treasury note that promises to pay $60 per year in interest payments plus the return of the investor's initial $1,000 in 24 months. As shown in Table 7.2, the economic value and market price of a promise

TABLE 7.3 Illustration of Interest-Rate Risk for Treasury Securities with a 6% Coupon Selling at Par of $1,000

		Decline in bond value following an increase in rates			Rise in bond value following a decrease in rates		
Bond Type	**Term-to-Maturity (years)**	+1%	+2%	+3%	−1%	−2%	−3%
Treasury bill (money market)	6 mo	0%	0%	0%	0%	0%	0%
Treasury note	2	−1.84%	−3.63%	−5.38%	1.88%	3.81%	5.78%
Treasury note	5	−4.16%	−8.11%	−11.87%	4.38%	8.98%	13.83%
Treasury bond	10	−7.11%	−13.59%	−19.51%	7.79%	16.35%	25.75%
Treasury bond	20	−10.68%	−19.79%	−27.60%	12.55%	27.36%	44.87%
Treasury bond	30	−12.47%	−22.62%	−30.96%	15.45%	34.76%	59.07%

to pay $60 per year for two years plus an additional $1,000 at the end of that period are mildly sensitive to interest rates. If interest rates rise, the market value of such a bond would fall to compete with newly issued bonds that pay higher interest. If interest rates fall, the value of such a bond would rise.

What many novice investors do not understand is how price sensitive bond prices can be to changing market conditions. If interest rates on newly issued two-year Treasury notes rise 1%, or from 6% to 7%, the value of older or seasoned notes must fall to provide subsequent investors with a competitive 7% yield-to-maturity. In the case of a two-year Treasury note, a 1% rise in rates causes a very modest 1.84% decline in the value of seasoned two-year Treasury notes. If interest rates rise by 3%, even very short-term two-year bonds suffer a meaningful 5.38% decline in market value.

The reaction of seasoned bond prices to changing interest rates becomes severe when longer maturity bonds are considered. The market price for a 30-year Treasury bond with a 6% coupon selling at par would fall by 12.47% following a 1% rise in market interest rates from 6% to 7%. If interest rates rise by as much as 3%, or from 6% to 9%, the value of such a 30-year bond would fall by a whopping 30.96%. Of course, the price volatility of long-term bonds can work to the advantage of bond investors when interest rates fall. If long-term interest rates fall by 1% from 6% to 5%, the value of a seasoned 6% bond selling at par would rise by 15.45%. The value of such a 30-year bond would rise a whopping 59.07% following a 3% fall in interest rates from 6% to 3%.

Notice that the percentage rise in bond value following a decline in rates is not symmetric with the percentage decline in bond value incurred following a rise in rates. This stems from the fact that while increases in bond prices are theoretically unlimited, no bond can decline by more than 100% in value. Remember, if an investor experiences a 33% decline in the value of a bond investment following a rise in market interest rates, it takes a 50% increase in the bond's price to restore its original value.

To be sure, a 1% change in market interest rates is a big change that is not commonly seen on a daily or monthly basis. Over the course of an entire year, however, a 1% change in long-term interest rates is not that unusual. Over longer time frames, changes in long-term interest rates of as much as 2–3% are sometimes experienced. During the late 1990s, for example, long-term interest rates fell precipitously. In December 1994, the yield on the 30-year Treasury bond exceeded 8%. In October of 1998, the yield on the long bond touched a low of 4.69%. As seen in Figure 7.1, over one-year periods, long-term rates can and do demonstrate a high degree of volatility. During periods of rapidly changing interest rates, long-term bonds can become extremely volatile assets.

Because changes in bond yields tend to be fairly small over daily, weekly, or monthly time frames, changes in bond yields are typically quoted in terms of **basis points,** one basis point equaling 1/100th of 1%. Thus, a 1.25% rise in rates translates into a rise of 125 basis points in yield. A 0.30% fall in yield represents a 30-basis point decline in rates.

basis points
1/100th of 1%. For example, 50 basis points = 0.5%.

Factors That Change Prevailing Interest Rates

The most important cause of fluctuations in the bond market is a change in prevailing interest rates. Interest rates change in response to changes in supply and

FIGURE 7.1 **Market Interest Rates for 30-Year U.S. Treasury Bonds, 1995–Present**

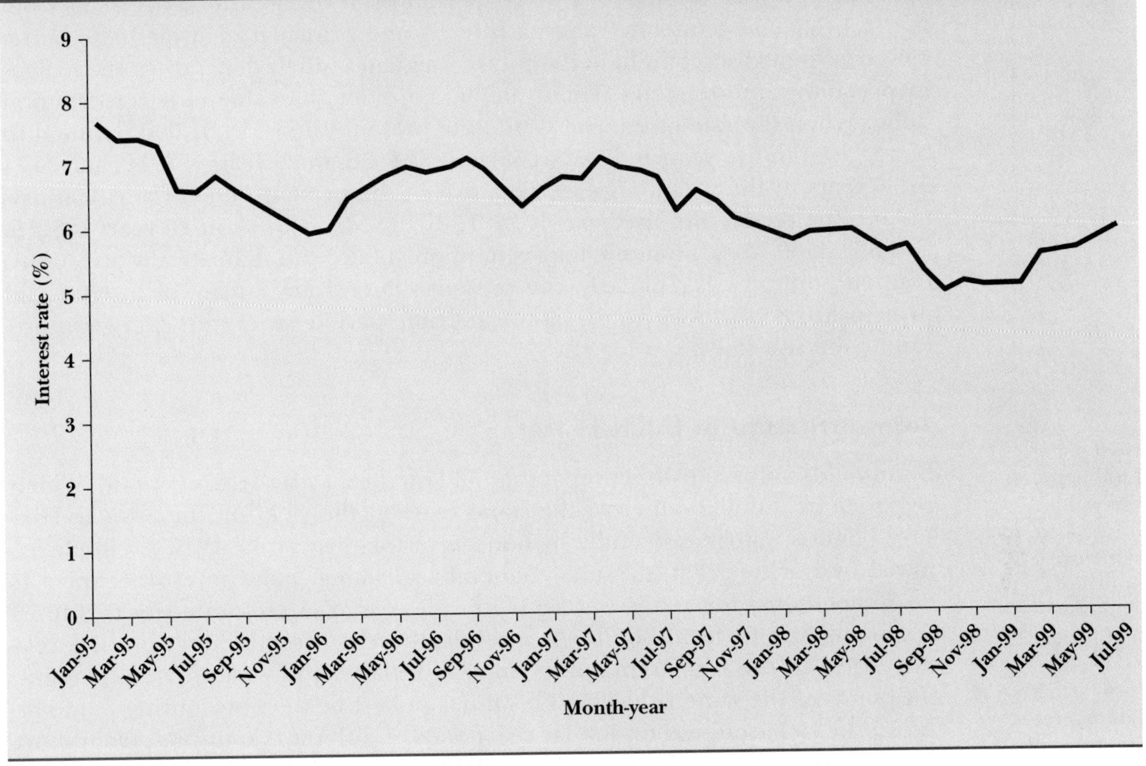

demand for credit, Federal Reserve policy, fiscal policy, exchange rates, economic conditions, market psychology, and, most important for the bond market, changes in expectations about inflation. The general public is sometimes puzzled by the fact that the bond prices typically react negatively to positive economic news.

The simple explanation is that the bond market acts as a barometer for inflationary expectations. An increase in inflation is feared by bond investors because it reduces the buying power of future interest and principal payments. As a result, an increase in the expected rate of inflation tends to increase the market rate of interest and lowers the value of outstanding bonds. Any economic report that raises the possibility of higher future inflation, raises interest rates and lowers bond prices. Thus, "good" economic news, such as lower unemployment or higher retail sales, is "bad" for bonds and tends to weaken bond market prices. However, "bad" economic news, such as higher unemployment or weak economic growth, tends to reduce inflationary expectations and is "good" for bonds. When inflationary expectations abate, bond prices tend to rise. Remember, bond prices and yields move in opposite directions. Because bond yields tend to move up during "good" economic conditions, a booming economy can be "bad" for bond prices. Because bond yields tend to move down during "bad" economic conditions, a poor economic environment can actually be "good" for bond prices.

As discussed in Chapter 6, changes in interest rates do not affect all bonds the same. Generally speaking, the longer it takes for a bond to mature, the greater is the risk of price fluctuations in the period prior to maturity. This stems from the fact that the economic value of interest and principal repayments to be received at some distant point in the future fluctuates widely depending on changes in prevailing interest rates. For example, consider the value of a zero coupon bond. When the rate of interest is 6%, the present value of a $1,000 payment to be received in five years is $747, in 10 years is $558, in 20 years is $312, and $174 in 30 years. If the prevailing rate rises to 8%, the present value of a $1,000 payment to be received in five years is $681, in 10 years is $480, in 20 years is $215, and $99 in 30 years. Modest changes in interest rates can dramatically affect zero coupon bond prices. Similarly, the present value of any stream of interest and principal to be received over a significant time period varies with change in prevailing interest rates.

Term Structure of Interest Rates

yield curve
Line between the yields offered on similar-risk bonds of different maturities.

term structure of interest rates
Interest-rate relation among bonds with the same credit quality but different maturities.

liquidity preference hypothesis
Theory that rising yield curves give long-term bond investors a holding-period risk premium.

segmented market hypothesis
Theory that yield curves reflect the hedging and maturity needs of institutional investors.

Bond yields follow the direction of the yield on the 30-year Treasury bond. Widely regarded as the bellwether of the bond market, the yield on the 30-year Treasury bond is watched carefully by bond investors just as the DJIA is closely followed by stock market investors. Generally speaking, bond investors expect to be compensated for taking on the higher degree of interest-rate risk tied to investments in long-term bonds. As a result, there is often a direct positive relation between the term-to-maturity (in years) and yield-to-maturity (in percent) for bonds of the same risk class. This link can best be seen by drawing a line between the yields offered on similar risk bonds of different maturities, from shortest to longest. Such a line is called a **yield curve** and describes the **term structure of interest rates.**

Figure 7.2 illustrates the typically upward-sloping yield curve for Treasury securities, as was prevalent during February 1999. Although a yield curve could be drawn for any risk-class segment of the bond market, it is most commonly drawn for the U.S. Treasury market. The U.S. Treasury offers securities of virtually every maturity length, and all such issues enjoy the full-faith backing of the federal government and the highest credit ranking. By watching changes in the yield curve over time, as reported in the financial press, bond investors gain a sense of where the market perceives interest rates to be headed.

The so-called term structure of interest rates displays the relation between yield-to-maturity and term-to-maturity for bonds of a given risk class. The **liquidity preference hypothesis** posits that the typically rising yield curve gives long-term bond investors a holding-period risk premium. This explanation of the prevailing term structure of interest rates is widely supported in academia and in the professional world. Another point of view, called the **segmented market hypothesis,** suggests that yield curves reflect the hedging and maturity needs of institutional investors. It posits a strong clientele effect explanation for the sometimes anomalous result that short-term bonds offer the same rate of interest, or even higher rates of interest, than long-term bonds.

A normal yield curve shows a fairly steep rise in yields between short-term and intermediate-term issues and a less pronounced rise between intermediate-term and long-term issues. The generally upward-sloping nature of the yield

FIGURE 7.2 **Term Structure of Interest Rates Shows Yield as a Function of the Term-to-Maturity**

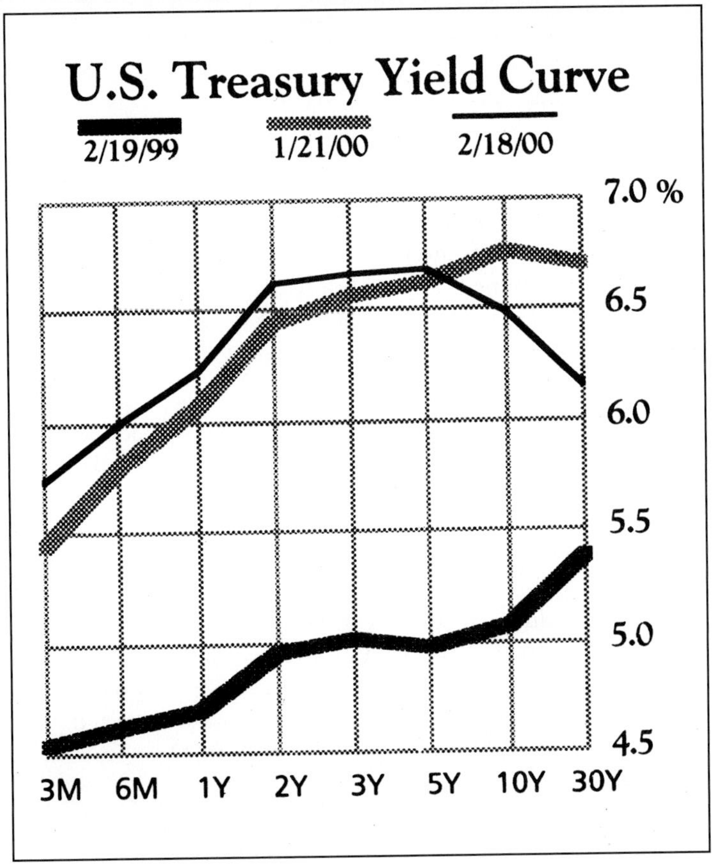

Source: *Barron's,* February 21, 2000, MW13.

curve reflects the fact that longer-term bonds are exposed to relatively greater interest-rate risk, and bond investors typically require an interest-rate premium to invest in long-term bonds. If the yield curve is said to be "steep," yields on short-term bonds are relatively low when compared with long-term bonds. A steep yield curve implies bond investors can obtain significantly increased income (yield) by buying longer as opposed to shorter maturities. If the yield curve is relatively "flat," the difference between short-term and long-term rates is relatively small. This means that the reward for extending maturities is relatively small, and relatively risk-adverse bond investors often choose to stay at the short end of the maturity range.

When yields on short-term bonds are higher than those on longer-term bonds, the yield curve is said to be "inverted." This unusual situation was prevalent during January and February 2000, as shown in Figure 7.2. As in the case of a relatively flat yield curve, an inverted yield curve suggests that bond investors expect interest rates to decline. An inverted yield curve reflects a particularly aggressive expectation of declining rates and is sometimes considered a precursor to economic recession.

Duration and Convexity

Duration Concept

The term-to-maturity of a bond is the amount of time required before all promised interest and principal payments are paid in full. Holding all else equal, the longer the term-to-maturity, the more sensitive bond prices are to changes in prevailing interest rates. However, term-to-maturity is an imperfect measure of bond risk because it ignores the valuation effects of differences in interest coupon and principal payment schedules.

duration
Economic life of a bond measured by the weighted-average time to receipt of interest and principal payments.

To provide a more direct measure of the risk to bondholders from changes in market interest rates, a financial economist by the name of Frederick R. Macaulay conceived of a measure of the economic life of a bond called **duration.** Duration is an estimate of the economic life of a bond measured by the weighted average time to receipt of interest and principal payments. In the duration calculation, each cash payment is weighted by its present value percentage of the bond's total market value. A bond's duration, measured in years, tells bondholders how sensitive the bond's price is to changes in prevailing interest rates. The shorter is duration, the less sensitive is a bond's price to fluctuations in market interest rates. The longer the duration, the more a bond's price will fluctuate when prevailing interest rates rise or fall. The formula used to calculate duration, sometimes referred to as Macaulay duration, is

$$\text{Duration} = \frac{\sum_{j=1}^{T} \dfrac{t_j \cdot \text{Cash Payment}_t}{(1+\text{Yield})^{t_j}}}{\sum_{j=1}^{T} \dfrac{\text{Cash Payment}_j}{(1+\text{Yield})^{t_j}}} \tag{7.4}$$

where t_j is the amount of time until receipt of the jth cash flow and the amount of yield is for one time period. Although this formula appears complicated, keep in mind that the numerator is simply the present value of cash flows weighted by (or multiplied by) their year of receipt. The denominator of this equation is the present value of the bond's future interest and principal payments. Therefore, the denominator also equals the bond's current market price.

Duration and Bond Prices

Although maturity factors into the calculation of duration, so do other variables. Duration is a way to compare the economic risk of bonds that differ in face amount, coupon, and/or term-to-maturity. Because maturity is only part of the duration equation, bonds with the same maturity but different coupons or call provisions will have different durations. Risk from fluctuating prices and reinvestment rates is eliminated—thus immunizing bondholders from risk—when duration equals the bond investor's investment horizon, or planning period. Banks and other financial institutions use this concept to match the duration of their financial assets and liabilities and lock in a profit margin on their loan portfolios. A prime use of the duration concept is for **risk immunization.**

risk immunization Elimination of interest rate risk by matching duration of financial assets and liabilities.

From Equation 7.4, it is clear that the duration period depends on the bond's term-to-maturity, size of promised cash payments, and the yield-to-maturity (or market interest rate). These relationships are illustrated further through examples provided in Table 7.4. As seen through these examples, longer maturities generally mean longer duration and, therefore, greater risk. The coupon interest rate on a bond helps determine duration because when greater interest income is received, the bond investor more quickly recoups the amount originally invested. Therefore, higher coupons help shorten duration. All else being equal, callable bonds will also tend to have shorter duration than noncallable bonds. At the heart of the duration concept is a simple notion that the quicker a bond investor recoups the amount invested, the less risky is the investment.

As shown in Table 7.4, the duration of a bond that pays coupon interest is always less than its term-to-maturity. Duration typically increases with term-to-maturity but at a slower rate. For zero coupon bonds, the bond investor receives no interest or principal payments until maturity. For zeros, such as those shown in columns (1) and (4), duration is exactly equal to the length of term-to-maturity. If two bonds have the same coupon rate and yield, the bond with the greater maturity has the greater duration. If two bonds have the same yield and maturity, the bond with the lower coupon rate has the greater duration. Duration also decreases with an increase in coupon payments or in the yield-to-maturity.

TABLE 7.4 Duration Depends on the Bond's Term-to-Maturity, Size of Promised Cash Payments, and the Yield-to-Maturity

	Bond Type				
	(1)	(2)	(3)	(4)	(5)
Face amount	$1,000	$1,000	$1,000	$1,000	$1,000
Semiannual interest	$0.00	$37.50	$25.00	$0.00	$35.00
Coupon interest rate	0.00%	7.50%	5.00%	0.00%	7.00%
Yield (market interest rate)	6.00%	6.75%	7.00%	8.25%	7.50%
Issue date	1/26/97	6/30/75	4/9/93	9/12/89	10/12/01
Settlement date (purchase date)	1/26/01	6/30/00	1/2/01	7/16/01	10/13/01
Maturity date	1/26/02	6/30/05	4/20/14	9/12/19	10/13/31
Term-to-maturity (years)	1.0	5.0	13.3	18.2	30.0
Bond price (% of par)	94.26	103.14	82.86	23.04	94.07
Bond valuation	$942.60	$1,031.38	$828.61	$230.44	$940.66
Duration (years)	1.0	4.3	9.4	18.2	12.5
Modified duration	1.0	4.1	9.0	17.4	12.0

modified duration Percentage change in bond price for each percentage point change in market interest rates.

The duration concept can be modified to measure sensitivity of bond prices to changes in yield-to-maturity. **Modified duration** is simply duration divided by 1 plus the yield-to-maturity:

$$\text{Modified duration} = \frac{\text{Duration}}{1 + \left(\dfrac{\text{Yield}}{\text{Coupon Payments per Year}}\right)} \tag{7.5}$$

Modified duration is a direct estimate of the percentage change that will occur in a bond's market price for each percentage point change in market interest rates. In the case of the bond depicted in column (4) of Table 7.4, for example, modified duration of 17.4 means that this zero coupon bond's price would fall roughly 17.4% with a 1% rise in interest rates, or rise by a commensurate amount if prevailing rates fell by 1%.

Duration is a powerful concept and an effective tool when used properly. It is important to keep in mind, however, that duration will not tell bond investors when market interest rates will move, by how much, or in which direction. Understanding the duration concept does help manage investment risk. Bond investors able to understand the duration concept are able to assess the risk of fixed-income investments and take on only as much risk as is appropriate for their situation.

For individual bonds, duration calculations such as those displayed in Table 7.4 can be made quickly and easily by using financial formulas found in leading spreadsheet software programs, such as Microsoft Excel. Fortunately for bond investors, it is also seldom necessary to make the complex calculation necessary to derive duration for a large bond portfolio. Leading bond mutual fund families, such as the Vanguard Group of Investment Companies, calculate and publish duration statistics for their bond mutual funds. Other printed publications, including *Morningstar Mutual Funds* and *The Value Line Mutual Fund Survey,* also report bond fund duration information. For many large mutual funds, detailed bond portfolio performance and risk information, including average maturity and duration, are also available on the Internet. For example, Vanguard's Bond Index–Total Bond Market Portfolio seeks to match the investment performance of the Lehman Brothers Aggregate Bond Index, a broad market-weighted index that encompasses U.S. Treasury and agency securities, corporate investment-grade bonds, and mortgage-backed securities. As shown in Figure 7.3, investors are able to access up-to-date return and risk information for this fund on Yahoo!'s excellent financial Web site.

Convexity

convexity Sensitivity of modified duration to changes in yield-to-maturity.

Modified duration measures the sensitivity of bond prices to changes in yield-to-maturity. **Convexity** measures the sensitivity of modified duration to changes in yield-to-maturity. If modified duration can be thought of as the "speed" of bond price changes from yield changes, then convexity is the rate of "acceleration" in bond price changes tied to yield changes. The convexity concept can be depicted in Table 7.5, which shows yield-to-maturity, bond price and modified duration for two bonds over a range of interest rates. Data are given for a 30-year, 6% coupon bond, and for a five-year, 6% coupon bond. Notice how the price of the 30-year bond appears to be more sensitive to yield changes than is the price of the five-

FIGURE 7.3 **Vanguard's Total Bond Market Index Gives Mutual Fund Investors a Means for Participating in the Bond Market**

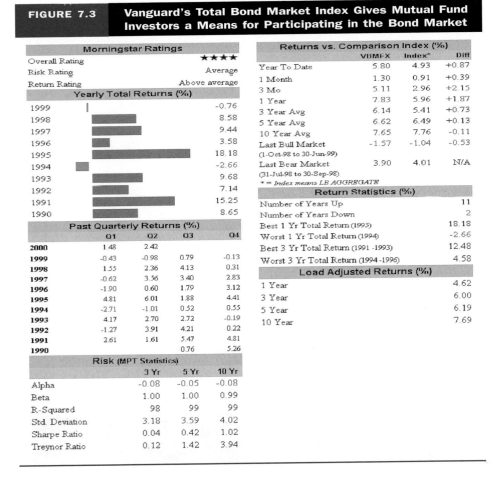

Morningstar Ratings	
Overall Rating	★★★★
Risk Rating	Average
Return Rating	Above average

Yearly Total Returns (%)	
1999	-0.76
1998	8.58
1997	9.44
1996	3.58
1995	18.18
1994	-2.66
1993	9.68
1992	7.14
1991	15.25
1990	8.65

Past Quarterly Returns (%)	Q1	Q2	Q3	Q4
2000	1.48	2.42		
1999	-0.43	-0.98	0.79	-0.13
1998	1.55	2.36	4.13	0.31
1997	-0.62	3.56	3.40	2.83
1996	-1.90	0.60	1.79	3.12
1995	4.81	6.01	1.88	4.41
1994	-2.71	-1.01	0.52	0.55
1993	4.17	2.70	2.72	-0.19
1992	-1.27	3.91	4.21	0.22
1991	2.61	1.61	5.47	4.81
1990			0.76	5.26

Risk (MPT Statistics)	3 Yr	5 Yr	10 Yr
Alpha	-0.08	-0.05	-0.08
Beta	1.00	1.00	0.99
R-Squared	98	99	99
Std. Deviation	3.18	3.59	4.02
Sharpe Ratio	0.04	0.42	1.02
Treynor Ratio	0.12	1.42	3.94

Returns vs. Comparison Index (%)	VBMFX	Index*	Diff
Year To Date	5.80	4.93	+0.87
1 Month	1.30	0.91	+0.39
3 Mo	5.11	2.96	+2.15
1 Year	7.83	5.96	+1.87
3 Year Avg	6.14	5.41	+0.73
5 Year Avg	6.62	6.49	+0.13
10 Year Avg	7.65	7.76	-0.11
Last Bull Market (1-Oct-98 to 30-Jun-99)	-1.57	-1.04	-0.53
Last Bear Market (31-Jul-98 to 30-Sep-98)	3.90	4.01	N/A

* = *Index means LB AGGREGATE*

Return Statistics (%)	
Number of Years Up	11
Number of Years Down	2
Best 1 Yr Total Return (1995)	18.18
Worst 1 Yr Total Return (1994)	-2.66
Best 3 Yr Total Return (1991 -1993)	12.48
Worst 3 Yr Total Return (1994 -1996)	4.58

Load Adjusted Returns (%)	
1 Year	4.62
3 Year	6.00
5 Year	6.19
10 Year	7.69

year bond. Also see how modified duration for the 30-year bond appears to be more sensitive to yield changes than is the modified duration of the five-year bond.

This relationship can also be shown graphically. In Figure 7.4, the *y*-axis is bond price expressed as a percentage of par value, and the *x*-axis is yield-to-maturity in percentage terms. Price-yield curves are shown for both the 30-year bond and for the five-year bond. Price-yield curves show the effects on bond prices of changes in the yield-to-maturity and are convex to (bend away from) the origin. Thus, the degree of convexity describes the degree of bend in the price-yield curve.

Relatively low convexity in the price-yield relationship for the short-term five-year bond is reflected in a comparatively straight downward-sloping price-yield curve. High convexity in the price-yield relationship for the long-term 30-year bond is reflected in a more sharply curved downward-sloping price-yield curve. In this example, the long-term 30-year bond is said to be more convex than the short-term five-year bond.

Convexity arises in the price-yield curve because, as yields change, the weights given to cash flow timing fluctuate more than yields. In general, convexity increases

TABLE 7.5 **The Percentage Impact on Bond Prices from Yield Changes Depends on the Yield-to-Maturity**

	30-year, 6% Bond		5-year, 6% Bond	
Yield (%)	**Price**	**Modified Duration**	**Price**	**Modified Duration**
1.00	$229.3139	19.4162	$124.3260	4.4447
1.50	208.3901	18.8549	121.5991	4.4266
2.00	189.9101	18.2890	118.9426	4.4086
2.50	173.5605	17.7205	116.3547	4.3906
3.00	159.0704	17.1514	113.8333	4.3726
3.50	146.2050	16.5839	111.3765	4.3547
4.00	134.7609	16.0199	108.9826	4.3367
4.50	124.5617	15.4615	106.6497	4.3188
5.00	115.4543	14.9104	104.3760	4.3009
5.50	107.3057	14.3687	102.1600	4.2830
6.00	100.0000	13.8378	100.0000	4.2651
6.50	93.4966	13.3193	97.8944	4.2472
7.00	87.5276	12.8145	95.8417	4.2294
7.50	82.1966	12.3245	93.8404	4.2115
8.00	77.3765	11.8503	91.8891	4.1937
8.50	73.0090	11.3926	89.9864	4.1759
9.00	69.0430	10.9519	88.1309	4.1581
9.50	65.4335	10.5287	86.3214	4.1403
10.00	62.1414	10.1231	84.5565	4.1225

FIGURE 7.4 **Price-Yield Curve for a 30-Year 6% Bond Is More Convex to the Origin than the Price-Yield Curve for a 5-Year 6% Bond**

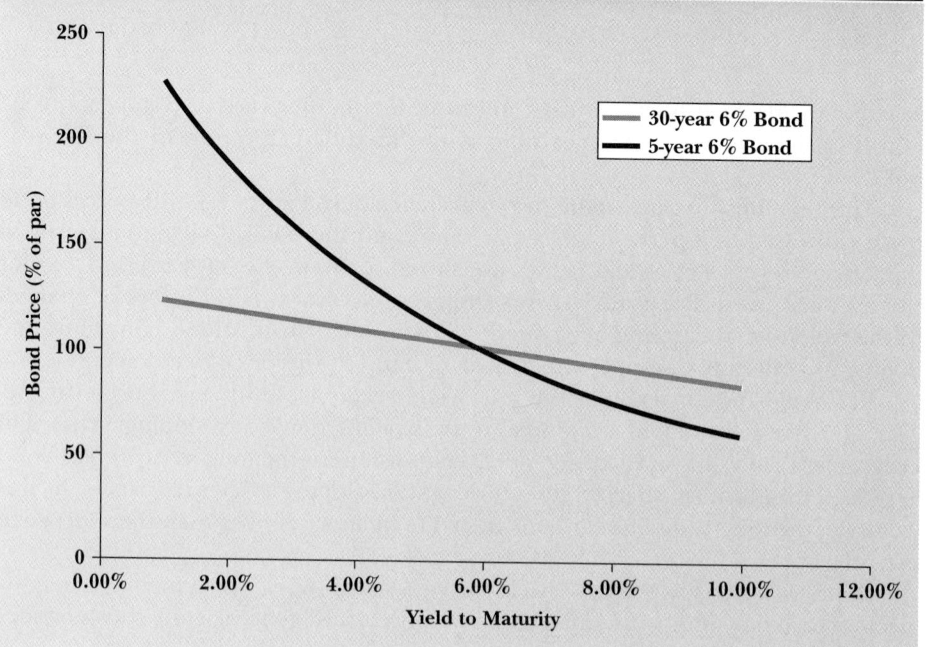

with a lower coupon, longer term-to-maturity, and lower yield. For very low-yield, long-term bonds, small changes in a low yield-to-maturity can lead to big changes in bond prices. For high-yield, short-term bonds, it can take a very big change in a high yield-to-maturity to measurably affect the bond's price. Convexity is simply another useful way of characterizing bond risk.

WALL STREET WISDOM 7.2

Junk Bonds Are Back!

NorthPoint Communications Group Inc. brought in a meager $21.1 million in revenue during 1999 and reported a net loss of $184 million. Who would lend $400 million to such a company? You and I might not, but it turns out that lots of bond investors are more than eager to lend money to such high-risk companies. Even as stable and profitable industrials experienced a tough time selling debt securities, media and telecom debt issues were hot with bond investors. In the case of NorthPoint, the company was able to double the planned size of a $200 million high-yield, or junk, bond offering led by Goldman Sachs and Morgan Stanley.

This is the bond market's equivalent of the bifurcated, or two-tiered, market that has confounded equity investors throughout 1999 and early 2000. During this period, high-tech stock market investors flipped over the "New Economy" concept and leapt at the opportunity to pay stunning market valuations for nascent companies with little revenues, profits, or tangible assets. The relatively staid bond world has taken on a similar skew. Bond investors literally threw millions of dollars in debt financing at media and telecom companies with huge losses. At the same time, junk bond investors appeared to refuse to fund just about anything else. As in the stock market, in which technology shares soared as everything else sputtered, the junk bond world became divided into the haves and have-nots. According to Goldman Sachs, telecom, media, and technology companies soaked up almost 90% of the $9.5 billion in worldwide junk bond issues during the first quarter of 2000. That compared with less than one-half of the $13.3 billion raised during the same period of 1999.

Bond investor cravings for original-issue junk bonds' dubious economic underpinnings is a troubling reminder of problems encountered more than a decade ago. During the 1980s and early 1990s, similar issues foundered and left bond investors with billions of dollars in losses. In the bond market, prices can quickly plummet when market interest rates rise or an issuer's credit quality deteriorates. If an aggressive bond investor builds a portfolio of seasoned junk bonds, many issues will be purchased for only pennies on the dollar. Some may be obtained for only 30%, 40%, or 50% of the original face amount. Of course, many such issuers will default, and bond investors may ultimately recoup much less than the original face amount or nothing. It is a dream come true for the junk bond investor when an issuer recovers its financial health, and an issue bought for only a small fraction of par value ultimately rebounds to make full interest and principal payments. The profit earned on such "home runs" makes up for returns from issues that result in modest profits or entail a loss.

The basic problem with original-issue junk bonds is that such bonds do not have the potential to give bond investors a home run when a depressed bond price fully recovers. Like almost all bonds, original-issue junk bonds have call provisions that allow the issuer to repurchase the bond on favorable terms. If credit quality improves for the issuer of an original-issue junk bond, the bond is apt to be called and refinanced with another bond that pays lower interest consistent with the issuer's now higher credit rating. The issuer, not the junk bond owner, is thus able to benefit from the firm's improvement in credit quality. Similarly, if market interest rates fall, junk bond issuers are likely to seek refinancing at the now-lower market interest rate. The issuer, not the junk bond owner, captures the benefit from a decline in interest rates. In the junk bond market, buyers of original-issue junk bonds have the odds stacked against them.

If credit quality improves, or market interest rates fall, original-issue junk bonds are refinanced to the issuer's benefit. If credit quality deteriorates or market interest rates rise, junk bond prices fall and the bond buyer gets stuck. Too often, the original-issue junk bond market is a "heads they win, tails I lose" proposition for bond investors.

See: Paul M. Sherer, " Bond World Pours Money into Telecom Companies," *The Wall Street Journal,* February 23, 2000, C1, C22.

Credit-Quality Risk

Bond Ratings

When a bond is issued, the issuer is responsible for providing details concerning its financial soundness. This information is contained in an offering circular known as the bond prospectus. Bond dealers and investment representatives are required by law to provide all buyers of newly issued bonds with a copy of the prospectus prior to the point of initial purchase. Nevertheless, it remains difficult for an individual investor to know if a given company or government entity has the capability to make promised interest and principal payments 10, 20, or even 30 years from the date of issue. For this reason, independent **bond-rating** agencies assess bond risk at the time of issue and monitor developments during the bond's lifetime. Securities firms and banks also maintain research staffs to monitor the creditworthiness of various issuers.

bond rating Credit quality.

Credit quality risk is the chance of investment loss due to the inability of a bond issuer to make timely interest and principal payments. Bond credit quality ranges from the highest-quality U.S. Treasury securities, backed by the full faith and credit of the U.S. government, to **below-investment-grade bonds,** or **junk bonds,** which are considered highly speculative. Because a long-term bond may not be redeemed or reach maturity for 10, 20, or even 30 years, credit quality is a prime consideration for bond investors. Prestigious bond credit-rating agencies in the United States include Moody's Investors Service, Standard & Poor's Corporation (S&P), Fitch IBCA Inc., and Duff & Phelps Credit Rating Co. Each of these credit analysis firms assign ratings based on a detailed analysis of the issuer's financial condition, general economic and credit market conditions, and the economic value of any underlying collateral. As shown in Table 7.6, highest credit-quality ratings are AAA (for S&P, Fitch, and Duff & Phelps) and Aaa (for Moody's). Bonds rated BBB or higher are generally considered investment-grade with little chance of impairment in the ability of the issuer to make promised interest and principal payments. Bonds

credit-quality risk Chance of loss due to the inability of a bond issuer to make timely interest and principal payments.

below-investment-grade bonds Junk bonds.

junk bonds Highly speculative debt securities.

TABLE 7.6 Bond Credit Ratings Distinguish Investment Grade Bonds from High-Yield or "Junk" Bonds

Credit Risk	Moody's	Standard & Poor's	Fitch/IBCA	DCR
Investment Grade				
Highest quality	Aaa	AAA	AAA	AAA
High quality (very strong)	Aa	AA	AA	AA
Upper medium grade (strong)	A	A	A	A
Medium grade	Baa	BBB	BBB	BBB
Below Investment Grade				
Somewhat speculative	Ba	BB	BB	BB
Speculative	B	B	B	B
Highly speculative	Caa	CCC	CCC	CCC
Most speculative	Ca	CC	CC	CC
Imminent default	C	D	C	C
Default	C	D	D	D

Data source: Bond Market Association.

rated BB and below are considered junk bonds, **high-yield bonds,** or simply below-investment-grade bonds. Experience has shown that broadly diversified portfolios of below-investment-grade bonds face only a modest risk from default, but these risks can be high for investors in individual junk bonds. Such risks are especially important when a reduction in credit rating signals a deterioration in credit quality.

high-yield bonds Below-investment-grade bonds.

Credit-quality assessment agencies signal they are considering a rating change by placing an individual bond, or all the bonds of a given issuer, on CreditWatch (S&P), under "review" (Moody's), on "rating alert" (Fitch IBCA), or on "rating watch" (Duff & Phelps). Rating agencies make their ratings information available to the public through their ratings information desks. In addition to published reports, ratings are made available in many public libraries and over the Internet.

Yield Spreads

The term structure of interest rates shows differences in the yield-to-maturity for bonds that have the same credit risk but differing terms to maturity. As such, the term structure of interest rates shows the risk premium earned by long-term bonds that involve greater interest-rate risk than short-term bonds. During recent years, the yield-to-maturity on long-term bonds has averaged 2½–3% per year higher than the return on very short-term notes. This return premium for long-term versus short-term equal-grade bonds constitutes the bond investors' compensation for the greater interest-rate risk of long-term bonds.

In addition to interest-rate risk, bond investors are also subject to credit risk, or the chance bond issuers will fail to make timely interest and principal payments. **Yield spreads** show the difference in yield for bonds with the same term-to-maturity but different credit risks. Differences in default risk are a prime source of yield spreads among general classes of debt securities, such as between government and corporate bonds. Coupon reinvestment risk is another source of yield spreads, particularly between conventional bonds versus zero coupon bonds.

yield spreads Difference in yield for bonds with the same term-to-maturity but different credit risks.

Figure 7.5 gives an example of yield spread comparisons that are printed on a daily basis in leading financial publications such as *The Wall Street Journal.* For example, notice that the 6.94% yield-to-maturity for 10-plus-year federal agency securities is 0.46%, or 46 basis points, higher than the 6.48% yield-to-maturity for 10-plus-year Treasury securities. This modest risk premium is slightly smaller than that observed between federal agency securities and AAA, or high-quality, corporate bonds. During early 2000, high-quality corporate bonds with 10-plus years to maturity paid a yield-to-maturity of 7.64%, and 0.70%, or 70 basis points, more than federal agency securities, and 1.16%, or 116 basis points, more than 10-plus-year Treasury securities.

Also notice in Figure 7.5 the very low rates of return earned on tax-exempt securities of various terms-to-maturity. These low rates reflect the stable payment history of municipal bonds and their tax-exempt status. Remember, with a 40% marginal income tax for high-income individuals, 12–22-year high-grade municipal bonds paying 5.90% give a tax-equivalent yield of 9.83% [$= 5.90\%/(1 - 0.4)$]. This represents a yield spread of 3.35%, or 335 basis points, over the 6.48% yield-to-maturity for 10-plus-year Treasury securities. When calculating yield spreads for municipal bonds, it is important to adjust for their tax-exempt status.

FIGURE 7.5 Yield Comparisons

YIELD COMPARISONS

Based on Merrill Lynch Bond Indexes, priced as of midafternoon Eastern time.

	2/18	2/17	–52 Week– High	Low
Corp.-Govt. Master	7.04%	7.10%	7.15%	5.59%
Treasury 1-10yr	6.63	6.69	6.71	4.98
10+ yr	6.48	6.55	6.93	5.60
Agencies 1-10yr	7.19	7.26	7.26	5.55
10+ yr	6.94	7.01	7.34	5.94
Corporate				
1-10 yr High Qlty	7.45	7.52	7.55	5.68
Med Qlty	7.83	7.90	7.94	6.15
10+yr High Qlty	7.64	7.71	7.85	6.41
Med Qlty	8.01	8.07	8.24	6.87
Yankee bonds(1)	7.69	7.75	7.79	6.41
Current-coupon mortgages (2)				
GNMA 7.50%	7.99	8.04	8.05	6.37
FNMA 7.50%	8.01	8.05	8.05	6.42
FHLMC7.50%	8.03	8.08	8.08	6.42
High-yield corporates	11.19	11.20	11.21	9.74
Tax-Exempt Bonds				
7-12-yr G.O. (AA)	5.30	5.30	5.36	4.16
12-22-yr G.O. (AA)	5.90	5.91	6.04	4.62
22+yr revenue (A)	6.22	6.24	6.35	4.93

Note: High quality rated AAA-AA; medium quality A-BBB/Baa; high yield, BB/Ba-C.

(1) Dollar-denominated, SEC-registered bonds of foreign issuers sold in the U.S. (2) Reflects the 52-week high and low of mortgage-backed securities indexes rather than the individual securities shown.

Source: *The Wall Street Journal*, February 22, 2000, C33.

As shown in Figure 7.6, money rates on all the various types of fixed-income securities reflect differences in interest-rate risk measured by term-to-maturity and credit risk measured by yield spreads. In characterizing interest-rate differentials, bond investors must be aware of both.

Bond Insurance

The credit quality of individual bonds can be enhanced when the issuer pays an independent third-party provider of bond insurance. Specialized insurance firms serve the fixed-income market by guaranteeing the timely payment of principal and interest on bonds issued by others. In the United States, major bond insurers include MBIA Inc., AMBAC Financial Group, Inc., and Financial Security Assurance Holdings, Inc. Leading bond insurers have a AAA rating attesting to their

FIGURE 7.6 **Short-Term Interest Rates Vary According to Credit Quality**

MONEY RATES

Monday, February 21, 2000

The key U. S. and foreign annual interest rates below are a guide to general levels but don't always represent actual transactions.

EURO COMMERCIAL P APER: placed directly by General Electric Capital Corp.: 3.38% 30 days; 3.48% two months; 3.56% three months; 3.62% four months; 3.69% five months; 3.72% six months.

LONDON LATE EURODOLLARS: 5.88% - 5.75% one month; 6.00% - 5.88% two months; 6.13% - 6.00% three months; 6.19% - 6.06% four months; 6.25% - 6.13% five months; 6.38% - 6.25% six months.

LONDON INTERBANK OFFERED RATES (LIBOR): 5.88000% one month; 6.11000% three months; 6.35375% six months; 6.85125% one year. No Fixing for Dec 27 and Dec 28. British Banker's Association average of interbank offered rates for dollar deposits in the London market based on quotations at 16 major banks. Effective rate for contracts entered into two days from date appearing at top of this column.

EURO LIBOR: 3.43000% one month; 3.61313% three months; 3.80375% six months; 4.21063% one year. British Banker's Association average of interbank offered rates for euro deposits in the London market based on quotations at 16 major banks. Effective rate for contracts entered into two days from date appearing at top of this column.

EURO INTERBANK OFFERED RATES (EURIBOR): 3.429% one month; 3.612% three months; 3.803% six months; 4.208% one year. European Banking Federation-sponsored rate among 57 Euro zone banks.

Friday, February 18, 2000

The key U. S. and foreign annual interest rates below are a guide to general levels but don't always represent actual transactions.

PRIME RATE: 8.75% (effective 02/03/00). The base rate on corporate loans posted by at least 75% of the nation's 30 largest banks.

DISCOUNT RATE: 5.25% (effective 02/02/00). The charge on loans to depository institutions by the Federal Reserve Banks.

FEDERAL FUNDS: 5 7/8 % high, 5 5/8 % low, 5 3/4 % near closing bid, 5 7/8 % offered. Reserves traded among commercial banks for overnight use in amounts of $1 million or more. Source: Prebon Yamane(U.S.A) Inc. FOMC fed funds target rate 5.75% effective 2/2/00.

CALL MONEY: 7.50% (effective 02/03/00). The charge on loans to brokers on stock exchange collateral. Source: Reuters.

COMMERCIAL PAPER: placed directly by General Electric Capital Corp.: 5.76% 30 to 49 days; 5.83% 50 to 74 days; 5.90% 75 to 109 days; 5.92% 110 to 140 days; 6.00% 141 to 162 days; 6.03% 163 to 209 days; 6.08% 210 to 270 days.

EURO COMMERCIAL PAPER: placed directly by General Electric Capital Corp.: 3.30% 30 days; 3.40% two months; 3.49% three months; 3.54% four months; 3.62% five months; 3.69% six months.

DEALER COMMERCIAL PAPER: High-grade unsecured notes sold through dealers by major corporations: 5.78% 30 days; 5.83% 60 days; 5.90% 90 days.

CERTIFICATES OF DEPOSIT: 5.35% one month; 5.45% two months; 5.52% three months; 5.83% six months; 6.25% one year. Average of top rates paid by major New York banks on primary new issues of negotiable C.D.s, usually on amounts of $1 million and more. The minimum unit is $100,000. Typical rates in the secondary market. 5.83% one month; 6.03% three months; 6.30% six months.

BANKERS ACCEPTANCES: 5.77% 30 days; 5.82% 60 days; 5.88% 90 days; 5.93% 120 days; 5.98% 150 days; 6.00% 180 days. Offered rates of negotiable, bank-backed business credit instruments typically financing an import order.

LONDON LATE EURODOLLARS: 5.88% - 5.75% one month; 6.00% - 5.88% two months; 6.13% - 6.00% three months; 6.19% - 6.06% four months; 6.25% - 6.13% five months; 6.38% - 6.25% six months.

LONDON INTERBANK OFFERED RATES (LIBOR): 5.8800% one month; 6.1100% three months; 6.3550% six months; 6.86125% one year. British Banker's Association average of interbank offered rates for dollar deposits in the London market based on quotations at 16 major banks. Effective rate for contracts entered into two days from date appearing at top of this column.

EURO LIBOR: 3.35500% one month; 3.54313% three months; 3.75000% six months; 4.16000% one year. British Banker's Association average of interbank offered rates for euro deposits in the London market based on quotations at 16 major banks. Effective rate for contracts entered into two days from date appearing at top of this column.

EURO INTERBANK OFFERED RATES (EURIBOR): 3.346% one month; 3.531% three months; 3.746% six months; 4.157% one year. European Banking Federation-sponsored rate among 57 Euro zone banks.

FOREIGN PRIME RATES: Canada 6.75%; Germany 3.25%; Japan 1.375%; Switzerland 4.375%; Britain 6.00%. These rate indications aren't directly comparable; lending practices vary widely by location.

TREASURY BILLS: Results of the Monday, February 14, 2000, auction of short-term U.S. government bills, sold at a discount from face value in units of $1,000 to $1 million: 5.510% 13 weeks; 5.760% 26 weeks.

OVERNIGHT REPURCHASE RATE: 5.64%. Dealer financing rate for overnight sale and repurchase of Treasury securities. Source: Reuters.

FREDDIE MAC: Posted yields on 30-year mortgage commitments. Delivery within 30 days 8.41%, 60 days 8.46%, standard conventional fixed-rate mortgages: 6.875%, 2% rate capped one-year adjustable rate mortgages. Source: Reuters.

FANNIE MAE: Posted yields on 30 year mortgage commitments (priced at par) for delivery within 30 days 8.47%, 60 days 8.55%, standard conventional fixed-rate mortgages; 7.45%,6/2 rate capped one-year adjustable rate mortgages. Source: Reuters.

MERRILL LYNCH READY ASSETS TRUST: 5.33%. Annualized average rate of return after expenses for the past 30 days; not a forecast of future returns.

CONSUMER PRICE INDEX: January, 168.7, up 2.7% from a year ago. Bureau of Labor Statistics.

Source: *The Wall Street Journal,* February 22, 2000, C33.

financial soundness. As a result, insured bonds receive the same AAA rating based on the insurer's creditworthiness and claims-paying resources. Although the focus of bond insurer activities has historically been in municipal bonds, bond insurers also provide guarantees in the mortgage and asset-backed securities markets. During recent years, bond insurers have begun to move into other more exotic fixed-income securities as well.

High-Yield Bonds

Risk Characteristics

Companies that offer high-yield bonds do so because they have no other choice. Any corporation that issues bonds is borrowing money. Like anyone who borrows money, corporations want to pay the lowest possible interest rate. Small, relatively new, or financially ailing corporations must offer high yields to compensate investors for the higher risks involved with buying their bonds. After all, corporate bond investors have a variety of safe but lower-yielding options for their investments. For example, safe but low-yield corporate bonds issued by the likes of International Business Machines, General Motors, or Citigroup are backed by the full faith and credit of some of the most creditworthy corporate bond issuers in the world.

High-yield bonds are sometimes referred to as junk bonds because they carry a relatively high risk of default. When an issuer defaults, bond investors fail to receive timely interest and principal payments. In extreme circumstances, interest and principal payments are never paid. In the eyes of bond investors, the big question is whether the higher yield offered by junk bonds is sufficient to compensate for the higher risk of default. This is a question that can only be answered over many years as economic and corporate events unfold to determine which bonds will pay their obligations and which ones will default.

Classifications of debt obligations as high-yield or junk are largely made on the basis of the issuing firm's credit rating. Credit ratings are independent judgments about the likelihood that a bond issuer will make good on its promise to make interest and principal payments. As shown in Table 7.6, Moody's and S&P are among the best known of the independent companies that assign these bond credit ratings. Their ratings are influenced by such factors as a company's financial strength (e.g., cash on hand, ratio of current assets to current liabilities, profitability) and its past record of repaying debts.

Investment Experience

The health of the U.S. economy also plays an important role in the junk bond market. A vibrant economy provides an excellent climate for high-yield bonds because it reduces the risk of default. In a weak economy, high-yield bonds lose their luster because the risk of default rises. To guard against hard-to-predict downturns in the overall economy, many junk bond investors seek the relative safety of investing in portfolios of high-yield bonds. Broadly diversifying across several bond issuers can help reduce, but does not eliminate, the relatively higher default risk of junk bonds.

Note in Figure 7.5, the relatively large yield spread between Treasury securities and high-yield bonds. Remember, high-yield corporate bonds entail substantial risk of default and must offer a substantial risk premium for bond investors to justify their purchase. In the example shown, an 11.19% yield-to-maturity for high-yield bonds represents a whopping 4.71%, or 471-basis-point, yield spread over the 6.48% yield-to-maturity for 10-plus-year Treasury securities. A wide gap in the yield-to-maturity for such securities is fairly common and actually grows during periods of bond market turmoil.

Table 7.7 shows the total rate of return earned on high-yield bonds since 1984, when investment interest in the high-yield bond market first exploded. These total rates of return include interest income plus any capital gain or loss earned by high-yield bond investors. As illustrated by the figures in Table 7.7, economic conditions can cause sharp fluctuations in high-yield bond returns. Consider the four-year time frame from 1989 to 1992. The Lehman High-Yield Index returned a scant 0.8% in 1989 and posted a negative return of −9.6% in 1990. Although such under-performance is discouraging for high-yield bond market investors, such periods are often followed by periods of outstanding returns. For example, the Lehman High-Yield Index earned a return of 46.2% in 1991 and 15.8% in 1992.

When considering high-yield bonds, it is important to remember that like all fixed-income securities their price will fall with a general increase in interest rates. The relatively higher default risk of junk bonds adds to the conventional interest-rate risk borne by all debt securities. The knowledgeable investor weighs such risks and decides on an appropriate risk-return trade-off. High-yield bonds are only appropriate for investors who are comfortable with the knowledge that the values of such bonds sometimes decline sharply.

TABLE 7.7 Total Returns on High-Yield or Junk Bonds, 1984–Present

Year	Total Return (%) on the Lehman High-Yield Bond Index
1984	9.70
1985	25.64
1986	17.45
1987	4.99
1988	12.53
1989	0.83
1990	−9.59
1991	46.19
1992	15.75
1993	17.11
1994	−1.03
1995	19.23
1996	11.35
1997	12.76
1998	1.60
1999	2.39

Data source: <http://www.vanguard.com>.

convertible bond Debt that can be exchanged into more junior securities.

indenture agreement Bond contract.

conversion ratio Number of junior securities per bond after conversion.

conversion price Amount per unit of the junior security that the company is willing to accept in trade per bond.

conversion value Worth of a bond as a junior security if converted at the present time.

common stock equivalent value Worth of a bond as common stock if converted at the present time.

premium to conversion Percentage over conversion value at which a convertible bond trades.

break-even time Number of years over which the conversion premium can be recovered by the increased income of the senior security over the junior security.

Convertible Bonds

Convertible Bond Features

A **convertible bond** is a special type of corporate bond that can be exchanged under certain circumstances into some more junior grade of securities. For example, many convertible bonds are sold that can be converted into common stock. Terms of the conversion option are set forth in the **indenture agreement,** or bond contract, and may be exercised at the discretion of the bondholder. Convertible bonds involve a combination of a straight financial instrument *plus* an option. Convertibles are hybrid securities.

For example, the conversion option might specify that a $1,000 bond is convertible into 25 shares of stock. In this case, the **conversion ratio** is simply 25:1. In other instances, the conversion option may be specified in terms of a **conversion price.** The conversion price is the price per share that the company is willing to accept in trade for the bond. For example, if the indenture states that the conversion price is $40 per share, a $1,000 bond is convertible into 25 (= $1,000/$40) shares of stock. This is equivalent to a 25:1 conversion ratio. In some instances, the convertible bond indenture might state that the conversion ratio changes through the years. The conversion price might be $40 for the first five years, $50 for the next five years, and so on. The purpose behind such a sliding scale is to force quick conversion of the bond and thereby reduce corporate interest expenses. To protect bondholders, convertible bonds typically have antidilution features. If the corporation were to split its stock 2:1 and the conversion ratio was 25:1 prior to the split, after the split the conversion ratio would be adjusted to 50:1. Stock dividends have a similar effect on the conversion ratio or conversion price.

Conversion value is the worth of a convertible as a junior security if converted at the present time. For bonds convertible into common stock, conversion value is often expressed as the bond's **common-stock equivalent** value. Because convertible bonds offer an income premium to the amount that would be earned on the junior security, they tend to sell in the marketplace at some premium to the common stock equivalent value. **Premium to conversion** is the percentage over conversion value at which the convertible trades. **Break-even time** is the number of years over which the conversion premium can be recovered by the increased income of the senior security over the junior security.

Convertible Bond Valuation Example

Suppose that the common stock of XYZ, Inc., pays a 25¢ dividend and has a market price of $20 per share. Also assume that XYZ's 7% convertible bond sells at 80 (or $800) and is convertible into common at $40 per share. Bond prices are always quoted in terms of a percentage of par, so 80 implies a bond price of $800 (= 80% × $1,000). See Table 7.8 for details.

In this case, conversion value is the number of equivalent common shares multiplied by the current share price or $500 = ($1,000/$40) × $20. Alternatively, with a par of $1,000 and a conversion price of $40 per share, each convertible bond has a conversion ratio of 25:1 (= $1,000/$40). This means that each bond represents an ownership interest equivalent to 25 shares of common stock. With a common share price of $20, each bond has a common stock–equivalent value of $500 (= 25 × $20).

TABLE 7.8 Convertible Bond-Pricing Example

Bond par value = \$1,000
Bond market value = \$800
Conversion price = \$40
Market price of XYZ common = \$20
Common dividend per share = \$0.25
Common dividend yield = \$0.25/\$20 = 1.25%
Conversion ratio = Par value ÷ Conversion price = \$1,000/\$40 = 25:1
Conversion value = Common stock equivalent × Common price = 25 × \$20 = \$500

$$\text{Premium to conversion} = \frac{\text{Bond market value} - \text{Conversion value}}{\text{Conversion value}} = \frac{\$800 - \$500}{\$500} = 60\%$$

$$\text{Break-even time} = \frac{\$800 - \$500}{\$70 - (\$800 \times 1.25\%)} = 5 \text{ years}$$

Because the convertible bond offers superior interest income to an equivalent amount invested in the company's common stock, the convertible bond typically sells at a premium to its common stock–equivalent value. Premium to conversion value is the percentage by which the current market value of the convertible bond exceeds the underlying common stock–equivalent value. In this case, the market value of the bond is \$800, or \$300 more than the bond's \$500 common stock–equivalent value. This means that the bond's premium to conversion value is 60% (= (\$800 − \$500)/\$500).

Finally, break-even time is the number of years needed to recover the conversion premium with the convertible's higher income. In this case, a \$20 stock paying a 25¢ dividend offers a 1.25% yield to common shareholders. On an \$800 investment in the company's common stock, a stockholder would earn \$10 of dividend income. By contrast, a convertible bondholder would earn \$70 of interest income on a similar \$800 investment in one bond. On an annual basis, the convertible bondholder earns \$60 in additional income. With a conversion premium of \$300, it would take the convertible bondholder five years to recoup the conversion premium. In this case, break-even time is five years (= \$300/\$60).

Convertible bonds appeal to patient long-term investors. If an investor expects to buy and hold a given security for an extended period, convertible bonds can prove to be a cost-effective investment. In the present example, if an investor wanted to buy and hold stock in XYZ for more than five years, buying the convertible bond would be preferable to buying the common stock. This is particularly true if the convertible bond can be held in a tax-sheltered retirement account, such as a 401-k or IRA, in which high interest income would not lead to higher income taxes.

Bond Investment Strategies

Why Invest in Bonds?

Bonds make attractive investments for two key reasons: stable income and diversification. The interest income earned on bonds is generally higher and more stable than the interest earned by investments such as money market funds, certificates

WALL STREET WISDOM 7.3

Amazing Amazon.com Converts

Amazon.com, Inc., is an online retailer that offers books, music CDs, videos, DVDs, computer games, and toys. The company sources products from a network of distributors, publishers, and manufacturers. Although Amazon.com carries its own inventory, it relies on rapid fulfillment from major distributors and wholesalers that carry a broad selection of titles. Amazon.com has offered books for sale since July 1995 and expanded its product offerings to music (June 1998), videos, and other holiday gifts (November 1998). On Wall Street, the company's stock has been an investment phenomenon, rising from a split-adjusted $1.50 in 1997 to $88.88 per share in early 1999.

In early 2000, Amazon.com made some noise when it announced a number of promising partnership arrangements with other Web sites, such as Drugstore.com, Audible.com, and Living.com. In total, these Web sites agreed to pay Amazon.com more than $100 million over the next few years. To many stock and bond investors, such cross-promotion deals appear to validate Amazon.com's business model of seeking to become a leading general-purpose retailer or shopping mall on the Internet.

Of course, several curious investors wondered out loud where such embryonic dot.coms could get the financial wherewithal to make multimillion-dollar marketing arrangements with Amazon.com. Eyebrows were raised when it was revealed that Amazon.com itself was the source of these monies. In what appear to be quid pro quo deals, Amazon.com buys equity in various dot.com start-ups and then requires them to pay fees that show up as revenues on Amazon.com's books. Amazingly, normally conservative bond investors are the ones Amazon.com has been relying on to fund such relationships.

In February 2000, Amazon.com sold 600 million euros ($586 million) of convertible bonds to British, German, and other European investors. This amount is in addition to the $1.25 billion Amazon.com raised in the U.S. bond market during 1999 to fund the company's expansion plans and mushrooming operating losses. At the end of 1999, Amazon.com had roughly $700 million in cash and marketable securities on hand. Amazon.com's euro bond deal was unusual because of its gigantic size and because of various unusual enticements designed to make the bond attractive to usually temperate bond investors. Like most convertible bond offerings, Amazon.com's deal allows investors to convert the bonds into Amazon.com stock at a later date at a price greater than Amazon.com's current market price. However, in a highly unusual twist, if Amazon.com's stock falls in either of the first two years, the company will lower the bondholder's conversion price.

To optimists, this unique inducement was seen as evidence of the confidence Amazon.com executives had in the continued strength of the company and its stock price. Less ebullient investors noted that such a provision puts Amazon.com's current stockholders at risk of substantial future dilution in their ownership position. Another troubling sign of a lack of confidence in Amazon.com's future is provided by the fact that the bonds could only be placed after offering investors a juicy coupon of about 7.13%, among the highest interest rates paid on convertible bonds issued by a major corporation.

Apparently, more than a few bond investors are concerned that Amazon.com's investments in Internet start-ups will become worthless unless such partners are able to quickly build viable business models. More skeptical investors argue that Amazon.com's partnership funding practices cause revenues to be wildly overstated and undermine confidence in the validity of Amazon.com's own business model. After all, how robust is demand for Amazon.com's products if the company has to "buy" revenues? To some investors, Amazon.com's revenue-building relationships are reminiscent of practices at Boston Chicken, Inc., in which intracompany transactions were used to build revenue and profit growth for a company that, in the end, proved not to be viable on an economic basis.

Going forward, it will be interesting to learn if Amazon.com's innovative convertible bond funding and revenue recognition practices are just the typical growing pains of a rapidly evolving industry leader or instead indicators of more basic flaws in the company's business model.

See: William Peske, Jr., "Unreliable Vehicles," *Barron's*, May 1, 2000, 32.

of deposit (CDs), or bank passbook accounts. However, the added income potential of bonds comes with some added risk. Unlike bonds, passbook accounts and bank CDs are guaranteed within limits by an agency of the federal government. Many investors, and particularly retirees who need current income, use bonds for a substantial part of their investment portfolios. Many investors in the stock market also hold bonds to help smooth out the inevitable fluctuations in the value of their overall investment portfolios. Although bond prices fluctuate in value, they do not always move in the same direction or to the same degree as stocks. Some affluent investors also use municipal bond funds as a source of tax-exempt interest income. Because municipal bonds tend to have lower before-tax yields than taxable bonds, such investments are usually appropriate only for investors in high tax brackets. Finally, investors may use short-term, high-quality bond funds as an alternative to money market funds. Although this strategy can provide higher interest income, it does entail the risk that the investor could lose some principal because of fluctuating bond prices.

Most financial advisors recommend that investors maintain a diversified investment portfolio consisting of stocks, bonds, and cash reserves, depending on individual circumstances and objectives. Because bonds typically produce a predictable stream of interest and principal payments, many investors are attracted to them as a means to preserve capital and to receive dependable interest income. Bond investing is often useful when saving for children's college education, a new home, or retirement income. This is especially true in the case of retirement planning. During recent years, traditional fixed-benefit retirement plans have increasingly been replaced by defined contribution programs, such as 401-k plans. Although such plans offer great freedom in selection, investors must be self-reliant in securing their retirement lifestyles. The broad diversity of fixed-income securities presents investors with a variety of choices to tailor investments to individual financial objectives.

Asset Allocation

Because risk is inescapable when investing in common stocks, bonds, and money market instruments, investors are best served by using time-tested strategies for risk management. An important element in managing risk is the knowledge that long-term returns are driven by economic fundamentals, but that fear and greed can hold sway over brief periods. When emotion runs high during rampant bull markets, such as during the late 1990s, an investor must maintain the discipline of not getting carried away and becoming overly aggressive. Similarly, the successful long-term investor avoids panic in the face of a sharp downturn in stock prices, such as occurred during October 1987. How would you react to a typical bear market decline of 20–25% in the overall market? Would you be more inclined to buy or sell during such a period? It is best to ask such questions before the fact. To be forewarned is to be forearmed.

To keep an appropriate economic and emotional balance through both bull and bear markets, the long-term investor must construct an investment portfolio that balances the risk characteristics of stocks, bonds, and cash investments against a realistic expectation of expected returns. Although some investors may want a portfolio that consists of only one class of assets, such as stocks, many investors prefer a portfolio that includes more than one type of asset, such as stocks, bonds, and money market instruments. Bonds, depending on their quality and maturity characteristics, have the potential to offer high income and principal stability. Bonds often offer investors a safety net that comes in handy during bear markets. Although the level of income provided by money market instruments is generally lower than the income provided by intermediate-term and long-term bonds, money market investments provide necessary liquidity for short-term obligations and emergencies. For some investors, holding a portion of their portfolio in bonds and cash makes it easier—financially and psychologically—to endure market downturns without selling stocks at depressed prices.

asset allocation Process of diversifying an investment portfolio across various asset categories, such as stocks, bonds, and cash.

Figure 7.7 shows the investment results for a series of **asset allocation** decisions that investors might make to balance the risk/reward trade-off among stocks, bonds, and cash investments. From 1950 to the present, it shows the average annual return, the number of years with a loss, and the worst annual loss for various portfolios consisting of stocks, long-term Treasury bonds, and short-term Treasury bills. Annual returns on four different asset allocation portfolios are compared with an "aggressive growth" portfolio composed solely of common stocks. In a "growth" portfolio, 80% is devoted to stocks and 20% to Treasury bonds. A "growth and income" portfolio contains 60% stocks and 40% Treasury bonds. The remaining two asset allocation portfolios are a "balanced portfolio," containing 40% stocks, 40% Treasury bonds, and 20% Treasury bills, and an "income" portfolio, consisting of 20% stocks, 20% Treasury bonds, and 60% Treasury bills.

In analyzing the effects of various asset allocation decisions on the balance between risk and return, it is obvious that the prime benefit of asset allocation is measured in terms of risk reduction. When risk is measured by the volatility of annual returns, the income portfolio has roughly one-half of the annual return volatility experienced by the aggressive growth (all-stock) portfolio. Such an impressive reduction in risk is costly, however, in that the income portfolio has a mean annual rate of return that is also roughly one-half that of the aggressive growth portfolio. Interestingly, a 100% allocation to common stocks gives the highest annual rate of return for all portfolios in 66% of the years since 1950. The income portfolio is the top-performing mix in 28% of the years studied. Investors interested in maximizing annual rates of return should obviously focus their long-term investment portfolios on common stocks. However, investors especially concerned about the potential for substantial year-to-year volatility might find appropriate an asset allocation that is similar to the income portfolio. Since 1950, the −26.47% worst annual rate of return on common stocks was experienced in 1974. During that year, the income portfolio lost a mere −1.08%. The worst year for the income portfolio was 1994, when a loss of only −3.62% was experienced.

An important lesson to be gained from the data presented in Figure 7.7 is that even a modest amount of diversification can sharply dampen portfolio risk measured by the chance of significant loss during a given year. Another important lesson is that broad diversification entails widespread diversification within each specific asset type, such as common stocks, and among classes of investment assets. Diversification within asset type (common stocks, etc.) can be achieved by investing in common stock index funds designed to mimic the performance of the S&P Stock Index. Diversification among asset types can be achieved by constructing an investment portfolio made up of a variety of index funds. A popular misconception is that broad diversification requires a large variety of investment vehicles. In

FIGURE 7.7 **Asset Allocation Can Help Achieve a Balance between Risk and Return, 1950–Present**

Asset Allocation	Annual Return	Risk (St. Dev.)	Risk-Reward (Coef. Var.)	How Often the Best Mix?	Years with Loss	Worst Loss (Year)
Aggressive Growth 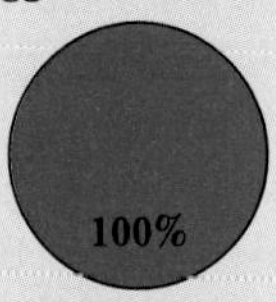	13.61%	16.45%	1.21	66%	20%	−26.47% (1974)
Growth 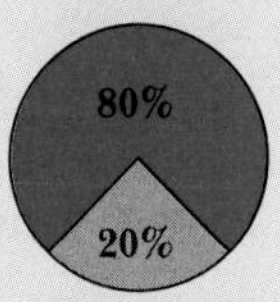	12.91%	14.21%	1.10	0%	22%	−20.31% (1974)
Growth & Income 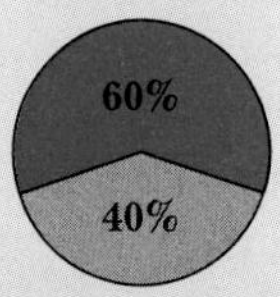	11.25%	11.94%	1.06	4%	18%	−14.14% (1974)
Balanced Portfolio 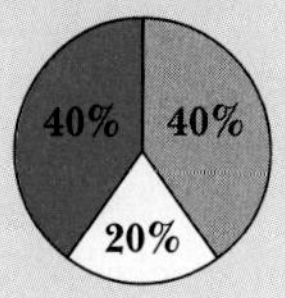	9.41%	8.88%	0.94	2%	16%	−7.25% (1974)
Income 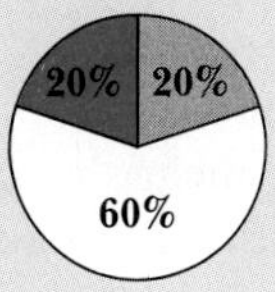	7.53%	8.08%	1.07	28%	14%	−3.62% (1994)

Legend: Common Stocks (S&P 500); Long-Term Treasury Bonds; Short-Term Treasury Bills

Data source: *Federal Reserve Bulletin.*

fact, broad diversification can be easily and cheaply obtained by investing in just three mutual funds: a common stock index fund, a bond market fund, and a money market fund. By changing the mix of the portfolio invested in stocks, bonds, and money markets, just three mutual funds, the investor can fashion an infinite variety of risk profiles. When low-cost index funds are relied on, the costs of broad diversification can be minimal. Furthermore, it is often easy to change your portfolio mix.

The specific asset allocation that is most appropriate depends on a number of factors. The appropriate investment strategy for dealing with risk must be based on personal objectives, time horizon, risk tolerance, and financial circumstances. It must not be wholly determined by the near-term direction of the financial markets or the opinions of various financial "experts." If an investor decides to liquidate a portion of his or her portfolio or to shift the mix between stocks and bonds, it is often best to make such changes gradually through a regular series of transactions. This strategy can substantially reduce the risk of buying or selling any particular asset class at the worst possible moment. Finally, perhaps the best advice for mitigating investment risk is to remind the investor to be patient. Successful long-term investors have three things in common: They tend to be smart, lucky, and *old.*

Who Has the Best Blend?

One of the most interesting Wall Street rituals is the quarterly publication of recommended asset allocation blends by major brokerage houses. Figure 7.8 shows asset allocation recommendations by 13 major Wall Street firms for periods ended December 31, 1999. As is often the case, a striking diversity of opinion is evident regarding the best mix of stocks, bonds, and cash.

Lehman Brothers, a perennial Wall Street bull, thought a mix of 80% stocks, 10% bonds, and 10% cash looked about right for the low-inflation and rapid-earnings growth environment that it foresaw as the millennium approached. Merrill Lynch was "a breed apart" in suggesting an extremely defensive position vis-à-vis the U.S. market with a position of only 26% in domestic stocks, 14% in international stocks, 55% in bonds, and 5% in cash. Investors who found Lehman's bullish mix too "hot" but were left "cold" by Merrill's bearish stance might adopt a consensus mix of 60% stocks, 35% bonds, and 5% cash.

Every three months, *The Wall Street Journal* tracks the performance of the asset allocation recommendations of 13 brokerage firm strategists as a means of communicating the success of the investment professionals in forecasting broad investment trends. The quarterly survey seeks to determine how an investor would fare by following advice from each firm's investment strategist on dividing a portfolio among stocks, bonds, cash, and other alternatives. As can be seen from the data in Figure 7.8, investors who followed the advice of Wall Street's best investment strategists would have vastly underperformed a fully invested 100% stock position over the past five years. The rip-roaring bull market of the 1990s is one that caught investment professionals by surprise, obviously. At the same time, several investment strategists' recommendations did somewhat better than a "fixed blend" of 55% stocks, 35% bonds, and 10% cash.

The lesson communicated by the asset allocation information contained in Figure 7.8 is twofold. First, the diversity of investment opinion common among

FIGURE 7.8 **Wall Street Brokerages Routinely Publish Recommended Blends of Stocks, Bonds, and Cash**

Who Has the Best Blend?

Performance of asset-allocation blends recommended by 13 major brokerage houses in periods ended Dec. 31, 1999. Figures do not include transaction costs.

	PERFORMANCE			BLEND RECOMMENDED NOW		
BROKERAGE FIRM	**3-MONTH**	**1-YEAR**	**5-YEAR**	**STOCKS**	**BONDS**	**CASH**
Lehman Brothers	12.25%	**14.62%**	169.75%	80%	10%	10%
Morgan Stanley D.W.	10.68	**14.35**	161.66	70[1]	20	10
Edward D. Jones	10.98	**13.86**	149.55	71[2]	24	5
Prudential Securities[3]	11.46	**13.36**	154.09	75	5	15
Goldman Sachs[4]	10.38	**12.98**	159.19	70	27	0
Raymond James[5]	8.33	**10.18**	112.42	55	15	20
A.G. Edwards	8.51	**10.04**	142.49	60	35	5
Paine Webber	7.66	**9.44**	146.42	48	37	15
Credit Suisse F.B.	8.06	**9.33**	142.18	55	30	15
J.P. Morgan	7.48	**9.13**	N.A.	50	25	25
Bear Stearns	7.93	**8.75**	141.52	55	35	10
Salomon Smith Barney	8.65	**8.57**	130.4	55	35	10
Merrill Lynch	5.76	**5.15**	104.15	40[6]	55	5
BENCHMARKS						
Stocks	15.49%	**20.37%**	254.20%	100%	0	0
Bonds	- 1.45	**- 7.65**	47.73	0	100	0
Cash	1.14	**4.57**	30	0	0	100
Fixed blend	7.93	**8.43**	139.24	55	35	10

[1]11% in international stocks [2]12% in international stocks [3]5% in real estate [4]3% in commodities [5]10% in real estate; 6% international stocks [6]14% in international stocks

Sources: Wilshire Associates, Carpenter Analytical Services, the companies

Source: *The Wall Street Journal,* February 17, 2000, C1.

individual investors is also typical among investment professionals on Wall Street. Asset allocation is an essentially personal decision that reflects each individual investor's risk preferences. When it comes to asset allocation, a "one-size-fits-all" approach is never appropriate. And second, any asset allocation decision that dramatically reduces the amount of an investment portfolio devoted to stocks is apt to have a significant cost in terms of reducing the investor's long-term rate of return.

Maturity-Based Strategies

A bond portfolio consisting solely of short-term securities would have a high degree of price stability but earn only a modest yield. Conversely, a bond portfolio invested exclusively in long-term securities has a relatively high expected yield but can be subject to volatile price swings. Bond investors seeking greater interest income with minimum price volatility can do so with a maturity-based strategy called **laddering.**

laddering
Portfolio allocation into bonds with a steplike sequence of maturity dates.

When an investor constructs a portfolio by using bonds with a series of targeted maturities, thus resembling a bond maturity "ladder," the risk of loss due to fluctuating interest rates can be reduced or eliminated. For example, suppose an investor had projected financial needs in two, four, six, eight, and ten years. A laddered portfolio would be constructed by buying an appropriate amount of bonds with identical two-, four-, six-, eight-, and ten-year maturities. At the end of each two-year period, sufficient bonds would mature to take care of immediate financial needs. No bonds would ever need to be sold prior to maturity, and the risk of loss due to fluctuating market conditions would be eliminated. The advantages of bond laddering are obvious. The return on a laddered portfolio is higher than one composed solely of short-term issues. Such a portfolio also entails less risk than one including only a single maturity bond or long-term issues.

barbell strategy
Bond portfolio concentration at both the short and long ends of the maturity spectrum.

A **barbell** strategy also involves investing in securities of more than one maturity to limit the risk of fluctuating prices. Instead of dividing a portfolio into a series of bonds that mature over time, as with a laddered portfolio, a barbell strategy involves portfolio concentration at both ends of the maturity spectrum. For example, a barbell strategy might involve portfolio concentration in six-month Treasury bills and 30-year Treasury bonds. Such a portfolio might have a weighted-average time to maturity of eight to ten years and entail relatively high interest income with moderate price volatility.

bond swap
Simultaneous sale and purchase of fixed-income securities to achieve some investment purpose.

Bond investors also use swaps to realize a variety of benefits. A **bond swap** involves the simultaneous sale and purchase of fixed-income securities. Bond swaps are sometimes motivated by an investor's desire to change the portfolio's average maturity, credit quality, current income, or other objectives. A common motivation for bond swaps is to achieve tax savings. Any investor who owns bonds selling below their purchase price has suffered a paper loss that might be used to offset other capital gains or up to $3,000 per year in ordinary income on a joint return. In a bond swap transaction, such an investor might sell a bond that is worth less than the price paid and simultaneously purchase a similar bond at approximately the same price. By swapping such securities, the investor converts the paper loss into an actual loss, which can be used to offset capital and ordinary income. At the same time, the investor maintains a bond portfolio with the same essential expected return and risk characteristics.

Summary

- Economic characteristics of any bond include the bond's interest payment obligation, price, yield, maturity, redemption features, and credit quality. In combination with the level of prevailing **market interest rate,** these factors determine bond value and determine the degree to which it matches the financial objectives of any given investor. Interest rates on floating-rate bonds are reset periodically to keep in line with changes in an underlying **benchmark interest rate.** Rates on short-term Treasury bills or 30-year Treasury bonds are popular interest rate benchmarks. For another popular bond type, called **zero coupon bonds,** the bond investor receives one single payment at the time of maturity that equals a return of the original purchase price (or principal) plus the total interest earned. Zeros are attractive to long-term bond investors because they eliminate **interest reinvestment risk,** the chance that a subsequent rise in interest rates will reduce the amount earned on reinvested interest income. Prices for **seasoned bonds** depend on a number of factors, including prevailing market interest rates, the supply and demand for similar types of bonds, credit quality, and the term-to-maturity and tax status of individual bonds.

- A bond's **settlement date** is the date on which the buyer takes effective possession of the security. The **maturity date** is the date when the security expires or ceases to accrue interest. Another important component of bond valuation is the **bond coupon rate,** expressed as a percentage of par value. **Bond redemption value** is the amount to be received from the issuer on the maturity date. This amount is usually equal to par value, which is typically $1,000. Most bonds pay **semiannual interest** in two equal installments. In the United States, it is conventional to calculate bond interest rates on the **day count basis** of 30 days per month and 360 days per year. Some bonds, especially mortgage-backed securities, are typically priced and traded on the basis of an expected **average life** rather than on the basis of any stated term-to-maturity.
- Most bonds have **call provisions** that allow the issuer to repay the investors' principal at a specified date and price and thereby redeem the bond prior to scheduled maturity. **Call protection** is the amount of time before a newly issued bond is callable. Other refinancing options also exist. For lightly traded issues, the company might make a formal **bond tender offer** announcement in large financial newspapers. This type of transaction is called a **refunding** and is designed to reduce financing costs or improve financial flexibility.
- **Yield-to-maturity** or **yield-to-call** calculations tell bond investors the total rate of return that might be expected if such an investor were to buy and hold the bond until it matures or is called away by the issuer. Some **bond put provisions** give investors the option to require issuers to repurchase bonds when interest rates have risen, when the credit quality of the issuer has deteriorated, or when a serious threat of credit-quality deterioration is present.
- Because all long-term bonds are priced, at least in part, within the context of aggregate credit market conditions, all long-term bonds are sensitive to market-wide changes in interest rates. This is called **interest-rate risk.** Because changes in bond yields tend to be fairly small over daily, weekly, or monthly time frames, bond yield changes are typically quoted in terms of **basis points,** in which each basis point equals $1/100^{th}$ of 1%.
- A line between the yields offered on similar-risk bonds of different maturities, from shortest to longest, is called a **yield curve** and describes the **term structure of interest rates.** The **liquidity preference hypothesis** posits that the typically rising yield curve gives long-term bond investors a holding-period risk premium. This explanation of the prevailing term structure of interest rates is widely supported. Another point of view, called the **segmented market hypothesis,** suggests that yield curves reflect the hedging and maturity needs of institutional investors. **Duration** is an estimate of the economic life of a bond measured by the weighted-average time to receipt of interest and principal payments. The longer the duration, the more a bond's price will fluctuate when

prevailing interest rates rise or fall. Banks and other financial institutions match the duration of their financial assets and liabilities and thereby "lock in" a profit margin on their loan portfolios. A prime use of the duration concept is for such **risk immunization. Modified duration** is simply duration divided by 1 plus the yield-to-maturity. Modified duration is a direct estimate of the percentage change that will occur in a bond's market price for each percentage point change in market interest rates. **Convexity** measures the sensitivity of modified duration to changes in yield-to-maturity. If modified duration can be thought of as the "speed" of bond price changes from yield changes, then convexity is the rate of "acceleration" in bond price changes tied to yield changes.

- Independent **bond-rating** agencies assess bond risk at the time of issue and monitor developments during the bond's lifetime. **Credit-quality risk** is the chance of investment loss due to the inability of a bond issuer to make timely interest and principal payments. Bond credit-quality ranges from the highest-quality U.S. Treasury securities, backed by the full faith and credit of the U.S. government, to **below-investment-grade bonds,** or **junk bonds,** that are considered highly speculative. **Yield spreads** show the difference in yield for bonds with the same term-to-maturity but different credit risks. Companies that offer **high-yield** bonds do so because they have no other choice. High-yield bonds are sometimes referred to as junk bonds because they carry a relatively high risk of default.
- A **convertible bond** is a special type of corporate bond that can be exchanged under certain circumstances into a junior grade of securities. Terms of the conversion option are set forth in the **indenture agreement,** or bond contract, and may be exercised at the discretion of the bondholder. For example, a $1,000 bond convertible into 25 shares of stock has a **conversion ratio** of 25:1. The **conversion price** is the price per share that the company is willing to accept in trade for the bond. **Conversion value** is the worth of a convertible as a junior security if converted at the present time. For bonds convertible into common stock, conversion value is often expressed as the bond's **common stock equivalent** value. **Premium to conversion** is the percentage over conversion value at which the convertible trades. **Break-even time** is the number of years over which the conversion premium can be recovered by the increased income of the senior security over the junior security.
- **Asset allocation** decisions are made by investors to balance the risk/reward tradeoff among stocks, bonds, and cash investments. Asset allocation is simply the process of diversifying an investment portfolio across various asset categories, such as stocks, bonds, and cash. Bond investors seeking greater interest income with minimum price volatility can do so with a maturity-based strategy called **laddering.** Instead of dividing a portfolio into a series of bonds that mature over time, as with a laddered portfolio, a **barbell strategy** involves portfolio concentration at both ends of the maturity spectrum. A **bond swap** involves the simultaneous sale and purchase of fixed-income securities.

Questions

1. When the yield-to-maturity for short-term bonds exceeds that for long-term bonds, yield spreads are said to be
   a. inverted.
   b. flat.

c. normal.

d. none of these.

2. An original-issue deep-discount bond that pays no interest is called a

a. zero.

b. asset-backed mortage.

c. payment-in-kind bond.

d. convertible bond.

3. Zero coupon bonds

a. eliminate reinvestment rate risk.

b. are free from taxes until maturity.

c. must be issued at face (or par) value.

d. are free from price volatility.

4. The coupon divided by the current price of a bond is called the

a. yield-to-maturity.

b. approximate yield-to-maturity.

c. current yield.

d. internal rate of return.

5. The relation of yield-to-maturity with term-to-maturity at a given point in time is called the

a. yield spread.

b. term structure of interest rates.

c. liquidity preference hypothesis.

d. segmented market hypothesis.

6. Yield spreads rise with a

a. fall in term-to-maturity.

b. rise in term-to-maturity.

c. rise in coupon reinvestment risk.

d. fall in coupon reinvestment risk.

7. High-yield subordinated securities of less than investment grade are called

a. forwards.

b. junk bonds.

c. barbell bonds.

d. callable bonds.

8. The duration of a bond

a. is always less than the term-to-maturity for bonds paying coupon interest.

b. is directly related to coupon yield.

c. decreases with maturity.

d. is directly related to its yield-to-maturity.

9. Which of the following bond relationships is *not* inverse?
   a. duration and maturity.
   b. coupon and duration.
   c. duration and yield-to-maturity.
   d. interest rate changes and bond prices.
10. Yield spreads do *not* reflect differences in
    a. maturity.
    b. quality.
    c. marketability.
    d. coupon rates.
11. As the coupon on a bond increases, the
    a. percentage change in price for a given change in yield falls.
    b. percentage change in price for a given change in yield rises.
    c. dollar price change for a given change in yield rises.
    d. dollar price change for a given change in yield falls.
12. Which of the following statements about duration is *false?*
    a. Duration is a complete measure of bond risk.
    b. Duration reflects coupon and maturity.
    c. Bond price changes are directly related to duration.
    d. Modified duration equals duration divided by $(1 + r)$.
13. The price of an 8% coupon bond with semiannual discounting, three years to maturity, and a market return of 6% is
    a. $105.38.
    b. $1,000.
    c. $1,260.
    d. $125.88.
14. If the *y*-axis is the percentage change in bond price and the *x*-axis is the yield-to-maturity, a line that represents the price response to a given change in yield is
    a. convex to (bends away from) the origin.
    b. concave to (bends away from) the origin.
    c. concave to (bends toward) the origin.
    d. convex to (bends toward) the origin.
15. Modified duration measures the sensitivity of bond prices to changes in
    a. yield-to-maturity.
    b. Macaulay duration.
    c. the sensitivity of modified duration to changes in yield-to-maturity.
    d. the sensitivity of modified duration to changes in term-to-maturity.
16. The yield curve would "flatten" with a rise in the
    a. T-bill rate.

b. long-term bond rate.

c. equity risk premium.

d. yield spread.

17. Holding all else equal, bond investment risk increases with an unexpected rise in

a. inflation.

b. credit quality.

c. bond demand.

d. liquidity.

The common stock of ABC, Inc., pays no dividend and has a market price of 80. ABC's 8% convertible bond sells at 128 and is convertible into common at a stock price of $100 per share. Use this information to answer the succeeding three questions.

18. The conversion value of ABC's convertible bond is

a. $1,280.

b. $1,024.

c. $1,000.

d. $800.

19. The percent premium to conversion value for ABC's convertible bond is

a. 375%.

b. 160%.

c. 100%.

d. 60%.

20. The breakeven time for ABC's convertible bond is

a. 16 years.

b. 10 years.

c. 6 years.

d. 3.5 years.

Investment Application

How to Buy Bonds

Individual and institutional investors have an enormous variety of individual securities from among which they can make their bond investment selections. Most individual bonds are bought and sold in the over-the-counter (OTC) market, but some corporate bonds are also listed on the New York Stock Exchange. Like the OTC stock market, the OTC bond market includes hundreds of dealers who trade with individual and institutional investors by phone or electronically. Some bond dealers keep an inventory of bonds and make markets in them. Others act only as brokers, and buy or sell to dealers in response to specific requests on behalf of customers.

Bond investors interested in purchasing a new bond issue receive an offering statement, or prospectus. This document explains the bond's terms and features, as well as risks that investors should know about before investing. Most bond trading occurs in the secondary market. In the secondary bond market, dealers keep inventories of outstanding bonds. Bond prices quoted to investors normally include a dealer markup used to cover dealer costs and provide for a profit margin. If a broker or dealer has to seek out a specific bond that is not in inventory for a customer, a commission may be added to compensate for the costs and efforts of serving the customer's special needs. Each bond dealer or broker establishes her or his own markup, which may vary depending on the size of the transaction, the type of bond, and the amount of service provided. Bond investors rely on competition between various dealers and brokers to keep reasonable markups and commissions.

There are a number of services to help investors compare current prices for bonds of various types. For municipal bond prices, benchmark yields are available on the Internet and in newspapers through The Bond Market Association/Bloomberg National Municipal Yield Table. For a nominal fee, investors can also obtain current dealer prices or evaluations by subscribing to a service provided by S&P and The Bond Market Association. The telephone number for this service is 1-800-BOND INFO (800-266-3463). Rules issued by the Municipal Securities Rulemaking Board make prices of actively traded municipal bonds widely available, and these prices are sometimes reported in the financial press. For Treasury securities and corporate bonds, several media sources and vendors provide current pricing information. The Bond Market Association Web site provides links to multiple services providing price-yield information on all market segments. Bond investors can also compare prices for specific fixed-income securities by getting bids from several brokers and dealers. See <http://www.bondmarket.com>.

Bond Funds and Unit Investment Trusts

Bond mutual funds offer small investors an efficient way to invest in the bond markets. Bond funds, like stock funds, offer professional selection and management of a diversified portfolio of securities. They allow bond investors to diversify risks across a broad range of issues and offer a number of other conveniences, such as the option of having interest payments reinvested. Bond funds tend to be actively managed, with securities added or eliminated from the portfolio in response to market conditions and investor demand. They have no specific maturity date. With conventional mutual funds, bond investors are able to buy or sell fund shares at any time. Because the market value of outstanding bonds fluctuates on a daily basis, bond fund values also change from day to day. As a result, when an investor chooses to sell shares in a bond fund, the value of such an investment may be higher or lower than at the time of purchase.

Most bond funds charge annual management fees averaging 1%. Some also impose initial sales charges up to 5% or fees for selling shares. Because the annual management fees and sales commissions lower investment returns, bond fund investors need to be aware of them when calculating their overall expected return. The minimum initial investment in bond mutual funds is usually between $1,000 and $2,500 and $500 for retirement accounts.

Bond unit investment trusts are another investment alternative for bond investors that have certain similarities to bond mutual funds. Bond unit investment trusts offer a fixed portfolio of investments in government, municipal, mortgage-backed, or corporate bonds, which are professionally selected and remain constant throughout the life of the trust. The benefit of a unit trust is that investors know exactly how interest income will be earned because the composition of the portfolio remains stable. Another advantage is that because unit trusts are not an actively managed pool of assets, there is usually no management fee. Investors can earn interest income during the life of the trust and recover their principal as securities within the trust are redeemed. The trust typically ends when the last investment matures. Investors pay sales charges plus a small annual fee to cover supervision, evaluation expenses, and trustee fees. The minimum initial investment in bond unit investment trusts is usually between $1,000 and $5,000.

Money market mutual funds, as the name implies, are pooled investments in short-term, highly liquid fixed-income securities. These securities include short-term Treasury securities, municipal bonds, certificates of deposit issued by major commercial banks, and commercial paper issued by established corporations. Generally, these funds consist of securities having maturities of three months or less and offer interest rates roughly comparable with bank certificates of deposit. However, whereas the interest rate on a certificate of deposit is usually fixed, money market interest rates rise when prevailing interest rates go up or fall when interest rates decline. Money market mutual funds also offer convenient liquidity, because most allow investors to withdraw their funds at any time. The minimum initial investment is usually between $3,000 and $5,000.

Savings Bonds

For many small investors, U.S. savings bonds offer an attractive combination of safety, market-based yields, and tax benefits. Savings bonds can be purchased for small amounts. The minimum investment is only $25 when buying through financial institutions. They are lower risk than most investments because both principal and interest are guaranteed by the full faith and credit of the United States, and lost, stolen, or destroyed bonds can be replaced. They are also convenient. Savings bonds can be bought through most financial institutions and through payroll savings plans. There are no commissions or similar fees. Interest is exempt from state and local income tax, and federal income taxation can be postponed until you cash your bond or until it stops earning interest in 30 years. Education Savings Bonds may provide further tax savings when used to finance higher education.

Many savings bonds are bought through local banks. Banks forward savings bond applications and payments to a Federal Reserve Bank where the bonds are issued and mailed to the owner. Bonds are delivered within 15 business days. The bond's issue date reflects the date of application, so no interest is lost. Banks also have gift certificates that bond purchasers can give to gift recipients to let them know that a bond has been ordered for them. Finally, it is worth noting that savings bonds are designed as a savings instrument only. Savings bonds are legally not permitted to be used as collateral for a loan or as security for the performance of any obligation. Information about savings bonds can be obtained from the Bureau of the Public Debt, P.O. Box 1328, Parkersburg, WV 26106-1328.

There are numerous sources of mutual fund and unit investment trust information available for bond investors, including *The Wall Street Journal* and *Barron's*.

Major financial publications such as *Forbes, Business Week,* and *Money* magazine also provide regular in-depth coverage. Well-known mutual fund research firms, such as Morningstar Inc. and Lipper Analytical Services, also provide detailed analyses by subscription and on the Internet. The Vanguard Group of Investment Companies has excellent bond investment and asset allocation information on the Internet at <http://www.vanguard.com>. (Chapter 15 discusses mutual fund investment options in detail.) Investors interested in savings bonds should consult <http://www.publicdebt.treas.gov/sav/sav.htm>.

A. Under what circumstances might an investor prefer bond mutual funds to bond unit investment trusts?

B. Are savings bonds obsolete?

Selected References

Asness, Clifford S. "Stocks versus Bonds: Explaining the Equity Risk Premium." *Financial Analysts Journal* 56 (March/April 2000): 96–113.

Ball, Clifford A., and Walter N. Torous. "The Stochastic Volatility of Short-Term Interest Rates: Some International Evidence." *Journal of Finance* 54 (December 1999): 2239–2359.

Chakrabarti, Rajesh. "Just Another Day in the Inter-Bank Foreign Exchange Market." *Journal of Financial Economics* 56 (April 2000): 3–28.

Chapman, David A., and Neil D. Pearson. "Is the Short Rate Drift Actually Nonlinear?" *Journal of Finance* 55 (February 2000): 355–388.

Crack, Timothy Falcon, and Sanjay K. Nawalkha. "Interest Rate Sensitivities of Bond Risk Measures." *Financial Analysts Journal* 56 (January/February 2000): 34–43.

Das, Sanjiv Ranjan, and Rangarajan K. Sundaram. "Of Smiles and Smirks: A Term Structure Perspective." *Journal of Financial and Quantitative Analysis* 34 (June 1999): 211–239.

de Haan, Jakob, and Willem J. Kooi. "Does Central Bank Independence Really Matter?" *Journal of Banking and Finance* 24 (April 2000): 643–664.

Duan, Jin-Chuan, and Min-The Yu. "Capital Standard, Forbearance and Deposit Insurance Pricing under GARCH." *Journal of Banking and Finance* 23 (November 1999): 1691–1706.

Green, Richard C., and Kristian Rydqvist. "Ex-Day Behavior with Dividend Preference and Limitations to Short-Term Arbitrage: The Case of Swedish Lottery Bonds." *Journal of Financial Economics* 53 (August 1999): 145–187.

Gupta, Anurag, and Marti G. Subrahmanyam. "An Empirical Examination of the Convexity Bias in the Pricing of Interest Rate Swaps." *Journal of Financial Economics* 55 (February 2000): 239–279.

Hong, Gwangheon, and Arthur Warga. "An Empirical Study of Bond Market Transactions." *Financial Analysts Journal* 56 (March/April 2000): 32–46.

Nickell, Pamela, William Perraudin, and Simone Varotto. "Stability of Rating Transitions." *Journal of Banking and Finance* 24 (January 2000): 203–227.

Rudolph-Shabinsky, Ivan, and Francis H. Trainer, Jr. "Assigning a Duration to Inflation-Protected Bonds." *Financial Analysts Journal* 55 (September/October 1999): 53–59.

Treacy, William F., and Mark Carey. "Credit Risk Rating Systems at Large U.S. Banks." *Journal of Banking and Finance* 24 (January 2000): 167–201.

Wang, Hung-Jen. "Symmetrical Information and Credit Rationing: Graphical Demonstrations." *Financial Analysts Journal* 56 (March/April 2000): 85–95.

PART 4

Common Stock Analysis

CHAPTER 8

Common Stock Basics

On March 7, 2000, Old Economy stalwart Procter & Gamble (P&G) rattled financial markets with an earnings warning, and the Dow Jones Industrial Average (DJIA) tumbled 374.47 points, the fourth biggest point drop on record. When P&G said its earnings-per-share growth would come in at 7% for the year, below Wall Street expectations of 13% growth, investors marked down its shares from $87.44 to $60.13, a stunning drop of 31%. That shaved more than $35.5 billion dollars off P&G's market capitalization and left investors wondering if there was any such thing as a "safe" stock. After all, if moderate earnings disappointment could chop almost one-third off P&G's already depressed stock price, what would happen if truly bad news hit?

Wall Street's reaction to P&G's earnings announcement may be a disheartening prelude to what lies in store for shareholders of other slow-growing companies. Even after its stunning one-day drop, P&G was still selling for roughly 34 times earnings. This is a stiff premium to pay for a slow-growing leader in mature markets. Historically, such slow-growing companies have seldom commanded a price-earnings ratio that greatly exceeds the earnings-per-share growth rate. In the case of P&G and other slow-growth consumer products stalwarts such as Gillette, Coca-Cola, and Clorox, further price erosion may still lie ahead.[1]

This chapter looks at common stock valuation within the context of the firm's economic fundamentals. In the short run, stock prices change in mysterious ways. In the long run, however, stock prices rise only with basic improvement in the firm's earnings capacity. Without growth in earnings and earnings potential, stock prices wither and fade.

Buying Part of a Business

Business Valuation

In the United States, common stocks have vastly outperformed all other types of financial assets during the 20th century. As shown in Chapter 5, rates of return on

[1] See: E. S. Browning, "Blue Chips Plunge 374.47 on P&G News," *The Wall Street Journal,* March 8, 2000, C1, C23.

common stocks have averaged roughly 12–14% per year during the post–World War II period. Bond and money market instrument returns averaged closer to 5–6%. After taxes and inflation, bonds and money market instruments are losing propositions, whereas stocks are big winners.

There are simple, yet powerful economic reasons for this phenomenon. Whenever a company issues debt securities, the rate of interest paid is less than the expected rate of return on investment. It has to be. If the rate of interest offered was greater than the expected rate of return on investment, the company could not make required interest and principal payments. In the long run, such a company would go broke. The rate of interest paid is typically much less than the expected rate of return on investment to provide a margin of safety, or required profit margin. Because the long-run rate of return on common stocks is 12–14% per year, the long-term average rate of return on investment also falls in the range between 12 and 14%. If a 6% interest rate is paid on long-term corporate bonds, the company's expected profit margin on borrowed funds is in the range of 6–8%, or 12–14% minus 6%. These figures are important because they establish reasonable expectations for long-term investors. They also explain why long-term investors in common stocks fair better than long-term investors in bonds. Simply put, they have to.

Unlike corporate bonds, which represent debt, common stocks represent part ownership in a corporation. Holders of common stock are actual owners of the issuing corporation. Their part ownership in the company is in direct proportion to the relative amount of shares owned. If a given investor owns 1% of the total number of outstanding shares, such an investor owns 1% of the company. When considering the advantages or disadvantage of share ownership, investors must keep firmly in mind the idea that they are buying or selling part of a real business. In the long run, the prospects for profiting from stock market investing are tied directly to the real economic prospects of the underlying business. If an investor buys and holds stock in an attractive business with large and rapidly growing profits, long-term investment success will follow. If an investor buys and holds shares in companies with inherently poor economic prospects, sub-par investment returns are ensured.

In the same way, if someone seeks to "time the market" through quick in-and-out trading activity, the higher transaction costs and taxes tied to such speculation guarantee sub-par long-term results. In the late 1990s, rapid information flow and cheap commission rates on the Internet have created explosive growth in stock market speculation. Some speculators pride themselves on their ability to quickly profit from the hard-to-predict swings in volatile markets. Unfortunately, the spectacular success enjoyed when a company's stock price unexpectedly skyrockets tends to be matched by spectacular losses when share prices unexpectedly plummet. Nobody in his or her right mind would buy a new car in the morning with the idea of quickly selling it before noon, only to repurchase it before closing time. Similarly, no investor would contemplate buying a stock in the morning with the idea of selling it before noon, only to repurchase it at the market close. In the short run, speculators sometimes profit from the impossible-to-predict short-run twists and turns in the market. In the long run, investors always profit when they buy and hold shares in attractive businesses.

Investment versus Speculation

stock market investment Process of buying and holding stock for dividend income and long-term capital appreciation.

stock market speculation Purchase or sale of securities on the expectation of short-term trading profits from share price fluctuations tied to temporary good fortune.

Stock market investment is the process of buying and holding for dividend income and long-term capital appreciation the shares of companies with inherently attractive economic prospects. Investors seek to profit by sharing in the normal and predictable good fortune of such companies. **Stock market speculation** is the purchase or sale of securities on the expectation of capturing short-term trading profits from share-price fluctuations tied to the perhaps temporary good fortune of a given company. Speculators depend on a short-term or fundamental change in the economic prospects facing a company.

Success in the investment process depends on a careful examination of the essential economic characteristics of business and stock market investing. However, successful speculation depends on hard-to-predict changes in basic economic conditions, investor psychology, and luck. The focus of this chapter, indeed the focus of this entire book, is the investment process. In the process of deciding the investment merit of a given company, the investor must face a number of questions tied to determining the investment merit of a given situation.

In the long run, stock market investors can do no better than the companies in which they invest. If share ownership is maintained in highly profitable companies that grow, a growing stream of dividend income and capital appreciation can be anticipated. If shares are bought in companies with inferior rates of profitability and poor growth prospects, poor investor returns are ensured.

Although every stock market investor must be concerned with company profitability and growth prospects, the first criteria defining an attractive investment must be a superior rate of profitability. An "all-you-can-eat" diner with large portions but bad food is no bargain. Similarly, a rapidly growing company with poor profits in a bad business is a poor investment choice. Thus, investors must be able to discern corporate profitability prior to making an appropriate investment decision. The most important question that must be answered by investors is disarmingly simple: Is this a good business?

net income Difference between revenues and expenses, often expressed after taxes.

earnings per share Net income divided by the number of shares outstanding.

basic earnings per share Earnings per share.

fully diluted earnings per share Net income divided by the number of shares outstanding after consideration for the possible conversion of stock options.

Measuring Profitability

Absolute Measures

The most useful indicator of business quality is a consistently high level of profitability. More precisely, a good business returns consistently high profits relative to the amount of capital used. Ideally, a high and growing stream of business profits over time would not require additional capital resources. The best businesses are self-financing in the sense that sufficient profits are generated to fund all investment needs. Very few good businesses require substantial capital investment prior to the receipt of significant revenues and cash-flow income. However, mediocre businesses commonly require significant up-front capital investment.

When evaluating business profits, many investors refer to the amount of **net income** generated, or **earnings per share.** Of course, net income is simply the difference between revenues and expenses, often expressed on an after-tax basis. **Basic earnings per share** is simply net income after taxes divided by the number of outstanding shares. **Fully diluted earnings per share** is the amount of net income

WALL STREET WISDOM 8.1

Dot.con?

What is the most valuable invention of all time? Suppose you measured value in terms of economic betterment to humankind. In that case, you might choose something that has made life easier for millions, such as electricity, or cures for widely dreaded diseases, such as insulin or penicillin. In terms of revenues and profits generated, the safety razor, television, and xerography would be high on anyone's list of the most valuable inventions. Going back even further, how about the printing press? With the printing press, wide dissemination of news and knowledge first became available. As the masses became better educated and better informed, the age of royalty came to a screeching halt. In the United States, the wild and wooly West was not only tamed by law-abiding citizens, but better communication made it impossible for notorious outlaws to escape punishment and "fade into the sunset." History books credit Pat Garrett for bringing to an end the rampage of "Billy the Kid" in the New Mexico Territory on July 14, 1881, but Billy's days were numbered when reliable photographs became available.

So just how big is the potential of the Internet? No one knows for sure, but the possibilities are enormous. With the Internet, the flaws and costs of poorly designed and executed government policies are quickly exposed. Similarly, consumers are better able to make informed judgments about product quality and pricing. Like the printing press, but even more so, the Internet is the enemy of despots, price gouging, and excess profits.

With all the hoopla, it is tough to sort out what is real and what is Internet hype. For companies, building a publishing-only Web site is the first step to becoming an e-business. This is a step that most businesses have already taken. That is fine as far as it goes; it is an extremely cost-efficient way to distribute basic information. However, the payoff for business starts with "self-service" Web sites in which customers can do things such as check the status of an account or trace a package online (e.g., at FedEx). The real payoff begins with transaction-based Web sites that go beyond just buying and selling to create a dynamic and interactive flow of information.

An e-business is created when companies put their core processes online to improve service, cut costs, or boost revenue. For example, IBM helped Charles Schwab Web-enable their brokerage systems for online trading and customer service. Since opening, Schwab's Web service has generated more than one million online accounts, totaling more than $68 billion in assets. And e-business economics are compelling. According to Booz-Allen & Hamilton, a traditional bank transaction costs $1.07; the same transaction over the Web costs about 1¢. A traditional airline ticket costs $8 to process; an e-ticket costs just $1. Customers love the convenience; management loves the lower costs.

Although several companies have already used the Web to further exploit long-standing competitive advantages, it is not certain if they can use the Web to *create* such benefits. Hoping to stand out from the crowd, budding Internet merchants are devoting as much as 70% of total revenues to advertising in a mad scramble to create a brand-name image that they hope will provide shelter from an onslaught of competitors. None is more active in this regard than online bookseller Amazon.com, which offers more than 2.5 million in-print and out-of-print titles. Well aware of the threat posed by Amazon.com, book-selling chain giants Barnes & Noble, Inc., and Borders Group, Inc., are moving fast to establish online businesses of their own. With powerful Internet search engines, consumers can easily find the cheapest price for any title in print. Thus, although online book sales are growing rapidly from a very small base, neither Amazon.com, Barnes & Noble, nor Borders has any immediate hope of generating an online profit.

From an economic standpoint, the Internet is already huge, and it is going to get bigger. However, economic importance is a necessary but not sufficient condition for investment merit. Obviously, the Internet is a powerful information device. What remains to be seen is how it can be used to generate profits.

See: Suzanne McGee, "With IPO Theater Shuttered, Dot-Coms Act Out Cash Pleas for Private Patrons," *The Wall Street Journal,* May 18, 2000, C1, C21.

divided by the number of shares outstanding after consideration for the possible conversion of stock options.

As shown in Table 8.1, panel A, General Electric, Microsoft, and Ford are among the most profitable firms in the United States when profitability is measured by net income. These are highly profitable corporate giants. However, although net income is an obviously useful indicator of profit-generating ability, it has equally obvious limitations. For example, net income will grow with a simple increase in the scale of the operation. A 2% savings account will display growing interest income over time but would scarcely represent a good long-term investment. Similarly, a company that generates profit growth of only 2% per year would seldom turn out to be a good investment.

In the same way, investors must be careful in their interpretation of earnings-per-share numbers. These numbers are artificially affected by the number of outstanding shares. Following a 2:1 stock split, for example, the number of shares outstanding will double, while share price and earnings per share will fall by one half. However, such a stock split neither enhances nor detracts from the economic appeal of a company. Because the number of outstanding shares is wholly determined by vote of the company's stockholders, the specific earnings-per-share number for any given company at any point in time is somewhat arbitrary. Earnings-per-share numbers are only significant on a relative basis. For example, the growth in earnings per share over time is a fundamentally important determinant of future share prices.

Relative Measures

Absolute measures, like net income, paint only an incomplete picture of corporate profitability. To provide insight concerning business profit rates, various relative measures of profitability are relied on by investors. First among these is the rate of return on sales, or **profit margin,** defined as accounting net income expressed as a percentage of sales revenue. Profit margins show the amount of profit earned per dollar of sales. When profit margins are high, the company is operating at a high level of efficiency, competitive pressure is modest, or both. Table 8.1, panel B, shows that software-maker Microsoft, chewing tobacco manufacturer UST Inc., and drug powerhouse Amgen are among the most profitable companies in the United States, when profitability is measured by profit margin.

profit margin Profit earned per dollar of sales.

Business profit rates are also measured by the accounting rate of **return on stockholders' equity**. Simply referred to as ROE, the return-on-stockholders'-equity measure is defined as net income divided by the book value of **stockholders' equity,** which is the book value of total assets minus total liabilities. ROE tells how profitable a company is in terms of each dollar invested by shareholders. A limitation of ROE is that it can sometimes be unduly influenced by share buybacks and other types of corporate restructuring. According to generally accepted accounting principles (GAAP), the book value of stockholders' equity is simply the amount of money committed to the enterprise by stockholders. It is calculated as the sum of paid-in capital and retained earnings, minus any amount paid for share repurchases. When "extraordinary" or "unusual" charges are significant, the book value of stockholders' equity is reduced, and ROE can become inflated. Similarly, when share repurchases are at market prices that exceed the book value per share, book value per share falls and ROE rises.

return on stockholders' equity Net income divided by the book value of stockholders' equity.

stockholders' equity Total assets minus total liabilities.

TABLE 8.1 **Profitability Is Measured by Net Income, Net Profit Margin, Return on Equity (ROE), and Return on Assets (ROA)**

Company Name	Ticker	Industry	Net Income ($ millions)	Net Profit Margin (%)	ROE (%)	ROA (%)
A. Most Profitable Firms by Net Income						
Genl Electric	GE	Electrical Equipment	9,296.00	18.03	23.91	12.44
Microsoft Corp.	MSFT	Computer Software & Svcs.	7,625.00	38.61	27.67	20.51
Ford Motor	F	Auto & Truck	6,570.00	4.55	28.17	2.77
Bank of America	BAC	Bank	6,490.00		14.09	1.05
Exxon Mobil Corp.	XOM	Petroleum (Integrated)	6,440.00	6.40	14.73	6.95
Citigroup Inc.	C	Financial Svcs. (Div.)	6,342.00		15.16	0.94
Intl Business Mach.	IBM	Computer & Peripherals	6,328.00	7.75	32.88	7.34
Intel Corp.	INTC	Semiconductor	6,178.00	23.52	26.42	19.62
Philip Morris	MO	Tobacco	5,372.00	7.22	33.17	8.96
Merck & Co.	MRK	Drug	5,248.20	19.51	41.00	16.48
Averages			**6,588.92**	**15.70**	**25.72**	**9.71**
B. Most Profitable Firms by Profit Margin						
Microsoft Corp.	MSFT	Computer Software & Svcs.	7,625.00	38.61	27.67	20.51
UST Inc.	UST	Tobacco	455.28	31.99	97.21	49.85
Amgen	AMGN	Drug	863.20	31.76	33.68	23.51
BMC Software	BMCS	Computer Software & Svcs.	391.07	29.99	29.30	17.12
Transocean Sedco Forex	RIG	Oil Field Svcs./Equip.	297.32	28.33	15.02	9.15
Franklin Resources	BEN	Financial Svcs. (Div.)	500.44	27.92	21.94	14.38
Carnival Corp.	CCL	Recreation	835.88	27.78	19.50	11.64
Computer Associates	CA	Computer Software & Svcs.	1,301.00	24.77	47.67	16.12
Yahoo! Inc.	YHOO	Internet	49.93	24.56	9.31	8.02
Lilly (Eli)	LLY	Drug	2,174.80	23.54	49.10	17.26
Averages			**1,449.39**	**28.93**	**35.04**	**18.76**
C. Most Profitable Firms by ROE						
Unisys Corp.	UIS	Computer & Peripherals	387.00	5.37	289.18	6.94
US WEST Inc.	USW	Telecom. Svcs.	1,508.00	12.18	199.74	8.18
Avon Products	AVP	Toiletries/Cosmetics	392.80	7.54	137.78	16.14
Sara Lee Corp.	SLE	Food Processing	1,147.50	5.73	108.84	10.91
Jostens Inc.	JOS	Diversified Co.	59.07	7.66	100.89	16.12
Hilton Hotels	HLT	Hotel/Gaming	198.50	11.22	100.79	5.03
UST Inc.	UST	Tobacco	455.28	31.99	97.21	49.85
US Airways Group	U	Air Transport	538.00	6.19	89.70	6.83
Bestfoods	BFO	Food Processing	662.00	7.90	78.76	10.28
SLM Holding	SLM	Financial Svcs. (Div.)	449.00		68.65	1.20
Averages			**579.71**	**10.64**	**127.15**	**13.15**
D. Most Profitable Firms by ROA						
UST Inc.	UST	Tobacco	455.28	31.99	97.21	49.85
Parametric Technology	PMTC	Computer Software & Svcs.	197.65	19.42	60.35	23.73
Amgen	AMGN	Drug	863.20	31.76	33.68	23.51
Guidant Corp.	GDT	Medical Supplies	361.10	19.04	65.18	23.01
Tellabs Inc.	TLAB	Telecom. Equipment	374.30	22.55	27.19	23.00
Schering-Plough	SGP	Drug	1,756.00	21.74	43.88	22.39
Price (T. Rowe) Assoc.	TROW	Financial Svcs. (Div.)	174.14	19.65	28.35	21.85
Dell Computer	DELL	Computer & Peripherals	1,460.00	8.00	62.89	21.23
Compuware Corp.	CPWR	Computer Software & Svcs.	349.86	21.35	32.40	20.87
Gap (The) Inc.	GPS	Retail (Special Lines)	824.54	9.11	52.39	20.80
Averages			**681.61**	**20.46**	**50.35**	**25.02**

Data source: *Value Line Investment Survey for Windows,* January 2000.

As shown in Table 8.1, panel C, truly extraordinary ROE can be reported by companies that have recently undergone significant corporate restructuring, such as toiletries and cosmetics giant Avon Products, food products leader Sara Lee, and travel and entertainment powerhouse Hilton Hotels. Similarly, highly leveraged companies such as U.S. Air Group can report robust ROE during periods of growing revenues or declining fuel prices. ROE can also be boosted to extraordinary levels for companies such as computer services company Unisys Corp., in which book values have been depleted by significant operating losses during recent years.

return on assets Net income divided by the book value of total assets.

Given the difficulty of interpreting ROE for companies that have undergone significant restructuring and for highly leveraged companies, some investors focus on the **return on assets** (ROA), or net income divided by the book value of total assets. Like ROE, ROA captures the effects of managerial operating decisions. ROA also tends to be less affected than ROE by the amount of financial leverage used. As such, ROE has some advantages over ROA as a fundamental measure of business profits. Irrespective of whether net income, profit margin, ROE, ROA, or some other measure of business profits is used, consistency requires using a common basis for between-firm comparisons.

In Table 8.1, panel D, it is clear that various software companies and computer manufacturers have been able to generate stellar profit rates, when profitability is measured by ROA. Obviously, UST Inc. is also an enormously profitable company. It is worth noting, however, that the financial statements of this company do not reflect the hard-to-measure extent of future liabilities tied to its tobacco sales. Similarly, the enormous profit rates reported by drug industry leaders such as Amgen and Schering-Plough may be somewhat overstated because they fail to reflect the asset value created by patents and long-standing research and development programs.

On an overall basis, it is clear that each respective measure of profitability captures a slightly different important dimension of profitability. All such profit numbers are reported on a regular basis because each provides slightly different insight concerning corporate profitability.

Elements of ROE

Despite its limitations, many investors continue to regard ROE as the best single indicator of corporate profitability because it reflects the company's use of both operating leverage and financial leverage. To illustrate the various elements that go into a high ROE, Table 8.2 shows ROE calculations for the 30 large companies that together comprise the DJIA. ROE calculations for such a diverse list of companies show the wide variation in relative profitability that exists, even among the largest and most successful companies in the economy. As seen in Table 8.2, ROE can be described as the simple product of three common accounting ratios. ROE equals the firm's profit margin multiplied by the total asset turnover ratio, all times the firm's leverage ratio:

$$\begin{aligned} \text{ROE} &= \frac{\text{Net Income}}{\text{Equity}} \qquad (8.1) \\ &= \frac{\text{Net Income}}{\text{Sales}} \times \frac{\text{Sales}}{\text{Total Assets}} \times \frac{\text{Total Assets}}{\text{Equity}} \\ &= \text{Profit Margin} \times \begin{matrix}\text{Total Asset}\\ \text{Turnover}\end{matrix} \times \text{Leverage} \end{aligned}$$

When profit margins are high, robust demand or stringent cost controls, or both, allow the firm to earn a significant profit contribution. Holding capital requirements constant, the firm's profit margin is a useful indicator of managerial efficiency in responding to rapidly growing demand and/or effective measures of cost containment. The outstanding profit margins reported by Merck, Coca-Cola, and P&G are interesting examples of well-run firms. However, rich profit margins do not necessarily guarantee a high rate of return on stockholders' equity. Despite high profit margins, firms in mining, construction, heavy equipment manufacturing, cable TV, and motion picture production often earn only modest rates of return on equity because significant capital expenditures are required before meaningful sales revenues can be generated. Thus, it is vitally important to consider the magnitude of capital requirements when interpreting the size of profit margins for a firm or an industry.

total asset turnover Sales revenue divided by the book value of total assets.

Total asset turnover is sales revenue divided by the book value of total assets. When total asset turnover is high, the firm makes its investments work hard in the sense of generating a large amount of sales volume. Grocery and apparel retailing are good examples of industries in which high rates of total asset turnover can allow efficient firms to earn attractive rates of return on stockholders' equity despite modest profit margins. Among firms found in the DJIA, retail juggernauts Wal-Mart and Home Depot and aerospace leader Boeing all feature above-average rates of total asset turnover. However, Boeing has been unable to turn this advantage into above-average ROE. Unfortunately, operating problems tied to the introduction of new aircraft types during the past few years have introduced production inefficiencies that the company has yet to eliminate.

leverage Total assets divided by stockholders' equity. It reflects the extent to which debt and preferred stock are used in addition to common stock financing.

Leverage is often defined as the ratio of the book value of total assets divided by stockholders' equity. It reflects the extent to which debt and preferred stock are used in addition to common stock financing. Leverage is used to amplify firm profit rates over the business cycle. During economic booms, leverage can dramatically increase the firm's profit rate; during recessions and other economic contractions, leverage can just as dramatically decrease realized rates of return, if not lead to losses. Despite ordinary profit margins and modest rates of total asset turnover, ROE in the automobile, financial services, and telecommunications industries can sometimes benefit through use of a risky financial strategy that uses significant leverage. Among DJIA companies, financial service giants Citigroup and J. P. Morgan and auto manufacturing giant General Motors display above-average financial leverage. However, it is worth remembering that a risky financial structure can lead to awe-inspiring profit rates during economic expansions, such as that experienced during the mid-1990s, but it can also lead to huge losses during economic contractions or recessions, such as that experienced during 1991. In the financial services sector, high rates of financial leverage can boost profits during periods of declining interest rates but cause extreme financial distress during periods of rapidly fluctuating interest rates.

What Is a Typical ROE?

For large publicly traded companies in the United States, such as those found on the New York Stock Exchange and Nasdaq, ROE has fluctuated in a broad range between 8 and 16% during the post–World War II period. During economic recessions, many firms report operating losses, and the average ROE dives below 10%. During uninterrupted economic expansions, such as that experienced during the

TABLE 8.2 ROE Is Determined by Profit Margin, Total Asset Turnover, and Financial Leverage

Company Name	Ticker	Industry	Net Income ($ millions)	Common Equity ($ millions)
AT&T Corp.	T	Telecom. Svcs.	5,235	25,522
Alcoa Inc.	AA	Aluminum	853	6,000
Amer. Express	AXP	Financial Svcs. (Div.)	2,201	9,698
Boeing	BA	Aerospace/Defense	1,120	12,316
Caterpillar Inc.	CAT	Machinery	1,513	5,131
Citigroup Inc.	C	Financial Svcs. (Div.)	6,342	40,395
Coca-Cola	KO	Beverage (Soft Drink)	3,533	8,403
Disney (Walt)	DIS	Entertainment	1,383	20,975
Du Pont	DD	Chemical (Basic)	2,923	13,717
Eastman Kodak	EK	Precision Instrument	1,419	3,988
Exxon Mobil Corp.	XOM	Petroleum (Integrated)	6,440	43,645
Genl Electric	GE	Electrical Equipment	9,296	38,880
Genl Motors	GM	Auto & Truck	3,662	14,983
Hewlett-Packard	HWP	Computer & Peripherals	3,065	16,919
Home Depot	HD	Retail Building Supply	1,614	8,740
Honeywell Intl	HON	Diversified Co.	1,331	5,297
Intl Business Mach.	IBM	Computer & Peripherals	6,328	19,186
Intl Paper	IP	Paper & Forest Products	308	8,902
Intel Corp.	INTC	Semiconductor	6,178	23,377
Johnson & Johnson	JNJ	Medical Supplies	3,678	13,590
McDonald's Corp.	MCD	Restaurant	1,769	9,465
Merck & Co.	MRK	Drug	5,248	12,802
Microsoft Corp.	MSFT	Computer Software & Svcs.	7,625	27,458
Minnesota Mining	MMM	Chemical (Diversified)	1,526	5,936
Morgan (J. P.) & Co	JPM	Bank	1,067	10,567
Philip Morris	MO	Tobacco	5,372	16,197
Procter & Gamble	PG	Household Products	4,148	10,277
SBC Communication	SBC	Telecom. Svcs.	4,117	12,780
United Technologies	UTX	Diversified Co.	1,255	3,998
Wal-Mart Stores	WMT	Retail Store	4,430	21,112
Averages			**3,499**	**15,675**

Data source: *Value Line Investment Survey for Windows,* January 2000.

1990s, the average ROE for publicly traded companies can soar above 20% for industry leaders and as high as 16% per year for all companies. For a typical year during the post–World War II period, the average ROE tends to fall in a range between 12 and 14%. This average ROE comprises a typical profit margin on sales revenue of roughly 5%, a standard total asset turnover ratio of 1.05 times per year, and a common leverage ratio of roughly 2.5:1:

$$\begin{aligned}\text{Typical ROE} &= \text{Profit Margin} \times \text{Total Asset Turnover} \times \text{Leverage} \\ &= 5\% \times 1.05 \times 2.5 \\ &= 12\% \text{ to } 14\%\end{aligned} \quad \textbf{(8.2)}$$

ROE is an attractive measure of firm performance because it shows the rate of profit earned on funds committed to the enterprise by its owners, the stockhold-

TABLE 8.2 ***(continued)***

Sales ($ millions)	Total Assets ($ millions)	ROE	Profit Margin (Net Income/ Sales)	Total Asset Turnover (Sales/ Total Assets)	Leverage (Total Assets/ Common Equity)
53,223	59,550	20.5%	9.8%	0.89	2.33
15,340	17,463	14.2%	5.6%	0.88	2.91
19,026	126,933	22.7%	11.6%	0.15	13.09
56,154	36,672	9.1%	2.0%	1.53	2.98
20,977	25,128	29.5%	7.2%	0.83	4.90
	668,641	15.7%			16.55
18,813	19,145	42.0%	18.8%	0.98	2.28
23,402	43,679	6.6%	5.9%	0.54	2.08
24,767	38,536	21.3%	11.8%	0.64	2.81
13,406	14,733	35.6%	10.6%	0.91	3.69
100,697	92,630	14.8%	6.4%	1.09	2.12
51,546	74,670	23.9%	18.0%	0.69	1.92
161,315	257,389	24.4%	2.3%	0.63	17.18
47,061	33,673	18.1%	6.5%	1.40	1.99
30,219	13,465	18.5%	5.3%	2.24	1.54
15,128	15,560	25.1%	8.8%	0.97	2.94
81,667	86,100	33.0%	7.7%	0.95	4.49
19,541	26,356	3.5%	1.6%	0.74	2.96
26,273	31,471	26.4%	23.5%	0.83	1.35
23,657	26,211	27.1%	15.5%	0.90	1.93
12,421	19,784	18.7%	14.2%	0.63	2.09
26,898	31,853	41.0%	19.5%	0.84	2.49
19,747	37,156	27.8%	38.6%	0.53	1.35
15,021	14,153	25.7%	10.2%	1.06	2.38
	261,067	10.1%			24.71
74,391	59,920	33.2%	7.2%	1.24	3.70
38,125	32,113	40.4%	10.9%	1.19	3.12
28,785	45,066	32.2%	14.3%	0.64	3.53
25,715	18,375	31.4%	4.9%	1.40	4.60
137,634	49,996	21.0%	3.2%	2.75	2.37
42,177	**75,916**	**23.8%**	**10.8%**	**1.00**	**4.75**

ers. When ROE is at or above 12% per year, the rate of profit is generally sufficient to compensate investors for the risk involved with a typical business enterprise. When ROE consistently falls far below 12% per year, profit rates are generally insufficient to compensate investors for the risks undertaken. Of course, when business risk is substantially higher than average, a commensurately higher rate of return is required. When business risk is somewhat lower than average, a somewhat below-average profit rate is adequate.

This naturally suggests an important question: How is it possible to know if business profit rates in any given circumstance are sufficient to compensate investors for the risks undertaken? The answer to this difficult question turns out to be rather simple: Just ask current and potential shareholders and bondholders. Although it is difficult to accurately assess business risk and the problem of accurately measuring profit rates is always vexing, shareholders and bondholders implicitly inform management of their risk/return assessment of the firm's performance on a daily basis. If performance is above the minimum required, the firm's bond and stock prices will rise; if performance is below the minimum required, bond and stock prices will fall. For privately held companies, the market's risk/return assessment comes at infrequent intervals, such as when new bank financing is required. If performance is above the minimum required, bank financing will be easy to obtain; if performance is below the minimum required, bank financing will be difficult or impossible to procure. Therefore, as a practical matter, firms must consistently earn a business profit rate or ROE of at least 12% per year to grow and prosper. If ROE consistently falls below this level, sources of financing tend to dry up and the firm withers and dies. If ROE consistently exceeds this level, new debt and equity financing is easy to obtain, and growth by new and established competitors is rapid.

Finally, although ROE may indeed be the most useful accounting indicator of business profits, other accounting data should also be used to compare profit rates across different lines of business, companies, and industries. In particular, investors must be cautious in evaluating companies that report lofty ROE but only moderate profit margins and low ROA.

Firm Size Measures

Market Capitalization

What is the single most important number to an investor? That is a tough question. In terms of accounting data, it is possible that ROE is most important. Many traditional accountants might quibble with that suggestion and argue total assets, the book value of shareholders' equity, or net income are just as important. However, financial economists might suggest that the total market capitalization of common stock, or **market cap** for short, is the best available indicator of future profits. In financial theory, the market capitalization of the firm equals the discounted net present value of all future profits. Market capitalization is synonymous with the value of the firm.

market cap
Market value of the firm.

Table 8.3 shows the largest firms in the United States, in which firm size is captured by four common measures. Notice the enormous market caps for Microsoft and General Electric. Based on market capitalization, Microsoft is roughly twice the size of IBM, the number three company. Whereas General Electric has a long corporate history that traces back more than 100 years to Thomas Edison, Microsoft is a relative newcomer.

Microsoft was founded on April 4, 1975, and moved from Albuquerque, New Mexico, to Bellevue, Washington, on January 1, 1979. On August 12, 1981, IBM introduced its personal computer, with Microsoft's 16-bit operating system, MS-DOS 1.0. On February 26, 1986, Microsoft moved its operations to its corporate campus in Redmond, Washington. It was only on March 13, 1986, less than 14 years from the millennium, that Microsoft sold stock to the public. The rest is the stuff of stock market lore. Since its inception, Microsoft's mission has been to create software for the personal computer that empowers and enriches people in the workplace, at school, and at home. Microsoft's early vision of a computer on every desk and in every home is coupled today with a strong commitment to Internet-related technologies that

TABLE 8.3 **Firm Size as Measured by Market Capitalization, Sales, Net Worth, or Total Assets**

Company Name	Ticker	Industry	Market Cap ($ millions)	Sales ($ millions)	Net Worth ($ millions)	Total Assets ($ millions)
A. Largest Firms by Market Capitalization						
Microsoft Corp.	MSFT	Computer Software & Svcs.	588,884	19,747	28,438	37,156
Genl Electric	GE	Electrical Equipment	470,140	51,546	38,880	74,670
Cisco Systems	CSCO	Computer & Peripherals	347,897	12,154	11,678	14,725
Wal-Mart Stores	WMT	Retail Store	280,586	137,634	21,112	49,996
Exxon Mobil Corp.	XOM	Petroleum (Integrated)	280,388	100,697	43,750	92,630
Intel Corp.	INTC	Semiconductor	279,457	26,273	23,377	31,471
Lucent Technologies	LU	Telecom. Equipment	222,904	38,303	13,584	38,775
Intl Business Mach.	IBM	Computer & Peripherals	209,14	81,667	19,433	86,100
Citigroup Inc.	C	Financial Svcs. (Div.)	171,610		42,708	668,641
America Online	AOL	Internet	166,823	4,777	3,033	5,348
Averages			**301,784**	**52,533**	**24,599**	**109,951**
B. Largest Firms by Sales						
Genl Motors	GM	Auto & Truck	45,855	161,315	14,984	257,389
Ford Motor	F	Auto & Truck	57,776	144,416	23,409	237,545
Wal-Mart Stores	WMT	Retail Store	280,586	137,634	21,112	49,996
Exxon Mobil Corp.	XOM	Petroleum (Integrated)	280,388	100,697	43,750	92,630
Royal Dutch Petr.	RD	Petroleum (Integrated)	128,122	93,692	54,962	110,068
Intl Business Mach.	IBM	Computer & Peripherals	209,148	81,667	19,433	86,100
Philip Morris	MO	Tobacco	55,604	74,391	16,197	59,920
Boeing	BA	Aerospace/Defense	39,835	56,154	12,316	36,672
AT&T Corp.	T	Telecom. Svcs.	162,765	53,223	25,522	59,550
Genl Electric	GE	Electrical Equipment	470,140	51,546	38,880	74,670
Averages			**173,022**	**95,474**	**27,057**	**106,454**
C. Largest Firms by Net Worth (Book Value)						
Royal Dutch Petr.	RD	Petroleum (Integrated)	128,122	93,692	54,962	110,068
Bank of America	BAC	Bank	79,569		45,938	617,679
MCI WorldCom	WCOM	Telecom. Svcs.	143,995	17,678	45,801	86,401
Exxon Mobil Corp.	XOM	Petroleum (Integrated)	280,388	100,697	43,750	92,630
Citigroup Inc.	C	Financial Svcs. (Div.)	171,610		42,708	668,641
Genl Electric	GE	Electrical Equipment	470,140	51,546	38,880	74,670
Microsoft Corp.	MSFT	Computer Software & Svcs.	588,884	19,747	28,438	37,156
Amer. Intl Group	AIG	Financial Svcs. (Div.)	153,044		27,531	194,398
AT&T Corp.	T	Telecom. Svcs.	162,765	53,223	25,522	59,550
Chase Manhattan Corp.	CMB	Bank	58,632		23,838	365,875
Averages			**223,715**	**56,097**	**37,737**	**230,707**
D. Largest Firms by Total Assets						
Citigroup Inc.	C	Financial Svcs. (Div.)	171,610		42,708	668,641
Bank of America	BAC	Bank	79,569		45,938	617,679
Fannie Mae	FNM	Thrift	58,061		15,453	485,014
Chase Manhattan Corp.	CMB	Bank	58,632		23,838	365,875
Freddie Mac	FRE	Thrift	30,348		10,835	321,421
Morgan S. Dean Witter	MWD	Securities Brokerage	68,093	31,131	14,519	317,590
Merrill Lynch & Co.	MER	Securities Brokerage	26,845	35,853	10,132	299,804
Bank One Corp.	ONE	Bank (Midwest)	34,580		20,560	261,496
Morgan (J. P.) & Co	JPM	Bank	20,628		11,261	261,067
Genl Motors	GM	Auto & Truck	45,855	161,315	14,984	257,389
Averages			**59,422**	**76,100**	**21,023**	**385,598**

Data source: *Value Line Investment Survey for Windows,* January 2000.

expand the power and reach of the PC. As the world's leading software provider, Microsoft strives to produce innovative products that meet customers' evolving needs. Microsoft products include operating systems for personal computers, server applications for client/server environments, business and consumer productivity applications, interactive media programs, and Internet platform and development tools. Microsoft also offers online services, sells personal computer books and input devices, and researches and develops advanced technology software products. Microsoft products, available in more than 30 languages and sold in more than 50 countries, are available for most PCs, including Intel microprocessor-based computers and Apple computers. Obviously, Bill Gates and his talented staff of software engineers have created staggering stock market wealth by making powerful user-friendly software that transforms the desktop computer into a marvelous device for computing and communication.

Accounting Indicators

sales
Gross receipts.

revenue
Sales.

net worth
Sum of common plus preferred stockholders' equity.

book value per share
Common shareholders' equity divided by the number of shares outstanding.

total assets
Stockholders' equity plus total liabilities.

Despite its enormous stock market capitalization, Microsoft is still of relatively modest size in terms of **sales** or **revenue.** With roughly \$20 billion in sales, Microsoft has less than one-eighth of the revenue of GM, the largest generator of total revenue, and is only about 40% the size of GE, the 10th largest company according to sales. Top auto manufacturers, retailers, and oil companies all dwarf Microsoft in terms of sales revenue. The key to success for Microsoft is clearly its ability to generate enormous profit margins on its rapidly growing sales revenue.

Neither market cap nor sales statistics capture the gigantic size of several companies with huge investments in natural resources, plant, and equipment. The world's largest integrated oil companies, such as Royal Dutch Petroleum and Exxon Mobil, are among the largest companies according to **net worth.** Net worth is the sum of common plus preferred stockholders' equity. It includes all intangible assets, such as goodwill and deferred charges, less current liabilities and long-term debt. It is a common measure of financial soundness because it measures the total amount committed to the enterprise by equity investors. **Book value per share,** calculated as common shareholder equity divided by the number of outstanding shares, measures the contribution of common stockholders. Notice that lists of the largest firms by net worth and **total assets** include a number of giant financial institutions such as Citigroup and Bank of America. Banks and other financial institutions such as investment bankers and brokers hold enormous inventories of bonds, mortgages, and other financial assets. This makes them very large companies when size is measured by net worth and total assets.

Does Size Matter?

All this information about firm size begs a very important question: So what? From an investor's perspective, is firm size an important consideration? The answer is yes. Large companies with market capitalizations greater than, say, \$5 billion are generally considered less risky than mid-cap or small-cap stocks. This is because there is a large liquid market for their shares and a longer history of earnings and dividend growth. Such companies have not only stood the test of time, they typically have a portfolio of different lines of business and operate in a variety of domestic and global markets.

When an investor buys stock in a large financial institution such as Citigroup, for example, the investor buys stock in a virtual financial supermarket. The only truly global consumer bank, Citibank is meeting the banking needs of a middle class that is rapidly growing throughout the world. There are more than 20 million Citibank customers in more than 40 countries. Citigroup is also big in investment banking and brokerage services. One of every six affluent individual investors in the United States is a Salomon Smith Barney client. Assets in customer accounts approach $1 trillion. In addition to stock brokerage and an extensive array of mutual funds, annuities, and investment products, Citigroup's Private Client Group offers a wide spectrum of retirement and estate-planning services for high-net-worth individuals. An undisputed leader in the credit card business, Citibank has more than 50 million card member accounts worldwide. Growth has continued through the acquisition of the AT&T Universal Card Services business, introduction of the Driver's Edge and Sony Citibank cards, and expansion of the Citibank–American Airlines partnership. Citigroup's consumer finance company, Commercial Credit, has been serving middle-income and lower-income Americans with loans since 1912. The company pioneered automobile financing in the United States. Through Travelers Insurance, Citigroup offers a variety of financial products, including property and casualty insurance, life insurance, annuities, and long-term care insurance.

Finally, when considering the obvious advantages of large firm size, it is important for investors to recognize that large size tends to limit opportunities for above-average future growth. If an investor had been so fortunate so as to invest $10,000 in Microsoft at the time it first went public, such an investment would have grown to almost $5 million within 15 years. Because of its enormous success during the 1980s and 1990s, there is simply no way that Microsoft can duplicate this feat. With its current market cap in excess of $500 billion, a 500:1 payoff over the next 15 years would imply a market cap for Microsoft of more than $250 trillion. This is roughly 10 times the current market cap of all companies traded on all global equity markets. With its enormous strengths, Microsoft may well enjoy notable success during the next 15 years, but it will never repeat the stock market success it enjoyed during the 1980s and 1990s. Elephants do not run like jackrabbits.

Valuation Indicators

P/E Ratio

Not all stocks carry the same degree of risk. Some stocks are "priced for perfection" and bid up to lofty levels on the basis of equally lofty expectations for future earnings growth. If such growth does not materialize, stock prices crumble. Similarly, some stocks linger at meager valuations on the basis of a pessimistic consensus concerning the company's economic prospects. Moreover, the overall stock market is not always priced the same. At times, a cheery consensus regarding favorable future earnings growth and moderate inflation causes investors to bid up stock prices. At other times, a gloomy consensus, perhaps caused by the onset of an economic recession or an unexpected upward spike in interest rates, causes investors to dump stocks, and prices in general fall sharply.

Stock analysts and investors use various valuation measures to arrive at what they think is a reasonable price for a given stock or for stocks in general. Just as you would not pay $100,000 for a Chrysler minivan, neither would a knowledgeable investor pay $100 for a share of stock that, by most reasonable assumptions, has an economic value closer to $15 or $20 per share.

WALL STREET WISDOM 8.2

Intel: Running Fast to Stay in Place

Intel is the dominant and most profitable maker of integrated circuits, the microscopic pieces of silicon chips used to power electronic computers, calculators, video games, and a burgeoning array of other products. The trademark *intel inside*™ is a valued one that identifies products made by a company whose microprocessors are the brains of more than 100 million IBM-compatible personal computers, more than five times that of its nearest rival. So complete has been Intel's grip on the PC market that its sales are expected to surge from $2.9 billion in 1988 to roughly $55 billion in 2003, while profits explode from $452.9 million in 1988 to roughly $15 billion in 2003. Meanwhile, Intel's stock price skyrocketed from a split-adjusted $1.13 to more than $130 by early 2000.

Despite this enviable record of success and despite obvious strengths, Intel's core business is facing its biggest challenge in a decade. Led by Advanced Micro Devices, Inc., Cyrix Inc., International Business Machines, Inc., Texas Instruments, Inc., and a handful of foreign firms, competitors are rushing to produce competitors of Intel chips. High-quality clones can quickly erode the profits of early innovators such as Intel, a company that has come to count on giant-sized operating margins of +40%. During recent years, both investors and market analysts have posed an important question: Is Intel's dominance of the integrated circuits market coming to an end?

Not without a fight, it won't. Intel is led by visionary Chairman Andrew S. Grove, author of the 1997 best-seller *Only the Paranoid Survive,* and his hand-picked successor Craig R. Barrett, president/CEO. Driven by paranoia, Intel is striking back at competitors on multiple fronts, dragging competitors into court for patent infringement, slashing prices, and advertising its products on national television. Intel's strategic vision has also been revamped to focus on computer microprocessor products, the core of its business. Perhaps most important, Intel has launched a campaign to speed product development and to thereby expand the potential market for its products. Gordon Moore founded Intel with Robert Noyce, the co-inventor of the integrated circuit. Moore is credited with a prescient prediction in 1975, now referred to as "Moore's Law," that the power of state-of-the-art computer chips would double every *18 months.* If anything, the pace of that advance is quickening. Intel is no longer satisfied to introduce one or two new generations of chips annually and new microprocessor families every three or four years. In 1992, for example, it marketed roughly 30 variants of its cutting-edge 486 chip. By the summer of 1992, several months ahead of schedule, it unveiled its next-generation product, the Pentium microprocessor, a veritable one-chip mainframe that is roughly 30% faster than an i486 chip. In 1997, Grove confidently predicted that by the year 2011 Intel chips will contain *one billion* transistors (up from today's 5.5 million) and feature a clock speed of 10 gigahertz (or 10,000 megahertz, up from today's 800 megahertz standard).

Intel seems to be on track. On Monday, March 6, 2000, AMD introduced the first one-gigahertz processor. The new "Athlon" chip can process information at 1,000 megahertz, or one billion, bits of information a second. The Athlon chip will make computers 10 times faster than they were six years ago. Unfortunately, AMD did not get to gloat long over its achievement. Arch rival Intel launched its own one-gigahertz chip, the Pentium III, just two days later. AMD and Intel analysts will probably still be arguing about which gigahertz chip, the Athlon or the Pentium III, is faster until the two-gigahertz chip is introduced.

This blistering tempo of technological innovation is one that Intel hopes will keep competitors in a perpetual catch-up mode. In the years ahead, Intel hopes to become a force in supercomputers, interactive digital video, and flash memory, a semiconductor alternative to storing data on magnetic disks. But none of these new products will have the support needed to bring them to market unless Intel can protect its main turf from increasingly aggressive rivals.

See: "Chipset for Cellular Phones is Planned with Mitsubishi," *The Wall Street Journal,* May 17, 2000, B6.

Perhaps the most common valuation yardstick used to measure relative value is the **price/earnings ratio,** or stock price divided by earnings per share. Major financial publications, such as *The Wall Street Journal,* and most major daily newspapers report P/E ratio information alongside daily stock price quotes. The intuition behind the popularity of P/E ratio information is disarmingly simple. A P/E ratio of 20:1, for example, means that an investor buying at the current market price is paying $20 for $1 in earnings per share. Similarly, when a P/E ratio of 20:1 is paid, the **earnings yield,** or E/P ratio, is 5%. Why would a present-day investor pay a P/E of 20:1, or settle for an earnings yield on their investment of only 5%, in a market environment in which risk-free short-term Treasury bills also pay roughly 5%? Obviously, it only makes sense to pay a P/E of 20:1 when underlying earnings per share are expected to grow rapidly. Just how rapidly earnings have to grow to justify paying a given P/E ratio depends on the amount of future earnings growth anticipated and level of investor confidence.

price/earnings ratio Stock price divided by earnings per share.

earnings yield E/P, or earnings/price, ratio.

For example, Sara Lee Corp. is a diversified international manufacturer of branded consumer products such as Sara Lee baked goods, Hillshire Farms specialty meats, and Champion apparel (Figure 8.1). There exists a high level of investor confidence in the company's ability to deliver dependable modest earnings per share growth of roughly 11% per year. As a result, investors are typically willing to pay an average P/E ratio in the range of 18:1 for Sara Lee Corp. common stock. Investors are much less certain about the ability of Countrywide Credit Industries, Inc., to deliver similarly modest earnings-per-share growth (Figure 8.2). Countrywide is the nation's largest independent residential mortgage provider and servicing agent. Although Countrywide is expected to grow roughly as fast as Sara Lee, investors are much less confident in making this projection. As a result, Countrywide typically sells at an average P/E ratio in the 12:1 range.

Table 8.4 shows frequently analyzed valuation ratios for common stocks as represented by the DJIA from 1950 to the present. P/E ratios in 1982–83 and 1991–92 have been adjusted for massive losses at component firms (see Table 5.2 for unadjusted data). In both instances, the DJIA's P/E skyrocketed when an economic downturn caused earnings to collapse for DJIA component companies. After adjustment, notice that the average P/E ratio for the DJIA of 14.7 is roughly the same as the median (or middle) P/E ratio for the DJIA of 15. In the normal course of events, the DJIA's P/E usually falls between 10:1 and 20:1. In only a handful of instances during the past 50 years, the DJIA's P/E closed the year at or below the 10:1 mark. Similarly, in only a handful of instances, the DJIA's P/E closed the year at or above the 20:1 mark. Thus, many investors regard stock prices as high when P/Es are greater than 20:1 and cheap when P/Es are less than 10:1. The P/E ratio on the DJIA has rarely been as high as it was at the start of 2000.

P/B Ratio and Dividend Yield

Although the measure is much less popular than the P/E ratio, many investors judge whether a stock is expensive on the basis of its current market price relative to the accounting book value per share. The **price/book ratio** (P/B) shows the relationship between a stock's current price and its accounting net worth, in which accounting book value is simply total assets minus total liabilities. Of course, accounting book values are historical measures of identifiable worth as mandated by GAAP. Despite compelling logic and consistency, GAAP book value numbers

price/book ratio Stock price divided by accounting net worth.

FIGURE 8.1 Sara Lee Offers Investors Stable EPS Growth

SARA LEE NYSE-SLE

RECENT PRICE 27 | P/E RATIO 20.6 (Trailing: 21.8, Median: 18.0) | RELATIVE P/E RATIO 1.36 | DIV'D YLD 2.0% | VALUE LINE

TIMELINESS 4 Raised 10/8/99
SAFETY 1 Raised 2/12/99
TECHNICAL 4 Raised 9/3/99
BETA .70 (1.00 = Market)

2002-04 PROJECTIONS

	Price	Gain	Ann'l Total Return
High	40	(+50%)	*12%*
Low	35	(+30%)	*9%*

Insider Decisions

	D	J	F	M	A	M	J	J	A
to Buy	0	0	0	0	1	0	0	0	1
Options	0	1	2	0	0	0	2	1	2
to Sell	1	1	0	1	0	0	4	0	2

Institutional Decisions

	4Q1998	1Q1999	2Q1999
to Buy	297	322	230
to Sell	284	300	370
Hld's(000)	507258	512665	498286

	1987	1988	1989	1990	1991	1992	1993	1994	1995	1996	1997	1998	1999
High:	6.4	8.4	8.3	14.5	16.3	15.6	13.0	16.9	20.3	28.9	31.8	29.0	
Low:	4.1	5.4	6.0	7.4	11.7	10.5	9.7	12.1	14.9	18.3	22.2	21.2	

Target Price Range 2002 | 2003 | 2004

% TOT. RETURN 10/99

	THIS STOCK	VL ARITH. INDEX
1 yr.	-7.7	13.4
3 yr.	62.1	49.9
5 yr.	145.3	107.3

1983	1984	1985	1986	1987	1988	1989	1990	1991	1992	1993	1994	1995	1996	1997	1998	1999	2000	© VALUE LINE PUB., INC.	02-04
7.12	7.92	9.48	9.29	10.34	11.79	12.89	12.60	13.30	13.80	15.02	16.16	18.43	19.20	20.54	21.72	22.64	*23.55*	Sales per sh A	*30.10*
.31	.35	.39	.42	.49	.58	.73	.85	.95	1.10	1.23	1.31	1.43	1.56	1.72	1.84	1.90	*2.10*	"Cash Flow" per sh	*2.90*
.18	.20	.23	.25	.29	.35	.43	.48	.54	.62	.70	.74	.81	.92	1.02	1.11	1.21	*1.35*	Earnings per sh B	*2.10*
.07	.08	.09	.10	.12	.14	.17	.20	.23	F.31	.28	.31	.34	.37	.41	.45	.49	*.54*	Div'ds Decl'd per sh C■	*.70*
.20	.18	.29	.26	.32	.51	.60	.65	.56	.53	.75	.65	.50	.56	.57	.51	.61	*.65*	Cap'l Spending per sh	*.70*
1.01	1.00	1.10	1.35	1.60	1.78	1.72	2.12	2.38	3.18	3.33	3.14	3.79	4.16	4.17	1.69	1.17	*1.00*	Book Value per sh D	*3.95*
923.39	883.99	856.14	854.11	885.79	884.47	909.34	921.36	930.74	959.45	970.76	961.53	961.31	970.11	960.55	921.33	883.78	*870.00*	Common Shs Outst'g E	*830.00*
7.2	7.8	9.4	12.7	16.3	14.0	13.6	15.4	15.2	19.5	19.9	16.2	15.4	17.0	18.5	24.1	21.8		Avg Ann'l P/E Ratio	*18.0*
.61	.73	.76	.86	1.09	1.16	1.03	1.14	.97	1.18	1.18	1.06	1.03	1.06	1.07	1.25	1.20		Relative P/E Ratio	*1.20*
5.5%	5.0%	4.1%	3.0%	2.5%	2.9%	3.0%	2.8%	2.8%	2.5%	2.0%	2.6%	2.7%	2.4%	2.2%	1.7%	1.9%		Avg Ann'l Div'd Yield	*1.8%*

CAPITAL STRUCTURE as of 10/2/99
Total Debt $3870 mill. **Due in 5 Yrs** $2800 mill.
LT Debt $2140 mill. **LT Interest** $175.0 mill.
Incl. $60.0 mill. capitalized leases. Incl. $253.0 mill. ESOP loan guarantee.
(LT interest earned: 10.2x; total interest coverage: 7.8x) (55% of Cap'l)

Pension Liability None
Pfd Stock $265.0 mill. **Pfd Div'd** $19.9 mill.
Incl. 3,654,073 shs. 7.5% ESOP pfd. cv. into 8 com. shs. (7% of Cap'l)
Common Stock *880,740,000* shs. (38% of Cap'l)
MARKET CAP: $23.8 billion (Large Cap)

1989	1990	1991	1992	1993	1994	1995	1996	1997	1998	1999	2000		02-04
11718	11606	12381	13243	14580	15536	17719	18624	19734	20011	20012	*20500*	Sales ($mill) A	*25000*
9.0%	10.4%	10.9%	11.5%	11.6%	11.8%	11.3%	11.7%	11.8%	11.9%	11.5%	*12.0%*	Operating Margin	*13.0%*
280.0	351.4	393.8	472.0	522.0	568.0	606.0	634.0	680.0	618.0	553.0	*565*	Depreciation ($mill)	*580*
399.2	470.3	535.0	620.0	704.0	729.0	804.0	916.0	1009.0	1102.0	1147.5	*1250*	Net Profit ($mill)	*1830*
37.6%	34.1%	35.5%	34.9%	34.9%	35.0%	34.0%	33.5%	32.0%	31.0%	28.7%	*27.0%*	Income Tax Rate	*27.0%*
3.4%	4.1%	4.3%	4.7%	4.8%	4.7%	4.5%	4.9%	5.1%	5.5%	5.7%	*6.0%*	Net Profit Margin	*7.3%*
224.3	385.5	393.5	395.0	d293.0	d450.0	84.0	439.0	375.0	d513.0	d966.0	*d1000*	Working Cap'l ($mill)	*1550*
1488.2	1523.9	1399.1	1389.0	1164.0	1496.0	1817.0	1842.0	1933.0	2270.0	1892.0	*1800*	Long-Term Debt ($mill)	*2000*
2097.4	2629.5	2894.8	3733.0	3908.0	3657.0	4273.0	4658.0	4522.0	1866.0	1299.0	*1335*	Shr. Equity ($mill)	*3750*
12.7%	12.8%	13.8%	13.3%	14.8%	15.2%	14.5%	15.3%	16.6%	28.5%	38.7%	*42.5%*	Return on Total Cap'l	*33.0%*
19.0%	17.9%	18.5%	16.6%	18.0%	19.9%	18.8%	19.7%	22.3%	59.1%	88.3%	*94.0%*	Return on Shr. Equity	*49.0%*
14.6%	12.5%	12.5%	11.4%	12.3%	13.2%	12.2%	12.9%	14.4%	42.0%	66.1%	*69.5%*	Retained to Com Eq	*35.0%*
43%	48%	48%	F44%	43%	46%	45%	43%	43%	41%	40%	*39%*	All Div'ds to Net Prof	*33%*

CURRENT POSITION ($MILL.)	1998	1999	10/2/99
Cash Assets	273.0	279.0	169.0
Receivables	1800.0	1744.0	1998.0
Inventory (FIFO)	2882.0	2643.0	2751.0
Other	265.0	321.0	332.0
Current Assets	5220.0	4987.0	5250.0
Accts Payable	2003.0	1782.0	1482.0
Debt Due	807.0	1503.0	1730.0
Other	2923.0	2668.0	2692.0
Current Liab.	5733.0	5953.0	5904.0

ANNUAL RATES of change (per sh)	Past 10 Yrs.	Past 5 Yrs.	Est'd '97-'99 to '02-'04
Sales	6.5%	7.5%	*5.5%*
"Cash Flow"	11.5%	8.5%	*8.0%*
Earnings	12.0%	10.0%	*11.0%*
Dividends	12.0%	8.5%	*7.5%*
Book Value	3.5%	-6.0%	*9.0%*

Fiscal Year Ends	QUARTERLY SALES ($ mill.) A Sep.Per	Dec.Per	Mar.Per	Jun.Per	Full Fiscal Year
1996	4656	4898	4443	4627	18624
1997	4886	5269	4649	4930	19734
1998	4893	5279	4736	5103	20011
1999	4860	5286	4664	5202	20012
2000	4950	*5400*	*4800*	*5350*	*20500*

Fiscal Year Ends	EARNINGS PER SHARE A B Sep.Per	Dec.Per	Mar.Per	Jun.Per	Full Fiscal Year
1996	.19	.29	.19	.25	.92
1997	.21	.32	.21	.28	1.02
1998	.22	.35	.23	.31	1.11
1999	.25	.39	.26	.31	1.21
2000	.28	*.42*	*.30*	*.35*	*1.35*

Calendar	QUARTERLY DIVIDENDS PAID C■ Mar.31	Jun.30	Sep.30	Dec.31	Full Year
1995	.085	.085	.085	.085	.34
1996	.095	.095	.095	.095	.38
1997	.105	.105	.105	.105	.42
1998	.115	.115	.115	.115	.46
1999	.115	.125	.125	.125	

BUSINESS: Sara Lee Corporation is a diversified international manufacturer and marketer of branded consumer products with operations in coffee, specialty meats, baked goods, foodservice distribution, household/personal care, and apparel. Food group includes: *Douwe Egberts, Hillshire Farms, Jimmy Dean, Ball Park, Kahn's, Mr. Turkey, Sara Lee.* Consumer products group includes *Hanes, L'eggs, Kiwi, Bali, Champion, Playtex, Coach,* and *Dim.* Foreign operations: 39% of sales; 39% of pretax income. '99 depreciation rate: 11.1%. Estimated plant age: 7 years. Has 138,000 employees, 85,100 common stockholders. Chairman: John H. Bryan, Jr. Incorporated: Maryland. Address: Three First National Plaza, Chicago, IL 60602. Tel.: 312-726-2600. Internet: www.saralee.com.

Results at Sara Lee's Foods division will probably continue to be constrained in the first half of fiscal 2000 (year ends June 30th), as the unit still realizes the effects of a processed-meat recall in December of 1998. The second-half performance should show a dramatic improvement, however, as we expect the division to increase its plant-capacity utilization from the current 55% level back to nearly 100%.

We look for Sara Lee to earn about $1.35 this fiscal year. That figure represents a 12% increase over last year's bottom line, despite what we believe will only be a moderate increase in sales. The top line may well be restrained by sluggish growth at the Sara Lee Foods and the Coffee and Tea divisions, where sales dropped 8% and 1%, respectively, in the first quarter. Increased marketing expenses will probably continue to eat into profit margins, as the company rebuilds brand equity in its Packaged Meats area. We believe, though, that these issues will be offset by strong showings from Sara Lee's other units, including the Household and Body Care division, which showed internal growth of 15% over the first fiscal quarter of 1999, excluding companies acquired. Also posting strong showing in the first period of this year were Intimate Apparel, up 12%, and Knit Products, up 14%, excluding acquisitions. Earnings should be further supported by a lower tax rate and an ongoing share-buyback program.

In fiscal 2001, we look for similar growth in share earnings, which should expand at a slightly faster pace than sales. Our earnings estimate for next year is currently $1.50 a share, based on sales of about $22 billion.

Sara Lee completed its acquisition of Chock Full o'Nuts during the recent quarter. SLE issued about 9.7 million common shares to CHK stockholders. The addition of Chock's approximately $350 million in sales will have little effect on Sara Lee's share earnings in 2000.

Sara Lee shares' capital-appreciation potential to 2002-2004 is subpar. Given the Timeliness rank of 4 (Below Average), investors should wait until the stock's share price and earnings momentum improves before committing.

Dylan D. Cathers *November 12, 1999*

(A) Fiscal year ends on Sat. closest to June 30.
(B) Primary egs. until fiscal '97. Diluted egs. beg. fiscal '98. Excl. net nonrecurr. items: '89, 2¢; '92, 15¢; '94, d55¢; '98, d$1.73; '99, 5¢.
Next earnings report due late January.
(C) Next div'd mtg. abt. Jan. 30th. Next ex-div'd date abt. Nov. 30th. Approx. div'd pymt. dates: 1st of Jan., Apr., July, Oct. ■ Div'd reinvestment plan avail.
(D) Incl. intang. In '98: $3,178 mill.; $3.45/sh.
(E) In mill., adj. for stk. splits.
(F) Incl. special div'd, 6¢/sh.

Company's Financial Strength	A+
Stock's Price Stability	85
Price Growth Persistence	75
Earnings Predictability	100

©1999 Value Line Publishing, Inc.

FIGURE 8.2 Countrywide Credit EPS Growth Changes with Interest Rates

COUNTRYWIDE CRED. NYSE-CCR | RECENT PRICE **29** | P/E RATIO **8.1** (Trailing: 8.3 Median: 11.0) | RELATIVE P/E RATIO **0.54** | DIV'D YLD **1.4%** | VALUE LINE

TIMELINESS **3** Lowered 5/7/99
SAFETY **3** Raised 3/7/97
TECHNICAL **3** Raised 11/19/99
BETA 1.55 (1.00 = Market)

	1987	1988	1989	1990	1991	1992	1993	1994	1995	1996	1997	1998	1999	2000
High:		3.8	4.3	4.0	17.7	19.9	23.3	19.1	26.8	30.3	43.3	56.3	51.4	
Low:		2.1	2.6	2.3	3.7	10.8	15.2	12.4	12.6	19.8	24.4	28.6	28.5	

Target Price Range 2002 | 2003 | 2004

2002-04 PROJECTIONS

	Price	Gain	Ann'l Total Return
High	80	(+175%)	*30%*
Low	55	(+90%)	*18%*

Insider Decisions

	J	F	M	A	M	J	J	A	S
to Buy	0	0	0	0	0	0	0	0	1
Options	2	1	0	0	2	1	0	0	2
to Sell	2	0	0	0	0	0	1	1	0

Institutional Decisions

	4Q1998	1Q1999	2Q1999
to Buy	152	160	137
to Sell	98	105	122
Hld's(000)	93093	91922	91820

1983	1984	1985	1986	1987	1988	1989	1990	1991	1992	1993	1994	1995	1996	1997	1998	1999	2000	© VALUE LINE PUB., INC.	02-04
1.34	1.56	2.22	3.70	3.48	3.52	4.41	5.10	4.13	7.84	11.33	9.56	11.17	13.47	13.82	17.05	*19.00*	*20.10*	Revenues per sh A	*24.00*
.20	.15	.21	.58	.58	.54	.45	.61	.79	1.73	2.14	1.26	2.21	2.81	3.57	3.89	*4.15*	*4.50*	"Cash Flow" per sh	*6.00*
.17	.11	.18	.49	.35	.27	.31	.48	.88	1.52	1.94	.96	1.95	2.42	2.76	3.29	*3.60*	*4.00*	Earnings per sh B	*5.50*
.07	.06	.05	.09	.11	.12	.11	.12	.16	.22	.28	.31	.32	.32	.32	.32	*.40*	*.40*	Div'ds Decl'd per sh C	*.40*
.94	.96	1.06	1.51	2.54	2.69	2.90	3.22	7.00	8.30	9.67	10.35	12.91	15.19	19.12	18.92	*21.70*	*24.80*	Book Value per sh	*36.80*
252%	176%	202%	303%	160%	101%	116%	100%	163%	189%	201%	141%	148%	163%	155%	212%	*135%*	*120%*	%Price To Book	*150%*
27.13	28.53	29.86	29.94	39.22	40.35	40.56	40.89	79.50	83.50	91.06	91.06	102.24	106.10	109.21	112.90	*113.50*	*115.00*	Common Shares Outst'g D	*125.00*
13.6	14.8	11.9	9.2	11.8	10.1	10.8	6.8	12.9	10.3	10.0	15.2	10.8	10.5	10.9	13.4	*Bold figures are*	*Value Line*	Avg Ann'l P/E Ratio	*12.0*
1.15	1.38	.97	.62	.79	.84	.82	.51	.82	.62	.59	1.00	.72	.66	.63	.70		*estimates*	Relative P/E Ratio	*.80*
3.0%	3.7%	2.4%	2.0%	2.7%	4.4%	3.4%	3.7%	1.4%	1.4%	1.4%	2.1%	1.5%	1.3%	.9%	.7%			Avg Ann'l Div'd Yield	*.6%*

CAPITAL STRUCTURE as of 8/31/99
Total Debt $11284.0 mill.

Total Interest $695.0 mill. (78% of Cap'l)
Leases, Uncapitalized Annual rentals $22.8+ mill.

Pension Liability None

Pfd Stock $500.0 mill.

Common Stock 113,058,030 shs. (22% of Cap'l)
MARKET CAP:$3.3 billion (Mid cap)

1989	1990	1991	1992	1993	1994	1995	1996	1997	1998	1999	2000		02-04
179.0	208.4	328.1	654.3	1031.5	870.4	1142.3	1429.2	1509.0	1979.0	*2150*	*2310*	Revenues ($mill) A	*3000*
3640	4577	12156	32388	52459	27866	34584	37811	48772	92881	*75000*	*70000*	Loan Production ($mill)	*70000*
32.6	42.3	72.7	140.1	227.7	199.1	286.9	424.3	424.3	669.7	*720*	*745*	Salary Expense ($mill)	*1100*
10.8	13.1	60.2	140.1	179.5	88.4	195.7	257.4	345.0	385.4	*400*	*430*	Net Profit ($mill)	*725*
40.0%	40.0%	40.0%	40.0%	40.0%	40.0%	40.0%	39.0%	39.0%	39.0%	*37.5%*	*37.5%*	Income Tax Rate	*40.0%*
7.3%	10.7%	18.3%	21.4%	17.4%	10.2%	17.1%	18.0%	22.9%	19.5%	*18.6%*	*18.6%*	Net Profit Margin	*24.0%*
12515	15684	27456	54484	84678	113111	136835	158585	182888	215489	*250000*	*285000*	Mortgages Serviced	*425000*
436.9	588.7	1306.9	1943.5	3859.2	3963.1	6097.5	5013.0	7475.2	9935.8	*12250*	*14250*	Total Debt ($mill)	*22000*
117.5	171.6	596.2	718.9	880.1	942.6	1319.8	1611.5	2587.9	3018.9	*3375*	*3725*	Shr. Equity ($mill) E	*6000*
9.1%	7.8%	5.8%	6.0%	6.4%	4.5%	4.5%	21.7%	3.4%	4.5%	*5.0%*	*5.0%*	Return on Total Cap'l	*4.5%*
11.1%	13.0%	10.1%	19.5%	20.4%	9.4%	14.8%	16.0%	13.3%	12.8%	*12.0%*	*11.5%*	Return on Shr. Equity	*12.0%*
7.3%	11.5%	8.5%	16.8%	17.5%	6.4%	12.5%	13.9%	14.9%	14.1%	*13.0%*	*12.5%*	Retained to Com Eq	*13.0%*
35%	32%	22%	17%	14%	32%	16%	13%	10%	10%	*10%*	*10%*	All Div'ds to Net Profit	*7%*

MORTGAGE BANKING ($Mil.)

	1996	1997	1998
Loan Originations	37810.8	48771.0	92881.0
Revenue From:			
Mortgage Originations	440.5	455.5	617.2
Mortgage Servicing	547.0	547.0	654.0
Balances—End of Period:			
Servicing Portfolio	158585	182888	215489
Loans-In-Process	4677.0	12622.0	14645.0

ANNUAL RATES of change (per sh)	Past 10 Yrs.	Past 5 Yrs.	Est'd '96-'98 to '02-'04
Revenues	15.0%	17.5%	*6.5%*
"Cash Flow"	20.0%	22.5%	*10.0%*
Earnings	22.0%	21.5%	*11.0%*
Dividends	14.0%	14.0%	*4.0%*
Book Value	25.0%	20.5%	*12.0%*

Fiscal Year Begins	QUARTERLY REVENUES ($ mill.) A May 31	Aug.31	Nov.30	Feb.28	Full Fiscal Year
1996	340.4	347.0	358.7	383.1	1429.2
1997	318.6	404.3	375.2	410.9	1509.0A
1998	450.3	482.2	514.2	532.3	1979.0
1999	537.0	537.0	*533*	*543*	*2150*
2000	*570*	*575*	*575*	*590*	*2310*

Fiscal Year Begins	EARNINGS PER SHARE A B May 31	Aug.31	Nov.30	Feb.28	Full Fiscal Year
1996	.58	.60	.62	.62	2.42
1997	.64	.67	.71	.74	2.76
1998	.78	.81	.84	.86	3.29
1999	.88	.91	*.90*	*.91*	*3.60*
2000	*1.00*	*1.00*	*1.00*	*1.00*	*4.00*

Cal-endar	QUARTERLY DIVIDENDS PAID C Mar.31	Jun.30	Sep.30	Dec.31	Full Year
1995	.08	.08	.08	.08	.32
1996	.08	.08	.08	.08	.32
1997	.08	.08	.08	.08	.32
1998	.08	.08	.08	.08	.32
1999	.08	.10	.10	.10	

BUSINESS: Countrywide Credit Industries, Inc. is the nation's largest independent residential mortgage lender and servicer with offices nationwide. The company subsequently securitizes and sells its loan production (6% marketshare) to investors, retaining the servicing rights (5% marketshare). It conducts business through roughly 400 branch offices. Also operates an insurance agency and a securities broker-dealer. As of 2/28/99, the mortgage servicing portfolio was $236.5 billion; delinquency, 3.11%; pipeline $10.6 bill). Has 2,653 shrhldrs. Officers & dirs. own 5.8% of stock; Neuberger & Berman, 14.0%; Oppenh., 8.0%; (6/99 Proxy). Chrmn. & Pres.: David S. Loeb. Inc.: DE. Addr.: 155 North Lake Ave., Pasadena, CA 91101. Tel.: 818-304-8400. Internet: http://www.countrywide.com

It's hard to make a compelling near-term case for Countrywide Credit's neutrally-ranked stock during a period when pressure on production is so severe and profit comparisons are difficult. Still, a modest premium to book value seems like a good entry point for long-term investors. We think there is little risk to book value in the way of investment writedowns and restructuring charges. We view the intangible value of the franchise as substantially more than the market is assessing it at (recent apparent market share losses in the ARM segment notwithstanding). That said, history is useful for gauging the market's willingness to pay up for earnings, which are highly cyclical, until proven otherwise. The company has a track record of top-line, earnings, and book value growth that is, for all intents and purposes, the best in its class. Some other diversification initiatives are bearing fruit, and the purchase of a British unit seems like a nice platform for expansion in Europe. That gives us confidence that the long-term upwards earnings trajectory is on course. Setbacks in the fixed income markets (such as in 1990) and several times since the Seventies shows that the insulation from interest rate swings is only partial (thanks to hedging instruments). In fact, the downswing in demand during periods of higher rates is too great to be offset through financial engineering. We view the floor for the stock at book value, which is about 25% from the current price. The equity has less downside risk than some of the thrifts and financials with substantially more balance sheet uncertainty, while the long-term debt overstates true leverage since the loans are held for sale.

With refinancings slowing to a trickle, the recurring portion of revenues is higher due to less amortization of the servicing right. Although the company will have to realign expenses with new production levels, a lot of the costs are variable. Prepayment rates have slowed meanwhile. And, while the robustness of the economy will provide some cushion for production through next year, the growth of the servicing asset, barring significant wholesale purchases, will be in the high single digits.

Peter Azcue *December 3, 1999*

(A) Fiscal year ends Feb. 28 of following calendar year. Total Revenue as reported beginning in '97. (B) Fully diluted earnings from '92. Next earnings report due late Dec. Excludes extraordinary gain: '88, 9¢. (C) Next dividend meeting about Dec. 10th. Goes ex about Jan. 12th. Approximate dividend payment dates: Jan. 31, Apr. 30, Jul. 31, Oct. 31. Plus stock: '86; 2%, '87; 2%, '88; 2%, '89; 5%. (D) In millions, adjusted for stock splits. (E) Incl. pfd. sub. trust.

Company's Financial Strength	B+
Stock's Price Stability	40
Price Growth Persistence	90
Earnings Predictability	50

©1999 Value Line Publishing, Inc.

TABLE 8.4 Valuation Ratios for the Dow Jones Industrial Average, 1950–Present

Year	Year's Close	P/B Ratio	P/E Ratio	% Dividend Yield
1950	235.41	1.21	7.7	6.85%
1951	269.23	1.33	10.1	6.07%
1952	291.90	1.37	11.8	5.29%
1953	280.90	1.15	10.3	5.74%
1954	404.39	1.62	14.4	4.32%
1955	488.40	1.80	13.7	4.42%
1956	499.47	1.75	15.0	4.60%
1957	435.69	1.46	12.1	4.96%
1958	583.65	1.88	20.9	3.43%
1959	679.36	2.00	19.8	3.05%
1960	615.89	1.67	19.1	3.47%
1961	731.14	1.90	22.9	3.11%
1962	652.10	1.63	17.9	3.57%
1963	762.95	1.79	18.5	3.07%
1964	874.13	2.09	18.8	3.57%
1965	969.26	2.14	18.1	2.95%
1966	785.69	1.65	13.6	4.06%
1967	905.11	1.90	16.8	3.34%
1968	943.75	1.81	16.3	3.32%
1969	800.36	1.48	14.0	4.24%
1970	838.92	1.46	16.4	3.76%
1971	890.20	1.47	16.2	3.47%
1972	1020.02	1.59	15.2	3.16%
1973	850.86	1.23	9.9	4.15%
1974	616.24	0.83	6.2	6.12%
1975	852.41	1.09	11.3	4.39%
1976	1004.65	1.26	10.4	4.12%
1977	831.17	0.99	9.3	5.52%
1978	805.01	0.90	7.1	6.03%
1979	838.74	0.98	6.7	6.08%
1980	963.99	1.04	7.9	5.64%
1981	875.00	0.90	7.7	6.43%
1982	1046.54	1.19	9.2	5.17%
1983	1258.64	1.42	11.1	4.48%
1984	1211.57	1.32	10.7	5.00%
1985	1546.67	1.64	16.1	4.01%
1986	1895.95	1.92	16.4	3.54%
1987	1938.83	1.92	14.6	3.67%
1988	2168.57	2.02	10.1	3.67%
1989	2753.20	2.16	12.4	3.74%
1990	2633.66	1.98	15.3	3.94%
1991	3168.83	2.44	18.4	3.00%
1992	3301.11	2.88	19.2	3.05%
1993	3754.09	3.36	25.6	2.65%
1994	3834.44	2.94	15.0	2.76%
1995	5117.12	3.83	16.5	2.28%
1996	6448.27	4.56	18.2	2.03%
1997	7908.25	4.96	20.2	1.72%
1998	9181.43	5.43	23.6	1.67%
1999	11497.10	6.81	24.8	1.34%
Average		**1.9**	**14.7**	**4.00%**
Median		**1.6**	**15.0**	**3.75%**

Data source: Dow Jones & Company.
Note: P/E ratios in 1982–83 and 1991–92 have been adjusted for massive losses at component firms.

often neglect to include important intangible assets such as valuable brand names, copyrights, or patents. As such, it is common to find that stock prices exceed accounting book values, and P/B ratios typically average more than 1:1. As shown in Table 8.4, P/B ratios are commonly found in the range near 1.5:1 to 2:1. Rarely has the year-end P/B ratio for the DJIA fallen below 1:1. At such times, stock prices must be regarded as unusually cheap. In only a few instances since 1950 has the year-end P/B ratio for the DJIA exceeded 3:1. At such times, stock prices must be regarded as unusually expensive. The P/B ratio on the DJIA has seldom been as high as it was at the start of 2000.

dividend yield Dividend income expressed as a percentage of the amount paid for a stock.

Dividend yield is a third popular measure of relative valuation. This measure tells investors the amount of dividend income, in which dividend income is expressed as a percentage of the amount paid for a stock. If a company's stock is selling for $40 per share and it pays a 25¢ quarterly dividend, or $1 per year, dividend yield is 2.5% (= $1/$40) per year. Investors must not ignore the power of dividends in overall stock market performance because dividends play an important role in determining the investor's **total return,** which is the sum of dividend income plus capital appreciation. The compounding effect of dividends over time is also impressive. Over the long term, dividend income represents between one-third and one-half of the total return earned on common stocks. Since 1950, for example, DJIA companies have paid an average 4% dividend and provided capital appreciation of roughly 8% per year. This means that one-third of the long-term investor's total return has come from dividend income. To provide a competitive long-term rate of return, a riskier stock that paid no dividends would have to grow by 12% per year, or fully 50% faster than the 8% growth typical of the average DJIA stock. Dividend yields on DJIA stocks have never been as low as they were at the start of 2000.

total return Sum of dividend income plus capital appreciation.

Figure 8.3 shows the profile of a typical high-yield stock. Most investors are familiar with WD-40, or "water-displacement formula 40," a petroleum-based spray lubricant used to prevent rust. Many do not realize that the WD-40 Company has publicly traded common stock. The company has high and stable profit margins but enjoys only modest growth opportunities given its 80% market share. As a result, WD-40 pays out a substantial share of its income to shareholders in the form of cash dividends. With a roughly 5% dividend yield, WD-40 represents the type of high-yield company that investors like because high dividends serve as a protective cushion when the overall market declines. With expected earnings per share growth on the order of 9% per year, WD-40's 5% dividend gives investors the opportunity to earn a very competitive total return on the order of 14% per year.

Are Stock Prices Too High?

A cursory examination of the data in Table 8.4 suggests that P/E and P/B ratios for the DJIA rose to historic highs during the late 1990s, and dividend yield has plummeted to historic lows. These trends for the DJIA are depicted in Figure 8.4. Take away the surge in P/E ratios tied to the economic recessions of 1982–83 and 1991–92, and P/E ratios on the DJIA have never been higher than at the start of the new millennium. Over the entire post–World War II period, P/B ratios have never been higher and dividend yield has never been more modest. Against this backdrop, many investors and stock market analysts are now prone to ask: Are stock prices too high?

FIGURE 8.3 **WD-40 Offers Investors Significant Dividend Income**

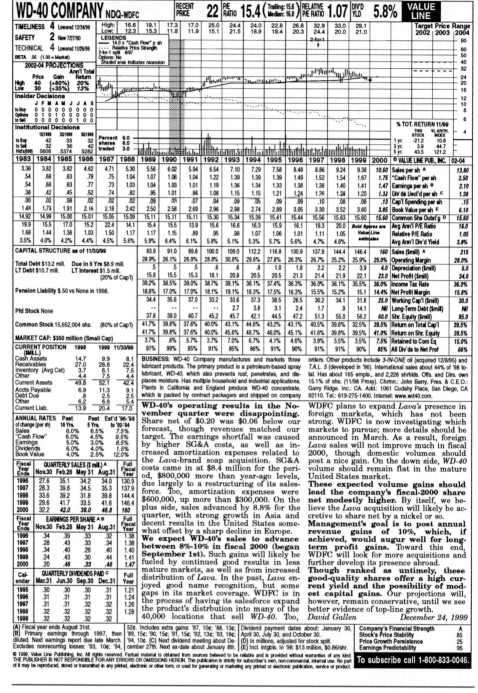

WD-40 COMPANY NDQ-WDFC

RECENT PRICE **22** | P/E RATIO **15.4** (Trailing: 15.6 Median: 16.0) | RELATIVE P/E RATIO **1.07** | DIV'D YLD **5.8%** | **VALUE LINE**

TIMELINESS **4** Lowered 12/24/99
SAFETY **2** New 7/27/90
TECHNICAL **4** Lowered 11/26/99
BETA .50 (1.00 = Market)

	High:	16.6	19.1	17.3	17.0	25.0	24.4	24.0	22.8	26.6	32.9	33.0	29.1			Target Price Range
	Low:	12.3	15.3	11.8	11.9	15.1	21.5	18.9	19.4	20.3	24.4	20.0	21.0			2002 | 2003 | 2004

2002-04 PROJECTIONS

	Price	Gain	Ann'l Total Return
High	40	(+80%)	20%
Low	30	(+35%)	13%

Insider Decisions

	J	F	M	A	M	J	J	A	S
to Buy	0	0	0	0	0	0	0	0	0
Options	0	1	0	1	0	0	0	0	0
to Sell	0	0	0	0	0	0	1	0	0

Institutional Decisions

	1Q1999	2Q1999	3Q1999
to Buy	42	33	32
to Sell	32	36	42
Hld's(000)	5608	5374	5282

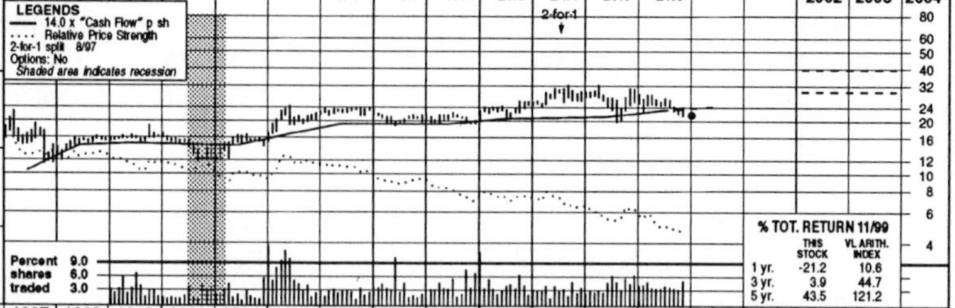

% TOT. RETURN 11/99

	THIS STOCK	VL ARITH. INDEX
1 yr.	-21.2	10.6
3 yr.	3.9	44.7
5 yr.	43.5	121.2

1983	1984	1985	1986	1987	1988	1989	1990	1991	1992	1993	1994	1995	1996	1997	1998	1999	2000	© VALUE LINE PUB., INC.	02-04
3.36	3.82	3.82	4.62	4.71	5.30	5.56	6.02	5.94	6.54	7.10	7.29	7.58	8.48	8.86	9.24	9.38	*10.60*	Sales per sh A	*13.80*
.54	.68	.63	.78	.75	1.04	1.07	1.06	1.04	1.22	1.39	1.39	1.39	1.49	1.52	1.54	1.67	*1.75*	"Cash Flow" per sh	*2.50*
.54	.68	.63	.77	.73	1.03	1.04	1.03	1.01	1.19	1.36	1.34	1.33	1.38	1.38	1.40	1.41	*1.47*	Earnings per sh B	*2.10*
.38	.42	.45	.52	.74	.82	.95	1.01	.86	1.08	1.15	1.15	1.21	1.24	1.26	1.28	1.20	*1.32*	Div'ds Decl'd per sh C	*1.38*
.00	.02	.08	.02	.02	.02	.09	.03	.07	.04	.09	.05	.09	.09	.10	.08	.08	*.13*	Cap'l Spending per sh	*.15*
1.48	1.73	1.91	2.16	2.18	2.42	2.50	2.58	2.69	2.96	2.98	2.74	2.89	3.05	3.30	3.52	3.60	*3.85*	Book Value per sh E	*6.10*
14.92	14.99	15.00	15.01	15.05	15.09	15.11	15.11	15.11	15.30	15.34	15.39	15.41	15.44	15.56	15.63	15.60	*15.60*	Common Shs Outst'g D	*15.60*
19.9	15.5	17.0	15.2	22.4	14.1	15.4	15.5	13.9	15.6	16.6	16.3	15.9	16.1	19.3	20.0	*Bold figures are*		Avg Ann'l P/E Ratio	*16.0*
1.68	1.44	1.38	1.03	1.50	1.17	1.17	1.15	.89	.95	.98	1.07	1.06	1.01	1.11	1.05	*Value Line*		Relative P/E Ratio	*1.05*
3.5%	4.0%	4.2%	4.4%	4.5%	5.6%	5.9%	6.4%	6.1%	5.8%	5.1%	5.3%	5.7%	5.6%	4.7%	4.6%	*estimates*		Avg Ann'l Div'd Yield	*3.8%*
						83.9	91.0	89.8	100.0	109.0	112.2	116.8	130.9	137.9	144.4	146.4	*160*	Sales ($mill) A	*215*
						28.9%	26.1%	26.9%	28.8%	30.8%	29.6%	27.8%	26.3%	26.7%	25.2%	25.9%	*25.0%*	Operating Margin	*28.0%*
						.5	.5	.5	.6	.6	.8	1.0	1.8	2.2	2.2	3.9	*4.0*	Depreciation ($mill)	*5.0*
						15.8	15.5	15.3	18.1	20.8	20.5	20.5	21.3	21.4	21.9	22.1	*23.0*	Net Profit ($mill)	*34.0*
						39.2%	38.5%	39.0%	38.7%	39.1%	38.1%	37.4%	36.3%	36.0%	36.1%	35.5%	*36.0%*	Income Tax Rate	*36.0%*
						18.8%	17.0%	17.0%	18.1%	19.1%	18.3%	17.5%	16.3%	15.5%	15.2%	15.1	*14.4%*	Net Profit Margin	*15.8%*
						34.4	35.6	37.0	33.2	33.6	37.3	38.5	26.5	30.2	34.1	31.8	*25.0*	Working Cap'l ($mill)	*30.0*
						--	--	--	--	2.7	3.8	3.1	2.4	1.7	.9	14.1	*Nil*	Long-Term Debt ($mill)	*Nil*
						37.8	39.0	40.7	45.2	45.7	42.1	44.5	47.2	51.3	55.0	56.2	*60.0*	Shr. Equity ($mill)	*95.0*
						41.7%	39.8%	37.6%	40.0%	43.1%	44.8%	43.2%	43.1%	40.5%	39.6%	32.5%	*39.5%*	Return on Total Cap'l	*39.5%*
						41.7%	39.8%	37.6%	40.0%	45.6%	48.7%	46.0%	45.1%	41.6%	39.8%	39.5%	*41.0%*	Return on Shr. Equity	*39.5%*
						3.7%	.6%	5.7%	3.7%	7.0%	6.7%	4.1%	4.6%	3.9%	3.5%	3.5%	*7.5%*	Retained to Com Eq	*15.0%*
						91%	99%	85%	91%	85%	86%	91%	90%	91%	91%	90%	*85%*	All Div'ds to Net Prof	*66%*

CAPITAL STRUCTURE as of 11/30/99

Total Debt $13.2 mill. **Due in 5 Yrs** $8.9 mill.
LT Debt $10.7 mill. **LT Interest** $1.5 mill.
(20% of Cap'l)

Pension Liability $.50 vs None in 1998.

Pfd Stock None

Common Stock 15,652,004 shs. (80% of Cap'l)

MARKET CAP: $350 million (Small Cap)

CURRENT POSITION ($MILL.)	1998	1999	11/30/99
Cash Assets	14.7	9.9	8.1
Receivables	27.0	28.6	22.4
Inventory (Avg Cst)	3.7	6.1	7.5
Other	4.4	7.5	4.4
Current Assets	49.8	52.1	42.4
Accts Payable	6.9	11.3	9.1
Debt Due	.8	2.5	2.5
Other	6.2	6.6	5.4
Current Liab.	13.9	20.4	17.0

ANNUAL RATES of change (per sh)	Past 10 Yrs.	Past 5 Yrs.	Est'd '96-'98 to '02-'04
Sales	6.0%	6.5%	*7.5%*
"Cash Flow"	6.0%	4.5%	*9.5%*
Earnings	5.0%	3.0%	*8.5%*
Dividends	6.0%	4.0%	*1.5%*
Book Value	4.0%	2.5%	*12.0%*

Fiscal Year Ends	QUARTERLY SALES ($ mill.) A Nov.30	Feb.28	May 31	Aug.31	Full Fiscal Year
1996	27.6	35.1	34.2	34.0	130.9
1997	28.3	39.8	34.5	35.3	137.9
1998	33.6	39.2	31.8	39.8	144.4
1999	29.6	41.7	33.5	41.6	146.4
2000	32.2	*42.0*	*39.0*	*46.8*	*160*

Fiscal Year Ends	EARNINGS PER SHARE A B Nov.30	Feb.28	May 31	Aug.31	Full Fiscal Year
1996	.34	.39	.33	.32	1.38
1997	.28	.43	.33	.34	1.38
1998	.34	.40	.26	.40	1.40
1999	.24	.43	.30	.44	1.41
2000	.20	*.46*	*.33*	*.48*	*1.47*

Cal-endar	QUARTERLY DIVIDENDS PAID C Mar.31	Jun.30	Sep.30	Dec.31	Full Year
1995	.30	.30	.30	.31	1.21
1996	.31	.31	.31	.31	1.24
1997	.31	.31	.32	.32	1.26
1998	.32	.32	.32	.32	1.28
1999	.32	.32	.32	.32	

BUSINESS: WD-40 Company manufactures and markets three lubricant products. The primary product is a petroleum-based spray lubricant, *WD-40*, which also prevents rust, penetrates, and displaces moisture. Has multiple household and industrial applications. Plants in California and England produce WD-40 concentrate, which is packed by contract packagers and shipped on company orders. Other products include *3-IN-ONE* oil (acquired 12/8/95) and *T.A.L. 5* (developed in '96). International sales about 44% of '98 total. Has about 165 empls., and 2,226 shrhlds. Offs. and Dirs. own 15.1% of shs. (11/98 Proxy). Chrmn.: John Barry. Pres. & C.E.O.: Garry Ridge. Inc.: CA. Add.: 1061 Cudahy Place, San Diego, CA 92110. Tel.: 619-275-1400. Internet: www.wd40.com.

WD-40's operating results in the November quarter were disappointing. Share net of $0.20 was $0.06 below our forecast, though revenues matched our target. The earnings shortfall was caused by higher SG&A costs, as well as increased amortization expenses related to the *Lava*-brand soap acquisition. SG&A costs came in at $8.4 million for the period, $800,000 more than year-ago levels, due largely to a restructuring of its salesforce. Too, amortization expenses were $600,000, up more than $300,000. On the plus side, sales advanced by 8.8% for the quarter, with strong growth in Asia and decent results in the United States somewhat offset by a sharp decline in Europe.

We expect WD-40's sales to advance between 8%-10% in fiscal 2000 (began September 1st). Such gains will likely be fueled by continued good results in less mature markets, as well as from increased distribution of *Lava*. In the past, *Lava* enjoyed good name recognition, but some gaps in its market coverage. WDFC is in the process of having its salesforce expand the product's distrbution into many of the 40,000 locations that sell *WD-40*. Too, WDFC plans to expand *Lava's* presence in foreign markets, which has not been strong. WDFC is now investigating which markets to pursue; more details should be announced in March. As a result, foreign *Lava* sales will not improve much in fiscal 2000, though domestic volumes should post a nice gain. On the down side, *WD-40* volume should remain flat in the mature United States market.

These expected volume gains should lead the company's fiscal-2000 share net modestly higher. By itself, we believe the *Lava* acquisition will likely be accretive to share net by a nickel or so.

Management's goal is to post annual revenue gains of 10%, which, if achieved, would augur well for long-term profit gains. Toward this end, WDFC will look for more acquisitions and further develop its presence abroad.

Though ranked as untimely, these good-quality shares offer a high current yield and the possibility of modest capital gains. Our projections will, however, remain conservative, until we see better evidence of top-line growth.

David Gallen *December 24, 1999*

(A) Fiscal year ends August 31st.
(B) Primary earnings through 1997, then diluted. Next earnings report due late March. Excludes nonrecurring losses: '93, 10¢; '94, 52¢. Includes extra gains: '87, 10¢; '88, 13¢; '89, 15¢; '90, 15¢; '91, 15¢; '92, 13¢; '93, 18¢; '94, 10¢. (C) Next dividend meeting about December 27th. Next ex-date about January 8th. Dividend payment dates about: January 30, April 30, July 30, and October 30.
(D) In millions, adjusted for stock split.
(E) Incl. intgbls. In '98: $13 million, $0.86/shr.

Company's Financial Strength	A
Stock's Price Stability	85
Price Growth Persistence	25
Earnings Predictability	95

FIGURE 8.4 **DJIA Is at All-Time Highs Compared with Earnings, Book Values, and Dividends**

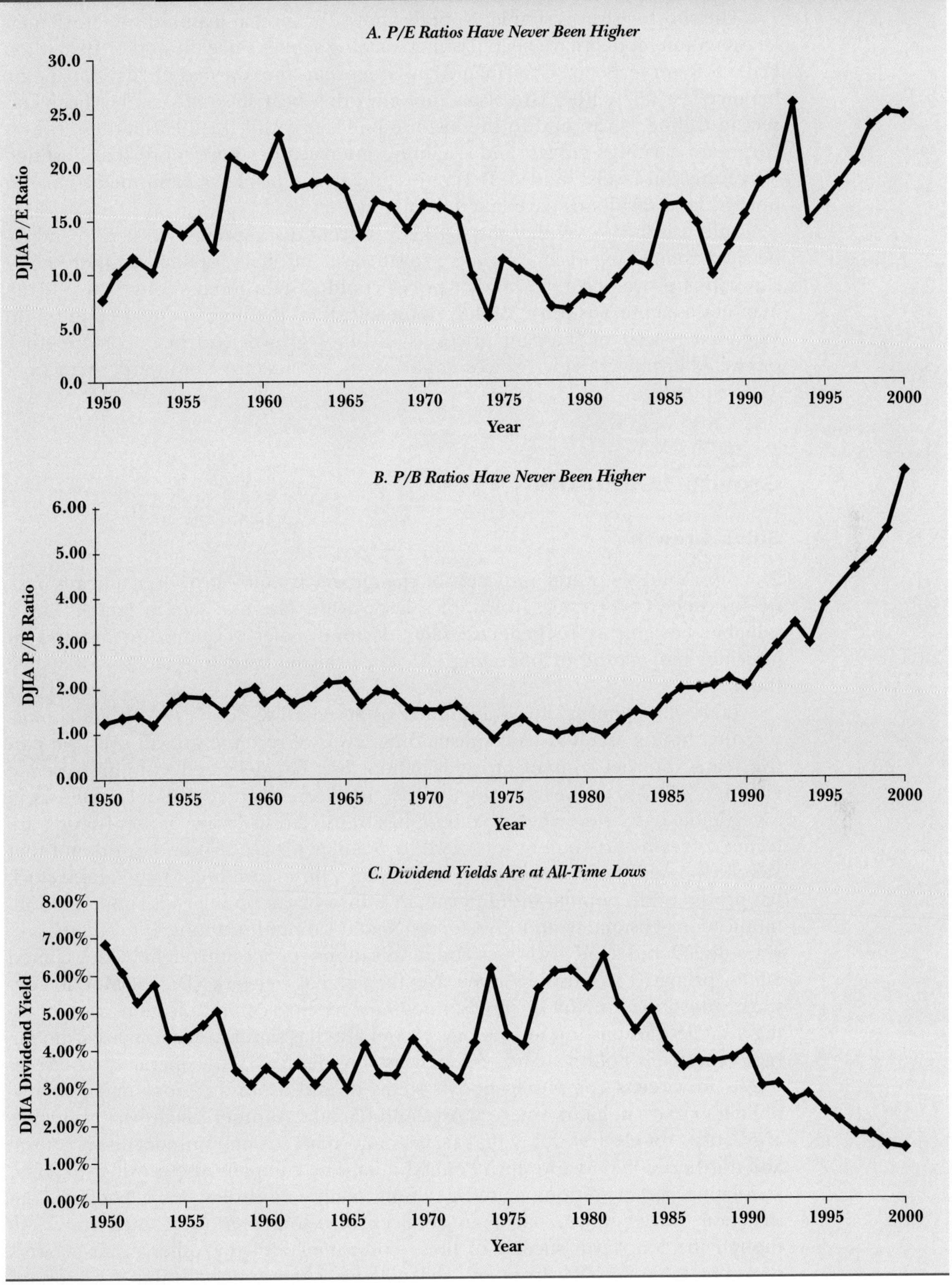

Data source: Dow Jones & Company.

The short answer is simple: Nobody knows for sure, at least not yet. Stock market valuation models have been flashing warning signals since the end of 1996 when Federal Reserve Board Chairman Alan Greenspan first warned of "irrational exuberance." So far, neither Greenspan nor any other bearish soothsayer has been correct in calling for an end to the historic bull market of the 1990s. So far, robust corporate earnings growth and declining interest rates have more than justified lofty valuation levels. Indeed, P/E ratios and P/B ratios have continued to march upward, and dividends have fallen to minimal levels.

Still, it is fair to say that the market's current assumptions about risk, and especially about long-term earnings growth, are unusually optimistic. If these assumptions prove accurate, market prices could sustain today's lofty levels. If the market's assumptions prove unduly optimistic, then the market could be in for an extended period of stagnant prices as earnings growth "catches up" with stock prices. Alternatively, stock prices could be in for a sharp downward correction. Time will tell.

Growth Indicators

Sales Growth

The most valuable overall indicator of change or "top-line" growth in a firm's business prospects is revenue growth or sales growth. The first step in establishing a valuable business is to generate sales. Without sales revenue, no amount of judicious cost-cutting or operating efficiency can be used to establish a valuable franchise.

Table 8.5, panel A, shows a number of Standard & Poor's (S&P) 500 companies that have generated truly outstanding levels of revenue growth over the past five years. Internet content provider Yahoo! Inc. has delivered stunning revenue growth of 173.1% per year during the past five years. Granted, Yahoo! started from a negligible base. Nevertheless, Yahoo! has translated its brand of user-friendly Internet software and content into a wildly popular service. No one can doubt that Yahoo! is popular with Internet users. Similarly, none can doubt that Yahoo! stock has proved wildly popular with Internet investors. Just as popular with both telecommunications customers and investors is Nextel Communications, Inc. Nextel provides digital and analog wireless communications services throughout the United States, primarily to business users. Nextel's digital network (Digital Mobile Network) constitutes one of the largest integrated wireless communications systems using a single transmission technology. Nextel also has significant specialized mobile radio spectrum holdings and, through its subsidiaries, owns, operates, or has interests in wireless communications systems in and around various major metropolitan markets in Latin America, Asia, and Canada. Another fast grower is FirstEnergy Corp., an electric utility that serves more than 5.5 million persons in central and northern Ohio and western Pennsylvania. The company also provides heating, ventilating, air conditioning, refrigeration, facility control systems, roofing construction, and energy management services to customers in the United States. Although the long-term success of these companies and the other rapid growers shown in Table 8.5 is far from ensured, all have taken important first steps toward developing valuable franchises.

Not too long ago, the suggestion that building revenue is the necessary first step toward corporate success would have seemed an innocuous premise. Since the advent of the Internet, however, even this simple idea appears to have been shaken. During the late 1990s, for example, "dot.com mania" resulted in billions of dollars of market value being accorded to companies with little or no revenues. Of course, Netscape Communications, now part of America Online, Inc., started the business model of a company giving away its products in the hope of building customer loyalty and "eventually" figuring out a way of charging customers. Even Microsoft proudly points to widespread use of its products in China and other Asian countries where software piracy is rampant and little, if any, current revenues are generated. Before judging all Internet investors as crazy, however, it is important to keep in mind that there is a big difference between products that are unable to generate much in the way of current revenues and products that have little or no hope of *ever* generating sales. If users of free computer software become loyal adopters of continuing product upgrades, for example, it can be a prudent business plan to give away early versions (i.e., "freeware"). Similarly, if an Internet service provider (ISP) can capture dedicated user "eyeballs" for extended periods, even free ISP service can become profitable, like broadcast TV, on the basis of advertising revenues.

EPS Growth

When an investor purchases a share of stock, part ownership of the corporation is established. From the investor's standpoint, it is what happens to the value of that part ownership that is most important. Because firm value can be thought of as the discounted net present value of all future profits, the rate of earnings-per-share (EPS) growth is a vital determinant of the value of the firm. If long-term investors identify and hold companies with above-average EPS growth, such investors can anticipate above-average long-term rates of return. If long-term investors identify and purchase companies with below-average EPS growth, they will realize mediocre returns, at best.

Table 8.5, panel B, shows a number of S&P 500 companies that have produced excellent EPS growth over the past five years. A favorite computer manufacturer and e-commerce retailer, Dell Computer, leads the list. Dell has generated stunning EPS growth of 86% per year over the past five years, and Dell customers and shareholders have benefited mightily from the company's astounding performance. Although other companies listed in Table 8.5 have also generated stunning EPS growth, it is worth emphasizing that Dell's EPS growth has been accompanied by sparkling revenue growth. This means that Dell's EPS growth has not simply reflected a sharp turnaround from large write-offs or a single year's bad operating performance. This was the case for Coastal Corp. Coastal is a Houston, Texas-based natural gas transmission and storage company. Coastal is also involved with petroleum refining, marketing, and distribution; gas and oil exploration and production; chemicals; and coal mining and power.

Dividend and Book Value Growth

One of the most powerful benefits of common stock ownership is a large and growing stream of dividend income. As shown in Table 8.5, panel C, life-insurer Conseco Inc., computerized payroll-service provider Paychex Inc., and soft drink bottling

TABLE 8.5 **Historical Growth Is Measured by Change in Sales, Earnings per Share, Dividends, and Book Value**

Company Name	Ticker	Industry	Market Cap ($ millions)
A. Top 5-Year Sales Growth			
Yahoo! Inc.	YHOO	Internet	105,405
Nextel Communic. 'A'	NXTL	Telecom. Svcs.	29,213
FirstEnergy Corp.	FE	Electric Util. (Central)	5,330
Texas Utilities	TXU	Electric Util. (Central)	9,968
Waste Management	WMI	Environmental	10,766
CenturyTel Inc.	CTL	Telecom. Svcs.	6,104
AES Corp.	AES	Electric Util. (Central)	14,524
Watson Pharmac.	WPI	Drug	3,304
Network Appliance	NTAP	Computer & Peripherals	11,532
BMC Software	BMCS	Computer Software & Svcs.	12,012
Averages			**20,816**
B. Top 5-Year EPS Growth			
Dell Computer	DELL	Computer & Peripherals	127,437
America Online	AOL	Internet	166,823
Coca-Cola Enterprises	CCE	Beverage (Soft Drink)	8,393
Coastal Corp.	CGP	Natural Gas (Diversified)	7,084
N.Y. Times	NYT	Newspaper	7,690
Tellabs Inc.	TLAB	Telecom. Equipment	24,790
Deere & Co.	DE	Machinery	10,238
KLA-Tencor	KLAC	Precision Instrument	8,666
Brunswick Corp.	BC	Recreation	1,934
Applied Materials	AMAT	Semiconductor Cap Equip.	43,802
Averages			**40,686**
C. Top 5-Year Dividend Growth			
Conseco Inc.	CNC	Insurance (Life)	5,540
Paychex Inc.	PAYX	Computer Software & Svcs.	9,662
Coca-Cola Enterprises	CCE	Beverage (Soft Drink)	8,393
Molex Inc.	MOLX	Electronics	3,811
Caterpillar Inc.	CAT	Machinery	17,418
Intel Corp.	INTC	Semiconductor	279,457
Cummins Engine	CUM	Machinery	1,930
Schwab (Charles)	SCH	Securities Brokerage	30,134
Archer Daniels Midland	ADM	Food Processing	7,111
Dollar General Corp.	DG	Retail Store	5,767
Averages			**36,922**
D. Top 5-Year Book-Value (Net Worth) Growth			
Clear Channel	CCU	Entertainment	28,762
America Online	AOL	Internet	166,823
Cisco Systems	CSCO	Computer & Peripherals	347,897
EMC Corp.	EMC	Computer & Peripherals	104,803
Safeway Inc.	SWY	Grocery	18,220
MCI WorldCom	WCOM	Telecom. Svcs.	143,995
Bed Bath & Beyond	BBBY	Retail (Special Lines)	4,387
Oracle Corp.	ORCL	Computer Software & Svcs.	145,215
Kohl's Corp.	KSS	Retail Store	11,152
Viacom Inc. 'A'	VIA	Entertainment	7,151
Averages			**97,841**

Data source: *Value Line Investment Survey for Windows,* January 2000.

TABLE 8.5 ***(continued)***

Sales Growth 5-Year (%)	EPS Growth 5-Year (%)	Dividend Growth 5-Year (%)	Book-Value Growth 5-Year (%)
173.1			
132.8			29.0
101.7	3.0		3.0
89.3		−7.0	−1.5
74.0	21.0		20.5
73.1	18.5	4.5	20.5
64.9	24.0		37.0
61.4			
60.9			
55.7	29.0		32.0
88.7	**19.1**	**−1.3**	**20.1**
49.9	86.0		34.0
46.6	76.5		61.0
14.5	74.0	38.5	7.0
−24.2	72.5	1.0	8.5
9.0	69.0	3.0	4.5
28.9	68.0		38.0
16.0	63.5	4.5	8.5
−28.7	59.5		30.0
4.7	53.0	2.5	8.0
−1.0	51.0		38.0
11.6	**67.3**	**9.9**	**23.8**
	10.5	56.5	24.5
20.2	36.5	50.0	29.0
14.5	74.0	38.5	7.0
4.8	17.0	38.5	11.5
14.2		38.5	14.5
2.9	34.0	38.0	28.0
11.4	15.5	37.5	17.0
18.2	26.5	35.0	32.0
−13.8	−2.0	33.0	8.0
21.6	31.5	31.0	26.5
10.5	**27.1**	**39.7**	**19.8**
44.4	46.0		89.5
46.6	76.5		61.0
37.3	49.0		60.0
33.4	50.5		48.5
5.8	38.5		45.0
19.1	19.5		41.5
29.8	34.0		40.0
26.1	43.5		39.5
19.8	27.5		39.0
−6.7	−10.0		38.5
25.5	**37.5**		**50.3**

WALL STREET WISDOM 8.3

What'n Heck Is a FASB?

The Financial Accounting Standards Board (FASB) is a nongovernmental body empowered by the Securities and Exchange Commission with responsibility for determining the nature and scope of accounting information. Started in 1973 as the logical successor to the Accounting Principles Board, the FASB develops new accounting standards in an elaborate process that reflects the views of accountants, business executives, security analysts, and the public. As a result, the FASB plays a key role in defining the specific information that must be incorporated in published corporate financial statements. FASB provides essential input concerning the framework for accounting balance sheets that define the current financial status of a company ("where it is") and for accounting income statements that show changes in a company's financial performance ("where it is going"). By standardizing the content and format of such reports, FASB helps managers run their businesses better and helps investors monitor their investments.

The FASB is also instrumental in the resolution of a broad range of important and controversial accounting issues. For example, the FASB plays a key role in the debate over accounting policy issues, including the controversy on whether to require firms to use current market values rather than historical-cost book values for accounts receivables, bonds, and intangible assets such as brand names and patents. This is a highly controversial issue, because the market-value approach would lead to a much different picture of corporate assets and liabilities for many companies.

Corporate executives typically resist the FASB's efforts to install new accounting rules, citing the higher operating expenses sometimes required to meet new guidelines. Most new standards require the capture of new data or the reworking of existing accounting information. At times, however, more subtle unspoken interests may be responsible for corporate opposition to new FASB standards. During inflationary periods, as has been the case in the United States since World War II, the use of historical book values tends to overstate net income numbers and to understate the value of tangible plant and equipment.

As a result, reported profit rates, such as the key return-on-stockholders'-equity measure, can be inflated when book-value data are used. Because of the effects of inflation, a market-value standard provides a more meaningful picture of "true" corporate profitability, but it typically results in lower profit rates. The fact that a market-value standard lowers reported profits is an important concern to many executives, especially those with compensation plans tied to reported profits.

One of the most important accounting innovations promoted by the FASB during recent years involves the cash-flow statements that all companies are now required to provide. By minimizing distortions that are sometimes introduced by imperfect accrual accounting methods, cash-flow data are intended to provide a clearer picture of current corporate performance. Needless to say, many corporations oppose cash-flow reporting requirements, especially when meeting them causes perceived (reported) performance to falter.

On Wall Street, some observers view ongoing disputes between the FASB and the corporate community on the accounting treatment of executive stock options, for example, as being based on a rather myopic view of the information-processing capability of both professional and institutional investors. Clearly, the takeover and corporate restructuring boom of the late 1980s was based on a sophisticated awareness of corporate cash flows, an awareness that preceded FASB cash-flow reporting requirements. Still, cash-flow statements help individual investors by providing them with another low-cost basis for evaluating corporate performance, whereas new reporting requirements allow investors to determine the economic impact of executive stock option grants.

Given the wide range of important accounting issues being addressed, the role played by the FASB has grown steadily. At times, the public perception of the FASB has failed to match this pace. This is changing as the FASB's public visibility increases. FASB-inspired guidelines allow companies to report assets and incomes that are closer to real economic values. For investors, more detailed disclosure of income, assets, and liabilities is an important benefit of standardized accounting rules.

See: Jim McTague, "Congress Could Block Move to Sink Pooling," *Barron's Online*, May 15, 2000. <http://www.wsj.com>

giant Coca-Cola Enterprises have notched stellar dividend growth during the past five years. However, just as EPS growth statistics can be distorted by one-time write-offs, dividend growth data can be overstated following dividend interruptions or initiations. It is imperative that investors consider these data carefully.

Finally, the rate of change in accounting book value per share over time is another useful indicator of corporate growth. Book-value growth generated internally stems from a rapid buildup in retained earnings. Investors must be cautious when book-value growth merely stems from accounting adjustments or other external factors. For example, rapid book-value growth sometimes simply reflects the effects of mergers or other corporate acquisitions. When book-value growth is accompanied by rapid sales growth, a favorable indication of the buildup in corporate value is provided. For example, fast book-value and sales revenue growth at radio, television, and billboard operator Clear Channel Communications, Inc., reflects dynamic growth in the scale of the operation. Similarly, vigorous book-value and revenue growth are evident for Cisco Systems and data storage behemoth EMC Corp.

Financial Statement Analysis

Balance Sheet

balance sheet "Snapshot" information about company financial well-being at a specific point in time.

Fruitful in-depth analysis of a given company starts with study of the firm's **balance sheet.** To see what is involved, consider the balance sheet and stockholders' equity statements for Microsoft Corp. given in Table 8.6. These data were obtained on the Internet from Microsoft's home page. Complete balance sheet information can be obtained from the company's annual report to shareholders or from Microsoft's annual 10-k report to the Securities and Exchange Commission (SEC). As is typical, Microsoft's annual report is available for viewing at the company's home page on the Internet. SEC reports for Microsoft and other publicly traded companies can be downloaded from the SEC's Internet Web site or <http://www.edgar.com>.

Microsoft's balance sheet information gives a "snapshot" of the company's financial well-being at a specific point in time. In this case, fiscal year-end information for 1998 and 1999 is provided, so some idea of the rate of change in financial condition is also given. Of course, according to accounting convention, total assets always equal the sum of total liabilities and stockholders' equity.

In terms of total assets, an important contribution from current assets, including cash and cash equivalents and inventories, can be detected. Total current assets account for more than one-half of Microsoft's total assets. Any rapid decline in cash or short-term investments might suggest problems with collections or accrual accounting problems with the estimation of operating expenses. Similarly, any rapid increase in accounts receivable would normally be cause for concern, especially if a buildup in older accounts receivable suggested collection problems. An unwanted rapid buildup in finished goods inventory might also be problematic. Such changes sometimes suggest softening product demand. However, no such problems are detected in the case of Microsoft. Microsoft has a very healthy balance sheet.

Also notice from Microsoft's balance sheet that stockholders' equity accounts for the bulk of company financing. Funds received from the sale of common stock, retained earnings, and miscellaneous accumulated income account for the

TABLE 8.6 Balance Sheet and Stockholders Equity Statements for Microsoft Corp., 1998–99 ($ millions)

A. Balance Sheet Statements, June 30	**1998**	**1999**
Assets		
Current assets:		
Cash and short-term investments	$13,927	$17,236
Accounts receivable	1,460	2,245
Other	502	752
Total current assets	15,889	20,233
Property and equipment	1,505	1,611
Equity and other investments	4,703	14,372
Other assets	260	940
Total assets	$22,357	$37,156
Liabilities and stockholders' equity		
Current liabilities:		
Accounts payable	$759	$874
Accrued compensation	359	396
Income taxes payable	915	1,607
Unearned revenue	2,888	4,239
Other	809	1,602
Total current liabilities	5,730	8,718
Commitments and contingencies		
Stockholders' equity:		
Convertible preferred stock—shares authorized 100; shares issued and outstanding 13	980	980
Common stock and paid-in capital—shares authorized 12,000; shares issued and outstanding 4,940 and 5,109	8,025	13,844
Retained earnings, including other comprehensive income of $666 and $1,787	7,622	13,614
Total stockholders' equity	16,627	28,438
Total liabilities and stockholders' equity	$22,357	$37,156

B. Stockholders' Equity Statements, Year Ended June 30	**1998**	**1999**
Convertible preferred stock		
Balance, beginning of year	$980	$980
Convertible preferred stock issued	—	—
Balance, end of year	980	980
Common stock and paid-in capital		
Balance, beginning of year	4,509	8,025
Common stock issued	1,262	2,338
Common stock repurchased	(165)	(64)
Structured repurchases price differential	328	(328)
Proceeds from sale of put warrants	538	766
Reclassification of put warrant obligation	—	—
Stock option income tax benefits	1,553	3,107
Balance, end of year	8,025	13,844
Retained earnings		
Balance, beginning of year	5,288	7,622
Net income	4,490	7,785
Other comprehensive income:		
Net unrealized investment gains	627	1,052
Translation adjustments and other	(124)	69
Comprehensive income	4,993	8,906
Preferred stock dividends	(28)	(28)
Common stock repurchased	(2,631)	(2,886)
Reclassification of put warrant obligation	—	—
Balance, end of year	7,622	13,614
Total stockholders' equity	$16,627	$28,438

Data source: Microsoft Corp.

financing of more than two-thirds of total assets. Total liabilities, including accounts payable, accrued compensation, income taxes payable, and unearned revenue, were used to finance less than one-third of the total assets. On an overall basis, Microsoft's use of financial leverage can be considered conservative.

Income and Cash-Flow Statements

income statement Ongoing view of dynamic change.

Whereas balance sheet information shows company financial well-being at a specific point in time, the company's **income statement** gives an ongoing view of dynamic change. If the balance sheet provides a snapshot of financial performance, then income and cash-flow statements provide the "video." In the case of Microsoft, operating information is provided in Table 8.7 for 1998–99. This is a standard format that gives investors an opportunity to judge the rate of change occurring in company operating performance.

The income statement begins with net revenues, typically defined as gross revenues minus returns, discounts, and allowances. Operating net income is the simple difference between net revenues and operating costs and expenses. In the case of Microsoft, major operating expense categories include research and development, sales and marketing, and general and administrative. Operating net income is increased by net interest income and other minor adjustments to arrive at net income before taxes.

After taxes have been deducted, net after-tax income is divided by the number of shares outstanding to arrive at basic earnings per share. This is an important indication of earnings-per-share performance but can sometimes prove misleading when a company issues a significant number of stock options to top executives and other employees. In Microsoft's case, management and employee stock options are

TABLE 8.7 **Income Statements for Microsoft Corp., 1998–99 ($ millions, except for per-share data)**

Year Ended June 30	1998	1999
Revenue	$15,262	$19,747
Operating expenses:		
Cost of revenue	2,460	2,814
Research and development	2,601	2,970
Acquired in-process technology	296	—
Sales and marketing	2,828	3,231
General and administrative	433	689
Other expenses	230	115
Total operating expenses	8,848	9,819
Operating income	6,414	9,928
Investment income	703	1,803
Gain on sale of Softimage, Inc.	—	160
Income before income taxes	7,117	11,891
Provision for income taxes	2,627	4,106
Net income	$4,490	$7,785
Earnings per share[1]:		
Basic	$0.92	$1.54
Diluted	$0.84	$1.42

[1]Earnings per share have been restated to reflect a two-for-one stock split in March 1999.
Data source: Microsoft Corp.

an important component of total compensation. As such, the potential dilution to the ownership position of current shareholders is significant. When the use of stock options is significant, investors focus their attention on diluted earnings-per-share numbers, rather than basic earnings per share.

To calculate the number of fully diluted shares, the company calculates the number of shares that would be outstanding if all stock options were converted into equity at the start of the year. It then assumes that proceeds received from management and other employees from the option exercise process would be used to repurchase stock at current market prices. Because the net effect of option exercises on the number of shares outstanding is always positive, the number of fully diluted shares is always greater than the number of shares outstanding. To calculate fully diluted earnings-per-share numbers, after-tax net income is simply divided by the number of fully diluted shares. In Microsoft's case, there is a measurable difference between basic earnings-per-share and diluted earnings-per-share numbers. Such differences can be even greater in the case of other high-tech compa-

TABLE 8.8 Cash-Flow Statements for Microsoft Corp., 1998–99 ($ millions)

Year Ended June 30	1998	1999
Operations		
Net income	$4,490	$7,785
Depreciation and amortization	1,024	1,010
Write-off of acquired in-process technology	296	—
Gain on sale of Softimage, Inc.	—	(160)
Unearned revenue	3,268	5,877
Recognition of unearned revenue from prior periods	(1,798)	(4,526)
Other current liabilities	208	966
Accounts receivable	(520)	(687)
Other current assets	(88)	(235)
Net cash from operations	6,880	10,030
Financing		
Common stock issued	959	1,350
Common stock repurchased	(2,468)	(2,950)
Put warrant proceeds	538	766
Preferred stock issued	—	—
Preferred stock dividends	(28)	(28)
Stock option income tax benefits	1,553	3,107
Net cash from (used for) financing	554	2,245
Investing		
Additions to property and equipment	(656)	(583)
Cash portion of WebTV purchase price	(190)	—
Cash proceeds from sale of Softimage, Inc.	—	79
Purchases of investments	(19,114)	(36,441)
Maturities of investments	1,890	4,674
Sales of investments	10,798	21,080
Net cash used for investing	(7,272)	(11,191)
Net change in cash and equivalents	162	1,084
Effect of exchange rates on cash and equivalents	(29)	52
Cash and equivalents, beginning of year	3,706	3,839
Cash and equivalents, end of year	3,839	4,975
Short-term investments	10,088	12,261
Cash and short-term investments	$13,927	$17,236

Source: Microsoft Corp.

nies that make even more extensive use of management and employee stock options. In any event, investors must focus on fully diluted numbers and beware of companies that aggressively dilute their ownership position through the granting of stock options.

Finally, although the income statement provides a vital measure of ongoing performance, accrual accounting errors or bias sometimes reduces its value as a measure of economic performance. In such instances, investors often look to the **cash-flow statement** for an interesting perspective on change in the company's economic position. As shown in Table 8.8, cash flow has three primary sources. Net cash is provided by operating, financing, and investing activities. Operating cash flow is the change in company liquidity as captured by net income plus noncash charges, such as depreciation and amortization. Adjustments to reconcile net income to cash provided by operating activities also include various changes in assets and liabilities. Cash flows provided by or used for financing activities include transactions involving purchase and/or sale of the company's own stocks and bonds. Cash flows provided by or used for investing activities include additions to plant and equipment, changes in short-term investments, and mergers and acquisitions. Taken together with the income statement, the cash-flow statement gives investors a clear view of the health of the company's ongoing operations.

cash-flow statement Change in the company's cash position.

Problems with Accounting Information

Historical Focus Problem

Accounting information is compiled in a logistical and consistent framework. Balance sheet data provide a historical record of the firm's past investments and the decisions made to finance those investments. Income statement information gives insight concerning the present flow of revenues and costs, as measured by using GAAP. Although such information is compiled in a coherent manner across firms and industries, the reliance on historical rather than forward-looking perspectives can sometimes create problems for investors.

When costs are calculated for a firm's income tax returns, the law requires use of the actual dollar amount spent to purchase the labor, raw materials, and capital equipment used in production. For tax purposes, **historical cost,** or actual cash outlays, is the relevant cost. This is also generally true for annual 10-k reports to the SEC and for reports to stockholders. Despite their usefulness, historical costs are not appropriate as a sole basis for many investment decisions. Current costs are typically much more relevant. **Current cost** is the amount that must be paid under prevailing market conditions. Current cost is influenced by market conditions measured by the number of buyers and sellers, the present state of technology, inflation, and so on. For assets purchased recently, historical cost and current cost are typically the same. For assets purchased several years ago, historical cost and current cost are different. Since World War II, inflation has been an obvious source of large differences between current and historical costs throughout most of the world. With an inflation rate of roughly 5% per year, prices double in less than 15 years and triple in roughly 22 years. Land purchased for $50,000 in 1970 often has a current cost in excess of $200,000. In California, Florida, Texas, and other rapidly growing areas, current costs run much higher. Just as no homeowner would sell his

historical cost Actual cash outlay.

current cost Amount that must be paid under prevailing market conditions.

or her home for a lower price based on lower historical costs, no firm can afford to sell assets or products for less than current costs. Similarly, investors must be able to adjust historical accounting information to account for the presence of undervalued or overvalued assets on the firm's balance sheet.

Historical costs provide a measure of the market value of an asset at the time of purchase. Current costs are a measure of the market value of an asset at the present time. Traditional accounting methods and the IRS rely heavily on the historical cost concept because it can be applied consistently across firms and is easily verifiable. However, when historical and current costs differ markedly, reliance on historical costs sometimes leads to investment decisions with disastrous consequences. The U.S. savings and loan (S&L) industry debacle during the late 1980s is a clear case in point. On a historical cost basis, almost all thrifts appeared to have solid assets to back up liabilities. On a current cost basis, however, many S&Ls proved insolvent because assets had a current market value below the current market value of liabilities. The move by federal and state bank regulators toward market value–based accounting methods is motivated by a desire to avoid S&L-type disasters in the future.

Although current costs usually exceed historical costs, this is not always the case. Computers and many types of electronic equipment cost much less today than they did just a few years ago. In many high-tech industries, the rapid advance of technology has overcome the general rate of inflation. As a result, current costs are falling. Current costs for computers and electronic equipment are determined by what is referred to as **replacement cost,** or the cost of duplicating productive capability by using current technology. For example, the value of used personal computers tends to fall by 25–30% per year. When investors value such assets, the appropriate measure is the much lower replacement cost—not the historical cost. Similarly, if a company holds electronic components in inventory, the relevant cost for pricing purposes is replacement cost.

replacement cost Cost of duplicating productive capability by using current technology.

Just as investors must be on the lookout for hidden "diamonds" on the company's balance sheet, so too must they take care not to miss hidden "lumps of coal." Corporate restructuring often involves eliminating nonstrategic operations to redeploy assets and strengthen core lines of business. When nonessential assets are disposed of in a depressed market, there is typically no relation between low "fire sale" proceeds and book value, historical cost, or replacement cost. Conversely, when assets are sold to others who can more effectively use such resources, sale proceeds can approximate replacement value and greatly exceed historical costs and book values. Even under normal circumstances, the link between economic and accounting values can be tenuous. Economic worth as determined by profit-generating capability, rather than accounting value, is always the most vital consideration when determining the investment value of specific assets.

The Problem of Overlooking Intangible Assets

Investors have come to learn that many of the most valuable assets owned by some corporations are its **intangible assets.** They have come to place an increasingly high value on corporate assets that can be neither seen nor touched, such as company reputation, brand names, patents, and copyrights. Over time, the physical plant and equipment recognized by traditional accounting methodology have become much less important, at least on a relative basis. During recent years, there has developed

intangible assets Valuable holdings that have no physical form.

a yawning gap between stock prices and the accounting book value of the firm. By the end of 1999, the P/B ratio for the S&P 500 Index exceeded a stunning 6.96:1. This means that investors place a value on the average S&P 500 stock that is almost seven times higher than the accountant's measure of book value. In other words, the accounting profession is struggling mightily to measure less than 15% of the assets judged important by investors.

In the case of large high-tech firms, the gap between stock prices and book values per share is even wider. For example, Microsoft Corp. has the largest market cap among the S&P 500 and sells at a P/B ratio of 19.3:1, GE's P/B is 11.8:1, Cisco's P/B is 24.8:1, and Wal-Mart sells at a P/B of roughly 11.6:1 (see Table 8.9). The average P/B ratio among the S&P market cap leaders is more than 14.5:1. This implies that for these gigantic corporations, accounting book values capture less than 7% of what investors value.

The failure of accounting methodology to capture investment value is even more apparent when one considers how common truly lofty P/B and P/E ratios are among high-tech companies included in the S&P 500. Even aside from the astronomic P/B ratios of the small-cap Internet and high-tech favorites, P/B ratios average almost 50:1 for rapidly growing firms that have captured the imagination of growth stock investors. What is especially noteworthy is the significant market

TABLE 8.9 Price-Book and Price-Earnings Ratios Are at Lofty Levels for the Largest Firms by Market Capitalization

Company Name	Ticker	Industry	Market Cap ($ millions)	P/B Ratio	P/E Ratio
Microsoft Corp.	MSFT	Computer Software & Svcs.	588,884	19.3	69.0
Genl Electric	GE	Electrical Equipment	470,140	11.8	41.9
Cisco Systems	CSCO	Computer & Peripherals	347,897	24.3	
Wal-Mart Stores	WMT	Retail Store	280,586	11.6	45.0
Exxon Mobil Corp.	XOM	Petroleum (Integrated)	280,388	4.5	26.0
Intel Corp.	INTC	Semiconductor	279,457	9.6	34.3
Lucent Technologies	LU	Telecom. Equipment	222,904	16.5	51.2
Intl Business Mach.	IBM	Computer & Peripherals	209,148	10.7	30.8
Citigroup Inc.	C	Financial Svcs. (Div.)	171,610	3.8	17.2
America Online	AOL	Internet	166,823	43.3	
AT&T Corp.	T	Telecom. Svcs.	162,765	2.2	26.0
Merck & Co.	MRK	Drug	158,508	12.3	26.0
SBC Communications	SBC	Telecom. Svcs.	153,301	10.0	20.2
Amer. Intl Group	AIG	Financial Svcs. (Div.)	153,044	4.7	28.7
Oracle Corp.	ORCL	Computer Software & Svcs.	145,215	41.5	88.7
MCI WorldCom	WCOM	Telecom. Svcs.	143,995	2.9	32.4
Coca-Cola	KO	Beverage (Soft Drink)	140,591	14.9	40.4
Home Depot	HD	Retail Building Supply	137,922	12.1	62.0
Procter & Gamble	PG	Household Products	135,524	12.8	31.6
Royal Dutch Petr.	RD	Petroleum (Integrated)	128,122		25.1
Dell Computer	DELL	Computer & Peripherals	127,437	29.6	60.9
Pfizer Inc.	PFE	Drug	120,737	13.7	33.2
Johnson & Johnson	JNJ	Medical Supplies	120,664	7.8	28.7
Nortel Networks	NT	Foreign Telecom.	119,283		78.2
Bristol-Myers Squibb	BMY	Drug	116,915	13.9	27.4
Averages			**203,274**	**14.5**	**40.2**

Data source: *Value Line Investment Survey for Windows,* January 2000.

capitalization of many of these high P/B ratio and P/E ratio stock market darlings. At the start of the new millennium, many investors have clearly decided that historical accounting book value and earnings information have little role to play in assessing the investment merit of individual issues.

To be fair, obvious practical problems involved with identifying and measuring intangible assets make setting clear and appropriate accounting standards difficult. Ultimately, the existence of intangible assets is measured by future economic benefits, not by any costs that might have been incurred at some point in the past. Anything that is commonly bought and sold has future economic benefit. For example, can you imagine an acquirer purchasing the trucks and distribution network of the Coca-Cola Company without also buying the rights to sell Coca-Cola? For the Coca-Cola Company, the Coca-Cola brand name is clearly its most valuable asset. Coca-Cola's flawless brand-name reputation explains the company's sterling profits and explains why the company sells at a P/B ratio of 14.9 : 1. Somehow, the accountant's book value of zero for the Coca-Cola brand name seems a little low.

Because advertising and research and development expenditures are immediately expensed rather than capitalized and written off over their useful lives, intangible assets can be grossly understated for many companies. The balance sheet of P&G does not reflect the hundreds of millions of dollars spent to establish and maintain the good reputation of Tide, just as Merck's balance sheet fails to reflect research dollars spent to develop important product names such as Mevacor, Prinivil, and Vasotec. As a result, accounting balance sheet information and income and cash-flow statements offer only a distorted view of true economic performance for many companies. Savvy investors become adept at carefully analyzing and adjusting traditional accounting statements for important "off balance sheet" and "off income statement" information.

Summary

- **Stock market investment** is the process of buying and holding for dividend income and long-term capital appreciation the shares of companies with inherently attractive economic prospects. Investors seek to profit by sharing in the normal and predictable good fortune of such companies. **Stock market speculation** is the purchase or sale of securities on the expectation of capturing short-term trading profits from share-price fluctuations tied to the perhaps temporary good fortune of a given company. Speculators depend on a short-term or fundamental change in the economic prospects facing a company.
- When evaluating business profits, many investors refer to the amount of **net income** generated, or **earnings per share.** Of course, net income is simply the difference between revenues and expenses, often expressed on an after-tax basis. Earnings per share is simply net income divided by the number of shares outstanding, referred to as **basic earnings per share,** or the amount of net income divided by the number of shares outstanding after consideration for the possible conversion of stock options, called **fully diluted earnings per share.**
- **Profit margins** show the amount of profit earned per dollar of sales. When profit margins are high, the company is operating at a high level of efficiency, competitive pressure is modest, or both. The **return on stockholders' equity** is defined as net income divided by the book value of **stockholders' equity,** which is

the book value of total assets minus total liabilities. ROE tells how profitable a company is in terms of each dollar invested by shareholders. Some savvy investors focus on the **return on assets,** or net income divided by the book value of total assets.

- **Total asset turnover** is sales revenue divided by the book value of total assets. When total asset turnover is high, the firm makes its investments work hard in the sense of generating a large amount of sales volume. **Leverage** is often defined as the ratio of the book value of total assets divided by stockholders' equity. It reflects the extent to which debt and preferred stock are used in addition to common stock financing.
- Financial economists suggest that the total market capitalization of common stock, or **market cap** for short, is the best available indicator of future profits. Firm size is also measured by **sales** or **revenue. Net worth** is the sum of common plus preferred stockholders' equity. It includes all intangible assets, such as goodwill and deferred charges, less current liabilities and long-term debt. It is a common measure of financial soundness because it measures the total amount committed to the enterprise by equity investors. **Book value per share,** calculated as common shareholder equity divided by the number of shares outstanding, measures the contribution of common stockholders. The largest firms by net worth and **total assets** include a number of giant financial institutions.
- The most common valuation yardstick used to measure relative value is the **price/earnings ratio,** or stock price divided by earnings per share. When a P/E ratio of 20:1 is paid, the **earnings yield,** or E/P ratio, is 5%. The **price/book ratio** shows the relationship between a stock's current price and its accounting net worth, in which accounting book value is simply total assets minus total liabilities. **Dividend yield** tells investors the amount of dividend income, which is expressed as a percentage of the amount paid for a stock. Dividends play an important role in determining the investor's **total return,** which is equal to the sum of dividend income plus capital appreciation.
- Whereas **balance sheet** information shows company financial well-being at a specific point in time, the company's **income statement** gives an ongoing view of dynamic change. Although the income statement provides a vital measure of ongoing performance, accrual accounting errors or bias sometimes reduces its value as a measure of economic performance. In such instances, investors often look to the **cash-flow statement** for an interesting perspective on change in the company's economic position.
- When costs are calculated for a firm's income tax returns, the law requires use of the actual dollar amount spent to purchase the labor, raw materials, and capital equipment used in production. For tax purposes, **historical cost,** or actual cash outlays, is the relevant cost. This is also generally true for annual 10-k reports to the SEC and for reports to stockholders. Despite their usefulness, historical costs are not appropriate as a sole basis for many investment decisions. Current costs are typically much more relevant. **Current cost** is the amount that must be paid under prevailing market conditions. Current cost is influenced by market conditions measured by the number of buyers and sellers, the present state of technology, inflation, and so on. Current costs for computers and electronic equipment are determined by what

is referred to as **replacement cost,** or the cost of duplicating productive capability by using current technology. Increasingly, investors have come to learn that the most valuable assets owned by corporations are its **intangible assets.**

Questions

1. Holding all else equal, ROE will fall with a rise in
   a. the book value of stockholders' equity.
   b. profit margin.
   c. sales.
   d. leverage.
2. An attractive measure of the firm's success in managing operating and financial leverage is the rate of
   a. return on assets.
   b. return on equity.
   c. return on sales.
   d. earnings-per-share growth.
3. ROE will fall with a rise in
   a. profit margin.
   b. total asset turnover.
   c. leverage.
   d. net worth.
4. Assume EPS = \$1, P = \$15, and P/B = 3. A retention rate of 60% implies sustainable growth of
   a. 6.7%.
   b. 12%.
   c. 40%.
   d. 60%.
5. Assume EPS = \$1, P = \$15, P/B = 3, and zero dividends. EPS in the coming year will equal
   a. \$1.20.
   b. \$1.00.
   c. \$3.00.
   d. \$2.00.
6. One of the problems with accrual accounting is that revenue can be reported without any increase in
   a. debt.
   b. cash.
   c. sales.
   d. accounts receivable.

7. Holding all else equal, the rate of growth made possible by internally generated funds rises with
   a. an increase in dividends.
   b. an increase in the Treasury bill rate.
   c. a decrease in total asset turnover.
   d. an increase in EBIDTA.
8. Free cash flow falls with a rise in
   a. depreciation.
   b. amortization.
   c. capital expenditures.
   d. sales.
9. Net income divided by the number of shares outstanding after consideration for the possible conversion of stock options is called
   a. earnings per share.
   b. basic earnings per share.
   c. fully diluted earnings per share.
   d. none of these.
10. Corporate restructuring charges can have the effect of boosting
    a. profit margins.
    b. net income.
    c. return on equity.
    d. stockholders' equity.
11. Select the one *true* statement from among the following:
    a. Following a 2:1 stock split, the market capitalization of the firm doubles.
    b. Following a 2:1 stock split, the market capitalization of the firm falls by one-half.
    c. Stock splits enhance the economic returns of a company.
    d. The earnings-per-share number at any point in time is somewhat arbitrary.
12. For a typical year during the post–World War II period, the average ROE tends to fall in a range between
    a. 4% and 6%.
    b. 8% and 10%.
    c. 12% and 14%.
    d. 20% and 25%.
13. Capital appreciation potential tends to be greater for firms with high
    a. earnings growth.
    b. price/earnings ratios.
    c. market cap.
    d. total assets.

14. Investor risk tends to rise with an increase in
    a. total asset turnover.
    b. earnings yield.
    c. price-earnings ratios.
    d. profit margins.
15. Over the long term, dividend income represents approximately what share of the total return earned on common stocks?
    a. nil.
    b. 12–14%.
    c. 33–50%.
    d. 75%.
16. A "snapshot" of the company's financial well being at a specific point in time is given by the
    a. balance sheet.
    b. income statement.
    c. cash-flow statement.
    d. none of these.
17. The cost of duplicating productive capability by using current technology is called
    a. historical cost.
    b. replacement cost.
    c. current cost.
    d. opportunity cost.
18. Price/earnings ratios for the market in general tend to fall in a range from
    a. 1–3%.
    b. 1:1 to 3:1.
    c. 5:1 to 10:1.
    d. 10:1 to 20:1.
19. At the start of the new millennium, the price/book ratio for the Standard & Poor's 500 Index
    a. equaled roughly 7:1.
    b. exceeded 32:1.
    c. was below historical norms.
    d. was near historical norms.
20. At the start of the new millennium, price/book ratios for Standard & Poor's 500 companies tended to be highest for firms with the highest
    a. dividend yields.
    b. market capitalization.
    c. sales.
    d. earnings yields.

Investment Application

Is Coca-Cola the "Perfect" Business?[2]

One of the most basic principles of investing is that, in the long run, investors can do no better than the businesses in which they invest. Common stock represents share ownership in the corporation and entitles the owner to a proportionate share of the company's earnings, dividends, and/or any proceeds in the event of a merger or dissolution. To make above-normal returns, investors must identify and invest in companies with above-normal business prospects. Moreover, these above-normal prospects must not be recognized in the marketplace and already be factored into the company's stock price. Ideally, one would like to identify and purchase shares in an undiscovered "perfect business." Thus, a fundamental question for any investor is simply: "What does a perfect business look like?"

For Warren Buffett and his partner Charlie Munger, vice chairman of Berkshire Hathaway, Inc., it looks a lot like Coca-Cola. To see why, imagine going back in time to 1885, to Atlanta, Georgia, and trying to invent something from scratch, a beverage perhaps, that would make you, your family, and all your friends rich.

Your beverage would be nonalcoholic to ensure widespread appeal among both young and old alike. It would be cold rather than hot so as to provide relief from climatic effects. It must be ordered by name—a trademarked name. Nobody gets rich selling easy-to-imitate generic products. It must generate a lot of repeat business through what psychologists call conditioned reflexes. To get the desired positive conditioned reflex, you will want to make it sweet, rather than bitter, with no aftertaste. Without any aftertaste, consumers will be able to drink as much of your product as they like. By adding sugar to make your beverage sweet, it gains food value in addition to a positive stimulant. To get extra-powerful combinatorial effects, you may want to add caffeine as an additional stimulant. Sugar and caffeine combine to give more than the sum of their parts—what Munger calls a "lollapalooza" effect. Additional combinatorial effects could be realized if you design the product to appear exotic. Coffee is another popular product, so making your beverage dark in color seems like a safe bet. By adding carbonation, a little fizz can be added to your beverage's appearance and its appeal.

To keep the lollapalooza effects coming, you will want to advertise. If people associate your beverage with happy times, they will tend to reach for it whenever they are happy or want to be happy. (Isn't that always, as in "Always Coca-Cola?") Make it available at sporting events, concerts, the beach, and at theme parks—wherever and whenever people have fun. Enclose your product in bright, upbeat colors that customers tend to associate with festive occasions (another combinatorial effect). Red and white packaging would be a good choice. Also, make sure that customers associate your beverage with festive occasions. Well-timed advertising and price promotions can help in this regard—annual price promotions tied to the Fourth of July holiday, for example, would be a good idea.

To ensure enormous profits, profit margins and the rate of return on invested capital must both be high. To ensure a high rate of return on sales, the price

---

[2]See Charles T. Munger, "How Do You Get Worldly Wisdom?," *Outstanding Investor Digest,* December 29, 1997, 24–31.

charged must be substantially above unit costs. Because consumers tend to be least price sensitive for moderately priced items, you would like to have a modest "price point," say, roughly \$1–\$2 per serving. This is a big problem for most beverages because water is a key ingredient, and water is very expensive to ship long distances. To get around this cost-of-delivery difficulty, you will not want to sell the beverage itself, but a key ingredient, such as syrup, to local bottlers. By selling syrup to independent bottlers, your company can also better safeguard its "secret ingredients." This also avoids the problem of having to invest a substantial amount in bottling plants, machinery, delivery trucks, and so on. This minimizes capital requirements and boosts the rate of return on invested capital. If you correctly price the key syrup ingredient, you can ensure that the enormous profits generated by carefully developed lollapalooza effects accrue to your company and not to the bottlers. Of course, you want to offer independent bottlers the potential for highly satisfactory profits to provide the necessary incentive for them to push your product. You not only want to "leave something on the table" for the bottlers in terms of the bottlers' profit potential, but they in turn must be encouraged to "leave something on the table" for restaurant and other customers. This means that you must demand that bottlers deliver a consistently high-quality product at carefully specified prices if they are to maintain their valuable franchise to sell your beverage in the local area.

If you had indeed gone back to 1885, to Atlanta, Georgia, and followed all of these suggestions, you would have created what you and I know as The Coca-Cola Company. To be sure, there would have been surprises along the way. Take widespread refrigeration, for example. Early on, Coca-Cola management saw the fountain business as the primary driver in cold carbonated beverage sales. They did not foretell that widespread refrigeration would make grocery store sales and in-home consumption popular. Still, much of Coca-Cola's success has been achieved because its management had, and still has, a good grasp of both the economics and the psychology of the beverage business. By getting into rapidly growing foreign markets with a winning formula, they hope to create local brand-name recognition, scale economies in distribution, and other "first-mover" advantages like the ones they have nurtured in the United States for more than 100 years.

As shown in Figure 8.5, in a world where the typical company earns 12–14% rates of return on invested capital, Coca-Cola earns three and four times as much. Typical profit rates, let alone operating losses, are unheard-of at Coca-Cola. It enjoys large and growing profits and requires practically no tangible capital investment. Almost its entire value is derived from brand equity derived from generations of advertising and carefully nurtured, positive lollapalooza effects. On an overall basis, it is easy to see why Buffett and Munger regard Coca-Cola as a "perfect" business.

A. One of the most important skills to learn in investments is the ability to identify a good business. Discuss at least four characteristics of a good business.

B. Identify at least four companies that you regard as having the characteristics listed above. Suppose you bought common stock in each of them. Three years from now, how would you know if your analysis was correct? What would convince you that your analysis was wrong?

FIGURE 8.5 **Is Coca-Cola the Perfect Business?**

COCA-COLA NYSE-KO

RECENT PRICE **57** | P/E RATIO **43.2** (Trailing: 46.0 Median: 26.0) | RELATIVE P/E RATIO **2.84** | DIV'D YLD **1.2%** | VALUE LINE

TIMELINESS 5 Lowered 3/5/99
SAFETY 1 New 7/27/90
TECHNICAL 4 Lowered 11/12/99
BETA 1.05 (1.00 = Market)

2002-04 PROJECTIONS

	Price	Gain	Ann'l Total Return
High	90	(+60%)	*13%*
Low	60	(+5%)	*3%*

Insider Decisions

	D	J	F	M	A	M	J	J	A
to Buy	1	0	0	0	0	0	0	0	0
Options	1	0	1	0	0	0	0	0	0
to Sell	2	0	1	0	1	0	0	1	0

Institutional Decisions

	4Q1998	1Q1999	2Q1999
to Buy	435	466	423
to Sell	455	451	483
Hld's(000)	1225717	1145400	1251705

High:	5.7	10.1	12.3	20.4	22.7	22.5	26.7	40.2	54.3	72.6	88.9	70.9
Low:	4.4	5.4	8.2	10.7	17.8	18.8	19.4	24.4	36.1	50.0	53.6	47.3

Target Price Range 2002 | 2003 | 2004

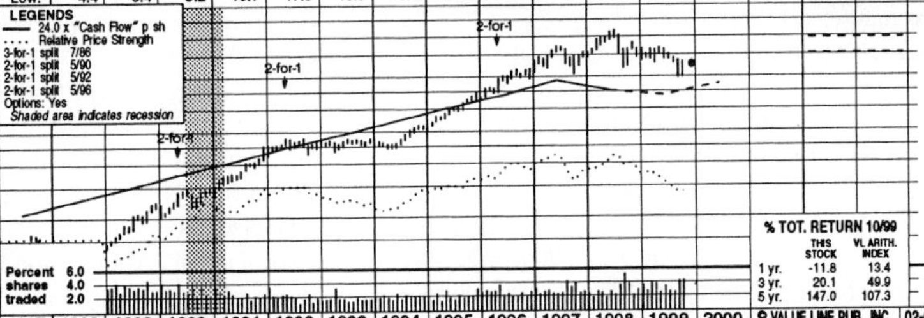

% TOT. RETURN 10/99

	THIS STOCK	VL ARITH. INDEX
1 yr.	-11.8	13.4
3 yr.	20.1	49.9
5 yr.	147.0	107.3

1983	1984	1985	1986	1987	1988	1989	1990	1991	1992	1993	1994	1995	1996	1997	1998	1999	2000	© VALUE LINE PUB., INC.	02-04
2.09	2.35	2.56	2.81	2.57	2.94	3.33	3.83	4.05	5.00	5.38	6.34	7.19	7.48	7.64	7.63	*8.00*	*8.55*	Sales per sh [A]	*11.70*
.22	.25	.28	.31	.36	.43	.50	.60	.71	.84	.98	1.16	1.37	1.60	1.92	1.69	*1.60*	*1.85*	"Cash Flow" per sh	*2.75*
.17	.20	.22	.26	.30	.36	.42	.51	.61	.72	.84	.99	1.19	1.40	1.64	1.42	*1.30*	*1.52*	Earnings per sh [B]	*2.35*
.11	.12	.12	.13	.14	.15	.17	.20	.24	.28	.34	.39	.44	.50	.56	.60	*.64*	*.68*	Div'ds Decl'd per sh [C] ■	*.92*
.12	.11	.16	.12	.10	.14	.17	.22	.30	.41	.31	.34	.37	.40	.44	.35	*.55*	*.60*	Cap'l Spending per sh	*.70*
.89	.88	.96	1.14	1.08	1.07	1.18	1.41	1.67	1.49	1.77	2.05	2.15	2.48	2.96	3.41	*3.40*	*3.45*	Book Value per sh [D]	*5.00*
3272.5	3139.8	3087.9	3080.1	2978.8	2838.3	2696.1	2673.0	2657.9	2613.7	2594.9	2551.9	2504.6	2481.0	2470.6	2465.5	*2460*	*2430*	Common Shs Outst'g [E]	*2360*
12.6	12.2	13.6	17.3	18.0	13.9	17.8	20.4	24.4	28.7	25.1	22.5	26.8	32.8	38.1	51.3	***Bold figures are Value Line estimates***		Avg Ann'l P/E Ratio	*30.0*
1.07	1.14	1.10	1.17	1.20	1.15	1.35	1.52	1.56	1.74	1.48	1.48	1.79	2.05	2.20	2.67			Relative P/E Ratio	*2.00*
5.2%	4.8%	4.2%	2.9%	2.6%	3.0%	2.3%	1.9%	1.6%	1.4%	1.6%	1.7%	1.4%	1.1%	.9%	.8%			Avg Ann'l Div'd Yield	*1.3%*
						8965.8	10236	11572	13074	13957	16172	18018	18546	18868	18813	*19700*	*20800*	Sales ($mill) [A]	*27600*
						21.3%	21.4%	22.3%	23.7%	24.8%	25.5%	25.2%	23.7%	29.8%	29.8%	*27.5%*	*28.5%*	Operating Margin	*30.5%*
						183.8	243.9	261.4	321.9	360.0	411.0	454.0	479.0	626.0	645.0	*700*	*750*	Depreciation ($mill)	*875*
						1192.8	1381.9	1618.0	1883.8	2188.0	2554.0	2986.0	3492.0	4129.0	3533.0	*3240*	*3740*	Net Profit ($mill)	*5620*
						32.4%	31.4%	32.1%	31.4%	31.3%	31.5%	31.0%	24.0%	31.8%	32.0%	*31.5%*	*31.5%*	Income Tax Rate	*31.5%*
						13.3%	13.5%	14.0%	14.4%	15.7%	15.8%	16.6%	18.8%	21.9%	18.8%	*16.4%*	*18.0%*	Net Profit Margin	*20.4%*
						d54.4	d153.7	26.6	d1056	d737.0	d972.0	d1898	d1496	d1410	d2260	*d2800*	*d3450*	Working Cap'l ($mill)	*d3000*
						548.7	535.9	985.3	1120.1	1428.0	1426.0	1141.0	1116.0	801.0	687.0	*785*	*875*	Long-Term Debt ($mill)	*1085*
						3485.5	3849.2	4425.8	3888.4	4584.0	5235.0	5392.0	6156.0	7311.0	8403.0	*8365*	*8350*	Shr. Equity ($mill)	*11715*
						30.2%	32.2%	30.6%	38.4%	37.7%	39.3%	46.5%	48.5%	51.2%	39.1%	*36.5%*	*41.5%*	Return on Total Cap'l	*45.0%*
						34.2%	35.9%	36.6%	48.4%	47.7%	48.8%	55.4%	56.7%	56.5%	42.0%	*38.5%*	*44.5%*	Return on Shr. Equity	*48.0%*
						22.0%	22.0%	22.1%	29.5%	28.5%	29.6%	34.8%	36.5%	37.5%	24.4%	*20.0%*	*25.0%*	Retained to Com Eq	*29.5%*
						41%	40%	40%	39%	40%	39%	37%	36%	34%	42%	*49%*	*44%*	All Div'ds to Net Prof	*39%*

CAPITAL STRUCTURE as of 6/30/99
Total Debt $6207.0 mill.
LT Debt $1104.0 mill. **LT Interest** $60.0 mill.
(Total interest coverage: 20x)
(10% of Cap'l)

Pension Liability None

Pfd Stock None

Common Stock 2,469,000,000 shs.
(90% of Cap'l)

MARKET CAP: $141 billion (Large Cap)

CURRENT POSITION ($MILL.)	1997	1998	6/30/99
Cash Assets	1843.0	1807.0	2364.0
Receivables	1639.0	1666.0	1913.0
Inventory (Avg Cst)	959.0	890.0	937.0
Other	1528.0	2017.0	1910.0
Current Assets	5969.0	6380.0	7124.0
Accts Payable	3249.0	3141.0	3228.0
Debt Due	3074.0	4462.0	5103.0
Other	1056.0	1037.0	1211.0
Current Liab.	7379.0	8640.0	9542.0

ANNUAL RATES of change (per sh)	Past 10 Yrs.	Past 5 Yrs.	Est'd '96-'98 to '02-'04
Sales	10.5%	9.0%	*7.5%*
"Cash Flow"	17.0%	15.5%	*8.0%*
Earnings	17.0%	15.5%	*8.0%*
Dividends	14.5%	14.0%	*9.0%*
Book Value	10.5%	12.5%	*9.0%*

Calendar	QUARTERLY SALES ($ mill.) Mar.31	Jun.30	Sep.30	Dec.31	Full Year
1996	4194	5253	4656	4443	18546
1997	4138	5075	4954	4701	18868
1998	4457	5151	4747	4458	18813
1999	4428	5379	5195	*4698*	*19700*
2000	*4700*	*5700*	*5450*	*4950*	*20800*

Calendar	EARNINGS PER SHARE [B] Mar.31	Jun.30	Sep.30	Dec.31	Full Year
1996	.28	.42	.39	.31	1.40
1997	.39	.52	.40	.33	1.64
1998	.34	.48	.36	.24	1.42
1999	.30	.38	.32	*.30*	*1.30*
2000	*.32*	*.47*	*.40*	*.33*	*1.52*

Calendar	QUARTERLY DIVIDENDS PAID [C] ■ Mar.31	Jun.30	Sep.30	Dec.31	Full Year
1995	--	.11	.11	.22	.44
1996	--	.125	.125	.25	.50
1997	--	.14	.14	.28	.56
1998	--	.15	.15	.30	.60
1999	--	.16	.16	.16	

BUSINESS: The Coca-Cola Company is the world's largest soft drink company. Distributes major brands (*Coca-Cola, Sprite, Fanta, TAB*, etc.) through bottlers throughout the world. Business outside North America accounted for 63% of net sales and 73% of profits in 1998. Food division, world's largest distributor of juice products (*Minute Maid, Five Alive, Hi-C*, etc.). Coca-Cola Enterprises, 45%-owned soft drink bottler. Advertising costs, 8.5% of sales. Has approximately 29,500 employees; 366,000 stockholders. Berkshire Hathaway owns 8.1% of stock (3/99 Proxy). 1998 depr. rate: 11.3%. Chrmn. and Chief Exec. Officer: M. Douglas Ivester. Inc.: Delaware. Address: One Coca-Cola Plaza, Atlanta, Georgia 30313. Tel.: 404-676-2121. Internet: www.thecoca-colacompany.com.

Coca-Cola's earnings were down again in the September quarter, as we had expected, but comparisons should begin to pick up before 1999 ends. Results this year have been hurt by the weak economic situation in much of the world (unit case sales of Coca-Cola's products were down in both the first and second quarters, but picked up in the third), by the continuing strength of the dollar, by quality control problems and related adverse publicity in Europe, and by extra marketing efforts to boost the company's business in European markets.

In June, the company's Belgian bottler recalled products after receiving reports that people had become sick from drinking Coca-Cola soft drinks. No one was reported to be severely ill, but quality control problems were discovered at two plants. Efforts to maintain quality have since been considerably strengthened, but lost sales were costly, expenses of the recall and subsequent marketing efforts have been high, and consumer confidence obviously suffered. It is impossible to say when confidence may be restored, but our assumption is that it will be sometime in 2000 before business returns to normal.

Our profit forecasts for both 1999 and 2000 have been coming down. We now think that Coke will earn $1.30 a share this year and that profits will rebound somewhat, probably to just over $1.50 a share, next year.

Looking out to 2002-2004, we think that Coke will again have steady earnings growth. While revenue growth in the U.S. will probably be in the 2%-4% range, we think Coke will have 8%-10% volume gains outside the U.S. There are still vast untapped markets in much of the world, and Coke has the experience, financial strength, and marketing capabilities to develop those markets. The recent purchase of many of Cadbury Schweppes' brands outside the U.S. will strengthen the breadth of the product line. With steady volume gains, moderate price increases, and a continuing stock buyback program, annual share earnings should rise 15%, or more. The stock's Timeliness rank remains low, however, because of the recent earnings shortfalls.

Stephen Sanborn, CFA November 12, 1999

(A) Includes Columbia Pictures: 1/83-12/86. (B) Based on primary shs. thru '96, diluted shs. thereafter. Next earnings report due mid-Jan. Excludes special gain: '86, 8¢; disc. op. gains (loss): '83, (1¢); '85, 2¢; '89, 2¢; nonrec. gain (loss): '89, 36¢; '92, (8¢). (C) Next div'd meeting about Feb. 22. Goes ex about Nov. 29. Div'd payment dates: April 1, July 1, Oct. 1, Dec. 15. ■ Div'd reinvestment plan avail. (D) Incl. intangibles. In '98: $547.0 mill., 22¢/sh. (E) In millions, adj. for stock splits.

Company's Financial Strength	A++
Stock's Price Stability	85
Price Growth Persistence	95
Earnings Predictability	80

©1999 Value Line Publishing, Inc.

Selected References

Ahn, Hee-Joon, and Yan-Leung Cheung. "The Intraday Patterns of the Spread and Depth in a Market without Market Makers: The Stock Exchange of Hong Kong." *Pacific-Basin Finance Journal* 7 (December 1999): 539–556.

Ang, James S., Rebel A. Cole, and James Wuh Lin. "Agency Costs and Ownership Structure." *Journal of Finance* 55 (February 2000): 81–106.

Arnold, Tom, and Jerry James. "Finding Firm Value without a Pro Forma Analysis." *Financial Analysts Journal* 56 (March/April 2000): 77–84.

Chordia, Tarun, Richard Roll, and Avanidhar Subrahmanyam. "Commonality in Liquidity." *Journal of Financial Economics* 56 (April 2000): 3–28.

Demirgüç-Kunt, Asli, and Vojislav Maksimovic. "Institutions, Financial Markets, and Firm Debt Maturity." *Journal of Financial Economics* 53 (July 1999): 295–336.

Deng, Zhen, Baruch Lev, and Francis Narin. "Science and Technology as Predictors of Stock Performance." *Financial Analysts Journal* 55 (May/June 1999): 20–32.

Dow, James, and Rohit Rahi: "Should Speculators Be Taxed?" *Journal of Business* 73 (January 2000): 89–107.

Goldstein, Michael A., and Kenneth A. Kavajecz. "Eighths, Sixteenths, and Market Depth: Changes in Tick Size and Liquidity Provision on the NYSE." *Journal of Financial Economics* 56 (March 2000): 125–149.

Griffiths, Mark D., Brian F. Smith, D. Alasdair, S. Turnbull, and Robert W. White. "The Costs and Determinants of Order Aggressiveness." *Journal of Financial Economics* 56 (April 2000): 65–88.

Hanson, Robert C., and Moon H. Song. "Managerial Ownership, Board Structure, and the Division of Gains in Divestitures." *Journal of Corporate Finance* 6 (March 2000): 55–70.

Lee, Charles M. C., and Bhaskaran Swaminathan. "Valuing the Dow: A Bottom-Up Approach." *Financial Analysts Journal* 55 (September/October 1999): 4–23.

Leibowitz, Martin L. "Franchise Labor." *Financial Analysts Journal* 56 (March/April 2000): 68–76.

Lim, Kian-Guan, Kie-Ann Wong, Wee-Yong Yeo, and Soo-Chen Wong. "Information and Liquidity Effects of Government Approved Stock Investments." *Pacific-Basin Finance Journal* 7 (December 1999): 523–538.

Linsmeier, Thomas J., and Neil D. Pearson. "Value at Risk." *Financial Analysts Journal* 56 (March/April 2000): 47–67.

Slovin, Myron B., Marie E. Sushka, and John A. Polonchek. "An Analysis of Contagion and Competitive Effects at Commercial Banks." *Journal of Financial Economics* 54 (October 1999): 197–225.

CHAPTER 9

Investment Environment

Wall Street economists make a living trying to forecast the economic environment in which the financial markets operate. During an economic expansion, sales increase, profits grow, and stock prices march upward. Interest rates also tend to rise during economic booms as firms increase their demand for credit to finance expanding inventories and capital spending for new plant and equipment. Technology stocks and cyclical stocks do especially well during periods of robust economic activity. During an economic downturn, the reverse happens, and both stock prices and interest rates usually move lower. As a result, accurate economic forecasts are powerful tools for investors.

Unfortunately, forecasting the link between the stock market and the economy has become especially difficult during recent years. Economists have come to appreciate that not only does a booming economy boost the stock market, but a booming stock market also boosts the overall economy. For several decades, many economists have accepted the idea that when investors see their wealth increase because of rising stock market or real estate values, they tend to spend somewhere between 2 and 4% of that new wealth the following year. Economists call this the "wealth effect." As the stock market roughly doubled during the late 1990s, the value of household wealth in equities also doubled. Even if investors still spend the same portion of each new dollar of wealth, the stock market has twice the impact on consumer spending as it did in 1995.

For much of the 19th century, the value of the stock market was mainly a reflection of the vigor and growth in the overall economy. In the new millennium, the wealth created by the stock market is both a reflection of the overall economy and a prime contributor to future growth.[1]

Dimensions of the Economy

Macroeconomic Environment

macroeconomics Study of aggregate measures of economic activity.

Macroeconomics is the study of aggregate measures of economic activity at the international, national, regional, or state level. Predictions of Gross Domestic Product (GDP), unemployment, and interest rates by "blue-chip" business economists

[1]See: Todd Buchholz, "How High Can Rates Go?," *The Wall Street Journal*, May 16, 2000, A26.

are examples of macroeconomic forecasts that capture the attention of national media, businesses, government, and investors on a daily basis. GDP measures the final market value of goods and services produced by all labor and property located in the United States. As such, GDP is a measure of aggregate business activity during a given period by both domestic and foreign-owned enterprises. Years ago, aggregate economic activity was measured by using Gross National Product (GNP), which is the value at the final point of sale of all goods and services produced in the United States by *domestic* firms. GNP does not reflect domestic production by foreign-owned firms (e.g., Toyota Camrys produced in Kentucky) and is a less useful measure of economic activity in the modern global economy.

Other macroeconomic forecasts commonly reported in the press include predictions of consumer spending, business investment, home building, exports, imports, federal purchases, and state and local government spending. These macroeconomic predictions are important because they are used by businesses and individuals to make day-to-day and long-term investment decisions. If interest rates are projected to rise, homeowners may rush to refinance fixed-rate mortgages, while businesses float new bond and stock offerings to refinance existing debt or take advantage of investment opportunities. When such predictions are accurate, significant cost savings or revenue gains become possible. When such predictions are inaccurate, higher costs and lost marketing opportunities occur.

Despite the obvious potential for significant benefits from accurate macroeconomic forecasts, many obstacles can limit its usefulness. The accuracy of any forecast is subject to the influence of controllable and uncontrollable factors. In the case of macroeconomic forecasting, uncontrollable factors loom large. Take interest rate forecasting, for example. The demand for credit and short-term interest rates rise if businesses seek to build inventories or expand plant and equipment or if consumers wish to increase installment credit. The supply of credit rises and short-term interest rates fall if the Federal Reserve System acts to increase the money supply or if consumers cut back on spending to increase savings rates. Interest rate forecasting is made difficult by the fact that business decisions to build inventory, for example, are largely based on the expected pace of overall economic activity—which itself depends on interest-rate expectations. The macroeconomic environment is interrelated in ways that are unstable and cannot be easily predicted. Even policy decisions are hard to predict. For example, Federal Reserve System policy meeting minutes are confidential until months after the fact. Is it any wonder that "Fed watching" is a favorite pastime of business economists?

Microeconomic Environment

microeconomics Study of economic data at the industry, firm, plant, or product level.

Microeconomics is the study of economic data at the industry, firm, plant, or product level. Unlike predictions of GDP growth, which are widely followed in the press, the general public often ignores microeconomic forecasts of scrap prices for aluminum, the demand for new cars, or production cost for Crest toothpaste. It is unlikely that the *CBS Evening News* will ever be interrupted to discuss an upward trend in used car prices, even though these data are excellent predictors of new car demand. When used car prices surge, new car demand often grows rapidly; when used car prices sag, new car demand typically drops. The fact that used car prices and new car demand are closely related is not surprising, given that new cars and used cars have a strong substitute-good relationship.

Trained and experienced analysts often find it easier to accurately forecast microeconomic trends, such as the demand for new cars, than macroeconomic trends, such as GDP growth. This is because microeconomic forecasts abstract from the profusion of important variables and variable interrelationships that together determine the macroeconomy. With specialized knowledge about changes in new car prices, car import tariffs, car loan rates, and used car prices, among other factors, it is possible to focus on the fairly narrow range of important factors that influence new car demand. By contrast, a similarly precise model of aggregate economic demand in the macroeconomy might involve literally thousands of economic variables and hundreds of functional relationships. This is not to say that microeconomic forecasting is easy and that forecast results are always precise. In late 1993, for example, the head of Ford forecast 1994 new car and truck demand of 14.5 million units, the head of General Motors forecast 14 million units, whereas the head of Chrysler forecast 16 million units. According to industry surveys, the actual number of new vehicles sold in 1994 was 15.4 million units. This was up from 14.2 million units in 1993 and roughly the same as industry sales of 15.5 million units in 1995 and 15 million units in 1996. Accurate auto and truck demand forecasting is tough even for industry experts.

Macroeconomic Forecasting

Business Cycles

The prime advantage gained from common stock investing is that it gives investors the opportunity to share in the benefits provided by economic growth. The profit and sales performance of all companies depends to a greater or lesser extent on the vigor of the overall economy. As shown in Figure 9.1, business activity in the United States expands at a rate of roughly 7.5% per year when measured in terms of GDP. With recent inflation averaging 4.5% per year, business activity has expanded at a rate of roughly 3% per year when measured in terms of inflation-adjusted, or real, dollars. During robust expansions, the pace of growth in real GDP can increase to an annual rate of 4–5% or more for brief periods. During especially severe recessions, real GDP can actually decline for an extended period. In the case of firms that use significant financial and operating leverage, a difference of a few percentage points in the pace of overall economic activity can make the difference between vigorous expansion and gut-wrenching contraction.

One of the most important economy-wide considerations for investors is the **business cycle,** or rhythmic pattern of contraction and expansion observed in the overall economy. Table 9.1 shows the pattern of business-cycle expansion and contraction that has been experienced in the United States throughout the post–World War II period. Between October 1945 and March 1991, there have been nine complete business cycles. The average duration of each cyclical contraction is 11 months when duration is measured from the previous cyclical peak to the low point or trough of the subsequent business contraction. The average duration of each cyclical expansion is 50 months, as measured by the amount of time from the previous cyclical trough to the peak of the following business expansion. Clearly, periods of economic expansion predominate, which indicates a healthy and growing economy.

business cycle Rhythmic pattern of contraction and expansion in the overall economy.

FIGURE 9.1 Gross Domestic Product, 1959–Present

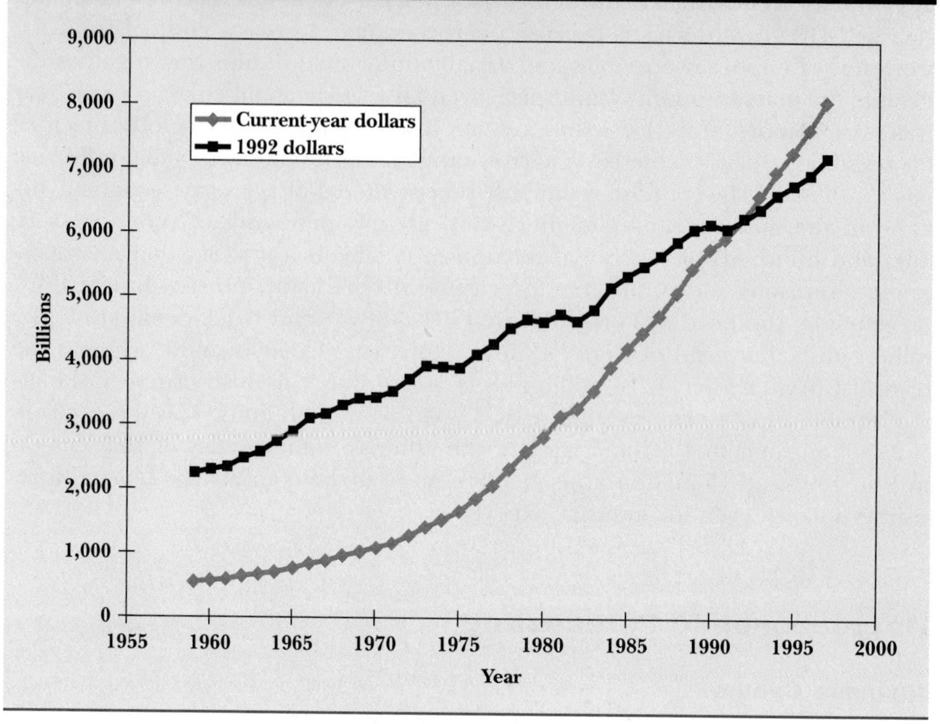

Data source: *Economic Report of the President,* February 2000.

TABLE 9.1 U.S. Business Cycle Expansions and Contractions

Post–WW II Period

Business Cycle Reference Dates		Duration in Months			
Trough	**Peak**	**Contraction**	**Expansion**	**T-T**	**P-P**
October 1945	November 1948	8	37	—	45
October 1949	July 1953	11	45	48	56
May 1954	August 1957	10	39	55	49
April 1958	April 1960	8	24	47	32
February 1961	December 1969	10	106	34	116
November 1970	November 1973	11	36	117	47
March 1975	January 1980	16	58	52	74
July 1980	July 1981	6	12	64	18
November 1982	July 1990	16	92	28	108
March 1991		8	—	100	—
Average, 1945–1991 (9 cycles)		**11**	**50**	**61**	**61**

Data source: The Conference Board Web site at <http://www.conferenceboard.org>.

On any given business day, a wide variety of news reports, press releases, and analyst comments can be found concerning the current state and future direction of the overall economy. The reason for intense interest is obvious. Whether the current economy is in a state of boom, moderate expansion, moderate contraction, or outright recession, there is sure to be widespread disagreement among analysts concerning current or future business prospects. This reflects the fact that, despite intense interest and widespread news coverage, the causes of economic contractions and expansions remain something of a mystery. *Why* the economy shifts from boom to bust and how such shifts might be predicted and controlled are still largely beyond our knowledge. Hopefully, the ever-increasing quality of economic data and the amazing power of computer hardware and software will unlock further mysteries of the business cycle during the next few years. In the meantime, changes in the pattern and pace of economic activity remain a matter for intense debate and conjecture.

Economic Indicators

Whereas cyclical patterns in most economic time series are erratic and make simple projection a hazardous short-term forecasting technique, a relatively consistent relation often exists among various economic variables over time. Even though many series of economic data do not exhibit a consistent pattern over time, it is often possible to find a high degree of correlation *across* these series. Should the forecaster have the good fortune to discover an economic series that leads the one being forecast, the leading series can be used as a barometer for forecasting short-term change, just as a meteorologist uses changes in a mercury barometer to forecast changes in the weather.

The Conference Board, a private research group, provides extensive data on a wide variety of **economic indicators,** or data series that successfully describe the pattern of projected, current, or past economic activity. Table 9.2 lists 10 leading, four roughly coincident, and seven lagging economic indicators of business-cycle peaks that are broadly relied on in business-cycle forecasting. Figure 9.2 shows the pattern displayed by composite indexes of these leading, coincident, and lagging indicators throughout the 1980s and 1990s. A **composite index** is a weighted average of leading, coincident, or lagging economic indicators. Combining individual data into a composite index creates a forecasting series with less random fluctuation, or noise. These composite series are smoother than the underlying individual data series and less frequently produce false signals of change in economic conditions. Notice how the composite index of leading indicators consistently turns down just prior to the start of each recessionary period. Similarly, notice how this data series bottoms out and then starts to rise just prior to the start of each subsequent economic expansion. Just as leading indicators seem to earn that description based on their performance, coincident and lagging indicators perform as expected over this period.

economic indicators
Data series that successfully describe the pattern of projected, current, or past economic activity.

composite index
Weighted average of leading, coincident, or lagging economic indicators.

The basis for some of these leads and lags is obvious. For example, building permits precede housing starts, and orders for plant and equipment lead production in durable goods industries. Each of these indicators directly reflects plans or commitments for the activity that follows. Other barometers are not directly related to the economic variables they forecast. An index of common stock prices is a good leading indicator of general business activity. Although the causal linkage may not

TABLE 9.2 Leading Economic Indicators and Related Composite Indexes

Composite indexes of leading, coincident, and lagging indicators are summary statistics for the U.S. economy. They are constructed by averaging individual components to smooth out the volatility of the individual series. Cyclical turning points in the leading index traditionally occur before those in aggregate economic activity. Cyclical turning points in the coincident index tend to occur at about the same time as those in aggregate economic activity, and cyclical turning points in the lagging index generally occur after those in aggregate economic activity.

Leading Index (10 Indicators)	**Standardization Factor (weight)**
Average weekly hours, manufacturing	.181
Average weekly initial claims for unemployment insurance	.025
Manufacturers' new orders, consumer goods and materials	.049
Vendor performance, slower deliveries diffusion index	.027
Manufacturers' new orders, nondefense capital goods	.013
Building permits, new private housing units	.018
Stock prices, 500 common stocks	.032
Money supply, M2	.308
Interest rate spread, 10-year Treasury bonds less federal funds	.329
Index of consumer expectations	.018
Coincident Index (4 Indicators)	
Employees on nonagricultural payrolls	.485
Personal income less transfer payments	.274
Industrial production	.131
Manufacturing and trade sales	.110
Lagging Index (7 Indicators)	
Average duration of unemployment	.038
Inventories to sales ratio, manufacturing and trade in 1992 dollars	.122
Labor cost per unit of output, manufacturing	.062
Average prime rate	.243
Commercial and industrial loans	.130
Consumer installment credit to personal income ratio	.218
Consumer price index for services	.187

be readily apparent, stock prices reflect aggregate profit expectations by investors and thus give a consensus view of the likely course of future business conditions. Thus, at any point in time, stock prices both reflect and anticipate changes in aggregate economic conditions. All of this makes macroeconomic forecasting particularly nettlesome for investors.

Information about Economic Trends

Investors commonly rely on surveys of business activity in various sectors of the economy to make informed judgments about vital economic trends. Surveys of business intentions to expand plant and equipment are conducted by the U.S. Department of Commerce, the Securities and Exchange Commission, the National Industrial Conference Board, and McGraw-Hill Inc., among others. Several trade associations also publish expenditure surveys for specific industries.

Some of the most readily available survey information is published regularly on the Internet and in leading business newspapers and magazines. For example, Figure 9.3 shows the range of useful information published on a weekly basis in

FIGURE 9.2 **Composite Indexes of 10 Leading, Four Coincident, and Seven Lagging Indicators (1987 = 100) (Shaded regions indicate an economic recession.)**

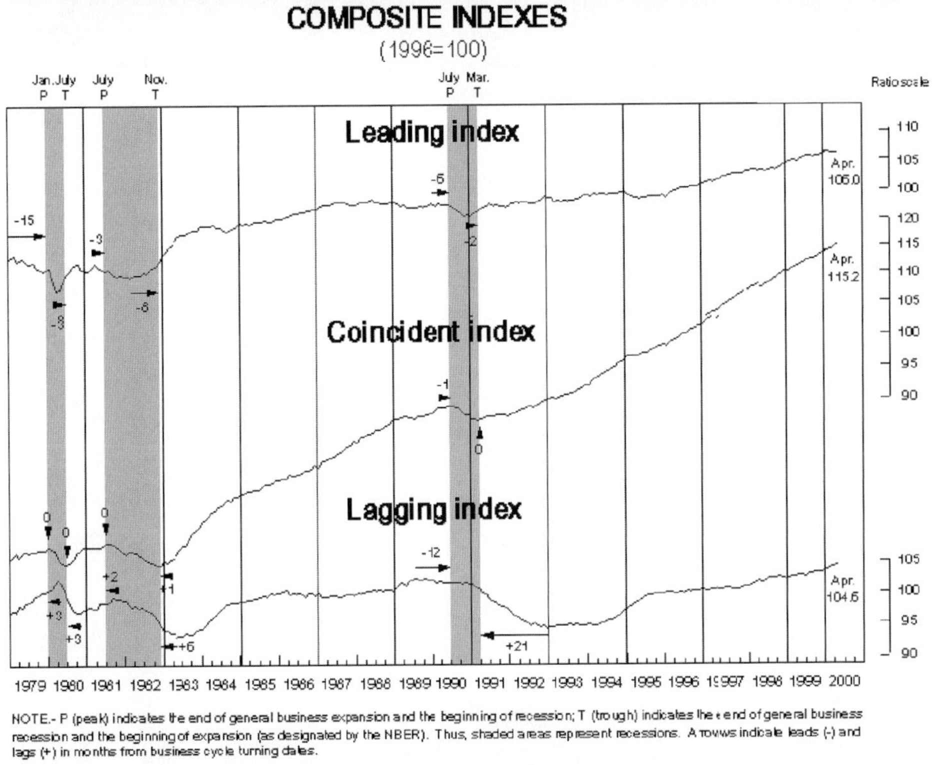

Source: The Conference Board Web site at <http://www.conference-board.org>.

Barron's business and financial weekly. *Barron's* "market laboratory" of economic indicators depicts the rate of change in the overall level of economic activity as indicated by GDP, durable and nondurable manufacturing, factory utilization, and other statistics. Also provided are specific data on the level of production in a wide range of basic industries such as autos, electric power, paper, petroleum, and steel. Data published weekly in *Barron's* include not only the level of production (what is made) but also distribution (what is sold), inventories (what is on hand), new orders received, unfilled orders, purchasing power, employment, and construction activity. *Forbes* magazine publishes its own biweekly index of economic activity using government data on consumer prices, manufacturers' new orders and inventories, industrial production, new housing starts, personal income, new unemployment claims, retail sales, and consumer installment credit. To measure these eight elements of the *Forbes Index,* 10 series of U.S. government data are monitored over a 14-month period.

Fortune and *Business Week* magazines also offer regular coverage of data on current and projected levels of economic activity. For instance, the quarterly *Fortune Forecast* of economic activity is based on a proprietary econometric model developed by the company's own staff economists. The forecast data and analysis published in

FIGURE 9.3 ***Barron's* Publishes Economic Indicator Data on a Weekly Basis**

MARKET LABORATORY • ECONOMIC INDICATORS

FEDERAL RESERVE DATA BANK

Member Bank Reserve Chgs. (Mil. $)	Latest Week	Prev. Week Change	Year Ago Change
One week ended March 1, 2000:			
U.S. Gov't securities:			
Bought outright	501,486	-707	+40,169
Held under repurch	....	....	-4,805
Federal agency secur:			
Bought outright	150	....	-186
Held under repurch	....	....	-3,478
Reserve bank credit:			
Adjustment credit	31	-11	+19
Seasonal borrowgs	+57	+5	+43
Extended credit	....	....	....
Float	903	-110	+1,223
Other F.R. Assets	32,793	+247	-1,425
Total Fed Credit #	556,770	-281	+52,912
Gold stock	11,048	....	+1
SDR Certif. Accounts	6,200	....	-3,000
Treas. Curr. Outst.	28,125	+14	+1,617
Total Acceptances	602,143	-268	+51,530
Currency in circ	563,836	-1,697	+51,329
Treas. Cash Hldgs	162	....	+41
Treas. Fed Deposits	5,090	-244	+116
Foreign Fed Deposits·	92	+11	-96
Other Fed Deposits	245	+7	-9
Serv Related bal.	6,917	-42	-113
Other FR liab/cap	18,807	-16	+2,287
Total factors	595,148	-1,983	+53,554
Reserves F.R. banks	6,995	+1,715	-2,024
Forgn hold U.S. debt	r704,579	+4,442	N.A.

Reserve Aggregates (Mil. $ sa)			
Two Weeks Ended March 1, 2000:			
Total Reserves	41,144	42,699	43,984
Nonborrowed Res#	41,045	42,585	43,872
Required Res##	39,952	41,552	42,751
Excess Reserves	1,192	1,147	1,232
Borrowed Reserves	100	114	112
Free Reserves###	1,092	1,033	1,120
Monetary Base	571,177	575,511	520,984

#Fed supply of permanent reserves provided.
##Demand for reserves to back deposits.
###Free reserves equal excess reserves minus discount window borrowings other than extended credit. Free reserves are a shorthand method of determining the degree of ease of Fed policy, or when they are negative net borrowed reserves, tightness.
r-Revised by Fed to include Federal Agency Securities in addition to U.S. Government Securities.

FEDERAL RESERVE KEY ASSETS & LIABILITIES

U.S. Banks (Bil. $)	Latest Week	Prev. Week Change
Week ended February 23, 2000:		
Key Assets:		
Bank Credit	3,567.9	+ 14.9
Comm/industrial loans	1,027.7	+ 5.0
Loans to individuals	504.7	+ 1.4
Real estate loans	1,507.8	+ 5.3
Home equity loans	113.0	+ 0.7
US Govt securities	804.2	+ 7.1
Other securities	453.6	+ 2.6
Key Liabilities:		
Transaction deposits	632.4	+ 25.2
Savings/other deposits	2,938.6	− 12.7
Includes large deposits	849.0	− 9.6

MONEY SUPPLY

Money Supply(Bil.$ sa)	Latest	Prev.	Yr. Ago
Week ended Feb 21:			
M1 (seas. adjusted)	1105.6	1101.8	1098.8
M1 (not adjusted)	1094.8	r1090.9	1084.7
M2 (seas. adjusted)	4691.8	r4687.1	4459.7
M2 (not adjusted)	4684.7	r4692.0	4437.5
M3 (seas. adjusted)	6546.7	r6532.1	6101.2
M3 (not adjusted)	6559.4	r6562.5	6092.7

Monthly Money Supply	Latest	Prev.	Yr. Ago
Month ended Jan:			
M1 (seas. adjusted)	1122.0	r1125.4	1090.4
M2 (seas. adjusted)	4684.3	r4661.2	4425.1
M3 (seas. adjusted)	6523.1	r6479.4	6030.4

ST. LOUIS FED MONETARY BASE

Monetary Base (Bil. $)	Latest 2 Wks	Prev. 2 Wks	Year Earlier
Two Weeks Ended Feb 21:			
Monetary Base	592.262	592.271	537.544

ADJUSTABLE MORTGAGE BASE RATES

	Feb 25	Feb 18	Yr. Ago
1-Year Treas Bills	6.22	6.23	4.82
2-Year Treas Notes	6.54	6.65	5.05
3-Year Treas Notes	6.57	6.71	5.09
5-Year Treas Notes	6.59	6.74	5.11
10-Year Treas Notes	6.38	6.55	5.18
30-Year Treas Bonds	6.13	6.23	5.49
11th District %Jan	4.901	4.852	4.608
FHFB Contract Rate	7.79	7.79	6.77
SAIF Cost-of-Funds	4.60	4.60	4.74

Source: Fed annualized yields adjusted for constant maturity. FHRB-Federal Housing Finance Board. SAIF-Savings Association Insurance Fund.

MONEY FUND REPORT

Taxable Funds Feb 29	Last Week	Prev. Week	Year Ago
Asset Levels, Bil $	1,430.97	1,425.04	1,224.97
Maturity, days	49	49	61
7-day comp yld,%	5.40	5.37	4.47
7-day simple yld,%	5.27	5.23	4.37
30-day comp yld,%	5.36	5.32	4.46
30-day simple yld,%	5.22	5.19	4.36

Tax-Exempts Feb 28	Last Week	Prev. Week	Year Ago
Asset Levels, Bil $	208.78	209.06	195.05
Maturity, days	39	41	42
7-day comp yld,%	3.17	3.07	2.45

Source: IBC Financial Data, Inc., a subsidiary of IBC USA (Publications) Inc. 290 Eliot Street, Ashland, Mass. 01721 800-343-5413.

Money Market Funds# (Bil.$)	Latest Week	Prev. Week	Year Ago
Total Assets Mar 1	1,679.0	r1,679.3	1,456.0

Source: Investment Company Institute, 1401 H Street NW, Suite 1200, Washington, D.C. 20005-2148 (202) 326-5800.

MONEY RATES

	Latest Week	Prev. Week	Yr Ago Week
Discount Rate(NY)	5¼	5¼	4½
Prime Rate(base)	8¾	8¾	7¾
Fed Funds Rate			
Avg effective offer	5⅞	5¾	5
Avg weekly auction-c	5.72	5.75	4.75
T-Bills Rate			
13 weeks, Coupon Yield	5.831	5.818	4.70
13 weeks, Auction Rate	5.67	5.64	4.57
26 weeks, Coupon Yield	6.022	6.038	4.772
26 weeks, Auction Rate	5.765	5.765	4.585
52 weeks, Coupon Yield	6.197	6.287	4.918
52 weeks, Auction Rate	5.84	5.905	4.665
Avg weekly auction-c	5.62	5.55	4.53
Broker Call Rate	7½	7½	6½
CD's Rate			
3 months	5.43	5.53	4.73
6 months	5.71	5.80	4.98
Commercial Paper Rate			
Dealer-placed			
1 month	5.80	5.78	4.85
2 months	5.88	5.85	4.85
3 months	5.92	5.90	4.85
Directly placed (GE Capital)			
30 to 46 days	5.80	5.76	4.83
221 to 270 days	6.07	6.07	4.85
Bankers Acceptances			
1 month	5.83	5.77	4.80
2 months	5.88	5.86	4.80
3 months	5.93	5.89	4.81
6 months	6.06	6.02	4.85
Libor Eurodollar Rate			
3 months	6.12	6.10125	5.03
6 months	6.34	6.3325	5.12688
12 months	6.76375	6.795	5.42875
Foreign Prime Rates			
Canada	6.75	6.75	6.75
Germany	3.25	3.25	3.08
Japan	1.375	1.375	1.50
Switzerland	3.625	3.75	3.25
Britain	6.00	6.00	5.50
Other Money Rates			
Eurodollar avg.-c	6.02	6.00	4.88
Freddie Mac Home Loan-b:			
30-Year Fixed Conv	8.16	8.28	7.07
1-Year Adjust Mtg	6.875	6.875	5.625
Fannie Mae Home Loan-b:			
30-Year Fixed Conv	8.28	8.32	7.06
1-Year Adjust Mtg	7.40	7.40	5.95
Merrill Ready Assets	5.34	5.33	4.46
Bank money market-z	2.07	2.07	2.14
Interest Checking	0.83	0.84	0.97
6-Month Certif-z	4.74	4.70	4.07
12-Month Certif-z	5.11	5.10	4.25
30-Month Accounts-z	5.41	5.40	4.30
5-Year Certificates-z	5.71	5.67	4.44
U.S. Savings EE Bonds:			
Long-Term (5 yrs+)	5.19	5.19	4.60

Sources: a-Prebon Yamane (USA) Inc. b-Telerate. c-Annualized yields, adjusted for constant maturity reported by the Federal Reserve on a weekly average basis. z-Bank Rate Monitor.

INVESTOR SENTIMENT READINGS

In Investors Intelligence's poll, the correction figure represents advisers who are basically bullish, but are looking for some sort of short-term weakness. High bullish readings in that poll, in Consensus Inc., or in Market Vane's usually are signs of market tops; low ones, market bottoms.

Investors Intelligence

	Last Week	Two Weeks Ago	Three Weeks Ago
Bulls	52.2%	51.8%	53.7%
Bears	28.3	28.6	26.9
Correction	19.5	19.6	19.4

Source: Investors Intelligence, 30 Church Street, New Rochelle, N.Y. 10801 (914) 632-0422.

Consensus Index

Bullish Opinion	27%	27%	35%

Source: Consensus Inc., 1735 McGee Street, Kansas City, Mo. 64108 (816) 471-3862.

AAII Index

Bullish	37%	41%	27%
Bearish	23	31	24
Neutral	40	28	48

Source: American Association of Individual Investors, 625 N. Michigan Ave., Chicago, Ill 60611 (012) 200-0170.

Market Vane

Bullish Consensus	34%	30%	41%

Source: Market Vane, P.O. Box 90490, Pasadena, CA 91109 (626) 395-7436.

BARRON'S GOLD MINING INDEX

12-month High	12-month Low		3/02	2/24	Year Ago	Week % Chg.
433.68	297.75	Gold mining	304.02	323.28	310.66	−5.96

GOLD & SILVER PRICES

Handy & Harman	3/03	2/25	Year Ago
Gold, troy ounce	288.50	294.00	287.90
Silver, troy ounce	5.08	5.13	5.22

Base for pricing gold or silver contents of shipments and for making refining settlements.

Coins	Price	Premium $	Premium %
Krugerrand	290.30	2.00	.69
Maple Leaf	291.30	3.00	1.04
Mexican Peso	349.30	1.40	.49
Austria Crown	284.60	2.00	.71
Austria Phil	291.30	3.00	1.04
U.S. Eagles	291.30	3.00	1.04

Premium is the amount over the value of the gold content in the coin.
ScotiaMocatta Bullion spot gold price 288.30

PLATINUM COIN PRICES

Coins	Coin Price Per Ounce	Premium $	Premium %
Australian Koala	468.50	5.00	1.08
Canadian Maple Leaf	468.50	5.00	1.08
Isle of Man Noble	468.50	5.00	1.08
Amer. Eagle Bullion	473.50	10.00	2.16

Premium is the amount over the value of the platinum content in the coin.
Spot platinum price 463.50. Source: Goldline Int'l, Santa Monica, CA. 800-827-4653
www.GoldlineInternational.com

TOP SAVINGS DEPOSIT YIELDS

Money Market Account[1]

Institution	Location	Telephone No.	Min. Deposit	Recent % Rate		Effect. % Yield
Heritage Bk, N.A.	Willmar,MN	(800)344-7048	75000	5.93	(CM)	6.10
Resource Bank	Virginia Bch	(877)726-5463	10000	5.90	(CM)	6.06
Cross Country Bank	Wilmingtn,DE	(800)334-3180	25000	5.89	(CM)	6.05
Bankfirst	Sioux Fls,SD	(800)328-2411	15000	5.85	(CM)	6.01
BankDirect	Dallas,TX	(877)839-2737	500	5.83	(CD)	6.00

One-Year CDs

Institution	Location	Telephone No.	Min. Deposit	Recent % Rate		Effect. % Yield
BankDirect	Dallas,TX	(877)839-2737	2000	6.67	(CD)	6.90
Net.Bnk&@	Atlanta,GA	(888)256-6932	1000	6.64	(CD)	6.86
Advanta Ntl Bank	Wilmingtn,DE	(800)441-7306	10000	6.63	(CD)	6.85
Bank Caroline	Greenville,S	(877)692-2765	500	6.63	(CD)	6.85
AcaciaBank	San Mateo,CA	(888)837-7400	10000	6.61	(CD)	6.83

Five-Year CDs

Institution	Location	Telephone No.	Min. Deposit	Recent % Rate		Effect. % Yield
Provident Bank	Cincinnati,O	(800)335-2220	1000	7.32	(CD)	7.70
Key Bank USA	Albany,NY	(800)872-5553	5000	7.30	(CD)	7.57
Providian Bank	Manchstr,NH	(800)414-9693	10000	7.26	(CD)	7.53
Providian Natl Bk	Tilton,NH	(800)821-9049	10000	7.26	(CD)	7.53
Savingsbot.com	Las Vegas,NV	(877)833-4248	10000	7.18	(CD)	7.44

Six-Month CDs[2]

Institution	Location	Telephone No.	Min. Deposit	Recent % Rate		Effect. % Yield
Bank Caroline	Greenville,S	(877)692-2765	500	6.30	(CD)	6.50
BankDirect	Dallas,TX	(877)839-2737	2000	6.30	(CD)	6.50
First Internet Bk of	Indianapolis	(888)873-3424	1000	6.25	(CM)	6.43
New South Fed	Birminghm,AL	(800)366-3030	5000	6.30	(SI)	6.40
Arkansas Ntl Bank	Bentnville,A	(501)271-2800	10000	6.25	(CD)	6.40

2½-Year CDs

Institution	Location	Telephone No.	Min. Deposit	Recent % Rate		Effect. % Yield
Key Bank USA	Albany,NY	(800)872-5553	5000	7.05	(CD)	7.30
Providian Bank	Manchstr,NH	(800)414-9693	10000	6.93	(CD)	7.18
Providian Natl Bk	Tilton,NH	(800)821-9049	10000	6.93	(CD)	7.18
Advanta Ntl Bank	Wilmingtn,DE	(800)441-7306	10000	6.91	(CD)	7.15
Net.Bnk&@	Atlanta,GA	(888)256-6932	1000	6.91	(CD)	7.15

90-Day Jumbo CDs

Institution	Location	Telephone No.	Min. Deposit	Recent % Rate		Effect. % Yield
NextBank, N.A.	San Francisc	(877)879-3353	100000	6.50	(SI)	6.66
Bluebonnet Savings	Dallas,TX	(800)892-6151	50000	6.28	(CM)	6.46
New South Fed	Birminghm,AL	(800)366-3030	50000	6.15	(SI)	6.29
BSB Bank & Trust	Binghmtn,NY	(888)245-7272	95000	6.11	(SI)	6.29
Providian Bank	Manchstr,NH	(800)414-9693	95000	5.94	(CD)	6.12

Rates are the highest yields on six types of accounts offered by federally-insured banks and savings associations nationwide. Yields are based on the stated rate and compounding method in effect Friday and are subject to change. Phone to verify before investing or sending money.

(CC) Compounded continuously
(CD) Compounded daily
(CM) Compounded monthly
(CQ) Compounded quarterly
(CSA) Compounded semiannually
(CA) Compounded annually
(SI) Simple interest

[1]Including passbook, statement savings, and bank-offered liquid asset accounts.
[2]Six-month CD yields assume reinvestment of principal and interest at the same rate for an additional six month.
Source: RateGram, a publication of the Bradshaw Financial Network. P.O.Box 9104, Ashland, MA 01721-9104. On The internet at www.ibcdata.com CompuServe: Go RateGram.

Source: *Barron's Market Week,* March 6, 2000, MW73.

these leading business periodicals provide investors with a useful starting point in the development of their own future expectations.

Problem of Changing Expectations

A subtle problem that bedevils both macroeconomic and microeconomic forecasting is the problem of changing expectations. If business purchasing agents are optimistic about future trends in the economy and boost inventories in anticipation of surging customer demand, the resulting inventory buildup can itself contribute to economic growth. Conversely, if purchasing agents fear an economic recession and cut back on orders and inventory growth, they themselves can be main contributors to any resulting economic downturn. The expectations of purchasing agents and other managers can become a self-fulfilling prophecy because the macroeconomic environment represents the sum of the investment and spending decisions of business, government, and the public. Indeed, the link between expectations and realizations has the potential to create an optimistic bias in government-reported statistics.

Government economists are sometimes criticized for being overly optimistic about the rate of growth in the overall economy, the future path of interest rates, or the magnitude of the federal deficit. As consumers of economic statistics, investors must realize that it can pay for government economists or politically motivated economists to be optimistic. If business leaders can be led to make appropriate decisions for a growing economy, their decisions can, in fact, help lead to a growing economy. Unlike many business economists from the private sector, government-employed and/or politically motivated economists often actively seek to manage the economic expectations of business leaders and the general public.

It is vital for investors to appreciate the link between economic expectations and realizations and to be wary of the potential for forecast bias.

Population Growth and Demographics

Population Growth

The growing value of the stock market is tied to economic growth, and population growth is a prime contributor to economic growth. As shown in Figure 9.1, GDP in the United States expands at a rate of roughly 7.5%. With 4.5% inflation, real business activity expands about 3% per year. Historically, about one-third of the annual rate of expansion in real GDP, or 1% of GDP growth per year, can be explained by population growth. The remaining two-thirds, or 2%, of GDP growth per year, is explained by productivity growth. Productivity growth is simply technical change as captured by the ability of a fixed amount of labor, capital, and equipment to produce a growing amount of output. Before turning our attention to productivity growth, it is important to understand population growth as an important component of understanding what makes the economy and the stock market grow over time.

Today, the world population is roughly six billion persons. A large number of these, perhaps 3.5 billion, live in Asia. More than 700 million individuals live in Africa and in Europe. Another 325 million or so live in South America. In North

WALL STREET WISDOM 9.1

The New Economy

It used to be that an economic recession might come along about once every five years or so. In 1990, the overall economy went into a short mild recession caused by high oil prices and economic uncertainty tied to the Gulf War Crisis. The economy then boomed and a typical economic recovery ensued. By 1994–95, it would have been common to expect another business slowdown as inflation heated up and rising interest rates began to choke off new investment. However, powerful new microprocessors led to a burst of innovation from the computer industry and throughout all industry as businesses began to take advantage of powerful new desktop computers. In the normal course of events, this would merely postpone the onset of the next recession for a few years, to say 1998–99. Then, something wonderful happened. Another new burst of business productivity tied to the growing public use of the Internet extended an already very long economic recovery. The result? Instead of slowing down, the economy continued to chug along, spurred by unprecedented gains in productivity. By February 2000, the United States marked a new economic era—the longest economic expansion in history. Robust economic growth and full employment without inflation. This was not an Old Economy, or even a Cinderella Economy; this was the New Economy.

Has a technological revolution truly created a New Economy? Maybe, maybe not. To be sure, computers and automation have allowed even old-style companies to become more productive with fewer employees. Moreover, it seems that even as those old-style companies fire unneeded or unwanted employees, new high-tech and entrepreneurial organizations are taking up the slack. Even in the midst of dramatic corporate restructuring, employment stays high, consumers remain confident, and spending continues to be robust, at least for the time being. However, it is important to recognize that the laws of demand and supply have not been repealed. It is also worth remembering that economic shocks tied to unexpected interruptions in supply still lead to dislocations that can create economic imbalances. Without seeking to appear ominous, it is perhaps worth recalling the supreme confidence of the 1920s, which led to widespread belief that good times could go on forever. That also was a time of a momentous technological revolution.

The introduction of electricity into everyday lives is perhaps the single most important business innovation to date. It was clearly more important and exciting than the introduction of personal computers and the Internet. Electricity brought a huge boost in productivity when factories could run day and night with powerful new machinery. It also made the assembly-line concept a reality for thousands of new workers. Fewer employees could produce a seemingly endless supply of new consumer goods. More than 3,000 new automobile companies were launched, and a continuous stream of new electric products improved life for both rural dwellers and city-bound consumers. The catch phrase of the day was "New Era," and economists proudly proclaimed a new era of sustained economic prosperity. Without minimizing the wondrous benefits brought by the technological revolution of the 19th century, it is important to remember that it created both longer economic booms and more extreme excesses. Fortuitous investment often gave way to rampant speculation. Sharp declines in financial markets were experienced as those excesses were eliminated.

In the new millennium, it is perhaps worth remembering that economic change is typically accompanied by hard-to-predict shifts in the competitive environment and financial markets. Although everyone seems well aware of what happens to Old Economy companies that fail to keep up, New Economy technology-related companies are especially susceptible to change in the competitive landscape. Mature companies that ignore the Internet and other means of serving customers better, cheaper, and faster invite daunting competition. Like dinosaurs, they wither and die. For high-tech companies, the "survival of the fittest" process is approaching warp speed.

Are we in a New Economy? Of course we are. The economy is in a constant process of dynamic change and revitalization. To be successful, investors must be aware of the opportunities presented, and the risks.

See: Robert McGough, "New Economy Looks at Old and Sees Gold," *The Wall Street Journal,* March 17, 2000, C1, C2.

America, which includes the United States, Canada, and Mexico, the population is roughly 450 million persons.

The world's population exceeded five billion persons for the first time in 1987 and is rising at about 1.7% a year. At this rate of growth, the global population will exceed 10 billion by the year 2030. This rapid rate of growth is often referred to as the world's population explosion. However, population growth rates vary dramatically over different parts of the world. In developing continents, such as Africa, the average age is very young and the population is growing at about 3% per year. In Europe, where population is growing little if at all, the average age of the population is much older. In the United States, the population is growing at a rate of about 1.1% a year.

In 1790, the first population census of the United States discovered about four million persons living in the country. Today, the U.S. population is roughly 265 million, or about 5% of the world's population. The growth of our population was most rapid during the 1790–1860 period. Another time of rapid growth was from 1946 to 1964, when the growth rate reached as high as 1.8% per year. This latter period is often referred to as the "Baby Boom" generation. Baby Boomers totaled about 76.8 million births, followed by 52.4 million in "Generation X" (1965–78) and more than 78 million in "Generation Y" (since 1979). As today's rate of growth of 1.1% per year, about one-third of the growth in U.S. population over time comes from immigration.

Although rapidly growing populations generally have the effect of boosting economic progress, many have been worried about population growth. For example, in the late 1700s, a famous economist by the name of Thomas Malthus was concerned that the population might increase beyond the limits of the earth's ability to support it. Malthus predicted that famine and war would become common unless the world's population was controlled. Since Malthus's dire prediction, the world's population has grown by some four billion persons while economic well-being has increased dramatically. It is easy to see why. The production of food, raw materials, and finished products has grown at a rate faster than the rate of growth in the overall population. So long as economic growth exceeds population growth, economic betterment results.

Demographics

One of the most important trends to affect the economy over the next generation is the graying of America. By the year 2020, the nation's Baby Boomers will range in age from 56 to 74. The benefits of a maturing population in terms of increased savings and added productivity are obvious, but some stock-market prognosticators have raised concern that a demographic "time bomb" is set to explode. Some have raised the concern that Boomers will cause a market crash as they dump stocks and bonds to finance their retirement and strain Social Security and Medicare to the breaking point.

Although such a grim scenario for the economy and stock and bond markets is remotely possible, current trends make such an outcome extremely unlikely. The most likely scenario is that Boomers will play a joke on the pundits by refusing to retire at 65 or earlier. In fact, the whole concept of retirement as we now know it may go out of style. Leading demographers predict that the number of working Boomers will achieve such critical mass that even subtle age discrimination in employment will end. Many Boomers are apt to stay on the payroll because they like to work. More will find that they cannot afford to retire. Even a slight delay in the average retirement age would result in a large tax windfall for Social Security and Medicare and huge benefits for stock and bond markets and the overall economy.

If they delay retirement, Boomers can also be expected to delay selling financial assets. As it is, the Internal Revenue Service offers senior citizens huge incentives to avoid realizing capital gains. Under current tax law, the tax basis or theoretical cost for those who inherit stocks and bonds is set at the point of death for the person making the inheritance. This means that any capital gains tax liability owned on highly appreciated stocks and bonds is effectively wiped out when such assets are retained until death. Heirs pay capital gains taxes only on any appreciation earned after the time of inheritance. This means that the dreaded selling wave for stock and bonds may be postponed until after the Boomers have departed this world and, with improved health and longevity, even that departure is expected to be delayed.

If Boomers delay their retirement, the combined output of millions of experienced workers could keep fueling economic growth. *Barron's* reports that more than 80% of all Baby Boomers plan to remain employed for financial reasons or simply because they enjoy working. For many, the plan to keep working reflects poor financial planning. Most have set aside far too little to fund a comfortable retirement. At the same time, the age at which one qualifies for full Social Security System benefits is gradually rising. Anyone born from 1943 to 1954 will not qualify until age 66. For anyone born in 1960 or later, the minimum age requirement will be 67. And while 62 will still be the earliest age at which one can collect reduced benefits, a 62-year-old will eventually receive only 70% of full benefits, rather than the current 80%. Moreover, Social Security is creating new incentives for older people to keep working. The age at which recipients could earn any amount without loss of benefits was reduced from 72 to 70 in 1983. In 1990, there was a reduction in the benefit loss, from 50 to 33 cents, for each dollar earned over the exempt amount among recipients over the customary retirement age of 65. Since 2000, full benefits are received after age 65 irrespective of earned income.

For many senior citizens, the "golden years" concept is long dead. Most demand a vital role in American life. As shown in Figure 9.4, labor force participation rates among older men have halted their long-term decline. For most older women, they have recently been on the increase. Long-term projections assume that by the year 2020, participation rates for men will have climbed back to 1964 levels, and that for women, rates will equal 1999 rates for men. These projections are conservative in that they fall well below the percentage of Baby Boomers who say they plan to work in their retirement years. Chances are that economy-wide labor shortages will become a semipermanent fact of life, providing aging Boomers with another reason to stay on the payroll. By 2020, there will be several million fewer persons aged 35–54 than there are today, even though many more jobs will need to be filled. This will motivate companies to make accommodations to attract and keep older employees. All in all, it is a safe bet that negative economic and

FIGURE 9.4 **Labor Force Participation Rates Are Apt to Soar as Baby Boomers Postpone Retirement**

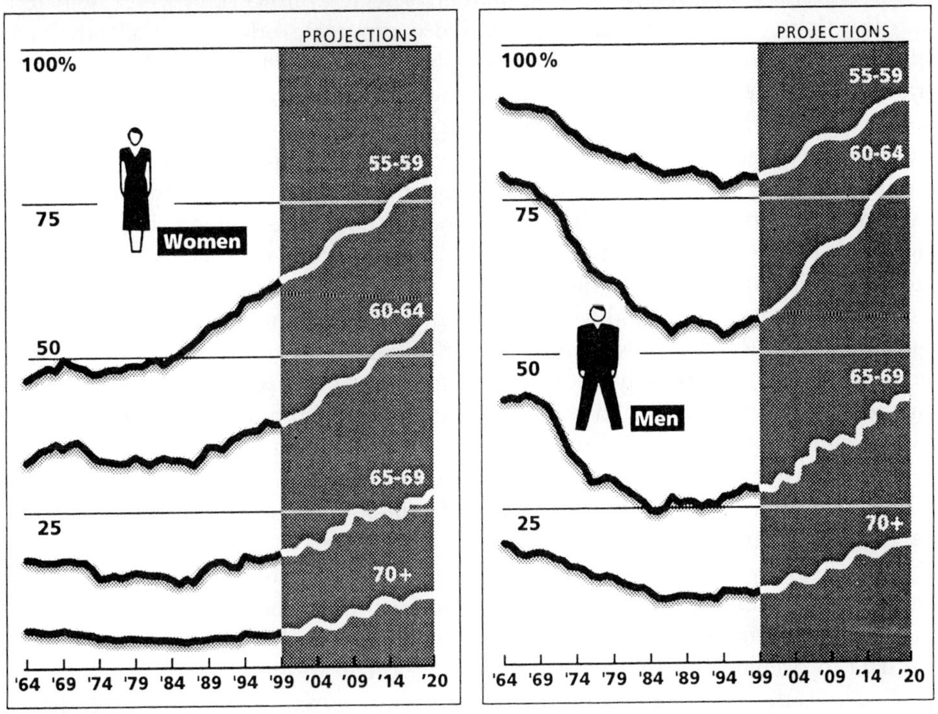

Source: *Barron's,* September 6, 1999: 28.

financial market effects tied to the aging of the Baby Boom generation have been greatly exaggerated.

Productivity Growth

Productivity Surveys

To provide detailed annual statistics on the location, activities, and products of U.S. manufacturers, the U.S. Commerce Department conducts mandatory annual surveys. Coverage is comprehensive. The total value of shipments (or sales revenue) by manufacturing establishments covered in the *Annual Survey of Manufacturers* is \$3 trillion, or roughly one-half of the GDP. Basic data obtained include kind of business, location, ownership, value of shipments, payroll, and employment. Also collected are data on the cost of materials, inventories, new capital expenditures, fuel and energy costs, hours worked, and payroll supplements.

The *Annual Survey of Manufacturers* has been a prominent feature of the federal government's annual data gathering activity since 1949. This annual study takes the form of a mail survey of roughly 55,000 selected manufacturing establishments.

This information is supplemented with administrative data for small employers and new businesses. Roughly 25,000 large establishments of multidivisional companies with shipments worth at least $500 million are selected with certainty. Also selected with certainty are manufacturers of selected computer products and all other establishments with at least 250 employees each. Another 30,000 establishments, generally with 20–250 employees per establishment, are selected with a probability that is proportional to each unit size's rate of occurrence in the overall population of manufacturers. Sometimes called a "stratified sample," representation within this group of 30,000 selected establishments is such that the collected manufacturing data will be representative of the entire cross section of manufacturing establishments. To ensure representative coverage, the mail survey universe is updated annually by using Internal Revenue Service administrative records.

Statistics collected for industry groups and industries include the value of shipments, value added (or sales minus the cost of goods sold), inventories, materials, employment, hours, and payroll. Geographic area reports provide additional data for the United States and each state. So-called value of shipments reports estimate sales revenues for about 1,750 product classes and multi-industry products, with a delay of approximately 12 months. Reports on exports from manufacturing establishments estimate the value of exports and related employment by industry and state, with a delay of about 36 months.

These survey data have many uses. The Bureau of Labor Statistics uses this information to calculate annual productivity series, update producer price indexes, and calculate weights for new index components. The Federal Reserve Board uses the data to prepare the Index of Industrial Production; the Bureau of Economic Analysis uses the data to prepare annual GDP updates and weights for GDP deflators. The Department of Commerce's International Trade Administration uses the export data to evaluate and forecast industrial activity. State and local agencies use the data to design trade and economic policies. Private industry and trade associations use it to plan operations, analyze markets, and make investment and production decisions.

Changes in Productivity Growth

productivity growth
Pace of economic betterment.

One of the most prominent uses of economic survey information is to track the pace of economic betterment, or **productivity growth,** in the overall economy. Productivity growth is the rate of increase in output per unit of input. For example, if the amount of output produced in the economy were to grow by 5% following only a 2% increase in the quantity of inputs used, then the overall rate of productivity growth would be roughly 3%. When productivity growth is robust in the overall economy, economic welfare per capita rises quickly. When productivity growth is sluggish, economic welfare improves slowly. If productivity growth is robust for individual companies or within specific industry groups, superior efficiency is suggested and exceptional profitability often ensues. Thus, the rate of productivity growth is important both for managers and investors in individual companies and for decision makers in the public sector.

Productivity growth has been relatively slow in the United States since the early 1970s (see Figure 9.5). From the mid 1970s to the mid 1990s, annual rises in nonfarm business productivity averaged only 1.1%, a drastic decline from the previously typical annual rate of roughly 3%. This slowdown is similar in timing and

FIGURE 9.5 **Actual and Trend Labor Productivity**

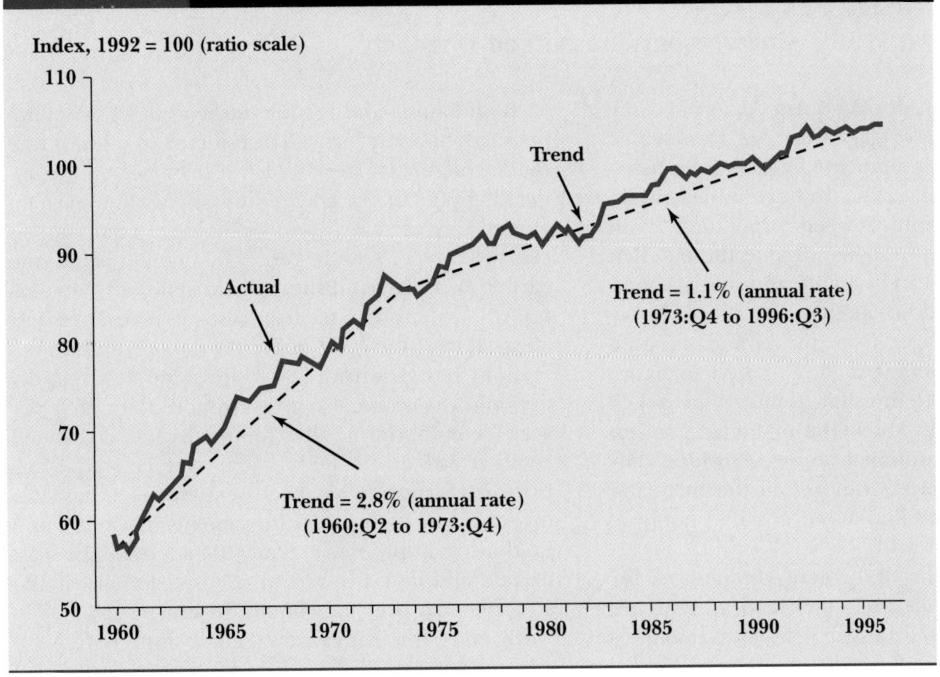

Data source: *Economic Report of the President* (U.S. Government Printing Office, Washington, D.C., 1997): 29.

magnitude in many advanced industrial economies. As a result, it cannot be explained by purely domestic factors.

Slower growth of inputs, both physical and human capital, is not a major cause of the productivity slowdown. The U.S. capital-labor ratio has grown a bit more slowly since 1973, but only enough to account for roughly one-tenth of the approximately 2% decrease in productivity growth. Moreover, the rate of increase of human capital, as measured by the average education level and experience of workers, has actually increased since the 1950s and 1960s. Human capital growth is now responsible for roughly one-quarter of total productivity growth, up from only 3% during prior periods. Although policies to increase investment, education, and training are important, they do not address the underlying causes of the recent productivity slowdown.

From an accounting perspective, almost the entire productivity slowdown in the United States is attributable to a decrease in the efficiency with which capital and labor are used. During the 1950s and 1960s, abnormally rapid productivity growth stemmed from the civilian use of government-funded innovation inspired by the World War II effort. Important examples include the digital computer, advances in electronics, and nuclear energy. Increased investment in science, such as the Internet and communications technology in general, is an effective means for helping increase the nation's productivity. Currently, hopes run high that the Internet-based burst in productivity (3%-plus per year in the late 1990s) will prove lasting.

WALL STREET WISDOM 9.2

Government-Guaranteed Oligopoly

The Federal National Mortgage Association and the Federal Home Loan Mortgage Corp., or Fannie Mae and Freddie Mac, enjoy immense benefits from being government-sponsored entities that are also for-profit, publicly traded, stockholder-owned corporations. Both are huge and highly profitable, despite the fact that they operate in a relatively simple and low-risk business. Fannie and Freddie purchase roughly $500 billion in home mortgages from thrifts and other financial institutions every year. Most of these loans are packaged and resold to investors as mortgage-backed securities, thus enabling home buyers to tap pension funds and other institutional money. Provided they qualify, U.S. home buyers can get all the financing they need in the most liquid and efficient home finance market in the world.

Fannie and Freddie are potent competitors for banks, savings and loans, and other lenders. Both are considering expansion into such markets as home equity lending and housing for the elderly, and Fannie has test-marketed construction lending programs for home builders. Fannie has also lent millions of dollars in home equity conversion loans, or "reverse mortgages," to people over 62 who have paid off most of their original mortgages. Fannie has also begun financing developers in the construction of single-family and multifamily homes. It is no surprise that competing financial institutions are unhappy about continued Fannie and Freddie expansion. They claim that the firms compete unfairly because they get a subsidy from the U.S. government.

Fannie and Freddie, as government-sponsored enterprises, get noncash subsidies worth *billions* of dollars per year. Both have implied U.S. government guarantees on all their liabilities. This earns them the highest possible credit ratings on their debt securities and allows them to attract institutional investors at the lowest possible interest rate. Although the U.S. government charges nothing for its implied credit guarantee, Fannie and Freddie together reap more than $10 billion per year in profits. In no small part, the amazingly good profit performance of Fannie and Freddie comes from the fact that they enjoy much lower interest costs on borrowed funds than the amount paid by their purely private-sector competitors.

Both Fannie and Freddie make a profit by selling packages of home loans to investors at an interest rate that is roughly 1% per year lower than that on the underlying pool of mortgages. In so doing, they earn an annual rate of return on stockholders' equity in excess of 20% per year, or nearly double the profit rate earned by financial institutions in general. These extraordinary profit rates have also remained remarkably stable as the scale of Fannie's and Freddie's operations has grown rapidly. During the past decade, earnings per share also grew by more than 15% per year for both; during the coming decade, continued profit growth of 15–18% per year is anticipated. Stock price performance has been sensational. Long-term investors saw their initial investments in Fannie and Freddie multiply more than 10-fold over the past decade and look forward to continued gains of 12–15% per year over the coming 10-year period.

By congressional charter, Fannie and Freddie are supposed to provide liquidity to the mortgage market and help low-income and moderate-income families purchase adequate housing. Indeed, Fannie Mae has committed to guarantee loans to low-income renters with excellent credit. At the same time, to ensure a rapidly growing market for their services, Congress has allowed Fannie and Freddie to underwrite single-family home mortgages in excess of $200,000 each. This angers private-sector competitors because, in effect, taxpayers are subsidizing households that make more than $100,000 a year and can afford $250,000 homes. The fact that Fannie's and Freddie's implicit federal subsidies are "off the books" also concerns budget watchers concerned with the federal deficit.

In light of such criticism, Congress is pushing stronger capital requirements for Fannie and Freddie and asking them to earmark more loans for low-income and moderate-income families. Despite such limits, Fannie and Freddie are likely to continue to prosper. There are clearly tangible rewards to government-guaranteed oligopoly!

See: Allison Krampf, "Fannie Mae, Freddie Mac Regulatory Worries Overdone," *Barron's Online*, May 15, 2000. (See <http://www.wsj.com>).

Competitive Environment

Investment Strategy in Hotly Competitive Markets

The firm's competitive environment is described by the **market structure** it faces. Market structure includes the number and size distribution of buyers and sellers, degree of product differentiation, **potential entrants,** cost of information about product price and quality, and conditions of entry and exit. Effects of market structure are measured in terms of firm profits and investor rates of return, prices paid by consumers, availability and quality of output, and the pace of product innovation, among other factors. Generally speaking, the greater the number of market participants, the more vigorous is price and product quality competition. Similarly, the more even the balance of power between sellers and buyers, the more likely it is that the competitive process will result in meager business profits and poor investor returns.

market structure Important industry characteristics.

potential entrants Individuals or firms posing a sufficiently credible threat of market entry to affect the price/output decisions of incumbant firms.

The most typical source of above-normal profits in perfectly competitive industries is called **disequilibrium profits.** Disequilibrium profits are above-normal returns earned in the interval between the time when a favorable influence on industry demand or cost conditions first occurs and when competition fully develops. **Disequilibrium losses** are below-normal returns suffered in the time interval that can arise between when an unfavorable influence on industry demand or cost conditions first transpires and when exit or downsizing finally occurs. When barriers to entry and exit are minimal, competitor reactions tend to be quick and disequilibrium profits are fleeting. When barriers to entry and exit are significant, competitor reactions tend to be slow and disequilibrium profits can persist for extended periods. In the quintessential perfectly competitive industry, disequilibrium profits are quickly dissipated. In real-world markets, disequilibrium profits can persist over an entire business cycle even in the most competitive industries. In retailing, for example, labor and inventory costs have been cut dramatically following the introduction of computerized price scanners. Despite the vigorously price-competitive nature of the retailing business, early innovators who first adopted the bar code technology were able to earn above-normal profits for a number of years. Innovative grocery retailers have enjoyed dramatically lower costs and profit margins on sales of 2–3.5%, versus a more typical 1%, over a decade and more.

disequilibrium profits Above-normal returns earned in the interval between a favorable change in the economic climate and full competitor response.

disequilibrium losses Below-normal returns earned in the interval between a favorable change in the economic climate and full competitor response.

As shown in Table 9.3, hotly competitive markets offer investors the potential for a normal risk-adjusted rate of return on investment during typical market conditions. If many capable competitors offer identical products, vigorous price competition tends to eliminate above-average profits. The only exception to this rule is that superior efficiency can sometimes lead to superior profits, even in perfectly competitive markets. Hamburger chain McDonald's Corp. and discount retailer Wal-Mart Stores, Inc., for example, have succeeded in providing investors with above-average rates of return in vigorously competitive industries. However, they are the exception. How many restaurant chains can you name that have achieved outstanding long-term success for investors? How many local and regional retailers has Wal-Mart put out of business?

Investment Strategy in Imperfectly Competitive Markets

Most industries and lines of business offer some blend of competition and **monopoly;** they represent business opportunities in imperfectly competitive markets. Developing and implementing an effective investment strategy in imperfectly

monopoly A single seller.

TABLE 9.3 Market-Structure Characteristics in Hotly Competitive and Imperfectly Competitive Markets

	Hotly Competitive	Imperfectly Competitive
Number of actual or potential competitors	Many sellers	Only one or few sellers whose decisions are directly related to those of competitors
Product differentiation	Consumers perceive few differences among the products of various competitors	Usually high, but depends on entry and exit conditions
Information	Low-cost or free information on price and product quality	Restricted access to price and product-quality information; cost and other data are often proprietary
Conditions of entry and exit	Easy entry and exit	High entry or exit barriers because of economies of scale, capital requirements, advertising, research and development, or other factors
Profit potential	Above-normal profits in short run only; normal profit in long run	Potential for economic (above-normal) profits in both short and long run
Examples	Clothing, consumer financial services, professional services, restaurants, retailing, information on the Internet	Automobiles, aluminum, soft drinks, investment banking, long-distance telephone service, pharmaceuticals

competitive markets involves a never-ending search for uniquely attractive products. Not all industries offer the same potential for sustained profitability; not all firms are equally capable of exploiting the profit potential that is available.

It is always helpful to consider the number and size distribution of competitors, degree of product differentiation, level of information available in the marketplace, and conditions of entry when assessing the investment merits of a given company. Unfortunately, these and other readily obtained data are seldom definitive. Conditions of entry and exit are subtle and dynamic, as is the role of unseen potential entrants. All this contributes to the difficulty of correctly assessing the profit potential of current products or prospective lines of business.

competitive advantage
Unique ability to create, distribute, or service products.

An effective investment strategy in imperfectly competitive markets must be based on the search for firms with a clear **competitive advantage.** A competitive advantage is a unique or rare ability to create, distribute, or service products valued by customers. Just as all industries are not alike in terms of their inherent profit potential, all firms are not alike in terms of their capacity to exploit available opportunities. In the business world, long-lasting above-normal rates of return require a sustainable competitive advantage that, by definition, cannot be easily duplicated.

Nike's use of basketball superstar Michael Jordan as the focal point of its extensive media advertising and product development campaign during the 1990s is an interesting case in point. Like other highly successful and innovative advertising campaigns, the Nike promotion captured the imagination of consumers and put competitors such as Reebok at a distinct disadvantage. After all, there is only one Michael Jordan. Nike sales surged as consumers got caught up in the enthusiasm of Jordan's amazing basketball prowess, and the excitement generated as the

Jordan-led Chicago Bulls marched to NBA championships. However, Jordan's popularity and Nike sales plummeted following Jordan's surprise retirement from basketball during the summer of 1993, only to surge once again on his triumphant return. Meanwhile, Reebok, the second largest basketball shoe manufacturer in America, sought to capture consumers' interest with the "Shaq Attack," an extensive media promotion and product development strategy built around NBA star Shaquille O'Neal. The risks of star-based advertising became even more readily apparent following the well-documented failure of Pepsi's sponsorship of musical legend Michael Jackson during the mid-1990s. Pepsi not only lost the millions of dollars it spent on an obviously ineffective Michael Jackson–based advertising campaign, but it also lost valuable market share to rival Coca-Cola.

This is not to suggest that advertising and other nonprice methods of competition have not been used to great advantage by many successful firms in imperfectly competitive markets. In fact, these techniques are often a primary force in developing a strong basis for product differentiation. Table 9.3 summarizes major characteristics of imperfectly competitive monopoly and **oligopoly** market structures. Although business and investor success is possible in hotly competitive markets, only difficult-to-enter monopoly and oligopoly markets hold the potential for long-lasting above-normal returns.

oligopoly
Few sellers.

How Are Markets Measured?

Economic Census

The **economic census** is the primary source of detailed public facts about the nation's economy. Economic censuses are taken at five-year intervals during years ending with the digits 2 and 7—for example, 1992, 1997, 2002, and 2007. Companies use census data to lay out territories, allocate advertising, and locate new stores or offices. Firms supplying goods and services to other businesses also use census data to target industries for business-to-business marketing. Manufacturers look at statistics on materials consumed to learn more about industries that use their products and to gain insight concerning industry growth potential. Investors compare operating ratios to census averages to see how they stack up against competitive norms. Consultants, government researchers, and job seekers use census data to analyze changes in industrial structure, location, and the pace of growth in job opportunities. Both state and federal regulators use census data to monitor business activity as captured by fluctuations in monthly retail sales, GDP, and other such measures. Industry trade associations and news media study census data to learn key business facts and to project trends.

economic census
Comprehensive statistical profile of the economy from the national, to the state, to the local level.

Industry statistics contained in the 1997 Economic Census are classified by using a new **North American Industry Classification System (NAICS)**. To a lesser extent, the classification of some industries is based on the old 1987 Standard Industrial Classification (SIC) system that was used in previous censuses. Both NAICS and SIC categorize establishments by the principal activity in which they are engaged. The NAICS, developed in cooperation with Canada and Mexico, classifies North America's economic activities at two-, three-, four-, and five-digit levels of detail. The U.S. version of NAICS further defines some industries to a more precise sixth digit of detail. Table 9.4 illustrates how the entire scope of economic activity

North American Industry Classification System (NAICS)
Method for categorizing establishments by the principal economic activity in which they are engaged.

TABLE 9.4 North American Industry Classification Systems (NAICS)

The NAICS classifies North America's economic activity.

NAICS Codes	Economic Sector
11	Agriculture, Forestry, Fishing and Hunting *(Separate census of agriculture, conducted by the Department of Agriculture, covers farming but excludes agricultural services, forestry, and fisheries.)*
21	Mining
22	Utilities
23	Construction
31–33	Manufacturing
42	Wholesale Trade
44–45	Retail Trade
48–49	Transportation and Warehousing *(Census excludes U.S. Postal Service, large certificated passenger air transportation, and all rail transportation.)*
51	Information
52	Finance and Insurance *(Census excludes funds and trusts.)*
53	Real Estate and Rental and Leasing
54	Professional, Scientific, and Technical Services *(Census excludes landscape architecture and veterinary services.)*
55	Management of Companies and Enterprises
56	Administrative and Support, Waste Management and Remediation Services *(Census excludes landscaping services.)*
61	Educational Services *(Census excludes elementary and secondary schools, colleges, and professional schools.)*
62	Health Care and Social Assistance
71	Arts, Entertainment, and Recreation
72	Accommodation and Food Services
81	Other Services (except Public Administration) *(Census excludes pet care; labor, political, and religious organizations; and private households.)*
92	Public Administration *(Separate census of governments does not present data according to NAICS or SIC systems.)*
99	Nonclassifiable *(not covered)*

is subdivided into sectors described by two-digit classifications. Below the two-digit major group or sector level, the NAICS system proceeds to desegregated levels of more narrowly defined activity.

To illustrate, Table 9.5 shows the breakdown that occurs as one moves from the two-digit "information" sector to the six-digit U.S. "paging" industry. Econo-

TABLE 9.5 Example Illustrating the NAICS Hierarchic Structure

	Example	
NAICS Level	**NAICS Code**	**Description**
Sector	51	Information
Subsector	513	Broadcasting and telecommunications
Industry group	5133	Telecommunications
Industry	51332	Wireless telecommunications carriers, except satellite
U.S. industry	513321	Paging

NAICS codes describe economic activity with increasing precision as one moves from the two-digit (sector) to six-digit (U.S. industry) levels of detail.

mists generally agree that five-digit or six-digit classifications correspond closely with the economic definition of a market. Establishments grouped at the five-digit or six-digit levels produce products that are ready substitutes and thus function as competitors. Investors who analyze census data to learn about the number and size distribution of actual and potential competitors focus their attention primarily on data provided at the five-digit or six-digit levels. The Census Bureau also classifies products. In the case of manufacturing and mining industries, products are classified in a manner consistent with the NAICS structure. The first six digits of the 10-digit product code are normally the same as the NAICS code for the industry with which the product is most frequently associated. Broad product or service lines also are provided for retail and wholesale trade and other service industries.

Concentration Ratios

Table 9.6 shows census information on the number of competitors, industry sales, and leading-firm market share data for a small sample of industries. Industries that contain a large number of firms of roughly equal sizes are generally regarded as vigorously competitive. Questions about the intensity of competition sometimes arise when only a limited number of competitors are present or when only a handful of large firms dominates the industry.

As shown in Table 9.6, the economic census uses two different methods to describe the degree of competitor size inequality within an industry. The most

TABLE 9.6 Number of Firms and Concentration Ratios for a Representative Sample of Industries from the U.S. Economic Census

The number of firms, concentration ratios, and the HHI give differing insight on the extent of competition as captured by the size distribution of competitors.

			Percentage of Sales Accounted for by:				
Industry	Number of Firms	Industry Sales ($ Millions)	Top 4 Firms (CR_4)	Top 8 Firms (CR_8)	Top 20 Firms (CR_{20})	Top 50 Firms (CR_{50})	Herfindahl Hirschmann Index (HHI)
Meat Packing Plants	1,296	$6,958.7	50	66	79	88	777
Pickles, Sauces, and Salad Dressings	332	6,398.0	41	56	72	89	661
Cereal Breakfast Foods	42	9,798.6	85	98	99	100	2,253
Dog, Cat, and Other Pet Food	102	7,023.0	58	77	92	99	1,229
Candy and Chewing Gum	705	10,207.1	45	59	75	86	699
Roasted Coffee	134	5,294.6	66	75	89	96	1,501
Fur Goods	211	205.4	32	40	55	75	403
Apparel Belts	245	639.6	33	47	67	82	422
Paper Mills	127	32,786.4	29	49	77	94	392
Newspapers	6,761	33,879.5	25	37	54	70	241
Saw Blades and Handsaws	128	847.2	45	59	80	96	685
Motor Vehicles and Car Bodies	398	151,711.9	84	91	99	99	2,676
Aircraft	151	62,937.7	79	93	99	99	2,717
Boat Building and Repairing	2,376	4,623.5	32	38	48	61	383
Burial Caskets	195	1,053.3	64	72	82	92	2,149

Note: All figures are from the 1992 census of manufacturers and were obtained on February 22, 1998, from <http://www.census.gov/mcd/mancen/download/mc92cr.sum>.

commonly used group measures of leading-firm market share data are calculated from sales information for various clusters of top firms. These group market share data are called **concentration ratios (CR)** because they measure the percentage market share concentrated in (or held by) an industry's top four (CR_4), eight (CR_8), 20 (CR_{20}), or 50 (CR_{50}) firms. Thus, the concentration ratio for a group of n leading firms is defined in percentage terms as:

concentration ratios
Data that show the percentage market share held by a group of leading firms.

$$CR_n = \frac{\sum_{i=1}^{n} \text{Firm Sales}_i}{\text{Industry Sales}} \times 100 \tag{9.1}$$

where i refers to an individual firm.

Concentration ratios can range between $CR_n = 0$ for an industry with a massive number of small competitors, to $CR_n = 100$ for an industry represented by a single monopolist. In the manufacturing sector in which concentration tends to be highest, four-firm concentration ratios tend to fall in a broad range between $CR_4 = 20$ and $CR_4 = 60$; eight-firm concentration ratios often lie in a range between $CR_8 = 30$ and $CR_4 = 70$. When concentration ratios are low, industries tend to include many firms and competition tends to be vigorous. Industries in which the four leading firms are responsible for less than 20% of total industry sales (i.e., $CR_4 < 20$) are highly competitive and approximate the perfect competition model. However, when concentration ratios are high, leading firms dominate following firms in terms of size, and leading firms may have more potential for pricing flexibility and economic profits. Industries in which the four leading firms control more than 80% of total industry sales (i.e., $CR_4 > 80$) are often described as highly concentrated. Industries with a $CR_4 < 20$ or $CR_4 > 80$, however, are rare. Three-quarters of all manufacturing activity takes place in hotly competitive industries with concentration ratios falling in the range $20 \leq CR_4 \leq 80$.

Herfindahl Hirschmann Index

By definition, concentration ratios rise with greater competitor size inequality within a given industry. Concentration ratios, however, are unaffected by the degree of size inequality within each respective group of leading firms. This can create problems because competition within industries featuring a handful of large competitors can be much more vigorous than in those in which a single dominant firm faces no large adversaries. For example, although $CR_4 = 100$ would signal monopoly in the case of a single dominant firm, it might describe a vigorously competitive industry if each of the leading four firms enjoys roughly equal market shares of 25%. The **Herfindahl Hirschmann Index (HHI)**, named after the economists who invented it, is a popular measure of competitor size inequality that reflects size differences among large and small firms. Calculated in percentage terms, the HHI is the sum of the squared market shares for all n industry competitors:

Herfindahl Hirschmann Index (HHI)
Sum of squared market shares for all n industry competitors.

$$HHI = \sum_{i=1}^{n} \left(\frac{\text{Firm Sales}_i}{\text{Industry Sales}} \right) \times 100^2 \tag{9.2}$$

For example, a monopoly industry with a single dominant firm is described by a $CR_4 = 100$ and a $HHI = 100^2 = 10{,}000$. A vigorously competitive industry in which each of the leading four firms enjoy market shares of 25% is also described by a $CR_4 = 100$ but features a $HHI = 25^2 + 25^2 + 25^2 + 25^2 = 2{,}500$. Like concentration ratios, the HHI approaches zero for industries characterized by a large number of very small competitors.

Limitations of Concentration Ratios and HHI Information

A major weakness of census concentration ratio and HHI information is that they ignore domestic sales by foreign competitors (imports) as well as exports by domestic firms. Only data on domestic sales from *domestic production,* not total domestic sales, are reported. This means, for example, that if foreign imports have a market share of 25%, the four leading domestic automobile manufacturers account for 63% (= 84% of 75%) of total U.S. car sales, rather than the entire 84%, as Table 9.6 suggests. For industries with significant import competition, concentration ratios and HHI data significantly overstate the relative importance of leading domestic firms. Concentration ratios and HHI information also overstate market power for several industries in which increasing foreign competition has been responsible for the liquidation or merger of many smaller domestic firms with older, less efficient production facilities. Despite reduced numbers of domestic firms and the consequent rise in concentration, an increase in foreign competition often makes affected industries more efficient and more competitive rather than less. The impact of foreign competition is important in many industries, but it is particularly so in manufacturing industries such as apparel, steel, automobiles, cameras, copiers, motorcycles, and television sets.

Another limitation of concentration ratio data is that they are *national totals,* whereas a relevant economic market may be national, regional, or local in scope. If high transportation costs or other product characteristics keep markets regional or local rather than national in scope, concentration ratios can significantly understate the relative importance of leading firms. For example, the leading firm in many metropolitan newspaper markets often accounts for 90% or more of the total market advertising and subscription revenues. Thus, a national CR_4 level for newspapers of 25% significantly understates local market power in that industry. Whereas national concentration ratios in the 25% range usually suggest, a highly competitive market structure, the local or regional character of some markets can make national concentration figures meaningless. Other examples of products with local or regional rather than national markets include milk, bread and bakery products, commercial printing, and ready-mix concrete.

Considering concentration ratio and HHI data in isolation can also lead to erroneous conclusions regarding the vigor of competition. Under certain circumstances, even a few large competitors can compete vigorously. For example, the market for large commercial and military aircraft is viciously competitive despite being dominated by only two global competitors: Boeing, from the United States, and Airbus Industrie, the European multinational consortium. In addition to considering the number and size distribution of competitors, investors must judge the competitive environment in the light of foreign competition, transportation costs, regional product differences, likely potential entrants, advertising, customer loyalty, research and development, demand growth, and economies of scale in production, among other factors, to make accurate pricing and output decisions. All these features constitute important elements of market structure.

establishment Geographic location for economic activity.

And finally, economic census statistics are collected and published at the **establishment** level of aggregation. An establishment is a business or industrial unit

FIGURE 9.6 Dow Jones Total Market Industry Group Components

MW70 BARRON'S • MARKET WEEK February 21, 2000

MARKET LABORATORY • STOCKS

DOW JONES TOTAL MARKET INDUSTRY GROUP COMPONENTS

The following list includes all the companies in the various industry groups. The list will be updated as conditions warrant.

BASIC MATERIALS

Chemical, Commodity:
- Chirex
- Du Pont Co
- Dow Chemical
- Georgia Gulf
- Hercules
- Millennium Chemicals
- Olin Corp
- Schulman (A)
- Union Carbide

Chemical, Specialty:
- Air Products & Chem
- Avery Dennison
- Borden Chem/Plas
- Cabot
- Calgon Carbon
- Chemed
- CK Witco
- Cytec Industries
- Dexter
- Engelhard
- Ecolab
- Eastman Chemical
- Ethyl Corp
- Foamex Intl
- Ferro
- Fuller (H B)
- Great Lakes Chem
- Geon Co
- Grace (W R)
- Mississippi Chem
- IMC Global
- Lesco
- Lubrizol
- Hanna (M A)
- MacDermid
- OM Group
- Praxair
- Rohm & Haas
- R P M
- RTI Intl Metals
- Sigma-Aldrich
- Solutia
- Wellman

Forest Products:
- Georgia-Pacific
- Louisiana-Pacific
- Rayonier
- Timber Group GP
- Willamette Industries
- Weyerhaeuser

Paper Products:
- Boise Cascade
- Bowater Inc
- Consolidated Papers
- Champion International
- Caraustar Industries
- Chesapeake Cp VA
- International Paper
- Lydall Inc
- Mead Corp
- Mail-Well Inc
- Pope & Talbot
- Westvaco Corp
- Wausau-Mosinee Paper

Aluminum:
- Alcoa
- Commonwealth Ind
- Kaiser Aluminum
- Maxxam
- Reynolds Metals

Mining, Diversified:
- Cleveland Cliffs
- Stillwater Mining

Other Non-ferrous:
- Allegheny Technol
- Freeport-McM C&G "B"
- Mueller Industries
- Phelps Dodge

Precious Metals:
- Battle Mountain Gold
- Echo Bay Mines
- Homestake Mining
- Newmont Mining

Steel:
- AK Steel Holding
- Bethlehem Steel
- Carpenter Technology
- Intermet
- LTV Corp
- Nucor
- Oregon Steel Mills
- Ryerson Tull
- Texas Industries
- WHX Corp
- Worthington Industries
- USX-US Steel

CONSUMER, CYCLICAL

Advertising:
- Doubleclick
- HA-LO Industries
- Interpublic Group
- Lamar Advertising
- ModemMedia Poppe
- Omnicom Group
- Snyder Comm.
- Student Advantage
- 24/7 Media
- Telespectrum Worldwide
- TMP Worldwide
- True North Comm
- Young & Rubicam

Broadcasting:
- Adelphia Comm "A"
- AMFM Inc
- American Tower "A"
- CBS
- Chris-Craft Ind
- Clear Channel Comm
- Citadel Comm
- Comcast Corp "A"
- Comcast Corp "A Spl"
- Cox Comm "A"
- Cablevision Systems
- Cox Radio "A"
- Echostar Comm
- Emmis Comm "A"
- Entercom Comm "A"
- Hispanic Broadcasting
- Hearst-Argyle Tele
- Jones Intercable "A"
- Sinclair Broadcast "A"
- Sirius Satellite Radio
- Source Media
- UnitedGlobalCom "A"
- Mediaone Group
- USA Networks
- Univision Comm "A"
- Valuevision Intl "A"
- Young Broadcasting "A"

Publishing:
- American Greetings "A"
- Belo (A.H.) Corp "A"
- Dow Jones & Co
- Central Newspapers Inc
- Gannett Co
- Harte-Hanks Inc
- Hollinger Int'l "A"
- Houghton Mifflin Co
- iVillage Inc
- Wiley (John) & Sons
- Knight-Ridder Inc
- Meredith Corp
- Media General Inc
- McGraw-Hill Cos
- McClatchy Co "A"
- NewsEdge Corp
- New York Times "A"
- OnHealth Network Co
- Primedia Inc
- Readers Digest "A"
- R.H. Donnelley Corp
- Scholastic Corp
- Scripps (E.W.) "A"
- Times Mirror Co "A"
- Nelson (Thomas) Inc
- Track Data Corp
- Tribune Co
- Valassis Comm
- Washington Post "B"
- Ziff-Davis Inc

Automobile Mfctrs:
- Ford Motor
- General Motors

Automobile Parts & Eqp:
- Arvin Industries
- Borg-Warner Auto
- Dana Corp.
- Delphi Automotive
- Dura Automotive
- Exide Corp.
- Federal-Mogul
- Genuine Parts
- Johnson Controls
- Lear Corp.
- Lo-Jack Corp.
- Modine Mfg.
- Meritor Automotive
- Mascotech Inc.
- Simpson Industries.
- Snap-On Inc.
- Superior Industries
- T B C Corp.
- Tenneco Automotive
- Tower Automotive

Casinos:
- Aztar Corp
- Harrah's Entertain
- Mandalay Resort
- MGM Grand
- Mirage Resorts
- Players Intl
- Park Place Entertain
- Anchor Gaming
- Station Casinos

Entertainment:
- ACTV Inc
- Metro-Goldwyn-Mayer
- Metromedia Int'l Grp
- Network Event Theater
- Pixar
- Time Warner
- Viacom "A"
- Viacom "B"

Recreation Products:
- Arctic Cat Inc
- Action Performance Cos
- AMC Entertainment
- American Classic Voy
- Brunswick Corp
- Bally Total Fitness
- Carnival Corp
- Coachmen Industries
- Dave & Busters Inc
- Disney (Walt) Co
- Eastman Kodak Co
- Callaway Golf Co
- Fleetwood Enterprises
- Ascent Entertainment Gr
- Harley-Davidson Inc
- Int'l Game Technology
- Int'l Speedway Corp "A"
- K2 Inc
- Vail Resorts Inc
- National R.V. Holdings
- Penn National Gaming
- Polaris Industries
- AMF Bowling Inc
- Premier Parks Inc
- Polaroid Corp
- Royal Carribean Cruises
- Boca Resorts Inc "A"
- SFX Entertainment "A"
- Scientific Games Hldg
- Speedway Motorsports
- Winnebago Industries
- WMS Industries Inc

Restaurants:
- Applebee's Int'l
- Avado Brands Inc
- Evans (Bob) Farms
- Buffets Inc
- Cheesecake Factory
- CBRL Group Inc
- CEC Entertainment Inc
- CKE Restaurants Inc
- Darden Restaurants Inc
- Brinkler Int'l Inc
- IHOP Corp
- Jack In The Box Inc
- Landry's Seafood Rest
- McDonald's Corp
- Outback Steakhouse
- Papa John's Int'l Inc
- Rainforest CafÈ Inc
- Ryan Family Steak
- Sonic Corp
- Lone Star Steakhouse
- Wendy's Int'l Inc
- Tricon Global Rest

Toys:
- Acclaim Entertainment
- Electronic Arts
- Hasbro
- Jakks Pacific
- Mattel
- THQ Inc
- Take-Two Interactive

Home Construction:
- Champion Enterprises
- Clayton Homes
- Centex
- Horton (D R)
- Kaufman & Broad
- Lennar
- Oakwood Homes
- Pulte Corp
- Toll Brothers
- U.S. Home

Home Furnishings:
- Black & Decker
- Bassett Furniture Ind
- Allen (Ethan) Interiors
- Furniture Brands
- Fedders Corp
- Interface "A"
- Leggett & Platt
- Mohawk Industries
- Miller (Herman)
- Maytag
- Steelcase "A"
- Shaw Industries
- Sunbeam
- Whirlpool

Retailers, Apparel:
- American Eagle Outfit
- Abercrombie & Fitch "A"
- AnnTaylor Stores
- Cato Corp. "A"
- Charming Shoppes
- Claire's Stores
- Dress Barn
- Delia*s Inc.
- Finish Line "A"
- Footstar
- Goody's Family Clothing
- Gap Inc.
- Gymboree Corp.
- Harcourt General
- Intimate Brands "A"
- Nordstrom
- Kohl's Corp
- Lands' End
- Limited Inc
- Children's Place Retail
- Pacific Sunwear Calif
- Ross Stores
- TJX Cos
- Wet Seal "A"

Retailers, Broadline:
- Ames Department St
- BJ's Wholesale Club
- Dillard's Inc
- Dollar General Corp
- Federated Department
- Family Dollar Stores
- Penney (JC) Inc
- Kmart Corp
- May Department Stores
- Sears Roebuck & Co
- Shopko Stores Inc
- Saks Inc
- Stein Mart Inc
- Target Corp
- Wal-Mart Stores Inc

Retailers, Drug-based:
- AmeriSource Health "A"
- Cardinal Health Inc
- CVS Corp
- Duane Reade Inc
- Longs Drug Stores Corp
- McKesson HBOC Inc
- Rite Aid Corp
- Walgreen Co

Retailers, Specialty:
- Americredit
- Amazon.com
- AutoNation Inc.
- AutoZone Inc
- Bombay Co
- Bed Bath & Beyond
- Best Buy Co
- Borders Group
- Barnes & Noble
- Building Materials Hldg
- Barnesandnoble.com
- Beyond.com
- Circuit City Stores
- Cdnow Inc
- CDW Computer Ctrs
- Compucom Systems
- Consolidated Stores
- Cyberian Outpost
- Costco Wholesale
- CompUSA Inc
- Cost Plus Inc
- Dollar Tree Stores
- Egghead.com
- Etoys Inc
- Fastenal Co
- Friedman's Inc
- Guitar Center Inc
- Homebase
- Home Depot Inc
- Hollywood Entertainmnt
- Heilig-Meyers
- Linens 'N Things
- Lowe's Cos
- Michaels Stores
- NBTY Inc
- Insight Enterprises
- Office Depot Inc
- U.S. Office Products
- OfficeMax Inc
- O'Reilly Automotive
- Pep Boys Manny M&Jk
- Petco Animal Supplies
- PetsMART Inc
- Pier 1 Imports
- Pomeroy Computer Res
- Pre-Paid Legal Services
- Payless Shoesource
- Sunglass Hut Int'l
- Rent-A-Center Inc
- RoweCom Inc
- Shop At Home Inc
- Starbucks Corp
- Staples Inc
- Tandy Corp
- Tiffany & Co
- Toys R US Inc
- Trans World Entertnmt
- Ugly Duckling
- United Stationers
- West Marine
- Williams-Sonoma
- Venator Group
- Zale Corp

Clothing/Fabrics:
- CYRK
- Fossil
- Fruit of the Loom
- Genesco
- Guilford Mills
- Oshkosh B'Gosh "A"
- Jones Apparel
- Kellwood
- Liz Claiborne
- Movado Group
- Nautica Enterprises
- Oakley
- Phillips-Van Heusen
- Polo Ralph Lauren
- Russell
- Springs Industries
- Tarrent Apparel
- Unifi
- Y F Corp
- Warnaco Group "A"
- Westpoint Stevens
- Quiksilver

Footwear:
- Cole (Kenneth) "A"
- Nike Inc
- Reebok Intl
- Stride Rite
- Timberland "A"
- Vans Inc
- Wolverine World Wide

Airlines:
- Airtran Holdings
- Atlantic Coast Air Hld
- Alaska Air Group
- AMR Corp.
- Continental Airlines
- Delta Air Lines
- Southwest Airlines
- Northwest Airlines
- Skywest Inc.
- Trans World Airlines
- US Airways Grp
- UAL Corp.

Lodging:
- Extended Stay America
- Hilton Hotels
- Hospitality Properties
- Marriott Int'l "A"
- Sunterra Corp
- Prime Hospitality
- Trendwest Resort
- Winston Hotels

CONSUMER, NONCYCLICAL

Consumer Services:
- Autobytel.com
- America Online
- Apollo Group
- Ask Jeeves
- EXCITE@Home
- Avis Rent A Car
- Budget Group
- Sothebys Holdings "A"
- About.com
- CareInsite Inc.
- Cendant Corp
- CPI Corp
- Cheap Tickets Inc
- DeVry Inc
- eBay Inc
- Earthlink Inc
- Goto.com
- Block (H & R)
- Hertz Corp
- High Speed Access
- Infospace.com
- Lycos Inc
- NBC Internet
- Priceline.com
- Protectionone
- Preview Travel
- Regis Corp
- Sylvan Learning Sys
- Sportsline.com
- Service Corp Intl
- Stewart Ent "A"
- Stamps.com
- Starmedia Network
- Theglobe.com
- Ticketmaster Online "B"
- uBid Inc
- United Rentals
- Veterinary Centers
- Yahoo!Inc

Cosmetics/Personal Care:
- Alberto-Culber
- Avon Products
- EsteeLauder "A"
- Gillette Co
- Helen of Troy
- Herbalife Intl "A"
- Intl Flavors&Fragrances
- Nature's Sunshine
- Revlon "A"
- Windmere Durable Hldg

Distillers & Brewers:
- Brown-Forman "B"
- Anheuser-Busch
- Canandaigua Brands
- Coors (Adolph) "B"

Food:
- Archer-Daniels-Midland
- BestFoods
- Ben&Jerrys "A"
- ConAgra
- NorthlandCranberries"A"
- Campbell Soup
- Corn Products Intl
- Chiquita Brands
- Celestial Seasonings
- Dean Foods
- Dole Food
- Dreyer's Grand IceCrm
- Earthgrains
- Flowers Industries
- General Mills
- Hain Food Group
- Heing (H J)
- Hormel Foods
- Hershey Foods
- Interstate Bakeries
- IBP Inc
- Imperial Sugar
- International Multifoods
- J&J Snack Foods
- Kellogg
- Keebler Foods
- Lancaster Colony
- Michael Foods
- McCormick & Co
- Nabisco Holdings "A"
- Nabisco Grp Holdings
- Quaker Oats
- American Ital'n Pasta"A"
- Ralcorp Holdings
- Ralston-Ralston Purina
- Rexall Sundown
- Smithfield Foods
- Smucker (J M)"A"
- Sara Lee
- Suiza Foods
- Tyson Foods "A"
- Twinlab
- WLR Foods
- Wrigley (William) Jr.
- Zapata

Soft Drinks:
- Coca-Cola Enterprises
- Coca Cola Co
- Pepsi Bottling Group
- Pepsico Inc
- Triarc Cos "A"
- Whitman

Food Retailers:
- Albertson's
- Casey's General Stores
- Delhaize America "A"
- Delhaize America "B"
- Fleming Cos
- Great Atlantic & Pacific
- Hannaford Brothers
- Kroger
- Wild Oats Markets
- Performance Food
- Smart & Final
- Supervalu
- Safeway
- Sysco
- U.S. Foodservice
- United Natural Foods
- Whole Foods Market
- Winn-Dixie Stores
- Weis Markets

House-Durable:
- Department 56
- Fortune Brands
- Libbey
- Newell Rubbermaid
- Tupperware

House-Non-Durable:
- Blyth Industries
- Central Garden & Pet
- Colgate-Palmolive
- Clorox
- Dial Corp
- Fort James
- Kimberly-Clark
- Procter & Gamble
- Scotts
- Valence Technology

Tobacco:
- Dimon
- Morris (Philip) Cos
- R J Reynolds Tob Hold
- UST Inc
- Universal Corp Holding

ENERGY

Coal:
- Consol Energy

Oil, Drilling:
- Atwood Oceanics
- Diamond Offshore Drill
- ENSCO Intl
- Evergreen Resources
- R&B Falcon
- Global Marine
- Helmerich & Payne
- Marine Drilling
- Nabor Industries
- Noble Drilling
- Pride Intl
- Parker Drilling
- Patterson Energy
- Rowan Cos.
- Transocean Sedco
- Santa Fe Intl
- Weatherford Intl

Oil, Integrated Majors:
- Atlantic Richfield
- Chevon Corp
- USX-Marathon
- Phillips Petroleum
- Texaco Inc
- Unocal Corp
- Exxon Mobil Corp

Oil, Secondary:
- Amerada Hess
- Apache Corp
- Anadarko Petroleum
- Ashland Inc
- Burlington Resources
- Barrett Resources
- Basin Exploration
- Conoco Inc "A"
- Cabot Oil & Gas "A"
- Devon Energy
- EEX Corp
- EOG Resources
- Forest Oil
- Harken Energy
- Kerr-Mcgee
- Dreyfus (Louis) Natural
- Murphy Oil
- Noble Affiliates
- NewField Exploration
- Occidental Petroleum
- Plains Resources
- Pennzoil-Quaker State
- Range Resources
- Santa Fe Snyder
- Stone Energy
- Sunoco Inc
- Titan Exploration
- Brown (Tom) Inc
- Meridian Resource
- Tosco Corp
- Tesoro Petroleum
- Ultramr Diamond Shmrk
- Union Pacific Resources
- Valero Energy
- Vintage Petroleum
- Vastar Resources
- W-D 40 Co.

Oil, Eqp. & Services:
- Baker Hughes
- B J Services
- Cooper Cameron
- Friede Goldman Intl
- Global Industries
- Halliburton Co
- IRI International
- Input/Output
- Lone Star Technologies
- Maverick Tube
- Newpark Resources
- Oceaneering Intl
- Seitel
- Superior Energy
- Smith International
- Schlumberger
- Tuboscope
- Trico Marine Services
- Varco International
- Veritas DGC

Pipelines:
- Coastal Corp
- El Paso Energy
- Kinder Morgan
- Ocean Energy
- Plains All Amer Pipeline
- Western Gas Resources
- Williams Cos

FINANCIAL

Banks:
- Amcore Financial
- Associated Banc
- Amsouth Bancorp
- Bank of America
- BB&T Corp
- Bank of New York
- Banknorth Group
- Bankunited Fincl "A"
- Bank United Corp.
- Pacific Century Fin
- BSB Bancorp
- Bancwest Corp.
- Carolina First
- Centura Banks
- Commerce Bancorp
- Commerce Bancshrs
- Compass Bancshrs
- CCB Financial
- CommunityFstBankshr
- Cullen-Frost Bankers
- Chittenden Corpo.
- Comerica
- Chase Manhattan
- Colonial Bancgroup
- Columbia Banking Sys
- Century South Banks
- City National
- F N B Corp
- Fleetboston Fincl
- First Charter Corp
- Firstfed Fincl
- Fifth Third Bancorp
- First Midwest Bancorp
- Firstmerit Corp
- First Republic
- First Security
- Firstar Corp.
- First Tenn Natl
- First Union
- First Virginia Banks
- Greater Bay Bancorp
- GBC Bancorp
- Gold Banc
- Hamilton Bancorp
- Haven Bancorp
- Huntington Bancshares
- Hibernia Corp
- Hudson United Banc
- Indepen Comm Bank
- Imperial Bancorp
- Indepen Bank
- Interwest Bancorp
- Morgan (J P) & Co
- Keycorp
- MBNA Corp
- Keystone Fincl
- Mellon Fincl
- Marshall & Ilsley
- Mercantile Bankshr
- M & T Bank Corp.
- Natl Commerce Banc
- National City
- North Fork
- Northern Trust
- Old Kent Fincl
- Old Natl Bancorp
- Bank One Corp.
- One Valley Bancorp
- People's Bk (Bridgeport)
- Provident Bankshr
- Pacific Bank
- Provident Fincl
- Peoples Heritage Fincl
- PNC Bank
- Republic Bancorp
- Reliance Bancorp
- Republic Bancshares
- Regions Fincl
- R & G Financial "B"
- Riggs National
- Pacific Capital Banc
- Sterling Bancshares
- State Financial Serv
- Silicon Valley Bancshr
- Synovus Financial
- Southtrust Corp
- Suntrust Banks
- State Street Corp
- Summit Bancorp
- Susquehanna Bancsh
- Southwest Bancorp Tx
- TCF Financial
- Texas Regional Banc "A"
- Trustmark
- Trustco Bancorp
- Unionbancal
- USBancorp
- United Bankshr WV
- UCBH Holdings
- FirstUnited Bancsh
- Union Planters
- US Bancorp
- US Trust Corp
- Valley Natl Banc
- WestAmeica Banc
- Wachovia Corp
- W Holding C
- West Coast Banc
- Westcorp
- Wells Fargo
- Wilmington Trust
- WSFS Financial
- Zions Bancorp

Insurance, Full Line:
- Allmerica Financial
- American International
- AON Corp
- Brown & Brown Inc
- CIGNA Corp
- CAN Financial
- E M C Insurance Grp
- Hartford Financial Svc
- Lincoln Nat'l (Indiana)
- StanCorp Financial
- Unitrin Inc

Insurance, Life:
- AFLAC Inc
- American General
- Amerus Life Hldgs "A"
- AXA Financial
- Conseco Inc
- Fremont General
- Hartford Life "A"
- Mann (Horace)
- Jefferson-Pilot
- Nationwide Financial "A"
- Protective Life
- Presidential Life
- Reinsurance Grp Amer
- Reliastar Financial
- Torchmark
- UICI
- UNUM Provident

Insurance, Property & Cas:
- American Financial
- Gallagher (Arthur J.)
- Allstate Corp
- Berkley (W.R.)
- Chubb Corp
- Cincinnati Financial
- Chicago Title
- Erie Indemnity "A"
- Blanch (E.W.) Holdings
- First American Finl
- Foremost Corp. Amer
- FPIC Insurance Group
- Financial Sec Assurance
- Frontier Insurance
- HCC insurance Holdings
- Harleysville Group
- HSB Group
- LandAmerica Financial
- Loews Corp
- Leucadia National
- MBIA Inc
- Mercury General
- Mutual Risk Managemt
- Ohio Casualty
- Old Republic Int'l
- Progressive Cp (Ohio)
- PXRE Group
- Everest Reinsurance
- Reliance Group Hldgs
- Renaissancere Holdings
- Safeco Corp
- Selective Insurance
- SCPIE Holdings
- St. Paul Cos
- Transatlantic Hldgs
- Trenwick Group

Real Estate Investment:
- Associated Estates Rlty
- Apartment Inv & Mgmt
- AMB Property Corp
- Arden Realty Group
- Archstone Communities
- AvalonBay Communities
- Brandywine Realty Trust
- Pinnacle Holdings Inc
- Building One Services
- Burnham Pacific Prop
- BRE Properties
- Boston Properties
- CBL & Associates Prop
- Chelsea GCA Realty
- Catellus Development
- Crescent Real Estate
- Mack Cali Realty Corp
- Colonial Properties Tr
- Cornerstone Properties
- Camden Property Trust
- Carramerica Realty
- Cousins Properties
- Crown Am Realty Trust
- Developers Div Realty
- Duke-Weeks Realty
- Equity Inns Inc
- Equity Office Prop Trust
- Equity Resident Prop Tr
- Felcor Lodging Trust
- Fairfield Communities
- Fidelity Nat Financial
- First Industrial Rlty Tr
- Federal Realty Inv Tr
- First Union RE Eq&Mort
- General Growth Prop
- Glenborough Realty Tr
- Health Care R E I T Inc
- Health Care Prop Inv
- Highwoods Properties
- Home Properties of NY
- Host Marriott (REIT)
- Starwood Hotels/Resorts
- Hollywood Park
- Healthcare Realty Tr
- HRPT Properties Trust
- Imperial Credit Cmrcl
- Insignia Financial Group
- I R T Property Co
- St Joe Co
- Koger Equity Inc
- Kimco Realty Corp
- Kilroy Realty Corp
- LNR Property Corp
- Liberty Property Trust
- Macerich Co
- Manufactured Home
- Mills Corp
- Meditrust Corp
- IndyMac Mort Holdings
- Newhall Land & Farming
- New Plan Excel Rlty Tr
- ProLogis Tr SBI
- Prentiss Prop Trust SBI
- Post Properties Inc
- Public Storage Inc
- Reckson Associates
- RFS Hotel Investors
- Rouse Co
- Redwood Trust Inc
- Security Capital Gr "B"
- Starwood Financial Inc
- Shurgard Storage
- SL Green Realty Corp
- Simon Property Group
- Spieker Properties Inc
- Storage USA Inc
- Town & Country Trust
- Thornburg Mort Asset
- Urban Shopping Centers
- Vornado Realty Trust
- Ventas Inc
- Webb (Del) Corp
- Walden Residential Prop
- Weingarten Realty Inv

Financial Services, Diversified:
- Arcadia Financial
- Ambac Financial
- American Capital Strat
- Advanta "A"
- Advanta "B"
- Associates First Cap "A"
- Allied Capital
- Affiliated Managers
- American Express
- Franklin Resources
- BISYS Group
- SierraCities.com
- Citigroup
- Credit Acceptance
- Countrywide Credit
- CIT Group "A"
- Capital One Financial
- E-Loan
- Federal Investors "B"
- Fannie Mae
- Finova Group
- Freddie Mac
- Heller Financial "A"
- Household International
- Imperial Credit Ind
- Investors Financial Serv
- Marsh & McLennan
- MGIC Investment
- Metris Cos
- NextCard
- Ocwen Financial
- Pioneer Group
- PMI Group
- Providian Financial
- Phoenix Invest Partners
- Radian Group
- SEI Investment
- SLM Holding
- Medallion Financial
- Triad Guaranty
- TerraNova (Bermuda)"A"
- Total System Services
- United Asset Mgt
- Unicapital Corp
- World Acceptance

Savings and Loans:
- Anchor Bancorp WI
- Astoria Financial Corp

Source: *Barron's Market Week,* February 21, 2000, MW70–MW71

FIGURE 9.6 ***(continued)***

MARKET LABORATORY • STOCKS

DOW JONES TOTAL MARKET INDUSTRY GROUP COMPONENTS

BankAtlantic Bancorp"A"
Bay View Capital Corp
Coastal Bancorp
Charter One Financial
Commercial Federal
Commonwealth Bancorp
Community Sav Bank
Dime Community Banc
Dime Bancorp
Downey Financial
First Essex Bancorp
Flagstar Bancorp
First Sentinel Bancorp
First Washn Bancorp
Golden West Financial
Greenpoint Financial
Golden State Bancorp
Harbor Florida Bancsh
JSP Financial
MAF Bancorp
Mech Financial Inc
Net.Bank Inc
OceanFirst Financial
PBOC Holdings
PFF Bancorp
PennFed Financial
Queens County Bancorp
Richmond County Finan
Republic Security Finan
Roslyn Bancorp
Staten Island Bancorp
Sovereign Bancorp
Webster Financial
Washington Federal
Washington Mutual

Securities Brokers:
Edwards (A G) Inc
Ameritrade Holding "A"
Bear Stearns Cos
Donaldson Lufkin & Jen
E*Trade Group
Eaton Vance
Lehman Bros Holdings
Legg Mason
Merrill Lynch
Morgan Keegan
Morgan Stan Dean Wit
Natl Discount Brokers
Knight/Trimark
PaineWebber Group
Raymond James Finan
Schwab (Charles)
Siebert Financial
Southwest Securities
T. Rowe Price Assoc

HEALTHCARE

Healthcare Providers:
Advance Paradigm
Aetna Inc
Apria Healthcare Group
Caremark Rx
Columbia/HCA Health
Coventry Health Care
Express Scripts "A"
Manor Care
Health Management "A"
Healthsouth
Humana
LCA-Vision
Lincare Holdings
Laser Vision Centers
MedQuist
Mid Atlantic Medical
Orthodontic Centers
Oxford Health Plans
Pediatrix Medical Grp
Pacific Health Systems
Phycor
Per-Se Technologies
Quorum Health
Renal Care
Sierra Health
Sunrise Assisted Living
Trigon Healthcare "A"
Tenet Healthcare
Universal Health Ser "B"
United Healthcare
US Oncology
Wellpoint Health Netwks

Advanced Medical Devices:
Acuson Corp
Affymetrix Inc
Arthrocare
Summit Technology
Becman Coulter
Biomet Inc
Coherent Inc
Cyberonics
Cygnus Inc
Eclipse Surgical Tech
Guidant Corp
Gliatech Inc
IGEN International
Imatron Inc
Kopin Corp
Medtronic Inc
Minimed Inc
Novoste Corp
Respironics Inc
Sunrise Technologies
St. Jude Medical
Stryker Corp
Dentsply International

Medical Supplies:
Abbott Laboratories
Baxter International
Bard (C.R.)
Becton, Dickinson
Bausch & Lomb
Boston Scientific
Closure Medical
Cytyc Corp
Datascope Corp
Haemonetics Corp
Hillenbrand Industries
Schein (Henry)
Invacare Corp
Mallinckrodt
Mentor Corp
Noven Pharmaceuticals
Omincare Inc
Owens & Minor
Osteotech Inc
Patterson Dental
Polymedica Corp
Syncor International
Spacelabs Medical
I-STAT Corp
Steris Corp
Sybron International
VISX Inc
Wesley Jessen Visioncr
Xceed Inc

Biotechnology:
Alkermes
Alliance Pharm
Amgen
Advanced Tissue Sci
Biogen
Bio-Tech General
Biomatrix
Chiron
COR Therapeutics
Delta and Pine Land
Dionex
Dura Pharm
Enzo Biochem
Enzon
Genzyme General
Gilead Sciences
Human Genome Sci
ICOS Corp
IDEC Pharm
Idexx Labs
Imclone Systems
Immune Response
Immunex
Incyte Pharm
Ligand Pharm "B"
Medimmune
Millennium Pharm
Monsanto
Myriad Genetics
NABI
Northfield Labs
Organogenesis
Protein Design Labs
PE Corp-PE Biosystems
Pharm Prod Dev
Parexel Intl
Regeneraon Pharm
Scios
Theragencis
Vertex Pharm
XOMA

Pharmaceutical:
Amdrx Corp
Allergan
American Home Prod
Alpharma "A"
Alza Corp
Bristol-Myers Squibb
Cephalon
Coulter Pharm
Columbia Labs
Emisphere Tech
Entremed
Forest Labs
Guilford Pharm
ICN Pharm
Inhale Therapeutics
IVAX Corp
Jones Pharma
Johnson & Johnson
King Pharm
KOS Pharm
Liposome Co
Lilly (Eli) & Co.
Macrochem
Merck & Co
Miravant Med Tech
Medicis Pharm "A"
Mylan Labs
Anesta
Pharmacyclics
Pfizer Inc
Pathogenesis
Pharmacia & Upjohn
Sangstat Medical
Sicor
Sepracor
Schering-Plough
Supergen
ViroPharma
Warner-Lambert
Watson Pharma

INDUSTRIAL

Aerospace & Defense:
AAR Corp.
Aeroflex
Alliant Techsystems
Boeing Co.
BE Aerospace
Cordant Tech
Fairchild Corp.
General Dynamics
Goodrich (BF)
Gencorp
Howmet Intl
Kaman Corp "A"
Litton Industries
Lockheed Martin
Northrop Grumman
Netoptix Corp.
Orbital Sciences
Precision Castparts
Raytheon Co. "A"
Raytheon Co. "B"

Building Materials:
Armstrong World Ind.
Apogee Enterprises
Dal-Tile Intl
Elcor Corp.
Genlyte Group
Hughes Supply
Johns Manville
Justin Industries
Lafarge Corp.
Lilly Industries "A"
Masco Corp.
Martin Marietta Mat
NCI Building Systems
Owens Corning
Southdown Inc.
Sherwin-Williams
USG Corp.
US Plastic Lumber
Valspar Corp.
Vulcan Materials

Heavy Construction:
Astec Industrial
Dycom Industries
EMCOR Group
Fluor Corp
Foster Wheeler
Granite Construction
Jacobs Engineering
Morrison Knudsen

Containers & Packaging:
Aptargroup
Ball Corp
Bemis Co
Crown Cork & Seal
EarthShell Container
Gaylord Container "A"
Owens-Illinois
Sealed Air
Sonoco Products
Smurfit-Stone Contain
Shorewood Packaging
Temple-Inland

Industrial Diversified:
ACX Technologies "A"
Albany Intl
Barnes Group
Briggs & Stratton
Cooper Industries
Crane Co
Carlisle Cos.
Catalytica Inc
Danaher Corp
Dover Corp
Flowserve Corp
F M C Corp
General Electric
Griffin Corp
Gentex Corp
Honeywell International
ITT Industries
Ionics Inc
Ingersoll Rand
Illinois Tool Works
Kaydon Corp
Kennametal Inc
Kroll O'Gara Co
National Service Ind
OEA Inc
Parker-Hannifin
Pentair Inc
P P G Industries
Paxar Corp
Roper Industries
Scott Technologies
SPS Technologies
Stanley Works
Commercial Intertech
Timken Co
Textron Inc
Tyco International
U.S. Industries
Wolverine Tube
Watts Industries

Electrical Components & Eqp:
American Power Conver
American Standard
Artesyn Tech
Avid Tech
Avnet
AVX Corp
Burr-Brown
General Cable
B M C Industries
C-COR.Net
C&D Technologies
Checkpoint Systems
Cohu
Cree Inc
CTS Corp
Commscope
Emerson Electric
Grainger (W W)
Hadco
Hubbell "B"
ITI Technologies
Kent Electronics
LSI Industries
MagneTek Inc
Methode Electronics "A"
Molex
Molex "A"
Pioneer Standard Elect
Park Electrochemical
Plexus
Recoton
Rare Medium Group
Sawtek
SLI Inc
Solectron
SPX Corp
Thomas & Betts
Technitrol
Vicor Corp
Audiovox "A"
Vishay Intertechnology
World Access
Encore Wire

Factory Equipment:
York International
Flow International
Gardner Denver
Innovex
Kulicke & Soffa
Milacron
Nordson
Regal-Beloit

Heavy Machinery:
AGCO Corp
Applied Power "A"
Caterpillar Inc
Deere & Co
Manitowoc Co
Terex Corp

Industrial Technology:
Alpha Industries
Aware Inc
CACI International "A"
Cognex Corp
Cymer Inc
Diebold
DII Group
Electro Scientific
Esterline Technologies
Etec Systems
Eaton Corp
Corning Inc
Helix Technology
Intergraph Corp
Mark IV Industries
JDS Uniphase
Kollmorgen
Littelfuse
Millipore Corp
Minn Mining & Mfg
MTI Technology
M T S Systems
Macrovision Corp
Maxwell Technologies
PerkinElmer Inc
Pall Corp
PRI Automation
Presstek Inc
Remec Inc
Rockwell International
Symbol Technologies
S C I Systems
SpeedFam IPEC
Tektronix
Teleflex
Tekelec
Thermo Electron
Trimble Navigation
T R W Inc
UCAR International
United Technologies
Veeco Instruments
Waters Corp
Wave Systems "A"
X-Rite Inc
Zebra Technologies "A"
Zygo Corp
Zoltek Cos

Industrial & Commercial Svcs:
Affiliated Cmptr "A"
Acxiom Corp
Advo Inc
Applied Graphics Tech
American Mgt Systems
Answerthink Consulting
APAC Customer
AppNet Int
ACNielsen
Arrow Electronics
Automatic Data Process
Billing Concepts
Banta Corp
Bowne & Co
Century Business Serv
CIBER Inc.
Complete Business Solu
Comdisco
Concord EFS
Brightpoint Inc.
Ceredian Corp
Consolidated Graphics
Checkfree Holdings
Cellstar
CMGI Inc
Concentric Network
CNET Inc
Copart Inc
Critical Path
PE - Celera Genomics
Computer Sciences
CSG Systems
Cintas
Covance
Convergys
Data Broadcasting
DBT Online
Deluxe Corp
Dun & Bradstreet
Donnelley (R R) & Sons
Digital River
DST Systems
Data Transmission Net
Diamond Tech "A"
Electronic Data Sys
Equifax
eLoyalty
Exodus Comm
First Data
First Health Group
Fiserv
Getty Images
G&K Services "A"
Galileo Intl
G A T X
Go2net Inc.
Healtheon/WebMD
Inacom Corp
IDT Corp
IDX Systems
IXL Enterprises
Ingram Micro "A"
Internet.com
Information Resources
Interim Services
Gartner Group
Intelligroup
Intraware
Intervu Inc.
Harland (John H)
Kelly Services
Romac International
Labor Ready
Lason Inc.
Learning Tree Int'l
Manpower Inc.
Multex.com
Metamor Worldwide
Media Metrix
Modis Professional Svcs
Marketing Services Grp
MSC Industrial Dir "A"
Mastec Inc
Navigant Consulting
NCO Group
National Data
Nova Corp (Georgia)
Network Solutions
Offshore Logistics
Paychex Inc
Perot Systems "A"
Personnel Group Amer
Primark
Prime Medical Services
Catalina Marketing
ProBusiness Services
Profit Recovery Grp
Prodigy Communicatns
Precision Response
PSINet Inc.
PSS World Medical
Proxicom
Pittston Brink's Grp
QRS Corp
Quintiles Transnational
Ryder System
Renaissance Worldwide
Reynolds Reynolds "A"
Half (Robert) Int'l
IMS Health
Scient Corp
Sodexho Marriott Svcs
SunGard Data Systems
Safeguard Scientifics
Sensormatic Electronics
StaffMark
Stewart Information
ServiceMaster
Sykes Enterprises
Syntel Inc.
Tech Data Corp
Sabre Holdings
Teletech Holdings
WSWeb Corp
VerticalNet Inc
Viant Corp
Verio Inc
Viad Corp
Wallace Computer Svcs
Coinmach Laundry
WebTrends Corp
Wackenhut Corrections
Whittman-Hart
Workflow Management

Pollution Control/
Waste Mgmt:
Allied Waste Industries
Casella Waste Sys "A"
Donaldson Co
IT Group Inc
Republic Services Inc
Safety-Kleen Corp
Stericycle Inc
U.S. Liquids Inc
Tetra Tech Inc
Waste Connections Inc
Waste Management

Air Freight/Couriers:
Airborne Freight
Atlas Air
Expeditors Intl Wash
FedEx Corp.

Marine Transportation:
Alexander & Baldwin
Seacor Smit
Overseas Shipholding
Tidewater Inc

Railroads:
Burlington Northern SF
C S X Corp
Kansas City Southern
Norfolk Southern Corp
Union Pacific Corp
Wisconsin Central Trans

Trucking:
Arkansas Best
CNF Transportation
Hunt (J B) Transport
Landstar System
Roadway Express
Swift Transportation
USFreightways
Werner Enterprises
Yellow Corp

Transportation Equipment:
ABC-NACO Inc
Cummins Engine
Detroit Diesel
Miller Industries
Monaco Coach
Navistar International
Paccar Inc.
Stewart & Stevenson
Trinity Industries
Titan International
Wabash National

TECHNOLOGY

Communications Technology:
Adaptive Broadband
A D C Telecomm
Advanced Fibre Comm
Allen Telecom
ANADIGICS
Ancor Comm
Andrew
ANTEC
Apex
Aspect Comm
Black Box
Carrier Access
Cable Design Tech
Ciena
Clarent
Copper Mtn Networks
Comverse Tech
3Com
Cabletron Systems
Cisco Systenms
Davox
DIGI International
Ditech Comm
Digital Microwave
EMS Tech
e.spire comm
E-Tek Dynamics
Exar Corp
Extreme Networks
Glenayre Tech
Harmonic
Harris Corp
ICG Comm
Inter-Tel
Intervoice-Brite
Loral Space & Comm
Lucent Tech
Level 3 Comm
Metricom
Metromedia Fiber Net
Motorola
MRV Comm
Northeast Optic Net
Northpoint Comm
Netopia
Network Eq Tech
NEXTLINK Comm "A"
Omnipoint
Pairgain Tech
P-Com
PictureTel
Polycom
Proxim
Premiere Tech
Powerwave Tech
Qualcomm
Razorfish
Redback Networks
RCN Corp
Rhythms Netconn
Scientific-Atlanta
Standard Microsystems
Spectrian
PanAmSat
Symmetricom
Terayon Comm Sys
Tellabs
Teltrend
TutSystems
TV Guide "A"
Crown Castle Intl
WAVO Corp
Westell Tech "A"
Xircom

Computers:
Apple Computer
Adaptec
Auspex Systems
Brocade Comm Sys
Computer Network Tech
Compaq Computer
Dell Computer
Digital Lightwave
EMC Corp
Emulex
Evans & Sutherland
Exabyte Corp
Globix Corp
Gateway Inc
HMT Technology
Hutchinson Tech
Hewlett-Packard
IBM
Inet Tech
Iomega Corp
Komag Inc
Micron Electronics
Maxtor
NCR
National Computer Sys
Qlogic Corp
Read-Rite Corp
Radisys Corp
SCM Microsystems
Seagate Technology
Silicon Graphics
Sandisk Corp
Storage Technology
Sum Microsystems
Unisys Corp
Western Digital

Office Equipment:
Brooktrout Inc
Electronics For Imaging
In Focus Systems
Lexmark Int'l "A"
Micros Systems
Pitney Bowes Inc
Xerox Corp

Semiconductor & Related:
Actel
Analog Devices
Alliance Semiconductor
Altera
Applied Materials
Applied Micro Circuits
Advanced Micro Devices
Amkor Technology
Asyst Technologies
Atmel Corp
Broadcom "A"
Brooks Automation
Credence Systems
Conexant Systems
C-Cube Microsystems
Cypress Semiconductor
DSP Group
Electroglas
ESS Technology
FSI International
Globespan
HI/FN In.
Integrated Device Tech
Intel
Jabil Cirbuit
KLA-Tencor
Linear Technology
Lam Research
Lattice Semiconductor
L S I Logic
L T X Corp
Microchip Technology
Micrel
MMC Networks
Micron Technology
Maxim Integrated Prod
NeoMagic
National Semiconductor
Novellus Systems
Oak Technology
Photronics
PMC-Sierra
RF Micro Devices
Rambus
Sanmina Corp
SDL
S3 Inc
Semtech
Silicon Valley Group
3DFX Interactive
Teradyne
Triquint Semiconductor
Transwitch
Texas Instruments
Ultratech Stepper
Vitesse Semiconductor
Xilinx Inc
Zixit Corp
Zoran Corp

Software:
Abode Systems
Autodesk
Allaire Corp
Ariba
Ardent Software
Aspect Development
Activision
Avant!Corp
Axent Technologies
Aspen Technology
BEA Systems
BMC Software
Broadvision
Computer Associates
Caere Corp
Cambridge Tech Part
Concord Comm
Cadence Design Sys
Cerner
Computer Horizons
Clarify
Clarus
Commerce One
Concur Technologies
Compuware
Citrix Systems
Cybersource
Documentum
Amdocs
Dendrite International
Engineering Animation
eFax.com
Entrust Technologies
Epicor Software
F5 Networks
Filenet
HNC Software
Harbinger
Hyperion Solutions
Informix
IMRGlobal
Infocure
Inktomi
Inprise
Intuit
Digital Island
ISS Group
I1 Technologies
JDA Software Group
J D Edwards
Juniper Networks
Keane
Legato Systems
LHS Group
Macromedia
Manugistics Group
MetaCreations
TSI International Soft
Mentor Graphics
Mercury Interactive
Medical Manager
Microsoft
MicroStrategy
Micromuse
New Era of Networks
Network Associates
NetManage
Net Perceptions
Novell
Netspeak
Network Appliance
Nvidia
Open Market
Oracle
Phone.com
Parametric Technology
Peregrine Systems
Portal Software
Project Software/Dev
Peoplesoft
Puma Technology
Quadramed
Rational Software
Remedy
RealNetworks
RSA Security
Sapient
Sanchez Computer
Systems & Compu Tech
Structural Dynamics
Sterling Commerce
Siebel Systems
Silknet Software.com
Synopsys
S1 Corporation
Spyglass
Sterling Software
Software.com
Sybase
Symantec
Transaction Sys Arch
Unify
USInternetWorking
Vignette
Verisign
Veritas Software
Verity
Wind River Systems

TELECOMMUNICATIONS

Fixed Line Communications:
Adelphia Business
Allegiance Telecom
Alltel Corp
Bell Atlantic
BellSouth
Broadwing
US LEC Corp "A"
Covad Comm
Caprock Comm
Citizens Utilities
Sprint Corpo. (FON)
G T E Corp
Global Telesystems
ITC Deltacom
McLeodUSA "A"
MGC Comm
Network Plus
NTL Inc
Pacific Gateway Exch
Primus Telecomm
Qwest Communications
SBC Comm
Startec Global Comm
Star Telecomm
AT&T Corp
Talk.com
Telephone & Data Sys
U S West
Ursus Telecom
Viatel
Winstar Comm
MCI Worldcom

Wireless Communications:
Aerial Comm
Arch Communications
CenturyTel Inc
Intermedia Comm
InterDigital Comm
Leap Wireless Intl
Nextel Comm
Sprint Comp. (PCS Grp)
Powertel
Rural Cellular "A"
American Mobile Satel
Teligent "A"
U.S. Cellular
VoiceStream Wireless
WebLink Wireless
Western Wireless "A"

UTILITIES

Electric:
Ameren
American Electric Power
AES Corp
Avista
Allegheny Energy
Constellation Energy
Cinergy Corp
Connectiv
CMS Energy
Cleco Corp
Carolina Power&Light
Calpine
Central & South West
CMP Group
Dominion Resources
DPL Inc
DQE
DTE Energy
Duke Energy
Dynegy Inc. "A"
Consolidated Edison
El Paso Electric
Edison International
Enron Corp
Entergy Corp
FirstEnergy
Florida Progress
F P L Group
GPU Inc
Hawaiian Electric
IdaCORP
Ipalco Enterprises
Kansas City P&L
KeySpan Corp
LG&E Energy
Alliant Energy
MidAmerican Energy
Montana Power
New Century Energies
Energy East
New England Electric
NiSource Inc
Niagara Mohawk
Northern States Power
Northeast Utilities
OGE Energy
Otter Tail Power
PG&E Corp
PECO Energy
Public Serv Enterprise
Public Serv New Mexico
Pinnacle West Capital
Potomac Electric Power
PPL Corp
Puget Sound Energy
Reliant Energy
RGS Energy Group
SCANA WI
Southern Co.
Sempra Energy
Sierra Pacific Resources
TECO Energy
T N P Enterprises
Texas Utilities
Unicom Corp
Utilicorp United
Unisource Energy
Wisconsin Energy
Western Resources

Gas:
AGL Resources
Columbia Energy
Eastern Enterprises
Equitable Resources
Nicor
MCN Energy
National Fuel Gas
N U I Corp
Northwest Natural Gas
Oneok
Peoples Energy
Piedmont Natural
Questar
Southern Union
Southwest Gas
WICOR Inc.
Yankee Energy System

Water:
American Water Works
American States Water
Azurix
Calif Water Service
E'Town
Philadelphia Suburban
United Water Resources

FIGURE 9.7 **Market Industry Group Performance Is Widely Followed**

March 6, 2000 BARRON'S • MARKET WEEK MW71

MARKET LABORATORY • STOCKS

DOW JONES U.S. TOTAL MARKET INDUSTRY GROUPS

Groups are weighted by capitalization. 52-week highs and lows are based on daily closes. December 31, 1991=100. In the U.S. listings, % vol chg column shows the change from previous 65-day moving average. Volume figures do not reflect extended trading hours.

	Volume (thous)	%Vol Chg	Value	% Change and Ranking: Week	Rank	Yr Ago	Rank	Yr to Date	Rank	52 Week High	52 Week Low
BASIC MATERIALS	**199,475**	**− 4**	**147.38**	**+ .52**		**+ .52**		**− 21.26**		**199.52**	**140.13**
Chemicals	82,946	0	158.30	+ .37	[74]	− 1.39	[44]	− 20.03	[76]	218.87	147.91
Chem-Commodity	36,741	− 2	191.88	− .08	[76]	+ .54	[40]	− 22.09	[84]	269.67	176.35
Chem-Speciality	46,205	+ 2	124.98	+ 1.19	[69]	− 3.30	[48]	− 16.08	[65]	170.86	120.14
Forest Products	20,421	− 7	170.78	+ 6.07	[31]	− 2.76	[47]	− 24.57	[90]	236.22	161.01
Paper Products	36,872	+ 7	149.78	+ .25	[75]	+ 2.95	[38]	− 25.41	[91]	207.75	144.38
Aluminum	15,790	− 7	280.38	− 3.50	[91]	+ 62.80	[13]	− 18.81	[72]	357.63	164.99
Mining, Diversified	1,284	− 22	198.23	+ .40	[72]	+ 13.50	[28]	+ 4.56	[19]	251.53	131.99
Other Non-ferrous	7,998	− 2	114.53	+ 2.94	[53]	+ 8.65	[31]	− 27.26	[93]	163.54	107.02
Precious Metals	11,561	− 30	45.64	− 4.05	[93]	− 5.95	[53]	− 13.22	[55]	67.34	40.49
Steel	22,603	− 7	89.63	+ 2.84	[55]	− 7.20	[54]	− 24.20	[87]	125.76	87.16
CONSUMER,CYCLICAL	**1,417,489**	**+ 11**	**300.18**	**+ 5.44**		**+ 2.71**		**− 12.20**		**343.02**	**280.08**
Advertising	75,065	+ 11	682.84	+ 6.77	[27]	+ 38.81	[22]	− 16.67	[66]	819.41	462.43
Broadcasting	196,289	+ 64	824.56	+ 4.82	[39]	+ 53.13	[16]	− 4.41	[28]	888.50	544.52
Publishing	49,888	− 3	246.06	+ 6.28	[28]	+ 7.60	[33]	− 15.78	[64]	292.15	225.43
Automobile Mfctrs	34,413	+ 16	428.81	− 1.06	[85]	− 10.55	[58]	− 9.49	[39]	552.59	404.72
Automobile Parts & Eqp	32,469	− 1	187.02	− .38	[77]	− 1.67	[46]	− 12.45	[51]	231.20	149.13
Casinos	29,244	+ 11	152.61	− 2.22	[89]	+ 5.18	[37]	− 15.48	[63]	196.68	140.37
Entertainment	47,514	− 5	527.02	+ 2.11	[60]	+ 31.33	[23]	+ 7.76	[18]	562.03	382.97
Recreation Products	110,539	+ 21	256.83	+ 5.78	[34]	− 4.88	[52]	− 3.47	[27]	295.29	230.94
Restaurants	50,107	− 5	207.45	+ 1.73	[64]	− 32.43	[84]	− 20.47	[79]	319.13	203.92
Toys	48,820	+ 6	159.42	+ 10.65	[8]	− 20.65	[70]	− 5.04	[29]	244.00	140.15
Home Construction	8,472	− 18	119.15	+ 3.88	[47]	− 31.43	[83]	− 12.59	[52]	189.74	111.52
Home Furnishings	30,370	− 6	140.47	+ 1.95	[63]	− 27.05	[80]	− 22.72	[85]	230.89	137.78
Retailers	614,898	+ 91	284.75	+ 7.88	[23]	− 1.32	[43]	− 17.41	[67]	344.77	262.43
Retailers, Apparel	87,194	+ 3	248.66	+ 4.41	[44]	− 10.57	[59]	− 8.52	[36]	323.21	223.13
Retailers, Broadline	147,031	+ 29	290.47	+ 15.82	[5]	+ 0.13	[35]	− 21.96	[83]	373.35	250.80
Retailers, Drug-based	58,310	+ 10	230.75	− 8.30	[94]	− 44.64	[92]	− 19.09	[73]	412.88	229.94
Retailers, Specialty	322,363	− 2	328.44	+ 4.75	[40]	+ 9.65	[30]	− 14.04	[58]	382.10	272.43
Clothing/Fabrics	23,539	− 8	77.39	+ 10.35	[11]	− 21.72	[71]	− 6.03	[33]	113.99	65.24
Footwear	10,994	+ 3	88.53	+ 9.88	[12]	− 35.18	[89]	− 33.34	[94]	171.78	80.57
Airlines	36,545	− 7	168.19	+ 4.39	[45]	− 20.60	[69]	− 10.27	[42]	238.90	156.94
Lodging	21,641	+ 66	191.38	− 1.92	[87]	− 29.09	[81]	− 18.02	[70]	312.42	191.38
CONSUMER,NON-CYCLICAL	**693,744**	**+ 6**	**203.93**	**+ .82**		**− 12.80**		**− 16.64**		**255.15**	**201.22**
Consumer Services	297,918	− 7	898.24	− .72	[82]	+ 38.94	[21]	− 17.92	[69]	1176.43	583.66
Cosmetics/Personal Care	38,706	+ 55	192.90	+ 1.32	[67]	− 34.20	[85]	− 14.36	[60]	319.11	183.82
Distillers & Brewers	8,473	+ 8	198.76	+ 2.47	[57]	− 19.44	[68]	− 13.10	[53]	256.85	190.11
Food	94,718	+ 9	110.22	− .78	[83]	− 30.63	[82]	− 20.43	[78]	162.41	109.14
Soft Drinks	54,617	+ 18	237.60	+ .38	[73]	− 18.83	[65]	− 12.09	[50]	322.18	228.84
Food Retailers	64,832	+ 16	158.59	− .59	[79]	− 36.88	[90]	− 13.97	[57]	262.72	157.55
Consumer Products	67,381	+ 13	259.13	+ 4.54	[43]	− 4.06	[49]	− 19.48	[75]	335.34	247.87
House-durable	8,335	− 28	73.78	+ 2.06	[62]	− 39.70	[91]	− 21.58	[80]	140.07	71.18
House-non-durable	59,046	+ 24	298.01	+ 4.70	[42]	+ .20	[42]	− 19.30	[74]	386.89	284.63
Tobacco	67,100	+ 23	67.83	+ 3.05	[51]	− 46.56	[93]	− 13.15	[54]	139.93	64.16
ENERGY	**436,929**	**+ 67**	**219.55**	**+ 9.74**		**+ 30.10**		**− .07**		**238.66**	**178.48**
Coal	242	− 29	32.77	− .54	[78]	− 18.22	[64]	− 24.54	[89]	59.51	32.42
Oil & Gas	436,686	+ 52	219.99	+ 9.75	[13]	+ 30.15	[24]	− .05	[23]	239.04	178.78
Oil, Drilling	120,842	+ 81	388.22	+ 21.19	[1]	+ 186.10	[2]	+ 26.94	[7]	396.87	153.39
Oil, Integrated Majors	72,543	+ 10	222.14	+ 6.10	[30]	+ 14.33	[27]	− 8.90	[37]	265.11	204.02
Oil, Secondary	107,834	+ 60	106.30	+ 10.55	[9]	+ 25.22	[25]	− 5.78	[32]	132.09	88.62
Oilfield, Eqp. & Services	106,441	+ 72	255.11	+ 17.70	[2]	+ 74.92	[11]	+ 27.58	[6]	262.90	162.88
Pipelines	29,027	+ 8	421.32	+ 14.02	[6]	+ 46.77	[18]	+ 32.20	[4]	421.32	293.71
FINANCIAL	**983,386**	**+ 17**	**312.13**	**+ 4.93**		**− 14.25**		**− 11.96**		**407.74**	**297.45**
Banks	335,340	+ 3	292.41	+ 2.31	[59]	− 26.11	[78]	− 14.51	[61]	431.14	285.82
Insurance, Composite	137,920	+ 15	234.39	+ 1.47	[66]	− 23.97	[75]	− 21.93	[82]	330.51	230.99
Insurance, Full Line	40,323	+ 9	359.21	+ 2.49	[56]	− 12.09	[61]	− 21.92	[81]	473.71	350.49
Insurance, Life	40,873	+ 5	231.48	+ 1.57	[65]	− 34.57	[87]	− 26.51	[92]	372.54	227.91
Insurance, Property & Cas	56,724	+ 30	142.10	− .99	[84]	− 34.77	[88]	− 17.51	[68]	231.47	142.10
Real Estate Investment	60,893	0	123.37	+ .72	[71]	− 8.93	[56]	− 1.91	[25]	152.00	114.17
Specialty Finance	449,233	+ 32	483.42	+ 9.72	[14]	+ 6.70	[34]	− 5.51	[30]	549.26	422.31
Financial Services, Diversified	196,515	+ 19	437.58	+ 7.36	[26]	+ .28	[41]	− 11.93	[48]	528.09	407.59
Savings and Loans	56,780	+ 4	225.36	+ 2.92	[54]	− 34.51	[86]	− 13.70	[56]	371.90	217.82
Securities Brokers	195,938	+ 61	846.97	+ 16.18	[4]	+ 41.34	[19]	+ 12.84	[12]	904.30	528.64
HEALTHCARE	**845,396**	**− 3**	**273.31**	**+ 21.38**		**− 1.30**		**+ 3.68**		**299.91**	**225.16**
Healthcare Providers	148,219	+ 14	133.32	+ 10.54	[10]	− 11.78	[60]	− 9.31	[38]	187.09	118.95
Medical Products	90,051	− 58	229.81	+ 4.70	[41]	+ 2.37	[39]	+ 10.40	[14]	248.97	191.54
Advcd Medical Devices	41,992	− 59	358.81	+ 7.91	[22]	+ 51.87	[17]	+ 37.60	[3]	358.81	219.74
Medical Supplies	48,059	− 58	162.01	+ 1.28	[68]	− 25.04	[76]	− 9.67	[41]	243.37	157.12
Pharmaceutical & Biotech	573,514	+ 4	325.59	+ .89	[70]	− 1.40	[45]	+ 3.24	[21]	360.06	291.11
Biotechnology	278,667	0	738.65	+ 5.65	[36]	+ 182.25	[3]	+ 53.85	[2]	738.65	264.46
Pharmaceuticals	294,848	+ 8	279.61	− .69	[81]	− 19.39	[67]	− 7.53	[35]	376.55	278.57
INDUSTRIAL	**1,153,772**	**+ 5**	**300.83**	**+ 6.28**		**+ 26.27**		**− 2.39**		**308.19**	**239.41**
Aerospace & Defense	43,963	− 23	154.60	− 3.55	[92]	− 25.51	[77]	− 15.36	[62]	263.00	154.60
Building Materials	26,306	+ 6	163.93	− .69	[80]	− 26.91	[79]	− 20.37	[77]	263.44	163.65
Heavy Construction	12,137	+ 20	108.94	+ 2.10	[61]	+ 10.26	[29]	− 9.61	[40]	125.62	86.32
Containers & Packaging	46,807	+ 70	105.38	+ 4.05	[46]	− 22.19	[73]	− 24.44	[88]	174.10	100.21
Industrial Diversified	141,998	+ 10	494.09	+ 8.28	[21]	+ 23.31	[26]	− 10.57	[45]	554.43	404.50
Industrial Equipment	322,659	+ 14	380.38	+ 8.59	[19]	+ 85.35	[10]	+ 18.13	[11]	380.38	202.71
Electrical Components & Eqp	114,178	+ 10	313.07	+ 3.66	[49]	+ 53.50	[15]	− 2.36	[26]	328.87	200.52
Factory Equipment	5,229	− 9	242.44	+ 8.49	[20]	+ 98.15	[9]	+ 22.25	[9]	242.44	112.45
Heavy Machinery	22,645	+ 21	248.53	− 1.69	[86]	− 9.36	[57]	− 23.78	[86]	377.21	240.07
Industrial Technology	180,606	+ 17	432.30	+ 8.87	[16]	+ 116.70	[7]	+ 31.55	[5]	432.30	196.47
Industrial & Commercial Svcs	469,853	− 3	284.11	+ 5.53	[38]	+ 39.96	[20]	+ 4.33	[20]	284.11	186.24
Pollution Control/Waste Mgmt	25,249	+ 1	41.09	− 3.06	[90]	− 53.41	[94]	− 18.37	[71]	111.98	40.05
Industrial Transportation	53,625	+ 19	145.30	+ 5.91	[32]	− 17.69	[63]	− 11.94	[49]	215.74	137.19
Air Freight/Couriers	8,931	− 10	302.76	+ 5.53	[37]	− 19.05	[66]	− 14.04	[59]	473.21	283.41
Marine Transportation	5,780	+ 47	119.00	+ 9.33	[15]	+ 54.32	[14]	− 6.96	[34]	127.90	82.12
Railroads	31,463	+ 32	133.70	+ 6.16	[29]	− 22.02	[72]	− 11.87	[47]	215.00	125.51
Trucking	7,452	+ 3	117.13	+ 3.03	[52]	− 12.14	[62]	− 10.32	[44]	145.13	109.39
Transportation Equipment	11,176	+ 3	170.77	+ 7.47	[25]	− 8.57	[55]	− 10.83	[46]	236.73	158.27
TECHNOLOGY	**3,733,632**	**+ 21**	**1438.98**	**+ 8.30**		**+ 123.22**		**+ 21.07**		**1438.98**	**654.80**
Hardware & Equipment	2,544,876	+ 29	1434.68	+ 8.63	[18]	+ 130.06	[6]	+ 26.79	[8]	1434.68	632.25
Communications Technology	1,094,204	+ 42	2734.48	+ 8.87	[17]	+ 155.19	[4]	+ 18.27	[10]	2734.48	1092.47
Computers	668,247	+ 18	839.45	+ 5.68	[35]	+ 73.31	[12]	+ 10.57	[13]	839.45	461.22
Office Equipment	35,771	+ 11	334.01	+ 5.86	[33]	− 23.32	[74]	+ 8.06	[17]	497.54	272.19
Semiconductor & Related	746,654	+ 24	3438.92	+ 11.04	[7]	+ 211.94	[1]	+ 61.06	[1]	3438.92	1132.07
Software	1,188,756	+ 7	1451.51	+ 7.53	[24]	+ 107.81	[8]	+ 8.81	[16]	1451.51	694.60
TELECOMMUNICATIONS	**632,784**	**+ 25**	**354.47**	**+ 14.93**		**+ 12.79**		**− .70**		**371.56**	**308.42**
Fixed Line Communications	507,288	+ 22	334.06	+ 16.83	[3]	+ 8.03	[32]	− 1.38	[24]	353.45	285.93
Wireless Communications	125,496	+ 36	1114.00	+ 3.77	[48]	+ 153.03	[5]	+ 9.95	[15]	1139.17	435.69
UTILITIES	**180,284**	**+ 10**	**120.76**	**+ 3.30**		**− 3.93**		**+ 2.24**		**138.37**	**113.04**
Electric	164,763	+ 8	116.64	+ 3.47	[50]	− 4.71	[51]	+ 3.21	[22]	135.12	107.67
Gas	13,555	+ 56	164.60	+ 2.42	[58]	+ 6.03	[36]	− 5.57	[31]	185.47	148.03
Water	1,966	− 7	189.51	− 2.19	[88]	− 4.15	[50]	− 10.31	[43]	234.46	185.20

144 FILINGS

SEC Form 144 must be filed by holders of restricted securities (also called letter stock) who intend to sell shares. Shares Indicated: the number to be sold. Sales Date: the approximate date of the sale. (Sometimes, shares aren't sold, even though their owner has filed a Form 144.) Title: AF: affiliated person; AI: affiliate of investment adviser; B: beneficial owner of at least 10% of a security; BC: beneficial owner as custodian; BT: beneficial owner as trustee; CB: chairman of the board; CP: controlling person; D: director; DO: director and beneficial owner; DS: indirect shareholder; GP: general partner; H: officer, director and beneficial owner; IA: investment adviser; LP: limited partner; MC: member of committee or advisory board; O: officer; OB: officer and beneficial owner; OD: officer and director; OS: officer of subsidiary; OX: divisional officer; P: president; R: retired, resigned, deceased, no longer with the company; SH: shareholder; T: trustee; UN: unknown; VP: vice president and VT: voting trustee.

Company	Shares Indicated	$ Value	Sale Date	Seller	Title
Appnet Inc	4,798	254,294	2/9/00	Canfield, Mary B	AF
Appnet Inc	8,500	484,500	2/15/00	Ducharme, Bryan	O
Appnet Inc	15,000	841,875	2/16/00	Hallett, Jonathan	O
Appnet Inc	20,000	1,113,125	2/16/00	McBeth, John T	OX
Appnet Inc	7,500	433,125	2/15/00	McCalley, Robert D	VP
Appnet Inc	5,000	285,000	2/15/00	Middlebrook, William D	O
Appnet Inc	2,500	144,375	2/15/00	Middlebrook, William D	O
Appnet Inc	3,500	210,875	2/15/00	Rauh, Thomas H	VP
Appnet Inc	103,291	5,784,296	2/15/00	Rauner, Bruce V	D
Appnet Inc	6,500	370,500	2/15/00	Silvanic, Anthony	O
Art Technology Group	105,169	12,288,590	2/9-14/00	Jones, Scott A	D
Art Technology Group	150,000	15,786,435	2/9/00	Matlack, Thomas N	AF
Broadcom Corp	6,659	1,143,683	2/15/00	Fernandez, Aurelio E	OX
Broadcom Corp	1,000	167,500	2/7-16/00	Ruehle, William J	O
Broadcom Corp	11,000	2,435,250	2/7-16/00	Ruehle, William J	O
Copper Mountain Networks	4,317	306,507	2/7/00	Bensky, Robert C	AF
Copper Mountain Networks	10,000	700,000	2/15-16/00	Creelman, John	VP
Copper Mountain Networks	15,000	1,133,000	2/15-16/00	Creelman, John	VP
Copper Mountain Networks	30,000	2,400,000	2/16/00	Gilbert, Richard S	OP
Copper Mountain Networks	3,105	216,574	2/7/00	Hamilton, Frederic C	D
Copper Mountain Networks	75,000	5,850,000	2/8-16/00	Handzel, Mark	VP
Copper Mountain Networks	25,000	1,875,000	2/8-16/00	Handzel, Mark	VP
Copper Mountain Networks	20,000	1,427,188	2/4/00	Helfrich, Diana	O
Copper Mountain Networks	30,000	2,190,000	2/9/00	Hunt, Steven	VP
Copper Mountain Networks	60,000	4,620,000	2/16/00	Long, Bryan	VP
Copper Mountain Networks	25,000	1,925,000	2/7-16/00	Markee, Joseph D	CB
Copper Mountain Networks	50,000	3,509,275	2/7-16/00	Markee, Joseph D	CB
Internet Capital Group	5,008	565,904	2/2/00	Kennedy, Justin	IA
McLeodUSA Inc	4,510	307,808	2/7-11/00	Collins, Thomas M	D
McLeodUSA Inc	61,345	4,186,796	2/7-11/00	Collins, Thomas M	D
McLeodUSA Inc	24,000	1,733,000	2/10-17/00	Currey, Robert J	D
McLeodUSA Inc	10,000	682,500	2/16/00	Dewyngaert, Susan K	AF
McLeodUSA Inc	11,705	798,867	2/7-11/00	Fisher, Blake O	D
McLeodUSA Inc	100,000	6,825,000	2/14/00	Gray, Stephen C	P
McLeodUSA Inc	10,000	682,500	2/1/00	Keon, Joseph J	AF
McLeodUSA Inc	10,000	682,500	2/16/00	Keon, Margaret L	MC
McLeodUSA Inc	267,500	18,725,000	2/8/00	Lumpkin, Elizabeth A	AF
McLeodUSA Inc	732,500	51,275,000	2/8/00	McLeod, Clark E	CB
McLeodUSA Inc	2,575	175,744	2/7-18/00	Patrick, J L	AF
McLeodUSA Inc	15,000	1,245,000	2/7-18/00	Patrick, J L	AF
McLeodUSA Inc	7,180	490,036	2/7-18/00	Patrick, J L	OX
McLeodUSA Inc	7,525	513,582	2/7-11/00	Rhines, Paul D	D
McLeodUSA Inc	29,055	1,983,003	2/7-11/00	Rhines, Paul D	D
McLeodUSA Inc	2,920	199,380	2/7-11/00	Shirar, Steven J	O
McLeodUSA Inc	5,855	399,604	2/7-11/00	Shirar, Steven J	VP

NYSE PROGRAM TRADING

Program trading is the purchase or sale of at least 15 different stocks with a total value of $1 million or more. Stock-index arbitrage is defined as the sale or purchase of derivatives such as stock-index futures, to profit from the price difference between the basket and the derivatives. Under Rule 80A, when the DJIA moves 50 points or more from the previous day's close,index arbitrage orders in stocks of the Standard & Poor's 500 are subject to a special tick test.

Week Ended February 25, 2000

(Volume Mil. Shares)	2/25 Week	2/18 Week	2/11 Week
NYSE avg daily	1063.4	1023.0	1026.0
NYSE prog trad	211.0	184.5	162.9
Buy programs	100.8	97.3	78.5
Sell programs	110.2	88.1	84.4
Program % NYSE	19.8	18.1	15.9
Index Arbitrage,%	2.99	3.55	1.89
Other 80A trades,%	0.10	0.20	0.21
Other trading,%	16.71	14.35	13.80

The Top Program Traders

(Mil. shrs)	Index Arbitrage	Derivative-Related-z	Other Strategies	Total
Morgan Stanley	11.6	....	125.1	136.7
Deutsche Bank Sec	20.6	....	84.1	104.7
RBC Dominion	43.7	....	26.5	70.2
BNP Securities	....	....	59.1	59.1
TLW Securities	3.6	1.6	52.7	57.9
First Boston	6.1	....	47.8	53.9
CIBC World Mkts	18.5	....	32.7	51.2
Goldman Sachs	....	....	34.1	34.1
Salomon Smith B	....	....	33.4	33.4
Bear Stearns	....	....	30.6	30.6
OVERALL TOTAL	127.9	4.0	712.3	844.2

z-Other derivative-related strategies besides index arbitrage
Source: New York Stock Exchange

EARNINGS SCOREBOARD

Last Week's Major Surprises

Company	Period	Cons. Est.[1]	Actual Net Per Share
Positive			
Steven Madden	4Q	0.20	0.33
World Wrestli	3Q	0.18	0.23
Dycom Industr	2Q	0.25	0.31
Hooper Holmes	4Q	0.17	0.20
Michaels Stor	4Q	1.25	1.41
PG & E Corp	4Q	0.72	0.81
Pall Corp	2Q	0.24	0.27
Factory 2-U S	4Q	0.63	0.70
Negative			
Smithfield Fo	3Q	0.57	0.36
Barrett Resou	4Q	0.19	0.14
Ritchie Bro	4Q	0.52	0.47
Wind River Sy	4Q	0.21	0.19

[1]Latest consensus estimate among industry analysts, as compiled by First Call/Thomson Financial (www.firstcall.com) before actual earnings were reported.

Last Week's Major Estimate Changes

Company	FY End	Prev. Fri. Cons.	Last[1] Fri. Cons.
Positive			
Citadel Commu	Dec-00	−0.68	−0.45
Steven Madden	Dec-00	0.95	1.07
Lehman Brothe	Nov-00	7.74	8.64
Ameritrade	Sep-00	−0.18	−0.16
Autodesk Inc	Jan-01	1.78	1.96
Genesco Inc	Jan-01	1.12	1.20
Michaels Stor	Jan-01	2.21	2.36
Dycom Industr	Jul-00	1.26	1.34
OM Group Inc	Dec-00	2.67	2.81
Semtech Corp	Jan-01	1.30	1.36
Goldman Sachs	Nov-00	5.04	5.26
Negative			
QLT Photother	Dec-00	−0.15	−0.26

[1]Latest consensus estimate among industry analysts, as compiled by First Call/Thomson Financial (www.firstcall.com)

Source: *Barron's Market Week,* March 6, 2000: MW71

at a single physical location that produces or distributes goods or performs services. For example, a single store or factory constitutes a single establishment under the census system. Of course, many companies own or control more than one establishment, and those establishments may be located in different geographic areas. They are often also engaged in different kinds of business activity. When data are collected at the establishment level, it becomes difficult to assess operating performance and the level of competition facing large, widely diversified firms. Because of this, most comparisons of operating performance for widely diversified firms involve firms that may be dissimilar in a number of significant ways but remain important competitors across a variety of important lines of business. Figure 9.6 (pages 354–355) shows industry group categories for a number of large firms as assembled by the Dow Jones News Service, in which industry group definitions loosely follow census criteria. Investors can find operating information on such groups of competitors in leading financial publications, such as *Barron's* (see Figure 9.7). On the Internet, industry group operating statistics are available without charge at <http://finance.yahoo.com> and on a fee basis at <http://www.hoovers.com>.

Legal Environment

Regulation of the Competitive Environment

regulation Government control.

Although all sectors of the U.S. economy are regulated to some degree, the method and scope of **regulation** vary widely. Most companies escape price and profit restraint, except during periods of general wage-price control, but they are subject to operating regulations governing pollution emissions, product packaging and labeling, worker safety and health, and so on. Other firms, particularly in the financial and the public utility sectors, must comply with financial regulation in addition to such operating controls. Banks and savings and loan institutions, for example, are subject to state and federal regulation of interest rates, fees, lending policies, and capital requirements. Unlike firms in the electric power and telecommunications industries, banks and savings and loans face no explicit limit on profitability.

Although the direct costs of regulation are immense, they may be less than hidden or indirect costs borne by consumers, employees, and investors. For example, extensive reporting requirements of the Occupational Safety and Health Administration (OSHA) drive up administrative costs and product prices. Consumers also bear the cost of auto emission standards mandated by the Environmental Protection Agency (EPA). Recent studies put direct and indirect expenses tied to federal regulation at roughly $2,500 per year for every man, woman, and child in the United States. Local and state regulations already cost consumers billions of dollars; new federal regulations on health care, worker safety, and the environment will add billions more.

The enormous and rapidly growing costs of regulation is an important concern for all investors (see Figure 9.8). Investment success requires finding opportunities in which the potential for debilitating regulatory costs can be avoided.

Antitrust Policy

antitrust policy Laws and rules designed to promote competition.

A significant recent challenge for **antitrust policy** has been the dramatic rise in merger activity. A skyrocketing stock market caused business mergers to leap

FIGURE 9.8 **Total Direct and Indirect Costs of Federal Government Regulations**

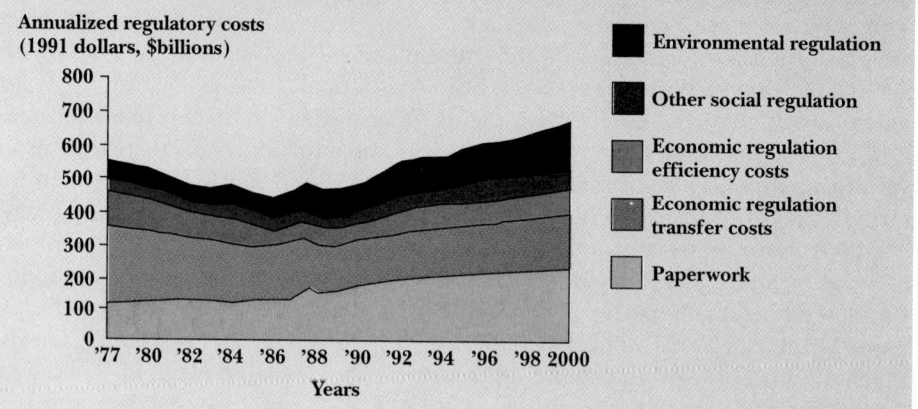

Data source: Department of Commerce.

during the late 1990s. Both 1996 and 1997 saw new records for the number of merger filings. In evaluating these mergers, enforcement agencies must strike a fine balance between expected cost savings and possible harm to competition. Both present-day and potential competitors must be considered. The impact on competition is particularly difficult to evaluate in industries experiencing rapid structural and technological change. Enforcement agencies must balance concerns about market power against the efficiencies that mergers can make possible.

The relevant market is generally the smallest group of products and geographic area in which a hypothetical monopolist could raise prices. Typically, the narrower the relevant market, the more likely it is that a merger will be investigated. For example, in 1997 the Federal Trade Commission (FTC) challenged the merger of Staples Inc. and Office Depot, Inc., because it believed that the relevant product market was "the sale of consumable office supplies through office superstores," and these firms were the two largest in that market.[2] Staples countered that the relevant market was all sales of office products, including sales by discount stores, drugstores, and wholesale clubs. The combined firm would have accounted for less than 6% of this broader market and would not be in a position to raise prices if this market definition were indeed correct. The FTC maintained, however, that the inventory selection offered by office superstores distinguish them from other office supply retailers. The FTC's statistical analysis showed that, when the presence of other potential competitors was controlled for, Staples' prices were more than 5% higher in cities where it did not face competition from other office supply superstores. The FTC took this as evidence that nonsuperstore sellers of office supplies do not constrain superstore prices. This evidence led the court to accept the FTC's market definition and conclude that the Staples–Office Depot merger would be

[2]For further details on the Staples Inc. and Office Depot, Inc., merger, and on other recent antitrust initiatives, see the *Economic Report of the President,* U.S. Government Printing Office, 1998.

anticompetitive. Rather than fight a protracted battle with the government, Staples and Office Depot abandoned their merger plans.

Present merger guidelines recognize that mergers may lessen competition through either collusion or unilateral effects. One recent example in which the analysis of unilateral effects suggested significant harm to competition is the acquisition of Continental Baking Co. by Interstate Bakeries Corp. Continental's Wonder Bread brand competed against various Interstate brands in several regions. Although these two firms were clearly not the only producers of white bread in these regions, the Justice Department concluded that white bread is a highly differentiated product, with significant customer loyalty. Simulations based on estimated demand elasticities helped convince the Justice Department that significant price increases would likely follow the merger. To avoid these price increases, the Justice Department entered into a consent decree requiring the merged firm to divest a brand of bread in each of five geographic regions.

Sometimes, antitrust authorities limit a merged firm's ability to raise prices without requiring divestiture. In 1995, Time Warner, Inc., proposed to acquire Turner Broadcasting System, Inc., in a deal valued at more than $7 billion. Both companies were important providers of programming to local cable system operators. Time Warner owned Home Box Office (HBO), the leading cable movie channel, and Turner owned Cable News Network (CNN). Both are "marquee" channels that cable operators must carry to attract and retain subscribers. The FTC was concerned that if Time Warner controlled both of these marquee channels it would increase prices charged to cable operators. To limit the anticompetitive effects of the merger, the FTC's consent order prohibited Time Warner from "bundling" HBO with Turner channels and CNN with Time Warner channels. The bundling restriction required that the Time Warner and Turner channels be offered separately at prices that do not depend on whether the other is purchased.

Of course, merger policy and analysis must reflect the fact that nonleading-firm growth or new entry can constrain the merged firm's ability to raise prices. To pose a significant competitive threat, entry must be timely, likely, and sufficient to counter the merger's adverse competitive effects. A recent merger in which the government concluded that entry seemed unlikely to offset the effects of increased concentration was the proposed 1995 acquisition of Intuit Inc. by Microsoft Corp. At that time, each of these two software companies produced a popular personal finance program: Microsoft's Money and Intuit's Quicken. Together, they accounted for more than 90% of the personal finance software market. The question faced by the Justice Department was whether other firms were likely to enter this market in sufficient force to constrain Microsoft's market power once it owned both programs. In the Justice Department's opinion, two important features of software markets limited the likelihood of entry: the importance of reputation and the "lock-in effect." Purchasers of personal finance software generally prefer a product that is widely accepted as reliable and successful and that has a reputation for performance and customer support. It can take many years and a significant investment to develop such a reputation. Even Microsoft had considerable difficulty overcoming the initial success of Intuit. After four years of effort, the market share of Microsoft's Money remained far less than that of Quicken, and Microsoft had yet to achieve a positive return on its investment. The fact that consumers have to put considerable time and effort into learning to use a given program gives rise to the lock-in effect. Users of existing software may be reluctant to incur the switching costs of learning another program. To make the deal acceptable to antitrust authorities, Microsoft planned to transfer part of its assets in Money to another software developer. Still, the Justice Department believed that the importance of reputation and the lock-in effect meant that entry could not be relied on to offset the high concentration that a merger of Microsoft and Intuit would have caused. The merger was challenged, and Microsoft decided not to pursue it.

The final major step in the review of competitive practices and mergers is to consider promised efficiencies as a possible offset to anticompetitive consequences. Two cases that the Justice Department recently filed and settled—one against a group of U.S. airlines and the other against so-called market makers who execute over-the-counter stock trades—highlight a straightforward problem with electronic commerce. Although computers increase the information available in the marketplace, they also make more information available to producers and other sellers. Sellers may be able to use this wealth of information to form or maintain cartels. For a cartel to raise prices successfully, members must come to agreement about what prices to charge and figure out a way to police that agreement. The airline and stock trading cases illustrate how computer networks can sometimes help a cartel solve both problems.

In 1994, the Justice Department reached a settlement in a price-fixing case involving eight major airlines and the Airline Tariff Publishing Company (ATP). According to the Justice Department, the airlines had used ATP's computerized fare dissemination services to negotiate increases in fares and to trade fare changes in certain markets for changes in other markets. Each airline submitted fare changes or planned changes to ATP. In turn, ATP reported the changes to other airlines. The resulting database was enormous. Each airline offered numerous fares, under various terms and conditions, on each of thousands of city pairs. Moreover, these fares changed frequently. In such a complex system, it would seem difficult for the airlines to negotiate or maintain any price-fixing agreement. With so many interrelated fares and fare changes, one might ask how one airline would distinguish whether another's price change was an attempt to cheat on a collusive agreement, a punishment of a third airline for deviating from an agreement in another market, or simply a normal response to increased costs. The Justice Department alleged that such confusion was avoided by linking fare changes with alphanumeric footnote designators and by the judicious use of first ticket dates. Because the ATP data were computerized, this mass of information could be analyzed by sophisticated computer programs each day. Aided by these computer analyses, airlines could engage in intricately camouflaged negotiations and monitor cheating on agreements. The settlement that the Justice Department entered into with the airlines barred them from using footnote designators, first ticket dates, and other devices to communicate with each other. According to one study, price leadership in the airline industry cost air travelers $365 million per year during the 1980s. Others have estimated that the cost of such behavior in the airline industry, had it been left unchecked, could have reached several billion dollars per year. These figures suggest that the Justice Department's attempts to eliminate anticompetitive practices in the airline industry could yield large dividends for consumers.

The stock trading case, which resulted in a 1996 consent decree, involved transactions in over-the-counter stocks over the automated quotation system operated by the National Association of Securities Dealers (the Nasdaq system). This case also revealed how computerized information networks can sometimes make it easier for firms to maintain agreements to sell at high prices. When an investor places a buy or sell order for shares of a company traded on Nasdaq, special traders called "market makers" typically execute the trade. These intermediaries make their profits from the bid-ask spread, the difference between the price at which they buy a stock and the price at which they sell it. In the Nasdaq case, the Justice Department alleged that Nasdaq market makers had agreed to a strategy of maintaining large bid-ask spreads. Working to support the agreement was the fact that the Nasdaq computer network provided sellers with instantaneous information about the strategies other sellers were using to quote prices. Market makers that were observed to deviate from the convention were harassed by other market makers and threatened with economic harm. In 1996, Nasdaq market makers agreed not to fix prices in the future and to commit resources to an ongoing monitoring effort to ensure that they adhere to the antitrust laws.

As these examples illustrate, antitrust policy is complex, and generalizations are difficult. Nevertheless, because antitrust policy constitutes a serious constraint to many business decisions, antitrust considerations are an important, if nebulous, aspect of the investment environment.

Corporate Governance

Corporate Governance inside the Firm

In recent years, investors have become increasingly concerned that top management of some companies is not sufficiently sensitive to shareholder interests. As a result, investors tend to favor companies with strong controls that help the firm effectively manage, administer, and direct its economic resources. If any corporation fails to effectively command its economic resources, this corporate failure can often be blamed on a similar failure of its **corporate governance** mechanisms. Corporate control mechanisms inside the firm are useful means for eliminating any potential divergence of interests between managers and stockholders. The degrees of vertical integration and horizontal scope of the corporation are examples of essential organization design characteristics. When inputs can be reliably obtained from suppliers operating in perfectly competitive markets, it is seldom attractive to produce such components in-house. Simple market procurement tends to work better. Similarly, when important economies of scale in production are operative, it is preferable to obtain inputs from large specialized suppliers. A high degree of vertical integration makes sense only when input production is within the firm's core competency and supply is erratic or suppliers charge excessive markups. In such instances, vertical integration can result in better coordination of the production process and thereby protect the firm's tangible and intangible investments.

corporate governance Control system that helps corporations effectively administer economic resources.

Vertical integration is sometimes seen as a useful means for deterring competitor entry into a company's primary market. Years ago, IBM made a huge strategic error in licensing Intel Corp. to manufacture key components for the personal

WALL STREET WISDOM 9.3

Institutional Investors Are Corporate Activists

On the morning of May 28, 1998, at a Holiday Inn in Lubbock, Texas, something extraordinary took place. Fed up with deteriorating operating performance and a declining stock price, pension-fund giant Teachers Insurance and Annuity Association of America-College Retirement Equities Fund (TIAA-CREF) spearheaded a stockholder rebellion that resulted in the ouster of the entire board of directors at Furr's/Bishop's Inc., a struggling cafeteria company. Although TIAA-CREF and other pension funds have sometimes been successful in supporting individual candidates for election to various company boards, this is the first time that an entire board has been replaced by a slate recommended by institutional investors.

What was the problem at Furr's/Bishop's? For starters, operating performance languished with anemic sales growth and deteriorating profit margins. TIAA-CREF also charged Furr's/Bishop's management with a failure to provide effective leadership, wasteful consulting and real estate contracts, and excessive executive compensation. All this was reflected in the company's stock price, which consistently declined and set an all-time low during 1998, while the overall market and industry competitors continued to set new highs.

The Furr's/Bishop's ouster could be a watershed event and mark the emergence of institutional investors as a strong force in corporate governance in the United States. Common sense suggests that institutional shareholders have the potential to become effective monitors of corporate performance. Institutional investors have significant financial and information resources at their disposal and are well positioned to obtain a clear picture of absolute and relative corporate performance. Corporate management also tends to be responsive to the questions and suggestions of institutional shareholders that control a meaningful percentage of company stock. Much institutional involvement has already taken the form of what is sometimes referred to as relationship investing. This occurs when an institutional shareholder with a significant stake in the corporation plays an active role in monitoring its activities and those of its board. Dissatisfaction among institutional shareholders can lead to a falling stock price—or worse still, quick support for an unfriendly takeover bid. As a result, corporate management and boards of directors have found themselves the recipient of increasingly detailed advice from institutional shareholders.

For example, the Council of Institutional Investors announces an annual list of companies it says have significant performance problems. The council's Focus List highlights 20 companies in the S&P 500 that most underperform industry averages in one-year, three-year, and five-year total shareholder returns. Separately, the California Public Employees Retirement System (CalPERS) gives companies letter grades on each board's performance in terms of corporate governance issues. As a means of applying pressure on individual directors, CalPERS has gone so far as to publish lists naming those persons who have served most often on the boards of underperforming companies. Such pressure tactics appear to work. Shareholder wealth tends to increase for responsive firms that adopt CalPERS suggestions; shareholder wealth decreases for unresponsive firms that reject CalPERS recommendations.

A growing role for institutional investors in corporate governance is much more than an American experience, it is a worldwide phenomenon. Institutional investors in Canada are abandoning purely passive investment strategies and have shown an increased willingness to take on management. In France, institutional investors have recently expressed their ire at bylaw changes that reduce the possibility for unfriendly takeovers. In most Italian companies, there is a major shareholder, or coalition of shareholders, who exercise majority control on the firm and are thus able to choose and remove management. In New Zealand, following changes in the Companies Act, company directors and executives face potentially tough new challenges from investing groups. Australian institutional investors have also discovered shareholder activism and are widely expected to become much more actively involved in corporate governance issues.

Thus, the ouster of Furr's/Bishop's Inc.'s underperforming board of directors may represent much more than just a precedent-setting victory for institutional investors. It may signal the dawn of a new era in corporate governance marked by activist institutional investors. If so, it will indeed be a new millennium in terms of corporate governance.

See: David Franecki, "TIAA-CREF Urges Cablevision to Add Independent Directors," *The Wall Street Journal, Interactive Edition,* May 2, 2000. <http://www.wsj.com>.

computer. Intel started out as simply a microprocessor manufacturer supplying the "brains" to manufacturers of personal computers and other "smart" electronics. Today, Intel dominates that business with a market share in excess of 85% and enjoys sky-high margins and an enviable rate of return on investment. To spur future growth, Intel is now branching out into the production of other PC components such as modems and networking equipment. Soon, the famous trademark "Intel Inside" may have to be replaced with "Intel Inside *and* Outside." Meanwhile, IBM earns only anemic returns in the PC business. All manufacturers would do well to contemplate IBM's experience with Intel before licensing the production of key components to others.

Another useful means for controlling the flow of corporate resources is provided by internal markets established among divisions to better balance the supply and demand conditions for divisional goods and services. Incentive compensation is another obvious corporate governance mechanism inside the firm. In many circumstances, the proper design and implementation of an appropriate **incentive pay** plan is the most fundamental determinant of whether corporate resources will be administered effectively. Like any effective corporate governance mechanism inside the firm, such arrangements must further the objective of minimizing transaction costs by effectively joining decision authority with the system of performance evaluation and rewards. Investors can easily obtain information about a company's incentive pay plan from the company's Annual Proxy Statement filed with the Securities and Exchange Commission. Table 9.7 shows a sample of such information for the Coca-Cola Company.

incentive pay Compensation according to measurable performance.

TABLE 9.7 Ownership of Equity Securities by Top Management and Members of the Directors in the Coca-Cola Company (as of 2/21/00)

Name	Aggregate Number of Shares Beneficially Owned	Percent of Outstanding Shares
Herbert A. Allen	9,214,823	*
Ronald W. Allen	14,410	*
Cathleen P. Black	17,778	*
Warren E. Buffett	200,006,622	8.1
Susan B. King	14,231	*
Donald F. McHenry	30,490	*
Sam Nunn	4,227	*
Paul F. Oreffice	90,778	*
James D. Robinson III	18,088	*
Peter V. Ueberroth	90,956	*
James B. Williams	105,665,419	4.3
M. Douglas Ivester	4,400,120	*
Douglas N. Daft	978,544	*
Jack L. Stahl	1,327,687	*
Joseph R. Gladden, Jr.	806,203	*
James E. Chestnut	476,282	*
All Directors and Executive Officers as a Group (20 Persons)	324,678,444	13.1

Data source: The Coca-Cola Company, Proxy Statement, March 3, 2000, 10.

Ownership Structure

capital structure Breakdown of debt and equity used to finance total assets.

ownership structure Divergent claims on the value of the firm.

inside equity Common stock held by management and other employees.

institutional equity Common stock held by mutual funds, pension plans, and other large investors.

The **capital structure** of the firm has been traditionally described in terms of the share of total financing obtained from equity investors versus lenders (debt). Today, interest has shifted from capital structure to **ownership structure,** as measured along a number of important dimensions, including inside equity, institutional equity, widely dispersed outside equity, bank debt, and widely dispersed outside debt. Among these, the percentage of **inside equity** financing receives the most attention. Inside equity is the share of stock closely held by the firm's chief executive officer (CEO), other corporate insiders including top managers, and members of the board of directors. Employees are another important source of inside equity financing, perhaps as part of an employee stock ownership plan (ESOP). The balance of equity financing is obtained from large single-party outside shareholders, mutual funds, insurance companies, pension funds, and the general public. Investors can easily obtain information about the amount of insider holdings from the company's Annual Proxy Statement filed with the Securities and Exchange Commission. Table 9.8 shows a sample of such information for the Coca-Cola Company.

When the share of insider holdings is "large," a similarly substantial self-interest in the ongoing performance of the firm can be presumed. Managers with a significant ownership interest have an obvious incentive to run the firm in a value-maximizing manner. Similarly, when ownership is concentrated among a small group of large and vocal institutional shareholders, called **institutional equity,** managers often have strong incentives to maximize corporate performance. However,

TABLE 9.8 Total Compensation for the Five Top Paid Executives of the Coca-Cola Company

		Annual Compensation		Long-Term Compensation			
Name and Principal Position	Year	Salary	Bonus	Restricted Stock Awards	Securities Underlying Options/SAR Awards	LTIP Payouts	All Other Compensation
M. Douglas Ivester	1999	$1,354,167	$0	$0	250,000	$0	$17,819,697
Former Chairman of the	1998	1,250,000	1,500,000	16,875,000	0	702,000	142,799
Board and Chief	1997	856,250	2,000,000	8,840,625	0	1,072,855	102,857
Executive Officer							
Douglas N. Daft	1999	459,833	0	0	125,000	0	33,932
Chairman of the Board	1998	415,250	275,000	2,700,000	0	351,900	33,749
and Chief Executive Officer	1997	385,000	315,000	0	87,000	440,568	31,941
Jack L. Stahl	1999	485,000	0	0	125,000	0	63,566
President and Chief	1998	465,000	275,000	2,700,000	0	429,300	61,716
Operating Officer	1997	452,250	315,000	0	87,000	659,547	61,663
Joseph R. Gladden, Jr.	1999	412,916	0	0	62,500	0	24,434
Executive Vice President	1998	390,000	175,000	0	50,000	261,900	20,442
and General Counsel	1997	381,833	205,000	0	32,000	421,544	21,443
James E. Chestnut	1999	400,000	0	543,125	117,500	0	25,529
Executive Vice President	1998	365,000	275,000	2,531,250	0	351,900	28,125
	1997	338,750	300,000	707,250	55,000	544,968	18,413

Data source: The Coca-Cola Company, Proxy Statement, March 3, 2000, p. 16.

TABLE 9.9 Insider and Institutional Stock Ownership among S&P 500 Firms

Company Name	Ticker	Industry	Market Capitalization ($ millions)	Insider Holdings (%)	Institutional Holdings (%)
A. High Market Capitalization Companies					
Microsoft Corp.	MSFT	Computer Software & Svcs.	588,884	36.0	41.5
Genl Electric	GE	Electrical Equipment	470,140	1.0	52.0
Cisco Systems	CSCO	Computer & Peripherals	347,897	3.0	60.8
Wal-Mart Stores	WMT	Retail Store	280,586	40.0	35.6
Exxon Mobil Corp.	XOM	Petroleum (Integrated)	280,388		45.2
Intel Corp.	INTC	Semiconductor	279,457		53.0
Lucent Technologies	LU	Telecom. Equipment	222,904	1.0	41.1
Intl Business Mach.	IBM	Computer & Peripherals	209,148	1.0	51.5
Citigroup Inc.	C	Financial Svcs. (Div.)	171,610		61.8
America Online	AOL	Internet	166,823	9.0	43.4
AT&T Corp.	T	Telecom. Svcs.	162,765		44.8
Merck & Co.	MRK	Drug	158,508		53.7
SBC Communications	SBC	Telecom. Svcs.	153,301		46.9
Amer. Intl Group	AIG	Financial Svcs. (Div.)	153,044		57.2
Oracle Corp.	ORCL	Computer Software & Svcs.	145,215	20.0	47.5
Averages			**252,711**	**13.9**	**49.1**
B. High Inside Ownership Companies					
Molex Inc.	MOLX	Electronics	3,811	73.0	21.6
NIKE Inc. 'B'	NKE	Shoe	8,632	56.0	44.7
Campbell Soup	CPB	Food Processing	15,440	52.0	26.3
Nortel Networks	NT	Foreign Telecom.	119,283	52.0	27.4
Coors (Adolph) 'B'	RKY	Beverage (Alcoholic)	1,864	50.0	40.3
Yahoo! Inc.	YHOO	Internet	105,405	47.0	22.5
Danaher Corp.	DHR	Diversified Co.	6,450	47.0	48.7
Alberto Culver 'B'	ACV	Toiletries/Cosmetics	799	47.0	35.9
Franklin Resources	BEN	Financial Svcs. (Div.)	7,974	43.0	40.2
Wal-Mart Stores	WMT	Retail Store	280,586	40.0	35.6
Times Mirror Co.	TMC	Newspaper	2,668	39.0	43.5
Schwab (Charles)	SCH	Securities Brokerage	30,134	38.0	44.6
Seagram Co.	VO	Beverage (Alcoholic)	20,619	37.0	27.4
Microsoft Corp.	MSFT	Computer Software & Svcs.	588,884	36.0	41.5
Dell Computer	DELL	Computer & Peripherals	127,437	35.0	41.6
Averages			**87,999**	**46.1**	**36.1**
C. High Institutional Ownership Companies					
Consol. Stores	CNS	Retail Store	1,659		97.4
Lockheed Martin	LMT	Aerospace/Defense	8,340		97.4
Bed Bath & Beyond	BBBY	Retail (Special Lines)	4,387		95.7
TJX Companies	TJX	Retail (Special Lines)	5,795	2.0	92.4
MGIC Investment	MTG	Financial Svcs. (Div.)	5,708	2.0	91.8
Solectron Corp.	SLR	Electronics	23,725	5.0	90.8
BMC Software	BMCS	Computer Software & Svcs.	12,012	1.0	90.5
Ceridian Corp.	CEN	Computer Software & Svcs.	3,001	2.0	90.0
AMR Corp.	AMR	Air Transport	9,450	1.0	89.8
Teradyne Inc.	TER	Semiconductor Cap Equip.	10,025	4.0	89.5
SLM Holding	SLM	Financial Svcs. (Div.)	6,035		89.4
WellPoint Health Ntwks	WLP	Medical Svcs.	4,439		89.2
Champion Int'l	CHA	Paper & Forest Products	6,108	1.0	89.1
PE Biosystems Group	PEB	Precision Instrument	11,132	1.0	89.0
MBIA Inc.	MBI	Financial Svcs. (Div.)	4,935	1.0	88.9
Averages			**7,783**	**2.0**	**91.4**
Averages for the S&P 500			**23,569**	**5.5**	**64.0**
Median for the S&P 500			**7,552**	**1.0**	**65.5**

Data source: *Value Line Investment Survey for Windows,* January 2000.

when the amount of closely held stock held is "small" and equity ownership is instead dispersed among a large number of small individual investors, top management can sometimes become insulated from the threat of stockholder sanctions following poor operating performance.

To get some direct insight on ownership structure among large firms, Table 9.9 shows insider and institutional stock ownership for the Standard & Poor's (S&P) 500 large-cap companies. These companies have an average market capitalization of $23.6 billion. This average is skewed upward by the enormous size of firms found at the top of the firm size distribution. The typical or median S&P 500 company has a size of $7.6 billion. The CEO, other members of top management, and members of the board of directors together own an average 5.5% of the corporations they lead. Inside ownership is skewed toward small levels, so the median inside ownership for S&P 500 companies is only 1.0%. Institutions own an average 64.0% of these companies, and the median institutional ownership is 65.5%. Because insider holdings tend to be relatively large when institutional holdings are relatively small, and vice versa, the percentage of closely held shares, or insider plus institutional holdings, has a mean of 69.5% and a median of 70.9%. This implies that roughly 30% of a typical S&P 500 company's common stock is widely dispersed among members of the general public.

Notice how the share of insider and institutional share ownership tends to vary according to firm size, even among corporate behemoths. Among true corporate giants, such as GE, Cisco, and Lucent, insiders own little stock in their employer when insider ownership is measured on a percentage basis. For them, insider ownership is much smaller than institutional ownership. Still, insider holdings of roughly 1% at GE, for example, represent an equity commitment of $4.7 billion—more than enough to provide Chairman Jack Welch and his crew with strong incentives to operate efficiently. Thus, even though the percentage of common stock held by insiders is relatively low among most corporate giants, the dollar values involved can be more than sufficient to provide necessary incentives for value maximization.

Data described in Table 9.9 reflect a well-established trend toward replacement of small atomistic shareholders by large institutional investors. Because this trend toward institutional share ownership is relatively recent in the United States, the economic advantages it entails may be relatively unappreciated. Clearly, the probability that outside investors will discover evidence of managerial inefficiency or malfeasance is increased when institutional ownership is substantial. Many institutional investors are forced to liquidate their holdings in the event of dividend omissions or bankruptcy filings. As a result, institutional investors are especially sensitive to such possibilities. Fiduciary responsibility also forces many institutional investors to tender their shares in the event of an above-market tender offer or takeover bid. At the same time, when institutional share ownership is high, the costs of proxy solicitations are reduced. Thus, managers of firms with high institutional ownership are relatively more susceptible to unfriendly takeover bids. Insider and institutional stock ownership appear to represent alternative forms of ownership concentration that combine to form an effective method for ensuring that managers of large corporations are sensitive to investor interests.

Summary

- **Macroeconomics** is the study of aggregate measures of economic activity at the international, national, regional, or state level. **Microeconomics** is the study of economic data at the industry, firm, plant, or product level. One of the most important economy-wide considerations for investors is the **business cycle,** or rhythmic pattern of contraction and expansion observed in the overall economy. The Conference Board, a private research group, provides extensive data on a wide variety of **economic indicators,** or data series that successfully describe the pattern of projected, current, or past economic activity. A **composite index** is a weighted average of leading, coincident, or lagging economic indicators.

- One of the most prominent uses of economic survey information is to track the pace of economic betterment, or **productivity growth,** in the overall economy. Productivity growth is the rate of increase in output per unit of input. When productivity growth is robust in the overall economy, economic welfare per capita rises quickly. When productivity growth is sluggish, economic welfare improves slowly. Firms responsible for high rates of productivity growth are investor favorites.
- **Market structure** is typically characterized on the basis of four important industry characteristics: the number and size distribution of active buyers and sellers and potential entrants, the degree of product differentiation, the amount and cost of information about product price and quality, and conditions of entry and exit. A **potential entrant** is an individual or firm posing a sufficiently credible threat of market entry to affect the price/output decisions of incumbent firms.
- An important source of above-normal profits in hotly competitive industries is **disequilibrium profits.** Disequilibrium profits are above-normal returns earned in the interval between when a favorable influence on industry demand or cost conditions first transpires and when competition fully develops. **Disequilibrium losses** are below-normal returns suffered in the time interval between when an unfavorable influence on industry demand or cost conditions occurs and when exit or downsizing finally transpires.
- An effective investment strategy in imperfectly competitive markets must be based on the search for firms with a clear **competitive advantage.** A competitive advantage is a unique ability to create, distribute, or service products valued by customers. Although business and investor success is possible in hotly competitive markets, only difficult-to-enter **monopoly** and **oligopoly** markets hold the potential for long-lasting above-normal returns.
- The **economic census** is the primary source of detailed public facts about the nation's economy. Economic censuses are taken at five-year intervals during years ending with the digits 2 and 7—for example, 1992, 1997, 2002, and 2007. Industry statistics contained in the 1997 Economic Census are classified by using a new **North American Industry Classification System (NAICS).**
- Leading-firm market share data are calculated from sales information for various clusters of top firms called **concentration ratios (CR)** because they measure the percentage market share concentrated in (or held by) an industry's top four (CR_4), eight (CR_8), 20 (CR_{20}), or 50 (CR_{50}) firms. The **Herfindahl Hirschmann Index (HHI)**, named after the economists who invented it, is a popular measure of competitor size inequality that reflects size differences among large and small firms. When investors use these census data, it is important to keep in mind that these data are collected at the **establishment** level of aggregation. Many companies own or control more than one establishment.

- Although all sectors of the U.S. economy are regulated to some degree, the method and scope of **regulation** vary widely. Most companies escape price and profit restraint, except during periods of general wage-price control, but they are subject to operating regulations governing pollution emissions, product packaging and labeling, worker safety and health, and so on. A significant recent challenge for **antitrust policy** has been the dramatic rise in merger activity.
- Investors tend to favor companies with controls that help manage, administer, and direct its economic resources. If any corporation fails to effectively command its economic resources, this corporate failure can often be blamed on a similar failure of its **corporate governance** mechanisms. In many circumstances, the design and implementation of an appropriate **incentive pay** plan are the most fundamental determinants of whether corporate resources will be administered effectively.
- **Capital structure** has been traditionally described in terms of the share of total financing obtained from equity investors versus lenders (debt). Today, interest has shifted from capital structure to **ownership structure,** as measured along a number of important dimensions, including inside equity, institutional equity, widely dispersed outside equity, bank debt, and widely dispersed outside debt. Among these, the percentage of **inside equity** financing receives the most attention. Inside equity is the share of stock closely held by the firm's chief executive officer (CEO), other corporate insiders including top managers, and members of the board of directors. When ownership is concentrated among a small group of large and vocal institutional shareholders, called **institutional equity,** managers often have strong incentives to maximize corporate performance.

Questions

1. An industry in which each of the leading four firms enjoys market shares of 25% is described by a
   a. $CR_4 = 25$.
   b. HHI = 25.
   c. $CR_4 = 100$ and an HHI = 2,500.
   d. $CR_8 = 100$ and an HHI = 25.
2. The North American Industry Classification System does *not*
   a. pertain to the United States, Canada, and Mexico.
   b. give timely insight regarding economic activity at the firm level.
   c. provide multiple levels of economic aggregation.
   d. draw on government and industry resources for collection and dissemination.
3. The required rate of return is *not* composed of the
   a. dividend yield.
   b. real risk-free rate.
   c. expected inflation rate.
   d. required risk premium.

4. Economic growth makes common stocks a
   a. zero-sum game before commissions and taxes.
   b. zero-sum game after commissions and taxes.
   c. positive-sum game after commissions and taxes.
   d. positive-sum game before commissions and taxes.
5. Microeconomics is used to predict
   a. inflation.
   b. unemployment.
   c. firm profits.
   d. GDP.
6. Business cycles traditionally occur about once every
   a. millennium.
   b. 12 months.
   c. five years.
   d. decade.
7. A popular leading indicator of economic activity is provided by the trend in
   a. the prime rate.
   b. industrial production.
   c. commercial and industrial loans.
   d. stock prices.
8. In the United States, business activity measured in real dollars expands at an annual rate of roughly
   a. 0%.
   b. 7.5%.
   c. 3%.
   d. 12–14%.
9. Macroeconomic forecasting is made difficult by
   a. low but stable interest rates.
   b. changing expectations.
   c. economic growth.
   d. high but stable interest rates.
10. Roughly two-thirds of real economic growth is explained by
    a. increasing productivity.
    b. growth in labor force participation.
    c. inflation.
    d. population growth.
11. When barriers to entry and exit are minimal, competitor reactions tend to be quick and disequilibrium profits are
    a. positive.
    b. temporary.
    c. negative.
    d. none of these.

12. Monopoly describes a market environment with
    a. few sellers of a differentiated product.
    b. many sellers of a differentiated product.
    c. few sellers of a homogeneous product.
    d. none of these.
13. A rare ability to create, distribute, or service products valued by customers is called a
    a. barrier to entry.
    b. barrier to exit.
    c. competitive disadvantage.
    d. competitive advantage.
14. Productivity growth, or the pace of economic betterment, in the United States
    a. averages 12–14% per year.
    b. is reduced by population growth.
    c. is measured by the rate of technical change.
    d. has been helped by the Internet.
15. A vigorously competitive industry composed of five leading firms of equal features is described by
    a. $CR_4 = 100$.
    b. HHI = 20%.
    c. HHI = 2,000.
    d. none of these.
16. HHI information overstates market power for industries with
    a. foreign competition.
    b. regional markets.
    c. domestic competition.
    d. high barriers to entry.
17. Economic census statistics are collected and published at the
    a. firm level of aggregation.
    b. establishment level of aggregation.
    c. industry level of aggregation.
    d. state level of aggregation.
18. Select the one *true* statement about the relevant market.
    a. The relevant market is generally the largest group of products for which a hypothetical monopolist could raise prices.
    b. The relevant market is generally the largest geographic area in which a hypothetical monopolist could raise prices.
    c. The impact of mergers on competition is particularly easy to evaluate in high-tech industries.

d. Typically, the narrower the relevant market, the more likely it is that a merger will be investigated.

19. Organization design does *not* involve
    a. planning the regulatory environment.
    b. corporate governance.
    c. incentive pay plans.
    d. contractual specifications.
20. Information about the firm's ownership structure can typically be obtained from the
    a. annual report.
    b. proxy statement.
    c. 10-report to the SEC.
    d. quarterly report.

Investment Application

Lies, Damn Lies, and Government Statistics

Once a reliable source of timely and accurate statistics on the U.S. economy, the federal government's system for gathering and interpreting economic data has fallen on hard times. To illustrate, consider an admittedly tough question: How much have prices risen or fallen lately?

When prices rise, there is the always hard-to-decipher problem of sorting out payments for quality improvements versus simply higher prices. Think about how much more you are paying for monthly long-distance telephone service and you will see what economists mean when they complain about adjusting for quality improvements. Chances are that your monthly long-distance bill is higher today than it was five years ago, but your use of telephone services has changed dramatically over time.

Ten years ago, one of the most innovative uses of the telephone centered on FAX services. Commercial and personal use of FAX services has skyrocketed as lawyers, for example, routinely send clients legal documents via FAX for their signature. Although FAX services may sometimes be more expensive than traditional "snail mail," how does one value the benefits achieved in terms of more timely client service?

Over the next few years, a large chunk of your phone bill will be accounted for by new charges for Internet connections and various other services. How does one adjust Internet service provider (ISP) charges for the value added by faster and more reliable ISP service? When telephone service is delivered by traditional cable television companies, how do you adjust the amount of your phone bill for the added benefit of "pay-per-view" movies and the added convenience of having phone and cable bills combined? Even measuring the cost of long-distance phone service becomes difficult when local and long-distance services are combined and offered by a single provider, as they will be in the years ahead. Every year, long-distance phone service customers make more frequent and longer phone conversations. The monthly bill paid by consumers continues to rise, but the cost per minute for long-distance phone service has fallen precipitously for decades. So tell me, is the cost of long-distance telephone service going up or down?

How about the cost for a personal computer? While the average price paid by consumers for a desktop PC has fallen from roughly $3,000 to $1,500 during the past decade, computer costs fell even faster than you think. Dramatic improvements in computing power and ease of use makes comparing computer hardware and software prices over time difficult, at best. The fact is that your desktop computer is several times more powerful and easier to use than a roomful of computers in the 1970s.

Problems judging the pace of productivity growth and price changes for telephone service and personal computers are only two examples of the many difficulties confronted by government statisticians. As the high-tech sector grows in importance over time, such difficulties are bound to escalate. Even in low-tech sectors in which product or service quality change little, consumers adapt buying habits to moderate the effects of price increases. How do you account for the fact that consumers bring their cars in between 7:00 and 9:00 in the morning to save $6 off the regular $28.95 price of an oil change at Jiffy Lube? How do you account for the fact that shoppers shift to apples when oranges jump from 79¢ to 89¢ per pound? When buyers shift their buying habits to save money, are such shifts relevant when calculating the pace of inflation?

For another illustration, consider the problems faced by the Bureau of Labor Statistics (BLS). The BLS's attempts to measure unemployment by monthly surveys of some 60,000 representative households are bedeviled by demographic and structural shifts. Among the important questions that the survey cannot answer are: How many of the "unemployed" work in the underground economy? What proportion of the roughly 85 million Americans putting in 35 or more hours a week and counted as full-time workers actually hold two or more part-time jobs? What about laid-off managers who adopt the label "consultant" to mask the reality of joblessness? Until these questions are answered, the true unemployment rate could be higher, or lower, than the official numbers.

The problem is that admittedly imperfect government-provided estimates increasingly involve errors and bias. Government statisticians are slow to recognize the effects of new technology and better products. Efforts to reduce the burden of paperwork on business have also made it more difficult to gather detailed data in a timely fashion. With help from leading manufacturers, the BLS revised its methods for calculating computer price indexes by taking into account increases in computing speed. As a result, computer prices adjusted for quality changes are plunging at a double-digit rate per year. In most other areas, the task of adjusting price indexes for changes in product quality is woefully inadequate. The producer price index, which contains thousands of values for products such as bolts and valves, still has no accurate measure for semiconductors or for communications equipment, arguably the biggest category of producer durables.

The rapidly expanding service sector has created almost all the economy's new jobs, and productivity measurement in services is treacherously difficult. Banks have been quick to apply computer technology to back-office operations and install automated teller machines. The resulting productivity gains go largely unmeasured.

In the securities industry, the number of shares traded per day on the New York Stock Exchange has jumped from 8 to 10 million during the 1960s to an average in excess of one billion shares per day at the start of the new millennium. Moreover, this surge in industry output has occurred despite a modest increase in industry employment.

A. What should be done to ensure that government statistics better measure productivity and price changes?

B. Detailed concentration ratio and HHI information for 1997 will not become available until mid-2000, at the earliest. Explain how this limits the usefulness of these data for investors, and what investors can do to remedy thc problem.

Selected References

Asness, Clifford S. "Stocks versus Bonds: Explaining the Equity Risk Premium." *Financial Analysts Journal* 56 (March/April 2000): 96–113.

Brown, David T. "Liquidity and Liquidation: Evidence from Real Estate Investment Trusts." *Journal of Finance* 55 (February 2000): 469–485.

Comerton-Forde, Carole. "Do Trading Rules Impact on Market Efficiency? A Comparison of Opening Procedures on the Australian and Jakarta Stock Exchanges." *Pacific-Basin Finance Journal* 7 (December 1999): 495–521.

Granito, Michael R. "Efficient Asset Management: A Practical Guide to Stock Portfolio Optimization and Asset Allocation." *Financial Analysts Journal* 55 (May/June 1999): 101–102.

Hanson, Robert C., and Moon H. Song. "Managerial Ownership, Board Structure, and the Division of Gains in Divestitures." *Journal of Corporate Finance* 6 (March 2000): 55–70.

Hermes, Niels, and Robert Lensink. "Financial System Development in Transition Economies." *Journal of Banking and Finance* 24 (April 2000): 507–524.

Hirschey, Mark, Vernon J. Richardson, and Susan Scholz. "How 'Foolish' Are Internet Investors?" *Financial Analysts Journal* 56 (January/February 2000): 62–69.

Hovakimian, Armen, and Edward J. Kane. "Effectiveness of Capital Regulation at U.S. Commercial Banks, 1985 to 1994." *Journal of Finance* 55 (February 2000): 451–468.

Jones, David. "Emerging Problems with the Basel Capital Accord: Regulatory Capital Arbitrage and Related Issues." *Journal of Banking and Finance* 24 (January 2000): 35–58.

Kim, E. Han, and Vijay Singal. "Stock Market Openings: Experience of Emerging Economies." *Journal of Business* 73 (January 2000): 25–66.

Krishnaswami, Sudha, and Venkat Subramaniam. "Information Asymmetry, Valuation, and the Corporate Spin-Off Decision." *Journal of Financial Economics* 53 (July 1999): 73–112.

Linsmeier, Thomas J., and Neil D. Pearson. "Value at Risk." *Financial Analysts Journal* 56 (March/April 2000): 47–67.

Olsen, Robert A. "Are Risk Premium Anomalies Caused by Ambiguity?" *Financial Analysts Journal* 56 (March/April 2000): 24–31.

Scholtens, Bert. "Financial Regulation and Financial System Architecture in Central Europe." *Journal of Banking and Finance* 24 (April 2000): 525–553.

Wilner, Benjamin S. "The Exploitation of Relationships in Financial Distress: The Case of Trade Credit." *Journal of Finance* 55 (February 2000): 153–178.

PART 5

Common Stock Selection

CHAPTER 10

Growth Stock Investing

Does the hot market for high-tech stocks reflect "irrational exuberance," as Federal Reserve Chairman Alan Greenspan has suggested, or are conventional views of the economy not exuberant enough? To many growth stock investors, the explosive rise of young high-tech stocks is a sign of economic prosperity and not a worrisome indicator of an overvalued market. If the stock market provides a forecast of future events, then a dramatic upswing in the financial markets represents a rosy forecast of higher output, productivity growth, and future profits. Some see evidence of technological change that amounts to another industrial revolution.[1]

Despite its 1999 makeover that added high-tech darlings Intel and Microsoft, the Dow Jones Industrial Average (DJIA) is dominated by Old Economy stalwarts such as Honeywell, J. P. Morgan, and Philip Morris. Many newer and faster growing companies that make up the Nasdaq 100 are surpassing DJIA behemoths. In March 2000, for example, the market value of the Nasdaq's 100 largest nonfinancial companies stood at more than $6 trillion and eclipsed the $3.8 trillion market capitalization of the DJIA. New Economy high-tech stocks, such as Cisco Systems, JDS Uniphase, and Qualcomm, typify the types of companies that investors seem to crave: leading companies in rapidly growing sectors that change like quicksilver.

Historically, it has been very tough to pinpoint "permanent winners" among rapidly evolving tech stocks. At the height of the "Nifty 50" era in 1972, for example, so-called one-decision stocks crumbled by 70% and more in the ensuing market downturn. Seasoned observers wonder: How will "Cisco and the Kids" fare when they encounter their first recession?

growth stock investing Investment approach that focuses on companies expected to have above-average rates of growth in earnings and dividends.

Growth Stocks

Forward-Looking Analysis

Portfolio management is often described according to the investment philosophy or "style" of stock selection used. Most methods build on one of the two most common approaches to equity investing. **Growth stock investing** involves focusing on

[1]See: Susan Pulliam, "Good News Is No News for Tech Stocks," *The Wall Street Journal*, May 24, 2000, CI,

companies expected to have above-average rates of growth in earnings and dividends. Another popular approach, **value investing,** involves focusing on securities considered to be temporarily undervalued or unpopular for various reasons. In both cases, investors seek bargains selling at prices below their actual **economic value.** In the case of value investing, bargains are typically described in terms of a market price that is below the economic value of assets in place. In the case of growth stock investing, bargains are defined in terms of securities selling for prices below the value of future growth opportunities.

value investing Investment approach that concentrates on securities considered to be temporarily undervalued or unpopular for various reasons.

economic value Value determined by economic prospects.

Table 10.1 illustrates the challenge faced by growth stock investors. There is often little relation between projected earnings per share (EPS) growth and historical EPS growth. When it comes to stock valuation, it is future earnings growth that matters.

Growth stock investors use differing criteria to identify attractive candidates for purchase. Some look for companies with three or more consecutive years of above-average growth in both per-share earnings and revenues. Others look for firms with high profit margins and projected earnings increases of 10–15% (or more) for three to five years. Still others look for earnings growth at a rate that is at least twice that of the average company represented by the Standard & Poor's (S&P) 500 Index. Growth stock investors also look beyond earnings-per-share numbers to gauge whether a company can prudently sustain rapid growth.

An important consideration is whether a growth company has sufficient resources to finance future growth internally or will need to borrow funds. Ideally, growth companies generate sufficient funds for above-average growth from retained earnings. In those instances in which growth companies cannot be self-financing, they are expected to have healthy balance sheets with equity levels that are at least twice the level of debt. In any event, companies with burdensome levels of debt financing are to be avoided.

The quality of management is also a key concern to growth stock investors. Do managers have the experience and know-how to cope with rapid growth? Are management and employee compensation plans in place to provide appropriate incentives for high-margin growth? If the answers to both questions are yes, then a rapidly growing company may indeed be appropriate for investment.

Seeking Opportunity

Growth stock investors favor aggressive companies that sell at premium valuations when value is measured in terms of conventional P/E ratios. Dividend income is typically a secondary consideration, if relevant at all. Such investors are usually willing to accept far larger than typical levels of risk in the pursuit of above-average long-term investment results.

Many growth stock investors focus first on a company's external economic environment. Does the company operate in a fast-growing economic sector, such as telecommunications equipment during the 1990s, in which a "rising tide lifts all boats"? Alternatively, does the company occupy a lucrative niche in an otherwise slow-growth market? Is the niche market expanding? If the company is in a market experiencing explosive growth, will large and small new entrants diminish or eliminate future profit opportunities?

Pinpointing the source of recent and expected earnings growth is crucial. Ideally, rising sales and earnings growth should be accompanied by higher profit

TABLE 10.1 Little Relation Often Exists between Projected EPS Growth and Historical EPS Growth

Company Name	Ticker	Industry	Market Cap ($ millions)	P/E Ratio	EPS Growth 5-Year (%)	Projected EPS Growth (%)	Projected 3–5 Year Return (%)
A. Top Projected EPS Growth							
America Online	AOL	Internet	166,823		76.5	92.5	9.0
Yahoo! Inc.	YHOO	Internet	105,405			70.5	−11.0
Amerada Hess	AHC	Petroleum (Integrated)	4,807	16.0		66.0	8.0
Inco Limited	N	Metals & Mining (Div.)	4,480	88.4		63.0	2.0
Network Appliance	NTAP	Computer & Peripherals	11,532			61.0	14.0
Qualcomm Inc.	QCOM	Telecom. Equipment	100,461			58.0	−17.0
Viacom Inc. 'A'	VIA	Entertainment	7,151	74.9	−10.0	48.0	4.0
Novell Inc.	NOVL	Computer Software & Svcs.	11,657	51.5	−27.0	45.0	5.0
Champion Intl	CHA	Paper & Forest Products	6,108	20.5		44.5	11.0
Unisys Corp.	UIS	Computer & Peripherals	8,987	18.1	24.0	40.5	15.0
MCI WorldCom	WCOM	Telecom. Svcs.	143,995	32.4	19.5	38.5	18.0
EMC Corp.	EMC	Computer & Peripherals	104,803	83.1	50.5	36.5	5.0
Best Buy Co.	BBY	Retail (Special Lines)	11,290	34.4	27.5	35.0	4.0
Dell Computer	DELL	Computer & Peripherals	127,437	60.9	86.0	34.5	12.0
Providian Finl	PVN	Financial Svcs. (Div.)	11,500	18.3		34.0	21.0
Averages			**55,096**	**45.3**	**30.9**	**51.2**	**6.7**
B. Top Historical 5-Year EPS Growth							
Dell Computer	DELL	Computer & Peripherals	127,437	60.9	86.0	34.5	12.0
America Online	AOL	Internet	166,823		76.5	92.5	9.0
Coca-Cola Enterprises	CCE	Beverage (Soft Drink)	8,393	63.7	74.0	19.0	14.0
Coastal Corp.	CGP	Natural Gas (Diversified)	7,084	13.4	72.5	13.0	12.0
N.Y. Times	NYT	Newspaper	7,690	25.2	69.0	13.0	6.0
Tellabs Inc.	TLAB	Telecom. Equipment	24,790	41.4	68.0	24.5	3.0
Deere & Co.	DE	Machinery	10,238	35.9	63.5	7.0	19.0
KLA-Tencor	KLAC	Precision Instrument	8,666	51.9	59.5	20.0	−7.0
Brunswick Corp.	BC	Recreation	1,934	8.3	53.0	11.0	26.0
Applied Materials	AMAT	Semiconductor Cap Equip.	43,802	39.6	51.0	20.0	−7.0
EMC Corp.	EMC	Computer & Peripherals	104,803	83.1	50.5	36.5	5.0
Union Carbide	UK	Chemical (Basic)	8,533	34.1	50.0	11.5	8.0
Cisco Systems	CSCO	Computer & Peripherals	347,897		49.0	25.5	−8.0
Clear Channel	CCU	Entertainment	28,762		46.0	22.5	6.0
Parametric Technology	PMTC	Computer Software & Svcs.	5,385	26.7	45.5	14.0	11.0
Averages			**60,149**	**40.3**	**60.9**	**24.3**	**7.3**

Data source: *Value Line Investment Survey for Windows*, January 2000.

margins. When rapid earnings growth is accompanied by stagnant or falling profit margins, negative implications for future growth opportunities often emerge. For example, if rising earnings are due to higher unit sales only made possible by expanding the number of retail stores, established stores may be losing momentum in fully saturated markets. Alternatively, if sales growth is only made possible by steep price cuts, future earnings growth may be constrained by product market competition. Worse still is the situation in which earnings growth is only achieved by a one-shot boost, such as a well-timed merger or a dip in the company's effective tax rate.

Financial maneuvering is a poor substitute for economic growth and a common precursor to poor future results.

Growth Stock Characteristics

Essential Features

Growth stock investing focuses on well-managed companies whose earnings and dividends are expected to grow faster than both inflation and the overall economy. In the late 1930s, Thomas Rowe Price, founder of Baltimore, Maryland–based mutual fund company T. Rowe Price and Associates, Inc., was a pioneer of the growth stock approach to investing. T. Rowe Price saw the test for a growth company as its ability to sustain earnings momentum even during economic slowdowns. He predicted that such companies would provide above-average long-term growth of earnings, dividends, and capital, thus preserving the investor's purchasing power against erosion from the effects of continuing inflation.

According to T. Rowe Price, growth stocks display a number of attractive economic characteristics:

- Growth stocks display high profit margins, an attractive return on total assets (ROA), and consistent earnings-per-share growth and use low levels of debt financing.
- Growth stocks lack cutthroat competition.
- Growth stocks have superior research to develop distinctive products and new markets.
- Growth stocks have low overall labor costs but pay high wages to talented employees.
- Growth stocks are immune from regulation.

At any point in time, it would be rare to find several growth stock investment opportunities that embody all these essential features. Still, prudence requires at least some diversification. Phillip Fisher, another famous early proponent of growth stock investing, was so focused on buying the best companies in the best industries that he often advocated an investment portfolio of as few as three to five well-chosen industry leaders. Although T. Rowe Price was also a fierce advocate of buying the best companies in the best industries, his investment approach advocated broader diversification and often included as many as 20–25 individual positions.

Although the late T. Rowe Price has not been active in the fund's management for more than 30 years, the investment philosophy that he developed remains in place today at the T. Rowe Growth Stock Fund. As shown in Figure 10.1, New York

FIGURE 10.1 **Freddie Mac Is a Top Holding of the T. Rowe Price Growth Stock Fund**

FREDDIE MAC NYSE-FRE

RECENT PRICE **48** | P/E RATIO **15.9** (Trailing: 17.3 Median: 12.0) | RELATIVE P/E RATIO **1.07** | DIV'D YLD **1.4%** | **VALUE LINE**

TIMELINESS 3 Lowered 6/25/99
SAFETY 2 Raised 5/2/97
TECHNICAL 3 Lowered 7/9/99
BETA 1.30 (1.00 = Market)

High:	4.2	8.7	6.8	11.6	12.3	14.2	15.7	20.9	29.0	44.6	66.4	65.3
Low:	1.0	4.1	2.5	3.7	8.4	11.3	11.8	12.5	19.1	26.8	38.7	45.4

Target Price Range 2002 | 2003 | 2004

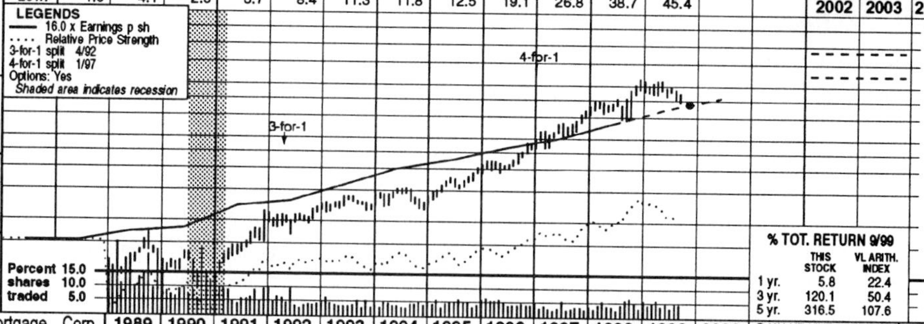

2002-04 PROJECTIONS

	Price	Gain	Ann'l Total Return
High	95	(+100%)	19%
Low	70	(+45%)	14%

Insider Decisions

	D	J	F	M	A	M	J	J	A
to Buy	0	0	0	0	0	0	0	0	0
Options	0	0	0	0	0	0	0	0	0
to Sell	0	0	0	0	0	0	0	0	0

Institutional Decisions

	4Q1998	1Q1999	2Q1999
to Buy	317	305	316
to Sell	223	263	242
Hld's(000)	547929	545697	543535

% TOT. RETURN 9/99

	THIS STOCK	VL ARITH. INDEX
1 yr.	5.8	22.4
3 yr.	120.1	50.4
5 yr.	316.5	107.6

Federal Home Loan Mortgage Corp. (Freddie Mac) was created by an Act of Congress in 1970. In 1984, it issued approx. 15 mill. shs. of participating pfd. stk. to FHLB-member S&Ls. Trading was generally limited to FHLB members and mkt. makers. In 8/88, co. offered for each pfd. share plus $7, 4 shares of freely transferable senior part. pfd., which began "when-issued" trading on the NYSE in 12/88. In 8/89, the FIRREA law converted these shs. into voting com. shs. All of the share figures shown assume the prior cv. of pfd. stock into voting com., adj. for the 4-for-1 exchange.

1989	1990	1991	1992	1993	1994	1995	1996	1997	1998	1999	2000	© VALUE LINE PUB., INC.	02-04
.55	.58	.77	.82	1.02	1.27	1.42	1.65	1.90	2.31	*2.90*	*3.30*	Earnings per sh A	*5.20*
.13	.13	.17	.19	.22	.26	.30	.35	.40	.48	*.60*	*.70*	Div'ds Decl'd per share B	*1.00*
2.66	2.96	3.56	4.92	4.95	5.95	6.99	7.68	8.74	11.54	*12.20*	*14.55*	Book Value per sh	*26.70*
721.03	720.43	720.24	721.33	722.57	723.05	715.16	694.48	678.89	695.18	*700.00*	*700.00*	Common shs Outs'g C	*700.00*
10.9	9.0	9.3	12.8	12.5	11.0	11.6	13.6	18.0	21.4	*Bold figures are*	*Value Line*	Avg Ann'l P/E Ratio	*16.0*
.83	.67	.59	.78	.74	.72	.78	.85	1.04	1.12	*estimates*		Relative P/E Ratio	*1.05*
2.2%	2.6%	2.3%	1.8%	1.7%	1.9%	1.8%	1.5%	1.2%	.9%			Avg Ann'l Div'd Yield	*1.2%*
21852	21858	26809	33665	55476	72693	107424	137755	164421	255009	*330000*	*370000*	Mortgage Loans ($mill)	*450000*
272870	316359	359163	407514	439029	460656	459045	554260	554260	646459	*755000*	*820000*	PCs Outs'g ($mill)	*1000000*
517.0	619.0	683.0	695.0	852.0	1155	1542	1882	1882	1927	*2525*	*2800*	Net Int Income ($mill)	*3500*
572.0	654.0	792.0	936.0	1033	1108	1087	1249	1249	1307	*1390*	*1475*	Guaranty Fees ($mill)	*1650*
10.00%	9.42%	8.35%	6.69%	6.70%	6.31%	7.15%	6.94%	7.01%	6.77%	*6.75%*	*6.85%*	Avg Portfolio Yield D	*7.10%*
9.49%	8.82%	7.81%	6.65%	6.68%	5.54%	5.93%	5.95%	6.42%	6.23%	*6.15%*	*6.15%*	Avg Interest Paid D	*6.40%*
30.4%	29.5%	30.6%	31.0%	30.3%	30.7%	31.2%	30.0%	29.0%	29.0%	*31.0%*	*31.0%*	Income Tax Rate	*30.0%*
437.0	414.0	555.0	622.0	786.0	983.0	1091.0	1243.0	1395.0	1700.0	*2150*	*2425*	Net Profit ($mill)	*3750*
16673	19959	17839	12854	17999	47307	62141	80105	85128	193871	*175000*	*190000*	Short-Term Debt ($mill)	*375000*
9474	10982	12423	16777	31994	45972	57820	76876	83446	93363	*170000*	*200000*	Long-Term Debt ($mill)	*250000*
1916	2136	2566	3570	4437	5162	5863	6731	7521	10835	*11350*	*13000*	Shr. Equity ($mill)	*21500*
5.4%	5.3%	5.5%	6.0%	5.3%	4.9%	4.3%	3.9%	3.9%	3.4%	*3.5%*	*3.5%*	Shr. Eq. to Total Assets	*3.5%*
1.23%	1.02%	1.18%	1.05%	.94%	.93%	.80%	.72%	.72%	.70%	*.65%*	*.60%*	Return on Total Assets	*.70%*
22.8%	19.4%	21.6%	17.4%	17.7%	19.0%	18.6%	18.5%	18.5%	15.7%	*16.5%*	*17.0%*	Return on Shr. Equity (E)	*18.0%*
17.3%	14.9%	17.0%	12.8%	16.1%	17.0%	16.2%	17.3%	17.3%	14.8%	*15.5%*	*15.5%*	Retained to Com Eq	*16.5%*
24%	23%	22%	27%	27%	26%	26%	26%	26%	27%	*25%*	*26%*	All Div'ds to Net Prof	*25%*

CAPITAL STRUCTURE as of 6/30/99
ST Debt $173.6 bill. (49% of Cap'l)
LT Debt $167.5 bill. (47% of Cap'l)
Pension Liability None
Pfd Stock $3207.0 mill. **Pfd Div'd** $150.0 mill. (1% of Cap'l)
Common Stock 695,180,000 shs. (3% of Cap'l)
MARKET CAP: $33.4 Billion (Large Cap)

ASSETS ($bill.)	1997	1998	9/30/99
Mortgages	164.3	255.3	314.5
Investments	20.8	44.8	23.4
Other	9.5	20.7	24.9
LIABILITIES ($bill.)			
Short-Term Debt	85.1	193.9	173.6
Long-Term Debt	84.0	93.4	167.5
Due PC Investors	11.0	19.4	7.5
Other Liab.	7.0	3.3	4.7
Net Worth	7.5	10.8	11.1
Total	194.6	320.8	364.4
PCs Outstanding	579.0	646.5	738.6

ANNUAL RATES of change (per sh)	Past 10 Yrs.	Past 5 Yrs.	Est'd '95-'97 to '02-'04
Mortgage Lns	28.5%	39.0%	*21.0%*
Savings Dep	--	--	--
Earnings	17.0%	18.0%	*17.5%*
Dividends	14.0%	16.5%	*13.0%*
Book Value	41.0%	15.5%	*16.5%*

Cal-endar	LOANS OUTSTANDING ($ bill.) Mar.31	Jun.30	Sep.30	Dec.31
1996	117.4	123.7	129.2	137.5
1997	144.4	149.1	157.0	164.3
1998	186.1	196.8	216.6	255.0
1999	277.7	299.0	314.5	*330*
2000	*340*	*345*	*360*	*370*

Cal-endar	EARNINGS PER SHARE A Mar.31	Jun.30	Sep.30	Dec.31	Full Year
1996	.40	.41	.41	.43	1.65
1997	.44	.46	.49	.51	1.90
1998	.54	.57	.58	.62	2.31
1999	.68	.74	.74	*.74*	*2.90*
2000	*.79*	*.81*	*.84*	*.86*	*3.30*

Cal-endar	QUARTERLY DIVIDENDS PAID B Mar.31	Jun.30	Sep.30	Dec.31	Full Year
1995	.075	.075	.075	.075	.30
1996	.088	.088	.088	.088	.35
1997	.10	.10	.10	.10	.40
1998	.12	.12	.12	.12	.48
1999	.15	.15	.15		

BUSINESS: Freddie Mac (known formally as Federal Home Loan Mortgage Corp.), maintains a secondary market in residential mortgages, primarily by securitizing and guaranteeing such loans. Also maintains a portfolio of residential mortgages for its own account. Debt enjoys favorable "government-agency" status, but is not explicitly backed by the full faith and credit of the U.S. government. Pres. of the U.S. appoints 5 dirs. to 18-member board. Subject to explicit federal regulation. Has about 3,200 emplys. Fidelity controls 12.1% of stk.; Berkshire Hathaway, 8.7%; Oppenheimer, 5.3%; offrs. & dirs., less than 1% (4/99 proxy). Chrmn. & C.E.O.: Leland C. Brendsel. Pres.: David W. Glenn. Inc.: U.S. Addr.: 8200 Jones Branch Dr., McLean, VA 22102. Tel.: 703-903-2000.

Freddie Mac, which has seen its stock's price momentum falter, is starting to face difficulties in its core mortgage market. Wall Street is factoring in a deceleration in earnings for the year ahead, a fact that will probably keep most performance-oriented accounts on the sidelines. The stock's premium P/E and price/book multiples have narrowed, while the prospects for regaining premiums to the market multiples seem less likely now that the pipeline of mortgages has diminished considerably. The earnings surprise factor had worked in the stock's favor for a while. But, the disappointment on the net-interest margin in the third period, and seemingly less reliability of the recurring portion of income, suggests some caution going forward. Some of the margin compression was offset by fee income from hedging activities, though the magnitude of the shortfall is what has alarmed some investors.

Although the company met consensus estimates in the period, the components of the earnings equation were not to Wall Street's liking. First, the compression of the margin, which is partially attributable to some re-weighting of short- and long-term debt, has provided evidence that managing for a stable margin will prove more trying. During periods of unusual volatility, Freddie Mac can use its financial muscle and liquidity to get better spreads, though its hedging activities come at a higher cost than would be the case otherwise because of the embedded risk premium. And though the changing risk profile of the mortgage portfolio should allow some reductions in provisioning for loan losses, we think the non recurring portion of the credit benefits (roughly $0.06-a-share quarterly) is not sustainable. Meanwhile, our estimates are below the Wall Street consensus. Yet, we still like the long-term fundamentals. In fact, Freddie Mac continues to increase its share of a strong market, and is using the Internet to complement its existing distribution channels. Still, finding an entry point during a period of rising rates may prove difficult, suggesting investors stay on the sidelines for now with respect to this neutrally ranked issue.

Peter Azcue *October 29, 1999*

(A) Based on avg. voting common/preferred shrs. outstanding; before 1990, in accordance with the preference in dividend distribution. Includes extraordinary losses: '93, 3¢; '94, 6¢; '96, 2¢. Next earnings report due mid-Jan. (B) Next div'd meeting mid-Dec. Goes ex about Dec. 12. Approx. dividend payment dates: Mar. 31, June 30, Sep. 30, Dec. 31. (C) In mill., adj. for exchange and splits. (D) Yield on interest earning assets and liabilities from 1998. (E) Includes preferred.

Company's Financial Strength	A+
Stock's Price Stability	65
Price Growth Persistence	95
Earnings Predictability	100

Source: Value Line Publishing, Inc.

Stock Exchange (NYSE)–listed Federal Home Loan Mortgage Corp. (or "Freddie Mac") is a favorite holding. Freddie Mac is a stockholder-owned corporation, created in 1970 and chartered by Congress to increase the supply of funds that mortgage lenders, such as commercial banks, mortgage bankers, savings institutions, and credit unions, can make available to home buyers. The company buys mortgages from lenders, packages these mortgages into securities, and sells them to investors. Freddie Mac guarantees these securities while mortgage lenders sell their loans to Freddie Mac and use the proceeds to fund new mortgages. This process increases the available credit for home buyers and makes Freddie Mac a solid growth stock. Freddie Mac earns an enviable 18% ROE, uses modest financial leverage, and is expected to enjoy solid revenue growth and rising profit margins in the years ahead. As such, Freddie Mac is a typical example of the type of stock favored by a growth stock investment philosophy.

A defining characteristic of growth stock investing is that it focuses first and foremost on the inherent economic quality of a given investment opportunity. Notice how none of T. Rowe Price's essential growth stock characteristics speak to the question of valuation. Little guidance is offered to help investors answer the question, How much is a growth stock worth? Growth stock investing is sometimes referred to as "one-decision" investing. Once the decision to buy has been made, a true growth stock investor is content to maintain a holding for years and years. Selling is only contemplated in the event of a rapid deterioration in the favorable economic characteristics of a given company. If a growth stock investor has done his or her homework well, sell decisions should be rare and portfolio turnover rates should be minimal.

Fertile Fields for Growth

From T. Rowe Price's investment selection criteria, it is clear that the first requirement for sustainable growth is that the company must be involved in an inherently appealing business. High profit margins and an above-average rate of return on total assets (ROA) are the most basic growth stock investment criteria. High profit margins signal relatively low levels of price competition in the company's main product lines and/or superior levels of operating efficiency. When either or both of these forces are at work, the groundwork is laid for superior long-term investment returns.

Growth stock investors typically shun companies toiling in viciously competitive markets. Such companies are seldom able to maintain long-lasting above-normal rates of return. For example, companies in basic industries in which it is tough to add value, such as mining, paper, petroleum, and steel, seldom qualify as growth stocks. Although there are obvious exceptions, such as Nucor Corp. in the steel industry, growth companies rarely find sustainable above-average growth in stagnant industries with poor economic characteristics. Easy entry and imitation also make it difficult to maintain sustainable above-average growth in a number of large industries such as medical services, restaurants, and retailing.

Sustainable above-average growth is much more likely for distinctive industry leaders in fertile competitive environments described by attractive growth, lucrative profit margins, and significant barriers to entry. As shown in Table 10.2, the total return earned by stock market investors over five-year and 10-year periods tend to be highest for companies in industries that earn above-average accounting

TABLE 10.2 **Industries That Feature High Rates of Return on Assets Represent Fertile Fields for Growth**

Industry Name	ROA %	ROE %	Total Return 1995–99	Total Return 1990–99	Industry Name	ROA %	ROE %	Total Return 1995–99	Total Return 1990–99
Toiletries/Cosmetics	10.50	31.26	21.62	17.70	Diversified Co.	4.37	14.81	25.96	16.97
Drug	10.42	22.51	48.84	29.00	Telecom. Equipment	4.34	10.30	81.92	41.15
Cement & Aggregates	10.21	18.80	21.63	13.24	Petroleum (Integrated)	4.28	9.85	33.89	20.43
Electrical Equip.	9.92	20.69	43.51	27.29	Newspaper	4.20	11.51	25.53	16.04
Retail Building Supply	9.74	16.71	51.32	41.18	Electronics	4.19	9.47	64.91	39.81
Semiconductor Cap Equip.	9.39	13.47	72.06	52.95	Air Transport	4.11	17.25	66.03	29.03
Household Products	8.93	30.16	29.37	21.69	Beverage (Alcoholic)	4.00	10.21	29.49	18.68
Medical Supplies	8.83	21.57	35.59	25.04	Healthcare Info. Systems	3.95	7.86	61.86	40.76
Furn./Home Furnishings	8.43	18.10	25.53	19.86	Aerospace/Defense	3.93	12.67	25.60	17.96
Computer Software & Svcs.	8.36	17.14	76.17	42.62	Advertising	3.68	16.96	48.08	21.30
Apparel	7.94	16.85	18.68	15.24	Aluminum	3.68	10.78	32.82	18.17
Semiconductor	7.42	12.76	61.53	46.92	Electric Utility (East)	3.54	11.41	15.76	12.02
Oilfield Services/Equip.	7.33	15.50	34.01	14.77	Food Wholesalers	3.49	12.14	39.76	22.88
Beverage (Soft Drink)	7.26	29.07	24.40	21.82	Environmental	3.47	12.53	28.11	12.04
Manuf. Housing/Rec. Veh.	7.19	15.65	19.49	23.29	Auto Parts (OEM)	3.43	14.05	14.05	12.56
Shoe	7.08	13.56	21.25	18.07	Textile	3.39	11.85	−75.03	−47.90
Metal Fabricating	7.00	14.97	23.00	18.31	Hotel/Gaming	3.37	10.48	17.24	12.30
Computer & Peripherals	6.91	17.57	92.29	49.95	Trucking/Transp. Leasing	3.22	13.66	18.66	15.88
Educational Svcs.	6.88	11.14	26.32	12.26	Water Utility	3.10	10.07	25.35	16.33
Retail (Special Lines)	6.51	14.47	56.73	31.55	Copper	3.02	8.18	11.25	8.71
Precision Instrument	6.50	16.64	34.27	23.06	Railroad	2.91	9.41	10.07	10.05
Tire & Rubber	6.44	16.26	5.26	11.39	Electric Utility (West)	2.87	11.06	14.91	10.07
Food Processing	6.37	18.55	27.41	18.72	Electric Util. (Central)	2.83	10.66	15.13	10.50
Restaurant	6.33	16.10	22.65	16.11	Auto & Truck	2.62	14.44	49.11	28.01
Tobacco	6.29	40.56	22.28	20.62	Telecom. Svcs.	2.62	8.22	43.54	22.45
Building Materials	6.28	21.46	15.80	11.24	Packaging & Container	2.47	10.05	14.04	11.86
Drugstore	5.95	14.96	39.45	24.38	Natural Gas (Distrib.)	2.37	6.66	20.78	13.07
Chemical (Basic)	5.88	19.60	27.55	18.62	Maritime	2.37	6.86	17.00	11.49
Chemical (Specialty)	5.83	16.94	−15.93	−2.48	Auto Parts (Replacement)	2.27	6.95	16.29	13.67
Machinery	5.74	16.96	26.28	18.28	Alternative Energy	2.25	16.60	42.41	18.76
Retail Store	5.58	15.83	45.95	26.36	Natural Gas (Diversified)	1.94	7.86	29.46	15.87
Office Equip. & Supplies	5.50	19.41	30.89	20.96	Paper & Forest Products	1.87	5.04	17.81	13.16
Home Appliance	5.36	21.23	22.11	14.69	Medical Services	1.70	9.32	19.28	17.99
Foreign Telecom.	5.34	13.49	34.44	25.75	Gold/Silver Mining	1.61	2.45	14.86	10.07
Recreation	5.25	11.69	27.85	18.11	Canadian Energy	1.57	3.97	16.04	9.21
Steel (Integrated)	5.25	15.50	17.36	13.88	Metals & Mining (Div.)	1.43	3.29	110.48	44.28
Chemical (Diversified)	4.95	15.03	29.87	20.76	Entertainment	1.36	2.41	43.22	29.51
Industrial Svcs.	4.83	11.66	30.18	18.83	Foreign Electron./Entertn.	0.48	1.19	32.45	15.56
Publishing	4.79	17.75	29.89	18.95	Petroleum (Producing)	−0.28	−1.02	18.19	14.69
Grocery	4.78	15.84	25.52	17.26	Cable TV	−6.48	−64.12	69.81	33.08
Homebuilding	4.69	14.06	39.91	20.56	Internet	−7.40	−18.46		
Steel (General)	4.50	9.96	9.64	11.65	**Averages**	**6.87**	**17.89**	**32.19**	**22.15**

Data source: *Value Line Investment Survey for Windows,* January 2000.

rates of return. For example, industry leaders, such as Coca-Cola and Pepsico in the soft drink industry, have effectively used economies of scale in distribution and advertising to build customer loyalty, brand-name awareness, and dominant market positions. Impressive barriers to entry shield these leaders from competition and protect historically high profit margins and impressive growth opportunities in domestic and foreign markets. Similarly, industry leaders in toiletries and cosmetics, drugs, and medical supplies use advertising and research and development to create "bulletproof" growth stock franchises.

Only growth companies that produce unique products or services have the potential to create sustainable above-average profits for investors. To maintain above-average profits, imitation must be prevented by advertising, patents, copyrights, or other means. Although a few growth companies have been able to dominate large or rapidly growing markets, most have been able to maintain their superior investment status through the successful exploitation of a **market niche.** A market niche is a segment of a market that can be successfully exploited through the special capabilities of a given firm. To be durable, above-normal profits derived from a market niche must not be vulnerable to imitation by competitors.

market niche Market segment that can be successfully exploited through the special capabilities of a given firm.

For example, Avon Products, Inc., is rightly famous for its veritable army of door-to-door sales representatives. "Avon Calling!" is a greeting that has long generated huge cash returns for the company in the United States and abroad. In Japan, for example, Avon's profit rate and popularity are even greater than that enjoyed in the United States. Avon has succeeded where others have failed because it has developed and nurtured the market for in-home cosmetic sales. Better than anyone else, Avon knows cosmetics, toiletries, costume jewelry, and other products that many women want and knows how much they are willing to pay for them. Avon keeps on growing despite numerous assaults from would-be competitors and regular predictions that its primary market is a sure-fire casualty of dual-income households. Indeed, its domestic and foreign business is so profitable that Avon has been the subject of repeated takeover speculation. To thwart such advances, the company has initiated a dramatic program to streamline operations in an effort to enhance already high profits. In the meantime, Avon keeps on dominating its market niche.

Another interesting example of a financial services firm that successfully exploits a profitable market niche is the Templeton Group of mutual funds. Templeton has a dominant and extraordinarily profitable market niche in the worldwide mutual fund business. Founder John Templeton was a pioneer of the global diversification concept for mutual fund investors. Not only has the idea proved popular to U.S. investors, but Japanese and European investors have jumped on the Templeton bandwagon as well. As a result, Templeton, now a subsidiary of mutual fund giant Franklin Resources, Inc., enjoys double-digit growth, profit margins that average in excess of 35% of sales and an ROA of more than 50% per year.

Avon Products and the Templeton Group are only two examples of the many firms that enjoy tremendous success through market niche dominance. To attain similar success, a firm must first recognize the attractiveness of the market niche and then successfully apply the concept to its own business. Few firms achieve any great measure of success in trying to be all things to all customers. Lasting success requires exploitation of those segments of the market that can be best served by using the special capabilities of a given firm.

Conservative Financial Structure

An obvious advantage of investing in growth stocks with high profit margins and high ROA is that companies with these characteristics are often freed from the need to raise debt or equity financing. An ongoing need to raise equity financing through the sale of common stock dilutes the ownership position of current equity holders and makes it much more difficult to achieve above-average EPS growth. T. Rowe Price was also leery of investing in companies that use extremely high levels of financial leverage. Of course, the problem with debt financing is that, during times of financial distress, lenders sometimes tend to be inflexible. Warren Buffett, multibillionaire chairman of Omaha-based Berkshire Hathaway, Inc., shares Price's aversion to debt financing. According to Buffett, "Bankers always want their loans repaid at the least convenient time." Such an aversion to debt appears old-fashioned when measured against popular perceptions that financial leverage is an attractive means for magnifying investor returns from good investment decisions.

In fact, it is startling to note the low levels of financial leverage used by some of the most profitable firms in the S&P 500 Index. Table 10.3 shows the amount of financial leverage used by the 15 firms with the highest ROA in the S&P 500 and ROA for the 15 firms with the lowest levels of financial leverage in the S&P 500. In Table 10.3, two related measures of financial leverage are depicted. The percentage of long-term debt to total capital illustrates the firm's use of leverage as a permanent source of financing plant and equipment. When long-term debt plus short-term debt is substantial, debt as a percentage of total assets becomes high, and there is significant risk of financial distress in the event of an economic downturn.

Despite the attractive simplicity of using long-term debt as a financial leverage indicator, investors sometimes fail to recognize that short-term debt can also pose a severe constraint on financial and operating decision flexibility. For this reason, it is appropriate to consider the effects of leverage as measured by the total amount of debt used to finance company operations. Only when the use of both long-term and short-term debt is modest can companies maintain the highest level of financial flexibility. Remember that net worth consists of the amount of equity committed to the enterprise by common and preferred stockholders. The difference between net worth and total assets can be accounted for by accounts payable, other current liabilities, and all forms of long-term debt financing. Because the percentage of debt to total assets is 48.7% for smokeless tobacco producer UST Inc., less than one-half of that company's total assets are financed by debt of all kinds.

S&P 500 firms with the highest ROA display total debt divided by net worth that averages only 40.4%. This means that debt of all kinds is used to finance only 40.4% of total assets for some of the most profitable firms in the United States. Many such firms use no long-term debt whatsoever. Notice how these conservatively financed high-profit firms are still able to exploit attractive long-term growth opportunities.

It is natural for investors to ask why such well-run and highly profitable firms use such modest financial leverage. For example, why doesn't Microsoft Corp. have *any* long-term debt? Why would a company worth more than $500 billion choose to use *no* long-term debt? Surely, Microsoft Corp. could borrow as much as $100 to $250 billion at very attractive interest rates. Presumably, the rate of interest paid would reflect Microsoft's gilded reputation and compare favorably with the rate

TABLE 10.3 Return on Assets (ROA) and Financial Leverage among the S&P 500

Company Name	Ticker	Industry Name	ROA (%)	% LTD to Capitalization	% Debt to Total Assets	Proj. EPS Growth (%)
A. Financial leverage is low among the most profitable firms.						
UST Inc.	UST	Tobacco	49.9	47.3	48.7	3.0
Parametric Technology	PMTC	Computer Software & Svcs.	23.7		60.7	14.0
Amgen	AMGN	Drug	23.5	6.9	30.2	15.5
Guidant Corp.	GDT	Medical Supplies	23.0	44.0	64.7	20.5
Tellabs Inc.	TLAB	Telecom. Equipment	23.0	0.2	15.4	24.5
Schering-Plough	SGP	Drug	22.4		49.0	16.0
Price (T. Rowe) Assoc.	TROW	Financial Svcs. (Div.)	21.9		22.9	16.5
Dell Computer	DELL	Computer & Peripherals	21.2	10.6	66.3	34.5
Compuware Corp.	CPWR	Computer Software & Svcs.	20.9	34.4	35.6	33.5
Gap (The) Inc.	GPS	Retail (Special Lines)	20.8	29.7	60.3	27.0
Microsoft Corp.	MSFT	Computer Software & Svcs.	20.5		23.5	25.0
Intel Corp.	INTC	Semiconductor	19.6	2.9	25.7	15.0
Wrigley (Wm.) Jr.	WWY	Food Processing	19.6		23.9	8.5
Bristol-Myers Squibb	BMY	Drug	19.3	13.6	53.4	13.5
Medtronic Inc.	MDT	Medical Supplies	18.6	0.5	25.0	18.0
Averages			**23.2**	**19.0**	**40.4**	**19.0**
B. Profitability is low among firms with high levels of financial leverage.						
Owens Corning	OWC	Building Materials	4.0	173.7	122.2	8.5
TRICON Global Rest's	YUM	Restaurant	9.8	131.0	125.7	
US Airways Group	U	Air Transport	6.8	96.5	92.5	
Hilton Hotels	HLT	Hotel/Gaming	5.0	93.0	95.3	9.0
Genl Mills	GIS	Food Processing	13.7	88.6	96.0	10.5
Genl Motors	GM	Auto & Truck	1.4	88.1	94.2	12.0
Campbell Soup	CPB	Food Processing	13.9	85.4	95.8	6.5
Allied Waste	AW	Environmental	3.4	85.2	75.2	22.0
Household Intl	HI	Financial Svcs. (Div.)	2.2	84.5	89.0	14.0
Ford Motor	F	Auto & Truck	2.8	83.9	90.2	8.5
Nextel Communic. 'A'	NXTL	Telecom. Svcs.	−13.1	82.6	84.4	
Equifax Inc.	EFX	Industrial Svcs.	10.6	82.6	80.0	11.5
Merrill Lynch & Co.	MER	Securities Brokerage	0.5	82.1	96.6	13.0
Assoc. First Capital	AFS	Financial Svcs. (Div.)	1.6	81.9	88.7	19.5
Lehman Bros. Holdings	LEH	Securities Brokerage	0.5	81.8	96.5	14.0
Averages			**4.2**	**94.7**	**94.8**	**12.4**

Data source: *Value Line Investment Survey for Windows,* January 2000.

paid on Treasury securities with similar maturities. Even if Microsoft had no immediate investment need for the funds, it could use the proceeds from a debt issue to retire common stock and thereby leverage future returns for stockholders.

The precise reason that Microsoft has chosen such a conservative financial structure is known only by company insiders. However, it is clear that the company has chosen to focus on making new and exciting software products rather than be distracted by **financial engineering.** Like many other highly successful firms depicted in Table 10.3, Microsoft has striven to dominate a business with the potential to generate huge amounts of cash flow with little need for investment in tangible plant and equipment. When software engineers and other key employees are paid in the form of stock options and other incentive-based compensation, Microsoft is able to tightly control out-of-pocket costs and generate astounding pretax profit margins.

financial engineering Sophisticated manipulation of the balance sheet through use of exotic forms of debt and equity financing.

The lesson for investors about the relationship between financial leverage and business quality seems simple. Enormous financial leverage cannot transform a mediocre business into a wonderful franchise. A wonderful business, such as computer software, is relatively self-financing. If a high degree of financial leverage is used in a wonderful business, the potential for leverage-induced benefits is obtained only at the risk of a reduction in financial and operating decision flexibility. In a mediocre business, such as paper and forest products, the use of financial leverage can magnify investor upside potential only at the risk of a similar magnification of downside risk. In mediocre businesses, such as agriculture, there is an old saying that investors best heed: "If you continue to bet the farm, eventually you'll lose the farm."

Pitfalls to Growth

Customer Loyalty Risk

One of the most prized possessions of any successful company is a large and growing body of satisfied customers. Customer loyalty built through years of dedicated service is often a wellspring of future business opportunity for both established and new products. Not only does a company have superior insight about the special needs and price sensitivity of established customers, long-standing business relationships built on trust and friendships are hard to beat when it comes to looking for new business. Stealing satisfied customers is never easy, but it is sometimes impossible for smaller competitors or start-ups. New entrants seeking a foothold by simply offering "me-too" products at a lower price are seldom successful against larger and more established competitors with deep pockets. Successful entry in stable or slow-growing markets with established competitors requires products and services that are substantially better, notably cheaper, or delivered much faster than the competition.

Entry in fast-growing markets is another matter, however. When new markets are undergoing explosive growth, few competitors need fear the problem of overcoming long-established customer loyalty. By definition, everything is up for grabs in a new market. As a result, **customer loyalty risk** is high and market share stability is low in rapidly growing markets. Rapidly growing markets are filled with risk and opportunity for companies and their investors. Sometimes, early movers are able to achieve durable advantages over subsequent competitors. More often, however, quick and unpredictable changes in the marketplace leave both companies and their investors looking for answers. In the realm of desktop computers, for example, early winners such as Atari, Digital Equipment, and Apple have given way to Dell, Compaq, Hewlett-Packard, and an ever-changing roster of capable competitors.

customer loyalty risk
Chance of losing customers to established competitors or new entrants.

Just as growth in mere size is no guarantee of growing EPS or growing stock value, growth that is simply tied to an expanding overall market is no guarantee of long-term success. In fact, rapid industry growth sometimes guarantees that new and highly capable competitors will quickly be attracted. In the early 1990s, for example, Snapple Beverage Company caused a stir by inventing the "New Age" beverage industry with a range of healthful noncola soft drinks. At first, Coca-Cola and Pepsico seemed amused by this upstart's irreverence and shunned tea and

WALL STREET WISDOM 10.1

What's in a Name?

Although the power of brand-name advertising has long been measured in the traditional broadcast and print media, upstarts such as America Online (AOL), Netscape, and Yahoo! have also made brand-name advertising a key competitive strategy in cyberspace. AOL seeks to be seen everywhere, and its ubiquitous "carpet bombing" of computer users with promotional diskettes seems to have achieved that purpose. Similarly, from irreverent advertising to the choice of its own moniker, Yahoo! seeks to create the perception of carefree fun for the antiestablishment crowd, and on the Internet, who is not antiestablishment? On Main Street, companies that do not spend enough on advertising to support valuable brand-name assets, and the products that carry them, are losing their premium status. On the Internet, upstarts routinely "bet the company" in a mad dash to create brand-name awareness before being buried by competitors.

The effect of brand-name advertising is sometimes so persuasive that it is almost too powerful. When words become unforgettably associated with innovative new products, the result can spell trouble. Aspirin, cellophane, and linoleum, the escalator, brassiere, yo-yo, and zipper are all products that lost distinctiveness because their trademarks fell into common usage. All suffered from *too much* success. Either their product was as new and innovative as its name, or the trademark seemed to be especially well suited to the underlying product. Owners of such modern-day trademarks as Astroturf, Coke, Frisbee, Kleenex, Kitty Litter, Styrofoam, Walkman, and Xerox employ a veritable army of lawyers in an endless struggle against "generic" treatment. Actually, this threat is remote, at least in the United States and Canada. The courts and Congress bend over backward to preserve trademarks for companies that advertise or otherwise expend significant effort and funds to establish and maintain distinctive product recognition.

One of the most stunning bits of new evidence on the value of name brand recognition was provided in March 2000 by VeriSign Inc.'s $17 billion purchase of Network Solutions, Inc., the longtime source of Internet domain names. Network Solutions began as a telecommunications consultancy in 1979. In 1992, Network Solutions landed a five-year contract with the National Science Foundation to develop a domain-name registration for the Internet. The contract gave Network Solutions the sole authority to issue Web addresses ending with ".com," ".net," ".org," ".edu," and ".gov." Network solutions has already issued more than nine million dot-com addresses, and VeriSign looks to provide similar addresses for up to 160 million new businesses.

The $17 billion VeriSign deal represented a stunning price for a company that had reported net income of only $26.9 million on revenues of $220.8 million during the prior fiscal year. A purchase price of more than 75 times revenue and 630 times profits hardly seems cheap. This is especially true in light of the fact that Network Solutions no longer has a monopoly on issuing new Internet addresses. Network Solutions charges $35 for each domain name it issues and gets $6 to register names issued by other companies in its database. As other companies race into the address-issuing business, proposals to create new .biz or .shop suffixes for Web names has the potential to threaten Network Solutions's mainstay business.

The $17 billion VeriSign deal also represented an astonishing return on a $4.5 million investment in 1995 when Science Applications International Corp., a closely held defense contractor, bought the company. In fact, it may be one of the largest payoffs in Internet history. The VeriSign deal, clearly one of the largest ever by a Silicon Valley company, underscores the increasing value placed on personal and corporate identity on the Web. As merchants and consumers rush online, VeriSign and Network Solutions hope to become a central location to establish and verify the identities of Internet buyers and sellers.

Although VeriSign and Network Solutions are among a select group of Internet companies that actually made money last year, it remains to be seen if VeriSign's stockholders will be so lucky.

See: Don Clark and Julia Angwin, "For the Keeper of Web Names, a $17 Billion Deal," *The Wall Street Journal,* March 8, 2000, B1, B4.

fruit-flavored beverages as a mere fad. Once Snapple and a host of imitators demonstrated that significant market demand existed for such products, Coke and Pepsi brought out their own offerings and crushed Snapple's business.

Merger Risk

A true growth company is able to profitably supply distinctive products and services to a rapidly growing marketplace. A vital determinant of a growth company's long-term success is the extent to which the company is able to maintain its ability to produce distinctively appealing products and services. True growth is based on the creative capability enjoyed by the firm and the creative differences enjoyed by its customers. The creative capability that gives rise to true growth is inherent to the firm or comes from within.

For example, Wal-Mart Stores, Inc., has enjoyed stunning success operating discount department stores (Wal-Mart), warehouse membership clubs (Sam's Clubs), and combination full-line supermarket and discount department stores (Wal-Mart Supercenters) in the United States and foreign markets. All Wal-Mart shoppers are aware of Sam Walton's legendary prowess as a merchandiser. Relatively few recognize that the company's amazing success is largely due to a state-of-the-art internal communications network ("Intranet") that efficiently communicates buyer decisions to Wal-Mart's suppliers. Wal-Mart beats the competition because it precisely meets customer needs while minimizing inventory and merchandising costs. Although Kmart was the first to popularize the discount retailer concept, Wal-Mart used communications technology to perfect it. Wal-Mart has succeeded because of its innate ability to meet customer needs quicker and cheaper than the competition.

Although Wal-Mart has built its success on an innate ability to exploit communications technology, other growth companies have built their success on a variety of inherent capabilities. Coca-Cola's long-standing success as a growth stock is based on the company's legendary advertising capability and its tremendous economies of scale in distribution. Computer microprocessor titan Intel Corp. and pharmaceutical giant Merck & Co. have built long-term success on the basis of amazing research and development capability that helps produce an ongoing string of products and product lines that shape and reshape important industries. The Walt Disney Company has built a diversified worldwide entertainment growth company specializing in creative content, broadcasting (ABC and ESPN), and theme parks and resorts. What is Disney's most precious asset? It is as small as a mouse. In fact, it is a mouse: Mickey Mouse.

Notice that all these great growth companies have built from within. None are the result of an ongoing series of mergers or acquisitions. The reason for this is simple. Acquired companies often underperform as divisions of larger companies. Employees that flourish in the entrepreneurial environment of a start-up or smaller company often chafe in the more structured atmosphere of a larger company. Following settlement of major mergers, key employees often leave the acquirer to start anew. When key employees leave following a merger or acquisition, their loss often represents more than just an important loss of the acquired firm's intellectual capital. Lost key employees often form the basis for new and vibrant competitors. As a result, it is seldom true that growth through merger and acquisition leads to durable long-term business success or investor prosperity. More typical is the case in which companies fall victim to **merger risk** and suffer merger indigestion and investor disappointment.

merger risk
Economic loss stemming from failure to achieve merger benefits.

On Wall Street, a **roll-up** is a company that grows through a constant acquisition binge. Fans view roll-ups as a way to bring economies of scale, management discipline, and superior access to low-cost capital into industries dominated by inefficient, undercapitalized mom-and-pop operations. For example, Wayne Huizenga reached hero status on Wall Street as he built an empire consolidating local garbage haulers into Waste Management, Inc., and independent video stores into Blockbuster Entertainment. Others have rolled up everything from funeral homes to rental businesses to Internet service providers. Skeptics view roll-ups as a game of financial engineering. Using highly valued stock as cheap currency to buy smaller companies, roll-ups use an ongoing string of mergers to produce a continuing boost to earnings per share. However, critics contend that when roll-up companies stop the process of constant acquisition, they often fail to deliver operating efficiencies.

roll-up
Company that grows through constant acquisition.

Houston-based Waste Management, Inc., provides a classic example. Waste Management offers a variety of integrated waste management services, including collection, transfer, disposal, recycling, and resource recovery services. The company also provides hazardous waste handling services to commercial, industrial, municipal, and residential customers. Until mid-1999, Waste Management was a Wall Street darling and showed stunning revenue and profit growth from acquisitions, internal growth, and lower general and administrative expenses. Investors prospered. As shown in Figure 10.2, Waste Management stock increased roughly 10:1 during the 1990s. In July 1999, the Waste Management story hit a speed bump. Hoped-for operating efficiencies failed to materialize, and the company began to strain under a daunting load of debt. Within weeks of announcing operating disappointments, the stock collapsed from $60 to less than $20 per share, thus wiping out years of investor gains.

Unfortunately, disappointing investor experience with roll-ups does not end with the Waste Management story. Spectacular belly flops by roll-ups have occurred in the funeral services industry, noteworthy for its stable revenues and high profit margins. Canadian entrepreneur Ray Loewen built The Loewen Group into the continent's second-largest funeral home operator through a series of acquisitions during the 1990s. At its height, Loewen operated more than 1,100 funeral homes and 400 cemeteries in North America. The company also operated three lucrative insurance subsidiaries. Once the pace of acquisitions tapered off, the company quickly fell apart. From a peak of $42.63 in October 1996, Loewen stock plummeted to less than a dollar per share and corporate bankruptcy within only 2½ years. Funeral services industry leader Service Corp. International suffered a similar, although less spectacular fate. After experiencing operating problems similar to Loewen's, Service Corp. began to struggle under a daunting debt burden during the summer of 1999 and saw its stock price collapse more than 90%, from more than $40 to roughly $3 per share.

The lesson for investors is simple but important. Growth made possible by superior capabilities that are innate to the firm provides an attractive basis for sustainable above-average investor returns. When growth depends on a continuing series of beneficial mergers and acquisitions, the risk of eventual loss and investor disappointment is significant.

Regulation Risk

According to T. Rowe Price, it is necessary to seek out fertile fields for economic growth to succeed in common stock investing. Risk can be reduced, but not

FIGURE 10.2 **Growth through Acquisition Led to Problems at Waste Management, Inc.**

WASTE MANAGEMENT NYSE-WMI

RECENT PRICE	16	P/E RATIO	9.2 (Trailing: 7.5 Median: 23.0)	RELATIVE P/E RATIO	0.63	DIV'D YLD	0.1%	VALUE LINE

TIMELINESS **5** Lowered 9/17/99
SAFETY **3** New 9/20/96
TECHNICAL **5** Lowered 10/8/99
BETA 1.10 (1.00 = Market)

High:	5.2	3.2	6.2	18.0	18.5	15.0	15.1	22.5	34.3	44.1	58.2	60.0
Low:	2.3	1.5	1.4	5.4	10.5	9.8	10.4	10.0	17.3	28.6	34.4	14.0

LEGENDS
— 8.0 x "Cash Flow" p sh
.... Relative Price Strength
Options: Yes
Shaded area indicates recession

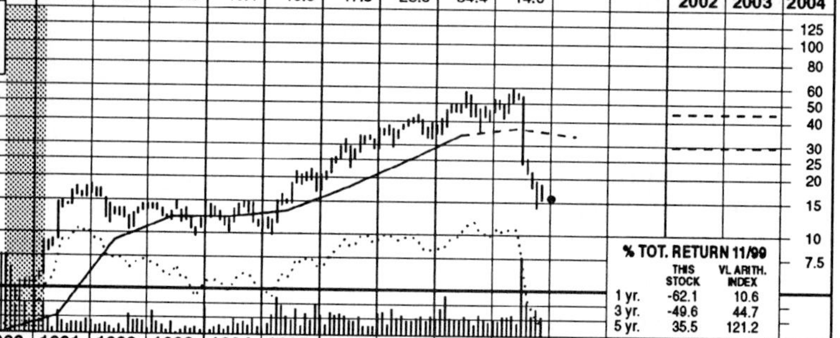

% TOT. RETURN 11/99

	THIS STOCK	VL ARITH. INDEX
1 yr.	-62.1	10.6
3 yr.	-49.6	44.7
5 yr.	35.5	121.2

2002-04 PROJECTIONS

	Price	Gain	Ann'l Total Return
High	45	(+180%)	*30%*
Low	30	(+90%)	*17%*

Insider Decisions

	J	F	M	A	M	J	J	A	S
to Buy	0	0	0	0	0	0	0	0	0
Options	0	0	1	0	10	6	0	0	1
to Sell	0	0	2	0	13	7	0	0	0

Institutional Decisions

	4Q1998	1Q1999	2Q1999
to Buy	263	289	284
to Sell	197	224	213
Hld's(000)	475611	505293	540128

USA Waste Services, the predecessor to Waste Management, was formed in 1987 and became a publicly held company on June 2, 1988. The I.P.O. price was $5, and the lead underwriter was R. B. Marich. The stock was traded on the over the counter market until July 20, 1993, when it began trading on the N.Y.S.E. The company has since grown rapidly through an aggressive acquisition program (see business description and footnote A).

1989	1990	1991	1992	1993	1994	1995	1996	1997	1998	1999	2000	© VALUE LINE PUB., INC.	02-04
1.00	.98	1.96	4.97	6.77	7.81	6.94	9.41	12.00	20.88	*21.45*	*18.65*	Sales per sh A	*23.00*
.17	.23	.46	1.16	1.54	1.55	1.68	2.23	3.04	4.28	*4.65*	*4.25*	"Cash Flow" per sh	*5.15*
.03	.08	.32	.65	.80	.75	.98	1.13	1.62	1.82	*1.90*	*1.90*	Earnings per sh B	*2.60*
--	--	.08	--	--	--	--	--	--	--	*.02*	*.01*	Div'ds Decl'd per sh C	*.05*
.77	.20	.46	.59	1.95	1.81	1.29	2.50	2.00	2.71	*1.50*	*1.50*	Cap'l Spending per sh	*2.00*
1.89	2.50	3.10	3.79	4.04	4.78	6.12	8.28	12.07	7.19	*7.60*	*9.50*	Book Value per sh D	*16.65*
2.81	3.95	9.91	10.51	11.55	22.58	65.84	139.59	217.78	608.31	*620.00*	*622.00*	Common Shs Outst'g E	*630.00*
76.5	44.9	37.9	21.2	15.8	17.2	16.6	24.2	23.3	25.0	*Bold figures are*	*Value Line estimates*	Avg Ann'l P/E Ratio	*14.5*
5.79	3.33	2.42	1.29	.93	1.13	1.11	1.52	1.34	1.32			Relative P/E Ratio	*1.05*
--	--	.7%	--	--	--	--	--	--	--			Avg Ann'l Div'd Yield	*Nil*
2.8	3.9	19.4	52.2	78.1	176.2	457.1	1313.4	2613.8	12703	*13300*	*11600*	Sales ($mill) A	*14500*
19.6%	27.7%	40.5%	36.5%	35.7%	29.3%	30.9%	34.1%	37.6%	31.6%	*32.0%*	*33.0%*	Operating Margin	*33.0%*
.4	.7	1.6	4.8	8.2	18.8	56.4	153.2	303.2	1498.7	*1625*	*1475*	Depreciation ($mill)	*1600*
.1	.2	3.0	7.3	9.6	16.3	54.0	157.9	358.4	1105.1	*1170*	*1180*	Net Profit ($mill)	*1650*
--	--	32.2%	35.0%	36.3%	35.8%	--	39.9%	40.0%	42.9%	*41.5%*	*41.0%*	Income Tax Rate	*40.0%*
3.2%	6.0%	15.3%	14.1%	12.3%	9.2%	11.8%	12.0%	13.7%	8.7%	*8.8%*	*10.2%*	Net Profit Margin	*11.4%*
1.0	1.6	2.8	9.4	.3	8.6	14.9	20.0	86.7	d412.3	*d800*	*d650*	Working Cap'l ($mill)	*d200*
.7	2.6	22.9	49.3	93.6	147.0	334.9	1158.3	2724.4	11114	*8700*	*7600*	Long-Term Debt ($mill)	*5800*
5.3	9.9	30.7	39.9	46.7	108.0	402.9	1155.3	2629.0	4372.5	*4700*	*5900*	Shr. Equity ($mill)	*10500*
3.1%	2.5%	7.2%	10.1%	9.0%	8.4%	9.4%	8.2%	7.9%	9.3%	*11.5%*	*11.0%*	Return on Total Cap'l	*11.5%*
1.7%	2.3%	9.7%	18.4%	20.5%	15.1%	13.4%	13.7%	13.6%	25.3%	*25.0%*	*20.0%*	Return on Shr. Equity	*15.5%*
1.7%	2.3%	7.6%	18.4%	20.5%	15.1%	13.4%	13.7%	13.6%	25.3%	*24.5%*	*20.0%*	Retained to Com Eq	*15.0%*
--	--	22%	--	--	--	--	--	--	--	*1%*	*1%*	All Div'ds to Net Prof	*2%*

CAPITAL STRUCTURE as of 9/30/99
Total Debt $11403.2 mill. **Due in 5 Yrs** $6800 mill.
LT Debt $8713.5 mill. **LT Interest** $610.0 mill.
Incl. two conv. debs./notes due 2001 and 2005 totaling $992 mill., conv. into 22.8 mill. common shares at an avg. rate of $43.51/sh.
(Total interest coverage: 4.4x) (66% of Cap'l)
Leases, Uncapitalized Annual rentals $142.4 mill.
Pension Liability $153 mill. in '98 vs. none in '97.
Pfd Stock None.

Common Stock 619,629,770 shs. (34% of Cap'l) **as of 11/9/99**
MARKET CAP: $9.9 billion (Large Cap)

CURRENT POSITION ($MILL.)	1997	1998	9/30/99
Cash Assets	51.2	88.7	221.9
Receivables	442.3	2246.0	1934.6
Other	161.9	1546.7	2640.8
Current Assets	655.4	3881.4	4797.3
Accts Payable	237.2	1040.6	1097.9
Debt Due	39.3	583.7	2689.7
Other	292.2	2669.4	2095.7
Current Liab.	568.7	4293.7	5883.3

ANNUAL RATES of change (per sh)	Past 10 Yrs.	Past 5 Yrs.	Est'd '96-'98 to '02-'04
Sales	35.5%	25.5%	*8.5%*
"Cash Flow"	37.0%	25.0%	*8.5%*
Earnings	36.0%	21.0%	*9.0%*
Dividends	--	--	*Nil*
Book Value	17.5%	20.5%	*10.5%*

Cal-endar	QUARTERLY SALES ($ mill.) A Mar.31	Jun.30	Sep.30	Dec.31	Full Year
1996	282.5	327.7	352.8	350.4	1313.4
1997	460.5	656.2	761.8	735.3	2613.8
1998	2969.4	3250.8	3244.2	3239.1	12703.5
1999	3070.6	3334.6	3385.3	*3509.5*	*13300*
2000	*2800*	*2900*	*2950*	*2950*	*11600*

Cal-endar	EARNINGS PER SHARE B Mar.31	Jun.30	Sep.30	Dec.31	Full Year
1996	.20	.29	.32	.32	1.13
1997	.29	.41	.47	.45	1.62
1998	.34	.41	.49	.58	1.82
1999	.55	.50	.44	*.41*	*1.90*
2000	*.42*	*.46*	*.51*	*.51*	*1.90*

Cal-endar	QUARTERLY DIVIDENDS PAID C ■ Mar.31	Jun.30	Sep.30	Dec.31	Full Year
1995	--	--	--	--	--
1996	--	--	--	--	--
1997	--	--	--	--	--
1998	--	--	--	--	--
1999	.01	--	--	.01	

BUSINESS: Waste Management is the largest solid-waste disposal company in No. America. USA Waste Services, the surviving entity (name changed), and Waste Management merged in July, 1998. Other major acquisitions incl.: Western Waste (5/96), Sanifill (9/96), and United Waste Systems (8/97). It operates about 320 landfills, 650 collection operations and 340 transfer stations in No. Amer.; rev. mix consists of collection (about 55%), landfill fees (30%), other (15%). Foreign and misc. domestic opers. account for about 22% of total revs. Has about 68,000 employees. Offs./dirs. own less than 1% of stock (5/99 proxy). Chairman and C.E.O.: A. Maurice Myers. Inc.: DE. Address: 1001 Fannin, Suite 4000, Houston, TX 77002. Tel.: 713-512-6548. Internet: www.wm.com

Waste Management has faced a number of serious problems this year. As a result of the discovery in July that first-quarter earnings included some previously undisclosed one-time gains, the directors hired two C.P.A firms to simultaneously conduct an audit. (Our earnings presentation for the first two quarters of 1999 have been adjusted for their findings.) Consequently, the company recorded pre-tax charges of almost $1.8 billion (equivalent to $1.98 a share), including a $420 million writedown of assets held for sale, in the third period. Of particular concern was the disclosure that the inadequacy of the management information system was a prime cause of $211 million in downward accounts receivable adjustments. In light of the above, as well as a medical problem affecting the former C.E.O., WM's senior management team resigned in mid-1999. These positions have recently been filled; the new C.E.O., Maurice Myers, previously held that position at Yellow Services, one of the nation's largest freight companies.

One of the company's key near-term objectives is improving the financial structure ... In conjunction with the July, 1998 merger of the "old" Waste Management, total debt jumped by about 150%. In order to reduce the debt, the new management team plans to sell the international subsidiaries and a number of non-core domestic operations. (At September 30th, "assets held for sale" totaled $2.1 billion.) This measure, though, would likely not boost earnings, since related interest-expense reductions would be offset by the absence of the underlying profits of those businesses. Finally, the company has scaled back its acquisition program, which has focused on the addition of waste-collection routes and transfer stations within existing markets.

... and another vital goal is the installation of a new management information system. Towards this end, Mr. Myers just hired the Chief Information Officer at Yellow Services. At this juncture, it is difficult to ascertain the timing of the system implementation.

This depressed stock is untimely. And we suggest that most investors await signs of tangible financial and MIS improvements before committing to these shares.

David R. Cohen *December 17, 1999*

(A) 1997 revenues include United Waste as of 1/1/97. 1998 revs. incl former Waste Management and Eastern Environmental as of 1/1/98. (B) Based on diluted earnings. Next earnings report due mid-Feb. Excludes extraord. losses: '92, $1.45; '93, $0.18; '94, $1.85; '95, $0.43; '96, $0.89; '97, $0.39; '98, $3.14;. '99-Q1-3, $2.05. (C) Last div. paid 10/19/99. At present, the timing of the next divident payment is uncertain. (D) Incl. intangs. At 9/30/99: $5317.2 mill., $8.58/sh. (E) In mills.

Company's Financial Strength	B
Stock's Price Stability	30
Price Growth Persistence	85
Earnings Predictability	75

Source: Value Line Publishing, Inc.

eliminated, when growth stock investors buy and hold for long-term appreciation and future income the best companies in the best industries. A host of important problems can also be avoided when investors seek to minimize **regulation risk.**

regulation risk Chance of investor loss due to burdensome government rules and regulations.

At the start of a new millennium, it is easy to predict that an aging population is apt to place increasing burdens on health care services. Over time, the demand for health care services, drugs, and medical supplies is sure to grow. Unfortunately, as demand skyrockets, so too does the demand for federal and state regulation to contain the upward spiral in health care costs. In the late 1990s, strong regulatory and cost-containment efforts were directed at hospitals and health maintenance organizations (HMO). Investors in hospital chains and HMOs have suffered accordingly. Like investors in public utilities, investors in important sectors of the health care sector have come to learn that booming revenues can lead to a profitless prosperity when the industry is subject to onerous regulation. It is no wonder that growth stock investors seek companies in industries that are not natural targets of regulation.

Although most investors are aware that health care demands will soar with an aging population, some neglect to consider other obvious implications of this demographic shift. Another byproduct of an aging population is that savings rates will rise sharply in the years ahead, and the demand for distinctive financial services will soar. Spending on leisure activities will also grow as aging Baby Boomers pursue what promises to be an active retirement. A lot of money will be made by leisure time companies whose distinctive products and services appeal to highly educated and high-income retirees. Helping customers have fun has long been a good way to turn an attractive profit in the broadcasting, lodging, entertainment, and theme park/gaming industries. Companies that specialize in providing tools for productivity enhancement will also benefit as an aging population puts a strain on labor productivity. Many aggressive growth stock investors seek out companies in the vanguard of important new innovations, such as the advent of the Internet. Savvy growth stock investors also look for companies that benefit from new communications and computer technology.

Price Risk

One of the most important potential pitfalls tied to growth stock investing is that the approach seldom offers clear guidance about how much is too much to pay for a stock with attractive growth prospects. The lack of a strict buying discipline leaves growth stock investors open to **price risk,** or the chance of overpaying for attractive companies, and the risk of suffering gut-wrenching devastation to their investment portfolios after even modest temporary declines in the overall market. For example, one of the most successful and popular growth stock mutual funds during the 1990s bull market was the Janus Twenty Fund, Inc. The Janus Twenty Fund seeks capital appreciation by investing in a concentrated portfolio of between 20 and 30 common stocks. To select its investments, the fund's manager evaluates improvement in profit margins, earnings, and unit growth to detect the fundamental investment value of the security.

price risk Chance of overpaying for attractive companies.

Like most successful growth stock investors during the late 1990s, the Janus Twenty Fund focuses on leading-edge companies in rapidly emerging high-tech industries, such as America Online, Inc. (AOL), and the Internet communications and services industry (Figure 10.3). Notice how this focus on leading-edge

FIGURE 10.3 **Janus Twenty Fund Focuses on Leading Edge High-Tech Companies**

Portfolio Composition (%)	
Stocks	74.01
Bonds	1.15
Preferred	N/A
Convertibles	N/A
Cash	2.20

Sector Weightings (%)	
Financials	3.30
Industrial Cyclicals	3.64
Consumer Durables	1.21
Services	25.83
Retail	3.47
Health	3.21
Technology	59.34

Top Holdings	Symbol	% Assets	YTD Return
Nokia Cl A ADR	N/A	10.86	-6.86
Cisco Sys	CSCO	9.76	22.17
Sun Microsystems	SUNW	8.26	36.16
America Online	AOL	6.40	-29.82
Time Warner	TWX	5.29	6.17
Sprint (PCS Group)	PCS	4.90	7.80
EMC/Mass	EMC	4.00	55.61
Microsoft	MSFT	3.81	-40.20
General Elec	GE	3.45	0.78
Vodafone Airtouch ADR	N/A	2.73	-12.70
% Fund Assets in Top Ten Holdings			59.46

Quotes for Top Holdings

Equity Holdings	
Avg. Price/Earnings	54.51
Avg. Price/Book	16.80
Median Market Cap	150.46 B

Bond Holdings	
Avg. Duration (Years)	N/A
Avg. Maturity (Years)	N/A
Avg. Maturity as of	N/A
Avg. Coupon	N/A
Avg. Quality	N/A

high-tech companies has resulted in a fund investment profile that includes an average price/earnings (P/E) ratio in excess of 54 : 1 and a price/book (P/B) ratio average of almost 17 : 1. As shown in Figure 10.4, which displays the funds' performance as of August 2000, such a high-risk stance served fund investors well during the nonstop bull market of the 1990s but began declining in early 2000. It remains to be seen how fund investors will hold up during the inevitable market corrections, in which major stock market averages fall 10% or more, and the occasional bear markets, in which downturns of 20% and more are experienced. During market downturns, it would be typical to see growth stock portfolios, such as the Janus Twenty Fund, decline two or three times as much as the market averages. Experienced risk-tolerant investors may be willing to ride out such adverse markets or even add to their positions. Less experienced investors, or less risk-tolerant investors, may panic during adverse market conditions and thereby incur devastating market losses.

It is now appropriate to consider important questions tied to how investors can appropriately value growth stocks. Various discount models offer simple and broadly appealing methods for valuing any stock based on the discounted present value of future cash flows.

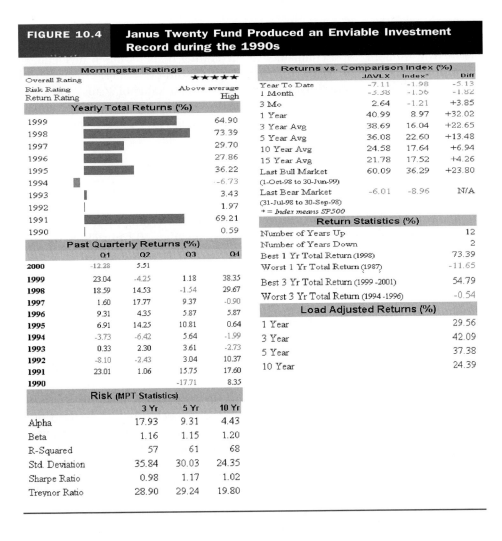

FIGURE 10.4 Janus Twenty Fund Produced an Enviable Investment Record during the 1990s

Morningstar Ratings	
Overall Rating	★★★★★
Risk Rating	Above average
Return Rating	High

Yearly Total Returns (%)	
1999	64.90
1998	73.39
1997	29.70
1996	27.86
1995	36.22
1994	-6.73
1993	3.43
1992	1.97
1991	69.21
1990	0.59

Past Quarterly Returns (%)	Q1	Q2	Q3	Q4
2000	-12.28	5.51		
1999	23.04	-4.25	1.18	38.35
1998	18.59	14.53	-1.54	29.67
1997	1.60	17.77	9.37	-0.90
1996	9.31	4.35	5.87	5.87
1995	6.91	14.25	10.81	0.64
1994	-3.73	-6.42	5.64	-1.99
1993	0.33	2.30	3.61	-2.73
1992	-8.10	-2.43	3.04	10.37
1991	23.01	1.06	15.75	17.60
1990			-17.71	8.35

Risk (MPT Statistics)	3 Yr	5 Yr	10 Yr
Alpha	17.93	9.31	4.43
Beta	1.16	1.15	1.20
R-Squared	57	61	68
Std. Deviation	35.84	30.03	24.35
Sharpe Ratio	0.98	1.17	1.02
Treynor Ratio	28.90	29.24	19.80

Returns vs. Comparison Index (%)	JAVLX	Index*	Diff
Year To Date	-7.11	-1.98	-5.13
1 Month	-3.38	-1.56	-1.82
3 Mo	2.64	-1.21	+3.85
1 Year	40.99	8.97	+32.02
3 Year Avg	38.69	16.04	+22.65
5 Year Avg	36.08	22.60	+13.48
10 Year Avg	24.58	17.64	+6.94
15 Year Avg	21.78	17.52	+4.26
Last Bull Market (1-Oct-98 to 30-Jun-99)	60.09	36.29	+23.80
Last Bear Market (31-Jul-98 to 30-Sep-98)	-6.01	-8.96	N/A

* = *Index means SP500*

Return Statistics (%)	
Number of Years Up	12
Number of Years Down	2
Best 1 Yr Total Return (1998)	73.39
Worst 1 Yr Total Return (1987)	-11.65
Best 3 Yr Total Return (1999 -2001)	54.79
Worst 3 Yr Total Return (1994 -1996)	-0.54

Load Adjusted Returns (%)	
1 Year	29.56
3 Year	42.09
5 Year	37.38
10 Year	24.39

Discounted Present Value

DPV Model

Consider the simple case of valuing a stock that an investor expects to hold for a limited investment horizon of one year. The **discounted present value** (DPV), P_0, or real economic value, of one share is the present value of the dividend to be received at the end of the first year, D_1, and the expected sales price in one year, P_1. It is important for investors to keep in mind that future stock prices and dividend payments cannot be known with certainty. Whenever investors deal with future stock prices and dividend payments, they are dealing with **expected values,** not certain sums. The per-share value of a stock to be sold in one year is the DPV of future dividends and the price to be received at the point of sale.

discounted present value Current worth of future cash flows after adjusting for risk and the time value of money.

expected values Anticipated amounts.

$$P_0 = \frac{D_1 + P_1}{1 + k} \quad (10.1)$$

risk-adjusted discount rate Investor's required return.

In Equation 10.1, the **risk-adjusted discount rate** k, or required return, is the interest rate required to fairly compensate investors for the risk involved with making their investment. Most companies loathe cutting their promised dividend, so estimating dividends one year in advance is seldom difficult. Thus, Equation 10.1 offers a useful means for estimating the true economic value of a stock, provided that the year-end stock price can be estimated with similar precision. To estimate the year-end stock price, P_1, Equation 10.1 again comes into play. Using the same logic as used to estimate P_0, the year-end value P_1 will be

$$P_1 = \frac{D_2 + P_2}{1 + k} \tag{10.2}$$

If investors can assume that the stock in question will be selling for its actual value next year, Equation 10.2 can be substituted into Equation 10.1 to yield

$$P_0 = \frac{D_1}{1 + k} + \frac{D_2 + P_2}{(1 + k)^2} \tag{10.3}$$

This equation gives the DPV of dividends plus sale proceeds for a stock that an investor expects to hold for two years. Notice that the expression beneath the second term on the right-hand side of Equation 10.3 is raised to the second power. This reflects the fact that two years will elapse before second-year dividends and stock sale proceeds will be received.

The logic evident in Equation 10.3 can be repeated for any number of years in an investor's expected holding period. For an expected holding period of n years, the inherent economic value of a stock as measured by the present value of dividends over the n years, and the ultimate sales price, P_n, is

$$P_0 = \frac{D_1}{1 + k} + \frac{D_2}{(1 + k)^2} + \cdots + \frac{D_n + P_n}{(1 + k)^n} \tag{10.4}$$

It is worth emphasizing that this formula involves both future dividend payments and proceeds from the stock's sale. As such, it incorporates both dividend income and capital appreciation, or loss. Although the DPV approach can be described as a type of dividend discount model, it involves full consideration of both major components of the investor's **total return** from investment.

total return Dividend income plus capital appreciation.

Observe the similarity between Equation 10.4 and the bond valuation formula developed in Chapter 7. From an economic standpoint, the present-value calculation for a stock or a bond is similar. Both values relate to the present value of a stream of future payments. The present value of a stock equals the present value of a series of dividend payments plus the final sales price. The present value of a bond equals the present value of a series of interest payments plus a final redemption value (or sales price).

The only difference between the valuation of a stock and the valuation of a bond relates to the degree of certainty tied to future dividend and interest payments. Because stock prices and dividend payments tend to be less predictable than bond interest payments and redemption values, the appropriate discount rate on common stock investing tends to be higher than the appropriate discount rate for bonds.

DPV for Dividend-Paying Stocks

To depict the use of the DPV model for dividend-paying stocks, consider the case of the General Electric Company (GE). With leading market positions in appliances, engines, lighting, power systems, and technical products, GE is one of the largest and most diversified companies in the world. As shown in Figure 10.5, GE has been a standout performer in the 1990s stock market. A DPV analysis for GE will suggest whether GE remains an attractive bargain for long-term investors or whether its current price more than amply reflects its near-term growth prospects.

To illustrate, consider the economic value for GE stock based on its expected dividend and stock price performance over the five-year 2000–2005 period. GE's dividends have been growing at a low double-digit rate during recent years. The highly respected *Value Line Investment Survey* projects 13% per year dividend growth for GE over the near term and EPS growth of 14% per year. These expected growth rates can be taken as good approximations for the consensus forecast GE growth rate. To conduct a DPV analysis for GE, its stock price must also be projected. According to *Value Line,* GE typically enjoys a P/E ratio of roughly 25:1. Once EPS has been forecast for 2005, GE's typical P/E ratio can be used to estimate its stock price in 2005. Then, GE's projected stock price for 2005 must be discounted back to the present by using an appropriate risk-adjusted discount rate. Thus, a vital component of DPV analysis is the calculation of an appropriate risk-adjusted discount rate.

In a common approach, the appropriate risk-adjusted rate of return on any common stock investment depends on the relative risk of the stock, in which relative risk is measured in terms of stock price volatility relative to the overall market. In this approach, stock risk is often described by using the Greek letter beta, or β. For the overall market, $\beta = 1$, and the expected rate of return is the long-term average rate of return of 12–14%. Of this amount, roughly 4–6% represents the expected rate of inflation, and 6–8% represents a required risk premium. For simplicity, let's assume an expected rate of return for the overall market of 13%, consisting of an 8% risk premium and a risk-free rate of 5%. If an individual stock has a $\beta = 1$, it is said to have market-like risk, and it too would have an expected rate of return equal to the long-term stock market average of roughly 13%. If an individual stock has a $\beta = 2$, meaning that it is twice as risky as the overall market, it would command twice the overall market's required risk premium. When $\beta = 2$, the required annual rate of return is 21% (= 5% + 2 × 8%). If an individual stock has a $\beta = 0.5$, meaning that it is one-half as risky as the overall market, it would command one-half of the overall market's risk premium. When $\beta = 0.5$, the required annual rate of return is 9% (= 5% + 0.5 × 8%).

For argument's sake, let's assume that GE is slightly more risky than the typical stock. *Value Line* projects a $\beta = 1.25$ for GE, meaning that the company has 125% of the risk of the overall market. This means that GE is roughly 25% more risky than the overall market, when risk is measured in terms of stock price volatility. With a risk premium of 8%, a stock that is 1.25 times as risky as the market as a whole would command 1.25 times the market risk premium. Under these circumstances, an appropriate risk premium for GE would not be 8%, but 1.25 times 8%, or 10% (= 1.25 × 8%). If you add the required risk premium of 10% to the 5% risk-free rate of interest, a reasonable risk-adjusted discount rate of 15% (= 5% + 1.25 × 8%) is suggested for GE. At the present time, GE pays a 1.3% dividend yield. If GE's EPS, dividend, and stock price are all expected to grow at

FIGURE 10.5 **GE Stockholders Enjoyed Stunning Growth during the 1990s**

GENERAL ELECTRIC NYSE-GE

RECENT PRICE **120** | P/E RATIO **36.1** (Trailing: 38.7 / Median: 15.0) | RELATIVE P/E RATIO **2.41** | DIV'D YLD **1.3%** | **VALUE LINE**

TIMELINESS **2** Raised 10/15/99
SAFETY **1** New 7/27/90
TECHNICAL **3** Lowered 4/2/99
BETA 1.25 (1.00 = Market)

	1988	1989	1990	1991	1992	1993	1994	1995	1996	1997	1998	1999
High:	12.0	16.2	18.9	19.5	21.9	26.8	27.4	36.6	53.1	76.6	103.9	125.2
Low:	9.6	10.9	12.5	13.3	18.2	20.2	22.5	24.9	34.8	47.9	69.0	94.1

Target Price Range 2002 | 2003 | 2004

2002-04 PROJECTIONS

	Price	Gain	Ann'l Total Return
High	150	(+25%)	7%
Low	125	(+5%)	3%

Insider Decisions

	N	D	J	F	M	A	M	J	J
to Buy	0	0	0	0	0	0	0	0	0
Options	0	0	1	1	0	4	0	0	2
to Sell	1	0	1	1	0	3	0	0	7

Institutional Decisions

	4Q1998	1Q1999	2Q1999
to Buy	578	578	544
to Sell	558	586	594
Hld's(000)	1670751	1669454	1669749

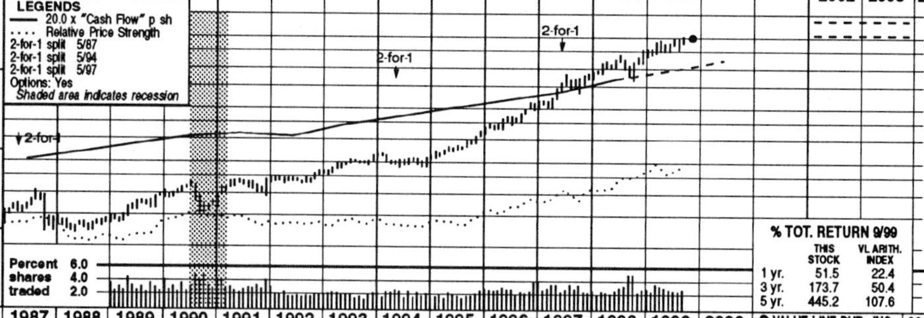

% TOT. RETURN 9/99

	THIS STOCK	VL ARITH. INDEX
1 yr.	51.5	22.4
3 yr.	173.7	50.4
5 yr.	445.2	107.6

1983	1984	1985	1986	1987	1988	1989	1990	1991	1992	1993	1994	1995	1996	1997	1998	1999	2000	© VALUE LINE PUB., INC.	02-04
7.37	7.68	7.75	9.65	10.89	10.76	11.33	12.32	12.47	11.09	11.08	11.62	12.91	14.02	14.99	15.76	**16.90**	**18.00**	Sales per sh A	**21.90**
.85	.93	.98	1.08	1.23	1.36	1.51	1.67	1.75	1.69	1.97	2.19	2.45	2.71	3.01	3.54	**3.95**	**4.50**	"Cash Flow" per sh	**6.35**
.56	.63	.64	.68	.80	.94	1.09	1.21	1.28	1.26	1.52	1.73	1.95	2.20	2.50	2.80	**3.22**	**3.70**	Earnings per sh B	**5.50**
.24	.26	.28	.30	.33	.37	.43	.48	.52	.58	.65	.75	.85	.95	1.08	1.25	**1.40**	**1.60**	Div'ds Decl'd per sh C■	**2.20**
.47	.68	.56	.55	.49	.51	.61	.61	.65	.42	.47	.51	.55	.73	.67	.63	**.75**	**.85**	Cap'l Spending per sh	**1.10**
3.10	3.46	3.81	4.14	4.56	5.12	5.77	6.21	6.27	6.86	7.56	7.73	8.88	9.46	10.55	11.89	**13.15**	**14.70**	Book Value per sh D	**10.75**
3637.0	3639.0	3647.8	3647.2	3611.8	3608.5	3610.1	0492.5	3456.5	3421.7	3414.6	3411.9	3333.0	3289.1	3264.6	3271.3	**3250.0**	**3250.0**	Common Shs Outst'g E	**3200.0**
11.9	10.9	12.1	14.2	16.5	11.4	12.2	12.9	13.7	15.5	15.5	14.3	15.1	19.4	25.1	30.3	*Bold figures are Value Line estimates*		Avg Ann'l P/E Ratio	**25.0**
1.01	1.01	.98	.96	1.10	.95	.92	.96	.88	.94	.92	.94	1.01	1.22	1.45	1.60			Relative P/E Ratio	**1.65**
3.6%	3.7%	3.6%	3.1%	2.5%	3.4%	3.2%	3.1%	3.0%	3.0%	2.8%	3.0%	2.9%	2.2%	1.7%	1.5%			Avg Ann'l Div'd Yield	**1.6%**

CAPITAL STRUCTURE as of 6/30/99
Total Debt $2883 mill. A Due in 5 Yrs $2206 mill.
LT Debt $677 mill. A LT Interest $40.0 mill.
(Total interest coverage: 17.4x) (2% of Cap'l)

Leases, Uncapitalized None
Pension Liability None
Pfd Stock None

Common Stock 3,280,189,000 shs (98% of Cap'l)

MARKET CAP: $394 billion (Large Cap)

1989	1990	1991	1992	1993	1994	1995	1996	1997	1998	1999	2000		02-04
41019	43017	43089	37943	37822	39630	43013	46119	48952	51546	**55000**	**58500**	Sales ($mill) A	**70000**
15.0%	15.2%	15.0%	15.0%	16.9%	17.4%	18.0%	18.3%	19.0%	21.2%	**22.0%**	**22.0%**	Operating Margin	**23.0%**
1524.0	1534.0	1607.0	1483.0	1631.0	1545.0	1581.0	1635.0	1622.0	2292.0	**2400**	**2500**	Depreciation ($mill) F	**2800**
3939.0	4303.0	4435.0	4305.0	5102.0	5915.0	6573.0	7280.0	8203.0	9296.0	**10500**	**11900**	Net Profit ($mill)	**17500**
28.3%	26.4%	26.7%	25.0%	24.4%	24.1%	23.9%	24.0%	24.0%	23.3%	**25.0%**	**25.0%**	Income Tax Rate	**25.0%**
9.6%	10.0%	10.3%	11.3%	13.5%	14.9%	15.3%	15.8%	16.8%	18.0%	**19.1%**	**20.3%**	Net Profit Margin	**25.0%**
1683.0	857.0	d79.0	d822.0	d419.0	544.0	204.0	d2147	d4881	d6708	**d3900**	**d2000**	Working Cap'l ($mill)	**1500**
3947.0	4048.0	4333.0	3420.0	2413.0	2699.0	2277.0	1710.0	729.0	681.0	**500**	**400**	Long-Term Debt ($mill) A	**Nil**
20890	21680	21683	23459	25824	26387	29609	31125	34438	38880	**42800**	**47700**	Shr. Equity ($mill)	**65000**
16.9%	17.8%	18.1%	17.0%	18.6%	20.9%	21.6%	22.9%	24.2%	23.5%	**23.5%**	**25.0%**	Return on Total Cap'l	**27.0%**
18.9%	19.8%	20.5%	18.4%	19.8%	22.4%	22.2%	23.4%	23.8%	23.9%	**24.5%**	**25.0%**	Return on Shr. Equity	**27.0%**
11.5%	12.0%	12.1%	10.1%	11.4%	13.1%	12.8%	13.6%	13.9%	13.8%	**14.0%**	**14.5%**	Retained to Com Eq	**16.0%**
39%	39%	41%	45%	42%	42%	42%	42%	42%	42%	**44%**	**42%**	All Div'ds to Net Prof	**42%**

CURRENT POSITION A ($MILL.)	1997	1998	6/30/99
Cash Assets	1422	1434	1830
Receivables	9054	8483	8186
Inventory (LIFO)	5109	5305	5894
Current Assets	15585	15222	15910
Accts Payable	4779	4845	4730
Debt Due	3629	3466	2206
Other	12058	13619	15328
Current Liab.	20466	21930	22264

ANNUAL RATES of change (per sh)	Past 10 Yrs.	Past 5 Yrs.	Est'd '96-'98 to '02-'04
Sales	3.5%	5.5%	5.5%
"Cash Flow"	9.5%	11.5%	13.0%
Earnings	12.0%	13.0%	14.0%
Dividends	12.5%	13.5%	13.0%
Book Value	8.5%	9.0%	11.0%

Cal-endar	QUARTERLY SALES ($ mill.) A Mar.31	Jun.30	Sep.30	Dec.31	Full Year
1996	9742	11520	11478	13379	46119
1997	10522	12620	11698	14112	48952
1998	11408	13217	12075	14846	51546
1999	11796	13966	13228	*16010*	*55000*
2000	*12600*	*15000*	*14300*	*16600*	*58500*

Cal-endar	EARNINGS PER SHARE B Mar.31	Jun.30	Sep.30	Dec.31	Full Year
1996	.46	.58	.54	.62	2.20
1997	.51	.66	.62	.71	2.50
1998	.57	.74	.69	.80	2.80
1999	.65	.85	.80	*.92*	*3.22*
2000	*.75*	*.95*	*.93*	*1.07*	*3.70*

Cal-endar	QUARTERLY DIVIDENDS PAID C■ Mar.31	Jun.30	Sep.30	Dec.31	Full Year
1995	.205	.205	.205	.205	.82
1996	.23	.23	.23	.23	.92
1997	.26	.26	.26	.26	1.04
1998	.30	.30	.30	.30	1.20
1999	.35	.35	.35		

BUSINESS: General Electric Co. is one of the largest & most diversified industrial cos. in the world. Indus. segments incl. Aircraft Engines (19% of '98 revs.; 18% of oper. pfts.), Appliances (11%, 8%), Broadcasting (10%, 13%), Indus. Pdts. & Systems. (21%, 19%), incl. lighting, locomotives, motors, indus. systems; Materials (13%, 16%), mainly plastic; Power Generation (16%, 13%), turbine-generators; Technical Pdts. & Svcs. (10%, 11%), medical systems, computer svcs. Also has GE Capital (provided $3.8 bill. in other inc.) Fgn.: 48% of sls.; R&D, 3%. Has abt. 293,000 empls., 534,000 stkhldrs. Off./Dir. own less than 1% of stk. (3/99 Proxy) Chrmn. & C.E.O.: J.F. Welch, Jr. Inc.: NY. Add.: 3135 Easton Turnpike, Fairfield, CT 06431. Tel.: 203-373-2211. Web: www.ge.com.

The operating environment remains favorable for General Electric. Earnings grew at a 16% year-over-year clip during the September quarter. Revenues increased at all of the company's eight operating segments, with the exception of a modest downturn at Appliances, which has been under competitive pressure for some time now. GE's appliances have long had a reputation for quality, and innovative new products that are in the works give us confidence the problems are of the short-term variety. Operating earnings at Power Systems, on the other hand, increased 51% on 28% sales growth in the quarter, and a hefty backlog indicates this trend is likely to persist.

Quality-control initiatives are powering much of the earnings growth at GE. Indeed, the company maintains executive management positions with the sole responsibility of improving quality across all operations. The ongoing process involves rigorous statistical analysis, with the goal of eventually minimizing the number of errors in any manufacturing or service activity to 1 in 3.4 million. Although this is difficult to measure, let alone achieve, we believe the program is approaching $2 billion in annual savings.

Services are becoming increasingly important to the bottom line. GE Capital, the company's financial services arm, currently accounts for about one-third of pretax profits, and this number is likely to continue to increase. But manufacturing service revenues are also growing rapidly. With the company's excellent reputation for quality, it is not difficult to sell service contracts along with an order for high-tech medical equipment, for instance. Moreover, these contracts provide a high-margin, recurring-revenue stream, which should help minimize the effect of economic downturns on the bottom line.

GE shares are timely. However, investors with an eye to 2002–2004 will probably want to wait for a pullback in the stock price before making new commitments. Earnings growth will likely remain in the mid-teens for the foreseeable future, but the relatively high P/E multiple currently accorded the stock leaves scant margin for error in the event of a rise in interest rates or a general market correction.

Noah Goldner *October 22, 1999*

(A) Revs. and balance-sheet data excl. fin. serv. sub.; revs. also excl. other inc. (B) Based on avg. shs. Excl. nonrecur. losses: '91, 52¢; '93, 26¢. Excl. gains (loss) from disc. oper.: '92, 13¢; '93, 22¢; '94, (35¢). Next egs. rpt. due late Jan. (C) Next div'd mtg. abt. Dec. 20th. Goes ex abt. Dec. 26th. Approx. div'd. pymt. dates: 25th of Jan., April, July, Oct. ■ Div'd reinvest. plan. (D) Incl. intang.: in '98: $9,996 mill., $3.06/sh. (E) In mill., adj. for stk. splits. (F) Mostly on an accelerated basis.

Company's Financial Strength	A++
Stock's Price Stability	90
Price Growth Persistence	100
Earnings Predictability	100

Source: Value Line Publishing, Inc.

approximately the same rate, a dividend yield of 1.3% can be anticipated over the coming five-year period. In terms of the 15% rate of return that is required by GE stockholders, 1.3% can be expected in the form of dividend income, and 13.7% can be anticipated in the form of stock price appreciation (capital gains).

Table 10.4, panel A, shows a DPV analysis for GE based on the assumption of variable EPS growth rates but a constant risk-adjusted discount rate. In each case, EPS in 2000 of $3.70 is the starting point for the analysis. For example, with 12% per year EPS growth over the five-year 2000–2005 period, GE's EPS in 2005 is projected to be $6.52. At 25 times earnings, this implies a 2005 stock price of $163.02. Discounting this price back to the present by using a risk-adjusted discount rate of 15% minus the 1.3% dividend yield, or 13.7% per year, gives an economic value of $85.79 for GE at the present time. Using alternate 14% and 16% per year EPS growth rate assumptions, economic values of $93.73 and $102.24 are calculated.

Table 10.4, panel B, shows a DPV analysis for GE based on the alternate assumption of constant EPS growth but variable risk-adjusted discount rates. Once again, EPS in 2000 of $3.70 is the starting point for the analysis. Here, 14% per year EPS growth and a typical P/E ratio of 25 times earnings are presumed. A range of economic values for GE from $85.90 to $102.42 is calculated based upon a range of risk-adjusted discount rates from 13% to 15%.

Therefore, based on a range of reasonable EPS growth rate and risk-adjusted discount rate assumptions, a range from $85.79 to $102.42 is calculated for the economic value of GE. Admittedly, this is a broad range. However, it provides investors with useful information if the current price of GE is well below or well above these levels. If GE's current stock price were well below $85.79, then GE would represent a bargain. If GE's current stock price were well above $102.42, then GE would be overpriced and should be avoided. In fact, a GE stock price of 120 seems too high in the light of dividend income and capital appreciation that can be reasonably anticipated over the near term.

DPV for Non–Dividend-Paying Stocks

DPV analysis can also be fruitfully used in the case of non–dividend-paying stocks, such as Waste Management, Inc., (WMI) depicted in Figure 10.2.

WMI has been built through a series of mergers over the years. After a battery of restructuring charges, earnings are expected to surge during the next few years. *Value Line* projects a sharp jump in earnings in 2000 and then more modest earnings growth going forward. Taking account of both, it seems reasonable to project an average 9% per year rate of EPS growth from a base year 2000 EPS of $1.90. *Value Line*'s projection of a typical 14.5:1 P/E ratio for WMI also seems appropriate. It also seems legitimate to accord a relatively high rate of risk adjustment to these projections, given that the expected earnings surge has not yet materialized. WMI also uses high financial leverage and would be extremely sensitive to changes in market interest rates. If WMI can be expected to be twice as risky as the average company ($\beta = 2$), investors would command twice the market risk premium. Under these circumstances, a reasonable risk-adjusted discount rate of 21% ($= 5\% + 2 \times 8\%$) is suggested for WMI. Notice that WMI pays no material dividend income and probably will not over the 2000–2005 time frame.

Against this backdrop of information, Table 10.4, panel C, shows a DPV analysis for WMI based on the assumption of varying EPS growth rates but a constant

TABLE 10.4 Discounted Present Value (DPV) Analysis

Intrinsic Economic Value of Stock $(1) = (6)/[1 + (8)^5]$	Current EPS (2)	Expected EPS Growth (3)	Expected EPS in 5 Years $(4) = EPS\ (1 + g)^5$	Expected P/E Ratio (5)	Expected Stock Price in 5 Years $(6) = (4) \times (5)$	Risk-Adjusted Discount Rate, *k* (7)	Discount Rate Minus Dividend Yield $(8) = (7) - 1.3\%$
A. GE valuation with different growth rates and a constant risk-adjusted discount rate (1.3% dividend).							
85.79	3.70	12.0%	6.52	25.0	163.02	15.0%	13.7%
93.73	3.70	14.0%	7.12	25.0	178.10	15.0%	13.7%
102.24	3.70	16.0%	7.77	25.0	194.28	15.0%	13.7%
B. GE valuation with constant growth and different risk-adjusted discount rates (1.3% dividend).							
102.42	3.70	14.0%	7.12	25.0	178.10	13.0%	11.7%
93.73	3.70	14.0%	7.12	25.0	178.10	15.0%	13.7%
85.90	3.70	14.0%	7.12	25.0	178.10	17.0%	15.7%
C. WMI valuation with different growth rates and a constant risk-adjusted discount rate (no dividend).							
14.90	1.90	7.0%	2.66	14.5	38.64	21.0%	21.0%
16.34	1.90	9.0%	2.92	14.5	42.39	21.0%	21.0%
17.90	1.90	11.0%	3.20	14.5	46.42	21.0%	21.0%
D. WMI valuation with constant growth and different risk-adjusted discount rates (no dividend).							
18.53	1.90	9.0%	2.92	14.5	42.39	18.0%	18.0%
16.34	1.90	9.0%	2.92	14.5	42.39	21.0%	21.0%
14.46	1.90	9.0%	2.92	14.5	42.39	24.0%	24.0%

risk-adjusted discount rate. In each case, EPS in 2000 of $1.90 is the starting point for the analysis. For example, with 7% per year EPS growth, WMI's EPS in 2005 is projected to be $2.66. At 14.5 times earnings, this implies a 2005 stock price of $38.64. Discounting this price back to the present by using a risk-adjusted discount rate of 21% per year gives an economic value of $14.90 for WMI at the present time. Using alternate 9% and 11% per year EPS growth rate assumptions, economic values of $16.34 and $17.90 are calculated. Based on the alternate assumption of constant EPS growth but variable risk-adjusted discount rates, a range of economic values for WMI from $18.53 to $14.46 is calculated, based upon a range of risk-adjusted discount rates from 18% to 24% (see Table 10.4, panel D).

Based on a range of reasonable EPS growth rate and risk-adjusted discount rate assumptions, a range from $14.46 to $18.53 is calculated for the economic value of WMI. This broad range gives useful investment information if the current price of WMI is well below or well above these levels. A WMI stock price well below $14.46 would signal a bargain; a stock price well above $18.53 would indicate that WMI is overpriced. In early 2000, WMI actually sold for a price below $14 per share. As such, it appeared attractive, assuming that its future earnings prospects remain intact.

Dividend Discount Models

Variable Growth Model

For a common stock investor with an indeterminate investment horizon, stock prices at any point in time can be described as the present value of all expected future dividends.

When one continues to substitute for stock price in Equation 10.4, the value of a stock is the present value of all future dividends into perpetuity:

$$P_0 = \frac{D_1}{1 + k} + \frac{D_2}{(1 + k)^2} + \frac{D_3}{(1 + k)^3} + \cdots \tag{10.5}$$

This formula is called the **dividend discount model** of stock prices. It is easy to misinterpret this model as implying that capital gains are not important. Although the dividend discount model focuses exclusively on future dividend income, future stock prices at any point in time will also be determined by anticipated dividend income. Expected capital gains are explicitly incorporated in the dividend discount model, but their influence is captured in terms of anticipated future dividend income.

dividend discount model Stock valuation approach based on expected dividend income and risk considerations.

The fact that only dividends appear in the dividend discount model does not imply that common stock investors should ignore capital gains in their buy/sell decisions. It simply means that capital gains will be determined by dividend forecasts made by other investors at the time the stock is sold. This is why stock prices at any point in time can be described as the present value of dividends plus sales price for *any* investment horizon. P_n is the present value at time n of all dividends expected to be paid after that point in time.

In today's investment environment, asserting that stock prices are wholly determined by future dividend income might strike aggressive investors as somewhat odd. After all, aren't some of the best recent performers in the stock market non–dividend-paying stocks such as Microsoft, Cisco Systems, Dell, and Intel? The answer is yes, of course, but it is important to note that these stocks fail to pay

WALL STREET WISDOM 10.2

Cisco's Urge to Merge

In the Internet infrastructure business, Cisco Systems, Inc., is the worldwide leader. Cisco creates hardware and software solutions that link computer networks so that people have easy access to information without regard to differences in time, place, or type of computer system. Cisco's strategy is to provide end-to-end networking solutions to help its customers improve productivity and gain a competitive advantage.

Cisco has enjoyed stunning business success. From a 1990 base of less than $70 million, revenues exploded to $16 billion by 2000. This represents a 36.9% compound annual rate of growth. Over this same time frame, profits jumped from $13.9 million to $3.2 billion, a 72.5% annual rate of growth. By 2003, sales are expected to leap to $35 billion, and profits are expected to vault to $6.6 billion. Clearly, Cisco has prospered as the main seller of the infrastructure or "plumbing" required to run the Internet.

More impressive than Cisco's business success is its accomplishment in the stock market. Cisco was formed in 1984 by computer scientists from Stanford University to commercialize the technology used in developing a campus-wide network. Its first multiprotocol routers were shipped in March 1986. On February 16, 1990, Morgan Stanley & Co. and Smith Barney, Harris Upham & Co. managed the initial public offering of 271.2 million shares at $0.09375 per share (adjusted for splits). By mid-2000, Cisco shares exceeded $80 per share, representing a return of more than 850:1 and a compound annual rate of return to investors of 96.3% per year! With a market capitalization of roughly $500 billion, Cisco represents one of the most stunning success stories in stock market history. With a price/sales ratio of more than 35:1 and a price/earnings ratio of more than 210:1, investors in mid-2000 were clearly looking for a sustained period of dazzling growth.

How did Cisco do it? The answer may surprise you. In technology, rapid firm growth is typically based on superior research capabilities and innovative new products. Protected by patents and committed to path-breaking research, companies such as Microsoft, IBM, and Motorola have enjoyed long-term success in the typically hazardous high-tech sector. Cisco is different. Rather than inventing new and innovative products, Cisco has a long-time strategy of simply buying other companies. Cisco has built its empire by methodically digesting more than 50 companies in the late 1990s and more than 20 per year during the past couple of years. Not every Cisco deal is a winner, but the company has succeeded in using acquisitions to reshape itself and plug holes in its product line. For example, Cisco bought Crescendo Communications, Inc., in 1993 for $95 million in stock. Today, Crescendo's switches, along with products from later acquisitions, are the heart of a unit with nearly $7 billion in annual sales.

Now, Cisco's Chairman John Chambers vows to accelerate the pace to as many as 25 acquisitions per year. According to Chambers, technology is advancing so rapidly that Cisco cannot do everything itself. As a result, the company plans to grow by buying the products and technology it cannot or does not want to develop. For example, in August 1999, Cisco bought Cerent Corp., a fiberoptics equipment maker, for $7.2 billion. The negotiations took only 2½ hours over three days. Cerent was bigger and more mature than most Cisco acquisitions. Still, Cerent had only 266 employees, including a manufacturing team and a sales force, and had generated less than $10 million in sales in its entire operating history.

In March 2000, Cisco acquired two closely held technology companies to extend its reach into nontraditional markets, including information appliances and wireless phones. Cisco acquired InfoGear Technology Corp. and its 74 employees for about $301 million in stock and JetCell Inc. and its 46 employees for about $200 million in stock. At the time, skeptics inquired about Cisco's "hiring policy" of paying more than $4 million per employee for companies that generate little or no revenues. Meanwhile, Cisco's stock price rose 2.31% on the news.

See: Thomas G. Donlan, "Cisco's Bids," *Barron's*, May 8, 2000, 31–34.

dividends only in the near term. Although speculators may find it tempting to ignore dividends or dividend paying potential, stock prices are determined ultimately by the cash flows generated for stockholders. Those cash flows may be regular cash payments in the form of dividends or irregular cash payments in the form of share buybacks. A company without the capability of making future cash payments to shareholders is properly worth zero.

Would any investor be enthusiastic about buying a business, such as a restaurant, that *never* provided a cash return? No, of course not. Similarly, common stock in a company that has no reasonable prospect of *ever* paying a dividend is worth very little. Although hope springs eternal and tends to boost stock prices for companies with scant future prospects, a company that will never provide a cash return to investors is worthless.

Constant Growth Model

The dividend discount model shown in Equation 10.5 is difficult to apply because it requires a precise estimate of annual dividends for every year into the indefinite future.

To simplify matters, growth stock investors often make the simple assumption of a constant rate of dividend growth. This **constant growth model** for growth stock valuation can be written:

constant growth model
Stock valuation method based on constantly growing dividends and risk considerations.

$$P_0 = \frac{D_0(1+g)}{1+k} + \frac{D_0(1+g)^2}{(1+k)^2} + \frac{D_0(1+g)^3}{(1+k)^3} + \cdots \qquad \textbf{(10.6)}$$

This equation can be simplified to

$$P_0 = \frac{D_0(1+g)}{k-g} = \frac{D_1}{k-g} \qquad \textbf{(10.7)}$$

This constant growth model is sometimes referred to as the **Gordon growth model,** after financial economist Myron J. Gordon who popularized its use.

Gordon growth model
Another name for the constant growth model.

An equivalent way of expressing the constant growth model in Equation 10.7 is to show how it describes the components of the required rate of return. After manipulation, Equation 10.7 can be used to identify the risk-adjusted discount rate as consisting of a dividend yield (or "bird in the hand") plus growth (capital appreciation):

$$k = \frac{D_1}{P_0} + g \qquad \textbf{(10.8)}$$
$$= \text{Dividend Yield} + \text{Capital Gain}$$

This version of the constant growth model offers investors a simple means for calculating the required rate of return k. For any common stock selling at its economic value, the investor's expected rate of return is equal to the risk-adjusted discount rate. This means that $k = D_1/P_0 + g$. By observing the indicated dividend yield, D_1/P_0 and estimating the growth rate of dividends, an investor can compute k. For example, if a company is presently paying a 2% dividend yield and that dividend yield is growing at 10% per year, the investor's required rate of return is 12%. This is also the risk-adjusted discount rate.

Valuation Using the CGM

The constant growth model (CGM) is simple to apply. Consider the case of a preferred stock that pays a simple cash dividend of \$2.40. Without any prospects for growth, the value of preferred stock is directly determined by the appropriate discount rate *k*. For simplicity, assume that the appropriate risk-adjusted discount rate for such a preferred stock is 6%. Based on Equation 10.7, the value of such a preferred stock is \$40 [= \$2.40/(0.06 − 0)]. If the discount rate for such a preferred stock falls to 4%, its value would rise to \$60 [= \$2.40/(0.04 − 0)]. If the discount rate for such a preferred stock rises to 8%, its value would fall to \$30 [= \$2.40/(0.08 − 0)]. Notice how the value of such a preferred stock rises and falls with changes in interest rates, just like a bond.

Now consider a common stock paying a \$2.40 dividend that grows by 2% per year. This means that at the end of year 1 the expected dividend rises to \$2.448 (= \$2.40 × 1.02), at the end of year 2 the expected dividend rises to \$2.497 (= \$2.40 × 1.02^2), and so on. Such a stock would obviously be worth more to investors than the no-growth preferred stock. Using the CGM, it is easy to determine exactly how much more. Using Equation 10.7, a common stock paying a \$2.40 dividend growing 2% per year is worth \$40 [= \$2.40/(0.08 − 0.02)] when the required rate of return is 8%, and \$60 [= \$2.40/(0.06 − 0.02)] when the required rate of return is 6%.

In the CGM approach, notice that the value of a growth stock will rise with an increase in the expected dividend per share or in the expected dividend growth rate. The value of a growth stock is inversely related to the risk-adjusted discount rate, *k*. The value of a growth stock falls with an increase in *k* and will rise as *k* decreases. Notice that any increase in the expected dividend growth rate has a valuation effect that is identical to that resulting from a decrease in the risk-adjusted discount rate. Also notice that the CGM implicitly assumes that the stock price will grow at the same constant rate as dividends.

Table 10.5 gives further insight concerning the CGM. When the CGM is used to value GE, the expected dividend during the coming year should be used. For simplicity, let us assume this amount is \$1.60. Once again, a reasonable choice for the risk-adjusted discount rate is 15%. When GE's dividend is expected to grow by precisely 13% per year, the CGM estimate of GE's real economic value per share is \$80. With 12% expected dividend growth, for example, the economic value of GE falls to \$53.33, or by a whopping one-third. Therefore, if a projected dividend growth rate of 13% per year is accurate, GE would appear to be only modestly overvalued at a price of \$120. If a projected dividend growth rate of 12% per year is accurate, however, GE would be substantially overvalued at a price of \$120.

Unfortunately, it usually is not possible to know whether GE will be able to grow its dividend by 13% versus 12%. A dividend growth forecast of 13% per year would be rightly viewed as accurate if actual dividend growth came in at 12%. Similarly, a dividend growth forecast of 12% per year would be on target if actual dividend growth came in at 13%. It simply is not realistic to expect to estimate dividend growth within ±1% per year for GE, or any such company, over any five-year period. Most investors would be happy if they could simply identify moderate dividend growers (4–8% per year) from more attractive fast dividend growers (12–15% per year).

As shown in Table 10.5, CGM estimates of the inherent value per share vary widely with small changes in dividend growth rate estimates. This is especially true as the expected dividend growth rate, *g*, approaches the risk-adjusted cost of capital, *k*. Notice that actual value is undefined when the expected dividend growth rate

TABLE 10.5 GE Valuation Using the Constant Growth Model

Intrinsic Economic Value of Stock $V_0 = D_1/(k - g)$	Expected Dividend, D_1	Expected Dividend Growth, g	Risk-Adjusted Discount Rate, k
22.86	1.60	8.0%	15.0%
26.67	1.60	9.0%	15.0%
32.00	1.60	10.0%	15.0%
40.00	1.60	11.0%	15.0%
53.33	1.60	12.0%	15.0%
80.00	1.60	13.0%	15.0%
160.00	1.60	14.0%	15.0%
—	1.60	15.0%	15.0%

exceeds the risk-adjusted cost of capital. Theoretically, an investor would be willing to pay *any* price for a stock capable of growing dividends faster than the required rate of return. In the very long run, rapid growth offsets even ridiculously high purchase prices. This line of reasoning has gotten many growth stock investors into trouble. The problem lies in the fact that high dividend growth rates are seldom sustainable for extended periods. When dividend growth begins to falter, as it inevitably does, high valuations become unsustainable and growth stock prices crash.

A final obvious problem with the CGM is that the approach is silent on the important subject of how to value non–dividend-paying stocks. As such, the CGM is a useful, although clearly imperfect tool for growth stock valuation.

Growth Stock Investment Strategies

PEG: Growth at a Reasonable Price

Determining a reasonable price to pay for any growth stock is always difficult. To deal effectively with the uncertainties involved, growth stock investors have developed various simple valuation devices. An **investment rule of thumb** is a simple guide to investment valuation that has served the test of time.

investment rule of thumb
Simple guide to investment valuation that has served the test of time.

For example, legendary mutual fund investor Peter Lynch is famous for developing the so-called P/E-to-growth ratio, or **PEG ratio.** *The Motley Fool's* David and Tom Gardner <http://www.fool.com> have done a lot to popularize its use. The PEG ratio is simply the P/E ratio divided by the EPS growth rate. If a company has a P/E of 20 and is expected to enjoy EPS growth of 20% per year, the company's PEG ratio would be 1. Generally speaking, a stock is fully valued if it sports a PEG ratio of 1 or more. If the PEG ratio is less than 1, the stock is worthy of investment consideration. The PEG ratio rule of thumb goes something like this:

PEG ratio
P/E divided by the expected EPS growth rate.

- If PEG $\leq$ 1, the stock may be worthy of investment attention and possible purchase.
- If PEG $\leq$ 0.5, the stock is definitely worthy of investment attention and may represent a very attractive investment.
- If PEG $\leq$ 0.33, the stock is apt to represent an extraordinarily attractive investment opportunity.

Momentum Strategies

upticks Minimal increases in stock price.

downticks Minimal decreases in stock price.

During rampant bull markets, such as that experienced during the late 1990s, momentum-based investment strategies flourish. In this approach to growth stock investing, stocks that have high volume on **upticks** and low volume on **downticks** are said to be benefiting from a positive inflow of investment funds. An uptick is an increase in price associated with a buy execution at the ask price immediately following a sell execution at the bid price. For example, suppose that the sale of 100 shares caused the IBM stock price to fall by ⅛ of a point. If the next transaction was a purchase of 2,500 shares that caused the stock to go back up ⅛ of a point to the original price, then IBM's trading activity would exhibit a net inflow of investment funds.

Some growth stock investors favor buying stocks with net cash inflows and advocate selling or avoiding stocks with net cash outflows. This type of "go-with-the-flow" growth stock investment strategy is based on a simple demand/supply view of equity investing. Net cash inflows are thought to be positive because they suggest significant demand and emerging upward price pressure. Net cash outflows are thought to be negative because they suggest significant supply and emerging downward price pressure.

As shown in Figure 10.6, prominent money flow numbers for NYSE stocks are published on a daily basis in *The Wall Street Journal.* These money flow figures are the dollar value of uptick trades minus the dollar value of downtick trades. The up-down ratio reflects the value of uptick trades relative to the value of downtick trades. Although the *Journal* publishes only limited information for companies with significant money flow imbalances, detailed information about money flows can be obtained from a number of sites on the Internet. Such data are intensively relied on by day traders and other short-term speculators who use various types of technical analysis to guide their stock picking. For example, Figure 10.7 shows a typical "pick-of-the-day" selection from Harry Aloof's *Wall Street Trader's Column* on the Internet <http://www.wstraders.com>. Like most such analyses, money flow numbers play a prominent role in identifying short-term buy/sell candidates.

Of course, investment professionals who use momentum-based investment strategies remain the minority on Wall Street. Investment professionals who focus on fundamental determinants of investment value, such as earnings, book value, and dividends, are quick to point out that momentum stocks get crushed during market corrections, such as that experienced during the fall of 1998 and the spring of 2000. Experience shows that liquidity may drive stock prices in the short run. In the long run, however, it is EPS growth that counts. It is worth emphasizing that sustained earnings growth is difficult even among the largest and most powerful corporations. As shown in Table 10.7, the largest corporations according to market capitalization often stumble and fall. Even for those corporations able to maintain gigantic market capitalizations over decades, few offer above-average long-term rates of return for investors. Remember, the fact that aggregate market capitalization has grown over time does not ensure that long-time investors have prospered. It is common for the market value of the firm to grow faster than stockholder rates of return. Shares issued to complete mergers and acquisitions, fund new plant and equipment, and fulfill employee stock option compensation plans can cause rapid market value growth even for firms with slowly growing share prices. This is worth remembering during an era when investors cannot imagine sub-par rates of return from investments in current stock market favorites such as Microsoft, GE, and Cisco

FIGURE 10.6 Money-Flow Numbers Show Near-Term Demand/Supply Forces

MONEY FLOW: UPTICK VS. DOWNTICK TRADING BY DOLLAR VOLUME

Thursday, March 9, 2000, 4:00 p.m. Eastern time

MARKET	Money Flow (in millions)	Money Flow Prev. Day	Up/Dn Ratio	MARKET	Money Flow (in millions)	Money Flow Prev. Day	Up/Dn Ratio
DJIA *	+ 22.7	– 71.2	101/100	S&P 500 *	+ 575.3	+ 166.4	105/100
Blocks	+ 72.3	– 389.5	105/100	Blocks	+ 672.7	– 235.8	109/100
DJ Global-US *	+ 504.9	+ 175.8	103/100	Russell 2000 *	– 53.0	– 94.5	99/100
Blocks	+ 303.7	– 583.5	103/100	Blocks	– 86.9	+ 261.4	94/100

MONEY FLOW - ISSUE GAINERS AND DECLINERS

GAINERS	Close	Money Flow (in millions)	Up/Dn Ratio	DECLINERS	Close	Money Flow (in millions)	Up/Dn Ratio
AmOnline (N)	61.000	+ 348.9	203/100	CiscoSys (Nq)	139.313	– 229.1	83/100
DellCptr (Nq)	50.438	+ 265.6	141/100	Motorola (N)	161.750	– 201.0	44/100
NASDAQ100 (A)	229.656	+ 240.2	127/100	OracleCp (Nq)	84.000	– 124.2	83/100
TycoInt (N)	44.625	+ 208.5	220/100	Tellabs (Nq)	54.625	– 116.2	56/100
LSI Logic (N)	83.125	+ 138.0	299/100	JDS Uniphs (Nq)	272.500	– 103.1	89/100
Merck (N)	61.000	+ 134.2	198/100	Intel (Nq)	118.375	– 100.3	84/100
TimeWarn (N)	86.875	+ 114.8	221/100	VeritasSftwr (Nq)	162.938	– 92.6	67/100
IBM (N)	107.500	+ 113.2	168/100	NtwkSol (Nq)	494.500	– 84.5	84/100
BrisMyrsSqb (N)	53.750	+ 110.9	184/100	Nokia (N)	214.438	– 75.4	68/100
QwestComm (N)	57.125	+ 87.2	154/100	ProctGamb (N)	57.375	– 73.0	76/100
HewlettPk (N)	151.875	+ 86.6	151/100	Verisign (Nq)	240.750	– 60.3	93/100
WarnerLamb (N)	91.375	+ 78.2	196/100	Ariba (Nq)	320.875	– 58.7	86/100
Pfizer (N)	34.188	+ 74.4	169/100	SunMicrsys (Nq)	97.250	– 58.6	82/100
Corning (N)	194.875	+ 59.6	147/100	NTL Inc (Nq)	96.500	– 48.7	49/100
Disney (N)	36.063	+ 58.8	347/100	LibertyM A (N)	51.438	– 45.8	29/100

Source: Dow Jones * - without block trades.
Moneyflow figures are the dollar value of composite uptick trades minus the dollar value of downtick trades. The up/down ratio reflects the value of uptick trades relative to the value of downtick trades.

Source: *The Wall Street Journal,* March 10, 2000, C4.

Systems. Historically, such high-priced behemoths tend to underperform over the very long run.

Technology Stock Investing

Many growth stock investors display asset category preferences reflecting strong underlying beliefs about where the best growth opportunities can be found. In the late 1990s, many such investors have come to display a strong preference for **technology stocks** at the vanguard of important new innovations in laptop computers, portable communications devices, cellular telephone technology, digital cameras and video disks, and the Internet. Companies expected to benefit from growth tied to the Internet have become a special focus. Important new areas for Internet-related growth include Internet infrastructure building and development (e.g., Cisco Systems, Inc.), Internet access and content (e.g., AOL), and e-commerce (e.g., Amazon.com).

technology stocks
Shares in companies at the vanguard of important new innovations.

FIGURE 10.7 Money-Flow Numbers Drive "Pick-of-the-Day" Selections

Buy Alert! EBAY INC (EBAY) Nasdaq

Report No. 1049 **Analysis by: Harry Aloof** **JUNE 5, 2000**

EBAY INC (EBAY-Nasdaq): ***Technical Viewpoint:*** From a low of $55 1/2 on May 10, 2000 prices rallied, reaching a high of $69.84 on May 22, 2000. A decline saw prices pull back, reaching a low of $56 3/4 on May 24, 2000. Another rally saw prices penetrate resistance line "A", closing 6/2/00 at $77.19. **Technicals: Momentum Index (MTM):** A Buy Alert! was given on May 24, 2000 when the solid line crossed the dotted line to the upside. **Support:** Remains at $57.00. **Resistance**: Is at $81.00. **Point & Figure**: Reversed to the upside on May 25, 2000. A **P&F** downside reversal takes place at $66.00. **Summary**: Technical indicators have turned bullish. BUY! EBAY INC (EBAY-Nasdaq) @ $77 3/8 **Stop:** Use a protective stop of $74 1/2. ***EBAY INC*** *is currently trading @ $77.19 plus $9.81 on Jun 2, 2000.* **Price Objective:** $106.00. **Risk/Reward:** $2 7/8 VS. $28 5/8. **Today's Risk Reward Ratio**: 10:1

Three Part
Technical Chart

Daily Candle Stick Chart
Point & Figure Chart
Technical Study

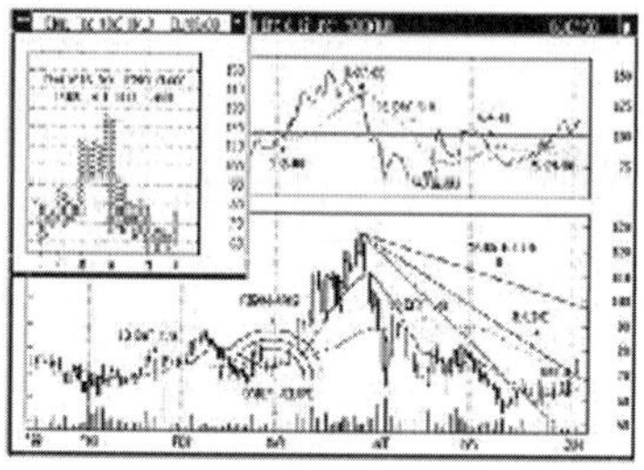

View full size chart

Price Objective:
$106.00

Risk/Reward:
$2 7/8 VS. $28 5/8

Risk/Reward Ratio:
10:1

Source: <http://www.wstraders.com>.

Despite the recent focus by technology stock investors on the Internet, high-tech stocks can be found across a broad spectrum of industry. Basic, diversified, and specialized chemical companies devote an enormous amount of spending to research and development (R&D) and are responsible for a continuing stream of important new inventions and innovations. Some of the most profitable applications from such discoveries are found in related areas such as pharmaceutical drugs, toiletries, and cosmetics. Of course, the biotechnology industry, the focus of intense speculative interest in the early 1990s, is now coming into its own with a string of important new pharmaceutical therapies and other bioengineered products, such as disease-resistant crops. R&D spending is also significant across a broad range of industrial machinery and equipment industries, including: computers, electronic devices, measuring instruments, medical devices, telecommunications, and transportation equipment. Of course, computer software and services are areas of large and growing importance for R&D.

The allure of technology stock investing during the late 1990s is obvious. Technology stocks tend to do well during economic expansions as capital spending rises,

TABLE 10.7 Over Decades, Turnover Is Significant among the Largest Corporations ($ billions)

1980			1990			2000		
Rank	Company	Market Value	Rank	Company	Market Value	Rank	Company	Market Value
1	IBM	39,626	1	IBM	64,567	1	Microsoft Corp.	588,884
2	AT&T Corp.	36,137	2	Exxon Corp.	64,449	2	GE	470,140
3	Exxon Corp.	34,837	3	GE	50,095	3	Cisco Systems	347,897
4	Amoco Corp.	23,352	4	Philip Morris Corp.	47,932	4	Wal-Mart Stores	280,586
5	Schlumberger Ltd.	22,347	5	Bank Tokyo	45,273	5	ExxonMobil Corp.	280,388
6	Shell Oil	17,999	6	Royal Dutch Petroleum	42,149	6	Intel Corp.	279,457
7	Standard Oil	17,685	7	Toyota Motors	38,840	7	Lucent Technologies	222,904
8	Mobil Corp.	17,167	8	AT&T Corp.	38,415	8	IBM	209,148
9	Cheveron Corp.	17,020	9	British Telecom	35,328	9	Deutsche Telekom	205,256
10	BP Amoco	15,582	10	Bristol Myers Squibb	35,096	10	Nokia Corp.	199,796
11	Atlantic Richfield	15,126	11	Merck & C0.	34,781	11	BP Amoco	196,450
12	GE	13,951	12	BP Amoco	34,367	12	Toyota Motor	174,870
13	GM	13,321	13	Wal-Mart	34,234	13	Citigroup Inc.	171,610
14	Royal Dutch Petroleum	13,067	14	Coca-Cola	31,073	14	America Online	166,823
15	Texaco, Inc.	12,891	15	Procter & Gamble	30,040	15	AT&T Corp.	162,765
16	Shell	12,222	16	Shell	29,140	16	Merck & Co.	158,508
17	Eastman Kodak	11,258	17	Hitachi Ltd.	26,457	17	SBC Communications	153,301
18	Halliburton	9,828	18	Bellsouth Corp.	26,388	18	Amer. Int'l Group	153,044
19	Phillips Petroleum Co.	8,941	19	Amoco Corp.	26,290	19	Oracle Corp.	145,215
20	Gulf Corp.	8,492	20	GTE Corp.	25,519	20	British Telecom	144,272
21	Unocal Corp.	7,743	21	Cheveron Corp.	25,477	21	MCI WorldCom	143,995
22	Union Pacific	7,559	22	Du Pont	24,617	22	Vodafone AirTouch	143,088
23	Getty Oil	7,548	23	Matsushita Electric	24,547	23	Coca-Cola	140,591
24	Conoco	7,049	24	Glaxo-Welcome	24,505	24	Home Depot	137,922
25	Minnesota Mining	6,921	25	Johnson & Johnson	23,898	25	Procter & Gamble	135,524

Data sources: 1980, 1990 data from *Compustat PC+*; 2000 data from *Value Line Investment Survey for Windows*, January 2000.

and the U.S. economy was on a nonstop tear throughout the 1990s. Fundamentally important new innovations during the 1990s have also contributed to the explosion of interest in high-tech stocks. First, the advent of amazingly powerful microprocessors transformed the PC into a mighty tool for business calculations. Then, the advent of the Internet and even more powerful microprocessors made it possible for the PC to become the focus of a communications industry revolution. What used to be called cameras, cellular phones, computers, copy machines, fax machines, printers, telephones, and televisions are quickly converging toward multicapability communications devices.

Huge potential rewards await those companies able to successfully navigate in such a rapidly changing environment. Somewhat less understood are the equally enormous risks facing companies unable to successfully anticipate and adapt to such challenges. Table 10.8 illustrates the rapidly changing landscape for high-tech companies in the computer networking equipment and computer software industries. Notice how few industry giants have been able to stay atop their competitors. Although IBM has been able to remain a force in the production of computers and peripheral equipment, no other company has been able to maintain a top 10 position in the industry for 20 years. Present-day giants, such as Cisco Systems, Inc., founded in 1984, have literally come out of nowhere. Similarly, Microsoft Corp., founded in 1975, has come out of nowhere to dominate the important computer software and services industry. Rather than assume that Cisco and Microsoft, for

TABLE 10.8 High-Tech Market Capitalization Rankings Change Dramatically over Time ($ millions)

	1980		1990		2000	
A. Computers and Peripheral Equipment						
1	IBM	$39,625.9	IBM	$64,567.2	Cisco Sys.	$347,897.3
2	Computer Sciences Corp.	240.4	Computer Sciences Corp.	1,071.4	IBM	209,148.0
3	American Management Sys.	53.9	American Management Sys.	175.4	Dell Computer	127,437.4
4	CGA Computers Inc.	34.3	Computer Task Group Inc.	62.8	Sun Microsystems	111,242.8
5	Hadron Inc.	32.6	BRC Holdings Inc.	55.2	Hewlett-Packard	109,277.4
6	Computer Task Group Inc.	20.5	Data Transmission Network	39.1	EMC Corp.	104,803.0
7	Dyatron Corp.	17.1	Medstat Group Inc.	33.0	Compaq Computer	47,600.0
8	BRC Holdings Inc.	12.7	National Information Group	30.9	Gateway Inc.	18,042.5
9	Cerplex Group, Inc.	6.3	Cerplex Group, Inc.	21.0	Apple Computer	16,731.5
10	Auxton Computer Enterprises	5.7	Mpsi Systems, Inc.	19.0	3Com Corp.	15,203.0
B. Computer Software and Services						
1	Computervision Corp.	1,206.2	Microsoft Corp.	8,641.1	Microsoft Corp.	588,884.1
2	Wang Labs, Inc.	875.0	Novell Inc.	1,742.7	Oracle Corp.	145,214.6
3	Cullinet Software, Inc.	196.5	Computer Associates Intl, Inc.	1,615.4	Computer Associates	33,864.2
4	UCCEL Corp.	190.9	Autodesk Inc.	1,110.7	VERITAS Software	32,736.7
5	Tyler Technologies, Inc.	150.3	BMC Software, Inc.	1,030.1	Automatic Data Proc.	32,193.1
6	Banctec Inc.	78.8	Oracle Corp.	1,022.2	Electronic Data Sys.	28,070.4
7	Intelligent Sys. Corp.	51.3	Lotus Development Corp.	844.4	First Data Corp.	20,567.2
8	Informatics General Corp.	51.0	Inprise Corp.	807.9	Intuit Inc.	14,646.2
9	Comshare Inc.	45.7	Policy Management Sys. Corp.	801.1	Siebel Sys.	13,810.7
10	Continuum Inc.	37.7	Cadence Design Sys. Inc.	713.0	Computer Sciences	13,778.9

Data sources: 1980, 1990 data from *Compustat PC+*; 2000 data from *Value Line Investment Survey for Windows*, January 2000.

example, will naturally dominate such a quickly changing landscape for the next 20 years, long-term investors may want to consider what will happen to their stock prices if (or when) they stumble.

WALL STREET WISDOM 10.3

The 1990s Were the Best of Times

Even novice investors are aware of the stock market crash of 1929 and the role it played as a signal of the onset of the Great Depression. However, many are not aware that stock prices actually continued to fall until 1932 as economic conditions worsened. The Dow Jones Industrial Average (DJIA) hit rock bottom on July 8, 1932, at 41.22, a breathtaking drop of 89.2% from the market peak of 381.71 reached on September 3, 1929. Wouldn't it have been nice to be a long-term buy-and-hold investor with funds to invest on that fateful day? Suppose you had indeed bought stocks at the very bottom on July 8, 1932, and held them until the end of 1949. You would have been delighted to have earned a more-than-satisfactory 12.8% per year rate of return on your investment. Even through the Great Depression and World War II, long-term investors did well.

Now, let's go forward in time to August 12, 1982, and the start of the Great Bull Market of the last part of the 20th century. On that day, the DJIA closed at 776.92. Assume that you had bought stocks on that fateful day and held them through the end of 1999. You would have then earned more than 18.9% per year, almost one and one-half times the annual rate of return earned by investors who bought at the pit of the Great Depression

There has never been a basketball player like Michael Jordan, and there has never been a stock market like the 1990s. We saw history being made. There has never been a bull market like it. Not in gains made. Not in duration or relative safety. Throughout the Great Bull Market of the 1990s, there were no truly serious corrections or bear markets. Panics and depressions have been typical throughout our economic history, at least until fairly recently. For more than 100 years, economic recessions and daunting bear markets seemed to come along about twice a decade. That no longer seems to be the case, at least it was not true during the late 1980s and the 1990s. Never before have conditions combined so beneficially for the market. There is nothing the stock market likes better than declining inflation, falling interest rates, rising worker productivity, and easy money from a friendly Federal Reserve. We have got a finely tuned economy in a world at peace. Not only is the world at peace, the popularity of capitalism and democracy has never been higher around the globe. The world seems to be scrambling to open markets, invest in the future, and create even more economic prosperity. It seems to be a golden age.

By the end of 1999, inflation, interest rates, and the unemployment rate had fallen to 30-year lows. Corporate earnings skyrocketed as companies restructured to focus on bottom-line profitability. In addition, we have enjoyed positives that only come along every few decades. An unprecedented technology-led revolution in worker and company productivity has boosted both worker incomes and corporate profits. Computers and automation have allowed old-line companies to produce more goods with fewer employees. Even as old-line companies downsized to improve earnings, the proliferation of new companies more than filled the employment gap. Not surprisingly, low interest rates and full employment pushed consumer confidence to record highs, and consumer spending has been robust.

All these beneficial economic and social changes led to a truly extraordinary period for investors. The long bull market has been fueled by growing investor optimism and an unprecedented boom in investor demand. Money has made it into the stock market that used to be earmarked for bank accounts, CDs, new homes, and other forms of investment, such as art and collectibles.

In August 12, 1982, the DJIA was at 776.92, unloved and unwanted. In early 2000, as the DJIA marched onward toward 12,000 and Nasdaq 5,000 captured the imagination of investors everywhere, a simple question came to mind.

Can it get any better than this?

See: E. S. Browning, "Old Economy Rally: Is It Repeating Its Fade?" *The Wall Street Journal,* May 22, 2000, C1, C2.

Is AOL a Growth Stock?

Comparing AOL to Microsoft

Investors in AOL and Microsoft Corp. enjoyed stellar stock market returns over the 1995–99 period. Both were among the top performers in a robust stock market environment. In evaluating the forward-looking investment potential for AOL, sometimes referred to as the "king of cyberspace," it is interesting to compare AOL to Microsoft, clearly the most successful technology stock of our lifetime.

After considering the effects of stock splits but ignoring nonrecurring charges, AOL had an EPS of 20¢ during 1999 (see Figure 10.8). AOL's 1999 EPS of 20¢ was very similar to 1993 earnings results achieved by Microsoft. As shown in Figure 10.9, Microsoft also made 20¢ per share in 1993. Also notice that AOL sales revenue in 1999 of $4.8 billion was much higher than Microsoft's $3.8 billion in revenues during 1993. This reflects the fact that Microsoft typically earns much higher profit margins than does AOL.

For argument's sake, let's assume that AOL enjoys stellar EPS growth over the 1999–2006 seven-year period. In fact, let's assume that AOL duplicates the unprecedented success that Microsoft enjoyed during the 1993–2000 period. If AOL grows at a Microsoft-like rate, AOL will report 2006 EPS of $1.65, a level that coincides with Microsoft's estimated earnings during 2000.

On a split-adjusted basis, AOL sold as high as $95.81 during December 1999. At that price, AOL was trading at a P/E = 479:1, when measured against 1999 earnings. Assuming that AOL is as successful in growing its earnings over the 1999–2006 period as Microsoft was at a similar stage in its life, a 1999 price of $95.81 for AOL implies a P/E = 58:1 against expected earnings of $1.65 in 2006.

At its share-price peak of $95.81 in December 1999, AOL's valuation looks expensive when compared with Microsoft. Over the 1993–2000 period, Microsoft's P/E ratio climbed with growing investor optimism regarding the company's future growth prospects. From an average P/E of roughly 26.8:1 in 1993, Microsoft's P/E reached roughly 55.6:1 by late 1999.

For argument's sake, let's assume that this optimistic valuation for Microsoft represents an appropriate valuation for a dominant high-tech leader. Let's also assume that such a valuation is appropriate for AOL. This means that one might assume a P/E in the range of 55:1 will be appropriate for AOL in 2006. In the opinion of *The Value Line Investment Survey,* an appropriate 2002–2004 P/E for AOL is, in fact, 55:1. At a 1999 price of $95.81 and a P/E = 58:1 against 2006 earnings, AOL was selling for more than its appropriate valuation in 2006 for a dominant high-tech leader. In other words, over the 1999–2006 period, AOL would have to grow its EPS faster than Microsoft grew its earnings over the 1993–2000 period to justify a 2006 stock price of $95.81!

Of course, current investors in AOL would be disappointed if its stock price failed to advance over the 1999–2006 time frame. If a typical AOL investor was looking for a 20% annual rate of return from such a high-risk stock, an investment in AOL at $95.81 in 1999 would need to grow to roughly $345 by 2006 to provide a satisfactory return. To justify such a price, AOL's earnings would have to grow at roughly 77% per year over the 1999–2006 time period. This is a substantial premium over the 42.1% annual earnings growth achieved by Microsoft over the 1993–2000 time frame or at a similar stage in its development.

FIGURE 10.8 Rise of AOL Is One of the Most Amazing Stories in Stock Market History

AMERICA ONLINE NYSE-AOL

RECENT PRICE	58	P/E RATIO	NMF (Trailing: NMF; Median: NMF)	RELATIVE P/E RATIO	NMF	DIV'D YLD	Nil	VALUE LINE	2215

TIMELINESS 2 Lowered 3/3/00

SAFETY 3 Raised 3/3/00

TECHNICAL 2 Raised 1/21/00

BETA 1.75 (1.00 = Market)

2002-04 PROJECTIONS

	Price	Gain	Ann'l Total Return
High	115	(+100%)	*19%*
Low	75	(+30%)	*7%*

Insider Decisions

	A	M	J	J	A	S	O	N	D
to Buy	0	0	0	0	0	0	0	0	0
Options	0	2	0	5	5	0	0	0	1
to Sell	0	0	0	10	5	0	8	0	0

Institutional Decisions

	1Q1999	2Q1999	3Q1999
to Buy	501	432	497
to Sell	217	315	278
Hld's(000)	1106700	925644	960618

	1992	1993	1994	1995	1996	1997	1998	1999
High:	0.2	0.5	0.9	2.9	4.4	5.7	40.0	95.8
Low:	0.1	0.1	0.4	0.8	1.4	2.0	5.2	32.5

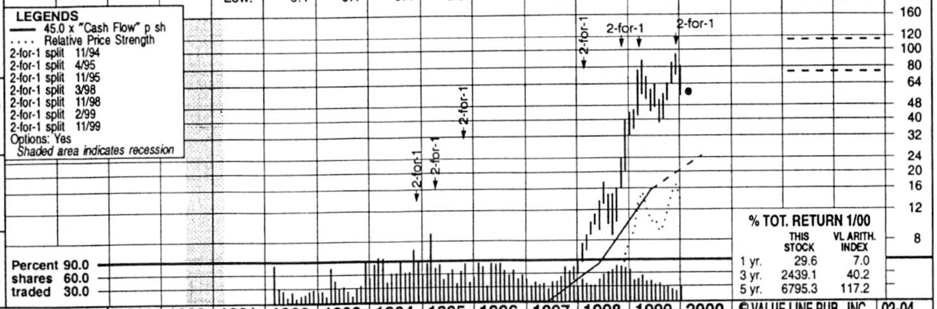

America Online was incorporated in Delaware in 1985. The company was listed on the Nasdaq in March, 1992 in connection with an initial public offering co-managed by Alex. Brown and Robertson, Stephens; two million common shares were tendered to the public at $0.09 apiece. In December, 1996, the company adopted a simplified, competitive pricing structure (currently $21.95 per month for unlimited access) and user-friendly interface, which helped to accelerate already-rapid revenue growth.

1989	1990	1991	1992	1993	1994	1995	1996	1997	1998	1999	2000	© VALUE LINE PUB., INC.	02-04
--	--	.14	.04	.05	.11	.33	.74	1.05	1.48	2.17	*2.90*	Revenues per sh A	*6.40*
--	--	.02	.00	.01	.01	.03	.04	.00	.13	.35	*.55*	"Cash Flow" per sh	*2.10*
--	--	.00	.00	.00	.01	.01	.02	d.05	.07	.20	*.38*	Earnings per sh A	*1.75*
--	--	--	--	--	--	--	--	--	--	--	*Nil*	Div'ds Decl'd per sh	*Nil*
--	--	.00	.00	.00	.02	.05	.03	.09	.20	.14	*.25*	Cap'l Spending per sh	*.45*
--	--	d.06	.03	.03	.11	.18	.35	.08	.34	1.38	*1.75*	Book Value per sh B	*5.40*
--	--	155.51	701.54	754.18	927.42	1201.8	1482.0	1603.0	1757.1	2201.8	*2300.0*	Common Shs Outst'g C	*2600.0*
--	--	--	32.3	48.7	79.8	60.7	NMF	NMF	NMF	NMF		Avg Ann'l P/E Ratio	*55.0*
--	--	--	1.96	2.88	5.23	4.06	NMF	NMF	NMF	NMF		Relative P/E Ratio	*3.65*
--	--	--	--	--	--	--	--	--	--	--		Avg Ann'l Div'd Yield	*Nil*
--	--	21.4	26.6	40.0	104.4	394.3	1093.9	1685.2	2600.0	4777.0	*6650*	Revenues ($mill) A	*16700*
--	--	14.9%	17.1%	14.9%	10.1%	11.1%	9.0%	NMF	11.9%	17.9%	*24.5%*	Operating Margin	*50.0%*
--	--	1.7	1.2	1.5	2.5	11.1	33.4	64.6	100.0	287.0	*300*	Depreciation ($mill)	*530*
--	--	.9	2.2	3.1	6.2	18.9	29.8	d71.5	132.6	486.0	*970*	Net Profit ($mill)	*5000*
--	--	38.2%	38.1%	38.2%	38.1%	44.5%	52.2%	41.0%	39.8%	39.3%	*39.0%*	Income Tax Rate	*39.0%*
--	--	4.4%	8.3%	7.7%	5.9%	4.8%	2.7%	NMF	5.1%	10.2%	*14.5%*	Net Profit Margin	*30.0%*
--	--	.2	14.8	16.8	64.9	d.4	d19.3	d231.0	36.0	254.0	*595*	Working Cap'l ($mill)	*7850*
--	--	.2	--	--	5.8	19.5	19.3	50.0	372.0	348.0	*390*	Long-Term Debt ($mill)	*510*
--	--	3.5	18.9	23.8	98.9	217.9	512.5	128.0	598.0	3033.0	*4000*	Shr. Equity ($mill)	*14000*
--	--	25.3%	11.7%	12.9%	5.9%	8.2%	5.7%	NMF	14.1%	14.6%	*22.5%*	Return on Total Cap'l	*34.5%*
--	--	26.6%	11.7%	12.9%	6.3%	8.7%	5.8%	NMF	22.2%	16.0%	*24.5%*	Return on Shr. Equity	*35.5%*
--	--	--	NMF	12.9%	6.3%	8.7%	5.8%	NMF	22.2%	16.0%	*24.5%*	Retained to Com Eq	*35.5%*
--	--	--	NMF	--	--	--	--	--	--	--	*Nil*	All Div'ds to Net Prof	*Nil*

CAPITAL STRUCTURE as of 12/31/99
Total Debt $1581.0 mill. **Due in 5 Yrs** $800.0 mill.
LT Debt $1581.0 mill. **LT Interest** $70.0 mill.
(20% of Cap'l)

Leases, Uncapitalized Annual rentals $262.0 mill.
Pension Liability None - No defined benefit plan.

Common Stock 2,281,767,899 shs. (80% of Cap'l) as of 1/31/00

MARKET CAP: $132.3 billion (Large Cap)

CURRENT POSITION ($MILL.)	1998	1999	12/31/99
Cash Assets	631.0	1424.0	3053.0
Receivables	104.0	402.0	483.0
Other	195.0	153.0	280.0
Current Assets	930.0	1979.0	3816.0
Accts Payable	87.0	74.0	65.0
Debt Due	--	--	--
Other	807.0	1651.0	2097.0
Current Liab.	894.0	1725.0	2162.0

ANNUAL RATES of change (per sh)	Past 10 Yrs.	Past 5 Yrs.	Est'd '97-'99 to '02-'04
Revenues	--	87.5%	*33.0%*
"Cash Flow"	--	98.0%	*68.0%*
Earnings	--	76.5%	*90.0%*
Dividends	--	--	*Nil*
Book Value	--	61.0%	*55.0%*

Fiscal Year Ends	QUARTERLY REVENUES ($ mill.) A Sep.30	Dec.31	Mar.31	Jun.30	Full Fiscal Year
1996	197.9	249.2	312.3	334.5	1093.9
1997	350.0	409.4	450.1	475.7	1685.2
1998	522.0	592.0	694.0	792.0	2600.0
1999	999.0	1147	1253	1378	4777
2000	1467	1510	*1743*	*1930*	*6650*

Fiscal Year Ends	EARNINGS PER SHARE A Sep.30	Dec.31	Mar.31	Jun.30	Full Fiscal Year
1996	d.01	.01	.01	.01	.02
1997	.01	d.06	--	--	d.05
1998	.01	.01	.02	.03	.07
1999	.04	.05	.05	.06	.20
2000	.08	.09	*.10*	*.11*	*.38*

Cal-endar	QUARTERLY DIVIDENDS PAID Mar.31	Jun.30	Sep.30	Dec.31	Full Year
1996	NO CASH DIVIDENDS BEING PAID				
1997					
1998					
1999					
2000					

BUSINESS: America Online, Inc. is the leading provider of online information services, with over 21 million subscribers (includes AOL and CompuServe). Offers electronic mail and conferencing, online forums and classes, interactive newspapers and magazines, and access to the Internet. Has strategic alliances with dozens of cos. incl. ABC, Viacom, American Express, IBM, and Bertelsmann. Has about 8500 employees, 240,000 shareholders. Acq'd WAIS, Inc., 5/95; Medior, Inc., 5/95; GNN, 6/95; Ubique Ltd., 9/95; Compuserve, 2/97; Netscape, 3/99. Officers and Directors own 2.4% of common (9/99 Proxy). Chairman & CEO: Stephen M. Case. Incorporated: DE. Address: 8619 Westwood Center Dr., Vienna, VA 22182. Telephone: 703-448-8700. Internet: www.aol.com.

America Online is on track to acquire Time Warner. The deal would provide Time Warner shareholders 1.5 AOL shares for each share of TWX (AOL stockholders would receive 1.0 shares in the new company). Subject to normal shareholder and regulatory approval, the acquisition—the second-largest in history—will likely be finalized late this year.

Combined, the companies have much to offer each other. One major benefit is that AOL would be able to offer high-speed Internet services over television cables. This should provide a more enjoyable Internet experience; enable the digital distribution of new services for interactive entertainment, information, and e-commerce; and facilitate the operation of these services on everything from desktop computers to television sets and handheld devices. Another benefit should come from gains in advertising. Linking AOL's strength in this area to Time Warner's entertainment sites holds sizable potential. And AOL's services should benefit Time Warner's operations as well. The CNN cable network, owned by Time Warner, stands to gain from the promotional strength provided by AOL's 24 million subscribers. And Time Warner's music division would gain from AOL's ability to deliver music online.

The company's Internet prospects remain substantial. Over the past year, AOL's net subscriber base has increased over 55%, to 24 million. Currently, about a third of all U.S. households have Internet access, and penetration appears likely to double by 2003. Meanwhile, advertising and commerce revenues should climb at an even higher rate, reaching about five times current levels, benefiting from the overwhelming size of AOL's audience.

The pending acquisition should modestly enhance appreciation potential from timely AOL stock's standalone prospects. The investment community has largely shied away from shares in AOL, as it hitches its growth possibilities to Time Warner's tangible, more mature assets. The combination would generate large amounts of cash flow, though, and, as noted, would have significant avenues for business investment. (Note: we will update our projections once the acquisition has been completed.)

Stephen E. Jones *March 3, 2000*

(A) Fiscal year ends June 30th. Based on diluted earnings, primary through '95. Excludes gains arising from net operating loss carryforward: '91, 1¢; '92, 1¢; '93, 1¢. Excludes nonrecurring charges: '97: 30¢; '98, 2¢; '99, 14¢. Next earnings report due early May.
(B) Includes intangibles. In '99: $454.0 million, 20¢/share.
(C) In millions, adjusted for stock splits.

Company's Financial Strength	A
Stock's Price Stability	10
Price Growth Persistence	100
Earnings Predictability	40

Source: Value Line Publishing, Inc.

FIGURE 10.9 **Microsoft Has Enjoyed Stunning Long-Term Success**

MICROSOFT NDQ-MSFT

RECENT PRICE	94	P/E RATIO	56.0 (Trailing: 58.7 Median: 28.0)	RELATIVE P/E RATIO	4.18	DIV'D YLD	Nil	VALUE LINE	2194

TIMELINESS	2	Lowered 6/4/99
SAFETY	2	Raised 12/8/95
TECHNICAL	2	Raised 2/4/00

BETA 1.10 (1.00 = Market)

2002-04 PROJECTIONS

	Price	Gain	Ann'l Total Return
High	130	(+40%)	*9%*
Low	95	(Nil)	*1%*

Insider Decisions

	A	M	J	J	A	S	O	N	D
to Buy	0	0	0	0	0	0	0	0	0
Options	2	2	0	2	4	0	0	1	2
to Sell	3	3	0	5	6	0	0	2	0

Institutional Decisions

	1Q1999	2Q1999	3Q1999
to Buy	612	633	628
to Sell	499	449	435
Hld's(000)	1911464	2011456	2118434

	1988	1989	1990	1991	1992	1993	1994	1995	1996	1997	1998	1999
High:	1.0	1.2	2.2	4.7	5.9	6.1	8.1	13.7	21.5	37.7	72.0	119.9
Low:	0.6	0.6	1.2	2.0	4.1	4.4	4.9	7.3	10.0	20.2	31.1	68.0

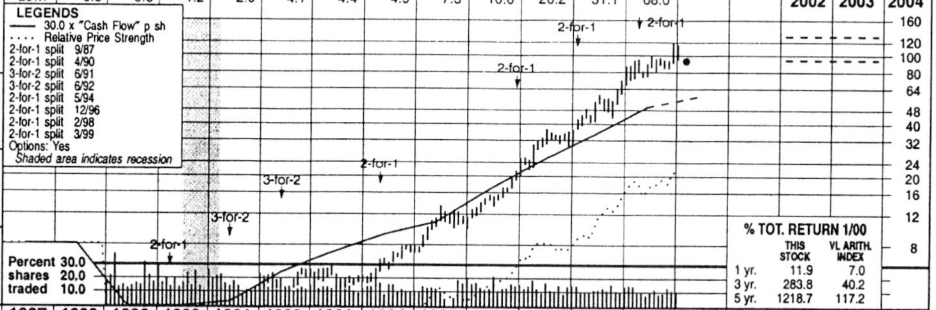

1983	1984	1985	1986	1987	1988	1989	1990	1991	1992	1993	1994	1995	1996	1997	1998	1999	2000	© VALUE LINE PUB., INC.	02-04
.02	.03	.05	.05	.09	.15	.20	.29	.44	.63	.83	1.00	1.26	1.84	2.36	2.93	3.87	*4.60*	Sales per sh [A]	*8.80*
--	--	.01	.01	.02	.04	.05	.08	.13	.19	.24	.31	.37	.56	.83	1.17	1.68	*1.95*	"Cash Flow" per sh	*3.35*
--	--	.01	.01	.02	.03	.04	.07	.10	.15	.20	.25	.29	.43	.66	.89	1.39	*1.68*	Earnings per sh [B]	*3.00*
--	--	--	--	--	--	--	--	--	--	--	--	--	--	--	--	--	*Nil*	Div'ds Decl'd per sh	*Nil*
--	--	--	--	.02	.02	.02	.04	.06	.07	.05	.06	.11	.11	.10	.13	.11	*.10*	Cap'l Spending per sh	*.15*
--	.01	.02	.04	.06	.10	.14	.22	.32	.50	.72	.96	1.13	1.47	2.03	3.17	5.37	*7.00*	Book Value per sh	*14.65*
3077.1	3061.5	3100.8	3674.9	3795.3	3863.7	3930.2	4093.2	4181.6	4354.2	4512.0	4648.0	4704.0	4704.0	4816.0	4940.0	5109.0	*5200.0*	Common Shs Outst'g [C]	*5000.0*
--	--	17.7	19.6	19.9	25.2	17.8	19.9	22.6	28.5	26.8	21.4	28.2	29.1	33.0	42.8	49.8		Avg Ann'l P/E Ratio	*38.0*
--	--	1.44	1.33	1.33	2.09	1.35	1.48	1.44	1.73	1.58	1.40	1.89	1.82	1.90	2.23	2.73		Relative P/E Ratio	*2.55*
--	--	--	--	--	--	--	--	--	--	--	--	--	--	--	--	--		Avg Ann'l Div'd Yield	*Nil*

CAPITAL STRUCTURE as of 12/31/99

Total Debt None

Leases, Uncapitalized $85.0 mill.
Pension Liability None - No defined benefit pension plan.

Pfd Stock None

Common Stock 5,204,853,333 shs. (100% of Cap'l)
as of 1/31/00
MARKET CAP: $490 billion (Large Cap)

1989	1990	1991	1992	1993	1994	1995	1996	1997	1998	1999	2000	© VALUE LINE PUB., INC.	02-04
803.5	1183.4	1843.4	2758.7	3753.0	4649.0	5937.0	8671.0	11358	14484	19747	*23800*	Sales ($mill) [A]	*44000*
33.2%	37.1%	39.4%	40.2%	39.4%	42.2%	38.9%	41.0%	50.1%	55.0%	56.0%	*55.5%*	Operating Margin	*51.5%*
24.2	46.3	75.8	112.3	151.0	237.0	269.0	480.0	557.0	1024.0	1010.0	*1025*	Depreciation ($mill)	*1290*
170.5	279.2	462.7	708.1	953.0	1210.0	1453.0	2176.0	3454.0	4786.0	7625.0	*9235*	Net Profit ($mill)	*15515*
32.0%	32.0%	31.0%	32.0%	32.0%	33.2%	32.9%	35.0%	35.0%	35.4%	35.0%	*35.0%*	Income Tax Rate	*35.0%*
21.2%	23.6%	25.1%	25.7%	25.4%	26.0%	24.5%	25.1%	30.4%	33.0%	38.6%	*38.8%*	Net Profit Margin	*35.3%*
310.1	533.1	735.1	1322.8	2287.0	3399.0	4273.0	5414.0	6763.0	10159	11515	*19465*	Working Cap'l ($mill)	*57895*
--	--	--	--	--	--	--	--	--	--	--	*Nil*	Long-Term Debt ($mill)	*Nil*
561.8	918.6	1350.8	2193.0	3242.0	4450.0	5333.0	6908.0	10777	16627	28438	*36340*	Shr. Equity ($mill)	*73240*
30.3%	30.4%	34.3%	32.3%	29.4%	27.2%	27.2%	31.5%	32.0%	28.8%	26.8%	*25.5%*	Return on Total Cap'l	*21.0%*
30.3%	30.4%	34.3%	32.3%	29.4%	27.2%	27.2%	31.5%	32.0%	28.8%	26.8%	*25.5%*	Return on Shr. Equity	*21.0%*
30.3%	30.4%	34.3%	32.3%	29.4%	27.2%	27.2%	31.5%	35.1%	30.4%	27.7%	*25.5%*	Retained to Com Eq	*21.0%*
--	--	--	--	--	--	--	--	--	1%	NMF	*Nil*	All Div'ds to Net Prof	*Nil*

CURRENT POSITION ($MILL.)	1998	1999	12/31/99
Cash Assets	13927	17236	17843
Receivables	1460	2245	3284
Inventory	--	--	--
Other	502	752	893
Current Assets	15889	20233	22020
Accts Payable	759	874	1233
Debt Due	--	--	--
Other	4971	7844	9271
Current Liab.	5730	8718	10504

ANNUAL RATES of change (per sh)	Past 10 Yrs.	Past 5 Yrs.	Est'd '97-'99 to '02-'04
Sales	35.0%	30.0%	*24.5%*
"Cash Flow"	42.5%	37.5%	*25.5%*
Earnings	41.5%	37.5%	*29.0%*
Dividends	--	--	*Nil*
Book Value	42.5%	37.0%	*37.0%*

Fiscal Year Ends	QUARTERLY SALES ($ mill.) [A] Sep.30	Dec.31	Mar.31	Jun.30	Full Fiscal Year
1996	2016	2195	2205	2255	8671
1997	2295	2680	3208	3175	11358
1998	3130	3585	3774	3995	14484
1999	4193[D]	5195[D]	4595[D]	5764	19747
2000	5384	6112	*5800*	*6504*	*23800*

Fiscal Year Ends	EARNINGS PER SHARE [A B] Sep.30	Dec.31	Mar.31	Jun.30	Full Fiscal Year
1996	.10	.11	.11	.11	.43
1997	.12	.14	.20	.20	.66
1998	.18	.21	.25	.25	.89
1999	.28	.36	.35	.40	1.39
2000	.38	.47	*.41*	*.42*	*1.68*

Cal-endar	QUARTERLY DIVIDENDS PAID Mar.31	Jun.30	Sep.30	Dec.31	Full Year
1996					
1997	NO CASH DIVIDENDS BEING PAID				
1998					
1999					
2000					

BUSINESS: Microsoft Corp. is the largest independent maker of software. Revenue sources in fiscal 1999: Windows Platforms 43% (operating systems and server applications and Internet products). Productivity Applications and Developer 45% (desktop applications, server applications, and developer tools). Consumer, Commerce, and Other 12% (learning and entertainment software, PC input devices, fees, consulting, and online services). R&D: 15.1% of sales. Has 31,400 employees and 92,170 stockholders. William H. Gates owns 15.3% of stock, other officers & directors 10.2% (9/99 proxy). Chairman: William H. Gates. President and CEO: Steven A. Ballmer. Inc.: WA. Address: One Microsoft Way, Redmond, WA 98052-6399. Tele.: 425-882-8080. Internet: www.microsoft.com.

Microsoft finally rolled out its next generation operating system (OS), *Windows 2000*. The upgrade to the company's *Windows NT* OS was released February 17th to generally favorable reviews. It offers better performance, scalability, security, and resource management than *Windows NT*. The new system is at the center of Microsoft's effort to extend its operating system hegemony from the desktop to high-end servers. Businesses are likely to take their time, and not rush to embrace the new OS. There reportedly will be a steep learning curve for information support personnel, and there may be incompatibility problems with some existing applications. Still, we expect the product to be very popular, given its improvements over *Windows NT*, and it should help boost the company's revenues and earnings for the next two or three years.

A further wave of new products should lead to continued good earnings gains. *Windows 2000* will be the base on which Microsoft builds a whole group of products. In April, it is scheduled to unveil its blueprint for Internet services. And, this summer, the company is scheduled to roll out upgrades for its database product, *SQL Server 2000* and its *Exchange Server 2000* messaging server, as well as an upgrade (*Millennium*) to the *Windows 98* OS. Then, too, the company is moving into new areas, such as television set-top boxes, and is investing in other businesses, such as cable operators. True, there is the possibility that Internet appliances, which access the Internet without the need for a personal computer, will become more common, cutting into Microsoft's sales. All told, though, we think the company's broad, growing product line and marketing efforts will lead to strong annual share-net growth out to 2002-2004.

Microsoft shares are timely. But the current price largely discounts the good earnings gains we forecast for the years ahead. Too, the company is the subject of several lawsuits, including one brought by the Department of Justice. Microsoft does not expect the actions to lead to any material adverse effects on it or its financial condition, but the uncertainties caused by the actions could lead to greater-than-usual stock-price volatility.

George A. Niemond *March 3, 2000*

(A) Fiscal year ends June 30th. (B) Primary earnings through fiscal '97, then diluted. Excludes nonrecurring losses: '94, 1¢;'98, 6¢; '00, 3¢; gains, '99, 3¢; '00, 2¢. Next earnings report due mid-April. (C) In millions, adjusted for stock splits and dividends. (D) Restated

Company's Financial Strength	A++
Stock's Price Stability	60
Price Growth Persistence	95
Earnings Predictability	85

Source: Value Line Publishing, Inc.

Of course, whether AOL will be able to achieve such stunning levels of earnings growth is a matter for conjecture. One thing is for certain, however. Investors in AOL are counting on truly unprecedented success in terms of AOL's future earnings growth.

AOL Risk Assessment

Another straightforward way of valuing AOL is to look at the company's projected EPS growth and attempt to discount such earnings at an appropriate risk-adjusted discount rate.

For argument's sake, let's assume that AOL is more risky than the typical stock. The *Value Line Investment Survey* projects a $\beta = 1.75$ for AOL, meaning that the company has 175% of the risk of the overall market. This means that AOL is roughly 75% more risky than the overall market, when risk is measured in terms of stock price volatility. With a risk premium of 8%, a stock that is 1.75 times as risky as the market as a whole would command 1.75 times the market risk premium. Under these circumstances, an appropriate risk premium for AOL would not be 8%, but 1.75 times 8%, or 14% (= 8% × 1.75). If you add the required risk premium of 14% to 5%, the risk-free rate of interest, you would get a reasonable discount rate for AOL in the range of 19% (= 5% + 1.75 × 8%).

Keep in mind that a 19% expected rate of return for AOL represents a fairly low expectation, given that the stock has virtually skyrocketed during recent years. It is reasonable to expect that many of AOL's present shareholders would be very disappointed with a 19% annual rate of return. They are looking at the recent history of AOL, in which it split its stock several times and jumped more than 20:1 over the 1997–98 time frame.

AOL Growth Expectations

The *Value Line Investment Survey* projects stunning AOL EPS growth of 90% per year over the three- to five-year period ending in 2002–2004. From 1999 levels, the consensus forecast earnings growth rate for AOL falls in a range near 50% per year.

Two things make it difficult to estimate earnings per share growth for AOL. First, EPS projection requires an accurate forecast of revenues and costs. Second, in the light of future earnings, an accurate estimate of EPS requires an accurate forecast of the likely growth in the number of outstanding shares. In early 2000, AOL had about 2.2 billion shares outstanding. *After* adjusting for splits, the number of outstanding shares for AOL has gone up by a factor of more than 14:1 since AOL first went public. Since first going public, AOL has used its stock for mergers, such as the merger with Netscape Communications in 1999, and for newly issued stock tied to options granted to top executives and other employees. A tremendous number of new shares will also be issued if the merger with Time Warner, Inc., goes through as planned.

Over the 1991–99 period, the number of AOL's split-adjusted shares outstanding grew from 155 million to 2.2 billion, or at a rate of roughly 39% per year. Of course, just because AOL has grown the number of shares outstanding by 39% a year for the past decade does not mean that they are going to grow the number of shares outstanding by 39% per year going forward. Still, it seems fair to suggest that AOL will, in fact, be issuing more shares over the coming decade to reward top-performing employees and executives and to pay for mergers in the ever-escalating telecommunications industry mating game. Given AOL's history, it seems conservative to assume that the company will increase the number of outstanding shares by at least 10% per year.

Over the three-year 1996–99 period, the number of AOL's split-adjusted shares outstanding grew from 1.5 billion to 2.2 billion or at a rate of roughly 14% per year. If AOL is able to grow earnings by 50% per year but the number of outstanding shares grows by 14% per year, the net growth in EPS will average much less than 50% per year. In fact, with earnings growth of 50% per year and annual growth in the number of shares outstanding of 14%, EPS growth will average only 31.5% (= 1.50/1.14) per year.

If AOL is, in fact, able to grow its earnings by 50% per year and only suffers dilution of 10% per year from new stock issues, AOL's EPS will grow by roughly 36% (= 1.5/1.1) per year. That is an optimistic EPS growth rate because it discounts the onslaught of competition that AOL is going to face from the likes of AT&T, with its @Home Internet service, among others.

AOL Valuation

With optimistic EPS growth of 36% per year from a 1999 base of 20¢, AOL's expected EPS in 2006 would total $1.72 (= $1.36^7 \times$ 20¢). To project a reasonable price for AOL in 2006, it is simply necessary to multiply that amount by a reasonable P/E ratio.

Fidelity Mutual Fund guru Peter Lynch is famous for saying that an appropriate P/E ratio should be no higher than the EPS growth rate. Using a P/E ratio of 36, a reasonable price for AOL in 2006 would be roughly $61.92 (= 36 × $1.72). However, today's stock market seems willing, if not eager, to pay premium P/E multiples for what many regard as "bulletproof" franchises. Microsoft has enjoyed a bulletproof software franchise for the desktop computer and enjoys a P/E multiple in the range of 55 : 1. If AOL is accorded a similar multiple, a reasonable price for AOL in 2006 would be roughly $94.60 (= 55 × $1.72). Therefore, based on admittedly rough assumptions regarding what might constitute an appropriate P/E multiple for AOL, a broad range from $61.92 to $94.60 is calculated as a reasonable AOL price in 2006.

How much was a stock that might sell for $61.92 to $94.60 in the year 2006 worth in the year 1999? The answer depends on the appropriate risk-adjusted discount rate. Using a 19% risk-adjusted rate of return, $1 will grow to $3.38 in seven years. In other words, the future value of a present sum of $1 growing at 19% for seven years is $3.38. The present value of $3.38 to be received in seven years is $1, when the interest rate is 19%.

In the case of AOL, the present value of a $61.92 stock price in 2006 is $18.32 [= $61.92/($1.19^7$)] when an appropriate risk-adjusted discount rate is 19%. Similarly, the present value of a $94.60 stock price in 2006 is $27.99 [= $94.60/($1.19^7$)] when the appropriate risk-adjusted discount rate is 19%. Based on a reasonable assessment of AOL's future growth prospects and after adjusting for the above-average risk tied to Internet stocks in general and AOL in particular, a reasonable 1999 price range for AOL would fall in the range between $18.32 and $27.99.

In the light of these numbers, how is one to interpret a 1999 stock price for AOL of $95.81? Two possibilities exist. On the one hand, widely accepted estimates of AOL's EPS growth prospects may have been far too conservative. Alternatively,

AOL's stock price of $95.81 may simply have been too high. To be sure, AOL's stock did spectacularly well during the 1995–99 period. Going forward, it will be interesting to learn if AOL bulls or bears were right about its 1999 stock price being too low (the bull case) or too high (the bear case). It might well be the case that buying AOL for $95.81 in 1999 was like buying the best farmland in Iowa and paying $7,500 per acre. When interest rates are 6% to 8% per year, it is an obvious no-win situation if you pay $7,500 an acre for farmland that generates only $150 per year in profits (see Chapter 1). In Iowa, anyone who pays $20,000 per acre for land to grow corn is going to get shelled. Similarly, in the stock market, anyone who pays $95.81 for stock worth $18.32 to $27.99 is going to get shelled. Within months of reaching $95.81, AOL stockholders did in fact get shelled. AOL's mid-2000 stock price plummeted to less than $50 per share, a mind-numbing loss of roughly *$100 billion* in market capitalization.

Summary

- One of the most popular investment philosophies or "styles" for stock selection is called **growth stock investing,** which involves focusing on companies expected to have above-average rates of growth in earnings and dividends. Another popular approach, **value investing,** involves focusing on securities considered to be temporarily undervalued or unpopular for various reasons. In both cases, investors seek bargains selling at prices below their real **economic value.**
- Few growth companies have been able to dominate large or rapidly growing markets. Most have been able to maintain their superior investment status through the successful exploitation of a **market niche.** A market niche is a segment of a market that can be successfully exploited through the special capabilities of a given firm. Highly successful companies focus on making new and exciting products rather than be distracted by **financial engineering,** or the sophisticated manipulation of the balance sheet through use of exotic forms of debt and equity financing.
- Growth stock investors face a variety of important pitfalls to growth. **Customer loyalty risk** is high and market share stability is low in rapidly growing markets. Acquired companies often underperform as divisions of larger companies. Many rapidly growing companies fall victim to **merger risk** and suffer merger indigestion and investor disappointment. On Wall Street, a **roll-up** is a company that grows through a constant acquisition binge. Critics contend that when roll-up companies stop the process of constant acquisition, they often fail to deliver operating efficiencies. A host of important problems can also be avoided when investors seek to minimize **regulation risk.** One of the most important potential pitfalls tied to growth stock investing is that the approach seldom offers clear guidance about how much is too much to pay for a stock with attractive growth prospects. The lack of a strict buying discipline leaves growth stock investors open to **price risk,** or the chance of overpaying for attractive companies.
- The **discounted present value,** or actual economic value, of a company is determined by prospects for future cash flows received by investors in the form of regular cash dividends or share repurchases. Whenever investors deal with future stock prices and dividend payments, they are dealing with **expected values,** not certain sums. The **risk-adjusted discount rate,** or required return, is the

interest rate required to fairly compensate investors for the risk involved with making their investment. Although the discounted present-value approach can be described as a type of dividend discount model, it involves full consideration of both major components of the investor's **total return** from investment, defined as dividend income plus capital appreciation.

- The **dividend discount model** focuses exclusively on future dividend income, but future stock prices at any point in time will also be determined by anticipated dividend income. Expected capital gains are explicitly incorporated in the dividend discount model, but their influence is captured in terms of anticipated future dividend income. The **constant growth model** for growth stock valuation is sometimes referred to as the **Gordon growth model,** after financial economist Myron J. Gordon who popularized its use. The constant growth model gives investors a simple means for calculating the required rate of return as the sum of dividend income and growth (capital gains).
- Determining a reasonable price to pay for any growth stock is always difficult. To deal effectively with the uncertainties involved, growth stock investors have developed various simple valuation devices. An **investment rule of thumb** is a simple guide to investment valuation that has served the test of time. Legendary mutual fund investor Peter Lynch is famous for developing the so-called P/E-to-growth or **PEG ratio.** Generally speaking, a stock is fully valued if it sports a PEG ratio of 1 or more. Strict **growth-at-a-reasonable-price investors** seldom, if ever, buy growth stocks with PEG ratios greater than 1.
- To effectively use the PEG ratio approach, investors must come up with simple but effective means for predicting EPS growth. In a common approach, growth stock investors focus on retained earnings as the primary source of internally generated funds for investment. The **retention rate** is the share of earnings retained to fund investment. The rate of growth made possible by internally generated funds is calculated as the retention rate multiplied by ROE. Whereas the retention rate is the share of earnings retained to fund investment, the **dividend payout ratio** is the percentage of income paid out in the form of dividends. Holding all else equal, an appropriate P/E ratio will fall with an increase in the dividend payout ratio or a rise in the risk-adjusted required rate of return. The appropriate P/E ratio will rise with an increase in the ROE.
- During rampant bull markets, such as that experienced during the late 1990s, momentum-based investment strategies flourish. In this approach to growth stock investing, stocks that have high volume on **upticks,** and low volume on **downticks** are said to be benefiting from a positive inflow of investment funds. Experience shows that liquidity may drive stock prices in the short run. In the long run, however, it is EPS growth that counts.
- In the late 1990s, many growth stock investors have come to display a strong preference for **technology stocks** at the vanguard of important new innovations. Huge potential rewards await those companies able to successfully navigate in such a rapidly changing environment. Somewhat less understood are the equally enormous risks facing those companies unable to successfully anticipate and adapt to such challenges.

Questions

1. MBI has a current price of \$36, an expected dividend per share of \$0.90, expected EPS of \$5.50, expected EPS growth of 10% per year, and a typical P/E ratio of 13.5. According to the discounted present-value model, what is the expected price for MBI in five years?
   a. \$119.56.
   b. \$74.25.
   c. \$57.94.
   d. \$133.81.

2. MBI has a current price of \$36, an expected dividend per share of \$0.90, expected EPS of \$5.50, expected EPS growth of 10% per year, and a typical P/E ratio of 13.5. According to the discounted present-value model, what is the expected rate of return on MBI over the next five years?
   a. 29.6%.
   b. 22.3%.
   c. 27.1%.
   d. 18.1%.

3. MBI has a current price of \$36, an expected dividend per share of \$0.90, expected EPS of \$5.50, expected EPS growth of 10% per year, and a typical P/E ratio of 13.5. According to the discounted present-value model, MBI is overvalued if investors have a risk-adjusted required return of
   a. 29.6%.
   b. 27.1%.
   c. 22.3%.
   d. none of the above.

4. BEN has a current price of \$25, is expected to pay a 25¢ dividend next year, and grow dividends at a rate of 15% for the foreseeable future. According to the dividend discount model, the required rate of return for BEN investors is
   a. 15%.
   b. 16%.
   c. 12%.
   d. 1%.

5. BEN has a current price of \$25, is expected to pay a 25¢ dividend next year, and grow dividends at a rate of 15% for the foreseeable future. According to the dividend discount model, BEN is
   a. overvalued if investors require a 15% rate of return.
   b. undervalued if the actual dividend next year is 26¢.
   c. overvalued if the actual rate of growth is 18%.
   d. worth \$50 if investors require a 15.5% rate of return.

6. The constant growth version of the dividend valuation model is
   a. $D_1/(k - g)$.
   b. $D_1/(k + g)$.
   c. $D_0/(k + g)$.
   d. $D_0/(k - g)$.
7. As the required rate of return increases, the P/E ratio
   a. decreases.
   b. increases.
   c. is not affected.
   d. first rises, then falls.
8. The P/E ratio is inversely related to the
   a. payout ratio.
   b. required rate of return.
   c. expected growth of dividends.
   d. expected growth of earnings.
9. The estimated value of a stock with current dividends of $1, 20% expected dividend growth, and a 22% required return is
   a. $60.
   b. $50.
   c. $46.75.
   d. $5.
10. According to T. Rowe Price, above-average returns stem from
    a. creative differences.
    b. nonleading firm growth in low-profit industries.
    c. nonleading firm growth in high-profit industries.
    d. growing competition.
11. According to Philip Fisher, superior profits can be made by investing in companies
    a. that shun high-tech industries.
    b. with the potential to become market leaders.
    c. with capable management.
    d. that are broadly diversified.
12. According to T. Rowe Price, a growth stock benefits through
    a. synergistic mergers.
    b. brand-name recognition.
    c. product standardization.
    d. leverage.
13. According to T. Rowe Price, growth prospects suffer if companies
    a. are subject to government regulation.
    b. have well-paid employees.

c. engage in substantial research to develop products and markets.

d. lack cutthroat competition.

14. Customer loyalty risk is high when

a. market expansion is rapid.

b. market share stability is high.

c. profit margins are high.

d. barriers to entry are high.

15. A company that grows through constant acquisition is called

a. vertically integrated.

b. horizontally integrated.

c. a roll-up.

d. none of these.

16. According to the discounted present value model, the value of the firm does *not* depend on

a. expected dividends.

b. current dividends.

c. the risk-adjusted discount rate.

d. the required return.

17. According to the constant growth model, when $g > k$, the value of the firm is

a. equal to the current price.

b. less than the current price.

c. equal to $D_1 \times (k - g)$.

d. infinite.

18. The constant growth model

a. is well suited to valuing non–dividend-paying stocks.

b. is simple to apply.

c. uses a variable discount rate assumption.

d. is insensitive to growth rate assumptions.

19. According to the PEG ratio rule of thumb, if PEG ≥ 1, then a stock

a. may be worthy of investment attention and possible purchase.

b. is definitely worthy of investment attention and may represent a very attractive investment.

c. is apt to represent an extraordinarily attractive investment opportunity.

d. none of these.

20. Holding all else equal, the retention rate will rise with an increase in

a. dividends.

b. ROE.

c. the payout ratio.

d. net income.

Investment Application

The "Nifty 50"

Not since the early 1970s has a small group of favored stocks come close to dominating investor interest like "Cisco and the Kids" have during the late 1990s. Those were the days when stocks such as Coca-Cola, Disney, Eastman Kodak, McDonald's, and Philip Morris achieved price/earnings multiples as high as 95:1. All were visible components of the so-called "Nifty 50."

The Nifty 50 was a group of 50 premier growth stocks that became stock-market darlings during the early 1970s. At the market peak in 1972, the group of Nifty 50 stocks sold at a P/E ratio of 41.9:1, or more than double the market average of 18.1:1. Each of these stocks had proven growth in revenues, earnings, and dividends. Virtually none had experienced a dividend cut during the post–World War II period. All had sufficiently large market capitalizations to allow large institutional investors to buy as much of them as their portfolios could hold. They represented the ultimate in one-decision stock investing. An investor simply had to buy and hold. No matter how high Nifty 50 stock prices seemed relative to revenue, earnings, or any other fundamental factors, any perception of being overvalued was sure to be temporary. Superior rates of growth would bail out any buyer, no matter how high the price seemed at the time of purchase. Nifty 50 investors could not lose, or so the story went, until the vicious bear market of 1972–74.

From a bull market peak of 1036.27 on December 11, 1972, the DJIA crashed to 577.60 on December 6, 1974. This bone-chilling drop of 44.3% for the market was relatively mild when compared with the devastation suffered by "Nifty 50" darlings. Coca-Cola dove 66.9% from $149.75 to $49.63, Disney cascaded down 91.3% from $236.75 to $20.50, Eastman Kodak tumbled 58.9% from $149.25 to $61.25, McDonald's plunged 63.2% from $77.38 to $28.50 while Philip Morris plummeted 59.4% from $118.25 to $45. The devastation experienced by stockholders of these Nifty 50 companies does not represent the worst of the story. Although some are no longer considered great growth stocks, all have continued as successful pillars of corporate America. All are now members of the DJIA. Some other former Nifty 50 companies and their shareholders did not fare so well. Former Nifty 50 companies, such as Burroughs, Digital Equipment, Joseph Schlitz Brewing, and MGIC Investment are gone. Their status as "bulletproof" growth stocks not only failed to protect them from disturbing volatility in a full-fledged bear market; for them it was down and out.

The plunge in prices for the original Nifty 50 during the severe bear market correction of 1972–74 has long been viewed as just punishment for absurdly valued stocks and the naive investors willing to buy them. Until recently, no one rose to defend such excesses. No one, that is, until Jeremy Siegel, a professor of finance at the University of Pennsylvania's Wharton School, became part of the Nifty 50 story in 1994 when he published an eminently readable book on the stock market titled *Stocks for the Long Run.* In his book, Siegel laid out a bullish argument for equity investing and calculated that an investor paying top dollar for the Nifty 50 in late 1972 would have earned nearly the same returns over the next 25 years as someone holding the S&P 500. Siegel calculates that the original Nifty 50 produced a 12.5% annualized return, slightly behind the 12.7% for the S&P 500. "Good growth stocks are expensive, but they can be worth the price," said Siegel.

TABLE 10.9 Nifty Fifty: Were They Worth It?

Listed below are the Nifty Fifty of 1972, along with their annualized return to shareholders through August 1998. Next come their 1972 price/earnings ratios. The last column shows the P/E ratios that were warranted back in 1972, based on the stocks' subsequent performance.

	Annualized Return (%)	1972 P/E Ratio	Warranted P/E Ratio		Annualized Return(%)	1972 P/E Ratio	Warranted P/E Ratio
Philip Morris	18.8	24.0	68.5	AMP	9.7	42.9	25.0
Pfizer	18.1	28.4	72.3	Texas Instruments	9.1	39.5	20.2
Bristol-Byers	16.8	24.9	49.8	3M	8.5	39.0	20.2
Gillette	16.8	24.3	45.4	Baxter	8.1	71.4	29.6
Coca-Cola	16.2	46.4	82.3	ITT	8.0	15.4	8.6
Merck	15.9	43.0	76.3	IBM	7.7	35.5	17.1
Heublein	15.7	29.4	47.0	J.C. Penney	7.3	31.5	14.8
General Electric	15.7	23.4	37.8	Sears Roebuck	7.3	29.2	14.2
Schering-Plough	15.7	48.1	79.8	Intl Flavors & Fragrances	7.0	69.1	27.7
Squibb Corp.	15.5	30.1	48.7	Jos. Schlitz Brewing	6.6	39.6	15.6
Pepisco	15.0	27.6	41.1	Xerox	6.5	45.8	19.4
Eli Lilly	14.0	40.6	50.4	Halliburton	6.3	35.5	12.7
American Home Products	13.8	36.7	43.6	Lubrizol	6.0	32.6	12.1
Procter & Gamble	13.2	29.8	32.4	Eastman Kodak	5.5	43.5	16.1
Revlon	13.1	25.0	26.9	Simplicity Patterns	5.3	50.0	8.7
Johnson & Johnson	12.6	57.1	56.6	Digital Equipment	5.2	56.2	9.7
Anheuser-Busch	12.5	31.5	30.8	Avon Products	5.0	61.2	24.2
Chesebrough Ponds	12.5	39.1	38.2	Louisiana Land & Expl.	4.4	26.6	8.6
McDonalds	12.1	71.0	63.2	Black & Decker	2.8	47.8	10.5
First Natl City (Citigroup)	11.4	20.5	16.9	Kresge (Kmart)	2.1	49.5	10.1
Walt Disney	11.3	71.2	53.6	Burroughs	−0.4	46.0	6.6
American Express	10.8	37.7	28.0	Polaroid	−1.0	94.8	11.9
Dow Chemical	10.6	24.1	17.7	Emery Air Freight	−1.9	55.3	8.0
American Hospital Supply	10.6	48.1	33.1	MGIC Investment	−8.6	68.5	4.8
Schlumberger	10.2	45.6	28.6	**Nifty Fifty**	**12.5**	**41.9**	—
Upjohn	10.0	38.8	25.3	**S&P 500**	**12.7**	**18.9**	—

Data source: *Barron's,* March 15, 1999, 21–22.

Siegel's book added fuel to the firestorm of controversy surrounding valuations of the 1990s version of the Nifty 50, the high-flying high-tech stocks, especially those tied to the Internet. When asked what he thinks of the new Nifty 50, Siegel hedges. The notion that good growth companies can be worth more than 50 times earnings has been proven by the facts. In Table 10.9 (page 423), Siegel shows the "warranted" P/E of the original Nifty 50, using a stock price then that would result in a return equal to the S&P 500 over the ensuing 25-plus years. Coca-Cola, for example, traded for a P/E of 46.4:1 in late 1972 but was actually worth a P/E of 82.3:1 given its market-beating results since then. That being said, it is clear that some of the best performances turned in by former Nifty 50 stocks have been generated by lower-multiple consumer products companies, such as Gillette, Pfizer, and Philip Morris. Nearly all the superhigh P/E stocks lagged behind, including Avon, International Flavor & Fragrances, and Polaroid. Siegel proclaims that only a handful of the best growth stocks in the past has been worth more than 70 times earnings. Microsoft is one stock that could well live up to its lofty P/E of 70, yet it is worth remembering that IBM was once thought to be invincible. Of course, that was when Microsoft was a baby.

A. Siegel's research shows that technology companies have had a tough time maintaining their edge over the long run. Why is that?

B. Back in 1972, the Nifty 50 represented an important group of stocks, but the market was dominated by non-Nifty industrials such as General Motors and Ford. Today, the market is dominated by the largest technology stocks, such as $450 billion market cap Microsoft Corp. (P/E = 65:1), $215 billion Cisco Systems, Inc. (P/E = 100:1), and $195 billion Lucent Technologies, Inc. (P/E = 75:1). Describe how the enormous size of these high-tech giants limits their future growth opportunities.

Selected References

Andersen, Torben M., and Morten Hviid. "Prices and Information under Imperfect Competition." *Scottish Journal of Political Economy* 46 (August 1999): 245–259.

Arnold, Tom, and Jerry James. "Finding Firm Value without a Pro Forma Analysis." *Financial Analysts Journal* 56 (March/April 2000): 77–84.

Block, Stanley B. "A Study of Financial Analysts: Practice and Theory." *Financial Analysts Journal* 55 (July/August 1999): 86–95.

Campbell, John Y., and John H. Cochrane. "By Force of Habit: A Consumption-Based Explanation of Aggregate Stock Market Behavior." *Journal of Political Economy* 107 (April 1999): 205–251.

Ciccotello, Conrad S., and Martin J. Hornyak. "Cooperation via Contract: An Analysis of Research and Development Agreements." *Journal of Corporate Finance* 6 (March 2000): 1–24.

Davis, James L., Eugene F. Fama, and Kenneth R. French. "Characteristics, Covariances, and Average Returns: 1929 to 1997." *Journal of Finance* 55 (February 2000): 389–406.

Deng, Zhen, Baruch Lev, and Francis Narin. "Science and Technology as Predictors of Stock Performance." *Financial Analysts Journal* 55 (May/June 1999): 20–32.

Dhatt, Manjeet S., Yong H. Kim, and Sandip Mukherji. "The Value Premium for Small-Capitalization Stocks." *Financial Analysts Journal* 55 (September/October 1999): 60–68.

Fisher, Kenneth L., and Meir Statman. "Investor Sentiment and Stock Returns." *Financial Analysts Journal* 56 (March/April 2000): 16–23.

Gompers, Paul, and Josh Lerner. "Money Chasing Deals? The Impact of Fund Inflows on Private Equity Valuation." *Journal of Financial Economics* 55 (February 2000): 281–325.

Hong, Harrison, Terence Lim, and Jeremy C. Stein. "Bad News Travels Slowly: Size, Analyst Coverage, and the Profitability of Momentum Strategies." *Journal of Finance* 55 (February 2000): 265–295.

Leibowitz, Martin L. "Franchise Labor." *Financial Analysts Journal* 56 (March/April 2000): 68–76.

Spiess, D. Katherine, and John Affleck-Graves. "The Long-Run Performance of Stock Returns Following Debt Offerings." *Journal of Financial Economics* 54 (October 1999): 45–73.

Zhou, Chunsheng. "Informational Asymmetry and Market Imperfections: Another Solution to the Equity Premium Puzzle." *Journal of Financial and Quantitative Analysis* 34 (December 1999): 445–464.

CHAPTER 11

Value Investing

In 1934, Benjamin Graham and David L. Dodd published a book with the modest title Security Analysis. *At the time, Graham was an investment advisor and lecturer in finance at Columbia University, where Dodd was an associate professor. Together, Graham and Dodd laid down the essential standards for value investing, an investment approach aimed at identifying stock market bargains. More than 70 years later, the principles laid down by Graham and Dodd have been proved, and Security Analysis remains perhaps the most influential book ever written on investments.*

In Omaha, Nebraska, near the first Monday in May, Graham's most famous and successful student, Warren Buffett, preaches the gospel according to Ben at Berkshire Hathaway's annual meeting. As chairman and CEO of Berkshire, Buffett has amassed a personal fortune approaching $30 billion and made scores of believers into multi-millionaires. It is easy to see why literally thousands of well-heeled investors make the annual pilgrimage to Omaha to hear Buffett speak. Inevitably, the crowd roars as Buffett skewers commonly held beliefs about stock market speculation. Concept stock investors, momentum players, and day traders all feel his sharp tongue.

In the light of Buffett's astounding success and enormous popularity, one might think that the value approach would be generally accepted and adopted by the overwhelming majority of investors. Surprisingly, it is not. Value investing involves dedication and patience that is too often missing among present-day investors. If day trading and playing initial public offerings of Internet stocks are the investment equivalent of rap music, then value investing and the tenets of Benjamin Graham are the counterpart of Mozart and Beethoven. Today, rap and momentum investing are popular. Classical music and value investing seem strangely out of step.[1]

Value Stocks

Conservative Stock Investing

Value investors like bargains. Whereas growth stock investors seek companies with the potential for above-average rates of growth in earnings and dividends, value in-

[1]See: Georgette Jason, "Picking Stocks? Don't Look to Pros for Consensus," *The Wall Street Journal*, August 3, 2000, C1, C17.

vestors seek companies whose stock prices have been unfairly beaten down in price. In both cases, investors seek bargains selling at prices below their real economic value, but differences in investment philosophy lead to distinctive investment decisions.

Growth stock investors sometimes buy stocks selling at very high prices relative to earnings and book values when they perceive that even high price/earnings (P/E) and price/book (P/B) ratios fail to fully reflect the superior capabilities of leading firms in dynamic industries. Aggressive stock picking by growth stock investors contrasts sharply with the conservative stock-picking style of value investors.

In the case of value investing, bargains are often measured in terms of market prices that are below the estimated economic value of tangible and intangible assets. Most value investors focus on rather easily measured tangible assets such as plant, equipment, common stock or other financial holdings in subsidiaries or other companies, and real estate. A bargain is discovered when market prices are temporarily depressed below a conservative estimate of the current market value of tangible assets. When the gap between stock market prices and the market value of tangible assets is great, an attractive candidate for purchase is discovered.

Of course, it is reasonable to ask how the market value of the firm in the eyes of stock market investors could fall to a significant discount to the value of the firm's tangible assets. One possibility is that stock market investors value firm assets in the light of the ability of present management to realize their full economic potential. Stock prices become depressed when entrenched management is inefficient or guilty of self-dealing, as measured by overly generous cash or stock option–based compensation for top managers. Value investors with the ability to wrest corporate control from the hands of inefficient or self-interested managers have the potential to cause a dramatic upturn in stock prices as they force a convergence between the firm's stock market valuation and the value of the firm's tangible assets. When naive investors unfairly discount the potential for a beneficial change in corporate control, value stock investors are able to earn an above-average rate of return on their bargain purchase price investments.

Another possible source of above-average returns for value investors depends on their ability to accurately perceive the near-term potential for a favorable change in regulation or public policy. For example, many value investors were attracted by the long-term investment potential of cable television providers and network broadcasters during the mid-1990s. At that time, onerous local regulation of cable television service prices led to below-average rates of return on investment capital, and the widespread perception that the industry's long-term growth potential would be unfairly limited. At the same time, onerous federal regulation limited the ability of broadcasters to buy local stations and to develop and market their own programming. As a result, cable television and network broadcasting companies were perceived as having poor growth prospects in the mid-1990s, and their common stocks fell to bargain levels.

Savvy value investors correctly perceived that rapid technological advances would force a convergence of the telephone, satellite broadcasting, and cable television industries. Although this ongoing convergence has the long-term potential to increase competitive rivalry and thereby limit industry prices and profitability, it had the very beneficial near-term effect of eliminating the rationale for much historical regulation. In the short run, cable television and network broadcasting regulation has eased, and their common stock prices have soared. In the long run, cable television company stocks will continue to prosper so long as such companies retain their superior ability to deliver a widening array of local and long-distance telephone service, video or "pay-per-view" movies, broadcast and cable television programming, Internet access, and content services. Similarly, network broadcasters will continue to flourish so long as they are able to provide a wide variety of quality programming.

Value investors tend to argue that overly emotional investors cause stock prices to be moved by "fear" and "greed" to levels that are sometimes too low or too high based on the economic fundamentals. As a result, value investors adopt a **contrarian investment philosophy** based on the premise that investors can profit by betting against the overly emotional crowd. According to practitioners of contrarian investment strategies, investors can profit if they are able to withstand the peer group and psychological pressures tied to common stock investing. To be successful, contrarian investors argue that one must "buy fear" and "sell greed."

contrarian investment philosophy
Investment strategy based on the premise that investors can profit by betting against the overly emotional crowd.

What Is a Value Stock?

Traditional **value investors** seek out-of-favor stocks selling at a discount to the overall market, in which such discounts are measured in terms of low P/E and P/B ratio and/or high dividend yield. These investment criteria often result in an investment preference for basic industry stocks, financial service companies, and utilities.

value investors
Investors who seek out-of-favor stocks selling at a discount to the overall market.

So-called **deep-value investors** favor indisputably cheap stocks. Some focus on companies at the brink of bankruptcy or in the midst of bankruptcy proceedings. Cyclical stocks also become a favorite of value investors when recession hits and economically sensitive stocks get hammered by short-term investors who focus on temporarily adverse sales and earnings information.

deep-value investors
Investors who focus on very cheap stocks.

During recent years, finding attractive companies with good economic prospects at low P/E ratios has become difficult. As a result, some value investors have used yardsticks based on new valuation criteria tied to cash flows or the rate of return on assets. This approach leads them to buy stocks that do not appear cheap by traditional P/E, P/B, or dividend yield standards. Such an approach also allows them to hang onto stocks that have racked up big gains, whereas a more traditional value investor would commonly unload stocks that have jumped sharply in price.

In judging the investment merit of the value approach, it is important to recognize that, by themselves, low stock prices do not necessarily signal attractive value any more than low prices signify attractive value at a department store or grocery store. No reasonable shopper would go into a grocery store and restrict buying to items selling for less than \$1, \$5, or \$10. Similarly, no reasonable value investor would restrict buying interest to stocks selling for less than \$1, \$5, or \$10. Even sharply marked down produce represents no real bargain when it is well past its prime and spoilage is at hand. A savvy produce shopper looks for bargain prices on fruits and vegetables that are in the peak of condition. Similarly, a savvy value investor looks for quality companies selling at unusually attractive prices when compared with conventional P/E, P/B, and/or dividend yield criteria.

There are often good economic reasons when a stock sells at a sharp discount to the market, and conservative investors must be wary to avoid being stuck with a real **dog.** In investment jargon, a dog is a company facing a fundamental deterio-

dog
Company facing a fundamental deterioration in its basic earnings power.

ration in its basic earnings power. Even industry leaders can become permanently impaired when industry fundamentals are undermined by adverse changes in government regulation, an onslaught of foreign or domestic competition, or a permanent shift in buyer preferences. Self-dealing by incompetent management can also permanently impair a company's earnings growth prospects and lead to a severe downturn in stock prices. In a permanently depressed industry, prospects for future growth in earnings and dividends also become depressed, and historical rates of return provide little guide to what investors might be able to expect going forward.

Value investors look for companies selling at sharp discounts to the market or a company's own historical valuations provided that such discounts cannot be explained by a parallel deterioration in the firm's economic fundamentals. For example, stock prices are sometimes low relative to company fundamentals simply because companies are relatively obscure. This is often true of small companies whose stocks may not be followed by research analysts. Wall Street analysts follow companies with ongoing investor interest and a continuing need for new debt and equity financing. Many institutional investors shun stocks with low market capitalizations or even stock priced at less than $10. As a result, research analysts often neglect to cover such companies, and the resulting lack of accessible information may create a bargain for the diligent investor.

Attractive stock market values can also be created when an entire industry falls into disfavor and investors tar all industry participants with the same brush. Companies that may be only marginally or temporarily affected by the industry problems can become **undervalued** in the marketplace. Some years ago, for example, investors turned their backs on the steel industry when big U.S. producers lost their ability to compete in world markets. Nevertheless, some small and highly efficient specialty steel mills proved to be excellent investments for discriminating investors. Radical changes facing the health care and financial services industries have also created opportunities for savvy value investors able to identify bargains amid the general uncertainty over the future of these businesses.

undervalued
A stock priced below real economic value.

Although the basic principle of value investing is easy to grasp, identifying undervalued opportunities requires considerable know-how and investments research. Low prices alone do not indicate an undervalued asset. Fundamentally sound economic prospects and quality management are equally important. Accurately assessing economic prospects and management quality requires a thorough understanding of the company—its business, balance sheet, and future prospects.

S&P/BARRA Value and Growth Indexes

During the 1990s, value investors found that when the stock market is very strong, conservative stock picking can lead to below-average rates of return. In a period of uninterrupted economic expansion, capital spending rises, productivity gains are created, and technology spending booms. These basic economic trends favor growth-oriented companies and penalize investors in the basic industry stocks often considered most attractive by value investors. As a result, value investing, which typically focuses on out-of-favor stocks, has itself been out of favor. True to their contrarian roots, value investors stubbornly cling to the notion that market conditions will turn in their favor at the start of the new millennium.

The relative performance shortfall facing value investors reached historic proportions during the late 1990s. To see that this is indeed the case, it is necessary for investors to have a benchmark to measure rates of return on value versus growth stocks. In 1992, Standard & Poor's (S&P) and BARRA Inc. began a collaboration to produce value and growth subsets of S&P's industry-leading equity indexes. Academic research pioneered by Nobel Laureate William Sharpe, and continued by Eugene Fama, Kenneth French, and others, has confirmed the validity of the value/growth distinction in terms of differential returns over time. The S&P/BARRA Value and Growth Indexes are constructed by dividing the stocks in an S&P index into two mutually exclusive groups according to the firm's P/B ratio. The Value Index contains firms with lower P/B ratios, and the Growth Index has firms with higher P/B ratios. Like other S&P indexes, the S&P/BARRA Value and Growth Indexes are weighted in proportion to the market capitalization of component firms. Although there is no definitive way to characterize "value" versus "growth" stocks, reliance on P/B ratios has the advantage of being simple and easy to understand, is mutually exclusive, and captures a fundamental difference between companies generally regarded as value companies versus growth companies. In addition, P/B ratios tend to be more stable over time than alternative measures, such as P/E ratios, earnings growth rates, or rates of return on stockholders' equity (ROE). As a result, S&P/BARRA Value and Growth Indexes have relatively low turnover over the course of a year and provide a useful basis for comparison between rates of return earned on value and growth stocks.

Companies in the S&P/BARRA Growth Index tend to have higher market capitalizations, on average, than those in the associated Value Index. As a result, there are many more companies in the S&P/BARRA Value Index than in the Growth Index. Generally speaking, companies in the Value Index also exhibit characteristics associated with "value" stocks, such as low P/E ratios, higher dividend yields, and lower historical and predicted earnings growth. At times, however, large losses at component firms can cause surprisingly high P/E ratios for the Value Index. From September 1993 through January 1994, for example, the P/E ratio for the Value Index based on 12-month trailing earnings was higher than that of the Growth Index because several large low-P/B stocks (e.g., General Motors) reported large losses. These losses were sufficiently large to push the P/E ratio of the Value Index temporarily above that of the Growth Index. On an overall basis, the Value Index can be described as more heavily concentrated in the energy, utility, and financial services sectors. Conversely, the Growth Index is usually more heavily weighted in the consumer noncyclicals and technology sectors. The stock price beta risk factor of the Growth Index is typically larger than that of the Value Index. As a result, the Growth Index tends to outperform the Value Index during periods of robust stock market returns. The Value Index tends to do relatively well during periods of tepid stock market returns.

As shown in Table 11.1, S&P/BARRA Value and Growth Indexes have been developed for stocks in the S&P 500, S&P MidCap 400, and S&P SmallCap 600. Performance data are available for the S&P 500/BARRA Growth and Value Indexes since December 31, 1974, for the MidCap 400/BARRA Growth and Value Indexes since May 31, 1991, and the SmallCap 600/BARRA Growth and Value Indexes since December 31, 1993. All S&P/BARRA Growth and Value Indexes are rebalanced semiannually on January 1 and July 1. The sole criteria for the growth/value split is book value divided by the market capitalization of the firm. Values used at the time of rebalancing are the equity's position at the close of trading on the prior November 30 and May 31. This one-month lag makes it possible for index funds

TABLE 11.1 Annual Returns Can Vary Widely for Value and Growth Components of the S&P 500

Year	S&P 500	S&P 500 Growth	S&P 500 Value	S&P MidCap 400	S&P MidCap 400 Growth	S&P MidCap 400 Value	S&P SmallCap 600	S&P SmallCap 600 Growth	S&P SmallCap 600 Value
1975	37.23%	31.72%	43.38%						
1976	23.93%	13.84%	34.93%						
1977	−7.16%	−11.82%	−2.57%						
1978	6.57%	6.78%	6.16%						
1979	18.61%	15.72%	21.16%						
1980	32.50%	39.40%	23.59%						
1981	−4.92%	−9.81%	0.02%						
1982	21.55%	22.03%	21.04%						
1983	22.56%	16.24%	28.89%						
1984	6.27%	2.33%	10.52%						
1985	31.73%	33.31%	29.68%						
1986	18.67%	14.50%	21.67%						
1987	5.25%	6.50%	3.68%						
1988	16.61%	11.95%	21.67%						
1989	31.69%	36.40%	26.13%						
1990	−3.11%	0.20%	−6.85%						
1991	30.47%	38.37%	22.56%						
1992	7.62%	5.06%	10.52%	25.14%	22.40%	26.45%			
1993	10.08%	1.68%	13.61%	13.95%	13.67%	13.43%			
1994	1.32%	3.13%	−0.64%	−3.58%	−6.98%	−0.57%	−4.77%	−5.47%	−4.52%
1995	37.58%	38.13%	36.99%	30.95%	27.30%	34.04%	29.96%	29.07%	30.69%
1996	22.96%	23.97%	22.00%	19.20%	18.41%	19.40%	21.32%	16.09%	26.10%
1997	33.36%	36.52%	29.98%	32.25%	30.28%	34.38%	25.58%	15.65%	36.45%
1998	28.58%	42.16%	14.67%	19.12%	34.86%	4.67%	−1.31%	2.29%	−5.06%
1999	21.04%	28.25%	12.72%	14.72%	28.74%	2.32%	12.40%	19.57%	3.03%
Geometric Mean	**17.26%**	**16.77%**	**17.31%**	**18.46%**	**20.39%**	**16.03%**	**13.09%**	**12.28%**	**13.16%**
Median	**21.04%**	**15.72%**	**21.16%**	**19.16%**	**24.85%**	**16.42%**	**16.86%**	**15.87%**	**14.56%**

Data source: <http://www.barra.com>.

to invest in the indexes as of the rebalancing dates because new constituent lists are known well in advance. Each index is initially designed so that approximately 50% of the market capitalization of the combined index is in the Value Index and 50% is in the Growth Index. During intervening months, of course, the relative weights of each index drift away from a 50-50 split as a result of market changes. Although wholesale changes in the indexes are made every six months, modest adjustments are made on a monthly basis to reflect additions and deletions to the larger indexes. At each semiannual rebalancing, a cutoff P/B value is determined for the "last" company in each Value Index. Subsequent additions to the relevant S&P index are made to the Growth Index if its P/B ratio is higher than the most recent semiannual cutoff value. Otherwise, it is added to the Value Index. When companies are deleted from the larger S&P index, they are also dropped from the relevant Value and Growth Index.

The short time frame covered by the S&P 500/BARRA Growth and Value Indexes for the S&P MidCap 400 and S&P SmallCap 600 make meaningful comparisons difficult. However, returns for the S&P/BARRA Value and Growth components of the S&P 500 have now been computed over a quarter century. As shown in Figure 11.1, over the 25-year period from 1975 to 1999, total rates of return have been similar for the value and growth components of the S&P 500. This means that a long-term investor could expect to receive similar rates of return on value and growth stocks.

value stocks
Low P/E and P/B and high-dividend stocks selling at bargain prices.

growth stocks
High P/E and P/B stocks with good prospects for above-average earnings increases.

This is despite the fact that there clearly are periods when either the value or growth style of investing is favored in the equity market. During the late 1970s, for example, **value stocks** clearly outperformed **growth stocks** (see Figure 11.2). Conversely, during the late 1990s, growth stocks just as clearly outperformed value stocks. Indeed, the annual rate of return advantage for growth stocks over value stocks has never been greater than during the 1998–99 period. Of course, contemplating what happened during the past is interesting, but what happens next

FIGURE 11.1 Growth and Value Stocks Have Similar Long-Run Cumulative Returns

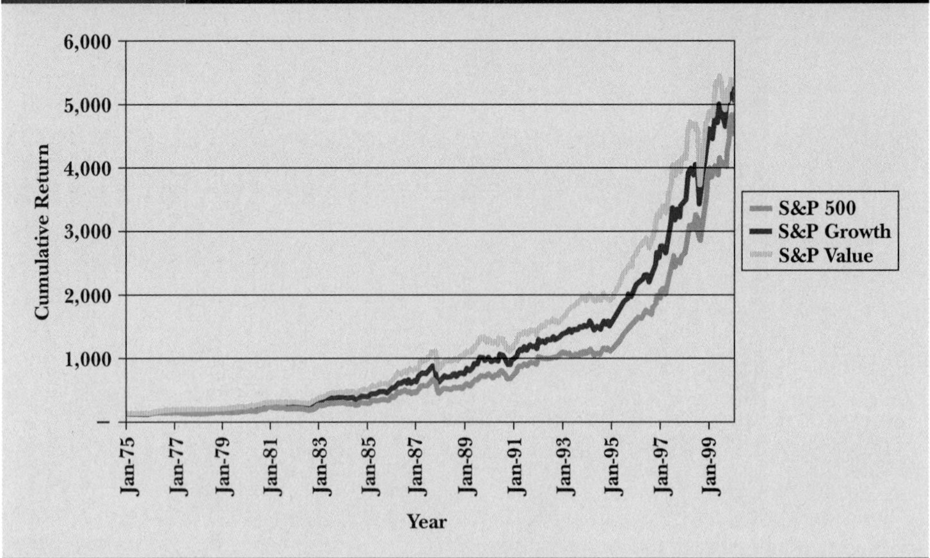

FIGURE 11.2 **Growth Outperformed Value during the Late 1990s**

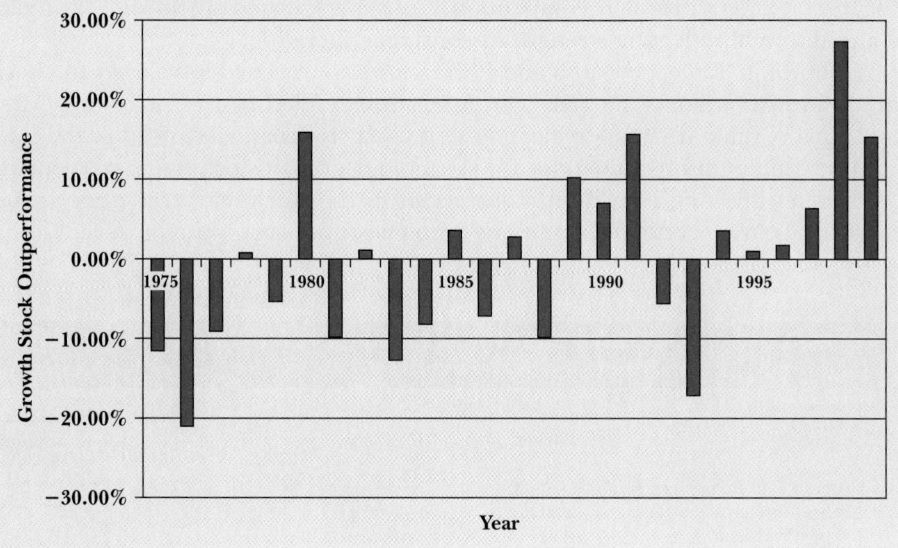

is of most importance to investors. Although it is difficult to predict when value investing will return to favor among investors, there is reason to believe that value stocks will do well during the start of the new millennium.

As shown in Figure 11.2, investor appetite for growth versus value stocks tends to run in cycles. During the late 1970s, a period of sluggish economic performance caused investors to favor conservative value stocks. During the late 1990s, unprecedented economic growth emboldened typically risk-averse investors to seek the greater potential rewards tied to growth stock investing. Such rewards are not without risk, however. In 1998, for example, stocks rose strongly during the first half of the year. After hitting a record high on July 17, the S&P 500 Index fell by 19.2% during the following six weeks. Declines were even steeper for most small stocks. The Russell 2000 Index fell nearly 40% from its peak in April before climbing back during the fourth quarter. The summer slump in stock prices reflected several factors that raised anxiety among investors and prompted a reconsideration of risk that extended past stocks to bonds. Among such factors were deteriorating corporate earnings, Russia's default on its debts, sharp swings in currency exchange rates, and lingering economic weakness in Asia. Although these sources of uncertainty remained as the year went on, many investors reacted by selecting large, well-known stocks perceived as reliable vehicles for long-term growth.

Throughout the late 1990s, technology stocks have led the market's advance. Investors have become convinced that consumers and businesses will keep spending freely on computer software and services. Speculation also played a role. Flourishing activity on the Internet has sent many "dot.com" stocks skyrocketing, even those with no hint of revenues nor profitability. Many confirmed value investors compare the bulge in Internet stock prices with such historical asset "bubbles" as the Japanese stock market in the late 1980s and Holland's tulip bulb mania in the

1630s. Health care and telecommunications stocks also soared more than 40%. Both sectors benefited from rising demand and a perception that they are somewhat insulated from foreign competition. Consumer-related stocks such as retailers also did well, reflecting strength in consumer spending.

As shown in Table 11.2, P/B and P/E ratios have reached lofty levels for stock market favorites among the S&P 500. After an extended run of superior performance, many value investors regard these growth stocks as overpriced at the start of the new millennium. Valuations for technology growth stocks seem particularly stretched. In the long run, if the value sector of the stock market is to do better on a relative basis, economic conditions facing basic industry must improve. Within

TABLE 11.2 Price Book and Price Earnings Ratios are at Lofty Levels for Stock Market Favorites

Company Name	Ticker	Industry	Market Cap ($ millions)
A. Highest P/B Ratio Firms in the S&P 500			
Yahoo! Inc.	YHOO	Internet	105,405
Avon Products	AVP	Toiletries/Cosmetics	7,360
Genl Mills	GIS	Food Processing	10,255
Qualcomm Inc.	QCOM	Telecom. Equip.	100,461
Campbell Soup	CPB	Food Processing	15,440
America Online	AOL	Internet	166,823
Oracle Corp.	ORCL	Computer Software & Svcs.	145,215
Quaker Oats	OAT	Food Processing	8,512
Network Appliance	NTAP	Computer & Peripherals	11,532
US Airways Group	U	Air Transport	2,175
Harcourt General	H	Publishing	1,952
Dell Computer	DELL	Computer & Peripherals	127,437
EMC Corp.	EMC	Computer & Peripherals	104,803
Cisco Systems	CSCO	Computer & Peripherals	347,897
Sun Microsystems	SUNW	Computer & Peripherals	111,243
Averages			**84,434**
B. Highest P/E Ratio Firms in the S&P 500			
Oracle Corp.	ORCL	Computer Software & Svcs.	145,215
Inco Limited	N	Metals & Mining (Div.)	4,480
Sun Microsystems	SUNW	Computer & Peripherals	111,243
Seagate Technology	SEG	Computer & Peripherals	8,671
EMC Corp.	EMC	Computer & Peripherals	104,803
Nortel Networks	NT	Foreign Telecom.	119,283
Viacom Inc. 'A'	VIA	Entertainment	7,151
Baker Hughes	BHI	Oilfield Svcs./Equip.	6,708
Microsoft Corp.	MSFT	Computer Software & Svcs.	588,884
PE Biosystems Group	PEB	Precision Instrument	11,132
Coca-Cola Enterprises	CCE	Beverage (Soft Drink)	8,393
Niagara Mohawk	NMK	Electric Utility (East)	2,599
Xilinx Inc.	XLNX	Semiconductor	14,249
Anadarko Petroleum	APC	Petroleum (Producing)	4,240
Home Depot	HD	Retail Building Supply	137,922
Dell Computer	DELL	Computer & Peripherals	127,437
Rowan Cos.	RDC	Oilfield Svcs./Equip.	1,619
Solectron Corp.	SLR	Electronics	23,725
Homestake Mining	HM	Gold/Silver Mining	2,033
Placer Dome	PDG	Gold/Silver Mining	3,378
Averages			**70,583**

Data source: *Value Line Investment Survey for Windows,* January 2000.

any historical context, the market is very richly valued. On the one hand, this may be rational because global business fundamentals are probably as sound as they have ever been. On the other hand, valuations are so stretched for premier growth stocks that the odds against satisfactory long-term results from current price levels seem high. No one would doubt that Microsoft Corp. is a superior organization. However, with a late-1990s valuation of approximately 4% of the entire S&P 500, Microsoft enjoys the same market capitalization as all the publicly traded industrial cyclical stocks *combined.* This creates an interesting hypothetical question: Can the stock of a premier growth company such as Microsoft *ever* be too high? To a value investor, the answer is yes.

TABLE 11.2 ***(continued)***

P/B Ratio	P/E Ratio	Average Annual P/E Ratio	Projected EPS Growth Rate	Proj. 3–5-Yr. Avg. Return
122.0		209.7	70.5	−11.0
120.3	18.0	25.3	12.5	16.0
94.6	16.8	20.4	10.5	14.0
71.3		32.4	58.0	−17.0
66.5	18.2	27.8	6.5	9.0
43.3		185.0	92.5	9.0
41.5	88.7	26.9	25.0	−7.0
41.2	21.6	24.3	11.5	6.0
32.0		72.9	61.0	14.0
31.5		11.4		30.0
29.6	21.6	27.4	8.0	16.0
29.6	60.9	49.7	34.5	12.0
24.6	83.1	33.6	36.5	5.0
24.3		62.2	25.5	−8.0
21.9	84.6	30.3	20.0	−12.0
52.9	**45.9**	**56.0**	**33.8**	**5.1**
41.5	88.7	26.9	25.0	−7.0
	88.4	−17.8	63.0	2.0
21.9	84.6	30.3	20.0	−12.0
2.8	83.3	−24.9	15.5	8.0
24.6	83.1	33.6	36.5	5.0
	78.2	27.9	25.5	−6.0
3.3	74.9	54.7	48.0	4.0
2.1	72.8	28.8	11.0	33.0
19.3	69.0	49.8	25.0	−2.0
18.3	65.5	31.1	20.5	
2.8	63.7	123.9	19.0	14.0
0.8	63.1	107.8	−4.0	2.0
14.0	62.9	30.1	30.0	3.0
3.2	62.7	205.8	24.0	14.0
12.1	62.0	40.1	25.0	−1.0
29.6	60.9	49.7	34.5	12.0
2.4	60.7	13.9	8.0	14.0
8.5	60.2	40.5	29.0	−4.0
2.7	60.1	−89.5		20.0
	57.6	35.5	14.5	14.0
9.2	**65.0**	**50.0**	**22.1**	**8.4**

WALL STREET WISDOM 11.1

Buffettology

Warren E. Buffett, then 34 years old, gained control of textile manufacturer Berkshire Hathaway in 1965. Buffett gradually built Berkshire into a conglomerate with a string of property casualty insurance companies, *See's Candies*, the *Buffalo News*, *World Book Encyclopedia*, and so on. During more than 25 years of Buffett's stewardship, Berkshire's net worth per share has compounded at 24% per year. In an era when median Fortune 500 companies count themselves lucky to earn half that much, Buffett's accomplishment can only be viewed as amazing—especially for a debt-free company.

In addition to being uniquely capable as an investor and manager, Buffett has the uncommon ability to communicate his insights on management in a disarmingly modest and humorous fashion that is equally important for stock market investors and experienced business managers. Among the most important dos and don'ts learned by Buffett are the following 10 lessons.

- *It is far better to buy a wonderful company at a fair price than a fair company at a wonderful price.* In a difficult business, no sooner is one problem solved than another surfaces. "There is never just one cockroach in the kitchen."
- *When a management with a reputation for brilliance tackles a business with a reputation for bad economics, it is the reputation of the business that remains intact.* According to Buffett, attractive economics include a 20% plus rate of return on capital without leverage or accounting gimmicks, high margins, high cash flow, low capital investment requirements, a lack of government regulation, and strong prospects for continuing growth. "Good jockeys do well on good horses," Buffett says, "but not on broken down old nags."
- *Management does better by avoiding dragons, not slaying them.* Buffett attributes his success to avoiding, rather than solving, tough business problems. As Buffett says, "We have been successful because we concentrated on identifying one-foot hurdles that we could step over, rather than because we acquired any ability to clear seven-footers."
- *As if governed by Newton's first law of motion, an institution will resist any change in its current direction.* Too often, the call for necessary change is blithely ignored.
- *Just as work expands to fill available time, corporate projects or acquisitions will materialize to soak up available funds.* Even when plainly called for, dividends or share buybacks are seldom seen as the best use of funds.
- *Any business craving of the leader, however foolish, will be quickly supported by detailed rate-of-return and strategic studies prepared by the troops.* Rationality frequently wilts when the institutional imperative comes into play.
- *The behavior of peer companies, whether they are expanding, acquiring, setting compensation, or whatever, will be mindlessly imitated.* Institutional dynamics often set management on a misguided course.
- *It is not a sin to miss a business opportunity outside one's area of expertise.* By inference, it is a sin to miss opportunities that you are fully capable of understanding.
- *If your actions are sensible, you are certain to get good results.* Leverage moves things along faster but at the unavoidable risk of anguish or default.
- *Do not join with managers who lack admirable qualities, no matter how attractive the prospects of their business.* When searching for businesses to buy, Buffett looks for first-class businesses accompanied by first-class management.

How well do these capital allocation rules work in practice? Consider that when Buffett gained control of Berkshire Hathaway in 1965 the company had a stock price of $12 per share. By mid-2000, Berkshire's stock price had risen to a high of more than $80,000 per share, making Buffett's personal stake worth about *$30 billion*. All in all, not too shabby!

See: Warren E. Buffett, *Berkshire Hathaway Annual Report*, Omaha, Neb., March 2000; <http://www.berkshirehathaway.com>.

Graham and Dodd Approach

Benjamin Graham

For many investors, the value investing concept is synonymous with the name of Benjamin Graham. Graham started his Wall Street career in 1914 as a brokerage firm messenger for $12 per week. From that position, he quickly rose to writing research reports. In 1920, at the young age of 26, Graham took his place as a full partner in the Wall Street firm of Newburger, Henderson & Loeb, having proved his ability to manage complex investment strategies. During the early 1920s, Graham searched for companies with understated earnings and hidden assets. In 1923, Graham left Newburger to start his own firm. He started a hedge fund focused on buying deeply undervalued securities, shorting overvalued stocks, or taking advantage of profitable hedging opportunities. By 1929, Graham was making $600,000 per year and so confident of success for his Graham-Newman partnership, operated with the help of his friend Douglass Newman, that he turned down an offer to become partners with Wall Street legend Bernard M. Baruch.

As it turned out, the tide was about to turn for Graham and his investment prowess. Between 1921 and 1929, the market surged 450%. Stock price manipulation was widespread, and margin buying with only 10% down fueled a meteoric rise. In retrospect, with short-term interest rates at 8%, it made little sense to buy stocks in such a "New Era" when the Dow Jones Industrial Average (DJIA) offered only a 2% dividend yield. In the ensuing stock market crash, the DJIA fell a mind-numbing 89.1%, from 381.17 on September 3, 1929, to 41.22 on July 8, 1932. So complete was the devastation that it would be 25 years before the 1929 peak was surmounted. Meanwhile, Graham's heavy reliance on financial leverage brought heavy losses. Despite savvy stock selections, Graham was ruined.

Although Graham's enormous stock market profit from the "Roaring 20s" was gone, Graham-Newman managed to stay in business and slowly rebound. Graham learned that the true measure of stock market values came not from price movements alone but from earnings, dividends, future prospects, and asset values. With the stock market in collapse and the economy in depression, Graham devoted increased effort to his "hobby" of teaching college students about investing. In 1928, to help organize and formalize his theories about the market, Graham had begun to teach a night class at Columbia University in New York titled "Advanced Security Analysis." This course became an enduring hit with students and Wall Street professionals who sat in on the class to get valuable tips about investment prospects. In May 1934, Graham teamed up with David. L. Dodd, an associate professor of finance at Columbia, to publish *Security Analysis*. Compiled from class notes, *Security Analysis* has gone on to become one of the most famous investments books of all time. Today, it is commonly referred to as the "bible" of value investing. Because of this work and another easy-to-read version titled *The Intelligent Investor*, published in 1949, Graham has come to be considered the "Dean of Financial Analysis." Value investors who follow Graham's conservative approach to stock picking are called **Graham and Dodd** investors.

Graham and Dodd Coauthors of *Security Analysis*, the value investor's bible.

margin of safety Positive difference between price and appraised value.

Investment Philosophy

Like any other investment philosophy, value investing resists being easily summarized. Still, the most important idea for a value investor is the **margin of safety** concept.

According to Graham and Dodd, the margin-of-safety idea becomes evident when applied to undervalued or bargain securities. By definition, bargains reflect a favorable difference between price and indicated or appraised value. That difference is the margin of safety. It is available for absorbing the effect of miscalculations or bad luck. Bargain buyers place particular emphasis on the ability of a given investment to withstand adverse developments.

The growth stock investor seeks investment opportunities with expected earnings growth that is greater than historical averages. A growth stock approach entails a dependable margin of safety only if future calculations are conservatively made. According to Graham and Dodd, the danger in growth stock investing lies in the tendency to pay high prices for stocks with questionable growth prospects. A basic rule of prudent investment is that all estimates must err on the side of understatement. Thus, the implicit margin of safety is large when a low price is paid for a company with robust growth prospects. The margin of safety will be lower at higher prices and nonexistent at some yet higher price.

From this perspective, the objective of security analysis is to obtain a true picture of the company as a going concern over a representative time period. Analysts search for an informed judgment of future profitability and growth. Analysts also seek to arrive at company valuations, which, on average, prove more reliable than the marketplace. The goal of enlightened stock analysis is to identify underpriced securities and to enjoy excess returns following the market's subsequent upward revaluation to a price consistent with **intrinsic value.** The intrinsic value of a stock is justified by assets, earnings, dividends, sure prospects, and management. According to Graham and Dodd, intrinsic values and current market prices rarely coincide given the effects of investor pessimism and euphoria.

intrinsic value
Real economic value.

Graham and Dodd drew parallels between stock market investing and partnership arrangements. Suppose you are in business with someone named **Mr. Market.** Without fail, Mr. Market appears every day to buy your share of the business or to sell you his. When optimistic, Mr. Market is motivated by greed to offer a very high price for your share of the business. When pessimistic, Mr. Market is overwhelmed by fear and offers to sell you his part of the business at a very low price. Mr. Market has the endearing characteristic of constantly revising his bid and ask prices. If you do not like today's numbers, just wait; he will be back tomorrow with new information.

Mr. Market
Graham and Dodd's metaphor for day traders and stock speculators.

The message from the fable of Mr. Market is simple. In the words of Graham and Dodd, the market is simply there to facilitate the investor's interest in buying or selling securities. At any point in time, market prices may be above or below the intrinsic economic value of the firm. For the investor capable of discerning a company's true intrinsic value, dealing with Mr. Market can become a profitable proposition. When market prices are too high, the discerning investor will choose to sell or wait for better bargains. When market prices are too low, the discerning investor takes advantage of the situation by snapping up the best bargains available.

liquidation value
Company worth measured in terms of scrap value.

net working capital
Current assets minus *all* liabilities, including long-term debt and preferred stock.

working capital
Current assets minus current liabilities.

Stock Selection Criteria

Graham and Dodd looked to find bargain basement stocks selling at prices below **liquidation value.** Remember that this was an investment philosophy born during the Great Depression. They sought stocks selling at a price below **net working capital. Working capital** is conventionally defined as current assets minus current liabilities. Net working capital equals current assets minus *all* liabilities, including long-term debt and preferred stock:

$$\text{Net Working Capital} = \text{Current Assets} - \text{Total Liabilities} \tag{11.1}$$

Net working capital shows what an investor would end up with if the company was converted into cash after paying off all short-term and long-term debt but ignoring noncurrent assets. Long-term assets are generally the hardest things to value on a balance sheet. Net working capital concentrates on easy-to-value cash holding, marketable securities, inventory, and so on. Obviously, the intrinsic economic value of a business is more than just the cash on hand minus all that is owed. Intangible assets such as brand names, patents, and copyrights are also important. To Graham and Dodd investors, however, the future is notoriously uncertain. Net working capital is a conservative guide to investing because it only considers what a company has on the books right now. Any future profits and growth are just gravy.

To Graham and Dodd investors, the ratio of price to net working capital is a handy comparative valuation measure, in which

$$\frac{\text{Price}}{\text{Net Working Capital}} = \frac{\text{Market Cap}}{(\text{Current Assets} - \text{Total Liabilities})} \tag{11.2}$$

For example, Figure 11.3 shows a list of "bargain basement stocks" published on a weekly basis in *The Value Line Investment Survey*. These are stocks with current price/earnings multiples and price/"net" working capital ratios that are in the bottom quartile of the 1,700-plus stocks covered by *Value Line*. Notice how Blair Corp. and a few others feature stock prices that are below the value of net working capital. Blair Corp. is a catalog retailer of fashion apparel for men and women and a limited range of home products. Blair also operates two retail stores and two outlet stores. During recent years, revenue growth has tailed off and net income has plummeted with rising advertising and other expenses.

Scanning the list of bargain basement stocks shown in Figure 11.3 points to two obvious difficulties tied to a strict Graham and Dodd approach. In today's investment environment, only a few companies qualify under the criteria of only buying stocks selling at prices below net working capital. In a world of Internet access to widespread investments information, such bargains seldom remain undiscovered. In addition, most companies selling for bargain-basement prices have obvious difficulties. Large operating losses or significant off-balance sheet liabilities are common. Most such companies are mediocre performers in mediocre industries. Few if any would ever qualify as wonderful businesses, as measured by high average rates of return on investment capital.

A significant problem tied to strict Graham and Dodd investing is that many stocks priced at or below net working capital are businesses that the typical investor might not want to own. For example, Beazer Homes USA, Inc., shown in Figure 11.3, designs, constructs, markets, and sells single-family homes in Arizona, California, Florida, and six other southern states. Although revenues and net income surged during mid-1999, the stock dove 40% amid complaints about management, quality of materials, and warranty problems. All this occurred against an industry backdrop of rising interest rates and heightened competition.

To lessen the risk inherent in companies with low price/net working capital ratios, Graham suggested buying dozens of such cheap stocks so that losses in a few stocks might be offset by gains in others. Of course, the scarcity of true Graham and Dodd bargains often makes broad diversification using the technique difficult.

FIGURE 11.3 **Graham and Dodd "Bargain-Basement" Stocks Are Listed in the *Value Line Investment Survey***

March 10, 2000 **SUMMARY AND INDEX • THE VALUE LINE INVESTMENT SURVEY**

HIGH RETURNS EARNED ON TOTAL CAPITAL

Stocks with high average returns on capital in last 5 years ranked by earnings retained to common equity

Page No.	Stock Name	Recent Price	Avg. Retained to Com. Eq.	Avg. Return On Cap.	Time-liness	Safety Rank	Beta	Current P/E Ratio	% Est'd Yield	Industry Group	Industry Rank
1038	Plantronics Inc.	80	521%	48%	2	3	0.90	19.5	NIL	Electronics	3
1234	Georgia Gulf	22	280%	31%	2	4	0.85	12.2	1.5	Chemical (Basic)	65
867	USG Corp.	33	125%	29%	3	3	1.10	3.7	1.8	Building Materials	73
1478	Gen'l Mills	33	118%	30%	4	2	0.65	16.2	3.4	Food Processing	78
833	Avon Products	30	67%	89%	4	3	1.00	17.0	2.7	Toiletries/Cosmetics	69
1467	Campbell Soup	29	58%	36%	4	2	0.90	14.6	3.3	Food Processing	78
741	Billing Concepts	5 13/16	54%	48%	4	4	0.70	32.2	NIL	Telecom. Services	28
2188	Gartner Group 'A'	15	52%	30%	3	3	1.20	18.8	NIL	Computer Software & Svcs	9
2180	Computer Associates	66	48%	33%	1	3	1.20	22.3	0.2	Computer Software & Svcs	9
1093	Dell Computer	43	48%	44%	3	3	1.35	58.9	NIL	Computer & Peripherals	10
1582	UST Inc.	20	47%	95%	3	2	0.70	7.4	8.8	Tobacco	84
1689	Dollar Tree Stores	36	45%	35%	2	3	1.35	22.1	NIL	Retail (Special Lines)	16
1703	Intimate Brands	33	45%	40%	3	3	1.10	17.1	1.7	Retail (Special Lines)	16
2204	SEI Investments	94	42%	40%	2	3	1.15	22.2	0.5	Computer Software & Svcs	9
782	Lucent Technologies	68	39%	34%	3	3	1.40	48.6	0.1	Telecom. Equipment	7
226	Ocular Sciences	14	39%	32%	2	4	1.25	8.1	NIL	Medical Supplies	21
2199	Parametric Technology	30	38%	38%	3	3	1.35	60.0	NIL	Computer Software & Svcs	9
764	TV Guide 'A'	45	38%	31%	–	4	0.85	NMF	NIL	Telecom. Services	28
2177	Ceridian Corp.	20	37%	36%	5	3	1.00	20.6	NIL	Computer Software & Svcs	9
2206	Sterling Commerce	44	36%	36%	–	4	1.50	25.4	NIL	Computer Software & Svcs	9
1027	Gemstar Int'l	72	35%	37%	1	4	1.60	NMF	NIL	Electronics	3
2198	Oracle Corp.	72	35%	32%	1	3	1.35	NMF	NIL	Computer Software & Svcs	9
1243	Amgen	65	34%	31%	2	3	1.00	60.7	NIL	Drug	11
1276	Schering-Plough	34	34%	53%	3	1	1.30	21.4	1.6	Drug	11
1542	Coca-Cola	51	33%	45%	4	1	1.10	37.0	1.3	Beverage (Soft Drink)	62
2174	BMC Software	50	32%	32%	3	3	1.45	36.2	NIL	Computer Software & Svcs	9
345	Catalina Marketing	84	32%	32%	2	3	1.25	28.2	NIL	Industrial Services	61
136	Dionex Corp.	31	31%	31%	3	3	0.90	18.9	NIL	Precision Instrument	15
1091	Cisco Systems	66	30%	30%	1	3	1.45	NMF	NIL	Computer & Peripherals	10
2194	Microsoft Corp.	91	30%	29%	2	2	1.05	53.5	NIL	Computer Software & Svcs	9
1064	Intel Corp.	116	29%	29%	2	3	1.05	43.4	0.1	Semiconductor	2
1663	Kenneth Cole 'A'	51	29%	28%	1	3	1.05	25.4	NIL	Shoe	42
1550	Champion Enterprises	6 1/4	28%	28%	5	3	1.30	5.3	NIL	Manuf. Housing/Rec Veh	82
1068	Maxim Integrated	64	28%	28%	1	3	1.45	69.6	NIL	Semiconductor	2
1695	Gap (The), Inc.	48	27%	28%	2	3	1.45	32.9	0.2	Retail (Special Lines)	16
1776	Callaway Golf	12	26%	31%	3	3	1.05	11.7	2.3	Recreation	40
1487	Kellogg	24	25%	30%	4	2	0.80	14.9	4.2	Food Processing	78
189	Abbott Labs.	34	24%	34%	4	1	1.00	20.0	2.2	Medical Supplies	21
1855	ADVO, Inc.	27	23%	36%	2	4	0.80	12.9	NIL	Advertising	4
2162	Price (T. Rowe) Assoc.	33	22%	28%	2	3	1.50	15.7	1.6	Financial Svcs. (Div.)	33
2152	Gallagher (Arthur J.)	25	21%	33%	3	2	0.70	13.5	3.7	Financial Svcs. (Div.)	33
1247	Bristol-Myers Squibb	51	20%	38%	3	1	1.15	23.0	1.9	Drug	11
2200	Paychex, Inc.	49	20%	30%	1	3	1.00	65.3	0.8	Computer Software & Svcs	9
1834	Reuters ADR	139	20%	35%	3	3	1.00	46.3	1.2	Publishing	34
1266	Merck & Co.	60	18%	29%	3	1	1.15	22.2	2.0	Drug	11
1593	Jostens, Inc.	24	14%	42%	–	3	0.85	20.5	3.7	Diversified Co.	63
1507	Wrigley (Wm.) Jr.	66	14%	28%	4	1	0.95	23.4	2.2	Food Processing	78
1369	Oakley Inc.	8 1/8	13%	29%	3	4	0.80	19.3	NIL	Diversified Co.	63
1325	Helix Technology	70	11%	29%	2	4	1.40	48.3	1.2	Machinery	53
796	Cable & Wireless HKT ADR	29	9%	35%	–	2	0.90	30.5	3.8	Foreign Telecom.	6

Source: Value Line Publishing, Inc.

Investment Fundamentals

Widely Available Value Indicators

fundamental value
Worth of a stock derived from a company's assets in place, sure prospects, and durable strengths.

Value investors rely on a variety of tangible indicators of a stock's **fundamental value.** Fundamental value is the worth of a stock derived from a company's assets in place, sure prospects, and durable strengths.

The search for value almost always starts with a review of basic financial information, such as P/E and P/B ratios and dividend yields. Remember, dividing a stock's price per share by its earnings per share gives you its P/E ratio. For example, a company that earned \$5 per share over the past year whose stock price is \$50 has a P/E of 10:1. This means that investors are willing to pay \$10 for each \$1 of earnings. P/E multiples are also frequently based on projected (or "forward") earnings over the next 12 months. A stock whose P/E is significantly below that of its peers, the market as a whole, or its own historical norm may represent a relative bargain. Of course, careful research is necessary to determine if a low P/E

FIGURE 11.3 ***(continued)***

BARGAIN BASEMENT STOCKS

Stocks with current price-earnings multiples and price-to-"net" working capital ratios that are in the bottom quartile of the Value Line universe

("Net" working capital equals current assets less all liabilities including long-term debt and preferred)

Page No.	Stock Name	Recent Price	Percent Price-to "Net" Wkg. Capital	Current P/E Ratio	Percent Price-to Book Value	Time-liness	Safety Rank	Beta	% Est'd Yield	Industry Group	Industry Rank
869	Beazer Homes USA	18	80%	4.0	58%	3	3	1.10	NIL	Homebuilding	26
873	Hovnanian Enterpr. 'A'	5⅞	85%	3.8	45%	3	4	1.05	NIL	Homebuilding	26
1699	Hancock Fabrics	2 13/16	87%	8.0	64%	4	3	0.55	3.6	Retail (Special Lines)	16
1678	Blair Corp.	18	90%	8.1	62%	3	3	0.55	3.3	Retail (Special Lines)	16
887	HomeBase, Inc.	2 11/16	98%	7.9	25%	4	4	0.90	NIL	Retail Building Supply	13
1364	Kaman Corp.	10	99%	7.2	68%	3	3	0.75	4.4	Diversified Co.	63
510	NCH Corp.	40	108%	7.9	86%	3	2	0.60	3.5	Chemical (Specialty)	50
1620	Oxford Inds.	17	128%	5.6	79%	4	3	0.85	4.9	Apparel	52
881	U.S. Home	35	130%	6.2	71%	–	3	1.20	NIL	Homebuilding	26
879	Standard Pacific Corp.	10	136%	4.3	70%	2	3	1.25	3.2	Homebuilding	26
1666	Stride Rite Corp.	5	138%	7.2	79%	3	3	0.75	4.0	Shoe	42
880	Toll Brothers	18	139%	5.8	91%	2	3	1.15	NIL	Homebuilding	26
1692	Enesco Group	6⅛	143%	4.8	76%	–	3	0.60	18.4	Retail (Special Lines)	16
1785	K2, Inc.	7 7/16	150%	6.9	53%	3	3	0.80	NIL	Recreation	40
1552	Coachmen Ind.	12	163%	6.7	70%	5	3	1.05	1.7	Manuf. Housing/Rec Veh	82
1690	Dress Barn	14	175%	7.8	101%	3	3	0.85	NIL	Retail (Special Lines)	16
1343	Tecumseh Products 'A'	44	177%	6.4	75%	3	2	0.65	3.0	Machinery	53
122	TBC Corp.	5⅛	188%	5.2	60%	3	3	0.90	NIL	Tire & Rubber	86
1682	Burlington Coat	11	198%	7.9	84%	3	3	1.05	0.2	Retail (Special Lines)	16
900	Bassett Furniture	14	207%	8.8	60%	4	3	0.75	5.7	Furn./Home Furnishings	49
836	Helen of Troy Ltd.	6¾	207%	8.5	78%	4	3	1.40	NIL	Toiletries/Cosmetics	69
1409	Bear Stearns	42	215%	7.1	107%	2	3	1.65	1.4	Securities Brokerage	8
1618	Nautica Enterprises	11	227%	8.5	115%	3	3	1.30	NIL	Apparel	52
1616	Kellwood Co.	16	234%	5.5	77%	3	3	0.65	4.3	Apparel	52
1408	Advest Group	17	235%	8.9	104%	3	3	1.30	1.4	Securities Brokerage	8
518	Schulman (A.)	13	236%	8.4	105%	4	3	0.60	4.2	Chemical (Specialty)	50
1555	Thor Inds.	25	250%	7.7	147%	2	3	0.75	0.3	Manuf. Housing/Rec Veh	82
343	CDI Corp.	19	262%	6.9	104%	3	3	1.00	NIL	Industrial Services	61
1551	Clayton Homes	8 1/16	267%	6.9	104%	3	3	1.05	0.8	Manuf. Housing/Rec Veh	82
1114	Tech Data	22	274%	8.2	94%	3	4	1.25	NIL	Computer & Peripherals	10
1780	Handleman Co.	10	289%	7.1	105%	2	4	1.10	NIL	Recreation	40
888	Hughes Supply	19	292%	6.2	76%	3	3	0.90	1.9	Retail Building Supply	13
585	Ampco-Pittsburgh	12	301%	7.3	70%	3	3	0.65	3.7	Steel (General)	48
1665	Reebok Int'l	8	309%	8.3	76%	4	3	1.00	NIL	Shoe	42
573	Fansteel Inc.	3⅜	310%	8.7	53%	4	3	0.75	NIL	Metal Fabricating	47
1419	Raymond James Fin'l	20	319%	8.3	143%	3	3	1.45	1.5	Securities Brokerage	8
1729	Trans World Entertain	11	320%	6.8	102%	2	4	1.00	NIL	Retail (Special Lines)	16
330	Schlotzsky's, Inc.	6⅞	325%	9.1	58%	4	3	0.95	NIL	Restaurant	58
871	Centex Corp.	20	327%	4.7	71%	4	3	1.20	0.9	Homebuilding	26
116	Wynn's Int'l	14	333%	8.0	137%	4	3	0.85	2.0	Auto Parts (Replacement)	88

indicates fundamental business problems, temporary difficulties, or just a lack of knowledge about the company. P/E ratios are perhaps the most widely used measure of fundamental value, in which low P/E ratios signal relatively cheap stocks and high P/E ratios signal relatively expensive stocks.

As discussed in Chapters 5 and 8, the market-wide average for P/E ratios tends to fall between 10 : 1 and 20 : 1, with a typical average of roughly 15 : 1. In today's market, a P/E ratio for the DJIA of roughly 24 : 1 signals that the market is at an historic high in terms of relative valuation. In today's market, P/E ratios below 15 : 1 for individual stocks are relatively low. P/E ratios above 30 : 1 are relatively high. *The Wall Street Journal* and most newspapers list P/E ratios for individual companies alongside daily stock quotations.

P/B ratios are calculated by dividing a stock's price by its book value per share. This ratio tells investors the extent to which a stock's price closely reflects the historical accounting value of the company's tangible and financial assets per share. A P/B ratio of 1 : 1 means a stock's price equals the historical accounting value of the company's assets. A P/B ratio below 1 : 1, or below industry or company norms, could indicate a cheap stock. The market-wide average P/B ratio tends to fall between 1 : 1 and 2 : 1, with a typical average of roughly 1.6 : 1. In today's market, a P/B ratio for the DJIA of roughly 6 : 1 again signals that the market is at a historic high in terms of relative valuation. In today's market, P/B ratios below 2 : 1 for individual stocks are relatively low. P/B ratios above 6 : 1 are relatively high. Again, research is necessary to find out if assets are valued accurately on the books. P/B ratios are not listed with stock quotes in newspaper tables but are available on the Internet at Yahoo.com and many other sites and in reference materials published by Standard & Poor's, Moody's, Value Line, and others.

Many present-day followers of Graham and Dodd seek opportunities for mispriced equities among stocks with low P/E and P/B ratios. Real bargains also may be found among small and/or misunderstood stocks that have the potential to be temporarily underpriced. Unfortunately, companies with low P/E ratios often face a dramatic downturn in earnings or poor future growth prospects (see Figure 11.4). Similarly, low P/B ratio companies often have assets with values that are difficult to realize during present market conditions (see Figure 11.5). Retailers with obso-

FIGURE 11.4 **Low P/E Stocks Often Have Poor Growth Prospects**

March 10, 2000 **SUMMARY AND INDEX • THE VALUE LINE INVESTMENT SURVEY**

LOWEST P/Es

Stocks with the lowest estimated current P/E ratios

Page No.	Stock Name	Recent Price	Current P/E Ratio	Timeliness	Safety Rank	Industry Group	Industry Rank
865	Owens Coming	15	3.0	4	3	Building Materials	73
112	Federal-Mogul	14	3.6	3	3	Auto Parts (Replacement)	88
1345	Terex Corp.	12	3.6	3	3	Machinery	53
855	Armstrong World Inds.	19	3.7	5	2	Building Materials	73
878	Ryland Group	17	3.7	2	3	Homebuilding	26
867	USG Corp.	33	3.7	3	3	Building Materials	73
1464	Aurora Foods	3 1/4	3.8	–	3	Food Processing	78
873	Hovnanian Enterpr. 'A'	5 7/8	3.8	3	4	Homebuilding	26
882	Webb (Del) Corp.	15	3.9	3	3	Homebuilding	26
869	Beazer Homes USA	18	4.0	3	3	Homebuilding	26
877	Pulte Corp.	17	4.0	3	3	Homebuilding	26
278	Arkansas Best	9 1/2	4.1	1	4	Trucking/Transp. Leasing	23
892	Centex Construction	23	4.1	3	3	Cement & Aggregates	38
1321	Foster Wheeler	5 3/16	4.1	5	3	Machinery	53
872	D.R. Horton	12	4.3	–	4	Homebuilding	26
879	Standard Pacific Corp.	10	4.3	2	3	Homebuilding	26
372	Safety-Kleen	4 3/8	4.4	4	4	Environmental	89
862	Johns-Manville	8 5/16	4.5	3	5	Building Materials	73
1583	Universal Corp.	16	4.6	4	2	Tobacco	84
871	Centex Corp.	20	4.7	4	3	Homebuilding	26
825	Meritor Automotive	14	4.7	3	3	Auto Parts (OEM)	60
1628	Burlington Inds.	3 1/16	4.8	5	4	Textile	55
1692	Enesco Group	6 1/8	4.8	–	3	Retail (Special Lines)	16
1377	Service Corp. Int'l	3 13/16	4.8	5	3	Diversified Co.	63
814	Arvin Ind.	19	4.9	4	3	Auto Parts (OEM)	60
1482	IBP, Inc.	14	4.9	4	3	Food Processing	78
874	Kaufman & Broad Home	19	5.1	2	3	Homebuilding	26
894	Lafarge Corp.	21	5.1	3	3	Cement & Aggregates	38
1492	Pilgrim's Pride 'B'	7 7/16	5.1	4	3	Food Processing	78
932	Republic Group	11	5.1	3	3	Paper & Forest Products	36
830	Tower Automotive	12	5.1	3	3	Auto Parts (OEM)	60
276	AMERCO	17	5.2	3	4	Trucking/Transp. Leasing	23
1662	Brown Shoe	11	5.2	3	3	Shoe	42
1631	Dixie Group	6 1/16	5.2	3	4	Textile	55
1553	Fleetwood Enterprises	15	5.2	4	3	Manuf. Housing/Rec Veh	82
822	Lear Corp.	22	5.2	3	3	Auto Parts (OEM)	60
122	TBC Corp.	5 1/8	5.2	3	3	Tire & Rubber	86
884	Building Materials	10	5.3	2	3	Retail Building Supply	13
1550	Champion Enterprises	6 1/4	5.3	5	3	Manuf. Housing/Rec Veh	82
1350	York Int'l	18	5.3	4	3	Machinery	53
816	Dana Corp.	22	5.4	4	3	Auto Parts (OEM)	60
1168	Golden State Bancorp	13	5.4	2	3	Thrift	76
1581	R.J. Reynolds Tobacco	18	5.4	–	3	Tobacco	84
298	Sea Containers Ltd. 'A'	24	5.4	3	3	Maritime	39
1791	Topps Co.	7 3/8	5.4	1	3	Recreation	40
583	Trinity Inds.	22	5.4	3	3	Metal Fabricating	47
120	Cooper Tire & Rubber	11	5.5	4	3	Tire & Rubber	86
1616	Kellwood Co.	16	5.5	3	3	Apparel	52
1368	Nortek, Inc.	23	5.5	3	4	Diversified Co.	63
115	Tenneco Automotive	7 7/16	5.5	–	3	Auto Parts (Replacement)	88
1162	Astoria Financial	24	5.6	3	3	Thrift	76
1165	Dime Bancorp, Inc.	13	5.6	3	3	Thrift	76
271	Northwest Airlines 'A'	17	5.6	3	3	Air Transport	83
1620	Oxford Inds.	17	5.6	4	3	Apparel	52
1567	Rank Group ADR	5 1/8	5.6	3	3	Foreign Electron/Entertn	29
1395	AK Steel Holding	8 1/16	5.7	5	3	Steel (Integrated)	54
411	Holly Corp.	14	5.7	3	3	Petroleum (Integrated)	51
582	TransTechnology	12	5.7	4	3	Metal Fabricating	47
265	Alaska Air Group	27	5.8	4	4	Air Transport	83
2142	CIT Group 'A'	14	5.8	4	3	Financial Svcs. (Div.)	33
563	Moog Inc. 'A'	18	5.8	3	3	Aerospace/Defense	71
1371	Park-Ohio	8 3/4	5.8	4	4	Diversified Co.	63
1580	Philip Morris	20	5.8	4	3	Tobacco	84
880	Toll Brothers	18	5.8	2	3	Homebuilding	26
1208	UNUMProvident Corp.	15	5.8	5	3	Insurance (Life)	75
1200	Conseco, Inc.	15	5.9	5	3	Insurance (Life)	75
945	Crown Cork	14	5.9	4	3	Packaging & Container	64
657	Magellan Health Svcs.	5 5/8	5.9	2	4	Medical Services	30
327	Piccadilly Cafeterias	3	5.9	5	3	Restaurant	58
1657	Shopko Stores	17	5.9	3	3	Retail Store	41
1626	Warnaco Group 'A'	11	5.9	4	3	Apparel	52
704	CMS Energy Corp.	17	6.0	4	3	Electric Util. (Central)	87
1907	Grace (W. R.)	9 15/16	6.0	–	3	Chemical (Diversified)	59
1170	GreenPoint Fin'l	16	6.0	3	3	Thrift	76
1176	Sovereign Bancorp	7 1/2	6.0	4	3	Thrift	76
1380	Stewart Enterpr. 'A'	4 1/8	6.0	5	3	Diversified Co.	63
853	Ameron Int'l	34	6.1	3	3	Building Materials	73
815	Borg-Warner Auto	33	6.1	4	3	Auto Parts (OEM)	60
565	Northrop Grumman	44	6.1	4	3	Aerospace/Defense	71
497	Ethyl Corp.	3 3/16	6.2	4	3	Chemical (Specialty)	50
888	Hughes Supply	19	6.2	3	3	Retail Building Supply	13
875	Lennar Corp.	17	6.2	3	3	Homebuilding	26
561	Litton Inds.	30	6.2	4	2	Aerospace/Defense	71
881	U.S. Home	35	6.2	–	3	Homebuilding	26
671	US Oncology Inc.	4 1/16	6.2	3	4	Medical Services	30
1178	Washington Mutual	22	6.2	4	3	Thrift	76
1772	Action Performance	8 1/2	6.3	5	4	Recreation	40
1578	British Amer Tobacco ADR	8 7/8	6.3	–	3	Tobacco	84
268	Delta Air Lines	45	6.3	4	3	Air Transport	83
821	Intermet Corp.	12	6.3	3	3	Auto Parts (OEM)	60
1784	Johnson Outdoors	6 7/8	6.3	3	3	Recreation	40
926	Mail-Well, Inc.	8 3/8	6.3	2	4	Paper & Forest Products	36
106	Navistar Int'l	34	6.3	3	4	Auto & Truck	37
108	PACCAR Inc.	43	6.3	3	3	Auto & Truck	37
1238	Solutia Inc.	14	6.3	4	3	Chemical (Basic)	65
1644	Dillard's, Inc.	17	6.4	4	3	Retail Store	41
1360	GenCorp Inc.	7 1/16	6.4	–	3	Diversified Co.	63
1525	Nash Finch Co.	7 7/8	6.4	3	3	Food Wholesalers	17
614	Old Republic	11	6.4	5	3	Insurance(Prop/Casualty)	90
595	Steel Technologies	9 5/8	6.4	1	3	Steel (General)	48

Source: Value Line Publishing, Inc.

lete inventory are a prime example. Graham and Dodd investors depend on their specialized expertise to separate the wheat from the chaff and uncover the real bargains among low P/E and low P/B companies. Such investors also depend on the notion that the overall market is primarily rational, and price tends to converge on intrinsic value over time. In their view, their sound valuation will be *eventually* validated in an efficiently functioning marketplace.

One of the most important indicators of fundamental value is a company's **free cash flow.** Free cash flow consists of earnings before interest, taxes, depreciation, and amortization, sometimes referred to as **EBITDA,** minus necessary capital expenditures. Free cash flow is a basic measure of profitability that often foreshadows earnings improvement. Similar to the P/E ratio, the price/cash flow ratio measures the relationship between a company's stock price and cash flow or the amount of cash generated by company operations. For example, a firm that generates $10 per share in cash flow and whose stock price is $50 has a price/cash flow ratio of 5:1 and a cash-on-cash rate of return of 20%. Companies with low price/cash flow ratios may end up as takeover targets or restructuring candidates. As shown in Figure 11.6, Value Line regularly publishes valuable information on free cash flow

free cash flow
Earnings before depreciation, interest, taxes, and amortization, minus necessary capital expenditures.

EBITDA
Earnings before interest, taxes, depreciation, and amortization.

FIGURE 11.4 ***(continued)***

HIGHEST P/Es

Stocks with the highest estimated current P/E ratios

Page No.	Stock Name	Recent Price	Current P/E Ratio	Timeliness	Safety Rank	Industry Group	Industry Rank
800	Nortel Networks	117	96.7	1	3	Foreign Telecom.	6
1248	Chiron Corp.	65	91.5	2	3	Drug	11
195	ArthroCare Corp.	118	90.8	1	4	Medical Supplies	21
797	Deutsche Telekom ADR	88	90.7	3	3	Foreign Telecom.	6
1007	Corning Inc.	203	90.2	1	3	Electrical Equipment	35
431	Gulf Canada Res.	3 9/16	90.0	3	5	Canadian Energy	25
2191	Intuit Inc.	48	87.3	1	4	Computer Software & Svcs	9
1336	PRI Automation	82	86.3	2	4	Machinery	53
1090	Cabletron Sys.	48	85.7	2	4	Computer & Peripherals	10
1078	Xilinx Inc.	75	85.2	1	3	Semiconductor	2
1094	EMC Corp.	118	84.9	1	3	Computer & Peripherals	10
1106	Newbridge Networks	36	83.7	–	3	Computer & Peripherals	10
1076	Texas Instruments	164	80.8	1	3	Semiconductor	2
131	Agilent Technologies	109	80.7	–	3	Precision Instrument	15
1891	Smith Int'l Inc.	65	78.3	3	4	Oilfield Services/Equip.	45
1110	Seagate Technology	51	77.3	3	3	Computer & Peripherals	10
2178	Cognizant Technology	54	77.1	–	3	Computer Software & Svcs	9
135	Coherent, Inc.	100	76.9	2	3	Precision Instrument	15
1115	3Com Corp.	104	76.5	3	3	Computer & Peripherals	10
798	Ericsson ADR	99	75.6	1	3	Foreign Telecom.	6
239	Techne Corp.	88	75.2	1	3	Medical Supplies	21
1890	Schlumberger Ltd.	81	74.3	–	2	Oilfield Services/Equip.	45
1565	NEC Corp. ADR	122	73.5	3	3	Foreign Electron/Entertn	29
1302	AGCO Corp.	11	73.3	3	4	Machinery	53
788	Scientific Atlanta	114	72.6	1	3	Telecom. Equipment	7
799	Nokia Corp. ADR	202	72.1	1	3	Foreign Telecom.	6
1056	Analog Devices	162	72.0	1	3	Semiconductor	2
1884	Nabors Inds.	38	71.7	3	3	Oilfield Services/Equip.	45
1797	Chris-Craft	68	71.6	3	2	Entertainment	57
1047	Symbol Technologies	100	71.4	1	3	Electronics	3
604	CNA Fin'l	27	71.1	4	2	Financial Svcs. (Div.)	33
1561	Hitachi, Ltd. ADR	132	71.0	3	3	Foreign Electron/Entertn	29
1806	Viacom Inc. 'A'	56	70.0	–	3	Entertainment	57
1068	Maxim Integrated	64	69.6	1	3	Semiconductor	2
1566	Pioneer Corp. ADR	34	69.4	2	3	Foreign Electron/Entertn	29
1879	Global Inds.	11	68.8	3	3	Oilfield Services/Equip.	45
1563	Kyocera Corp. ADR	183	68.3	2	3	Foreign Electron/Entertn	29
1564	Matsushita Elec. ADR	298	67.7	3	2	Foreign Electron/Entertn	29
1893	Transocean Sedco Forex	42	67.7	3	3	Oilfield Services/Equip.	45
1058	C-Cube Microsystems	96	67.1	–	4	Semiconductor	2
1055	Altera Corp.	85	66.4	1	4	Semiconductor Cap Equip	1
571	Allied Products	3 5/16	66.0	3	5	Metal Fabricating	47
1057	Atmel Corp.	51	65.4	2	4	Semiconductor	2
1066	LSI Logic	70	65.4	1	4	Semiconductor	2
2200	Paychex, Inc.	49	65.3	1	3	Computer Software & Svcs	9
769	Western Wireless 'A'	56	65.1	–	4	Telecom Services	28
1860	WPP Group ADR	101	64.7	1	3	Advertising	4
1183	Cambridgr Shop. Ctr.	8 3/8	64.6	3	4	R.E.I.T.	56
462	Williams Cos.	45	63.4	4	3	Natural Gas(Diversified)	32
843	Comcast Corp.	41	63.1	2	3	Cable TV	31
1245	Biogen Inc.	110	61.8	1	3	Drug	11
1243	Amgen	65	60.7	2	3	Drug	11
2199	Parametric Technology	30	60.0	3	3	Computer Software & Svcs	9
1049	Titan Corp	36	60.0	1	5	Electronics	3
1053	Advanced Energy	73	59.8	2	4	Semiconductor	2
1071	Motorola, Inc.	170	59.6	2	3	Semiconductor	2
1779	Electronic Arts	95	59.4	1	3	Recreation	40
1067	Linear Technology	102	59.0	1	3	Semiconductor	2
1093	Dell Computer	43	58.9	3	3	Computer & Peripherals	10
1262	IVAX Corp.	27	58.7	1	4	Drug	11
578	Lone Star Techn.	39	58.2	2	3	Metal Fabricating	47
2170	Adobe Systems	100	57.8	1	3	Computer Software & Svcs	9
1085	Teradyne Inc.	90	57.0	1	3	Semiconductor Cap Equip	1
141	KLA-Tencor	75	56.8	2	3	Precision Instrument	15
1256	Glaxo Wellcome ADR	50	56.2	4	2	Drug	11
154	Veeco Instruments	98	55.1	2	4	Precision Instrument	15
1420	Schwab (Charles)	45	54.9	2	3	Securities Brokerage	8
229	ResMed Inc.	40	54.8	1	3	Medical Supplies	21
787	Salient 3 Communic.	12	54.5	3	3	Telecom. Equipment	7
1862	Anadarko Petroleum	31	54.4	3	3	Petroleum (Producing)	18
1875	BJ Services	62	53.9	2	3	Oilfield Services/Equip.	45
745	Citizens Utilities	15	53.6	3	2	Telecom. Services	28
2196	Network Assoc.	30	53.6	3	4	Computer Software & Svcs	9
1850	Thomson Corp.	52	53.6	4	3	Newspaper	46
2194	Microsoft Corp.	91	53.5	2	2	Computer Software & Svcs	9
1881	Halliburton Co.	41	53.2	4	3	Oilfield Services/Equip.	45
1916	Phosphate Resource	8 1/2	53.1	4	3	Chemical (Diversified)	59
772	ADC Telecom.	45	52.9	1	3	Telecom. Equipment	7
795	Cable & Wireless ADR	69	52.3	3	3	Foreign Telecom.	6
1263	Jones Pharma	45	52.3	1	3	Drug	11
1889	Rowan Cos.	26	52.0	3	4	Oilfield Services/Equip.	45
1253	Forest Labs.	67	51.9	3	3	Drug	11
452	Enron Corp.	69	51.5	2	2	Natural Gas(Diversified)	32
332	Starbucks Corp.	35	51.5	2	3	Restaurant	58
1721	Sotheby's Holdings 'A'	23	51.1	5	3	Retail (Special Lines)	16
1081	Electro Scientific	58	50.4	1	3	Semiconductor Cap Equip	1
793	BCE Inc.	114	50.0	1	2	Foreign Telecom.	6
449	Dynegy, Inc. 'A' Hldg.	48	50.0	–	3	Natural Gas(Diversified)	32
1026	Flextronics Int'l	61	50.0	1	4	Electronics	3
1650	Kohl's Corp.	79	48.8	2	3	Retail Store	41
886	Home Depot	56	48.7	2	2	Retail Building Supply	13
1877	Diamond Offshore	34	48.6	3	3	Oilfield Services/Equip.	45
782	Lucent Technologies	68	48.6	3	3	Telecom. Equipment	7
1325	Helix Technology	70	48.3	2	4	Machinery	53
223	Medtronic, Inc.	49	48.0	2	3	Medical Supplies	21
1799	Disney (Walt)	35	47.9	3	2	Entertainment	57
759	PanAmSat Corp.	46	47.9	3	3	Telecom. Services	28
1080	Applied Materials	185	47.8	1	3	Semiconductor Cap Equip	1
1558	Canon Inc. ADR	42	47.7	3	2	Foreign Electron/Entertn	29
1083	MKS Instruments	49	47.6	–	3	Semiconductor Cap Equip	1

To subscribe call 1-800-833-0046.

FIGURE 11.5 Low P/B Stocks Often Have Assets with Hard-to-Realize Values

WIDEST DISCOUNTS FROM BOOK VALUE

Stocks whose ratios of recent price to book value are lowest

Page No.	Stock Name	Recent Price	Book Value Per sh.*	Percent Price-to-Book Value	Timeliness	Safety Rank	Beta	P/E Ratio	% Est'd Yield	Industry Group	Industry Rank
1632	Galey & Lord	1 13/16	8.80	20%	3	5	0.75	NMF	NIL	Textile	55
1554	Oakwood Homes	2 9/16	11.20	23%	5	4	0.90	NMF	1.5	Manuf. Housing/Rec Veh	82
1398	LTV Corp.	3 3/8	14.15	24%	4	4	0.80	NMF	3.5	Steel (Integrated)	54
1628	Burlington Inds.	3 1/16	12.55	25%	5	4	0.75	4.8	NIL	Textile	55
887	HomeBase, Inc.	2 11/16	10.85	25%	4	4	0.90	7.9	NIL	Retail Building Supply	13
1723	Sports Authority	2 1/8	8.50	25%	4	5	1.30	35.0	NIL	Retail (Special Lines)	16
279	Budget Group	5 13/16	20.75	28%	3	4	0.95	11.6	NIL	Trucking/Transp. Leasing	23
1377	Service Corp. Int'l	3 13/16	13.35	28%	5	3	1.20	4.8	NIL	Diversified Co.	63
1918	Terra Inds.	2 3/8	8.15	29%	3	5	0.55	NMF	NIL	Chemical (Diversified)	59
233	Sola Int'l	5 1/8	17.20	30%	4	4	1.25	6.8	NIL	Medical Supplies	21
592	Oregon Steel Mills	4 1/4	13.75	31%	5	4	1.15	NMF	1.9	Steel (General)	48
372	Safety-Kleen	4 3/8	13.95	32%	4	4	1.20	4.4	NIL	Environmental	89
238	Sunrise Medical	4 3/16	12.70	33%	3	3	0.65	13.1	NIL	Medical Supplies	21
1701	Heilig-Meyers	3 3/16	8.95	36%	4	4	1.05	9.4	2.5	Retail (Special Lines)	16
1661	Barry (R.G.)	2 15/16	7.85	37%	5	3	0.95	NMF	NIL	Shoe	42
566	Precision Castparts	25	67.75	37%	4	3	1.10	7.2	1.0	Aerospace/Defense	71
351	Fairchild Corp. 'A'	6 13/16	17.80	38%	4	4	1.00	NMF	NIL	Industrial Services	61
646	Beverly Enterprises	3 1/4	8.40	39%	4	4	1.30	11.0	NIL	Medical Services	30
1321	Foster Wheeler	5 3/16	13.40	39%	5	3	1.00	4.1	4.6	Machinery	53
1635	Pillowtex Corp.	4 5/8	11.85	39%	4	5	1.05	NMF	NIL	Textile	55
327	Piccadilly Cafeterias	3	7.45	40%	5	3	0.55	5.9	NIL	Restaurant	58
1380	Stewart Enterpr. 'A'	4 1/8	10.40	40%	5	3	1.05	6.0	1.9	Diversified Co.	63
320	Landry's Seafood	6 15/16	16.80	41%	2	4	1.25	9.3	1.2	Restaurant	58
112	Federal-Mogul	14	33.15	42%	3	3	1.30	3.6	0.1	Auto Parts (Replacement)	88
174	Green Mountain Pwr.	8 1/4	19.70	42%	4	4	0.45	7.2	6.6	Electric Utility (East)	85
1715	Pep Boys	6	13.75	44%	4	3	0.90	6.8	4.7	Retail (Special Lines)	16
201	Bergen Brunswig	5 1/8	11.40	45%	5	3	1.25	9.3	5.9	Medical Supplies	21
873	Hovnanian Enterpr. 'A'	5 7/8	13.15	45%	3	4	1.05	3.8	NIL	Homebuilding	26
281	Consol. Freightways	6 1/4	13.60	46%	4	4	1.10	35.0	NIL	Trucking/Transp. Leasing	23
594	Ryerson Tull	14	30.30	46%	–	3	0.85	7.6	1.4	Steel (General)	48
1614	Hartmarx Corp.	3 3/16	6.80	47%	3	4	0.65	10.3	NIL	Apparel	52
1784	Johnson Outdoors	6 7/8	14.70	47%	3	3	0.76	6.3	NIL	Recreation	40
644	Alterra Healthcare	5 15/16	12.10	49%	4	4	1.25	NMF	NIL	Medical Services	30
340	Angelica Corp.	9 3/16	18.60	49%	5	3	0.70	11.6	10.4	Industrial Services	61
604	CNA Fin'l	27	55.55	49%	4	2	1.00	71.1	NIL	Financial Svcs. (Div.)	33
1648	Hudson's Bay Co.	14	28.80	49%	3	3	0.80	14.1	2.6	Retail Store	41
582	TransTechnology	12	24.65	49%	4	3	0.70	5.7	2.2	Metal Fabricating	47
276	AMERCO	17	34.20	50%	3	4	1.20	5.2	NIL	Trucking/Transp. Leasing	23
321	Lone Star Steakhouse	8 15/16	17.70	50%	3	3	1.00	9.9	NIL	Restaurant	58
316	CKE Restaurants	6 1/4	12.40	51%	4	4	1.05	16.6	1.3	Restaurant	58
1633	Guilford Mills	9 3/16	17.95	51%	3	3	0.70	16.7	4.8	Textile	55
1630	Culp Inc.	6 1/16	11.80	52%	3	3	0.90	7.5	2.3	Textile	55
945	Gibson Greetings	8 1/8	15.60	52%	–	4	0.95	NMF	NIL	Packaging & Container	64
582	KLM Royal Dutch	19	36.80	52%	4	3	1.00	23.5	5.6	Air Transport	83
316	Ohio Casualty	12	23.05	52%	4	3	0.85	19.0	8.0	Insurance(Prop/Casualty)	90
276	Wolohan Lumber	11	21.00	52%	3	3	0.65	11.2	2.5	Retail Building Supply	13
536	Birmingham Steel	4 7/16	8.35	53%	4	4	0.60	NMF	NIL	Steel (General)	48
1631	Dixie Group	6 1/16	11.50	53%	3	4	1.20	5.2	NIL	Textile	55
573	Fansteel Inc.	3 3/8	6.40	53%	4	3	0.75	8.7	NIL	Metal Fabricating	47
653	HEALTHSOUTH Corp.	5 3/16	9.90	53%	4	4	1.55	8.1	NIL	Medical Services	30
1785	K2, Inc.	7 7/16	14.00	53%	3	3	0.80	6.9	NIL	Recreation	40
1525	Nash Finch Co.	7 7/8	14.95	53%	3	3	0.80	6.4	4.6	Food Wholesalers	17
878	Ryland Group	17	32.30	53%	2	3	1.20	3.7	0.9	Homebuilding	26
671	US Oncology Inc.	4 1/16	7.75	53%	3	4	1.40	6.2	NIL	Medical Services	30
1644	Dillard's, Inc.	17	31.75	54%	4	3	1.00	6.4	0.9	Retail Store	41
1634	Interface Inc. 'A'	4 7/16	8.10	54%	3	3	1.20	8.1	4.1	Textile	55
341	AutoNation, Inc.	7 1/4	13.30	55%	4	5	1.20	9.7	NIL	Industrial Services	61
1123	Gen'l Binding	7	12.70	55%	5	4	0.35	NMF	NIL	Office Equip & Supplies	67
614	Old Republic	11	20.00	55%	5	3	1.05	6.4	5.3	Insurance(Prop/Casualty)	90
602	Berkley (W.R.)	16	28.65	56%	5	3	0.85	NMF	3.3	Insurance(Prop/Casualty)	90
884	Building Materials	10	17.70	56%	2	3	0.85	5.3	NIL	Retail Building Supply	13
619	SAFECO Corp.	21	37.75	56%	5	2	1.00	11.3	7.2	Insurance(Prop/Casualty)	90
1345	Terex Corp.	12	21.50	56%	3	3	1.20	3.6	NIL	Machinery	53
731	Western Resources	16	28.65	56%	5	3	0.35	9.1	7.5	Electric Util. (Central)	87
711	Entergy Corp.	20	35.35	57%	5	3	0.55	8.4	6.0	Electric Util. (Central)	87
1371	Park-Ohio	8 3/4	15.40	57%	4	4	1.05	5.8	NIL	Diversified Co.	63
1376	Sequa Corp. 'A'	37	65.00	57%	4	3	0.70	17.7	NIL	Diversified Co.	63
421	Tesoro Petroleum	9 7/16	16.40	57%	4	3	1.05	NMF	NIL	Petroleum (Integrated)	51
882	Webb (Del) Corp.	15	26.10	57%	3	3	1.15	3.9	NIL	Homebuilding	26
869	Beazer Homes USA	18	31.10	58%	3	3	1.10	4.0	NIL	Homebuilding	26
120	Cooper Tire & Rubber	11	18.85	58%	4	3	1.00	5.5	4.2	Tire & Rubber	86
607	Fremont Gen'l	6 1/2	11.25	58%	5	3	0.90	9.8	4.9	Insurance(Prop/Casualty)	90
1128	Nashua Corp.	8	13.70	58%	5	3	0.60	44.4	NIL	Office Equip & Supplies	67
330	Schlotzsky's, Inc.	6 7/8	11.85	58%	4	3	0.95	9.1	NIL	Restaurant	58
1208	UNUMProvident Corp.	15	25.95	58%	5	3	1.35	5.8	4.0	Insurance (Life)	75
572	Amcast Industrial	12	20.35	59%	4	3	0.80	6.7	4.7	Metal Fabricating	47
1550	Champion Enterprises	6 1/4	10.70	59%	5	3	1.30	5.3	NIL	Manuf. Housing/Rec Veh	82
588	Cleveland-Cliffs	24	40.75	59%	4	2	0.85	8.9	6.3	Steel (General)	48
1704	Jo-Ann Stores	9 5/8	16.35	59%	3	3	0.75	6.6	NIL	Retail (Special Lines)	16
1654	Penney (J.C.)	16	27.35	59%	5	3	0.90	10.4	7.2	Retail Store	41
567	Raytheon Co. 'A'	20	34.10	59%	5	3	1.00	15.9	4.0	Aerospace/Defense	71
811	Rite Aid Corp.	7	11.85	59%	5	3	0.85	36.8	NIL	Drugstore	80
900	Bassett Furniture	14	23.30	60%	4	3	0.75	8.8	5.7	Furn./Home Furnishings	49
162	Cen. Vermont Pub. Serv.	10	16.75	60%	3	4	0.65	8.4	8.8	Electric Utility (East)	85
1649	Kmart Corp.	8 11/16	14.45	60%	3	3	1.05	7.4	NIL	Retail Store	41
618	Reliance Group Holdings	5 1/8	8.45	60%	3	3	1.10	NMF	NIL	Insurance(Prop/Casualty)	90
122	TBC Corp.	5 1/8	8.55	60%	3	3	0.90	5.2	NIL	Tire & Rubber	86
1136	TAB Products	5 7/8	9.85	60%	3	3	0.75	NMF	3.4	Office Equip & Supplies	67
315	CBRL Group	8 15/16	14.55	61%	5	3	1.00	7.4	0.2	Restaurant	58
2142	CIT Group 'A'	14	23.05	61%	4	3	1.10	5.8	2.9	Financial Svcs. (Div.)	33
945	Crown Cork	14	22.80	61%	4	3	1.00	5.9	7.1	Packaging & Container	64
2202	Policy Mgmt. Sys.	8 5/8	14.05	61%	5	3	0.90	11.5	NIL	Computer Software & Svcs	9
877	Pulte Corp.	17	28.00	61%	3	3	1.05	4.0	1.1	Homebuilding	26
1678	Blair Corp.	18	29.20	62%	3	3	0.55	8.1	3.3	Retail (Special Lines)	16
1134	Standard Register	13	21.10	62%	5	3	0.55	8.6	7.1	Office Equip & Supplies	67
830	Tower Automotive	12	19.35	62%	3	3	1.10	5.1	NIL	Auto Parts (OEM)	60
311	Avado Brands	4 1/8	6.50	63%	–	4	0.85	6.6	1.5	Restaurant	58
859	Int'l Aluminum	19	30.25	63%	5	2	0.55	15.3	6.3	Building Materials	73
1127	Moore Corp	4 1/2	7.20	63%	4	3	0.80	9.6	4.4	Office Equip & Supplies	67
1131	OfficeMax	6 11/16	10.65	63%	3	3	1.25	18.1	NIL	Office Equip & Supplies	67

***If fiscal 2000 Book Value not available, estimate used.**

Source: Value Line Publishing, Inc.

FIGURE 11.6 **Companies with Free Cash Flow Often Make Attractive Takeover Candidates**

BIGGEST "FREE FLOW" CASH GENERATORS

Stocks of companies that have earned more "cash flow" in the last 5 years than was required to build plant and pay dividends

Page No.	Stock Name	Recent Price	Ratio "Cash Flow" To Cash Out	Timeliness	Safety Rank	Industry Group	Industry Rank
1832	Playboy Enterprises 'B'	23	32.57	3	3	Publishing	34
880	Toll Brothers	18	18.23	2	3	Homebuilding	26
881	U.S. Home	35	13.49	–	3	Homebuilding	26
877	Pulte Corp.	17	12.25	3	3	Homebuilding	26
241	VISX, Inc.	17	11.06	3	3	Medical Supplies	21
2180	Computer Associates	66	10.92	1	3	Computer Software & Svcs	9
2217	CMGI, Inc.	128	10.56	2	3	Internet	5
804	Telefonica SA ADR	87	8.98	2	3	Foreign Telecom.	6
136	Dionex Corp.	31	8.26	3	3	Precision Instrument	15
2194	Microsoft Corp.	91	8.16	2	2	Computer Software & Svcs	9
2149	Eaton Vance Corp.	42	8.01	2	3	Financial Svcs. (Div.)	33
1387	Thermo Instrument	16	7.49	3	3	Diversified Co.	63
1038	Plantronics Inc.	80	7.32	2	3	Electronics	3
2196	Network Assoc.	30	7.19	3	4	Computer Software & Svcs	9
2182	Compuware Corp.	22	7.13	2	3	Computer Software & Svcs	9
2199	Parametric Technology	30	7.10	3	3	Computer Software & Svcs	9
2144	Cendant Corp.	17	6.63	1	4	Financial Svcs. (Div.)	33
373	Tetra Tech	26	6.49	2	3	Environmental	89
357	Modis Professional	16	6.37	3	4	Industrial Services	61
214	Enzo Biochem	82	6.26	2	4	Medical Supplies	21
228	Patterson Dental	35	6.09	2	3	Medical Supplies	21
1022	Arrow Electronics	31	6.05	2	3	Electronics	3
1253	Forest Labs.	67	5.84	3	3	Drug	11
672	WellPoint Health Ntwks	62	5.76	2	3	Medical Services	30
1384	Thermedics Inc.	8 13/16	5.42	3	3	Diversified Co.	63
1386	Thermo Fibertek	7 3/16	5.25	3	3	Diversified Co.	63
282	Heartland Express	14	5.21	3	3	Trucking/Transp. Leasing	23
2162	Price (T. Rowe) Assoc.	33	5.15	2	3	Financial Svcs. (Div.)	33
675	Health Mgmt. Systems	4 15/16	5.00	3	4	Healthcare Information	81
2174	BMC Software	50	4.94	3	3	Computer Software & Svcs	9
1091	Cisco Systems	66	4.91	1	3	Computer & Peripherals	10
662	PacifiCare Health	46	4.82	3	3	Medical Services	30
1093	Dell Computer	43	4.72	3	3	Computer & Peripherals	10
1252	Elan Corp. ADR	42	4.71	2	3	Drug	11
194	AmeriSource Health 'A'	15	4.68	2	3	Medical Supplies	21
764	TV Guide 'A'	45	4.68	–	4	Telecom. Services	28
1555	Thor Inds.	25	4.67	2	3	Manuf. Housing/Rec Veh	82
1280	Watson Pharmac.	39	4.67	3	3	Drug	11
1797	Chris-Craft	68	4.63	3	2	Entertainment	57
873	Hovnanian Enterpr. 'A'	5 7/8	4.57	3	4	Homebuilding	26
784	PairGain Technology	18	4.55	–	4	Telecom. Equipment	7
871	Centex Corp.	20	4.35	4	3	Homebuilding	26
1338	Roper Inds.	27	4.34	2	3	Machinery	53
645	Apria Healthcare	15	4.29	2	5	Medical Services	30
2188	Gartner Group 'A'	15	4.21	3	3	Computer Software & Svcs	9
1683	CDW Computer Ctrs	62	4.14	1	3	Retail (Special Lines)	16
1794	AMFM Inc.	64	4.13	–	4	Entertainment	57
874	Kaufman & Broad Home	19	4.13	2	3	Homebuilding	26
789	Tellabs, Inc.	52	4.10	2	3	Telecom. Equipment	7
1661	Barry (R.G.)	2 15/16	4.08	5	3	Shoe	42
1058	C-Cube Microsystems	96	4.03	–	4	Semiconductor	2
1615	Jones Apparel Group	26	4.01	2	3	Apparel	52
1500	Tootsie Roll Ind.	29	4.01	4	1	Food Processing	78
1078	Xilinx Inc.	75	3.99	1	3	Semiconductor	2
1104	MICROS Systems	51	3.98	1	3	Computer & Peripherals	10
209	Cooper Cos.	27	3.92	2	3	Medical Supplies	21
654	Humana Inc.	7 3/4	3.92	4	3	Medical Services	30
507	MacDermid Inc.	35	3.92	2	3	Chemical (Specialty)	50
2211	Transaction Sys. 'A'	46	3.90	3	3	Computer Software & Svcs	9
651	First Health Group	25	3.87	3	3	Medical Services	30
879	Standard Pacific Corp.	10	3.83	2	3	Homebuilding	26
151	Sybron Int'l	28	3.75	3	3	Precision Instrument	15
2166	United Asset Mgmt.	15	3.73	4	3	Financial Svcs. (Div.)	33
2171	Autodesk, Inc.	45	3.68	3	3	Computer Software & Svcs	9
1332	Lindsay Mfg.	17	3.67	3	3	Machinery	53
1074	QLogic Corp.	149	3.60	1	4	Semiconductor	2
2177	Ceridian Corp.	20	3.57	5	3	Computer Software & Svcs	9
1468	Celestial Seasonings	28	3.56	2	3	Food Processing	78
838	Playtex Products	13	3.54	3	3	Toiletries/Cosmetics	69
892	Centex Construction	23	3.52	3	3	Cement & Aggregates	38
1081	Electro Scientific	58	3.52	1	3	Semiconductor Cap Equip	1
2170	Adobe Systems	100	3.49	1	3	Computer Software & Svcs	9
2161	Power Corp.	21	3.49	3	3	Financial Svcs. (Div.)	33
1798	Clear Channel	69	3.43	3	3	Entertainment	57
208	Conmed Corp.	28	3.43	3	4	Medical Supplies	21
1138	United Stationers	27	3.43	2	3	Office Equip & Supplies	67
1791	Topps Co.	7 3/8	3.42	1	3	Recreation	40
205	Biomet	32	3.36	2	3	Medical Supplies	21
2198	Oracle Corp.	72	3.36	1	3	Computer Software & Svcs	9
1112	Storage Technology	12	3.34	4	4	Computer & Peripherals	10
1263	Jones Pharma	45	3.33	1	3	Drug	11
1665	Reebok Int'l	8	3.32	4	3	Shoe	42
2175	BARRA, Inc.	36	3.31	2	3	Computer Software & Svcs	9
1092	Compaq Computer	26	3.30	3	3	Computer & Peripherals	10
1088	Amer. Power Conv.	32	3.27	1	3	Computer & Peripherals	10
361	Robert Half Int'l	44	3.25	2	3	Industrial Services	61
236	Stryker Corp.	55	3.25	2	3	Medical Supplies	21
1883	Input/Output	5 15/16	3.24	3	4	Oilfield Services/Equip.	45
2208	SunGard Data Sys.	33	3.24	3	3	Computer Software & Svcs	9
134	Cognex Co.	45	3.23	2	3	Precision Instrument	15
1663	Kenneth Cole 'A'	51	3.20	1	3	Shoe	42
343	CDI Corp.	19	3.19	3	3	Industrial Services	61
1694	Fossil Inc.	23	3.19	2	4	Retail (Special Lines)	16
2202	Policy Mgmt. Sys.	8 5/8	3.16	5	3	Computer Software & Svcs	9
1067	Linear Technology	102	3.14	1	3	Semiconductor	2
1094	EMC Corp.	118	3.13	1	3	Computer & Peripherals	10
211	Datascope Corp.	40	3.11	2	3	Medical Supplies	21
2147	Countrywide Credit	25	3.10	4	3	Financial Svcs. (Div.)	33
212	Dentsply Int'l	26	3.10	3	3	Medical Supplies	21
1084	Novellus Sys.	60	3.10	1	3	Semiconductor Cap Equip	1

BEST PERFORMING STOCKS

(Measured by Price Change in the Last 13 Weeks)

Page No.	Stock Name	Recent Price	Percent Change In Price	Timeliness	Safety Rank
146	Newport Corp.	171	567.7%	2	4
758	Paging Network	3	340.9%	–	5
1429	TIBCO Software	130	336.8%	–	4
776	Ciena Corp.	177	305.2%	2	4
778	E-TEK Dynamics	297	288.3%	–	3
1257	Human Genome	225	272.7%	3	4
135	Coherent, Inc.	100	268.4%	2	3
1073	PMC-Sierra	195	267.4%	1	4
1430	Westell Techn. 'A'	33	243.8%	2	4
2229	Ventro Corp.	226	239.3%	–	3
1261	Inhale Therapeutic	102	231.8%	3	4
1260	Immunex Corp.	219	224.7%	1	4
1021	ANADIGICS Inc.	95	222.9%	2	4
1422	Cephalon Inc.	70	221.7%	2	5
214	Enzo Biochem	82	212.2%	2	4
525	Network Appliance	190	204.1%	1	4
1753	Ariba, Inc.	280	197.7%	–	3
2173	BEA Systems	126	190.4%	2	4
1925	Verisign Inc.	251	174.5%	–	4
1056	Analog Devices	162	166.9%	1	3
1075	SDL Inc.	444	165.9%	1	4
1267	Millennium Pharmac.	256	165.2%	3	4
783	Oak Technology	18	165.1%	3	4
1074	QLogic Corp.	149	164.4%	1	4
1020	Adaptive Broadband	102	161.5%	2	4
1115	3Com Corp.	104	156.3%	3	3
147	PE Biosystems Group	106	155.7%	1	3
131	Agilent Technologies	109	154.1%	–	3
2230	VerticalNet, Inc.	115	149.8%	–	3
1787	PhotoWorks	7 1/2	144.9%	2	4
1030	JDS Uniphase	281	144.7%	1	4
296	OMI Corp.	3 15/16	142.3%	3	4
154	Veeco Instruments	98	138.9%	2	4
1259	IDEC Pharmac.	147	137.0%	2	4
1755	Harmonic, Inc.	141	128.1%	1	4
1097	Identix Inc.	20	127.3%	3	5
1066	LSI Logic	70	126.7%	1	4
1082	Kulicke & Soffa	80	124.7%	2	4
1033	Micrel Inc.	114	123.8%	1	4
373	Tetra Tech	26	123.7%	2	3
1077	Vitesse Semiconductor	106	121.1%	1	3

WORST PERFORMING STOCKS

(Measured by Price Change in the Last 13 Weeks)

Page No.	Stock Name	Recent Price	Percent Change In Price	Timeliness	Safety Rank
241	VISX, Inc.	17	–78.7%	3	3
233	Sola Int'l	5 1/8	–63.6%	4	4
1464	Aurora Foods	3 1/4	–63.4%	–	3
1506	Vlasic Foods Int'l	2 7/8	–62.3%	–	5
372	Safety-Kleen	4 3/8	–62.2%	4	4
237	Summit Technology	7 5/8	–60.0%	3	4
1281	E-LOAN, Inc.	9 5/8	–58.4%	–	5
1345	Terex Corp.	12	–57.3%	3	3
1691	drugstore.com	19	–57.1%	–	4
2202	Policy Mgmt. Sys.	8 5/8	–57.1%	5	3
1672	AnnTaylor Stores	19	–56.8%	4	4
1670	Abercrombie & Fitch	15	–53.9%	3	3
1688	Cost Plus Inc.	19	–53.1%	2	3
1208	UNUMProvident Corp.	15	–53.1%	5	3
658	Manor Care	9 3/8	–51.8%	–	3
1673	Ashford.com	9 13/16	–51.5%	–	4
1395	AK Steel Holding	8 1/16	–50.0%	5	3
1712	O'Reilly Automotive	12	–49.6%	3	3
1592	G&K Services 'A'	17	–49.4%	5	3
1139	Wallace Computer Serv.	10	–49.2%	5	3
1321	Foster Wheeler	5 3/16	–49.1%	5	3
1692	Enesco Group	6 1/8	–49.0%	–	3
641	U.S. Bancorp	18	–48.6%	4	3
1772	Action Performance	8 1/2	–48.3%	5	4
704	CMS Energy Corp.	17	–48.2%	4	3
2203	Red Hat, Inc.	56	–48.1%	–	4
352	Galileo Int'l	17	–47.9%	4	3
592	Oregon Steel Mills	4 1/4	–47.7%	5	4
1726	Tandy Corp.	40	–47.7%	2	3
1624	Tommy Hilfiger	14	–47.5%	5	3
1377	Service Corp. Int'l	3 13/16	–47.4%	5	3
1671	Amer. Eagle Outfitters	26	–47.1%	2	3
633	FirstMerit Corp.	14	–46.7%	3	3
957	Dial Corp.	15	–46.4%	3	3
1018	Thomas & Betts	23	–45.5%	4	2
631	First Tenn. National	18	–44.8%	5	2
1708	Linens'n Things	19	–43.8%	3	3
1339	Sauer Inc.	7 1/2	–43.7%	–	3
126	Maytag Corp.	27	–43.2%	4	3
947	Owens-Illinois	14	–42.8%	5	3
855	Armstrong World Inds.	19	–42.1%	5	2

Source: Value Line Publishing, Inc.

TABLE 11.3 **Common Criteria for Value Stocks**

Ample cash reserves (cash >10% of market cap)
Ample free cash flow to fund necessary investment (EBIDTA> capital spending)
Conservative dividend payout policy (dividend <75% of EPS)
Conservative financial structure (debt <50% of market cap)
Conservative issuance of common stock to managers and other employees (constant or falling number of shares outstanding)
Low price/book ratio relative to the market and a company's own history (P/B <75% of S&P 500 average)
Low price/cash flow ratio relative to the market and a company's own history (P/CF <75% of S&P 500 average)
Low price/earnings ratio relative to the market and a company's own history (P/E <75% of S&P 500 average)
Negative investor sentiment as reflected in poor financial ratings (S&P rating of B− or worse)
Significant dividend income (yield >150% of S&P 500 average)

generators, or companies that generate more cash flow than the amount required to build and expand plant and equipment investment.

Another widely available indicator of fundamental value is dividend yield, found by dividing a stock's annual cash dividend by its price. For example, a stock selling for $20 with a dividend of 50¢ has a 2.5% yield. As discussed in Chapters 5 and 8, the market-wide average dividend yield has tended to fall between 3% and 6%, with a typical average of roughly 4%. In today's market, the DJIA dividend yield of roughly 1.3% is a historic low. An individual company paying a dividend yield significantly above its own historic norm, or that of its peer group, might be deemed attractive. However, more information is needed to determine whether such a company is indeed a relative bargain. Is the company paying out more than is prudent? Does the high yield reflect a relatively low price? If so, why is the price depressed? What is the outlook for a dividend cut? *The Wall Street Journal* and most daily newspapers include dividend information in their daily stock price tables.

Table 11.3 shows a summary of commonly used financial criteria for identifying value stocks using widely available financial data. Although any single value stock would seldom embody all such criteria, most will fit the definition of a value stock on multiple dimensions.

Other Value Indicators

private-market value
Price that a knowledgeable private buyer would pay for the entire franchise.

Another useful indicator of fundamental value is **private-market value.** Private-market value is the price a knowledgeable private buyer would pay for the entire franchise. As such, it reflects on–balance sheet and off–balance sheet assets and liabilities. Private-market value is sometimes referred to as potential transaction price or acquisition value. It is often a more accurate reflection of fundamental value than stated book value, especially if a company is very conservative in its application of accounting principles. Unrecognized private-market value may prompt management to buy back the company's stock or seek a friendly suitor. During recent years, asset plays have not generated much interest among investors who seem to prize profit growth above all else.

An example of what sometimes occurs is provided by the Associated Group, a low-profile Pittsburgh holding company with stakes in AT&T, Liberty Media, and

Teligent, a wireless telecommunications company, worth considerably more than its stock price. In mid-1999, Associated Group's class B shares traded near $45 per share, giving the company a market value of $1.7 billion. At that time, a report issued by Deutsche Bank Securities calculated that Associated Group's interests in the above three companies was worth about $70 per Associated Group share. Associated also owns True Position, a leader in developing the technology to pinpoint the location of mobile phones. This business has strong growth prospects because of a federal mandate requiring the cellular phone industry to be able to locate two-thirds of 911 calls to within 125 meters by October 2001. Including True Position, Deutsche Bank valued Associated Group's assets at $78 per share.

Associated Group traded at such a deep discount to its asset value because the company had huge embedded capital gains on its equity holdings. The company, controlled by the Berkman family, was an early investor in Tele-Communications Inc., which merged into AT&T. Its equity stakes had a cost basis of just $7 million. Deutsche Bank said that even if the company's portfolio was discounted at 20% to account for capital gains taxes, that still left a value of $64 per Associated Group share.

Interestingly, this "undervalued situation" did not last long. On June 1, 1999, just days after the favorable Deutsche Bank report, Associated Group announced that it had entered into a merger agreement with AT&T and its Liberty Media Corporation subsidiary. Management of both companies decided that such a combination was the most tax-efficient manner of realizing the value of Associated's holdings because, in effect, AT&T and Liberty could buy back their own stock at a discount. (Companies pay no taxes on capital gains realized when they buy back their own stock.) Interestingly, shortly after the AT&T and Liberty Media offer was announced, the price of Associated Group's stock rose to $64 per share.

Liquidation value reflects the value of a company's assets if the company ceased operations as a going concern. For example, how much could trucks, tankers, or idle real estate fetch in a "fire sale"? Perhaps a warehousing company is in decline, but its buildings are on valuable property; is this reflected in the stock price? Important intangible assets are also sometimes neglected by the market. Monopolies or near-monopolies sometimes have well-known brand names that are not reflected on company balance sheets or in stock prices. If these unrecognized assets could be used to generate strong sales and cash flow, the stock may be cheap. Perhaps the company's "true" value can be realized by a change in management or ownership. Thus, the relationship between intangibles, cash flow, and profits is of interest to value investors.

enlightened corporate governance Knowledgeable management that shares stockholder interests in value maximization.

Enlightened corporate governance is another fundamental value indicator. Value investors want to know that management shares stockholder interests in value maximization. It is always relevant to ask if management is knowledgeable to act in shareholder interests. Similarly, it is worthwhile to investigate the extent to which stock options and insider ownership give managers strong incentives to maximize the value of the firm. Many value investors would shun investment alternatives in which top managers have little or no ownership interest in the company.

value catalyst Any stimulus that will help close any discount between market cap and private-market value.

Finally, the concept of a **value catalyst** is often important in value investing. A value catalyst is an inside or outside stimulus that will help close any discount between the current market price of a stock and the prorated value of the company based on its private-market value. A crucial question often revolves around the timing of the value catalyst. Is it predictable?

Examples of value catalysts might include changes in regulation, such as the recent change in federal limitations on local television station ownership that allowed broadcasters to buy more local affiliates. Prices for local television stations surged in the aftermath. Pending changes in the rules governing local versus long-distance telephone service are sure to affect competition in the blossoming markets for wireless communications, data storage and retrieval, video on demand, Internet access and content, and so on. In other instances, a value catalyst might involve a change in corporate control that ousts inefficient managers in favor of shareholder-friendly management.

WALL STREET WISDOM 11.2

Nasdaq: The Lake Woebegone Market

On March 9, 2000, the technology-dominated Nasdaq Composite Index rolled through the 5000 mark, stunning bulls and bears alike. Nobody expected anything like that, not so soon after first piercing the 4000 level on December 29, 1999. It was only on November 3, 1999, that Nasdaq first breached the 3000 mark. Nasdaq 2000 fell on July 16, 1998, and Nasdaq 1000 was only reached on July 17, 1995. Never in stock market history has so rampant a bull market run wild, and never has the action been as wild as on Nasdaq.

Traditional valuation metrics have been thrown out the window, if not thrown forcefully *through* the window. At the end of February 2000, the price/earnings ratio on the Nasdaq reached the nosebleed level of 245.7 : 1. Think of it, at the end of the most rampant bull market in stock market history, the P/E on Nasdaq is more than 10 times higher than the P/E of the Dow Jones Industrial Average! Throw out talk of New Economy/Old Economy stocks; this is a market in which economic considerations do not matter. Throw out talk of a Tech Bubble and Tulip Mania. Do not even mention 1989 and the Japanese Nikkei Index at 39,500 and more than 100 times earnings. At 5000, Nasdaq valuation is bigger than the Japanese market, and P/E levels are not even close. Nothing is close to Nasdaq's recent performance in stock market history.

In 2000, Nasdaq defied almost all expectations by adding to its historic 86% gain in 1999 with an even stronger start to the year. Surprisingly, Nasdaq accomplished this without depending on a handful of stalwarts. Nasdaq's biggest market value gainers from 4000 to 5000 include Intel, up 41% to $395 billion; Juniper Networks, up 150% to $43 billion; and PMC-Sierra Inc., up 230% to $33 billion. None were among the top 10 contributors to the Nasdaq's move from 3000 to 4000. Move over traditional high-tech stalwarts such as Microsoft, Cisco, and Dell, the new leaders are Veritas, JDS Uniphase, and Qualcomm. As these high-tech upstarts have soared, they have sucked the air out from under the rest of the market. As shown in the figure opposite, the P/E for tech stocks in the S&P 500 is more than 40, while the rest of the market languishes at a P/E of 12.5.

There is only one possible explanation.

Nasdaq is a Lake Woebegone market. Author and humorist Garrison Keillor is famous for his nationally syndicated PBS radio program titled "A Prairie Home Companion." Broadcast live from St. Paul, Minnesota, Prairie Home Companion is heard each week by 2.6 million listeners on more than 450 public radio stations. The show is set in the fanciful locale of Lake Woebegone, where all "the men are good looking, the women are strong, and all the children are above average." In the light of investors current love affair with Nasdaq and all things technology related, one can only conclude that all such stocks are not only above average, they are at least 10 times above average.

See: E. S. Browning, "Nasdaq Index Skids 199.66 Points, Spooked by Interest-Rate Concerns," *The Wall Street Journal,* May 24, 2000, C1, C12.

Looking at a Market Without Tech Stocks

The value, as measured by the price-to-earnings ratio, for the Standard & Poor's 500 Index would be significantly less if technology stocks were excluded. P/E ratio* for S&P technology issues and for all other issues.

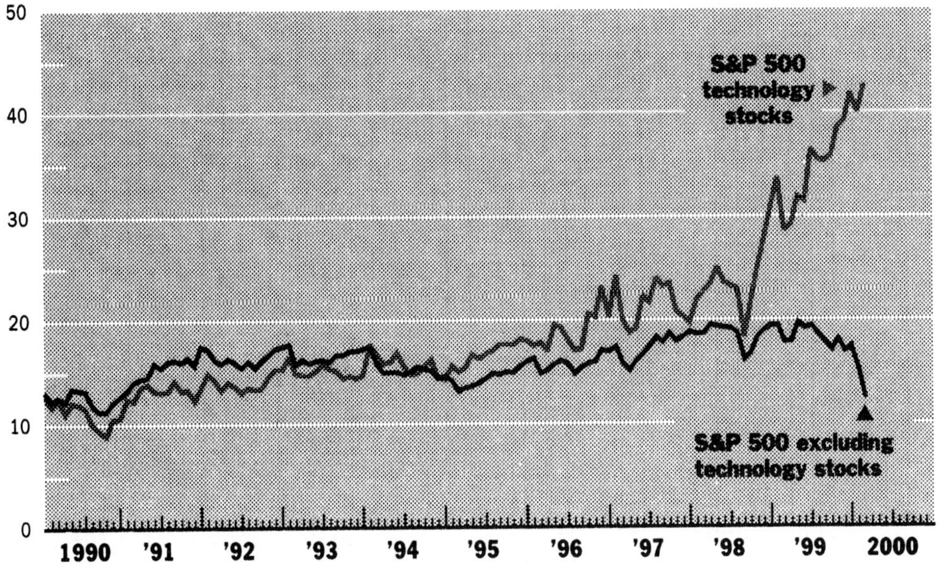

*Based on ratio of median company share price to IBES estimated 12-month earnings for the coming year.

Source: Wells Capital Management

Source: *The Wall Street Journal,* March 13, 2000, C1.

Dividends and Value Investing

Dividends Mitigate Risk

The goal of conservative stock investing is to achieve satisfactory long-term growth of capital without the extreme fluctuations that sometimes cause investors to cash out at just the wrong time. A hallmark of conservative stock portfolios is an emphasis on established companies with above-average dividend yields and dividend growth rates. Focusing on "cheap" stocks with secure dividends allows investors to participate in bull markets while minimizing the potential for loss tied to the market's inevitable downturns. To value investors, limiting downside risk is an important component of long-term value maximization.

Financial economist Myron Gordon is famous for declaring that dividends are the proverbial "bird in the hand" for stock market investors. When the dividend yield on an investor's portfolio is above average, the investor is guaranteed that at least one of the two components of investment return will be positive. The other, the change in portfolio market value, can be positive or negative. For example, a stock purchased at $40 per share that pays an annual dividend of $2 provides a 5%

annual yield (= \$2/\$40). If the stock's price grows 10%, or \$4, during the year, the total return to investors will equal 15%, or the dividend yield of 5% plus capital appreciation of 10%. If the share price declines 10%, a 5% dividend will offset one-half of the decline and cut the investor's overall loss to 5%. Because companies are extremely reluctant to cut dividends, the dividend yield tends to be much more predictable than capital gains. They constitute an important steadying influence on investor returns. The advantage of having dividend income play a prominent role in an investor's stock selection strategy is that such an approach reduces the risk of overpaying for a stock. This tends to lower downside risk and increase upside potential.

As shown in Figure 11.7, dividend yields have been in a long-term decline across all major segments of the U.S. market. From a market-wide perspective, the long-term decline in dividend yields reduces an important source of long-term returns on common stocks. During the 19th century, dividend yield constituted approximately 45–50% of the total rate of return earned by common stockholders. During the post–World War II period, dividend yield has accounted for approximately 25% of total returns. Historically, the best time to buy common stocks has been during periods when dividend yields were above average, such as 1982 when the dividend yield on the S&P 500 stood at roughly 6%. Below-average long-term rates of return typically follow periods of below-average dividend yields, such as 1972 when the dividend yield on the S&P 500 stood at roughly 3%. This should make investors cautious about long-term rates of return on common stocks at the start of the new millennium. A dividend yield of only 1.6% on the S&P 500 seems to portend an anemic expected rate of return on common stocks over the next several years. If dividends currently represent one-half of the expected rate of return on the S&P 500, the investor's expected return is only 3.2% per year (= 1.6%/0.5). If dividends presently represent one-quarter of the expected rate of return on common stocks, the investor's expected rate of return is only 6.4% per year (= 1.6%/0.25). In either event, the historically low dividend yields presently offered on common stocks suggests that investors should remain cautious.

Dividend Growth

For many investors, a portfolio of income-producing stocks is appealing because it has the potential to generate more stable income than a portfolio of bonds or money market securities. In an investment environment of declining interest rates, the proceeds from maturing bonds or called issues are reinvested at increasingly lower yields. This tends to reduce the income potential of fixed-income securities over time.

More important, dividend-paying stocks have the compelling virtue of offering income-motivated investors the opportunity for growing levels of dividend income over time. Dividend income for the S&P 500 has historically grown faster than the rate of inflation. Over time, rising dividend income on S&P 500 stocks has enabled investors to preserve and increase the buying power of their dividend income. If income-motivated investors are willing to accept some price fluctuation, owning stocks for dividend income is a viable long-term strategy. The key to this strategy's success is staying the course. An investor must remain invested in stocks for a number of years to see dividend income rise above the level of interest income that would have been earned on a similar fixed-income investment.

FIGURE 11.7 Dividend Yields Are at Historic Lows across All Market Segments

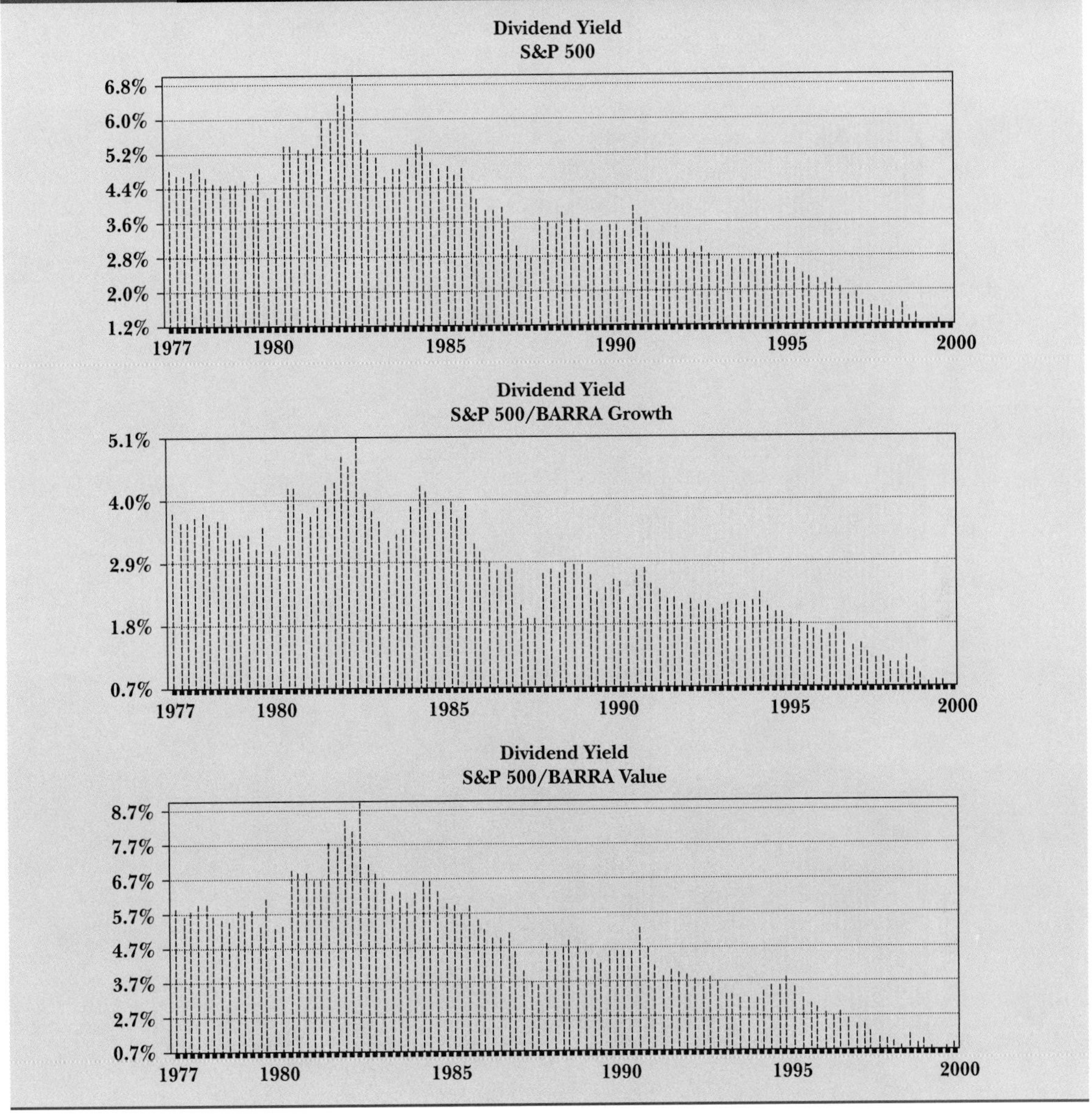

Data source: <http://www.barra.com>.

(continued)

For example, suppose an investor pays $50 for a share of stock in a company that pays a current dividend of $1 per share. Under these circumstances, the investor's dividend yield is 2%. If the company prospers and continues to pay out a similar share of its rising income stream, the cash dividend paid to investors will increase steadily. This dividend growth will provide investors with ever higher income on the original $50 investment. If dividend income grows by a modest 8%

FIGURE 11.7 ***(continued)***

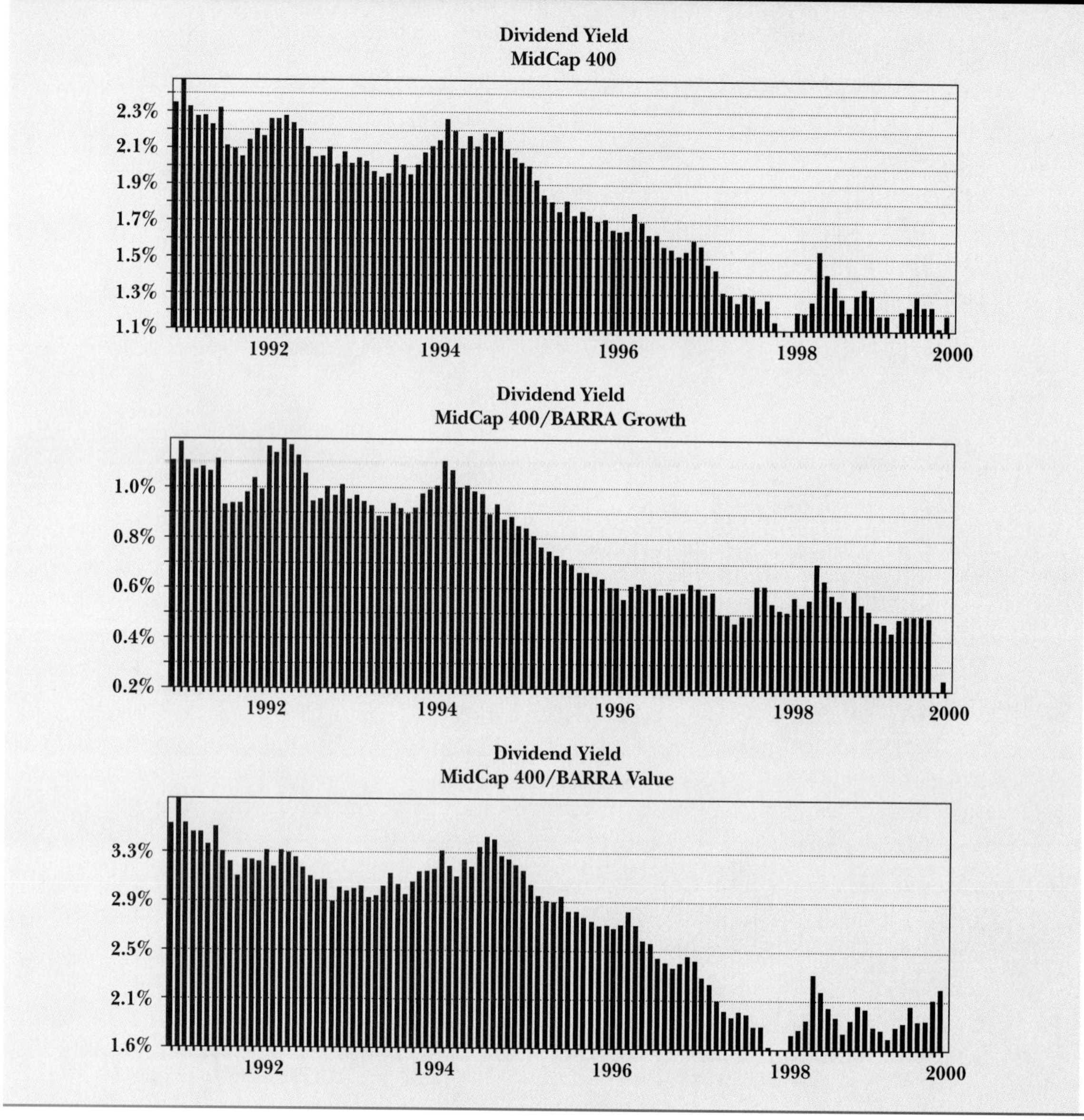

growth-and-income investors Investors who seek a relative balance between the goals of high and stable income and long-term capital growth.

per year, the dividend paid will rise to $6.85 per share in 25 years. As shown in Table 11.4, investors would then earn a 2% annual dividend on a stock price that has appreciated to $342.42 and a dividend yield of 13.7% on the original amount invested.

Notice how well **growth and income investors** fare when compared with the fixed-income investor. Even a below-market total return of 10% per year results in a substantial investment advantage over the 6% interest income earned by the fixed-income investor. In addition to substantial capital gains, notice how the stock

FIGURE 11.7 ***(continued)***

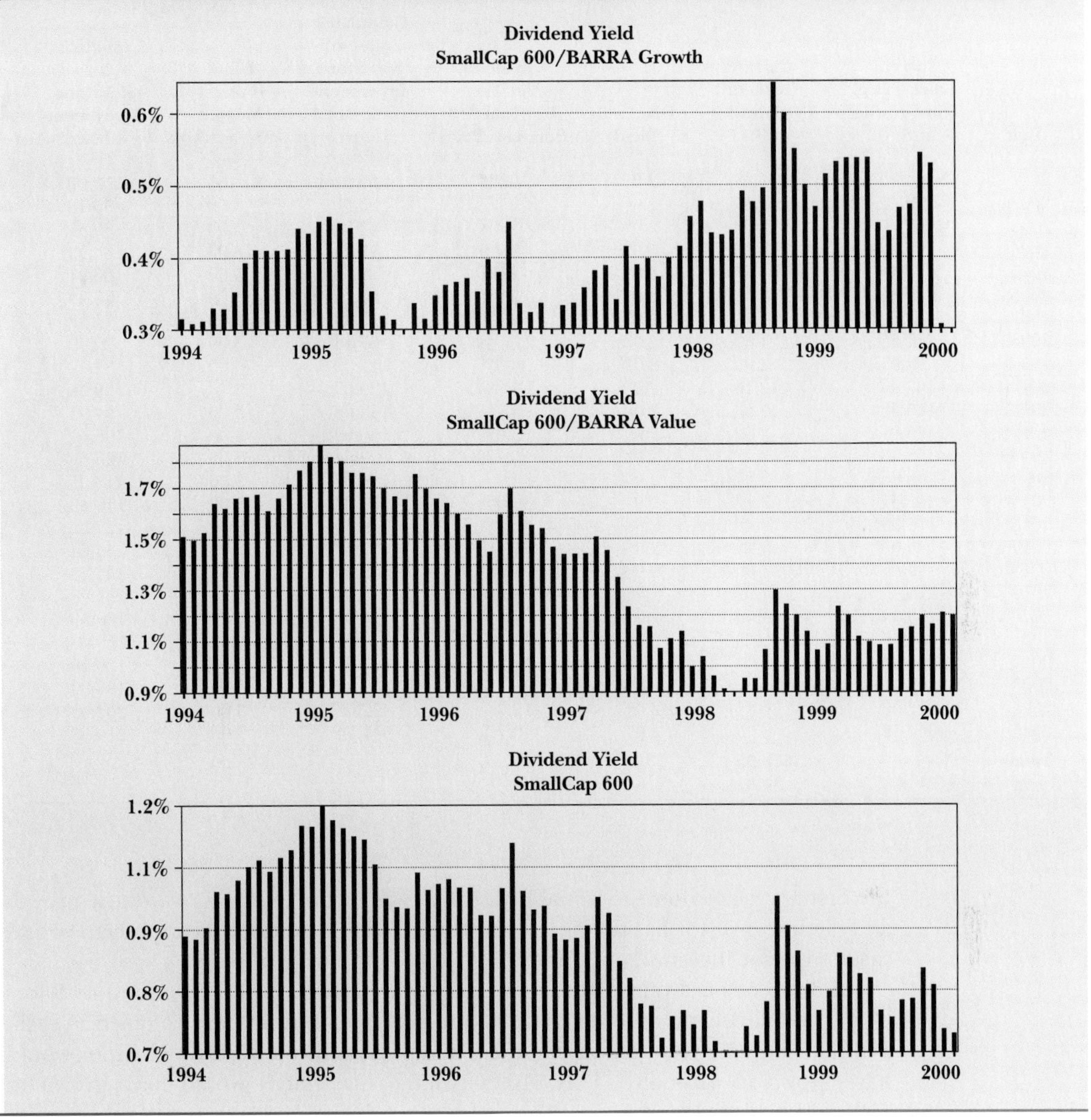

Data source: <http://www.barra.com>.

investor's dividend income exceeds the interest income earned by the fixed-income investor. Over this time frame, the growth and income investor gets to have his or her "cake" (capital gains) and "eat it" (dividend income) too! Observe how modest dividend growth of 8% per year has allowed a modest initial dividend yield of 2% per year to overcome the substantial interest income advantage initially enjoyed by a 6% bond. Of course, in the present example, the fixed-income investor would have the modest advantage of having received greater investment income during

TABLE 11.4 Dividend Growth Leads to a Rising Stream of Investment Income

Year	Current Stock Price ($50 Growing at 8%)	Current Dividend ($1 Growing at 8%)	Dividend Yield	Dividend Yield on Original $50 Purchase Price	Cumulative Value of $50 Stock Investment (10% Total Return)	Bond Interest Income ($50 at 6%)	Cumulative Value of $50 Bond Investment (6% Interest)
2001	$ 54.00	$ 1.08	2.0%	2.2%	$ 55.00	$ 3.00	$ 53.00
2002	58.32	1.17	2.0%	2.3%	60.50	3.00	56.18
2003	62.99	1.26	2.0%	2.5%	66.55	3.00	59.55
2004	68.02	1.36	2.0%	2.7%	73.21	3.00	63.12
2005	73.47	1.47	2.0%	2.9%	80.53	3.00	66.91
2006	79.34	1.59	2.0%	3.2%	88.58	3.00	70.93
2007	85.69	1.71	2.0%	3.4%	97.44	3.00	75.18
2008	92.55	1.85	2.0%	3.7%	107.18	3.00	79.69
2009	99.95	2.00	2.0%	4.0%	117.90	3.00	84.47
2010	107.95	2.16	2.0%	4.3%	129.69	3.00	89.54
2011	116.58	2.33	2.0%	4.7%	142.66	3.00	94.91
2012	125.91	2.52	2.0%	5.0%	156.92	3.00	100.61
2013	135.98	2.72	2.0%	5.4%	172.61	3.00	106.65
2014	146.86	2.94	2.0%	5.9%	189.87	3.00	113.05
2015	158.61	3.17	2.0%	6.3%	208.86	3.00	119.83
2016	171.30	3.43	2.0%	6.9%	229.75	3.00	127.02
2017	185.00	3.70	2.0%	7.4%	252.72	3.00	134.64
2018	199.80	4.00	2.0%	8.0%	278.00	3.00	142.72
2019	215.79	4.32	2.0%	8.6%	305.80	3.00	151.28
2020	233.05	4.66	2.0%	9.3%	336.37	3.00	160.36
2021	251.69	5.03	2.0%	10.1%	370.01	3.00	169.98
2022	271.83	5.44	2.0%	10.9%	407.01	3.00	180.18
2023	293.57	5.87	2.0%	11.7%	447.72	3.00	190.99
2024	317.06	6.34	2.0%	12.7%	492.49	3.00	202.45
2025	342.42	6.85	2.0%	13.7%	541.74	3.00	214.59
Totals		**$78.95**				**$75.00**	

the first few years after the initial investment was made. Going forward, the growth and income investor has the dual advantages of significant capital appreciation and vastly superior investment income.

If dividends are reinvested, they can play a powerful role in helping investors build capital. During the past 25 years, for example, if dividends are taken in cash, a $10,000 initial investment in the stocks comprising the S&P 500 Stock Index would have grown to $214,681. This $10,000 initial investment would have grown to $535,749 if all dividends were reinvested. Over this period, the total value of reinvested dividends was $321,068. As shown in Figure 11.8, reinvested dividend income accounts for more than one-half of the total return earned by long-term investors on the S&P 500 during this 25-year period.

Obviously, high and growing dividend income makes an important contribution to the long-term return achieved from common stock investments.

Dividends and Corporate Health

Dividends are also a useful indication of corporate profitability. Corporations are not obligated to share earnings with stockholders. This makes voluntary cash dividends a useful indicator of the size and likely persistence of company profitability.

FIGURE 11.8 **Reinvested Dividends Are a Big Part of Total Return for the S&P 500 (1975–Present)**

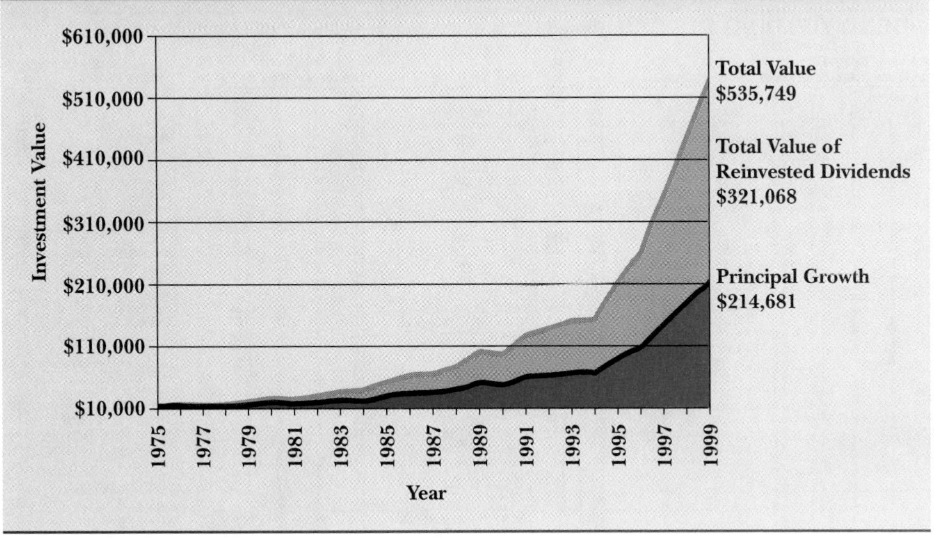

Data source: <http://www.barra.com>.

Obviously, cash dividends cannot be paid unless they are funded through current earnings, asset liquidations, or increased indebtedness. If a company is able to pay a $1 cash dividend without reducing company assets or taking on additional debt, this cash dividend represents a conservative assessment of corporate profitability during the period. This suggests that only highly profitable companies are able to pay high dividends. Moreover, because companies are loath to cut their dividend, a corporate policy of paying high dividends suggests that management has an optimistic view of the future. To the extent that rising dividends reflect rising profits, companies that consistently increase their dividends should enjoy rising share prices over time.

To be sure, dividend yields must be analyzed carefully. In assessing dividend yields, investors must be careful to search for yields that are both comparatively high and relatively safe. Most industrial companies distribute less than 50% of earnings in the form of cash dividends. They reinvest the rest in plant and equipment to facilitate future growth. Some solid utilities with scant growth prospects may pay out as much as 60–70% of total earnings in the form of dividend income. When the dividend payout ratio is much higher than that, the culprit may be transient earnings problems. In that case, company performance must be monitored to ensure that earnings problems are only temporary. If a permanent deterioration in the fundamental earning power of the company is evident, then a dividend cut is in the offing. In late 1999, escalating legal troubles suggested that the tobacco companies will have a difficult time maintaining the generous payouts shown in Figure 11.9.

equity-income investors Investors who stress income first and long-term capital growth second.

So-called **equity-income investors** stress income first and long-term capital growth second. Such portfolios have few, if any, equity holdings that do not provide significant dividend income. Capital appreciation is typically expected to result

FIGURE 11.9 High Current Dividends May Not Be Sustainable

Page 32 SUMMARY AND INDEX • THE VALUE LINE INVESTMENT SURVEY March 10, 2000

HIGHEST DIVIDEND YIELDING STOCKS (Based upon estimated year-ahead dividends per share)

Page No.	Stock Name	Recent Price	Timeliness	Safety Rank	Current P/E Ratio	% Est'd Yield	Industry Group	Industry Rank
1692	Enesco Group	6 1/8	–	3	4.8	18.4	Retail (Special Lines)	16
1581	R.J. Reynolds Tobacco	18	–	3	5.4	17.2	Tobacco	84
973	First Australia Prime	4 15/16	4	3	NMF	13.3	Investment Co.	68
970	ACM Gov't Income Fund	7	3	2	NMF	12.9	Investment Co.	68
977	Kemper High Income	7 7/8	4	4	NMF	12.3	Investment Co.	68
918	Crown Pacific Part.	19	3	3	16.4	12.0	Paper & Forest Products	36
1188	New Plan Excel R'lty	14	4	2	9.2	11.8	R.E.I.T.	56
386	Spain Fund	16	3	3	NMF	11.6	Investment Co.(Foreign)	14
590	G't Northern Iron	52	3	3	8.5	11.5	Steel (General)	48
1189	Penn. R.E.I.T.	17	4	3	10.6	11.1	R.E.I.T.	56
1193	United Dominion R'lty	9 3/4	3	3	25.8	11.0	R.E.I.T.	56
1578	British Amer Tobacco ADR	8 7/8	–	3	6.3	10.8	Tobacco	84
855	Armstrong World Inds.	19	5	2	3.7	10.5	Building Materials	73
928	Plum Creek Timber	23	4	3	15.5	10.3	Paper & Forest Products	36
976	Hancock (J) Patriot Div	7 3/4	4	2	NMF	10.1	Investment Co.	68
1235	Lyondell Chemical	8 7/8	4	3	11.4	10.1	Chemical (Basic)	65
1580	Philip Morris	20	4	3	5.8	10.0	Tobacco	84
1186	Federal Rlty. Inv. Trust	19	3	2	15.2	9.6	R.E.I.T.	56
979	MFS Multimarket Income	6	3	4	NMF	9.5	Investment Co.	68
1749	Puget Sound Energy	20	4	2	10.1	9.2	Electric Utility (West)	79
732	Wisconsin Energy	17	4	2	8.8	9.2	Electric Util. (Central)	87
972	Duff & Phelps Utilities	8 5/8	4	2	NMF	9.1	Investment Co.	68
1745	New Century Energies	26	–	2	8.2	9.0	Electric Utility (West)	79
183	RGS Energy Group	20	4	2	7.7	9.0	Electric Utility (East)	85
1567	Rank Group ADR	5 1/8	3	3	5.6	9.0	Foreign Electron/Entertn	29
342	Buckeye Partners L.P.	27	3	2	10.7	8.9	Industrial Services	61
1741	Hawaiian Elec.	28	4	2	9.5	8.9	Electric Utility (West)	79
471	KeySpan Corp.	20	–	2	11.2	8.9	Natural Gas (Distrib.)	70
730	WPS Resources	23	4	1	9.9	8.9	Electric Util. (Central)	87
1579	Gallaher Group ADR	17	4	3	7.8	8.8	Tobacco	84
1191	Simon Property Group	23	3	2	21.1	8.8	R.E.I.T.	56
1582	UST Inc.	20	3	2	7.4	8.8	Tobacco	84
173	GPU, Inc.	25	5	3	9.2	8.7	Electric Utility (East)	85
158	Amer. Elec. Power	28	4	2	12.3	8.6	Electric Utility (East)	85
706	Cinergy Corp.	21	4	2	8.6	8.6	Electric Util. (Central)	87
719	Northern States Power	17	5	1	10.2	8.6	Electric Util. (Central)	87
703	Ameren Corp.	30	5	1	10.4	8.5	Electric Util. (Central)	87
718	NiSource Inc.	13	4	1	8.7	8.5	Electric Util. (Central)	87
1184	Duke-Weeks R'lty	19	3	2	13.8	8.4	R.E.I.T.	56
181	Potomac Elec. Power	20	5	2	11.3	8.3	Electric Utility (East)	85
164	Consol. Edison	27	5	1	8.4	8.1	Electric Utility (East)	85
2134	Alliance Capital Mgmt.	37	2	3	12.3	8.0	Financial Svcs. (Div.)	33
1181	Archstone Communities	20	3	2	17.2	8.0	R.E.I.T.	56
613	Ohio Casualty	12	4	3	19.0	8.0	Insurance(Prop/Casualty)	90
712	FirstEnergy Corp.	19	3	3	7.3	7.9	Electric Util. (Central)	87
485	UGI Corp.	19	3	3	11.0	7.9	Natural Gas (Distrib.)	70
1195	Weingarten Realty	38	4	2	16.7	7.9	R.E.I.T.	56
1185	Equity Residential	40	3	3	26.8	7.8	R.E.I.T.	56
497	Ethyl Corp.	3 3/16	4	3	6.2	7.8	Chemical (Specialty)	50
1187	Kimco Realty	34	3	2	12.6	7.8	R.E.I.T.	56

Page No.	Stock Name	Recent Price	Timeliness	Safety Rank	Current P/E Ratio	% Est'd Yield	Industry Group	Industry Rank
721	OGE Energy	17	4	2	8.3	7.8	Electric Util. (Central)	87
723	Reliant Energy	20	3	2	8.5	7.8	Electric Util. (Central)	87
441	TransCanada Pipe.	6 7/8	–	3	10.6	7.8	Canadian Energy	25
1583	Universal Corp.	16	4	2	4.6	7.8	Tobacco	84
161	CH Energy Group	28	5	2	9.4	7.7	Electric Utility (East)	85
727	Texas Utilities	32	4	3	9.5	7.7	Electric Util. (Central)	87
1778	Cedar Fair L.P.	19	4	2	10.0	7.6	Recreation	40
1194	Washington R.E.I.T.	16	3	2	15.1	7.6	R.E.I.T.	56
729	UtiliCorp United	16	4	3	8.7	7.5	Electric Util. (Central)	87
731	Western Resources	16	5	3	9.1	7.5	Electric Util. (Central)	87
1182	BRE Properties	23	3	2	14.6	7.4	R.E.I.T.	56
182	Public Serv. Enterprise	29	4	2	8.6	7.4	Electric Utility (East)	85
1484	Int'l Multifoods	11	5	3	8.2	7.3	Food Processing	78
160	Carolina Power & Lt.	29	4	1	9.9	7.2	Electric Utility (East)	85
167	Dominion Resources	36	3	2	14.2	7.2	Electric Utility (East)	85
1909	Imperial Chem. ADR	32	3	3	11.3	7.2	Chemical (Diversified)	59
715	Kansas City Power & Lt.	23	4	2	13.9	7.2	Electric Util. (Central)	87
717	Minnesota Power	15	4	2	9.5	7.2	Electric Util. (Central)	87
1654	Penney (J.C.)	16	5	3	10.4	7.2	Retail Store	41
619	SAFECO Corp.	21	5	2	11.3	7.2	Insurance(Prop/Casualty)	90
186	TECO Energy	19	4	1	12.0	7.2	Electric Utility (East)	85
702	Alliant Energy	28	–	2	12.3	7.1	Electric Util. (Central)	87
945	Crown Cork	14	4	3	5.9	7.1	Packaging & Container	64
709	DTE Energy	29	5	2	8.7	7.1	Electric Util. (Central)	87
1751	Sierra Pacific Res.	14	–	3	9.9	7.1	Electric Utility (West)	79
1134	Standard Register	13	5	3	8.6	7.1	Office Equip & Supplies	67
440	TransAlta Corp.	14	5	2	26.4	7.1	Canadian Energy	25
2127	Union Planters	28	4	3	8.8	7.1	Bank	77
157	Allegheny Energy	25	4	1	9.0	7.0	Electric Utility (East)	85
610	HSB Group	25	5	2	12.5	7.0	Insurance(Prop/Casualty)	90
802	Telecom N. Zealand ADR	34	3	2	15.8	7.0	Foreign Telecom.	6
187	United Illuminating	41	3	2	11.1	7.0	Electric Utility (East)	85
627	Bank One Corp.	26	5	3	7.3	6.9	Bank (Midwest)	72
467	Cascade Natural Gas	14	3	3	10.8	6.9	Natural Gas (Distrib.)	70
127	National Presto Ind.	32	4	2	11.0	6.9	Home Appliance	66
479	Peoples Energy	29	4	1	10.5	6.9	Natural Gas (Distrib.)	70
482	SEMCO Energy	12	3	3	11.2	6.9	Natural Gas (Distrib.)	70
465	Atmos Energy	17	5	2	9.4	6.8	Natural Gas (Distrib.)	70
266	British Airways ADR	47	4	3	NMF	6.8	Air Transport	83
502	Hercules Inc.	16	4	3	7.1	6.8	Chemical (Specialty)	50
472	Laclede Gas	20	3	1	12.8	6.8	Natural Gas (Distrib.)	70
2115	KeyCorp	17	5	2	7.4	6.7	Bank	77
980	Nuveen Muni Value Fund	8 1/8	4	2	NMF	6.7	Investment Co.	68
523	WD-40 Co.	19	5	2	12.9	6.7	Chemical (Specialty)	50
1139	Wallace Computer Serv.	10	5	3	NMF	6.6	Office Equip & Supplies	67
477	Northwest Nat. Gas	19	3	2	11.6	6.5	Natural Gas (Distrib.)	70
1172	People's Bank	18	4	3	9.7	6.5	Thrift	76
464	AGL Resources	17	3	2	14.8	6.4	Natural Gas (Distrib.)	70
163	Conectiv	14	–	3	7.9	6.4	Electric Utility (East)	85
710	Empire Dist. Elec.	20	–	2	13.1	6.4	Electric Util. (Central)	87

Source: Value Line Publishing, Inc.

as individual holdings move from undervalued to fairly valued following an improvement in investor sentiment. Dividend growth is not expected to stem from rapid earnings gains by portfolio companies. Equity-income portfolios typically have dividend yields considerably higher than that of the overall market. They have strong appeal for retired investors seeking added income.

Growth and income investors seek a relative balance between the goals of high and stable income and long-term capital growth. Although growth and income portfolios have dividend yields that generally exceed that earned by the overall market, some stocks may be chosen primarily for their growth potential. If so, other holdings are typically selected to compensate on the income side. Stocks with relatively little current dividend income may be deemed attractive to a growth and income investor if the potential for future dividend growth is especially strong. The combination of lower current income and a greater emphasis on earnings growth tends to make growth and income investing somewhat more volatile than equity-income investing.

dividend-growth investors Investors who place primary emphasis on the potential for dividend growth in their stock selection strategy.

Dividend-growth investors place primary emphasis on the potential for dividend growth in their stock selection strategy. Consistent dividend growth is often associated with companies able to grow earnings faster than the rate of inflation.

FIGURE 11.9 ***(continued)***

STOCKS WITH HIGHEST 3- TO 5-YEAR PRICE APPRECIATION POTENTIAL

Some of the stocks tabulated below are very risky and appreciation potentialities tentative. Please read the full-page reports in Ratings & Reports to gain an understanding of the risks entailed. Some of these stocks may not be timely investment commitments. (See the Performance Ranks below.)

Page No.	Stock Name	Recent Price	3- to 5-year Potential	Timeliness	Safety Rank	Industry Group	Industry Rank
1464	Aurora Foods	3 1/4	580%	–	3	Food Processing	78
1377	Service Corp. Int'l	3 13/16	560%	5	3	Diversified Co.	63
1554	Oakwood Homes	2 9/16	535%	5	4	Manuf. Housing/Rec Veh	82
358	Navigant Consulting	9 13/16	510%	–	3	Industrial Services	61
112	Federal-Mogul	14	490%	3	3	Auto Parts (Replacement)	88
1321	Foster Wheeler	5 3/16	475%	5	3	Machinery	53
1717	PETsMART Inc.	3 3/8	475%	3	4	Retail (Special Lines)	16
1098	Ingram Micro 'A'	11	470%	4	3	Computer & Peripherals	10
836	Helen of Troy Ltd.	6 3/4	450%	4	3	Toiletries/Cosmetics	69
1715	Pep Boys	6	440%	4	3	Retail (Special Lines)	16
1208	UNUMProvident Corp.	15	435%	5	3	Insurance (Life)	75
2202	Policy Mgmt. Sys.	8 5/8	425%	5	3	Computer Software & Svcs	9
1661	Barry (R.G.)	2 15/16	415%	5	3	Shoe	42
1628	Burlington Inds.	3 1/16	415%	5	4	Textile	55
2228	theglobe.com	7 3/4	415%	–	4	Internet	5
153	Tokheim Corp.	2 7/8	415%	4	5	Precision Instrument	15
1772	Action Performance	8 1/2	400%	5	4	Recreation	40
2183	Corel Corp.	15	400%	3	5	Computer Software & Svcs	9
1701	Heilig-Meyers	3 3/16	400%	4	4	Retail (Special Lines)	16
781	Loral Space & Commun.	15	400%	3	3	Telecom. Equipment	7
1733	Wet Seal 'A'	11	400%	5	4	Retail (Special Lines)	16
854	Apogee Enterprises	4 7/16	390%	5	3	Building Materials	73
855	Armstrong World Inds.	19	385%	5	2	Building Materials	73
233	Sola Int'l	5 1/8	380%	4	4	Medical Supplies	21
311	Avado Brands	4 1/8	375%	–	4	Restaurant	58
279	Budget Group	5 13/16	375%	3	4	Trucking/Transp. Leasing	23
1869	Pioneer Natural Res.	8 7/16	375%	3	4	Petroleum (Producing)	18
671	US Oncology Inc.	4 1/16	375%	3	4	Medical Services	30
274	US Airways Group	19	360%	4	5	Air Transport	83
1484	Int'l Multifoods	11	355%	5	3	Food Processing	78
372	Safety-Kleen	4 3/8	355%	4	4	Environmental	89
1137	U.S. Office Products	2 3/4	345%	–	4	Office Equip & Supplies	67
1345	Terex Corp.	12	340%	3	3	Machinery	53
1550	Champion Enterprises	6 1/4	335%	5	3	Manuf. Housing/Rec Veh	82
281	Consol. Freightways	6 1/4	335%	4	4	Trucking/Transp. Leasing	23
139	Gerber Scientific	15	335%	2	3	Precision Instrument	15
1212	Battle Mtn. Gold Co.	2 1/16	330%	3	5	Gold/Silver Mining	43
1812	Hilton Hotels	7	330%	–	4	Hotel/Gaming	27
811	Rite Aid Corp.	7	330%	5	3	Drugstore	80
389	Templeton Emerg'g	11	330%	3	4	Investment Co.(Foreign)	14
1102	Key Tronic	3 3/8	325%	3	5	Computer & Peripherals	10
1139	Wallace Computer Serv.	10	325%	5	3	Office Equip & Supplies	67
315	CBRL Group	8 15/16	320%	5	3	Restaurant	58
862	Johns-Manville	8 5/16	320%	3	5	Building Materials	73
873	Hovnanian Enterpr. 'A'	5 7/8	315%	3	4	Homebuilding	26
276	AMERCO	17	310%	3	4	Trucking/Transp. Leasing	23
1672	AnnTaylor Stores	19	310%	4	4	Retail (Special Lines)	16
341	AutoNation, Inc.	7 1/4	310%	4	5	Industrial Services	61
133	Checkpoint Systems	7 7/8	310%	3	3	Precision Instrument	15
1692	Enesco Group	6 1/8	310%	–	3	Retail (Special Lines)	16

Page No.	Stock Name	Recent Price	3- to 5-year Potential	Timeliness	Safety Rank	Industry Group	Industry Rank
331	Shoney's Inc.	1 1/8	310%	4	5	Restaurant	58
834	Chattem Inc.	18	305%	3	4	Toiletries/Cosmetics	69
351	Fairchild Corp. 'A'	6 13/16	305%	4	4	Industrial Services	61
1907	Grace (W. R.)	9 15/16	305%	–	3	Chemical (Diversified)	59
1492	Pilgrim's Pride 'B'	7 7/16	305%	4	3	Food Processing	78
326	Papa John's Int'l	25	300%	3	3	Restaurant	58
567	Raytheon Co. 'A'	20	300%	5	3	Aerospace/Defense	71
1720	Ross Stores	15	300%	3	3	Retail (Special Lines)	16
1638	Unifi, Inc.	8 11/16	300%	3	3	Textile	55
2142	CIT Group 'A'	14	295%	4	3	Financial Svcs. (Div.)	33
945	Crown Cork	14	295%	4	3	Packaging & Container	64
666	Sunrise Asst. Living	12	295%	4	4	Medical Services	30
1506	Vlasic Foods Int'l	2 7/8	295%	–	5	Food Processing	78
1704	Jo-Ann Stores	9 5/8	290%	3	3	Retail (Special Lines)	16
1567	Rank Group ADR	5 1/8	290%	3	3	Foreign Electron/Entertn	29
665	Renal Care Group	18	290%	2	3	Medical Services	30
1680	Borders Group	13	285%	2	3	Retail (Special Lines)	16
1249	Covance Inc.	13	285%	3	3	Drug	11
607	Fremont Gen'l	6 1/2	285%	5	3	Insurance(Prop/Casualty)	90
1124	Hunt Corp.	9 3/4	285%	3	3	Office Equip & Supplies	67
926	Mail-Well, Inc.	8 3/8	285%	2	4	Paper & Forest Products	36
324	NPC Int'l	8 7/16	285%	3	3	Restaurant	58
327	Piccadilly Cafeterias	3	285%	5	3	Restaurant	58
1107	Quantum DSS Group	11	285%	–	3	Computer & Peripherals	10
371	Republic Services	11	285%	–	3	Environmental	89
207	Cardinal Health	39	280%	3	3	Medical Supplies	21
1644	Dillard's, Inc.	17	280%	4	3	Retail Store	41
504	Int'l Specialty Prod.	6 9/16	280%	4	3	Chemical (Specialty)	50
1923	Pittston Brink's	17	280%	3	3	Diversified Co.	63
1170	GreenPoint Fin'l	16	275%	3	3	Thrift	76
1665	Reebok Int'l	8	275%	4	3	Shoe	42
365	UniFirst Corp.	10	275%	4	3	Industrial Services	61
1395	AK Steel Holding	8 1/16	270%	5	3	Steel (Integrated)	54
278	Arkansas Best	9 1/2	270%	1	4	Trucking/Transp. Leasing	23
343	CDI Corp.	19	270%	3	3	Industrial Services	61
1258	ICN Pharmaceuticals	21	270%	3	4	Drug	11
1597	Rent Way Inc.	17	270%	2	3	Retail (Special Lines)	16
1724	TJX Companies	17	270%	3	3	Retail (Special Lines)	16
1670	Abercrombie & Fitch	15	265%	3	3	Retail (Special Lines)	16
490	Airgas Inc.	6 11/16	265%	3	3	Chemical (Specialty)	50
277	Amer. Freightways	11	265%	2	4	Trucking/Transp. Leasing	23
822	Lear Corp.	22	265%	3	3	Auto Parts (OEM)	60
865	Owens Corning	15	265%	4	3	Building Materials	73
1716	PETCO Animal Supplies	11	265%	1	4	Retail (Special Lines)	16
1178	Washington Mutual	22	265%	4	3	Thrift	76
1009	Federal Signal	16	260%	4	2	Electrical Equipment	35
1632	Galey & Lord	1 13/16	260%	3	5	Textile	55
1784	Johnson Outdoors	6 7/8	260%	3	3	Recreation	40
1497	Smithfield Foods	16	260%	4	3	Food Processing	78
1675	Barnes & Noble	17	255%	3	3	Retail (Special Lines)	16

Although such companies tend to pay out a relatively small percentage of their earnings at any given point, earnings growth typically leads to higher dividend income over time. Chances are that company share prices will also rise with earnings growth and thereby create capital gain opportunities. Dividend-growth investors are typically satisfied with dividend yields that match or fall slightly below the dividend yield on the overall market. Although dividend-growth investors enjoy a greater potential for long-term capital appreciation than other value investors, such an investment philosophy involves the potential for relatively high share-price volatility.

Implementing a Value Strategy

What Is a Value Line?

New York City–based Value Line, Inc., is one of the oldest and most widely respected independent providers of investment information, analysis, and research. Founded in 1931 by Arnold Bernard, Value Line is best known for *The Value Line*

Investment Survey, the world's most widely read investment information service. The *Investment Survey* provides detailed quarterly coverage on roughly 1,700 companies. These quarterly data are published in 13 editions per year. Each week, or 52 times per year, the *Investment Survey* publishes a new edition that gives comprehensive financial information on a subset of the companies it covers. Investment ratings and **computer stock screens** on all 1,700 companies are published weekly. These stock screens identify companies with interesting investment potential according to various profit, growth, or dividend criteria.

computer stock screens Computerized sorts of companies according to financial characteristics.

Value Line's founder, Arnold Bernard, believed that the intrinsic value of a stock was determined by its fundamental business prospects. In turn, the fundamental business prospects of a company's stock could be described by per-share growth in revenues, cash flow, earnings, dividends, and so on. Bernard was a pioneer in the use of statistical analysis for stock research. The **value line** is a *regression line* that best describes or "fits" the 60-month or five-year stock price history of a company's stock. When this regression line is combined with estimated sales, cash-flow, earnings, and dividend information for some future point in time, the projected value for a given stock can be calculated. If the present stock price is sufficiently low when compared with this projected value, the stock would be considered "timely" for purchase. If the present stock price is relatively high when compared with this projected value, the stock would be considered "untimely" and should be avoided.

value line Regression line that best describes or "fits" the 60-month or five-year stock price history of a company's stock.

A typical company page in the *Investment Survey* contains a helpful combination of graphic and tabular information. In addition to current-year data, historical and projected values are also depicted. This makes it possible to identify trends in earnings per share, cash flows, and other operating data. This also makes it easy to compare a company's current valuation against historical norms. To illustrate, assume that a typical ratio of price to cash flow for Coca-Cola is 24:1, as shown in Figure 11.10. Also assume that estimated cash flow per share in three to five years is $2.75. This gives a projected price in three to five years for Coca-Cola of $66 (= 24 × $2.75). When compared with a current market price of 57, realizing a projected price of 66 in, say, four years, would give less than a 4% per year annual rate of capital appreciation. In reality, the *Investment Survey* estimates a value line for companies such as Coca-Cola based on estimated growth in sales, cash flow, earnings, dividends, and a wealth of related information. Then, it uses projected future values for such financial information to make a future stock price projection. In the case of Coca-Cola, *Value Line* projects a range from 60 to 90 for a reasonable 2002–2004 stock price.

Value Line data can be used to identify ("screen for") stocks that meet various valuation criteria. Perhaps one of the most interesting computer stock screens reported in the *Investment Survey* is the list of companies with "high returns earned on total capital" (see Figure 11.3). These are wonderful businesses that display consistently high profitability on assets and stockholders' equity. These companies also display consistently high rates of earnings reinvestment, which often portends profitable future growth. The list of "biggest "free flow' cash generators" (see Figure 11.6) helps investors adjust for accrual accounting methods that often leave room for accounting manipulation and bias. A focus on "free cash flow" eliminates accrual accounting problems. Remember, "free cash flow" is the amount of cash generated that is not required to run and grow the business (e.g., EBITDA minus capital expenditures). Another useful screen is the *Investment Survey*'s "highest growth stocks" (see Figure 11.11). This list identifies companies with rapid projected growth in earnings per share. By showing current P/E ratio information, this list can also be used to identify companies selling at reasonable prices relative to projected growth.

FIGURE 11.10 In Late 1999, Coca-Cola's Stock Price Was above the Value Line

COCA-COLA NYSE-KO

RECENT PRICE **57** | P/E RATIO **43.2** (Trailing: 46.0 / Median: 26.0) | RELATIVE P/E RATIO **2.84** | DIV'D YLD **1.2%** | **VALUE LINE**

TIMELINESS 5 Lowered 3/5/99

SAFETY 1 New 7/27/90

TECHNICAL 4 Lowered 11/12/99

BETA 1.05 (1.00 = Market)

2002-04 PROJECTIONS

	Price	Gain	Ann'l Total Return
High	90	(+60%)	*13%*
Low	60	(+5%)	*3%*

Insider Decisions

	D	J	F	M	A	M	J	J	A
to Buy	1	0	0	0	0	0	0	0	0
Options	1	0	1	0	0	0	0	0	0
to Sell	2	0	1	0	1	0	0	1	0

Institutional Decisions

	4Q1998	1Q1999	2Q1999
to Buy	435	466	423
to Sell	455	451	483
Hld's(000)	1225717	1145400	1251705

	1988	1989	1990	1991	1992	1993	1994	1995	1996	1997	1998	1999
High:	5.7	10.1	12.3	20.4	22.7	22.5	26.7	40.2	54.3	72.6	88.9	70.9
Low:	4.4	5.4	8.2	10.7	17.8	18.8	19.4	24.4	36.1	50.0	53.6	47.3

Target Price Range 2002 | 2003 | 2004

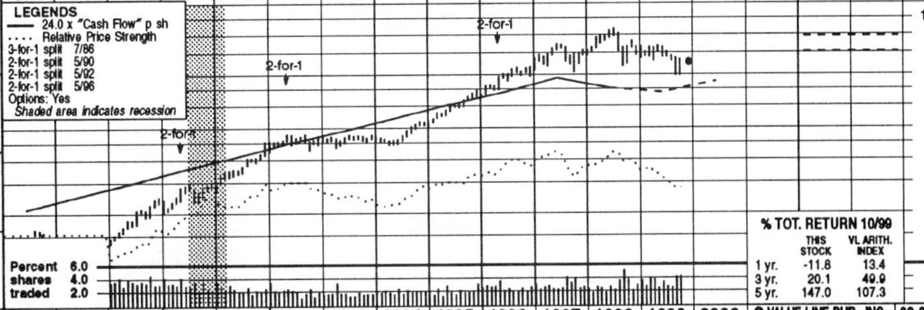

% TOT. RETURN 10/99

	THIS STOCK	VL ARITH. INDEX
1 yr.	-11.8	13.4
3 yr.	20.1	49.9
5 yr.	147.0	107.3

1983	1984	1985	1986	1987	1988	1989	1990	1991	1992	1993	1994	1995	1996	1997	1998	1999	2000	© VALUE LINE PUB., INC.	02-04
2.09	2.35	2.56	2.81	2.57	2.94	3.33	3.83	4.35	5.00	5.38	6.34	7.19	7.48	7.64	7.63	*8.00*	*8.55*	Sales per sh A	*11.70*
.22	.25	.28	.31	.36	.43	.50	.60	.71	.84	.98	1.16	1.37	1.60	1.92	1.69	*1.60*	*1.85*	"Cash Flow" per sh	*2.75*
.17	.20	.22	.26	.30	.36	.42	.51	.61	.72	.84	.99	1.19	1.40	1.64	1.42	*1.30*	*1.52*	Earnings per sh B	*2.35*
.11	.12	.12	.13	.14	.15	.17	.20	.24	.28	.34	.39	.44	.50	.56	.60	*.64*	*.68*	Div'ds Decl'd per sh C ■	*.92*
.12	.11	.16	.12	.10	.14	.17	.22	.30	.41	.31	.34	.37	.40	.44	.35	*.55*	*.60*	Cap'l Spending per sh	*.70*
.89	.88	.96	1.14	1.08	1.07	1.18	1.41	1.67	1.49	1.77	2.05	2.15	2.48	2.96	3.41	*3.40*	*3.45*	Book Value per sh D	*5.00*
3272.5	3139.8	3087.9	3080.1	2978.8	2838.3	2696.1	2673.0	2657.9	2613.7	2594.9	2551.9	2504.6	2481.0	2470.6	2465.5	*2460*	*2430*	Common Shs Outst'g E	*2360*
12.6	12.2	13.6	17.3	18.0	13.9	17.8	20.4	24.4	28.7	25.1	22.5	26.8	32.8	38.1	51.3	*Bold figures are*		Avg Ann'l P/E Ratio	*30.0*
1.07	1.14	1.10	1.17	1.20	1.15	1.35	1.52	1.56	1.74	1.48	1.48	1.79	2.05	2.20	2.67	*Value Line*		Relative P/E Ratio	*2.00*
5.2%	4.8%	4.2%	2.9%	2.6%	3.0%	2.3%	1.9%	1.6%	1.4%	1.6%	1.7%	1.4%	1.1%	.9%	.8%	*estimates*		Avg Ann'l Div'd Yield	*1.3%*

1989	1990	1991	1992	1993	1994	1995	1996	1997	1998	1999	2000		02-04
8965.8	10236	11572	13074	13957	16172	18018	18546	18868	18813	*19700*	*20800*	Sales ($mill) A	*27600*
21.3%	21.4%	22.3%	23.7%	24.8%	25.5%	25.2%	23.7%	29.8%	29.8%	*27.5%*	*28.5%*	Operating Margin	*30.5%*
183.8	243.9	261.4	321.9	360.0	411.0	454.0	479.0	626.0	645.0	*700*	*750*	Depreciation ($mill)	*875*
1192.8	1381.9	1618.0	1883.8	2188.0	2554.0	2986.0	3492.0	4129.0	3533.0	*3240*	*3740*	Net Profit ($mill)	*5620*
32.4%	31.4%	32.1%	31.4%	31.3%	31.5%	31.0%	24.0%	31.8%	32.0%	*31.5%*	*31.5%*	Income Tax Rate	*31.5%*
13.3%	13.5%	14.0%	14.4%	15.7%	15.8%	16.6%	18.8%	21.9%	18.8%	*16.4%*	*18.0%*	Net Profit Margin	*20.4%*
d54.4	d153.7	26.6	d1056	d737.0	d972.0	d1898	d1496	d1410	d2260	*d2800*	*d3450*	Working Cap'l ($mill)	*d3000*
548.7	535.9	985.3	1120.1	1428.0	1426.0	1141.0	1116.0	801.0	687.0	*785*	*875*	Long-Term Debt ($mill)	*1085*
3485.5	3849.2	4425.8	3888.4	4584.0	5235.0	5392.0	6156.0	7311.0	8403.0	*8365*	*8350*	Shr. Equity ($mill)	*11715*
30.2%	32.2%	30.6%	38.4%	37.7%	39.3%	46.5%	48.5%	51.2%	39.1%	*36.5%*	*41.5%*	Return on Total Cap'l	*45.0%*
34.2%	35.9%	36.6%	48.4%	47.7%	48.8%	55.4%	56.7%	56.5%	42.0%	*38.5%*	*44.5%*	Return on Shr. Equity	*48.0%*
22.0%	22.0%	22.1%	29.5%	28.5%	29.6%	34.8%	36.5%	37.5%	24.4%	*20.0%*	*25.0%*	Retained to Com Eq	*29.5%*
41%	40%	40%	39%	40%	39%	37%	36%	34%	42%	*49%*	*44%*	All Div'ds to Net Prof	*39%*

CAPITAL STRUCTURE as of 6/30/99
Total Debt $6207.0 mill.
LT Debt $1104.0 mill. **LT Interest** $60.0 mill.
(Total interest coverage: 20x)
(10% of Cap'l)

Pension Liability None

Pfd Stock None

Common Stock 2,469,000,000 shs.
(90% of Cap'l)

MARKET CAP: $141 billion (Large Cap)

CURRENT POSITION ($MILL.)	1997	1998	6/30/99
Cash Assets	1843.0	1807.0	2364.0
Receivables	1639.0	1666.0	1913.0
Inventory (Avg Cst)	959.0	890.0	937.0
Other	1528.0	2017.0	1910.0
Current Assets	5969.0	6380.0	7124.0
Accts Payable	3249.0	3141.0	3228.0
Debt Due	3074.0	4462.0	5103.0
Other	1056.0	1037.0	1211.0
Current Liab.	7379.0	8640.0	9542.0

ANNUAL RATES of change (per sh)	Past 10 Yrs.	Past 5 Yrs.	Est'd '96-'98 to '02-'04
Sales	10.5%	9.0%	*7.5%*
"Cash Flow"	17.0%	15.5%	*8.0%*
Earnings	17.0%	15.5%	*8.0%*
Dividends	14.5%	14.0%	*9.0%*
Book Value	10.5%	12.5%	*9.0%*

Cal-endar	QUARTERLY SALES ($ mill.) Mar.31	Jun.30	Sep.30	Dec.31	Full Year
1996	4194	5253	4656	4443	18546
1997	4138	5075	4954	4701	18868
1998	4457	5151	4747	4458	18813
1999	4428	5379	5195	*4698*	*19700*
2000	*4700*	*5700*	*5450*	*4950*	*20800*

Cal-endar	EARNINGS PER SHARE B Mar.31	Jun.30	Sep.30	Dec.31	Full Year
1996	.28	.42	.39	.31	1.40
1997	.39	.52	.40	.33	1.64
1998	.34	.48	.36	.24	1.42
1999	.30	.38	.32	*.30*	*1.30*
2000	*.32*	*.47*	*.40*	*.33*	*1.52*

Cal-endar	QUARTERLY DIVIDENDS PAID C ■ Mar.31	Jun.30	Sep.30	Dec.31	Full Year
1995	--	.11	.11	.22	.44
1996	--	.125	.125	.25	.50
1997	--	.14	.14	.28	.56
1998	--	.15	.15	.30	.60
1999	--	.16	.16	.16	

BUSINESS: The Coca-Cola Company is the world's largest soft drink company. Distributes major brands (*Coca-Cola, Sprite, Fanta, TAB*, etc.) through bottlers throughout the world. Business outside North America accounted for 63% of net sales and 73% of profits in 1998. Food division, world's largest distributor of juice products (*Minute Maid, Five Alive, Hi-C*, etc.). Coca-Cola Enterprises, 45%-owned soft drink bottler. Advertising costs, 8.5% of sales. Has approximately 29,500 employees; 366,000 stockholders. Berkshire Hathaway owns 8.1% of stock (3/99 Proxy). 1998 depr. rate: 11.3%. Chrmn. and Chief Exec. Officer: M. Douglas Ivester. Inc.: Delaware. Address: One Coca-Cola Plaza, Atlanta, Georgia 30313. Tel.: 404-676-2121. Internet: www.thecoca-colacompany.com.

Coca-Cola's earnings were down again in the September quarter, as we had expected, but comparisons should begin to pick up before 1999 ends. Results this year have been hurt by the weak economic situation in much of the world (unit case sales of Coca-Cola's products were down in both the first and second quarters, but picked up in the third), by the continuing strength of the dollar, by quality control problems and related adverse publicity in Europe, and by extra marketing efforts to boost the company's business in European markets.

In June, the company's Belgian bottler recalled products after receiving reports that people had become sick from drinking Coca-Cola soft drinks. No one was reported to be severely ill, but quality control problems were discovered at two plants. Efforts to maintain quality have since been considerably strengthened, but lost sales were costly, expenses of the recall and subsequent marketing efforts have been high, and consumer confidence obviously suffered. It is impossible to say when confidence may be restored, but our assumption is that it will be sometime in 2000 before business returns to normal.

Our profit forecasts for both 1999 and 2000 have been coming down. We now think that Coke will earn $1.30 a share this year and that profits will rebound somewhat, probably to just over $1.50 a share, next year.

Looking out to 2002-2004, we think that Coke will again have steady earnings growth. While revenue growth in the U.S. will probably be in the 2%-4% range, we think Coke will have 8%-10% volume gains outside the U.S. There are still vast untapped markets in much of the world, and Coke has the experience, financial strength, and marketing capabilities to develop those markets. The recent purchase of many of Cadbury Schweppes' brands outside the U.S. will strengthen the breadth of the product line. With steady volume gains, moderate price increases, and a continuing stock buyback program, annual share earnings should rise 15%, or more. The stock's Timeliness rank remains low, however, because of the recent earnings shortfalls.

Stephen Sanborn, CFA November 12, 1999

(A) Includes Columbia Pictures: 1/83-12/86. (B) Based on primary shs. thru '96, diluted shs. thereafter. Next earnings report due mid-Jan. Excludes special gain: '86, 8¢; disc. op. gains (loss): '83, (1¢); '85, 2¢; '89, 2¢; nonrec. gain (loss): '89, 36¢; '92, (8¢). (C) Next div'd meeting about Feb. 22. Goes ex about Nov. 29. Div'd payment dates: April 1, July 1, Oct. 1, Dec. 15. ■ Div'd reinvestment plan avail. (D) Incl. intangibles. In '98: $547.0 mill., 22¢/sh. (E) In millions, adj. for stock splits.

Company's Financial Strength	A++
Stock's Price Stability	85
Price Growth Persistence	95
Earnings Predictability	80

Source: Value Line Publishing, Inc.

FIGURE 11.11 Sustained Growth Is a Key Attribute of Attractive Investments

HIGHEST GROWTH STOCKS

(To be included, a company's annual growth of sales, cash flow, earnings, dividends and book value must together have averaged 13% or more over the past 10 years and be expected to average at least 13% in the coming 3-5 years.)

Page No.	Stock Name	Recent Price	Growth Past 10 Years	Est'd Growth 3-5 Years	Time-liness	Safety Rank	Beta	Current P/E Ratio	% Est'd Yield	Estimated 3-5 Year Price Appreciation	Industry Group	Industry Rank
772	ADC Telecom.	45	20%	22%	1	3	1.50	52.9	NIL	90-165%	Telecom. Equipment	7
1087	Adaptec Inc.	39	32%	17%	1	4	1.35	19.0	NIL	55-130%	Computer & Peripherals	10
2170	Adobe Systems	100	27%	17%	1	3	1.25	57.8	0.1	N- N%	Computer Software & Svcs	9
1055	Altera Corp.	85	30%	24%	1	4	1.35	66.4	NIL	N- 5%	Semiconductor Cap Equip	1
1241	ALZA Corp.	39	19%	17%	3	3	1.05	29.8	NIL	30- 90%	Drug	11
2138	Amer. Int'l Group	90	15%	15%	2	2	1.35	25.2	0.2	20- 65%	Financial Svcs. (Div.)	33
1056	Analog Devices	162	14%	19%	1	3	1.50	72.0	NIL	N- N%	Semiconductor	2
1080	Applied Materials	185	32%	19%	1	3	1.60	47.8	NIL	N- N%	Semiconductor Cap Equip	1
1305	Applied Power	23	14%	14%	3	3	1.10	9.6	0.3	115-205%	Machinery	53
2171	Autodesk, Inc.	45	15%	14%	3	3	1.25	22.5	0.5	35-110%	Computer Software & Svcs	9
1674	AutoZone Inc.	23	32%	17%	2	3	1.15	11.5	NIL	95-205%	Retail (Special Lines)	16
1244	Barr Labs.	47	22%	15%	3	3	0.80	20.1	NIL	40-100%	Drug	11
1677	Best Buy Co.	55	27%	26%	2	3	1.25	32.2	NIL	25- 80%	Retail (Special Lines)	16
556	Bombardier Inc. 'B'	30	19%	19%	2	3	0.95	25.0	0.8	N- 35%	Aerospace/Defense	71
313	Brinker Int'l	22	18%	14%	2	3	1.05	12.6	NIL	60-150%	Restaurant	58
207	Cardinal Health	39	19%	19%	3	3	1.05	14.6	0.3	210-350%	Medical Supplies	21
1777	Carnival Corp.	27	15%	16%	3	3	1.50	14.4	1.6	65-160%	Recreation	40
744	CenturyTel Inc.	34	17%	18%	3	2	0.90	18.2	0.6	75-135%	Telecom. Services	28
674	Cerner Corp.	34	22%	15%	3	4	0.95	NMF	NIL	N- 20%	Healthcare Information	81
347	Cintas Corp.	27	18%	17%	3	3	0.90	22.9	0.7	50-120%	Industrial Services	61
1685	Circuit City Group	38	18%	15%	2	3	1.25	23.0	0.2	30-110%	Retail (Special Lines)	16
1686	Claire's Stores	17	20%	21%	3	3	1.00	8.5	1.1	195-310%	Retail (Special Lines)	16
1798	Clear Channel	69	33%	22%	3	3	1.40	NMF	NIL	30- 95%	Entertainment	57
1092	Compaq Computer	26	26%	15%	3	3	1.30	31.0	0.4	35- 90%	Computer & Peripherals	10
2180	Computer Associates	66	23%	20%	1	3	1.20	22.3	0.2	45-105%	Computer Software & Svcs	9
2181	Computer Sciences	75	14%	17%	2	3	0.95	27.2	NIL	35-100%	Computer Software & Svcs	9
2146	Concord EFS	19	38%	32%	2	3	1.35	24.1	NIL	110-240%	Financial Svcs. (Div.)	33
120	Cooper Tire & Rubber	11	15%	15%	4	3	1.00	5.5	4.2	175-310%	Tire & Rubber	86
1643	Costco Wholesale	47	25%	14%	2	3	1.30	33.6	NIL	N- 30%	Retail Store	41
1061	Cypress Semiconductor	43	14%	15%	1	4	1.10	32.6	NIL	5- 75%	Semiconductor	2
1062	Dallas Semiconductor	41	22%	14%	2	3	1.20	32.0	0.3	N- N%	Semiconductor	2
1093	Dell Computer	43	48%	34%	3	3	1.35	58.9	NIL	50-120%	Computer & Peripherals	10
136	Dionex Corp.	31	15%	16%	3	3	0.90	18.9	NIL	75-160%	Precision Instrument	15
1645	Dollar General Corp.	20	23%	21%	3	3	1.20	21.5	0.7	75-150%	Retail Store	41
1094	EMC Corp.	118	35%	36%	1	3	1.35	84.9	NIL	90-185%	Computer & Peripherals	10
2149	Eaton Vance Corp.	42	16%	29%	2	3	0.80	14.0	1.4	30-100%	Financial Svcs. (Div.)	33
1252	Elan Corp. ADR	42	41%	24%	2	3	0.95	28.8	NIL	30- 80%	Drug	11
1779	Electronic Arts	95	30%	20%	1	3	1.25	59.4	NIL	N- 20%	Recreation	40
798	Ericsson ADR	99	17%	16%	1	3	1.25	75.6	0.3	N- N%	Foreign Telecom.	6
1646	Family Dollar Stores	18	14%	19%	3	3	0.95	18.0	1.3	40- 95%	Retail Store	41
885	Fastenal Co.	45	32%	23%	2	3	1.35	22.4	0.2	35-100%	Retail Building Supply	13
2187	Fiserv Inc.	28	19%	15%	2	3	1.00	22.6	NIL	80-150%	Computer Software & Svcs	9
2151	Franklin Resources	27	22%	16%	2	3	1.55	12.3	0.9	65-140%	Financial Svcs. (Div.)	33
1167	Freddie Mac	41	22%	17%	3	2	1.30	12.7	1.8	70-130%	Thrift	76
1695	Gap (The), Inc.	48	23%	28%	2	3	1.45	32.9	0.2	55-140%	Retail (Special Lines)	16
819	Gentex Corp.	29	34%	19%	3	3	0.90	30.9	NIL	5- 40%	Auto Parts (OEM)	60
1781	Harley-Davidson	69	22%	19%	2	3	1.15	34.8	0.3	N- 40%	Recreation	40
1325	Helix Technology	70	14%	15%	2	4	1.40	48.3	1.2	N- 0%	Machinery	53
886	Home Depot	56	32%	24%	2	2	1.30	48.7	0.3	5- 45%	Retail Building Supply	13
1258	ICN Pharmaceuticals	21	16%	18%	3	4	1.55	11.6	1.5	185-350%	Drug	11
575	Illinois Tool Works	53	15%	14%	3	2	1.10	16.0	1.4	90-155%	Metal Fabricating	47
1064	Intel Corp.	116	31%	15%	2	3	1.05	43.4	0.1	N- 5%	Semiconductor	2
1813	Int'l Game Tech.	18	26%	14%	3	3	1.00	12.4	NIL	65-150%	Hotel/Gaming	27
1329	JLG Industries	8⅜	23%	14%	5	3	0.90	6.8	0.5	140-255%	Machinery	53
860	Jacobs Engineering	28	23%	14%	3	3	0.95	10.4	NIL	80-170%	Building Materials	73
1263	Jones Pharma	45	31%	21%	1	3	1.00	52.3	0.2	N- 20%	Drug	11
141	KLA-Tencor	75	17%	17%	2	3	1.65	56.8	NIL	N- N%	Precision Instrument	15
1082	Kulicke & Soffa	80	15%	23%	2	4	1.75	26.7	NIL	N- 20%	Semiconductor Cap Equip	1
907	Leggett & Platt	16	15%	14%	3	3	1.25	10.0	2.5	120-215%	Furn./Home Furnishings	49
1067	Linear Technology	102	32%	23%	1	3	1.40	59.0	0.2	55-125%	Semiconductor	2
889	Lowe's Cos.	48	16%	22%	2	3	1.30	23.3	0.3	90-170%	Retail Building Supply	13
507	MacDermid Inc.	35	14%	16%	2	3	0.95	17.4	0.2	15- 70%	Chemical (Specialty)	50
1068	Maxim Integrated	64	33%	20%	1	3	1.45	69.6	NIL	N- N%	Semiconductor	2
223	Medtronic, Inc.	49	19%	14%	2	3	1.15	48.0	0.4	N- 35%	Medical Supplies	21
2194	Microsoft Corp.	91	42%	24%	2	2	1.05	53.5	NIL	10- 50%	Computer Software & Svcs	9
659	Omnicare, Inc.	9¹⁄₁₆	21%	15%	3	3	1.30	9.6	1.0	120-235%	Medical Services	30
2198	Oracle Corp.	72	34%	24%	1	3	1.35	NMF	NIL	N- 5%	Computer Software & Svcs	9
2200	Paychex, Inc.	49	26%	26%	1	3	1.00	65.3	0.8	10- 65%	Computer Software & Svcs	9
1036	Pioneer-Standard	18	14%	14%	2	4	1.05	13.4	0.7	0- 65%	Electronics	3
1039	Plexus Corp.	56	25%	18%	1	3	1.15	29.5	NIL	25-115%	Electronics	3
2162	Price (T. Rowe) Assoc.	33	22%	19%	2	3	1.50	15.7	1.6	50-110%	Financial Svcs. (Div.)	33
1719	Quiksilver Inc.	14	17%	20%	3	4	1.15	10.4	NIL	80-220%	Retail (Special Lines)	16
1419	Raymond James Fin'l	20	23%	16%	3	3	1.45	8.3	1.5	75-175%	Securities Brokerage	8
361	Robert Half Int'l	44	24%	17%	2	3	1.20	25.7	NIL	0- 60%	Industrial Services	61
1042	SCI Systems	44	16%	14%	1	3	1.80	32.6	NIL	N- 0%	Electronics	3
1276	Schering-Plough	34	16%	16%	3	1	1.30	21.4	1.6	75-105%	Drug	11
949	Shorewood Pack'g	21	14%	15%	–	3	0.70	16.2	NIL	45- 90%	Packaging & Container	64
272	Southwest Airlines	18	16%	17%	4	3	1.25	19.4	0.2	40-120%	Air Transport	83
2123	State Street Corp.	72	15%	14%	3	3	1.35	22.2	0.9	20- 75%	Bank	77
236	Stryker Corp.	55	23%	17%	2	3	0.95	26.4	0.3	65-145%	Medical Supplies	21
1113	Sun Microsystems	98	24%	20%	1	3	1.30	NMF	NIL	N- 0%	Computer & Peripherals	10
2208	SunGard Data Sys.	33	16%	15%	3	3	1.00	21.7	NIL	65-160%	Computer Software & Svcs	9
1047	Symbol Technologies	100	21%	16%	1	3	0.90	71.4	NIL	N- N%	Electronics	3
1528	Sysco Corp.	33	14%	15%	2	1	0.75	25.8	1.5	35- 50%	Food Wholesalers	17
1114	Tech Data	22	28%	15%	3	4	1.25	8.2	NIL	125-265%	Computer & Peripherals	10
239	Techne Corp.	88	37%	17%	1	3	0.90	75.2	NIL	N- 10%	Medical Supplies	21
805	Telefonos de Mexico ADR	69	20%	16%	1	3	1.25	20.7	1.0	10- 65%	Foreign Telecom.	6
789	Tellabs, Inc.	52	28%	24%	2	3	1.70	33.3	NIL	25- 85%	Telecom. Equipment	7
1555	Thor Inds.	25	15%	15%	2	3	0.75	7.7	0.3	100-200%	Manuf. Housing/Rec Veh	82
1727	Tiffany & Co.	69	15%	19%	1	3	1.40	32.1	0.4	N- N%	Retail (Special Lines)	16
880	Toll Brothers	18	16%	15%	2	3	1.15	5.8	NIL	120-235%	Homebuilding	26
2165	Total System Svcs.	16	21%	14%	3	3	1.00	37.2	0.3	55-120%	Financial Svcs. (Div.)	33
1389	Tyco Int'l Ltd.	39	14%	20%	3	2	1.10	19.5	0.1	55-105%	Diversified Co.	63
1138	United Stationers	27	15%	15%	2	3	0.95	10.5	NIL	50-120%	Office Equip & Supplies	67
806	Vodafone AirTouch ADR	57	30%	24%	3	3	1.10	NMF	0.5	N- 40%	Foreign Telecom.	6
366	Volt Info. Sciences	29	16%	17%	2	3	1.20	11.7	NIL	90-175%	Industrial Services	61
1659	Wal-Mart Stores	50	22%	20%	2	2	1.10	35.2	0.5	40- 80%	Retail Store	41
812	Walgreen Co.	26	14%	15%	2	2	1.20	35.6	0.5	15- 55%	Drugstore	80
291	Werner Enterprises	13	16%	14%	4	3	0.80	9.8	0.8	130-245%	Trucking/Transp. Leasing	23
1734	Williams-Sonoma	33	22%	21%	2	3	1.65	24.8	NIL	80-160%	Retail (Special Lines)	16

Source: Value Line Publishing, Inc.

Contrarian Investment Strategies

A contrarian investment philosophy is a strategy of systematically selecting stocks that are underanalyzed, less understood, and otherwise unpopular on Wall Street.

One of the more interesting points documented by academic research is that investors tend to place too much weight on Wall Street analyst forecasts that prove to be inherently unreliable. Analysts commonly overestimate favorable earnings growth, just as they overcompensate for expected downturns. Analyst forecasting errors have made earnings "surprises" common. In *Contrarian Investment Strategies: The Next Generation,* money manager David Dreman documents that only 47% of analyst quarterly earnings-per-share estimates are within plus or minus 10% of actual results. Between 1973 and 1996, the average amount of error was 44%. Reviewing 90,000 earnings estimates, Dreman found only a one in seven chance of some company going four consecutive quarters or one fiscal year without a negative earnings surprise. Over 10 quarters, or 2½ years, the odds of avoiding a negative surprise are 1 in 140. Over a five-year period, the odds of avoiding some negative earnings surprise falls to 1 in 20,000.

Because investors place too much faith in flawed Wall Street analyst forecasts, stocks with optimistic forecasts tend to be overpriced. Stocks with low expectations tend to be bargains. Dreman shows a big impact of positive earnings surprises on out-of-favor stocks with low P/E or P/B ratios. For 500 large companies between 1973 and 1995, Dreman found that low P/E stocks rose an average of 5.7% in the year following a positive earnings surprise. High P/E stocks rose only 0.5% on such news. Furthermore, Dreman found that negative earnings news has little influence on out-of-favor companies. Such news generally has a significant impact on high P/E companies. Dreman showed that low price/earnings stocks fell only 0.5% in the 12 months following a negative earnings surprise, whereas popular high price/earnings stocks fell 7.4%.

Dreman and some other contrarian investors believe that investors tend to overreact to good news and bad news. They argue that such overreaction is especially evident in the technology sector and among small-cap stocks. Dreman considers Internet stocks such as America Online (AOL) and Yahoo! to be overpriced based on overly optimistic forecasts that are apt to be wrong. Dreman believes AOL's 1999 stock market valuation could only be justified by a sustained period of 50% annual earnings per share (EPS) growth. To deliver those profits, Dreman estimates that AOL will need to increase its customer base to about 18 billion, or more than three times the current global population. As for Yahoo!, Dreman estimates that hyper EPS growth can only justify a small fraction of Yahoo!'s current stock price.

Stocks favored by a contrarian investment strategy are, by definition, bargain-basement stocks. Stocks with low price/net working capital ratios (see Figure 11.3), or low P/E ratios (see Figure 11.4), reflect companies suffering from investor despair. Similarly, stocks with low P/B ratios reflect investor skepticism regarding the quality and durability of company assets and earnings power (see Figure 11.5). Noted value investor Sir John Templeton built an enviable investment record on the simple premise of seeking investment bargains on a global basis. According to Sir John, earnings follow book values and stock prices follow earnings. Thus, to achieve superior returns, an investor had to focus on low P/B ratio stocks. Unfortunately for Sir John and other value investors, bargains sometimes continue to get cheaper and cheaper. So-called "turnaround" stocks do not always recover or turn around.

All the various manifestations of a contrarian investment strategy depend on the regression-to-the-mean concept introduced in Chapter 1 and illustrated in Figure 11.12. At any point in time, firm and industry profit rates vary widely. Over

FIGURE 11.12 **Profit Rates and Stock Returns Display a Regression to the Mean over Time**

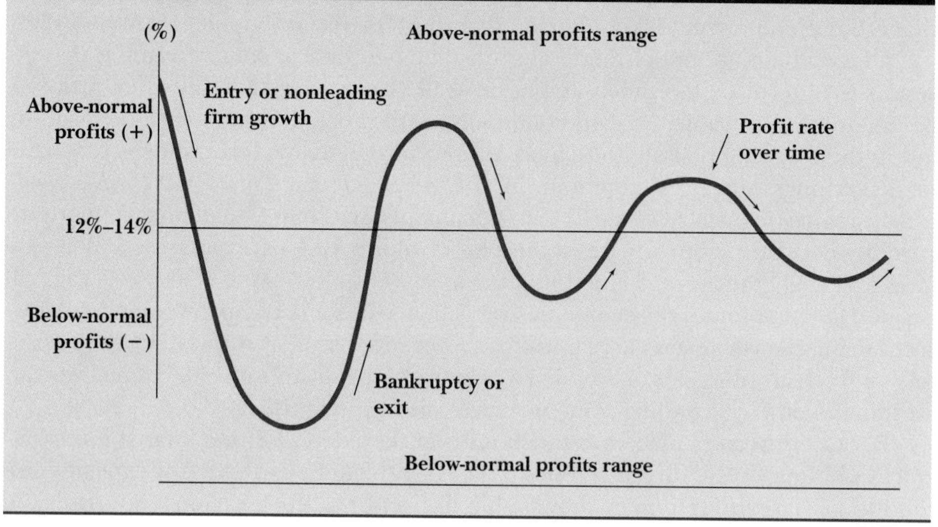

Over time, entry and nonleading firm growth causes above-normal profits to regress toward the mean. Similarly, bankruptcy or exit by weak competitors boosts profits for depressed industries. As a result, firm profits and stock-market returns converge toward the long-term average of 12–14% per year.

time, however, these profit rates tend to converge toward the overall average of 12–14% per year. Experienced investors know that competitor entry and growth in highly profitable industries cause above-normal profits to regress toward the mean. Conversely, bankruptcy and exit allow the below-normal profits of depressed industries to rise toward the mean.

For example, drugs, health care services, and medical supplies were among our most profitable industries during the late 1980s as an aging population and government-sponsored health programs caused the demand for health care to skyrocket. In the late 1990s, however, a proliferation of new drug therapies, cost-containment measures, and government regulations conspired to limit profit-making opportunities in health care. As a result, profit and sales growth in health care turned downward. Over the next decade, it is not likely that health care industry profits and stock gains will dramatically exceed all-industry averages. In that event, they will have regressed toward the mean profit level. At the same time, major air carriers such as United, American, and Delta typically earn meager profits, at best, because they operate in an industry with a homogeneous product (safe air travel) and huge fixed costs. As a result, price competition is vicious. Nevertheless, profit rates and stock prices for the airlines were bound to rise during the late 1990s because the industry could not continue to sustain the enormous losses incurred during the early 1990s. Bankruptcy and exit will allow prices and profits to rise toward a risk-adjusted normal rate of return for survivors.

Regression-to-the-mean theory suggests that companies with flawless histories have defective futures. Companies with defective histories tend to have less defective, if not flawless, futures. If both good and bad news is already in stock prices, investors should buy downtrodden low P/E stocks of "reversal of fortune" companies. If current P/E ratios are determined by backward-looking investors, low P/E stocks will outperform the market. High P/E stocks will underperform. Table 11.5

TABLE 11.5 Companies with Stellar Historical Stock Market Performance Often Face the Prospect of Lower Future Gains

Company Name	Ticker	Industry	Market Cap ($ millions)	EPS Growth 5-Year	Current P/E Ratio	Projected EPS Growth (%)	Projected 3–5-Year Return (%)	Historic Return 5-Year
A. Companies with High 5-Year Historical Returns								
America Online	AOL	Internet	166,823	76.5		92.5	9.0	145.6
Dell Computer	DELL	Computer & Peripherals	127,437	86.0	60.9	34.5	12.0	140.0
Qualcomm Inc.	QCOM	Telecom. Equip.	100,461			58.0	−17.0	125.8
Sun Microsystems	SUNW	Computer & Peripherals	111,243	39.5	84.6	20.0	−12.0	103.5
Cisco Systems	CSCO	Computer & Peripherals	347,897	49.0		25.5	−8.0	94.0
EMC Corp.	EMC	Computer & Peripherals	104,803	50.5	83.1	36.5	5.0	81.9
Microsoft Corp.	MSFT	Computer Software & Svcs.	588,884	37.5	69.0	25.0	−2.0	72.5
Schwab (Charles)	SCH	Securities Brokerage	30,134	26.5	53.3	23.0	−9.0	72.3
Clear Channel	CCU	Entertainment	28,762	46.0		22.5	6.0	69.7
Solectron Corp.	SLR	Electronics	23,725	35.0	60.2	29.0	−4.0	69.1
Gateway Inc.	GTW	Computer & Peripherals	18,042		36.3	26.5	5.0	67.9
Oracle Corp.	ORCL	Computer Software & Svcs.	145,215	43.5	88.7	25.0	−7.0	66.4
Nortel Networks	NT	Foreign Telecom.	119,283	14.0	78.2	25.5	−6.0	66.0
Applied Materials	AMAT	Semiconductor Cap Equip.	43,802	51.0	39.6	20.0	−7.0	64.4
BMC Software	BMCS	Computer Software & Svcs.	12,012	29.0	23.1	28.0	22.0	62.3
Averages			**131,235**	**44.9**	**61.5**	**32.8**	**−0.9**	**86.8**
B. Companies with High 3–5-Year Projected Returns								
Service Corp. Intl	SRV	Diversified Co.	1,786	17.0	8.1	8.5	50.0	−11.8
Pep Boys	PBY	Retail (Special Lines)	470	3.0	8.8	11.5	44.0	−21.2
IKON Office Solution	IKN	Office Equip. & Supplies	979	−2.0	9.1	10.0	44.0	−22.2
Washington Mutual	WM	Thrift	13,603	6.5	6.5	20.5	37.0	14.0
Conseco Inc.	CNC	Insurance (Life)	5,540	10.5	6.3	10.5	37.0	11.7
Milacron Inc.	MZ	Machinery	553		7.7	10.0	37.0	−6.5
Raytheon Co. 'A'	RTNA	Aerospace/Defense	2,545		27.2	11.0	35.0	
Toys 'R' Us	TOY	Retail (Special Lines)	3,254	2.5	8.3	9.5	34.0	−14.1
Humana Inc.	HUM	Medical Svcs.	1,309		13.5	8.5	34.0	−18.4
Baker Hughes	BHI	Oilfield Svcs./Equip.	6,708	10.5	72.8	11.0	33.0	4.6
Armstrong World Inds.	ACK	Building Materials	1,269	24.0	5.1	7.5	33.0	0.0
Dillard's Inc.	DDS	Retail Store	2,080	2.5	7.1	10.5	33.0	−5.0
Kmart Corp.	KM	Retail Store	4,765	−17.5	7.9	21.0	33.0	−4.0
Consol. Stores	CNS	Retail Store	1,659	23.5	14.8	15.0	32.0	6.4
Reebok Intl	RBK	Shoe	461	−7.5	9.4	2.5	32.0	−23.4
Hilton Hotels	HLT	Hotel/Gaming	3,007	10.5	10.1	9.0	31.0	−9.8
Averages			**3,409**	**5.8**	**14.7**	**11.2**	**34.6**	**−5.1**

Data source: *Value Line Investment Survey for Windows*, January 2000.

shows how companies with stellar historical stock market performance often face the prospect of lower future gains.

A logical explanation for the success of noted value investors such as Benjamin Graham, David Dreman, and Sir John Templeton is that they all use investment selection criteria designed to identify "survivors" in industries undergoing extreme hardship. By withstanding extreme hardship that eliminates notable competitors, such companies are poised to enjoy a favorable reversal of fortune when industry conditions improve. At the same time, by avoiding high P/E stocks with ebullient expectations, value investors avoid the types of earnings and stock price disappointments tied to an emergence of competition in high-profit and high-profile industries.

Quality at a Reasonable Price

Determining a reasonable price to pay for any stock is always difficult. To deal effectively with the uncertainties involved, some value investors rely on a simple investment rule of thumb called the **value of ROE,** or VRE for short.

value of ROE ROE percentage divided by the P/E ratio.

The VRE ratio is simply the return on equity or ROE percentage divided by the P/E ratio. If a company is expected to enjoy a ROE of 20% and has a P/E ratio of 20, the company's VRE ratio would be 1. Generally speaking, according to value investors, a stock is fully valued if it sports a VRE ratio of less than 1. If the VRE ratio is greater than 1, the stock is worthy of investment consideration. The VRE ratio rule of thumb goes something like this:

- If VRE ≥ 1, the stock may be worthy of investment attention and possible purchase.
- If VRE ≥ 2, the stock is definitely worthy of investment attention and may represent a very attractive investment.
- If VRE ≥ 3, the stock is apt to be an extraordinarily attractive investment opportunity.

Needless to say, the investment merit of a stock increases with an increase in the VRE ratio. Strict **quality-at-a-reasonable-price investors** seldom, if ever, buy value stocks with VRE ratios less than 1.

quality-at-a-reasonable-price investors Investors who seldom buy value stocks with VRE ratios less than 1.

As shown in Table 11.6, the attractiveness of a stock increases with an increase in the VRE ratio. Of course, it is important to adjust the VRE ratio for stocks with little or no stockholders' equity. In such circumstances, ROE can become wildly overstated, and it is perhaps prudent to substitute the return on assets (ROA) measure for ROE in the VRE calculation. In such circumstances, it is important to keep in mind that ROA tends to be lower than ROE, so companies with ROA that exceeds their P/E ratio are apt to be rare. In short, stocks with high VRE that is *sustainable* are attractive. Investors should be suspicious of stocks with towering VRE measures.

Advantages and Limitations

Like all strategies, value investing has its advantages and limitations. A principal advantage is that careful stock selection should limit downside risk. When an investor buys stocks that are already cheap, they should be less vulnerable to market

TABLE 11.6 Value of ROE Rankings Identify Highly Profitable Companies Selling at Reasonable Prices

Company Name	Ticker	Industry	Market Cap ($ millions)	ROE (%)	P/E Ratio	Value of ROE (ratio)	Projected 3–5-Yr Return (%)
A. High Value of ROE Firms							
Unisys Corp.	UIS	Computer & Peripherals	8,987	289.2	18.1	16.0	15.0
UST Inc.	UST	Tobacco	4,224	97.2	9.5	10.3	11.0
US WEST Inc.	USW	Telecom. Svcs.	33,540	199.7	20.0	10.0	6.0
Hilton Hotels	HLT	Hotel/Gaming	3,007	100.8	10.1	10.0	31.0
Avon Products	AVP	Toiletries/Cosmetics	7,360	137.8	18.0	7.7	16.0
Jostens Inc.	JOS	Diversified Co.	799	100.9	13.8	7.3	14.0
Sara Lee Corp.	SLE	Food Processing	18,379	108.8	15.4	7.1	17.0
SLM Holding	SLM	Financial Svcs. (Div.)	6,035	68.7	11.6	5.9	22.0
Armstrong World Inds.	ACK	Building Materials	1,269	29.9	5.1	5.9	33.0
Tupperware Corp.	TUP	Household Products	955	50.9	10.1	5.0	21.0
Navistar Intl	NAV	Auto & Truck	2,803	37.6	7.7	4.9	18.0
Philip Morris	MO	Tobacco	55,604	33.2	6.9	4.8	29.0
Maytag Corp.	MYG	Home Appliance	3,667	55.3	12.2	4.5	16.0
Equifax Inc.	EFX	Industrial Svcs.	3,023	52.8	12.9	4.1	25.0
Bestfoods	BFO	Food Processing	13,964	78.8	19.4	4.1	12.0
Averages			**10,908**	**96.1**	**12.7**	**7.2**	**19.1**
B. Low Value of ROE Firms							
Owens Corning	OWC	Building Materials	1,041	−18.0	3.8	−4.7	31.0
Dun & Bradstreet	DNB	Industrial Svcs.	4,404	−71.2	16.3	−4.4	14.0
TRICON Global Rest's	YUM	Restaurant	5,666	−38.3	10.5	−3.6	21.0
Freept-McMoRan C&G	FCX	Copper	2,049	−46.5	26.3	−1.8	17.0
National Semiconductor	NSM	Semiconductor	6,861	−24.6	30.8	−0.8	−9.0
Union Pacific Res.	UPR	Natural Gas (Diversified)	3,040	−22.0	29.4	−0.7	24.0
Amerada Hess	AHC	Petroleum (Integrated)	4,807	−7.4	16.0	−0.5	8.0
Cummins Engine	CUM	Machinery	1,930	−1.6	7.9	−0.2	17.0
Seagate Technology	SEG	Computer & Peripherals	8,671	−9.5	83.3	−0.1	8.0
Micron Technology	MU	Semiconductor	18,451	−1.7	23.3	−0.1	5.0
Homestake Mining	HM	Gold/Silver Mining	2,033	−3.5	60.1	−0.1	20.0
Union Pacific	UNP	Railroad	10,688	−0.7	12.7	−0.1	22.0
Inco Limited	N	Metals & Mining (Div.)	4,480	−5.0	88.4	−0.1	2.0
Polaroid Corp.	PRD	Precision Instrument	838	−0.6	12.9	0.0	20.0
Cabletron Sys.	CS	Computer & Peripherals	4,390	−1.3	56.5	0.0	1.0
Averages			**5,290**	**−16.8**	**31.9**	**−1.1**	**13.4**

Data source: *Value Line Investment Survey for Windows,* January 2000.

downdrafts than stocks that are richly valued. This is especially true when value stocks offer above-average dividend yields, as is true for many large companies that fall within the value stock category. Because dividend income always makes a positive contribution to total return, large dividends tend to cushion falling stock prices.

A possible impediment to adopting a value investment philosophy is the difficulty involved with obtaining relevant investments information. Although good financial data are readily available, detailed knowledge of a company's business and market environment is needed to interpret that data correctly. For instance, does a low P/E ratio indicate that a company is temporarily undervalued or permanently impaired? Because many low P/E and low P/B stocks are neglected by Wall Street analysts, finding out about many value stocks is a time-consuming and arduous task. This is especially true for the stocks of small companies, in which investment information is often scarce.

Another potential disadvantage is that value investing is not necessarily a buy-and-hold strategy. It implies constant recycling of stocks through the portfolio as their value is recognized by the market. This means that value investors face the need for constant research and monitoring. Such vigilance may be difficult for an individual investor. Also bear in mind that the value approach involves buying unpopular stocks with a checkered operating and financial history. A successful value investor is a contrarian in the truest sense of the word. Buying a stock when the market is pessimistic and selling when the market is optimistic is a psychological challenge. All of us enjoy being popular, and buying stocks that are unpopular in the market is a sure way to invite criticism.

Finally, it is important to recognize the complex problem faced by simple investment strategy rules of thumb, such as the PEG ratio in Chapter 10 and the value of ROE in this chapter. The usefulness of simple rules is apt to be frustrated by their own popularity. If low P/E stocks as a group tended to consistently outperform the market, such stocks would become popular with investors. They would then lose their bargain-basement status, and their P/E ratios would rise. In the world of investments, popular investment strategies *cannot* lead to superior profitability. If an investor chooses the same investment strategy as everyone else, that investor is bound to get the same rate of return as everyone else. Only by choosing a different investment strategy can an investor hope to obtain different returns. Only by choosing a superior strategy can investors hope to obtain superior investment returns.

Is AOL a Value Stock?

Industry Transactions

A sensible way for attempting to arrive at an economic value per share for AOL is to consider the prices paid for related businesses by knowledgeable industry insiders.

For example, on May 5, 1999, AT&T Corp. won the takeover fight to become the nation's largest cable TV company, with a complicated $54 billion bid to acquire MediaOne Group, Inc., the nation's fourth largest cable company. In the deal, AT&T, whose initial $62 billion bid topped Comcast's $48 billion offer, swapped cable systems that could result in Comcast gaining an extra 2 million customers and AT&T receiving up to $9.2 billion. Like AT&T, Comcast agreed to pay roughly $4,600 per subscriber for the cable customers being acquired. The amount paid per subscriber is a huge premium to the level paid only months earlier by AT&T for the cable operations of Tele-Communications Inc., the second largest cable provider. In 1998, the going rate was $2,500 per subscriber.

To justify such a premium price, AT&T plans to offer all its 16 million cable TV customers a broad array of telephone, Internet, and TV services. Customers will only need one cable into their homes and will receive one lower-priced bill, according to the company. AT&T claims it can save consumers 20–25% off their cable and telephone bills. The expanded service will include local, intrastate, and

WALL STREET WISDOM 11.3

Intrinsic Value

Suppose that you had just taken a new job and were looking for a car to provide transportation to work. Furthermore, assume that a trusted friend and classmate was also in the job market. As it turns out, she has a car that she is willing to sell to you at a mutually agreed-on price. Not being an expert on the value of used cars, you get on the Internet and go to a handful of sites that give unbiased advice on suggested retail and wholesale (trade-in) prices for used cars. For the car your friend has for sale, the suggested retail price is $6,000, and the suggested wholesale price is $4,500. Not being an expert on gauging the condition of used automobiles, you decide to pay $50 to have a mechanic look over the vehicle and give you his recommendation. After a thorough inspection, the mechanic tells you that the car is not only in good running condition, it appears to be in excellent condition.

If your friend offers to sell the vehicle at the wholesale price of $4,500, the only reasonable conclusion is that the car represents a good value at that price. You should buy it. But wait, it gets better. Assume that on the night before you are planning to tell your friend that you are willing to buy her car for $4,500, she gets a sales job in a distant city. Her new job includes a car, and she must report to work in just a couple of days. As a result, she wants to dump her current vehicle quickly and offers it to you for the bargain-basement price of $2,500.

Should you buy it? Of course you should. It is a real bargain. You know it is a bargain because you have checked prices for comparable vehicles and obtained an independent assessment of its quality from an expert. Having done your homework, you are in a position to make a reasonable purchase decision.

Assessing the investment merit of individual stocks and bonds involves a similar process. In the case of stocks, it is reasonable to check for typical earnings growth, dividends, price/earnings ratios, and so on. If a stock is presently selling at a P/E ratio that is significantly below historical norms, it may represent a real investment bargain provided that there has been no material deterioration in the company's competitive position. Conversely, in the absence of important new fundamental developments, if a stock is presently selling at a P/E ratio that is significantly above historical norms, it may be prudent to avoid new commitments until such a time as a more favorable price can be obtained.

Many individual investors become frustrated with their lack of investment success simply because they fail to use simple common sense in their assessment of a company's investment merit. In many cases, individual investors fail to reach their investment objectives because they are not willing to invest the time necessary to appropriately gauge a company's economic prospects. More basically, investors sometimes fail because they simply do not realize that they lack the skill, education, or experience necessary to measure the intrinsic economic value of a given company. Few investors are equipped to play the role of doctor, lawyer, and investment professional. At the same time, in their investment decisions they act as if they somehow have the skills to effectively assess companies in the pharmaceutical, networking equipment, and investment banking businesses.

Warren Buffett is fond of saying that successful investors do not need a wide "circle of competence." However, to become successful, it is extremely important to stay within the boundaries of that circle. Most stock market fortunes have been made by investors who held stocks in relatively few companies for a very long time. They bought stocks of companies in good businesses that they understood. Armed with such knowledge, they held them.

Lasting stock market success does not depend on grasping the art of speculation. It depends on learning the craft of valuation.

See: Gregory Zuckerman, "How Soros Funds Lost Game of Chicken against Tech Stocks," *The Wall Street Journal*, May 22, 2000, A1, A19.

---

long-distance phone calls, cable, and Internet access for a flat monthly fee. Extra services, such as call waiting and caller ID, may also be included. AT&T says it may only charge customers between $4 and $6 for an extra line for a fax or computer, compared with the $17 charged by some phone companies.

For purposes of illustration, let's assume that a typical AT&T customer is used to paying $30 per month for local phone service and another $70 per month for intrastate and long-distance phone calls. Let's also assume that 60% of these phone customers pay another $30 per month for cable TV service and that the market will grow to the point at which a similar 60% would be willing to pay $20 per month for Internet access. (Of course, Internet access penetration of the overall market is presently way behind cable TV's penetration, but the number of residences logging onto the Internet is growing fast.) Before discounting, this all adds up to $130 per month for a "typical" AT&T "service package" customer. After discounting, let's assume $110 per month, or $1,320 per year, for a "typical" AT&T service-bundle customer. This means that AT&T and Comcast appear willing to pay in the neighborhood of 3.5 times anticipated annual revenue per customer. Remember, customer revenues are before variable and fixed charges, which will be substantial.

According to Merrill Lynch, a typical monthly bill in 2002 could read as follows: $44 for basic cable, $12 for premium channels, $16 for digital channels, $35 for Internet access, and $70 for phone service. This adds up to $177 per month, or $2,124 per year in 2002. Under these assumptions, AT&T and Comcast appear to be willing to pay in the neighborhood of two times anticipated annual revenue per customer in the year 2002.

This means that a reasonable private-market value estimate of the value of AOL customers should be based on a number that is between two and 3.5 times anticipated annual revenue per customer.

AOL Customer Value

In late 1999, AOL operated two worldwide Internet services: the AOL service, with more than 20 million members, and the CompuServe service, with approximately 2.2 million members. Customers pay AOL under a variety of different plans anywhere from $4.95 per month to as much as $24.95 per month. AOL's most popular plan costs $21.95 per month. In addition to online service revenues, AOL generates revenue from advertising and online commerce. Presently, such revenues are about 25% of online service revenues but growing fast.

Let's take the optimistic view that AOL will be able to maintain online service revenue of roughly $20 per month despite heightening competition. Being optimistic, let's also assume that advertising, commerce, and other revenue will soon grow to 50% of online revenues, or $10 per month per AOL subscriber. This allows AOL to expect total revenue of $30 per month, or $360 per year, for each of some 22.2 million subscribers. This means that the anticipated annual revenue from AOL's 1999 customer base of roughly 22.2 million customers is $8 billion (= $360 × 22.2 million).

At a conservative two times anticipated annual revenue, the total value of AOL's 1999 customer base was $16 billion (= 2 × $8 billion). Using a more aggressive 3.5 times anticipated annual revenue, the total value of AOL's customer base in 1999 was $28 billion (= 3.5 × $8 billion).

Private-Market Value

In addition to its customer or subscriber base, AOL also operates AOL Studios, a leading creator of original interactive content; AOL.com, the world's most accessed Web site from home; Digital City, Inc., a leading local content network and community guide on AOL and the Internet; AOL NetFind, AOL's comprehensive guide to the Internet; AOL Instant Messenger, an instant messaging tool available on both the AOL service and the Internet; ICQ, an instant communications and chat technology on the Internet; and Netscape Communications, Inc.

Placing a value on such disparate operations is made difficult by the fact that they presently generate little in the way of revenues and profits. Optimistically, let's assume that these ancillary operations are worth $5 billion in total.

Taken as a whole, the analysis presented here suggests that an optimistic private-market value estimate for AOL at the end of 1999 would fall in the range between $21 billion (= $5 + $16) and $33 billion (= $5 + $28). With roughly 2.28 billion outstanding shares, this implies an optimistic private-market value for AOL of between $9.21 (= $21/2.28) and $14.47 (= $33/2.28) per share. Admittedly, this is a broad range and reflects the difficulties involved with valuing such a dynamic business. Still, these numbers can become useful when compared with AOL's December 1999 price of $95.81. Based on evidence from recent industry mergers, AOL seems way overpriced at that level.

Value of AOL-Time Warner

Several high-profile mergers have involved Internet companies of late, and more such mergers are sure to follow. However, few are apt to capture the imagination of investors like the proposed marriage between AOL, the largest Internet-access provider, and media powerhouse Time Warner, the world's leading media and entertainment company. The merger is expected to be completed in late 2000, assuming that it is approved by the Federal Trade Commission. Time Warner classifies its business interests into four fundamental areas: cable network programming (e.g., CNN), book and magazine publishing (e.g., *Time*), entertainment (Warner film studios), and cable services. The proposed merger excited investors because it held the promise of allowing AOL to provide high-speed Internet access over Time Warner's television cable systems, while enabling Time Warner to feed its film library and news content to AOL's large customer base. At the same time, the proposed merger between AOL and Time Warner raised some concern among Internet investors because they feared that the combined company would be valued using the metric of a large and mature media conglomerate rather than a New Economy superstar.

Around the time the merger was announced in January, 2000, Time Warner's stock spiked up from the high 60s to 102, while AOL's stock jumped from near 70 to $95.81. However, in the ensuing period, both stocks embarked on a sharp correction as investors scrambled to value the new company. During recessions, when advertising revenues taper off and earnings turn soft, media stocks have been traditionally valued in the stock market at roughly 8 to 10 times cash flow. During economic booms, such as that experienced during the late 1990s, advertising revenues and earnings jump, and media stocks can sell for premium prices of 12–15 times cash flow.

In the case of AOL-Time Warner, the $250 billion question is: What is a reasonable cash-flow expectation, and what is an appropriate multiple? Merrill Lynch's Internet software and services analyst Henry Blodget is famous for being an early bull on AOL. On February 23, 2000, Blodget put out a wildly bullish report on the proposed merger titled *AOL Time Warner: You've Got Upside!* In that report, Blodget

TABLE 11.7 Cash Flow and Stock Price Estimates for the Combined AOL–Time Warner

A. EBIDTA Cash-Flow Estimates (in $ billions)

EBIDTA Growth Rate	Conservative 10%	15%	20%	25%	Aggressive 30%
2000	7.7	8.1	8.4	8.8	9.1
2001	8.5	9.3	10.1	10.9	11.8
2002	9.3	10.6	12.1	13.7	15.4
2003	10.2	12.2	14.5	17.1	20.0
2004	11.3	14.1	17.4	21.4	26.0
2005	12.4	16.2	20.9	26.7	33.8

B. AOL–Time Warner Stock Price Estimates with Various EBIDTA Multiples

EBIDTA Multiple	Conservative 10%	15%	20%	25%	Aggressive 30%
2000	15.4	24.2	33.6	43.8	54.6
2001	16.9	27.8	40.3	54.7	71.0
2002	18.6	31.9	48.4	68.4	92.3
2003	20.5	36.7	58.1	85.4	120.0
2004	22.5	42.2	69.7	106.8	155.9
2005	24.8	48.6	83.6	133.5	202.7

wrote: "We also do not believe that an appropriate comparable or valuation metric for this company exists—and it could be that new valuation metrics arise that justify much higher targets than we are contemplating. This said, at $49.63, AOL seems undervalued by almost any measure." Blodget argued that the combined company would be able to grow EBITDA at an annual rate of 20% per year over the 2000–2005 five-year period and that a target EBITDA multiple could reach 28 times cash flow, if not higher. Within two trading days, AOL shot up to over 60, a gain of more than 20%!

Of course, it will be years before investors know if the AOL–Time Warner merger was able to capture all the synergies envisioned by investors during December 1999. Table 11.7 shows valuation scenarios for the combined company based on various EBITDA estimates and price-EBITDA multiples. With 22% growth and a cash-flow multiple of 28:1, Blodget foretold a stock price for the combined company of 90 per share by the end of 2002. Notice from Table 11.7 that Blodget's assumptions are at the most optimistic end of the cash-flow growth and price–cash flow multiple spectrums. Also notice how more modest expectations yield much lower stock price estimates.

Check out AOL's price history on Yahoo! How accurate was Henry Blodget back in February 2000 when he predicted a 2002 price for AOL of 90 per share?

Summary

- Value investors adopt a **contrarian investment philosophy** based on the premise that investors can profit by betting against the overly emotional crowd. According to practitioners of contrarian investment strategies, investors can profit if they are able to withstand the peer group and psychological pressures tied to common stock investing. To be successful, contrarian investors argue that one must "buy fear" and "sell greed." Traditional **value investors** seek out-of-favor stocks selling at a discount to the overall market, in which such discounts are measured in terms of low P/E and P/B ratio and/or high dividend yields. **Deep-value investors** dig deeper to find indisputably cheap stocks. Some focus on companies at the brink of bankruptcy or in the midst of bankruptcy proceedings.

- There are often good economic reasons when a stock sells at a sharp discount to the market, and conservative investors must be wary to avoid being stuck with a real **dog,** or a company facing a fundamental deterioration in its basic earnings power. Companies that may be only marginally or temporarily affected by the industry problems can become **undervalued** in the marketplace. Typically, **growth stocks** are defined as the 250 S&P 500 stocks with the highest P/B ratios. **Value stocks** are the remaining 250 S&P 500 stocks with relatively lower P/B ratios.
- Value investors who follow the conservative stock-picking style of Benjamin Graham are called **Graham and Dodd** investors, in reference to Graham and his *Security Analysis* coauthor David L. Dodd. This book is perhaps the most famous investment book of all time. One of the most important ideas for a value investor is the **margin of safety** concept. By definition, bargains reflect a favorable difference between price and appraised value. That difference is the margin of safety. It is available for absorbing the effect of miscalculations or bad luck. The goal of enlightened stock analysis is to identify underpriced securities and to enjoy excess returns following the market's subsequent upward revaluation to a price consistent with **intrinsic value.** The intrinsic value of a stock is justified by assets, earnings, dividends, sure prospects, and management.
- Graham and Dodd drew parallels between stock market investing and partnership arrangements. In the words of Graham and Dodd, the market simply facilitates the investor's interest in buying or selling securities. At any point in time, market prices may be above or below the intrinsic economic value of the firm. For the investor capable of discerning a company's true intrinsic value, dealing with **Mr. Market** can become a profitable proposition.
- Graham and Dodd looked to find bargain-basement stocks selling at prices below **liquidation value.** Remember that this was an investment philosophy born during the Great Depression. They sought stocks selling at a price below **net working capital. Working capital** is conventionally defined as current assets minus current liabilities. Net working capital equals current assets minus *all* liabilities, including long-term debt and preferred stock.
- Value investors rely on a variety of tangible indicators of a stock's **fundamental value.** Fundamental value is the worth of a stock derived from a company's assets in place, sure prospects, and durable strengths. One of the most important indicators of fundamental value is a company's **free cash flow.** Free cash flow consists of earnings before interest, taxes, depreciation, and amortization, sometimes referred to as **EBITDA,** minus necessary capital expenditures.
- Another useful indicator of fundamental value is **private-market value.** Private-market value is the price a knowledgeable private buyer would pay for the entire franchise. **Enlightened corporate governance** is another fundamental value indicator. Value investors want to know that management shares stockholder

interests in value maximization. It is always relevant to ask if management is knowledgeable to act in shareholder interests and has strong incentives to maximize the value of the firm. Finally, the concept of a **value catalyst** is often important in value investing. A value catalyst is an inside or outside stimulus that will help close any discount between the current market price of a stock and the prorated value of the company based on its private-market value.

- **Growth-and-income investors** seek a relative balance between the goals of high and stable income and long-term capital growth. **Equity-income investors** stress income first and long-term capital growth second. Such portfolios have few, if any, equity holdings that do not provide significant dividend income. **Dividend-growth investors** place primary emphasis on the potential for dividend growth in their stock selection strategy. Consistent dividend growth is often associated with companies able to grow earnings faster than the rate of inflation.
- *The Value Line Investment Survey* is the world's most widely read investment information service. The *Investment Survey* provides detailed quarterly coverage on roughly 1,700 companies. These quarterly data are published in 13 editions per year. Each week, or 52 times per year, the *Investment Survey* publishes a new edition that gives comprehensive financial information on a subset of the companies it covers. Investment ratings and **computer stock screens** on all 1,700 companies are published weekly. These stock screens identify companies with interesting investment potential according to various profit, growth, or dividend criteria. The **value line** is a *regression line* that best describes or "fits" the 60-month or five-year stock price history of a company's stock. When this regression line is combined with estimated sales, cash-flow, earnings, and dividend information for some future point in time, the projected value for a given stock can be calculated.
- All the various contrarian investment strategies depend on the regression-to-the-mean concept. Experienced investors know that competitor entry and growth in highly profitable industries cause above-normal profits to regress toward the mean. Conversely, bankruptcy and exit allow the below-normal profits of depressed industries to rise toward the mean. If both good and bad news is already in stock prices, investors should buy downtrodden low P/E stocks of "reversal of fortune" companies.
- Some value investors rely on a simple investment rule of thumb called the **value of ROE,** or VRE for short. The VRE ratio is simply the return on equity or ROE percentage divided by the P/E ratio. The investment merit of a stock increases with an increase in the VRE ratio. Strict **quality-at-a-reasonable-price investors** seldom, if ever, buy value stocks with VRE ratios less than 1.

Questions

1. S&P/BARRA Value and Growth Indexes are constructed by dividing stocks in an S&P index into two mutually exclusive groups according to the firm's
   a. dividend yield.
   b. price/earnings ratio.
   c. price/book ratio.
   d. earnings-per-share growth rate.

2. Which among the following statements is *true?*
   a. S&P/BARRA Value and Growth Indexes have relatively high turnover over the course of a year.
   b. Companies in the S&P/BARRA Value Index tend to have higher market capitalizations, on average, than those in the associated Growth Index.
   c. There are many more companies in the S&P/BARRA Growth Index than in the Value Index.
   d. Large losses at component firms can cause surprisingly high P/E ratios for the Value Index.
3. Which among the following statements is *false?*
   a. A long-term investor should expect to receive similar rates of return on value and growth stocks.
   b. During the late 1970s, value stocks outperformed growth stocks.
   c. Superior rates of earnings per share growth leads to consistently above-average rates of return for growth stocks.
   d. During the late 1990s, growth stocks outperformed value stocks.
4. Reversion to the mean theory predicts lower expected returns for stocks with low
   a. price/book ratios.
   b. price/sales ratios.
   c. historical returns.
   d. earnings/price ratios.
5. Holding all else equal, EBITDA will rise with a rise in
   a. interest rates.
   b. taxes.
   c. depreciation charges.
   d. sales revenue.
6. Private market value is *not* dependent on
   a. earnings per share.
   b. earnings and price momentum.
   c. cash flow.
   d. management quality.
7. A value catalyst is
   a. an inside or outside stimulus that will help close any discount between the current market price of a stock and the prorated value of the company based on its private-market value.
   b. favorable micro trend.
   c. favorable macro trend.
   d. earnings uptrend.
8. According to *Security Analysis,* a sound investment strategy requires
   a. broad diversification.

b. a price per share in excess of net current assets.
c. the prudent use of margin borrowing.
d. heavy reliance on bond investments.

9. Benjamin Graham did not believe the stock market crash of 1929 was due to
   a. stock manipulation by the exchanges and investment firms.
   b. margin borrowing for stock purchases.
   c. excessive optimism.
   d. economic prosperity.
10. The theory of reversion (regression) to the mean argues that the potential of low-profit firms is amplified by
    a. entry.
    b. imitation.
    c. exit.
    d. regulation.
11. According to Graham and Dodd, intrinsic value
    a. cannot be justified by assets, earnings, dividends, sure prospects, or management.
    b. can be justified by dividends and expected capital gains.
    c. and current market price typically coincide.
    d. and current market price rarely coincide given investor pessimism and euphoria.
12. According to Graham and Dodd,
    a. investors are rarely rational.
    b. intrinsic value tends to converge on price over time.
    c. a sound valuation is eventually validated in an efficiently functioning marketplace.
    d. a sound valuation is quickly validated in an efficiently functioning marketplace.
13. According to Graham and Dodd, the objective of security analysis is to
    a. seek company valuations, which, on average, prove more reliable than the marketplace.
    b. form an informed opinion of historical profitability and growth.
    c. picture the company as a going concern over all business conditions.
    d. identify overpriced securities and enjoy excess returns following the market's subsequent upward revaluation to a price consistent with intrinsic value.
14. The value of ROE is calculated as the ratio of
    a. ROE divided by P/E.
    b. the EPS growth rate divided by P/E.
    c. P/E divided by ROE.
    d. P/E divided by the EPS growth rate.

15. High dividend yields are typically associated with stocks that display
    a. below-average risk.
    b. below-average total returns.
    c. above-average total returns.
    d. below-average dividend payout ratios.
16. Holding all else equal, an increase in dividend payments results in higher
    a. EBIDTA.
    b. cash flow.
    c. free cash flow.
    d. none of these.
17. In a *Value Line* regression, the relevant *Y*-variable is
    a. stock price.
    b. earnings per share.
    c. stockholders' equity.
    d. expected total return.
18. *Value Line* outliers identify
    a. the fundamental business prospects of a company.
    b. the intrinsic value of a stock.
    c. the regression line that best describes (fits) the 60-month stock price history of a company.
    d. underpriced (timely) stocks or overpriced (not timely) stocks.
19. Wall Street research shows that
    a. positive-earnings surprises boost the share price of high P/E stocks more than in the case of low P/E stocks.
    b. negative-earnings surprises harm the share price of low P/E stocks more than in the case of high P/E stocks.
    c. security analyst forecasts of earnings per share tend to become more accurate over longer as opposed to shorter time periods.
    d. security analyst forecasts of earnings per share are rarely accurate.
20. Graham and Dodd investment bargains tend to
    a. have large operating losses or significant off–balance sheet liabilities.
    b. be plentiful.
    c. represent high profit-margin businesses.
    d. have low current assets relative to total liabilities.

Investment Application

Should You Buy Stock in a Mickey Mouse Organization?

The Walt Disney Company is one of the best-known and best-managed entertainment companies in the world. As the cornerstone of a carefully integrated entertainment marketing strategy, the company owns and operates the world's most acclaimed amusement parks and entertainment facilities. Some of the best-known and most successful among these are Disneyland, California, and Walt Disney World, Florida—an immense entertainment center that includes the Magic Kingdom, Epcot Center, and Disney-MGM Studios. During recent years, the company has extended its amusement park business to foreign soil with Tokyo Disneyland and Euro Disneyland, located just outside of Paris, France. Disney's foreign operations provide an interesting example of the company's shrewd combination of marketing and financial skills. To conserve scarce capital resources, Disney was able to entice foreign investors to put up 100% of the financing required for both the Tokyo and Paris facilities. In turn, Disney is responsible for the design and management of both operations, retains an important equity interest, and enjoys significant royalties on all gross revenues. Disney's innovative means for financing foreign operations has enabled the company to greatly expand its revenue and profit base without any commensurate increase in capital expenditures. As a result, the success of its foreign operations has allowed the company to increase its already enviable rate of return on stockholders' equity.

Disney is also a major force in the movie production business with Buena Vista, Touchstone, and Hollywood Pictures, in addition to the renowned Walt Disney Studios. The company is famous for recent hit movies such as *Beauty and the Beast, The Lion King,* and *Pocohantas,* in addition to a film library including hundreds of movie classics such as *Fantasia, Snow White,* and *Mary Poppins.* Disney uses an aggressive and highly successful video marketing strategy for new films and rereleases from the company's extensive film library. The Disney Store, a chain of retail specialty shops, profits from the sale of movie tie-in merchandise, books, and recorded music. Also making a significant contribution to the bottom line are earnings from the cable TV Disney Channel. In 1996, the Disney empire grew further with the acquisition of Capital Cities/ABC, a print and television media behemoth, for stock and cash. The company's family entertainment marketing strategy is so broad in its reach that Disney characters such as Mickey Mouse, Donald Duck, and Goofy have become an integral part of U.S. culture. Given its ability to turn whimsy into outstanding operating performance, the Walt Disney Company is one firm that does not mind being called a "Mickey Mouse Organization."

Table 11.8 shows a variety of accounting operating statistics, including revenues, cash flow, capital spending, dividends, earnings, book value, and year-end share prices for the Walt Disney Corporation during the 1980–97 period. All data are expressed in dollars per share to illustrate how individual shareholders have benefited from the company's consistently superior rates of growth. During this time frame, for example, revenue per share grew at an annual rate of 18.8% per year and earnings per share grew by 14.6% per year. These performance measures exceed industry and economy-wide norms by a substantial margin. Disney employees, CEO Michael D. Eisner, and all stockholders have profited greatly from the company's outstanding performance. Over the 1980–97 period, Disney common stock exploded in price from $1.07 per share to 33, after adjusting for stock splits. This represents more than a 22.3% annual rate of return and makes Disney one of the truly outstanding stock market performers during recent years.

Of course, present-day investors want to know how the company will fare during coming years. Will the company be able to continue sizzling growth, or like many companies, will Disney find it impossible to maintain such stellar performance? On the one hand, Tokyo Disneyland and Euro Disneyland promise significant future

TABLE 11.8 Operating Statistics for the Walt Disney Company (all data in dollars per share)

Year	Revenues	Cash Flow	Capital Spending	Dividends	Earnings	Book Value	Year-End Share Price
1980	$0.59	$0.11	$0.10	$0.02	$0.09	$0.69	$1.07
1981	0.65	0.10	0.21	0.02	0.08	0.75	1.09
1982	0.64	0.09	0.38	0.03	0.06	0.80	1.32
1983	0.79	0.11	0.20	0.03	0.06	0.85	1.10
1984	1.02	0.13	0.12	0.03	0.06	0.71	1.25
1985	1.30	0.18	0.12	0.03	0.11	0.76	2.35
1986	1.58	0.24	0.11	0.03	0.15	0.90	3.59
1987	1.82	0.34	0.18	0.03	0.24	1.17	4.94
1988	2.15	0.42	0.37	0.03	0.32	1.48	5.48
1989	2.83	0.55	0.46	0.04	0.43	1.87	9.33
1990	3.70	0.65	0.45	0.05	0.50	2.21	8.46
1991	3.96	0.58	0.59	0.06	0.40	2.48	9.54
1992	4.77	0.72	0.35	0.07	0.51	2.99	14.33
1993	5.31	0.78	0.49	0.08	0.54	3.13	14.21
1994	6.40	0.97	0.65	0.10	0.68	3.50	15.33
1995	7.70	1.15	0.57	0.12	0.84	4.23	19.63
1996	10.50	1.32	0.86	0.14	0.74	7.96	23.83
1997	11.10	1.51	0.95	0.17	0.92	8.54	33.00
2001–2003*	20.25	2.90	1.70	0.38	1.90	14.95	

*Indicates Value Line estimates from 1998.
Data sources: *The Value Line Investment Survey* (various years); *Compustat PC+,* January 1998.

revenues and profits from previously untapped global markets. Anyone with young children who has visited Disneyland or Disney World has seen their delight and fascination with Disney characters. It is also impossible not to notice how much foreign travelers to the United States seem to enjoy the Disney experience. Donald Duck and Mickey Mouse will do a lot of business abroad. Future expansion possibilities in Malaysia, China, or the former Soviet Union also hold the potential for rapid growth into the next century. On the other hand, growth of 20% per year is exceedingly hard to maintain for any length of time. At that pace, the 108,000 workers employed by Disney in 1998 would grow to more than 155,000 by the year 2000 and to roughly one million by the year 2010. Maintaining control with such a rapidly growing workforce would be challenging, to say the least; maintaining Disney's high level of creative energy might not be possible.

Given the many uncertainties faced by Disney and most major corporations, long-term forecasts of operating performance by industry analysts are usually restricted to a fairly short time perspective. *The Value Line Investment Survey,* one of the most widely respected forecast services, focuses on a three- to five-year time horizon. To forecast performance for any individual company, Value Line starts with an underlying forecast of the economic environment three to five years hence. During mid-1998, for example, Value Line forecasted a 2001–2003 economic environment in which unemployment will average 5.5% of the workforce, compared with 4.6% in 1998. Industrial production will be expanding about 2.5% per year; inflation measured by the consumer price index will continue at a modest 2.8% per year. Long-term interest rates are projected to be about 6.5%, and gross domestic product will average about $10 trillion in the years 2001 through 2003, or about 25% above the 1999 level of $8 trillion. As Value Line states, things may turn out differently, but these plausible assumptions offer a fruitful basis for measuring the relative growth potential of various firms such as Disney.[2]

The most interesting economic statistic for Disney stockholders is, of course, its stock price during some future period, say 2001–2003. In economic terms, stock prices represent the net present value of future cash flows, discounted at an appropriate risk-adjusted rate of return. To forecast Disney's stock price during the 2001–2003 period, an investor might use some or all the data in Table 11.8. Historical numbers for a recent period, such as 1980–98, often represent a useful context for projecting future stock prices. For example, Fidelity's legendary mutual fund investor Peter Lynch argues that stock prices are largely determined by the future pattern of earnings per share. Stock prices typically rise following an increase in earnings per share and plunge when earnings per share plummet. Another justly famous value investor, Sir John Templeton, the father of global stock market investing, focuses on book value per share. Templeton contends that future earnings are closely related to the book value of the firm, or accounting net worth. According to Templeton, "bargains" can be found when stock can be purchased in companies that sell in the marketplace at a significant discount to book value, or when book value per share is expected to rise dramatically. Both Lynch and Templeton have built a large following among investors who have profited mightily using their stock market selection techniques.

As an experiment, it will prove interesting to use the data provided in Table 11.8 to estimate regression lines that can be used to forecast the average common stock price for Walt Disney Company over the 2001–2003 period.

A. A simple regression model applied to data from the 1980–97 period, where the dependent *Y*-variable is the Disney year-end stock price and the independent *X*-variable is Disney's earnings per share, reads as follows (*t*-statistics in parentheses):

$$\begin{array}{l} P_t = \$-1.838 + \$30.153 EPS_t + u_t \quad \bar{R}^2 = 90.4\% \\ \qquad\;\; (-1.66) \qquad (12.71) \end{array}$$

Use this model to forecast Disney's average stock price for the 2001–2003 period by using the Value Line estimate of Disney's average earnings per share for 2001–2003. Discuss this share-price forecast.

B. A simple regression model applied to data from the 1980–97 period, where the *Y*-variable is the Disney year-end stock price and the *X*-variable is Disney's book value per share, reads as follows (*t*-statistics in parentheses):

$$\begin{array}{l} P_t = \$0.116 + \$3.727 BV_t + u_t \quad \bar{R}^2 = 93.0\% \\ \qquad\;\; (0.14) \qquad (15.10) \end{array}$$

Use this model to forecast Disney's average stock price for the 2001–2003 period by using the Value Line estimate of Disney's average book value per share for 2001–2003. Discuss this share-price forecast.

---

[2]See "Economic Series," *The Value Line Investment Survey*, July 31, 1998, 1160.

C. A multiple regression model applied to data from the 1980–97 period, where the *Y*-variable is the Disney year-end stock price and the *X*-variables are Disney's earnings per share and book value per share, reads as follows (*t*-statistics in parentheses):

$$P_t = -\$1.404 + \$14.442EPS_t + \$2.175BV_t + u_t \quad \bar{R}^2 = 97.9\%$$
$$\quad (-2.67) \quad (6.11) \qquad\qquad (7.55)$$

Use this model to forecast Disney's average stock price for the 2001–2003 period by using the Value Line estimate of Disney's average earnings per share and book value per share for 2001–2003. Discuss this share-price forecast.

D. A multiple regression model applied to data from the 1980–97 period, where the *Y*-variable is the Disney year-end stock price and *X*-variables include the accounting operating statistics shown in Table 11.8, reads as follows (*t*-statistics in parentheses):

$$P_t = -\$2.562 - \$3.708REV_t + \$21.3CF_t - \$4.448CAPX_t + \$112.0DIV_t$$
$$\quad (-2.95) \quad (-1.89) \quad (0.82) \quad (-1.41) \quad (2.43)$$
$$+ \$5.21EPS_t + \$2.837BV_t + u_t \quad \bar{R}^2 = 98.3\%$$
$$(0.24) \qquad (2.50)$$

Use this model and Value Line estimates to forecast Disney's average stock price for the 2001–2003 period. Discuss this share-price forecast.

Selected References

Aggarwal, Rajesh K., and Andrew A. Samwick. "Executive Compensation, Strategic Competition, and Relative Performance Evaluation: Theory and Evidence." *Journal of Finance* 54 (December 1999): 1999–2043.

Arnold, Tom, and Jerry James. "Finding Firm Value without a Pro Forma Analysis." *Financial Analysts Journal* 56 (March/April 2000): 77–84.

Balvers, Ronald, Yangru Wu, and Erik Gilliland. "Mean Reversion across National Stock Markets and Parametric Contrarian Investment Strategies." *Journal of Finance* 55 (April 2000): 745–772.

Bittlingmayer, George, and Thomas W. Hazlett. "DOS Kapital: Has Antitrust Action against Microsoft Created Value in the Computer Industry?" *Journal of Financial Economics* 55 (March 2000): 329–359

Davis, James L., Eugene F. Fama, and Kenneth R. French. "Characteristics, Covariances, and Average Returns: 1929 to 1997." *Journal of Finance* 55 (February 2000): 389–406.

Denis, David J., and Timothy A. Kruse. "Managerial Discipline and Corporate Restructuring following Performance Declines." *Journal of Financial Economics* 55 (March 2000): 391–424.

Desai, Hemang, and Prem C. Jain. "Firm Performance and Focus: Long-Run Stock Market Performance following Spinoffs." *Journal of Financial Economics* 54 (October 1999): 75–101.

Fisher, Kenneth L., and Meir Statman. "Investor Sentiment and Stock Returns." *Financial Analysts Journal* 56 (March/April 2000): 16–23.

Fridson, Martin S. "Value Investing: A Balanced Approach." *Financial Analysts Journal* 55 (September/October 1999): 92–93.

Hirschey, Mark, Vernon J. Richardson, and Susan Scholz. "How 'Foolish' Are Internet Investors?" *Financial Analysts Journal* 56 (January/February 2000): 62–69.

Kahle, Kathleen M. "Insider Trading and the Long-Run Performance of New Security Issues." *Journal of Corporate Finance* 6 (March 2000): 25–53.

La Porta, Rafael, Florencio Lopez-de-Silanes, Andrei Shleifer, and Robert W. Vishny. "Agency Problems and Dividend Policies around the World." *Journal of Finance* 55 (February 2000): 1–33.

Leibowitz, Martin L. "Franchise Labor." *Financial Analysts Journal* 56 (March/April 2000): 68–76.

Lewellen, Jonathan. "The Time-Series Relations among Expected Return, Risk, and Book-to-Market." *Journal of Financial Economics* 54 (October 1999): 5–43.

Olsen, Robert A. "Are Risk Premium Anomalies Caused by Ambiguity?" *Financial Analysts Journal* 56 (March/April 2000): 24–31.

PART 6

Efficient Markets

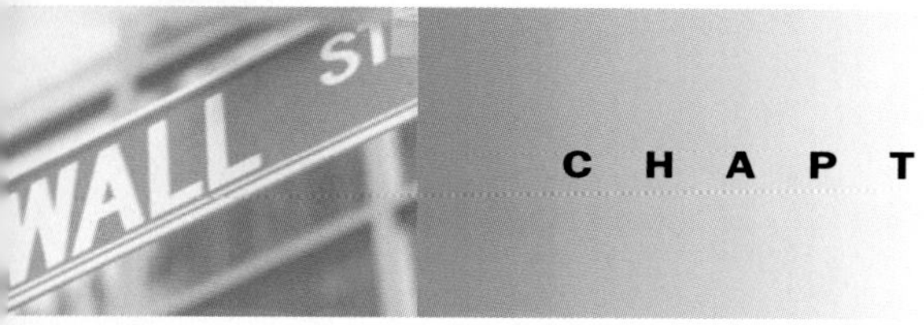

CHAPTER 12

Efficient Market Hypothesis

The ever-popular Motley Fool Web site <http://www.fool.com> aggressively pushes investing guides, investing tools, books, subscriptions, and even apparel and other "foolish" paraphernalia. They are especially proud of their new book, The Foolish Four: How to Crush Your Mutual Funds in 15 Minutes a Year with *** FREE SHIPPING! ***

> Are you outperforming the stock market? The Foolish Four is. It's so easy it takes only 15 minutes a year. So powerful it has compounded at 22% annually over the past 25 years! So safe you only invest in top blue-chip companies like IBM, Johnson and Johnson, and General Electric. The Foolish Four is a mechanical system of investing so compelling that we think it should be a part of almost every investor's portfolio. We've "back-tested" the approach more than 30 years, so it's a proven strategy.[1]

Boy, this sounds great! It is the most exciting "sure-fire" investment book since The Beardstown Ladies Investment Guide. *Oops! I guess that is the point. The Beardstown Ladies were a quaint group that purported to beat the market with another simple investment strategy. The Ladies' fame and book sales plummeted when journalists from* The Wall Street Journal *discovered that they had grossly overstated their investment returns. The Foolish Four strategy suffers from the same malady. When the Motley Fool says they have back-tested the Foolish Four approach, that means historical returns look good if you ignore taxes, commissions, and other real-world expenses. After taxes, commissions, and other trading costs that large and small investors must pay, Foolish Four stocks now underperform the stodgy old Dow Jones Industrial Average (DJIA).*

In the stock market, promised returns that look too good to be true are, in fact, too good to be true. Wall Street is not littered with $100 bills for the taking.

Efficient Market Concept

Treatise on Coin Flipping

Millions of stock-market investors and tens of thousands of professional money managers and security analysts around the globe seek stock-market bargains in a

[1]See: Foolmart: a foolish place to shop. <http://www.foolmart.com>.

24-hour trading day. Knowledgeable professional and individual investors comb through reams of widely available financial information looking for clues about how much to pay for what and when. Enterprising professionals and amateurs alike look for valuable unpublished information that "The Street" does not already know. The daily level of activity is feverish. It seems like serious business because it is. Any edge, ever so slight, can lead to enormous profits when sufficient leverage is used. And in a world filled with millions of investors hungry for stock market profits, enormous leverage will be brought to bear whenever valuable new information is discovered.

Investing in the stock market is taken seriously by millions of global investors. If anyone approaches investing as anything less than serious, millions of investors worldwide stand ready to take your money, and they will. Nobody should ever compare investing in the stock market with less serious pursuits such as gambling. Or should they? Of course not, at least when it comes to long-term investing. In the long run, the expected rate of return on common stocks in general falls in a range from 12 to 14% per year. These returns are tied to economic growth and the overall rate of inflation. In buying stocks, long-term investors are participating in the process of raising and committing capital for productive investment. Without equity and fixed-income investors, capital raising and our economic system would flounder.

Short-term speculation in the stock and bond markets is another thing altogether. In fact, it is well worth asking if short-term speculation in the stock market is the "blue-suit" equivalent of buying lottery tickets.

Imagine a global **coin-flipping contest** in which all six billion people in the world stand up and flip a dollar coin. Everybody whose coin comes up "heads" gets to remain standing and keep playing. Those whose coin comes up "tails" are out of the game and have to sit down. The losers' coins get contributed to a pot to be won by those lucky enough or able enough to keep flipping heads. The game ends whenever all remaining players agree to stop playing, or when only one player remains standing, whichever comes first.

coin-flipping contest Investment metaphor for gambling.

After round one, three billion players remain standing. These flippers were lucky enough to flip heads and are thus able to remain in the game. After 10 rounds, about six million coin flippers remain standing. These are among the luckiest coin flippers one has ever seen. They have flipped heads an astounding 10 times in a row. At this point, the good fortune enjoyed by the lucky coin flippers begins to give way to the perception that these folks are talented coin flippers.

Have you ever flipped 10 straight heads? Probably not. Among the crowd, the reasoning goes that these individuals must be unusually adept at coin flipping. Players begin to listen to the growing crowd. Some flippers are noticed for practicing their art with flair and charisma; others are noted for the cool patience and steadiness with which they approach the science of coin flipping. Some players will even begin to fashion themselves as "experts" in the art and science of coin flipping. To be sure, anyone who has flipped 10 heads in a row begins to get noticed.

After 10 more rounds, the elite circle of successful coin flippers has shrunk to roughly 6,000 persons worldwide. These people have flipped heads an unbelievable 20 times in a row. If there was any doubt whatsoever that they knew how to flip coins, that doubt has now been firmly and absolutely dispelled. Local notoriety has given way to large and growing regional reputations. Charming newspaper articles begin to appear about the humble roots of some, the hard luck stories of others, and how still others have been blessed since birth.

Half of these amazing success stories falter and fade on the next round when they inexplicably toss tails. Although some among the crowd utter their astonishment about how a talented favorite had lost his or her touch, attention quickly returns to the winners. It is more fun to watch the winners, and the pot to be shared by the winners is growing steadily.

After 25 rounds, only about 180 coin flippers remain standing worldwide. If the game stopped now, these coin flippers would each earn $33.3 million for their "efforts." For the first time, discussion begins among the winning coin flippers about whether they should call off the game, let each player collect his or her winnings, and go home. The conservatives get hooted down by more aggressive players. After all, these are among the most talented coin flippers of our generation. Books get written about them. Some establish schools designed to develop coin-flipping talent among the young and to spread interest in their particular approach. Others begin to make plans to endow such schools with their projected winnings. Of course, the winners vote to continue playing the game. Why stop now? After all, these players are *good* at flipping coins.

With only five more tosses, the ranks of the winners are further decimated. Now only six remain standing. If the game stopped now, each of these best coin flippers in the world would collect a cool $1 billion for their efforts. Discussion about the merits of continuing the game gets heated. However, the expected gain from continuing to play is greater than the anticipated loss, and the game goes on.

It takes only 32 tosses to reduce the number of winners to a single, solitary coin flipper. With a 50/50 chance of flipping heads, the chance of flipping heads 32 times in a row is roughly one in six billion. Thus, after about 32 tosses of a coin, a single solitary coin flipper, the one who has never flipped tails, walks off with a cool $6 billion.

Efficient Markets

At this point, it becomes intriguing to compare coin flippers with stock market speculators. There are literally millions of speculators and stock pickers trying to beat the stock market on a daily basis. Based on the laws of probability, many will be successful in significantly outperforming the market. The relevant question is: Are successful stock pickers equivalent to lucky coin flippers?

An important point to realize is that a long run of strong investment performance does not necessarily signify skill. This is especially true when it comes to the feverishly quick in and out trading typical of day traders and other short-term speculators. There are tens of thousands of money managers, mutual funds, and other professional market "players" constantly trying to beat the market. Investors who ignore mathematical probabilities run the risk of investing based on previous successes that are the result of nothing more than random chance. A "hot" mutual fund manager may be nothing more than lucky. Many stock market investors infer that they are smart when they buy a stock and it goes up. They tend to regard themselves as unlucky if they buy a stock and it goes down. This is a dangerous pattern of beliefs to fall into. In fact, an investor can be judged neither correct nor incorrect based on whether the market agrees with her or him over the short term.

efficient market In an efficient stock market, the price for any given stock effectively represents the expected net present value of all future profits.

In the short term, theory and evidence tell us that stock prices are equally apt to rise or fall in an **efficient market.** In an efficient stock market, the price for any given stock effectively represents the expected net present value of all future profits. In this calculation, profits are discounted by using a fair or risk-adjusted rate of return. If the stock market is to be perfectly efficient, there must be a large number of buyers and sellers of essential identical securities, information must be free and readily available, and entry and exit by market players must be uninhibited.

On an overall basis, basic criteria for an efficient market seem easily met by the stock market. In the United States, there are literally thousands of actively traded securities that promise investors a wide array of capital gain–and dividend income–producing opportunities. For any given risk class, there are dozens of common stocks with essentially identical economic characteristics. Moreover, financial and nonfinancial stock market information is widely disseminated to individual investors in the financial press, on television and radio. Hard-to-find information that was sought and prized by professional investors only a decade ago is now instantly published and available to all on the Internet. And finally, not only are millions of eager investors available to bid up the prices of attractive securities, the supply of available securities quickly adjusts to meet investor demand. For example, following the amazing stock market success of Netscape Communications, America Online, Inc., and Amazon.com, a veritable flood of new issues raised the number of publicly traded Internet or "dot.com" companies to more than 200 by mid-1999.

At any point in time, prices in an efficient market reflect the interplay of demand and supply. Investors seeking bargains bid up the price of attractive securities. Companies with quickly deteriorating economic fundamentals see their stock price collapse as investors desert in droves. Thus, at any point in time, the price for any stock or bond reflects the collective wisdom of market buyers and sellers regarding the company's future economic prospects. As such, the market price for a stock is the best available estimate of the company's future economic prospects given all that is presently known in the market. This makes it tough for professionals and amateurs alike to beat the market, let alone "wrestle its scrawny little body to the ground and make it beg for mercy" (see Figure 12.1).

Efficient Market Hypothesis

Basic Premise

The **efficient market hypothesis (EMH)** states that security prices fully reflect all available information. The implications of this simple premise are truly profound.

efficient market hypothesis (EMH) Theory stating that security prices fully reflect all available information.

Individual and professional investors buy and sell stocks under the assumption that they have discovered a divergence between intrinsic value and market price. When market price is below perceived intrinsic value, buyers aggressively acquire and bid up the price of such securities. When market price is above perceived intrinsic value, sellers aggressively abandon such securities and prices fall.

However, it is worth remembering that every transaction includes both buyers and sellers. Through their market activity, each buyer and each seller is behaving in such a way as to imply that they somehow know more than the person acting on the other side of each transaction. If the stock and bond markets are perfectly efficient and current prices fully reflect all available information, then neither buyers nor sellers have an informational advantage. In an efficient market, both buyers and sellers have exactly the same set of information.

FIGURE 12.1 **"Beat the Market" Strategies Are Always Popular but Seldom Effective**

"I don't want to just beat the market. I want to wrestle its scrawny little body to the ground and make it beg for mercy."

$8 INTERNET TRADE UNLIMITED SHARES Ready to take on the stock market? Ameritrade makes it simple to trade. Not to mention inexpensive. Commissions for Internet equity market orders are only $8, no matter how many shares you buy or sell. Or trade with a broker for $18. Limit and stop orders are just $5 more. And with Ameritrade, you get the same research tools that many professionals use. So call or visit our Web site today and open your account. The sooner you do, the sooner you can show that weak-kneed, lily-livered stock market who's boss.

Special offer: Get three commission-free equity trades to use in your first 90 days as a customer when you open your account between 9/1/99–12/20/99. Call 1.800.326.7271 and mention offer code REC.

Ameritrade®

Believe in yourself℠

Visit www.ameritrade.com AOL keyword: ameritrade

Not valid with any other offer. Not available for IRA accounts. Market volatility and volume may delay system access and trade executions. Member NASD/SIPC. $2,000 minimum equity required to open your account. SIPC account protection is $500,000, including $100,000 cash claims. An additional $24.5 million in securities protection is provided.

©1999 Ameritrade. Source: *USA Today,* October 21, 1999.

WALL STREET WISDOM 12.1

The Market Knows

In an efficient market, all pertinent investment information is reflected in stock prices. Every stock at every point in time is judged to be an equally good candidate for purchase or sale. This means that share prices can be used as useful indicators of the value placed on hard-to-value information. For example, the market's wisdom, as reflected through share prices, often gives interesting clues as to what investors can expect with respect to mergers and acquisitions.

For example, on June 6, 1999, two giant financial institutions headquartered in Salt Lake City, Utah, issued a corporate press release to happily announce their "merger of equals:"

> Zions Bancorporation (Nasdaq: ZION) and First Security Corporation (Nasdaq: FSCO) today announced a strategic merger that will create a financial services enterprise uniquely positioned in the best growth markets in the country. With assets of approximately $40 billion, the combination will result in the nation's 20th largest bank holding company. Under the terms of a definitive merger agreement, the two companies will merge in a stock-for-stock transaction valued at approximately $5.9 billion. The new organization will be known as First Security Corporation and headquartered in Salt Lake City.
>
> Under the terms of the agreement, which has been approved by the boards of directors of both companies, First Security shareholders will receive 0.442 of a share of new First Security common stock for each share of First Security common stock and Zions shareholders will receive one share of new First Security common stock in exchange for each share of Zions common stock. . . . Based on Zions' closing common stock price on June 4, 1999, the transaction valued First Security at $28.90 per share, a premium of 55% to First Security's closing price of $18.38 on that date.

Unfortunately, as sometimes happens with noncorporate marriages, this proposed union hit a snag on its way to the altar. After the merger had been approved by regulators, Zions balked when First Security issued a profit warning on March 3, 2000. This led Zions' New York investment banking firm Goldman Sachs Group, Inc., to announce that it no longer considered the deal favorable to Zions shareholders. Zions wanted a lower price, but First Security

(continued)

First Security: Taking It to the Bank

First Security's daily closing price

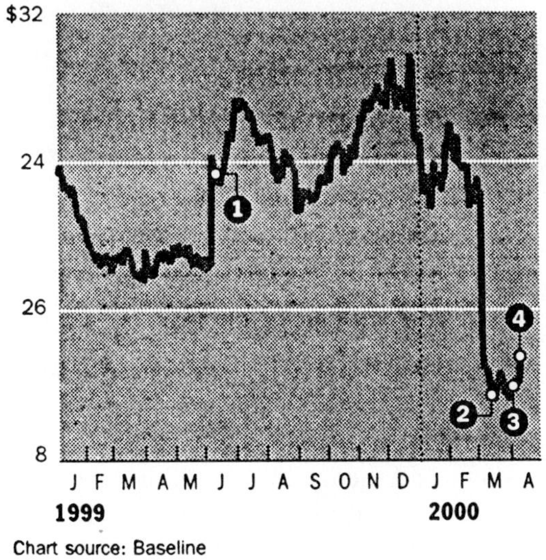

Chart source: Baseline

1. **June 6, 1999:** Zions Bancorp and First Security agree to merge in a $5.9 billion stock deal.
2. **March 13, 2000:** Goldman Sachs Group, financial adviser to Zions, says the exchange ratio in the proposed deal is unfair to Zions shareholders after First Security announces first-quarter earnings will not meet expectations.
3. **April 1:** First Security officially ends its attempt to merge one day after Zions shareholders reject the deal.
4. **April 10:** First Security is acquired by Wells Fargo in a stock pact value at around $2.9 billion.

(continued)

was not budging. On March 22, 2000, First Security approved the original terms of the merger agreement in preparation for a vote on the deal by Zions shareholders.

On March 30, 2000, the night before Zions shareholders' meeting, First Security's stock price closed at \$12; Zions closed at \$38.31. At that point in time, the expected value of First Security stock could be calculated based on its merger prospects. If the merger were voted on favorably by Zions shareholders, First Security would be worth \$16.93 (= 0.442 × \$38.31). If the merger were turned down, First Security would be worth some lesser amount as a stand-alone organization. Because First Security was selling for less than \$16.93, the market was telling investors that the merger had less than a 100% chance of being approved by Zions shareholders. The odds of the merger closing at the agreed-on terms were no better than 70.9% (= \$12/16.93).

As it turned out, Zions shareholders voted down the First Security merger. On next trading day, First Security stock closed at \$12.06, or up only six cents. This means that the market accurately predicted the Zions' merger vote. Only five trading days later, First Security moved up modestly to \$13.38 as the company okayed an alternative merger agreement with Wells Fargo. Apparently, the market also "knew" that another merger agreement was in the offing. As shown in the accompanying figure, merger news gets quickly and accurately reflected in stock prices.

See: Jonathan Eig, "Wells Fargo to Acquire First Security in Stock Deal Valued at \$2.89 Billion," *Wall Street Journal,* April 11, 2000, A3, A16.

In such circumstances, buying and selling securities in an attempt to outperform the market is a game of chance rather than skill. In other words, in an efficient market there is a 50-50 chance that the buyer will profit at the expense of the seller. Similarly, there is a 50-50 chance that the seller will profit at the expense of the buyer.

Within the context of the EMH, important characteristics of a perfectly competitive securities market include the following:

- New information arrives at the marketplace in an independent and random fashion.
- Investors rapidly adjust stock prices to reflect new information.
- Current stock prices reflect all relevant risk and return information.

The EMH can be viewed as a simple statement of the effectiveness with which financial securities such as stocks and bonds are priced. It implies that with the near-perfect distribution of financial information that is typical of our electronic society, stock prices accurately reflect everything that is known. As a result, stock prices only change when new information comes to the market. However, because new information cannot be anticipated, there is no way for the average investor to gain an edge.

Levels of Market Efficiency

Like any theory, the EMH is only useful to the extent that it can describe or predict real-world behavior. To the extent that the EMH accurately describes the configuration of securities prices, it can be useful in helping investors and others understand the price formation process. If the EMH does not yield useful insight concerning the security price formation process, it is bad theory and should be abandoned.

Because real-world securities markets are fraught with uncertainty, obtaining convincing evidence regarding the EMH is difficult. As a result, stock market analysts and financial economists have settled on three basic definitions or forms of market efficiency that can be studied independently of one another in an effort to learn the extent to which the EMH is a useful concept. Three alternative forms of the EMH can be described as:

- **Weak-Form Hypothesis**—current prices reflect all **stock market information.** Trading rules based on past stock market returns and trading volume are futile.
- **Semistrong-Form Hypothesis**—current prices reflect all **public information.** All trading rules based on public information are futile.
- **Strong-Form Hypothesis**—current prices reflect all public information and **nonpublic information.** All trading rules are futile.

weak-form hypothesis Premise that current prices reflect all stock market information.

stock market information Stock price and trading volume information.

semistrong-form hypothesis Premise that stock prices reflect all public information.

public information Freely shared knowledge.

strong-form hypothesis Premise that stock prices reflect all public information and nonpublic information.

nonpublic information Proprietary data.

Notice how each of these forms of the EMH involve slightly different assumptions regarding the level of information that is incorporated in security prices at any point in time.

The weak-form hypothesis involves the easiest or lowest hurdle that must be met for one to argue that the stock market is efficient. According to the weak-form hypothesis, stock and bond prices reflect all prior price and trading volume activity. As such, in an efficient stock market, it would not be possible to earn above-market returns by buying or selling stocks on the premise that they are going up on price momentum, or bound to rise on a quick reversal of "panic selling." In a market that is perfectly efficient, there is no such thing as panic selling, nor panic buying for that matter. All buying and selling are fully informed and unbiased in their assessment of the intrinsic value of the company's future prospects.

The semistrong-form hypothesis is somewhat more strict than the weak-form hypothesis. According to the semistrong-form hypothesis, no investor can obtain an edge by buying or selling stocks on the basis of any publicly available information. Of course, past stock market returns and trading volume activity are only a small part of this publicly available information. For example, at the moment unknown and unpredictable quarterly earnings information is released, stock prices quickly and accurately readjust so that subsequent investors earn only a risk-adjusted normal rate of return on their investment. Similarly, the moment a favorable report is issued by a leading Wall Street investment banker such as Merrill Lynch, stock prices react to incorporate that information. According to the semistrong-form hypothesis, anything you read in the newspaper, hear on television, or see on the Internet is already reflected in stock and bond prices.

The strong-form hypothesis is the toughest or highest hurdle that must be met for the stock market to be regarded as perfectly efficient. It encompasses all the various types of information considered by the weak-form and semistrong-form hypotheses and more. The securities market can be regarded as perfectly efficient only if all relevant information is accurately and instantaneously reflected in security prices. For example, to the extent that insiders such as the company chairman and CEO together earn above-normal rates of return on their stock market investments in the company, the market would not be judged as perfectly efficient according to the strong-form hypothesis. If such insiders do, in fact, earn above-normal rates of return, then one might conclude that they have profited by virtue of their access to superior or **insider information.**

insider information Proprietary data within the firm.

Notice how it might be possible to reject the notion of strong-form efficiency in favor of some weaker criteria such as semistrong-form efficiency. For example, if company insiders consistently earn above-normal rates of return, the concept of strong-form efficiency would be rejected. However, semistrong-form efficiency could still be maintained if investors fail to earn excess returns when they mimic insiders by basing buy and sell decisions on published reports of inside trading activity.

Time Series of Stock Prices

Indexes Are Correlated over Time

Most investors are well aware of the fact that stock market indexes move together over extended time frames. For example, during the five-year period from April 1, 1995, to March 31, 2000, the DJIA went on an unprecedented run from 4168.4 to 10921.9. This stunning advance of 162.0% represented a compound annual rate of growth before dividends of 21.2% per year. During this same time frame, the Standard & Poor's (S&P) 500 Index jumped from 501.9 to 1498.6, or 198.6% and 24.5% per year, while Nasdaq leapt from 818.1 to 4572.8, an astonishing run of 459.0%, or 41.1% per year.

As shown in Figure 12.2, the DJIA, S&P 500, and Nasdaq indexes move together over this time frame. Market indexes typically move up or down together. In statistical terms, these measures of overall market performance are correlated over time. Whenever the movement of stock prices over time is being analyzed, these

FIGURE 12.2 **Market Indexes Move Together over Time**

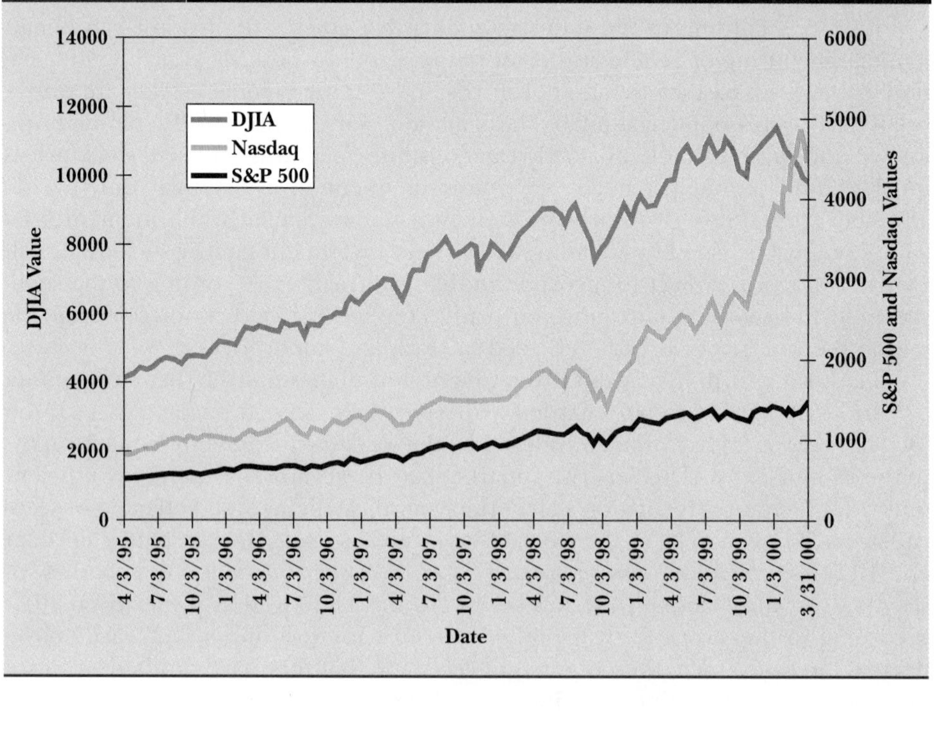

TABLE 12.1 Degree of Correlation Shows How Stock Market Indexes Move Together

	DJIA	S&P 500	Nasdaq
DJIA	100.00%		
S&P 500	93.72%	100.00%	
Nasdaq	66.12%	80.97%	100.00%

Note: Data are for the five-year period from 4/1/95 to 3/31/00.

data are described as a **time series** of market data. Correlation is said to be high and positive when large values of one index are associated with large values of another index. A correlation coefficient of +100% indicates perfect positive correlation. Correlation is said to be high and negative when large values of one index set are associated with small values of another index. A correlation coefficient of −100% indicates perfect negative or inverse correlation. When the values of market indexes are unrelated to each other, their correlation is near zero. A correlation coefficient of 0% indicates that two sets of data have no relation.

time series Data points over time.

Over this time frame, the correlation coefficient between daily returns for the DJIA and the S&P 500 is 93.72% (see Table 12.1). These two indexes closely capture movement among large-cap stocks and are similarly influenced by changes in interest rates and economic conditions. The correlation coefficient between daily returns for the DJIA and the Nasdaq is only 66.12%. This is consistent with the observation that over this period the DJIA and the Nasdaq indexes captured somewhat different aspects of the long-term advance in stock prices. The DJIA is dominated by established and diversified firms that represent a broad cross section of U.S. industry. By contrast, the Nasdaq index is dominated by large high-tech stocks such as Microsoft Corp., Intel Corp., Cisco Systems, Inc., MCI Worldcom, Inc., and Dell Computer Corp. These stocks also were important components of the S&P 500. But only two, Microsoft and Intel, were included in the DJIA, and for only part of this time frame. Thus, it comes as no surprise that the correlation of 80.97% between the S&P 500 and the Nasdaq tends to be somewhat greater than the correlation between the DJIA and Nasdaq.

Daily Returns

In any given year, the expected rate of return on a diversified portfolio of common stocks is roughly 12–14%, the long-term average rate of return. This means that market indexes, such as the DJIA and the S&P 500, typically advance at low double-digit rates. There are good economic reasons why stocks typically go up in price. Because stocks represent part ownership in real businesses, they benefit from economic growth made possible by technical progress and a growing population.

Although stocks can be counted on to advance over long periods of time, it is important to recognize that day-to-day changes in stock prices occur in an irregular and unpredictable pattern. Figure 12.3 shows the pattern of daily returns for the DJIA, S&P 500, and Nasdaq indexes over the five-year 4/1/95–3/31/00 period. Notice how closely centered these daily returns are around zero. In fact, the average daily return on the DJIA over this period was a scant 0.08%. During this same

FIGURE 12.3 **Daily Returns Are Noisy and Random around a Mean of Zero**

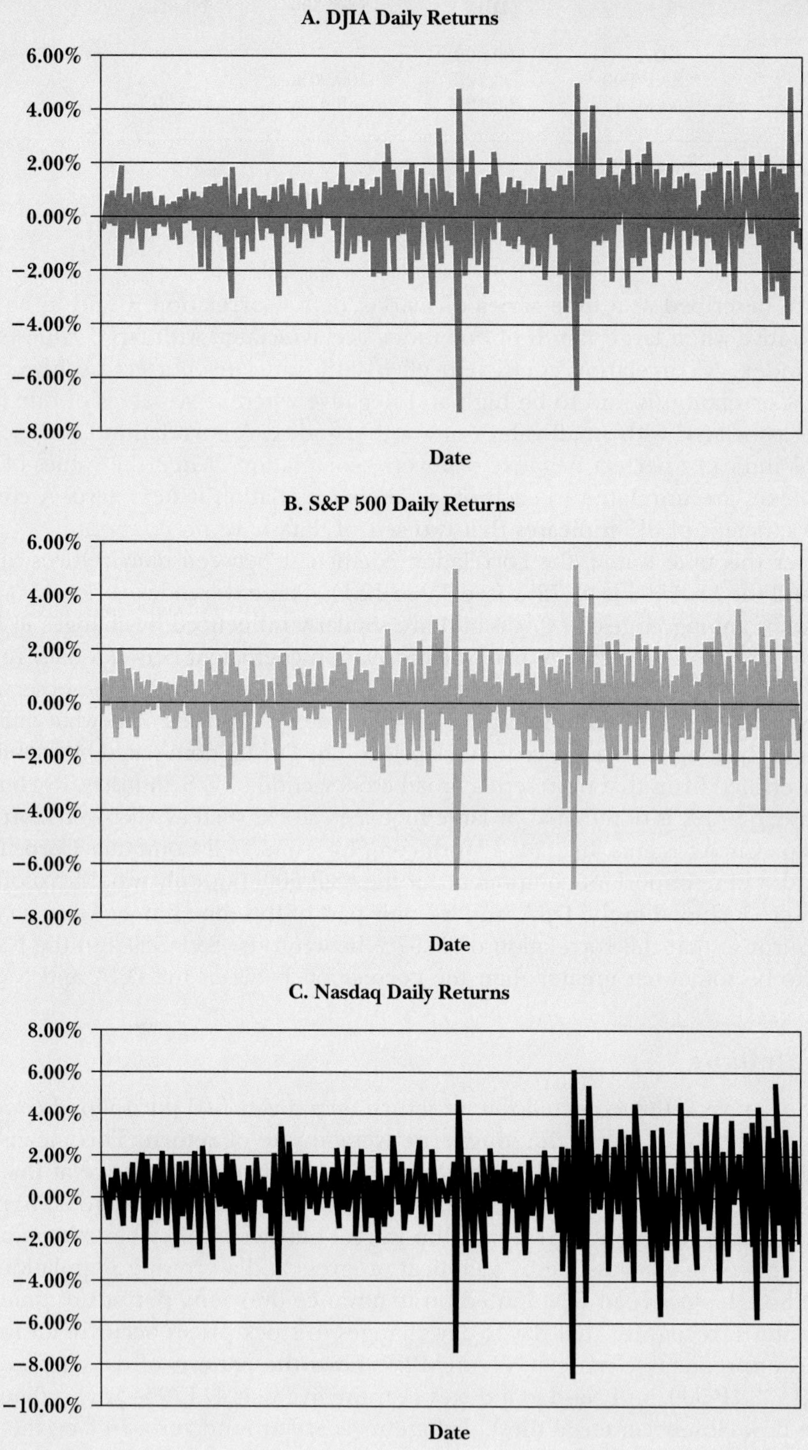

Note: Data are for the five-year period from 4/1/95 to 3/31/00.

period, the average daily return on the S&P 500 was 0.09% and on the Nasdaq Index was 0.15%. As Figure 12.2 shows, this was a period of unusually robust growth in the market, so the daily returns shown in the figure are well above historical norms, on average. In fact, these average daily returns were roughly double the long-term averages.

Even during a period of highly robust market returns, it is interesting to note how commonly negative-return days occur. With respect to the DJIA, for example, Table 12.2 shows that 679 of 1,261 trading days were positive-return days, and 579

TABLE 12.2 Daily Market Returns Fluctuate around a Mean of Roughly 0%

Bin	DJIA Frequency	S&P 500 Frequency	Nasdaq Frequency
−10.00%	0	0	0
−7.50%	0	0	1
−5.00%	2	2	3
−4.00%	1	0	5
−3.00%	6	7	22
−2.75%	4	3	9
−2.50%	4	8	14
−2.25%	10	2	15
−2.00%	12	15	11
−1.75%	13	20	22
−1.50%	23	20	34
−1.25%	26	31	35
−1.00%	36	30	36
−0.75%	78	63	53
−0.50%	78	90	87
−0.25%	126	117	92
0.00%	163	159	91
0.25%	157	158	117
0.50%	123	138	112
0.75%	99	114	112
1.00%	107	92	98
1.25%	71	65	76
1.50%	41	39	46
1.75%	23	29	43
2.00%	24	19	32
2.25%	12	13	22
2.50%	8	7	18
2.75%	4	9	17
3.00%	1	3	9
4.00%	5	4	19
5.00%	4	2	6
7.50%	0	2	4
10.00%	0	0	0
More	0	0	0
Average	**0.08%**	**0.09%**	**0.15%**
Standard deviation	**1.04%**	**1.05%**	**1.43%**
Positive	**679**	**694**	**731**
Negative	**579**	**566**	**530**
Unchanged	**3**	**1**	**0**
Total days	**1261**	**1261**	**1261**

Note: Data are for the five-year period from 4/1/95 to 3/31/00.

return days were negative. During one of the most robust five-year periods in stock market history, the DJIA experienced a downtick on 45.9% of all trading days! Significant volatility in the daily returns of the S&P 500 and the Nasdaq index are also evident over this period. On 566, or 44.9%, of all trading days, the S&P 500 experienced negative returns, whereas the Nasdaq index went down on 530, or 42.0%, of all trading days.

As depicted in Figure 12.3 and Table 12.2, there is significant day-to-day volatility in stock market returns. This means that there is a significant amount of dispersion around the average daily return. During this five-year time frame, the standard deviation of daily returns averaged more than 1%, or more than 10 times the average daily return. This means that the typical daily deviation in stock market

TABLE 12.3 Short-Term Price Changes in the Market Are Random and Unpredictable

Date	Open	High	Low	Close	Change	%	Prior Day	Following Day
A. Dow Jones Industrial Average Big Up-Days								
8-Sep-98	7964.9	8103.7	7779.0	8020.8	380.5	4.98%	−0.55%	−1.94%
16-Mar-00	10139.6	10716.2	10139.6	10630.6	499.2	4.93%	3.26%	−0.33%
28-Oct-97	7190.9	7553.6	6933.0	7498.3	337.1	4.71%	−7.18%	0.11%
15-Oct-98	7953.1	8375.6	7885.6	8299.4	330.6	4.15%	0.39%	1.41%
1-Sep-98	7583.1	7937.4	7379.7	7827.4	288.3	3.82%	−6.37%	−0.57%
2-Sep-97	7799.6	7903.5	7651.0	7879.8	257.4	3.38%	−0.94%	0.19%
15-Mar-00	9808.2	10294.6	9676.9	10131.4	320.2	3.26%	−0.46%	−1.87%
23-Sep-98	7988.6	8198.4	7891.8	8154.4	257.2	3.26%	0.82%	0.19%
3-Nov-97	7575.2	7709.0	7503.5	7674.4	232.3	3.12%	2.06%	−0.09%
5-Mar-99	9636.7	9799.9	9558.4	9736.1	268.7	2.84%	0.65%	0.68%
Averages						**3.84%**	**−0.83%**	**−0.22%**
B. Standard & Poors 500 Index Big Up-Days								
28-Oct-97	877.0	923.1	855.3	921.9	44.9	5.12%	−6.87%	−0.29%
8-Sep-98	973.9	1023.5	973.9	1023.5	49.6	5.09%	−0.85%	−1.69%
16-Mar-00	1392.2	1458.5	1392.2	1458.5	66.3	4.76%	2.43%	0.41%
15-Oct-98	1005.5	1053.1	1000.1	1047.5	42.0	4.17%	1.08%	0.85%
1-Sep-98	957.3	1000.7	940.0	994.3	37.0	3.86%	−6.80%	−0.38%
23-Sep-98	1029.6	1066.1	1029.6	1066.1	36.5	3.54%	0.56%	−2.19%
28-Oct-99	1296.7	1342.5	1296.7	1342.4	45.7	3.53%	1.15%	1.53%
2-Sep-97	899.5	927.6	899.5	927.6	28.1	3.13%	−0.46%	0.03%
11-Sep-98	980.2	1009.1	969.7	1009.1	28.9	2.95%	−2.58%	2.05%
3-Sep-99	1319.1	1357.7	1319.1	1357.2	38.1	2.89%	−0.90%	−0.50%
Averages						**3.90%**	**−1.32%**	**−0.02%**
C. NASDAQ Index Big Up-Days								
8-Sep-98	1,566.5	1,660.9	1,566.5	1,660.9	94.3	6.02%	−0.34%	−2.19%
24-Feb-00	4,583.9	4,620.0	4,495.2	4,617.7	235.5	5.37%	−0.67%	−0.59%
9-Oct-98	1,447.3	1,493.5	1,419.1	1,492.5	73.4	5.17%	−2.97%	3.59%
1-Sep-98	1,509.0	1,577.5	1,475.5	1,575.1	75.8	5.06%	−8.56%	1.13%
28-Oct-97	1,484.7	1,603.2	1,465.8	1,603.0	70.3	4.58%	−7.16%	−0.02%
15-Oct-98	1,541.8	1,611.4	1,538.6	1,611.0	70.0	4.55%	2.09%	0.62%
10-Jan-00	4,002.2	4,072.4	3,958.8	4,049.7	167.1	4.30%	4.17%	−3.17%
16-Jun-99	2,465.0	2,517.9	2,414.7	2,517.8	103.2	4.27%	0.68%	1.05%
7-Jan-00	3,711.1	3,882.7	3,711.1	3,882.6	155.5	4.17%	−3.88%	4.30%
11-Feb-99	2,339.0	2,405.8	2,326.2	2,405.6	96.1	4.16%	−0.06%	−3.48%
Averages						**4.77%**	**−1.67%**	**0.12%**

Note: Data are for the five-year period from 4/1/95 to 3/31/00.

returns tends to be far greater than the average daily return. No wonder day traders and other short-term speculators have a difficult time in deciphering the short-term direction of the market! Up-days seem to be closely followed by down-days in a day-to-day pattern that appears essentially chaotic.

As shown in Table 12.3, daily returns are clearly centered in the region around zero, with small positive daily returns on the order of 0.00–0.25% most common. Notice how the frequency of large up-days tends to diminish as the magnitude of the advance grows. Notice too how the frequency of declining markets tends to diminish with the size of the daily downtick. From a statistical perspective, the distribution of daily returns closely resembles a **normal distribution,** or bell-shaped curve, with an average daily return around zero.

normal distribution Bell-shaped curve.

TABLE 12.3 ***(continued)***

Date	Open	High	Low	Close	Change	%	Prior Day	Following Day
Dow Jones Industrial Average Big Down-Days								
27-Oct-97	7608.3	7717.4	7150.1	7161.2	−554.2	−7.18%	−1.69%	4.71%
31-Aug-98	8079.0	8149.0	7517.7	7539.1	−512.6	−6.37%	−1.40%	3.82%
27-Aug-98	8377.9	8448.7	8062.2	8166.0	−357.4	−4.19%	−0.92%	−1.40%
7-Mar-00	10197.6	10208.7	9651.8	9796.0	−374.5	−3.68%	−1.90%	0.62%
4-Aug-98	8859.9	8896.7	8463.4	8487.3	−299.4	−3.41%	−1.09%	0.70%
10-Sep-98	7680.4	7761.0	7469.0	7615.5	−249.5	−3.17%	−1.94%	2.36%
4-Jan-00	11349.8	11358.4	10907.0	10997.9	−359.6	−3.17%	−1.21%	1.13%
15-Aug-97	7851.0	7919.3	7685.1	7694.7	−247.3	−3.11%	0.17%	1.41%
8-Mar-96	5578.5	5612.8	5395.3	5470.5	−171.2	−3.03%	0.21%	2.02%
30-Sep-98	8025.4	8097.5	7775.4	7842.6	−237.9	−2.94%	−0.35%	−2.68%
Averages						**−4.03%**	**−1.01%**	**1.27%**
Standard & Poors 500 Index Big Down-Days								
27-Oct-97	941.6	941.6	876.7	877.0	−64.7	−6.87%	−0.95%	5.12%
31-Aug-98	1027.1	1033.5	957.3	957.3	−69.9	−6.80%	−1.48%	3.86%
27-Aug-98	1084.2	1084.2	1037.6	1042.6	−41.6	−3.84%	−0.79%	−1.48%
4-Jan-00	1455.2	1455.2	1397.4	1399.4	−55.8	−3.83%	−0.95%	0.19%
4-Aug-98	1112.4	1119.7	1071.8	1072.1	−40.3	−3.62%	−0.73%	0.87%
8-Mar-96	653.7	653.7	627.6	633.5	−20.2	−3.08%	0.25%	1.03%
30-Sep-98	1049.0	1049.0	1015.7	1017.0	−32.0	−3.05%	0.03%	−3.01%
18-Feb-00	1388.3	1388.6	1345.3	1346.1	−42.2	−3.04%	0.04%	0.45%
1-Oct-98	1017.0	1017.0	981.3	986.4	−30.6	−3.01%	−3.05%	1.64%
9-Jan-98	956.1	956.1	921.7	927.7	−28.4	−2.97%	−0.82%	1.24%
Averages						**−4.01%**	**−0.85%**	**0.99%**
NASDAQ Index Big Down-Days								
31-Aug-98	1,646.8	1,655.2	1,498.7	1,499.3	−140.4	−8.56%	−2.77%	5.06%
27-Oct-97	1,650.9	1,650.9	1,531.6	1,532.8	−118.2	−7.16%	−1.22%	4.58%
19-Apr-99	2,501.7	2,501.7	2,341.4	2,345.6	−138.4	−5.57%	−1.50%	2.73%
4-Jan-00	4,020.0	4,073.3	3,898.2	3,901.7	−229.5	−5.55%	1.52%	−0.62%
5-Oct-98	1,591.2	1,615.0	1,511.2	1,536.7	−78.3	−4.85%	0.16%	−1.68%
1-Oct-98	1,663.3	1,693.8	1,606.6	1,612.3	−81.5	−4.81%	−2.32%	0.16%
27-Aug-98	1,742.1	1,742.1	1,673.6	1,686.4	−81.7	−4.62%	−1.67%	−2.77%
14-Mar-00	4,997.3	5,013.5	4,706.6	4,706.6	−200.6	−4.09%	−2.80%	−2.63%
30-Mar-00	4,540.4	4,683.9	4,355.7	4,457.9	−186.8	−4.02%	−3.91%	2.58%
15-Jul-96	1,102.5	1,103.5	1,059.4	1,060.2	−43.3	−3.92%	−0.26%	−0.63%
Averages						**−5.32%**	**−1.48%**	**0.68%**

Booms and Busts

During recent years, investors have become increasingly interested in abruptly changing stock prices. In an Internet era of instant communication and low-cost stock trading, investor sentiment on the market can change suddenly and lead to sharp upswings or quick downturns in the market. Table 12.3 shows the 10 biggest up-days and the 10 biggest down-days in the DJIA, S&P 500, and Nasdaq indexes over the five-year 4/1/95–3/31/00 period.

Notice how often a big up-day for each respective market index was preceded by a day on which the index suffered negative returns. In the case of the DJIA, for example, six of 10 big up-days were preceded by negative-return days. In fact, the average rate of return on the day prior to a big up-day for the DJIA was −0.83%. Over this period, the pattern of a big up-day being preceded by a majority of down-days was also typical for the S&P 500 and Nasdaq indexes. The S&P 500 and the Nasdaq also experienced negative average returns on the day prior to big up-days.

Negative-return days just prior to big up-days may reflect a simple manifestation of the reversion-to-the-mean concept described in Chapter 5. Although such forces are surely at work, it is worth emphasizing that the magnitude of such daily return reversals is too small and too unpredictable to merit serious consideration as a day-to-day investment strategy. During this time frame, big up-days for the major market indexes averaged 3.84 to 4.77%. They were preceded by down-days that averaged only −0.83% to −1.67%. Notice from Table 12.2 how frequently such down-days were during this period of robust growth in the overall market. Literally dozens of substantial down-days are followed by up-days, down-days, or no change at all in the overall market.

For example, notice the muted response on days following big up-days in the overall market. The average market return ranged between −0.22% and 0.12% on the day just following big up-days in the major market indexes. In the case of big up-days, it is fair to say that the overall market hardly budged on the following day. This further undermines any case for attempting to use reversion-to-the-mean theory as a useful premise to guide day-to-day trading activity. Again, evidence suggests that the magnitude of daily return reversals is too small and too unpredictable to merit serious consideration of reversion to the mean as a day-to-day investment strategy.

A study of returns on the day just prior to and on the day just following big down-days in the overall market yields similar conclusions. In Table 12.3, notice how often the average down-day for each respective market index was preceded by a day on which the index also suffered negative returns. In the case of the DJIA, for example, eight of 10 big down-days were preceded by negative-return days. However, the average rate of return on the day prior to a big down-day in the DJIA was only −1.01%. Over this period, the pattern of big down-days being preceded by a majority of down-days was also typical for the S&P 500 and Nasdaq indexes. Again, the magnitude of such down-days was fairly small. Interestingly, each of the various major market indexes experienced modest up-days on the day following big down-days. However, as in the case of big up-days, evidence suggests that following big down-days, the magnitude of daily return reversals is too small and too unpredictable to merit serious consideration of the reversion-to-the-mean concept as a day-to-day investment strategy.

Random Walk Theory

Random Walk Concept

A **random walk** is an irregular pattern of numbers that defy prediction. With respect to the stock market, **random walk theory** asserts that stock price movements do not follow any pattern or trend. As a result, past price action cannot be used to predict future price movements. All subsequent price changes represent arbitrary departures from previous prices.

random walk Irregular pattern of numbers that defies prediction.

Random walk theory goes back a long way. Much of the random walk theory can be traced to a French mathematician named Louis Bachelier who wrote a famous Ph.D. dissertation titled *The Theory of Speculation* in 1900. Bachelier's work includes insights and commentary that are still remarkable today. A century ago, Bachelier came to the conclusion that the mathematical expectation of the speculator's profit is zero when stock prices follow a random walk. He described this market situation as a **fair game** in which the professional and the novice alike face exactly the same chance for success. Unfortunately, Bachelier's insights were so far ahead of the times that they went largely unnoticed for more than 50 years, until his work was rediscovered and eventually translated into English.

random walk theory Concept that stock price movements do not follow any patterns or trends.

fair game Even bet, or 50-50 chance.

The reasoning behind the random walk concept as it applies to the stock market is disarmingly simple. Securities markets are flooded with tens of thousands of intelligent, well-paid, and highly-educated professional investors and security analysts. Millions of similarly capable individual investors are also standing by. All such market participants are constantly seeking undervalued securities to buy and overvalued securities to sell. The more contestants in the market, the faster the dissemination of relevant information, and the more efficient the market becomes.

When information arises about a stock or the market as a whole, the news spreads very quickly and tends to be quickly reflected in security prices. The logic of the random walk idea is not that market prices are erratic. It is simply that when the flow of information is unimpeded, all of today's news is reflected in today's stock prices. Tomorrow's price changes reflect only tomorrow's news. By definition, news is unpredictable and random. Thus, price changes that result when news is released must also be unpredictable and random.

Although stocks can be expected to advance over long periods of time, day-to-day rates of return in the stock market can be expected to exhibit what might be called a **random walk with drift.** Daily rates of return on common stocks have a slight upward bias, or upward drift, given the long-term positive expectation for investor rates of return. Still, random walk theory asserts that the overwhelming characteristic of short-term rates of return in the stock market is their unpredictability.

random walk with drift Slight upward bias to inherently unpredictable daily stock prices.

As shown in Figure 12.4, the distribution of daily returns on major stock market indexes closely resembles a normal distribution, or bell-shaped curve, with an average daily return around zero. This is the essential characteristic of a daily return pattern that resembles the conceptual prediction of random walk theory.

Random Walk Research

The efficient market debate has resulted in literally thousands of empirical studies attempting to determine the extent to which specific markets can be judged efficient. Many amateur investors are surprised to learn that a tremendous amount of

FIGURE 12.4 **Frequency of Daily Returns Resembles a Bell-Shaped Curve**

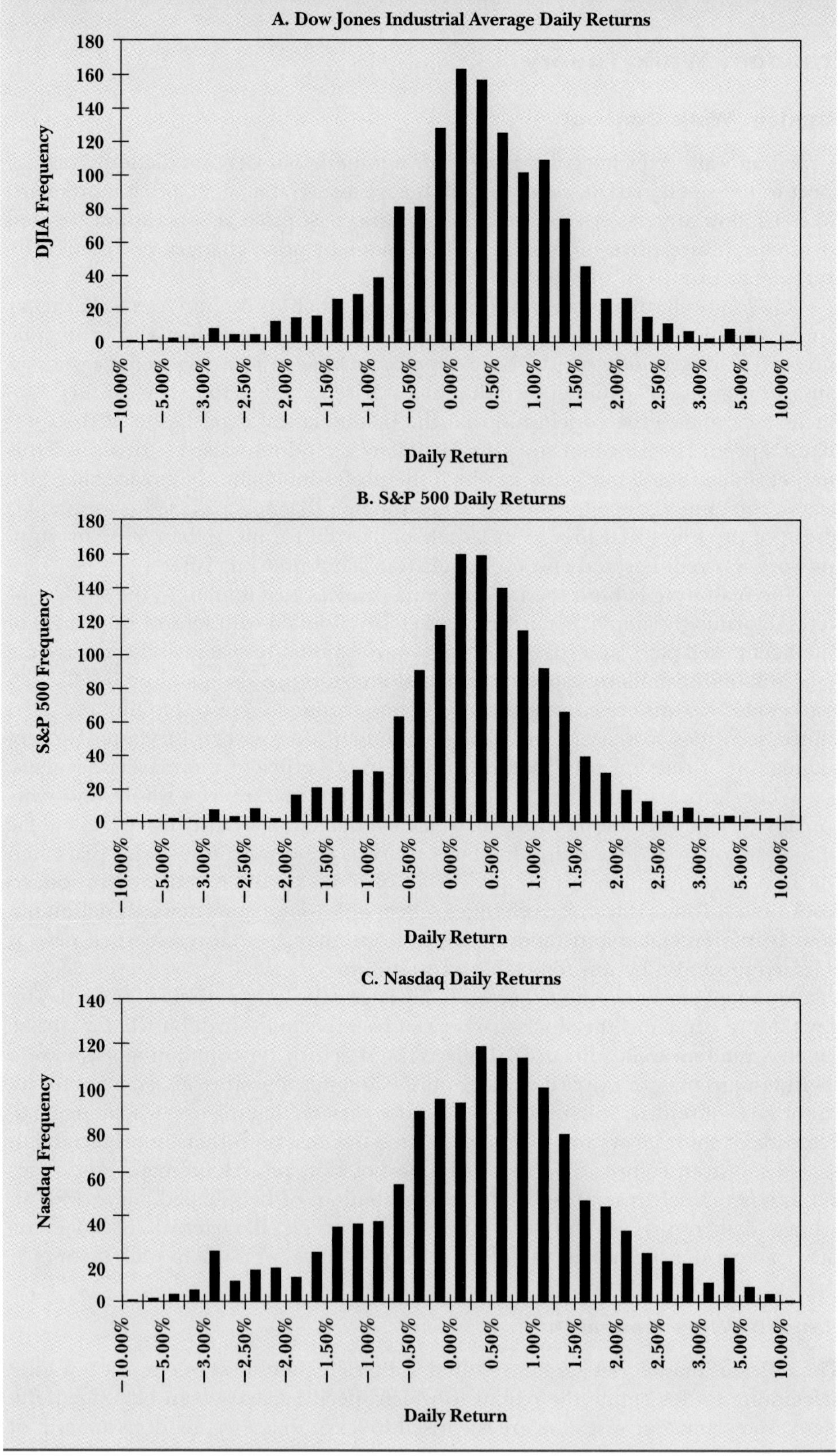

Note: Data are for the five-year period from 4/1/95 to 3/31/00.

stock market evidence has accumulated to support the notion that short-term stock prices follow a random walk. As such, many novice investors are unaware of the fact that significant evidence has accumulated to support the weak form of the EMH.

Early tests of the EMH focused on **technical analysis,** or the use of patterns in historical stock prices and trading volume activity to predict future stock prices. Common techniques include strategies based on relative strength, moving averages, and support and resistance. Practitioners of technical analysis, called **chartists,** are especially threatened by theory and empirical evidence that supports the EMH. If stock prices do indeed follow a random walk, then there are no predictable patterns or trends in stock prices and technical analysis is worthless. That is just what empirical evidence on technical analysis tends to suggest.

technical analysis Use of patterns in historical stock prices and trading volume activity to predict future stock prices.

chartists Practitioners of technical analysis.

Almost all studies on technical analysis have found that trading strategies based on past trends in prices and trading activity are completely useless. Even in those instances in which traders or stock analysts have detected inexplicable regularities in the pattern of historical stock market returns, transaction costs and/or tax penalties tend to reduce, if not eliminate, such advantages. The overwhelming majority of researchers who have tested technical trading systems and the weak-form EMH conclude that prices adjust rapidly to stock market information and that technical analysis provides no advantage to investors. As a result, it is generally accepted today that the central proposition of charting is absolutely false. Investors who follow technical trading rules to guide their buying and selling will accomplish nothing but to increase substantially the brokerage charges that they pay. Indeed, there has been remarkable uniformity in the conclusions of studies done on all forms of technical analysis. None has consistently outperformed a simple buy-and-hold strategy.

Failures of Technical Analysis

Data-Snooping Problem

A very few argue that there is at least some validity to technical trading strategies. In a 1992 study by William Brock, Josef Lakonishok, and Blake LeBaron, the authors analyzed moving averages and trading range breaks on the DJIA from 1897 to 1985.[2] The authors conclude that some well-known technical rules, such as buying on strength, have weak predictive power. However, even in that study, transactions costs prove to be a serious limiting factor and must be carefully considered before such strategies can be implemented. These authors conclude that previous judgments of technical analysis as useless are "premature."

Interestingly, a comprehensive follow-up study by Ryan Sullivan, Allan Timmerman, and Halbert White found that superior performance of the "best" technical trading rules are not repeated in an **out-of-sample experiment** covering the period 1987–96.[3] An out-of-sample experiment is a test of any historically useful

out-of-sample experiment Test of any historically useful technical trading rule over some new sample of data that was not used to derive it.

[2] William Brock, Josef Lakonishok, and Blake LeBaron, "Simple Technical Trading Rules and the Stochastic Properties of Stock Returns," *Journal of Finance* (December 1992): 1731–1764.

[3] Ryan Sullivan, Allan Timmerman, and Halbert White, "Data-Snooping, Technical Trading Rule Performance, and the Bootstrap," *Journal of Finance* (October 1999): 1647–1691.

WALL STREET WISDOM 12.2

Caveat Venditor!

On Wall Street, finding a way to make money with virtually no risk is everyone's top priority. Ira Gaines, a 50-year-old former copper wire salesman, appears to have figured it out. In an era when hot-shot Wall Street pros seek above-average profits by using complicated derivatives trading strategies, Mr. Gaines uses a remarkably simple system. Gaines simply offers to buy small stakes in publicly traded companies at prices that are well *below* current market prices. Amazingly, it is an offer that some unsophisticated investors accept.

Public awareness of the so-called below-market minitender offer emerged during the summer of 1998 when Gaines offered to buy less than 5% of Lexington Corporate Properties, Inc., a New York–based real estate investment trust. Gaines' bid was for $10 per share at a time when the stock was trading for about $12 each on the New York Stock Exchange. Gaines succeeded in getting 57,000 shares tendered to him. A month later, Mr. Gaines called Lexington's chairman and asked if they wanted to buy the shares back at $12.75. Later, Gaines told *The Wall Street Journal* that he realized a profit of more than $100,000 on the deal, and it cost him almost nothing to do it. Gaines does not even have to put up his own money to make the offers. In some cases, he has simply promised to pay investors within 30 days, giving him ample time to sell the shares that he receives and pocket the difference.

Below-market minitender-offers are the essence of simplicity. All one needs to do to make any tender offer is to send a letter to Depository Trust Co. (DTC), the nation's central securities depository based in New York. Then, the DTC electronically sends that information to more than 500 banks and brokerage firms nationwide. In turn, brokerage firms must send tender information to clients as part of their fiduciary responsibility to pass on any pertinent information regarding client holdings. Stockholders then get a brief letter describing a limited-time, first-come-first-served offer, with instructions to fill out, sign, and return quickly if interested. Under Security and Exchange Commission (SEC) rules, offers for fewer than 5% of a company's shares are not subject to the detailed and expensive reporting requirements of larger bids.

During recent months, these below-market minitender offers have been sent to shareholders of dozens of companies. In October 1998, for example, Gaines's IG Holdings offered to buy as much as 2% of catalog retailer Spiegel Inc. for $1.78 per share. At the time, Spiegel was trading on the Nasdaq Stock Market for $2.625, or 47% more. Also that month, IG Holdings offered $3.05 per share for up to 2% of Friendly Ice Cream Corp. During October 1998, Friendly traded between $5.875 and $6.375 a share, or roughly 50% above IG Holdings' offering price.

Who tenders shares for less than they could easily get in the open marketplace? According to critics of below-market minitender offers, elderly or unsophisticated shareholders tend to be victimized by such schemes. Although below-market offers are legal, targeted companies are exasperated by the mysterious offers and subsequent calls from confused shareholders asking whether they should tender their shares. Critics contend that companies making below-market tender offers typically use misleading information to trick investors into accepting lowball prices. A below-market bid can also raise fears that big buyers know of pending problems that might lead to lower stock prices. A further problem is that many investors believe that the tender offer is endorsed by the brokerage firm that holds their securities.

Below-market minitender offers have attracted the attention of the SEC, which is considering issuing disclosure guidelines to require current pricing and other information in such bids. Many target companies complain that lowball offers are especially confusing for shareholders of thinly traded stocks whose current market price may not be listed in the local newspaper.

Caveat emptor! is a famous Latin expression often used on Wall Street. It means "buyer beware." Based on the minitender episode, investors should also be advised *Caveat venditor!* (seller beware!).

See: Barbara Martinez, "Minitender King Gaines Finds Way to Make Money with Little Risk," *The Wall Street Journal,* January 28, 1999, C1, C24.

technical trading rule over some new sample of data that was not used to derive it. Using a comprehensive sample of roughly 8,000 technical trading rules over the 100-year period from 1897 to 1996, Sullivan et al. conclude that there is no robust statistical evidence that *any* technical trading rules will work to outperform the market.

Therefore, the empirical evidence strongly suggests that occasional "evidence" of investment merit for various technical trading rules is nothing more than the recurrent manifestation of the **data-snooping problem** in investment research. Given sufficient computer time, anyone is capable of finding some mechanical trading rule that would have provided superior investment returns over some historical time frame. This is true even when historical market returns resemble a table of random numbers. However, such **back testing,** or backward-looking analysis, is an unfair test of the usefulness of technical trading rules or any investment strategy. A fair test of any investment strategy involves a statement of the investment philosophy in such a way that it can be easily implemented and judged in actual practice. It is not surprising that there are inexplicable patterns in stock market returns over various historical time intervals. Historical patterns in stock market returns conflict with the EMH only when investors are able to exploit such regularities over some future time period.

data-snooping problem Reliance on chance observations in historical data as a guide to investment decision making.

back testing Backward-looking analysis.

Taken as a whole, empirical research from literally thousands of studies suggests that technical analysis does not work. Similarly, a simple inspection of day-to-day rates of return-on-stock-market indexes provides strong support for the notion that stock prices display a random walk over short time intervals. Evidence of a random walk in daily returns is simply overwhelming.

Believing-Is-Seeing Problem

Given the well-documented failures of technical analysis, it becomes interesting to ask why anyone still practices the "art" of technical analysis. Why do commentators who use technical analysis continue to merit coverage on CNNfn and CNBC? Why does *The Wall Street Journal* provide coverage of technical analysis? Why do various Internet sites offer detailed instruction on technical trading rules that consistently fail to provide documented evidence of investment merit?

From an economic perspective, the existence of technical analysts and popularity of technical analysis suggest that there is indeed an economic demand for technical analysis of the stock market. Even without investment merit, some demand for technical analysis may exist because of its entertainment value. Technical analysis of the stock market is complicated and interesting to anyone who is fascinated by inexplicable patterns of stock market returns. Of course, most practitioners would recoil at the suggestion that technical analysis has no real investment merit. In part, such individuals have succumbed to a type of **believing-is-seeing problem.** For many skeptical investors, "seeing is believing" when it comes to the investment merit of any given investment philosophy. For example, all wary individuals wait for documented evidence of superior stock-picking ability before committing investment funds to any given investment advisor. Unfortunately, some investors are eager to believe in the possibility of market-beating results. They "see" such results even when they do not truly exist. Any investor who believes he is "smart" when he buys a stock and it goes up, but merely "unlucky" when he buys a stock and it goes down, is guilty of succumbing to the believing-is-seeing problem.

believing-is-seeing problem Eager to believe in the possibility of market-beating results, investors sometimes "see" results that do not truly exist.

There is no doubt that many purveyors of technical trading advice are sincere in their belief that technical analysis can be used to enhance shareholder returns and/or limit investor risk. Similarly, there is no doubt that some of the picks recommended by technical traders, such as the *Wall Street Trader's Column* on the Internet, will yield spectacular results (see Figure 12.5). However, such anecdotal evidence in support of technical trading techniques is a very poor basis for an investment strategy. This is especially true when one remembers the overwhelming body of contrary evidence.

FIGURE 12.5 Technical Analysis Remains Popular Despite Its Ineffectiveness

See: <http://www.wstraders.com>.

Simply put, there is no robust evidence that technical trading rules can be used to enhance investor profits. A generation of sophisticated research by stock market analysts and financial economists is remarkably uniform in its support for the view of technical analysis expressed by Benjamin Graham in the *Intelligent Investor* more than 50 years ago:

> The one principal that applies to nearly all these so-called technical approaches is that one should buy *because* a stock or the market has gone up and one should sell *because* it has declined. This is the exact opposite of sound business sense everywhere else, and it is most unlikely that it can lead to lasting success in Wall Street. In our own stock market experience and observation, extending more than 50 years, we have not known a single person who has consistently or lastingly made money by thus "following the market." We do not hesitate to declare that this approach is as fallacious as it is popular.[4]

Measuring Relative Performance

Investment Dartboard

In 1973, Burton Malkiel published the first edition of *A Random Walk Down Wall Street,* one of the most famous books ever written about the stock market.[5] In that book, Malkiel argued that a blindfolded chimpanzee throwing darts at *The Wall Street Journal* could select a portfolio that would do as well as those of the experts. Of course, Malkiel's advice was really not that investors should select stocks by throwing darts nor that they should hire chimpanzees to do their stock selection. Malkiel's point was that investors should purchase an index fund that simply bought and held a widely diversified portfolio of common stocks.

The point that Malkiel was trying to make was made more forceful by his clever use of the dartboard metaphor. In fact, once a month *The Wall Street Journal* runs a popular contest called the "Investment Dartboard." In this regular feature, individual investors are invited to submit their best stock picks for an investment-holding period of six months. Stock picks submitted by four readers are selected in a drawing, and these picks are matched against stocks selected by four Wall Street professionals. Both sets of picks are also compared against four stocks randomly selected by *Journal* staffers.

To be eligible, individual investors need only send an e-mail message with the name of a stock pick to dartboard@interactive.wsj.com by the end of each month. Nonprofessional contestants provide only a name and home address, an e-mail address, and home and work phone numbers. They must also be willing to be interviewed. Among individual investor contestants, no brokers or other financial professionals are allowed. The *Journal* is looking for amateurs only.

Both amateur and professional participants are allowed to pick only one stock, either long or short. To weed out highly volatile penny stocks, the minimum market price for an eligible pick is $2. Each pick must be listed on the New York Stock Exchange, the American Stock Exchange, or the Nasdaq Stock Market. To weed out

---

[4] Benjamin Graham, *The Intelligent Investor,* 4th rev. ed. (New York: Harper & Row, 1973): x.

[5] Burton G. Malkiel, *A Random Walk Down Wall Street,* rev. ed. (New York: W. W. Norton, 1999).

thinly traded stocks, the minimum market capitalization allowed is $50 million, and average daily trading volume must be $100,000 or more. For simplicity, results are only measured in terms of capital gains or losses.

Stocks selected by both amateur and professional investors are measured against a four-stock portfolio selected at random by *Journal* staffers using darts and the investment pages of *The Wall Street Journal. Journal* staffers simply line up and toss four darts at the investment pages. The dartboard portfolio is selected on the basis of wherever the darts land.

How well do individual investors compete against the pros? Well, there is both good and bad news on that score. The good news is that stocks selected by amateur investors perform in line with those selected by the pros. In fact, you cannot reject the hypothesis that amateur stock selectors are as adept as the pros in their stock selections. The bad news is that stocks carefully selected by both the amateurs and the pros fail to outperform the dartboard portfolio.

Some might contend that results for such hypothetical buy/sell decisions prove nothing about the EMH or anything about the random nature of short-term price movements in the stock market. After all, there is no prize money given in the *Journal*'s monthly Investment Dartboard contest. There is just the glory, or the embarrassment, of publicly pitting one's stock-picking skills against the investment professionals and the forces of chance. However, even if many readers do not take the Investment Dartboard contest seriously, it is obvious that investment professionals take the contest very seriously. It gives them the chance to make a reputation for acuity in their stock-picking skills. Moreover, the failure of professional investors to outperform randomly selected portfolios is not limited to the *Journal*'s somewhat whimsical Investment Dartboard contest.

Investment professionals also fail to beat randomly selected investment portfolios when real money is on the line.

Benchmarks

Measuring the investment performance of investment professionals may be more difficult than you think. Consider the situation of a mutual fund manager whose income is determined by portfolio performance and the amount of money managed. Furthermore, assume that such a manager was selected to participate in *The Wall Street Journal*'s Investment Dartboard contest. The amount of free publicity tied to making a profitable pick is substantial and could translate into a significant amount of new mutual fund business. This could easily affect the fund manager's investment selection criteria. When real money is on the line, fund managers often focus on sensibly priced stocks with good growth prospects and solid loss protection. When no real money is on the line, or when the payoff for outstanding performance is dramatically more than the penalty for underperformance, a speculative choice with the potential for truly outstanding performance, or a spectacular flop, is often a better bet. Thus, it becomes hazardous to judge investment prowess on the basis of hypothetical results.

investment benchmark Investment standard.

Similarly, it is difficult to measure the success of professional investment management unless an appropriate **investment benchmark,** or investment standard, for expected investment risk and return is established. If the overall market rose 25%, the performance of an investment advisor would hardly be judged as spectacular if the advisor's portfolio returned a meager 15% rate of return. However, it would be cause for celebration if the overall market fell 10% and that same professional money manager earned 15%. Of course, it is not only necessary to consider investment performance relative to the overall market or an appropriate benchmark. It also is necessary to consider relative risk. For example, a professional investor who outperforms the overall market only by taking on above-market risk might very well fail to provide superior risk-adjusted performance. Any such investor could scarcely be described as beating the market. Beating the market requires superior rates of return for the same level of risk, or marketlike returns from a portfolio with below-market risk.

As shown in Table 12.4, performance benchmarks are commonly selected from among the wide variety of available market indexes. The DJIA may be the index that heads the stock market report on the news each evening, but few portfolio managers use the DJIA as a performance benchmark. The DJIA includes only 30 stocks that together represent roughly 30% of the overall market's capitalization and is barely indicative of the market's breadth. By far and away the most commonly accepted investment benchmark, or reference point for investment performance, is the S&P 500 Index. As a value-weighted index of 500 major companies chosen to be broadly representative of U.S. industry, the S&P 500 satisfies the need for a widely understood and comprehensive standard for investment performance. Despite its widespread appeal, the S&P 500 has a decidedly large-cap bias.

To measure the relative performance of portfolio managers who invest in the stocks of smaller companies, a number of more-specialized market indexes have been used as investment benchmarks. For mid-cap stocks, the Wilshire 4500 is often used, as measured by the Wilshire 500 total stock market index minus the large-cap S&P 500. A frequently used investment benchmark for small-cap stocks is the Russell 2000. When venturing outside the domestic U.S. equity market, the S&P 500 becomes even less relevant. For international equity investors, a commonly

TABLE 12.4 Major Indexes Make Useful Performance Benchmarks

Index	Key Facts
S&P 500	Market value–weighted index of 500 blue-chip stocks selected to be broadly representative of overall market. Median market capitalization of roughly $65 billion.
Wilshire 4500	Mid-cap proxy composed of Wilshire 5000 Index minus the S&P 500. Market-value weighted with a median market capitalization of roughly $1.8 billion.
Russell 2000	Small-cap proxy composed of smallest 2000 stocks in Russell 3000. Market-value weighted with a median market capitalization of roughly $725 million.
MSCI EAFE	Foreign-stock-market proxy. Market value–weighted index that includes major stock markets of Europe, Asia, and the Far East.
Lehman Brothers Aggregate Bond Index	Bond market proxy composed of roughly 6,000 government, corporate, mortgage, and asset-backed securities. Average maturity tends to be less than 10 years; average duration is less than five years.

relied-on investment benchmark is the Morgan Stanley Capital International, Inc., Europe, Asia, and Far East (EAFE) Index. Bond investment performance is typically judged relative to the performance of the Lehman Brothers Aggregate Bond Index.

Style Boxes

To judge portfolio performance, both risk and return must be considered. Unfortunately, although portfolio returns can be measured precisely at the end of any given performance period, portfolio risk and investment strategy risk are less easily measured. When it comes to risk, both seen and unseen danger must be considered. This presents a real challenge to determining relative portfolio performance. Not only must the amount of experienced volatility be considered, so too must the amount of unseen volatility be contemplated.

For example, suppose that it is wintertime and you take a crazy chance by walking out on the ice of a lake that has just frozen over. It is obvious that you have taken an absurd risk if the ice gives way and a rescue squad must be called to fish you out of the water. However, you took on significant risk even if the razor-thin ice does not give way and you return safely to shore.

Superior portfolio performance can be accomplished in one of two ways. Exceptional performance often involves beating the market in terms of earning above-market investment returns with marketlike risk. Alternatively, superior performance might involve earning marketlike returns from a portfolio with below-market risk. To help investors measure the risk and return performance of investment managers, the concept of a **style box** was implemented. A style box is simply a way of characterizing portfolio risk and return according to the investment characteristics of portfolio holdings.

style box Simple characterization of portfolio risk and return.

Table 12.5 illustrates the style box concept by using a methodology articulated by Chicago-based Morningstar Inc. Morningstar is a leading provider of mutual fund, stock, and variable-insurance investment information using both print media and the Internet (<http://www.morningstar.com>). Unlike Wall Street brokerages, Morningstar does not own, operate, or hold any interest in mutual funds, stocks, or insurance products. As such, investors have come to rely on Morningstar for unbiased data and analysis and candid editorial commentary. Rather than go by each fund's self-proclaimed investment objective, Morningstar assesses what each

TABLE 12.5 Morningstar's Innovative Nine-Part Style Boxes Allow Investors to Characterize Portfolio Risk and Return

	Value Strategy (Score < 1.75)	Blend ($1.75 \le$ Score ≤ 2.25)	Growth Strategy (Score > 2.25)
Large-cap (Top 5%)		S&P 500 Benchmark	
Mid-cap (Next 15%)		Wilshire 4500 Benchmark	
Small-cap (Bottom 80%)		Russell 2000 Benchmark	

fund actually owns. Traditionally, investors have tended to characterize stock portfolios as falling into one of four style boxes: large-company value, large-company growth, small-company value, and small-company growth. Company size is often an important risk consideration because larger companies typically have the diversification and financial strength necessary to fully exploit profitable opportunities and withstand severe economic hardship. Investment style is also an important risk consideration because growth stock investors are typically more adventuresome than conservative value investors. Over time, however, use of only four style boxes became too restrictive a means for classifying investment portfolios, and Morningstar innovated by introducing the concept of a nine-part style box.

Characterizing mutual funds and investment portfolios by market capitalization is easy. In the United States, the pool of the 5,000 largest companies together represent virtually the entire market capitalization of the stock market. Morningstar considers the top 250 companies by market capitalization to be large caps. The next 750 are classified as mid-caps. The remaining 4,000 companies are considered small-caps. Although these numbers may seem a bit lopsided, a relatively small number of big blue-chip stocks account for an overwhelming portion of the total amount of money invested in the market. The S&P 500 is an appropriate market benchmark for large-cap stocks. The performance standard for mid-cap portfolios is captured by the Wilshire 4500 Index, composed of the Wilshire 5000 minus the S&P 500. The Russell 2000 is an appropriate benchmark for small-cap stocks.

Morningstar calculates each fund's median market cap to determine which size category it belongs in. Of course, to determine a simple median, an investor would simply rank portfolio holdings from largest to smallest and pick out the one in the middle. However, if a fund holds a large number of relatively small positions at either end of the size scale, the market cap of the median holding might distort the size picture for the overall portfolio. Therefore, after ranking each portfolio from top to bottom, Morningstar measures the size of portfolio holdings by the weighted average market capitalization of stocks in the portfolio's third quintal, or middle segment. This is what statisticians call a trimmed median. This method smoothes out statistical aberrations that might distort a simple dollar-weighted median market cap.

To place funds along the horizontal axis of the style box, Morningstar determines how cheap or expensive portfolio holdings are relative to the overall market. Value stocks are typically defined as stocks that feature low price/earnings (P/E) and low price/book (P/B) ratios. Of course, absolute figures are less telling than relative numbers. Morningstar looks at P/E and P/B ratios relative to asset-weighted median multiples for each market-cap group. In other words, P/E and P/B ratios for a small-cap stock fund are compared with those for small-cap stocks in general and not against those of large blue-chip companies.

Thus, in the Morningstar style box system, each portfolio holding receives a relative P/E and relative P/B score. In both cases, a score of 1.00 indicates that a P/E or P/B ratio is exactly in line with the market-cap group norm. For each portfolio, Morningstar then calculates an asset-weighted average of the middle quintal for both the P/E and P/B ratios and adds these two results together. If a fund has a relative P/E score plus relative P/B score that exceeds 2.25, it falls into the growth column of the style box. If the combined scores fall below 1.75, the fund is considered a value fund. Anywhere in between, from 1.75 to 2.25, lands the fund in the blend column.

Armed with style box information, investors are capable of doing the fairest and most effective assessment possible of portfolio manager performance. For example, performance of funds in the large-company blend style box should be compared relative to the S&P 500 Index. The performance of large value stock portfolios can be compared with a low P/B portfolio derived from the S&P 500. The performance of large growth stock portfolios can be compared with a high P/B portfolio derived from the S&P 500. Funds and investment portfolios that find themselves in the mid-cap blend style box are most effectively compared with the Wilshire 4500 Index. Wilshire value and growth components can be used to measure the performance of mid-cap value and growth portfolios. The Russell 2000 proxy for the small-cap segment of the market is an appropriate performance benchmark for funds and portfolios in the small-cap blend style box. Similarly, value and growth components of the Russell 2000 can be used to measure the relative performance of small-cap value and growth portfolios.

Professional Investment Management

A Loser's Game?

John C. Bogle, founder of The Vanguard Group of Investment Companies, once made a tongue-in-cheek comparison between the Morningstar style box system and the children's game of tic-tac-toe. In fact, it is interesting that the Morningstar style box system has a configuration that is identical to a nine-box tic-tac-toe grid. In tic-tac-toe, two players take turns in placing an X or O in the tic-tac-toe grid. The object of the game is to get three X's or three O's across a single row, column, or diagonal line. Unfortunately, there is simply no winning strategy. Each player, in turn, simply blocks the other player's previous move. Even moves made by a genius can be blocked effectively by a player with only moderate intelligence. Of course, if one of the players is extremely dull witted or lacking in concentration, a loss is easily accomplished. Thus, it is fair to describe tic-tac-toe as a game that cannot be won. Because tic-tac-toe is a game that can be easily lost, it is the ultimate loser's game. In the light of the EMH, the similarity of the Morningstar style box system to a tic-tac-toe grid raises the interesting question: Is professional money management also a loser's game?

Of course, every amateur and professional investor wants to beat the market. Unfortunately, that is impossible. Investors as a whole make up the market, so as a group, investors can do no better than the market itself. If one investor outperforms the market, another must underperform it by a like amount. In an increasingly institutional market, it likewise becomes impossible for the average institutional investor to beat the market. If portfolio management had no cost, investors as a whole would just match the market's returns as measured by benchmark indexes such as the S&P 500. Of course, portfolio management is not costless; it typically involves management fees, operating expenses, transaction costs composed of brokerage commissions and bid-ask spreads, and marketing expenses, such as mutual fund load charges. After management fees, sales loads, operating expenses, and so on, investors as a group are bound to underperform conventional market indexes because index rates of return are calculated before costs.

WALL STREET WISDOM 12.3

Economic Forecasting: The Art and the Science

Accurate forecasts of future economic activity are valuable to firms making hiring, inventory, and other investment decisions. Consumers making purchase and career decisions also find accurate forecasts of short- and long-term economic trends exceptionally useful. Because firms and consumers base important decisions on expectations about the pace of future economic activity, a substantial demand for economic forecasts results. So extensive is this demand that the supply of economic forecasting services has exploded during recent years. Economic forecasts by academic, business, and government economists are prominently featured on television and radio and in the print media. The high level of business and consumer interest, and resulting media coverage, gives rise to a high level of visibility for economists who provide forecasting services.

This high level of visibility has focused attention on both the strengths and limitations of economic forecasting. In terms of limitations, the accuracy of economic forecasts is often criticized. For example, it is difficult to decipher if real economic growth will be 2.0% or 2.5%. The difference, although small, can be crucial for sectors such as capital equipment, in which business conditions are closely tied to aggregate economic activity. The demand for capital equipment might rebound vigorously with a 2.5% growth in gross domestic product (GDP) but remain sluggish with a 2.0% rise. Thus, a difference of only 0.5% in GDP growth might make a difference of millions of dollars in revenues and profits. If a weather forecast calls for sunny skies and a high of 75 degrees, the forecaster is applauded if sunny skies and a high of 80 degrees results. Not so with the economic forecaster. You and I may not notice any difference between 2.0% and 2.5% rates of economic growth, but companies blame (or fire) their economists when projections for robust economic growth fail to materialize and spending plans go awry. Patience with forecast error in business tends to be low.

Many of us also do not understand why disagreement among forecasting economists is common and why this disagreement can produce divergent economic forecasts. These concerns sometimes reflect too little appreciation of the difficulty of economic forecasting. In the real world, "all else held equal" does not hold very often, if ever. To forecast the future course of GDP, for example, one must be able to accurately predict the future pattern of government spending, tax and monetary policy, consumer and business spending, dollar strength against foreign currencies, weather, and so on. Although typical patterns can be inferred on the basis of past trends, atypical departures often have economic consequences that complicate matters. An unexpected drought, winter storm, or labor strike can disrupt economic activity and upset the accuracy of economic forecasts in the process.

In the light of the uncertainties involved, it seems reasonable that different forecasting economists would accord differing importance to a wide variety of economic influences. Just as individual forecasters assess different probabilities to an increase in government spending, they might also interpret consequences differently. Forecasters' judgment is reflected not only in the interpretation they give to the data generated by complex computer models but also in the models themselves. Computers may generate economic forecasts, but they do so on the basis of programs written by economists. Computer-generated economic forecasts are only as sophisticated as the data used, model analyzed, and the subsequent analysis.

Given the criticism often aimed at forecasters, it is ironic to note that the success of economic forecasting is responsible, at least in part, for some of its failures. Users have come to expect a nearly unattainable level of forecast accuracy. At the same time, users forget that forecasts can, by themselves, have important economic consequences. When consumers and businesses cut back on spending in reaction to the forecast of an impending mild recession, for example, they change the basis for the forecasters' initial prediction. By their behavior, they may also cause a steeper recession. This is the forecaster's dilemma: The future as we know it does not exist. In fact, it cannot.

See: Yochi J. Dreazen and Nicholas Kolish, "Data Suggests Economy May Be Slowing," *The Wall Street Journal*, June 1, 2000, A2, A6.

zero sum game
When one investor's gain is another investor's loss.

Figure 12.6 shows the dilemma faced by professional investment management. *Before* expenses, portfolio managers as a group can be expected to do no better than the overall market. When portfolio performance is measured relative to the market, beating the market becomes a **zero sum game.** For every investor who beats the market, some other investor underperforms. *After* expenses, portfolio managers as a group must be expected to underperform the overall market, when market performance is measured by conventional market indexes with rates of return calculated before investment costs.

From this perspective, professional portfolio management resembles the loser's game of tic-tac-toe. Competition among amateur and professional investors makes the market extremely efficient and greatly complicates the task of beating the market after expenses. By adopting a buy-and-hold investment philosophy with widespread diversification and careful expense control, investors can virtually assure themselves marketlike returns and above-average performance when compared with conventional high-cost investment strategies. In efficient stock and bond markets, investors can easily avoid losing vis-à-vis the overall market by investing in low-cost mutual funds that mimic market indexes. At the same time, winning vis-à-vis

FIGURE 12.6 **Managed Portfolios Underperform the Overall Market after Expenses**

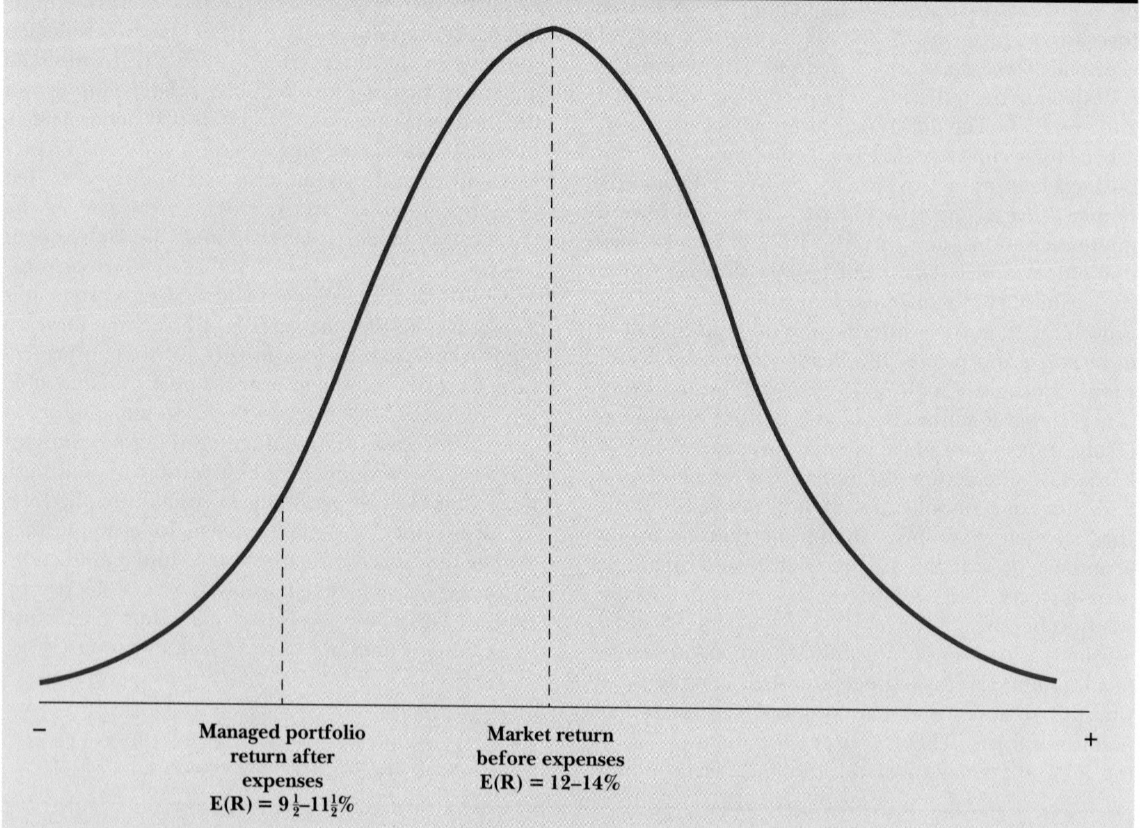

Source: *The Wall Street Journal.*

the overall market by adopting conventional high-cost investment strategies is extremely difficult. Professional investment management is a game that is easily lost. When it comes to professional investment management, to avoid losing is a winning investment strategy.

Managed Portfolio Performance

Financial information is so readily available about large U.S. companies that it becomes very tough for any professional portfolio manager to sustain a long-term performance edge. Although some parts of the capital market may be less than perfectly efficient, high transaction costs can erode investor advantages even in such pockets of opportunity. For example, global emerging markets are notoriously inefficient, as are parts of the U.S. small-capitalization market. In both instances, however, transaction costs are much higher than in the liquid market for large S&P 500–type companies.

Of course, some actively managed funds manage to beat the market over holding periods that may be several years in length. These are exceptional cases. More often than not, today's top-performing portfolio managers become tomorrow's average performers, or worse. Over time, the typical broadly diversified market index tends to outperform the strong majority of actively managed investment portfolios. Although it is unfair to compare the typical managed portfolio against the idealized performance of a market index, today's investor can choose among a broad range of so-called index funds, or passively managed portfolios. These portfolios seek to match the investment performance of a specific stock or bond benchmark performance index. Instead of actively trading securities in an effort to beat the market, an index fund manager simply holds a broadly representative sample of the securities in the index.

An index fund incurs minimal advisory fees, distribution charges, and other expenses. A low-cost index fund might have an expense ratio of 0.3% (or $3 per $1,000 invested). By comparison, the typical publicly traded mutual fund has operating expenses of roughly 1.25%. These expenses cover the costs of mailing out reports, auditing, management fees, and so on. In addition, the typical fund incurs advertising and marketing costs of roughly 0.3% per year. Finally, actively managed portfolios incur brokerage and other transaction costs that average as much as 1% per year of assets under management. Thus, it is unsurprising that the typical mutual fund underperforms on the order of 2–3% per year when measured against the appropriate benchmark.

For example, Lipper Inc., a mutual fund industry watchdog, reports that the average general equity mutual fund earned a cumulative return of 274.97% and a compound annual rate of return of 14.13% per year for the 10-year period ending December 31, 1999. During this same time frame, the S&P 500, a good proxy for the overall market, earned a cumulative return of 432.77%, or 18.21% per year. In terms of actual performance, the average general equity fund underperformed the appropriate performance benchmark by 4.08% (= 18.21% − 14.13%) per year. Although this may not seem like much in any given period, it mounts up over a long-term investment horizon. For example, a 4.08% per year return advantage from investing in an appropriate performance benchmark rather than in a professionally managed account is enough to double a given investment portfolio in roughly 17 years. In other words, the cost disadvantage involved with professional portfolio management versus a low-cost index fund is enough to cut by one-half the retirement portfolio of a typical investor.

Many index funds also have outperformed comparable actively managed portfolios across a spectrum of investment styles and market capitalizations. Table 12.6 uses the Morningstar style box to show the percentages of actively managed mutual funds that were outperformed by their relevant large-capitalization stock indexes over the 10-year period ending December 31, 1998. Relative performance by mid-cap and small-cap stock portfolios is shown over the five-year period ending December 31, 1998. Over this period, the cost disadvantage to active portfolio management results in 76–91% of large-cap funds underperforming their appropriate benchmark. Underperformance by mid-cap fund managers is of a similar order of magnitude, roughly 81–82%. Only in the case of small-cap growth funds does it seem that active management has led to superior performance during the late 1990s. Caution is advised in making any firm interpretations concerning this finding, however. Market outperformance by managed small-cap growth funds depends on the stunningly good performance of Internet stocks during this period. Time will tell if the superior performance of this sector of the market will continue.

Market underperformance by professionally managed funds presents investors with a conundrum. If you feel sick, it is always desirable to consult a medical doctor. No one would attempt to perform delicate surgery on his or her own abdomen, for example. In such cases, the money spent to retain a skilled surgeon is always well spent. Similarly, nobody would attempt to remove his or her own impacted wisdom teeth. A skilled oral surgeon can be a real blessing in such circumstances. However, when it comes to the case of active portfolio management, the average investment professional adds *no* value. The typical long-term investor is far better off investing in a market index fund than in the average professionally managed portfolio.

If an individual investor accepts the overwhelming evidence in favor of the EMH, the best investment strategy is to buy an index fund. Such a strategy is apt to earn the market return, and few actively managed funds will provide superior investment performance. The risk is much greater if an investor bets on market inefficiency rather than on market efficiency. No matter what investment risk profile is sought, an investor is well advised to seek low-cost index funds. A simpler course is to index an entire investment portfolio with a total stock market index.

TABLE 12.6 Percentage of Stock Funds Outperformed by Benchmarks

	Value Strategy	Blend	Growth Strategy
Large-cap	76%	91%	86%
Mid-cap	82%	82%	81%
Small-cap	64%	50%	28%

Data source: <www.vanguard.com>.

Role of Investment Professionals

Given empirical evidence suggesting that the stock market is extremely efficient, if not perfectly efficient, serious questions arise for investment professionals. What role do they play in the market? For what can they demand compensation?

For those who accept the logic and compelling evidence in support of the EMH, the primary role of a portfolio manager consists of analyzing and investing appropriately based on an investor's individual tax considerations and risk profile. Optimal portfolios for individual investors will vary according to factors such as age, tax bracket, risk aversion, and employment status. The role of the portfolio manager in an efficient market is to tailor a portfolio to those needs, rather than to beat the market.

Although proponents of the EMH do not believe it is possible to beat the market, some believe that stocks can be divided into categories based on risk factors and correspondingly higher or lower expected returns. For instance, some may believe that small stocks are riskier than the market as a whole and, therefore, might be expected to have higher nominal returns. Similarly, some may believe that growth stocks are riskier than value stocks and, therefore, tend to have higher expected returns. Of course, when faced with the inference that they cannot add value, many active portfolio managers argue that the markets are inefficient. Otherwise, their jobs and the jobs of thousands of investment professionals might be regarded as nothing more than superfluous.

Similarly, the investment media is generally ambivalent at best, and often outright hostile, toward the EMH because they make money supplying information to investors who believe that information is timely and valuable. A lot of people watch CNNfn or CNBC in the search for timely investment information that they act on. Others read *The Wall Street Journal* or *Barron's* seeking an edge. Others spend thousands of dollars per month to get up-to-the-minute news, information, and market diagnostics. If all investors came to believe that investment information is rapidly reflected in security prices, there would be no practical reason for them to seek out or purchase information about the securities markets. Without any investments or financial purpose, the only reason to follow the securities markets would be for fun or entertainment value. Although some might continue to tune into CNBC rather than *Monday Night Football* or *Friends,* many others would simply turn to other interests. This would be bad for the financial media business.

Investment professionals and the financial media offer an extremely valuable public service. Markets are efficient only because so many active investors and stock analysts are on the constant search for market-beating strategies. The paradox of the efficient market concept is that markets are only efficient when a sufficiently large number of market participants believe there are ample profit-making opportunities. If every investor believed the market was efficient, no one would analyze securities and the market would cease to be efficient. In effect, efficient markets depend on the large number of market participants who believe that the market is inefficient and actively trade securities in an attempt to beat the market.

Summary

- Short-term speculation in the stock and bond markets is akin to a **coin-flipping contest.** It is gambling, pure and simple. In the short term, theory and evidence tell us that stock prices are equally apt to rise or fall in an **efficient market.** In an efficient stock market, the price for any given stock effectively represents the expected net present value of all future profits. The **efficient market hypothesis (EMH)** states that security prices fully reflect all available information. In an efficient market, there is a 50-50 chance that the buyer will profit at the expense of the seller. Similarly, there is a 50-50 chance that the seller will profit at the expense of the buyer.

- Three alternative forms of the EMH exist. Under the **weak-form hypothesis,** current prices reflect all **stock market information.** Trading rules based on past stock market returns and trading volume are futile. The **semistrong-form hypothesis** asserts that prices reflect all **public information.** All trading rules based on public information are futile. The **strong-form hypothesis** posits that current prices reflect all public information and **nonpublic information.** In that case, all trading rules are futile.
- To the extent that insiders such as the company chairman and CEO earn above-normal rates of return on their stock market investments, the market would not be judged as perfectly efficient according to the strong-form hypothesis. If such insiders do, in fact, earn above-normal rates of return, then one might conclude that they have profited by virtue of their access to superior or **insider information.**
- Whenever the movement of stock prices over time is being analyzed, these data are described as a **time series** of market data. A correlation coefficient of +100% indicates perfect positive correlation. A correlation coefficient of −100% indicates perfect negative or inverse correlation. A correlation coefficient of 0% indicates that two sets of data have no relation. From a statistical perspective, the distribution of daily returns closely resembles a **normal distribution,** or bell-shaped curve, with an average daily return around zero.
- A **random walk** is an irregular pattern of numbers that defies prediction. With respect to the stock market, **random walk theory** asserts that stock price movements do not follow any patterns or trends. The mathematical expectation of the speculator's profit is zero when stock prices follow a random walk. This market is a **fair game** in which the professional and the novice face exactly the same chance for success. Although stocks can be expected to advance over long periods of time, day-to-day rates of return can be expected to exhibit what might be called a **random walk with drift.** Daily rates of return on common stocks have a slight upward bias, or upward drift, given the long-term positive expectation for investor rates of return. Still, random walk theory asserts that the overwhelming characteristic of short-term rates of return in the stock market is their unpredictability.
- Early tests of the EMH focused on **technical analysis,** or the use of patterns in historical stock prices and trading volume activity to predict future stock prices. Common techniques include strategies based on relative strength, moving averages, as well as support and resistance. Practitioners of technical analysis, called **chartists,** are especially threatened by theory and empirical evidence that supports the EMH. If stock prices do, indeed, follow a random walk, then there are no predictable patterns or trends in stock prices and technical analysis is worthless.

- Superior performance by the "best" technical trading rules is not repeated in **out-of-sample experiments.** An out-of-sample experiment is a test of any historically useful technical trading rule over some new sample of data that was not used to derive it. Occasional "evidence" of investment merit for various technical trading rules is nothing more than the recurrent manifestation of the **data-snooping problem** in investment research. Given sufficient computer time, anyone is capable of finding some mechanical trading rule that would have provided superior investment returns over some historical time frame. This is true even when historical market returns resemble a table of random numbers. However, such **back testing,** or backward-looking analysis, is an unfair test of the usefulness of technical trading rules or any investment strategy. It is not surprising that there are inexplicable patterns in stock market returns over various historical time intervals. Historical patterns in stock market returns conflict with the EMH only when investors are able to exploit such regularities over some future time period.
- Some individuals have succumbed to a type of **believing-is-seeing problem.** These investors are so eager to believe in the possibility of market-beating results that they "see" such results even when they do not truly exist.
- It is difficult to measure the success of professional investment management unless an appropriate **investment benchmark,** or investment standard, for expected investment risk and return is established. To help investors measure the risk and return performance of investment managers, the concept of a **style box** was implemented. A style box is simply a way of characterizing portfolio risk and return according to the investment characteristics of portfolio holdings.
- *Before* expenses, portfolio managers as a group can be expected to do no better than the overall market. When portfolio performance is measured relative to the market, beating the market becomes a **zero sum game.** For every investor who beats the market, some other investor underperforms.

Questions

1. The failure of technical analysis to provide market-beating results is support for the
   a. weak-form efficient market hypothesis.
   b. semistrong-form efficient market hypothesis.
   c. strong-form efficient market hypothesis.
   d. none of these.
2. An efficient market reflects
   a. past, current, and inferred information.
   b. future information.
   c. past and current information.
   d. current and inferred information.
3. An efficient market does *not* require that
   a. stock prices incorporate all company operating information.
   b. all past price information be reflected in current prices.

c. price adjustments occur very quickly.

d. each price adjustment be perfect.

4. Which of the following is a test of strong-form efficiency?

a. stock splits

b. accounting changes

c. insider transactions

d. dividend announcements

5. In which form of the efficient market hypothesis do security prices reflect only past stock price and volume information?

a. weak form

b. semistrong form

c. strong form

d. none of the above

6. "Filter rules" do not tend to be profitable because of

a. transaction costs.

b. market volatility.

c. trends in stock prices.

d. the fact that no rules outperform a buy-and-hold strategy, even for short periods.

7. Weak-form market efficiency

a. contradicts the random walk hypothesis.

b. incorporates semistrong-form efficiency.

c. is compatible with technical analysis.

d. involves only price and volume information.

8. Which of the following is not a test of semistrong-form efficiency?

a. stock splits

b. accounting changes

c. dividend announcements

d. insider transactions

9. The highest level of market efficiency is

a. strong-form efficiency.

b. weak-form efficiency.

c. semistrong-form efficiency.

d. random walk efficiency.

10. Statistically testing the independence of stock price changes is a test of

a. weak-form efficiency.

b. semistrong-form efficiency.

c. strong-form efficiency.

d. the seasonal effect.

11. An efficient market does not require that

a. stock prices incorporate all information.

b. all known information be reflected in prices.

c. the adjustments occur very quickly.

d. each adjustment be perfect.

12. A fully hedged position has a return potential that equals the

a. firm's dividend yield.

b. risk-free rate.

c. market return.

d. market risk premium.

13. In an efficient market, index options are priced so that a perfectly hedged portfolio earns

a. the market rate of return.

b. a zero rate of return.

c. the risk-free rate.

d. the zero-beta rate of return.

14. In an efficient market,

a. 50% of all investors will outperform the market average after expenses.

b. 50% of all investors will outperform the market average before expenses.

c. less than 50% of all investors will outperform the market average before expenses.

d. less than 50% of all investors will underperform the market average after expenses.

15. Which among the following pairs of returns on market indexes are most closely correlated?

a. DJIA and Nasdaq Composite

b. DJIA and S&P 500

c. S&P 500 and Nasdaq Composite

d. DJIA and the Russell 2000

16. Day traders and other short-term speculators have a difficult time profiting because the

a. average daily market return is positive.

b. average daily market return is negative.

c. standard deviation of daily market returns is relatively low.

d. standard deviation of daily market returns is relatively high.

17. On the day following big up-days, the DJIA tends to

a. rise substantially.

b. fall precipitously.

c. rise moderately.

d. none of the above.

18. Daily returns for the overall market are

a. skewed upward.

b. skewed downward.

c. normally distributed with a mean near zero.

d. normally distributed with a mean near 12–14%.

19. Which among the following statements is *not* consistent with random walk theory?

    a. Stock price movements do not follow any patterns or trends.

    b. Past price action cannot be used to predict future price movements.

    c. Price changes represent arbitrary departures from previous prices.

    d. Big up-days in the overall market tend to be followed by big down-days.

20. The data-snooping problem can be avoided by

    a. back testing.

    b. study of extensive samples of data.

    c. technical trading rules.

    d. out-of-sample experiments.

Investment Application

The 'Dogs of the Dow' Myth[6]

During August 1988, a fascinating article titled "Study of Industrial Averages Finds Stocks with High Dividends Are Big Winners" appeared in *The Wall Street Journal.*[7] In that article, analyst John Slatter, then of Prescott, Ball & Turben, Inc., in Cleveland, Ohio, proposed a simple and intuitively appealing investment approach. Later dubbed the "Dogs of the Dow" (or "Dow Dog") investment strategy, Slatter suggested that investors confine their stock market selections to the 10 top yielding stocks found among the 30 industrial giants included within the Dow Jones Industrial Averages (DJIA). According to Slatter, these "dogs" provide anything but doglike returns. He offered evidence that a portfolio of high-yielding Dow stocks outperforms the DJIA by an eye-popping 7.59% per year (see Table 12.7)!

Over the years, the Dow Dog approach has generated significant and growing interest among both institutional and individual investors. The only calculation required is to compute the current dividend yield for all 30 DJIA components on the first trading day of the year. Then, rank the 30 DJIA stocks in descending order by dividend yield, buy the top 10 yielding stocks, and maintain these holdings until the first trading day of the new year. At that point, this simple selection process is repeated. With an elementary dividend yield criterion, anyone can adopt the strategy. With only once-a-year rebalancing, transaction costs tied to brokerage commissions and capital gains taxes are kept at a minimum. Because membership on the list of high-yielding DJIA stocks tends to be stable, low portfolio turnover rates and modest transaction costs can be expected.

---

[6]For a complete review of this study, see Mark Hirschey, "The 'Dogs of the Dow' Myth," *Financial Review* 35, no. 2 (May 2000): 1–16.

[7]John R. Dorfman, "Study of Industrial Averages Finds Stocks with High Dividends Are Big Winners," *The Wall Street Journal,* August 11, 1988, 29.

Given the promise of huge excess returns, and its appeal as a simple-to-execute "contrarian" investment philosophy, the wide and still-growing popularity of the Dow Dog strategy is easy to understand. A number of best-selling books extolling the virtues of the approach have also served to speed its acceptance, for example, Michael O'Higgins and John Downs's *Beating the Dow* (1991), Harvey C. Knowles III and Damon H. Petty's *The Dividend Investor* (1992), and most important, David and Tom Gardner's *The Motley Fool Investment Guide* (1996). The Gardners have also been instrumental in extending the popularity of the Dow Dog strategy beyond the print media and into cyberspace. Today, more than 200,000 individual investors are said to follow the Dow Dog investment strategy by using the Motley Fool on America Online or the Internet.[8] In 1991, Merrill Lynch launched the *Defined Asset Funds: Select Ten Portfolio* to buy Dow Dogs and has attracted more than *$10 billion* in assets. With thousands of individual investors independently following the Dow Dog strategy, *Barron's* now estimates that as much as $20 billion, an amount larger than all but the top 15 mutual funds, is currently committed to the Dow Dog strategy.[9]

Companies included within the DJIA are among the largest, most liquid, and heavily analyzed on Wall Street. Moreover, the Dow Dog method is a very simple investment strategy that uses widely scrutinized public data. In short, the popular press suggests an *unbelievable* level of excess returns for the Dow Dog approach. How could the market be so inefficient?

A simple check of figures used in prior studies suggests that data errors, rather than market inefficiency, may provide at least a partial explanation for the perceived advantage of Dow Dogs. For example, Slatter shows a total return of 44.4% for the DJIA in 1974. This is plainly incorrect. The market did not go up in 1974; returns were negative as the market concluded a long and painful bear market. If numbers such as these are wrong, perhaps other less easily checked numbers are incorrect as well. There is troubling inconsistency in published estimates of Dow Dog returns *for identical time periods.* For example, Slatter's 27.3% annual rate of return for 1979 contrasts sharply with 1979 returns of 12.37%, 9.67%, 12.99%, and 8.24% reported elsewhere (see Table 12.8).[10] In 1987, Slatter's 17.3% conflicts with the 0.61%, 6.89%, 6.97%, and 9.09% related in other studies. These are not small differences in a market that averages 10.27% (1979) and 5.93% (1987), as measured by *Barron's* estimate of the annual rate of return for the DJIA (see Table 12.8). It is troubling when estimated returns for such an easily implemented strategy deviate wildly.[11]

---

[8]*The Motley Fool* is on the Internet at <http://www.fool.com>. *The Daily Dow,* a Web site devoted exclusively to promoting the Dogs of the Dow and various other investment strategies tied to the DJIA, is featured at <http://www.fool.com/DDow/DD>. Estimated usage is from Daniel Kadlec, "The Dow Dogs Won't Hunt," *Time,* December 8, 1997, 76.

[9]See Andrew Barry, "They Still Hunt," *Barron's,* January 5, 1998, 25–26.

[10]See John R. Dorfman, p. 29; Michael O'Higgins and John Downs, p. 191–192, as updated in Andrew Barry, "Canny Canines," *Barron's,* December 13, 1993, p. 14, and Andrew Barry, "Faithful Friends," *Barron's,* December 26, 1994, p. 14; Harvey C. Knowles III and Damon H. Petty, p. 30; Merrill Lynch, *Defined Asset Funds: Select Ten Portfolio, 1999,* promotional material; *The Daily Dow* Web site (address above); and <http://www.dogsofthedow.com/dogyrs.htm>.

[11]McQueen and Thorley, "Mining Fool's Gold," *Financial Analysts Journal* 55, no. 2 (March/April 1999): 61–72, discuss similar data errors in the "Foolish Four" investment strategy, which is based on a subset of the highest yielding stocks in the DJIA.

TABLE 12.7 Previously Estimated Annual Rates of Return for Equally Weighted Portfolios of "Dow Dogs" and the DJIA, 1961–98

Prior studies suggest above-market returns from an investment strategy that focuses on the 10 highest-yield components of the DJIA. However, data errors, rather than market inefficiency, may provide a partial explanation. Transactions

	Slatter		O'Higgins & Downs (as updated in Barron's)		Knowles & Petty	
Year	**Ten High-Yield**	**DJIA**	**Ten High-Yield**	**DJIA**	**Ten High-Yield**	**DJIA**
1961						
1962						
1963						
1964						
1965						
1966						
1967						
1968						
1969						
1970						
1971						
1972	3.30%	−14.40%			23.85%	18.10%
1973	−2.90%	−23.40%	3.94%	−13.12%	3.88%	−13.40%
1974	58.90%	44.40%	−1.28%	−23.14%	1.02%	−23.40%
1975	35.60%	22.30%	55.87%	44.40%	53.23%	44.40%
1976	1.10%	−13.20%	34.81%	22.72%	33.21%	22.30%
1977	3.30%	2.40%	0.93%	−12.71%	−1.03%	−13.20%
1978	12.70%	10.20%	−0.13%	2.69%	2.40%	2.40%
1979	27.30%	21.00%	12.37%	10.52%	9.67%	10.20%
1980	6.30%	−3.60%	27.23%	21.41%	27.53%	21.00%
1981	24.50%	26.00%	5.02%	−3.40%	2.68%	−3.60%
1982	41.10%	25.50%	23.58%	25.79%	20.68%	26.00%
1983	9.00%	9.00%	38.73%	25.65%	39.22%	25.50%
1984	23.30%	27.80%	7.64%	1.08%	6.27%	0.71%
1985	27.20%	26.60%	29.48%	32.78%	31.20%	31.14%
1986	6.30%	5.80%	32.08%	26.92%	28.12%	26.60%
1987	17.30%	6.40%	0.61%	6.02%	6.89%	5.80%
1988			26.14%	15.95%	18.22%	15.55%
1989			26.53%	31.71%	27.37%	30.75%
1990			−7.58%	−0.40%	−10.01%	−3.36%
1991			34.25%	23.91%		
1992			7.86%	7.44%		
1993			27.30%	16.80%		
1994			4.10%	4.90%		
1995			36.50%	36.40%		
1996			27.90%	28.60%		
1997			21.90%	24.90%		
1998			10.70%	17.75%		
Average	**18.39%**	**10.80%**	**18.71%**	**14.45%**	**17.07%**	**11.76%**
Std. Dev.	**16.92%**	**18.36%**	**15.91%**	**16.67%**	**16.41%**	**18.06%**

Note: The Motley Fool compares Dow Dog performance with returns for an equally weighted portfolio of DJIA stocks (the "Dow 30" portfolio).

TABLE 12.7 ***(continued)***

costs, such as brokerage commissions and bid-ask spreads, and higher tax consequences tied to the technique are more than enough to overcome any perceived advantage, especially during recent years.

Merrill Lynch		*The Motley Fool*	
Ten High-Yield	DJIA	Ten High-Yield	Dow 30
		26.91%	22.74%
		−0.14%	−7.37%
		19.57%	23.03%
		20.28%	19.64%
		18.26%	17.32%
		−13.92%	−15.10%
		25.81%	21.95%
		14.47%	10.04%
		−14.41%	−8.91%
		2.01%	4.82%
		6.20%	9.01%
23.26%	18.21%	23.90%	16.72%
−4.08%	−13.12%	3.89%	−10.86%
−2.40%	−23.14%	1.04%	−15.68%
55.65%	44.40%	50.99%	44.24%
33.25%	22.72%	33.24%	29.20%
−2.90%	−12.71%	1.17%	−12.41%
−1.91%	2.69%	2.55%	2.52%
10.48%	10.52%	8.24%	11.34%
24.69%	21.41%	31.23%	25.31%
5.51%	−3.40%	4.25%	−3.26%
23.79%	25.79%	20.85%	19.59%
36.93%	25.68%	39.22%	35.63%
5.41%	1.06%	6.36%	0.51%
27.00%	32.78%	30.50%	29.77%
32.96%	26.91%	26.20%	21.69%
5.06%	6.02%	9.09%	11.96%
22.44%	15.95%	17.96%	14.64%
25.65%	31.71%	29.68%	31.97%
−10.14%	−0.57%	−10.01%	−9.17%
31.81%	23.93%	43.95%	31.48%
6.44%	7.34%	6.24%	10.96%
25.30%	16.72%	23.68%	17.96%
1.95%	4.95%	2.43%	3.73%
34.97%	36.48%	37.16%	36.66%
26.34%	28.57%	27.47%	24.33%
19.92%	24.78%	20.39%	22.32%
8.55%	18.00%	11.66%	13.51%
17.26%	**14.58%**	**16.01%**	**13.21%**
15.98%	**16.38%**	**15.63%**	**15.67%**

TABLE 12.8 **Total Returns for the DJIA and "Dow Dog" Portfolios, 1961–98**

One cannot outperform a simple buy-and-hold strategy by focusing on high-yield stocks included within the DJIA. Much of the false impression of market outperformance by Dow Dogs is created by prior mistakes in rate-of-return calculations and the common failure to accurately reflect transaction costs and taxes.

			DD Advantage before Transaction Costs		
Year	DJIA Total Return (from Barron's)	"Dow Dogs" Total Return	Annual	5-year Periods	10-year Periods
1961	21.82%	26.06%	4.24%		
1962	−7.24%	−2.48%	4.76%		
1963	20.07%	19.03%	−1.04%		
1964	18.14%	19.23%	1.09%		
1965	13.83%	16.64%	2.81%		
1966	−14.88%	−14.22%	0.66%		
1967	18.53%	24.22%	5.69%		
1968	7.59%	13.78%	6.19%	3.26%	
1969	−10.95%	−15.92%	−4.97%		
1970	8.58%	0.57%	−8.01%		
1971	9.58%	4.88%	−4.70%		
1972	17.74%	22.70%	4.96%		
1973	−12.43%	0.32%	12.75%	−0.28%	
1974	−21.45%	−2.95%	18.50%		
1975	42.71%	47.28%	4.57%		
1976	21.98%	32.97%	10.99%		
1977	−11.76%	0.97%	12.73%		
1978	2.88%	1.15%	−1.73%	8.79%	4.15%
1979	10.27%	6.40%	−3.87%		
1980	20.57%	28.41%	7.84%		
1981	−2.81%	2.21%	5.02%		
1982	24.77%	17.66%	−7.11%		
1983	24.74%	37.97%	13.23%	2.75%	
1984	1.26%	4.85%	3.59%		
1985	31.67%	27.72%	−3.95%		
1986	26.12%	24.73%	−1.39%		
1987	5.93%	7.45%	1.52%		
1988	15.52%	17.71%	2.19%	0.36%	1.54%
1989	30.70%	27.62%	−3.08%		
1990	−0.40%	−12.95%	−12.55%		
1991	23.32%	34.34%	11.02%		
1992	7.22%	2.94%	−4.28%		
1993	16.37%	22.80%	6.43%	−0.84%	
1994	4.89%	0.73%	−4.16%		
1995	35.75%	35.17%	−0.58%		
1996	28.04%	27.25%	−0.79%		
1997	24.36%	19.80%	−4.56%		
1998	17.75%	10.97%	−6.78%	−3.40%	−2.13%
Arith. Avg.	**12.39%**	**14.16%**	**1.77%**		
Geo. Mean	**11.35%**	**13.13%**	**1.55%**		
Std. Dev.	**15.10%**	**15.33%**	**6.87%**		

Conceptual problems also may be responsible for at least some of the perceived premium earned by Dow Dogs. In the still-popular O'Higgins and Downs book, for example, the authors use arithmetic averages in the calculation of realized returns. In practice, return estimates tend to be biased upward when arithmetic averages are used to study highly volatile portfolios. This stems from the fact that upward performance is unlimited, whereas downward performance is limited to −100%.[12] Thus, annual rates of return for Dow Dogs as reported by O'Higgins and Downs, among others, are upwardly biased.

Results from prior studies are also suspect because they fail to reflect transaction costs. The Dow Dog strategy involves picking stocks with higher than typical dividend yields, by definition. Like any high-yield approach, the method will necessarily involve higher-than-average income taxes on dividends, and therefore higher taxes on total realized returns. Such a high-yield approach will also involve annual portfolio rebalancing and brokerage commissions, bid-ask spread costs, and capital gains taxes that could be avoided if a simple buy-and-hold investment strategy were used.

To conduct a fair test of the Dow Dog investment strategy, individual stocks were "purchased" without commissions on the first trading day of the year—January 2, 3, or 4—and formed into portfolios of 10 stocks each. The high-yield portfolio consists of the 10 highest yielding DJIA stocks. Dividends paid throughout the year, including extra or special dividends, are added to the year-end price and then this total is divided by the initial price to calculate total returns as $R_{it} = ([(P_{t+1} + D_t)/P_t] - 1)$. Stock dividends increase the number of shares sold at the end of the year. Spin-offs are recorded as if held from the time they were issued until the end of the year. Spun-off stocks are treated as if sold on the first trading day of the following year.

For the 38-year 1961–98 time frame, Table 12.8 shows arithmetic and geometric total returns for the DJIA, as reported in *Barron's*,[13] and for the Dow Dog portfolios. Before transactions costs, the geometric mean return for the Dow Dogs is 13.13%, or only 1.55% per year greater than the 11.35% annual return on the DJIA.[14] Notice that this very modest 1.55% excess return, calculated before taxes and transaction costs, is sharply lower than the Dow Dog return premium suggested in earlier studies (see Table 12.7). Much of the popularly perceived premium to Dow Dog investing appears due to data coding errors and to the bias of arithmetic averages.

For the moment, consider the possibilities facing tax-efficient and transactions cost–efficient institutional investors. A potential annual excess return of 1.55% could make the Dow Dog investment strategy worth pursuing if such advantages were stable and predictable. Unfortunately, they are not. As shown in Table 12.8,

---

[12]If a stock appreciates by 100% and then falls by 50%, the arithmetic average rate of return for two periods is 25% [= (100% − 50%)/2]. In reality, no net profit is made, and the actual geometric mean rate of return is 0%[= $(2.0 \times 0.5)^{0.5}$ − 1].

[13]See *Barron's*, January 2, 1995, MW 95, plus updates from recent issues.

[14]Here the geometric mean of the difference between Dow Dog returns and the DJIA is 1.55% per year, whereas the simple difference between the geometric mean returns for the Dow Dogs and the DJIA is 1.78% per year. Because of compounding, the geometric mean of the differences is less than the difference of the geometric means.

Dow Dogs outperform the DJIA portfolio in only 21 of 38 years during the 1961–98 period. Dow Dogs outperform the DJIA during only three of seven 5-year periods and exhibit an edge during two of three 10-year periods. This return pattern is typical of equally performing comparison portfolios. Interestingly, positive above-average returns for the Dow Dog strategy seem to be a thing of the past. During the most recent decade, for example, a total return penalty of 2.13% to Dow Dog investing is operative.

A. A fair test of the Dow Dog strategy would consider both transactions costs and tax penalties tied to its implementation. Could such expenses explain the perceived advantage of Dow Dog investing?

B. It is conceivable that the high-yield characteristic of Dow Dog stocks might make such an investment strategy perceptibly less risky than the DJIA portfolio. Use the evidence in Table 12.8 and simple logic to support or refute this assertion.

Selected References

Berk, Jonathan B. "Sorting Out Sorts." *Journal of Finance* 55 (February 2000): 407–428.

Bernstein, Peter L. "A New Look at the Efficient Market Hypothesis." *Journal of Portfolio Management* 25 (Winter 1999): 1–2.

Dutt, Swarna D., and Dipak Ghosh. "A Note on the Foreign Exchange Market Efficiency Hypothesis." *Journal of Economics and Finance* 23 (Summer 1999): 157–161.

Kan, Raymond, and Chu Zhang. "GMM Tests of Stochastic Discount Factor Models with Useless Factors." *Journal of Financial Economics* 54 (October 1999): 103–127.

Kaul, Aditya, Vikas Mehrotra, and Randall Morck. "Demand Curves for Stocks Do Slope Down: New Evidence from an Index Weights Adjustment." *Journal of Finance* 55 (April 2000): 893–912.

Kellard, Neil, Paul Newbold, Tony Rayner, and Christine Ennew. "The Relative Efficiency of Commodity Futures Markets." *Journal of Futures Markets* 19 (June 1999): 413–432.

Lee, Chun I., and Ike Mathur. "Efficiency Tests in the Spanish Futures Markets." *Journal of Futures Markets* 19 (February 1999): 59–77.

Lotz, Christopher, and Lutz Schlögl. "Default Risk in a Market Model." *Journal of Banking and Finance* 24 (January 2000): 301–327.

Loughran, Tim, and Jay R. Ritter. "Uniformly Least Powerful Tests of Market Efficiency." *Journal of Financial Economics* 55 (March 2000): 361–389.

Louis, Henock, Lloyd P. Blenman, and Janet S. Thatcher. "Interest Rate Parity and the Behavior of the Bid-Ask Spread." *Journal of Financial Research* 22 (Summer 1999): 189–206.

Malliaris, A. G., and Jerome L. Stein. "Methodological Issues in Asset Pricing: Random Walk or Chaotic Dynamics." *Journal of Banking and Finance* 23 (November 1999): 1605–1635.

Mookerjee, Rajen, and Qiao Yu. "An Empirical Analysis of the Equity Markets in China." *Review of Financial Economics* 8 (1999): 41–60.

Rajan, Raghuram, Henri Servaes, and Luigi Zingales. "The Cost of Diversity: The Diversification Discount and Inefficient Investment." *Journal of Finance* 55 (February 2000): 35–80.

Stonham, Paul. "Too Close to the Hedge: The Case of Long Term Capital Management LP—Part One: Hedge Fund Analytics." *European Management Journal* 17 (June 1999): 282–289.

Tse, Yiuman. "Round-the-Clock Market Efficiency and Home Bias: Evidence from the International Japanese Government Bond Futures Markets." *Journal of Banking and Finance* 23 (December 1999): 1831–1860.

CHAPTER 13

Capital Asset Pricing Theory

Modern portfolio theory has made a compelling contribution to our understanding of financial markets. Models of market efficiency help academics and practitioners understand the subtleties of risk-reward relationships and facilitate the construction of efficient portfolios. Beta is an accepted measure of stock market risk at research seminars, on the pages of financial publications, and in the boardrooms of corporate America. The concept of risk-adjusted performance is also broadly accepted. Portfolio managers and investors everywhere seek to earn the largest possible return, given a specified level of risk. Alternatively, portfolio managers and investors seek the lowest level of risk, given a specified required return.

Still, both academics and practitioners decry abuses that occur when overly enthusiastic theoreticians forget that their models describe asset-pricing behavior under idealized conditions that are seldom met in "messy" real-world stock and bond markets. Some practitioners have been known to cry out that the "b" in beta is for "baloney," because conventional risk-reward relationships have a way of becoming unconventional at crucial moments of high stock market volatility. Even the most elegant models of asset pricing leave ample room for improvement.[1]

In considering the merits and demerits of models of market efficiency such as the Capital Asset Pricing Model, investors should not reject the validity of the market efficiency concept just because a single characterization of that concept has obvious flaws. "The sunrise is in the east" is a useful concept despite the fact that during the course of the year its timing and geographic location vary. Alternative versions of the market efficiency concept are similarly useful despite obvious limitations.

Portfolio Theory

Basic Assumptions

investment portfolio
Collection of securities that together provide an investor with an attractive trade-off between risk and return.

Nobel Laureate Harry Markowitz, working in the early 1950s, was among the first to focus investor attention on the risks and returns of an **investment portfolio.** An investment portfolio is a collection of securities that together provide an investor

[1]See: Barry Henderson, "Divining the Storm," *Barron's,* July 31, 2000, 17.

portfolio theory Concept of making security choices based on portfolio expected returns and risks.

expected return Anticipated profit over some relevant holding period.

risk Return dispersion; usually measured by the standard deviation of returns.

probability distribution Apportionment of likely occurrences.

with an attractive trade-off between risk and return. Unlike investment theorists before him, Markowitz argued that the volatilities of individual securities are not the most important concern for investors. Of most consequence is how the expected return and volatility characteristics of individual securities affect the expected return and volatility of the overall portfolio. For example, most stock and bond prices tend to fall with an increase in the expected rate of inflation. However, gold mining and natural resource stocks tend to rise with an increase in inflationary expectations. Therefore, the price volatility of stocks in general and gold mining stocks are often inversely related. When inflationary expectations rise, gold stocks jump up while general stock prices decline. Thus, by adding volatile gold stocks to a broadly diversified investment portfolio, the price volatility of the overall portfolio can actually decline.

Portfolio theory is the simple concept of making security choices based on the expected return and risk of a collection of securities. **Expected return** is measured by the amount of profit anticipated over some relevant holding period. **Risk** is captured by return dispersion. Within this framework, investment alternatives are represented by the **probability distribution** of security returns over some future period. As shown in Figure 13.1, a probability distribution can be described as an

FIGURE 13.1 **Annual Rates of Return on Common Stocks Approximate a Normal Distribution, 1950–Present**

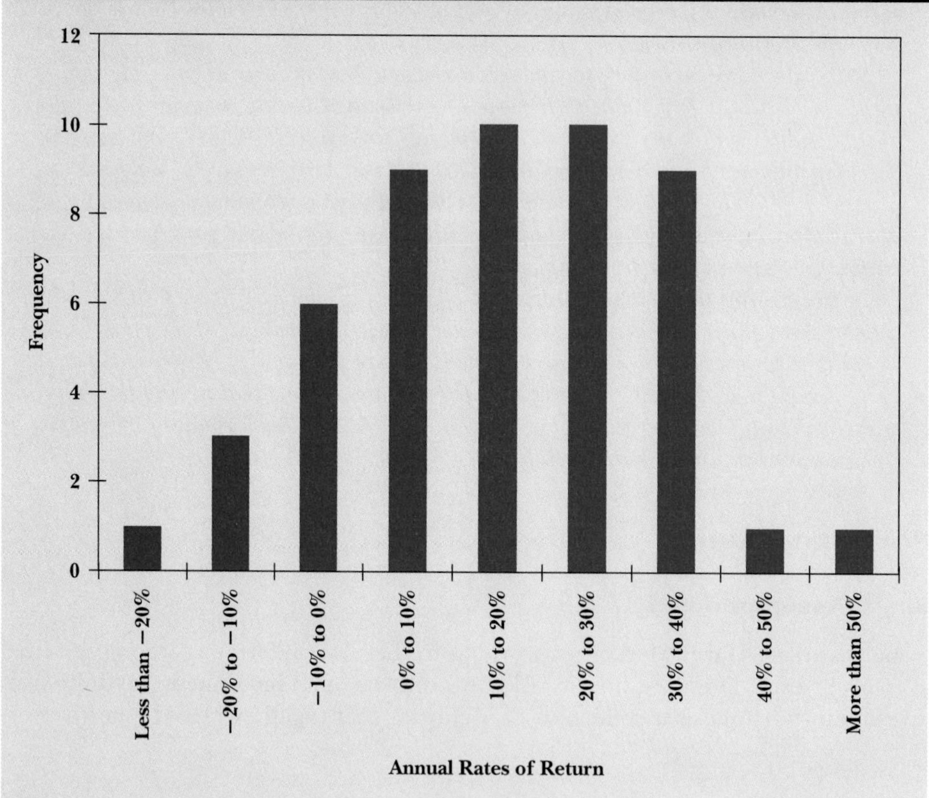

Data source: Federal Reserve (data shown for S&P 500 Index).

array of likely returns on a histogram. On the vertical axis is the annual rate of return, and on the horizontal axis is the frequency of annual occurrence. As reflected by the Standard & Poor's (S&P) 500 Index, the mean annual rate of return earned on common stocks has been 13.46% per year during the post–World War II period (also see Table 5.3). The median, or "middle," annual rate of return earned on common stocks during this time frame has been 16.81% per year. Notice that when the average and median rate of return are very close, as is the case here, the distribution of annual rates of return approximates a normal distribution, or a bell-shaped curve. Under such circumstances, the average or median annual rate of return can form a useful estimate for the anticipated or expected rate of return on common stocks.

A basic assumption of portfolio theory is that investors seek out investments with the potential to provide maximum benefits. They search for the highest expected rate of return for a given amount of risk, or the lowest amount of risk for a given expected rate of return. In other words, investors get positive benefit or **utility** out of an increase in the expected rate of return and suffer a psychic loss or **disutility** out of an increase in the amount of risk, or return volatility. This means that investors tend to be **risk averse.** They would prefer a cash payment of $100 to a bet with an expected payoff of $100. In selecting their investments, investors seek out investments with the characteristic of providing the maximum expected rate of return for a given level of risk, or the minimum anticipated volatility for a given expected rate of return.

utility
Positive benefit.

disutility
Psychic loss.

risk averse
Desire to avoid risk.

Notice that the portfolio theory concept of an optimal portfolio is based on the assumption that all the advantages of an investment portfolio can be summarized in terms of the expected rate of return. Similarly, all the disadvantages tied to an investment portfolio are summarized by the anticipated level of volatility. The sole motivation behind investment decisions is to maximize economic welfare. No nonpecuniary considerations are involved. This abstracts from the possibility that various investors may be motivated to buy stocks in "socially conscious" corporations. Portfolio theory is based on the concept that only monetary considerations are involved when an investor is making investment decisions.

To summarize, portfolio theory is based on three fundamental assertions:

- Investors seek to maximize utility.
- Investors are risk averse: Utility rises with expected return and falls with an increase in volatility.
- The optimal portfolio has the highest expected return for a given level of risk, or the lowest level of risk for a given expected return.

Portfolio Risk and Return

Investment alternatives involve distinct combinations of expected return and anticipated volatility. The relationship between the expected rate of return and risk can be depicted in a two-dimensional graph in which expected return is on the vertical axis and risk is on the horizontal axis, as shown in Figure 13.2. Risk is depicted by using the standard deviation measure of return volatility.

In Figure 13.2, panel A, each investment alternative is depicted as a simple dot in expected return-risk space. In other words, the desirability of each portfolio can be fully described as a simple combination of expected return and the standard

FIGURE 13.2 Expected Rate of Return and Risk Are Fundamental Economic Characteristics of Investment Opportunities

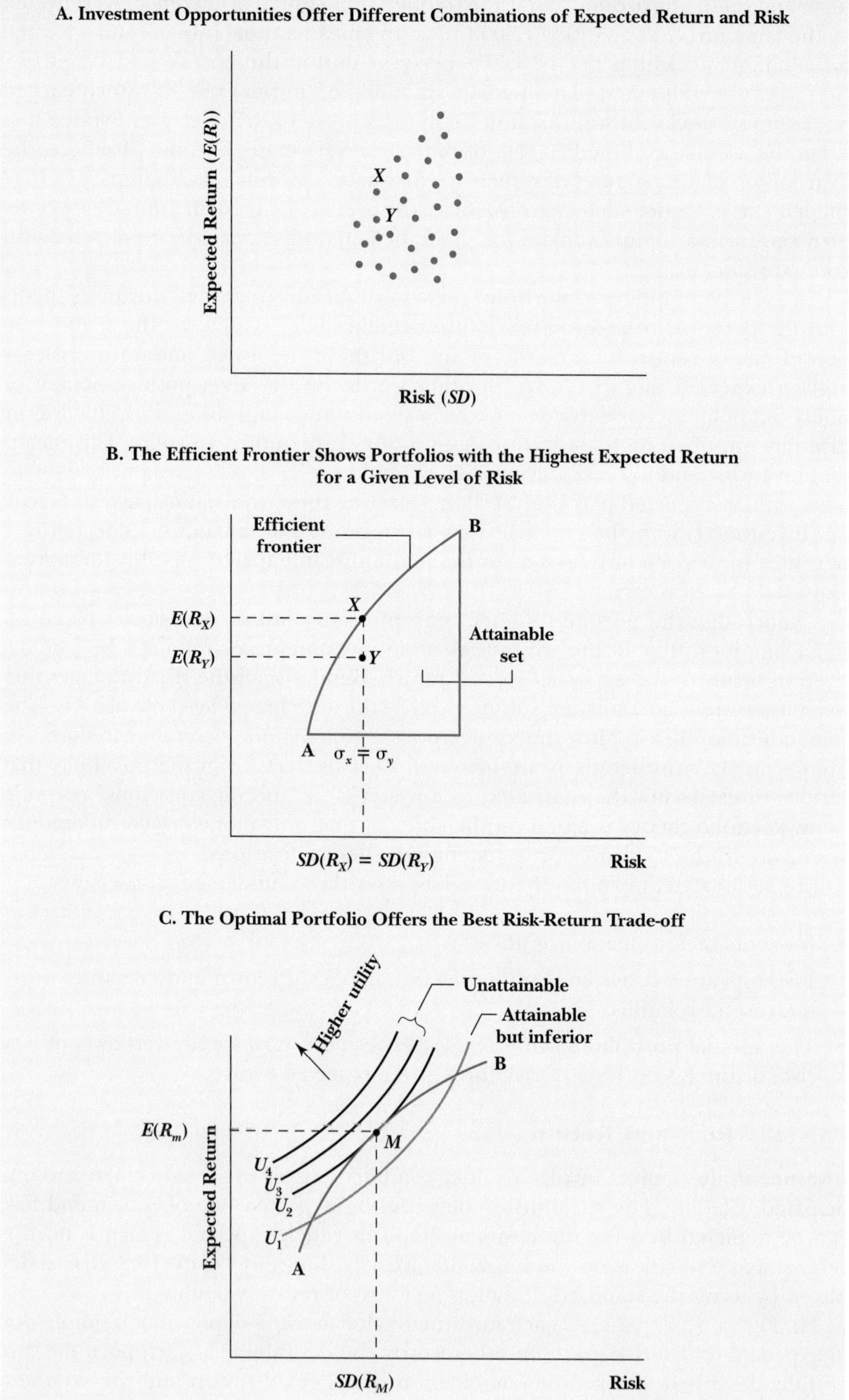

deviation of returns. Because investors favor investments with higher levels of expected return and lower levels of risk, investment opportunities tend to be regarded more favorably when they offer a higher level of expected return for a given level of risk.

The expected rate of return for each portfolio is simply

$$E(R_p) = \sum_{i=1}^{N} W_i E(R_i) \tag{13.1}$$

where W_i is the portfolio weight, or percentage, devoted to a given security i, and $E(R_i)$ is the expected rate of return on security i. For example, suppose an investor put 70% of a portfolio in a stock with an expected return of 12% and 30% in a stock with an expected return of 15%. The expected rate of return on the overall portfolio is a simple weighted sum of the portfolio percentage times the anticipated return on each respective holding. In this case, the expected rate of return on the portfolio is 12.9% [= 0.7(12%) + 0.3(15%)].

The standard deviation of a portfolio is calculated by using the expression

$$SD(R_p) = \sqrt{\sum_{i=1}^{N} W_i^2 \times VAR(R_i) + \sum_{i=1}^{N}\sum_{j=1}^{N} W_i \times W_j \times COV(R_i R_j)} \tag{13.2}$$

In this expression, $SD(R_P)$ is the portfolio standard deviation, W is the portfolio weight in securities i and j, respectively, $VAR(R_i)$ is the variance of returns for individual securities [and $SD(R_i) = VAR(R_i)^{1/2}$], and $COV(R_i R_j)$ is the covariance between the returns on securities i and j. Whereas standard deviation is a simple measure of return volatility, covariance is a measure of how rates of return on two individual securities vary together versus separately. Therefore, the standard deviation of a portfolio rises with an increase in the standard deviation or volatility of individual securities and to the extent these securities have high covariance or vary together.

The statistical concept of covariance can be thought of as an average of the products of the deviations from the means for each data point pair. Covariance is an absolute measure of comovement that varies between plus and minus infinity, $-\infty$ and $+\infty$. To calculate covariance by hand would be tedious. However, covariance is a standard statistical concept and can be easily computed by using common spreadsheet functions. The covariance concept can be used to determine the relationship between any two data sets. For example, labor economists use covariance to examine whether greater income accompanies higher levels of education. Financial economists use the covariance concept to study common characteristics in stock return data.

For example, Table 13.1 shows how monthly returns for leading auto manufacturers such as General Motors (GM) and Ford tend to move together. During the period in question, the covariance of monthly returns for these two competitors was 0.81%. High positive covariance diminishes the diversification advantage gained from combining these two stocks in a single portfolio. Notice the much lower level of stock return covariance for cigarette manufacturer Philip Morris and financial powerhouse Citigroup. Unlike GM and Ford, Philip Morris and Citigroup are in distinctly different businesses and have few common economic characteristics. As such, it is unsurprising that a relatively low level of negative

TABLE 13.1 Portfolio Risk Increases with the Volatility of Individual Holdings and the Extent to which Holdings Have High Covariance

Month	GM	Ford	Portfolio A	Philip Morris	Citigroup	Portfolio B
July '98	−19.1%	−21.7%	−20.4%	−5.1%	−34.0%	−20.9%
August	−5.6%	5.3%	−0.3%	12.4%	−15.5%	−2.5%
September	15.1%	16.5%	15.8%	10.5%	25.3%	17.7%
October	11.4%	1.5%	6.3%	9.4%	6.9%	8.2%
November	2.4%	6.6%	4.5%	−3.5%	−1.1%	−2.3%
December	25.4%	5.5%	15.0%	−12.4%	13.2%	−0.4%
January '99	−7.5%	−3.5%	−5.5%	−16.5%	4.8%	−6.5%
February	5.4%	−4.4%	0.4%	−9.1%	8.7%	−0.6%
March	2.4%	13.6%	7.8%	−0.4%	17.6%	8.2%
April	−5.8%	−10.7%	−8.3%	10.0%	−11.5%	−1.4%
May	−4.3%	−1.2%	−2.8%	5.3%	7.5%	6.4%
June	−7.4%	−13%	−10.4%	−7.3%	−5.9%	−6.6%
Mean	0.40%	−1.07%	−0.34%	−1.01%	0.03%	−0.49%
S.D.	12.30%	10.83%	10.51%	10.15%	16.78%	9.89%
Covariance		0.81%			−0.08%	

covariance exists between the monthly stock returns of Philip Morris and Citigroup. The low level of return covariance between Philip Morris and Citigroup has the effect of reducing portfolio risk when both stocks are combined in a single portfolio.

In the example shown, two different portfolios are formed on the assumption that one-half of each portfolio is invested in each pair of stocks. In portfolio A, 50% of the overall portfolio is initially invested in GM, and the remaining 50% is invested in Ford. Portfolio B is based on the assumption of an initial 50-50 split in the amount invested in Philip Morris and Citigroup. Portfolio standard deviation depends on the weight, standard deviation, and covariance of individual asset returns. As shown in Table 13.1, the relatively high positive covariance of 0.81% between GM and Ford stock returns has the effect of limiting the diversification advantage of combining both stocks in a single portfolio. Low covariance implies a much greater diversification advantage from combining two or more securities in a given portfolio. Notice the risk-reducing advantage of including Philip Morris and Citigroup in a single portfolio in the light of their negative return covariance of −0.08%.

It is important to keep in mind that an individual security's contribution to portfolio risk depends on the asset's weight in the portfolio, its standard deviation, and its covariance with other portfolio securities. An equal investment in two securities with the same expected return and standard deviation but a perfect inverse correlation, $r_{ij} = -1$, would yield a **zero-risk portfolio** in which $SD_P = 0$. Remember from Chapter 5 that correlation is a relative measure of comovement that falls between −1 and +1, or −100% and +100%. For security returns, it is calculated as the ratio of return covariance divided by the product of the return standard deviations for a pair of securities.

zero-risk portfolio
Constant-return portfolio.

To understand how the correlation concept relates to portfolio risk, consider a simple example. Suppose an investor owns a portfolio containing only two stocks priced at $40 per share. If one rose by $1 while the second fell by $1, portfolio value would remain unchanged. For an equal investment in two securities with the same expected return and standard deviation, $r_{ij} = -1$ implies that the returns on one security are perfect mirror images of the returns on the other held in the portfolio. Thus, an equal investment in two securities with the same expected return and standard deviation, but a perfect inverse correlation, will have a constant value over time. This is what is meant by a zero-risk portfolio. It never changes in value. For risky portfolios, asset covariance determines portfolio risk when the number of portfolio holdings is large.

Optimal Portfolio Choice

An **efficient portfolio** is one that provides maximum expected return for a given level of risk. Alternatively, an efficient portfolio is one that provides minimum risk for a given expected return. In Figure 13.2, panel A, it is important to keep in mind that the expected rate of return on a stock is calculated as the ratio of expected future cash flows divided by the investor's purchase price per share. If a given company were expected to generate $4 per share in future cash flows per year, an investor paying $40 would enjoy a 10% annual rate of return (10% = $4/$40). However, an investor who paid a price of $50 per share would have an expected rate of return of only 8% per year (8% = $4/$50).

efficient portfolio Portfolio with maximum expected return for a given level of risk, or minimum risk for a given expected return.

Consider portfolios X and Y depicted in Figure 13.2A and B. Suppose that they have the exact same level of risk $SD(R_X) = SD(R_Y)$ but that the expected rate of return on X is greater than on Y, or $E(R_X) > E(R_Y)$. In the real world, this would be an impossible situation. Under such circumstances, investors would naturally favor X over Y. They would sell Y and use the proceeds to buy X. This would cause the price of Y to decline until such point that it would offer investors exactly the same rate of return on investment as X. Remember, assuming future cash flows are constant, the expected rate of return on a security rises with a fall in the purchase price. In fact, the prices of X and Y will continue to adjust until $E(R_X) = E(R_Y)$ and each offers investors an expected rate of return commensurate with their level of risk.

The **efficient frontier** is the complete set of efficient portfolios. The efficient frontier includes all efficient portfolios that provide maximum expected return for a given level of risk. Alternatively, the efficient frontier depicts all efficient portfolios that entail minimum risk for a given expected return. It is shown by a curved line that is upward sloping to the right from *A* to *B* in Figure 13.2B. Portfolio A consists of auto stocks and offers a relatively low expected rate of return with modest risk; portfolio B is made up of biotech stocks and offers a relatively high expected rate of return with greater risk. Both represent efficient portfolios. The shape of the efficient frontier implies that there are diminishing returns to risk taking in the investment world. To gain ever higher expected rates of return, investors must be willing to take on ever-increasing amounts of risk. Relatively few investment opportunities in the economy offer investors the possibility of stupendous rates of return, and such opportunities entail equally stupendous amounts of risk.

efficient frontier Collection of all efficient portfolios.

The **optimal portfolio** is one that provides an investor with the highest level of expected utility. To be sure, optimal portfolio choice depends on individual risk

optimal portfolio Collection of securities that provides an investor with the highest level of expected utility.

preferences. Very risk-averse individuals may prefer a portfolio consisting of auto stocks, given their solid dividend income and high degree of price stability. Adventuresome investors may prefer a portfolio containing biotech stocks, given their enticing growth opportunities and potential for rapid price appreciation. Neither investor is wrong in making such choices. Each choice is appropriate given differences in individual risk preferences.

market portfolio All tradable assets.

As shown in Figure 13.2C, optimal portfolio choice involves a trade-off between that which is available, the efficient frontier, and that which is preferred, as determined by investor preferences. A key concept in portfolio theory is that the **market portfolio** is an efficient portfolio, as depicted by portfolio M in Figure 13.2C. This means that the market portfolio, as represented by the S&P 500 Index, for example, reflects an appropriate trade-off between risk and the expected rate of return.

Capital Asset Pricing Model (CAPM)

Basic Assumptions

capital asset pricing model (CAPM) Method for predicting how investment returns are determined in an efficient capital market.

Portfolio theory offers a fundamental framework within which financial economists and others can structure detailed tests of the efficient market hypothesis (EMH). The most detailed model or construct used to describe the efficient pricing of investment securities is called the **capital asset pricing model (CAPM)**. The CAPM is an elaborate attempt to provide a complete context for describing how investment returns are determined. At its most basic, CAPM is a method for predicting how investment returns are determined in an efficient capital market.

The CAPM entails a number of important underlying assumptions. These basic assumptions are that

- Investors hold efficient portfolios; higher expected returns involve higher risk.
- There are unlimited borrowing and lending at the risk-free rate.
- Investors have homogeneous expectations.
- There is a one-period time horizon.
- Investments are infinitely divisible.
- No taxes or transaction costs exist.
- Inflation is fully anticipated.
- Capital markets are in equilibrium.

Some criticize the CAPM for being based on such a restrictive set of underlying assumptions. After all, taxes and transaction costs exist in the real world. However, it is worth pointing out that a model can be a useful predictive device even if its underlying assumptions fail to be met. If a model such as the CAPM can be used to predict stock returns with a high degree of accuracy, then the restrictiveness of its underlying assumption is a mute point. Moreover, some might argue that CAPM assumptions are fairly innocuous. For example, individual retirement account (IRA) investors and pension funds often pay no taxes on capital gains or dividend income. When deep discount brokers on the Internet allow investors to buy and sell stocks for $8 and less per trade, transaction costs do, in fact, become minimal.

CAPM and Market Efficiency

Within the context of its underlying assumptions, the CAPM can be used as a tool to evaluate the EMH. According to the CAPM, the market is efficient if only risk-free assets give risk-free returns. If three-month Treasury bills yield 5%, then any security offering higher rates of return necessarily entails greater risk. The market is inefficient if risk-free assets or portfolios give above-risk-free returns.

By isolating deviations from predicted returns, CAPM has potential as a tool to help investors isolate instances in which the pricing of individual securities deviates from that predicted for a perfectly efficient capital market. Under such circumstances, portfolio managers might devise investment strategies to take advantage of unusual profit-making opportunities. Similarly, the CAPM has the potential to offer investors an effective means for risk assessment and management.

Based on the predictions of the CAPM, researchers and public officials might suggest reforms in market rules or regulations to speed the flow of timely information and improve capital market efficiency. For example, the CAPM predicts an improved functioning for capital markets when both bid and ask information is widely disseminated throughout the trading day. Trade and reporting rule innovations have, in fact, been based on such theoretical predictions.

In both situations, the CAPM offers investors and others a device that can be used to better understand the functioning of capital markets.

Lending And Borrowing

An important underlying assumption of the CAPM is that investors have the opportunity to lend or borrow at the risk-free rate. Lending occurs if a portion of the investor's portfolio is held in the risk-free asset. For example, an individual investor is lending at the risk-free rate when Treasury bills constitute an important part of the investor's portfolio. Borrowing or leverage is used when more than 100% of the investor's portfolio is invested in risky assets. Margin account customers do, in fact, have the opportunity to leverage their stock investments by borrowing at the broker loan rate. The broker loan rate is often the most attractive interest rate available to individual borrowers and is seldom much above the three-month Treasury bill rate. Presently, investors are able to purchase equity securities with an initial margin requirement of 50%. This means that investors with $10,000 of capital can buy as much as $20,000 worth of equity securities.

In Figure 13.3A, a straight line is drawn from the risk-free rate R_F to the market return R_M on the efficient frontier. At R_F, 100% of the investor's portfolio is invested in T-bills. At R_M, 100% of the investor's portfolio is invested in the market index. Between R_F and R_M, the investor's portfolio is invested in both. The closer to the vertical axis and R_F, the more that will be invested in T-bills. The closer to R_M, the more that will be invested in the market portfolio. At the midpoint of the line from R_F to R_M, the investor's portfolio is split 50-50 between T-bills and the market index. Indeed, it is interesting to see how an infinite variety of expected return profiles can be constructed by simply varying the amount of an entire investment portfolio that is held in the risk-free asset and the market portfolio. Investors need only two assets to construct an infinite variety of expected return-risk combinations.

It is interesting to note how a portfolio of risky assets with lending or borrowing at the risk-free rate can dominate many real-world investment alternatives.

FIGURE 13.3 Efficient Frontier becomes a Straight Line When Risk-Free Lending and Borrowing Is Possible

A. Expected Return with Lending Beats the Low-Risk Portfolio, $E(R_{A*}) > E(R_A)$; Expected Return with Borrowing Beats the High-Risk Portfolio, $E(R_{B*}) > E(R_B)$.

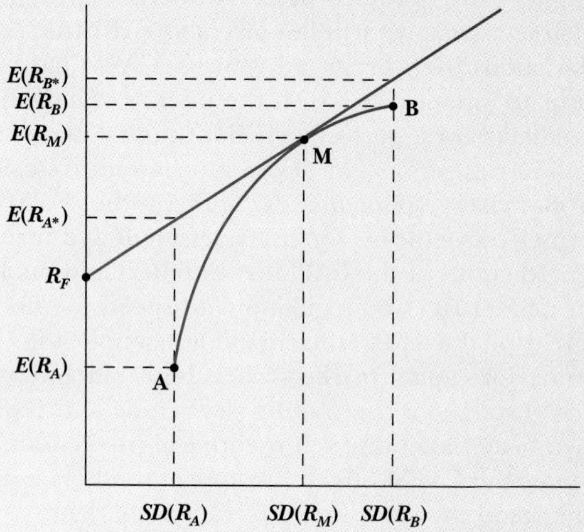

B. Lending Is Preferable to Low-Risk U_1 Investors; Borrowing Is Preferable to High-Risk U_2 Investors.

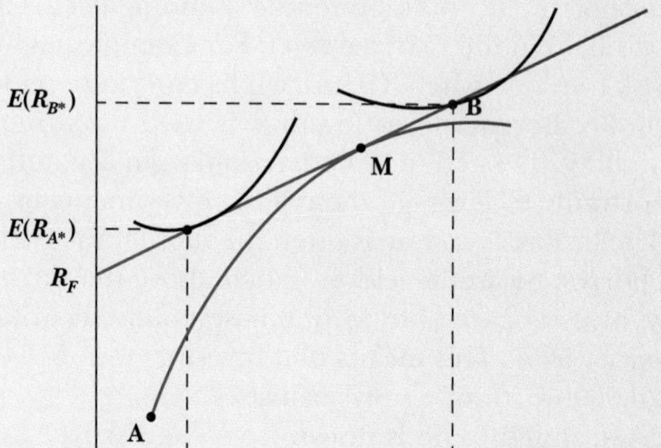

Notice how the expected return $E(R_{A*})$ on a portfolio containing the market index plus risk-free lending is higher than the expected return $E(R_A)$ on a portfolio of low-risk auto stocks. With the same level of risk $SD(R_A)$, the lending portfolio will be preferred by low-risk investors. Similarly, observe how the expected return $E(R_{B*})$ on a portfolio consisting of the market index plus risk-free borrowing (leverage) is higher than the expected return $E(R_B)$ on a portfolio of high-risk biotech stocks.

With the same level of risk $SD(R_B)$, the leverage portfolio will be preferred by high-risk investors.

Just as in the case of Figure 13.2 and the pricing of inefficient portfolios, the superior returns made possible through risk-free lending and borrowing have direct implications for all investors. Risk-free lending and borrowing changes the pricing of all investment portfolios. In Figure 13.3A the low-risk portfolio of auto stocks must fall in price to offer investors a higher competitive rate of return commensurate with the $E(R_{A*})$ produced by the lending portfolio. At the same time, the high-risk portfolio of biotech stocks must fall in price to offer investors a higher rate of return comparable with the $E(R_{B*})$ provided by the borrowing (leverage) portfolio. The opportunity for risk-free lending and borrowing collapses the efficient frontier from Figure 13.2 into the straight-line capital market line (CML) shown in Figure 13.3B. As shown in Figure 13.3B, depending on their risk preferences, investors choose individually optimal locations along the CML. Low-risk investors choose to invest in low-risk portfolios consisting of both T-bills and the market portfolio. High-risk investors choose to invest in high-risk portfolios combining the use of leverage with the market portfolio.

Expected Return and Risk

Capital Market Line

The CAPM describes three distinct relations between the expected rate of return and risk. The first of these is called the **capital market line (CML).** The CML shows the linear risk-return trade-off for all investment portfolios. It depicts a straight-line relation between the expected rate of return on a portfolio, $E(R_P)$, and portfolio risk, $SD(R_P)$, as measured by the standard deviation of portfolio returns:

capital market line (CML) Linear risk-return trade-off for all investment portfolios.

$$E(R_P) = R_F + \frac{E(R_M) - R_F}{SD(R_M)} SD(R_P) \qquad \textbf{(13.3)}$$

$$= R_F + \frac{SD(R_P)}{SD(R_M)} [E(R_M) - R_F]$$

As shown in Figure 13.4A, the CML asserts that the expected return on a portfolio is the risk-free rate R_F plus the relative risk of the portfolio, $SD(R_P) \div SD(R_M)$, times the market risk premium, $E(R_M) - R_F$.

During the post–World War II period, the expected rate of return on the U.S. market has been roughly 13% per year and the risk-free rate is roughly 5%. This implies that the market risk premium is 8% (= 13% − 5%). The CML identifies "reward for waiting" plus "reward for risk taking" components of expected return. In an overall market in which the expected rate of return is 13% per year, the risk-free rate of 5% can be thought of as the reward-for-waiting component of total return. The market risk premium of 8% can be thought of as the investor's reward for risk taking. The expected rate of return of 13% on the market portfolio represents both a reward for waiting and a reward for risk taking.

Market risk as measured by the standard deviation of annual returns falls in a range near 20% per year. According to the CML, a portfolio with twice the market risk level would need to provide investors with twice the standard risk premium of 8% per year. Therefore, a portfolio with $SD(R_P) = 40\%$ would have an expected

WALL STREET WISDOM 13.1

Dear Abby (Joseph Cohen)

Abby Joseph Cohen is known as one of Wall Street's most respected and influential stock market analysts. Cohen is managing director and chair of the Investment Policy Committee of Goldman, Sachs & Co. where she is responsible for the firm's U.S. portfolio strategy. Born in 1952 in Queens, New York, Cohen obtained a BA in 1973 from Cornell University in economics and computer science. She earned a MS degree in economics from George Washington University in 1976. In an industry in which chauffeured stretch limousines are the rule, the unpretentious and unassuming Cohen rises at 5:00 AM each workday and takes the city bus to work. Still, she logs more than 125,000 airline miles per year meeting with Goldman Sachs clients and gives more than 150 speeches per year to clients and other investors. Prior to joining Goldman Sachs in 1990, Cohen was with Wall Street firm Drexel Burnham Lambert for seven years, where she served as chief equity strategist. Earlier, she was an economist and quantitative research director for Baltimore, Maryland–based mutual fund powerhouse T. Rowe Price Associates. Cohen started her professional career as an economist with the Federal Reserve Board in Washington, D.C.

Cohen makes numerous television appearances and is frequently quoted in the financial press. If every bull market has its sage, the 1990s surely belonged to Cohen. She has been the bull market's most ardent supporter, explaining its every move to traders and urging them to believe it would continue its run. The higher stock prices soared in the 1990s, the more followers she won. When it was even rumored that she had turned bearish, stocks plummeted. In the summer of 1998, when valuations became stretched, Cohen declared stocks had become "fairly valued." She became bullish once again in the fall of 1998 after stocks turned lower, or "corrected" by more than 10%. This pattern repeated itself in the spring of 1999 when Cohen turned less bullish. After stocks fell dramatically in late summer and early fall, Cohen reiterated her faith in the bull market as stocks romped to new highs at the end of the year. On March 28, 2000, Cohen rocked the markets once again with her suggestion that investors raise cash and cut back on their portfolio allocation to stocks. A long-time bull on tech stocks, Cohen also recommended that investors begin to underweight technology in the stock portion of their portfolios. Market reaction was swift, as the tech-heavy Nasdaq composite fell more than 2.5% on its way to a correction, representing more than a 10% decline in the Nasdaq.

Using solid economic analysis, Cohen has been able to accurately predict the overall market's direction for more than a decade. Her success has convinced many that macroeconomic theory and analysis are vital tools for investment research. Cohen's bullish view on the stock market has been based on her perception of continuous improvement in the overall economy. For several years, the stock market has marched ahead as governments around the world have reduced budget deficits and cut taxes, corporations have closed businesses that did not make sense, and individuals have increased savings and investment. What drives the economy are consumption, employment, and income. According to Cohen, so long as the underlying economy remains strong, stock market investors will enjoy a favorable investment environment. Since a mild economic recession in the early 1990s, an uninterrupted economic expansion has blessed investors with the most favorable stock market environment in history. With low inflation, falling interest rates and robust economic growth, the backdrop for equity investors could not have been more favorable throughout the 1990s.

What might derail the longest economic expansion in history and the most vibrant bull market ever recorded? According to Cohen, favorable economic cycles and stock market environments do not end because they get "old." They end because business inventory becomes excessive, inflation becomes problematic, or the Federal Reserve raises interest rates too far or too fast.

See: E. S. Browning, "Nasdaq Surges 5.34% on Additional Signs of Slowing Economy as Bonds Advance," *The Wall Street Journal,* June 2, 2000, C1.

FIGURE 13.4 Capital Market Line (CML) Shows the Straight-Line Relation for Portfolio Expected Return and Risk

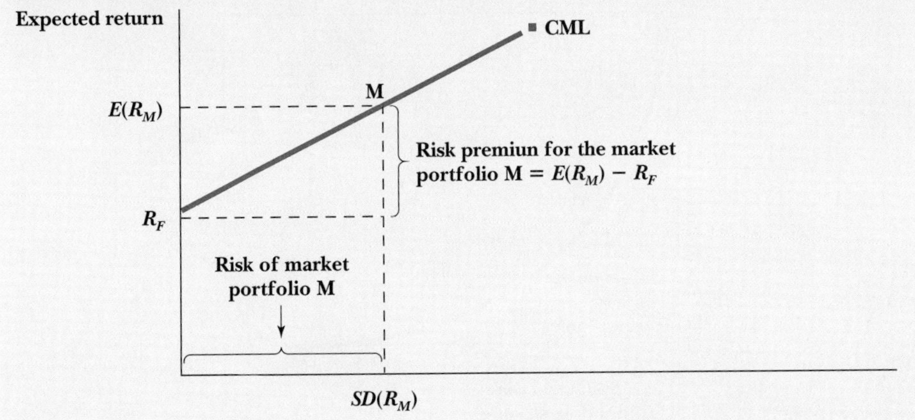

return of 21% [= 5% + (40%/20%) × (13% − 5%)]. A portfolio with one-half the market risk level would need to provide investors with one-half the standard risk premium of 8% per year. Thus, a portfolio with $SD(R_P)$ = 10% would have an expected return of 9% [= 5% + (10%/20%) × (13% − 5%)].

Thus, the CML depicts a linear risk-reward trade-off for all portfolios.

Security Market Line

The **security market line (SML)** characterizes a linear risk-return trade-off for individual stocks. In the case of individual securities, the SML shows how the expected rate of return $E(R_i)$ can be seen as a simple function of the amount of **systematic risk.** Systematic risk is a measure of return volatility in an individual stock that is tied to the overall market. **Unsystematic risk** is the amount of return volatility that is specific to an individual company. An example of unsystematic risk is the chance that a company's excessive use of leverage might lead to financial difficulties or bankruptcy.

Although both systematic risk and unsystematic risk contribute to the total amount of volatility experienced by investors, only systematic risk has a favorable influence on the expected rate of return. Investors cannot demand higher rates of expected return for unsystematic risk because such risk can be easily diversified away through the judicious selection of a diversified portfolio. Unsystematic risk is synonymous with **diversifiable risk.** As shown in Figure 13.5, the total amount of portfolio risk declines with an increase in the number of portfolio holdings. When the number of securities in some diversified portfolio approaches roughly 30, investors can virtually eliminate unsystematic risk. Notice that the Dow Jones Industrial Average (DJIA) includes 30 large companies, and the DJIA is often taken as a useful proxy for the overall market. However, even after unsystematic risk is eliminated through diversification, substantial systematic or **nondiversifiable risk** remains. Because systematic risk cannot be eliminated through diversification, investors must be rewarded for any increase in this form of risk to justify their investment in a particular stock or market sector.

security market line (SML)
Linear risk-return trade-off for individual stocks.

systematic risk
Return volatility tied to the overall market.

unsystematic risk
Return volatility specific to an individual company.

diversifiable risk
Unsystematic risk.

nondiversifiable risk
Systematic risk.

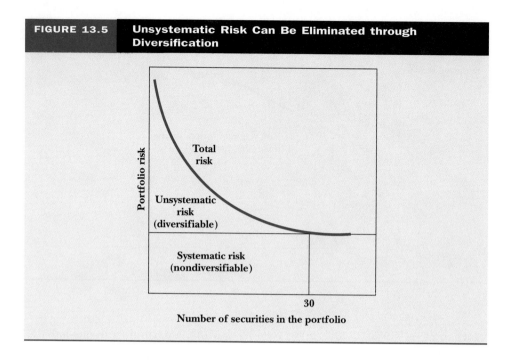

FIGURE 13.5 Unsystematic Risk Can Be Eliminated through Diversification

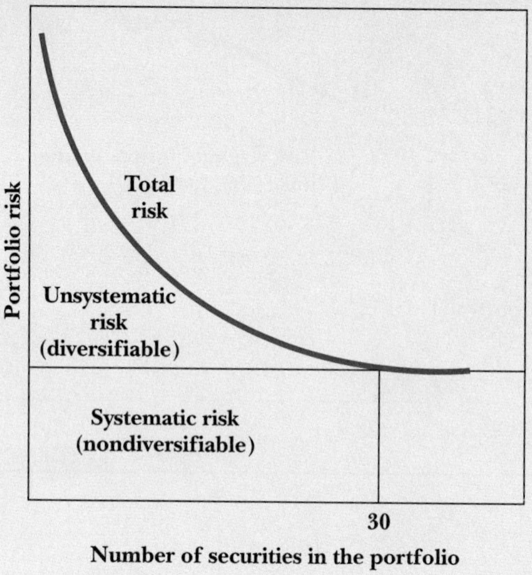

For example, tech stocks are especially volatile because few high-tech companies have durable advantages over dog-eat-dog competitors. A constant flow of inventions and new product introductions in the high-tech sector means that today's stock market winner may be tomorrow's also-ran. The fortunes of high-tech companies are also closely tied to interest rates and the pace of the overall economy. Thus, if the overall market goes up by 15% on the expectation of a decrease in interest rates, high-tech stocks as a group may rise by 20% or more. If the market in general dips 10% on the expectation of a sharp slowdown in economic growth and capital spending, high-tech stocks can drop 15% or more. Such systematic volatility is unavoidable when investing in high-tech stocks.

beta
Sensitivity of a security's returns to the systematic market risk factor.

Systematic risk is the amount of unavoidable volatility that is directly tied to the overall market. For an individual stock or investment portfolio, systematic risk is measured by **beta.** Statisticians use the Greek letter beta to signify the slope coefficient in a linear relation. Financial economists use this same Greek letter, β, to signify systematic risk because stock price betas are the slope coefficients in the linear SML. The SML relation can be written

$$\begin{aligned} E(R_i) &= R_F + \frac{R_M - R_F}{VAR(R_M)} \times COV(R_i R_M) \\ &= R_F + \frac{COV(R_i R_M)}{VAR(R_M)} \times (R_M - R_F) \\ &= R_F + \beta_i\,(R_M - R_F) \end{aligned} \tag{13.4}$$

As shown in Figure 13.6, the SML shows the straight-line relation between the expected rate of return and systematic risk for an individual security. In the SML, the expected rate of return is the risk-free rate plus relative risk, measured by β, multiplied by the market risk premium. Like the CML, the SML shows the reward-

FIGURE 13.6 **Security Market Line (SML) Shows the Straight-Line Relation between the Expected Rate of Return and Systematic Risk for an Individual Security**

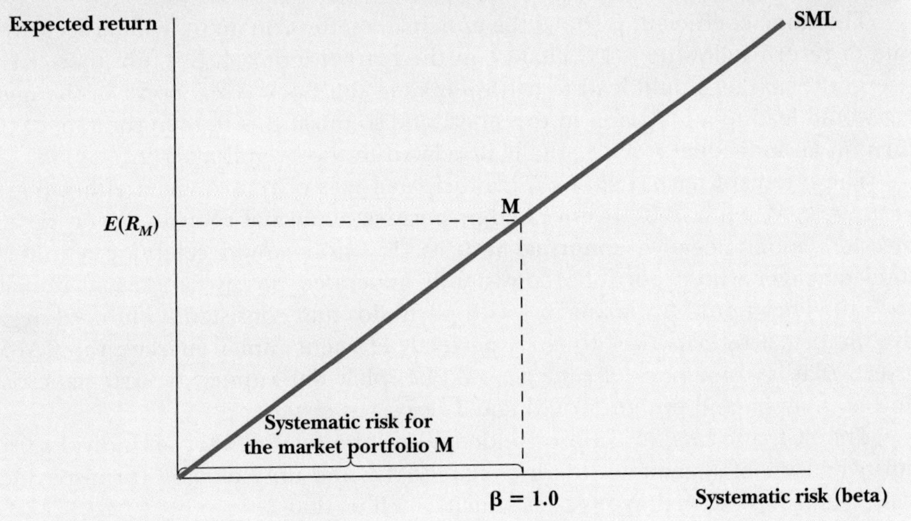

for-waiting and the reward-for-risk-taking parts of expected return. The difference lies in the fact that the CML deals with portfolios whereas the SML deals with individual securities.

β is a measure of relative risk, in which $\beta = 1$ for the overall market. $\beta = 2$ for a security with twice the systematic risk of the overall market, and $\beta = 0.5$ for a security with one-half the systematic risk of the market. As in the case of the CML, a fair estimate of the risk-free rate is 5%, and the expected rate of return on the market is 13%. This means that an individual security with $\beta = 2$ has an expected rate of return of 21% (= 5% + 2 × 8%). An individual security with $\beta = 0.5$ has an expected rate of return of 9% (= 5% + 0.5 × 8%).

Security Characteristic Line

The CML characterizes the relationship between the expected rate of return and risk for portfolios. It builds a link between the CAPM and traditional portfolio theory. The SML depicts the relationship between the expected rate of return and systematic risk for individual securities. By pertaining to individual securities held within well-diversified portfolios, the SML is somewhat more inclusive than the CML. The CAPM's third linear relationship between risk and return is called the **security characteristic line (SCL).**

security characteristic line (SCL) Linear relation between the return on individual securities and the overall market at every point in time.

The SCL shows the linear relation between the return on individual securities and the overall market at every point in time. The SCL is written:

$$R_{it} = \alpha_i + \beta_i R_{Mt} + \epsilon_i \qquad \textbf{(13.5)}$$

where R_{it} is the rate of return on an individual security i during period t, the intercept term is described by the Greek letter α (alpha), the slope coefficient is the

Greek letter β (beta) and signifies systematic risk (as before), and the random disturbance or error term is depicted by the Greek letter ϵ (epsilon). At any point in time, ϵ has an expected value of zero. This means that the expected return on an individual stock is determined by α and β.

The slope coefficient β shows the anticipated effect on an individual security's rate of return following a 1% change in the market index. If $\beta = 1.5$, then a 1% rise in the market would lead to a 1.5% hike in the stock, a 2% boost in the market would lead to a 3% jump in the stock, and so on. If $\beta = 0$, then the rate of return on an individual stock is totally unrelated to the overall market.

positive abnormal returns Above-average returns that cannot be explained as compensation for added risk.

negative abnormal returns Below-average returns that cannot be explained by below-market risk.

The intercept term α shows the anticipated rate of return when either $\beta = 0$ or $R_M = 0$. When $\alpha > 0$, investors enjoy **positive abnormal returns.** When $\alpha < 0$, investors suffer **negative abnormal returns.** Investors would celebrate a mutual fund manager whose portfolio consistently generated positive abnormal returns ($\alpha > 0$). They would fire managers with portfolios that consistently suffered negative abnormal returns ($\alpha < 0$). In a perfectly efficient capital market, the CAPM asserts that investor rates of return would be solely determined by systematic risk and both alpha and epsilon would equal zero, $\alpha = \epsilon = 0$.

The SCL also lays out in precise detail how the total risk for an individual security consists of systematic (market-related) risk and unsystematic (firm-specific) risk. When $R_{it} = \alpha_i + \beta_i R_{Mt} + \epsilon_i$, statisticians tell us that

$$\begin{aligned} VAR(R_i) &= VAR(\alpha_i + \beta_i R_M + \epsilon_i) \\ &= VAR(\alpha_i) + VAR(\beta_i R_M) + VAR(\epsilon_i) \\ &= 0 + \beta_i^2 VAR(R_M) + VAR(\epsilon_i) \end{aligned} \tag{13.6}$$

In turn, this implies that

$$\begin{aligned} \text{Total risk} &= \text{Systematic risk} + \text{Unsystematic risk} \\ SD(R_i) &= \sqrt{0 + \beta_i^2\ VAR(R_M) + VAR(\epsilon_i)} \end{aligned} \tag{13.7}$$

Empirical Implications of CAPM

The CAPM leads to several testable propositions. According to the CAPM, optimal portfolio choice depends on market risk-return trade-offs and the risk preferences of individual investors. Given individual differences in risk preferences, every investor can be expected to have a unique portfolio.

A fundamental assertion of the CAPM is that there is a linear relation between expected return and risk for all portfolios and all individual assets. Because it is costless to avoid unsystematic risk through diversification in a portfolio with as few as 30 stocks, only systematic risk-taking behavior is rewarded with higher expected returns. For all investment portfolios, the expected rate of return is the risk-free rate plus relative risk (β_p) times the market risk premium. High risk premiums will be earned by high beta portfolios. Low risk premiums will be earned by low beta portfolios. In equilibrium, the risk premium earned on any investment portfolio equals β_p times the market risk premium.

Most important, the CAPM asserts that stock price beta measures the relevant risk for individual securities. Beta measures the systematic risk contribution of any security to the riskiness of any portfolio. As such, high risk premiums will be earned by high-beta stocks, low risk premiums will be earned by low-beta stocks.

Empirical Criticisms of Beta

Model Specification Problems

One of the most telling criticisms of beta as a standard risk measure is that the CAPM provides only an incomplete description of return volatility. On a theoretical level, the SCL asserts that volatility in stock returns can be usefully described in terms of the volatility of the overall market. However, obvious problems emerge in empirical work that attempts to confirm or deny the hypothesis that the SCL offers a compelling method for describing and predicting return volatility.

An important problem is that return volatility for the overall market is very difficult to measure. On the nightly news, when commentators talk about the market being up or down, they often refer to moves in the DJIA. However, the DJIA includes only 30 component stocks representing roughly 30% of the value of all stocks traded on the New York Stock Exchange (NYSE), Nasdaq, and the American Stock Exchange. Although the DJIA offers good insight concerning changes in the prices of large blue-chip companies, it offers little insight concerning volatility in the returns earned by investors in smaller, high-tech stocks. From the perspective of many individual and institutional investors, the S&P 500 Index gives superior insight concerning moves in the overall market, but like the DJIA, the S&P 500 is dominated by large blue-chip companies. Although the Nasdaq and Russell 2000 indexes are popular measures of high-tech and smaller stocks, they are much less informative about changes in the overall market.

As shown in Figure 13.7, beta can be estimated for individual stocks by using a simple ordinary least-squares regression model. Although there is a high degree of correlation in rates of return earned on the DJIA, S&P 500, Nasdaq, and Russell 2000 indexes, slight differences can have meaningful effects on beta estimates. **Market index bias** is the distortion to beta estimates caused by the fact that market indexes are only imperfect proxies for the overall market. To illustrate the problem posed by imprecise proxies for rates of return earned by the overall market, four alternative stock price beta estimates are shown for Internet bellwether Yahoo! over the same one-year period. Yahoo!'s stock price beta is estimated as $\beta = 1.773$ when weekly rates of return on the DJIA are used as a proxy for rates of return on the overall market. When $\beta = 1.773$, the systematic risk of a stock is estimated to be 77.3% higher than that of the overall market. However, Yahoo!'s beta is estimated as $\beta = 1.955$ when weekly returns on the S&P 500 are used as a proxy for the overall market. In this case, Yahoo!'s systematic risk is estimated to be 95.5% higher than that of the overall market. By way of contrast, Yahoo!'s stock price beta is estimated as $\beta = 1.593$ when the Nasdaq is used as a market index, and $\beta = 1.497$ when the Russell 2000 small-cap index is used. Thus, the relative risk borne by Yahoo! shareholders is estimated to be anywhere from less than 1.5 times as risky as the overall market to almost twice as risky as the overall market, depending on the market index used, *during the same one-year period!*

market index bias
Distortion to beta estimates caused by the fact that market indexes are only imperfect proxies for the overall market.

The presence of market index bias makes it imperative that beta comparisons among individual companies reflect identical and appropriate market benchmarks. From a theoretical perspective, the most appropriate benchmark would be a market index that included *all* capital assets, including stocks, bonds, real estate, collectibles, and so on. Unfortunately, no such market index is available. To greater or lesser degree, this affects the accuracy of all beta estimates and undermines confidence in beta as an accurate measure of security risk.

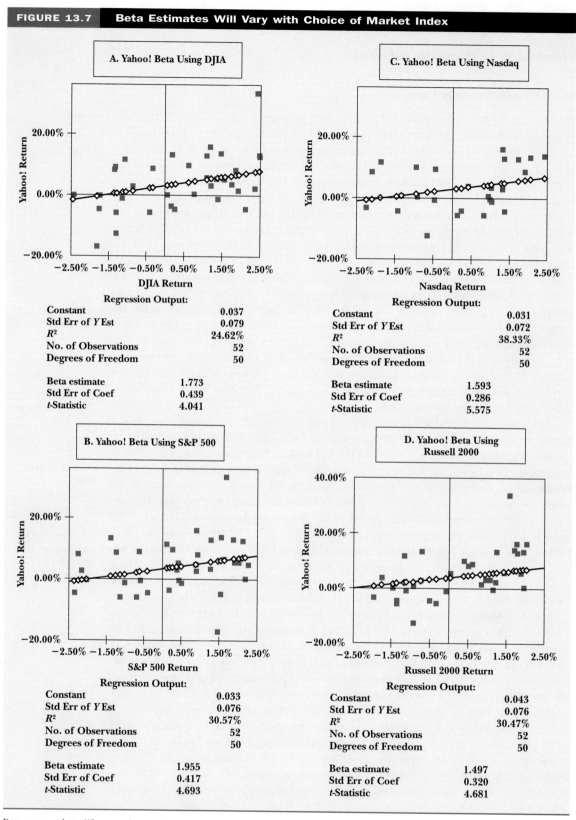

FIGURE 13.7 Beta Estimates Will Vary with Choice of Market Index

A. Yahoo! Beta Using DJIA

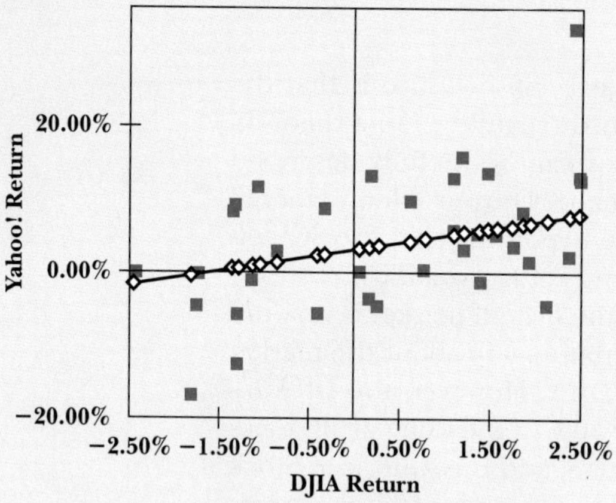

Regression Output:

Constant	0.037
Std Err of *Y* Est	0.079
R^2	24.62%
No. of Observations	52
Degrees of Freedom	50

Beta estimate	1.773
Std Err of Coef	0.439
t-Statistic	4.041

B. Yahoo! Beta Using S&P 500

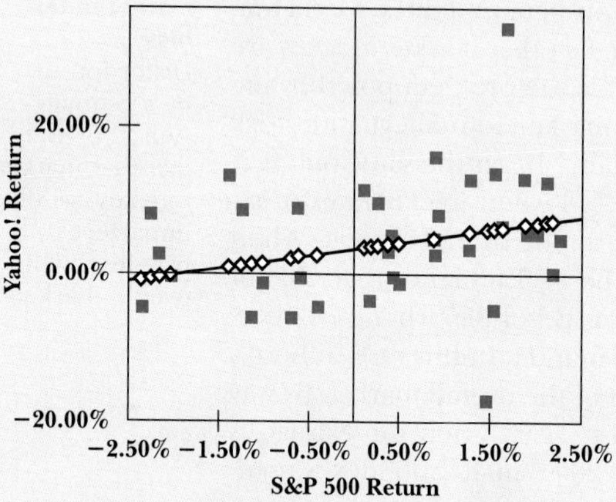

Regression Output:

Constant	0.033
Std Err of *Y* Est	0.076
R^2	30.57%
No. of Observations	52
Degrees of Freedom	50

Beta estimate	1.955
Std Err of Coef	0.417
t-Statistic	4.693

C. Yahoo! Beta Using Nasdaq

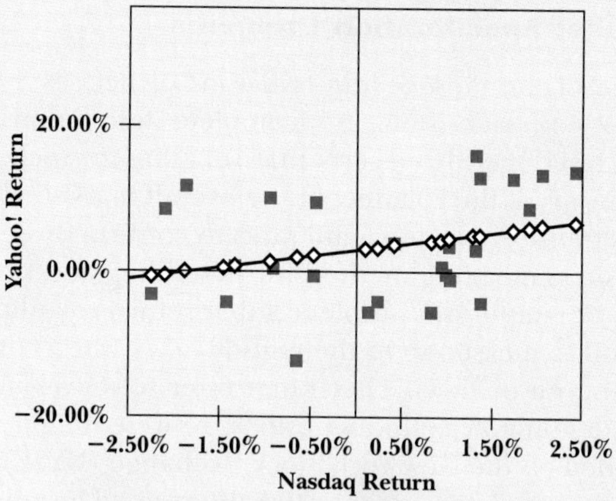

Regression Output:

Constant	0.031
Std Err of *Y* Est	0.072
R^2	38.33%
No. of Observations	52
Degrees of Freedom	50

Beta estimate	1.593
Std Err of Coef	0.286
t-Statistic	5.575

D. Yahoo! Beta Using Russell 2000

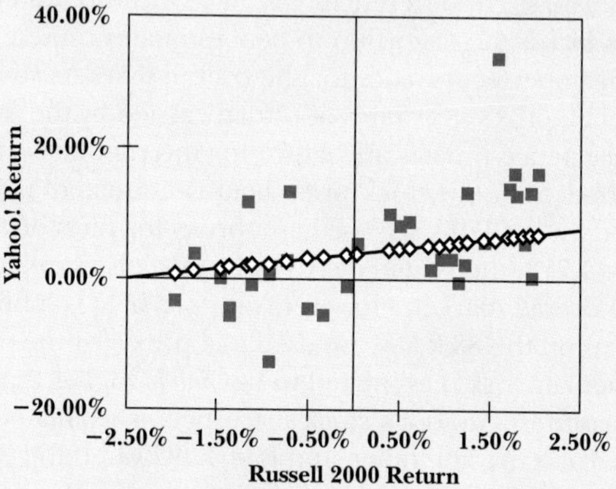

Regression Output:

Constant	0.043
Std Err of *Y* Est	0.076
R^2	30.47%
No. of Observations	52
Degrees of Freedom	50

Beta estimate	1.497
Std Err of Coef	0.320
t-Statistic	4.681

Data source: <http://finance.yahoo.com>.

Beta estimate variability is not only caused by underlying differences in each respective proxy for the overall market. It is also caused by the fact that other important but unmeasured sources of common stock volatility are at work. **Model specification bias** distorts beta estimates because the SCL fails to include other important systematic influences on stock market volatility. In the case of Yahoo!, for example, R^2 information shown in Figure 13.7 indicates that only 24.62–38.33% of the total variation in Yahoo! returns can be explained by variation in the overall market. This means that between 61.67% and 75.38% of the variation in the weekly returns for Yahoo! stock is unexplained by such a simple regression model. Although the amount of explained variation is statistically significant, it may not be economically meaningful in the sense of providing investors with useful risk information.

model specification bias Distortion to beta estimates because the SCL fails to include other important systematic influences on stock market volatility.

Data Interval Problems

Another problem faced in obtaining consistent and reliable beta estimates is the fact that these data are subject to estimation problems stemming from the length of time analyzed. **Time interval bias** exists because beta estimates are sensitive to the length of time over which stock return data are measured.

time interval bias Beta estimation problem derived from the fact that beta estimates depend on data interval studied.

Figure 13.8 shows beta estimates derived for the General Electric Company over the 1970–98 period. In all instances, returns on the S&P 500 Index are used as a proxy for the overall market. Using return data for 7,330 daily trading periods, $\beta = 1.169$. This daily return beta estimate is very close to the $\beta = 1.164$ estimated by using return data for 1,513 weekly periods, and the $\beta = 1.142$ estimated by using return data for 347 monthly periods. However, when annual return data are analyzed over this same 29-year period, $\beta = 1.431$. When beta estimates differ according to the time interval analyzed, the usefulness of beta as a consistent measure of risk is greatly diminished.

Nonstationary Beta Problem

An ideal measure of stock market risk would be stationary from one year to another. With an ideal risk measure, investors are able to control the risk exposure faced during volatile markets with well-targeted and well-timed investment buy/sell decisions. For example, suppose an elderly investor wants to maintain an exposure to the equity markets during retirement but wants to limit risk to regulate the possibility of devastating losses. With an ideal risk measure, retired investors could precisely tilt portfolio allocation toward securities with low risk characteristics. Alternatively, if an investor anticipated a surge in stock prices following a decline in interest rates, precise risk measures could help such an investor tilt an investment portfolio toward more volatile stocks.

The usefulness of stock market risk indicators diminishes to the extent that they fail to provide accurate and consistent measures of risk exposure from one year to another. In fact, an important limitation of risk estimators derived from the CAPM is that they vary from one period to another in ways that prove highly unpredictable. Table 13.2 shows alpha and beta estimates and R^2 information for the 30 stocks that together comprise the DJIA. These SCL-based estimates were derived over a one-year period by using 52 observations of weekly returns and the S&P 500 Index as an indicator of the overall market.

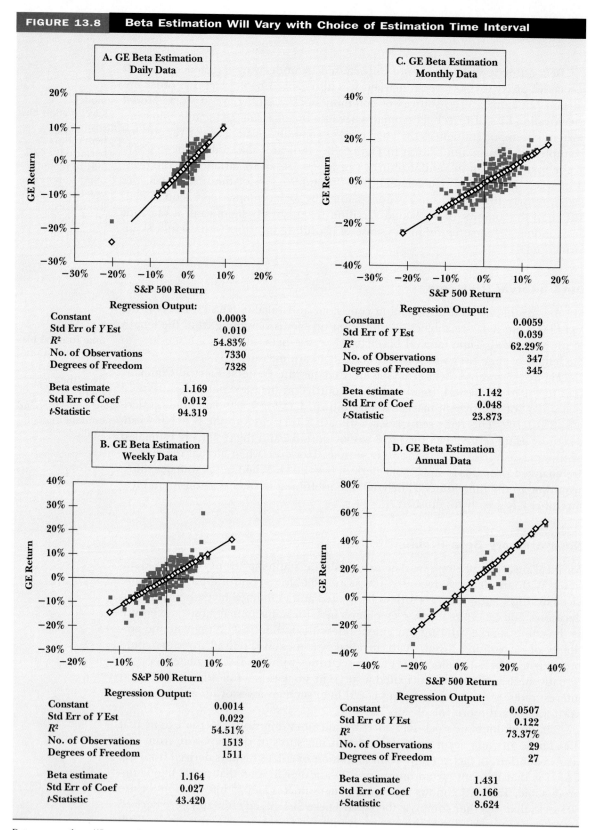

FIGURE 13.8 **Beta Estimation Will Vary with Choice of Estimation Time Interval**

A. GE Beta Estimation Daily Data

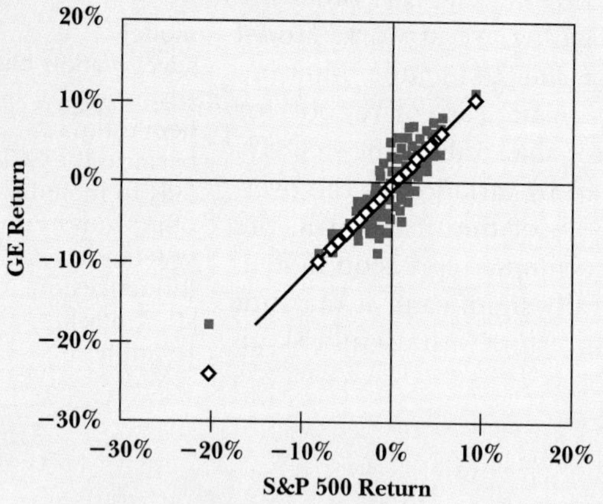

Regression Output:

Constant	0.0003
Std Err of *Y* Est	0.010
R^2	54.83%
No. of Observations	7330
Degrees of Freedom	7328
Beta estimate	1.169
Std Err of Coef	0.012
t-Statistic	94.319

C. GE Beta Estimation Monthly Data

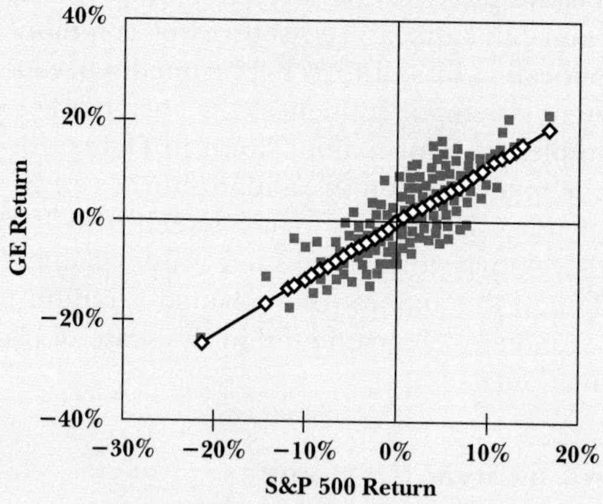

Regression Output:

Constant	0.0059
Std Err of *Y* Est	0.039
R^2	62.29%
No. of Observations	347
Degrees of Freedom	345
Beta estimate	1.142
Std Err of Coef	0.048
t-Statistic	23.873

B. GE Beta Estimation Weekly Data

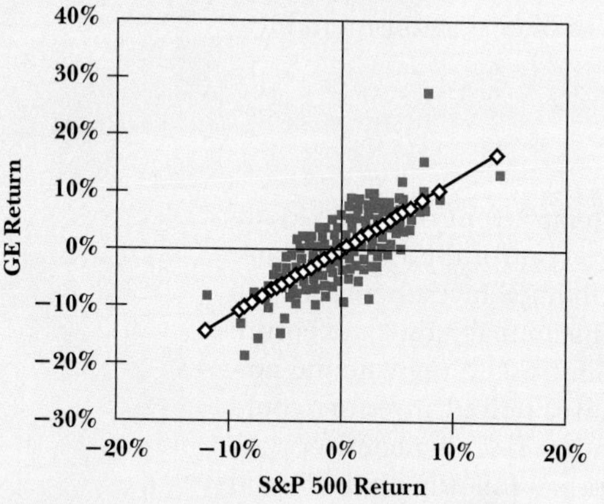

Regression Output:

Constant	0.0014
Std Err of *Y* Est	0.022
R^2	54.51%
No. of Observations	1513
Degrees of Freedom	1511
Beta estimate	1.164
Std Err of Coef	0.027
t-Statistic	43.420

D. GE Beta Estimation Annual Data

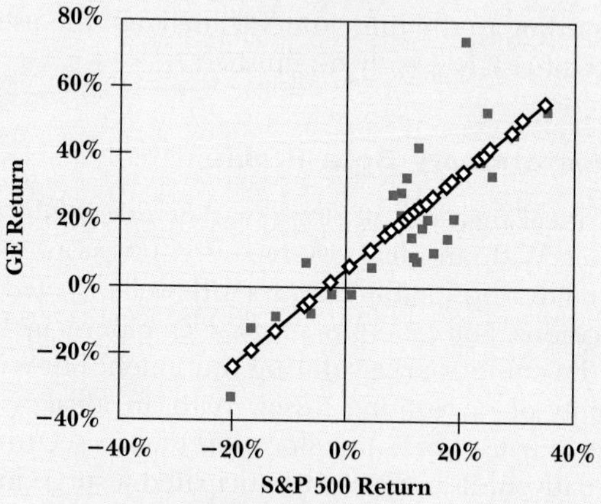

Regression Output:

Constant	0.0507
Std Err of *Y* Est	0.122
R^2	73.37%
No. of Observations	29
Degrees of Freedom	27
Beta estimate	1.431
Std Err of Coef	0.166
t-Statistic	8.624

Data source: <http://finance.yahoo.com>.

TABLE 13.2 Beta Estimation Using the Security Characteristic Line for 30 Industrial Leaders That Comprise the Dow Jones Industrial Average

Company Name (Ticker Symbol)	Alpha Estimate	*t*-Statistic	Beta Estimate	*t*-Statistic	R^2	*F*-Stat.	S.D.
Aluminum Co. of America (AA)	−0.008	−0.18	0.663	2.65	12.3%	7.03	4.83%
American Express Co. (AXP)	−0.392	−0.75	1.743	8.64	59.9%	74.56	5.76%
AT&T Corp. (T)	0.388	0.76	0.350	1.76	5.8%	3.10	3.71%
Boeing Company (BA)	−1.137	−1.53	1.143	3.97	23.9%	15.72	5.98%
Caterpillar Inc. (CAT)	−0.335	−0.51	0.697	2.72	12.9%	7.38	4.97%
Citigroup Inc. (C)	−0.410	−0.74	1.100	5.11	34.3%	26.10	4.80%
Coca-Cola Company (KO)	−0.967	−1.29	2.366	8.12	56.8%	65.86	5.13%
E. I. du Pont de Nemours and Company (DD)	−0.672	−0.97	1.203	4.49	27.3%	20.20	5.13%
Eastman Kodak Co. (EK)	0.296	0.46	0.079	0.32	0.2%	0.10	5.74%
Exxon Corp. (XON)	0.045	0.10	0.704	4.24	26.4%	17.97	4.49%
General Electric Co. (GE)	0.058	0.17	1.349	10.44	67.9%	108.93	3.51%
General Motors Corp. (GM)	−0.156	−0.32	1.181	6.23	43.7%	38.84	4.17%
Hewlett-Packard Co. (HWP)	−0.147	−0.21	0.826	3.03	15.5%	9.20	4.57%
Home Depot (HD)	0.009	1.65	1.304	5.92	41.2%	35.00	5.36%
Honeywell (HON)	−0.191	−0.41	1.045	5.84	40.5%	34.08	4.20%
Intel Corp. (INTC)	0.008	1.13	0.614	2.29	9.5%	5.25	5.20%
International Business Machines Corp. (IBM)	0.790	1.54	0.772	3.89	23.3%	15.15	5.10%
International Paper Co. (IP)	−0.321	−0.59	0.830	3.95	23.8%	15.59	4.10%
J.P. Morgan & Co., Inc. (JPM)	−0.676	−1.21	1.463	6.76	46.7%	45.68	4.36%
Johnson & Johnson (JNJ)	0.306	0.68	0.500	2.86	14.1%	8.18	3.41%
McDonald's Corp. (MCD)	0.592	1.00	0.925	4.01	24.3%	16.07	4.80%
Merck & Co., Inc. (MRK)	0.284	0.68	0.810	5.01	33.4%	25.10	3.59%
Microsoft Corp. (MSFT)	0.009	1.79	1.359	6.83	48.2%	46.59	5.01%
Minnesota Mining and Manufacturing Co. (MMM)	−0.579	−1.18	0.723	3.81	22.5%	14.51	3.90%
Philip Morris Companies, Inc. (MO)	0.244	0.48	0.294	1.49	4.3%	2.23	5.42%
Procter & Gamble Co. (PG)	0.069	0.13	0.497	2.47	10.9%	6.11	3.64%
SBC Communications (SBC)	0.006	1.01	0.540	2.52	11.3%	6.38	3.85%
United Technologies Corp. (UTX)	0.312	0.74	1.124	6.85	48.4%	46.91	4.11%
Wal-Mart Stores, Inc. (WMT)	0.916	2.06	1.229	7.14	50.5%	50.93	4.13%
Walt Disney Co. (DIS)	−0.559	−0.89	1.027	4.22	26.2%	17.79	4.43%
Averages	**−0.074**	**0.12**	**0.949**	**4.59**	**28.9%**	**26.22**	**4.58%**

Data source: <http://finance.yahoo.com> (1998 data).

Notice how the average alpha estimate of $\alpha = -0.074$ is very close to zero, as predicted for a perfectly competitive market by the CAPM. The average beta estimate of $\beta = 0.949$ means that a typical DJIA stock has risk characteristics that are representative of the overall market. As you recall, the overall market has a $\beta = 1$. Although the magnitude of these alpha and beta estimates for DJIA stocks are not surprising, it is unfortunate that the average $R^2 = 28.9\%$ when the SCL is estimated for DJIA stocks. This means that volatility in the overall market explains roughly one-quarter (28.9%) of the volatility in individual DJIA stocks, and roughly three-quarters (71.1%) of this volatility is left unexplained by a simple SCL regression model. Although there is a statistically significant link between the volatility of individual DJIA components and market volatility, a large portion of stock price volatility is left unaccounted for by the SCL.

According to the CAPM, the expected value for alpha is zero, $E(\alpha) = 0$. Notice from Figure 13.9A that alphas appear unstable from one year to the next. In

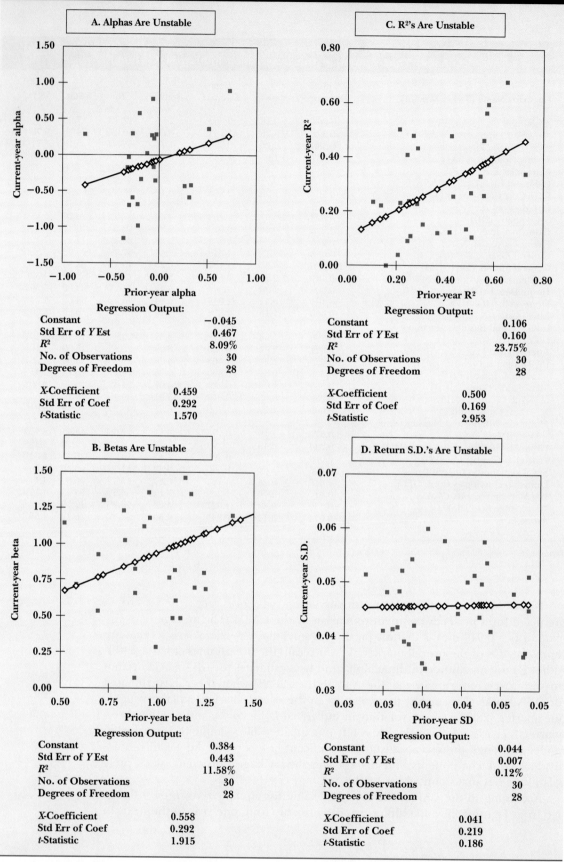

FIGURE 13.9 Alpha, Beta, R^2, and the Standard Deviation of Returns Cannot Be Predicted by Using Prior-Year Values

A. Alphas Are Unstable

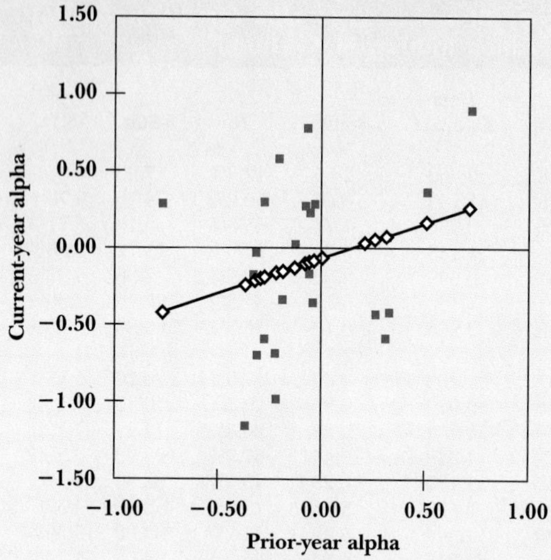

Regression Output:

Constant		−0.045
Std Err of *Y* Est		0.467
R^2		8.09%
No. of Observations		30
Degrees of Freedom		28
X-Coefficient	0.459	
Std Err of Coef	0.292	
t-Statistic	1.570	

C. R²'s Are Unstable

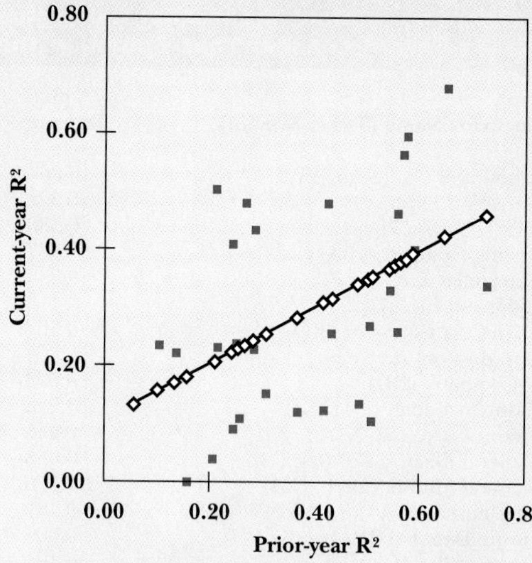

Regression Output:

Constant		0.106
Std Err of *Y* Est		0.160
R^2		23.75%
No. of Observations		30
Degrees of Freedom		28
X-Coefficient	0.500	
Std Err of Coef	0.169	
t-Statistic	2.953	

B. Betas Are Unstable

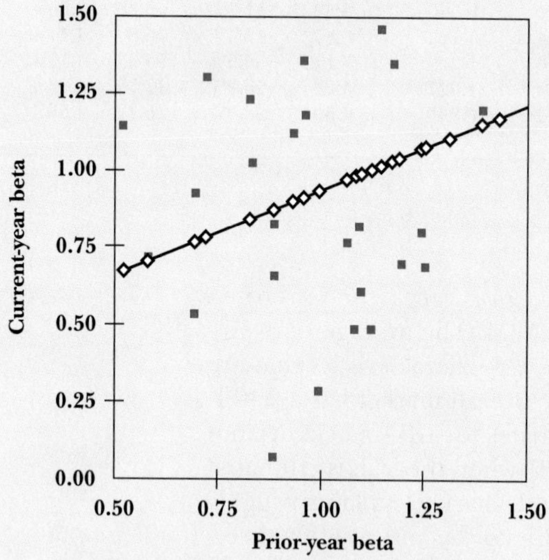

Regression Output:

Constant		0.384
Std Err of *Y* Est		0.443
R^2		11.58%
No. of Observations		30
Degrees of Freedom		28
X-Coefficient	0.558	
Std Err of Coef	0.292	
t-Statistic	1.915	

D. Return S.D.'s Are Unstable

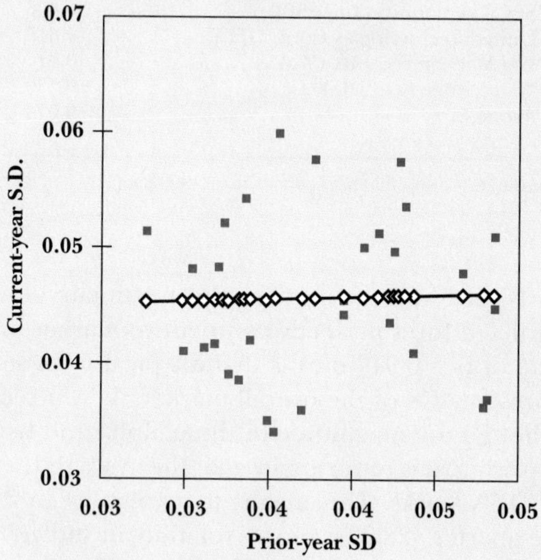

Regression Output:

Constant		0.044
Std Err of *Y* Est		0.007
R^2		0.12%
No. of Observations		30
Degrees of Freedom		28
X-Coefficient	0.041	
Std Err of Coef	0.219	
t-Statistic	0.186	

Data source: <http://finance.yahoo.com> (1997–98).

Figure 13.9A, alpha (intercept) coefficient estimates derived from SCL regressions for all 30 DJIA stocks are plotted against expected values based on prior-year information. Prior-year alphas are also used as independent variables in a simple regression model used to predict current-year alphas. Based on this analysis, it does not appear that prior-year alpha information can be used to predict alphas in the subsequent year. Only 8.09% of the variation in current-year alphas can be explained by variation in prior-years alphas; fully 91.91% of such variation is left unexplained. Alphas appear to change from one year to another in ways that cannot be predicted. The fact that alphas are unstable from one year to the next is consistent with the prediction of the CAPM for an efficient stock market.

Unfortunately, the fact that betas are also unpredictable is a problem for the CAPM. As shown in Figure 13.9B, betas are inherently unstable from one year to another. This is the **nonstationary beta problem.** For DJIA stocks, only 11.58% of the variation in current-year betas can be explained by variability in prior-year betas. This means that 98.42% of beta variation cannot be explained by prior-year information. When betas vary from one year to another in ways that are essentially random and unpredictable, betas fail to provide investors with a risk assessment tool that can be used to effectively manage portfolio risk. This is, in fact, what Figure 13.9B implies.

nonstationary beta problem Difficulty tied to the fact that betas are inherently unstable.

Figure 13.9C further suggests that the amount of information captured by the SCL from one year to another also varies in ways that are essentially random and unpredictable. In Figure 13.9C, the amount of stock return variation that can be explained by variation in the overall market(R^2) is plotted against prior-year R^2 information. For DJIA stocks, only 23.75% of the variation in current-year R^2 information can be explained by variability in prior-year R^2 information. This means that 76.25% of the variation in R^2 information cannot be explained by prior-year R^2 information. Similarly, as shown in Figure 13.9D, the standard deviation (SD) of annual returns for DJIA stocks vary in an unforeseeable way from one year to the next. Like the apparently random changes in betas, arbitrary year-to-year variation in R^2 and SD indicates that the CAPM fails to provide investors with practical risk assessment tools that can be used to effectively manage portfolio risk.

Arbitrage Pricing Theory

Limitations of CAPM

Main testable implications of the CAPM are that

- β, the slope of the regression of a security's return on the market return, is the only risk factor needed to explain expected return.
- There is a positive expected return premium for risk as captured by β.

Importantly, evidence of a positive relation between β and expected return can be taken as support for the CAPM only if β suffices as a valid risk indicator.

Unfortunately, information provided in Table 13.2 and Figures 13.7, 13.8, and 13.9 documents the fact that stock price betas explain relatively little of the variation in average returns, diverge according to the market index chosen, and vary over time (the nonstationary β problem). These findings are consistent with results from a recent series of studies on the subject by Professors Eugene Fama from the

University of Chicago and Kenneth French from Yale University. Fama and French demonstrate that there is no simple relation between average returns and CAPM market β's. Contrary to the predictions of the CAPM, β alone cannot explain expected return.[2]

In particular, firm size emerges as a consistently important risk indicator. When NYSE companies are formed into 10 portfolios based on market capitalization (price times number of outstanding shares), empirical research in financial economics clearly documents that firms in the smallest-firm decile consistently earn above-average rates of return. Above-average rates of return for small firms may simply reflect the greater risks associated with such companies. Small firms seldom feature extensive product lines, enjoy only narrow geographic dispersion, and often have only limited managerial and financial resources. Although it is understandable that investors in smaller firms face greater risks than investors in large companies, the failure of β to capture small-firm risk undermines the usefulness of CAPM as a practical tool for risk assessment and management. This also makes it difficult to use CAPM as a tool to test semistrong and strong forms of the EMH.

Interestingly, the fact that firm size adds to the explanation of average returns provided by β is not the only problem faced by the CAPM. Several studies in

[2]See Eugene F. Fama and Kenneth R. French, "The CAPM Is Wanted, Dead or Alive," *Journal of Finance* 51, no. 5 (December 1996), 1947–1958.

WALL STREET WISDOM 13.2

Market Models

Investment strategists use economic models to measure the attractiveness of the overall market in light of earnings growth expectations, interest rates, and so on. Some of these models are simple; some are complex. Data on earnings, dividends, interest rates, and risk are all used to derive a "fair value" for the stock market. If the Standard & Poor's (S&P) 500 or some other market index exceeds this number, then the market is overvalued and stocks should be avoided. If the S&P 500 is below "fair value," then stocks are undervalued and investors should load up on stocks. Since the start of 1999, most such market valuation models have been blinking red, warning of overvaluation. At the start of the new millennium, vocalized concern about overvaluation reached a crescendo. Using historical assumptions about risk, interest rates, and long-term earnings growth, stock prices seemed unduly optimistic. Based on the historical record, stock prices appeared headed for a big fall.

For example, Byron Wien, chief domestic strategist at Morgan Stanley Dean Witter, suggested that the S&P 500 should be trading at 945, roughly a third below where it stood on April 1, 2000 (see figure). According to Wien, equities were more richly priced at the start of 2000 than they were just before the stock market crash of 1987. Wein's model measures the relative appeal of stocks and bonds by using three key inputs: the level of interest rates, projected corporate profit growth, and a risk premium for stocks. With a Treasury yield of 6.7%, estimated profit growth of 10% per year, and a modest 2% risk premium for stocks, Wien calculates that stocks are more richly valued relative to bonds than at any time in the past 30 years. Although more bullish analysts project annual earnings growth of 17% for the next five years, Wien points out that the long-term average profit growth rate is only 7% per year for the S&P 500.

According to Wien, the prevailing view is that we will never again experience a serious economic recession or stock market correction. Stay tuned!

See: Andy Barry, "Model Behavior: Are Wall Street Market Models Passé or Are Stocks Headed for Fall?" *Barron's*, January 24, 2000, 22.

Flawed? Or Fearful?

▸ A predictive stock-market model used by Morgan Stanley strategist Byron Wien relies on two key inputs: Treasury yields and projected profits for the S&P 500 in the next 12 months. Based on the current Treasury yield of 6.70% and expected profits of $57.50 for the S&P, the model suggests the appropriate level for the S&P 500 Index is around 945, way below its current level of around 1455. The huge gap – as demonstrated in the matrix below, which shows appropriate levels for the S&P based on different combinations of rates and profits–suggests that either the model is flawed or stocks are greatly overvalued.

S&P EARNINGS	TREASURY YIELDS 3.50%	4.00%	4.50%	5.00%	5.50%	6.00%	6.50%	7.00%	7.50%
$53	1693	1505	1347	1214	1100	1002	917	842	776
54	1721	1529	1369	1233	1117	1017	930	854	787
55	1749	1554	1391	1253	1135	1033	944	867	798
56	1777	1578	1412	1272	1152	1048	958	879	810
57	1805	1603	1434	1291	1169	1064	972 ★	892	821
58	1833	1627	1455	1310	1186	1079	986	904	833
59	1861	1652	1477	1329	1203	1094	1000	917	844
60	1889	1676	1499	1349	1220	1110	1014	929	855
61	1917	1701	1520	1368	1238	1125	1028	942	867
62	1944	1725	1542	1387	1255	1141	1041	955	878

★ Current target of 945

Source: Morgan Stanley Dean Witter

Record Territory

▸ Based on the Wien model, stocks are overvalued by a record 54%, exceeding the prior peak of around 40% just before the 1987 market crash. The model had a pretty solid predictive record until the past year.

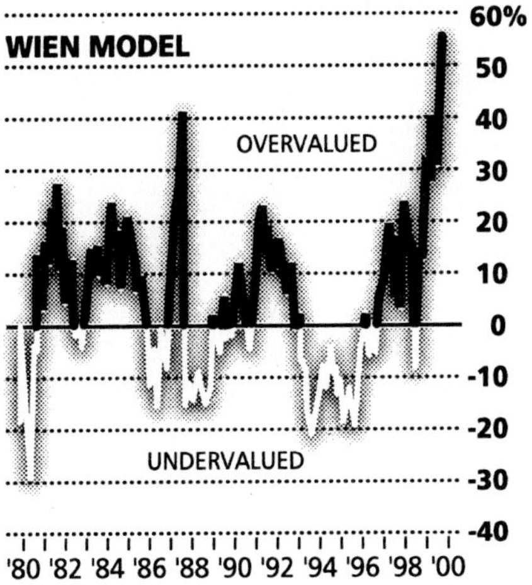

Source: Morgan Stanley Dean Witter

Optimistic Expectations

▸ A key reason that stocks remain at such lofty levels in the face of higher rates is that expectations of corporate growth have risen in recent years. The current projection among Wall Street analysts is that profits for the companies in the S&P 500 will rise by 17% annually over the next five years. As recently as 1996, the five-year growth expectation was around 12%.

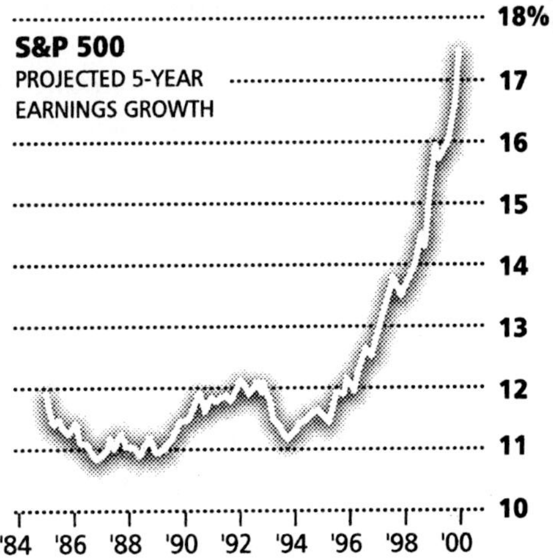

Sources: Goldman Sachs; I/B/E/S

Source: *Barron's.*

financial economics document higher long-term rates of return for stocks with low price/earnings, price/cash flow, and price/book ratios and low historical sales growth.[3] As predicted by contrarian value stock investors, such companies tend to be good candidates to benefit from the reversion-to-the-mean phenomenon. However, although higher expected returns for beaten-down stocks make economic sense, the failure to reflect such influences reduces the practical value of the CAPM.

APT Approach

CAPM assumes that a single market risk factor β is all that is required to measure the systematic risk of individual securities. Assuming that asset pricing is rational, average-return anomalies detected by using the CAPM may suggest that a multi-factor version of the model is more appropriate. Market β's might represent only one of the firm's many risk factors. For example, firm size might represent a second risk factor, price/earnings ratios a third, price/book ratios a fourth, and so on. In that case, a theoretical model of capital asset pricing that is capable of reflecting multiple aspects of risk would be preferable to the single risk factor CAPM approach.

arbitrage pricing theory (APT) Multifactor asset-pricing model that allows market β's to represent only one of the firm's many risk factors.

arbitrage Simultaneous buying and selling of the same asset.

On a theoretical level, a multiple risk factor approach called **arbitrage pricing theory** (APT) has the potential to provide a superior description of average returns. **Arbitrage** is simply the simultaneous buying and selling of the same asset. According to APT, a market is perfectly efficient if it is not possible to earn a risk-free arbitrage profit by simultaneously buying and selling the same asset. APT is a very simple model of security pricing. Its sole underlying assumption is that investors prefer more wealth to less wealth.

Whereas CAPM posits that asset returns are systematically affected by a single market risk factor β, APT suggests that asset returns might be affected by N risk factors:

$$R_i = a_i + b_{i1}F_1 + b_{i2}F_2 + \cdots + b_{iN}F_N + \epsilon_i \tag{13.8}$$

where F_i common risk factors affect security returns, and b_i represents the return sensitivity to a given risk factor. Notice the similarity of this equation to the SCL from the CAPM. The sole difference is that this APT approach allows for an unspecified number of important risk factors in addition to the CAPM's market β. Unfortunately, the fact that APT fails to specify the source or number of these unknown risk factors greatly diminishes its theoretical appeal.

APT versus CAPM

On an empirical level, some evidence seems to suggest that six-factor APT models are superior to the one-factor CAPM. Obvious candidates for fundamental risk factors include market β, firm size (market capitalization), price/earnings ratios, price/book ratios, price/cash flow ratios, and historical sales growth.

Unfortunately, just like the volatile returns attributable to market β, returns attributable to various APT risk factors are very unstable. Like the one-factor

[3]See Eugene F. Fama and Kenneth R. French, "Multifactor Explanations of Asset Pricing Anomalies," *Journal of Finance* 51, no. 1 (March 1996), 55–84.

WALL STREET WISDOM 13.3

Psychology and the Stock Market

How rational is the average stock market investor? In the past, academics and other observers of the stock market confidently assumed that buyers and sellers of equities and other securities maintained a rational perspective concerning investment values. However, in the light of the rampant bull market of the late 1990s and historic valuations for technology and Internet stocks, some academics are beginning to wonder if the bedrock principle of investor rationality can indeed be relied on.

Some academics now speculate that a shift in investor psychology has caused stock prices to race ahead of economic fundamentals and has set the market up for an unusually harsh decline. For example, Yale University's Robert J. Shiller, a highly respected specialist in behavioral finance, offers an unconventional interpretation of recent U.S. stock market performance in a controversial new book titled *Irrational Exuberance* (Princeton University Press). Shiller argues that Federal Reserve Chairman Alan Greenspan's term *irrational exuberance* is a good description of the current mood behind the market. Shiller warns that decidedly poorer stock market performance may be in the offing and credits an unprecedented confluence of events with driving stocks to uncharted and irrational heights. Shiller credits structural and psychological factors for explaining why the Dow Jones Industrial Average tripled between 1994 and 1999, a level of growth not reflected in any other sector of the economy. In contrast to many analysts, Shiller stresses circumstances that alter investors' perceptions of the market. These include the rise of the Internet, day trading, and the mistaken impression that budding investments by aging Baby Boomers provides a cushion of safety for equity investors. Shiller also considers the role of cultural factors, such as sports-style media coverage of the market's ups and downs and "new era" thinking about the "goldilocks" economy. The most controversial conclusion of the book is that the market that is wildly overvalued and unusually precarious. Shiller argues that policy makers should end what he calls perilous schemes to privatize social security, reconsider the usefulness of bonds in balanced investment programs, and urge financial institutions to use prudent risk management principles.

At the level of the individual investor, getting a handle on investor psychology can be tricky. As a rule, most investors are squeamish about taking risks but tend to be much less sensitive to losses if they have previously earned gains. Academics refer to this as the "house-money" effect. Like a casino gambler who gets lucky early in the evening and starts taking riskier bets because he "is playing with the house's money," investors who have enjoyed big gains often become less risk averse. It is not just that such investors put more money into the market; there is also a tendency to make riskier and riskier bets. Having earned a quick 50% on a $10,000 investment in Cisco Systems, for example, investors are more prone to make bigger and riskier bets on less solid investments, say, $50,000 in JDS Uniphase Corp. Analysts argue that a disproportionate amount of such "house money" has ended up in the "dot.com" and high-tech neighborhoods favored by novice investors.

This is not the only factor causing stock prices to overshoot economic fundamentals. The more stocks go up, the more novice investors think that they can continue to rise. For a time, such momentum-based investment strategies can become something of a self-fulfilling prophesy, especially when crowd psychology is involved. But that cannot go on forever; eventually there is no "greater fool" willing to pay still higher prices for stocks with questionable economic fundamentals.

The same psychological factors that may have propelled stock prices ahead of economic fundamentals can also cause stocks to overshoot on the way down. Suppose the Federal Reserve continues to ramp up interest rates, and the upward spiral in stock prices is broken. Then, stock prices may fall into a cascading downturn.

Momentum investors can push stocks up in a buying frenzy. They can also drive them down in a selling panic.

See: Phred Dvorak, "Japan Catches Investment Fever Again," *The Wall Street Journal*, April 10, 2000, A25–A30.

CAPM, even six-factor APT models explain very little of the variation in average returns.

Therefore, although both CAPM and APT theory and evidence confirm that risk and return *are* related, neither approach gives investors a precise tool for risk assessment and management. Similarly, although CAPM and APT theories provide useful guides for testing semistrong-form and strong-form versions of the EMH, neither approach is foolproof.

Summary

- An **investment portfolio** is a collection of securities that together provide an investor with an attractive trade-off between risk and return. **Portfolio theory** is the simple concept of making security choices based on expected portfolio returns and risks. **Expected return** is measured by the amount of profit anticipated over some relevant holding period. **Risk** is captured by return dispersion. Within this framework, investment alternatives are represented by the **probability distribution** of security returns over some future period. Investors get positive benefit or **utility** out of an increase in the expected rate of return and suffer a psychic loss or **disutility** out of an increase in the amount of risk, or return volatility. This means that investors tend to be **risk averse.**
- An equal investment in two securities with the same expected return and standard deviation, but a perfect inverse correlation, would create a constant return, or **zero-risk portfolio.** An **efficient portfolio** provides maximum expected return for a given level of risk. Alternatively, an efficient portfolio provides minimum risk for a given expected return. The **efficient frontier** includes all efficient portfolios that provide maximum expected return for a given level of risk. Alternatively, the efficient frontier depicts all efficient portfolios that entail minimum risk for a given expected return. The **optimal portfolio** provides an investor with the highest level of expected utility. A key concept in portfolio theory is that the **market portfolio** is an efficient portfolio.
- The most detailed model or construct used to describe the efficient pricing of investment securities is called the **capital asset pricing model (CAPM)**. The CAPM is a method for predicting how investment returns are determined in an efficient capital market.
- The CAPM describes three distinct relations between the expected rate of return and risk. The **capital market line (CML)** shows the linear risk/return trade-off for all investment portfolios. The **security market line (SML)** characterizes a linear risk/return trade-off for individual stocks.
- The SML shows how the expected rate of return can be seen as a simple function of the amount of **systematic risk.** Systematic risk is a measure of return volatility in an individual stock that is tied to the overall market. **Unsystematic risk** is the amount of return volatility that is specific to an individual company. Unsystematic risk is synonymous with **diversifiable risk.** Even after unsystematic risk is eliminated through diversification, substantial systematic or **nondiversifiable risk** remains. Because systematic risk cannot be eliminated through diversification, investors must be rewarded for any increase in this form of risk to justify their investment in a particular stock or market sector. Financial economists use the Greek letter **beta** (β) to signify systematic risk.

- The CAPM's third linear relationship between risk and return is called the **security characteristic line (SCL)**. The SCL shows the linear relation between the return on individual securities and the overall market at every point in time. The intercept term α shows the anticipated rate of return when either $\beta = 0$ or $R_M = 0$. When $\alpha > 0$, investors enjoy **positive abnormal returns.** When $\alpha < 0$, investors suffer **negative abnormal returns.** Investors would celebrate a mutual fund manager whose portfolio consistently generated positive abnormal returns ($\alpha > 0$). They would fire managers of portfolios that consistently suffered negative abnormal returns ($\alpha < 0$). $\beta > 1$ signifies above-market risk; $\beta < 1$ signifies below-market risk.
- One of the most telling criticisms of beta as a standard risk measure is that the CAPM provides only an incomplete description of return volatility. **Market index bias** is the distortion to beta estimates caused by the fact that market indexes are only imperfect proxies for the overall market. Beta estimate variability is caused by underlying differences in each respective proxy for the overall market. It is also caused by the fact that other important but unmeasured sources of common stock volatility are at work. **Model specification bias** distorts beta estimates because the SCL fails to include other important systematic influences on stock market volatility. **Time interval bias** exists because beta estimates are sensitive to the length of time over which stock return data are measured. The fact that betas are inherently unstable from one year to another is a further problem for the CAPM. This is the **nonstationary beta problem.**
- When the CAPM fails to precisely capture, or "model," stock market returns, model specification bias may be present. Market β's might represent only one of the firm's many risk factors. For example, firm size might represent a second risk factor, price/earnings ratios a third, and price/book ratios a fourth. In that case, what is called **arbitrage pricing theory** (APT) can provide a better description of average returns. **Arbitrage** is simply the simultaneous buying and selling of the same asset. According to APT, a market is perfectly efficient if it is not possible to earn a risk-free arbitrage profit by simultaneously buying and selling the same asset.
- CAPM and APT theory and evidence confirm that risk and return *are* related, but neither approach gives investors a precise tool for risk assessment and management. Similarly, although CAPM and APT theories provide useful guides for testing semistrong-form and strong-form versions of the EMH, neither approach is foolproof.

Questions

1. The optimal portfolio
   a. maximizes utility derived from nonmonetary and monetary rewards.
   b. has the lowest level of risk for a given expected return.
   c. is always the market portfolio.
   d. none of the above.
2. An $R^2 = 25\%$ in the stock price beta estimation for the Coca-Cola Company implies that 25% of the variation in the

a. return on Coca-Cola can be explained by variation in the S&P index return.

b. S&P index can be explained by variation in the Coca-Cola stock return.

c. Coca-Cola stock price can be explained by variation in the S&P index.

d. S&P index can be explained by variation in the Coca-Cola stock price.

3. In the stock price beta estimation for the Coca-Cola Company, the independent variable is the

a. value of the S&P 500 Index.

b. return on Coca-Cola.

c. return on the S&P 500.

d. price of Coca-Cola stock.

4. A stock with below-market risk involves

a. $\alpha < 1$.

b. $\beta < 0$.

c. $\beta < 1$.

d. $\alpha < 0$.

5. A risk-averse investor is one who will

a. assume risk only with adequate compensation.

b. sometimes assume risk for its own sake.

c. not assume risk.

d. not assume large risk.

6. *Ex ante,* the return/risk trade-off available to investors is

a. expected to be a horizontal line in return/risk space.

b. expected to be upward sloping in return/risk space.

c. indefinable as to its general shape.

d. downward sloping in return/risk space for risk averse individuals.

7. Asset prices are *not* determined by

a. future possibilities.

b. investor expectations.

c. historical experience.

d. future probabilities.

8. A security with a beta of 1.5 is

a. 150% more volatile than the overall market.

b. approximately as risky as the average security.

c. 50% more volatile than the overall market.

d. 50% less volatile than the overall market.

9. The chance of loss due to fluctuations in the stock market is

a. market risk.

b. interest rate risk.

c. business risk.

d. inflation risk.

10. The difference between the return on common stocks and the return on riskless assets is the
    a. total return.
    b. equity risk premium.
    c. systematic return.
    d. market model.
11. Total risk for common stocks is
    a. measured by beta.
    b. the sum of systematic risk and diversifiable risk.
    c. the sum of market risk and systematic risk.
    d. the sum of diversifiable risk and unsystematic risk.
12. The coefficient of variation is
    a. a relative risk/reward measure.
    b. the square root of variance.
    c. the chance of loss.
    d. the mean geometric return.
13. The CML is upward sloping because
    a. it shows the optimum combination of risky securities.
    b. it contains all securities weighted by their respective market values.
    c. investors are risk averse.
    d. it indicates the required return for each portfolio risk level.
14. If $R_m = 15\%$ and $R_F = 5\%$, which one of the following securities is undervalued?

	α_i	β_i	Required return
a. Security A	5	1.0	20.0%
b. Security B	7	1.2	25.5%
c. Security C	8	0.8	12.0%
d. Security D	4	0.7	14.5%

15. The slope of the CML is
    a. the market price of risk for efficient portfolios.
    b. the amount of return expected for bearing the risk of an individual portfolio.
    c. the market price of risk for any given security.
    d. none of the above.
16. The SML depicts the trade-off between risk and required return for
    a. inefficient portfolios.
    b. efficient portfolios only.
    c. individual securities only.
    d. all assets.
17. Using the Markowitz model, the efficient frontier is
    a. an upward-sloping straight line.
    b. a downward-sloping straight line.

c. an upward-sloping curved line.
d. a downward-sloping curved line.

18. The SCL is
    a. a downward-sloping curved line.
    b. a downward-sloping straight line.
    c. an upward-sloping straight line.
    d. an upward-sloping curved line.
19. Portfolio risk is reduced by combining securities with
    a. high standard deviations.
    b. low standard deviations.
    c. less than perfect correlation.
    d. perfect correlation.
20. A useful *relative* measure of the risk/reward relationship is provided by the
    a. covariance.
    b. standard deviation.
    c. correlation coefficient.
    d. coefficient of variation.

Investment Application

Long-Term Capital Management: How Do You Say "Oops"?

The best seller *Liar's Poker* chronicled the exploits of John Meriwether, a pioneer of fixed-income arbitrage at investment bank Salomon Brothers.[4] Meriwether made bond trading a huge money maker by using enormous leverage to exploit small price differences in various bond markets. When forced to resign from Salomon following a Treasury-bond bid-rigging scandal in 1991, Meriwether assembled an all-star lineup to form a new firm, called Long-Term Capital Management (LTCM).

Meriwether's group of heavy hitters included David Mullins, former Harvard Business School professor and vice chairman of the Federal Reserve Board, and Nobel Laureates Myron Scholes, from Stanford University, and Robert Merton, from MIT. Scholes and Merton won the 1997 Nobel prize in economics for their path-breaking work on how financial securities are priced in perfectly efficient capital markets. At LTCM, Scholes and Merton hoped to capture above-average returns for investors by exploiting tiny inefficiencies in world capital markets. With sterling academic credentials, broad industry experiences, and unbeatable contacts in industry and government, how could LTCM fail? Easy. LTCM was based on the faulty premise that capital markets were sufficiently inefficient to support immensely profitable risk-free arbitrage.

In the early to mid-1990s, LTCM's traders, economists, and mathematicians used computers to detect suspected mispricings, or anomalies, in the value of bonds

[4]See: Gregory Zuckerman, "Long-Term Capital Chief Acknowledges Flawed Tactics," *The Wall Street Journal,* August 21, 2000, C1, C2; Michael Lewis, *Liar's Poker: Rising through the Wreckage on Wall Street* (New York: Penguin Books, 1989).

and financial derivatives. In presentations before potential investors, Scholes, among others, described the firm's investment philosophy as "scouring world capital markets, looking for loose nickels." Even small mispricings in debt and equity securities could lead to big profits for LTCM if sufficient leverage was brought to bear. In the case of Scholes and his colleagues, enormous leverage was not to be feared. It was simply viewed as a tool that could be used to magnify gains. Unfortunately, just as massive leverage can magnify gains on the upside, it can exaggerate losses on the downside.

In U.S. equity markets, investors are limited by Federal Reserve regulations to use no more than 50% initial leverage. This means that $10 million worth of stock can be bought with as little as $5 million in equity. This implies a 2:1 leverage ratio because twice as much equity can be purchased relative to the amount of investment capital used. Because normally liquid U.S. Treasury securities enjoy the full faith and credit of the U.S. government, investors are able to buy them using anywhere from 10:1 to 20:1 leverage. As a result, normally low-risk Treasury securities have become the security of choice for investment funds such as LTCM who seek to profit from what they view as small pricing anomalies. In the case of LTCM, higher than typical leverage could be brought to bear because the firm made extensive use of options and other complicated financial derivatives. In its heyday, published reports asserted that LTCM may have used financial leverage as high as 40:1 or 50:1. Notice that when 50:1 leverage is used, a 1% increase in the value of an investment security will lead to a 50% increase in the investor's capital. Conversely, when 50:1 leverage is used, a 2% decrease in the value of an investment security will wipe out all the investor's capital.

In August 1998, LTCM made a gigantic bet that the interest-rate difference would narrow between U.S. Treasury bonds and riskier Danish Mortgage securities. Instead, interest-rate spreads widened, and LTCM lost—big time. To avert a wide-scale financial panic, Federal Reserve Board Chairman Allan Greenspan helped broker a $3.6 billion bailout led by 14 major Wall Street securities firms and banks. Although financial panic was averted, terms of the bailout effectively wiped out more than 90% of the value of the ownership interest held by Meriwether and his colleagues.

Four months after the closely held firm almost collapsed, two original partners of the once-highflying hedge fund, including Scholes, decided to take early retirement. Led by Meriwether, the firm began to ask investors for new money to buy out the consortium that had pumped in billions of dollars to save it. Although LTCM had assets of $4.7 billion as of January 1, 1999, doubt still remains as to whether the fund will be able to survive, let alone regain its former prominence. Meriwether has traveled as far as London, Geneva, and Asia to meet with potential investors and get the money Wall Street executives demand for him to regain control of LTCM. That could be an insurmountable challenge without Scholes's help.

In the early days of LTCM, Scholes, fellow Nobel Laureate Merton, and former Federal Reserve Vice Chairman Mullins were instrumental in securing an audience with foreign investors who were not familiar with Meriwether's track record or investment philosophy. With sterling academic credentials bolstered by Nobel prize recognition, LTCM could not lose when it came to garnering new business. Many of the pension funds and investment executives that LTCM called on had studied Scholes and Mertion's path-breaking research on market efficiency while in business school. It was required reading at all the top MBA programs around the world. If anyone knew how to exploit *almost* efficient markets, surely LTCM could. It obviously had the brainpower. Thus, Scholes' departure from LTCM is an especially telling blow to the company and its future prospects. It suggests that at least one of the core members of the group has lost faith in their ability to find successful risk-free arbitrage opportunities in the bond market. Although LTCM would obviously take exception to this suggestion, it is hard to think of Scholes's leaving as anything other than a vote of "no confidence."

Although Scholes has steadfastly declined to comment on his reasons for leaving LTCM, he plans to maintain his investment there as a limited partner. This means that Scholes has the potential to share in future partnership gains but is absolved from any day-to-day responsibility for making investment decisions. Scholes plans to return to occasional lecturing and writing at Stanford University, where he is an emeritus (retired) professor. Like other such professors at Stanford, Scholes will enjoy free office space but will not draw a salary. Instead, he will be paid on a per-lecture basis and serve as a consultant to a number of firms, including LTCM.

At this point, it is clear that LTCM faces an uphill battle. Meriwether and his colleagues are trying to sell investors on the idea that the interest-rate volatility that led to the firm's 1998 losses has created a significant investment opportunity. Published reports suggest that the fund has indeed made a small comeback since the 1998 bailout. Nevertheless, most investors remain skeptical. For some reason, investors were once eager to embrace the idea that razor-sharp academics would be able to translate abstract mathematical analysis into risk-free arbitrage profit opportunities. For obvious reasons, investors are now skeptical about anyone's ability to deliver above-average risk-adjusted profits in some of the largest and most liquid bond and equity markets in the world.

A. Many criticized the Federal Reserve's role in the LTCM bailout as a troubling signal to the capital markets. What do you think?

B. To the extent that the bailout averted even steeper losses for LTCM investors, who should share in such benefits?

Selected References

Bamber, Linda Smith, Orie E. Barron, and Thomas L. Stober. "Differential Interpretations and Trading Volume." *Journal of Financial and Quantitative Analysis* 34 (September 1999): 369–386.

Boyle, Phelim P., and Yisong Tian. "Pricing Lookback and Barrier Options under the CEV Process." *Journal of Financial and Quantitative Analysis* 34 (June 1999): 241–264.

Dimson, Elroy, and Mussavian Massoud. "Three Centuries of Asset Pricing." *Journal of Banking and Finance* 23 (December 1999): 1745–1769.

Doukas, John, Patricia H. Hall, and Larry H. P. Lang. "The Pricing of Currency Risk in Japan." *Journal of Banking and Finance* 23 (January 1999): 1–20.

Frankfurter, George M., and Elton G. McGoun. "Ideology and the Theory of Financial Economics." *Journal of Economic Behavior and Organization* 39 (June 1999): 159–177.

Grauer, Robert R. "On the Cross-Sectional Relation between Expected Returns, Betas, and Size." *Journal of Finance* 54 (April 1999): 773–789.

Jacobs, Kris. "Incomplete Markets and Security Prices: Do Asset-Pricing Puzzles Result from Aggregation Problems?" *Journal of Finance* 54 (February 1999): 123–163.

Jacoby, Gady, David J. Fowler, and Aron A. Gottesman. "The Capital Asset Pricing Model and the Liquidity Effect: A Theoretical Approach." *Journal of Financial Markets* 3 (February 2000): 69–81.

Kan, Raymond, and Chu Zhang. "Two-Pass Tests of Asset Pricing Models with Useless Factors." *Journal of Finance* 54 (February 1999): 203–235.

Kristensen, Henrik. "Does Fairness Matter in Corporate Takeovers?" *Journal of Economic Psychology* 21 (February 2000): 43–56.

Longstaff, Francis A. "Arbitrage and the Expectation Hypothesis." *Journal of Finance* 55 (April 2000): 989–994.

Los, Cornelis A. "Galton's Error and the Under-Representation of Systematic Risk." *Journal of Banking and Finance* 23 (December 1999): 1793–1829.

Stambaugh, Robert F. "Predictive Regressions." *Journal of Financial Economics* 53 (July 1999): 375–421.

van Wijnbergen, Sweder, and Antonio Estache. "Evaluating the Minimum Asset Tax on Corporations: An Option Pricing Approach." *Journal of Public Economics* 71 (January 1999): 75–96.

Wei, K. C. John, Cheng Lee, and Alice C. Lee. "Linear Conditional Expectation, Return Distributions, and Capital Asset Pricing Theories." *Journal of Financial Research* 22 (Winter 1999): 471–487.

CHAPTER 14

Stock Market Anomalies

QXL.com is a British-based online auction community that conducts business-to-consumer auctions in four languages and currencies. Like many Internet companies, QXL.com has little operating revenues, and profits are nonexistent. During 1999, its initial 12-month period, for example, revenues were a scant \$6.5 million, and operating losses were \$44.3 million. Cash reserves are sufficient to fund current operating losses for less than two years. Within that time frame, the company hopes to be able to turn a profit or convince stock and bond investors to inject more capital. Analysts expect the company to experience large and growing losses for the foreseeable future. How much would investors pay to get in on the "ground floor" of the "next Ebay"? A lot, it appears. In early 2000, the company sported a market capitalization in excess of \$3 billion.

QXL.com soared from an initial price of \$16.19 on October 4, 1999, to \$176.50 on February 24, 2000. On the eve of a 3:1 stock split, QXL.com was "only" \$67 on April 5, 2000. To jumpstart such "anemic" performance, Thomas Bock, a little-known Wall Street analyst with SG Cowen, issued a buy recommendation with an eye-popping price target of \$1,000! It is the latest stunt for obscure Wall Street analysts. Predict that the price of a hot stock will soar to unprecedented heights and create instant buzz around the shares—and yourself. In 1998, this "moonshot" strategy worked for Henry Blodget, who predicted a jump from \$230 to \$400 for Amazon.com. On cue, Amazon.com soared, as did Blodget's reputation.

Who says security analysis is a boring profession? It certainly is not boring. Based on some of the pure cheerleading going on, some are even questioning its credentials as a profession.[1]

Testing The EMH

Theory Is a Tool

The capital asset pricing model (CAPM) and arbitrage pricing theory (APT) can be used as tools to evaluate the efficient market hypothesis (EMH). According to

[1]See Robert McGough, "Merrill's Web Guru Blodget Downgrades," *The Wall Street Journal,* August 8, 2000, C1, C18.

the CAPM, the market is efficient if only risk-free assets give risk-free returns. If three-month Treasury bills yield 5%, then any security offering a higher expected rate of return necessarily entails greater risk. This simple message was ignored at their peril by Long Term Capital Management and its stable of Nobel prize–winning economists. Apparently, bond and equity markets are much more efficient than anticipated by those knowledgeable investors. The market can be judged inefficient only if risk-free assets or portfolios give above-risk-free returns. According to APT, a market is perfectly efficient if it is not possible to earn a risk-free arbitrage profit by simultaneously buying and selling the same asset. In the bond market, the market for Treasury bills is judged to be perfectly efficient if it is impossible to earn a risk-free arbitrage profit by buying and selling such securities to various investors at a given point in time.

By isolating deviations from predicted returns, CAPM and APT have potential as tools to help investors isolate instances in which the pricing of individual securities deviates from that predicted for a perfectly efficient capital market. Under such circumstances, portfolio managers might devise investment strategies to take advantage of unusual profit-making opportunities. In such situations, the CAPM and APT also offer investors and others mechanisms that can be used to better understand the functioning of capital markets.

A basic criterion used to measure the usefulness of the CAPM and APT, or any model for that matter, is their predictive capability. A fundamental test of the CAPM and APT is their ability to explain and predict real-world behavior. It is never fair to say, "that may work well in theory, but it doesn't work in practice." If financial theory, such as the CAPM and APT, does not predict security pricing in the real world, it must be rejected and the search must begin for better theory. When traders or stock analysts have detected inexplicable patterns in historical stock market returns, such regularities represent a challenge to the CAPM and APT concepts and to our understanding of market efficiency. For example, one must reject the EMH if tax-loss selling made it possible for investors to buy stocks with depressed share prices in late December, only to sell them at a risk-free profit in early January. However, one could not reject the EMH if transaction costs and/or tax penalties eliminated any perceived advantages to buying beaten-down stocks during December and selling them in January.

Joint Test Problem

Whenever inexplicable patterns of abnormal stock market returns are detected in empirical studies of the stock market, an **average-return anomaly** is said to be found. Important stock market anomalies are statistically significant, regular, and persistent abnormal returns that have no ready explanation in financial theory. Economically meaningful stock market anomalies are both statistically significant and offer a meaningful risk-adjusted economic reward to investors. By definition, statistically significant stock market anomalies have yet unknown economic and/or psychological explanations.

average-return anomaly Inexplicable pattern of abnormal stock market returns.

On the one hand, average-return anomalies may reflect some market inefficiency. For example, suppose stock prices tend to rise after widely anticipated stock split announcements. Abnormal returns tied to such public information are inconsistent with the semistrong form of the EMH. Similarly, if corporate insiders regularly earn above-market returns on insider buy/sell transactions, such abnormal returns are inconsistent with the strong form of the EMH.

On the other hand, abnormal returns detected when using the CAPM or APT as a measurement device may simply reflect the fact that these models fail to precisely capture the stock return generating process. In this case, abnormal returns reflect errors in the calculation of expected returns because some important determinant of stock market returns is left out of the analysis. When the CAPM or APT fail to precisely capture, or "model," stock market returns, model specification bias is present. If the amount of CAPM or APT specification bias is substantial, abnormal returns detected by using these models shed little useful light on questions of market efficiency.

There is something of a "chicken or the egg" problem when it comes to detailed tests of market efficiency. Suppose stock returns during late December and early January appear unusual given the predictions of the CAPM. This could mean that the stock market is, in fact, inefficient during the turn of the year. However, the CAPM may simply offer an incomplete picture of the stock return generating process. In other words, a **joint test problem** exists because anomalous evidence that is inconsistent with a perfectly efficient market could be evidence of market inefficiency or a simple failure of CAPM accuracy.

joint test problem
Anomalies indicate market inefficiency or market-model inaccuracy.

Practical Relevance

During recent years, the practical relevance of the joint test problem has become increasingly obvious.

In the 1960s and 1970s, many stock market analysts and financial economists became gradually convinced that CAPM and APT theory offered a reasonable view of highly liquid stock and bond markets. During the 1980s and 1990s, however, a number of inexplicable patterns in stock market returns emerged that caused some to actively question the appropriateness of CAPM and APT theory. Some of these have come to reject CAPM and APT while retaining the basic underlying premise offered by the EMH. Others have come to reject CAPM, APT, and the market efficiency concept.

At the same time, it is fascinating to note that during the 1980s and 1990s many individual investors came to appreciate the diversification advantages of low-cost index funds. Millions began to aggressively invest their retirement funds in indexed portfolios that seek to match the market without any active portfolio management whatsoever. As such, individual investors have entered their ringing endorsement for the simplest prescription of the EMH: A buy-and-hold strategy works best in an efficient stock and bond market.

This apparent divergence of opinion about the EMH is noteworthy. It is also important to recognize that one can reject CAPM and APT but still maintain the validity of the EMH concept. CAPM and APT are only two of many possible descriptions of a perfectly efficient capital market. Although the market could be deemed perfectly efficient if CAPM and APT were to hold, their failure does not necessarily mean that the market is inefficient. The market does not become inefficient because CAPM and APT fail to capture the essence of a perfectly efficient capital market. In short, do not reject the EMH just because CAPM and APT do not work. Do not throw the baby out with the bath water.

WALL STREET WISDOM 14.1

Is Bigger Better?

In the late 1990s, tech stocks led by Microsoft, Cisco Systems, and Intel soared to unprecedented valuations in terms of price earnings and price book ratios. "Buy the dip" was the battle cry of momentum traders who came to learn that bigger is always better. Looking forward, investors might want to ask: "Is Bigger Better?"

When economies of scale are substantial, larger firms are able to achieve lower costs of production or distribution than their smaller rivals. These cost advantages translate into higher and more stable profits and a permanent competitive advantage for larger firms in some industries. Diseconomies of large-scale organizations work in the opposite direction. When diseconomies of scale are operative, larger firms suffer a cost disadvantage when compared with their smaller rivals. Smaller firms are then able to translate the benefits of small size into a distinct competitive advantage. Rather than losing profits and sales opportunities to their larger rivals, these smaller firms can enjoy higher profit rates and a gain in market share over time.

In general, industries dominated by large firms tend to be those in which there are significant economies of scale, important advantages to vertical integration, and a prevalence of mass marketing. As a result, large organizations with sprawling plants emphasize large quantities of output at low production costs. Use of national media, especially TV advertising, is common.

By contrast, industries in which "small is beautiful" tend to be those characterized by diseconomies of scale, considerable advantages of subcontracting for "just-in-time" assembly and manufacturing, and niche marketing that emphasizes the use of highly skilled individuals adept at personal selling. Small factories with flexible production schedules are common. Rather than mass quantity, many smaller companies emphasize quality. Instead of the sometimes slow-to-respond hierarchical organizations of large companies, smaller companies feature "flat" organizations with decentralized decision making and authority.

Even though the concept of diseconomies of large size is well known, it is sometimes not appreciated how common the phenomenon is in actual practice. In many sectors, smaller companies have emerged as a dominant competitive force. In many industries offering business and consumer services, smaller firms are typically better able to quickly meet the specialized needs of their customers and have successfully met competition from large companies. Many sectors of industrial manufacturing have found that the highly flexible and customer-sensitive nature of many smaller companies can lead to distinct competitive advantages. For example, although early advances in large mainframe computers were historically the domain of larger companies such as IBM, the vast majority of innovations in the computer industry during the 1980s and 1990s—the personal computer, minicomputer, supercomputer, and user-friendly software—were started or commercialized by venture-backed entrepreneurial companies.

The villain sometimes encountered by large-scale firms is not any diseconomy of scale in the production process itself, but rather the burden that size places on effective management. Big often means complex, and complexity results in inefficiencies and bureaucratic snarls that can strangle effective communication. Many large organizations are now splitting assets into smaller independent operating units that can react quickly to customer needs without the long delays typical of large organizations. Corporate America is going through a metamorphism that will favor large organizations that are especially adept at reallocating capital among nimble entrepreneurial operating units.

In the 1960s and 1970s, when foreign visitors wanted to experience firsthand the latest innovations in U.S. business and administrative practice, they found it mandatory to stop and visit major corporations in Chicago, Detroit, New York, and Pittsburgh. In the new millennium, it is more likely that they would make stops at Boston's Route 128, California's Silicon Valley, North Carolina's Research Triangle, or Redmond, Washington.

For example, even the hugely successful software colossus Microsoft has found it necessary to decentralize decision making and push management autonomy down closer to the customer level. No longer the Bill (Gates) and Steve (Ballmer) show, Microsoft has found that rapid innovation and continued growth require a lean and responsive organization.

See: Scott Thurm, "Microsoft's Behavior Is Helping Cisco Learn How to Avoid Trouble," *The Wall Street Journal*, June 1, 2000, A1, A14.

Fundamental Anomalies

Small-Cap Effect (or Myth?)

When New York Stock Exchange (NYSE) companies are formed into portfolios based on market capitalization (price times number of outstanding shares), empirical research in financial economics documents the fact that firms in the smallest-firm decile consistently earn above-average rates of return. For example, Eugene F. Fama and Kenneth R. French estimate that small-cap stocks earned 7.02% per year more that the largest-cap decile over the 1928–93 period.[2] On an annual rate-of-return basis, large-cap stocks tended to earn annual rates of return significantly below those of small-cap stocks during much of the modern era on Wall Street.

In the eyes of many stock market participants, unusually large historical rates of return for small-cap investors suggests a size-related market inefficiency. However, by characterizing the small-cap effect as an anomaly, stock-market analysts and other researchers admit that these unusual patterns of abnormal returns remain unexplained.

small-cap effect Tendency for outperformance by small-capitalization stocks.

Table 14.1 and Figure 14.1 give interesting perspective on the **small-cap effect** phenomenon. Today, rates of return on small-cap stocks are typically measured by using the Russell 2000 Index. In 1984, Frank Russell Company created the Russell family of stock indexes to help investors monitor the performance of investment managers across various market segments. As you may recall from Chapter 3, the Russell 3000 Index measures the performance of the 3,000 largest U.S. companies based on total market capitalization and represents approximately 98% of the market value of all U.S. stocks. In early 2000, the average market capitalization of Russell 3000 stocks was approximately $4.4 billion, and the median market capitalization was roughly $701.7 million. At that time, companies in the Russell 3000 had a total market capitalization range of approximately $407.2 billion to $178.2 million. By contrast, the Russell 2000 Index measures the performance of the 2,000 smallest companies in the Russell 3000 Index and represents approximately 8% of the total market capitalization of the Russell 3000 Index. In early 2000, the average market capitalization of Russell 2000 stocks was almost $526.4 million, and the median market capitalization was about $428.0 million. At that time, the largest company in the Russell 2000 had a market capitalization of roughly $1,349.8 million. It is worth emphasizing that many small-cap stocks included within the Russell 2000 are apt to be underperforming "fallen angels," or companies with significant revenues and profitability that have fallen on hard times and seen their share prices collapse. In many cases, small-caps are not emerging growth stocks, at least not as conventionally defined in the financial press. Small-caps definitely do not include Internet stocks with enormous stock market capitalizations despite minuscule revenues and operating profits.

As shown in Table 14.1, from 1980 to 1999, the annual rate of return on small-cap stocks was 13.96% per year. The typical level of risk (return standard deviation [SD]) for small-cap stocks was 17.13% per year. During this time frame, the annual

---

[2]See Eugene F. Fama and Kenneth R. French, "The CAPM Is Wanted, Dead or Alive," *Journal of Finance* 51, no. 5 (December 1996), 1947–1958.

TABLE 14.1 Small-Cap Outperformance May Be a Thing of the Past

Year	Russell 2000	S&P 500	Small-Cap Premium (+) Deficit (−)
1980	38.58%	32.42%	6.16%
1981	2.03%	−4.91%	6.94%
1982	24.95%	21.41%	3.54%
1983	29.13%	22.51%	6.62%
1984	−7.30%	6.27%	−13.57%
1985	31.05%	32.16%	−1.11%
1986	5.68%	18.47%	−12.79%
1987	−8.77%	5.23%	−14.00%
1988	24.89%	16.81%	8.08%
1989	16.24%	31.49%	−15.25%
1990	−19.51%	−3.17%	−16.34%
1991	46.05%	30.55%	15.50%
1992	18.41%	7.67%	10.74%
1993	18.91%	9.99%	8.92%
1994	−1.82%	1.31%	−3.13%
1995	28.44%	37.43%	−8.99%
1996	16.49%	23.07%	−6.58%
1997	22.36%	33.36%	−11.00%
1998	−2.55%	28.58%	−31.13%
1999	21.26%	21.04%	0.22%
Mean Return	**13.96%**	**17.87%**	**−4.09%**
Standard Deviation	**17.13%**	**13.10%**	**11.89%**

Data source: <http://vanguard.com>.

FIGURE 14.1 Small-Caps Have Underperformed during Recent Years

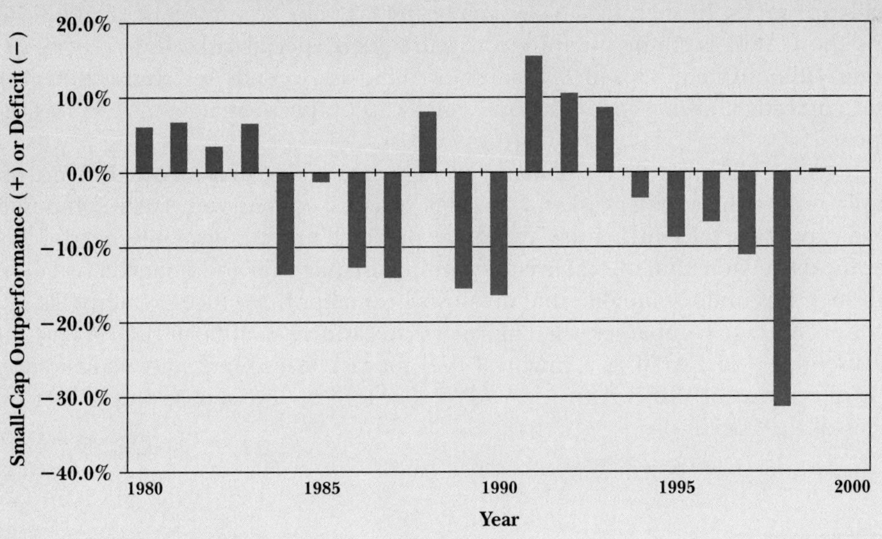

Data source: <http://www.nyse.com>.

rate of return on large-cap stocks, as captured by the Standard & Poor's (S&P) 500, was 17.87% per year (and SD = 13.10%). Thus, during the past 20 years, the annual return *deficit* from investing in small-cap versus large-cap stocks was 4.09% per year. By focusing their attention on historical data from the 1940s, 1950s, 1960s, and 1970s, many market observers have failed to notice that less-risky large-cap stocks have beaten small-caps since 1980! Perhaps the small-cap effect has gone away! In today's global economy, large-cap firms may be better equipped to compete with worldwide competitors. Alternatively, modern stock markets may simply be much more efficient than the stock markets of previous generations.

A number of researchers doubt the very existence of a long-term small-cap effect. Measurement errors rather than market inefficiency may explain the perceived outperformance of small-cap stocks. For example, recent studies suggest that previous research was biased in its focus on small-cap winners. By ignoring the effects of firms that are delisted for poor performance, previous studies may be infected with **delisting bias.** Small-caps that go bankrupt or otherwise disappear are often excluded from academic studies. By excluding small-cap losers from previous studies, the total returns earned on small-cap stocks may have been overstated. In an interesting article, Tyler Shumway and Vincent A. Warther document that delisting bias is highly correlated with size but not with other fundamental measures of firm value, such as price/book ratios.[3] For the smallest publicly traded companies, Shumway and Warther calculate that proper adjustment for the effects of delisting reduce annual returns by more than enough to account for the entire small-cap effect.

delisting bias Tendency to ignore the effects of firms that are delisted for poor performance.

Alternatively, above-average returns for small-cap stocks may simply reflect a necessary small-cap risk premium. Small-cap firms trade infrequently and market models such as the CAPM and APT can understate small-firm risk. For example, IBM stock trades every minute of every trading day. Its share price quickly reflects changes in economic expectations and investor psychology. Many small-cap tech stocks trade only a few times per day, if at all. This means that the return volatility of large-cap stocks tends to be more precisely measured than is the volatility of small-cap stocks. In such instances, small-caps may not be underpriced at all. Perhaps the CAPM is simply unable to capture their special risks (i.e., the *model* is wrong). Illiquid small-caps involve substantial bid-ask spreads and transaction costs. After correctly allowing for such costs, small-cap outperformance may, in fact, disappear.

It seems plausible that any above-average rates of return for small firms may simply reflect the greater risks or trading costs associated with such companies. Small-cap firms seldom feature extensive product lines, enjoy only narrow geographic dispersion, and often have only limited managerial and financial resources. Although it is understandable that investors in smaller firms face greater risks than investors in large companies, the failure of β to capture small-firm risk undermines the usefulness of CAPM as a practical tool for risk assessment and management. This also makes it difficult to use CAPM as a tool to test semistrong and strong forms of the EMH.

---

[3]Tyler Shumway and Vincent A. Warther, "The Delisting Bias in CRSP's Nasdaq Data and Its Implications for the Size Effect," *Journal of Finance* 54, no. 5 (December 1999), 2361–2379.

Value Effects

The fact that firm size adds to the explanation of average returns provided by β is not the only problem faced by the CAPM. Several studies in financial economics document higher long-term rates of return for stocks with low price/earnings, price/cash flow, and price/book ratios and low historical sales growth.[4] As predicted by contrarian value stock investors, such companies tend to be good candidates to benefit from the reversion-to-the-mean phenomenon. However, while higher expected returns for beaten down stocks make economic sense, the failure to reflect such influences in the CAPM reduces its practical value.

Despite lower risk, value stocks have ended to outperform growth stocks over sustained periods up to the 1990s. This **value effect** may be another manifestation of the small-cap effect. Beaten-down stocks have low prices and market values, by definition. As such, they also tend to have low price/earnings, price/cash flow, and price/book ratios. This is not to say that a value effect necessarily rules out a small-cap effect, or vice versa. Both can be present. Similarly, several Wall Street analysts have suggested superior performance for low price/sales ratio stocks, high dividend yield stocks, and neglected stocks that enjoy little coverage by Wall Street analysts. All such effects suggest that value stocks with low prices and low investor expectations tend to perform better than expected. Conversely, growth stocks with high prices reflecting optimistic investor expectations tend to underperform these high expectations.

value effect
Tendency for outperformance by value stocks.

Behavioral finance researchers use theories from the field of psychology to explain **investor overreaction** to both good and bad information. According to such reasoning, investors become too optimistic in the case of growth stocks and too pessimistic in the case of value stocks. As a result, investors in growth stocks tend to encounter operating experience that is poorer than the lofty expectations of growth stock investors and suffer stock market disappointment. Conversely, value stock investors tend to encounter operating experience that is better than the low expectations of value stock investors and enjoy better than anticipated stock market returns.

investor overreaction
When greed or fear pushes stock prices too high or too low.

Behavioral explanations of the value effect are compatible with economic explanations derived from the reversion-to-the-mean concept illustrated in Chapter 11. Experienced investors know that competitor entry and growth in highly profitable industries causes above-normal profits to regress toward the mean. Conversely, bankruptcy and exit allow the below-normal profits of depressed industries to rise toward the mean. Thus, superior performance for value stocks can be explained by economic reversion to the mean.

Of course, and as in the case of the small-cap effect, traditional market models such as the CAPM and APT may simply understate the higher risk associated with value stocks. In that case, superior rates of return would simply reflect the greater level of risk associated with value stocks, and no true value effect anomaly would be present. Again, the stock prices may be right, but popular asset-pricing models may be wrong.

Alternatively, perhaps perceived advantages for value and growth stocks may be the sorts of inexplicable and reversible patterns in annual rates of return that will be observed from time to time. As shown in Figure 14.2, like all investment

---

[4]See James L. Davis, Eugene F. Fama, and Kenneth R. French, "Characteristics, Covariances, and Average Returns: 1929 to 1997," *Journal of Finance* 55, no. 1 (February 2000): 389–406.

FIGURE 14.2 **Value Outperformed Growth during the 1970s and 1980s but Not during the Late 1990s**

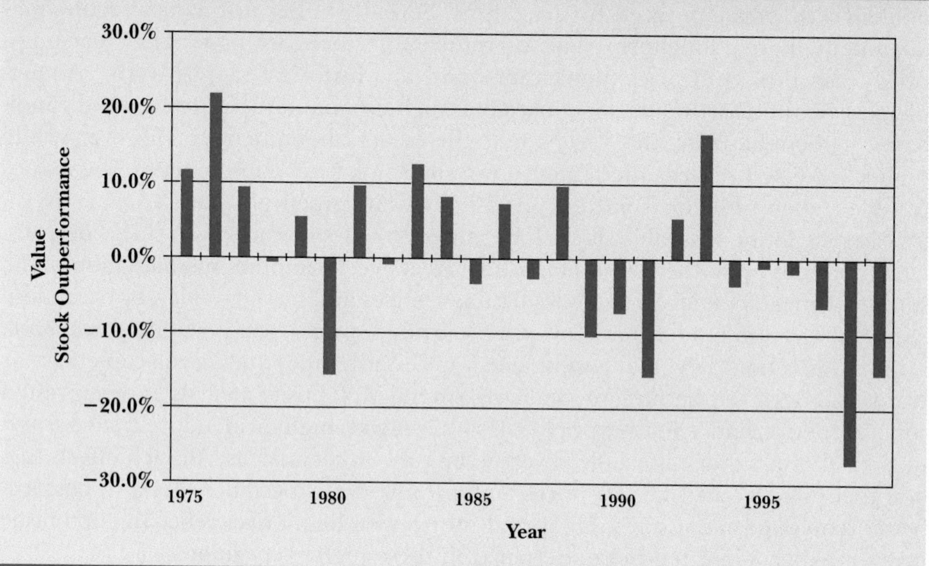

Data source: <http://barra.com>.

strategies, value and growth investment strategies go in and out of style at various points in time. Throughout the 1970s and 1980s, growth stocks were popular and contrarian strategies focusing on value stocks were profitable. During the 1990s, and after the sensibility of value stock investing became generally accepted among investors, value strategies began to underperform growth.

In the late 1990s, no investment strategy has been able to compete with a large-cap growth stock approach. As shown in Table 14.2, the best-performing Nasdaq stocks of late have been large-cap growth stocks. No doubt, researchers will begin to analyze and try to decipher these data. We may even see underreaction theories developed to explain this 1990s phenomenon in which investors came to prefer large-cap growth stocks such as Microsoft Corp., Intel Corp., and Cisco Systems, Inc. The recent disparity between growth and value stock valuations suggests that the odds are against a continuation of superior growth stock performance during the next few years. Value stocks tend to outperform when investors anticipate a new cycle of economic and corporate profit growth, because the earnings of economically sensitive companies can rise sharply from depressed levels. Rising interest rates can also change investment cycles, as investors become less willing to pay large premiums for future earnings growth and begin to look for less richly priced value stocks.

Experienced investors realize that you do not necessarily make above-average rates of return in the stock market by investing in companies with sterling historical performance. Investors make money by investing in companies that are better than the market thinks. Given the recent underperformance by small-cap and value stocks, a true contrarian strategy at the start of the new millennium would be to buy small-cap value stocks.

TABLE 14.2 Large-Cap Growth Stocks Have Performed Best on Nasdaq during the Late 1990s

A. 1999 Performance of Nasdaq National Market Common Stocks by Market Value

Market Value Range ($Millions)	Average Market Value ($Millions)	Number of Issues	Percentage Change in Mkt Value	Average Percentage Price Change
$0–49.9	$32.9	1,026	22.6	20.8
$50–99.9	$86.4	628	20.2	13.3
$100–199.9	$171.5	578	22.2	11.8
$200–499.9	$371.5	527	15.7	9.5
$500–999.9	$944.4	250	36.4	23.9
$1 billion +	$9,765.4	266	42.9	34.1

B. 1999 Performance Distribution of Nasdaq Market Common Stocks by Quartile

Criterion (December 31, 1998)	Quartile 1	Quartile 2	Quartile 3	Quartile 4	Total
Price/Earnings Ratio (over 100 excluded)					
Number of Securities	508	508	509	508	2,033
Average P/E Ratio	7.56	14.45	21.50	48.21	22.93
Range of Low/High	0.37/11.57	11.57/17.40	17.40/27.22	27.24/99.70	0.37/99.70
Average Price Performance	**13.56%**	**2.86%**	**1.73%**	**9.55%**	**6.93%**
Price/Book Ratio (over 50 excluded)					
Number of Securities	788	788	788	787	3,151
Average P/B Ratio	0.75	1.41	2.45	8.38	3.25
Range of Low/High	0.00/1.11	1.11/1.81	1.81/3.35	3.36/49.85	0.00/49.85
Average Price Performance	**11.12%**	**16.11%**	**15.87%**	**27.55%**	**17.66%**
Price Performance					
Number of Securities	807	807	807	806	3,227
Average Performance	−56.65%	−25.19%	0.04%	93.83%	3.01%
Range of Low/High	−98.92/−38.14	−38.11/−13.50	−13.49/18.30	18.42/966.21	−98.92/966.21
Average Price Performance	**27.12%**	**8.27%**	**9.66%**	**28.44%**	**18.37%**
Earnings Growth Rate (neg. earn. excl.)					
Number of Securities	506	506	506	506	2,024
Average Growth Rate	−31.02%	4.18%	23.76%	150.06%	36.75%
Range of Low/High	−99.38/−1.50	−1.38/9.70	9.73/49.00	49.05/500	−99.38/500
Average Price Performance	**8.60%**	**−1.20%**	**5.78%**	**16.79%**	**7.49%**

Data source: <http://nasd.com>.

Calendar Anomalies

January Effect

Seasonal variation in asset prices is inconsistent with the notion of an efficient market. Take the price of corn as an example. In the Midwest, corn is planted in May, grows to knee-high height by the Fourth of July, and is typically harvested in late September or early October. As a result, the supply of corn is at its highest in October and November. The amount of corn in storage is drawn down to its lowest level just prior to the next harvest. At the time of harvest, farmers will keep their corn off the market and store surplus grain if they believe they can obtain a future price that covers the cost of storage and provides a risk-adjusted normal rate of return. Otherwise, they will simply sell any surplus production at the time of harvest. As a result, the supply and demand for corn in the marketplace will exactly balance at prices that have no seasonal variation, even though the physical supply of corn obviously varies over the course of a year.

Similarly, time-related patterns in stock prices and security returns are inconsistent with the market efficiency concept. No seasonality exists in an efficient stock market. Therefore, it is surprising that a variety of academic studies have documented an inexplicable patter on abnormal returns tied to the turn of the year. The **January effect** has been documented in a number of studies that show unusually large positive rates of return for stocks during the first few trading days of the year. January seasonals have been noted in the rates of return earned on a variety of stock characteristics, including size, yield, and neglect. Small-cap stock performance is especially strong on the last trading day of the year and on the first four trading days of the new year. Such returns can be substantial.

January effect
Unusually large positive rates of return for stocks during the first few trading days of the year.

To illustrate the seasonal nature of monthly returns in the stock market, Figure 14.3 shows monthly average rates of return on the Dow Jones Industrial Average (DJIA) from 1900 to 1999. Over this full century of stock-market evidence, monthly rates of return tend to be highest in July (1.236%), December (1.186%), and January (1.074%). Monthly rates of return tend to be lowest in September (−1.180%), May (−0.244%), and February (−0.107%). Notice that monthly rates of return in January average somewhat less than the monthly rates of return for

FIGURE 14.3 **Monthly Returns Are High in January, July, and December**

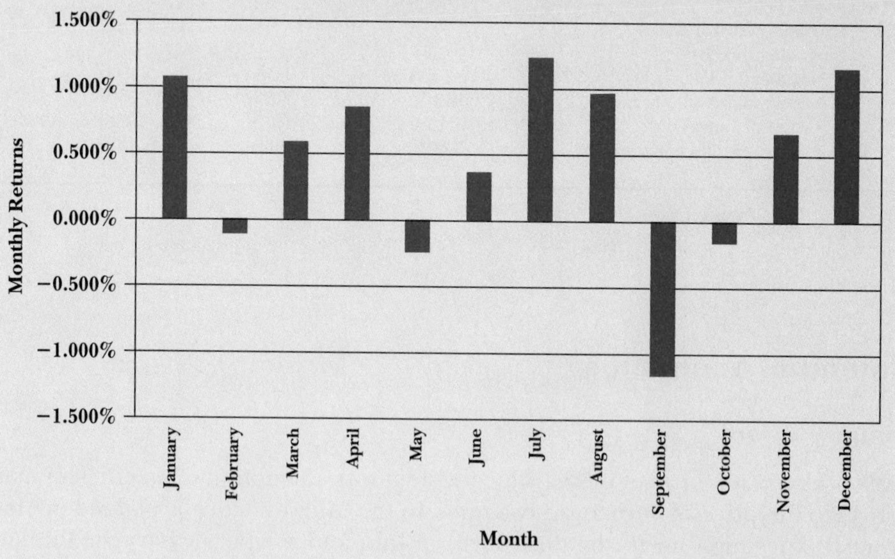

Data source: <http://nyse.com>.

July and December. The general perception of January as the most beneficial month for the stock market may stem from the fact that many researchers reported on the "January effect" phenomenon during the 1980s when January returns averaged 3.112%, the highest on record. During the 1990s, December (2.587%) and May (2.544%) rates of return were especially strong.

Because many top-performing small-caps in January have poor prior-year performance, a bounce-back from tax-loss selling is an often-used explanation for the January effect. Individual stocks depressed near year end are more likely to be sold for tax-loss recognition, whereas stocks that have run up are often held until after the new year so as to postpone capital gains taxes. However, this simplistic explanation defies equally simple logic. Suppose, for example, that there was indeed a dependable January effect. If investors knew that the stock market would rally in the first four trading days of the year, they would all rush to buy stocks during the last trading days of December, and then rush to sell them at the end of the fourth trading day of the new year. If a large number of investors were involved, the market would rally strongly during late December. Similarly, it would drop sharply at the end of the fifth trading day of the new year. To beat the crowd, investors would be forced to buy earlier and earlier in December and sell earlier and earlier in January. Eventually, the January effect would self-destruct.

In fact, the January effect has been very weak to nonexistent during recent years. Some investors now believe the January effect has moved into November and December as a result of investor buying in anticipation of January gains. Strong monthly returns in November (2.074%) and December (2.587%) during the 1990s tend to support this inference. Institutional factors may also be at work. Mutual funds must now pay out capital gain distributions prior to the end of the calendar year and might sell losers before year-end to minimize the amount of taxable distributions that must be paid. In any event, the once incredible January effect has diminished greatly in importance.

Turn-of-the-Month Effect

In the 1980s, a number of studies documented anomalous rates of return in the stock market at the turn of each month. Although not as dramatic as the January effect, the **turn-of-the-month** effect has been suggested as an important seasonality in stock market returns. As shown in Figure 14.4A, especially strong stock market returns are experienced on the last two trading days of the month and on the first three trading days of the new month. At the turn of the month, average daily rates of return are 0.099% (on the 30th), 0.089% (on the 31st), 0.133% (on the 1st), 0.145% (on the 2nd), and 0.103% (on the 3rd). During these five trading days, average daily returns are four to six times greater than the 0.026% average daily rate of return for all days.

turn of the month
Tendency for strong stock market returns on the last two trading days of the month and on the first three trading days of the new month.

The most convincing explanation for a turn-of-the-month effect is that pension funds receive significant new cash inflows at the end of each month from payroll savings plans, 401-k plans, and so on. However, as in the case of a January effect, it seems reasonable that investors would take advantage of any predictable turn-of-the-month effect by appropriately timing their buy and sell decisions. To enhance profits, investors would simply buy just prior to the end of the month and sell into the turn-of-the-month buying activity. Over time, such anticipatory buying and selling would tend to diminish, if not eliminate, the stock price effects of turn-of-the-month buying by pension funds.

FIGURE 14.4 **Daily Returns Are High at the Turn of the Month and on Days Preceding Market-Closing Holidays; Monday Is the Only Negative-Return Day**

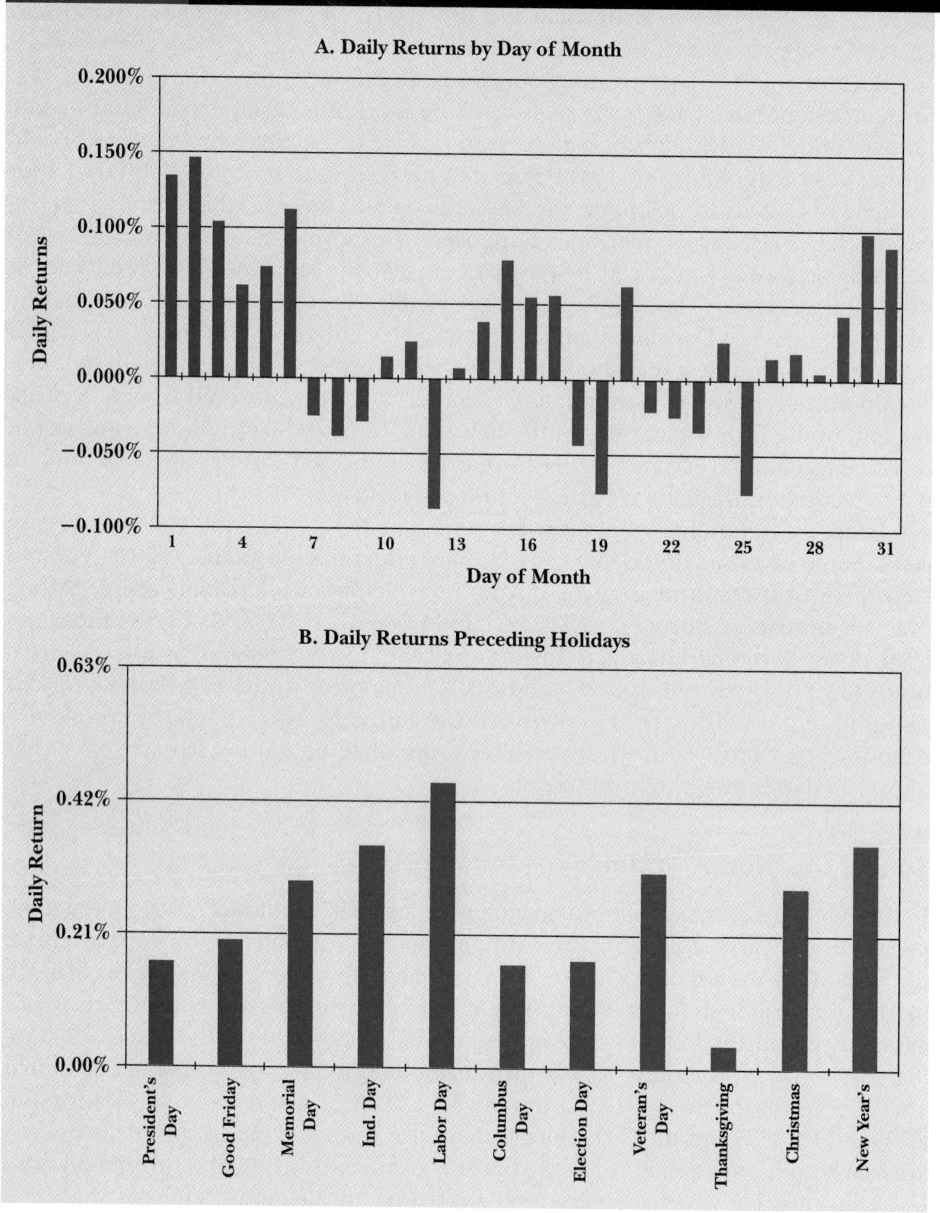

Day Effects

By definition, all anomalies tend to be unpredictable. Patterns of returns that are inexplicable often arise or go away in an inexplicable fashion. This indeed appears to be the case with day effects.

FIGURE 14.4 ***(continued)***

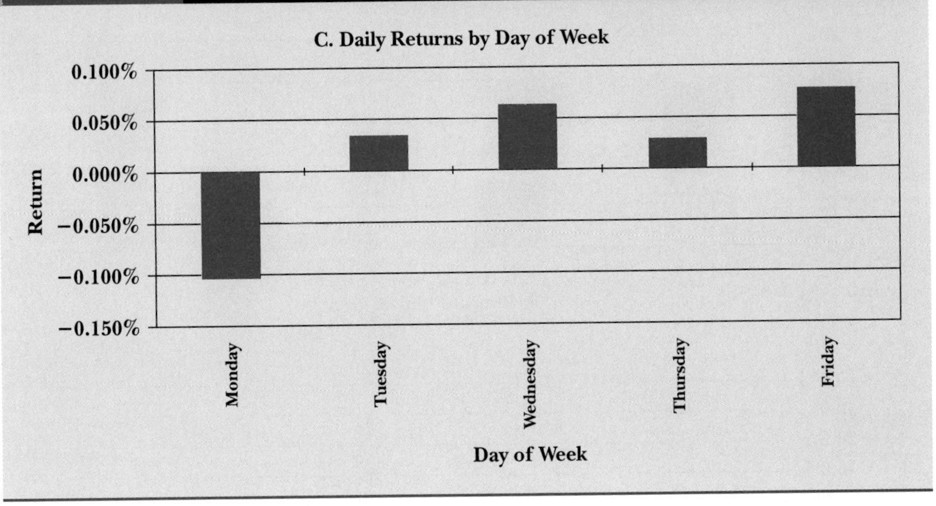

Data source: <http://nyse.com>.

holiday effects Regularity of unusually good performance for stocks on the day prior to market-closing holidays.

Monday effect Monday is the only day of the week that averages a negative rate of return.

beginning-of-day effect Stock prices usually rise the first 45 minutes of the trading day.

end-of-day effect Stock prices usually rise near the close of the trading day.

political-cycle effect During the first and last years of a new presidential administration, annual returns are abnormally high.

Unusually good performance for stocks on the day prior to market-closing holidays has been documented. Indeed, **holiday effects** have become an article of faith among practitioners. As shown in Figure 14.4B, daily rates of return appear abnormally high on the day before Labor Day (0.46%), New Year's Day (0.36%), the Fourth of July (0.35%), Memorial Day (0.30%), and Christmas Day (0.29%). Notice that each of these holidays is a major festive occasion that happens to occur near the turn of the month. Thus, both psychological and economic forces may be at work.

Weekends are often bad for stocks, possibly because companies and governments tend to release bad news on the weekends. As a result, Monday is the worst performing day of the week. In fact, as shown in Figure 14.4C, Monday is the only day of the week that averages a negative rate of return. Daily returns on Monday average an abysmal −0.102%. This **Monday effect** has given rise to the refrain: *Don't sell stocks on (blue) Monday!* Daily returns are especially strong on Wednesday (0.064%) and on Friday (0.077%), which is the best return day.

Some researchers have also detected a **beginning-of-day effect** and **end-of-day effect.** Tuesday through Friday, prices tend to rise during the first 45 minutes of the trading day, then trade flat until the last 15 minutes, at which point stocks tend to rally strongly to the close. Strong openings are usually attributed to the first few trades of the day. Strong closes are attributed to the last trade of the day. On Mondays, stocks tend to fall during the first 45 minutes of the trading day and then trade as on any other day of the week. There is little but conjecture to explain such patterns.

Yearly Seasonals

Finally, as shown in Figure 14.5, anomalous patterns in annual rates of return occur over the course of the political cycle. This **political-cycle effect** is statistically

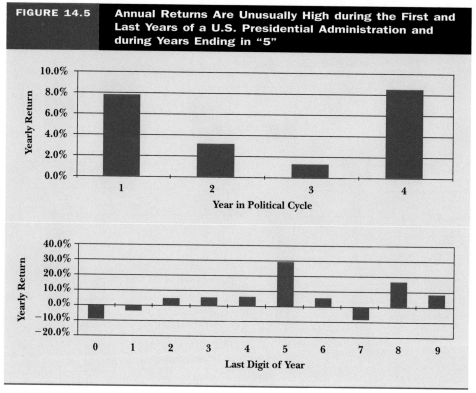

FIGURE 14.5 **Annual Returns Are Unusually High during the First and Last Years of a U.S. Presidential Administration and during Years Ending in "5"**

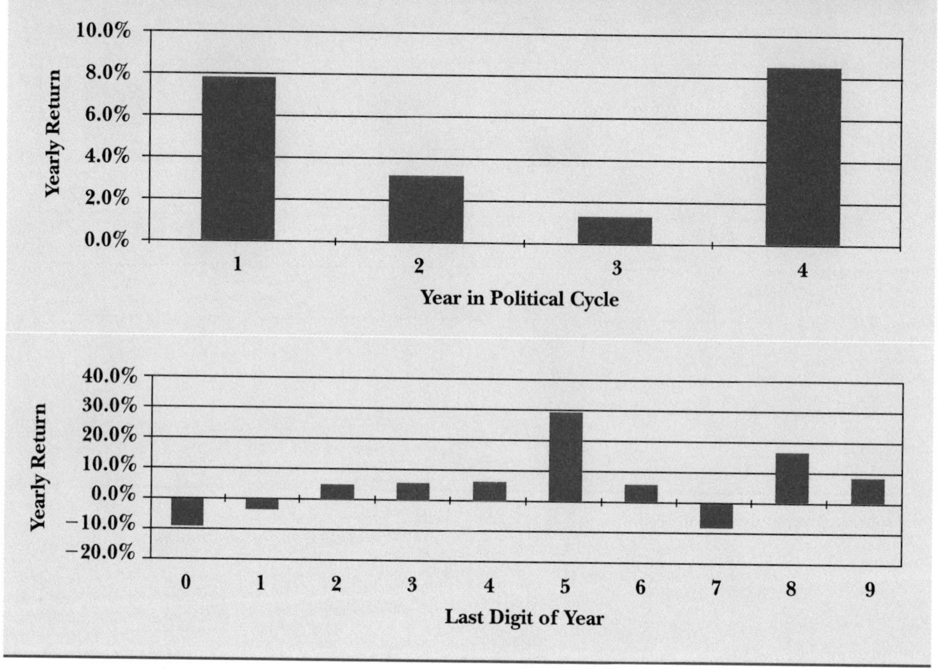

Data source: <http://nyse.com>.

significant. During the first (7.854%) and last (8.6%) years of a new presidential administration, annual returns before dividends are abnormally high. Annual returns before dividends appear abnormally low during the third (1.040%) year of a presidential administration. Common explanations center on political motives to make "tough" decisions after the election so that economic recovery and renewed prosperity can be ensured prior to the next election. Of course, nobody knows why voters and investors could be fooled by such a ruse year after year and from one administration to another.

Most inexplicable of all is why annual rates of return might be higher during years ending with the number 5, but they are. During years ending in the digit 5, annual returns average a whopping 28.962% before dividends. There is no rhyme nor reason to explain such an impact. In all likelihood, it is simply the type of inexplicable regularity that occurs when enormous volumes of historical rates-of-return data are studied.

Event Studies

Economic Events

According to the semistrong-form EMH, current stock prices reflect all public information. The strong-form hypothesis posits that current stock prices incorporate all public information and nonpublic information. In both instances, new information is instantaneously reflected in stock prices so that subsequent investors are able to earn just a risk-adjusted normal rate of return. Thus, an interesting test of the EMH is to consider a firm's stock market returns in the few days surrounding a cleanly identified date on which some important new information was communicated to the marketplace. In a perfectly efficient market, good news results in a sharp upward spike in shareholder returns on the announcement day. Bad news results in a downward spike in shareholder returns on the announcement day. In both instances, there should be no **postannouncement drift,** neither positive nor negative. In the postannouncement period, stock returns should be random.

postannouncement drift
Predictable returns in the postannouncement period.

Of course, in testing the importance of various new information, it is important to keep in mind that several influences affect stock prices on any given day. Stocks go up or down for reasons tied to the overall market, the industry in which the firm competes, and other firm-specific influences. Whether a given stock goes up or down on a given day proves nothing about the importance of a given piece of news. For any news item to represent an important **economic event,** it must change the underlying perceptions of investors and result in an unusual movement in the stock's price during the **announcement period. Event studies** measure abnormal returns surrounding significant news items that may have important economic consequences for the firm, such as earnings announcements, mergers, and the death of a CEO. It is the primary means by which semistrong-form and strong-form versions of the EMH are investigated.

economic event
Change in the underlying perceptions of investors.

announcement period
Time frame during which an economic event occurs.

event studies
Studies that measure abnormal returns surrounding significant news items that may have important economic consequences for the firm.

Many event studies begin with the simple underlying premise, or hypothesis, that stock market returns on individual companies can be usefully described by using the CAPM's SCL regression, in which

$$R_{jt} = \alpha_j + \beta_j R_{mt} + \epsilon_{jt} \qquad \textbf{(14.1)}$$

In this model, R_{jt} is the rate of return on the common stock of the jth firm on day t and R_{mt} is the market rate of return on day t. The market rate of return is typically described by the return on a broadly diversified market index, such as the S&P 500. Results from this SCL model are used to estimate **market-model abnormal returns,** *AR,* for the common stock of firm j on day t, such that

$$AR_{jt} = R_{jt} - (\alpha_j + \beta_j R_{mt}) \qquad \textbf{(14.2)}$$

market-model abnormal returns
Returns that cannot be explained by the CAPM.

Given the empirical limitations of the CAPM and SCL relation, abnormal returns are often also estimated by using two alternative methods.

In a second common approach, **market-adjusted abnormal returns** are estimated by subtracting the return on the market index for day t, R_{mt}, from the rate of return of the common stock of the jth firm on day t. Abnormal returns estimated by using market-adjusted returns are

market-adjusted abnormal returns
Above-market returns.

$$AR_{jt} = R_{jt} - R_{mt} \qquad \textbf{(14.3)}$$

A third common approach involves estimating **mean-adjusted abnormal returns** by subtracting the arithmetic mean return of the common stock of the jth firm computed over the estimation period, from its return on day t:

mean-adjusted abnormal returns
Above-average returns.

$$AR_{jt} = R_{jt} - \bar{R}_j \qquad \textbf{(14.4)}$$

In all instances, the relation between firm and market-wide returns is established over a significant period of time before some newsworthy item. For example, it is common to consider a 255-day estimation period that begins 300 trading days before the event date, $t = -300$, and ends 45 trading days before the event date, $t = -45$. This estimation period corresponds to roughly one calendar year in length. The event date, $t = 0$, is typically assumed to be the day a particularly newsworthy item is broadly disseminated, such as when a company news item first appears in *The Wall Street Journal.*

Daily abnormal returns are often averaged over a sample of N firms to yield average abnormal returns, AAR:

$$AAR_t = \frac{\sum_{j=1}^{N} AR_{jt}}{N} \tag{14.5}$$

cumulative abnormal returns Sum of abnormal returns over some event interval period, typically of one, two, or three days.

Cumulative abnormal returns (CARs) are then calculated over an event interval period, typically of one, two, or three days:

$$CAR_{T_1,T_2} = \frac{\sum_{j=1}^{N} \sum_{t=T_1}^{T_2} AR_{jt}}{N} \tag{14.6}$$

The statistical significance of CARs is typically established by comparing their size and variability in so-called t-tests. When the CAR for an individual news event affecting a given stock is large relative to its underlying variability, it is said to be statistically significant and different from zero. This means that the pattern of stock prices surrounding a given news item is indeed unusual, and the event has economic significance. When the CAR for an individual news event is small relative to its underlying variability, it is said to be insignificant and near zero. In this case, the pattern of stock prices surrounding a given news item is typical, and the incident in question has no economic significance.

CARs can also be used to identify groups of stocks with unusually attractive or unusually unattractive performance characteristics. When the CARs for a group of securities are large relative to their underlying variability, such securities exhibit better-than-expected performance and represent historical bargains in the eyes of investors. Conversely, when CARs for a group of securities are small relative to their underlying variability, such securities exhibit typical performance and represent opportunities that offer no better than a risk-adjusted or normal rate of return.

Event Study Illustration: How "Foolish" Are Internet Investors?[5]

One of the most popular Internet stock Web sites is The Motley Fool (http://www.fool.com), run by brothers David and Tom Gardner. These loquacious and irreverent investors advertise having in excess of 200,000 daily readers

[5]See Mark Hirschey, Vernon J. Richardson, and Susan Scholz, "How 'Foolish' Are Internet Investors?" *Financial Analysts Journal* 56, no. 1 (January/February 2000), 62–69.

who celebrate the virtues of interactive investment analysis. The popularity and high visibility of *The Motley Fool* makes it an attractive basis on which to analyze the ability of broadly advertised Internet stock advice to move share prices. To measure the impact of Internet stock advice, consider the magnitude of stock price reactions surrounding buy recommendations published in the nightly performance recap of The Motley Fool's *Rule Breaker Portfolio.*

Over the August 5, 1994, to December 31, 1998, period, The Motley Fool made 21 buy decisions involving typically small-cap growth stocks in *The Rule Breaker Portfolio.* For example, after the market close on July 1, 1998, at 6:00 PM EST, The Motley Fool announced its intention to buy Nasdaq-listed Starbucks Corp. At that time, The Motley Fool described Starbucks as a "mid-cap, high-growth world beater." In a loquacious buy announcement of 7,066 words in length, The Motley Fool extolled nontraditional virtues of investing in Starbucks, including its "new, hip, and refreshingly boppy iced Frappuccino."[6] On the first trading day following The Motley Fool buy announcement, Starbucks jumped $4, from $52.63 to $56.63, or 7.89%. This one-day return was comparable to price gains following other similarly effusive buy announcements for @Home and Amazon.com. On December 2, 1998, @Home jumped $4.06, or 7.68%, from $52.88 to $56.94. On September 9, 1997, Amazon.com jumped $2.88, or 7.99%, from $36 to $38.88. The biggest one-day gain following The Motley Fool buy announcement over this period came on January 6, 1998, for small-cap video chip manufacturer 3Dfx Interactive, which jumped $2.94, or 14.11%, from $20.81 to $23.75. Over this period, the weakest reaction to The Motley Fool buy announcement came on May 16, 1995, for portable disk-drive maker Iomega, which suffered a ¼ point, or 1.72%, loss from $14.75 to $14.50. A recent reaction to The Motley Fool buy announcement for large-cap growth stock Amgen was relatively muted. On the day following the December 15, 1998, buy announcement, Amgen rose a mere $2.81, or 2.15%.

Although unadjusted stock price reactions to The Motley Fool buy announcements suggests the possibility of market-moving ability, such a conclusion awaits a more-detailed abnormal returns analysis. Table 14.3 shows CARs for 21 small-cap buy announcements in *The Rule Breaker Portfolio* over the August 4, 1994, to December 31, 1998, period. CAR estimates are derived by using alternative mean-adjusted, market-adjusted, and market-model-adjusted abnormal return estimation methods. CARs are also estimated by using three alternative market indexes: the Russell 2000, S&P 500, and Wilshire 5000 value-weighted indexes. In all, seven different CAR estimates are provided for each event period. Of primary interest is the wealth effect observed over the day (0) event period. However, CARs are also reported for four additional event-period windows, including days (−1), (+1), (0, +1), and (−1, +1). Both mean (average) and median results are reported.

On average, The Motley Fool buy announcements have statistically significant positive wealth effects over the (0) event period of 3.36% (t = 3.26) to 3.72% (t = 3.63), depending on the estimation method. Weakly positive but statistically insignificant valuation effects on (+1) suggest that the influence of The Motley Fool buy announcements is quickly incorporated into target-company stock prices. What is intriguing about results reported in Table 14.3 is that stocks benefiting from The Motley Fool buy announcements also tend to rise significantly on the trading day

[6]See <http://www.fool.com/portfolios/RuleBreaker/Trades/RuleBreakerTrade_sbux980701.htm>.

TABLE 14.3 Cumulative Abnormal Returns for the Motley Fool *Rule Breaker Portfolio* Small-Cap Growth Stock Buy Announcements

This table presents cumulative abnormal returns (CARs) for five event periods following announcements of the intent to purchase in *The Rule Breaker Portfolio.* Three methods are used to estimate CARs: mean-adjusted returns, market-adjusted returns, and market-model-adjusted returns. Market-adjusted and market-model CARs are estimated by using three stock indexes: the Russell 2000, the S&P 500, and the Wilshire 5000. Mean (median) CARs and *t*-statistics (*z*-scores) are presented.

Event period: $n = 21$	−1	0	+1	0,+1	−1,+1
			Mean CAR (*t*-statistic)		
Mean-Adjusted Returns[a]					
	1.89%	3.48%	0.89%	4.38%	6.27%
	1.79*	3.31***	0.85	2.94***	3.43***
Market-Adjusted Returns					
Russell 2000	2.15%	3.72%	0.99%	4.71%	6.87%
	2.10**	3.63***	0.97	3.25***	3.86***
S&P 500	2.03%	3.64%	0.90%	4.55%	6.58%
	1.96**	3.52***	0.88	3.11***	3.67***
Wilshire 5000	2.07%	3.64%	0.92%	4.57%	6.64%
	2.01**	3.53***	0.90	3.13***	3.72***
Market-Model Adjusted Returns[a]					
Russell 2000	2.00%	3.57%	0.76%	4.34%	6.34%
	1.99**	3.55***	0.76	3.05***	3.64***
S&P 500	1.94%	3.36%	0.75%	4.11%	6.05%
	1.89**	3.26***	0.73	2.82***	3.39***
Wilshire 5000	1.99%	3.39%	0.69%	4.08%	6.08%
	1.95**	3.31***	0.67	2.82***	3.43***
			Median CAR (*z*-score)		
Mean-Adjusted Returns[a]					
	1.83%	2.70%	1.17%	1.91%	5.30%
	1.80**	1.80**	1.37*	2.24**	1.80**
Market-Adjusted Returns					
Russell 2000	2.22%	2.27%	0.68%	2.57%	4.60%
	1.45*	1.01	0.58	2.32**	2.32**
S&P 500	2.12%	2.24%	0.71%	1.95%	4.08%
	1.49*	2.36***	1.05	1.92**	1.92**
Wilshire 5000	1.93%	2.22%	0.53%	2.00%	4.13%
	1.50*	1.93**	1.06	1.93**	1.93**
Market-Model Adjusted Returns[a]					
Russell 2000	2.04%	1.96%	0.09%	1.85%	3.83%
	1.83**	1.83**	0.52	2.27**	1.83**
S&P 500	2.30%	2.06%	0.54%	1.88%	3.17%
	1.77**	2.65***	0.90	2.21**	2.21**
Wilshire 5000	2.02%	1.96%	0.36%	1.88%	2.79%
	1.80**	2.67***	0.92	2.23**	2.23**

* Indicates significance at the $\alpha = 0.10$ level.
** Indicates significance at the $\alpha = 0.05$ level.
*** Indicates significance at the $\alpha = 0.01$ level.
[a]Estimation period is day −295 to day −46 when returns are available.

before the announcement is made public on The Motley Fool Web site. Mean CARs over the (−1) event period are 1.89% ($t = 1.79$) to 2.15% ($t = 2.10$). This suggests that the possibility of some preannouncement "leakage" of The Motley Fool's buying intention. However, positive preannouncement returns may simply indicate that The Motley Fool uses a "momentum" style of investing. In any event, CARs over the entire (−1, +1) event period average a surprisingly high 6.05% (t = 3.39) to 6.87% (t = 3.86), depending on the estimation method.

In terms of relative magnitude, announcement period (0) stock price effects of *The Motley Fool* buy announcements appear to be somewhat larger than the stock returns of 2.35% tied to stock recommendations in *Business Week* magazine's "Inside Wall Street" column.[7] Similarly, these results are on the same order of magnitude as average positive abnormal returns of 4.06% in the period surrounding publication of analyst recommendations in the *Wall Street Journal*'s Dartboard column.[8] The magnitude of stock price effects tied to The Motley Fool buy announcements suggests that such information is more "newsworthy" than buy recommendations published in *Business Week* or *The Wall Street Journal.*

This evidence documents the fact that The Motley Fool's widely followed buy announcements for the *Rule Breaker Portfolio* are acted on by Internet investors. Buy announcements and stock advice on The Motley Fool move stock prices. These results are especially interesting given The Motley Fool's mission: "To educate, to enliven, and to enrich," in which "the whole point of Foolishness is to make your own decisions, sink or swim based on your own beliefs." In fact, The Motley Fool regularly derides small investors who follow the "Wise" buy/sell advice offered on Wall Street. In the letter case–specific world of The Motley Fool, following the stock-picking advice of others just is not Foolish (with an upper-case *F*). It is intriguing to learn that online readers of The Motley Fool closely follow and act on the stock-trading advice that they find there. If it is indeed foolish to mindlessly follow the stock-picking advice of novice investors, one can only describe The Motley Fool's own followers as foolish (with a lower-case *f*).

Announcement Anomalies

Earnings Announcements

Event study methodology has been used to discover inexplicable patterns in stock prices following announcements of important firm-specific information. One among the most important of these is tied to companies that report higher-than-expected earnings. Such companies are said to have a positive **earnings surprise.** Companies reporting better-than-expected earnings results typically see their stock price move up briskly. Underperforming companies that report less-than-expected earnings often see their stock sell off sharply. Because earnings announcements represent important economic information, there is nothing inconsistent with the EMH when stock prices react strongly to earnings announcements. Indeed, it would be inconsistent with the EMH if stock prices did not move when reported earnings differ greatly from the consensus earnings forecast. According to the semistrong-form EMH, current stock prices accurately reflect all public information. Thus, good news should push stock prices up, whereas bad news should cause affected stock prices to fall.

earnings surprise Different from expected earnings.

[7]See Ike Mathur and Amjad Waheed, "Stock Price Reactions to Securities Recommended in *Business Week*'s Inside Wall Street," *Financial Review* 30, no. 3 (August 1995), 583–604.

[8]See Brad M. Barber and Douglas Loeffler, "The 'Dartboard' Column: Second-Hand Information and Price Pressure," *Journal of Financial and Quantitative Analysis* 28, no. 2 (June 1993), 273–284.

WALL STREET WISDOM 14.2

Internut Mania

The bubble in Internet stocks showed signs of strain during late March 2000 when *Barron's* financial weekly issued a seething analysis of the economic underpinnings of several leading dot.com companies. According to *Barron's,* scores of Internet upstarts were then on the verge of running out of cash raised in the frothy IPO market of 1999. Although even top Internet companies such as Amazon.com have been vocal proponents of using investor cash to build market-leading positions, such risky business strategies are prone to falter if investors' patience wears thin, and Internet companies are no longer able to issue stocks or bonds to fund large and growing operating losses. Net music retailer CDNow (Nasdaq: CDNOW), medical advice website drkoop.com (Nasdaq: KOOP), and net grocery retailer Peapod (Nasdaq: PPOD) were singled out as well-known Internet companies in especially dire straits. Almost as if on cue, in the week following the *Barron's* article, auditors for each of these concerns issued warnings about the ability of each of these companies to continue as growing concerns.

Investor reaction was swift. The stock of CDNow, a leading online retailer of CDs and other music-related products, tumbled roughly 30% on the news from more than \$5 to \$3.50, a far cry from its April 8, 1998, high of \$37.13. This represented an astonishing reversal for a company that just two years earlier had been accorded a stock market capitalization of roughly \$1.3 billion. Despite sales revenue of nearly \$150 million per year, operating losses ate up more than \$10 million per month and created a severe cash bind for the company. The news was scarcely better for drkoop.com and Peapod.

drkoop.com was established as an Internet portal to provide health care content on a wide variety of subjects, including information on acute ailments, chronic illnesses, nutrition, and fitness. The site also supported more than 130 chat groups and tools to permit users to personalize their online experience and to purchase health care–related products and services online. The hallmark philosophy of the site was that "the best prescription is knowledge." Chairman of the board and philosophical leader of the company was the venerable Dr. C. Everett Koop, a former U.S. Surgeon General with more than 60 years' experience in health care, government, and industry. With sterling credentials and a growing market among tech-savvy Baby Boomers, early investors figured that drkoop.com was a can't-miss proposition. With 30.3 million shares outstanding, investors bid drkoop.com up to a stunning market capitalization of \$1.4 billion during July 1999, shortly after its warmly received IPO. Less than a year later, with annual revenues running below \$10 million per year and operating losses of more than \$80 million per year, the company foundered and the stock price plummeted from a high of \$45.75 to \$3.25, a stunning drop of 92.8%.

Peapod Inc. was another Internet start-up that seemed to have a can't-miss business plan. Peapod aimed to make its mark as an Internet grocer and provider of targeted media and research services. Peapod's "Smart Shopping for Busy People" concept was designed to provide consumers with time savings and convenience through a user-friendly and highly functional virtual supermarket. Peapod also hoped to appeal to advertisers by selling access to an extensive database created from the online shopping behavior, purchase histories, online attitudinal surveys, and demographic information. On the basis of these data, Peapod hoped to provide customized one-to-one advertising and promotions. Again, a seemingly plausible business model ran into a simple snag: it did not work. Although sales approached \$75 million per year, operating losses averaged more than 30% of sales and showed no signs of abating as the stock price crumbled from \$16.38 to \$2.50, thereby leaving investors \$300 million poorer for the experience.

Keep these spectacular Internet flame-outs in mind if someone suggests you do not need a solid business to support a sky-high stock market valuation. In the short run, speculators can push silly stock prices to extraordinary levels. In the long run, it is the company's earnings that matter.

See: Jack Willoughby, "Burning Up: Warning: Internet Companies Are Running Out of Cash—Fast," *Barron's,* March 20, 2000, 29–32.

For example, any stock with earnings that plummet is a disaster for investors. This is especially true for companies with high price/earnings ratios stemming from a consensus expectation of spectacular earnings growth. Aware of high investor expectations, growth stocks have been known to stretch accounting conventions so as to place company earnings performance in a favorable light. When the fundamental operations of highly esteemed growth stocks begin to deteriorate, "creative accounting" has sometimes given way to outright fraud. Several companies whose earnings literally "fell off a cliff" have later been found guilty of earnings manipulation, or worse. Companies that report earnings later than usual, or firms that report their earnings later than others in the industry, often have poor results to announce. Therefore, savvy investors often avoid companies with questionable reporting practices or ones that delay earnings reports. These types of earnings information are already reflected in the stock prices of companies set to report earnings results. It is only the "news" component of current earnings information that affects stock prices in a perfectly efficient market.

It is well known that Wall Street analysts systematically overestimate good earnings and systematically understate poor earnings performance. However, so long as investors correctly discount the earnings forecast information provided, analyst bias has no necessary influence on market efficiency. What is inconsistent with the EMH is evidence of a **postearnings announcement effect,** whereby price movements tied to earnings announcements can continue for several weeks after the earnings announcement. In such cases, investors have the potential to profit from previously disclosed public information by buying stocks in companies that report favorable results or selling companies that report sub-par results. In a perfectly efficient market, good and bad earnings information is instantaneously reflected in company stock prices so that subsequent investors earn only a risk-adjusted normal rate of return on their investment.

postearnings announcement effect
Stock price movements tied to earnings announcements that continue after the earnings announcement.

Some anecdotal evidence of earnings announcement effects is provided in Figure 14.6, which shows long downward drift in the stock prices of three major New York Stock Exchange (NYSE) companies following the widespread disclosure of major accounting irregularities. Despite these problems, all three continue in business today. Cendant Corp. operates in travel, real estate, alliance marketing, and other consumer and business services. Cendant offers services such as shopping, travel, car rental, tax services, and real estate brokerage services. McKesson HBOC, Inc., is a health care supply management company that also provides software solutions, technological innovations, and comprehensive services to the health care industry. Sunbeam Corp. manufactures, distributes, and markets durable household and outdoor leisure consumer products through mass market and other distribution channels. All three are major NYSE companies, and all three were the subject of extensive media coverage following the disclosure of accounting improprieties. Each was the subject of numerous front-page stories in *The Wall Street Journal.* Despite immediate and intense media coverage, the stock prices of all three companies continued to drift lower for months following the initial discovery of the accounting improprieties. Notice how each company's April disclosure of accounting improprieties led to a sharp sell-off in the stock, only to be followed by an equally agonizing decline over the subsequent six-month period. It remains a mystery why investors were so slow to realize the magnitude of the problems facing these companies.

FIGURE 14.6 **Investors Appear to Have Been Slow to React to Earnings Problems at These Major NYSE Companies**

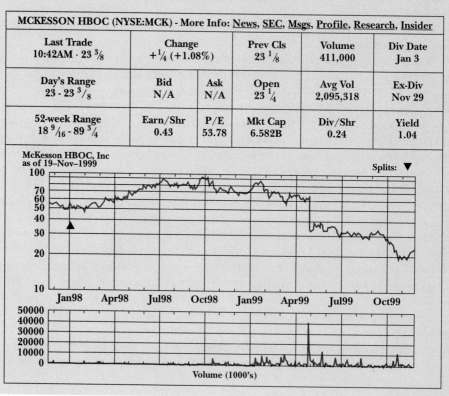

CENDANT CP (NYSE:CD) - More Info: News, Msgs, Profile, Research, Insider

Last Trade 10:42AM · $16\frac{3}{8}$	Change $+\frac{1}{16}$ (+0.38%)		Prev Cls $15\frac{3}{16}$	Volume 1,956,800	Div Date Oct 1996
Day's Range $16\frac{1}{4}$ - $16\frac{7}{8}$	Bid N/A	Ask N/A	Open $16\frac{1}{2}$	Avg Vol 3,009,954	Ex-Div Oct 1996
52-week Range $13\frac{5}{8}$ - $22\frac{5}{8}$	Earn/Shr 1.86	P/E 8.77	Mkt Cap 11.643B	Div/Shr N/A	Yield N/A

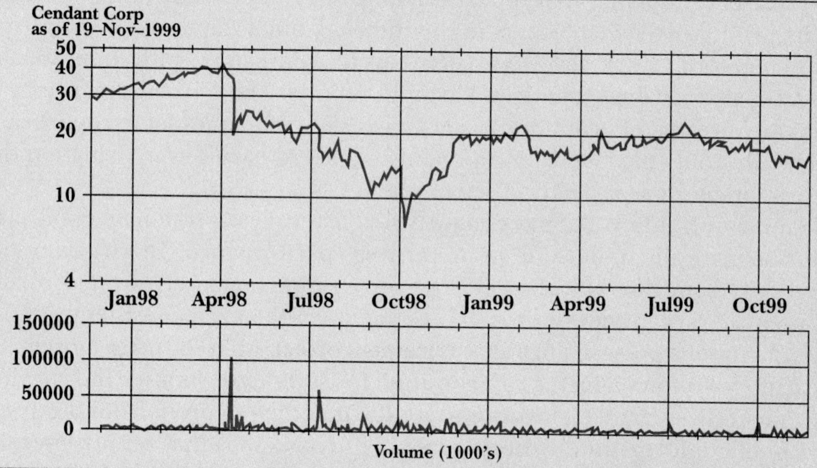

MCKESSON HBOC (NYSE:MCK) - More Info: News, SEC, Msgs, Profile, Research, Insider

Last Trade 10:42AM · $23\frac{3}{8}$	Change $+\frac{1}{4}$ (+1.08%)		Prev Cls $23\frac{1}{8}$	Volume 411,000	Div Date Jan 3
Day's Range 23 - $23\frac{3}{8}$	Bid N/A	Ask N/A	Open $23\frac{1}{4}$	Avg Vol 2,095,318	Ex-Div Nov 29
52-week Range $18\frac{9}{16}$ - $89\frac{3}{4}$	Earn/Shr 0.43	P/E 53.78	Mkt Cap 6.582B	Div/Shr 0.24	Yield 1.04

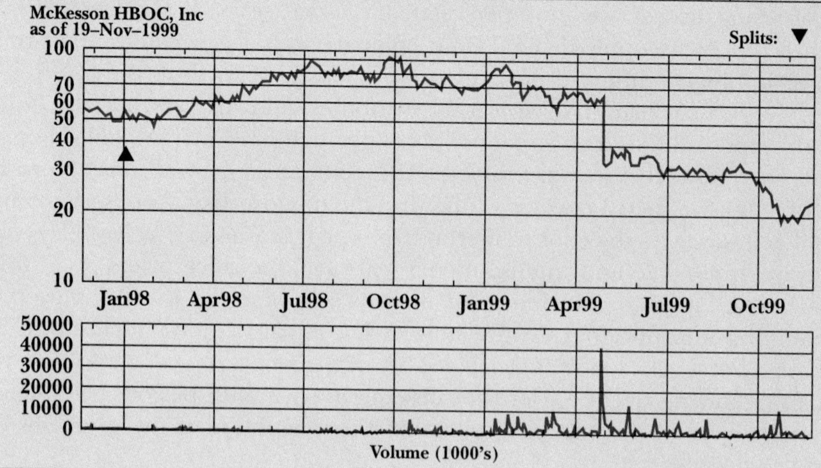

FIGURE 14.6 ***(continued)***

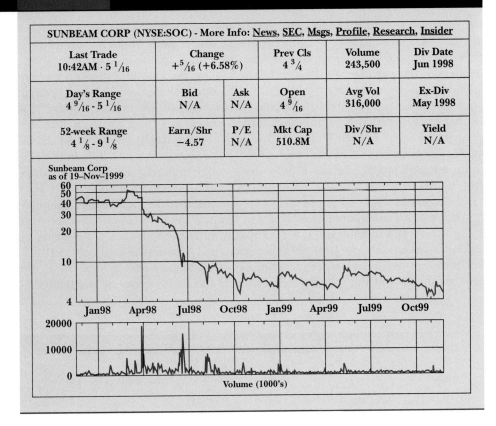

SUNBEAM CORP (NYSE:SOC) - More Info: News, SEC, Msgs, Profile, Research, Insider						
Last Trade 10:42AM · $5\frac{1}{16}$	Change $+\frac{5}{16}$ (+6.58%)		Prev Cls $4\frac{3}{4}$	Volume 243,500	Div Date Jun 1998
Day's Range $4\frac{9}{16}$ - $5\frac{1}{16}$	Bid N/A	Ask N/A	Open $4\frac{9}{16}$	Avg Vol 316,000	Ex-Div May 1998
52-week Range $4\frac{1}{8}$ - $9\frac{1}{8}$	Earn/Shr −4.57	P/E N/A	Mkt Cap 510.8M	Div/Shr N/A	Yield N/A

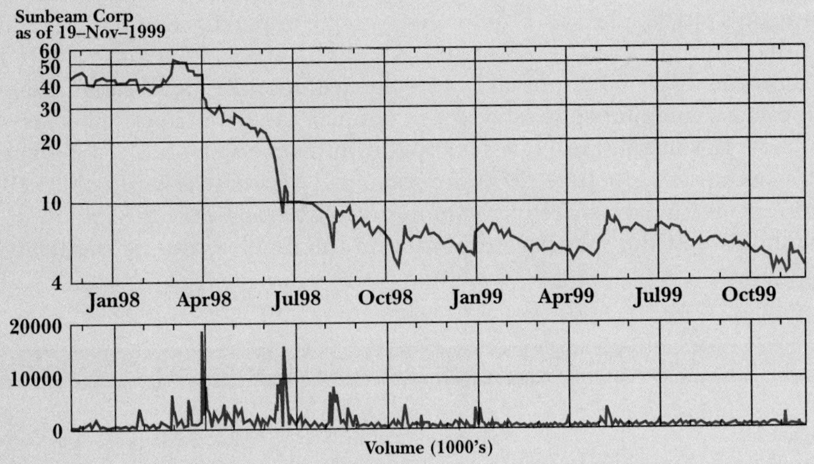

Stock Split Announcements

A wide body of research in financial economics agrees that, by themselves, stock split announcements have no effect on the market value of the firm. Stock splits are, in effect, stock dividends. They are one-time events paid out with additional shares, as opposed to the quarterly cash dividends many companies pay on a regular basis. On the face of it, stock splits appear to represent merely cosmetic changes because they increase the number of outstanding shares but have no direct effect on the market value of the firm. With a 2 : 1 stock split, for example, the investor comes to own twice as many shares as before the split, but the postsplit price falls by one-half. A traditional explanation for stock splits is that they increase the number of small shareholders. A possible reason for such an increase is stocks with lower prices tend to have higher percentage bid-ask spreads and give brokers more incentive to promote the stock.[9]

For example, Amgen Inc. made a 2 : 1 stock split announcement on Wednesday, October 20, 1999. Amgen Inc. is a global biotechnology company that discovers, develops, manufactures, and markets human therapeutics based on advances in

[9]See Paul Schultz, "Stock Splits, Tick Size and Sponsorship," *Journal of Finance* 55, no. 1 (February 2000), 429–450.

record date
Date on which a shareholder must be a registered owner to receive the benefit of a stock split (or other stockholder benefit).

announcement date
News publication date.

pay date
Date on which a split becomes effective.

ex-split date
Date on which the stock begins trading at the new postsplit price.

split ratio
Rate of increase in stock outstanding.

cellular and molecular biology. The **record date** of Friday, November 5, followed this **announcement date** by roughly two weeks, as is typical. Holders of record on November 5 received one additional share for every share owned on Friday, November 19, the **pay date.** In the case of stock splits, the **ex-split date** is on the day following the pay date. This means that buyers of the stock would pay the presplit price all the way up through the pay date. In the case of Amgen, on Monday, November 22, the exsplit date, the share price opened at $47.32, or one-half of the prior day close of $94.69. Thus, effective with the pay day, the number of shares held by each Amgen shareholder doubled but the share price split in half. In principle, Amgen's stock split was a nonevent with no repercussions for the market value of the firm.

As shown in Table 14.4, not all stock splits feature a 2:1 **split ratio.** Although 2:1 is the most common split ratio, other popular ratios for stock splits are 3:1, 3:2, and 5:4. In some instances, a stock split involves the spin-off of a subsidiary to current shareholders. In June 2000, for example, Hewlett-Packard split off 0.37 shares of Agilent for each share of common stock. Irrespective of the split ratio, the principle holds that the split has no impact on the market value of the firm. Fol-

TABLE 14.4 Two-for-One Stock Splits Are Most Common

Company	Split Ratio	Reported in *WSJ*	Record Date	Pay Date
C-Cube Microsystems, Inc. (split-off of shares in Cube Semiconductor)	1:1	4/7/00	5/2/00	6/2/00
Hewlett-Packard (split-off of shares in Agilent)	0.37:1	4/7/00	4/18/00	4/19/00
Nokia	4:1	4/7/00	4/18/00	4/19/00
ArmHoldgsPlc	5:1	4/7/00	4/18/00	4/19/00
Cognos Inc.	2:1	4/6/00	4/20/00	4/27/00
Philips Electron	4:1	4/6/00	4/14/00	4/17/00
Track Data Corp.	3:2	4/3/00	4/12/00	4/19/00
Fairchild Corp. (split-off of shares in Fairchild Corp.)	0.475:1	3/31/00	4/3/00	4/14/00
Micron Technology	2:1	3/30/00	4/18/00	5/1/00
Image Sensing System	6:5	3/29/00	4/17/00	5/1/00
Rogers Corp.	2:1	3/30/00	5/12/00	5/26/00
Sonic Foundry, Inc.	2:1	3/27/00	4/7/00	4/28/00
Hummingbird Communications	2:1	3/24/00	4/17/00	4/24/00
Clickaction Inc.	2:1	3/23/00	4/5/00	4/20/00
Credence Systems	2:1	3/23/00	5/1/00	5/17/00
QXL.com Plc.	3:1	3/23/00	4/3/00	4/6/00
Rimage Corp.	3:2	3/23/00	4/1/00	4/7/00
Chase Manhattan	3:2	3/22/00	5/17/00	6/9/00
Celgene Corp.	3:1	3/21/00	4/11/00	4/14/00
Hooper Holmes	2:1	3/21/00	4/12/00	4/26/00
Xcelera.com Inc.	2:1	3/21/00	4/10/00	4/28/00
Silicon Valley Bankshares	2:1	3/17/00	4/21/00	5/15/00
Broadbase Software	2:1	3/16/00	3/31/00	4/7/00
Finisar Corp.	3:1	3/16/00	3/27/00	4/12/00
Jabil Circuit	2:1	3/16/00	3/23/00	3/30/00
London Pacific	4:1	3/16/00	3/23/00	3/24/00
Amphenol Corp. A	2:1	3/15/00	3/23/00	4/25/00

Data source: <http://www.wsj.com>.

lowing any stock split, the quantity of shares increases, and the share price declines by a commensurate amount so that the net effect on the value of the firm is zero.

Nevertheless, many investors remain convinced that stock splits represent good news that tends to move the company's market value upward. Several investment newsletters and Web sites describe stock splits as one of the best marketing tools ever conceived by companies seeking to boost their market values. According to popular wisdom, stock splits create a positive feeling among shareholders. As the stock price drops as a result of a split, more retail investors jump on board. If retail investors are less easily shaken out on a downgrade or market jiggle, stock splits can tend to moderate share-price fluctuations. When a given market sector is hot, many stocks are setting new highs and become stock split candidates. Indeed, the 90-day period prior to a stock split announcement is one of the more profitable periods enjoyed by stocks. In the late 1990s, many individual investors have come to expect stock to shoot higher on the announcement of a stock split.

However, this popular perception that stock splits cause stocks to shoot higher is fallacious. As shown in Table 14.5, stocks tend to split *after* their share price has surged, not before. In the presplit period, 246 companies that split their stock

TABLE 14.4 ***(continued)***

Company	Split Ratio	Reported in *WSJ*	Record Date	Pay Date
United Pan-Europe	3:1	3/15/00	3/17/00	3/23/00
Vignette Corp.	3:1	3/15/00	3/27/00	4/13/00
Adaptive Broadband	2:1	3/14/00	3/23/00	3/30/00
Concord Camera	2:1	3/14/00	3/27/00	4/14/00
Datalink.net	2:1	3/14/00	4/10/00	4/26/00
NYFIX Inc.	3:2	3/14/00	3/24/00	4/4/00
Quanta Services	3:2	3/14/00	3/27/00	4/7/00
SERENA Software	3:2	3/14/00	3/21/00	3/29/00
Applied Micro Circuits	2:1	3/13/00	3/15/00	3/23/00
Commerce One Inc.	2:1	3/13/00	3/24/00	4/19/00
Datalink.net	2:1	3/13/00	3/26/00	4/10/00
Sony Corp.	2:1	3/13/00	3/30/00	5/24/00
Quest Software Inc.	2:1	3/10/00	3/20/00	3/31/00
Rambus Inc.	4:1	3/10/00	5/24/00	6/14/00
TrintechGrp PLC	2:1	3/10/00	3/20/00	3/22/00
Uniroyal Tech Corp.	2:1	3/10/00	3/20/00	4/5/00
BEA Systems Inc.	2:1	3/9/00	4/7/00	4/24/00
Interlink Electrons	3:2	3/9/00	3/20/00	4/7/00
NaviSite Inc.	2:1	3/9/00	3/22/00	4/5/00
Redback Networks	2:1	3/9/00	3/20/00	4/3/00
Comverse Technol	2:1	3/8/00	3/27/00	4/3/00
Engage Techs Inc.	2:1	3/8/00	3/20/00	4/3/00
Mechanical Tech	3:1	3/8/00	4/3/00	4/12/00
On Assignment Inc.	2:1	3/8/00	3/27/00	4/3/00
Breakaway Sols.	2:1	3/7/00	3/7/00	3/23/00
CT Communications	2:1	3/7/00	3/15/00	4/5/00
Covad Communications	3:2	3/7/00	3/17/00	3/31/00
Vitria Tech Inc.	2:1	3/7/00	3/22/00	4/5/00
Waddell & Reed Finl A	3:2	3/7/00	3/17/00	4/7/00
Waddell & Reed Finl B	3:2	3/7/00	3/27/00	4/7/00
Kohl's Corp.	2:1	3/6/00	4/7/00	4/24/00

TABLE 14.5 Stock Prices Tend to Rise before Stock Splits (1995–99)

	Stock	Index
A. Presplit Returns		
20-day percentage change ending on the last trade day of presplit prices: 246 higher, 139 lower, 7 unchanged	+4.35%	+1.33%
10-day percentage change ending on the last trade day of presplit prices: 231 higher, 149 lower, 12 unchanged	+1.34%	+0.63
On the final day of presplit trading: 217 higher, 137 lower, 38 unchanged	+0.56%	+0.08%
On the first day of postsplit prices: Split Day 220 higher, 152 lower, 20 unchanged	+0.82%	+0.18%
B. Postsplit Returns		
On the first day of postsplit prices: 168 higher, 119 lower, 17 unchanged	+1.12%	+0.19%
Split plus 10 trading days: 157 higher, 128 lower, 19 unchanged	+1.72%	+0.98%
Split plus 20 trading days: 169 higher, 127 lower, 8 unchanged	+3.08%	+1.96%
Split plus 30 trading days: 180 higher, 119 lower, 5 unchanged	+4.59%	+2.92%
Split plus 40 trading days: 177 higher, 123 lower, 4 unchanged	+4.66%	+3.52%
Split plus 50 trading days: 169 higher, 126 lower, 9 unchanged	+5.58%	+4.33%
Split plus 60 trading days: 168 higher, 132 lower, 4 unchanged	+5.55%	+5.21%
Split plus 88 trading days (4 months): 185 higher, 116 lower, 3 unchanged	+7.25%	+7.26%

Data source: <http://www.rightline.net>.

after January 1, 1995, saw their prices rise; prices fell for 139, and 7 were unchanged. In the postsplit period, prices rose for 185, prices fell for 116, and 3 were unchanged. Thus, companies that split their stock tend to do somewhat better than the overall market during the presplit period but perform in line with the overall market during the postsplit period. Moreover, it is not the stock split itself, or the expectation of a stock split, that causes stock prices to rise. Stocks tend to rise with the announcement of a stock split only if other favorable fundamental news is issued at the same time as the stock split announcement.

For instance, consider the company press release issued by Amgen, Inc., after the market close on Wednesday, October 20, 4:15 PM EST:

Amgen Announces Strong Third Quarter Financial Results, Stock Split and $2 Billion Stock Repurchase Plan

THOUSAND OAKS, Calif.—(BUSINESS WIRE)—Oct. 20, 1999—Amgen (Nasdaq:AMGN—news) today announced that earnings per share for the third quarter ended September 30, 1999, increased 33%, to $0.56 from $0.42 for the third quarter a year ago. Included in earnings for the third quarter is $49 million, or $0.06 per share, resulting from reduced uncertainties related to potential spillover liabilities to Johnson & Johnson. Without this item, earnings per share for the third quarter would have increased 19%.

Net income for the third quarter increased 36%, to $300 million from $221 million, including the reduction in the company's potential spillover liabilities. Without this item, net income would have increased 22%. Total product sales increased 20% in the third quarter, to $769 million from $642 million.

Sales of EPOGEN® (Epoetin alfa) increased 28%, to $449 million from $350 million, and sales of NEUPOGEN® (Filgrastim) increased 9%, to $313 million from $287 million.

Amgen also announced a two-for-one split of the company's common stock in the form of a 100% stock dividend. The dividend will be distributed on November 19, 1999, to stockholders of record on November 5, 1999.

Amgen's board of directors has authorized the repurchase of up to $2 billion in Amgen common stock between now and December 2000, replacing the remaining $127 million of the stock repurchase plan announced in October 1998.

Notice how the Amgen announcement cited exceptionally strong third-quarter financial results, a 2:1 stock split, and a $2 billion stock repurchase plan. Obviously, the company has been firing on all cylinders. Outstanding stock price performance and a subsequent stock split are in recognition of this outstanding historical performance. Amgen's stock split did not cause the company's outstanding prior operating results.

Companies sometimes announce **reverse stock splits,** in which the number of shares held by shareholders goes *down.* In a 1:3 reverse stock split, investors receive one share of stock for every three shares of stock held previously. Reverse stock splits are most common among companies with deteriorating fundamentals and a crumbling share price. To be sure, just as a stock split does not cause superior prior performance, reverse stock splits do not cause inferior prior performance.

reverse stock splits
Stock split that reduces the number of shares outstanding.

Finally, there is a type of anomaly associated with stock splits called the **spin-off anomaly.** A spin-off is the separation of a business from a diversified corporation, accomplished through the distribution of stock in the new entity to current shareholders. Spin-offs of smaller companies from larger organizations often lead to favorable stock market performance. A recent study by Hemang Desai and Prem C. Jain looked at 155 stock spin-offs and found that the best stock market performers were companies that dramatically improved their operating performance by more tightly focusing on their core operations.[10] In the first three years on their own, these newly minted companies earned an average abnormal return of 33.36% per year. Management analysts argue that before the spin-off, smaller companies do not get as much executive attention as necessary. After the spin-off, management of the smaller company tends to be much better focused, has the right incentives to maximize shareholder value, and the stock tends to move up substantially. What is not understood is why investors do not fully realize the operating and financial advantages of these small independent operations and fail to bid up parent stock prices following the spin-off announcements.

spin-off anomaly
Tendency of spinoffs of smaller companies from larger organizations to lead to favorable stock market performance.

[10]See Hemang Desai and Prem C. Jain, "Firm Performance and Focus: Long-Run Stock Market Performance following Spinoffs," *Journal of Financial Economics* 54, no. 1 (October 1999), 75–101.

S&P 500 Listing

index effect Tendency of stocks to jump when Standard & Poor's announces that they are about to be added to the S&P 500.

The S&P 500 is the most widely used benchmark for judging professional money managers, and some $700 billion is directly linked to it through index funds. Portfolio managers of S&P 500 Index funds must time their purchases and sales decisions to ensure a close correspondence between fund and index performance. Other fund managers whose performance is measured by the S&P 500 must also be sensitive to differences between the makeup of their portfolios and the S&P 500. As a result, S&P 500 additions and deletions have direct portfolio management implications that have given rise to an **index effect.** The index effect is the tendency of stocks to jump when S&P announces that they are about to be added to the S&P 500. A modest rise in price over a few days following the news is typical, although outsized gains associated with index additions are sometimes noted. Table 14.6 shows a sample of S&P 500 Index additions during the first half of 2000 and the price moves associated with such news. These price rises are generated by index funds buying the stock and by arbitrageurs trying to create a profitable market squeeze.

Of course, S&P does not want to move the market with its index change decisions. Several years ago, in an effort to reduce potential market impact, S&P began announcing its decisions a few days in advance. Index addition and deletion decisions are made by the S&P Index Committee. Neither companies nor any other

TABLE 14.6 Stocks Added to the S&P 500 Often Experience a Price Jump

Company	Ticker	Date Announced	Announcement-Day Closing Price
NCR Corp.	NCR	12/27/99	36.875
Young & Rubicam	YNR	12/29/99	62.563
Biogen Inc.	BGEN	1/24/00	85.188
Harley-Davidson	HDI	1/24/00	71.375
Conexant Systems	CNXT	1/26/00	74.313
Sabre Holdings Corp.	TSG	3/8/00	49.000
Pharmacia Corp.	PHA	3/27/00	47.359
Veritas Software	VRTS	3/27/00	168.438
Linear Technology	LLTC	3/27/00	51.031
Altera Corp.	ALTR	4/12/00	82.000
Siebel Systems, Inc.	SEBL	5/1/00	123.313
Maxim Integrated Products	MXIM	5/2/00	63.875
Sapient Corp.	SAPE	5/3/00	79.375
Agilent Technologies	A	5/25/00	68.750
American Power Conversion	APCC	5/26/00	30.875
Starbucks Corp.	SBUX	6/5/00	35.625
Average Price Change			
Median Price Change			
Percent Positive			

Note: All announcements are made after the market close, and percent change is from the announcement date share price.

S&P clients play a role in the decision-making process. The index is viewed as the leading companies in leading industries and an overall reflection of the U.S. stock market. Only U.S. companies are eligible for addition to the index. Turnover among S&P 500 companies averages roughly 25–50 firms per year, representing roughly 5–10% of the market capitalization of the index. As shown in Table 14.7, sector composition is a consideration, but when a stock is dropped from the index, its replacement will not necessarily come from the same sector. Closely held stocks in which a small group has control of a company will often be excluded from consideration. Finally, a rigorous fundamental analysis is performed. S&P seeks to add only relatively stable stocks to the S&P 500. Normally, announcements are made at about 5:15 PM New York time and are released to the public by the major wire services and posted on the S&P Index Services Web site (http://www.spglobal.com). Only after the public is informed are S&P clients or the affected companies notified.

The index effect can be explained as consistent with the EMH to the extent that it merely reflects the implicit endorsement of a company's future economic prospects by the S&P corporation. However, the index effect is inconsistent with the EMH to the extent that it suggests stock prices move for reasons that have nothing to do with the economic prospects of the companies involved.

TABLE 14.6 ***(continued)***

Next-Day Opening Price	Percent Change	Date Added to S&P 500	Date Added to S&P 500 Closing Price	Percent Change
36.875	0.00%	1/3/00	38.625	4.75%
71.000	13.49%	1/5/00	63.000	0.70%
93.250	9.46%	1/28/00	92.250	8.29%
77.000	7.88%	1/28/00	71.000	−0.53%
89.000	19.76%	1/28/00	86.500	16.40%
49.063	0.13%	3/15/00	48.375	−1.28%
46.625	−1.55%	3/31/00	51.500	8.74%
166.250	−1.30%	3/31/00	131.000	−22.23%
56.188	10.10%	3/31/00	55.000	7.78%
88.750	8.23%	4/17/00	84.438	2.97%
128.813	4.46%	5/4/00	130.453	5.79%
67.125	5.09%	5/9/00	63.641	−0.37%
91.438	15.20%	5/4/00	102.188	28.74%
67.000	−2.55%	6/2/00	81.750	18.91%
34.188	10.73%	5/31/00	35.438	14.78%
39.000	9.47%	6/7/00	34.563	−2.98%
	6.79%			**5.65%**
	8.06%			**5.27%**
	81.25%			**68.75%**

Data source: *The Wall Street Journal,* February 9, 1998, C1.

TABLE 14.7 Anomalous Stock Price Performance Is Associated with S&P Additions and Deletions

S&P 500 Index Changes 1999
(all changes effective after close of trading)

	Additions		Deletions	
Date	**Company**	**Ticker**	**Company**	**Ticker**
1/12	McKesson HBOC Inc.	MCK	HBO & Co.	HBOC
2/26	SouthTrust Corp.	SOTR	Oryx Energy	ORX
3/09	AmSouth Bancorporation	ASO	Tele-Communications	TCOMA
3/24	Century Telephone Enterprises	CTL	Rubbermaid Inc.	RBD
4/01	Kansas City Southern Ind.	KSU	AMP Inc.	AMP
4/09	Watson Pharmaceuticals	WPI	Aeroquip-Vickers Inc.	ANV
4/30	CMS Energy	CMS	Union Camp	UCC
5/27	Delphi Automotive Systems	DPH	Moore Corp.	MCL
5/27	AFLAC Corporation	AFL	Meyer (Fred) Inc.	FMY
6/03	Paine Webber Group	PWJ	Bankers Trust	BT
6/08	WellPoint Health Networks	WLP	Harnischfeger Indus.	HPH
6/14	Nabisco Group Holdings	NGH	RJR Nabisco Holdings Corp.	RN
6/21	Florida Progress	FPC	Morton International	MII
6/23	Office Depot	ODP	American Stores	ASC
6/24	Network Appliance	NTAP	Ascend Communications	ASND
6/29	Best Buy Co., Inc.	BBY	AirTouch Communications	ATI
6/30	Vulcan Materials	VMC	Provident Companies Inc.	PVT
7/21	QUALCOMM Inc.	QCOM	Transamerica Corp.	TA
7/30	Allied Waste Industries	AW	Browning-Ferris Ind.	BFI
7/30	ADC Telecommunications	ADCT	Nalco Chemical	NLC
8/06	Conoco Inc.	COC.B	Battle Mountain Gold	BMG
8/12	Lexmark Intl Group A	LXK	Raychem Corp.	RYC
9/17	Tosco Corp.	TOS	Mercantile Bancorp	MTL
9/28	Global Crossing	GBLX	Frontier Corp.	FRO
9/30	Adaptec, Inc.	ADPT	Fruit of the Loom	FTL
9/30	Bed Bath & Beyond	BBBY	BankBoston Corp.	BKB
10/1	Pinnacle West Capital	PNW	Pioneer Hi-Bred Intl	PHB
10/8	—	—	Ameritech	AIT
10/11	Analog Devices	ADI	—	—
10/12	T. Rowe Price Associates	TROW	Data General	DGN
10/15	Leggett & Platt	LEG	Cyprus Amax Minerals Co.	CYM
10/25	El Paso Energy	EPG	Sonat Inc.	SNT
10/26	Comverse Technology	CMVT	ASARCO Inc.	AR
11/04	Tenneco Packaging (name changed to Pactiv Corp.)	PTVwi	Tenneco Inc. (Old)	TEN
11/05	Xilinx, Inc.	XLNX	Harris Corp.	HRS
11/12	Teradyne, Inc.	TER	Case Corp.	CSE
11/15	Quintiles Transnational	QTRN	King World Productions	KWP
11/29	—	—	PacifiCorp	PPW
11/30	Molex Inc.	MOLX	—	—
11/30	Citrix Systems	CTXS	Mobil Corp.	MOB
12/01	Old Kent Financial	OK	Honeywell	HON
12/07	Yahoo! Inc.	YHOO	Laidlaw Inc.	LDW
12/30	Transocean Sedco Forex Inc.	RIG	Helmerich & Payne	HP
12/31	—	—	Republic New York	RNB

Note: AlliedSignal changed its name to Honeywell International, Inc., (HON) after acquiring Honeywell.
Data source: <http://www.spglobal.com>.

WALL STREET WISDOM 14.3

Message Board Fraud

Anyone who spends a significant amount of time on Internet financial sites eventually becomes attracted to the scuttlebutt bandied about on message boards or stock chat Web sites. Some posts offer new and interesting insight about the company in question, its products, or competitive position. Most posts on investment chat sites, however, involve little or no new information of investment value. They sometimes simply represent an entertaining form of diversion for those who like to sound off on topics of great or little import. In some instances, a darker purpose is served. The Internet has become a means for disseminating false or misleading information designed to manipulate stock price. "Pump-and-dump" schemes are plots by perpetrators who seek to pump up a stock price only to sell it at an inflated price to unwitting buyers, who are then stuck with losses as the overinflated stock price crashes. Another variety of this classic form of manipulation is to spread false or misleading information about a company in the effort to cause its price to fall, thereby creating profits for short sellers or buying opportunities for those who seek to add a given stock to their investment portfolios at bargain prices.

Sometimes, perpetrators of stock fraud on the Internet become so desperate that they fabricate authentic-looking but false "company press releases" that hoodwink unsuspecting investors into thinking that either favorable or unfavorable market-moving news has been issued by the company in question. A good example of stock market manipulation on the Internet was provided on March 30, 2000, when a day trader was arrested and charged with securities fraud for posting bogus information on the Yahoo! message board about Lucent Technologies, Inc. (NYSE: LU).

According to the U.S. attorney's office, Fred Moldofsky, 43, posted a fraudulent press release stating that Lucent expected an earnings shortfall. The ruse was successful. On the day after Moldofsky's posting, Lucent's stock price fell by 3.6%, or roughly $7.1 billion in market capitalization. Although Lucent quickly moved to assure investors that it anticipated meeting second-quarter earnings expectations, dismissing rumors that had been fueled by the fake press release proved nettlesome for the company. Even a temporary dip in the company's stock price can undermine investor confidence and create uncertainty. Of course, temporary dips hurt investors who sell at artificially depressed prices.

As it turns out, Moldofsky, who described himself on an Internet Web site as a "full-time online stock investor," allegedly traded 6,000 shares of Lucent stock the day he issued the bogus press release. According to *The Wall Street Journal,* Moldofsky identified himself by using the screen name "hot-like-wasabe" and sent a message captioned "LUCENT RELEASES EARNINGS WARNING! DAMN!" Attached to the message was a fake press release modeled after a legitimate release issued by Lucent on January 6 in which the company issued an earnings warning with respect to the first quarter of its fiscal year 2000. To bolster belief in the legitimacy of the bogus press release, Moldofsky posted more than 20 messages on the Lucent bulletin board using a wide variety of different aliases. Such messages included "links" that allowed readers to access the fraudulent press release. The messages were captioned with phrases such as "LUCENT WARNS! WE'RE ALL DOOMED TOMORROW!"

Law enforcement officials were able to identify Moldofsky, who lived in Houston, by collecting evidence from Yahoo!, America Online, and Moldofsky's Internet service provider. If convicted, Moldofsky faces a possible maximum sentence of 10 years in prison and a fine of $1 million. The Securities and Exchange Commission also filed related civil charges against Moldofsky in Manhattan federal court.

The lesson to be learned from such episodes of Internet fraud is simple. When it comes to investment advice, presume that bullish information posted on the Internet was authorized by someone who benefits if you buy. Bearish advice is posted by someone who benefits when you sell. Do not look to anonymous sources for valuable investment information.

See: "Day Trader Is Charged with Posting on Web False Lucent Information," *The Wall Street Journal,* March 31, 2000, C18.

Imperfections in Investment Information

Microcap Stocks

A fundamental requirement that must be met in perfectly competitive markets is the widespread availability of accurate investment information. Not only must accurate investment information be available, but investors must be sufficiently knowledgeable to properly interpret and act on such information. The disturbing recent prevalence of microcap and Internet stock fraud gives one pause in asserting that the entire stock market is perfectly efficient for all companies at all times. Around the edges of the public marketplace, evidence of market imperfections is common.

microcap stocks Companies with very small stock market capitalizations.

penny stocks Stocks that trade at prices below $1 and in low volumes.

OTC bulletin board OTC market for microcap stocks.

pink sheets Circular describing microcap stocks.

Accurate information about **microcap stocks,** or low-priced stocks issued by the smallest of companies, can be difficult to find. The term *microcap stock* applies to companies with very small stock market capitalizations. In recent cases in which the Securities and Exchange Commission (SEC) suspended trading in microcap stocks, the average company had only $6 million in net tangible assets. Nearly half had less than $1.25 million. Microcap companies often are **penny stocks** that trade at prices below $1 and trade in low volumes. Many microcap stocks trade in the over-the-counter market and are quoted on the **OTC Bulletin Board** (OTCBB) or the **pink sheets.** The OTCBB is an electronic quotation system that displays real-time quotes, last-sale prices, and volume information for many OTC securities not listed on the Nasdaq Stock Market. Brokers who subscribe to the system use the OTCBB to look up prices or enter quotes for OTC securities. Although the National Association of Securities Dealers oversees the OTCBB, the OTCBB is not part of the Nasdaq Stock Market. Stock con artists often claim that an OTCBB company is a Nasdaq company to mislead investors into thinking that the company is bigger than it really is. The pink sheets are a weekly publication of a company called the National Quotation Bureau and give a thumbnail sketch of information about a large number of thinly traded stocks (on pink paper). Although the pink sheets are updated electronically on a daily basis, it is often difficult to obtain timely intraday price and volume information on such companies.

The biggest difference between microcaps and other stocks is the amount of reliable public information about the company. Larger public companies file reports with the SEC that any investor can download for free from the SEC's Web site. Professional securities analysts also regularly provide research reports about larger public companies, and it is easy to find timely stock quotes on the Internet or in leading financial newspapers. By contrast, microcap information can be extremely scarce. Whereas companies with stock listed on major exchanges or the Nasdaq Stock Market must meet minimum financial standards, companies on the OTCBB or the pink sheets face no such requirements. Microcap companies tend to be new and often have no proven performance record. Some have products and services that are still in development or are untested in the marketplace; others have virtually no assets.

In general, a company must file reports with the SEC if it has 500 or more investors and $10 million or more in assets or if it lists its securities on a major stock exchange or Nasdaq. To prevent securities fraud, federal securities laws require all but the smallest of public companies to file regular comprehensive reports with the SEC. Microcap stocks fit this exception. Historically, only about one-half of the 6,500 companies whose securities are quoted on the OTCBB filed regular reports with the SEC. As of June 2000, however, companies on the OTCBB that refuse to file with the SEC, banking, or insurance regulators cannot remain on the OTCBB.

With few exceptions, companies that file reports with the SEC must do so electronically by using the SEC's EDGAR system. EDGAR stands for "electronic data gathering and retrieval." The EDGAR database is available on the SEC's Web site at <http://www.sec.gov>. Corporate filings in the EDGAR database include annual and quarterly reports and registration statements. Any investor can access and download this information for free from the SEC's Web site. By law, company reports filed with the SEC must be truthful and complete. However, the SEC does not guarantee the accuracy of filed company reports. Dishonest companies occasionally break the law and file false reports, thus triggering a SEC enforcement action.

Microcap stocks with less than $10 million in assets generally do not have to file reports with the SEC. Moreover, although most companies that want to sell securities to the public must register with the SEC, two common exemptions are designed to fit microcap companies:

- Reg. A Offerings: Companies raising less than $5 million in a 12-month period may be exempt from registering their securities under a rule known as Regulation A. Instead of filing a registration statement through EDGAR, these companies need only file a printed copy of an "offering circular" with the SEC containing financial statements and other information.
- Reg. D Offerings: Some smaller companies offer and sell securities without registering the transaction under an exemption known as Regulation D. Reg. D exempts from registration companies that seek to raise less than $1 million in a 12-month period. It also exempts companies seeking to raise up to $5 million, as long as the companies sell only to 35 or fewer individuals or any number of "accredited investors" who must meet high net-worth or income standards. In addition, Reg. D exempts some larger private offerings of securities. Although companies claiming an exemption under Reg. D do not have to register or file reports with the SEC, they must still file what is known as a Form D within a few days after they first sell their securities. Form D is a brief notice that includes the names and addresses of owners and stock promoters but little other information about the company.

Companies that are exempt from registration under Reg. A and Reg. D typically do not have to file public reports with the SEC.

Microcap Fraud

Most microcap companies that do not file reports with the SEC are legitimate businesses with real products or services. However, the lack of reliable available information about some microcap companies opens the door to fraud. It is simply far easier for stock promoters and con artists to manipulate a stock when there is little or no reliable public information about the company. Microcap fraud depends on spreading false information.

Stock con artists often issue press releases that contain exaggerations or outright lies about the microcap company sales, acquisitions, revenue projections, and new products or services. Some microcap companies also pay brokers and other stock promoters to recommend or "tout" its stock in supposedly independent and unbiased investment newsletters, research reports, or radio and television shows. Federal securities laws require that newsletters disclose who paid them, the amount, and the type of payment. Many illegal stock promoters mislead investors into believing that they are receiving independent advice.

cold calls Unrequested telephone solicitations.

Dishonest brokers and stock promoters also assemble small armies of high-pressure salespeople to make literally hundreds of telephone **cold calls** to potential investors. For many businesses, including securities firms, random telephone solicitations serve as a legitimate way to reach potential customers. In the securities business, however, unwitting investors sometimes suffer serious financial losses when dishonest brokers pressure them to make unsuitable investments.

three-call technique Cold call technique for gaining investor confidence.

A classic example of cold calling abuse in the securities business is the **three-call technique.** In the first call, the "warm-up," the broker tries to build investor trust and confidence by describing the broker's past successes and high-quality research. No solicitation for business is made at this time, the caller simply asks permission to call again if an "exciting" deal comes along. In their second call, the "set-up," dishonest brokers whet the investor's appetite by telling them about fabulous deals that they "think" they can get them into. In the third call, the "closer," dishonest brokers often frantically urge the investor to buy now or miss the opportunity of a lifetime.

What makes the cold calling efforts of dishonest brokers especially objectionable and illegal is their propensity for bait-and-switch tactics. Dishonest brokers often lure new customers by encouraging them to purchase well-known and widely traded "blue-chip" stocks but ultimately pressure them to invest in small or unknown companies with little or no earnings. Not only do such stocks tend to be very risky and thinly traded, dishonest brokers often work for firms that themselves own large amounts of the stock. The broker's employer may have been involved in the company's initial public offering (IPO) or may simply make a market in it. If only one dealer or a small group of dealers makes a market in a thinly traded stock, its price can often be easily manipulated. Some dishonest brokers overcharge their customers by adding an undisclosed markup to the price the broker's employer paid for the stock. Although it is illegal for brokers to charge excessive markups, some dishonest brokers mark up the prices of the stocks that they sell by 100% or more. Many investors find that once they buy a **house stock,** they cannot get what they paid for it, even if they decide to sell immediately. Some dishonest firms follow "no net sales" policies in which brokers cannot execute orders to sell house stocks unless they find a customer to buy an equal number of shares. Other dishonest firms discourage brokers from selling house stocks for customers by offering little or no commissions on such sales.

house stock Stock sponsored by a broker's employer.

The best way for an individual investor to fight microcap fraud is to become better armed with reliable information. Even when working with a broker or an investment adviser, investors should always obtain detailed written information about the company that they are investing in, its business plan, finances, and management. Company annual reports to shareholders often give a good overview of the company's historical performance and future prospects. Although the always colorful annual report is a promotional document that places the firm's performance in the most favorable light possible, the plain, black-and-white annual 10-k report to the SEC gives a much more guarded view of the company's operating strengths and weaknesses. The annual Proxy Statement (Def. 14A) also gives valuable insight concerning inside ownership and managerial compensation. Like virtually all SEC reports, most 10-k and Proxy Statement information can be downloaded for free at the EDGAR Web site. State regulators can also be a productive source of information, as are libraries and investments research Web sites on the Internet.

The SEC has recently increased its focus on microcap fraud in the Division of Enforcement in Washington, D.C., and in the regional and district offices around the country, to bring actions against fraudulent microcap companies, promoters, and brokers. In these microcap cases, the SEC seeks immediate relief, such as temporary restraining orders and asset freezes, as well as strong remedies such as permanent industry bars, registration revocations, and fines. In addition, the SEC has increased its use of trading suspensions to minimize investor harm by intervening early in ongoing market manipulations when there is misinformation about the issuer in the market.

Fraud on the Internet[11]

The Internet is a marvelous tool that allows investors to easily and inexpensively research investment opportunities. Unfortunately, the Internet is also an excellent tool for stock promoters and con artists. Increasingly, the Internet is a wild and wooly frontier for stock fraud and manipulation. The Internet allows individuals or companies to communicate with a large audience without spending a lot of time, effort, or money. Anyone can reach tens of thousands of individuals by building an Internet Web site, posting a message on an online bulletin board, entering a discussion in a live chat room, or sending mass e-mails. It is easy for con artists to make their messages look credible. At the same time, it is extremely difficult for investors to tell the difference between fact and fiction.

Hundreds of online investment newsletters have appeared on the Internet in recent years. Many appear to offer investors unbiased and free information about featured companies or stock picks. Although legitimate online newsletters can help investors gather valuable information, some are tools for fakes and swindlers. Companies sometimes pay the authors of online newsletters cash or securities to **tout** or aggressively recommend their stocks. Although legitimate companies pay public relations firms to promote their firm's image, federal securities laws require that all newsletters disclose who paid them, the amount, and the type of payment received. Illegal stock promoters and con artists fail to do so. Instead, they lie about payments received and their independence to bolster credibility with individual investors.

tout
Extravagantly praise.

Online bulletin boards on the Internet and proprietary networks, such as America Online, have become an increasingly popular forum for investors to share information. These bulletin boards typically feature "threads" of information focused on individual stocks or investment strategies. Although many messages reflect the sincere questions and opinions of individual investors, many are bogus and reflect the efforts of stock promoters and con artists who seek to use the Internet medium to widely spread false information. Fraudulent promoters sometimes pump up a company by pretending to reveal inside information about company management, new product announcements, mergers, acquisitions, or lucrative contracts. Deter-

[11]For up-to-the-minute information about the U.S. Securities and Exchange Commission and its Internet fraud enforcement activities, see the SEC's Web site at <http://www.sec.gov>.

mining the veracity of bulletin board information is made difficult by the fact that readers never know for certain with whom they are dealing. On bulletin boards, it is easy for those posting messages to hide behind multiple aliases. Persons claiming to be unbiased investors who have carefully researched a company may actually be insiders, disgruntled employees, large shareholders, or paid promoters. A single individual can easily create the illusion of widespread interest in small, thinly traded stocks by posting a series of messages under various aliases. Alternatively, a single individual can wrongly create a sense of widespread panic among shareholders by suggesting fraudulent behavior on the part of management, order cancellations, cost overruns, and so on.

Stock fraud on the Internet is a big problem. For example, on February 25, 1999, the SEC announced four enforcement actions against 13 individuals and companies, including one current and two former stock brokers, for committing fraud over the Internet. The filing of these cases followed the SEC's October 1998 Internet Sweep, the first orchestrated nationwide operation by the SEC to combat Internet fraud. These first Internet fraud cases involved a range of illicit Internet conduct including fraudulent spam (Internet junk mail), online newsletters, message board postings, and Web sites. The SEC's allegations include violations of the antifraud provisions and the antitouting provisions of federal securities laws. Suspected violations included making misrepresentations about company operations or failing to disclose adequately the nature, source, and amount of compensation paid by the touted company. Alleged creators of the fraudulent Internet touts purported to provide unbiased investment opinions, while at the same time receiving more than $450,000 in cash and approximately 2.7 million stock shares and options for their services.

pump-and-dump Market manipulation scheme in which promoters pump up a stock price so that they can sell their own inventories to unwitting investors.

scalping Fraudulent touting and sale of securities.

In a typical case, con artists sold their stock or exercised their options immediately following their buy recommendations. A classic **pump-and-dump** market manipulation scheme involved the securities of software developer Interactive Multi-Media Publishers, Inc. (IMP), of Akron, Ohio. The SEC alleged that corporate insider P. Joseph Vertucci and stockbroker Bruce Straughn sold to the public essentially worthless securities that were not registered with the SEC as required by federal securities laws. They also paid touters undisclosed compensation in the form of cheap or free stock to publicize IMP on the Internet and elsewhere. When IMP's price rose in the wake of these touts, Vertucci, Straughn, and the touters all sold their shares at a profit, a deceptive practice also known as **scalping.** Subsequently, IMP's stock price collapsed and the company ceased operations. The SEC sued the various participants involved for violations ranging from the fraudulent sale of securities to the fraudulent touting of securities. Enforcement remedies sought by the SEC included federal injunctions against further violations of federal securities laws, civil penalties, and disgorgement of ill-gotten gains.

One of the most compelling advantages of the Internet is that it allows the widespread dissemination of information on an almost cost-free basis. Electronic mail, or e-mail, is one of the Internet's most popular uses. However, like any inherently useful tool, the use of e-mail can be corrupted to serve illegal purposes. So-called e-mail spam is a favorite tool of con artists who seek to promote bogus investment schemes or to spread false information about a company over the Internet. Using low-cost but sophisticated software, spam artists can send literally thousands of e-mail messages to potential investors with a simple mouse click. E-mail spam allows the unscrupulous to target many more potential investors than ever could be reached by traditional cold-calling or mass-mailing techniques. In this way, the Internet has become a powerful new medium for illegal stock promotion and fraud.

To gain full advantage of the information-gathering potential of the Internet, investors must learn how to use this powerful new medium to invest wisely. To invest wisely and steer clear of Internet fraud, investors must rely on information reported by reputable individuals and institutions that can be independently verified. Investors should never make an investment decision based solely on what can be read in an online newsletter or bulletin board posting. This is especially true for investments in small, thinly traded companies that are not well known. No investor should contemplate investing in microcap stocks that do not file regular reports with the SEC unless such an investor is capable of independently investigating and verifying all pertinent financial and nonfinancial information.

Is the EMH Valid?

What Are the Riddles?

By the late 1970s, most financial economists had come to believe that the U.S. stock market is very efficient and that, apart from the long-term uptrend, stock prices were essentially unpredictable. But academics get their tenure by proving their elders wrong, and the thrust of much academic work during the 1980s and 1990s has been to search for cracks in the EMH. Some academic studies suggest predictable patterns in the stock market. Best-selling books continue to entice investors with stories of predictable stock market patterns that investors can exploit to earn extraordinary rates of return with low risk.

Over the years, several reputable studies have suggested anomalous patterns in stock market returns, such as the small-firm effect and the January effect. Stocks seem to do very well during the first few trading days of the new year. This appears especially true of small stocks. However, before rushing out to buy small stocks in late December, keep in mind that much of the apparent advantage of such bargain hunting can be offset by transactions costs. When these nonrandom effects are positive, they are small relative to the transaction costs involved with trying to exploit them. In addition, investors trying to exploit fundamental or announcement-related anomalies must be sensitive to problems tied to risk estimation. Small-company stocks tend to be riskier than large-company stocks, for example, and should give investors a greater reward. Moreover, the dependability of inexplicable return anomalies is notoriously poor. Just about the time investors recognize the potential for market-beating results, conditions change and profit-making opportunities tend to evaporate.

Researchers have used event study methodology for more than a generation to produce useful knowledge about how stock prices respond to new information. This approach works especially well when used to study ramifications of hard-to-anticipate economic events over brief periods of time. The underlying assumption is that stock prices should respond quickly and accurately to firm-specific information that is harmful or helpful. Any lag in the stock price response to important economic events should be short-lived. Long-lived price responses give investors the opportunity to profit from such information and are

TABLE 14.8 Event Studies Give Evidence That Is Reasonably Split between Underreaction and Overreaction

Event	Long-Term Preevent Return	Announcement Return	Long-Term Postevent Return
Earnings announcements	Not available	Positive	Positive
Dividend initiations	Positive	Positive	Positive
Dividend omissions	Negative	Negative	Negative
Initial public offerings	Not available	Positive	Negative
Mergers (acquiring firm)	Positive	Zero	Negative
New exchange listings	Positive	Positive	Negative
Proxy fights	Negative	Positive	Negative (or Zero)
Seasoned equity offerings	Positive	Negative	Negative
Share repurchases (open market)	Zero	Positive	Positive
Share repurchases (tenders)	Zero	Positive	Positive
Stock spin-offs	Positive	Positive	Positive (or Zero)
Stock splits	Positive	Positive	Positive

inconsistent with the EMH. The semistrong-form of the EMH is supported by literally hundreds of studies that document the absence of postannouncement abnormal returns tied to public announcements of important new information. Despite this, event study methodology has identified at least a dozen different types of important economic events for which there appears to be long-term underreaction or long-term overreaction. As shown in Table 14.8, the evidence in favor of semistrong-form and strong-form EMH appears somewhat mixed and controversial.[12]

However, in an efficient market, apparent underreaction will be about as frequent as apparent overreaction. If purported anomalies split about evenly between underreaction and overreaction, then taken as a whole, they are generally consistent with market efficiency. When analyzed one by one, stock market anomalies seem to give damning evidence about the reliability of the EMH. When viewed on an overall basis, the event study literature seems to provide evidence of return anomalies that can reasonably be attributed to chance.

Evidence in support of the strong form of the EMH is fairly weak. In favor of the strong-form EMH lies evidence that the overwhelming majority of professional money managers fail to beat a buy-and-hold strategy. Insider-based trading rules also do not work. However, at least some money managers consistently beat a buy-and-hold strategy (e.g., Warren Buffett). Insiders such as corporate officers, board members, and 10% equity holders appear to consistently earn abnormal returns. Stock exchange specialists also earn abnormal stock market returns based on their access to buy/sell information. Thus, although technical analysis is not productive, fundamental analysis may have modest potential for discovering bargains among small, low–price earnings, and neglected stocks. Still, such findings remain tenuous.

[12]See Eugene F. Fama, "Market Efficiency, Long-Term Returns, and Behavioral Finance," *Journal of Financial Economics* 49, no. 3 (September 1998), 283–306.

What Do We Know?

The clearest implication from the last half-century of stock market evidence is that a simple buy-and-hold strategy is the best portfolio management technique. Although some regular patterns appear in the stock market from time to time, they are not dependable. Some, such as the size effect, may simply reflect a better way of measuring risk than can be found with traditional measures. Others, such as popular calendar-related anomalies, come and go with unpredictable timing. Many so-called patterns in the stock market tend to self-destruct, as would be true in a perfectly efficient market. On an overall basis, stock market evidence strongly suggests that the weak form of the EMH is entirely valid. Technical analysis of the stock market is indeed worthless.

Despite obvious problems tied to the CAPM, APT, and other attempts to precisely measure the asset pricing process, investors must keep firmly in mind the evidence about how few professional investment managers seem capable of beating the unmanaged S&P 500 Index. When more than 90% of professional mutual fund managers fail to beat the market averages, one can only conclude that the market must be extremely efficient. The stock market may not be *perfectly* efficient, but it is *very* efficient. If it were easy to earn excess returns by exploiting predictable patterns in the stock market, a substantial number of talented investment professionals would do so. A true market inefficiency is an exploitable opportunity. If it is extraordinarily difficult to exploit stock market anomalies in a systematic way, then it is very hard to say that all available information is not properly incorporated into stock prices.

Psychology and the Stock Market

According to the EMH, current stock prices precisely reflect all relevant risk and return information. This implies that near-term stock price changes are random and independent. In a rational pricing environment, investing in the stock market is a "fair game" in which the expected excess return for each security is zero. Taken literally, this means that every stock at every point in time is an equally good buy or sell.

Billionaire investor George Soros, among others, disputes the notion that markets are perfectly efficient. Soros suggests that subtle psychological influences can help explain certain anomalous pricing situations. In the words of Soros, "Classical economic theory assumes that market participants act on the basis of perfect knowledge. That assumption is false. The participants' perceptions influence the market in which they participate, but the market action also influences the participants' perceptions. They cannot obtain perfect knowledge of the market because their thinking is always affecting the market and the market is affecting their thinking."[13]

Within this context, it becomes reasonable to regard the EMH as a working hypothesis regarding *primarily* rational investors that *typically* price securities in a rational fashion. Nevertheless, history seems to suggest that outbreaks of crowd behavior, typified by bouts of extraordinary optimism and extraordinary pessimism,

---

[13]See George Soros, *Soros on Soros: Staying Ahead of the Curve* (New York: John Wiley & Sons, 1995): 67.

can and do affect stock market prices. The age-old Wall Street adage to "buy fear and sell greed" reflects recognition that asset prices sometimes get out of whack with underlying economic fundamentals. Although most stocks appear to be fairly priced almost all the time, some stocks with hard-to-decipher economic characteristics will undoubtedly be mispriced from time to time. Similarly, manias and crashes sometimes occur when overall markets take leave of underlying economics.

Summary

- Whenever inexplicable patterns of abnormal stock market returns are detected in empirical studies of the stock market, an **average-return anomaly** is said to be found. A **joint test problem** exists because anomalous evidence that is inconsistent with a perfectly efficient market could be evidence of market inefficiency or a simple failure of CAPM or APT accuracy.
- On an annual rate-of-return basis, large-cap stocks tend to earn annual rates of return significantly below those of small-cap stocks during much of the modern era on Wall Street. This **small-cap effect** relates to companies listed on the New York Stock Exchange that rank in the bottom 20% in terms of market capitalization plus unlisted companies of comparable sizes. However, evidence of small-cap outperformance may be infected with **delisting bias.** By ignoring the effects of firms that are delisted for poor performance, many previous studies may have focused only on small-cap winners. Proper adjustment for the effects of delisting accounts for the entire small-cap effect.
- Despite lower risk, value stocks have ended to outperform growth stocks over sustained periods until the 1990s. This **value effect** may be another manifestation of the small-cap effect. Behavioral finance researchers use theories from the field of psychology to explain **investor overreaction** to both good and bad information. According to such reasoning, investors become too optimistic in the case of growth stocks and too pessimistic in the case of value stocks.
- The **January effect** has been documented in several studies that show unusually large positive rates of return for stocks during the first few trading days of the year. Although not as dramatic as the January effect, the **turn-of-the-month** effect has been suggested as an important seasonality in stock market returns. Especially strong stock market returns are experienced on the last two trading days of the month and on the first three trading days of the new month. Unusually good performance for stocks on the day prior to market-closing holidays has also been documented. Such **holiday effects** have become an article of faith among practitioners. Monday is the only day of the week that averages a negative rate of return. This **Monday effect** has given rise to the refrain: *Don't sell stocks on (blue) Monday!* Some researchers have also detected a **beginning-of-day effect** and **end-of-day effect.** Anomalous patterns in annual rates of return also occur over the course of the political cycle. This **political-cycle effect** is statistically significant. During the first and last years of a new presidential administration, annual returns before dividends are abnormally high.
- In a perfectly efficient market, good news results in a sharp upward spike in shareholder returns on the announcement day. Bad news results in a downward spike in shareholder returns on the announcement day. In both instances, there

should be no **postannouncement drift.** In the postannouncement period, stock returns should be random. For any news item to represent an important **economic event,** it must change the underlying perceptions of investors and result in an unusual movement in the stock's price during the **announcement period.** **Event studies** measure abnormal returns surrounding significant news items that may have important economic consequences for the firm. In event studies, the SCL is used to estimate **market-model abnormal returns,** or returns that cannot be explained by the CAPM. **Market-adjusted abnormal returns** are also estimated by subtracting the return on the market index from the rate of return on a given stock for a given day. A third common approach involves estimating **mean-adjusted abnormal returns** by subtracting the arithmetic mean return on a common stock from its daily return. **Cumulative abnormal returns** are the sum of abnormal returns over some event interval period, typically of one, two, or three days.

- Event study methodology has been used to discover inexplicable patterns in stock prices following announcements of important firm-specific information. Among the most important of these patterns is one tied to companies that report higher than expected earnings or a positive **earnings surprise.** Inconsistent with the EMH is evidence of a **postearnings announcement effect** whereby price movements tied to earnings announcements can continue for several weeks after the earnings announcement.
- Stock splits are merely cosmetic changes that increase the number of outstanding shares but have no direct effect on the market value of the firm. The **record date** is the date on which a shareholder must be a registered owner to receive the benefit of a stock split. This day follows the **announcement date** by roughly two weeks. The **pay date** is the date a split becomes effective. The **ex-split date** is the day following the pay date and marks the day on which the stock begins trading at the new postsplit price. Although 2:1 is the most common **split ratio,** other popular ratios for stock splits are 3:1, 3:2, and 5:4. Companies sometimes announce **reverse stock splits** in which the number of shares held by shareholders goes *down.* In a 1:3 reverse stock split, investors receive one share of stock for every three shares of stock held previously.
- There is a type of anomaly associated with stock splits called the **spin-off anomaly.** A spin-off is the separation of a business from a diversified corporation, in which the separation is accomplished through the distribution of stock in the new entity to current shareholders. Spin-offs of smaller companies from larger organizations often lead to favorable stock market performance. The **index effect** is the tendency of stocks to jump when Standard & Poor's announces that they are about to be added to the S&P 500.
- Accurate information about **microcap stocks,** or low-priced stocks issued by the smallest of companies, can be difficult to find. **Penny stocks** trade at prices below $1 and in low volumes. Many microcap stocks trade in the over-the-counter market and are quoted on the **OTC bulletin board** or the **pink sheets.**
- Dishonest brokers and stock promoters assemble small armies of high-pressure salespeople to make literally hundreds of telephone **cold calls** to potential investors. A classic example of cold calling abuse in the securities business is the **three-call technique.** Many investors find that once they buy a

house stock they cannot get what they paid for it, even if they decide to sell immediately.

- Companies sometimes pay the people who write online newsletters cash or securities to **tout** or aggressively recommend their stocks. In a typical case, con artists sold their stock or exercised their options immediately following their buy recommendations. A classic **pump-and-dump** market manipulation scheme is one in which promoters attempt to pump up a stock price so that they can sell their own inventories to unwitting investors. A deceptive practice also known as **scalping** involves the fraudulent touting and fraudulent sale of securities.

Questions

1. The bond market is perfectly efficient if
   a. it is possible to earn a risk-free arbitrage profit by simultaneously buying and selling the same asset.
   b. any security offering higher historical rates of return necessarily entails greater risk.
   c. any security offering a higher expected rate of return necessarily entails greater risk.
   d. only risk-free assets give a 0% expected rate of return.
2. By isolating deviations from predicted returns, CAPM and APT identify
   a. profit-making investment opportunities.
   b. proof of market inefficiency.
   c. market anomalies.
   d. proof that the market model is flawed.
3. A fundamental test of the CAPM is its
   a. ability to explain and predict investment rates of return.
   b. ability to explain the historical pattern of investment rates of return.
   c. logical and mathematical rigor.
   d. acceptance among academics and practitioners.
4. Meaningful stock market anomalies are
   a. easily explained by financial theory.
   b. seldom documented over extensive samples of data.
   c. statistically significant and offer meaningful risk-adjusted economic rewards to investors.
   d. related to above-average stock market risk.
5. The joint test problem results because
   a. CAPM specification bias is greater than that for APT.
   b. APT specification bias is greater than that for the CAPM.
   c. the market is sometimes inefficient.
   d. none of the above.

6. The popularity of low-cost index funds is a ringing endorsement of the
   a. EMH.
   b. joint test problem.
   c. investor's ability to profit from market anomalies.
   d. explanatory power of the CAPM.
7. Small-cap stocks tend to have low
   a. price/book ratios.
   b. sales revenues.
   c. book values.
   d. net income.
8. Superior rates of return on small-cap portfolios were most common during
   a. the late 1990s.
   b. the mid-1970s to mid-1980s.
   c. the 1920s.
   d. the most recent economic recessions.
9. Above-average rates of return for small cap stocks cannot be explained by
   a. delisting bias.
   b. required risk premiums.
   c. transaction costs.
   d. an apparent mania for Internet stocks.
10. A market anomaly is *not* associated with
    a. earnings announcements.
    b. a size effect.
    c. stock splits.
    d. a seasonal effect.
11. A well-known market anomaly is found between
    a. money supply growth and stock prices.
    b. P/E ratios and subsequent stock returns.
    c. P/E ratios and earnings momentum.
    d. stock prices and auditor changes.
12. To profit from time-related market anomalies, one might sell
    a. large-cap stocks prior to the turn of the year.
    b. small-cap stocks on the day after Labor Day.
    c. small-cap stocks at the open on Mondays.
    d. large-cap stocks one-half hour prior to the close.
13. The apparently superior long-term performance of small-cap stocks can be explained by
    a. lower systematic risk for small-cap stocks.

b. higher transaction costs for small-cap stocks.
c. lower unsystematic risk for small-cap stocks.
d. the risk-reducing advantages of diversification.

14. In the finance literature, small-cap stocks are small in terms of
    a. market value.
    b. sales.
    c. book value.
    d. all the above.
15. Transaction costs in the over-the-counter market are increased by
    a. payment for order flow.
    b. competition among multiple market makers.
    c. tight bid-ask spreads.
    d. the open outcry nature of this auction market.
16. The value effect
    a. can be explained as a necessary risk premium.
    b. suggests that dividend yield has become increasingly significant.
    c. describes outperformance by value stocks relative to growth stocks.
    d. has been especially prevalent during the late 1990s.
17. The investor overreaction hypothesis from behavioral finance can be used to explain superior performance by stocks with low
    a. dividend yields.
    b. earnings yields.
    c. revenue growth.
    d. P/E ratios.
18. In an efficient market, investor rates of return
    a. rise and fall with the economic cycle.
    b. rise gradually throughout the year.
    c. fall gradually throughout the year.
    d. none of the above.
19. Event studies provide evidence of market inefficiency when they detect
    a. positive abnormal returns during the announcement period.
    b. negative abnormal returns during the announcement period.
    c. no abnormal returns during the announcement period.
    d. postannouncement drift.
20. The CAPM is used to derive
    a. market-model abnormal returns.
    b. market-adjusted abnormal returns.
    c. mean-adjusted abnormal returns.
    d. none of the above.

Investment Application

How Much Is a Tulip Worth?[14]

During the 1600s, The Netherlands was a major sea power, accounting for roughly one-half of Europe's shipping trade. In 1602, Dutch firms trading with the East Indies combined to form the Dutch East India Company. The Dutch West India Company, founded in 1621, opened trade with the New World and western Africa. In 1624, the company colonized New Netherland, which consisted of parts of present-day New York, New Jersey, Connecticut, and Delaware. In 1626, Dutch colonists bought Manhattan Island from the Indians for goods worth about $24. They had established New Amsterdam (now New York City) the year before. Expanding trade and the international influence of a great colonial empire made Amsterdam a major commercial city and gave the Dutch one of the highest standards of living in the world. It was during this "golden age" that tulips were introduced to The Netherlands.

Conrad Gesner is credited with bringing the first tulip bulbs from Constantinople to Holland and Germany in 1559, where they became much sought after among the rich and well-to-do. By 1634, the rage for possessing tulips had spread to the middle classes of Dutch society. Merchants and shopkeepers began to vie with one another in the preposterous prices paid for simple tulip bulbs. Men became known to pay a fortune for a single bulb, not with the idea of reselling at a profit but simply for private admiration. Later, investors began to accumulate tulip bulbs for resale and trading profits.

Prices continued to rise until 1635 when persons were known to invest fortunes of as much as 100,000 florins in the purchase of 40 tulip bulbs. Various tulip bulbs fetched anywhere from 1,260 to 5,500 florins each. Of course, translating 17th-century prices in florins, or any early currency, into present-day values is made difficult by changing price levels and monetary systems. However, a present-day equivalent of 17th-century Dutch tulip prices can be estimated because an early account of the craze by Charles Mackay gives an example of a typical price, measured both in terms of florins and in terms of real goods received in trade.[15] This example, shown in Table 14.9, provides an opportunity to calculate a present-day equivalent price of the amount paid. Keep in mind throughout this example that one single tulip bulb was received in trade for *all* items listed.

The first item received in trade is two lasts of wheat. A last is a unit of weight or cubic measure that typically equals 4,000 pounds but can vary in different localities and for different loads.[16] Let's assume that 4,000 pounds is indeed the correct weight and that a bushel of wheat weighs 60 pounds, with the current price of wheat being roughly $3.30 per bushel. This gives a price of $440 for two lasts of wheat. Similarly, four lasts of rye at a price of $144.60 per ton, given 2,000 pounds per ton, are worth $1,152.

---

[14]For further details, see Mark Hirschey, "How Much Is a Tulip Worth?" *Financial Analysts Journal* 54, no. 4 (July/August 1998), 11–17.

[15]See Charles Mackay, *Memoirs of Extraordinary Popular Delusions and the Madness of Crowds* (London: Richard Bentley, 1841).

[16]*The World Book Dictionary,* vol. 2 (Chicago: Scott Fetzer, 1994): 1182.

TABLE 14.9 How Much Is a Tulip Worth?

	Holland price 1635 (in florins)	U.S. price 2000 (in dollars)
Two lasts of wheat	448	$440
Four lasts of rye	558	1,152
Four fat oxen	480	3,476
Eight fat swine	240	1,134
Twelve fat sheep	120	702
Two hogsheads of wine	70	4,792
Two tons of butter	192	7,571
Four tons of beer	32	6,109
One thousand pounds of cheese	120	6,980
A complete bed	100	1,410
A suit of clothes	80	750
A silver drinking cup	60	68
Total	2,500	$34,584

In 17th-century Holland, oxen were a valuable source of power in an agrarian economy. In the present-day United States, oxen have been replaced by a different kind of "animal," John Deere. To measure the current value in use of four fat oxen, one might reasonably measure the cost of a modest farm tractor, or a commensurate value of four fat beef animals, say, white-faced Herefords. Four Herefords are cheaper than a modest John Deere tractor and thus represent a conservative measure of the value represented by four fat oxen. With a typical weight of 1,100 pounds and an on-the-hoof price of $0.79 per pound, a conservative estimate of the value of four fat Herefords is $3,476. Similarly, the value of eight fat swine with an average weight of 225 pounds and an on-the-hoof price of $0.63 per pound is $1,134. The value of 12 fat sheep with an average weight of 65 pounds and an on-the-hoof price of $0.90 per pound is $702.

According to *The World Book Dictionary,* a hogshead is a large barrel or cask. In the United States, a hogshead holds from 63 to 140 gallons; in Great Britain it contains from 50 to 100 gallons.[17] Taking 75 gallons as a reasonable average, two hogsheads represent 150 gallons of wine. As a proxy for the cost of a medium-grade table wine, consider the $5.99 per bottle price for the 1996 Fetzer Vineyards Sundial Chardonnay (California). Each bottle holds 750 milliliters, and each liter equals roughly one quart. Taking four quarts to the gallon, this gives $4,792 as the present-day value of 150 gallons of wine.

Of course, a ton is a standard measure of weight, equal to 2,000 pounds (short ton) in the United States and Canada and equal to 2,240 pounds (long ton) in Great Britain. Thus, two long tons of butter at a retail price of $1.69 per pound has a value of $7,571. Popularly priced beer in 12-ounce cans, such as Budweiser, weighs 22 pounds per case. Given a typical retail price of $15 per case, this gives a price of $6,109 for four tons of beer.[18] A typical retail price for an 8-ounce brick

[17] *The World Book Dictionary,* vol. 1 (Chicago: Scott Fetzer, 1994): 1007.

[18] When used to measure liquids, a ton is sometimes measured by the volume of water that a ship will displace at sea level. The volume of a long ton of seawater is 35 cubic feet.

of Kraft Sharp Cheddar cheese is $3.49. This gives a present-day value of 1,000 pounds of cheese of roughly $6,980.

The present-day value of a complete bed, a suit of clothes, and silver drinking cups can vary widely, depending on personal preferences. For example, a typical retail price for a popular Serta Masterpiece Worthington queen-size foundation and mattress is $576. Frames usually run $59, with a headboard and footboard costing anywhere between $400 and $600, say, $500. Sheets, pillows, pillowcases, and a comforter might run an additional $275. This brings the present-day value of a complete bed to roughly $1,410. A moderately priced suit of clothes for a businessman or businesswoman might run $500–$1,000, say, $750. And finally, a moderately priced handmade *Alesandro* drinking cup made of sterling silver has a typical retail price of $68.

In sum, a representative calculation of the present-day price paid for a single Viceroy tulip bulb during 1635, near the height of the tulip mania in Holland, totals a whopping $34,584. Therefore, Mackay's example of individual tulip bulbs fetching anywhere from 1,260 to 5,500 florins implies a present-day price range from $17,430 to $76,085 each.

Mackay relates that interest in tulips grew so much that by 1636 regular marts for their sales were established on the Amsterdam Stock Exchange, in Rotterdam, Leyden, Alkmar, Hoorn, and other towns. Popular interest in tulips shifted from hobbyists and collectors to stock jobbers, speculators, and gamblers. People from all walks of life liquidated homes and real estate at ridiculously low prices to garner funds for tulip speculation. Tulip notaries and clerks were appointed to record transactions; intricate public laws and regulations were developed to control the tulip trade.

It was during the early autumn of 1636 that the more prudent began to liquidate their tulip holdings. Tulip prices began to weaken, slowly at first but then more rapidly. Soon, confidence was destroyed, and panic seized the market. Within six weeks, tulip prices crashed by 90% or more; widespread defaults on purchase contracts and liens were experienced. At first, the Dutch government refused to interfere and advised tulip holders to agree among themselves to some plan for stabilizing tulip prices and restoring public credit. All such plans failed. After much bickering, assembled deputies in Amsterdam agreed to declare null and void all contracts made at the height of the mania, or prior to the month of November 1636. Tulip contracts entered into subsequently to that date were to be settled if buyers paid 10% of earlier prices. However, this decision gave no satisfaction as tulip prices continued to fall, and the Provincial Council in The Hague was asked to invent some measure to stabilize tulip prices and public credit. Again, all such efforts failed. Tulip prices continued to crash even further. In Amsterdam, judges unanimously refused to honor tulip contracts on the grounds that those gambling obligations were not debts in the eyes of the law. No court in Holland would enforce payment. Dutch tulip collectors, stock jobbers, speculators, and gamblers who held tulips at the time of the collapse were left to bear ruinous losses. Those lucky enough to have profited were allowed to keep their gains. Tulip prices plunged to less than the present-day equivalent of one dollar each (or 10 guineas), and many of those who profited from the mania and the ensuing collapse apparently converted their gains into English or other funds to hide them from enraged countrymen. Commerce in Holland suffered a severe shock from which it took many years to recover.

A. Popular accounts of tulip bulb pricing in Holland during the 1634–36 period refer to the word *mania* when describing that episode. What is a mania?

B. Explain how crowd behavior can affect asset pricing and its implications for the EMH.

Selected References

Barberis, Nicholas. "Investing for the Long Run When Returns Are Predictable." *Journal of Finance* 55 (February 2000): 225–264.

Capaul, Carlo. "Asset-Pricing Anomalies in Global Industry Indexes." *Financial Analysts Journal* 55 (July/August 1999): 17–37.

Carpenter, Jennifer N., and Anthony W. Lynch. "Survivorship Bias and Attrition Effects in Measures of Performance Persistence." *Journal of Financial Economics* 53 (July 1999): 337–374.

Chordia, Tarun, and Bhaskaran Swaminathan. "Trading Volume and Cross-Autocorrelations in Stock Returns." *Journal of Finance* 55 (April 2000): 913–935.

Chow, Ying-Foon, and Ming Liu. "Long Swings with Memory and Stock Market Fluctuations." *Journal of Financial and Quantitative Analysis* 34 (September 1999): 341–367.

Dimson, Elroy, and Paul Marsh. "Murphy's Law and Market Anomalies." *Journal of Portfolio Management* 25 (Winter 1999): 53–69.

Hirschey, Mark. "How Much Is a Tulip Worth?" *Financial Analysts Journal* 54 (July/August 1998): 11–17.

Leibowitz, Martin L. "P/E Forwards and Their Orbits." *Financial Analysts Journal* 55 (May/June 1999): 33–47.

Lewellen, Jonathan. "The Time-Series Relations among Expected Return, Risk, and Book-to-Market." *Journal of Financial Economics* 54 (October 1999): 5–43.

Marshall, David A., and Nayan G. Parekh. "Can Costs of Consumption Adjustment Explain Asset Pricing Puzzles? *Journal of Finance* 54 (April 1999): 623–654.

Schultz, Paul. "Stock Splits, Tick Size and Sponsorship." *Journal of Finance* 55 (February 2000): 429–450.

Shumway, Tyler, and Vincent A. Warther. "The Delisting Bias in CRSP's Nasdaq Data and Its Implications for the Size Effect." *Journal of Finance* 54 (December 1999): 2361–2379.

Song, Moon H., and Ralph A. Walkling. "Abnormal Returns to Rivals of Acquisition Targets: A Test of the Acquisition Probability Hypothesis." *Journal of Financial Economics* 55 (February 2000): 143–171.

Starmer, Chris. "Experimental Economics: Hard Science or Wasteful Tinkering?" *Economic Journal* 109 (February 1999): F5–F15.

Zhou, Chunsheng. "Informational Asymmetry and Market Imperfections: Another Solution to the Equity Premium Puzzle." *Journal of Financial and Quantitative Analysis* 34 (December 1999): 445–464.

PART 7

Investment Management

Chapter 15 Mutual Funds
Chapter 16 Global Investing

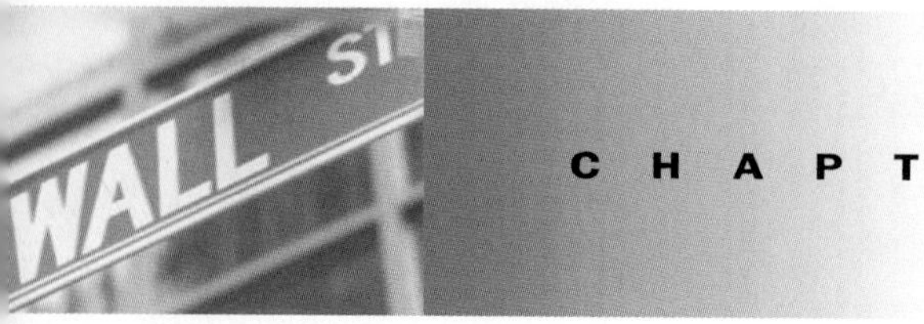

CHAPTER 15

Mutual Funds

Stock fund performance used to be evaluated on the simple basis of dividends plus realized and unrealized appreciation. Bond fund performance was measured by the percentage of interest income and capital appreciation or minus capital losses (if any). Now, the name of the game is risk-adjusted performance against a peer group of funds. Investors can choose among global flexible portfolio funds, international small-cap funds, Latin American funds, Pacific region funds, and Pacific region funds that exclude investments in Japan (called Pacific ex-Japan funds).

Unfortunately, when funds and fund managers are judged on the basis of peer-group performance, fund operators have incentives to seek peer-group classification with underperforming asset classes that might be misleading. For example, the rip-roaring bull market of the late 1990s paid handsome benefits to "growth" fund investors that bought companies with rapidly growing revenues or earnings growth potential. Badly underperforming were funds emphasizing "value," or stocks that look cheap on the basis of low price/earnings and low price/book value ratios. Value funds showed poor relative performance, and some value-fund managers scooped up growth stocks to boost returns relative to value funds.

To facilitate apples-to-apples performance comparisons, mutual fund watchdog Lipper Analytical Services, Inc., now places domestic stock funds into more than 20 different categories based on actual portfolio holdings and the riskiness of the investment style, rather than on investment objectives outlined in the mutual fund prospectus.[1] *This is important because, as every mutual fund shareholder knows, "actions speak louder than words."*

Mutual Fund Basics

What Is a Mutual Fund?

mutual fund Open-end investment company.

A **mutual fund** is an investment company that issues its shares to the public. The money it receives from shareholders is pooled and invested in a wide range of stocks, bonds, or money market securities to meet specific investment objectives.

[1] See Christopher Oster, "Most Big-Cap Growth Funds Return to Earth," *The Wall Street Journal,* August 18, 2000, C1, C22.

The various investments included in a fund's portfolio are handled by professional money managers in line with the stated investment policy of the fund. Some funds invest primarily in securities offering long-term growth, others in securities providing current income, and still others focus on particular industries or classes of securities. Many offer a combination of objectives.

As shown in Figure 15.1, mutual funds are a simple concept. In a mutual fund, groups of investors pool their financial resources to efficiently purchase various types of securities in the pursuit of a specific financial goal, such as building a substantial retirement nest egg. Each investor shares proportionately in the income and investment gains and losses that the fund's investments produce. Similarly, each investor shares proportionately in the brokerage expenses, management fees, and other operating costs incurred by the fund. In the most common type of mutual fund, investors can sell their shares or buy new shares each business day at the prorated per-share value of the fund's cash holdings and stock or bond investments. The per-share value of a mutual fund's stock, bond, and cash reserve holdings is called the fund's **net asset value.** Most mutual funds are also called **open-end investment companies** because the number of mutual fund shares issued at any point in time depends solely on investor demand. As investor demand grows, the number of shares issued by the fund and the dollar value of assets under management increase.

net asset value Per-share value of a mutual fund's stock, bond, and cash reserve holdings.

open-end investment companies Mutual funds that continuously offer to sell and buy shares.

All mutual funds have a portfolio manager, or investment advisor, who directs the fund's investments according to broadly recognized investment objectives. Common mutual fund objectives often include some combination of long-term growth, high current income, or stability of principal. Depending on its investment objective, mutual funds may invest in common stocks, various types of taxable and nontaxable bonds, or money market–type investments.

Mutual funds have been in existence for more than 75 years. The oldest mutual funds have survived a wide variety of turbulent economic and political conditions, including the Great Depression and World War II. Over their long history, mutual funds have never been more popular than they are today. According to the Investment Company Institute, investors in the United States have entrusted their advisors with more than $6 trillion in more than 10,000 mutual funds. Mutual fund assets account for roughly 20–25% of the total value of the stock and bond markets. The Investment Company Institute is a national trade association representing mutual funds, unit investment trusts, and closed-end funds. The institute is a nonprofit organization supported primarily by its membership. The purpose of the institute is to represent members and their shareholders in matters of legislation, regulation, taxation, public information, marketing, statistics, and economic and market research. The institute is also a clearinghouse for industry information and serves as spokesman and fact finder in many areas affecting its members, their shareholders, and the investing public.

FIGURE 15.1 Mutual Funds Are Cost-Efficient Financial Intermediaries

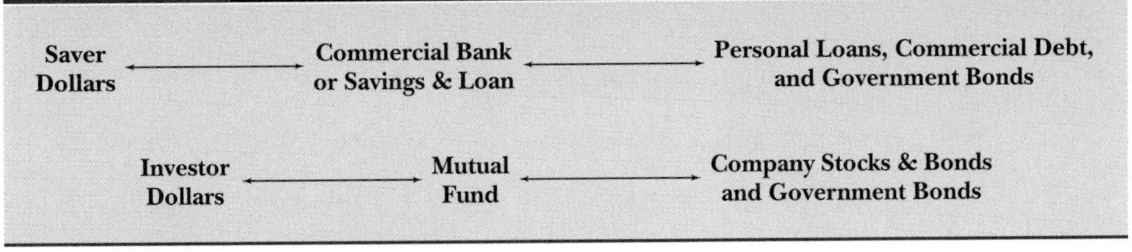

Mutual Fund Types

Investors have different objectives, so various types of mutual funds are needed to help them achieve their goals. Although there are thousands of funds to choose among, as shown in Table 15.1, most funds fit into one of three basic categories: money market, bond, and stock mutual funds.

TABLE 15.1 Types of Mutual Funds

Types of Mutual Funds	Investor Objective	What These Funds Hold	Capital Growth Potential	Current Income Potential	Stability of Principal
Money Market Funds					
Taxable money market	Current income, stability of principal	Cash investments	None	Moderate	Very high
Tax-exempt money market	Tax-free income, stability of principal	Municipal cash investments	None	Moderate	Very high
Bond Funds					
Taxable bond	Current income	Wide range of government and/or corporate bonds	None	Moderate to high	Low to moderate
Tax-exempt bond	Tax-free income	Wide range of municipal bonds	None	Moderate to high	Low to moderate
Common Stock Funds					
Balanced	Current income, capital growth	Stocks and bonds	Moderate	Moderate to high	Low to moderate
Equity income		High-yielding stocks, convertible bonds	Moderate to high	Moderate	Low to moderate
Value funds		Low P/E, P/B stocks	Moderate to high	Low to moderate	Low to moderate
Growth and income		Dividend-paying stocks	Moderate to high	Low to moderate	Low to moderate
Domestic growth	Capital growth	U.S. stocks with high potential for growth	High	Very low	Low
International growth		Stocks of companies outside U.S.	High	Very low to low	Very low
Aggressive growth	Aggressive growth of capital	Stocks with very high potential for growth	Very high	Very low	Very low
Small-cap		Stocks of small companies	Very high	Very low	Very low
Specialized		Stocks of industry sectors	High to very high	Very low to moderate	Very low to low

Money market mutual funds invest in cash reserves, or short-term IOUs issued by the government, corporations, or financial institutions. U.S. Treasury bills and bank certificates of deposit (CDs) that mature in 90 days or less are two popular types of cash investments. During recent years, money market mutual funds have become a popular alternative to bank checking and savings accounts.

money market mutual funds Funds that invest in cash reserves, or short-term IOUs.

Bond funds invest in debt instruments, or IOUs, issued by corporations or government agencies. In exchange for a bond investor's money, the issuer promises to repay the money at a specified date in the future and to make periodic interest payments. The amount of interest paid is fixed at the time of issue as a percentage of the amounts invested, which is why bonds are called fixed-income securities.

bond funds Funds that buy debt instruments.

Stock funds are one of the oldest and most popular types of mutual funds. Stocks represent equity ownership in corporations. Most successful corporations pay out at least some of their profits to stockholders in the form of dividends, although many reinvest most or all of their profits as they seek to increase future sales and profits. The primary goal of most common stock investors is to see the value of their shares increase over time through capital appreciation.

stock funds Funds that make equity investments.

Within each of these three broad categories are specific risk classes of funds. For example, stock funds range from relatively conservative equity income funds, to the mainstream growth and value funds, to aggressive small-company and international funds. Bond funds can be grouped according to short-term, intermediate-term, and long-term maturity and according to the credit quality or tax status of their holdings. Money market mutual funds have uniformly short-term portfolios but may specialize in government or corporate securities. **Index funds** closely track the performance of some broad stock or bond market benchmark.

index fund Mutual fund strategy designed to mimic the performance of some broad market benchmark.

Sources of Information

As might be expected for such a visible and rapidly growing industry, investors benefit from intensive coverage of mutual funds by the financial media. Several print publications such as *Smart Money* and *Forbes* offer intensive coverage and performance reviews on a semiannual basis. *Barron's* gives weekly financial commentary about the industry and up-to-date information about fund performance, management strategies, industry trends, and so on (Figure 15.2).

Lipper Inc., together with its affiliated companies, is the leading provider of data and analysis on the investment company business. As shown in Table 15.2, Lipper compiles extensive performance data on the mutual fund industry. Lipper currently tracks performance of approximately 32,000 funds worldwide with assets in excess of 6 trillion U.S. dollars. In the United States, Lipper clients include 96% of the fund management groups, which manage more than $2 trillion in assets. Elsewhere in the world, Lipper clients include the largest fund management groups that manage offshore and international investment funds worldwide. Lipper data are carried in more than 100 newspapers, in various magazines, on the radio, and on TV. In the United States, Lipper's media partners include *The Wall Street Journal, Barron's, USA Today,* CNN, CNBC, and *Forbes* magazine, among others. Internationally, Lipper data appear in *The Wall Street Journal Europe, Financial Times, The Asian Wall Street Journal, International Herald Tribune,* and so on. On the Internet at <http://www.lipperweb.com>, Lipper offers a multitude of useful tips and valuable information, including links to hundreds of useful mutual fund sites with information on mutual fund education, search tools, portfolio trackers, and asset allocators.

FIGURE 15.2 ***Barron's* Is a Top Source for Detailed Mutual Fund Industry Data, Commentary, and Analysis**

Source: *Barron's Mutual Funds,* July 10, 2000.

TABLE 15.2 ***Barron's* Publishes Detailed Weekly Information on More Than 10,000 Mutual Funds**

LIPPER MUTUAL FUND PERFORMANCE AVERAGES

Weekly Summary Report: Thursday, 4/06/2000
Cumulative Performances With Dividends Reinvested

NTA Mil.$	No. Funds		12/31/99- 04/06/00	03/30/00- 04/06/00	03/09/00- 04/06/00	01/06/00- 04/06/00	04/08/99- 04/06/00
General Equity Funds:							
362,604.3	446	Large-Cap Core Funds	+ 3.86%	+ 0.84%	+ 5.54%	+ 9.26%	+ 16.81%
493,231.2	511	Large-Cap Growth Funds	+ 6.45%	− 0.30%	− 0.16%	+ 14.19%	+ 29.70%
349,241.9	364	Large-Cap Value Funds	+ 1.73%	+ 1.70%	+ 8.95%	+ 5.27%	+ 6.92%
172,117.2	426	Multi-Cap Core Funds	+ 4.48%	+ 0.65%	+ 2.54%	+ 10.00%	+ 21.13%
521,011.2	411	Multi-Cap Growth Funds	+ 9.57%	− 0.95%	− 7.92%	+ 18.74%	+ 53.83%
163,021.8	518	Multi-Cap Value Funds	+ 2.02%	+ 2.01%	+ 10.05%	+ 5.25%	+ 6.95%
52,320.3	165	Mid-Cap Core Funds	+ 11.60%	− 0.21%	− 8.00%	+ 19.64%	+ 53.70%
120,178.3	245	Mid-Cap Growth Funds	+ 11.86%	− 1.76%	− 15.42%	+ 21.83%	+ 84.17%
32,124.1	194	Mid-Cap Value Funds	+ 4.42%	+ 1.14%	+ 4.28%	+ 8.80%	+ 19.57%
37,623.6	227	Small-Cap Core Funds	+ 8.99%	+ 0.00%	− 8.15%	+ 15.18%	+ 51.74%
78,987.0	282	Small-Cap Growth Funds	+ 10.83%	− 2.22%	− 17.08%	+ 19.69%	+ 85.84%
39,070.9	360	Small-Cap Value Funds	+ 4.97%	+ 1.29%	+ 2.26%	+ 8.85%	+ 24.67%
2,040.5	28	Specialty Dvsfd Eq Funds	+ 5.65%	+ 0.27%	− 1.23%	+ 5.79%	+ 10.21%
228,508.9	121	S&P 500 Funds	+ 2.34%	+ 0.92%	+ 7.14%	+ 7.14%	+ 12.39%
98,869.6	225	Equity Income Funds	+ 0.31%	+ 1.79%	+ 9.89%	+ 2.69%	+ 1.66%
2,750,950.8	4,523	Gen. Equity Funds Avg.	+ 5.67%	+ 0.41%	+ 0.33%	+ 11.54%	+ 30.78%
Other Equity Funds:							
39,650.0	70	Health/Biotechnology	+ 22.14%	+ 7.28%	− 7.06%	+ 22.95%	+ 49.72%
4,378.6	59	Natural Resources	+ 7.76%	− 0.05%	+ 6.02%	+ 8.19%	+ 32.45%
168,411.4	158	Science & Technol.	+ 11.51%	− 3.70%	− 17.77%	+ 23.05%	+ 111.54%
12,454.8	21	Telecommunication Funds	+ 6.93%	− 3.36%	− 12.13%	+ 15.77%	+ 54.32%
25,739.9	101	Utility Funds	+ 4.54%	− 1.21%	− 1.55%	+ 7.76%	+ 19.12%
11,166.7	76	Financial Services	− 0.13%	+ 1.80%	+ 16.52%	+ 5.35%	− 6.87%
7,520.7	149	Real Estate Fund	+ 3.47%	+ 2.19%	+ 6.97%	+ 3.86%	+ 5.07%
3,121.0	96	Specialty/Misc.	− 0.85%	+ 0.89%	+ 4.27%	+ 1.44%	+ 3.44%
1,804.7	36	Gold Oriented Funds	− 13.81%	+ 1.88%	− 5.06%	− 10.24%	− 2.96%
172,441.4	267	Global Funds	+ 1.81%	− 0.81%	− 1.54%	+ 7.92%	+ 31.08%
26,634.2	47	Global Small Cap Funds	+ 7.26%	− 2.84%	− 10.02%	+ 12.12%	+ 57.42%
258,969.9	704	International Funds	− 1.83%	− 1.82%	− 3.98%	+ 4.65%	+ 32.16%
14,921.6	77	Int'l Small Cap Funds	+ 7.45%	− 5.47%	− 13.57%	+ 11.60%	+ 76.05%
26,820.2	166	European Region Fds	+ 4.14%	− 1.41%	− 5.94%	+ 8.96%	+ 29.08%
8,591.1	60	Pacific Region Funds	− 7.41%	− 5.47%	− 4.90%	+ 0.51%	+ 55.92%
8,467.0	48	Japanese Funds	− 8.85%	− 4.34%	− 1.13%	+ 1.69%	+ 58.73%
5,703.3	88	Pacific Ex Japan Funds	− 3.28%	− 6.12%	− 7.27%	+ 0.37%	+ 55.27%
875.5	27	China Region Funds	+ 6.51%	− 7.60%	− 9.29%	+ 15.17%	+ 67.64%
23,217.5	196	Emerging Markets Funds	+ 0.51%	− 3.59%	− 8.22%	+ 2.50%	+ 53.49%
2,145.0	54	Latin American Funds	+ 2.53%	− 1.55%	− 8.06%	+ 9.81%	+ 41.08%
82.8	2	Canadian Funds	+ 10.51%	+ 0.22%	+ 3.21%	+ 16.16%	+ 44.05%
550,674.2	1,772	World Equity Funds Avg.	− 0.26%	− 2.42%	− 5.17%	+ 5.38%	+ 39.46%
3,574,068.1	7,025	All Equity Funds Avg.	+ 4.29%	− 0.30%	− 1.19%	+ 9.93%	+ 33.07%
Other Funds:							
66,588.6	244	Flexible Portfolio	+ 3.36%	+ 0.71%	+ 2.50%	+ 6.79%	+ 11.84%
22,766.0	112	Global Flex Port.	+ 1.23%	− 0.18%	− 0.08%	+ 5.48%	+ 18.72%
168,248.1	485	Balanced Funds	+ 2.68%	+ 0.87%	+ 4.09%	+ 5.67%	+ 8.01%
859.9	11	Balanced Target	+ 3.65%	+ 0.85%	+ 4.00%	+ 6.21%	+ 11.27%
8,806.8	65	Conv. Securities	+ 8.10%	− 0.41%	− 4.82%	+ 13.66%	+ 35.91%
39,903.4	104	Income Funds	+ 1.85%	+ 0.76%	+ 2.89%	+ 3.52%	+ 4.90%
20,988.9	262	World Income Funds	+ 1.18%	− 0.04%	+ 0.01%	+ 1.34%	+ 2.89%
451,738.8	2,187	Fixed Income Funds	+ 1.46%	+ 0.34%	+ 0.47%	+ 1.85%	+ 0.59%
4,353,968.6	10,495	Long-Term Average	+ 3.49%	− 0.07%	− 0.45%	+ 7.67%	+ 23.22%
N/A		Long-Term Median	+ 2.37%	+ 0.40%	+ 0.92%	+ 5.59%	+ 12.85%
N/A		Funds with a % Change	+ 10,210	+ 10,091	+ 10,164	+ 10,212	+ 9,585

(continued)

TABLE 15.2 ***(continued)***

NTA Mil.$	No. Funds	12/31/99-04/06/00	03/30/00-04/06/00	03/09/00-04/06/00	01/06/00-04/06/00	04/08/99-04/06/00
	Securities Market Indexes					
Value	**U.S. Equities:**					
532.50	Russell 2000 Index P	+ 5.50%	+ 0.14%	− 12.14%	+ 12.03%	+ 33.16%
658.79	NYSE Composite P	+ 1.31%	+ 2.03%	+ 9.25%	+ 4.98%	+ 5.53%
1,879.19	S&P Industrials	+ 2.02%	+ 0.71%	+ 5.04%	+ 6.90%	+ 16.22%
1,501.34	S&P 500 P	+ 2.18%	+ 0.90%	+ 7.11%	+ 6.97%	+ 11.71%
11,114.30	Dow Jones Ind. Avg. P	− 3.33%	+ 1.22%	+ 11.02%	− 1.23%	+ 8.99%
Value	**International Equities:**					
20,223.61	Nikkei 225 Average P	+ 6.81%	− 1.07%	+ 2.85%	+ 11.31%	+ 20.05%
6,451.14	FT S-E 100 Index	− 6.91%	+ 0.09%	− 1.24%	+ 0.06%	+ 0.21%
7,446.21	DAX Index	+ 7.01%	− 2.60%	− 6.33%	+ 15.00%	+ 46.90%
	Fund Management Companies					
Value:						
3,694.29	Stock-price Index	+ 14.61%	+ 0.40%	+ 10.27%	+ 19.47%	+ 33.87%

P-Price only index. Calculated without reinvestment of dividends. The Nikkei index value is divided by 10 due to space limitation. Source: Lipper Analytical Services Inc., Summit, New Jersey 07901

Source: *Barron's*, April 10, 2000, F127.

Chicago-based Morningstar.com is another leading provider of mutual fund, stock, and variable-insurance investment information. Morningstar does not own, operate, or hold any interest in mutual funds, stocks, or insurance products. As a result, investors have come to rely on Morningstar for unbiased data and analysis and candid editorial commentary. Morningstar was launched with the introduction of the *Mutual Fund Sourcebook* in 1984. At that time, mutual fund industry investment performance information was either unavailable or priced out of the reach of individual investors. Over the years, Morningstar has created a diversified selection of products and services aimed at individual investors and professionals. For example, financial planners and other investment professionals turn to Morningstar for tools helping them research, analyze, and support their investment ideas. Broadcast and cable television, newspapers, and magazines seek out Morningstar editors and analysts for authoritative commentary about breaking financial news on mutual funds. Morningstar was the first to track the performance of individual fund managers. Morningstar was also the first to calculate funds' price/earnings and price/book ratios and the first to do fundamental analysis on the underlying stocks held by various funds. Morningstar's investment style box and star rating system have become industry standards.

Morningstar.com (<http://www.morningstar.com>) is a perennial pick as a top Web site for investment information (Figure 15.3). Making a hit with cyber-investors has been easy with Morningstar.com's unique blend of proprietary reports with plenty of analysis, interactive tools, regular news updates and market reports, and a special investor-education section. Of course, the Internet has become a convenient source for timely information on individual mutual funds and an extraordinary amount of up-to-date information about mutual fund investing. Millions of investors rely on electronic media to obtain news and investment and

FIGURE 15.3 Morningstar.com Is a Top Choice for Mutual Fund Investor Information

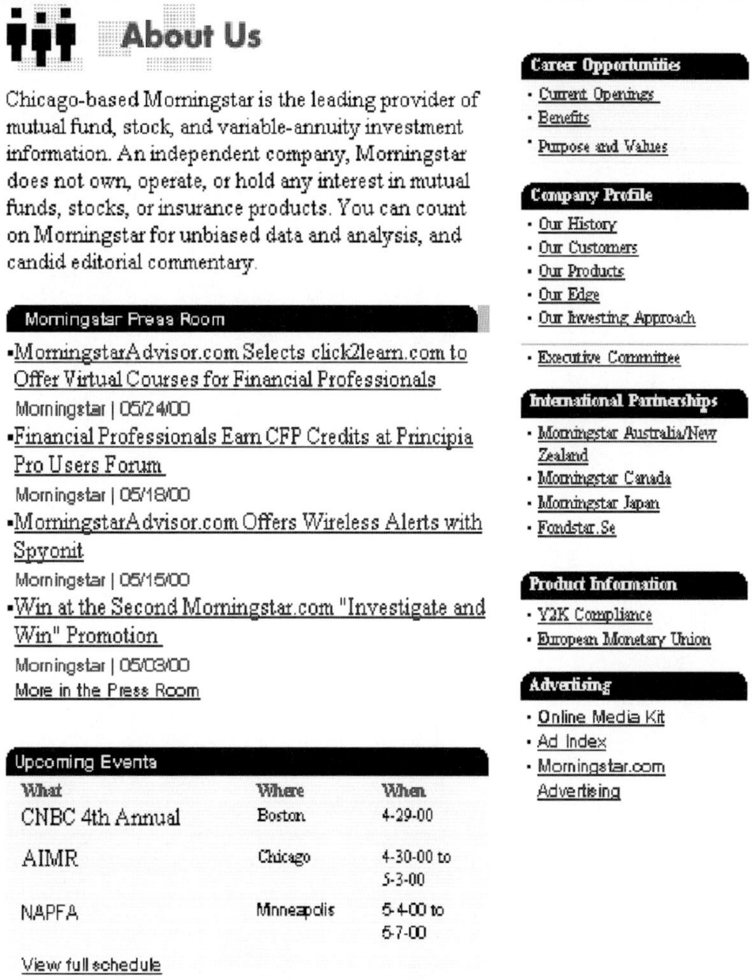
About Us
Chicago-based Morningstar is the leading provider of mutual fund, stock, and variable-annuity investment information. An independent company, Morningstar does not own, operate, or hold any interest in mutual funds, stocks, or insurance products. You can count on Morningstar for unbiased data and analysis, and candid editorial commentary.
Morningstar Press Room
•MorningstarAdvisor.com Selects click2learn.com to Offer Virtual Courses for Financial Professionals
Morningstar | 05/24/00
•Financial Professionals Earn CFP Credits at Principia Pro Users Forum
Morningstar | 05/18/00
•MorningstarAdvisor.com Offers Wireless Alerts with Spyonit
Morningstar | 05/15/00
•Win at the Second Morningstar.com "Investigate and Win" Promotion
Morningstar | 05/03/00
More in the Press Room
Upcoming Events
What | Where | When
CNBC 4th Annual | Boston | 4-29-00
AIMR | Chicago | 4-30-00 to 5-3-00
NAPFA | Minneapolis | 5-4-00 to 5-7-00
View full schedule
Career Opportunities
· Current Openings
· Benefits
· Purpose and Values
Company Profile
· Our History
· Our Customers
· Our Products
· Our Edge
· Our Investing Approach
· Executive Committee
International Partnerships
· Morningstar Australia/New Zealand
· Morningstar Canada
· Morningstar Japan
· Fondstar.Se
Product Information
· Y2K Compliance
· European Monetary Union
Advertising
· Online Media Kit
· Ad Index
· Morningstar.com Advertising

Source: <http://www.morningstar.com>.

account information. Some of the best sites for mutual fund investors are described in Table 15.3. Among these is <http://www.vanguard.com>, the investment Web site of the Vanguard Group of investment companies. Since its founding in 1974, Vanguard has emerged as a leader in the mutual fund industry by providing competitive investment performance, a diversity of fund alternatives, and the lowest operating expenses in the industry, 0.28% versus the fund industry average of 1.25% per year. It is uncommon, perhaps unprecedented, for a firm with what is generally regarded as the highest service quality to also be the lowest-cost provider of services. Vanguard has also taken the industry lead in full disclosure and investor education. This makes Vanguard's emphasis on candor a benefit to all mutual fund investors.

TABLE 15.3 Web Sites for the Ten Largest Mutual Fund Groups Give Investors Valuable Investment Tools

Fund Group	Internet Address	Online Trading	Portfolio Tracking	Interactive Planning Tools	Comments
American Century	<http://www.americancentury.com>	American Century funds; all securities via American Century Brokerage	Yes, all securities	Roth IRA conversion	Basic description of investment philosophy
Dreyfus	<http://www.dreyfus.com>	Yes, Dreyfus funds	No	Roth IRA conversion; investment calculator	Good basic investor information
Fidelity	<http://www.fidelity.com>	Fidelity funds, all securities via Fidelity Brokerage	Yes, all securities	College, asset allocation, retirement, estate, Roth IRA conversion	Extensive site, very user-friendly. One of the best on the Web
Janus	<http://www.janus.com>	Yes, Janus funds	Yes, Janus funds only	College, retirement, miscellaneous	Very basic
Charles Schwab	<http://www.schwab.com>	Schwab funds; all securities via Schwab brokerage	Yes, all securities	College, asset allocation, retirement, Roth IRA conversion	Broad investment site; lots of attractive features
Scudder	<http://www.scudder.com>	Scudder funds; all securities via Scudder Brokerage	Yes, all securities	College, asset allocation, retirement, estate, Roth IRA conversion, monthly budget	Wealth of investment information, accessible
Strong funds	<http://www.strong-funds.com>	Strong funds selected other funds	Yes, all securities	College, asset allocation, retirement, Roth IRA conversion	Features for investors of all ages
T. Rowe Price	<http://www.troweprice.com>	T. Rowe Price funds; all securities via T. Rowe Price brokerage	Yes, all mutual funds	College, Roth IRA conversion, portfolio review, retirement planner	Investment perspectives from fund managers. Very good site
TIAA-CREF	<http://www.tiaa.org>	Yes, TIAA funds	Yes, TIAA funds	College	Good basic site
Vanguard	<http://www.vanguard.com>	Vanguard funds; all securities via Vanguard Brokerage	Yes, all securities	College, asset allocation, retirement, estate Roth IRA conversion	Wonderful online library, extensive investment tools. Simply the best on the Web

Advantages and Disadvantages

Mutual Fund Advantages

Perhaps the preeminent advantage offered by mutual funds is broad diversification. Most mutual funds hold securities from literally hundreds of different issuers spread across a variety of asset categories. Diversified stock funds typically hold large- and small-company stocks broadly spread across a variety of industries and economic sectors. Diversified bond funds hold a wide assortment of bonds issued by numerous issuers with an eclectic mix of maturity structures, coupon payment patterns, and credit quality. By pooling their resources, shareholders in diversified stock and bond funds are able to achieve a level of diversification that few investors could achieve on their own. In the case of specialized stock and bond funds, portfolio holdings may be fairly uniform in terms of the general characteristics of issuing corporations, but a variety of issues is held to minimize the risk of adverse operating results at any single holding. When investors hold a carefully selected mix of specialized mutual funds, they are also able to spread their assets among many different securities and security asset classes. This also sharply reduces the risk of loss from problems with any one company or asset class of securities.

A second prime advantage enjoyed by mutual fund shareholders is the ability to retain professional investment management at reasonable cost. Professional investment managers make decisions about which securities to buy and sell based on extensive company research, market information, and insight provided by skilled securities traders. Professional management is a valuable service because few investors have the time or expertise to carefully investigate the tens of thousands of individual stocks and bonds available in the financial markets. Similarly, few individual investors have the time or patience to manage their personal investments on a daily basis.

Another advantage of investing in mutual funds is investor convenience. Open-end mutual funds are required to redeem their shares any business day for the net asset value per share. Using conventional surface (or "snail") mail, payment must be received within seven business days. Most mutual funds also offer investors the opportunity to buy and sell shares over the Internet or using toll-free telephone numbers. At many financial institutions offering a "family" of mutual funds, money can also be moved easily from one fund to another as investor needs or investment priorities change. Automatically investing a fixed amount per month, or redeeming a fixed amount per month, is made easy by electronic transfers of funds between the investor's bank account and several large mutual fund firms. At the investor's option, interest and dividend income can be paid directly to the mutual fund investor or automatically reinvested. Most mutual funds also provide extensive record-keeping services free of charge. This helps investors keep track of transactions, follow fund performance, and complete tax returns. Fund performance can easily be monitored in daily newspapers, such as *The Wall Street Journal,* by telephone, or at a number of interesting Web sites on the Internet.

Mutual Fund Disadvantages

Unlike federally insured bank deposits, the amount of money invested in a mutual fund is not insured or guaranteed by the Federal Deposit Insurance Corporation (FDIC) or any other agency of the U.S. government. The market value of any

FIGURE 15.4 **No-Load Mutual Funds Work Best for Small Investors, but Individual Stocks Can Be Cheaper for Large Investors**

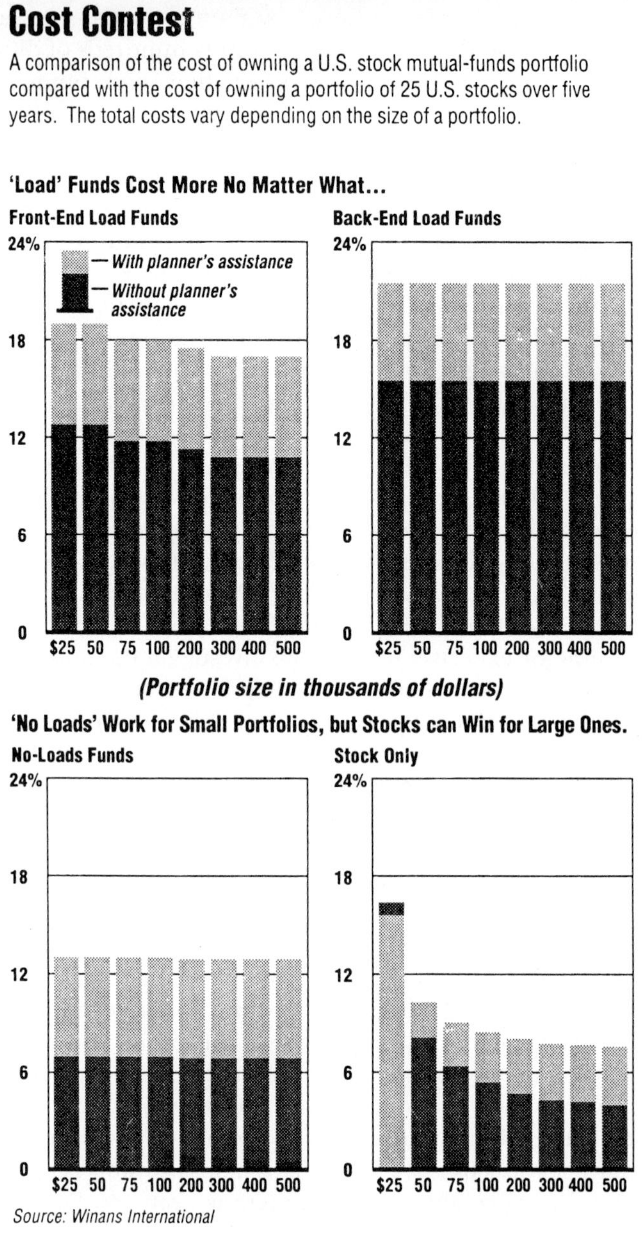

Source: *The Wall Street Journal,* August 14, 1998, C1.

mutual fund can fluctuate, even if the fund invests in low-risk government bonds or money market securities. Although mutual funds are extensively regulated by the U.S. Securities and Exchange Commission (SEC) and by state securities officials, such regulation is typically limited to the need to provide investors with full disclosure of information needed to make sound investment decisions. Mutual fund regulation does not eliminate the risk of an investment falling in value. Money invested in the stock and bond markets through mutual funds can be expected to vary on a day-to-day basis. At times, this volatility can be significant.

Because mutual funds typically hold a large number of securities, fund shareholders give up the chance to earn the sometimes-outstanding returns earned on individual stocks and bonds. Although diversification eliminates the risk of catastrophic loss from holding a single security, it also eliminates the potential for huge returns from a single holding whose value skyrockets. Anyone who bought Internet darlings such as Amazon.com, America Online, eBay, or Yahoo! and sold them at a profit knows how the meteoric rise in the stock of a single company can boost the rate of return earned on a small portfolio. It also is important to remember that diversification does not protect any investor from the risk of loss from an overall decline in financial markets. When investors fear the onset of economic recession, technology stocks tend to fall as companies cut back on orders for new plant and equipment. Although devastating losses from the decline in any single holding can be limited, mutual fund investors who invest in technology-sector mutual funds can anticipate significant losses following a severe downturn in the overall economy.

A final, but avoidable, disadvantage of investing through some mutual funds is related to high management fees and sales commissions. In most instances, mutual funds represent a low-cost way to buy securities when compared with buying individual stocks and bonds with the help of a traditional broker. However, as shown in Figure 15.4, mutual fund costs can sometimes greatly diminish after-tax returns on large investment portfolios of $100,000 and more. This is especially true of **load funds** purchased through retail brokers and investment professionals because most broker-sponsored mutual funds entail sales commissions totaling at least 1–3% to as much as 4–8½% of the amount invested. Sometimes, mutual fund commissions are repaid up front. Sometimes, they are deferred. In either case, sales commissions dramatically cut the total return earned by mutual fund shareholders. By contrast, **no-load funds** are sold directly by mutual fund management companies to investors without commission. High operating expenses at some funds can also offset the efficiencies expected through mutual fund ownership. It is vital that mutual fund shareholders carefully compare the costs of mutual fund alternatives to ensure an efficient selection.

load fund
Fund that charges shareholders a sales commission.

no-load fund
Fund sold without sales commission.

Mutual Fund Performance

Sources of Investment Return

Mutual fund performance is best measured by the fund's **total return** comprising dividend and interest income and realized and unrealized appreciation. A fund's total return is reflected by the change in the value of an investment in the fund over time.

total return
Dividend and interest income, and realized and unrealized appreciation.

WALL STREET WISDOM 15.1

Indexing: "If You Can't Beat 'em, Join 'em"

On April 6, 2000, the Vanguard 500 Index Fund surpassed Fidelity Magellan as the world's largest mutual fund. This event marked an important signpost in the history of investment management. Long a recognized investment strategy among institutional pension fund managers, the indexing concept has clearly caught on with mutual fund investors. Industry estimates place the total value of indexed assets at roughly 12% of the overall market, or in the range of $1.5 trillion. In the mutual fund industry, index funds claim roughly $250 billion, or less than 5% of the industry. Although somewhat small as a share of industry assets, indexing is rapidly growing in popularity.

Like the Vanguard 500 Index Fund, most popular index funds are designed to mimic the Standard & Poor's 500 Index. However, indexing can be used to match the returns of any stock or bond market benchmark, or index. When an index strategy is used, the portfolio manager is replaced by a computer staff that simply attempts to replicate the investment results of the target index by holding all or a representative sample of index securities. Index funds make no attempt to use stock selection or traditional active management techniques to beat the market. Similarly, index funds shun bets on individual stocks or narrow industry sectors in an attempt to outpace the overall market. Indexing can be described as a passive investment approach that emphasizes broad diversification and low portfolio-trading activity.

The popularity of indexing is derived from the intellectual foundation provided by the efficient market hypothesis. One simply cannot expect the average investor to outperform the market averages. Similarly, it is impossible for all mutual fund investors to outperform the overall stock market. For example, since World War II, the stock market has provided investors with an average return of 12–14% per year before expenses. Some investors, because of luck or skill, have earned more than average. Others have not fared as well. Yet the 12–14% historical average return is, by definition, the entire "pie" that investors are able to divide prior to the payment of investment costs. Investors who gain their fair share of the pie and pay typical mutual fund costs earn somewhat below the 12–14% market return.

Mutual fund costs come in the form of advisory fees, distribution charges, operating expenses, portfolio brokerage and other trading costs, 12b-1 charges, and sales commissions (for load funds). In 1999, Lipper Inc. reported that the average general equity fund had an annual expense ratio of 1.41% of investor assets. Traditional equity fund managers with a typical portfolio turnover rate of 85% per year incur portfolio brokerage and trading costs of 0.5–1% annually. When selling commissions and other costs are considered, it is easy to see how the typical equity mutual fund underperforms the broad market averages by 3–4% per year.

The key advantage of index fund investing is its relatively low cost. Index funds pay minimal advisory fees, if any, and also minimize operating expenses and portfolio transaction costs. The strategy is especially appropriate for long-term investors who seek a very competitive long-term investment return through broadly diversified portfolios. Because index funds are designed to provide returns that closely track returns on their benchmark indexes, index funds carry all the risks normally associated with the type of asset that the fund holds. For investors seeking small-capitalization stocks, the Russell 2000 Index is the most widely accepted benchmark. In often volatile developed and emerging global markets, indexing is a reliable way for reducing the impact of dramatic price swings and high trading costs. A strong case can also be made for indexed bond investments that follow specific maturity sectors, such as short-term, intermediate-term, or long-term.

In short, indexing is a time-tested investment strategy that offers long-term investors an efficient means for achieving market-matching results that typically beat professionally managed mutual funds.

See: Kay Larsen, "Fund Managers Show Optimism in Survey," *The Wall Street Journal,* June 14, 2000, C23.

Mutual funds produce current income for shareholders from investments in interest-bearing securities, such as short-term and long-term bonds, and from dividends paid on common stocks owned by the fund. After expenses, all mutual fund income must be paid out in full every year to fund shareholders in the form of income dividends. Depending on the type of fund, income dividends may be paid on a monthly basis for money market funds and short-term bond funds or on a quarterly, semiannual, or annual basis for stock and long-term bond funds. Fund shareholders can choose to receive income dividends in cash or to have their dividends reinvested in additional shares of the fund. Shareholders designate the method of dividend payment when an account is opened but may change their selection at any time.

Annual income produced by the fund, expressed as a percentage of the fund's current market value, is known as its yield. For example, a common stock fund with a share price, or net asset value, of $25 that pays out $1 per year in income has a yield of 4% (= $1 ÷ $25). Of course, not all mutual funds seek to produce investment income. Many stock funds, especially growth and aggressive-growth funds, primarily seek capital appreciation from the securities they hold and may produce little or no investment income.

When securities that a fund has purchased rise in value, the fund generates an unrealized capital gain. These **unrealized capital gains** raise the net asset value (or market value) of its shares. This gain remains unrealized until the fund or an individual sells his or her shares. If the fund itself sells securities at a profit, a taxable capital gain is realized. These realized capital gains are periodically paid out to mutual fund shareholders in the form of a **capital gains distribution.** When a fund pays out realized capital gains, the fund's share price is reduced by the amount of the distribution. As in the case of income dividends, capital gains distributions may be received by a shareholder in cash or reinvested for further appreciation. Of course, stocks and bonds can also fall in value, and funds periodically incur capital losses that reduce the market value of fund shares. Likewise, individual investors can suffer losses on their mutual fund investments by selling shares for a price lower than the investor paid for them.

unrealized capital gains Increase in fund value caused by a rise in the value of fund investments.

capital gains distribution Payment of realized capital gains.

Mutual Fund Expenses

All mutual funds have ongoing expenses that are deducted from interest and dividend income. Only after such expenses have been paid is any remaining net income passed along to mutual fund shareholders in the form of dividends. Basic mutual fund operating expenses include investment advisory fees and the costs of legal and accounting services, postage, printing, and related services. The total of these costs expressed as a percentage of the fund's average net assets during the year is called the fund's **operating expense ratio.**

operating expense ratio Operating expenses expressed as a percentage of fund assets.

Annual expense ratios typically range from a low of about 0.2% (or $20 per $10,000 in assets) to 2% ($200 per $10,000 in assets). Annual expense ratios are typically lowest for money market mutual funds and highest for stock funds. A conventional operating expense charge for money market funds falls in the range of 0.5% per year. For stock funds, operating expenses of 1.5% per year are common. Operating expense ratios for bond funds typically fall somewhere in the range between 0.5% and 1.5%, depending on fund size and investment philosophy. Operating expense ratios tend to be lowest for large funds that invest in the most actively traded (liquid) stocks and bonds. Operating expense ratios tend to be highest for small or specialized funds that invest in illiquid sectors of the market or in smaller and riskier foreign markets.

Regardless of the type of mutual fund, investors must be aware of fees and expenses because they directly affect the fund's total return. Those costs are important to money market fund and bond fund investors because they are the most important source of any differences in yield observed among comparable money market and bond funds. Once bond fund investors have chosen an acceptable level of credit quality and average maturity, most funds will have a similar gross yield before expenses. High expenses have the potential to consume a substantial portion of this amount. For example, if a short-term corporate bond fund has a gross yield of 6.5% and an industry-average expense ratio of 0.86%, its net yield to the investor is only 5.64%. If a similar but cost-efficient fund has the same gross yield but an expense ratio of only 0.3%, the net yield to the investor would be 6.2%. The interest income received by an investor in the low-cost fund is roughly 10% greater than that received by an investor in the fund of average efficiency. Compounding the problem of high-cost funds is the tendency of high-cost fund managers to take on additional risk in the hope of receiving higher returns. Low-cost funds have the potential to provide competitive returns with a lower level of risk than other funds.

load charges Sales commissions.

front-end loads Commissions paid at the time of fund purchase.

low-load funds Funds that charge sales fees ranging from 1% to 3%.

back-end load Commissions paid when a fund is sold.

12b-1 fees Marketing expenses.

level load Portion of a 12b-1 fee used to compensate brokers and investment advisers for selling shares of the fund.

Many mutual fund investors also pay one-time sales commissions, or **load charges.** Sales loads are often charged at the time of purchase as a simple percentage of the amounts invested. Such **front-end loads** typically range from 4% to 8.5% (or \$400–\$850 per \$10,000 invested). Funds that charge sales fees ranging from 1% to 3% (or \$100–\$300 per \$10,000 invested) are called **low-load funds.** Another form of sales charge is the **back-end load,** which is assessed when an investor sells fund shares. Back-end loads are sometimes called contingent deferred sales charges because their timing depends on the investor's sale decision. Back-end loads may be as high as 6% for redemptions that take place within one year of the original investment. These charges typically decline over time and may disappear by the seventh year after the original purchase of fund shares.

Some funds also charge investors an additional amount to cover marketing and distribution costs. These marketing charges are sometimes called **12b-1 fees,** after the 1980 U.S. SEC rule that permits this practice. According to SEC regulations, a fund is required to disclose a 12b-1 fee in its stated expense ratio. There is no legal limit to the 12b-1 fees that a fund may charge, but such fees normally run between 0.25% and 1% of the fund's average annual net assets. At 1%, the 12b-1 charge to the investor is \$100 per \$10,000 in fund assets per year. The term **level load** describes the portion of a 12b-1 fee used to compensate brokers and investment advisers for selling shares of the fund. If a fund charges a 12b-1 fee in excess of 0.25%, it may not call itself a no-load fund even if it has no other sales charges. Funds that are sold without front-end or back-end load charges are called no-load funds.

Like all operating expenses, 12b-1 fees are deducted directly from a fund's earnings. Some funds use 12b-1 charges instead of an up-front sales commission to compensate salespersons for marketing their products. For example, a broker or dealer might receive an annual 12b-1 fee equal to 0.25% of the mutual fund assets held by his or her customers as recurring compensation for promoting the fund, as well as ongoing compensation for answering mutual fund client questions. These charges are sometimes criticized because they represent a "hidden" charge against capital and adversely affect the fund's total return to shareholders. Many mutual fund investors are completely unaware of the existence of 12b-1 charges and their negative long-term effects on mutual fund performance.

Some mutual funds also charge a variety of miscellaneous fees. An **exchange fee** of $5–$25 per transaction may be assessed when an investor exchanges shares from one fund to another within the same fund family. All funds allow switches based on the investor's written instructions. Many funds also allow switches using the fund's toll-free telephone number or PC-based trading system on the Internet. In many cases, fees charged for Internet transactions are somewhat lower than those incurred using other mediums. Account **maintenance fees** of between $10 and $25 per year also may be assessed. Such charges are sometimes reserved for very small accounts having balances below a stated dollar level, such as $5,000–$10,000 in assets. Maintenance charges are designed to fairly apportion fixed costs associated with maintaining individual accounts.

exchange fee Charge assessed when an investor exchanges shares from one fund to another within the same fund family.

maintenance fees Bookkeeping charges.

Transaction fees of 1–2% of the amount transferred to another account may be assessed on redemptions, on initial purchases, or both. In most instances, these fees are not properly referred to as sales loads because they are not used to compensate salespeople. Transaction fees are paid directly to the fund itself to help defray brokerage and other costs associated with buying and selling securities. However, in the eyes of individual investors, transaction fees that are only weakly related to transaction costs can represent a real burden.

transaction fees Charges for redemptions or initial purchases.

How Mutual Fund Costs Affect Returns

The best resource to help investors determine mutual fund costs is the fund's **prospectus,** or offering circular, which must be given to all investors at or before the time of purchase. The SEC requires that information about mutual fund sales charges and operating expenses be spelled out in a fee table near the front of the prospectus. This information makes it easy to compare mutual fund costs and helps investors identify funds that can meet their investment objectives on a cost-efficient basis. This fee table includes all expenses that a hypothetical investor would pay assuming a 5% annual return on a $10,000 investment over investment horizons of one, three, five, and ten years. SEC regulations also make it easy for mutual fund shareholders to compare load charges and operating expense ratios across funds. Paying higher operating expenses or load charges might make sense if doing so were to lead to higher investor returns. Unfortunately, there is no evidence to suggest funds with higher expense ratios or load charges do better than cost-efficient no-load funds. To the contrary, simple logic confirms that cost-efficient no-load funds leave more dollars available to build long-term wealth for mutual fund investors.

prospectus Offering circular.

Representative prospectus fee tables are shown in Table 15.4, panel A. This table shows all fees and expenses assessed by three hypothetical mutual funds. First indicated is whether the fund imposes load charges on the initial amount invested and on reinvested dividends. Any redemption and exchange fees must also be indicated. Important components of the funds' annual fund operating expenses are also noted. The "bottom line" is the fund's total operating expense. Although this percentage can seem rather small, small savings add up to important amounts over extended time periods. The savings realized from using a cost-efficient stock fund can be impressive over time, as illustrated in Table 15.4, panel B.

TABLE 15.4 Mutual Fund Expenses Have a Dramatic Effect on Investor Returns

This table illustrates all expenses and fees that a shareholder of three hypothetical mutual funds would incur. The example also shows the expenses that investors would incur on a $10,000 investment over various time periods, assuming a 5% annual rate of return and redemptions at the end of each period.

A. Typical fee tables found in three different mutual fund prospectuses.

	Fund A	Fund B	Fund C
Shareholder Transaction Expenses			
Sales load imposed on purchases	None	None	4.75%
Sales load imposed on reinvested dividends	None	None	4.75
Redemption fees	None	None	None
Exchange fees	None	None	None
Annual Fund Operating Expenses			
Management and administrative expenses	0.22%	0.60%	0.70%
Investment advisory expenses	0.02	—	—
12b-1 marketing fees	—	0.30	—
Marketing and distribution costs	0.02	—	—
Miscellaneous expenses	0.03	0.32	0.26
Total Operating Expenses	**0.29%**	**1.22%**	**0.96%**
Expenses on a $10,000 Investment			
1 year	$30	$ 124	$ 587
3 years	93	387	823
5 years	63	670	1,077
10 years	368	1,477	1,805

B. The impact of equity mutual fund costs on long-term investor returns.

	Fund A	Fund B	Fund C
Initial investment	$ 10,000	$10,000	$10,000
Day 1	10,000	10,000	9,525
5 years	18,189	17,451	16,186
10 years	33,084	30,565	29,689
15 years	60,178	53,145	52,416
20 years	109,458	92,743	92,539
Gross return	13.00%	13.00%	13.00%
Operating expenses	0.29%	1.22%	0.96%
Net return	12.71%	11.78%	12.04%

Data source: <http://www.vanguard.com>.

In the hypothetical examples illustrated, fund A is a typical cost-efficient index fund designed to mimic the performance of a broad market index such as the Standard & Poor's (S&P) 500. Fund B is a conventional no-load stock mutual fund with typical operating expenses. Fund C is a low-load stock mutual fund with less than typical annual operating expenses. For simplicity, each fund is assumed to earn the market average of 13% per year before expenses. From these three examples, it becomes clear that high mutual fund costs are a significant but sometimes overlooked limiting force on long-term investment performance. Before investing in a mutual fund with a front-end or back-end load charge, the mutual fund investor must weigh these costs against the value of any investment advice received from the investment professional that helped with the transaction. Similarly valuable professional service must be rendered to justify investing in a fund that carries 12b-1 fees, as do about half the mutual funds tracked by Lipper Analytical Services, Inc. And finally, all mutual fund investors should consider the merits of investing in funds that have low expense ratios. High marketing and operating expenses reduce the mutual fund investor's total return and can only be justified by valuable professional services.

Mutual Fund Risk

Money Market Mutual Funds

Money market funds aim to provide current income while maintaining a constant $1 per-share net asset value. They strive to achieve this objective by investing in high-quality, short-term debt instruments such as CDs, U.S. Treasury bills, and commercial paper. Money market funds essentially make short-term loans with an average maturity of 90 days or less. Investment holdings of money market funds are generally of exceptionally high quality. The SEC requires that all taxable money market funds invest at least 95% of their assets in securities of the highest grade, as rated by major credit rating agencies such as Moody's Investors Service, Inc., or Standard & Poor's Corporation. Money market mutual funds that invest in municipal bonds to provide nontaxable income also seek out the highest-quality debt securities.

Although all money market funds expect to maintain a steady net asset value of $1 per share, there is no assurance that they will be able to do so under all types of market conditions. Under conditions of extreme duress, it is conceivable that a measurable share of the assets of any given money market fund might become impaired. Under extreme circumstances, it is conceivable that money market shareholders might face delays in processing their redemption requests or the risk of capital loss. Although no such circumstance has ever presented itself to date, it is also conceivable that shareholders in a given money market fund might be defrauded by unscrupulous management. Investments in money market mutual funds are neither insured nor guaranteed by the U.S. government.

One of the most obvious risks faced by money market mutual fund shareholders is the risk of purchasing power loss due to the ongoing effects of economy-wide inflation. Because money market funds produce lower rates of return when compared with stock and bond funds, money market funds often have a hard time keeping pace with inflation. **Inflation risk** is the chance that rising prices will erode real (or after-inflation) investment returns. Inflation risk is of particular interest to investors with long-term investment horizons, such as parents saving for a young child's college expenses or workers saving for retirement. As seen in Chapter 5, inflation has consumed much of the before-tax return earned by money market investors over the past 50 years.

inflation risk Chance that rising prices will erode real (or after-inflation) investment returns.

Bond Funds

Bond prices and bond mutual funds can be volatile. Since World War II, annual total returns on long-term bonds have fluctuated from roughly −8% to +10%. Such fluctuations in bond prices reflect interest rate risk. Remember, when interest rates rise, bond prices fall. Conversely, when interest rates decline, bond prices rise. This follows from the fact that when interest rates rise, the fixed interest payments on existing bonds become less valuable because new bonds may be purchased that pay higher interest yields. Investors wanting to sell older lower-yielding bonds discover that they will fetch a lower price than a newer bond. However, if interest rates decline, the fixed interest paid on older bonds is more attractive compared with lower rates on newly issued bonds. In this situation, the price of older bonds will rise. In general, the longer a bond's time to maturity, the more its price will fall in response to an increase in interest rates or rise in response to a drop in rates.

income risk Chance that the income from mutual fund investments will fluctuate.

Another type of risk borne by mutual fund investors is **income risk.** This is the chance that the income from various mutual fund investments will fluctuate. This risk is particularly important to retired investors who rely on their investment portfolios for income to cover living expenses. Income risk is greatest with money market securities and short-term bonds because interest payments on these instruments are fixed only for short periods. Income risk is moderate with long-term bonds because interest payments on long-term bonds are fixed for longer periods. Common stocks tend to have little income risk because dividends paid on broadly diversified portfolios of common stocks are remarkably stable and tend to rise over time.

Figure 15.5A shows the recent volatility of short-term and long-term bonds relative to the total stock market. Notice how long-term bonds can be just as volatile as stocks over brief holding periods. Notice too how long-term rates of return tend to be higher for long-term bonds and stocks. Finally, notice in Figure 15.5B how long holding periods "tame" stock and bond fund investor risk in the sense that good and bad years tend to average out so that investors are able to earn long-term market-average rates of return over extended investment horizons.

Stock Funds

market risk Change in value because prices of stocks and bonds fluctuate.

inferior management risk Chance that poor timing or substandard security selection will result in bad performance.

sector risk Chance of loss due to focus on some underperforming industry or industry group.

There are several kinds of risk to consider when investing in stock funds. The first and most obvious is **market risk.** Market risk exists because the prices of stocks and bonds fluctuate. It is the most obvious type of risk borne by mutual fund shareholders. Market risk is not the same as **inferior management risk,** or the chance that poor timing or substandard security selection will result in bad performance. Broadly diversified stock funds ordinarily will move in the same direction as the overall stock market, and the market is subject to wide fluctuations.

All mutual fund investors face the risk of loss or inferior short-term performance when specific asset classes suffer through the inevitable periods of underperformance. At times, such **sector risk** can be substantial. For example, on December 29, 1989, the Japanese Nikkei Index closed at 38,916, near an all-time high. At the start of the 1990s, the Japanese stock market was the world's largest. Japanese-style management and the thriftiness of the Japanese people were the envy of the world. The success of the Japanese stock market not only caused Japanese stock prices to skyrocket, international investing in established and emerging global stock markets became the rage in the mutual fund business. Then, the bubble burst. Nine years later, on December 30, 1998, the Nikkei Index closed at 13,842, reflecting a stunning decline of more than 65%. International funds that were sold to mutual fund investors on the basis of their ability to spread risks and increase rewards by investing in foreign stock markets such as Japan's suffered huge losses. Making matters worse is the fact that the domestic U.S. stock market soared during the 1990s. Today, international investing is often discredited. Sadly, despite attractive investment opportunities in many foreign markets, few mutual fund investors are now encouraged to adopt a global perspective.

FIGURE 15.5 Mutual Fund Investor Risk Is Tamed over Extended Holding Periods

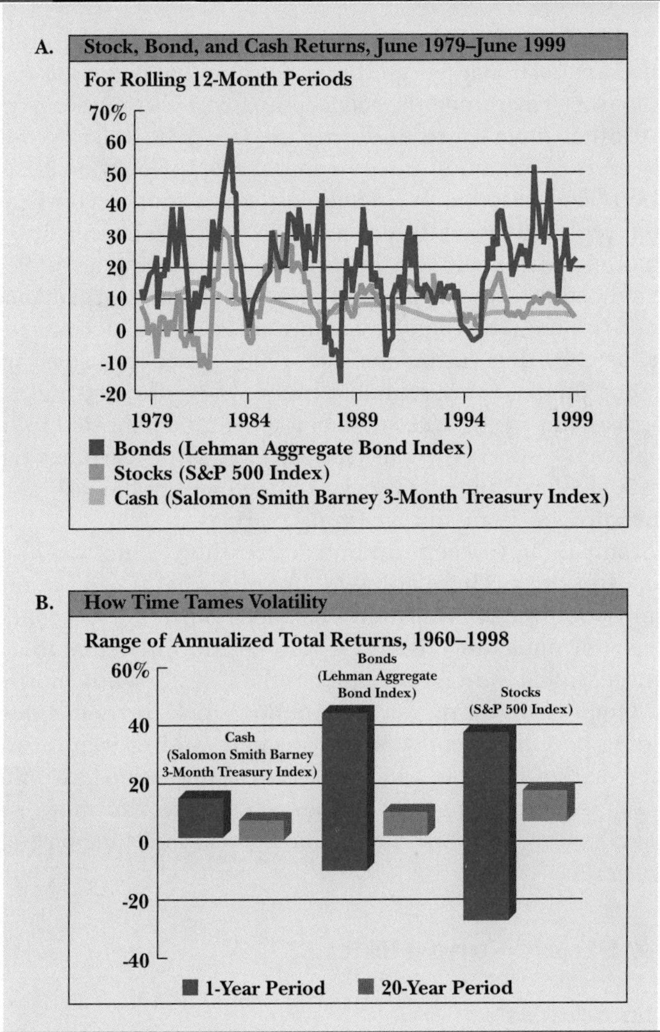

Source: <http://www.vanguard.com>.

Mutual fund investors also face the risk of loss or inferior short-term performance when valid investment styles suffer through inevitable periods of underperformance. **Style risk** can be substantial. In the late 1990s, for example, the conservative "value" style of investing fell into relative disfavor. Value investors favor low price/earnings or low price/book ratios on the premise that such companies often possess favorable risk/reward trade-offs. The more aggressive "growth" style of investing focuses on a company's potential for future earnings; current earnings and book values may be low or even nonexistent. During robust economic expansions, growth companies and growth-style mutual funds do well. During periods of tepid economic growth or economic recession, value mutual funds do better.

style risk
Chance of loss or inferior short-term performance when valid investment styles suffer through inevitable periods of underperformance.

Although over an entire economic cycle there is no significant advantage to either value or growth styles of investing, style risk can be substantial over extended periods.

When studying mutual fund performance, it is best to focus on long-term execution because financial markets go through cycles that can last for several years. During some market environments, small-company stocks outperform large-company stocks. At other times (such as during the late 1990s), large-company stocks are star performers. A common investor mistake is to focus on best-performing funds from the recent past. Unfortunately, last year's "hot" sector in the financial markets is often replaced by a different sector in the present year. Too often, many mutual fund companies encourage this practice by boasting about recent performance, while conceding (usually in small print) that past performance is no indication of future results. When large-company stock prices race ahead of business fundamentals, as they did during the late 1990s, price/earnings multiples and price/book ratios jump to unsustainable highs. Over the next decade, investors seeking better bargains in the U.S. stock market can be expected to turn their attention to small-caps, especially small-caps with low price/earnings ratios and low price/book ratios. Global investors may even rediscover the risk and return advantages of investing in Asian and emerging markets.

The important thing to keep in mind is that there is no way to eliminate all types of mutual fund risk. There are ways, however, that it can be mitigated. The simplest and most obvious way is to hold a balanced portfolio. A second and equally important means of mitigating risk is for mutual fund investors to adopt a long-term perspective. Mutual fund risk declines as the investor's time horizon increases because the chance of losing money in common stocks or bonds declines as the investor's holding period increases. Money needed within a year or two should remain in money market funds in which the risk of near-term price fluctuations is small. Money set aside for long time periods, say, 10 years or more, should be invested more aggressively, primarily in common stocks and long-term bonds.

Assessing Stock Fund Risk

Portfolio Characteristics

Common stock investors look to the company's annual report and 10-k report to the SEC as the first primary sources for information about the company's assets, earnings, management, and strategy. Both can be obtained free of charge from the company's investor relations department or downloaded from the Internet. In a similar fashion, mutual fund investors look to the fund's annual report to shareholders and its prospectus for information about the fund's investment holdings, historical rates of return, management, and investment philosophy. Like a company annual report, the mutual fund's annual report is a marketing document designed to place the fund's performance and prospects in their most favorable light. If an investor wants to get a better handle on historical risks, potential hazards, and operating expenses, the mutual fund's prospectus is required reading. Both the annual report and the prospectus provide valuable information that can help an investor understand fund performance and investment strategy.

A detailed sketch of mutual fund investment philosophy, performance, and portfolio holdings is also provided for many large mutual funds on the Internet at yahoo.com (see Figure 15.6). Together, this information can help answer such important questions as, How is the fund performing? What is the fund investing in? How risky is the fund? Is the fund a vehicle for cost-efficient investing?

When evaluating mutual funds, performance is always the bottom line. However, it is important to view performance in relative terms. Fund performance must always be viewed relative to an appropriate benchmark index and against peer-group competitor funds that have similar objectives and policies. Yahoo!'s mutual fund overview gives investors the information necessary to make detailed assessments of the fund's investment philosophy, relative performance, fees and expenses. For example, a large-cap fund that produced a 20% annual rate of return

FIGURE 15.6 Yahoo! Finance Gives Detailed Information about Mutual Fund Investment Information, Fees, and Expenses

Fund Background

Category	Large Value
Fund Family	Legg Mason Family of Funds
Net Assets (N/A)	$11.68 billion
Morningstar Rating	★★★★★
Year to Date Return	2.17%
Current Quote	LMVTX

Morningstar Style Box

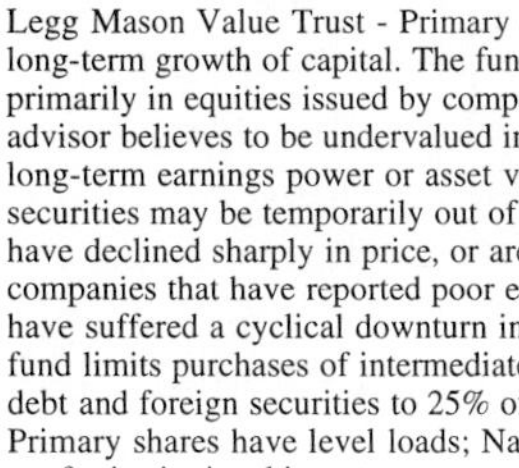

Category: Large Value

View top category funds

Style Box Definition

Legg Mason Value Trust - Primary Class seeks long-term growth of capital. The fund invests primarily in equities issued by companies that the advisor believes to be undervalued in relation to long-term earnings power or asset value. These securities may be temporarily out of favor and often have declined sharply in price, or are issued by companies that have reported poor earnings or that have suffered a cyclical downturn in business. The fund limits purchases of intermediate- and long-term debt and foreign securities to 25% of assets in each. Primary shares have level loads; Navigator shares are for institutional investors.

Fund Operations

Turnover (N/A)	19.30%
Last Dividend (22-May-97)	$0.04
Last Cap Gain (29-Jun-00)	$6.65
Inception:	16-Apr-82
Phone:	800-577-8589
Lead Manager:	William H. Miller III
Manager Since:	16-Apr-82

Returns (%)

	3mo	1yr	3yr avg	5yr avg
LMVTX	5.22	13.78	25.05	31.98
SP500	-1.21	8.97	16.04	22.60
Diff.	+6.43	+4.81	+9.01	+9.38

Chart

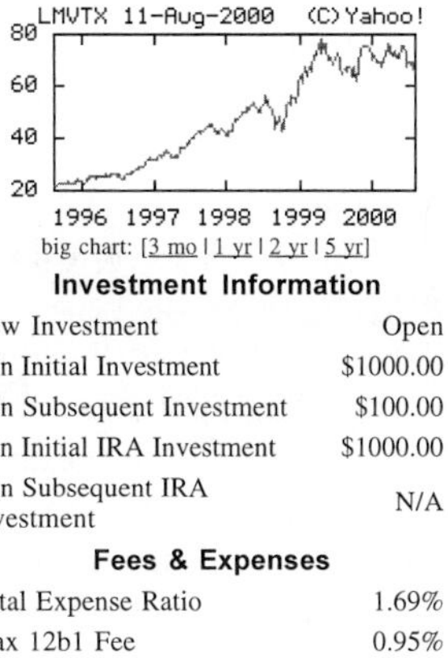

big chart: [3 mo | 1 yr | 2 yr | 5 yr]

Investment Information

New Investment	Open
Min Initial Investment	$1000.00
Min Subsequent Investment	$100.00
Min Initial IRA Investment	$1000.00
Min Subsequent IRA Investment	N/A

Fees & Expenses

Total Expense Ratio	1.69%
Max 12b1 Fee	0.95%
Max Front End Sales Charge	0%
Max Deferred Sales Charge	0%

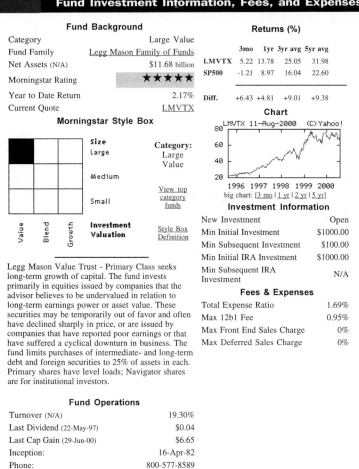

Data source: Legg Mason.

during the late 1990s produced a very attractive absolute return but still fell short of the S&P 500 Index, which earned more than 25% per year over this same time frame. Moreover, an individual investor's performance may not exactly mirror fund performance. Individual investor performance may differ, depending on when shares were purchased, the price paid, and whether dividends and capital gains are reinvested. Most mutual funds report total returns for specific one-, five-, and ten-year periods based on the assumption that all income plus capital gains are reinvested. Although mutual fund investors are right to focus on the "Performance Summary" section of the annual report and prospectus, it is equally important to focus on why the fund is performing the way it is. The annual report should offer a candid assessment of why the fund performed as it did. Did a stock fund lag the benchmark because it was overweighted in a market sector that faltered? Did a long-term bond fund fare well because interest rates declined? Such insights are important because they have the potential to directly influence the fund's potential for future performance.

One of the most interesting and potentially useful sections of a mutual fund's annual report is the listing of portfolio holdings. More than any general statement of fund investment philosophy or investment strategy, the portfolio listing helps to clarify a fund's investment policies. If a so-called value fund lists high-flying Internet stocks among its largest holdings, for example, one can be sure that the fund is exposed to significant downside risk in the event of an overall downturn in the market. Such a suggestion is far from pure fantasy. Yahoo!'s mutual fund holdings overview gives investors a helpful snapshot of investment philosophy and portfolio makeup for individual funds.

In the late 1990s, for example, Legg Mason Value Trust was a top performer among so-called value funds despite the fact that it holds a number of Internet and technology stocks in its portfolio. As shown in Figure 15.7, in mid 2000 Legg Mason Value Trust held an astounding 25.93% of its portfolio in such high-flying stocks as America Online (9.42%), Gateway (5.7%), MCI Worldcom (4.06%), Nextel (3.45%), and Nokia (3.30%). None of these stocks fits the conventional definition of what value funds look for in terms of low price/earnings or value stocks. With an average price/earnings ratio of 29.56 and an average price/book ratio of 8.46, holdings in the Legg Mason Value Trust scarcely fit the conventional definition of low price/earnings or low price/book stocks favored by value investors. Similarly, bond fund investors seeking the safety offered by U.S. Treasury securities want to be sure that U.S. Treasury bond funds hold all Treasury securities or invest only a small a portion of their assets in non-Treasury securities.

Prudent investors also look at the percentage of a stock fund's assets invested in the top 10 securities. This tells an investor the level of concentration in the portfolio. Although a concentrated fund may have 50% or more of its assets invested in its top 10 holdings, a more diversified fund may limit its top 10 holdings to no more than 30% of assets. For example, Figure 15.7 shows that in early 2000, the Legg Mason Value Trust held a whopping 42.96% of fund assets in only 10 securities.

Be sure to remember that a fund report, or snapshot such as that shown in Figure 15.7, gives only a one-time perspective on fund performance and risk. In assessing fund performance and risk, it is important to consider multiple inde-

FIGURE 15.7 **Yahoo! Finance's Mutual Fund Holdings Overview Gives a Helpful Snapshot of Investment Philosophy and Portfolio Makeup**

Portfolio Composition (%)

Stocks	84.39
Bonds	N/A
Preferred	N/A
Convertibles	N/A
Cash	2.66

Sector Weightings (%)

Financials	31.64
Industrial Cyclicals	3.20
Consumer Durables	4.67
Consumer Staples	0.97
Services	20.98
Retail	7.43
Health	5.76
Technology	25.35

Top Holdings

	Symbol	% Assets	YTD Return
America Online	AOL	9.42	-29.82
Gateway Inc	GTW	5.70	-23.42
MCI WorldCom	WCOM	4.06	-26.38
WPP Grp	N/A	3.67	N/A
UnitedHealth Grp	UNH	3.67	54.08
Waste Mgmt	WMI	3.55	8.00
Nextel Comms Cl A	NXTL	3.45	8.48
Nokia Cl A ADR	N/A	3.30	-6.86
Citigroup	C	3.22	27.29
MGIC Invest	MTG	2.92	-5.50
% Fund Assets in Top Ten Holdings			42.96

Quotes for Top Holdings

Equity Holdings

Avg. Price/Earnings	29.56
Avg. Price/Book	8.46
Median Market Cap	29.65 B

Data source: Legg Mason.

pendent periods. For example, it is never enough to consider fund performance over just the most recent one-, five-, and ten-year periods. Extraordinary one-year performance often leads to outsized returns for any performance period that includes the most recent year. A much more accurate perspective of risk and return is provided if one considers fund performance over each of the three most recent nonoverlapping three-year periods. Of course, historical performance is only a useful guide to expected risk and return if the fund's investment philosophy has not changed.

Alpha, Beta, and R^2

On a theoretical basis, remember from the Capital Asset Pricing Model (CAPM) discussed in Chapter 13 that the security market line (SML) posits a simple straight-line relation between the expected rate of return on a portfolio and systematic risk in which

$$E(R_P) = R_F + \beta_P(R_M - R_F) \tag{15.1}$$

In Equation 15.1, $E(R_P)$ is the expected return on a mutual fund portfolio, R_F is the risk-free rate, and R_M is the market return. Therefore, the difference $R_M - R_F$ is the risk premium earned by the overall market. The risk premium earned by a given mutual fund is expected to be proportional to the risk premium earned on the overall market, $R_M - R_F$.

On average, the risk premium earned by the typical mutual fund should be β_P times as great as the market risk premium, where β_P is the beta measure of portfolio systematic risk. It shows the systematic relation between the risk premium earned on the fund and on the overall market. If $\beta_P = 1.5$, the mutual fund portfolio is one and one-half times as risky as the overall market. In that case, investors should anticipate earning an annual rate of return equal to the risk-free rate plus one and one-half times the market risk premium. If $\beta_P = 0.5$, the mutual fund portfolio is only one-half times as risky as the overall market, and investors should anticipate earning an annual rate of return equal to the risk-free rate plus one-half the market risk premium. Finally, ϵ_{Pt} is a random error term with an expected value of zero. During the past 50 years in the United States, a fair estimate of the risk-free rate is 5%, and the expected rate of return on the market is roughly 13%. This means that a mutual fund with $\beta_P = 2$ has an expected rate of return of 21% (= 5% + 2 × 8%). A mutual fund with $\beta_P = 0.5$ has an expected rate of return of 9% (= 5% + 0.5 × 8%).

For any given mutual fund portfolio, Equation 15.1 can be used to identify any abnormal risk-adjusted performance. The Greek letter alpha (α_P) is used to signify the amount of annual return on the portfolio that cannot be tied to volatility in the overall market. Subtracting the risk-free rate R_F from each side of Equation 15.1 and adding α_P to signify abnormal return gives

$$E(R_P) - R_F = \alpha_P + \beta_P(R_M - R_F) \qquad \textbf{(15.2)}$$

If $\alpha_P > 0$ and statistically significant, a mutual fund portfolio has returned positive risk-adjusted performance to its shareholders, indicating superior historical portfolio manager performance (or good luck). If $\alpha_P < 0$ and significant, the mutual fund has underperformed the market on a risk-adjusted basis, and inferior historical performance (or bad luck) is demonstrated.

selectivity Stock-picking ability.

market timing Punctual purchase and sale of securities.

When $\alpha_P > 0$, portfolio performance is better than the theoretical expectation derived from the CAPM. Market-beating performance can be due to superior **selectivity,** or the selection of stocks with exceptionally good risk/reward characteristics. This is the hallmark of a good stock picker. Although few portfolio managers have demonstrated good stock-picking ability that has stood the test of time, there are some notable exceptions. Warren Buffett, Fidelity's Peter Lynch, and global investor John Templeton are some examples. Outstanding portfolio performance can also be due to astute risk management through careful **market timing.** Over the years, few have demonstrated superior stock market timing. Hedge fund manager George Soros is a possible exception.

When $\alpha_P < 0$, portfolio performance is worse than the theoretical expectation. In the case of inferior performance, bad stock picking or bad market timing is sometimes to blame. Most often, inferior mutual fund performance has a simpler explanation. Excessive operating expenses tied with extravagant portfolio manager compensation, or unreasonably high portfolio turnover, are often blamed for subpar results.

Although alpha is a measure of unexpectedly good or bad mutual fund performance, R^2 (like beta) is a measure of mutual fund volatility derived from the CAPM that has the potential to help investors put mutual fund performance in perspective. Beta measures how volatile a fund has been compared with a relevant benchmark. R^2 measures the degree to which volatility in a fund's return is explained by volatility in the overall market. The lower a fund's R^2, the more idiosyncratic is the fund's performance, and the more fund performance depends on the fund manager's timing and stock selection. If a stock fund has a low R^2, it is hard to predict how the fund will perform compared with the overall stock market. Also, keep in mind that the lower R^2 is, the less reliable beta is as an indicator of fund volatility.

Despite well-known problems with CAPM discussed in Chapters 12–14, it is now standard to include alpha, beta, and R^2 as measures of mutual fund risk derived from modern portfolio theory. As shown in Figure 15.8, the Legg Mason Value Trust displayed market-beating results over the past three-, five-, and ten-year periods. Over the past three-year period, an alpha of 3.64 means that the fund earned an abnormal return of 3.64% per year that could not be explained according to the CAPM. Similarly, $\alpha = 4.15$ over the past five-year period indicates above-average

FIGURE 15.8 **Yahoo! Finance's Mutual Fund Performance Overview Gives Detailed Perspective on Risk and Return**

Morningstar Ratings

Overall Rating	★★★★★
Risk Rating	Average
Return Rating	High

Yearly Total Returns (%)

1999	26.71
1998	48.04
1997	37.05
1996	38.43
1995	40.76
1994	1.39
1993	11.26
1992	11.44
1991	34.73
1990	-16.96

Past Quarterly Returns (%)

	Q1	Q2	Q3	Q4
2000	-3.31	-0.01		
1999	18.69	-0.58	-9.70	18.91
1998	17.20	5.23	-11.64	35.86
1997	3.40	18.05	16.49	-3.62
1996	7.15	3.64	8.83	14.54
1995	6.15	14.47	10.74	4.61
1994	-1.96	-1.52	6.11	-1.04
1993	3.25	-0.78	3.19	5.25
1992	0.26	-0.07	1.98	9.07
1991	13.01	0.85	11.51	6.01
1990			-21.31	5.71

Risk (MPT Statistics)

	3 Yr	5 Yr	10 Yr
Alpha	3.64	4.15	1.61
Beta	1.19	1.19	1.17
R-Squared	81	83	83
Std. Deviation	27.63	25.85	20.92
Sharpe Ratio	0.67	1.16	1.01
Treynor Ratio	14.80	23.90	17.24

Returns vs. Comparison Index (%)

	LMVTX	Index*	Diff
Year To Date	2.17	-1.98	+4.15
1 Month	-1.05	-1.56	+0.51
3 Mo	5.22	-1.21	+6.43
1 Year	13.78	8.97	+4.81
3 Year Avg	25.05	16.04	+9.01
5 Year Avg	31.98	22.60	+9.38
10 Year Avg	21.36	17.64	+3.72
15 Year Avg	17.68	17.52	+0.16
Last Bull Market (1-Oct-98 to 30-Jun-99)	67.24	36.29	+30.95
Last Bear Market (31-Jul-98 to 30-Sep-98)	-13.57	-8.96	N/A

* = *Index means SP500*

Return Statistics (%)

Number of Years Up	15
Number of Years Down	2
Best 1 Yr Total Return (1998)	48.04
Worst 1 Yr Total Return (1990)	-16.96
Best 3 Yr Total Return (1998 -2000)	41.09
Worst 3 Yr Total Return (1992 -1994)	7.63

Load Adjusted Returns (%)

1 Year	3.80
3 Year	26.75
5 Year	31.86
10 Year	21.17

Data source: Legg Mason.

returns of 4.15% that may be attributed to superior stock-picking ability or market timing. Over the past ten years, an alpha of 1.61, indicating 1.61% per year superior annual returns, is so small as perhaps due to chance. A range for beta from 1.17 to 1.19 (versus a market $\beta = 1$), and for standard deviation from 20.92% to 27.63% (versus a market 20%), means that this fund exhibits above-market levels of risk. Nevertheless, Legg Mason Value Trust was a standout performer during the 1990s.

Is Mutual Fund Alpha, Beta, and R^2 Information Useful?

Unfortunately, the usefulness of alpha, beta, and R^2 is diminished to the extent that the CAPM fails to accurately depict the risk/reward relationship for mutual funds over time. As discussed in Chapter 13, alpha, beta, and R^2 tend to be unstable when individual stocks such as the 30 stocks in the Dow Jones Industrial Average (DJIA) are considered. Table 15.5 suggests that the same seems to hold true when alpha, beta, and R^2 estimates for 30 of the largest common stock funds are

TABLE 15.5 Risk and Reward Performance Estimation for 30 Large Mutual Funds Using the S&P 500 as a Market Index

Mutual Fund	Ticker	Alpha Estimate	*t*-Statistic	Beta Estimate	*t*-Statistic	R^2	F-stat.	S.D.
AIM Equity Constellation A	CSTGX	−0.285	−1.50	1.226	16.63	84.7%	276.49	3.41%
American Century Ultra	TWCUX	−0.103	−0.51	1.094	14.02	79.3%	196.41	3.14%
Europacific Growth	AEPGX	−0.174	0.68	0.760	7.61	53.7%	57.96	2.66%
Fidelity Advisors Growth Opportunity	FAGOX	−0.081	−0.67	0.901	19.20	88.1%	368.69	2.46%
Fidelity Asset Manager	FASMX	−0.330	−1.00	0.517	4.04	24.6%	16.30	2.67%
Fidelity Blue Chip Growth	FBGRX	−0.037	−0.31	1.134	24.83	92.5%	616.50	3.02%
Fidelity Contrafund	FCNTX	0.070	0.60	0.997	22.04	90.7%	485.92	2.68%
Fidelity Equity-Income	FEQIX	−0.319	−2.90	0.945	22.13	90.7%	489.55	2.54%
Fidelity Equity-Income II	FEQTX	−0.187	−1.16	0.945	15.12	82.1%	228.67	2.67%
Fidelity Magellan Fund	FMAGX	−0.045	−0.47	1.111	29.97	94.7%	898.20	2.92%
Fidelity Puritan	FPURX	−0.276	−1.61	0.757	11.35	72.1%	128.90	2.28%
Fundamental Investors	ANCFX	−0.257	−1.38	0.779	10.75	69.8%	115.53	2.39%
Growth Fund of America	AGTHX	−0.105	−0.45	0.951	10.35	68.2%	107.15	2.95%
IDS New Dimensions	INNDX	−0.001	−0.80	1.020	20.91	89.7%	437.20	2.75%
Income Fund of America	AMECX	−0.202	−1.11	0.344	4.89	32.4%	23.94	1.55%
Investment Co. of America	AIVSX	−0.182	−1.00	0.800	11.36	72.1%	129.15	2.41%
Janus Fund	JANSX	0.042	0.24	1.183	17.10	85.4%	292.39	3.28%
Janus Twenty	JAVLX	0.541	2.55	1.153	14.03	79.7%	196.82	3.31%
Janus Worldwide	JAWWX	0.008	0.04	0.944	11.18	71.4%	125.08	2.86%
MSDW Dividend Growth B	DIVBX	−0.119	−1.12	0.759	18.53	87.3%	346.40	2.08%
New Perspectives Fund	ANWPX	−0.040	−0.19	0.787	9.71	65.3%	94.30	2.49%
Putnam Growth & Income A	PGIIX	−0.373	−1.92	0.922	12.21	74.9%	148.97	2.73%
Putnam Voyager A	PVOYX	−0.260	−1.27	1.164	14.69	81.2%	215.76	3.31%
T. Rowe Price Equity Income	PRFDX	−0.268	−1.83	0.627	11.04	70.9%	121.83	1.91%
Templeton Growth	TEGTX	−0.922	−2.16	0.715	4.31	27.1%	18.59	3.51%
Vanguard Windsor	VWNDX	−0.651	−2.55	1.062	10.72	69.7%	114.80	3.26%
Vanguard 500 Index	VFINX	0.006	0.31	0.990	135.56	99.7%	18375.38	2.54%
Vanguard Wellington	VWELX	−0.215	−1.01	0.452	5.45	37.3%	29.74	1.89%
Vanguard Windsor II	VWNFX	−0.292	−1.37	0.865	10.43	68.5%	108.83	2.68%
Washington Mutual	AWSHX	−0.176	−0.96	0.744	10.52	68.9%	110.75	2.29%
Averages		−0.174	−0.827	0.888	17.689	72.4%	829.206	2.69%

Data source: <http://finance.yahoo.com> (1998 data).

considered. These SCL-based estimates were derived over a one-year period by using 52 observations of weekly returns and the S&P 500 Index as an indicator of the overall market.

Notice how the average alpha estimate of $\alpha = -0.174$ is very close to zero, as predicted for a perfectly competitive market by the CAPM. The average beta estimate of $\beta = 0.888$ means that a typical large stock fund stock has risk characteristics that are fairly representative of the overall market. As you recall, the overall market has $\beta = 1$. Although the magnitude of these alpha and beta estimates for large stock funds is not surprising, it is unfortunate that the average $R^2 = 72.4\%$ when the SCLs are estimated for the 30 largest funds. This means that volatility in the overall market explains less than three-quarters (72.4%) of the volatility in large stock funds, and a bit more than one-quarter (27.6%) of this volatility is left unexplained by simple SCL regression models. Although there is a statistically significant link between the volatility of large common-stock funds and market volatility, a meaningful portion of stock fund price volatility is left unaccounted for by the SCL.

According to the CAPM, the expected value for alpha is zero, $E(\alpha) = 0$. Notice from Figure 15.9 that alpha, beta, and R^2 information appear unstable from

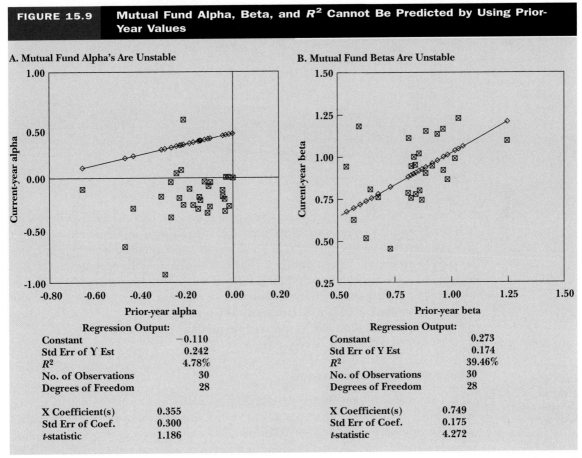

FIGURE 15.9 Mutual Fund Alpha, Beta, and R^2 Cannot Be Predicted by Using Prior-Year Values

A. Mutual Fund Alpha's Are Unstable **B. Mutual Fund Betas Are Unstable**

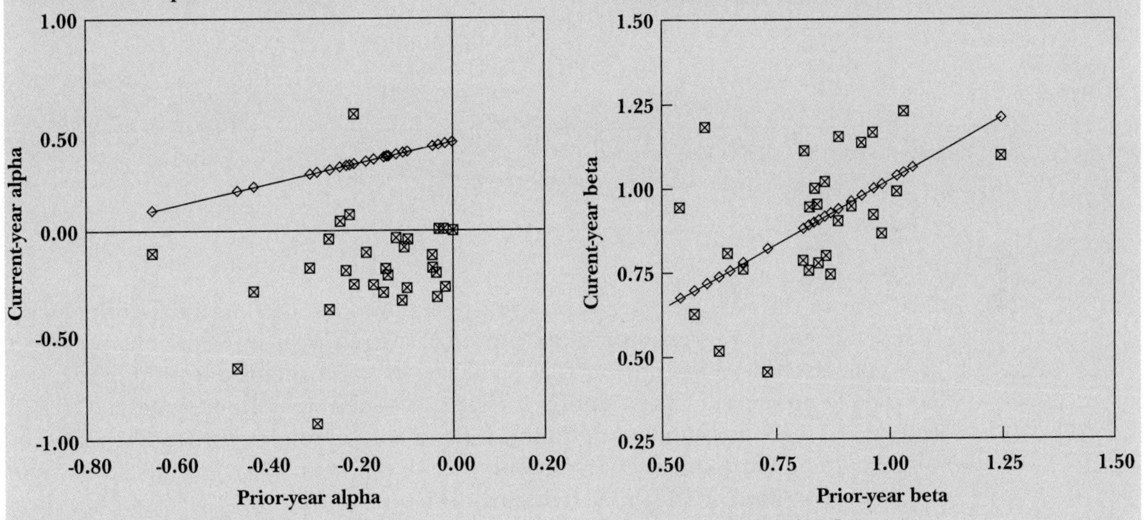

A. Regression Output:

Constant		−0.110
Std Err of Y Est		0.242
R^2		4.78%
No. of Observations		30
Degrees of Freedom		28
X Coefficient(s)	0.355	
Std Err of Coef.	0.300	
t-statistic	1.186	

B. Regression Output:

Constant		0.273
Std Err of Y Est		0.174
R^2		39.46%
No. of Observations		30
Degrees of Freedom		28
X Coefficient(s)	0.749	
Std Err of Coef.	0.175	
t-statistic	4.272	

(continued)

FIGURE 15.9 ***(continued)***

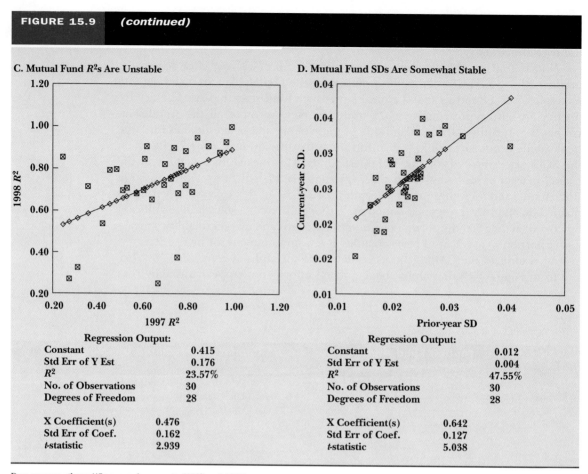

C. Mutual Fund R^2s Are Unstable

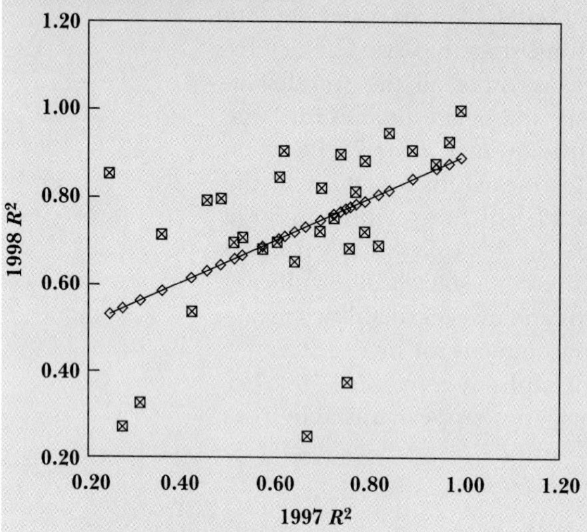

Regression Output:

Constant		0.415
Std Err of Y Est		0.176
R^2		23.57%
No. of Observations		30
Degrees of Freedom		28
X Coefficient(s)	0.476	
Std Err of Coef.	0.162	
t-statistic	2.939	

D. Mutual Fund SDs Are Somewhat Stable

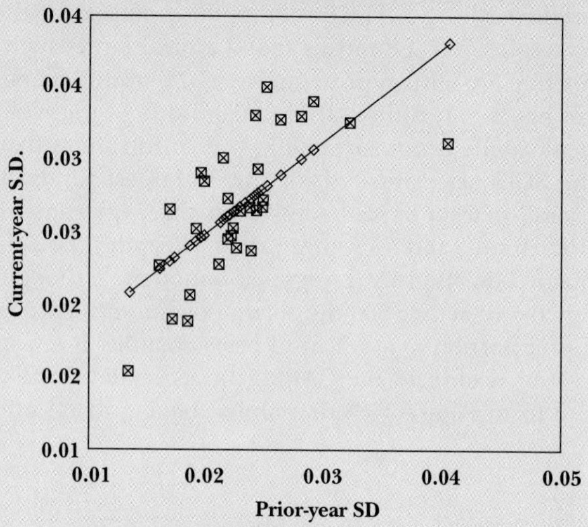

Regression Output:

Constant		0.012
Std Err of Y Est		0.004
R^2		47.55%
No. of Observations		30
Degrees of Freedom		28
X Coefficient(s)	0.642	
Std Err of Coef.	0.127	
t-statistic	5.038	

Data source: <http://finance.yahoo.com> (1997 and 1998).

one year to the next. In each case, prior-year values are used as independent variables in a simple regression model to predict current-year information. Based on this analysis, it does not appear that prior-year risk information from the SCL can be used to predict such information for the subsequent year. Interestingly, as shown in Figure 15.9D, the standard deviation (SD) of annual returns for large stock funds appears to be fairly consistent from one year to the next. These results offer some weak support for the idea that standard deviation can be used as a rough indicator of stock mutual fund risk that has some predictive power.

reward-to-variability measure (Sharpe ratio) Risk premium earned relative to total risk.

Risk-Adjusted Performance

Nobel Laureate William Sharpe developed a measure of risk-adjusted performance for mutual funds and other portfolios called the **reward-to-variability measure** (RVAR) (or **Sharpe ratio**). The RVAR measure can be used to provide a ranking of portfolios by the risk premium earned per unit of total systematic plus unsystematic risk. In other words, RVAR considers the ex-postrisk premium earned per unit of total risk:

$$RVAR = \frac{\bar{R}_P - \bar{R}_F}{SD(R_P)} \tag{15.3}$$

$$= \frac{\text{Excess return on portfolio } P}{\text{Total risk for portfolio } P}$$

In Equation 15.3, $\bar{R}_P$ is the average rate of return on portfolio P during period t, $\bar{R}_F$ is the average risk-free rate of return, and $SD(R_P)$ is the portfolio standard deviation during period t. Poor relative performance exists if RVAR > 0 and small, or if $\bar{R}_P < \bar{R}_F$ and the $SD_P > 0$ and RVAR < 0. Very good relative performance is indicated if RVAR > 0 and large.

Financial economist Jack Treynor developed an alternative measure of risk-adjusted performance for mutual funds and other portfolios called the **reward-to-volatility measure** (RVOL) (or **Treynor ratio**). The RVOL measure ranks portfolios by risk premium per unit of systematic risk. An increase in RVOL is preferred by all investors, regardless of risk preferences, in which

reward-to-volatility measure (Treynor ratio) Risk premium earned relative to systematic risk.

$$RVOL = \frac{\bar{R}_P - \bar{R}_F}{\beta_P} \tag{15.4}$$

$$= \frac{\text{Excess return on portfolio } P}{\text{Systematic risk for portfolio } P}$$

As before, $\bar{R}_P$ is the average rate of return on portfolio P during period t, $\bar{R}_F$ is the average risk-free rate of return. In Equation 15.4, β_P is the beta measure of systematic risk for the mutual fund or other investment portfolio. Poor relative performance exists if RVOL > 0 and small, or if $\bar{R}_P < \bar{R}_F$ and $\beta_P > 0$ and RVOL < 0. Good relative performance is indicated if RVOL > 0 and large, or RVOL < 0 and $\beta_P < 0$.

When comparing the RVAR and RVOL measures, it is important to recognize that they differ only in terms of the risk measure used. RVAR ranks portfolios according to the risk premium earned relative to total risk using $SD(\bar{R}_P)$, whereas RVOL ranks portfolios according to the risk premium earned relative to systematic risk using β_P. Rank orderings of various portfolios are often similar. As shown in Figure 15.8, over the past three years the Legg Mason Value Trust had a Sharpe ratio of 0.88, meaning that an annual risk premium of 0.88% was earned for each 1% of portfolio SD. For comparison purposes, it is perhaps worth noting that the overall market has earned an annual risk premium of roughly 8%, that is, a typical return of 13% minus the risk-free rate of 5%. With a 20% typical SD of annual returns, the Sharpe ratio for the overall market is roughly 0.4 (= 8%/20%). This means that Legg Mason Value has recently offered much better than a typical risk/reward trade-off.

Similarly, Legg Mason Value had a Treynor ratio of 23.13 over the past three years, meaning that a risk premium of 23.13% was earned for each unit of systematic risk as measured by β_P. With a market risk premium of 8% and a market-wide $\beta = 1$, the market's risk/reward trade-off is 8 (= 8%/1) using the Treynor ratio. As in the case of the Sharpe ratio, market-beating performance for Legg Mason Value is indicated when using the Treynor ratio.

WALL STREET WISDOM 15.2

Mutual Fund Myths

Mutual fund investment strategies are sometimes subject to myths that distort investor understanding about what can and cannot be expected from professional investment managers. Although mutual funds receive generally favorable coverage in the financial news media, some misconceptions exist that have the potential to lead to investor disappointment.

Myth #1: Indexing works best with large-cap domestic stocks.

Some investors mistakenly equate index investing with the Standard & Poor's (S&P) 500 Index. The S&P 500 is composed of blue-chip stocks that represent about 80% of the stock market's total value. Although the S&P 500 is by far the leading proxy targeted by index funds, the indexing concept is equally valid for small-caps, international equities, and fixed-income investing. During the 1990s, the S&P 500 outperformed almost every broad market index. While this has been of obvious benefit to index fund investors, outstanding absolute relative performance by large-cap growth stocks should not be expected indefinitely.

Outstanding relative results have sometimes been turned in by small-caps and foreign stocks, and indexing is an efficient means of participating in these market segments. In fact, because transaction costs tend to be higher for small-caps and in foreign markets, the low-cost advantage of indexing has the potential to be most important in these market sectors. Indexing is also an efficient means for fixed-income investing where active portfolio management holds only modest opportunity.

Myth #2: Index funds outperform the majority of actively managed stock funds every year.

Before expenses, 50% of the actively managed mutual funds will outperform broad market averages; 50% will underperform. After expenses, less than 50% of actively managed mutual funds in any asset class category will outperform the broad market averages. Over extended time periods, the low-cost advantage of indexing leads to huge investor savings and a significant premium over the average managed mutual fund. However, in any given year, the low-cost advantage of index fund investing may not be enough to overcome the effects of chance or skill as displayed by mutual fund managers in general.

For example, during the late 1990s, the S&P 500 Index outperformed between 75% and 90% of general equity funds each year. However, this was an unusually good period for large-cap growth stocks. During the mid-1990s, more than 50% of managed mutual funds beat S&P 500 index funds on an annual basis. In any one year, outperformance might be achieved by large-cap growth stocks. In another year, small-cap value stocks might shine. In a generally declining market, cash reserves held by managed mutual funds help them to do well vis-à-vis the market averages and index funds. However, cash reserves are an anchor that hurts the relative performance of managed funds during generally rising markets.

Over time, index funds can be expected to outperform the vast majority of actively managed funds. Stellar stock pickers sometimes emerge, and anything can happen during any given year.

Myth #3: Index funds are safer than actively managed funds.

Strong absolute and relative performance by index funds during recent years has led some investors to believe that index funds are less volatile than actively managed portfolios. This belief is wholly without merit. Index funds are not bulletproof. In a sharp market correction, index funds tend to be even more volatile than managed mutual funds. Cash positions held by actively managed funds cushion the effects of market declines. Fully invested index funds have no such cushion against a declining market.

Buy index funds because you want cost-efficient exposure to the overall market or a given market sector. In either event, be sure to know what you are buying.

See: Jonathan Clements, "Don't Use Index Funds as Sector Bets," *The Wall Street Journal,* June 20, 2000, C1.

Bond Fund Investing

Why Bonds?

Bond mutual funds play important roles in the portfolios of millions of individual and institutional investors. Although the stock market attracts more attention from the financial media, Americans have invested more than $850 billion in bond funds. Bond fund investments are attractive for two key reasons, stable income and diversification. Interest income earned in bond mutual funds is generally higher and more stable than the interest earned on investments in money market funds, CDs, or bank passbook accounts. As a result, investors such as retirees who need stable current income use bond funds for a substantial part of their investment portfolio. Many young investors in the stock market also hold bond funds to help smooth out fluctuations in the value of their overall investment portfolios. Although long-term bond funds fluctuate in value just as stock funds do, bond funds do not always move in the same direction or to the same degree as stock funds.

Some adventuresome investors may use short-term, high-quality bond funds as an alternative to money market funds. Although this strategy can provide higher returns, it does entail the risk that the investor could lose some principal because of fluctuating bond prices.

Finally, some affluent investors use municipal bond funds as a source of tax-exempt interest income. Because municipal bond funds tend to have lower before-tax interest yields than those on taxable bonds, this investment is usually appropriate only for people in high tax brackets.

Advantages of Investing in Individual Bonds

An investor may prefer to purchase individual bonds instead of a bond mutual fund for any number of reasons.

For example, an investor may have great confidence in the ability of a given bond issuer to make all promised interest payments and to repay the principal in full on maturity. This is like wanting to buy a favorite stock. By holding individual bonds, the investor also has the ability to choose when to buy or sell. This allows the investor to retain control over the timing and amount of any taxable capital gains or losses. By buying individual bonds rather than bond mutual funds, the investor also avoids paying fees for professional management or record keeping and is thus able to receive all the income produced by the bonds.

Finally, a bond investor may want assurance that the value of a given bond investment will be paid in full on a certain date so that it can be targeted to pay for anticipated living expenses or an expected cost such as college tuition. When bonds of different maturity dates are purchased to meet specific expenses, a technique called **laddering** is used. For example, if extra living expenses of $1,000 per year are anticipated over a 10-year period, a bond investor might buy an appropriate series of bonds of $1,000 par value each that would mature in sequence over that time frame. Because bond interest and principal payments can be precisely predicted at the time of purchase, an investor can closely estimate the value of bond investments at maturity. Consider a $1,000 bond that pays 6% interest and will mature in one year. If the bond is purchased today for $1,000, the investor receives $60 in interest and $1,000 in principal in the next year—for a total value of $1,060.

laddering
Bond investment strategy of buying bonds of different maturity dates meet specific investor needs.

Investors should keep in mind that they must pay brokerage commissions when buying or selling individual bonds. One exception to this rule is U.S. Treasury securities, which may be purchased without commissions through the Treasury Direct program of the Federal Reserve System.

Table 15.6, panel A, shows some of the pros and cons involved with buying individual bonds versus bond funds.

Advantages of Bond Funds

Although there are obvious advantages to purchasing individual bonds, there are equally obvious and compelling advantages to investing in bonds through a bond mutual fund. Many investors prefer to invest in bond mutual funds.

Like all mutual funds, a bond fund pools money from several investors and uses the money to buy securities that meet the fund's stated investment objectives and policies. Decisions to buy and sell individual bonds are made by a professional portfolio manager. A bond fund offers several important advantages to fixed-income investors.

TABLE 15.6 Bond Funds Help Investors Limit Investment Risk

A. Individual Bonds versus Bond Mutual Funds: Pros and Cons

A bond investor could choose to invest in either individual bonds or in bond mutual funds, depending on the relative benefits and drawbacks listed below. Investors should keep in mind that an investment in an individual bond or a small number of bonds may have greater credit risk than an investment in a diversified bond mutual fund.

	Individual Bonds*	Bond Mutual Funds
Principal stability	Yes, if held to maturity	No
Interest payments fixed	Yes	No
Risk diversification	No**	Yes
Professional management	No	Yes
Access to principal	Less convenient	Very convenient
Automatic dividend reinvestment	No	Yes

B. Interest Rate Risk: Bond Prices Fluctuate

The following table shows the percentage change in price for short-term, intermediate-term, and long-term bonds when interest rates increase or decrease by 1% and 2%. Bond price volatility increases with maturity. Short-term bonds are relatively stable, and long-term bonds have the greatest exposure to interest rate risk.

Percentage Change in the Price of a Bond Yielding 7% and Selling for Its Face Amount

	Increase in Rates		Decrease in Rates	
Bond Maturity	**+1%**	**+2%**	**−1%**	**−2%**
Short-term (2–5 years)	−2.2%	−4.4%	2.3%	4.6%
Intermediate-term (10 years)	−6.8	−13.0	7.4	15.6
Long-term (20 years)	−9.9	−18.4	11.6	25.1

*Assumes no risk of default.

**Unless you purchase a portfolio of many bonds.

Note: Bond trading results in brokerage fees and other transaction expenses, except for purchase of U.S. Treasury securities through the Treasury Direct program offered by the Federal Reserve System. The purchase or redemption of bond fund shares will also incur transaction expenses, except with shares of no-load mutual funds.

Data source: <http://www.vanguard.com>.

A prime advantage of investing through bond funds is the opportunity to derive a source of regular monthly interest income. A typical bond fund distributes virtually all its interest income in the form of dividends each month. Investors may choose to receive these dividends in the form of cash or decide to have them automatically reinvested. Individual bonds generally pay interest at six-month intervals, and such payments cannot automatically be reinvested.

Bond funds also appeal to small investors with limited amounts to invest. The minimum amount for an individual bond investment can be as much as $10,000. With such a high minimum, many individual bond investors lack the resources to build a broadly diversified bond portfolio. The minimum initial investment in a bond fund is often considerably lower. With only a few thousand dollars to invest, individual investors with limited funds can still participate in the bond market. For example, the minimum initial investment in most leading bond funds is as low as $3,000 per portfolio for a regular account or $1,000 for an individual retirement account (IRA). A mutual fund investor can also purchase additional fund shares in amounts far smaller than the cost of an individual bond. Minimum amounts for subsequent purchases can be as low as $100, and there is typically no minimum amount required for income reinvestment.

Perhaps the most compelling advantage offered by bond funds is the advantage of diversification. A typical bond fund may hold bonds from hundreds of different issuers. In such a broadly diversified bond fund, the failure of any single issuer to make timely interest or principal payments has only a slight effect on the overall portfolio. However, if the owner of only a few individual bonds faced default by a single issuer, the bond investor could face a catastrophic loss in the value of his or her portfolio.

Professional management is another advantage offered by bond mutual funds. A professional investment manager with access to extensive research, market information, and skilled securities traders is in a position to make informed trading decisions. Professional management can be a valuable service because few investors have the time or expertise to manage their personal investments on a daily basis or to investigate literally thousands of bonds available in the financial markets.

Finally, bond funds offer the advantage of ready liquidity. Shares in a bond mutual fund may be bought or sold whenever an investor chooses, and often using the fund's toll-free telephone number or Internet-based trading facility. Most bond funds also offer check writing redemption options that make bond investment and redemption extraordinarily convenient.

Providing modest offsets to these important advantages tied to bond fund investing are a few minor disadvantages. First, the dividend income paid by a bond fund tends to vary with the overall course of interest rates. It is not fixed, as it is with an individual bond. The actual interest income paid to the bond fund investor in the form of dividends may go up or down slightly as the fund buys and sells individual bonds. Second, unlike an individual bond, bond funds have no fixed maturity date. Instead, bond funds usually seek to maintain a fixed maturity structure by selling off aging bonds and buying newer ones and this may create unwanted taxable capital gains for the fund's shareholders. As a result, in 10 years, a five- to 10-year bond fund will still have a five- to 10-year average maturity, but a 10-year bond would have matured and been paid off. The owner of an individual bond has the option of holding any individual bond to maturity and receiving the face amount of the bond. The bond fund investor may have to redeem a bond mutual fund investment at a price higher or lower than the original purchase price, thus realizing a capital gain or loss.

Bond Fund Risks

Bond fund investors are subject to a variety of risks. Unlike bank savings deposits or money market funds, the value of a bond fund goes up and down with changes in credit market conditions. In 1999, for example, investors learned that bond funds can sometimes be as risky as stock funds, as a rapid rise in interest rates caused long-term bond funds to lose 8–10% of their value.

The market value of bond funds decreases in value when interest rates rise. This market value, or net asset value, increases when rates fall. The risk that a bond fund will rise or fall in value is known as interest rate risk. As shown in Table 15.6, panel B, the longer a bond fund's average time to maturity, the greater the interest rate risk. Bond fund investors also face the risk of short-term losses in income due to falling interest rates. In periods of declining market interest rates, a bond fund's interest income may fall. During periods of rising market interest rates, a bond fund's interest income can rise. Income risk is higher for short-term bond funds and lower for long-term funds. This follows from the fact that as interest rates change, short-term bonds mature and those assets can be reinvested at the new higher (or lower) interest rates. Investors can reduce interest rate risk by concentrating on short-term and intermediate-term bond funds. The only way to eliminate interest-rate risk is to fully invest in money market funds, but such funds have high income risk.

call risk
Chance of bond redemption when doing so would be economically advantageous to the issuer.

prepayment risk
Chance of mortgage-backed security redemption.

Investors in long-term bond funds also face the possibility that some bonds can be redeemed by the issuer before they mature if the issuer believes that doing so would be economically advantageous. This is **call risk.** If market interest rates have fallen or a bond issuer's credit rating has improved, bond issuers often have the opportunity to refinance their debt at a lower interest rate. By refinancing their older and higher interest-rate debt, the issuer benefits whereas the bond owner is faced with a potential loss in interest income. When a bond is refinanced by the issuer, bond holders must then reinvest their money at a lower yield. A similar risk, called **prepayment risk,** affects mortgage-backed securities such as Ginnie Maes (Government National Mortgage Association securities). When interest rates fall, homeowners often pay off their mortgages by refinancing. Securities backing those mortgages must also be paid off.

Bond investors can lose money if an issuer defaults or if a bond's credit rating is reduced. However, because a mutual fund invests in many bonds, the possibility that a single default would significantly impair the investor's overall portfolio is greatly reduced. Credit risk is lowest with U.S. Treasury bonds, followed by U.S. government agency bonds, then by corporate and municipal bonds that have high credit ratings. Investors in high-risk or junk bond funds are subject to significant credit risk, especially during economic downturns.

Finally, like all bond investors, bond mutual fund investors are exposed to inflation risk. Long-term bond investments lose purchasing power as prices rise. The risk of inflation is a serious concern for anyone relying on fixed-income securities to pay future expenses. With inflation of only 3% for five years, for example, the value of a $1000 bond principal is reduced to only $862 in actual purchasing power. Over significant periods of time, the long-run effects of inflation on the value of a bond portfolio can be devastating.

Specialized Funds

Exchange-Traded Funds (ETFs)

Some of the hottest new products to hit the mutual fund industry in decades are called **exchange-traded funds (ETFs).** ETFs offer investors a convenient means for investing in baskets of stocks that closely track any one of a large number of market indexes. ETFs are available that track the performance of broad market averages, such as the Standard and Poor's 500 Index; narrower market sectors, such as technology; or major stock markets from around the world, such as Japan. Unlike traditional index mutual funds that can be purchased or redeemed only at the end of the trading day, ETFs can be purchased or sold anytime the markets are open. Like stocks, ETFs can also be held for long-term capital appreciation. ETFs pay quarterly cash dividends from interest and dividend income, less fees and expenses that average only 0.18% to 0.25% per year.

exchange-traded funds (ETFs) Tradeable shares that represent proportional ownership in baskets of stocks.

Among the most popular ETFs are **Standard and Poor's Depository Receipts (SPDRs),** based on the S&P 500 (see Figure 15.10). SPDRs (called "spiders") are shares in a unit investment trust that holds shares of all the companies in the S&P 500. SPDRs closely track the price performance and dividend yield of the Index.

Standard and Poor's Depository Receipts (SPDRs) ETFs that track the price performance and dividend yield of the S&P 500 Index.

FIGURE 15.10 **Exchange-Traded Funds (ETFs) and Index Shares (iShares) Give Investors a Broad Range of Investment Opportunities**

Name	Symbol	Last Sale	Net Change	Volume
iShares MSCI - Australia	EWA	9.875	0.0625▼	5,000
iShares MSCI - Austria	EWO	8.25	0.375▲	5,200
iShares MSCI - Belgium	EWK	13.3125	0.125▼	3,300
iShares MSCI - Canada	EWC	18.875	0.125▼	6,700
iShares MSCI - France	EWQ	29.3125	0.3125▼	23,500
iShares MSCI - Germany	EWG	25.8125	0.0625▲	80,000
iShares MSCI - Hong Kong	EWH	12.0625	0.25▼	15,000
iShares MSCI - Italy	EWI	25.375	0.1875▼	900
iShares MSCI - Japan	EWJ	15.0625	0.0625▲	144,800
iShares MSCI - Malaysia (Free)	EWM	6.5625	0.0625▼	122,200
iShares MSCI - Mexico (Free)	EWW	15.75	0.6875▼	113,700
iShares MSCI - Netherlands	EWN	24.5	0.125▼	4,000
iShares MSCI - Singapore (Free)	EWS	7.375	0.0625▲	20,400
iShares MSCI - South Korea	EWY	20.75	0.25▼	10,200
iShares MSCI - Spain	EWP	26.875	0.25▼	8,100
iShares MSCI - Sweden	EWD	34	0.0625▲	6,600
iShares MSCI - Switzerland	EWL	16.0625	0.1875▲	20,200
iShares MSCI - United Kingdom	EWU	19.8125	0.125▼	26,600

Source: <http://nasdaq.com>.

Using SPDRs, investors can buy or sell the entire S&P 500 portfolio in a single transaction as easily as buying or selling shares of a single stock. ETFs have also been established to track the Dow Jones Industrial Average (called **DIAMONDS**), Nasdaq 100 Index (called **QQQs**), and the S&P MidCap 400 Index (called **MidCap SPDRs**). Also popular are **Select Sector SPDRs** that unbundle the S&P 500 Index and give investors ownership in a particular market sector or group of industries. At the present time, Select Sector SPDRs are offered for basic industries, consumer services, consumer staples, cyclicals/transportation, energy, financial services, industrials, technology, utilities, and so on.

DIAMONDS ETFs that track the price performance and dividend yield of the Dow Jones Industrial Average.

QQQs ETFs that track the price performance and dividend yield of the Nasdaq 100 Index.

MidCap SPDRs ETFs that track the price performance and dividend yield of the S&P MidCap 400 Index.

Select Sector SPDRs ETFs that track the price performance and dividend yield of particular industry groups.

iShares Index shares (ETFs) created by Barclays Global Investors.

Barclays Global Investors has been among the most innovative companies in the development of ETFs, and now offers more than 50 index portfolios, called **iShares,** or index shares. Using iShares, investors are able to trade portfolios that are constructed according to various broad market indexes, investing styles, market sectors, industries, and regions around the globe. With iShares, it's easy to add exposure to a wide variety of equity investment opportunities. For example, iShares are available for growth stock and value investors who want to track the performance of all the major U.S. market indexes and sector indexes produced by Dow Jones, Inc., Standard & Poor's Corp, and the Frank Russell Company. iShares are also available to track the performance of global stock markets, as reflected in 19 global indexes produced by Morgan Stanley Capital International. iShares allow investors to achieve broad geographic diversification with investments in developed global markets, such as Canada, Germany, and the United Kingdom, and in emerging markets, such as Hong Kong, Malaysia, and Mexico.

Traders and speculators like ETFs (including iShares) because they can be used to write covered options, can be purchased on margin, and, unlike common stocks, can be sold short on "downticks." Their ease of trading and broad liquidity have made ETFs a hit with day traders and other short-term speculators. While the typical mutual fund is owned for about 400 days, the typical ETF investor has a holding period of only 10 to 30 days, on average. In the case of ETFs based upon the enormously popular Nasdaq 100 Trust, the typical holding period is a mere *three days!* Many speculators face the obvious risk of losing the broad diversification and low-cost advantages of ETFs through risky rapid-fire trading strategies.

For long-term investors, ETFs and iShares represent valuable investment vehicles. ETFs and iShares can serve as the core position in an investor's portfolio by giving diversified exposure to one or more broad market indices. They can complement an existing core portfolio by enabling investors to add specific kinds of exposure, such as an aggressive sector play or a more conservative value tilt. They also make it easy for investors to add international exposure to domestic portfolios. Therefore, when judging the attractiveness of ETFs and iShares, long-term investors must keep in mind that the underlying investment concept is sound even though many ETF and iShare investors adopt short-term trading strategies that are speculative and counterproductive.

Closed-End Funds

closed-end funds Investment companies that issue a fixed number of shares at a given point in time.

A relatively small number of mutual funds, called **closed-end funds,** issue a fixed number of shares at a given point in time. They collect money from investors through an initial public offering (IPO) and use this money to invest in securities. The number of shares issued by the fund and the dollar value of assets under management are fixed at the time of the fund's IPO. Thereafter, total assets under management grow or decline depending on management's investment success. In some circumstances, closed-end fund assets can be increased following a secondary offering of shares to the general public. A closed-end fund is a publicly traded investment company. The shares of closed-end funds trade on exchanges such as the New York Stock Exchange (NYSE) and the American Stock Exchange (AMEX) or on the Nasdaq Stock Market.

Like other public corporations, closed-end funds have a board of directors elected by shareholders. The board appoints an investment advisor for investment research and portfolio management. The investment advisor employs a portfolio manager to make portfolio investment decisions in accordance with the guidelines listed in the prospectus issued during the IPO. Day-to-day administrative duties such as mailing shareholder reports or responding to shareholder concerns are performed by the investment advisor or a separate administrator.

As shown in Figure 15.11, closed-end funds offer a wide array of investment alternatives. Broadly diversified domestic funds reflect the portfolio managers' investment philosophy in their stock selection methods. Among U.S. equity funds, there are those that emphasize growth, value, market timing, blue chips, and small-caps. Many specialized closed-end funds focus on individual sectors such as banking and financial services, environmental, health care, media, and gold and natural resources. Other specialized closed-end funds focus on stocks in individual foreign countries such as Germany, India, Korea, Mexico, and Thailand. Some foreign closed-end funds focus on regions rather than individual countries. In addition to deciding which countries have particularly attractive investment environments, such funds also must decide how to allocate investments within each country. Examples include funds that focus on Africa, Asia, Europe, Latin America, and Africa. Other closed-end funds focus on emerging markets in developing nations. A few closed-end funds take a global perspective and invest in the securities of U.S. and international markets. Some of these global funds invest according to a specific theme, such as a global small-cap fund.

As for any typical mutual fund, net asset value is the current net worth per share of a closed-end fund. It is computed by deducting total liabilities from the current market value of securities held by the fund plus cash and dividing this result by the total number of outstanding shares. Closed-end fund shares trade openly on listed exchanges or in the over-the-counter market at prices that may exceed or fall short of net asset values. When the market price per share for closed-end funds exceeds its net asset value, the fund is selling at a **premium.** Closed-end funds sell at a premium to net asset value when investors are unusually optimistic about the fund's investment prospects. When the market price per share for a closed-end fund is less than its net asset value, the fund is selling at a **discount.** For example, if net asset value is $10 per share and the fund is selling on the NYSE for $12, the fund is selling at a 20% premium. If the same fund is selling for $8.50, the fund is selling at a 15% discount to net assets.

premium
When the market price per share for closed-end funds exceeds net asset value.

discount
When the market price per share for a closed-end fund is less than net asset value.

Closed-end mutual funds typically sell at a discount of 15–20% because there is no implicit agreement on the part of the fund advisor to redeem investor shares at net asset value. Closed-end funds also tend to sell at a discount because they operate in relative obscurity. Although most investors have heard about traditional open-end mutual funds, very few have heard about closed-end funds. Conventional mutual funds advertise extensively to attract new investors because fund managers

FIGURE 15.11 ***Barron's* Provides Coverage of the Closed-End Fund Industry**

F126 BARRON'S • Lipper Mutual Funds Quarterly July 10, 2000

WEEKLY CLOSED-END FUNDS

Closed-end funds sell a limited number of shares and invest in securities. Unlike open-end funds, closed-ends generally do not buy their shares back from investors who wish to sell. Instead, shares trade on a stock exchange. The following list, provided by Lipper, shows the ticker symbol and exchange where each fund trades (A: American; C: Chicago; N: NYSE; O: Nasdaq; T: Toronto; z: does not trade on an exchange). The data also include the fund's most recent net asset value (NAV), share price and the percentage difference between the market price and NAV (the premium or discount), unless indicated by a footnote otherwise. For equity funds, the final column provides 52-week returns based on market prices plus dividends; for bond funds, the past 12 months' income distributions as a percentage of the market price at last month's end. Footnotes: a: the Net Asset Value and the market price are ex dividend. b: the NAV is fully diluted. c: NAV is as of Thursday's close. d: NAV as of Wednesday's close. e: NAV assumes rights offering is fully subscribed. v: NAV is converted at the commercial Rand rate. y: NAV and market price are in Canadian dollars. NA: Information is not available or is not applicable. NS: Fund not in existence for whole period. ♣Free annual or semiannual reports are available by phoning 1-800-965-2929 or faxing 1-800-747-9384. Daily closed-end listings are available in The Wall Street Journal Interactive Edition at http://wsj.com on the Internet's World Wide Web.

Fund Name (Symbol)	Stock Exch	NAV	Market Price	Prem /Disc	52 week Market Return
Friday, July 07, 2000					
General Equity Funds					
Adams Express (ADX)	♣N	43.57	37 3/8	-14.2	35.7
Alliance All-Mkt (AMO)	N	47.88	41 11/16	-12.9	16.5
Avalon Capital (MIST)	O	17.24	15 7/16	-10.5	-17.1
Bergstrom Cap (BEM)	A	275.65	257 1/4	-6.7	48.2
Blue Chip Value Fd (BLU)	♣N	8.58	8 7/16	-1.6	-6.4
Boulder Tot Rtn (BTF)	♣N	13.03	10 5/8	-18.4	-2.4
Brantley Cap Corp (BBDC)	O	NA	9 1/8	NA	18.7
Central Secs (CET)	A	40.81	35 1/4	-13.6	42.4
Engex (EGX)	A	29.90	40 1/2	+35.5	362.9
Equus II (EQS)	♣N	16.88	10 11/16	-36.7	-8.3
Gabelli Equity Tr (GAB)	N	12.38	12 3/16	-1.5	18.4
General American (GAM)	♣N	43.03	39 1/2	-8.2	37.3
Librty AllStr Eq (USA)	♣N	14.35	12 11/16	-11.6	4.6
Librty AllStr Gr (ASG)	♣N	14.22	11 3/4	-17.4	18.4
MFS Special Value (MFV)	N	13.06	14 1/4	+9.1	-3.6
Morgan FunShares (MFUN)-c	O	7.84	7	-10.7	-6.7
Morgan Gr Sm Cap (MGC)	♣N	15.41	12 15/16	-16.0	34.8
NAIC Growth (GRF)-c	C	NA	11 3/4	NA	8.5
Royce Focus Trust (FUND)	O	6.11	5 1/32	-17.7	13.0
Royce Micro-Cap Tr (OTCM)	O	12.44	10 3/8	-16.6	29.9
Royce Value Trust (RVT)	N	16.52	13 15/16	-15.6	13.8
Salomon Brothers (SBF)	N	19.72	17 3/8	-11.9	3.8
Source Capital (SOR)	N	48.52	49	+1.0	16.0
Tri-Continental (TY)	♣N	32.20	25 9/16	-20.6	-5.9
Zweig (ZF)-a	♣N	11.38	9 13/16	-13.8	-0.3
Specialized Equity Funds					
ASA Limited (ASA)-c,q	N	19.14	15 11/16	-18.0	0.0
C&S Realty Inc (RIF)	♣A	7.35	6 7/8	-6.4	-14.4
Centrl Fd Canada (CEF)-cl	♣A	3.75	3 7/16	-8.3	12.4
Cohen&Steers TotRet (RFI)	♣N	12.07	11 11/16	-3.2	2.0
Duff&Ph Util Inc (DNP)	N	9.03	9 5/8	+6.6	-0.4
Dundee Prec Mtls (DPM.A)-cy	T	13.02	NA	NA	NA
First Financial (FF)	N	9.37	8 5/16	-11.3	-5.5
Gabelli Gl MltiMed (GGT)-f	N	19.08	14	-26.6	15.6
Gabelli Utility (GUT)	N	7.83	7 13/16	-0.3	-15.6
H&Q Health Inv (HQH)	♣N	43.96	32 7/8	-25.2	138.4
H&Q Life Sci Inv (HQL)	♣N	37.51	31	-17.4	152.6
INVESCO GloblHlth (GHS)	♣N	24.49	19	-22.4	33.6
J Han Bank (BTO)	♣N	8.41	6 7/8	-18.2	-20.3
LCM Internet Gro (FND)	A	11.74	9	-23.3	NS
Petroleum & Res (PEO)	♣N	44.74	36 1/4	-19.0	9.3
Seligman New Tech (N/A)	z	43.68	NA	NA	NS
SthEastrn Thrift (STBF)	♣O	16.28	13 1/4	-18.6	-19.2
Thermo Oppty (TMF)	A	13.39	13 3/8	-0.1	63.4
Tuxis Corp (TUX)	A	13.51	11 1/4	-16.7	0.8
meVC DFJ Fd I (MVC)	N	19.06	15 7/8	-16.7	NS
Income & Preferred Stock Funds					
Ghartwell Div&Inc (CWF)	♣N	12.51	11 5/8	-7.0	-4.1
Delaware Div&Inc (DDF)	N	12.49	11 7/16	-8.4	-16.7
Delaware Gl Div (DGF)	N	13.16	12	-8.8	-5.2
J Han Pat Globl (PGD)-a	♣N	12.58	10 13/16	-14.1	1.9
J Han Pat Pref (PPF)-a	♣N	11.86	10 3/8	-12.5	-3.0
J Han Pat Prm (PDF)	♣N	9.33	8 7/16	-9.5	2.2
J Han Pat Prm II (PDT)	♣N	11.32	9 3/8	-17.1	-5.3
J Han Pat Sel (DIV)-a	♣N	14.18	12 3/16	-14.0	-3.8
Preferred Inc Op (PFO)	♣N	10.45	9 1/2	-9.1	-7.5
Preferred Income (PFD)	♣N	13.19	12 1/8	-8.0	-2.0
Putnam Divd Inc (PDI)	N	10.45	9 1/8	-12.6	1.9
Convertible Sec's. Funds					
Bancroft Conv (BCV)	♣A	27.99	22 3/16	-20.7	12.6
Castle Conv (CVF)	A	28.44	21 15/16	-22.9	6.5
Ellsworth Conv (ECF)	♣A	11.87	9 3/16	-22.6	12.4
Gabelli Conv Sec (GCV)	N	11.25	9 7/8	-12.2	-6.7
Lincoln Conv (LNV)-c	♣N	22.55	18 7/16	-18.2	34.9
Putnam Conv Opp (PCV)	N	22.64	18 3/4	-17.2	-1.0
Putnam Hi Inc Cv (PCF)	N	8.17	7 9/16	-7.5	-5.8
Ren Cap G&I III (RENN)	O	12.99	12 5/8	-2.8	72.0
TCW Conv Secs (CVT)	♣N	12.85	10 5/8	-17.3	23.0
VK Conv Sec (VXS)	N	35.88	33 9/16	-6.5	57.0
World Equity Funds					
Argentina (AF)	N	16.12	10 13/16	-32.9	7.2
Asia Pacific (APB)	N	NA	9 13/16	NA	-7.0
Asia Tigers (GRR)	N	12.93	9 1/8	-29.4	-6.8
Austria (OST)	♣N	12.20	9 7/16	-22.6	11.8
Brazil (BZF)	N	25.07	18 1/8	-27.7	27.2
Brazilian Equity (BZL)	♣N	8.57	6 3/16	-27.8	30.3
Cdn Genl Inv (CGI)-y	♣T	18.57	11 1/2	-38.1	-3.1
Cdn Wrld Fd Ltd (CWF)-cy	♣T	7.23	4 19/32	-36.4	4.5
Central Eur Eqty (CEE)	♣N	19.85	14 5/8	-26.3	6.4
Central Euro Val (CRF)	N	14.07	10 7/8	-22.7	-9.3
Chile (CH)	♣N	13.77	10	-27.4	-14.2
China (CHN)	N	13.64	9 11/16	-29.0	-18.4
Clemente Str Val (CLM)	N	15.70	12 15/16	-17.6	11.6
Economic Inv Tr (EVT)-cy	T	170.27	95 1/2	-43.9	NA
Emer Mkts Grow (N/A)	z	69.89	NA	NA	NA
Emer Mkts Infra (EMG)	♣N	14.48	12 1/4	-15.4	33.1
Emer Mkts Tel (ETF)	♣N	20.14	15 1/2	-23.0	37.0
Europe Fd (EF)	♣N	20.95	17 11/16	-15.6	19.9
European Warrant (EWF)-c	N	19.67	14 13/16	-24.7	12.1
F&C Middle East (EME)-c	N	18.20	NA	NA	NA
Fidelty Ad Korea (FAK)	♣N	NA	11 15/16	NA	8.5
First Australia (IAF)	A	8.36	6 11/16	-20.0	-9.3
First Israel (ISL)	♣N	22.49	17 3/4	-21.1	34.6
First Philippine (FPF)	N	5.19	4 1/16	-21.8	-53.6
France Growth (FRF)-a	N	16.01	14 3/8	-10.2	44.7
Germany Fund (GER)	♣N	15.82	14	-11.5	9.4
Greater China (GCH)	♣N	12.55	9 1/16	-27.8	-9.4
Herzfeld Caribb (CUBA)	O	5.11	5 3/8	+5.3	-8.4
India Fund (IFN)	N	21.78	14 15/16	-31.4	35.8
India Growth (IGF)-d	N	18.47	11 5/8	-37.0	12.8
Indonesia (IF)	♣N	2.35	3 1/4	+38.3	-51.6
Irish Inv (IRL)	N	19.79	13 15/16	-29.6	-16.2
Italy (ITA)	N	21.27	19 1/4	-9.5	65.7
Jakarta Growth (JGF)	N	1.54	1 1/2	-2.6	-60.7
Japan Equity (JEQ)-c	♣N	9.54	7 5/8	-20.0	-22.2
Japan OTC Equity (JOF)	N	13.00	9 1/2	-26.9	-6.6
Jardine Fl China (JFC)	♣N	10.73	7 7/8	-26.6	-5.9
Jardine Fl India (JFI)-c	♣N	17.19	11 7/16	-33.5	52.5
Korea (KF)	N	20.34	14 1/2	-28.7	-12.8
Korea Equity (KEF)	N	NA	4	NA	-32.6
Korean Inv (KIF)	N	10.53	7 5/16	-30.6	-18.8
Latin Amer Disc (LDF)	N	14.89	11 1/16	-25.7	18.4
Latin Amer Eq (LAQ)	♣N	18.40	13 3/4	-25.3	32.5
Latin Amer Inv (LAM)	♣N	18.86	16	-15.2	49.6
MSDW Emg Mkts (MSF)	N	20.60	15 1/2	-24.8	25.3
MSDW Africa (AFF)	N	11.57	7 7/8	-31.9	-19.8
MSDW Asia-Pac (APF)	N	14.74	10 9/16	-28.4	5.0
MSDW E Europe (RNE)	N	20.22	17 1/4	-14.7	7.8
MSDW India (IIF)	N	18.25	11 11/16	-36.0	12.7
Malaysia (MF)	N	5.71	4 13/16	-15.8	-33.9
Mexico (MXF)-m	♣N	23.88	16 5/16	-31.7	-4.5
Mexico Eqty&Inc (MXE)-c	N	12.31	11 9/16	-6.1	45.4
New Germany (GF)	♣N	17.86	13 11/16	-23.4	19.2
Pakistan Inv (PKF)	N	3.58	2 1/2	-30.2	7.6
Portugal (PGF)	♣N	14.82	12 1/4	-17.3	2.9
ROC Taiwan (ROC)	N	10.32	8 3/8	-18.8	-4.2
Scudder New Asia (SAF)	N	20.16	14 7/8	-26.2	0.2
Singapore (SGF)-c	♣N	8.73	6 15/16	-20.5	-31.5
Southern Africa (SOA)	N	17.69	13 1/8	-25.8	12.7
Spain (SNF)	N	13.57	12 7/8	-5.1	12.5
Swiss Helvetia (SWZ)	♣N	18.86	15 1/4	-19.1	16.6
Taiwan (TWN)	N	23.04	18 3/8	-20.2	-6.3
Taiwan Equity (TYW)-c	♣N	NA	NA	NA	NA
Templeton China (TCH)-cl	N	10.79	8	-25.9	-9.7
Templeton Dragon (TDF)	N	11.64	8 3/4	-24.8	-9.2
Templeton Em App (TEA)-cl	N	13.64	9 7/8	-27.6	-15.6
Templeton Em Mkt (EMF)	N	11.96	9 3/4	-18.5	-30.8
Templeton Russia (TRF)-cl	N	15.41	16 3/4	+8.7	-11.8
Templeton Vietnm (TVF)	N	10.11	7 1/4	-28.3	-34.1
Thai (TTF)	N	3.91	5 1/16	+29.4	-53.5
Thai Capital (TC)-c	♣N	2.18	3 1/2	+60.6	-48.6
Third Canadian (THD)-cy	T	19.76	14	-29.2	-9.8
Turkish Inv (TKF)	N	19.67	15 5/8	-20.5	127.8
United Corps Ltd (UNC)-cy	T	79.52	42	-47.2	NA
Z-Seven (ZSEV)	O	8.28	8 5/32	-1.5	8.2

Tracking Closed-End Funds

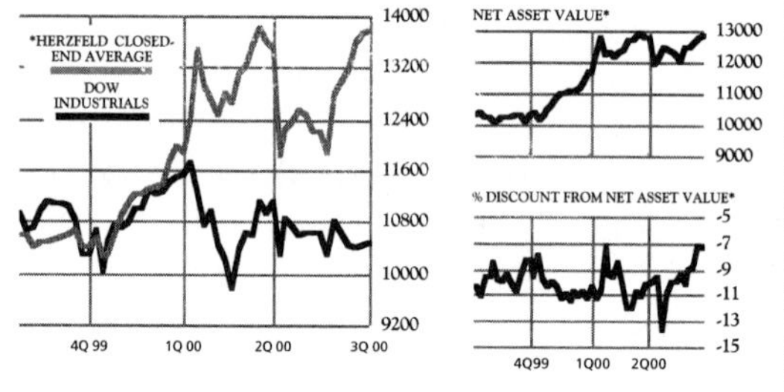

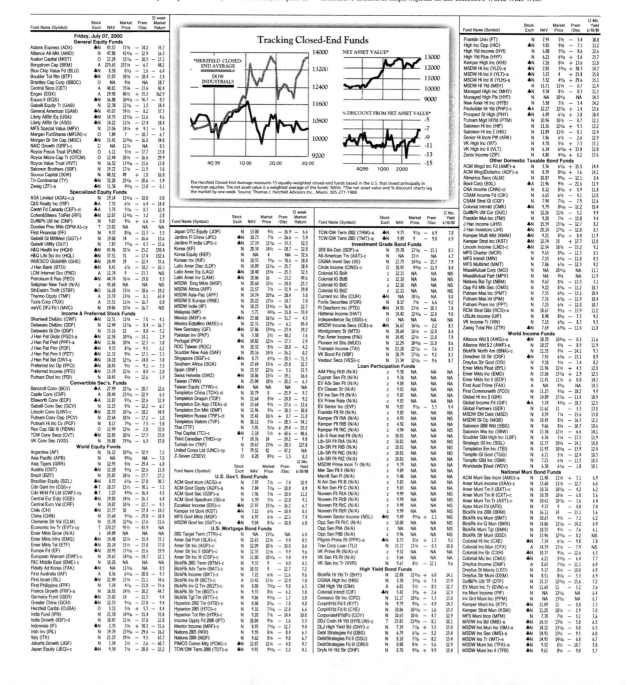

The Herzfeld Closed-End Average measures 15 equally-weighted closed-end funds based in the U.S. that invest principally in American equities. The net asset value is a weighted average of the funds' NAVs. *The net asset value and % discount charts lag the market by one week. Source: Thomas J. Herzfeld Advisors Inc., Miami. 305-271-1900

Fund Name (Symbol)	Stock Exch	NAV	Market Price	Prem /Disc	12 Mo. Yield 6/30/00
U.S. Gov't. Bond Funds					
ACM Govt Incm (ACG)-a	N	7.97	7 3/8	-7.4	10.9
ACM Govt Oppty (AOF)-a	N	7.84	7 1/16	-10.0	8.9
ACM Govt Sec (GSF)-a	N	7.96	7 1/8	-10.4	11.2
ACM Govt Spectrum (SI)-a	N	6.59	5 3/4	-12.8	9.1
Excelsior Income (EIS)-c	♣N	17.97	15 1/16	-16.2	6.7
Kemper Int Govt (KGT)	♣N	7.12	6 3/8	-10.4	8.5
MFS Govt Mkts (MGF)	N	6.97	6 1/8	-12.1	7.9
MSDW Govt Inc (GVT)-a	♣N	9.04	8 1/16	-10.8	6.8
U.S. Mortgage Bond Funds					
2002 Target Term (TTR)-c	N	NA	13 5/16	NA	6.4
Amer Sel Port (SLA)-c	N	12.63	11 3/8	-9.9	8.5
Amer Str Inc (ASP)-c	N	12.09	10 7/8	-10.0	8.6
Amer Str Inc II (BSP)-c	N	12.35	11 1/8	-9.9	9.6
Amer Str Inc III (CSP)-c	N	11.80	10 11/16	-9.4	9.9
BlckRk 2001 Term (BTM)-c	N	9.37	9	-4.0	4.1
BlckRk Adv Term (BAT)-c	N	10.31	9	-12.7	7.2
BlckRk Income (BKT)-c	N	7.22	6 3/8	-11.6	9.6
BlckRk Inv 09 (BCT)-c	A	13.41	11 3/4	-12.4	7.8
BlckRk Inv Q Tm (BQT)-c	N	8.80	7 15/16	-9.8	6.5
BlckRk Str Tm (BGT)-c	N	9.33	8 3/4	-6.2	5.8
BlckRk Tgt Tm (BTT)-c	N	9.86	9 11/16	-1.7	5.0
Hyperion 2002 Tm (HTB)-c	N	8.88	8 3/16	-7.8	4.8
Hyperion 2005 (HTO)-c	N	9.10	7 15/16	-12.8	6.6
Hyperion Tot Rtn (HTR)-c	N	9.20	7 7/8	-14.4	10.0
Income Oppty Fd 2000 (IFT)	N	10.04	9 7/8	-1.6	5.5
Mentor Income (MRF)-c	N	8.95	7 13/16	-12.7	9.4
Nations 2003 (NGI)	N	9.55	8 3/4	-8.4	6.3
Nations 2004 (NGF)	N	9.62	8 3/4	-9.0	6.7
PIMCO Comm Mtg (PCM)-c	♣N	12.87	12 1/4	-4.8	9.7
TCW/DW Term 2000 (TDT)-a	♣N	9.91	9 11/16	-2.2	4.1
TCW/DW Term 2002 (TRM)-a	♣N	9.73	9 1/16	-6.9	7.0
TCW/DW Term 2003 (TMT)-a	♣N	9.89	9	-9.0	6.9
Investment Grade Bond Funds					
1838 Bd-Deb (BDF)-a	N	19.78	17 3/16	-13.1	8.3
All-American Tm (AAT)-c	N	NA	11 1/2	NA	6.7
CIGNA Invmt Sec (IIS)	N	17.73	14 15/16	-15.7	7.9
Circle Income (CINS)-c	O	10.97	9 21/32	-11.9	8.4
Colonial IG BdA	z	12.11	NA	NA	NS
Colonial IG BdB	z	12.10	NA	NA	NS
Colonial IG BdC	z	12.10	NA	NA	NS
Colonial IG BdZ	z	12.11	NA	NA	NS
Current Inc Shs (CUR)	♣N	NA	10 3/16	NA	8.0
Fortis Securities (FOR)	N	8.17	7 5/8	-6.6	9.2
Ft Dearborn Inc (FTD)	♣N	14.91	13 3/8	-10.3	7.8
Hatteras Income (HAT)	N	14.42	12 11/16	-12.0	9.0
Independence Sq (ISIS)-c	O	NA	NA	NA	NA
MSDW Income Secs (ICB)-a	♣N	16.67	16 5/16	-2.2	8.3
Montgomery St (MTS)	N	18.64	16 1/4	-12.8	8.4
Pac Amer Income (PAI)	N	14.45	12 3/4	-11.8	7.9
Pioneer Int Shs (MUO)	N	12.29	10 15/16	-11.0	8.6
Transam Income (TAI)	N	23.28	22 7/16	-3.6	8.5
VK Bond Fd (VBF)	N	18.79	17 1/16	-9.2	8.3
Vestaur Secs (VES)-c	N	13.34	12 1/16	-9.6	8.7
Loan Participation Funds					
AIM Fltng Rt:B (N/A)	z	9.58	NA	NA	NA
Cyprstr Sen Flt (N/A)	z	9.76	NA	NA	NA
EV Adv Sen Flt (N/A)	z	9.84	NA	NA	NA
EV Classic Sr (N/A)	z	9.81	NA	NA	NA
EV Ins Sen Flt (N/A)	z	9.87	NA	NA	NA
EV Prime Rate (N/A)	z	9.83	NA	NA	NA
EV Senior Inc (EVF)	N	9.83	9 5/16	-5.3	9.4
Franklin Flt Rt (N/A)	z	9.85	NA	NA	NA
Kemper Flt RtA (N/A)	z	4.93	NA	NA	NS
Kemper Flt RtB (N/A)	z	4.92	NA	NA	NA
Kemper Flt RtC (N/A)	z	4.94	NA	NA	NS
Lib-S Roe Inst Flt (N/A)	z	10.01	NA	NA	NA
Lib-SR Flt RtA (N/A)	z	10.01	NA	NA	NS
Lib-SR Flt RtB (N/A)	z	10.01	NA	NA	NS
Lib-SR Flt RtC (N/A)	z	10.01	NA	NA	NS
Lib-SR Flt RtZ (N/A)	z	10.01	NA	NA	NA
MSDW Prime Incm Tr (N/A)	z	9.79	NA	NA	NA
Mer Sen Flt II (N/A)	z	9.89	NA	NA	NA
Merrill Sen Fl (N/A)	z	9.48	NA	NA	NA
N Am Sen Flt B (N/A)	z	9.83	NA	NA	NA
N Am Sen Flt C (N/A)	z	9.83	NA	NA	NA
Nuveen Flt Rt:A (N/A)	z	9.99	NA	NA	NS
Nuveen Flt Rt:B (N/A)	z	9.99	NA	NA	NS
Nuveen Flt Rt:C (N/A)	z	9.99	NA	NA	NS
Nuveen Flt Rt:R (N/A)	z	9.99	NA	NA	NS
Nuveen Senior Income (NSL)	♣N	9.49	9 11/16	+2.1	NS
Opp Sen Flt Rt:C (N/A)	z	10.00	NA	NA	NS
Opp Sen FltA (N/A)	z	NA	NA	NA	NS
Opp Sen FltB (N/A)	z	9.96	NA	NA	NS
Pilgrim Prime Rt (PPR)-a	♣N	8.75	8 7/8	+1.5	9.2
Trav Corp Loan (TLI)	N	15.17	13 7/8	-8.5	10.0
VK Prime Rt (N/A)-cl	z	9.52	NA	NA	NA
VK Sen Flt Rt (N/A)	z	9.64	NA	NA	NA
VK Sen Inc Tr (VVR)	N	9.67	8 1/2	-12.1	9.6
High Yield Bond Funds					
BlckRk Hi Yld Tr (BHY)	N	12.08	12 13/16	+6.0	14.1
CIGNA High Inc (HIS)	N	5.30	5 11/16	+7.4	13.9
CIM High Yld (CIM)	A	6.01	5 1/2	-8.5	12.7
Colonial Intmdt (CIF)	♣N	5.42	5 9/16	+2.6	12.3
Conseco Str Inc (CFD)	N	11.17	10 9/16	-5.5	13.8
CorpHiYld Fd II (KYT)	N	9.79	9 5/16	-4.9	14.3
CorpHiYld Fd III (CYE)	N	10.86	10 11/16	-1.6	13.5
CorporateHiYldFd (COY)	N	10.63	10 1/8	-4.7	12.9
DDJ Cndn Hi Yld (HYB.UN)-y	T	23.83	21 29/32	-8.1	10.1
DLJ High Yield Bd (DHY)-c	N	7.19	7 7/16	+3.5	13.4
Debt Strategies Fd (DBS)	N	6.79	6 7/16	-5.2	13.4
DebtStrategies Fd II (DSU)	N	8.10	7 7/16	-8.2	13.4
DebtStrategies Fd III (DBU)	N	8.88	8 3/8	-5.6	12.9
Dryfs Hi Yld Str (DHF)	N	8.70	9 9/16	+9.9	15.4
Franklin Univ (FT)	N	7.93	7 1/2	-5.4	10.8
High Inc Opp (HIO)	♣N	9.85	9 1/8	-7.3	11.2
High Yld Income (HYI)	N	6.08	5 9/16	-8.6	12.6
High Yld Plus (HYP)	N	6.21	6 9/16	+5.6	13.7
Kemper High Inc (KHI)	♣N	7.26	8 1/4	+13.6	11.8
MSDW Hi Inc (YLD)-a	♣N	2.85	3 15/16	+38.3	14.7
MSDW Hi Inc II (YLT)-a	♣N	3.23	4	+23.8	15.0
MSDW Hi Inc III (YLH)-a	♣N	3.52	4 9/16	+29.6	15.1
MSDW Hi Yld (MSY)	N	11.71	11 5/8	-0.7	11.4
Managed High Inc (MHY)	♣N	9.54	8 3/4	-8.3	11.3
Managed High Pls (HYF)	N	NA	10 9/16	NA	14.5
New Amer Hi Inc (HYB)	N	3.50	3 3/8	-3.4	14.2
Pacholder Hi Yld (PHF)-c	♣A	12.27	12 7/16	+1.4	13.6
Prospect St High (PHY)	♣N	6.09	6 7/16	+5.8	18.4
Putnam Mgd HiYld (PTM)	N	10.96	10 7/8	-0.7	12.1
Salomon Hi Inc (HIF)	N	11.26	12 5/16	+9.3	12.2
Salomon Hi Inc 2 (HIX)	N	11.89	11 7/8	-0.1	12.4
Senior Hi Incm Ptfl (ARK)	N	7.06	6 7/8	-2.6	12.9
VK High Inc (VIT)	N	4.78	5 1/8	+7.3	13.1
VK High Inc II (VLT)	N	6.14	6 15/16	+13.0	12.8
Zenix Income (ZIF)	N	4.80	4 13/16	+0.2	13.6
Other Domestic Taxable Bond Funds					
ACM Mngd Inc Fd (AMF)-a	N	5.36	6 3/16	+15.5	14.4
ACM MngdDollarInc (ADF)-a	N	8.39	8 11/16	+3.6	14.1
Allmerica Secs (ALM)	N	10.87	9 9/16	-12.1	8.4
Bexil Corp (BXL)	♣A	11.96	9 3/8	-21.6	11.9
CNA Income (CNN)-cl	N	8.12	8 3/16	+0.9	11.8
CSAM Income Fd (CIK)	N	6.65	6 3/8	-4.1	12.0
CSAM Strat Gl (CGF)	N	7.94	7 5/16	-7.9	12.6
Colonial Intrmkt (CMK)	♣N	9.79	8 11/16	-11.2	10.4
Duff&Ph Util Cor (DUC)	N	12.26	11 5/8	-5.1	9.9
Franklin Mul-Inc (FMI)	N	9.20	7 3/4	-15.8	9.4
J Han Income (JHS)	♣N	15.39	13 7/16	-12.7	8.2
J Han Investors (JHI)	♣N	20.14	17 9/16	-12.8	8.3
Kemper Multi Mkt (KMM)	♣N	9.21	8 7/16	-8.4	11.9
Kemper Strat Inc (KST)	♣N	12.74	15	+17.7	12.0
Lincoln Income (LND)-c	♣N	12.54	10 7/8	-13.2	9.2
MFS Charter (MCR)	N	9.65	8 9/16	-11.3	8.5
MFS Intmdt (MIN)	N	7.15	6 5/16	-11.8	8.5
MFS Multimkt (MMT)	N	7.06	6 3/16	-12.3	9.2
MassMutual Corp (MCI)	N	NA	20 11/16	NA	11.1
MassMutual Part (MPV)	N	NA	9 5/8	NA	11.9
Nations Bal Tgt (NBM)	N	9.67	8 3/8	-13.3	5.1
Opp Fd Mlti-Sec (OMS)	N	9.22	8 3/16	-11.2	10.3
Putnam Mas Inc (PMT)	N	7.55	6 9/16	-13.1	10.4
Putnam Mas Int (PIM)	N	7.31	6 7/16	-11.9	10.4
Putnam Prem Inc (PPT)	N	7.25	6 3/8	-12.0	10.7
RCM Strat Glbl (RCS)-a	N	10.67	9 3/16	-13.9	11.2
USLife Income (UIF)	N	8.98	8 5/16	-7.5	9.2
VK Income Tr (VIN)	N	7.15	6 9/16	-8.3	9.5
Zweig Total Rtn (ZTR)	♣N	7.69	6 13/16	-11.4	11.8
World Income Funds					
Alliance Wld $ (AWG)-a	♣N	10.70	10 11/16	-0.1	11.6
Alliance Wld $ 2 (AWF)-a	N	10.57	9 5/8	-8.9	11.9
BlckRk North Am (BNA)-c	N	11.35	9 3/4	-14.1	9.3
Dresdner Gl Str (DSF)	♣N	7.43	6 5/16	-15.1	8.9
Dreyfus Str Govt (DSI)	N	9.58	9 1/4	-3.4	8.2
Emer Mkts Float (EFL)	N	11.96	12 1/2	+4.5	12.8
Emer Mkts Inc (EMD)	N	13.06	13 7/16	+2.9	12.5
Emer Mkts Inc II (EDF)	N	11.41	11 1/2	+0.8	14.3
First Aust Prime (FAX)	A	NA	4 9/16	NA	14.5
First Commonwlth (FCO)	N	11.23	9 3/16	-18.2	9.9
Global Hi Inc $ (GHI)	N	14.89	13 3/16	-11.4	10.9
Global Income Fd (GIF)	♣A	5.74	4 11/16	-18.3	12.5
Global Partners (GDF)	N	11.62	11	-5.3	13.0
MSDW EM Debt (MSD)	N	8.59	7 1/4	-15.6	13.8
MSDW Gl Op (MGB)	N	10.45	8 3/4	-16.3	12.2
Salomon 2008 Wld (SBG)	N	9.66	8 5/8	-10.7	10.6
Salomon Ww Inc (SBW)	N	13.38	12 1/2	-6.6	14.1
Scudder Glbl High Inc (LBF)	N	6.36	5 1/4	-17.5	11.9
Strategic Gl Inc (SGL)	N	12.37	10 5/8	-14.1	10.8
Templeton Em Inc (TEI)	N	11.97	10 5/16	-13.9	12.4
Templtn Gl Govt (TGG)	N	6.71	5 7/8	-12.4	10.3
Templtn Glbl Inc (GIM)	N	7.21	6 3/8	-11.5	10.5
Worldwide $Vest (WDV)	N	6.30	6 3/16	-1.8	10.1
National Muni Bond Funds					
ACM Muni Sec Incm (AMU)-a	N	11.40	11 3/4	+3.1	6.9
Amer Muni Income (XAA)-c	N	13.60	11 7/8	-12.7	6.6
Amer Muni Tm II (BXT)-c	N	10.76	10 5/16	-4.2	6.2
Amer Muni Tm III (CXT)-c	N	10.78	10 1/8	-6.0	5.6
Amer Muni Tm Tr (AXT)-c	N	10.61	10 7/16	-1.6	6.4
Apex Muni Fd (APX)	N	9.37	9	-4.0	7.4
BlckRk Ins 2008 (BRM)	N	16.11	14	-13.1	5.6
BlckRk Ins Muni (BMT)	N	10.63	9 7/8	-7.1	6.2
BlckRk Inv Q Mun (BKN)	N	14.06	12 1/16	-14.2	6.9
BlckRk Muni Tgt (BMN)	N	10.55	9 3/4	-7.6	6.1
BlckRk Str Muni (BSD)	N	13.96	12 13/16	-8.2	NS
Colonial Hi Inc (CXE)	♣N	7.14	6 7/16	-9.8	7.8
Colonial Ins Mun (CFX)	A	14.39	13 1/4	-7.9	NS
Colonial Inv Gr (CXH)	♣N	10.37	9 1/16	-12.6	6.5
Colonial Mu Inc (CMU)	♣N	6.21	5 13/16	-6.4	7.7
Dreyfus Income (DMF)	A	8.65	7 11/16	-11.1	6.9
Dreyfus St Munis (LEO)	N	9.17	8 1/4	-10.0	6.9
Dreyfus Str Muni (DSM)	N	8.51	8 1/16	-5.3	6.9
Duff&Ph Util TF (DTF)	N	15.17	12 13/16	-15.6	7.2
EV Muni Inc Tr (EVN)-a	N	11.60	11	-5.2	7.6
Ins Muni Income (PIF)	N	NA	12 5/16	NA	6.4
Inv Grd Muni Inc (PPM)	N	NA	13 9/16	NA	6.7
Kemper Muni Inc (KTF)	♣N	11.09	11	-0.8	7.3
Kemper Strat Mun (KSM)	♣N	11.20	10 7/8	-2.9	7.0
MFS Muni Inco (MFM)	N	7.78	7 3/8	-5.1	7.6
MSDW Ins Bd (IMB)-a	♣N	14.35	13 5/8	-5.0	6.5
MSDW Ins Mun Inc (IIM)-a	♣N	14.12	13 7/16	-4.8	6.5
MSDW Ins Sec (IMS)-a	♣N	14.91	13 1/2	-9.5	6.0
MSDW Ins Tr (IMT)-a	♣N	14.95	14 1/16	-6.0	6.7
MSDW Muni Inc (TFA)-a	♣N	9.52	8 1/2	-10.7	5.8
MSDW Muni Inc II (TFB)	♣N	9.61	8 3/4	-9.0	5.7

FIGURE 15.11 ***(continued)***

July 10, 2000 BARRON'S • Lipper Mutual Funds Quarterly F127

WEEKLY CLOSED-END FUNDS

Fund Name (Symbol)	Stock Exch	NAV	Market Price	Prem /Disc	12 Mo. Yield 6/30/00
MSDW Muni IncIII (TFC)-a	♣N	9.48	8	-15.6	5.8
MSDW Muni Op (OIA)	♣N	7.87	8 5/16	+5.6	7.3
MSDW Muni Op II (OIB)-a	♣N	8.34	7 3/16	-13.8	6.9
MSDW Muni Op III (OIC)-a	♣N	9.32	8 1/8	-12.8	6.9
MSDW Muni Prem (PIA)-a	♣N	9.39	8 1/8	-13.4	6.8
MSDW Qual Inc (IQI)-a	♣N	15.01	13 3/4	-8.4	6.9
MSDW Qual Inv (IQT)-a	♣N	14.44	13 13/16	-4.4	6.8
MSDW Qual Sec (IQM)-a	♣N	13.94	12 1/8	-13.0	6.7
Managed Munis (MMU)	♣N	11.31	10 1/16	-11.1	6.1
Managed Munis 2 (MTU)	N	11.27	9 13/16	-13.0	6.3
Merrill Hi Inc (N/A)	z	9.41	NA	NA	NA
Merrill Mun Str (N/A)	z	8.74	NA	NA	NA
MnHldgs Fd (MHD)	N	13.38	13 5/8	+1.9	7.0
MnHldgs Fd II (MUH)	N	12.37	11 1/2	-7.0	7.3
MunHldgsIn (MUS)	N	12.67	11 7/8	-6.2	7.0
MunHldgsInII (MUE)	N	12.58	10 9/16	-16.1	7.5
MunHldgsInIII (MSR)	N	13.19	11 1/4	-14.7	7.4
MunHldgsInIV (MOU)	A	15.37	13 1/4	-13.8	NS
Muni Partners (MNP)	N	13.59	12	-11.7	6.8
Muni Partners II (MPT)	N	13.19	11 13/16	-10.5	6.5
MuniAssets Fd (MUA)	N	12.99	11 1/2	-11.5	7.2
MuniEnhancedFd (MEN)	N	10.71	9 5/8	-10.1	6.6
MuniInsured (MIF)	A	9.21	7 15/16	-13.8	5.7
MuniVest Fd (MVF)	A	8.87	7 15/16	-10.5	7.3
MuniVest Fd II (MVT)	N	13.10	11 13/16	-9.9	7.0
MuniYield Fd (MYD)	N	13.10	12 5/8	-3.6	7.2
MuniYield Ins Fd (MYI)	N	13.93	12 9/16	-9.8	6.9
MuniYieldQlty Fd (MQY)	N	13.91	12 3/16	-12.4	6.9
MuniYieldQlty Fd II (MQT)	N	12.25	11 9/16	-5.6	7.1
Municipal Adv (MAF)	N	13.50	11 9/16	-14.4	7.0
Municipal High (MHF)	♣N	8.81	7 7/8	-10.6	7.6
Nuveen Div Advtg (NAD)	N	13.21	12 1/2	-5.4	7.2
Nuveen Ins Opp (NIO)	♣N	14.48	13	-10.2	7.0
Nuveen Ins Pr 2 (NPX)	♣N	12.83	11 7/16	-10.8	6.5
Nuveen Ins Qual (NQI)	♣N	14.31	13 11/16	-4.3	7.0
Nuveen Inv Qual (NQM)	♣N	14.34	12 13/16	-10.7	7.3
Nuveen Muni Adv (NMA)	♣N	14.32	12 3/4	-11.0	7.6
Nuveen Muni Inc (NMI)	♣N	11.28	11 1/2	+2.0	6.1
Nuveen Muni Mkt (NMO)	♣N	14.30	13 5/16	-6.9	7.5
Nuveen Muni Val (NUV)	♣N	9.65	8 5/8	-10.6	6.0
Nuveen Perf Plus (NPP)	♣N	14.07	12 1/4	-12.9	7.3
Nuveen Pr (NPI)	♣N	13.91	12	-13.7	6.9
Nuveen Pr 2 (NPM)	♣N	14.61	13 5/16	-8.9	7.2
Nuveen Pr 4 (NPT)	♣N	13.59	12 1/4	-9.9	6.8
Nuveen Pr Ins (NIF)	♣N	14.50	13 5/16	-8.2	7.0
Nuveen Pr Mun (NPF)	♣N	14.33	13 1/2	-5.8	7.3
Nuveen Qual (NQU)	♣N	14.40	13 3/8	-7.1	7.5
Nuveen Sel Mat (NIM)	♣N	11.32	10 9/16	-6.7	5.9
Nuveen Sel Qual (NQS)	♣N	14.31	13 1/8	-8.3	7.3
Nuveen Sel TF (NXP)	♣N	14.91	14 5/8	-1.9	6.3
Nuveen Sel TF 2 (NXQ)	♣N	14.77	14 5/16	-3.1	6.2
Nuveen Sel TF 3 (NXR)	♣N	14.35	13 5/8	-5.0	6.1
Putnam Hi Yld (PYM)	N	8.13	7 7/8	-3.1	7.8
Putnam Inv Gr (PGM)	N	10.63	10	-5.9	9.2
Putnam Inv Gr II (PMG)	N	12.77	11 3/16	-12.4	7.4
Putnam Inv GrIII (PML)	A	12.36	11 1/16	-10.5	7.0
Putnam Mgd Inc (PMM)	N	8.42	9 3/16	+9.1	8.4
Putnam Muni Opp (PMO)	N	12.73	12 7/16	-2.3	7.5
Putnam TxFr Hlth (PMH)	N	13.35	12 1/4	-8.2	7.5
SB Intmdt Muni (SBI)	A	10.04	9	-10.4	6.0
SB Muni (SBT)	A	14.61	12 15/16	-11.4	6.0
Seligman Quality (SQF)	♣N	13.45	11 5/8	-13.5	6.5
Seligman Select (SEL)	♣N	11.06	9 9/16	-13.6	6.9
VK Adv Muni (VKA)	N	15.23	13 1/16	-14.3	7.0
VK Adv Muni II (VKI)	A	13.15	11 5/8	-11.6	6.7
VK Inv Gr Muni (VIG)	N	9.28	8 15/16	-3.7	7.3
VK Muni Inc Tr (VMT)	N	9.07	8 13/16	-2.9	7.0
VK Muni Opp II (VOT)	N	13.52	11 9/16	-14.5	6.9
VK Muni Opp Tr (VMO)	N	16.03	13 5/8	-15.0	6.6
VK Muni Trust (VKQ)	N	14.70	13 13/16	-6.1	7.2
VK Sel Sect (VKL)	A	12.67	10 15/16	-13.7	6.7
VK Strat Sec (VKS)	N	13.42	11 1/2	-14.3	6.8
VK Tr Ins Muni (VIM)	N	15.67	14 3/4	-5.9	6.7
VK Tr Inv Grd (VGM)	N	15.91	13 7/8	-12.8	7.4
VK Value Muni (VKV)	N	14.12	12 1/4	-13.2	6.9
Single State Muni Bond					
BlckRk CA Ins 08 (BFC)	N	16.36	14 9/16	-11.0	5.3
BlckRk CA Inv (RAA)	A	14.49	13 3/8	-7.7	6.4
BlckRk FL Ins 08 (BRF)	N	15.51	14 5/8	-5.7	5.8
BlckRk FL Inv (RFA)	A	14.49	13	-10.3	6.2
BlckRk NJ Inv (RNJ)	A	13.76	12 1/2	-9.2	5.9
BlckRk NY Ins 08 (BLN)	N	15.68	14 5/16	-8.7	5.8
BlckRk NY Inv (RNY)	A	14.34	13 1/8	-8.4	6.4
BlckRk PA Str (BPS)	A	14.02	13 3/4	-1.9	NS
Colonial CA Ins (CCA)	A	14.66	14 3/4	+0.6	NS
Colonial NY Ins (CNM)	A	14.50	14 5/8	+0.9	NS
Dreyfus CA Inc (DCM)	A	8.69	8 1/4	-5.1	6.6
Dreyfus NY Inc (DNM)	A	9.03	8 1/16	-10.7	6.3
EV CA Muni Inc (CEV)	A	12.26	11 1/4	-8.2	7.0
EV FL Muni Inc (FEV)	A	12.33	10 9/16	-14.4	7.1
EV MA Muni Inc (MMV)-a	A	11.71	11 5/16	-3.4	6.7
EV MI Muni Inc (EMI)-a	A	12.22	10 3/4	-12.0	7.1
EV NJ Muni Inc (EVJ)-a	A	12.00	10 15/16	-8.8	6.9
EV NY Muni Inc (EVY)-a	A	12.33	11	-10.8	7.2
EV OH Muni Inc (EVO)-a	A	12.29	11 1/2	-6.4	6.6
EV PA Muni Inc (EVP)-a	A	12.27	10 7/8	-11.3	7.0
Greenwich St CA (GCM)	A	13.45	11 11/16	-13.1	5.1
MA Hlth & Educ (MHE)	A	12.67	12 21/32	0.0	6.1
MSDW CA Ins (IIC)-a	♣N	13.97	13 3/16	-5.6	6.1
MSDW CA Qual (IQC)-a	♣N	13.55	12 15/16	-4.5	6.1
MSDW Ins CA (ICS)-a	♣N	14.88	13 3/4	-7.6	5.4
MSDW NY Qual (IQN)-a	♣N	13.47	12 9/16	-6.8	6.2
Minn Muni Income (MXA)-c	A	13.57	12 5/8	-6.9	6.3
Minn Muni Tm (MNA)-c	N	10.31	10 1/16	-2.4	6.4
Minn Muni Tm II (MNB)-c	A	10.17	10	-1.7	6.0
MnHdgs MI Ins Ii (MDH)	N	14.93	13 3/4	-7.9	NS
MnHldgs CA Ins Fd II (MUC)	N	13.47	12 3/8	-8.1	6.6
MnHldgs CA Ins V (CAF)	N	14.56	13 3/4	-5.6	NS
MnHldgs Fl Ins Fd (MFL)	N	13.40	11 3/16	-16.5	7.3
MnHldgs Fl Ins V (FDM)	N	14.11	12 3/4	-9.6	NS
MnHldgs NJ Ins (MUJ)	N	12.97	11 1/2	-11.3	7.0
MnHldgs NJ Ins IV (MHJ)	N	14.08	12 3/8	-12.1	NS
MnHldgs NY Ins (MHN)	N	13.71	11 15/16	-12.9	7.1
MnHldgs NY Ins IV (MNW)	N	14.01	12 3/4	-9.0	NS
MuniYield AZ (MZA)	A	12.88	11 1/8	-13.6	6.5
MuniYield CA Fd (MYC)	N	13.85	13 1/2	-2.5	6.2
MuniYield CA Ins Fd (MIC)	N	13.36	13 1/4	-0.8	6.2
MuniYield CA Ins Fd II (MCA)	N	13.87	13 1/2	-2.7	6.1
MuniYield FL (MYF)	N	13.60	11 1/2	-15.4	6.9
MuniYield FL Ins Fd (MFT)	N	13.72	12 1/4	-10.7	6.4
MuniYield MI Fd (MYM)	N	13.62	12 1/8	-10.9	6.8
MuniYield MI Ins Fd (MIY)	N	14.24	12	-15.7	6.8
MuniYield NJ Fd (MYJ)	N	13.64	13 1/8	-3.7	6.6
MuniYield NJ Ins Fd (MJI)	N	13.74	13 5/16	-3.1	6.3
MuniYield NY Ins (MYN)	N	13.50	11 11/16	-13.4	7.1
MuniYield PA Ins (MPA)	N	13.89	12 11/16	-8.6	6.6
Nuveen AZ Pr (NAZ)	♣N	14.17	14 1/2	+2.3	5.9
Nuveen CA Div Ad (NAC)	♣N	13.14	13 9/16	+3.2	6.5
Nuveen CA Inv Q (NQC)	♣N	14.46	15 1/16	+4.2	6.4
Nuveen CA Mkt (NCO)	♣N	14.64	15 1/4	+4.2	6.6
Nuveen CA Perf (NCP)	♣N	14.60	14 15/16	+2.3	6.6
Nuveen CA Pr (NCU)	♣A	12.93	13	+0.5	6.2
Nuveen CA Qual (NUC)	♣N	15.05	15 1/2	+3.0	6.3
Nuveen CA Sel (NVC)	♣N	14.57	14 11/16	+0.8	6.5
Nuveen CA Val (NCA)	♣N	9.62	9 1/8	-5.1	5.6
Nuveen CT Pr (NTC)	♣N	13.48	14 11/16	+9.0	5.7
Nuveen FL Inv Q (NQF)	♣N	14.35	14 3/8	+0.2	6.6
Nuveen FL Qual (NUF)	♣N	14.67	14 1/4	-2.9	6.4
Nuveen GA Pr (NPG)	♣A	13.39	13 7/16	+0.4	6.0
Nuveen Ins CA (NPC)	♣N	14.61	14 7/16	-1.2	5.8
Nuveen Ins CA 2 (NCL)	♣N	13.63	13 3/8	-1.8	6.0
Nuveen Ins Fl (NFL)	♣N	14.39	13 1/4	-7.9	6.1
Nuveen Ins NY (NNF)	♣N	14.16	13 3/8	-5.5	6.3
Nuveen InsCA Sel (NXC)	♣N	14.61	14 3/8	-1.6	5.5
Nuveen InsNY Sel (NXN)	♣N	14.35	13	-9.4	6.0
Nuveen MA Pr (NMT)	♣N	13.67	14 3/16	+3.8	6.0
Nuveen MD Pr (NMY)	♣N	13.35	13 13/16	+3.5	5.6
Nuveen MI Pr (NMP)	♣N	14.16	13	-8.2	6.5
Nuveen MI Qual (NUM)	♣N	14.45	14	-3.1	6.5
Nuveen MO Pr (NOM)	♣A	13.22	13 1/2	+2.1	5.8
Nuveen NC Pr Inc (NNC)	♣N	13.19	13 11/16	+3.8	5.9
Nuveen NJ Inv (NQJ)	♣N	14.54	14 1/16	-3.3	6.5
Nuveen NJ Pr (NNJ)	♣N	14.39	13 11/16	-4.9	6.4
Nuveen NY Div Ad (NAN)	♣N	13.28	12 15/16	-2.6	6.6
Nuveen NY Inv (NQN)	♣N	14.46	13 7/8	-4.0	6.8
Nuveen NY Perf (NNP)	♣N	14.59	13 13/16	-5.4	7.2
Nuveen NY Qual (NUN)	♣N	14.44	13 5/8	-5.6	6.8
Nuveen NY Sel (NVN)	♣N	14.59	13 7/8	-4.9	7.0
Nuveen NY Val (NNY)	♣N	9.52	8 9/16	-10.1	5.9
Nuveen OH Qual (NUO)	♣N	15.45	16 1/8	+4.4	6.2
Nuveen PA Inv (NQP)	♣N	14.49	14 9/16	+0.5	6.8
Nuveen PA Pr 2 (NPY)	♣N	13.60	12 9/16	-7.7	6.5
Nuveon TX Qual (NTX)	♣N	14.17	12 7/8	-9.1	7.1
Nuveen VA Pr (NPV)	♣N	13.85	14 5/16	+3.3	5.9
Putnam CA Inv Gr (PCA)	A	14.41	14 1/16	-2.4	6.4
Putnam NY Inv Gr (PMN)	A	13.05	12 11/16	-2.8	6.5
VK Adv PA Muni (VAP)	N	16.14	14 1/2	-10.2	6.7
VK CA Muni (VKC)	A	9.42	8 1/2	-9.8	6.3
VK CA Qual (VQC)	N	16.17	15 1/2	-4.1	5.9
VK CA Value (VCV)	N	15.55	14 1/4	-8.4	5.9
VK FL Muni Opp (VOF)	A	13.61	12	-11.8	6.2
VK FL Qual (VFM)	N	15.83	13 15/16	-11.9	7.1
VK Inv Grd CA (VIC)	N	15.51	15 3/4	+1.6	6.4
VK Inv Grd FL (VTF)	N	16.32	14 3/8	-11.9	6.9
VK Inv Grd NJ (VTJ)	N	16.34	15 1/16	-7.8	6.4
VK Inv Grd NY (VTN)	N	16.43	15 5/8	-4.9	6.5
VK Inv Grd PA (VTP)	N	16.50	14 3/4	-10.6	6.7
VK MA Value (VMV)	A	14.58	13 15/16	-4.4	5.9
VK NJ Value (VJV)	A	14.21	14	-1.5	6.0
VK NY Qual (VNM)	N	16.02	14 1/8	-11.8	6.5
VK NY Value (VNV)	N	14.66	13 3/8	-8.7	6.1
VK OH Qual (VOQ)	N	16.02	15 1/4	-4.8	6.6
VK OH Value (VOV)	A	14.09	12 5/8	-10.4	5.9
VK PA Qual (VPQ)	N	15.94	14 7/8	-6.7	6.9
VK PA Value (VPV)	N	14.65	12 15/16	-11.7	6.3
Voyageur AZ (VAZ)	A	14.00	13 3/16	-5.8	5.8
Voyageur CO Ins (VCF)	A	14.08	13 1/16	-7.2	5.6
Voyageur FL Ins (VFL)	A	14.48	12 5/16	-15.0	6.3
Voyageur MN I (VMN)	A	14.10	13	-7.8	6.8
Voyageur MN II (VMM)	A	13.65	12 7/8	-5.6	6.4
Voyageur MN III (VYM)	A	12.61	11 13/16	-6.3	6.3

f-Rights offering in process. g-Rights offering announced. h-Lipper data has been adjusted for rights offering. j-Rights offering has expired, but Lipper data not yet adjusted. l-NAV as of previous day. o-Tender offer in process.

Source: Lipper

Source: *Barron's,* July 10, 2000, F126.

receive a percentage of total assets under management. For conventional mutual funds, a growing pool of assets under management leads to higher fee income for the investment advisor. Closed-end funds, except under very rare circumstances, operate with a stable pool of investment money. Therefore, advertising or other promotion cannot be used to increase the asset base.

Some investment advisors recommend closed-end funds that trade at a significant discount. However, closed-end funds tend to sell at a wide discount only when they consistently underperform relevant benchmarks. Many older closed-end funds also sell at significant discounts because they have substantial capital gains tax liabilities tied to long-held equity positions. New investors who buy such funds may find themselves with a large capital gains tax liability if the fund unwinds some older and profitable positions. Closed-end funds that invest in private placements, provide venture capital, or invest in companies under bankruptcy reorganization also often sell at steep discounts. Such investments tend to be difficult to value, risky, and illiquid. On occasion, closed-end funds sell at significant premiums because they offer a unique vehicle for a particular type of investment opportunity. For example, countries such as Korea have historically limited investment opportunities for foreign investors, and The Korea Fund has often sold at large premiums to net asset value.

Closed-end funds seldom trade at a fixed discount or premium. More often, discounts and premiums trade around historical norms depending on liquidity and market sentiment. Discounts tend to grow during bear markets and fall during bull markets. Economic, social, or political developments can also affect the short-term outlook for various markets around the world, as well as discounts and premiums. The introduction of new closed-end funds with similar investment philosophies or investment objectives can also limit premiums or increase discounts by drawing away money that would otherwise have been committed to established funds.

In sum, closed-end funds offer long-term investors an investment alternative that may be well suited to specialized investing in small or illiquid markets in which portfolio turnover is harmful to long-term results. However, conventional mutual funds offer many of these same advantages with more flexibility at lower cost.

Hedge Funds

hedge funds Investment partnerships that use speculative investment techniques, such as leverage and short selling, that are very risky and commonly prohibited for mutual funds.

Hedge funds are similar to traditional mutual funds, but there are important differences in investment philosophy, investor suitability, and regulation. Like mutual funds, hedge funds represent a means for groups of investors to pool financial resources to efficiently purchase various types of securities in the pursuit of a specific financial goal. In the United States, however, hedge funds are typically organized as partnership arrangements available only to the wealthiest investors. They also have the flexibility to use speculative investment techniques, such as leverage and short selling, that are very risky and commonly are prohibited for mutual funds.

Unlike mutual funds, which are extensively regulated by the SEC, hedge funds are subject to only limited oversight because they ostensibly serve only financially sophisticated investors. U.S. mutual funds must register with the SEC, and they are subject to extensive reporting and operating requirements designed to protect investors. Virtually every aspect of mutual fund operations is subject to strict regulation under numerous federal and state laws, including the Securities Act of 1933, the Securities Exchange Act of 1934, the Investment Company Act of 1940, and the Investment Advisers Act of 1940. For example, mutual funds are strictly prohibited from investing more than 5% of fund assets in the securities of any single issuer. Another major area of mutual fund regulation is disclosure. Mutual funds are required to provide shareholders with regular information about fund management, investments, performance, fees, and expenses. Because hedge funds are largely unregulated, there is little reliable information about their operations. *Barron's* estimates there are as many as 4,000 domestic and offshore hedge funds with approximately $500 billion in investor equity.

Table 15.7 shows several important differences between the hedge funds and traditional mutual funds. Notice that almost 63 million Americans own mutual fund shares. The only financial qualification for investing in a typical mutual fund is having the minimum investment to open an account. This is often $1,000, or less. In the case of hedge funds, only sophisticated, high-net-worth individuals are eligible to invest. A typical hedge fund investor is a wealthy individual or institution with a minimum of $1 million to invest. Although annual expense ratios average only 1.24% of net mutual fund assets, hedge fund investors pay annual fees of 1–2% of net assets under management and 20% or more of hedge fund profits. Whereas securities laws restrict the ability of a mutual fund to use leverage or borrow against the value of securities in its portfolio, hedge funds face no such limitation. Many hedge funds use aggressive investment techniques such as stock and index options, futures and forward contracts, and short selling. In fact, the aggressive use of leverage and other such speculative techniques is a distinguishing characteristic of hedge funds and explains why many of their operations remain secret, even to long-term investors.

TABLE 15.7 Hedge Funds Differ from Mutual Funds in a Number of Ways

	Mutual Funds	Hedge Funds
Who Invests	Nearly 63 million Americans own mutual fund shares. The only qualification for investing is having the minimum investment to open an account with a fund company—often $1,000 or less.	Only sophisticated, high-net-worth investors are eligible to invest. The typical investor is a wealthy individual or an institution such as an endowment or foundation. A minimum investment of $1 million or more is required.
Fees	Mutual fund shareholders pay, on average, an annual expense ratio of roughly 1.5% of assets. Load charges can increase this to 2.5–5% per year. Funds must disclose fees and expenses in detail. Sales charges and other distribution fees are subject to specific regulatory limits.	Hedge fund investors often pay a portfolio management fee of 1–2% of net assets, plus a performance-based fee that can run as high as 10% per year, depending on performance. Fees are not subject to specific regulatory limits.
Investment Practices	Securities laws restrict a mutual fund's ability to leverage, or borrow against the value of securities in its portfolio. Funds that use options, futures, forward contracts, and short selling must "cover" their positions with cash reserves or other liquid securities. Investment policies must be fully disclosed to investors.	Leveraging strategies are hallmarks of hedge funds. Investment policies do not have to be disclosed, even to investors in the fund.
Pricing and Liquidity	Mutual funds must value their portfolio securities and compute their share price daily. They generally must also allow shareholders to redeem shares on at least a daily basis.	There are no specific rules on valuation or pricing. As a result, hedge fund investors may be unable to determine the value of their investment at any given time. In addition, new investors typically must pledge to keep their money in a hedge fund for at least one year.

Data source: Investment Company Institute.

Hedge fund regulation is a controversial topic of growing importance. For the latest information on this topic, and on securities regulation in general, see the SEC Web site at <http://www.sec.gov>.

Taxes

Taxes on Distributions

Mutual funds are not taxed on the income or capital gains earned on their investments so long as those earnings are fully passed along to shareholders in the form of dividends. Once income dividends and capital gains distributions have been received by shareholders, they must pay any taxes due when they file their income taxes with the Internal Revenue Service (IRS).

Income dividends are derived from all interest and dividend income earned from the fund's cash investments, bonds, and stock positions. The amount paid to shareholders is the fund's net income, after subtracting fund operating expenses. Capital gains distributions represent the net profit made during a given calendar year following sales of the fund's securities. When securities are sold at a price higher than the amount paid, the fund realizes a capital gain. When securities are sold at a lower price, the fund realizes a capital loss. If total capital gains exceed

WALL STREET WISDOM 15.3

Tiger Loses Its Growl

Hedge funds are loosely regulated investment vehicles for wealthy individuals and institutions that sometimes reap huge gains or suffer major losses. In most cases, investors are not obligated to pay a hedge fund for managing their money unless they recoup the losses of any previously reported period. Hedge funds are also noteworthy because they have the ability to adopt both long and short positions as means for controlling, or hedging, investor risk. In fact, most hedge funds seldom adopt conservative or risk-reducing investment strategies. Most are prone to make big market, interest rate, or foreign currency gambles given their unique performance reward system. Investors typically promise to pay the hedge fund manager a conventional share of typical investment profits but an outsized share of above-normal returns. This gives hedge fund managers a tremendous incentive to swing for the fences. Too often, hedge funds seem to be managed on a flip-of-a-coin basis: "Heads, and the hedge fund manager wins. Tails, and the hedge fund investors lose." There are important exceptions to this rule, of course.

For example, Warren Buffett got his start as the manager of an investment limited partnership. Buffett was paid 25% of any investment returns above an initial 6% return that was paid to each limited partner. Today, such an arrangement would be called a hedge fund. Notice how this type of incentive compensation gives the hedge fund manager strong incentives to take on above-normal risk in the search for above-normal profits. In the case of the Buffett partnership, initial investors who placed $10,000 with Buffett in 1956 collected about $293,738 when the partnership was dissolved in 1969. Over this 13-year period, the Buffett partnership earned investors 29.6% per year after fees and never had a down year. Initial investors who stuck with Buffett when he bought control of Berkshire Hathaway are now worth tens of millions of dollars. Such high returns from a low-risk investment strategy are seldom heard about anywhere, especially in the hedge fund industry.

The now retired Julian Robertson was an icon of the hedge fund industry. Alongside Buffett, Fidelity's Peter Lynch, and hedge fund manager George Soros, Robertson is one among very few that can claim market-beating results during a long string of bull and bear markets. Robertson, who earned more than 25% per year for more than 20 years, named his funds after wild jungle animals. He started the Tiger hedge fund in 1980 with $8 million in assets. Tiger grew in assets as Robertson gained in reputation as an astute stock picker. Ultimately, Tiger became Robertson's largest and most famous fund and had a well-deserved reputation for making huge bets. Jaguar was another famous Robertson hedge fund. Whether it was in stocks or foreign currencies, Robertson won big and lost big. In 1996, for example, Jaguar posted an eye-popping return of 50%, followed by an awesome 72% in 1997. At its peak, Robertson's Tiger fund rose to a stunning $22 billion in assets under management. Financial press coverage was laudatory, management fees raced into the hundreds of millions of dollars per year, and Robertson was worth billions.

After an unprecedented run of above-market returns, Robertson's investment performance turned sour in 1998 with huge losses on Japanese stocks and the yen. Humbled, Robertson returned to his roots to emphasize controversial and deeply discounted value stocks. As Robertson stuck by Old Economy stocks, his performance lagged badly and Tiger investors began to flee. Booming technology stocks were simply too hard to resist for institutional and individual investors riding the momentum of high-flying stocks.

By the end of March, 2000, Tiger's assets had dwindled from $22 billion to $6.5 billion, and Robertson threw in the towel. Blaming the craze over Internet, technology, and biotech stocks for overshadowing time-tested investment strategies, Robertson said he was withdrawing from an irrational market where earnings and price considerations take a backseat to "mouse clicks and momentum."

Ironically, Robertson quit just weeks before the bubble burst on many high-flying technology stocks.

See: Gregory Zuckerman and Paul Beckett, "Tiger Lies Down on a Day When Value Stocks Look Up," *The Wall Street Journal,* March 31, 2000, C1, C18.

total capital losses, the fund has net realized capital gains that must be fully distributed to its shareholders in the same calendar year. Net realized capital losses are not passed through to shareholders but are retained by the fund and may be used to offset future capital gains.

On occasion, mutual fund distributions may include a nontaxable return of capital. Returns of capital are generally not taxable because they are considered a return of a portion of the mutual fund shareholder's original investment. In that event, returns of capital are used to simply reduce the mutual fund shareholder's cost basis. The only exception occurs when the amount of capital returned exceeds the mutual fund shareholder's cost basis. In this situation, returns of capital include a capital gain, which is taxable as such to the individual shareholder.

All income and capital gains distributions are generally subject to local, state, and federal income taxes. Taxes must be paid on distributions regardless of whether they are received in cash or reinvested in additional shares. Exceptions to this rule include interest income derived from U.S. Treasury securities (T-bills and T-bonds), which is exempt from state and local income taxes. Municipal bond interest income is exempt from federal taxes. Municipal bond income is also typically exempt from state and local taxes for shareholders from that same tax jurisdiction. California residents do not pay state and local income taxes on interest income derived from bonds issued by California municipalities, for example. Nevertheless, any capital gains on U.S. Treasury securities or municipal bond funds are generally taxable.

Although the amount of interest income and capital gains received from a mutual fund is of obvious importance, another important consideration is the holding period for capital gains or losses. How long securities are held before they are sold or exchanged has direct implications for the amount of tax that must be paid. Gains or losses on securities held one year or less before they are sold or exchanged are categorized as short term. Short-term capital gains are taxed at ordinary income tax rates that vary with the level of earned income, in which the marginal tax rate can be as much as 39.6% at the federal level. State and local income taxes add to this amount. Long-term capital gains on securities held more than one year are taxable at a maximum federal tax rate of 20% and at only 10% for the lowest income tax bracket. The short-term versus long-term capital gains distinction is important because funds with a short-term orientation generate short-term capital gains, interest income, and dividends that are all taxed as ordinary income at the mutual fund shareholder's highest marginal tax rate.

The tax owed on mutual fund distributions may also depend on when shares are bought. Mutual fund distributions, whether from income or capital gains, are generally taxed in the year they are made. However, in certain circumstances, distributions declared during the last three months of a year and paid the following January are taxable in the year they were declared. Although money market funds pay dividends daily, stock and long-term bond funds pay dividend and capital gains distributions according to a regular schedule that might be on a quarterly, semiannual, or annual basis.

When a mutual fund makes a distribution, its share price and net asset value fall by the amount of the distribution. For example, the net asset value of a mutual fund that trades for $15 per share falls to $12.50 per share on the day its shareholders receive a distribution of $2.50, before accounting for any market activity on that day. The impact on the value of shares held is zero, but the fund shareholder owes taxes on the entire $2.50 distribution. As a result, before purchasing a fund, the buyer needs to know when the fund plans to make its next distribution. If a shareholder owns shares on the fund's record date, she or he will receive a distribution. Purchasing shares shortly before a distribution is made is called "buying the dividend" and exposes the buyer to taxes on the distribution received even though net asset value per share has fallen and no true gain has been realized. For fund shares purchased in an IRA, the timing of dividend payments is not relevant. But for taxable accounts, the timing of dividends is a valid consideration.

To help shareholders file their income taxes properly, mutual funds send out IRS Form 1099-DIV, which details income dividends and capital gains distributions that must be reported.

Influences on the Size of Distributions

Successful mutual funds generate lots of income and capital gains. All else equal, it is obviously preferable to own a fund that generates substantial distributions. At the same time, it is desirable to invest in funds that achieve shareholder objectives with a minimum of deadweight loss due to taxes. Thus, it becomes important for all mutual fund investors to consider tax efficiency as an important criterion in mutual fund selection.

Money market funds pay dividends on interest income that are fully taxable, except in the case of low-yield funds that invest in tax-exempt municipal bonds. However, because money market funds are designed to maintain a constant net asset value of $1 per share, they do not ordinarily generate capital gains or losses. Bond funds also typically produce relatively high levels of taxable income. The exception is, again, those bond funds that invest in tax-exempt securities. Over long periods, almost all the return from bond funds comes from dividend payments. Nevertheless, because the prices of long-term bonds and bond funds fluctuate in response to changing interest rates, it is common to generate taxable capital gains from investing in bond funds, even tax-exempt bond funds. Sometimes a fund will generate taxable capital gains distributions by selling bonds at a profit after a decline in interest rates. However, shareholders trigger a capital gain by selling bond fund shares at a price higher than original cost.

Stock funds generate income from dividends paid by common stocks held in the portfolio and from capital gains on sales of stock. Over time, however, most of the return earned from owning a common stock mutual fund comes in the form of stock price appreciation. Given the much greater volatility of stocks versus bonds, mutual fund investors are much more likely to realize a capital gain or loss when selling shares of a stock mutual fund than when selling shares of bond funds or money market funds. Because large and well-established "blue-chip" companies are more likely to pay dividends than smaller companies, mutual funds that emphasize large-company stocks usually generate more taxable dividend income than funds that emphasize small-company stocks.

turnover rate Common measure of a mutual fund's trading activity.

Because capital gains distributions result from the profitable sale of securities in the portfolio, frequent selling within a fund makes the fund more likely to produce taxable distributions than a fund that follows a "buy-and-hold" strategy. A common measure of a mutual fund's trading activity is the **turnover rate** expressed as a percentage of the fund's average assets. According to Lipper Analytical Services,

Inc., the industry-average turnover rate for U.S. stock mutual funds is 79%. This means that, over the course of a year, the typical stock fund sells and replaces securities with a value equal to 79% of the fund's average net assets. Another way of describing turnover of 79% is to say that the average fund holds a typical stock purchase for about 15 months (a 50% turnover rate implies a two-year holding period, and so on). Funds with high turnover generate lots of short-term gains and realized long-term gains and relatively higher taxes for mutual fund shareholders. Funds with low turnover generate mostly long-term gains and lots of unrealized long-term appreciation. This can result in an important tax advantage for mutual fund shareholders because unrealized gains are allowed to compound on a tax-free basis. Indeed, one of the most compelling advantages of simple buy-and-hold strategies is that they are a tax-efficient means of building mutual fund shareholder wealth.

Taxes on Sales and Exchanges

All capital gains from the sale of mutual fund shares are taxable, even those from the sale of shares in tax-exempt funds. Exchanging shares within a "family" of funds is considered a sale in the eyes of the IRS, even though all sale proceeds are used to buy shares in some other mutual fund. Writing a check against an investment in a short-term bond fund with a fluctuating share price also triggers a sale of shares and may expose the mutual fund investor to a tax on any resulting capital gains.

Although all capital gains realized on the sale of mutual funds generate a tax liability in the year realized, this is not necessarily true in the case of tax benefits generated by capital losses. Mutual fund investors can always use losses on the sale of shares to fully offset other capital gains on mutual funds, stocks, bonds, or other investments. After capital gains have been fully offset, mutual fund shareholders can also use up to $3,000 of net capital losses to offset ordinary income, such as salary or investment income, in any year. If an investor has a net capital loss of $2,500 following the unprofitable sale of mutual fund shares, for example, that loss can be used to reduce other taxable income. Capital losses that exceed $3,000 in any year can be carried forward to offset future capital gains and ordinary income.

A couple of cautionary comments about realizing capital losses are in order. If an investor redeems shares at a loss and purchases shares in the same fund within 30 days, the IRS considers the redemption a **wash sale.** In the eyes of the IRS, there was no effective sale of shares, and the investor may not be allowed to claim some or all of the realized losses on his or her tax return. If an investor redeems shares at a loss from a tax-exempt municipal bond fund by selling shares held for six months or less, a portion of the loss may also be disallowed. In such a case, the realized loss must be reduced by the tax-exempt income received from the shares. Moreover, if an investor realizes a short-term capital loss on shares held six months or less in an account that also received long-term capital gains distributions on those shares, the short-term loss must be reported as a long-term loss up to the amount of the capital gains distribution earned.

wash sale
When an investor redeems shares at a loss and purchases shares in the same fund within 30 days.

Tax rules governing taxable gains and losses can be complex, and individual investors may wish to consult with a tax adviser or tax preparer for guidance in dealing with these situations.

Summary

- A **mutual fund** is an investment company that issues its shares to the public. The money that it receives from shareholders is pooled and invested in a wide range of stocks, bonds, or money market securities to meet specific investment objectives. The per-share value of a mutual fund's stock, bond, and cash reserve holdings is called the fund's **net asset value.** Most mutual funds are also called **open-end investment companies** because as investor demand grows, the number of shares issued by the fund and the dollar value of assets under management increases.
- **Money market mutual funds** invest in cash reserves or short-term IOUs issued by the government, corporations, or financial institutions. **Stock funds** are one of the oldest and most popular types of mutual funds. Stocks represent equity ownership in corporations. **Bond funds** invest in debt instruments, or IOUs, issued by corporations or government agencies. In exchange for a bond investor's money, the issuer promises to repay the money at a specified date in the future and to make periodic interest payments. An **index fund** is a mutual fund designed to mimic the performance of some broad market index.
- Mutual fund performance is best measured by the fund's **total return,** comprising dividend and interest income and realized and unrealized appreciation. A fund's total return is reflected by the change in the value of an investment in the fund over time. When securities that a fund has purchased rise in value, the fund generates an unrealized capital gain. These **unrealized capital gains** raise the net asset value (or market value) of its shares. This gain remains unrealized until the fund or an individual sells his or her shares. If the fund itself sells securities at a profit, a taxable capital gain is realized. These realized capital gains are periodically paid out to mutual fund shareholders in the form of a **capital gains distribution.**
- All mutual funds have ongoing expenses that are deducted from interest and dividend income. The total of these costs expressed as a percentage of the fund's average net assets during the year is called the fund's **operating expense ratio.** Many mutual fund investors also pay one-time sales commissions, or **load charges.** Sales loads are often charged at the time of purchase as a simple percentage of the amounts invested. Such **front-end loads** typically range from 4% to 8.5%. Funds that charge sales fees ranging from 1% to 3% are called **low-load funds.** Another form of sales charge is the **back-end load,** which is assessed when an investor sells fund shares. Some funds also charge investors an additional amount to cover marketing and distribution costs. These marketing charges are sometimes called **12b-1 fees,** after the SEC rule that permits this practice. The term **level load** describes the portion of a 12b-1 fee used to compensate brokers and investment advisers for selling shares of the fund. A **load fund** is a mutual fund that charges significant sales commissions. If a fund charges a 12b-1 fee in excess of 0.25%, it may not call itself a **no-load fund** even if it has no other sales charges. Funds that are sold without front-end or back-end load charges are called no-load funds. An **exchange fee** of \$5–\$25 per transaction may be assessed when an investor exchanges shares from one fund to another within the same fund family. Account **maintenance fees** of between \$10 and \$25 per year also may be assessed. **Transaction fees** of 1–2%, of the amount transferred to another account may be assessed on redemptions, on

initial purchases, or both. The best resource to help investors determine mutual fund costs is the fund's **prospectus,** or offering circular, which must be given to all investors at or before the time of purchase.

- Because money market funds produce lower rates of return when compared with stock and bond funds, money market funds often have a hard time keeping pace with inflation. **Inflation risk** is the chance that rising prices will erode real (or after-inflation) investment returns. Another type of risk borne by mutual fund investors is **income risk.** This is the chance that the income earned from mutual fund investments will fluctuate. There are several additional risks to consider when investing in stock funds. The first and most obvious is **market risk.** Market risk exists because the prices of stocks and bonds fluctuate. **Sector risk** is the chance that some industry or industry group will underperform the overall market. Market risk is not the same as **inferior management risk,** or the chance that poor timing or substandard security selection will result in bad performance. **Sector risk** is the chance that some chosen industry or industry group will underperform the overall market. Mutual fund investors also face the risk of loss or inferior short-term performance when valid investment styles suffer through inevitable periods of underperformance. **Style risk** can be substantial.
- When $\alpha_P > 0$, portfolio performance is better than the theoretical expectation derived from the CAPM. Superior portfolio performance can be due to **selectivity,** or the selection of stocks with exceptionally good risk/reward characteristics. This is the hallmark of a good stock picker. Outstanding portfolio performance can also be due to astute risk management through careful **market timing.**
- Nobel Laureate William Sharpe developed a measure of risk-adjusted performance for mutual funds and other portfolios called the **reward-to-variability measure** (or **Sharpe ratio**). Financial economist Jack Treynor developed an alternative measure of risk-adjusted performance called the **reward-to-volatility measure** (or **Treynor ratio**). RVAR ranks portfolios according to the risk premium earned relative to total risk using $SD(R_P)$, whereas RVOL ranks portfolios according to the risk premium earned relative to systematic risk using β_P. Rank orderings of various portfolios are often similar under the two methods.
- When bonds of different maturity dates are purchased to meet specific expenses, a technique called **laddering** is used. Investors in long-term bond funds also face the possibility that some bonds can be redeemed by the issuer before they mature if the issuer believes that doing so would be economically advantageous. This is **call risk.** A similar risk, called **prepayment risk,** affects mortgage-backed securities such as Ginnie Maes (Government National Mortgage Association securities).
- Some of the hottest new products to hit the mutual fund industry in decades are called **exchange-traded funds (ETFs).** ETFs are tradable shares in baskets of stocks that closely track broad market averages, market sectors, or major stock markets from around the world. Among the most popular ETFs are **Standard and Poor's Depository Receipts (SPDRs)** (called "spiders") which closely track the price performance and dividend yield of the S&P 500 Index. ETFs have also been established to track the Dow Jones Industrial Average (called **DIAMONDS**), Nasdaq 100 Index (called **QQQs**), and the S&P MidCap 400 Index

(called **MidCap SPDRs**). Also popular are **Select Sector SPDRs** that unbundle the S&P 500 Index and give investors ownership in a particular market sector or group of industries. Barclays Global Investors has been among the most innovative companies in the development of ETFs, and offers more than 50 index portfolios called **iShares,** or index shares. ETFs and iShares represent valuable long-term investment vehicles.

- A relatively small number of mutual funds, called **closed-end funds,** issues a fixed number of shares at a given point in time. They collect money from investors through an initial public offering (IPO) and use this money to invest in securities. When the market price per share for closed-end funds exceeds its net asset value, the fund is selling at a **premium.** When the market price per share for a closed-end fund is less than its net asset value, the fund is selling at a **discount. Hedge funds** are similar to traditional mutual funds, but there are important differences in investment philosophy, investor suitability, and regulation.
- A common measure of a mutual fund's trading activity is the **turnover rate,** expressed as a percentage of the fund's average assets. According to Lipper Analytical Services, Inc., the industry-average turnover rate for U.S. stock mutual funds is 79%. This means that, over the course of a year, the typical stock fund sells and replaces securities with a value equal to 79% of the fund's average net assets.
- If an investor redeems shares at a loss and purchases shares in the same fund within 30 days, the IRS considers the redemption a **wash sale.** In the eyes of the IRS, there was no effective sale of shares, and the investor may not be allowed to claim some or all of the realized losses on their tax return.

Questions

1. In an efficient market, what percentage of mutual funds would outperform the market averages?
   a. 50% before expenses.
   b. 50% after expenses.
   c. 0% before expenses.
   d. 0% after expenses.
2. Investors in equity index funds avoid
   a. systematic risk.
   b. unsystematic risk.
   c. brokerage expenses.
   d. 12b-1 charges.
3. All no-load index funds entail
   a. 12b-1 charges.
   b. portfolio brokerage expenses.
   c. management fees.
   d. sales commissions.

4. Net asset value per share rises with an increase in
   a. the portfolio turnover rate.
   b. capital gains distributions.
   c. unrealized appreciation.
   d. none of the above.
5. Money market mutual funds are especially susceptible to
   a. systematic risk
   b. inflation risk.
   c. unsystematic risk.
   d. capital loss due to rising interest rates.
6. The average equity fund typically underperforms the S&P 500 because of
   a. excessive risk taking.
   b. insufficient cash balances.
   c. excessive portfolio turnover.
   d. insufficient diversification.
7. The amount of capital invested in the mutual fund industry is roughly
   a. $5 billion.
   b. $6 trillion.
   c. $14 trillion.
   d. $100 billion.
8. A money market mutual fund is
   a. a closed-end investment company.
   b. an index fund.
   c. a way to directly invest in stocks and bonds.
   d. an open-end investment company.
9. All managed mutual funds
   a. are open-end.
   b. charge a management fee.
   c. are closed-end.
   d. have shares traded on exchanges.
10. All open-end investment companies
    a. charge a sales fee.
    b. sell at a discount.
    c. have a Net Asset Value that remains constant across time.
    d. have a market capitalization that changes continually.
11. What percentage of the total value of the stock and bond markets can be account for by mutual funds?
    a. 80%
    b. 50%

c. 20–25%

d. 5%

12. An advantage of buying a no-load fund relative to a load fund is that

a. the management fee is avoided.

b. no-load funds can sometimes be bought at a discount.

c. administrative fees and transaction costs are avoided.

d. sales commissions are avoided.

13. In comparing the reward-to-variability measure (RVAR) and the reward-to-volatility measure (RVOL), it is important to remember that

a. RVAR is based on total risk whereas RVOL is based on systematic risk.

b. RVOL is based on total risk whereas RVAR is based on systematic risk.

c. RVAR is based on unsystematic risk whereas RVOL is based on systematic risk.

d. RVOL is based on systematic risk whereas RVAR is based on unsystematic risk.

14. The percentage of the variance in portfolio returns that is explained by the market returns is given by

a. the standard deviation.

b. beta.

c. the coefficient of determination.

d. alpha.

15. According to Jensen's differential return measure, alpha is

a. the intercept of the SML line.

b. the intercept of the CML line.

c. a means of identifying superior or inferior portfolio performance.

d. the actual excess return on a portfolio during one period.

16. If $R_F = 6\%$, $R_M = 12\%$, $\beta = 2$, portfolio performance of 18% is

a. a risk-adjusted market return.

b. 6% inferior.

c. 12% inferior.

d. 6% superior.

17. Which measure indicates the percentage of the variance in the portfolio's returns that is explained by the market's returns?

a. standard deviation.

b. coefficient of determination.

c. beta.

d. alpha.

18. Alpha measures

a. systematic risk.

b. market return.

c. the risk-free rate.

d. excess return.

19. A market price less than NAV can only exist for

a. a money market mutual fund.

b. an open-end investment company.

c. a common stock mutual fund.

d. a closed-end investment company.

20. Imitators who follow Warren Buffett's objective criteria are hampered by

a. the complex nature of Buffett's trading strategies.

b. the market illiquidity of Buffett's stock selections.

c. stock price reactions associated with announcements of Buffett's investment interest in a company.

d. the complexity of Buffett's investment criteria.

Investment Application

Warren Buffett: The 5σ Investor

Statisticians like to use Greek letters to symbolize statistical concepts. For example, the Greek letter mu(μ), is used to signify mean, or the central tendency of a population. The Greek letter sigma (σ), is used to represent standard deviation, or the degree of dispersion in the population. From a statistical view, portfolio returns that are as much as 5σ above the average market return (μ) are so rare as to be seldom, if ever, observed. Based on the evidence, Warren Buffett, chairman and CEO of Omaha-based Berkshire Hathaway, is a 5σ event.

Buffett started an investment partnership with $100 in 1956 and has gone on to accumulate a personal net worth in excess of $30 billion. Today, Buffett runs Berkshire like a closed-end mutual fund. He combines a stable of operating businesses, such as Geico Insurance, with a handful of core investment holdings, such as Coca-Cola. As shown in Table 15.8, Buffett has earned 24.9% annual returns in a typical market environment of 13.6% per year. Moreover, the S&P 500 numbers are pretax whereas the Berkshire numbers are after-tax. If a corporation such as Berkshire were simply to have owned the S&P 500 and accrued the appropriate taxes, its results would have lagged the S&P 500 in years when that index showed a positive return but would have exceeded the S&P in years when the index showed a negative return. Over the years, the tax costs would have caused the aggregate lag to be substantial. Even before adjusting for the significant tax burden borne by Berkshire over the years, Buffett has more than doubled the overall market's annual rate of return over an investment career involving the public's money that stretches for more than 34 years. In the world of investments, Buffett's performance is so outlandishly good as to defy description.

How does Buffett do it? Buffett's first rule is to not lose money. The second rule is: Don't forget the first rule. Buffett argues that is not terribly important to have a big circle of competence, but it is terribly important to know the boundaries of the circle you do have. Buy only what you know. Buffett has also been known to say that it is better to buy a wonderful company at a fair price than a fair

TABLE 15.8 Berkshire Hathaway's Performance Has Been Outstanding versus the S&P 500

	Berkshire's Book Value Growth (%)	S&P 500 Total Return (%)	Relative Performance (%)	Berkshire's Cumulative Value of $10,000	S&P 500 Cumulative Value of $10,000
1965	23.8	10.0	13.8	12,380	11,000
1966	20.3	(11.7)	32.0	14,893	9,713
1967	11.0	30.9	(19.9)	16,531	12,714
1968	19.0	11.0	8.0	19,672	14,113
1969	16.2	(8.4)	24.6	22,859	12,927
1970	12.0	3.9	8.1	25,602	13,432
1971	16.4	14.6	1.8	29,801	15,393
1972	21.7	18.9	2.8	36,268	18,302
1973	4.7	(14.8)	19.5	37,973	15,593
1974	5.5	(26.4)	31.9	40,061	11,477
1975	21.9	37.2	(15.3)	48,835	15,746
1976	59.3	23.6	35.7	77,793	19,462
1977	31.9	(7.4)	39.3	102,609	18,022
1978	24.0	6.4	17.6	127,236	19,175
1979	35.7	18.2	17.5	172,659	22,665
1980	19.3	32.3	(13.0)	205,982	29,986
1981	31.4	(5.0)	36.4	270,660	28,486
1982	40.0	21.4	18.6	378,925	34,582
1983	32.3	22.4	9.9	501,317	42,329
1984	13.6	6.1	7.5	569,496	44,911
1985	48.2	31.6	16.6	843,993	59,103
1986	26.1	18.6	7.5	1,064,276	70,096
1987	19.5	5.1	14.4	1,271,810	73,671
1988	20.1	16.6	3.5	1,527,443	85,900
1989	44.4	31.7	12.7	2,205,628	113,131
1990	7.4	(3.1)	10.5	2,368,845	109,624
1991	39.6	30.5	9.1	3,306,907	143,059
1992	20.3	7.6	12.7	3,978,209	153,931
1993	14.3	10.1	4.2	4,547,093	169,478
1994	13.9	1.3	12.6	5,179,139	171,681
1995	43.1	37.6	5.5	7,411,348	236,234
1996	31.8	23.0	8.8	9,768,157	290,567
1997	34.1	33.4	0.7	13,099,098	387,617
1998	48.3	28.6	19.7	19,425,962	498,475
1999	0.5	21.0	(20.5)	**19,523,092**	**603,155**
Average	**24.9**	**13.6**	**11.3**		
S.D.	**13.9**	**16.2**	**14.5**		
Median	**21.7**	**16.6**	**10.5**		

Data source: <http://berkshirehathaway.com>.

company at a wonderful price. Bargain purchases seldom turn out to be a steal. In a difficult business, no sooner is one problem solved than another surfaces. "Never is there just one cockroach in the kitchen." Although good jockeys will do well on good horses, nobody rides well on broken-down old nags. Buffett looks for first-class businesses and first-class management. "It is usually far more profitable to stick with the easy and obvious," says Buffett, "than it is to resolve the difficult."

Buffett looks for owner-oriented companies that enjoy strong franchises, pricing flexibility, high return on equity, high cash flow, owner-oriented management, and predictable earnings growth. Like T. Rowe Price, Buffett also looks for companies that are not natural targets of regulation. The Coca-Cola Company, one of Berkshire's biggest and most successful holdings, typifies the concept of a wonderful business. Coca-Cola enjoys perhaps the world's strongest franchise, owner-oriented management, and both predictable and growing returns. Also, the company is not subject to price or profit regulation. From the standpoint of being a wonderful business, Coca-Cola is clearly "the real thing." Berkshire also holds a large stake in The American Express Company, a premier travel and financial services firm that is strategically positioned to benefit from aging Baby Boomers. Banks and newspapers, such as M&T Bank, Wells Fargo & Company, and The Washington Post Company, can enjoy immense economies of scale and dominating competitive advantages that fit Buffett's criteria for wonderful businesses. In the case of the Federal Home Loan Mortgage Corporation, commonly referred to as Freddie Mac, a government charter that confers gigantic advantages gives Berkshire a dependable source of above-normal returns. Razors and toiletry juggernaut Gillette is another large holding. In the case of Gillette, above-normal returns stem from unique products that are designed and executed by extraordinarily capable management.

To be sure, above-normal returns from investing in wonderful businesses are only possible to the extent that such advantages are not fully recognized by other investors. Buffett has profited by taking major positions in wonderful companies that suffer from some significant, but curable, malady. In 1991, for example, Buffett made a huge investment in American Express when the company suffered unexpected credit card and real estate loan losses. When the company absorbed these losses without any lasting damage to its intrinsic profit-making ability, its stock price soared and Buffett cleaned up. Companies that are conservatively financed enjoy a similar ability to profit when an unexpected business downturn causes financially distressed rivals to sell valuable assets at bargain-basement prices.

The fact that Buffett has compiled his enviable record by buying large and well-known public companies makes his astounding success even more remarkable. Moreover, each year on the first Monday in May, Buffett teaches his investment philosophy to a crowd of thousands at Berkshire's annual stockholders' meeting. By mixing classic Ben Graham with the growth stock philosophies of T. Rowe Price and Phil Fisher, Buffett has fashioned a level of investment success that questions the veracity of the Efficient Markets Hypothesis.

A. Explain how Buffett's investment success can be interpreted within the context of the EMH.

B. Explain how Buffett's investment success might be described as a contradiction of the EMH.

Selected References

Bollen, Nicolas P. B., and Robert E. Whaley. "Do Expirations of Hang Seng Index Derivatives Affect Stock Market Volatility?" *Pacific-Basin Finance Journal* 7 (December 1999): 453–470.

Chow, George, Eric Jacquier, Mark Kritzman, and Kenneth Lowry. "Optimal Portfolios in Good Times and Bad." *Financial Analysts Journal* 55 (May/June 1999): 65–73.

Comerton-Forde, Carole. "Do Trading Rules Impact on Market Efficiency? A Comparison of Opening Procedures on the Australian and Jakarta Stock Exchanges." *Pacific-Basin Finance Journal* 7 (December 1999): 495–521.

Coval, Joshua D., and Tobias J. Moskowitz. "Home Bias at Home: Local Equity Preference in Domestic Portfolios." *Journal of Finance* 54 (December 1999): 2045–2073.

Edelen, Roger M. "Investor Flows and the Assessed Performance of Open-End Mutual Funds." *Journal of Financial Economics* 53 (September 1999): 439–466.

Faccio, Mara, and M. Ameziane Lasfer. "Do Occupational Pension Funds Monitor Companies in Which They Hold Large Stakes?" *Journal of Corporate Finance* 6 (March 2000): 71–110.

Fisher, Kenneth L., and Meir Statman. "A Behavioral Framework for Time Diversification." *Financial Analysts Journal* 55 (May/June 1999): 88–97.

Gallo, John G., and Larry J. Lockwood. "Fund Management Changes and Equity Style Shifts." *Financial Analysts Journal* 55 (September/October 1999): 44–52.

Indro, Daniel C., Christine X. Jiang, Michael Y. Hu, and Wayne Y. Lee. "Mutual Fund Performance: Does Fund Size Matter?" *Financial Analysts Journal* 55 (May/June 1999): 74–87.

Jain, Prem C., and Joanna Shuang Wu. "Truth in Mutual Fund Advertising: Evidence on Future Performance and Fund Flows." *Journal of Finance* 55 (April 2000): 937–958.

Klein, Peter. "The Capital Gain Lock-In Effect and Equilibrium Returns." *Journal of Public Economics* 71 (March 1999): 355–378.

Lin, Wenling. "Controlling Risk in Global Multimanager Portfolios." *Financial Analysts Journal* 56 (January/February 2000): 44–53.

Olsen, Robert A. "Are Risk Premium Anomalies Caused by Ambiguity?" *Financial Analysts Journal* 56 (March/April 2000): 24–31.

O'Neal, Edward S. "Mutual Fund Share Classes and Broker Incentives." *Financial Analysts Journal* 55 (September/October 1999): 76–87.

Su, Dongwei, and Belton M. Fleisher. "Why Does Return Volatility Differ in Chinese Stock Markets?" *Pacific-Basin Finance Journal* 7 (December 1999): 557–586.

CHAPTER 16

Global Investing

Asia, Europe, or Latin America? That is the question. At least, that is an important question on the minds of global investors.

In 1999, aggressive pension and hedge funds began unloading European stocks in favor of depressed Latin American and Japanese companies.[1] *European stock markets slipped in reflection of negative investor sentiment toward the euro, Europe's new cross-country currency. After a rousing welcome in currency markets at the start of 1999, the euro began to fall against the dollar because of problems with smoothly proceeding to a comprehensive European Union. For dollar-based investors, the euro's weakness is an important reason not to invest in Europe.*

Another is the relative attractiveness of the Brazilian and Japanese stock markets. In particular, the exciting potential for Japanese restructuring clearly has drawn the attention of many global investors. Missing out on a turnaround in the world's second-largest economy is just too risky for portfolio managers whose performance is judged on the basis of relative performance vis-à-vis global stock market indexes. Although domestic investors hold the bulk of European, Latin American, and Japanese shares, U.S. and other foreign investors are "swing" players who can shape trends. Foreigners have become net sellers of European shares and net purchasers of Asian and Latin American stocks. Some savvy investors are shifting toward Japan because companies there are finally focusing on profit margins, not market share. Also positive is the fact that the Japanese government seems intent on boosting its stagnant economy.

Stay tuned. Over the next five years, global investing could get exciting!

Tracking Global Markets

Morgan Stanley Capital International, Inc.

Morgan Stanley Capital International, Inc. (MSCI) is the leading provider of global stock market and bond market indexes and benchmark-related products to investors worldwide. MSCI is an affiliate of investment banker and stock brokerage giant Morgan Stanley Dean Witter & Co. Morgan Stanley, a global financial

[1]See Phred Dvorak and G. Thomas Sims, "Global Markets, Following U.S., Acquire Taste for Junk," *The Wall Street Journal,* August 14, 2000, C1, C21.

services firm and a market leader in securities, asset management, and credit services, is the majority shareholder of MSCI. The Capital Group Companies, Inc., a global investment management group, is a minority shareholder. MSCI is fully responsible for the design, maintenance, production, and distribution of its indexes. In the world of global investing, MSCI is the primary source of information about the size and performance of global financial markets.

MSCI indexes are the most widely used benchmarks measuring the performance of global portfolio managers. More than 1,200 clients worldwide presently use the MSCI benchmarks. In North America and Asia, more than 90% of institutional international equity assets are benchmarked to MSCI indexes. In Europe, more than half of Continental fund managers currently use MSCI indexes as their benchmark. Founded in 1968, no other benchmark provider has been monitoring and tracking the world's equity markets for as long as MSCI. With more than 30 years' experience, an extensive product line, and dedicated staff of more than 100 in offices around the globe, MSCI has built a dominant market position with investment professionals and individual investors who need to accurately compare the stock and bond markets of different countries. On the Internet, MSCI gives global investors an abundance of information about the global economic environment and the risk and return characteristics of global stock and bond markets (see <http://www.msci.com>).

The MSCI research database contains more than 24,000 equity securities covering more than 50 countries. There are presently more than 3,000 MSCI indexes calculated daily. To get some feel for how recent is investor interest in global investing, consider the fact that it was not until 1969 that MSCI introduced the first series of generally accepted measures of stock market performance for **developed markets** (Figure 16.1). Eighteen years later, in 1987, MSCI responded to the growth of interest in newer stock markets in developing economies with its series of measures designed to track the stock markets of **emerging markets.** In the 1990s, the pace of global benchmark index innovation quickened considerably. In 1995, MSCI introduced the All Country Series. In 1997, value indexes and growth indexes were added for developed and emerging markets. In 1998, small-cap, extended market, and fixed-income indexes were added. In 1999, a variety of euro indexes was introduced.

developed markets Securities markets in countries with advanced economies.

emerging markets Securities markets in countries with rapidly evolving economies.

MSCI indexes provide benchmarks for individual industries across eight major sectors, including energy, materials, capital equipment, consumer goods, services, finance, multi-industry, and gold mining. In addition to individual country coverage, MSCI compiles regional and composite indexes for developed markets (e.g., Europe, Australasia, Far East [EAFE]), emerging markets (e.g., Emerging Markets Free–Latin America), and all countries by region (e.g., All Countries—Europe). Prices and monthly returns are calculated in local currencies and U.S. dollars. Total return indexes for developed stock markets are calculated with and without dividends. Total returns for emerging stock markets include dividend income. MSCI calculates many indexes by using alternative weighting schemes. Country weights determined by market capitalization, although reflective of the actual investment capacity of the country, may be undesirable for some portfolio strategies. Thus, MSCI offers regional indexes using a gross domestic product (GDP)–weighting scheme. On a customized basis, MSCI also calculates indexes by using price-weighting and equal-weighting schemes.

Of course, many local information providers and stock exchanges also calculate their own stock market indexes. Global investors are familiar with Japan's Nikkei 225, the United Kingdom's FTSE 100, and Germany's DAX indexes, among oth-

FIGURE 16.1 MSCI Indexes Have Tracked the Growth of Global Equity Markets since 1969

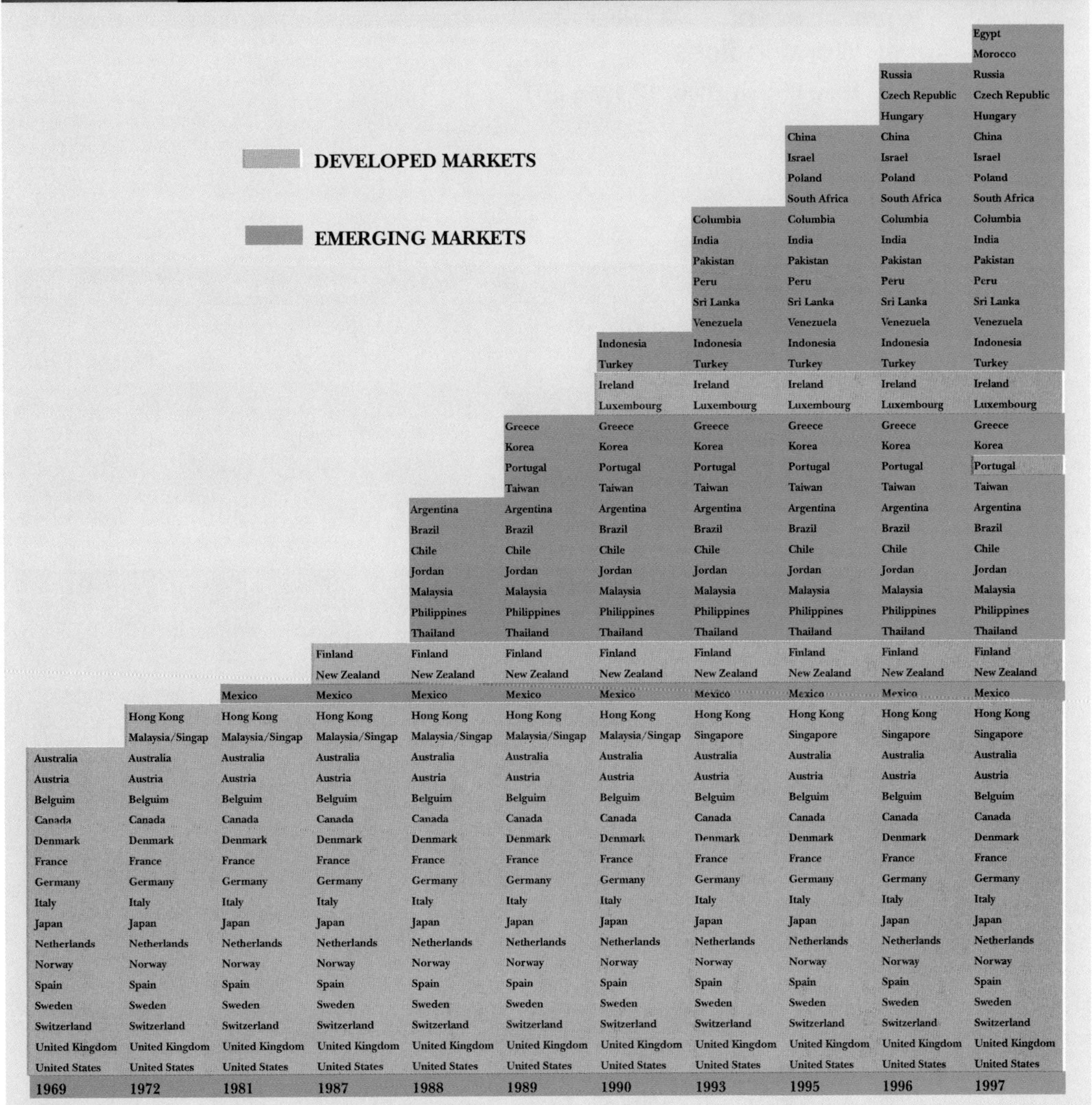

Note: Portugal was reclassified as a developed market as of the close of November 28, 1997.

Source: <http://www.msci.com>.

ers. However, as shown in Table 16.1, local indexes are generally not comparable across countries given global differences in market representation, mathematical formulas, base dates, and methods of adjusting for capital appreciation and depreciation. MSCI applies the same company selection criteria and calculation methodology across all markets for all indexes, developed and emerging. In fact, MSCI is the only provider of indexes consistently developed and applied across

TABLE 16.1 **Global Stock Market Performance Is Tracked by a Variety of Local Market Indexes**

World Indices

Mon, 05 Jun 2000, 12:49pm EDT

North/Latin America

Index	Value	Chg	Pct Chg	Date
DOW JONES INDUS. AVG (INDU)	10835.15	40.39	0.37%	12:46
S&P 500 INDEX (SPX)	1472.29	-4.97	-0.34%	12:46
NASDAQ COMB COMPOSITE IX (CCMP)	3833.91	20.53	0.54%	12:46
TSE 300 Index (TS300)	9716.60	-31.07	-0.32%	12:26
MEXICO BOLSA INDEX (MEXBOL)	6634.19	6.85	0.10%	12:25
BRAZIL BOVESPA STOCK IDX (IBOV)	16173.27	-49.21	-0.30%	12:45

Europe/Africa

Index	Value	Chg	Pct Chg	Date
BLOOMBERG EUROPEAN 500 (EURO500)	284.62	-2.48	-0.86%	12:45
FT-SE 100 Index (UKX)	6546.70	-79.70	-1.20%	11:36
CAC 40 INDEX (CAC)	6656.26	-17.26	-0.26%	11:54
DAX INDEX (DAX)	7411.45	-27.50	-0.37%	12:46
IBEX 35 INDEX (IBEX)	11004.20	-137.30	-1.23%	11:36
MILAN MIB30 INDEX (MIB30)	46894.00	-334.00	-0.71%	11:42
BEL20 INDEX (BEL20)	2891.73	-3.64	-0.13%	10:59
AMSTERDAM EXCHANGES INDX (AEX)	672.66	-5.26	-0.78%	10:30
SWISS MARKET INDEX (SMI)	7791.10	-50.50	-0.64%	11:01

Asia/Pacific

Index	Value	Chg	Pct Chg	Date
NIKKEI 225 INDEX (NKY)	17201.79	401.73	2.39%	2:03
HANG SENG STOCK INDEX (HSI)	15861.68	577.58	3.78%	4:05
ASX ALL ORDINARIES INDX (AS30)	3105.10	8.80	0.28%	6/2
SING: STRAITS TIMES INDU (STI)	1982.43	72.03	3.77%	5:01

Source: <http://www.bloomberg.com>.

developed and emerging markets (see Table 16.2). MSCI indexes are also notable for the depth and breadth of their coverage. MSCI's developed and emerging market indexes reflect stock market trends by representing the evolution of an

TABLE 16.2 MSCI Indexes Reflect a Consistent Methodology across All Markets

			LOCAL COUNTRY INDEX				MSCI			
Country Index	Weighting	Selection Criteria	Number Securities	Number Industries	YTD Local Return	Index % of Market	Number Securities	Number Industries	YTD Local Return	Index % of Market
Hong Kong Hang Seng	market cap	Companies must be among top 90% in terms of market cap and turnover.	33	10	11.9%	83.3%	35	16	5.4%	52.6%
Sweden OMX	market cap	Companies with highest trading value on Stockholm Stock Exchange	30	15	39.2%	63.7%	29	16	39.8%	58.5%
United Kingdom FTSE-100	market cap	100 highest capitalized companies on London Stock Exchange	100	27	27.3%	71.7%	132	33	26.6%	61.7%
Canada TSE-35	basket	Blue chips in Canada	35	16	15.4%	43.4%	83	24	18.9%	58.3%
Italy MIB 30	market cap	Largest 30 companies that are liquid.	30	13	52.1%	76.4%	53	19	47.2%	71.5%
Thailand SET 50	market cap	Top 50 companies in market cap and liquidity	50	15	-33.0%	90.4%	62	26	-32.0%	57.8%

Data as of 9/30/97.

Local stock exchange indices vary considerably and are not comparable to one another. MSCI Indices reflect a consistent methodology across all markets.

Source: <http://www.msci.com>.

unmanaged portfolio containing a broad selection of domestically listed companies. With a target market coverage of 60%, MSCI indexes balance the theoretical appeal of an "all share" index against the practical usefulness of a "blue-chip" index. Whereas all-share indexes have the appealing characteristic of reflecting market-wide movements, high transaction costs typically preclude their use as the basis for a practical investment vehicle. Conversely, blue-chip indexes that can be readily copied by professional and individual investors often fail to provide necessary market coverage. MSCI indexes avoid both problems and give investors a practical means for tracking market-wide movements and an appealing basis on which to build index-based investment strategies.

There is much better information available today about foreign stock markets than ever before. Because MSCI makes much of this information accessible for free on the Internet, both large and small investors have ready access to a wealth of information about global market risk and return characteristics. Even novice investors can investigate global investment opportunities with a level of insight that just a few years ago was available only to the most sophisticated professional managers.

Global Market Indexes

The MSCI World Index, the MSCI EAFE Index, and the MSCI Emerging Markets Free Index are the premier benchmarks used by investment managers to measure the performance of global stock markets. In addition, MSCI country indexes are commonly used to measure stock market investment performance in more than

50 countries around the world. Fixed-income indexes are also provided for more than 30 countries. The consistent construction methodology used for the various country indexes allows for simple aggregation of the country indexes to form 65 regional stock market indexes. Regional indexes published by MSCI represent investable areas as determined by global investment managers. Such regions are found within both developed and emerging markets. Investment-style indexes produced by MSCI include the MSCI value and growth indexes and are available for developed and emerging equity markets.

The MSCI indexes are generally calculated and disseminated on the Internet and to news services on a daily basis. However, the 15 MSCI European developed-market country indexes, as well as major MSCI European regional indexes, are calculated on a real-time basis and updated intraday every 60 seconds. Real-time index calculations, updated in 15-second intervals, are also available for MSCI Hong Kong, MSCI Taiwan, MSCI Singapore, and MSCI Euro and Pan-Euro indexes. Sector and industry indexes are available for the MSCI global equity benchmark series. There are presently eight MSCI sectors and 38 MSCI industry groups. The MSCI Euro Credit Index has nine sector indexes as part of its index series. Major regional MSCI indexes are shown in Table 16.3.

TABLE 16.3 MSCI Indexes Are Calculated across Developed Markets, Emerging Markets, and All Country Regions

Index Name	Description	Number of Countries
The World Index	All developed markets in the world	23
Kokusai (The World Index ex Japan)	All developed markets in the world excluding Japan	22
EAFE®	Europe, Australasia, Far East - developed markets only	21
EASEA (EAFE® ex Japan)	Europe and South East Asia - developed markets only	20
Europe	All developed markets in Europe	15
Pacific	All developed markets in the Pacific Rim	6
North America	USA and Canada	2
EM (Emerging Markets)	All emerging markets in the MSCI universe	26
EMF (Emerging Markets Free)	All emerging markets in the MSCI universe, with Free versions of countries where they exist	26
EMF Asia	All emerging markets in the Asian MSCI universe, with Free versions of countries where they exist	10
EMF Latin America	All emerging markets in the Latin American MSCI universe, with Free versions of countries where they exist	7
EM Europe	All emerging markets in the European MSCI universe	6
ACWI (All Country World Index)	All developed and emerging markets in the MSCI universe	48
ACWI Free ex USA	All developed and emerging markets in the MSCI universe excluding the USA, with Free versions of countries where they exist	47
ACWI Free ex Japan	All developed and emerging markets in the MSCI universe excluding Japan, with Free versions of countries where they exist	47
AC Europe	All developed and emerging markets in the European MSCI universe	21
AC Far East Free ex Japan	All developed and emerging markets in the Far Eastern MSCI universe excluding Japan, with Free versions of countries where they exist	9

MSCI Indices are calculated across developed markets, emerging markets, and All Country regions.

Source: <http://www.msci.com>.

full market capitalization weights Price multiplied by the number of outstanding shares.

All MSCI equity indexes are calculated using **full market capitalization weights,** with returns measured in local currency and in U.S. dollars. MSCI covers more than 60% of the market cap of global equities in developed and emerging markets. Its objective in doing so is to create a series of indexes that together replicate the investment opportunities available in all equity markets around the world, a true global portfolio. Nevertheless, MSCI performance calculations incorporate sophisticated dividend reinvestment assumptions, which, although relevant throughout the developed world, may be problematic in high-inflation emerging markets. Because some money managers prefer to use alternative weighting schemes, MSCI calculates regional indexes by using GDP weighting for individual emerging markets.

As shown in Table 16.4, the late 1990s marked a period of unprecedented stock market growth. As measured by the MSCI World Index, the return earned in U.S. dollars by equity investors during the 1995–99 period was a stunning 18.09% per year. Among major stock markets of the world, the late 1990s bull market was clearly led by the United States. In the United States, equity investors enjoyed an amazing 27.36% annual rate of return from 1995 to 1999. Not only was the performance of U.S. equities the best among major world markets during the late 1990s, this outstanding performance was in stunning contrast with anemic returns earned by some other world markets, particularly in Asia. In the Pacific region, annual rates of return for the 1995–99 period were a sickly 1.42%. Over the entire decade of the 1990s, equity investors actually lost money in the Pacific Region (−0.69% per year).

Figure 16.2 gives further perspective on the recently outstanding performance of U.S. equities vis-à-vis global equity markets by illustrating the compound return earned on the MSCI World Index, the MSCI World Index excluding the United States, and the U.S. equity index over the 1995–99 period. Notice how the 18.09% annual rate of return for the MSCI World Index compounded to earn a total of 229.7% over this five-year period. During this time frame, the 27.36% annual return earned by U.S. equities compounded to a total return of 335.3%, or more than double the 11.39% annual return and 171.6% total return earned by global equities excluding the United States.

During the late 1990s, the U.S. equities market was a world beater. Such stunningly good performance by a major world equity market is seldom encountered. In fact, the last major world market to turn in such amazingly good relative performance was the Japanese stock market during the 1980s. If you recall, this was a period when "Japan, Inc." and "Japan's long-term investment perspective" became standard topical fare in business schools around the country. The superiority of Japanese technology and innovation also became taken for granted. In the 1980s, enthusiasm for all things Japanese helped fuel a historical rise in Japan's stock market. As shown in Figure 16.3, Japan's Nikkei 225 Index reached a stunning peak of 38,957 on December 29, 1989, or more than triple the 11,543 level of January 1, 1985. At that point, typical price/earnings (P/E) ratios for Japanese blue chips exceeded 100 times earnings. Then, the bubble burst. It no longer seemed prudent to global investors to pay in excess of 100 times earnings for Japan's telecommunications giant NTT when America's telecommunications goliath AT&T could be had for a mere 15 times earnings. Japanese equity prices continued to crumble until October 9, 1998, when the Nikkei tumbled to 12,788, or fully 67.2% below the peak reached more than eight years earlier!

Of course, parallels between the late 1990s performance of the U.S. equities market and the performance of Japanese equities a decade earlier are not exact.

TABLE 16.4 **Global Equity Markets Earned Outstanding Rates of Return in the 1990s**

Performance | **Index Returns** | Index Values | Industries (New) | Industries (Old) | Constituents

Market: Developed Markets Style: Standard

Type: Price Index (official) Date: 01-Jan-2000 ... Submit

Print Preview Download as CSV Download into Excel

MSCI INDEX RETURNS

Developed Markets Price Index (official) as of 31-Dec-1999

IN LOCAL CCY ANNUAL RETURNS 1Y	3Y	5Y	10Y		IN US DOLLARS ANNUAL RETURNS 1Y	3Y	5Y	10Y
				INTERNATIONAL INDEXES				
26.27%	22.04%	19.62%	9.20%	THE WORLD INDEX	23.56%	20.11%	18.09%	9.61%
21.64%	26.63%	26.91%	15.68%	NORTH AMERICA	21.91%	26.51%	26.87%	15.53%
31.68%	17.67%	13.96%	4.82%	EAFE	25.27%	14.09%	11.14%	5.32%
37.47%	34.85%	26.55%	13.18%	EMU	17.35%	24.57%	21.14%	11.10%
27.92%	27.81%	23.04%	12.88%	EUROPE	14.12%	20.65%	19.84%	11.54%
40.99%	36.91%			EURO	20.35%	26.48%		
29.59%	29.57%			PAN-EURO	15.64%	22.39%		
104.86%	49.09%	37.34%	19.83%	NORDIC COUNTRIES	85.11%	37.66%	32.62%	16.84%
43.22%	2.76%	2.29%	(3.37%)	PACIFIC	56.17%	5.20%	1.42%	(0.69%)
47.81%	2.46%	1.92%	(3.87%)	FAR EAST	61.10%	5.78%	1.33%	(0.87%)
25.43%	22.21%	19.53%	8.66%	G7	24.55%	21.37%	18.52%	9.40%
				INTERNATIONAL FREE INDEXES				
26.16%	21.97%	19.58%	9.20%	THE WORLD INDEX FREE	23.45%	20.04%	18.06%	9.62%
31.43%	17.53%	13.91%	4.77%	EAFE FREE	25.03%	13.96%	11.10%	5.30%
42.29%	2.47%	2.19%	(3.42%)	PACIFIC FREE	55.20%	4.90%	1.34%	(0.72%)
31.40%	(1.07%)	4.53%	7.94%	PACIFIC FREE EX JAPAN	34.95%	(6.58%)	1.37%	6.49%
46.74%	2.14%	1.81%	(3.92%)	FAR EAST FREE	60.00%	5.46%	1.25%	(0.90%)
				SPECIAL AREAS				
32.12%	17.68%	14.13%	5.00%	WORLD EX USA	26.22%	14.17%	11.39%	5.39%
32.12%	17.68%	14.14%	5.00%	EAFE + CANADA	26.22%	14.17%	11.40%	5.39%
24.35%	25.42%	24.03%	14.04%	KOKUSAI INDEX (WORLD EX JAPAN)	19.43%	22.43%	22.66%	13.52%
28.55%	23.89%	20.54%	12.20%	EASEA INDEX (EAFE EX JAPAN)	15.90%	17.03%	17.35%	10.89%
35.55%	0.23%	5.13%	7.85%	PACIFIC EX JAPAN	39.35%	(5.34%)	1.95%	6.50%
27.78%	22.64%	20.02%	9.05%	WORLD EX UK	25.17%	20.75%	18.24%	9.53%
24.00%	19.73%	18.30%	8.50%	WORLD EX EMU	24.98%	19.28%	17.52%	9.33%
25.62%	19.67%	18.17%	7.83%	WORLD EX EUROPE	28.62%	20.05%	17.46%	8.95%
37.04%	17.91%	13.60%	3.73%	EAFE EX UK	29.63%	14.02%	10.01%	4.38%

Source: <http://www.msci.com>.

TABLE 16.4 ***(continued)***

34.91%	33.14%	26.37%	13.77%	EUROPE EX UK	16.00%	23.42%	21.18%	11.88%
30.32%	28.10%	22.93%	12.57%	EUROPE EX SWITZERLAND	16.75%	20.93%	19.93%	11.16%
17.13%	20.35%	19.14%	12.25%	EUROPE EX EMU	10.01%	16.18%	18.09%	11.72%
26.52%	22.24%	19.78%	9.24%	WORLD EX AUSTRALIA	23.67%	20.38%	18.28%	9.68%
				NATIONAL INDEXES				
7.97%	8.27%	8.76%	6.42%	AUSTRALIA	15.19%	1.49%	5.12%	4.44%
4.88%	4.08%	1.73%	(0.57%)	AUSTRIA	(10.47%)	(3.81%)	(2.84%)	(1.98%)
(1.33%)	24.94%	20.84%	9.87%	BELGIUM	(15.77%)	15.46%	15.30%	8.52%
43.41%	18.28%	18.84%	9.48%	CANADA	51.78%	16.04%	18.03%	7.03%
29.31%	26.04%	22.25%	10.57%	DENMARK	10.85%	16.73%	17.49%	9.24%
193.70%	101.74%	61.09%	31.91%	FINLAND	150.71%	85.45%	54.02%	26.95%
49.95%	35.65%	26.60%	12.71%	FRANCE	28.00%	25.62%	21.54%	11.32%
39.05%	33.43%	24.88%	12.38%	GERMANY	18.70%	23.33%	19.26%	10.79%
55.38%	2.18%	10.20%	15.97%	HONG KONG	54.85%	2.01%	10.10%	16.02%
0.72%	19.90%	19.29%	9.99%	IRELAND	(14.02%)	9.02%	14.77%	7.81%
15.41%	36.20%	21.21%	10.45%	ITALY	(1.48%)	25.75%	17.06%	5.89%
45.69%	3.84%	1.82%	(4.78%)	JAPAN	60.56%	8.29%	1.30%	(1.49%)
76.31%	25.73%	16.13%	11.74%	LUXEMBOURG	50.50%	16.18%	10.81%	10.37%
23.30%	25.38%	24.89%	15.34%	NETHERLANDS	5.25%	15.74%	19.12%	13.72%
11.12%	(2.56%)	2.22%	1.30%	NEW ZEALAND	9.70%	(11.95%)	(1.88%)	(0.03%)
36.62%	5.52%	8.01%	5.03%	NORWAY	29.52%	(2.27%)	4.35%	2.97%
4.43%	27.52%	21.11%	7.11%	PORTUGAL	(10.86%)	17.18%	15.71%	4.04%
98.99%	11.37%	5.06%	6.66%	SINGAPORE	97.08%	5.06%	2.29%	8.07%
59.97%	1.67%	2.14%	6.52%	SINGAPORE FREE	58.43%	(4.09%)	(0.55%)	7.93%
21.28%	34.00%	32.48%	14.80%	SPAIN	3.53%	23.53%	26.48%	10.11%
87.35%	40.91%	35.55%	20.29%	SWEDEN	77.76%	30.76%	31.83%	16.49%
7.44%	24.49%	23.32%	15.80%	SWITZERLAND	(7.81%)	17.40%	18.45%	15.36%
13.28%	16.82%	16.06%	10.59%	UNITED KINGDOM	9.74%	14.50%	16.75%	10.58%
20.86%	27.06%	27.36%	16.09%	USA	20.86%	27.06%	27.36%	16.09%

These data are based on information generally available to the public from sources believed to be reliable. No representation is made that it is accurate or complete. Certain assumptions may have been made in this analysis which have resulted in any returns detailed herein. No representation is made that any returns indicated will be achieved. Changes to the assumptions may have a material impact on any returns detailed. Past performance is not necessarily indicative of future returns. The foregoing has been prepared solely for informational purposes, and is not an offer to buy or sell or a solicitation of an offer to buy or sell any security or instrument or to participate in any particular trading strategy.

FIGURE 16.2 **Global Equity Markets Soared during the Late 1990s, Especially in the United States**

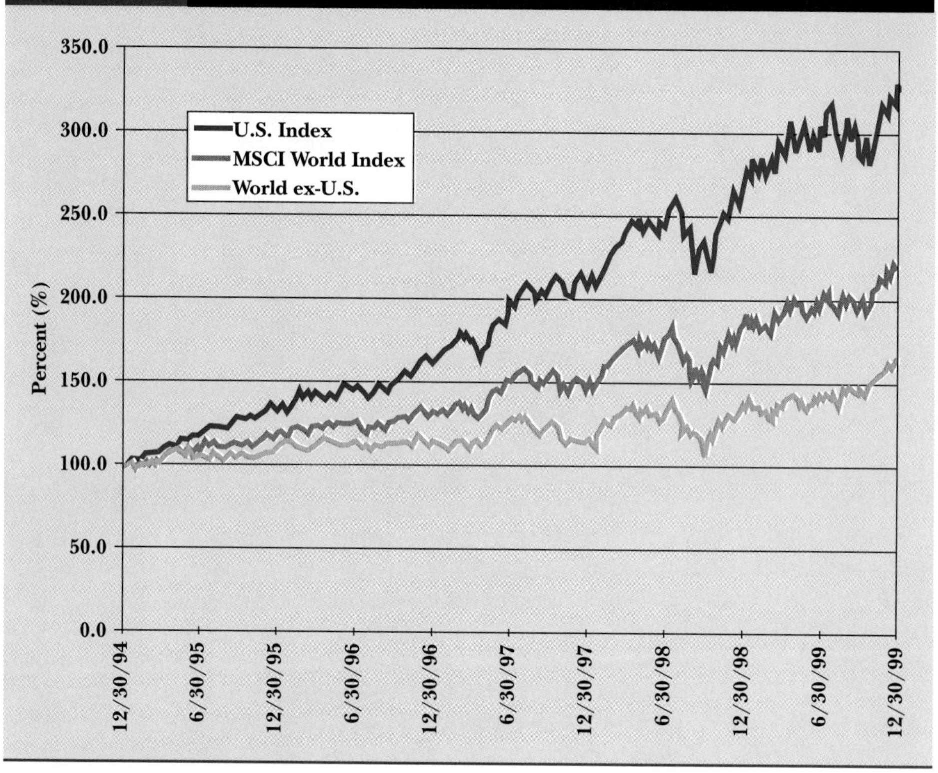

Data source: <http://www.msci.com>.

FIGURE 16.3 **Booming Japanese Stock Market in the 1980s Gave Way to a Stunning Collapse during the 1990s**

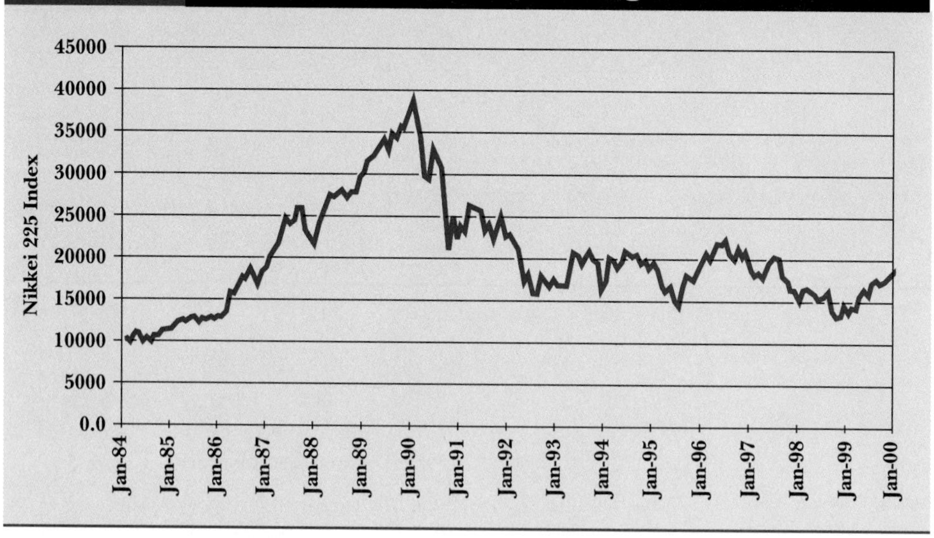

Data source: <http://finance.yahoo.com>.

Therefore, it is not fair to conclude that a collapse of the U.S. equities market is clearly imminent as we enter the new millennium. Still, the recent experience of the Japanese stock market illustrates the dangers involved with focusing one's entire investment portfolio on a single equity market that has enjoyed stunningly good recent performance. Global diversification has the potential to shield investors from the type of cataclysmic collapse experienced by Japanese investors during the 1990s. U.S. investors best take heed, especially in the light of estimates that placed the P/E ratio for Nasdaq companies at more than 200 at year-end 1999.

Developed and Emerging Markets

Established global stock markets in the United States, Japan, United Kingdom, Germany, and other countries hold investment potential for a variety of industries and companies. The emerging markets of countries such as Brazil, Mexico, South Africa, and Taiwan, among others, hold speculative potential and offer investors the opportunity to participate in dynamically growing economies. However, from an investment perspective, there are no economic characteristics that definitively identify an emerging market. Instead, emerging markets tend to share a variety of common economic characteristics. Modern equity and bond markets develop as economic growth accelerates, companies begin to raise capital, trading mechanisms are established, regulations are liberalized, and investor interest grows. Use of the word *emerging* to describe equity and bond markets connotes markets that are developing, unfolding, or maturing. It is important to recognize, however, that countries with emerging markets may or may not be successful in translating immense economic opportunities into lasting economic success. Some emerging stock markets such as Argentina, for example, have long histories of economic progress punctuated by bouts of economic turmoil and depression. As a result, it is important to recognize that some emerging markets may never, in fact, emerge like Portugal to join the ranks of developed markets.

Emerging markets share a number of common characteristics. They tend to be found in countries with GDP per capita substantially below the average for developed economies. The typical emerging market covered by MSCI has GDP per capita that is only one-fifth to one-sixth of that seen in countries with developed markets. In the United States, for example, GDP per capita averages roughly $30,000. In a typical emerging market, GDP per capita averages less than $5,000. Emerging markets also tend to have substantially greater government regulation of industry than that faced by companies in developed markets. This is despite the fact that emerging markets are often characterized by loose securities market regulation. In many emerging markets, local trading hours are irregular, clearing and trade settlement capabilities are antiquated, and shareholder reporting requirements are often lax. Emerging market countries also sometimes put limitations on share ownership by foreign investors or place restrictions on the repatriation of capital gains, dividends, or interest income.

free indexes Price performance for securities available to all investors.

As shown in Table 16.4, MSCI indexes give detailed coverage to developed and emerging equity markets. In some emerging markets, MSCI designates **free indexes** and **nonfree indexes.** A free index is one in which all component securities are available without restriction to foreign investors. A nonfree index includes various securities that are available only to domestic investors or are available to domestic investors on more favorable terms than those accessible to foreign investors. All MSCI indexes are considered free unless a nonfree index is also offered.

nonfree indexes Price performance for securities available on a preferential basis to domestic investors.

TABLE 16.5 Developed Markets Account for Much of Global Market Capitalization (12/31/99)

	Estimated Market Capitalization ($ billions)	Number of Companies	Percentage of Global Market Cap
Developed Markets			
Australia	$325,016	1,135	1.04
Austria	32,570	112	0.10
Belgium	185,842	140	0.60
Canada	725,203	1,194	2.33
Denmark	110,518	242	0.36
Finland	394,314	71	1.27
France	1,130,756	767	3.64
Germany	1,236,488	717	3.97
Hong Kong	442,073	545	1.42
Ireland	54,067	62	0.17
Italy	484,330	236	1.56
Japan	3,779,361	3,114	12.15
Malaysia	550,411	612	1.77
Netherlands	587,721	197	1.89
New Zealand	24,465	128	0.08
Norway	56,326	148	0.18
Portugal	47,166	158	0.15
Singapore	168,505	285	0.54
Spain	341,819	361	1.10
Sweden	520,016	223	1.67
Switzerland	654,048	261	2.10
United Kingdom	2,583,028	1,859	8.30
United States	14,693,494	7,663	47.24
EAFE	**$13,200,441**	**11,215**	**42.44**
All Developed Markets	**$29,127,538**	**20,230**	**93.64**
Emerging Markets*			
Argentina	$51,872	147	0.17
Brazil	245,253	550	0.79
Chile	62,047	290	0.20
China	66,633	532	0.21
Colombia	7,065	123	0.02
Czech Republic	14,546	1,628	0.05
Greece	79,838	218	0.26
Hungary	9,778	45	0.03
India	185,325	5,999	0.60
Indonesia	37,403	256	0.12
Israel	61,038	655	0.20
Jordan	4,051	133	0.01
Korea	207,629	760	0.67
Mexico	176,651	196	0.57
Pakistan	6,795	782	0.02
Peru	11,405	239	0.04
Phillippines	41,180	216	0.13
Poland	11,591	66	0.04
Russia	59,059	173	0.19
South Africa	232,069	636	0.75
Sri Lanka	1,331	235	0.00
Taiwan	283,691	382	0.91
Thailand	10,865	454	0.03
Turkey	104,010	228	0.33
Venezuela	8,293	89	0.03
All Emerging Markets	**$ 1,979,416**	**15,032**	**6.36**
All Countries	**$ 31,106,954**	**35,262**	**100.00**

*Note: No market cap data available on Luxembourg.
Data source: <http://www.msci.com>.

Table 16.5 and Figure 16.4 show the breakdown in global market capitalization in developed and emerging markets. In the developed market's universe, the U.S., U.K., and Japanese markets are dominant. With the stunning recent growth during the late 1990s, the U.S. market now represents roughly one-half of the total market capitalization of global equities. As shown in Figure 16.4, the U.K. and Japanese markets are of comparable size and constitute vibrant, broad, and liquid developed markets. Other developed markets, such as those found in Germany, France, Canada, and Switzerland, are much smaller than leading developed markets. In fact, the market value of a handful of leading U.S. companies often rivals, if not exceeds, the market capitalization of several important developed markets. For example, at the end of 1999, a list of the five U.S. companies with the largest market capitalizations read as follows: Microsoft Corp. ($604 billion), General Electric Co. ($507 billion), Cisco Systems, Inc. ($340 billion), Wal-Mart Stores, Inc.

FIGURE 16.4 **The United States, United Kingdom, and Japan Are Dominant Developed Markets; Brazil, Taiwan, and South Africa Are Major Emerging Markets**

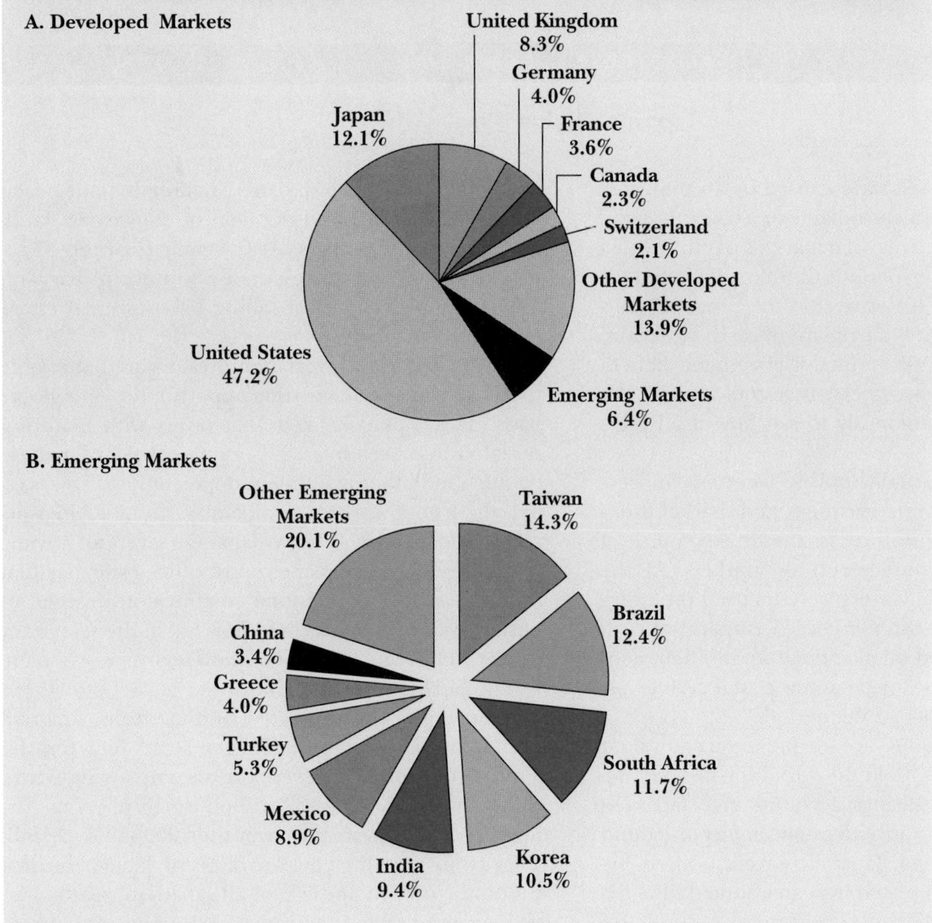

Data source: <http://www.msci.com>.

($308 billion), and Intel Corp. ($275 billion). Notice that major developed markets in continental Europe are scarcely larger that the market capitalization of two or three such goliaths from the United States. In many cases, a single industrial giant from the United States has a market capitalization that exceeds that of major developed markets. This has important implications for investors seeking to add an international dimension to their investment portfolios. Even in developed markets, global investors cannot expect to find a wide range of investment alternatives that have the breadth of market reach and economic might of industrial giants from the United States.

The global dominance of the U.S. market and the enormous size of industrial giants from the United States becomes even more obvious when one considers the fact that even the largest emerging markets fail to equal the market capitalization of a single top firm from the United States. Most emerging markets are characterized by only a handful of investment opportunities. In most cases, investment alternatives in emerging markets are limited to trading companies and infrastructure investments such as telecommunications, transportation, and electric utilities.

WALL STREET WISDOM 16.1

Japan's Rising Sun?

A tsunami is a huge sea wave caused by an undersea disturbance, such as an earthquake or a volcanic eruption. Most of the time, financial markets pay little heed to tsunamis and other natural disasters. This time is different. It is not a sea wave that the financial markets are focused on; it is a tsunami of cash. Moreover, it is not a disaster at all. In fact, it is a hugely beneficial event for Japanese savers. Investors around the globe are watching anxiously to see how it all plays out.

Global investors usually look to forecasts for economic growth, corporate earnings, and market interest rates when trying to forecast the future course of equity and fixed-income securities markets. At the start of 2000, global investors were focused on a very different catalyst for the markets. A tsunami of cash is going to be released on global equity and debt markets by the expiration of Japanese postal savings accounts during the 2000–2001 period.

Postal savings accounts are the Japanese equivalent of U.S. savings bonds. Sold door to door in small denominations, postal savings accounts give Japanese savers a risk-free alternative to public equity and bond markets. A decade ago, Japanese savers poured billions of dollars worth of yen into guaranteed time deposits paying 6% interest. Government controls on foreign investments by Japanese nationals made postal savings accounts the instrument of choice for "landlocked" Japanese savers. At the time, guaranteed interest rates of 6% represented a wonderful bargain, especially in the light of falling Japanese real estate and equity markets.

Today, Japanese savers and investors are better able to take advantage of investing opportunities on a global basis. This makes it likely that savers with maturing postal savings accounts will begin to consider Japanese equities and other investment opportunities. This is especially true given that comparable postal savings accounts today promise to pay Japanese savers an anemic 0.2% interest. The Japanese post office estimates that as much as 50% of the total amount now invested in postal savings accounts could flow out in the search for higher yields. Much of that outflow seems poised to enter the Japanese stock market.

How big is the projected outflow from Japanese postal savings accounts? To get some feel for the amount of money involved, the accompanying figure shows that as much as $2 trillion worth of postal savings accounts will mature over the 2000–2001 period. That is an amount equal to 20% of Japan's annual economic output and 5% of all Japanese wealth. Maturing postal savings accounts also represent close to

8% of the total value of global equities and as much as 40–50% of the total market capitalization of the Japanese stock market.

A host of international financial firms hope to cash in by selling Japanese investors various annuities, domestic and foreign stock mutual funds, and fixed-income securities. The same question is on everybody's mind: What will they buy?

See: Bill Spindle and Phred Dvorak, "Japan Inc. Seeks Advice of Wall Street Bankers," *The Wall Street Journal,* March 14, 2000, A21, A22.

Riding the Wave...

Amount in Japanese 10-year postal savings accounts maturing over the next two years; quarterly data, in billions of U.S. dollars, converted from yen at current rate

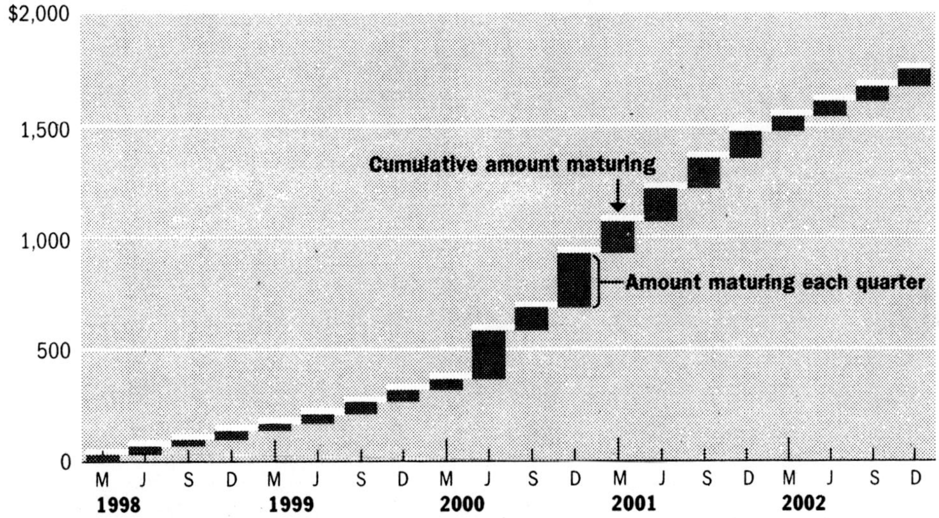

Source: Japan's Ministry of Posts and Telecommunications and Nikko Salomon Smith Barney

Source: *The Wall Street Journal,* March 24, 2000, C1.

Global Investing Risks

Market Volatility

Until the mid-1990s, there was a tremendous and growing amount of investor interest in global investment opportunities. This was particularly true of emerging markets. For example, in the United States there was spreading investor interest in Latin America, where investors saw the opportunity to profit from thriving economic cooperation between the United States and its Latin neighbors, as typified by the North American Free Trade Agreement (NAFTA).

As shown in Figure 16.5, emerging markets in Latin America, like emerging markets everywhere, can prove highly volatile. In January 1995, for example, Latin American markets, as measured by the MSCI Latin American Emerging Markets Index, began a sharp nosedive from 928. They reached a low point of 529 on March 9, 1995, a drop of roughly 45%. Then, in a quick turnabout, Latin American

FIGURE 16.5 **Emerging Markets in Latin America and Other Areas Tend to Be Highly Volatile**

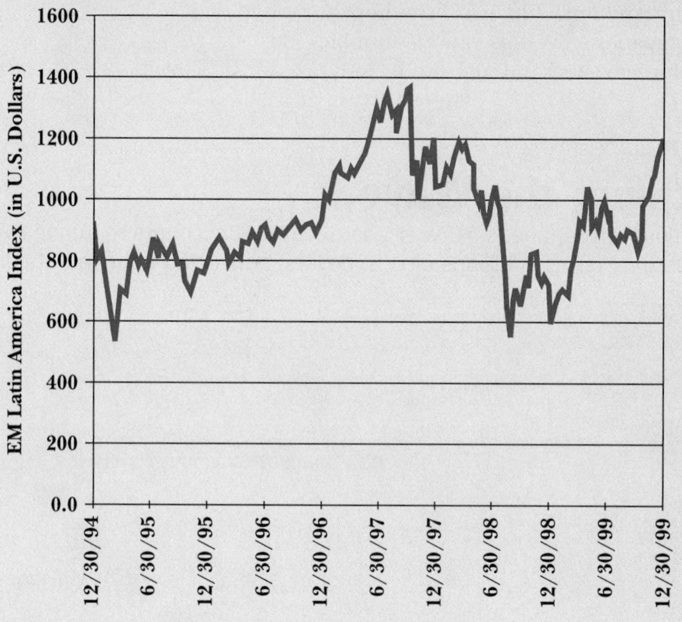

Data source: <http://www.msci.com>.

markets quickly recovered most of these losses before autumn, only to reverse once again to test previous lows during November 1995. At that point, Latin American markets took off on an enormous bull market run that brought regional markets to 1376 on July 10, 1997, a stunning 160% advance in only 28 months from the early 1995 low. However, the roller-coaster ride for Latin American investors did not stop there. In a gut-wrenching turn of events, Latin American markets broke sharply downward. Despite a brief recovery in early 1998, they dove to 532 on September 10, 1998, from which they bounced upward to almost 1200 by the end of 1999.

market volatility Change in security prices.

Experiences such as these have convinced many U.S. investors that global investing, particularly emerging markets investing, is not for them. Thus, it is important to keep in mind that investing in foreign markets, especially emerging ones, generally involves much higher **market volatility** than that associated with U.S. equities. The potential for above-average gains in foreign equity markets comes with the risk of similarly above-average losses in any given year. In fact, foreign stock market returns are often more volatile than domestic returns.

Table 16.6 shows the relative volatility of foreign markets as a whole relative to the U.S. market based on annual rates of return. Over the 15-year 1985–99

TABLE 16.6 Annual Returns in Foreign Markets Are More Volatile than in the U.S.

Year	Wilshire 5000	MSCI EAFE
1985	32.6%	56.7%
1986	16.0%	69.9%
1987	2.3%	24.9%
1988	18.0%	28.6%
1989	29.1%	10.8%
1990	−6.2%	−23.3%
1991	34.3%	12.5%
1992	9.0%	−11.8%
1993	11.2%	32.9%
1994	−0.1%	8.1%
1995	36.4%	11.6%
1996	21.3%	6.4%
1997	31.3%	2.1%
1998	23.4%	20.3%
1999	22.1%	25.3%
Mean	**18.0%**	**16.2%**
SD	**13.2%**	**23.7%**

Data sources: <http://www.vanguard.com> and <http://www.msci.com>.

period, for example, the average annual rate of return for U.S. equities as captured by the Wilshire 5000 Index was 18.0%. Over this time frame, the standard deviation of annual returns on U.S. equities was 13.2%. These figures compare with average annual rates of return on foreign stocks as captured by MSCI's EAFE Index of 16.2% per year and a standard deviation of 23.7% per year. Therefore, during recent years, foreign markets have tended to underperform the U.S. market while displaying a somewhat higher level of return volatility. No wonder backward-looking U.S. investors prefer to invest domestically rather than in foreign equities.

In terms of risk, the story gets worse for investing in the stocks of individual foreign markets. As described in Table 16.4, investors earned stunning rates of return in such developed markets as Finland (150.71%) and Singapore (97.08%) during 1999. At the same time, and despite a global boom in equity prices, investors lost money during 1999 in the stocks of countries such as Belgium (−15.77%), Ireland (−14.02%), and Portugal (−10.86%). Table 16.7 shows the relative volatility of national equities markets as a whole based on returns and return volatility for a recent five-year period. In the United States, a typical standard deviation of annual returns is in the range of 10% per year. Such return volatility is often more than twice as great in developed foreign markets such as Hong Kong (27.6%), Italy (26.4%), and Japan (21.9%). It is much higher still in emerging markets such as Turkey (55.9%), Brazil (36.6%), and Mexico (36.6%). Based on history, equity investors should expect substantially greater levels of market volatility when venturing abroad.

TABLE 16.7 Developed and Emerging Foreign Markets Are More Volatile than the U.S. Market

	5-Year Annualized Returns (%)	Annualized Monthly Standard Deviations (%)
Developed Markets		
Australia	15.7	16.7
Austria	2.8	14.5
Belgium	15.1	11.0
Canada	16.4	13.7
Denmark	18.6	14.8
Finland	46.5	28.3
France	11.3	15.7
Germany	16.8	14.8
Hong Kong	21.7	27.6
Ireland	22.9	15.0
Italy	19.2	26.4
Japan	3.7	21.9
Malaysia	3.5	28.8
Netherlands	24.0	14.1
New Zealand	24.3	19.6
Norway	22.2	17.7
Portugal	19.4	20.6
Singapore	9.9	18.6
Spain	24.8	20.0
Sweden	31.5	21.8
Switzerland	23.2	15.5
United Kingdom	17.6	12.7
United States	21.2	10.5
EAFE	12.7	13.4
Europe	18.5	11.6
The World Index	16.4	10.5
Kokusai Index (World Ex-Japan)	19.7	9.9
World Ex-U.K.	16.3	10.7
World Ex-U.S.	12.8	13.1

Note: n.a. means "not available."
Data source: <http://www.msci.com>.

Liquidity Risk

liquidity risk Loss potential tied to the fact that a stock can become difficult to buy or sell.

Liquidity risk refers to loss potential tied to the fact that a stock can become difficult to buy or sell. This problem is frequently greater in foreign stock markets than in U.S. equity markets. This is especially true of emerging markets. Foreign markets typically have modest daily trading activity when compared with the United States. In some countries, fewer than 200 stocks trade in quantities sufficient to support the interest of foreign investors. In many emerging markets, trading activity is dominated by a mere handful of investment opportunities. The problem of scarcity in global investment opportunities is exacerbated by the fact that countries with emerging markets often permit foreigners to buy only specific classes of shares for certain companies. Sometimes, quantities of such shares are strictly limited. Under these circumstances, a scarcity of investment opportunities leads to thin trading volume, increased market volatility, and exorbitant premiums for sought-after shares.

TABLE 16.7 ***(continued)***

	5-Year Annualized Returns (%)	Annualized Monthly Standard Deviations (%)
Emerging Markets		
Argentina	18.4	30.9
Brazil	34.8	36.6
Chili	17.3	22.6
China	n.a.	n.a.
Colombia	n.a.	n.a.
Czech Republic	n.a.	n.a.
Egypt	n.a.	n.a.
Greece	18.8	22.1
Hungary	n.a.	n.a.
India	n.a.	n.a.
Indonesia	2.6	32.2
Israel	n.a.	n.a.
Jordan	6.0	15.8
Korea	3.6	23.9
Malaysia	3.3	28.8
Mexico	10.1	36.6
Morocco	n.a.	n.a.
Pakistan	n.a.	n.a.
Peru	n.a.	n.a.
Philippines	1.7	32.3
Poland	n.a.	n.a.
Russia	n.a.	n.a.
South Africa	n.a.	n.a.
Sri Lanka	n.a.	n.a.
Taiwan	19.4	35.4
Thailand	−9.7	34.4
Turkey	24.8	55.9
Venezuela	n.a.	n.a.
AC Far East Free Ex-Japan	11.3	23.5
AC World Index	16.1	10.4
EMF (Emerging Mkts Free)	13.4	17.4

Thin trading activity in foreign developed and emerging markets often leads to higher **market impact costs.** Of course, high bid-ask spreads are the most obvious sign of low liquidity and significant market impact costs. In the United States, bid-ask spreads for highly liquid large-cap stocks listed on the New York Stock Exchange (NYSE) are commonly no more than 25 basis points (0.25%). For smaller and less liquid U.S. equities traded on Nasdaq, bid-ask spreads can easily top 2 to 3%, or eight to 12 times higher. In foreign markets, not only do bid-ask spreads tend to be higher than in the United States, large buyers and sellers are often not able to deal in quantity at posted prices. Buyers of large blocks of foreign equities, for example, often have to pay a price higher than the quoted ask price to complete a given purchase transaction. Sellers of large blocks of foreign equities often receive only a marked-down price that is lower than the quoted bid price.

market impact costs
Costs tied to changing market bid and ask prices.

Liquidity risks are especially high in emerging markets. Emerging markets are generally small, with fewer stocks listed and less trading activity than is common in developed countries. Not only can the entire market capitalization of an emerging market be less than that of a single large U.S. company, many companies in emerging markets are closely held family businesses. For example, as shown in Table 16.5, shares in only a couple hundred companies trade on a daily basis in leading European countries such as Italy, Sweden, and Switzerland. Some important emerging markets feature less than 100 investment opportunities. This contrasts with the United States, where more than 7,000 companies and close to two billion shares trade on a daily basis. The lower trading volumes characteristic of emerging markets mean that institutional investors may not be able to get fair and timely trade executions. During some financial crises, emerging markets have also been known to close for brief periods, such as in India where the Bombay Stock Exchange closed for three days in March 1995. Some foreign countries also restrict nondomestic investments. In Taiwan, for example, foreigners are permitted to own only certain classes of shares, which may be available in limited quantities. In Chile, nondomestic investors must wait at least one year to withdraw capital from the market. All such restrictions reduce market liquidity for nondomestic investors.

In addition to higher market impact costs in foreign markets, the special liquidity risks associated with investing in developed and emerging markets are accompanied by higher global equity transaction costs. **Brokerage commissions, exchange fees, currency translation costs,** and **custodial fees** tend to be substantially higher in emerging markets than in the developed markets of the United States and Europe. Several foreign governments also levy taxes based on the total value of equity purchase and sale transactions. For example, brokerage commissions and exchange fees total only five to 15 basis points (0.05–0.15%) of the total value of an equity purchase or sales transaction in the United States. In Brazil, one of the largest and most liquid emerging markets, brokerage commissions, exchange fees, and foreign currency translation costs average 0.60%. Similar costs are incurred by nondomestic equity investors in emerging Asian markets such as Indonesia (0.60%), Malaysia (0.55%), and the Philippines (0.75%). When such fees are combined with meaningful market impact costs, overall transaction costs for buying a basket of emerging market stocks can easily exceed 2% per year. If quoted historical rates of return on benchmark indexes for emerging market equities do not include such real-world costs, they systematically understate what can become a significant drag on investor returns.

brokerage commissions Sales charges.

exchange fees Trading cost imposed by organized trading system.

currency translation costs Expenses of converting host country currency into domestic currency of buyer or seller.

custodial fees Bookkeeping charges.

Political Risk

Many global markets are immature, vulnerable to scandal, subject to manipulation, and lacking in investor protections. This is especially true of emerging markets in which political events have the potential to threaten the stability of returns. Many countries with emerging markets are vulnerable to **political risk** stemming from coups, assassinations, or civil unrest, which increase market volatility and decrease investor returns. Some countries with emerging markets are governed by dictatorships with succession plans shrouded in secrecy and uncertainty. Governments of countries with emerging markets also tend to be moving toward democracy and struggling with long-standing political and social problems. Sudden retreats toward socialism are apt to occur, especially during periods of social unrest.

political risk Loss potential tied to government stemming from coups, assassinations, or civil unrest.

Economic progress can also be stalled by unexpected trade deficits that sometimes undermine currency stability. In 1997–98, for example, a local currency crisis contributed to severe economic upheaval in Malaysia, where economic controls were quickly put in place to restrict the repatriation of investment funds by nondomestic investors. **Government policy risk** is an important consideration for global investors. Nondomestic investors must always be on the lookout for policy changes that could become unfavorable. Such changes could include currency controls, changes in monopoly franchise agreements, and adverse revisions in the taxation of foreign investment. In a worst-case scenario, investors must be on the lookout for the potential expropriation of investments made by nondomestic investors. In an era of privatization of formerly public assets, investors tend to forget the **expropriation risk** that claimed the assets of global investors during the 1960s and 1970s.

government policy risk
Loss potential tied to changes in government rules and regulations.

expropriation risk
Loss potential tied to government confiscation of assets.

Currency Risk

When investors think of political risks, thoughts often turn to the potential loss of monopoly franchises, operating authorities, or tax abatements. Although such risks are always an important consideration, **currency risk** is the most pervasive political risk faced when making global investments.

currency risk
Loss potential tied to changing relative value of world currencies.

The U.S. dollar and all currencies fluctuate in value over time. Just like any commodity, the value of the dollar rises and falls according to the laws of supply and demand. In the domestic market for goods and services, when the supply of dollars rises faster than the rate of growth in goods and services, prices rise and inflation occurs. Inflation is measured by the rate of increase in prices. Inflation signifies a fall in the value of the dollar, when value is measured in terms of the amount of goods and services that can be purchased for $1. If prices drop, deflation occurs and the value of the dollar rises. Movements in the value of the dollar in foreign currency markets operate in a similar way. A **strong dollar** signifies an increase in the amount of foreign currency that can be purchased for $1. A **weak dollar** connotes a decrease in the amount of foreign currency that can be purchased for $1. When the dollar is strong, the dollar price of goods and services purchased from abroad falls. When the dollar is weak, the dollar price of goods and services purchased from abroad rises.

strong dollar
Increase in the amount of foreign currency that can be purchased for $1.

weak dollar
Decrease in the amount of foreign currency that can be purchased for $1.

Changes in the value of the dollar have obvious implications for U.S. consumers. For example, when the dollar strengthens, the dollar price of Toyotas made in Japan falls, and U.S. consumers snap up such foreign-produced bargains. When the dollar weakens, the dollar price of Toyotas made in Japan rises, and U.S. consumers tend to favor automobiles built in Detroit. On an overall basis, the balance of trade describes the balance between the amount of goods and services U.S. consumers purchase from foreign suppliers versus the amount foreign consumers buy from U.S. suppliers. A **trade deficit** occurs when U.S. consumers buy more goods and services produced abroad than the amount of U.S. goods and services bought by foreigners. A **trade surplus** occurs when U.S. consumers buy fewer goods and services produced abroad than the amount of U.S. goods and services bought by foreigners. When a trade deficit occurs, U.S. dollars pile up in the bank accounts of foreigners. As foreigners convert these dollars into local currencies, the dollar tends to weaken. If a trade surplus arises, foreign currencies pile up in U.S. banks. As these foreign currencies are converted into dollars, the dollar tends to strengthen.

trade deficit
Trade imbalance that occurs when U.S. consumers buy more foreign products than the amount of U.S. products bought by foreigners.

trade surplus
Trade imbalance that occurs when U.S. consumers buy fewer foreign products than the amount of U.S. products bought by foreigners.

Changes in the value of the dollar also have important implications for global investors. If stock prices in Japan rise by 10% but the dollar strengthens 3% against the Japanese yen, the net return earned by U.S. investors on their Japanese holdings

FIGURE 16.6 **In the Late 1990s, a Strong U.S. Dollar Reduced Returns on Foreign Securities**

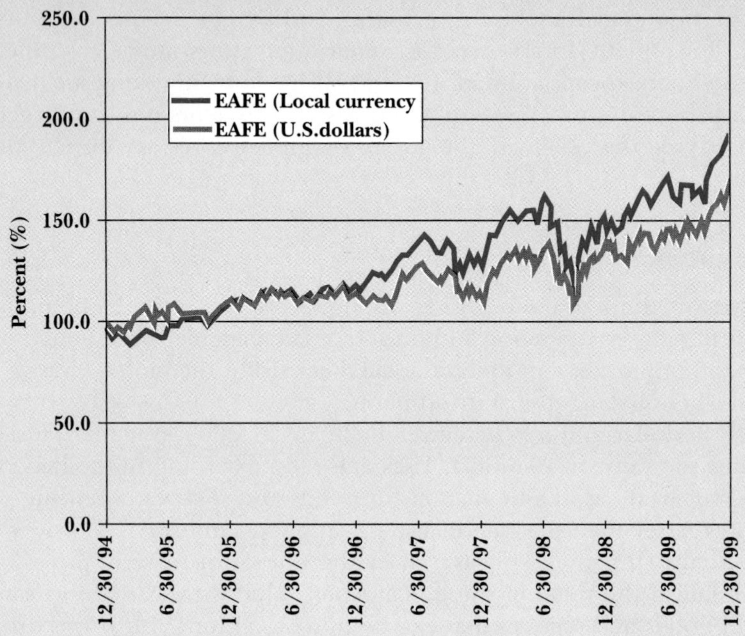

Data source: <http://www.msci.com>.

falls to 7%. However, if stock prices in Japan rise by 10% and the dollar weakens 3% against the Japanese yen, the net return earned by U.S. investors on their Japanese holdings jumps to 13%.

Fluctuations in world currency markets can have a dramatic effect on returns earned abroad. Table 16.4 shows a one-year return for MSCI's World Index of 26.27% when measured in terms of local currencies, but only 23.56% when measured using the U.S. dollar. The 2.71% difference reflects a general strengthening in the value of the dollar versus world currencies during 1999. During the 1990s, MSCI's World Index earned an average 9.20% annual rate of return when measured in terms of local currencies but 9.61% when measured using the U.S. dollar. This means that the 1999 strength of the U.S. dollar contrasts with decade-long weakness. On average, the dollar lost a modest 0.41% per year in value when measured against all other world currencies. The effects of rising or falling currencies can be much more dramatic when viewed on a country-by-country basis.

In Germany, for example, Table 16.4 shows that robust one-year gains of 39.05% were trimmed to only 18.70% for U.S. investors when the appreciation of the U.S. dollar versus the euro is taken into account. Similarly, stock market returns for other European countries were greatly diminished for U.S. investors when returns are measured in dollars versus the local currency. In some emerging markets, plunging local currencies have led to devastating losses for U.S. investors. High emerging market returns from rising stock prices can sometimes be turned into losses because of the falling value of local currencies. For example, during 1994, the Turkish stock market posted a strong one-year return of 31.5% when measured using the Turkish lira, but a sharp decline in the value of the lira created a net 50.5% loss when measured in U.S. dollars. Similarly, a 314.0% gain in Turkey during 1997 was reduced to only 118.1% after accounting for currency losses. When a developing nation's currency is devalued and its stock market declines, U.S. investors can suffer steep losses, as they did in Asia during late 1998.

A primary cause of currency risk in emerging markets has been runaway inflation. Annual inflation rates of 1,000% or more are not without precedent. Although there have been some notable successes in controlling global inflation recently—for example, in Argentina and Chile—a potential resurgence of inflation remains a threat to currency stability around the globe. As shown in Figure 16.6, a strengthening U.S. dollar during the late 1990s tended to reduce rates of return from global markets for U.S. investors. As a result, global investors must remain vigilant concerning the potential for losses stemming from currency risk.

Global Investing Benefits

Attractive Opportunities

The astonishing performance of large-cap U.S. stocks during the late 1990s has convinced many U.S. investors that domestic portfolios provide superior investment returns. Over the 1995–99 time frame, there is scarcely any investment strategy that could have beaten the Standard & Poor's (S&P) 500 and a simple buy-and-hold strategy. Why go abroad and invest in markets, companies, and currencies that you do not fully understand when you can stay home and buy the best-performing stocks in the world? The answer is simple: Global markets can give superior returns.

Despite recent experience, substantial evidence exists to suggest that a global investment strategy exposes investors to attractive investment opportunities. As shown in Table 16.8, although the United States is among the world leaders in providing a high standard of living for its citizens, the rate of economic growth, or economic betterment, in the United States is somewhat below the world average. Over time, some emerging markets have provided higher investment returns than the stock markets of developed nations, and many economists expect that to continue. Those higher returns reflect the greater potential for economic growth in developing countries, which should translate into higher personal incomes and greater corporate profits. Many developing economies continue to grow 6–7% per year, a rate far faster than the 2–3% that is typical for a healthy, developed economy. For a number of years, the rate of economic growth in the United States has been substantially below that found in smaller developed markets in Asia, such as China, Hong Kong, Malaysia, and Singapore. In the mid-1990s, for example, China enjoyed economic growth exceeding 10% per year, while some Latin American economies, such as Mexico's, shrank more than 6% in some years. By investing in rapidly growing foreign markets, U.S. investors enjoy the opportunity to share in the benefits provided by explosive economic growth. Moreover, the dramatic downturn in Asian and emerging markets that occurred in the late 1990s has left many global markets at valuation levels that are relatively attractive when compared with

TABLE 16.8 Gross Domestic Product and Economic Growth by Country

	Gross Domestic Product			Annual Compound Growth Rate 1986–1996		
Country	**US$ (billions)**	**US$ per Capita**	**Weight in GDP World**	**GDP (1)**	**GDP (2)**	**Market Capitalization**
United States	7,263	27,614	33.4%	2.3%	5.6%	13.3%
Japan	4,308	34,413	19.8	2.5	3.7	2.4
Germany	2,307	28,256	10.6	2.5	3.5	8.0
France	1,526	26,296	7.0	2.0	4.5	12.1
United Kingdom	1,253	21,507	5.8	2.0	6.7	12.7
Italy	1,221	21,350	5.6	1.9	6.2	7.5
Canada	575	19,421	2.6	2.0	4.7	10.6
Spain	571	14,566	2.6	2.8	8.6	14.3
Australia	397	21,976	1.8	3.2	7.2	12.7
Netherlands	384	24,833	1.8	2.7	4.2	15.4
Switzerland	272	38,638	1.3	1.2	4.0	9.4
Belgium	258	25,686	1.2	1.9	4.9	9.7
Sweden	249	28,221	1.1	1.6	5.6	17.5
Austria	223	26,197	1.0	2.6	5.3	16.9
Denmark	172	32,832	0.8	1.6	4.3	12.7
Norway	158	36,194	0.7	2.7	7.0	17.2
Hong Kong	155	24,119	0.7	5.7	14.2	21.5
Finland	123	24,135	0.6	1.5	4.5	17.7
Malaysia	99	4,918	0.5	8.2	11.0	34.3
Singapore	95	31,684	0.4	8.8	11.7	11.7
Ireland	73	20,411	0.3	5.8	7.7	N/A
New Zealand	66	18,735	0.3	1.9	5.3	8.5
Total/Average	**21,748**	**25,091**	**100.0%**	**3.1%**	**6.4%**	**13.6%**

1996 GDP estimates and 1996 total market capitalization are converted at year-end exchange rates. The annual compound growth rates are calculated in local currencies. (1) = at constant price. (2) = at current price.
Data source: <http://www.msci.com>.

the large-cap U.S. stocks that tend to dominate capitalization-weighted domestic market indexes such as the S&P 500.

Foreign markets have often outperformed U.S. stocks. From 1985 to 1999, for example, foreign stocks outpaced domestic stocks in seven out of 15 rolling three-year periods (1982–85, 1983–86, and so on), as shown in Figure 16.7. Although U.S. equities have had the upper hand during the late 1990s, there are important reasons to believe that this trend will reverse itself over the coming decade. During the 1990s, the rate of appreciation in U.S. stock prices outstripped the pace of growth in revenues, profits, and dividends. As a result, P/E ratios jumped and dividend yields plummeted as the decade wore on. During the late 1990s, the relative valuation of U.S. equities reached unprecedented proportions relative to the domestic market's historical norms and relative to valuations in foreign markets. Some savvy investors predict that this recent period of superior performance for U.S. equities is at an end.

In late 1999, for example, legendary investor Warren Buffett gave interesting insight concerning the relative valuation of U.S. equities at the start of the new millennium and, indirectly, gave a glimpse of the advantages to be gained through global diversification. From an investment perspective, it is fascinating to look back at the 17-year period from the end of 1964 through 1981. In that time interval, the

FIGURE 16.7 Foreign Stock Markets Often Provide Superior Returns

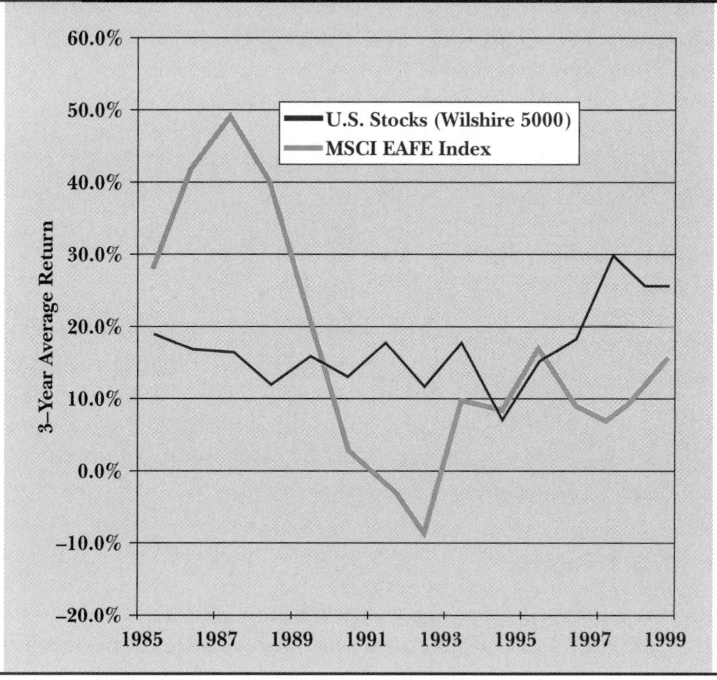

Data sources: <http://www.msci.com> and <http://www.vanguard.com>.

Dow Jones Industrial Average (DJIA) stagnated. On December 31, 1964, the DJIA was at 874.12. On December 31, 1981, it stood at 875.00. During that same 17-year period, the GDP of the United States almost quintupled, rising by 370%. Of course, during the 1964–81 period, there was a tremendous increase in long-term interest rates, from just more than 4% at year-end 1964 to more than 15% by late 1981. The negative effect on stock prices of this historical rise in interest rates fully offset the beneficial influence of rising economic activity, and U.S. stock prices went nowhere. In the early 1980s, this situation reversed itself. In the 17 years from 1982 through 1999, interest rates plummeted to 6.5%, the economy boomed, and the stock market soared. The DJIA closed at a then-record 11,497.12. The increase in U.S. equity value during the 1980s and 1990s beats anything in history. The rate of appreciation in U.S. equity values even surpasses what an investor would have realized if they had bought stocks at their Depression bottom on July 8, 1932 (when the DJIA was at 41.22) and held them for 17 years.

In short, the late 1990s was the sparkling culmination of a period that represented the very best of times for U.S. equity investors. Going forward, continuing double-digit returns for U.S. investors would require a further sharp drop in long-term interest rates to 3% or lower on 30-year bonds or an unprecedented rise in corporate profitability relative to GDP. Both are extremely unlikely. Much more probable is that the rate of return on U.S. equities will fall sharply over the coming decade. Looking ahead and assuming constant interest rates, 2% inflation, and robust real economic growth of 4% per year, Buffett has an expected total rate of return for U.S. equities of 6% per year at the start of the new millennium. Of course, such a return could be earned in a slow and steady progression from current levels or following a collapse and brisk rise from lower levels.

Although it may be tempting to dismiss the thoughts of this century's most renowned investor as old-fashioned, the data depicted in Figure 16.3 suggest ample reason for caution. Japanese equity investors, intently studying the road just traveled, bought right up and through the 1989 peak, only to experience devastating losses during the 1990s. At the end of the 1990s, Japanese equities were priced at bargain levels when compared with U.S. stocks. It is also worth remembering that Japan is the world's second largest economy, sits at the doorstep of rapidly growing Asian economies, has the world's largest pool of liquid savings, and is a country that emphasizes the benefits of capitalism, education, and hard work. Rather than focus on U.S. equities at historically high valuations, shrewd investors may be well advised to carefully consider the investment potential of attractive global markets such as Japan.

Diversification Benefits

Diversification is an important consideration in any prudent investment program. In addition to providing global investors with more and perhaps better investment opportunities, added diversification is a prime benefit that can be derived through adoption of a global investment strategy.

All global economies are directly affected by local economic conditions, and many experience economic cycles that differ from those experienced in the domestic market by U.S. investors. When the U.S. economy slows down or is in recession, some if not many foreign economies may continue to grow and prosper. As a result, foreign equity markets generally do not move in lockstep fashion with the U.S. equity market. As U.S. stock prices rise or fall, foreign stocks often move in some different increment or in the opposite direction. For example, as shown in Table 16.6, during 1994, the Wilshire 5000 Index fell by −0.1% while foreign equity markets as measured by the EAFE Index rose by 8.1%. Thus, global diversification has the potential to cushion investor portfolios from downward fluctuations in domestic markets. Similarly, domestic portfolios can cushion the fall sometimes experienced in foreign stock portfolios, as in 1992 when the Wilshire 5000 rose 9.0% while the EAFE fell 11.8%.

Studies show that adding foreign stocks to a well-rounded portfolio may enhance total returns while reducing overall volatility. By moderating downward swings, a modest allocation to foreign stocks can also make it easier for investors to ride out downturns in domestic markets. Given that foreign equity markets tend to be riskier that the U.S. market, it may not seem reasonable that adding international stocks to an investment portfolio could reduce overall risk. However, research shows that combinations of domestic and foreign equities often produce the lowest risk for a given expected level of return. Combinations of domestic and foreign equities often produce the highest expected rate of return for a given level of risk.

To illustrate the concept of an efficient portfolio with domestic and foreign stocks, Figure 16.8 plots both the expected rate of return and level of risk for var-

FIGURE 16.8 Efficient Portfolios Contain Domestic and Foreign Stocks (1985–99)

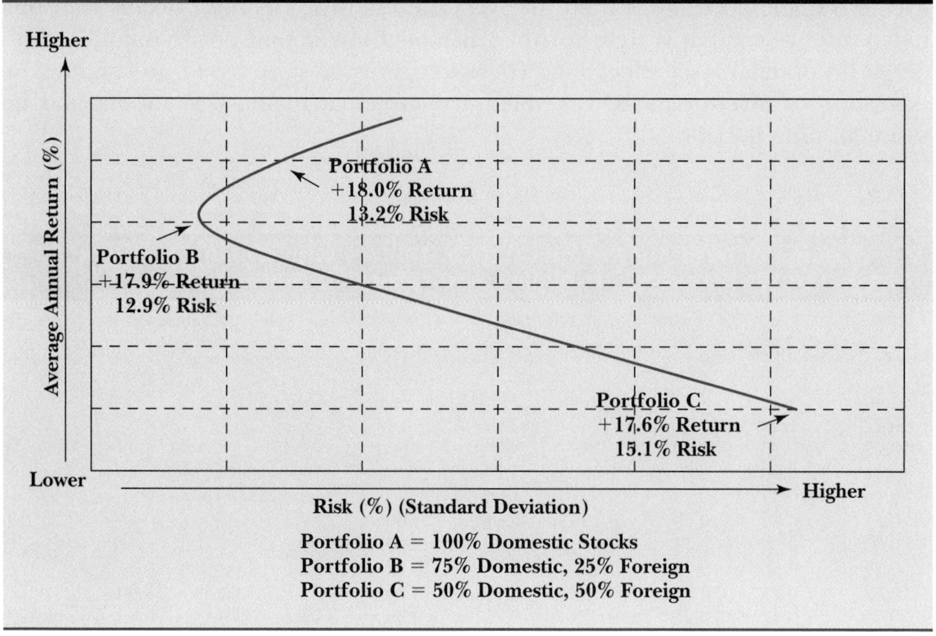

Data source: <http://www.vanguard.com>.

ious combinations of domestic and foreign equities. Portfolio A is 100% invested in U.S. stocks as represented by the Wilshire 5000 Index. As shown in Table 16.6, over the 15-year period ending December 31, 1999, such a portfolio produced an 18.0% average annual rate of return. Over this time frame, market volatility as captured by the standard deviation of annual returns was 13.2%. Portfolio B consists of 75% U.S. stocks and 25% foreign stocks as measured by the EAFE Index. Such a globally diversified portfolio produced a slightly lower 17.9% average annual rate of return but involved a somewhat lower risk level with a standard deviation of 12.9% per year. Globally diversified portfolio C, invested 50% in U.S. stocks and 50% in foreign stocks, produced a lower 17.6% annual rate of return with a higher risk level of 15.1%.

In short, the highest portfolio return for this 15-year period came from portfolio A, an entirely domestic portfolio. However, even during this period of unprecedented returns for U.S. investors, there were risk-reduction benefits to be had through global diversification. The 17.9% return from the globally diversified portfolio B was only slightly lower than the domestic portfolio A, but the risk of such a globally diversified portfolio was measurably lower than that for a domestic portfolio. Finally, portfolio C had not only the lowest average return (17.6%) but also the highest risk of all three sample portfolios. Consequently, portfolio B produced the lowest risk with a return only slightly lower than portfolio A.

The lesson learned from the simple example illustrated in Figure 16.8 is that global diversification has the potential to measurably reduce risk with only a modest reduction in the average annual rate of return. The proper amount of such diversification depends on investor risk attitudes and available investment alternatives. No single portfolio is right for everyone. All investors must decide the combination of assets that is right for their personal investment portfolio and how to derive an optimal asset allocation. These decisions must be based on careful consideration of investor goals, risk tolerance, personal financial situation, and investment time horizon.

TABLE 16.9 **Correlations of Monthly Returns in U.S. Dollars with Gross Dividends Reinvested for Selected Developed and Emerging Markets**

Developed Markets

	Australia	Austria	Belgium	Canada	Denmark	Finland	France	Germany	Hong Kong	Ireland
Australia	1.00									
Austria	0.72	1.00								
Belgium	0.59	0.25	1.00							
Canada	0.41	0.00	0.60	1.00						
Denmark	0.70	0.49	0.78	0.75	1.00					
Finland	0.51	0.62	0.49	0.15	0.61	1.00				
France	0.65	0.39	0.71	0.87	0.89	0.37	1.00			
Germany	0.72	0.56	0.78	0.47	0.90	0.72	0.77	1.00		
Hong Kong	0.89	0.71	0.48	0.55	0.73	0.36	0.73	0.64	1.00	
Ireland	0.74	0.42	0.73	0.67	0.71	0.53	0.77	0.73	0.65	1.00
Italy	0.75	0.59	0.33	0.19	0.57	0.45	0.46	0.52	0.64	0.43
Japan	0.54	0.58	−0.09	−0.29	−0.06	0.20	−0.05	0.11	0.37	0.24
Malaysia	0.76	0.74	0.24	0.10	0.35	0.41	0.39	0.37	0.75	0.57
Netherlands	0.64	0.34	0.82	0.79	0.86	0.54	0.87	0.89	0.59	0.86
New Zealand	0.80	0.83	0.48	0.19	0.57	0.78	0.50	0.70	0.67	0.73
Norway	0.75	0.69	0.66	0.44	0.82	0.84	0.70	0.86	0.65	0.78
Singapore	0.68	0.76	0.24	−0.29	0.16	0.48	0.04	0.36	0.50	0.33
Spain	0.65	0.24	0.62	0.88	0.87	0.23	0.90	0.71	0.73	0.63
Sweden	0.81	0.44	0.81	0.75	0.87	0.57	0.84	0.85	0.75	0.89
Switzerland	0.79	0.61	0.74	0.50	0.73	0.49	0.67	0.80	0.75	0.70
United Kingdom	0.53	0.24	0.70	0.91	0.90	0.49	0.90	0.79	0.62	0.74
United States	0.20	−0.23	0.61	0.88	0.59	0.03	0.67	0.50	0.26	0.53

Emerging Markets

	Argentina	Brazil	Chili	Greece	Indonesia	Jordan	Korea	Malaysia	Mexico	Phillipines
Argentina	1.00									
Brazil	0.71	1.00								
Chili	0.10	0.52	1.00							
Greece	0.58	0.42	0.20	1.00						
Indonesia	0.77	0.52	0.03	0.46	1.00					
Jordan	0.36	0.25	0.12	0.70	0.40	1.00				
Korea	0.05	0.23	0.68	−0.11	0.14	0.12	1.00			
Malaysia	0.52	0.49	0.26	0.21	0.87	0.23	0.33	1.00		
Mexico	0.92	0.64	−0.02	0.35	0.63	0.18	0.01	0.40	1.00	
Philippines	0.48	0.57	0.62	0.10	0.63	0.03	0.59	0.83	0.41	1.00
Portugal*	0.71	0.69	0.15	0.75	0.54	0.41	−0.31	0.38	0.52	0.22
Taiwan	0.43	0.72	0.50	0.05	0.15	−0.21	0.06	0.28	0.43	0.51
Thailand	0.04	0.10	0.48	−0.25	0.36	−0.03	0.85	0.61	0.00	0.74
Turkey	0.10	0.07	−0.20	0.47	0.35	0.70	−0.31	0.25	−0.10	−0.19

(Monthly correlations based on five years of data from 9/30/92 to 9/30/97.)
*Portugal is now classified as a developed market.
Data source: <http://msci.com>.

Finally, it is important to remember that effective global diversification involves investing in markets that have low correlation with market movements in the United States or even among themselves. In other words, when one market is falling, it is smart to be invested in another that is rising. Around the globe, assorted developed and emerging markets exhibit varying economic growth and equity market performance. As shown in Table 16.9, equities in certain markets such as Canada, move almost in lockstep fashion with the United States. Other equity

TABLE 16.9 ***(continued)***

Italy	Japan	Malaysia	Netherlands	New Zealand	Norway	Singapore	Spain	Sweden	Switzerland	United Kingdom	United States
1.00											
0.48	1.00										
0.48	0.57	1.00									
0.39	0.00	0.29	1.00								
0.52	0.57	0.81	0.58	1.00							
0.66	0.19	0.57	0.79	0.82	1.00						
0.49	0.76	0.72	0.16	0.77	0.48	1.00					
0.54	−0.05	0.25	0.79	0.32	0.57	−0.04	1.00				
0.51	0.13	0.49	0.91	0.69	0.79	0.32	0.81	1.00			
0.37	0.34	0.48	0.76	0.71	0.63	0.54	0.61	0.83	1.00		
0.29	−0.24	0.24	0.88	0.44	0.69	−0.08	0.85	0.85	0.64	1.00	
−0.07	−0.37	−0.21	0.73	0.00	0.23	−0.39	0.72	0.64	0.50	0.78	1.00

Portugal*	Taiwan	Thailand	Turkey
1.00			
0.49	1.00		
−0.33	0.00	1.00	
0.45	−0.20	−0.25	1.00

markets, such as Australia, display only a weak positive correlation with the U.S. market. Equities returns in some global markets, such as Italy, appear almost unrelated to U.S. equity returns. Some markets display an inverse correlation, such as Japan. When seeking to achieve the benefits of global diversification, investors must be careful to select investments in countries that offer significant potential for risk reduction. For U.S. investors, investments in Japanese equities are much more likely to yield risk-reduction benefits than a similar investment in Canadian securities.

The idea of spreading investments around the globe to reduce risk and enhance returns was very popular in the mid-1990s. Unfortunately, it is no longer generally accepted as valid by many U.S. investors. Not only have investors been mesmerized by recently exceptional returns on U.S. equities, they have been dissuaded from the global diversification concept by highly volatile foreign markets. This is a pity because history suggests that global diversification is an effective tool for risk reduction.

American Depositary Receipts

ADR Concept

American depositary receipts (ADRs) Negotiable instruments that represent ownership in the equity securities of a non-U.S. company.

American depositary shares (ADS) Foreign shares represented by a given ADR.

ADR ratio Number of underlying shares represented by one ADR.

American depositary receipts (ADRs) are negotiable instruments that represent ownership in the equity securities of a non-U.S. company. ADRs offer investors a convenient means for adding global exposure to domestic portfolios. Banking giant J. P. Morgan created the first ADR in 1927 to allow Americans to invest in the British retailer Selfridge's. Since that time, the ADR has evolved in sophistication and in importance. Generally speaking, ADRs are issued by U.S. commercial banks, such as J. P. Morgan, that function as the depositary institution. Each ADR is backed by a specific number of **American depositary shares (ADS)** in a non-U.S. company, usually referred to as the issuer. The number of underlying shares represented by one ADR is referred to as the **ADR ratio.** This ratio is typically depicted as 1:3, or one ADR per three underlying shares; 1:4, or one ADR per four underlying shares; and so on. Each ADR certificate identifies the account number, name(s) of registered owners, transaction or issue date, and the number of shares that the certificate represents. ADR certificates are negotiable documents and should be signed only in the event of a sale or transfer of ownership.

ADRs are transferable on the books of the sponsoring depositary institution. This greatly simplifies trading activity. ADRs can be listed on the NYSE or American Stock Exchange (AMEX) and may be quoted for trading on Nasdaq or the over-the-counter (OTC) market. They can also be privately placed and traded. The ADR concept has been extended to other geographic markets in the form of global depositary receipts (GDR), international depositary receipts (IDR), and European depositary receipts (EDR), which are traded in one or more global markets.

ADRs trade and settle according to U.S. market practices. ADR holders are generally entitled to the same corporate and economic rights as other shareholders, subject to the terms specified on the ADR certificate. Importantly, ADR holders are entitled to the same voting privileges and dividends as direct shareholders. When U.S. investors purchase ADRs, they eliminate the need for safekeeping charges in the issuer's home country and facilitate prompt dividend payments and corporate correspondence. They are quoted and traded in dollars and pay dividends in dollars. Record keeping and ADR custodial charges are deducted

WALL STREET WISDOM 16.2

Online Messages from the Boss's Kid?

A lively debate raged during the spring of 1999 on an otherwise quiet Yahoo! message board over the prospects of Franklin Resources (NYSE: BEN), a top global mutual fund management company.

On April 26, 1999, in a post derisively titled "I highly recommend this stock," a poster known only as "Trialballoon" said, "I can't think of a better company to get into. They have high fees, lousy fund performance, and they keep getting investors, I'm sure they will turn things around. And monkeys might learn how to use the Internet."

Trialballoon's negative post brought a quick response titled "Experience is King" by "FlmMkr9899," who shot back, "Value investing still has its place, especially for a company like Franklin with a 50-year history of beating the odds through conservative investing. I also find it hard to believe that you can find fault with Charles Johnson, a self-made billionaire elected by his peers in the industry to chairman of the NASD a few years ago. I believe that this stock will be 45 by mid-July; we have already seen the beginnings of a recovery in emerging markets as well as renewed respect for cyclicals and value investing as this market breadth widens." A market price of 45 was a bold call at the time. Franklin Resources had traded down from a 52-week high of $55\frac{1}{4}$ to only 36.

On April 27, 1999, "FlmMkr9899" was at it again, with scathing commentary for the company's critics. In "Hubris Is Tragedy," he said, "I don't understand how someone so obviously intelligent can have such poor judgment. You keep comparing BEN to companies such as Vanguard. They are totally different animals. The fact is no-load funds are inherently more unstable than load funds because of investor behavior during adverse market conditions. The distribution structure may seem archaic, and brokers may seem like dinosaurs, yet they tend to help counteract the more emotional impulses of new investors, especially during a market downturn. The Franklin Funds have amazing diversification in most investment sectors."

During the next few days, "FlmMkr9899" made 15 additional posts extolling the virtues of Franklin Resources and blasting its naysayers. All this came to a screeching halt on May 5, 1999, when "lardicksen" surprised everyone by posting "FlmMkr9899—Bill Johnson," which asked, "Do you want to properly identify yourself as the 36-year-old son of BEN's CEO, Charlie Johnson? I think this only fair to the board, in view of your family's controlling interest in the company."

Huh? Do you mean to say that "FlmMkr9899," the fellow who could not find fault with Charles Johnson, is the *son* of Charles Johnson? As *The Wall Street Journal* reported, "If defending your father is a virtue, William Johnson, 36, a film producer, is a very good son." Although family loyalty is very much to be admired, eyebrows were raised when a son anonymously endorsed Franklin, which is 35% owned by the Johnson family and traded on the New York Stock Exchange. Some were especially concerned that William Johnson boasted in the postings about how much money he was making on 750 call options (bets that the stock would rise). He also predicted a soon-to-be-released company report would be favorable.

In this particular case, there may have been no overt attempt at stock price manipulation. Unlike three of his siblings, William Johnson is not employed by Franklin. At the time, he said he simply was upset at others taking shots at his father and his dad's company. The Franklin Resources board on Yahoo! is relatively quiet with only 657 total messages between 11/26/97 and 5/10/99. By contrast, the Dell board on Yahoo! had a whopping 210,278 messages between 9/3/97 and 5/10/99. At a minimum, the Franklin Resources episode shows how investors often are clueless about the motives of those who post information on anonymous message boards.

At a minimum, investors had better take what they read on the Internet with more than a grain of salt.

See: Mitchell Pacelle and Patrick McGeehan, "Online Booster of Franklin Turns Out to Be Boss's Son," *The Wall Street Journal,* May 7, 1999, C1, C2.

from dividend payments. These charges are modest when one considers the many shareholder benefits obtained through ADR ownership. It is important to remember that although ADRs are dollar-denominated securities, they represent underlying shares in non-U.S. markets. Like any investors in foreign securities, ADR investors are exposed to foreign exchange risk.

As shown in Figure 16.9, the mechanics of ADR issuance and cancellation are simple. On behalf of customers, brokers and dealers can either purchase existing

FIGURE 16.9 ADR Purchase and Issuance Process: Three Scenarios

The ADR purchase and issuance process: three scenarios

Global Invest Direct

(A1) Investor enrolls and places order through J. P. Morgan's Global Invest Direct Program.

(A2) Morgan purchases ADRs in the applicable market.

(A3) Settlement of the ADRs and credit to the account of the Investor.

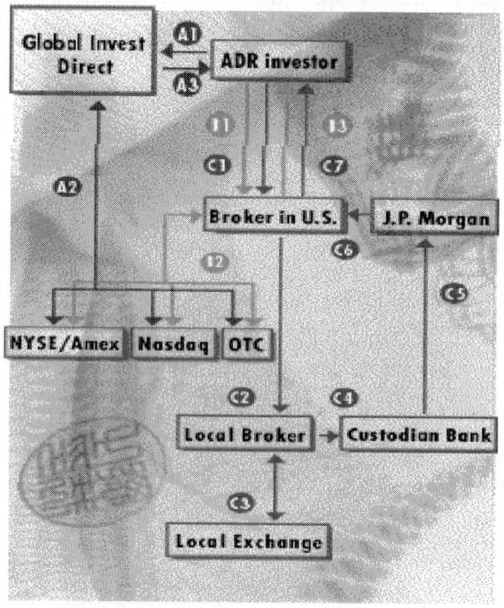

Existing ADRs

(B1) Investor places order with broker in the United States.

(B2) Broker in the United States purchases ADRs in the applicable market.

(B3) Settlement and delivery of the ADRs (In book-entry or certificate form).

New ADRs

(C1) Investor places order with broker in the United States.

(C2) Broker in the United States places order with local broker (outside U.S.) for equivalent shares.

(C3) Local broker purchases shares in local market.

(C4) Local shares are deposited with Morgan's custodian.

(C5) Morgan receives confirmation of share deposit.

(C6) Morgan issues new ADRs and delivers them to broker in the US.

(C7) Settlement and delivery of the ADRs (in book-entry or certificate form).

Issuance

1. To request the issuance of new ADRs, a broker needs to deposit the ADRs with JPMorgan and submit a cancellation request.
2. The shares are then deposited with the designated local custodian.
3. The custodian informs J.P. Morgan that the shares have been deposited in its account.
4. J.P. Morgan issues ADRs and delivers them through the Depositary Trust Company to the broker.

Cancellation

1. To cancel ADRs, a broker needs to own or purchase shares in the local market.
2. J.P. Morgan instructs the custodian to release the shares.
3. The custodian delivers the shares as instructed.

Source: <http://www.adr.com>.

ADRs in the United States or buy underlying shares in the issuer's home market and have new ADRs created. To create new ADRs, underlying shares are purchased in the issuer's home market and deposited with a custodian bank. The custodian bank then issues ADRs representing those shares. To cancel ADRs, underlying shares are obtained from the custodian bank and then sold in the issuer's home market. The custodian bank then cancels the ADRs representing those shares. Individual stockholders can also choose to convert foreign stock holdings into ADRs. To do so, they simply transfer underlying shares to the local correspondent bank of the ADR depositary institution. On receipt of the underlying shares, the depositary institution issues ADRs representing the newly deposited shares. To convert ADRs into underlying shares, stockholders merely instruct their broker to cancel the ADRs, and provide the broker with delivery instructions in the issuer's home country. Brokers and dealers decide whether to purchase existing ADRs or have new ones issued, depending on such factors as availability, pricing, and market conditions in the United States and the issuer's home market. Therefore, the pool of available ADRs is constantly changing according to market demand and supply conditions.

Investors can buy or sell ADRs through any registered broker or dealer. Investors can also buy some ADRs through J. P. Morgan's Shareholder Services Program (SSP), the first no-load ADR purchase program. This program provides first-time purchasers and existing shareholders with a convenient and inexpensive way to invest in many ADRs. Through the SSP, investors can buy or sell ADRs and reinvest dividends.

Market Dynamics

Issuers seeking the benefits of ADRs generally pursue what is called a **sponsored ADR program.** In a sponsored ADR program, companies initiate the ADR process and work with a depositary bank to actively manage the program. In general, only sponsored ADRs can be listed on major stock exchanges or quoted on the Nasdaq system. Although most new ADR programs are sponsored, some **unsponsored ADR programs** exist in which ADRs are created and offered to investors without the issuing company's active participation.

sponsored ADR program
ADR program conducted with the support of the foreign corporation whose shares are represented.

unsponsored ADR programs
ADR programs conducted without the support of the foreign corporation whose shares are represented.

There are many reasons why issuing corporations may want to launch and manage an ADR program. From the company's perspective, an ADR program can stimulate investor interest, enhance a company's visibility, broaden its shareholder base, and increase share liquidity. By enabling foreign companies to tap U.S. equity markets, ADRs offer an efficient means for raising new investment capital at competitive rates. For companies with a desire to build a stronger presence in the United States, ADRs can be used to help finance U.S. investments or acquisitions. ADRs can also be used to provide a means for more timely and effective communications with U.S. shareholders. ADRs also offer an easy way for U.S. employees of nondomestic companies to invest in employee stock purchase plans. Similarly, ADR dividend reinvestment programs offer a convenient means for ongoing investment.

Level I ADRs represent the most basic form of a sponsored ADR program. Level I is used when the issuer is not initially seeking to raise capital in the United States or list its ADRs on an exchange or Nasdaq. Level I ADR programs offer a relatively inexpensive way for issuers to gauge interest in its securities and begin building a presence in the U.S. securities markets. Level I ADRs are traded in the OTC market, with bid and ask prices published daily or posted on the OTC bulletin board (OTCBB). All nondomestic equities, including ADRs, must be registered with the Securities and Exchange Commission (SEC).

level I ADRs
ADRs issued when the issuer is not initially seeking to raise capital in the United States or list its ADRs on an exchange or Nasdaq.

level II ADRs ADRs issued when a company has no immediate financing needs and is listed on U.S. exchanges or quoted on Nasdaq.

level III ADRs ADRs issued when an issuer floats a public offering of ADRs in the United States and obtains listing on a major U.S. exchange or Nasdaq.

Level II ADRs are listed on U.S. exchanges or quoted on Nasdaq, thereby offering higher visibility in the U.S. market, active trading, and great liquidity. **Level III ADRs** are the highest-profile forms of sponsored ADR programs. In a level III ADR program, an issuer floats a public offering of ADRs in the United States and obtains listing on a major U.S. exchange or Nasdaq. During recent years, the amount of investment capital raised through level III ADRs has risen from roughly $5 billion to $15 billion per year. Level II and III ADR programs must comply with the full SEC registration and reporting requirements. Annual reports and interim financial statements must be submitted on a regular basis to the SEC and all registered public shareholders.

Table 16.10 illustrates the market dynamics for ADRs on a typical trading day. On any given trading day, shares in 250–300 different ADRs will trade in the United States on listed exchanges, Nasdaq, or the OTC market. Much of this trading activity takes place in the shares of large, well-known global leaders from developed countries. Popular issues at the top of ADR trading activity include oil industry goliaths such as Royal Dutch Petroleum (RD) and BP Amoco PLC (BPA) and telecommunications giants such as Nokia Corp. (NOK), Vodafone Airtouch PLC (VOD), and L. M. Ericsson, PLC (ERICY). ADRs in each of these companies give U.S. investors an attractive means for investing in established global leaders and an ap-

TABLE 16.10 ADRs Offer U.S. Investors an Effective Means for Investing in Top Foreign Companies

ADR trading data

Today As of 09:38 June 6, 2000	Total	Year to date As of 09:58 June 5, 2000	Total	Avg.daily
Share volume (thousand):	6,131	Share volume (thousand):	12,592,264	117,685
Value of trading (million of $US)	216	Value of trading (million of $US)	506,939	4,738
Issues up:	82	Issues up:	150	
Issues down:	72	Issues down:	252	
Issues unchanged:	23	Issues unchanged:	6	

Top 10 ADRs by volume Today | Year to Date

Symbol	Last	Change	% Change	Volume (thousand)
LM Ericsson Telephone Company [ERICY]	22 7/8	7/16	1.9	2,891.8
Nokia Corporation [NOK]	56 15/16	-1/16	-0.1	339.8
BP Amoco p.l.c. [BPA]	56 1/2	1/4	0.4	214.2
Royal Dutch Petroleum Company [RD]	62 7/16	11/16	1.1	180.2
Vodafone Airtouch Plc [VOD]	48 7/8	-1 1/8	-2.2	174.5
Baan Company N.V. [BAANF]	2 5/8	1/16	2.4	167.1
Alcatel Alsthom Compagnie Generale D'Electricite [ALA]	60 3/8	-1 3/8	-2.2	143.9
DaimlerChrysler [DCX]	57 1/2	1 1/16	1.9	137.9
chinadotcom corporation [CHINA]	27	3/16	0.7	89.7
Glaxo Wellcome plc [GLX]	52 7/8	-3/8	-0.7	87.2

Source: <http://www.adr.com>.

pealing method of adding global diversification to domestic portfolios. In all, there are more than 500 large nondomestic corporations with ADRs that trade on U.S. exchanges and Nasdaq. That number is projected to grow roughly 8–10% per year as U.S. investors increasingly turn their attention to global investment opportunities.

Multinational Investment Opportunities

Top U.S. Multinationals

Obvious benefits are to be gained by investing in U.S. companies that are global leaders. U.S. **multinational** giants set the pace for technology and innovation in aerospace, autos, telecommunications, computer software and engineering, and related fields. It is fair to say that throughout much of high-tech, U.S. multinationals are at the vanguard in meeting customer needs with new and exciting products.

multinational Corporation that conducts business in a number of host countries.

The importance of an effective global presence to lasting economic success is not fully appreciated by some investors. In most cases, companies that are highly successful in the U.S. market are also prosperous in a number of foreign markets. Even so-called domestic portfolios often have an important global perspective. For example, investors in the S&P 500 own a group of companies that are worldwide in their reach. In a typical year, about 40–45% of the profits earned by S&P 500 companies comes from foreign as opposed to U.S. operations. Foreign operations can be much higher for large-cap companies found at the top of the S&P 500. An investor that buys stock in Boeing, Coca-Cola, or GM establishes a position in some of the biggest and most successful companies in America and the world. By buying industrial giants found within the S&P 500, investors are getting an important exposure to global growth opportunities.

Multinational involvement is typically measured by the foreign percentage of corporate revenues, profits, or assets. These data are available from a number of sources, including *Forbes*'s annual survey of global business and investment opportunities. Table 16.11 shows that multinational involvement is high for leading firms in the auto, chemical, and consumer product industries, and high-tech sector. Technology companies such as Compaq Computer, Lucent Technologies, and Electronic Data Systems do particularly well overseas. For many such companies, market shares in foreign markets outstrip their market shares in the U.S. market. This stems from the fact that the United States is the largest free trade area in the world. The U.S. market is large enough to support a host of large and able competitors in most industries. By way of contrast, many foreign markets are relatively small and easily dominated by industrial and service goliaths from the United States. As Microsoft Corp. chairman Bill Gates is happy to point out, Microsoft's percentage share of the computer software market in Asian countries such as China is much higher than it is in the United States. Of course, Microsoft does not yet show up on lists as a large multinational because software piracy is rampant in foreign markets. Over time, as copyright and intellectual property rights become better enforced around the globe, the dominant role played by U.S. service providers in software and related services will become more apparent.

multinational involvement Foreign percentage of corporate revenues, profits, or assets.

TABLE 16.11 Top U.S. Multinationals Earn Large Profits on Foreign Operations

Rank	Company	Revenue					Net profit[1]			Assets	
		foreign ($mil)	% change	total ($mil)	% change	foreign as % of total	foreign ($mil)	total ($mil)	foreign as % of total	foreign ($mil)	total ($mil)
1	Exxon	80,705	−14.8	100,697	−16.3	80.1	4,193	6,440	65.1	40,094[2]	65,199[2]
2	IBM	46,364	1.1	81,667	4.0	56.8	4,359	6,328	68.9	16,653[2]	35,103[2]
3	Ford Motor	43,819	−6.8	144,416	−0.6	30.3	NA	5,939	NA	18,278[3]	44,039[3]
4	General Motors	40,918	−1.4	132,863	−9.5	30.8	2,142[4]	3,149[4]	68.0	13,514[3]	32,608[3]
5	Texaco	31,313[5]	−4.3	39,497[5]	−27.3	79.8	272	603	45.1	8,757[2]	15,007[2]
6	General Electric	31,278	15.9	100,469	10.6	31.1	3,634[6]	15,188[6]	23.9	128,823	355,935
7	Mobil	28,009[7]	−21.3	47,678[7]	−20.5	58.7	NA	1,704	NA	16,105[2]	24,727[2]
8	Citigroup	26,276	NA	76,431	5.7	34.4	NA	5,807	NA	281,619[8]	618,787[8]
9	Hewlett-Packard	25,531	7.2	47,061	9.7	54.3	2,257	2,945	76.6	19,757	33,673
10	Philip Morris Cos	19,814	0.1	57,813	3.0	34.3	2,373	5,372	44.2	6,508[2]	22,124[2]
11	Chevron 5	19,008	−17.6	40,216	−17.7	47.3	697	1,339	52.1	20,375	40,828
12	Procter & Gamble	17,928[9]	2.6	37,154	3.9	48.3	1,310	3,780	34.7	10,016[9]	30,966
13	American Intl Group	17,478[9]	6.2	33,296	8.8	52.5	NA	3,766	NA	75,815[9]	194,398
14	Compaq Computer	17,188	43.3	31,169	26.8	55.1	1,498	−2,743	P-D	1,053[2]	6,543[2]
15	Intel	14,610	4.2	26,273	4.8	55.6	2,177	6,068	35.9	3,533[3]	11,609[3]
16	Motorola	13,990E	3.8	29,398	−1.3	47.6	416	−962	P-D	10,887	28,728
17	Xerox	12,767[5]	3.2	22,854[5]	6.0	55.9	103[4]	556[4]	18.5	1,302[2]	3,397[2]
18	Wal-Mart Stores	12,247	62.9	137,634	16.7	8.9	551[6]	8,120[6]	6.8	9,537	49,996
19	Coca-Cola	11,721[9]	−4.0	18,813	−0.3	62.3	2,283	3,533	64.6	6,122[10]	12,459[10]
20	EI du Pont de Nemours	11,692	3.6	24,767	2.8	47.2	687[4]	1,672[4]	41.1	5,677[3]	14,131[3]
21	Halliburton	11,221	14.9	17,353	6.6	64.7	585[11]	279[11]	209.7	1,665[2]	4,098[2]
22	Johnson & Johnson	11,095	2.1	23,657	4.5	46.9	NA	3,059	NA	4,903[2]	13,187[2]
23	Dow Chemical	11,030	−2.1	18,441	−7.9	59.8	584[4]	1,327[4]	44.0	4,201[2]	8,447[2]
24	United Technologies	10,307[7]	1.8	25,715[7]	4.1	40.1	1,112[6]	2,167[6]	51.3	2,332[2]	6,015[2]
25	Caterpillar	10,107	7.1	20,977	10.8	48.2	247	1,509	16.4	1,828[3]	4,866[3]

Data source: *Forbes,* July 26, 1999, 202–206.

Multinational Investment Advantages

Investors are poised to capture a number of important investment advantages when they seek to add a global dimension to their investment portfolios by adding top U.S. multinationals. Too often, investors seem to take for granted the many investment advantages provided by the U.S. economic and legal environment. Stock options and well-developed mechanisms for corporate governance give U.S. managers strong incentives for value maximization that do not exist in some foreign markets. Securities laws, rules, and regulations also give U.S. investors more timely access to reliable information than is true in most parts of the world. Unlike foreign companies, U.S. firms have familiar, consistent, and open reporting standards. Many foreign countries have far different accounting conventions than familiar U.S. standards.

In Japan and East Asia, for example, auditors often do not challenge company executives over poor bookkeeping for fear of being impolite. Accounting practices for important cost categories such as retirement and health care benefits can also vary greatly. In Japan, for example, reported earnings for major automakers are overstated compared with their U.S. counterparts, largely because of differences in accounting for the cost of retirement benefits. Cross-border valuations everywhere will get easier once global market regulators adopt uniform accounting standards set by the International Accounting Standards Committee. In the meantime, investors can minimize the potential for accounting surprises by focusing their investment attention on U.S. multinationals.

Because U.S. multinationals can be efficiently purchased in the transparent and highly liquid U.S. equity market, investments in multinational companies enjoy an important transaction-cost advantage over investments in foreign securities that must be purchased in less liquid foreign markets. Large-cap U.S. multinationals can be purchased by investors with minimal brokerage fees and taxes. Shares in large-cap U.S. multinationals can also be easily purchased and sold in quantity by institutional and individual investors. These factors make a U.S. multinational investment strategy an efficient means for adding a global dimension to domestic investment portfolios.

Given the enormous size of top U.S. multinationals, a multinational investment strategy is also a cost-effective means for achieving broad diversification in a global investment portfolio. Not only do top U.S. multinationals operate in a wide array of world currencies and countries, they often participate in a broad market basket of individual product and service markets. For example, multinational giant Philip Morris is not only a global leader in the manufacture and sale of tobacco products (mainly cigarettes), it is also one of the world's largest processors and marketers of retail packaged food products, such as Kraft cheeses, Post cereals, Oscar Mayer packaged meat products, and Miller beer. Investors in Philip Morris own a veritable mutual fund of consumer products companies that earn revenues in a diversified portfolio of global currencies. As such, Philip Morris and other top U.S. multinationals give investors a cost-efficient method of global diversification.

Finally, it is worth noting that a significant global presence speaks well about the fundamental investment merit of top U.S. multinationals. Studies show that firms enjoy higher valuations in the stock market when they earn a significant portion of total profit from foreign versus domestic operations. Although foreign returns are sometimes protected by monopoly grants or operating authorities granted by foreign governments, barriers to entry, or little domestic competition, a large international presence speaks volumes about the global competitiveness of a firm's products. When a significant portion of total profit comes from abroad, there is less reason to fear that a company's competitive position in the domestic market is apt to be undermined by global competitors. Many top U.S. multinationals need not fear a competitive onslaught from the proverbial two-ton gorilla. *They* are a two-ton gorilla for their competitors!

Global Investing through Mutual Funds

Global Investment Options

Interest in international investing has grown dramatically among U.S. mutual fund investors during the 1990s. U.S. investors have poured nearly $100 billion into international stock funds over the past few years, and the assets of international stock funds approach $500 billion. International stock and bond mutual funds provide

WALL STREET WISDOM 16.3

NYSE Global Shares

With the globalization of financial markets, there has been a big increase in cross-border merger and acquisition activity. This trend has given rise to a growing demand for a single class of global equity securities that can be traded on a 24-hour-per-day basis around the world.

Traditionally, a non-U.S. company wishing to trade its shares in the United States converts its home market shares into American depositary receipts (ADR). ADRs are issued by a New York custodian bank, which holds the company's home market shares on deposit and distributes ADRs in place of local shares. These receipts must be converted into ordinary shares to trade in non-U.S. markets. By contrast, global shares are a fungible security, which can be traded on either the New York Stock Exchange (NYSE) or the home-country market without any need for conversion. Canadian companies have used this model to trade in the United States since 1883. By expanding the global share concept to leading multinationals with home countries in Europe or Asia, the NYSE hopes to create a class of "super equities." If successful, global shares will allow trading in European and Asian equities on the same terms as equities from North America. This is expected to offer compelling investment appeal to global investors both here and abroad. Global shares enable virtually seamless cross-border trading. This allows non-U.S. companies to increase liquidity and pricing efficiency in the U.S. market while permitting U.S. investors access to home-market shares on the same terms as local investors. NYSE-listed global shares may be used to raise investment capital or as currency for U.S. acquisitions.

NYSE trading in global shares is identical to trading U.S. shares. Global shares offer a number of key features that are certain to appeal to global investors:

- All shareholders have equal status and voting rights with respect to dividend payments, shareholder meeting invitations, rights offerings, and so on. Share certificates are identical across all markets and can be freely converted in all participating countries.
- The timing of corporate events, including dividend payments, occurs on the same day worldwide.
- Separate share registrars in the United States and home (or other) markets are electronically linked to constitute a single global share registry.
- A transfer agent, usually a New York bank, is used in the United States to facilitate payment of dividends and distribute shareholder information.
- Global shares registered in the United States are quoted, traded, and settled in the United States in dollars, and in local currencies elsewhere.

The merger between Daimler-Benz AG and Chrysler Corporation in November 1998 marked the first time a company based outside the United States or Canada directly listed the same common shares on a U.S. stock exchange and its home stock exchange. In the case of DaimlerChrysler (NYSE: DCX), global shares trade on the NYSE, the Frankfurt Stock Exchange, and multiple exchanges around the world. DaimlerChrysler shares are quoted in U.S. dollars on the NYSE and in local currencies on other markets. Dividends are payable in deutschmarks, euros, or U.S. dollars. For U.S. shareholders, a New York transfer agent handles the conversion and payment process. Separate transfer agents in the United States and Germany clear trades via a computer link between the New York custodian of shares (Depositary Trust Company) and the Frankfurt custodian (Deutsche Börse Clearing).

Trading in DaimlerChrysler shares since 1998 has demonstrated some of the benefits of the global share concept. The NYSE and home country constitute a single fungible market for shares with a resulting increase in share liquidity. Buyers also enjoy advantages by virtue of the fact that they get to directly purchase equity in the company without having to pay custodian fees to an intermediary, as would be true with ADRs.

Time will tell if other U.S. and foreign companies like the idea of going truly global!

See: Craig Karmin, "European Markets Rally after More Evidence That Slower U.S. Economy Could End Rate Cycle," *The Wall Street Journal*, June 15, 2000, C18.

small individual investors with a cost-efficient means for participating in foreign securities markets. For small individual investors, investing internationally through mutual funds provides an opportunity for better diversification and higher returns. Although investing in individual foreign securities gives investors greater diversification than if they were invested solely in U.S. securities, a mutual fund with an international perspective can spread its assets among many securities traded in a number of different countries. Brokerage fees for small foreign stock transactions can be high on a percentage basis, especially if issues purchased are not actively traded. Because mutual fund managers deal regularly and in large numbers of buy and sell transactions, they usually have the potential to be more cost-effective than small investors in foreign markets. Of course, mutual funds pay management fees and marketing costs that can offset these cost advantages.

World equity funds invest primarily in the stocks of foreign companies. An **emerging markets fund** invests predominately in the stocks of companies based in countries with developing economies. Investing in emerging markets is risky because many such countries experience great difficulty in evolving from an agricultural or socialist economy to an industrial free market. Notable examples of countries experiencing birth pains in the 1990s include Argentina, India, Indonesia, and Turkey. Of course, as an offset to their greater risks, emerging markets funds hold the potential for higher rates of economic growth than the more mature markets of the United States, western Europe, and Japan.

emerging markets fund Mutual fund that invests predominately in the stocks of companies based in countries with developing economies.

A mutual fund that invests in U.S. and foreign stock is known as a **global equity fund,** or world equity fund. Like international stock funds, global funds typically seek long-term growth. Because global funds can duplicate some U.S. stock holdings for domestic investors with broadly diversified holdings, some investors prefer funds that invest only in foreign stocks. A global equity fund invests in equity securities traded on a worldwide basis, including those of U.S. companies. An **international equity fund,** or foreign fund, invests in the equity securities of companies located outside the United States and generally is prohibited from investing in U.S. equities. The most popular and widely held international equity funds invest in the stocks of developed European markets such as the United Kingdom, Germany, and France and various Pacific Rim nations such as Japan, Hong Kong, and Australia. The investment objective of most broadly diversified international stock funds is long-term growth, although some value-oriented funds may place modest emphasis on current income.

global equity funds Mutual fund that invests in U.S. and foreign stocks.

international equity fund Mutual fund that invests in the equity securities of companies located outside the United States.

The investment strategies of international funds vary widely. Some funds emphasize investments in particular countries rather than individual stock selections, hoping to capitalize on those countries that will enjoy the highest future economic growth. Other funds use a more fundamental investment approach that focuses on the most promising companies, regardless of the countries in which they operate. Indexing is also becoming a popular investment strategy for international stock funds. When adopting an indexing strategy, most mutual funds seek to match the performance of a group of securities that form a recognized global market measure such as the EAFE Index.

An international fund that invests in companies from a particular geographic region, such as Europe or the Pacific Basin, is known as a **foreign regional fund.** By concentrating on a single region, these funds hope to capture the investment benefits derived from explosive economic growth tied to political changes, trade initiatives, or demographic trends. Share prices for regional funds typically fluctuate

foreign regional fund International funds that invest in the stocks of specific global areas.

single-country fund Mutual fund that invests in a sole foreign country.

more than the share prices of broadly diversified international stock funds. Even more volatile is a **single-country fund** that invests in a single foreign country, such as Hong Kong, Mexico, or Italy. Many single-country funds are closed-end mutual funds that trade on an exchange at sizable discounts or premiums relative to net asset value. Single-country funds can be extremely risky because of their narrow focus.

Most international funds assess a sales commission or sales load on purchases and redemptions. Front-end loads typically vary from 4% to 6% on initial purchases and are deducted before the investor's money is invested in the fund. Back-end loads typically range from 2% to 5% and are assessed when investors redeem their shares. Loads, operating expenses, and transaction costs all reduce investor returns and must be minimized to achieve a competitive rate of return.

International Index Funds

Courtesy of the Internet, today's amateur investor has much better global investment information than the pros did only a few years ago. In addition to better information, new and experienced investors have a wide choice of attractive global investment vehicles. If an individual investor wants to add a global dimension to stock and bond portfolios, there is ample variety of top-notch open-end and closed-end mutual funds managed by professionals with global expertise. There are also several industry-focused and country-specific mutual funds that offer investors intriguing global investment opportunities. It is easy to make the argument that today's investor is better informed and better prepared and has better investment alternatives to pursue global investment opportunities.

international index fund Mutual fund that seeks to match the performance of an international stock or bond benchmark.

Among the most useful innovations in global opportunities is the emergence of a vast array of global equity and fixed-income index funds. Given the added risks and high costs of international investing, index funds offer special advantages. Although some global stock and bond portfolios offer ample diversification, few managed portfolios can compete with the level of diversification provided by an **international index fund.** Most international index funds offer expansive diversification in a representative collection of industries over an assortment of countries. Importantly, international index funds offer these diversification benefits at shareholder costs that are much lower than the expenses tied to actively managed funds. Some international index funds have operating and transaction costs that average less than 1% a year, compared with roughly 4% for actively managed world equity funds.

On the face of it, a 3% annual cost advantage for passive international index funds versus actively managed world equity funds may not appear noteworthy. However, over a retirement portfolio investment horizon of 24 years, a 3% net return advantage leads to a *doubling* in retirement wealth. Given that few portfolio managers have displayed the ability to consistently beat global equity benchmarks, careful consideration of indexing alternatives for adding a global dimension to one's investment portfolio seems a prudent idea. This explains why international indexed mutual funds are rapidly growing in popularity among institutional and individual investors.

International iShares

As discussed in Chapter 15, Barclays Global Investors has been a leader in the development and marketing of index shares (called iShares) that offer investors the broad diversification of an index fund, and the trading flexibility of common stocks. In June 2000, Barclays introduced a broad new array of iShares that give investors simple ways to gain exposure to U.S. equity markets (by size, style, and sector) and many of the world's premier developed and emerging markets.

For the U.S. equity market, iShares are now available for investing in both large and small stocks as measured by all major indexes offered by Standard & Poor's, Dow Jones & Company, and the Frank B. Russell Company. For example, iShares are available to cover the large-cap S&P 500 and the S&P Midcap 400, which measures the performance of mid-sized U.S. companies. Certain iShares are also offered that allow investors to take different style slants to major value-oriented stocks in the S&P 500 or S&P 400 indices (see Figure 15.10, page 645).

Firm size and investment style are important investment considerations, but geographical diversification is another key factor. When added to the domestic investment opportunities available to the U.S. investors, **international iShares** that track market movements around the world offer investors a broader set of investment opportunities. International iShares also have the potential to add much needed diversification to domestic portfolios because global markets rarely move in lock-step fashion. With international iShares, global investors can add to their investment portfolios diversified baskets of stocks from any number of developed and emerging equity markets.

international iShares
Unit trusts that track the performance of an underlying international benchmark index.

Currently the most popular international iShares offered by Barclays are based upon well-known Morgan Stanley Capital International (MSCI) indexes. As mentioned previously, MSCI indexes have become the most widely used benchmarks for non-U.S. stock markets since 1969, when the firm launched its first developed-country indexes. In 1988, MSCI added emerging market indexes. Like the MSCI indexes, the objective of international iShares offered by Barclays is to track the performance of a given country's publicly traded equity securities. Like the underlying MSCI indexes, international iShares offered by Barclays typically reflect a market value–weighted exposure to approximately 60% of a country's stock market. Formerly known as WEBs (for "World Equity Benchmark Shares"), international iShares have been managed by Barclays Global Investors and traded on the American Stock Exchange since 1996. The most popular international iShares track MSCI indexes for major developed and emerging equity markets, including:

MSCI Australia
MSCI Austria
MSCI Belgium
MSCI Canada
MSCI France
MSCI Germany
MSCI Hong Kong
MSCI Italy
MSCI Japan
MSCI Malaysia
MSCI Mexico
MSCI Netherlands
MSCI Singapore
MSCI South Korea
MSCI Spain
MSCI Sweden
MSCI Switzerland
MSCI Taiwan
MSCI United Kingdom

Over time, Barclays and its competitors will add to this menu of country offerings as international iShare investing grows in popularity. Similarly, Barclays and its competitors are sure to add international iShares that give exposure to regional markets, such as the European Economic Community, or specific investment styles in country-specific markets, such as growth stocks in the United Kingdom, or Japanese technology stocks. As is the case with any foreign-market investment, investors in international iShares must be aware of the normal risks associated with equity investing, and that international investing involves the additional risk of capital loss due to unfavorable fluctuations in the currency markets. International iShare investors also face exposure to investment losses stemming from economic or political instability in other nations.

Investors with an interest in international iShares can learn more at the Barclays Web site, <http://www.ishares.com>.

Summary

- Morgan Stanley Capital International (MSCI) is the premier source of investment information about global equity markets. The MSCI research database contains more than 24,000 equity securities covering more than 50 countries. Established equity markets in leading advanced economies are called **developed markets.** Securities markets for countries with rapidly evolving economies are called **emerging markets.** All MSCI equity indexes are calculated by using **full market capitalization weights** (price multiplied by the number of outstanding shares). MSCI covers more than 60% of the market cap of global equities in developed and emerging markets. In some emerging markets, MSCI designates **free indexes** and **nonfree indexes.**
- Investing in foreign markets, especially emerging foreign markets, generally involves much higher **market volatility** than that associated with U.S. equities. The potential for above-average gains in foreign equity markets comes with the risk of similarly above-average losses in any given year. **Liquidity risk** refers to loss potential tied to the fact that a stock can become difficult to buy or sell. Thin trading activity in foreign developed and emerging markets often leads to higher **market impact costs.** Special liquidity risks associated with investing in developed and emerging markets are accompanied by higher global equity transaction costs. **Brokerage commissions, exchange fees, currency translation costs,** and **custodial fees** tend to be substantially higher in emerging markets than in the developed markets of the United States and Europe.
- Many countries with emerging markets are vulnerable to **political risk** stemming from coups, assassinations, or civil unrest, which increase market volatility and decrease investor returns. **Government policy risk** is an important consideration for global investors. Nondomestic investors must always be on the lookout for policy changes that could become unfavorable. In a worst-case scenario, investors must be on the lookout for the **expropriation risk** that claimed the assets of global investors during the 1960s and 1970s. **Currency risk** is the most pervasive political risk faced when making global investments.
- A **strong dollar** signifies an increase in the amount of foreign currency that can be purchased for $1. A **weak dollar** indicates a decrease in the amount of foreign currency that can be purchased for $1. When the dollar is strong, the dollar price of goods and services purchased from abroad falls. When the dollar is

weak, the dollar price of goods and services purchased from abroad rises. A **trade deficit** occurs when U.S. consumers buy more goods and services produced abroad than the amount of U.S. goods and services bought by foreigners. A **trade surplus** occurs when U.S. consumers buy fewer goods and services produced abroad than the amount of U.S. goods and services bought by foreigners.

- **American depositary receipts (ADR)** are negotiable instruments that represent ownership in the equity securities of a non-U.S. company. Each ADR is backed by a specific number of **American depositary shares (ADS)** in a non-U.S. company, usually referred to as the issuer. The number of underlying shares represented by one ADR is referred to as the **ADR ratio.** This ratio is typically depicted as 1:3, or one ADR per three underlying shares; 1:4, or one ADR per four underlying shares; and so on. Issuers seeking the benefits of ADRs generally pursue what is called a **sponsored ADR program.** Although most new ADR programs are sponsored, some **unsponsored ADR programs** exist in which ADRs are created and offered to investors without the issuing company's active participation.
- **Level I ADRs** are used when the issuer is not initially seeking to raise capital in the United States or lists its ADRs on an exchange or Nasdaq. **Level II ADRs** are issued when a company has no immediate financing needs and is listed on U.S. exchanges or quoted on Nasdaq. **Level III ADRs** are the highest-profile forms of sponsored ADR programs. In a level III ADR program, an issuer floats a public offering of ADRs in the United States and obtains listing on a major U.S. exchange or Nasdaq. Level II and III ADR programs must comply with full SEC registration and reporting requirements.
- **Multinational** giants set the pace for technology and innovation in aerospace, autos, telecommunications, computer software and engineering, and related fields. **Multinational involvement** is typically measured by the foreign percentage of corporate revenues, profits, or assets. Because U.S. multinationals can be efficiently purchased in the transparent and highly liquid U.S. equity market, investments in multinational companies enjoy an important transaction cost advantage over investments in foreign securities that must be purchased in less liquid foreign markets. A significant global presence also speaks well about the fundamental investment merit of top U.S. multinationals. When a significant portion of total profit comes from abroad, there is less reason to fear that a company's competitive position in the domestic market is apt to be undermined by global competitors.
- An **emerging markets fund** invests predominately in the stocks of companies based in countries with developing economies. A mutual fund that invests in U.S. and foreign stocks is known as a **global equity fund,** or world equity fund. An **international equity fund,** or foreign fund, invests in the equity securities of companies located outside the United States and generally is prohibited from investing in U.S. equities. An international fund that invests in companies from a particular geographic region, such as Europe or the Pacific Basin, is known as a **foreign regional fund.** Share prices for regional funds typically fluctuate more than the share prices of broadly diversified international stock funds. Even more volatile is a **single-country fund** that invests in a sole foreign country, such

as Hong Kong, Mexico, or Italy. Although some global stock and bond portfolios offer ample diversification, few managed portfolios can compete with the level of diversification provided by an **international index fund.** International index funds offer these diversification benefits at shareholder costs that are much lower than the expenses tied to actively managed funds.

- **International iShares** are unit portfolio trusts that track the performance of an underlying international benchmark index by holding proportionate interests in component shares. Many of the most popular international iShares follow country-specific MSCI indexes and are traded on the American Stock Exchange. International iShares are available for major developed and emerging markets. The investment objective of international iShares is to offer a cost-effective means for adding an international dimension to domestic investment portfolios.

Questions

1. When measured across various local stock markets, local indexes are generally comparable with respect to
   a. methods of adjusting for capital appreciation and depreciation.
   b. market representation.
   c. mathematical formulas.
   d. none of these.
2. In terms of market capitalization, the three largest local stock markets in the world do *not* include
   a. the United Kingdom.
   b. Japan.
   c. Germany.
   d. the United States.
3. The MSCI EAFE Index does not reflect stock market movements in
   a. Japan.
   b. Germany.
   c. Latin America.
   d. Australia.
4. All MSCI equity indexes are calculated by using
   a. market capitalization weights.
   b. GDP weights.
   c. price weights.
   d. an equally weighted arithmetic index.
5. During the 1990s, equity market returns were unusually high in
   a. Japan.
   b. the United States.
   c. Canada.
   d. none of these.

6. In a typical emerging market, annual GDP per capita averages
   a. $30,000.
   b. $20,000.
   c. $10,000.
   d. less than $5,000.
7. A MSCI nonfree index includes various securities that are available only to
   a. government institutions.
   b. institutional investors.
   c. domestic investors.
   d. foreign investors.
8. The emerging markets universe includes the country of
   a. Australia.
   b. Brazil.
   c. Japan.
   d. Portugal.
9. Few emerging markets are
   a. characterized by only a handful of investment opportunities.
   b. successful in translating immense economic opportunities into lasting economic prosperity.
   c. limited to trading companies and infrastructure investments.
   d. smaller than Microsoft Corp. in terms of market capitalization.
10. During the 1990s, emerging markets were characterized by
    a. uniformly high rates of investment return.
    b. high volatility.
    c. uniformly rapid economic growth.
    d. rapidly appreciating local currencies.
11. When compared with the United States, daily trading activity in other developed markets is
    a. much higher.
    b. somewhat higher.
    c. about the same.
    d. much, much lower.
12. Market impact costs tend to be reflected in
    a. high trading volume.
    b. low bid-ask spreads.
    c. high bid-ask spreads.
    d. rising institutional investor interest.

13. During the 1990s, a prevalent form of political risk in emerging markets was
    a. currency risk.
    b. privatization risk.
    c. expropriation risk.
    d. liquidity risk.
14. Assume a U.S. investor in a British stock enjoys capital appreciation of 20% but that the pound declines by 10% vis-à-vis the dollar. After accounting for currency risk, the investor enjoys
    a. an 8% gain.
    b. an 8% loss.
    c. a 10% loss.
    d. a 10% gain.
15. When the dollar is strong, the
    a. amount of foreign currency that can be purchased for $1 decreases.
    b. amount of dollars that can be purchased for ¥1 (one Japanese yen) increases.
    c. dollar price of goods and services purchased from abroad rises.
    d. none of these.
16. When a trade deficit occurs,
    a. U.S. consumers buy fewer goods and services produced abroad than the amount of U.S. goods and services bought by foreigners.
    b. U.S. dollars pile up in the bank accounts of foreigners.
    c. the dollar tends to strengthen.
    d. the net return earned by U.S. investors on foreign stock holdings tends to be favorably affected by changes in the rate of currency translation.
17. Over the past 30 years, foreign stock markets have
    a. never outperformed the U.S. market.
    b. always outperformed the U.S. stock market.
    c. offered modest opportunities for risk reduction.
    d. suffered because of generally declining economic growth in emerging markets.
18. Real economic growth in the United States can be expected on the order of
    a. 12–14% per year.
    b. 9% per year.
    c. 4% per year.
    d. 1–2% per year.
19. Which of the following statements is *not* descriptive of American depositary receipts (ADRs)?
    a. ADRs are negotiable instruments that represent ownership in the equity securities of a U.S. company.

b. ADR certificates are negotiable documents and should be signed only in the event of a sale or transfer of ownership.

c. ADRs are transferable on the books of a sponsoring *depositary* institution.

d. ADRs can be listed on the New York Stock Exchange and may be quoted for trading on Nasdaq.

20. ADR holders are not

a. owners of dollar-denominated securities.

b. entitled to the same voting privileges as direct shareholders.

c. exposed to foreign exchange risk.

d. responsible for safekeeping charges in the issuer's home country.

Investment Application

The Templeton Touch

Sir John Templeton is one of the 20th century's greatest investors. Back in the 1950s, long before it became fashionable, Templeton scoured the globe looking for investment opportunities. Templeton's investment strategy is contrarian and value-oriented. He is perhaps most famous for being among the first foreign investors to commit money to Japan.

In the early 1960s, the Tokyo market was selling for four times earnings versus the United States, where stocks were selling at 16 times earnings. At only one-fourth the average P/E ratio of the U.S. market, Templeton spied a bargain. He was able to buy some of the finest Japanese growth companies at only three times earnings. Of course, Templeton's strategy of buying Japanese bargains was criticized by U.S. investors who preferred market bellwether IBM, then a darling of growth stock investors and selling at a P/E ratio of 33 times earnings. Indeed, at the time, the market capitalization of the entire Japanese market was less than that accorded IBM. The consensus among professional money managers was that Japanese stocks were risky; IBM was viewed as a safe and secure blue chip. However, at only one-tenth the P/E of IBM, Templeton believed that outstanding Japanese growth stocks offered investors a significant investment opportunity. Templeton was right. Within a few years, the rest of the world caught on to the bargains represented by well-run Japanese companies, and the P/E ratio of a typical Japanese growth stock rose to 33 times earnings. By then, Templeton was off to other world markets seeking more and better bargains.

Today, Templeton is widely regarded as the dean of global investing even though he is no longer involved with active portfolio management. In 1992, Templeton retired after a 50-year career of helping investors manage their money and sold his huge mutual fund complex to Franklin Resources, Inc. Templeton now devotes all his energy to the John Templeton Foundation, a nonprofit organization devoted to the scientific study of world religions. Templeton's investment philosophy lives on with the Templeton Group of funds, a collection of global and world equity funds managed by investment professionals that Templeton hired. Moreover, Templeton is a frequent commentator on investment trends in the print and broadcast media, so investors are able to hear his ongoing advice on a regular basis.

Templeton's investment philosophy is based on four simple bedrock principles. The first of these is that the thrifty will eventually own the spendthrifts. More than just wanting to be rich, Templeton realized early that the only sure way to wealth is to save part of what you earn and invest the proceeds in securities that will make you wealthy. As a young man, Templeton and his wife decided to save a whopping 50% of their combined gross incomes. Even in the investment community, such thriftiness is rare. According to Templeton, few security analysts or Wall Street brokers ever become wealthy because few are thrifty. Although many on Wall Street make amazing incomes, often in the hundreds of thousands of dollars per year, few are sufficiently thrifty to become truly wealthy. Thriftiness is also important among nations. Where the people of a nation are most thrifty, that nation becomes prosperous and powerful. Where the people of a nation are spendthrifts, that nation declines toward poverty.

Templeton's second investment principle is that investors should buy at the point of maximum pessimism and sell at the point of maximum optimism. According to Templeton, it is only human nature to be afraid to buy when stories of failure abound. It is also human nature to cast caution to the wind when boastful stories of easy profits are common. The lowest price for any actively traded security can occur only at the point of maximum pessimism. Markets go up in anticipation of good news. It is the beginning of such anticipation, and not the good news itself, that causes prices to rise. Therefore, if you wait to see the light at the end of the tunnel, it is too late. Other investors have also seen the light, and prices have already begun to rise.

Templeton's third investment principle is that all assets are risky, including cash. When investors say that they are going to play it safe by selling stocks and holding cash, they are merely trading one risky class of assets for another. With inflation common around the globe, cash is losing purchasing power in virtually every nation. Income-producing assets such as common stocks maintain long-run value better than bonds, cash, collectibles, gold, real estate, or virtually any other asset. In every nation, purchasing power fluctuates widely and rapidly for every asset. Investors are fooling themselves to think that they are playing it safe to hold cash. Cash is a speculative investment that rarely holds its value.

Templeton's fourth principle is that outstanding relative performance requires a contrarian attitude. If an investor buys the same securities as everyone else, exactly the same investment results will be achieved. Superior investment performance requires investing differently from the crowd. If 10 medical doctors tell a patient to take a certain medicine, the patient is wise to follow their advice. However, if 10 investment advisors tell an investor to buy a given stock, that popularity will already be reflected in a high stock price. The investor would be wise to shun the overwhelming consensus of investment information.

How well has Templeton's common-sense approach to investing performed over the years? Quite well, as it turns out. As shown in Figure 16.10, a $10,000 investment in the Templeton Growth Fund made in 1954 would now be worth more than $4 million. Templeton investors have been well served by the global search for more and better investment bargains.

A. In your opinion, why do few high-income Wall Street professionals manage to accumulate significant personal wealth?

B. In today's investment environment, would it be difficult to duplicate Templeton's long-term success?

FIGURE 16.10 **"Mountain Chart" Shows the Growth in Shareholder Value over Time**

TEMPLETON GROWTH FUND

Class A

If you had invested $10,000 in Templeton Growth Fund—Class A at inception, it would have been worth more than $4.2 million on February 29, 2000. The chart below illustrates the cumulative total return of a hypothetical $10,000 investment in the Fund on November 29, 1954 (inception), with income from dividends and capital gains reinvested as shown through February 29, 2000.*

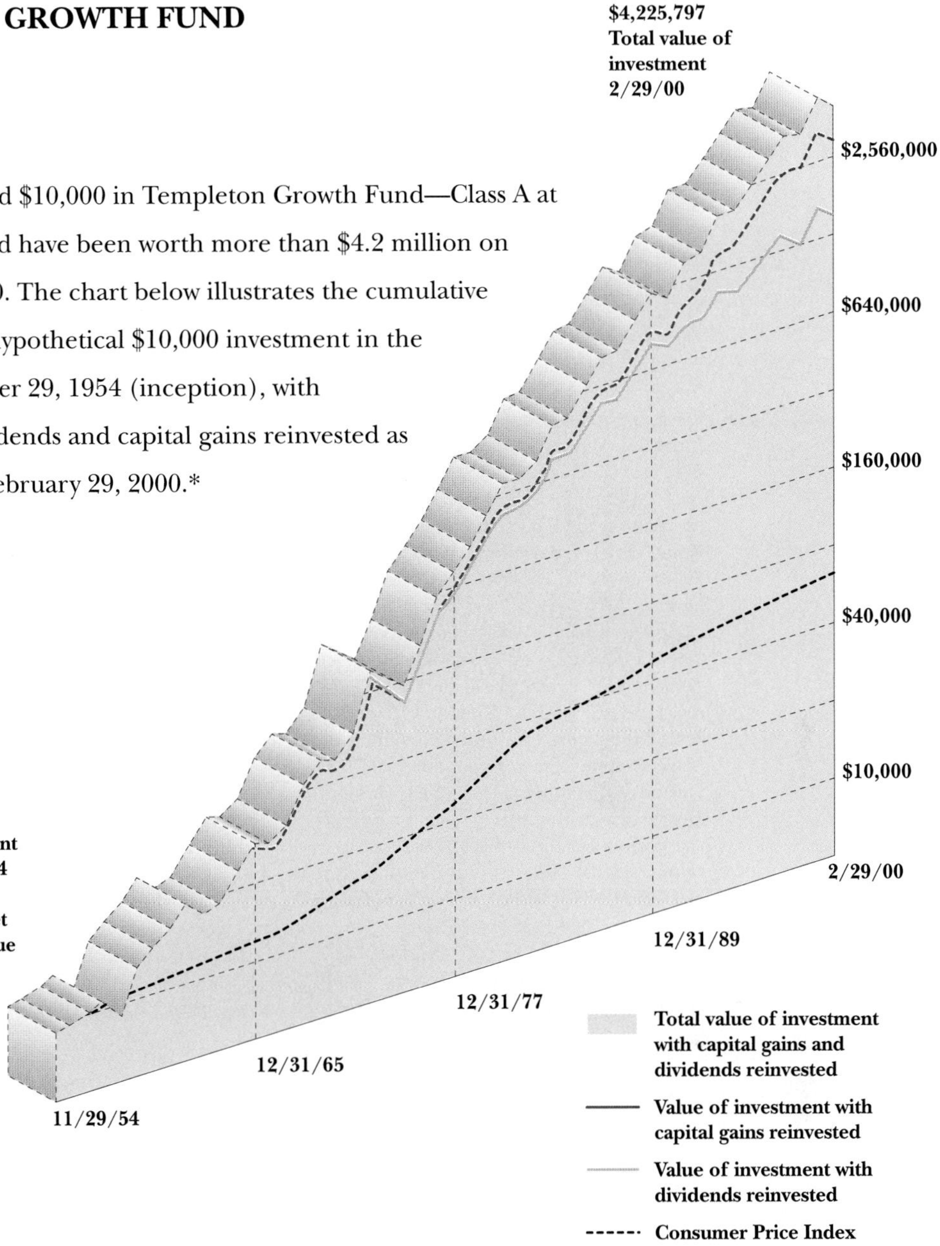

* Cumulative total return represents the change in value of an investment over the indicated period. All figures have been restated to reflect the current maximum 5.75% initial sales charge; thus, actual total return for purchasers of shares during the periods shown may differ. Prior to July 1, 1992, these shares were offered at a higher initial sales charge. On January 1, 1993, the Fund's Class A shares implemented a plan of distribution under Rule 12b-1, which will affect subsequent performance.

Except as noted, all figures assume reinvestment of dividends and capital gains at net asset value. Since markets can go down as well as up, investment return and principal value will fluctuate with market conditions, and you may have a gain or loss when you sell your shares.

The historical data shown above pertain only to Class A shares of the Fund. The Fund offers three other share classes, subject to different fees and expenses, which will affect their performance. Please see the prospectus for more details.

Past performance does not guarantee future results.

Source: <http://templeton.com>.

Selected References

Bailey, Warren, Peter Y. Chung, and June-Koo Kang. "Foreign Ownership Restrictions and Equity Price Premiums: What Drives the Demand for Cross-Border Investments?" *Journal of Financial and Quantitative Analysis* 34 (December 1999): 489–511.

Bekaert, Geert, and Campbell R. Harvey. "Foreign Speculators and Emerging Equity Markets, [Figures and Tables], [Supplement]." *Journal of Finance* 55 (April 2000): 565–613.

Bhattacharya, Utpal, Hazem Daouk, Brian Jorgenson, and Carl-Heinrich Kehr. "When an Event Is Not an Event: The Curious Case of an Emerging Market." *Journal of Financial Economics* 55 (January 2000): 69–101.

Chan, Yue-Cheong. "The Price Impact of Trading on the Stock Exchange of Hong Kong." *Journal of Financial Markets* 3 (February 2000): 1–16.

Charemza, Wojciech W., and Ewa Majerowska. "Regulation of the Warsaw Stock Exchange: The Portfolio Allocation Problem." *Journal of Banking and Finance* 24 (April 2000): 555–576.

Choe, Hyuk, Bong-Chan Kho, and René M. Stulz. "Do Foreign Investors Destabilize Stock Markets? The Korean Experience in 1997." *Journal of Financial Economics* 54 (October 1999): 227–264.

Coval, Joshua D., and Tobias J. Moskowitz. "Home Bias at Home: Local Equity Preference in Domestic Portfolios." *Journal of Finance* 54 (December 1999): 2045–2073.

Errunza, Vihang, Ked Hogan, and Mao-Wei Hung. "Can the Gains from International Diversification Be Achieved without Trading Abroad?" *Journal of Finance* 54 (December 1999): 2075–2107.

Froot, Kenneth A., and Emil M. Dabora. "How Are Stock Prices Affected by the Location of Trade?" *Journal of Financial Economics* 53 (August 1999): 189–216.

Green, Christopher J., Paolo Maggioni, and Victor Murinde. "Regulatory Lessons for Emerging Stock Markets from a Century of Evidence on Transactions Costs and Share Price Volatility in the London Stock Exchange." *Journal of Banking and Finance* 24 (April 2000): 577–601.

Henry, Peter Blair, "Stock Market Liberalization, Economic Reform, and Emerging Market Equity Prices." *Journal of Finance* 55 (April 2000): 529–564.

Kairys, Jr., Joseph P., Raimonds Kruza, and Ritvars Kumpins. "Winners and Losers from the Introduction of Continuous Variable Price Trading: Evidence from the Riga Stock Exchange." *Journal of Banking and Finance* 24 (April 2000): 603–624.

Khanna, Tarun, and Krishna Palepu. "Is Group Affiliation Profitable in Emerging Markets? An Analysis of Diversified Indian Business Groups." *Journal of Finance* 55 (April 2000): 867–891.

Lins, Karl, and Henri Servaes. "International Evidence on the Value of Corporate Diversification." *Journal of Finance* 54 (December 1999): 2215–2239.

Rouwenhorst, K. Geert. "European Equity Markets and the EMU." *Financial Analysts Journal* 55 (May/June 1999): 57–64.

PART 8

Financial Derivatives

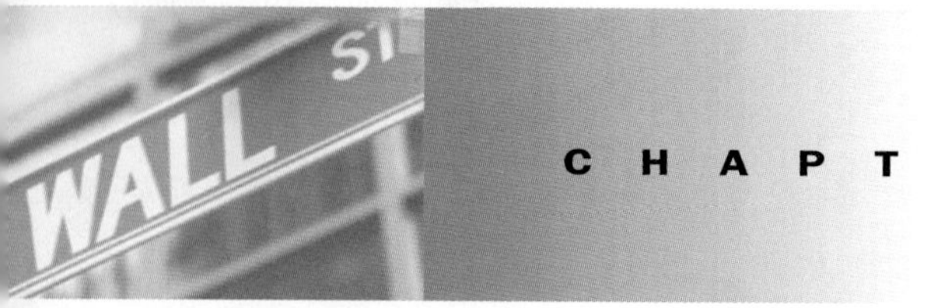

CHAPTER 17

Options Markets and Strategies

The options markets attract some surprising players. For example, the chief financial officers of Microsoft Corp. and Dell Computer, among other companies, have become regular sellers of put options on their own company's stock. Buyers of put options obtain the right to sell at a given price for a specified time period. Sellers of put options incur the obligation to buy at a fixed price for that same period. In the six-month period ending December 31, 1999, Microsoft pocketed $472 million from selling put options on its own stock, down from $355 million in the prior-year period. So long as Microsoft stock keeps rising at a torrid pace, such puts expire worthlessly and Microsoft pockets a tax-free gain. Corporations such as Microsoft are exempt from income taxes on trading gains derived from buying and selling their own stock.

In a rampant bull market, selling put options is easy money. Not only Microsoft has made millions; others such as Dell Computer have profited from hopping on the corporate put-selling bandwagon. In some quarters during the late 1990s, Dell made more money selling put options than it did selling computers. Unfortunately, bull markets always end, and in a bear market, selling put options becomes dangerous. As of December 31, 1999, Microsoft had 163 million put options outstanding with strike prices ranging from $69 to $78 per share. At that time, it seemed likely that Microsoft's stock would continue to skyrocket and that such puts would expire worthlessly. However, antitrust problems during early 2000 drove Microsoft's stock price downward and raised the possibility of millions of dollars in losses from Microsoft's put-selling strategy.[1]

There is a simple lesson here. In the options markets, there is no such thing as easy money.

Chicago Board Options Exchange (CBOE)
U.S. options market pioneer.

option contract
Right to buy or to sell a given amount or value of a particular asset at a fixed price until a given expiration date.

Options Markets

Origin and Evolution

On April 26, 1973, the **Chicago Board Options Exchange (CBOE)** pioneered the concept of standardized listed options to be traded in a centralized and regulated marketplace. An **option contract** is the right to buy or to sell a given amount or

[1]See Erin E. Arvedlund, "Microsoft's Other Business: Is Corporate Put-Selling Doomed?" *Barron's*, May 1, 2000, MW14.

value of a particular asset at a fixed price until a given expiration date. A **call option** gives the right to buy. A **put option** gives the right to sell. Options are **derivative securities** because their economic value is derived or stems from changes in the value of some other asset. Listing call options on just 16 common stocks, the CBOE traded a mere 911 contracts on its first day of business. Put options were introduced in 1977. In less than a generation, the CBOE has come a long way. The CBOE's present 45,000-square-foot trading floor opened for trading in February 1984. The exchange is now connected with more than 50,000 miles of electronic cable, most of it beneath the trading floor. There is enough cable at the CBOE to serve a city of 200,000 persons. At the CBOE, more information is displayed on computer screens than in any other building in the world.

call option
Right to buy.

put option
Right to sell.

derivative securities
Financial instruments with value stemming from changes in the value of some other asset.

Not only have times changed for the CBOE, active trading in equity and index options has also exploded on the American Stock Exchange (AMEX), New York Stock Exchange (NYSE), Pacific Exchange, and Philadelphia Stock Exchange. Many stock market investors remember 2000 as the year tech stocks continued to power the surging U.S. market as the Dow Jones Industrial Average (DJIA) broke through 11,750, and the Nasdaq Index surged past 5,100. In the options markets, participants watched in excitement as the use of equity options continued its exponential growth. Today, almost all actively traded equities have option contracts available. Trading volume has grown steadily. In 1999, for example, the option industry broke six daily volume records and five monthly volume records and surpassed its 1998 year-end volume by October. In December 1999, month-end equity volume was the highest ever, with 50.9 million contracts traded. This was a 67% increase over the same period in 1998 when 30.5 million contracts were traded and beat the previous month-end record set in November 1999 by 3.2 million contracts. As shown in Figure 17.1, cleared contract volume during 1999 for equities stood at

FIGURE 17.1 **Trading Activity in Equity Option Contracts Has Risen Sharply**

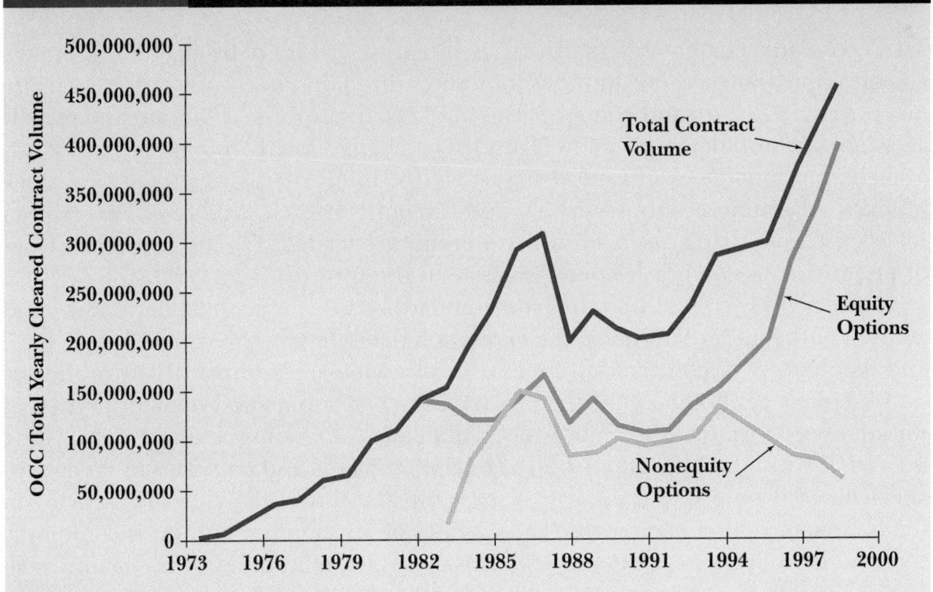

FIGURE 17.2 **Most Actively Traded Equity Issues Now Have Option Contracts Available**

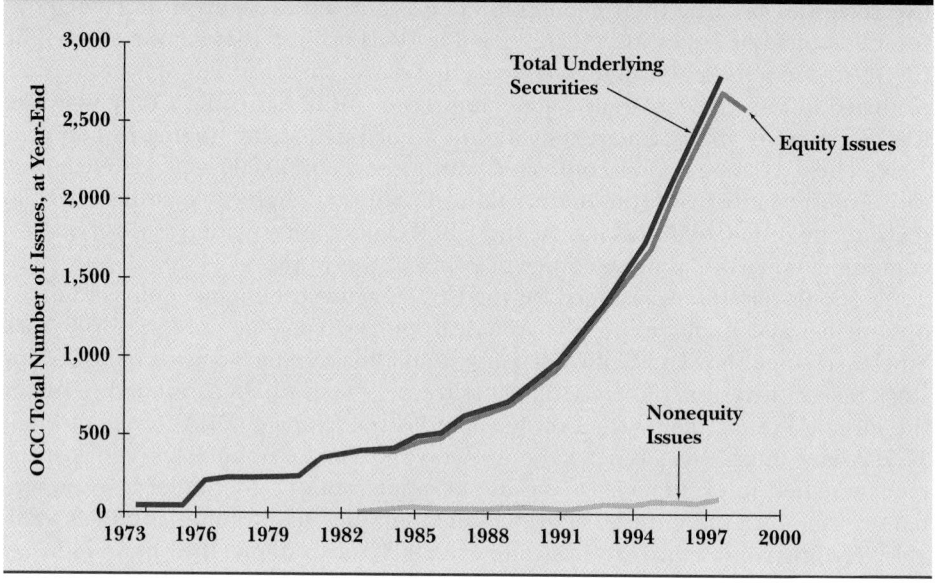

444.8 million, up from 329.6 million contracts a year earlier. Since 1992, equity option trading volume has jumped 318%. Over the past few years, equity options have grown from tools for professional investors to a variety of versatile instruments that can be used to help meet a wide range of individual investor needs. As shown in Figure 17.2, options are actively traded on more than 2,700 underlying equities and more than 100 nonequity securities.

Characteristics of Exchange-Traded Options

The economic resources and financial integrity provided by major option exchanges contribute the groundwork for standardized option contracts used to maintain orderly, efficient, and liquid options markets. In response to vibrant and rapidly growing investor demand, actively traded exchange-listed options are presently available on four types of underlying assets (or interests): equity securities, stock indexes, government debt securities, and foreign currencies. Each options market selects the underlying assets on which options are traded. Options on other types of underlying assets may become available in the future.

Most actively traded options have standardized terms such as the nature and amount of the underlying asset, the expiration date, the exercise price, option type, and the manner of contract fulfillment (or settlement). Trading activity in the options markets is wholly determined by the forces of supply and demand. Whereas the number of shares of common stock available for trading at any point in time is fixed, the number of options traded flexibly expands and contracts to meet market demand. Composite trading volume is the amount of daily trading activity on the five major option exchanges. The number of outstanding options is commonly referred to as **open interest** and depends solely on the number of buyers and sell-

open interest Number of outstanding options.

ers interested in receiving and conferring these rights. At any point in time, total open interest for equity options stands at roughly 35 million contracts representing 3.5 billion shares of common stock.

As seen in Figure 17.3, composite trading volume and open interest tend to be high for stock options tied to volatile common stocks with large numbers of

FIGURE 17.3 **Closing Quotes for Actively Traded Stock Options Can Be Obtained from *The Wall Street Journal* and Leading Newspapers**

LISTED OPTIONS QUOTATIONS

Wednesday, May 3, 2000

Composite volume and close for actively traded equity and LEAPS, or long-term options, with results for the corresponding put or call contract. Volume figures are unofficial. Open interest is total outstanding for all exchanges and reflects previous trading day. Close when possible is shown for the underlying stock on primary market. **CB**-Chicago Board Options Exchange. **AM**-American Stock Exchange. **PB**-Philadelphia Stock Exchange. **PC**-Pacific Stock Exchange. **NY**-New York Stock Exchange. **XC**-Composite. **p**-Put.

MOST ACTIVE CONTRACTS

Option/Strike				Vol	Exch	Last	Net Chg	a-Close	Open Int
AT&T	Jun	40		9,744	XC	2 15/16	− 1 5/16	39 13/16	27,588
AT&T	Jun	50		9,732	XC	⅝	− ¼	39 13/16	94,036
Maxim	May	60		9,686	XC	9	...	64⅛	326
Cisco	May	70		9,291	XC	2 5/16	− 9/16	66 1/16	110,940
go.com	May	12½	p	8,206	XC	⅜	− 7/16	14⅛	1,770
Wrn Lm	May	115		8,073	XC	4¼	− ¾	116½	663
Qualcom	May	115		7,789	XC	5¾	− ⅞	110 15/16	14,960
Citigrp	Jan 01	60		7,537	XC	9¾	− ⅜	60⅛	28,160
Compaq	May	25		7,331	XC	2 15/16	− 1 1/16	27 9/16	66,664
AT&T	Jan 01	45	p	7,004	XC	8⅝	+ 1¼	39 13/16	30,700
SiebelSys	May	150		6,337	XC	1 11/16	− 5/16	125⅜	20,936
AmOnline	May	55		5,657	XC	4¼	− ⅛	57⅛	75,704
MCI Wld	May	45		5,598	XC	15/16	− ⅛	42⅜	118,728
Ph Mor	May	25		5,417	XC	⅝	− ⅛	23¼	77,044
Microsft	Jan 01	60		5,179	XC	17⅞	+ 1¼	70 9/16	91,260
AmOnline	May	60		5,159	XC	1¾	− 3/16	57⅛	89,900
TycoLb	May	50		5,157	XC	13/16	− 5/16	46¾	48,572
Compaq	May	30		5,011	XC	7/16	− ¼	27 9/16	168,992
GenMotH	Jun	120		5,000	XC	1⅛	− ⅞	91 5/16	26,052
GenMotH	Jun	120	p	5,000	XC	29¾	+ 2¾	91 5/16	24,974

Option/Strike				Vol	Exch	Last	Net Chg	a-Close	Open Int
Cisco	May	65		4,895	XC	4¾	− ¾	66 1/16	74,968
TimeW	May	105		4,500	XC	¼	...	85 5/16	22,172
AT&T	Jun	40	p	4,428	XC	2¾	+ 13/16	39 13/16	25,336
Cisco	May	75		4,368	XC	1	+ 1/16	66 1/16	119,348
SunMicro	May	90		4,334	XC	3¾	− ¼	87⅜	52,076
AmOnline	Jul	90	p	4,325	XC	33½	+ 1½	57⅛	2,800
Gemstr	Jun	45		4,067	XC	5⅛	− ⅞	41 11/16	7,137
JohnJn	Jul	110		4,012	XC	¼	...	83¼	10,772
Genentc	May	130		4,009	XC	6	+ ⅝	123½	3,576
UtdhlthGr	Jun	55	p	4,008	XC	3	+ 1⅝	61¼	72
AT&T	Jun	45		3,989	XC	1¼	− ¾	39 13/16	24,224
GlblCrss	May	30		3,906	XC	5¼	+ 1¼	34⅛	24,584
AplMat	May	90		3,791	XC	10	− 1	94½	54,288
Intel	May	120		3,771	XC	5⅛	− ¾	119 1/16	40,544
Citigrp	Jan 01	60	p	3,740	XC	6⅞	+ ⅛	60⅛	40,596
Intel	May	125		3,690	XC	3⅛	− ⅜	119 1/16	50,904
Cisco	May	65	p	3,657	XC	3¼	+ 13/16	66 1/16	74,940
Citigrp	May	65		3,539	XC	⅝	− ⅛	60⅛	53,044
Cisco	May	62½		3,464	XC	6¼	− 1¼	66 1/16	102,456
Gen El	May	160		3,464	XC	4	− 2⅝	156 1/16	14,696

Complete equity option listings and data are available in The Wall Street Journal Interactive Edition at **http://wsj.com** on the Internet's World Wide Web.

Option/Strike		Exp.	Call Vol.	Call Last	Put Vol.	Put Last
ADC Tel	55	May	1545	5⅞	13	3⅛
58⅜	60	May	603	3¼	43	7
AES Cp	75	May	45	9/16	290	9/16
A S A	17½	May	70	⅜	300	1⅛
ASM Intl	35	Sep	520	5⅜	...	...
AT&T	40	Jun	9744	2 15/16	4428	2¾
39 13/16	45	Jun	3989	1¼	560	6¼
39 13/16	50	May	2187	⅛	174	10¼
39 13/16	50	Jun	9732	⅝	22	10⅜
39 13/16	55	May	427	1/16	299	15½
Abbt L	37½	May	36	1 9/16	525	1¼
37⅝	40	May	662	9/16	10	2⅞
AberFitch	22½	May	342	¾	90	⅞
Adelph	40	May	401	5⅜	...	...
AdobeS	115	May	358	7⅞	19	12
AdvFibCm	40	May	457	8⅝	31	1⅝
46 11/16	45	May	195	5⅜	486	4
46 11/16	50	Jun	294	4¼	...	...
A M D	70	May	307	16	45	1 1/16
87 9/16	80	May	320	10⅜	310	5⅛
87 9/16	80	Jun	760	14⅜	39	6⅝
87 9/16	85	May	1134	7	315	5⅞
87 9/16	90	May	2868	5¼	151	7⅞
87 9/16	90	Jun	459	9½	34	13
87 9/16	95	May	426	3¼	4	11⅛
87 9/16	95	Jun	321	6¼	...	...
87 9/16	100	May	835	2 1/16	13	14¼
Aetna	60	May	305	1⅛	...	...
AkamaiT	65	May	500	31	4	1
Alcatl	40	May	408	5⅜	...	...
45¼	45	May	1301	2 13/16	...	...
45¼	50	May	543	13/16	...	...
Alcoa	60	May	1041	4¼	4	⅞
AllRiser	20	May	340	1½	20	3½
Allste	25	Jun	349	1	10	2⅝
Altera	90	May	772	9½	181	3
96 9/16	105	May	349	2½	10	13½
Amazon	60	May	1644	2 1/16	146	8¼
54⅛	65	May	1014	1	63	12
AmOnline	50	May	134	8	3371	11/16
57⅛	50	Jul	40	10⅜	1226	2¾
57⅛	55	May	5657	4¼	1683	2
57⅛	55	Jun	194	5¾	293	3⅜
57⅛	60	May	5159	1¾	829	4⅜
57⅛	60	Jun	397	3¾	737	6⅜
57⅛	60	Oct	784	8¼	2	9¾
57⅛	65	May	1955	⅝	188	8⅜
57⅛	65	Jun	557	2 1/16	28	9½
57⅛	65	Jul	291	3½	66	10¾
57⅛	70	May	1393	¼	93	13
57⅛	70	Jun	553	1 3/16	67	13⅝
57⅛	70	Jul	1135	2 7/16	62	14⅛
57⅛	75	May	317	⅛	16	18¼
57⅛	75	Jul	491	1 7/16	20	18½
57⅛	85	May	10	⅛	300	28½
57⅛	90	May	...	...	1100	33½
57⅛	90	Jul	403	½	4325	33½
57⅛	95	Jul	18	5/16	2000	38½
57⅛	100	Jul	258	5/16	2000	43½
57⅛	110	Jul	...	...	300	53½
57⅛	120	May	...	...	400	63½
AmExpr	130	May	...	...	352	1 11/16
142	140	May	9	7½	449	4⅝
142	145	May	405	4⅛	158	7⅞
142	150	May	156	3⅛	383	10½
142	165	May	581	⅜	5	24
AmIntGp	105	May	600	7¼	90	2 5/16
109 9/16	110	May	321	3¾	141	3¾
109 9/16	115	May	144	1¾	500	6¼
109 9/16	115	Aug	601	7¾	...	...
APwrCv	40	Jun	675	¾	54	11¼
ATower	45	May	310	1¾	3	3⅞
Analog	75	May	909	1 15/16	5	12
68¼	90	May	482	¼	...	...
AncorCm	35	Jun	822	4	6	8⅞
AppleC	120	May	676	4	121	9⅜
115 1/16	125	May	1669	3⅝	20	12¼
115 1/16	130	May	463	2 1/16	...	...
AplMat	75	Jun	...	...	649	4⅜
94½	80	May	120	16¼	503	3⅛
94½	85	May	186	13⅜	280	3⅝
94½	90	May	3791	10	1166	5½
94½	95	May	875	7½	293	9⅝
94½	100	May	2382	5¼	174	10⅜
94½	100	Jun	453	9	30	13¼
94½	105	May	628	3¾	63	15⅛
94½	110	May	946	2¼	520	19½
94½	115	May	502	1 11/16	...	...
94½	120	May	208	¾	600	28
94½	125	May	51	11/16	902	34⅛
94½	130	Oct	279	8¼	...	...
94½	135	Jun	397	1½	...	...
94½	135	Oct	360	8⅜	...	...
Ariba	60	May	14	18⅞	744	⅞
78⅛	70	May	1196	11½	89	3¼
78⅛	80	May	396	6⅛	119	8⅝
AsiaPlp	7½	Dec	510	⅞	...	...
AscFCap	25	May	27	1	2305	2
24	25	Jun	10	1¾	300	2 7/16
AtHome	17½	May	1864	1¼	279	1⅜
17⅜	20	May	462	⅝	89	3⅛
17⅜	35	May	...	...	1000	18
17⅜	40	May	...	...	1000	23
17⅜	45	May	...	...	500	28
17⅜	45	Jul	29	¼	3416	26⅞
17⅜	50	Jul	200	¼	2506	33⅜
17⅜	52½	May	868	¼	...	...
17⅜	55	Jul	...	...	2500	37⅛
Atl R	100	Jul	300	1 13/16	...	...
Atmel	50	May	844	1⅛	100	6¼
45 3/16	55	May	653	⅝	...	...
AutoNatn	7½	May	700	1½	...	...
BEA Sys	40	May	451	8¼	138	1 7/16
47¾	40	Jun	13	8	506	3¼
47¾	45	Jun	143	6	374	6¼
47¾	50	May	421	3⅜	66	6⅛
BJ Svc	65	May	600	7½	...	...
70	75	May	846	2 1/16	200	7⅝
BMC Sft	50	Jun	767	2¼	...	...
BP Amoco	60	Jul	429	15/16	...	...
BakrHu	35	May	2873	1⅛	...	...
Bk of Am	45	Aug	253	6¾	1352	2 9/16
49	47½	May	313	2⅝	42	1 3/16
49	50	May	254	1½	425	2¼
49	55	May	979	¼	1	6¼
49	65	Aug	300	⅝	...	...
BarrLab	50	Jun	530	3⅛	...	...
BarickG	17½	May	1273	1¼	341	⅜
18 9/16	20	May	364	¼	23	2¼
18 9/16	20	Jul	670	1	10	2¾
Baxter o	70	May	324	3/16	...	...
BellSo	50	May	318	7/16	3	3
BestBuy	70	May	10	9¾	1207	1 11/16
80½	80	May	1038	3	298	4½
Bestfoods	50	May	306	11⅜	208	5/16
61¼	50	Jul	291	13⅞	111	1½
61¼	55	May	106	7⅛	505	⅞
61¼	55	Jun	2130	7¾	558	1 13/16
61¼	60	Jul	992	5⅜	92	4¾
61¼	65	Jul	291	3¼	59	7
Biogen	50	Jun	10	10½	500	3
55¾	55	Jul	341	8½	321	7½
55¾	65	May	678	¾	25	11½
55¾	100	Jul	308	⅞	...	...
55¾	110	Jul	300	½	...	...
BiotechT	130	May	501	11⅞	22	8
Boeing	40	May	82	½	554	3⅜
37 5/16	45	May	783	⅛	13	7½
BostSc	30	Aug	279	2½	45	5
BrMSq	50	May	170	2½	374	1 3/16
50¾	50	Jun	1273	4	27	2⅜
50¾	55	Jun	1269	1⅞	40	4¾
50¾	65	May	...	...	578	14¼
50¾	70	May	...	...	300	19¼
50¾	70	Jun	20	¼	500	19¼
50¾	75	Jun	1	¼	500	24¼
BroadVis	35	Sep	15	15⅞	708	7⅛
45 11/16	40	May	468	7⅛	352	1 9/16
45 11/16	45	May	1600	4⅞	278	3¾
45 11/16	50	May	1063	2 13/16	225	8
45 11/16	50	Jun	505	6⅜	1	10¼
45 11/16	55	May	433	1¼	26	11
45 11/16	60	May	325	¾	42	16⅜
45 11/16	60	Jun	696	3¼	15	17½
Broadcom	160	May	111	22⅝	722	5½
175 15/16	170	May	326	16⅜	241	10
175 15/16	210	May	663	3	...	...
175 15/16	240	Nov	1050	26⅜	...	...
BrcdeCo	100	May	412	22⅛	11	5¾
BurlRs	40	May	381	1	...	...
38⅝	42½	May	345	7/16	...	...
BurrBrn	55	May	1	11⅞	830	1 3/16
65 11/16	65	May	16	5⅜	608	4¼
CBS Cp	60	May	83	1 9/16	1500	2¾
CMGI Inc	40	Jun	40	24⅜	405	¾
62 1/16	70	Jun	593	5⅛	...	...
62 1/16	75	May	306	1¼	8	15
62 1/16	80	May	339	11/16	19	19⅞
62 1/16	115	May	...	...	400	53
62 1/16	120	May	...	...	400	58
62 1/16	150	Jun	6	⅛	500	88
62 1/16	155	Sep	...	...	610	8⅜
Cable&W	80	May	...	...	305	6¼
75⅛	80	Jun	...	...	325	8½
Cabltrn	30	May	699	½	...	...
Calpine	95	Jul	315	9⅝	...	...
CellGens	20	Jul	300	4¼	...	...
Cendant	15	May	58	⅝	627	1 1/16
14 35/64	15	Jun	575	1 1/16	25	1⅜
14 35/64	27½	Aug	...	...	300	12⅞
14 35/64	30	Aug	...	...	300	15⅜
ChamIn	60	May	300	6¾	...	...
66⅜	70	May	315	11/16	...	...
ChartCm	15	May	82	9/16	913	1½
ChaseM	65	May	...	...	1343	⅜
74¼	70	May	...	...	1405	1 5/16
74¼	70	Jun	...	...	312	2⅜
ChkPntSf	155	May	679	25	10	8
Chkfree	40	May	21	10	591	1¼
Chiron	30	May	49	5¼	396	1⅛
34 9/16	32½	May	...	...	1110	1 15/16
34 9/16	35	May	439	2 13/16	131	3
34 9/16	37½	May	1581	1 9/16	66	4½
34 9/16	40	May	557	1¼	20	6
CienaCp	110	May	793	19⅝	88	4
126 61/64	120	May	127	14½	538	7⅞
126 61/64	125	Jun	688	18¾	6	17¼
126 61/64	130	May	348	9⅜	105	12⅛
126 61/64	150	May	840	2½	11	27⅞
CirCty	55	May	72	5⅛	455	2 1/16
Cisco	47½	Jul	22	20½	620	2 1/16
66 1/16	50	May	163	15⅝	284	⅜
66 1/16	55	May	167	12	423	13/16
66 1/16	57½	May	45	9¼	1028	1⅛
66 1/16	60	May	2041	7⅞	1547	1¾
66 1/16	60	Jun	193	10	653	3⅛
66 1/16	60	Jul	152	12	1783	4½
66 1/16	62½	May	3464	6¼	1278	2¾
66 1/16	62½	Jul	66	10	279	5⅞
66 1/16	65	May	4895	4¾	3657	3¼
66 1/16	65	Jun	2115	6¼	1408	5½
66 1/16	67½	May	1674	3¼	598	4⅜
66 1/16	70	May	9291	2 5/16	1764	6
66 1/16	70	Jun	1444	4	58	8¾
66 1/16	70	Jul	1365	6	571	9
66 1/16	72½	May	1816	1⅜	14	8½
66 1/16	75	May	4368	1	146	9½
66 1/16	75	Jun	1306	2 3/16	13	12⅛
66 1/16	75	Jul	510	4⅛	24	12½
66 1/16	77½	May	406	⅝	34	11⅜
66 1/16	80	May	1190	⅜	161	14⅛
66 1/16	80	Jul	3088	2 13/16	20	16¾
66 1/16	80	Oct	2884	5¾	3	17⅜
66 1/16	85	May	283	⅛	...	...
66 1/16	85	Oct	357	3⅞	5	19¾
66 1/16	90	Jul	746	1 3/16	...	...
66 1/16	100	Jul	306	⅜	...	...
Citigrp	55	Jun	...	...	1894	1 7/16
60⅛	60	May	1703	2⅛	2794	1⅞
60⅛	60	Jun	74	3¾	595	3¼
60⅛	65	May	3539	⅝	53	5⅜
60⅛	65	Jun	285	1 11/16	23	6¼
CitrixSys	35	Jun	18	12	292	2½
44 9/16	45	May	675	5	798	3¾
44 9/16	45	Jun	280	8	127	7¼
44 9/16	50	May	784	2¾	118	6⅞
44 9/16	55	May	407	1¾	27	11¾
Coke	45	May	139	4	762	½
48½	50	May	1001	1⅛	479	2⅝
48½	50	Jun	580	2 1/16	432	3⅝
48½	55	May	21	¼	384	6¾
48½	55	Aug	197	1¾	292	7¾
ColumEn	65	Aug	300	2 3/16	5	2½
Com21	30	May	285	3⅛	5	3⅜
Comcst sp	35	Jun	14	2	1003	3⅜
ComOne	52½	May	810	5½	10	4½
55 11/16	60	May	421	3	77	8½
55 11/16	75	May	440	1	40	20⅜
Compaq	25	May	7331	2 15/16	2634	⅜
27 9/16	25	Jul	30	4¼	1084	1 11/16
27 9/16	27½	May	1692	1¼	1659	1⅛
27 9/16	30	May	5011	7/16	646	2¾
27 9/16	30	Jun	981	1⅛	80	3½
27 9/16	30	Jul	810	1 15/16	152	4
27 9/16	32½	May	785	⅛	182	5⅝
27 9/16	32½	Jun	501	9/16	50	4⅞
27 9/16	32½	Jul	514	1⅛	...	...
27 9/16	32½	Oct	391	2⅜	...	...
27 9/16	35	May	1428	1/16	9	7⅝
27 9/16	35	Jun	606	¼	...	...
27 9/16	35	Jul	940	⅝	10	7¾
CompAssoc	50	May	136	3	449	2⅞
Comvers	90	May	743	1⅜	10	12¾
Conexnt	55	May	1357	3½	46	6⅛
51 15/16	60	May	430	1 13/16	14	10¼
51 15/16	75	May	773	¼	43	25½
Cnseco	5	Jun	85	1¼	735	¾
6⅛	10	May	20	1/16	500	4⅜
Corning	160	May	437	24	180	2½
181	200	May	280	1	77	25¾
CovadCm	25	May	113	4½	744	2⅝
CrwnCstl	40	May	430	¼	...	...
CumMed	45	Jul	...	...	600	31¾
13 5/16	45	Oct	...	...	500	31¾
CypSem	50	May	2823	2⅞	91	4¼
49½	55	May	753	1⅝	16	9⅝
Dana	30	Oct	511	3⅜	2	3¾
DellCptr	35	May	17	14⅛	1130	⅛
49 5/16	42½	May	8	6¼	395	½
49 5/16	42½	Nov	...	...	1550	3⅞
49 5/16	45	May	2530	5¼	1124	⅞
49 5/16	45	Jun	303	6½	66	1 13/16
49 5/16	47½	May	291	3⅜	633	1 7/16
49 5/16	50	May	2293	2 1/16	1421	2 9/16
49 5/16	50	Jun	1105	3⅝	269	4½
49 5/16	55	May	1737	11/16	891	7¼
49 5/16	55	Jun	1733	1¾	7	8
49 5/16	60	May	310	3/16	60	11¼
49 5/16	60	Aug	310	2 3/16	26	12½
DelphiAu	20	Jun	755	1½	...	...
DeltaAr	60	Jul	280	3¼	...	...
Dexter	50	May	750	4⅛	15	15/16
Disney	37½	May	165	3⅛	1210	⅞
41	40	May	1841	2⅛	451	1 11/16
41	40	Jun	294	2 7/16	212	2 3/16
41	40	Oct	59	4¾	1011	4
41	42½	May	607	⅞	43	3
41	45	May	399	5/16	5	4¼
41	45	Jun	869	1	...	...
41	50	May	50	3/16	3043	10⅛
Dow Ch	90	Sep	502	29½	...	...
DuPont	50	May	1106	1 5/16	17	2½
ETradeGr	20	May	672	1¼	583	1 13/16
19 5/16	22½	May	395	⅜	30	3¾
19 5/16	22½	Jun	490	1¼	...	...
19 5/16	25	Jul	301	1⅜	20	7
eBay	230	May	40	1/16	288	5¼
ECI	30	May	522	1	42	2⅝
28⅜	30	Jun	320	2 1/16	...	...
EMC	130	May	655	10	847	3⅞
136¼	130	Jun	63	15	511	9⅛
136¼	135	May	1588	7	615	5⅞
136¼	140	May	1803	4½	404	9⅛
136¼	145	May	631	2 15/16	70	13½
136¼	150	May	1130	1⅝	42	14⅞
EchoStr	60	May	672	2 13/16	366	7⅛
Edwards	35	Jun	1000	2⅞	1500	1 7/16
EDS	75	May	34	3/16	1000	14½
Emulex	160	May	477	5¼	...	...
Enron	85	Jul	505	2⅞	...	...
ENSCO	30	May	1000	4⅝	500	⅝
EqOffPT	22½	May	310	4⅞	...	...
EricTel	90	May	318	3½	1434	7⅜
87	90	Jul	761	8¾	600	10⅜
87	100	Jun	647	3⅛	1	15¾
eToys	7½	May	26	13/16	296	1⅛
ExodsCm	85	May	544	9½	194	8¼
86⅞	85	Jun	415	15½	68	13⅛
86⅞	90	May	329	7⅛	32	11⅜
86⅞	100	May	754	4	25	19
86⅞	105	Jun	725	6¾	...	...
ExodsC	180	May	1149	12	310	5
FrchldS	50	May	279	1⅝	...	...
F N M	50	Jun	...	...	785	1 7/16
FMogul	10	Oct	800	4¼	...	...
12 15/16	12½	Oct	18	2 7/16	407	1½
12 15/16	17½	Oct	1000	1	...	...
FedInvst	35	Oct	1325	1¼	...	...
FstTenn	15	Aug	...	...	330	11/16
Flextrn	60	May	1090	2¾	113	5
58½	65	May	405	1 7/16	91	5¾
58½	70	May	281	11/16	11	12¼
FordMot	55	May	1143	⅝	175	2⅞
52 13/16	55	Jun	328	2	46	4¼
52 13/16	60	May	802	1/16	...	...
FHLB	45	Jun	900	2¾	75	3½
Gap	35	May	60	3½	655	1¼
37¼	35	Jun	12	4¾	2189	2
37¼	40	May	1137	1 3/16	97	4⅛
Gateway	50	May	53	3⅞	932	1½
Gemstr	40	May	60	3⅞	2315	3⅞
41 11/16	45	Jun	4067	5⅛	...	...
Genentc	110	May	1000	10½	53	2⅞
123½	125	May	313	6⅝	...	...
123½	130	May	4009	6	...	...
Gen El	115	Jun	3	42⅛	303	⅜
156 1/16	130	Jun	1	28⅜	1294	1 7/16
156 1/16	135	Jun	6	23⅝	298	2
156 1/16	140	May	13	17½	2105	1
156 1/16	145	May	35	13⅞	407	1⅝
156 1/16	150	May	167	9⅜	294	3
156 1/16	155	May	343	6⅜	494	4⅞
156 1/16	160	May	3464	4	171	7½
156 1/16	160	Jun	226	7⅝	418	10½
156 1/16	165	May	1038	2 7/16	259	10⅝
156 1/16	170	May	902	1 3/16	23	14¾
156 1/16	170	Jun	277	4	...	...
156 1/16	175	May	934	⅝	...	...
156 1/16	180	Jun	378	1½	...	...
GenlMotr	65	Jun	2920	25⅜	...	...
88 1/16	80	Jun	61	11¾	731	3¼
88 1/16	85	May	46	4⅛	1257	2 1/16
88 1/16	85	Jun	44	6¼	1091	5
88 1/16	90	May	382	2 3/16	359	4⅝
88 1/16	95	May	483	⅞	319	8⅛
88 1/16	100	May	390	5/16	5	11¾
88 1/16	100	Jun	134	2	1041	15¼
GenMotH	75	Jun	667	20⅜	2	2⅛
91 5/16	95	May	870	3⅛	...	...
91 5/16	120	Jun	5000	1⅛	5000	29¾
Gillet	35	Jun	487	2 7/16	17	1½
GlblCrss	30	May	3906	5¼	228	¾
34⅛	35	May	1828	1 15/16	443	3⅜
34⅛	35	Jun	432	3¾	56	4⅛
34⅛	40	May	619	⅜	20	6½
34⅛	40	Jul	335	2 13/16	3	9
GlobM	25	Jun	1000	1 7/16	...	...
Globalstr	15	May	276	15/16	1105	4¼
go.com	12½	May	...	...	8206	⅜
14⅛	15	May	498	⅞	175	1 9/16
GoldmnS	100	May	10	2 3/16	366	11¼
Gdrich	25	May	517	7½	...	...
Halbtn	50	Jun	730	1 13/16	...	...
HlthRh	7½	May	580	¾	...	...
7¾	10	Jun	560	3/16	...	...
Hewlet	65	Aug	315	6⅛	...	...
132½	120	May	50	15¾	449	3
132½	120	Aug	881	22⅞	66	11
132½	125	May	771	11	302	5½
132½	135	May	1553	6¾	905	10¾
132½	140	May	322	4¾	88	13
HighSpd	10	May	310	1½	...	...
BigEnt	17½	Aug	500	1 3/16	...	...
HomeDp	50	May	90	4½	928	1 5/16
54	55	May	1478	2¼	653	3¾
54	60	May	1440	⅝	603	6⅝
54	60	Jun	580	1⅞	40	7¼
54	65	Jun	287	½	...	...
54	70	May	387	⅛	5	15⅝
Homstk	7½	Jul	1519	⅝	125	1 7/16
Houshl	50	Jul	550	1 1/16	...	...
Humana	7½	May	521	3/16	20	13/16
ICN Phma	30	Sep	630	2 9/16	250	6
IDTCorp	35	May	377	1	...	...
IMS Hlth	15	May	800	2 1/16	...	...
16 7/16	17½	May	5	13/16	2010	1½
16 7/16	17½	Aug	...	...	2000	2 13/16
16 7/16	22½	May	...	...	1780	5⅜
16 7/16	22½	Aug	...	...	1780	6
IbisTech	135	May	310	4¼	2	3
Infocure	10	May	830	9/16	...	...
Infonet	17½	May	...	...	415	1¾
Infrmx	10	Aug	82	2 1/16	324	1 13/16
InfoSpce	90	Oct	520	10⅞	...	...
Inktomi	140	May	190	14⅛	601	9
IntgDv	30	May	287	12	...	...
44¼	40	May	427	5½	78	1⅜
44¼	45	May	501	2⅞	123	3⅛
44¼	50	May	338	1 5/16	113	7⅝
44¼	50	Jun	360	3	3	8½
44¼	50	Aug	284	6¾	...	...
Intel	90	May	40	27¼	564	¼
119 1/16	95	May	1	23½	721	7/16
119 1/16	100	May	1719	19¾	1032	½
119 1/16	105	May	2608	13⅝	1036	1
119 1/16	110	May	576	11⅝	1054	2
119 1/16	110	Jun	372	14⅝	202	5⅛
119 1/16	115	Jun	440	11⅜	582	6
119 1/16	120	May	3771	5⅛	1545	5⅝
119 1/16	120	Jun	1219	8⅜	672	8⅜
119 1/16	120	Jul	1363	12⅜	1053	11½
119 1/16	125	May	3690	3⅛	762	8½
119 1/16	125	Jun	559	6	37	11
119 1/16	130	May	3301	1⅝	158	12¼
119 1/16	130	Jun	1204	4¼	19	14½
119 1/16	135	May	1150	13/16	10	18⅜
119 1/16	135	Jun	594	3¼	48	20⅛
119 1/16	140	May	2265	5/16	31	24
119 1/16	140	Jul	536	4¾	...	...
119 1/16	145	May	641	3/16	6	27¼
119 1/16	145	Jul	678	3⅞	...	...
119 1/16	165	Oct	1080	3⅞	...	...
InterDig	30	May	401	1 9/16	20	6⅝
24⅞	35	May	421	⅝	...	...
I B M	100	May	143	9⅞	792	1⅛
108⅛	105	May	164	6⅛	653	2⅛
108⅛	105	Jun	22	7¾	462	4¼
108⅛	105	Jul	70	10⅞	543	6¾
108⅛	110	May	764	3¼	422	5¾
108⅛	110	Jul	98	7⅝	556	9
108⅛	115	May	1244	1⅝	997	7⅜
108⅛	120	May	1327	9/16	756	11¾
108⅛	120	Jul	1270	4¾	105	14
108⅛	130	Jul	509	2½	9	22
108⅛	140	Jul	320	1 1/16	...	...
IntHmFds	12½	May	427	2¾	...	...
ItrntCap	35	May	381	6⅛	102	2⅜
39⅝	45	May	318	2 5/16	...	...
39⅝	50	May	703	1 11/16	45	12
IntVceBr	15	May	281	1½	...	...

Source: *The Wall Street Journal,* May 4, 2000, C26.

exercise price Promised price for underlying asset. Also called a **strike price.**

at-the-money Option strike price equals current market price of underlying asset.

in-the-money Call (put) strike price is less (more) than the market price of the underlying security.

out-of-the-money Call (put) strike price is more (less) than the market price of the underlying security.

option series Options that have the same terms except for different strike prices.

holders Buyers.

writers Sellers.

contract period Time between when an option contract is established and when it expires.

option premium Option price.

institutional and individual shareholders. Notice, too, that activity in stock options tends to be highest for an **exercise price,** or **strike price,** that is near the current market price for the underlying common stock. The exercise price, or strike price, of an option is the designated price at which the shares of stock can be bought by the buyer of a call option or sold by the buyer of a put option. Strike prices are set at the time trading in an option is initiated. When the price of the underlying security is equal to the strike price, the option price is said to be **at-the-money.** A call option is **in-the-money** if the strike price is less than the market price of the underlying security. A put option is in-the-money if the strike price is greater than the market price of the underlying security. A call option is **out-of-the-money** if the strike price is greater than the market price of the underlying security. A put option is out-of-the-money if the strike price is less than the market price of the underlying security.

Strike prices are set at levels designed to satisfy the largest number of option buyers and sellers. Most stocks with actively traded options feature options with strike prices that are in-the-money, at-the-money, and out-of-the-money for various put and call options. For example, a given common stock trading at 49 might have stock options introduced with strike prices of 45, 50, and 55 to ensure market liquidity. Strike prices are determined when the underlying asset reaches a certain numeric value and trades consistently at or above that value. If a stock was trading at 49 and then moved up to hit a price of 50 and traded consistently at this level, the next highest strike price of 60 may be added (see Table 17.1).

To facilitate trading, strike prices are given alphanumeric codes that start with the letter *A*. As shown in Table 17.1, the letter *A* is used to indicate a strike price of \$5, *B* for a strike price of \$10, *C* for a strike price of \$15, and so on. A \$5 increment in strike prices is most common, but strike price increments of \$2½ are sometimes used for low-priced stocks or for stocks with unusually active option buyer and option seller interest.

Options that have the same standardized terms but different strike prices comprise an **option series.** The standardization of terms makes it more likely that there will be a secondary market in which **holders,** or buyers, and **writers,** or sellers, of options can close out their positions by offsetting sales and purchase transactions. It has become increasingly common that options of the same series are traded on more than one options market at the same time.

The length of time between when an option contract is established and when it expires is the **contract period.** The amount paid for the option is the **option premium.** The option premium is also the price at which the contract trades. The premium is the amount paid by the buyer to the writer, or seller, of the option. For this amount, the writer of the call option is obligated to deliver the underlying security if the call is exercised. Alternatively, the writer of a put option is required to buy the underlying security if the put is exercised. Writers keep the premium whether or not the option is exercised. It is simply a nonrefundable payment in full from the option holder to the option writer for the rights conveyed by the option. Premium amounts are subject to continuous change in response to the economic forces of supply and demand. Premiums are affected by the current value of the underlying asset, exercise price, values of related assets, expected volatility, and so on.

TABLE 17.1 **Call (put) options are in-the-money when the stock price exceeds (is less than) the strike price; call (put) options are out-of-the-money when the stock price is less than (exceeds) the strike price.**

	Call Option Strike Price			Put Option Strike Price		
Stock Price	**45**	**50**	**55**	**45**	**50**	**55**
45	**At the money**	Out of the money	Out of the money	**At the money**	In the money	In the money
46	In the money	Out of the money	Out of the money	Out of the money	In the money	In the money
47	In the money	Out of the money	Out of the money	Out of the money	In the money	In the money
48	In the money	Out of the money	Out of the money	Out of the money	In the money	In the money
49	In the money	Out of the money	Out of the money	Out of the money	In the money	In the money
50	In the money	**At the money**	Out of the money	Out of the money	**At the money**	In the money
51	In the money	In the money	Out of the money	Out of the money	Out of the money	In the money
52	In the money	In the money	Out of the money	Out of the money	Out of the money	In the money
53	In the money	In the money	Out of the money	Out of the money	Out of the money	In the money
54	In the money	In the money	Out of the money	Out of the money	Out of the money	In the money
55	In the money	In the money	**At the money**	Out of the money	Out of the money	**At the money**
56	In the money	In the money	In the money	Out of the money	Out of the money	Out of the money
57	In the money	In the money	In the money	Out of the money	Out of the money	Out of the money
58	In the money	In the money	In the money	Out of the money	Out of the money	Out of the money
59	In the money	In the money	In the money	Out of the money	Out of the money	Out of the money
60	In the money	In the money	In the money	Out of the money	Out of the money	Out of the money

Options can be usually bought with one of four expiration dates into the future from the **front month,** or the time when the option contract is originated. As shown in Table 17.2, options are traded in three sequential cycles starting in January, February, and March. In this table, the most recently added expiration month is listed in all caps. For example, at April expiration, the May options will become the new front month options while the expiration month JUNE is added to replace the expired April options. At May expiration, the June options will become the new front month options while the expiration month JULY is added to replace the expired May options. At June expiration, the July options will become the new front month options while the expiration month AUGUST is added to replace the expired June options. Notice how the most recently added expiration month will have either two months or eight months until its expiration.

front month Month in which contract period begins.

The most actively traded stock and index options tend to be calls with a short period of time until expiration. Buying calls tends to be more profitable than buying puts because stocks usually go up in price. Investor interest also tends to focus on short-term call options because they are more sensitive than long-term call options to near-term price changes in the underlying stock. In an effort to broaden the potential market for financial derivatives, option exchanges have introduced very long-term stock and index options called **long-term equity anticipation securities (LEAPS).** Like short-term options, LEAPS are available in two types—calls and puts. The main distinguishing feature of LEAPS is that they are available with expiration dates up to three years from the time they are initially issued. In addition, all LEAPS options expire on the third Friday of January. LEAPS

long-term equity anticipation securities (LEAPS) Long-term calls and puts.

TABLE 17.2 Option Series Are Issued in Sequential Cycles Beginning in January, February, and March

A. January Sequential Cycle (Symbol Guide Cycle #1)

Front Month	Available Expiration Months*			
January	Jan	FEB	Apr	Jul
February	Feb	MAR	Apr	Jul
March	Mar	Apr	Jul	OCT
April	Apr	MAY	Jul	Oct
May*	May	JUN	Jul	Oct
June	Jun	Jul	Oct	JAN
July	Jul	AUG	Oct	Jan
August	Aug	SEP	Oct	Jan
September	Sep	Oct	Jan	APR
October	Oct	NOV	Jan	Apr
November	Nov	DEC	Jan	Apr
December	Dec	Jan	Apr	JUL

B. February Sequential Cycle (Symbol Guide Cycle #2)

Front Month	Available Expiration Months*			
January	Jan	Feb	May	AUG
February	Feb	MAR	May	Aug
March	Mar	APR	May	Aug
April	Apr	May	Aug	NOV
May	May	JUN	Aug	Nov
June*	Jun	JUL	Aug	Nov
July	Jul	Aug	Nov	FEB
August	Aug	SEP	Nov	Feb
September	Sep	OCT	Nov	Feb
October	Oct	Nov	Feb	MAY
November	Nov	DEC	Feb	May
December	Dec	JAN	Feb	May

C. March Sequential Cycle (Symbol Guide Cycle #3)

Front Month	Available Expiration Months*			
January	Jan	FEB	Mar	Jun
February	Feb	Mar	Jun	SEP
March	Mar	APR	Jun	Sep
April	Apr	MAY	Jun	Sep
May	May	Jun	Sep	DEC
June	Jun	JUL	Sep	Dec
July*	Jul	AUG	Sep	Dec
August	Aug	Sep	Dec	MAR
September	Sep	OCT	Dec	Mar
October	Oct	NOV	Dec	Mar
November	Nov	Dec	Mar	JUN
December	Dec	JAN	Mar	Jun

*The most recently added expiration month is listed in all CAPS. For example, at June expiration, the July options will become the new "Front Month" options while the expiration month "AUGUST" is added to replace the expired June options. Notice how the most recently added expiration month will have either two months or eight months until its expiration.

TABLE 17.2 ***(continued)***

D. Expiration Month and Strike Price Codes

Expiration Months Code

	JAN	FEB	MAR	APR	MAY	JUN	JUL	AUG	SEP	OCT	NOV	DEC
Calls	A	B	C	D	E	F	G	H	I	J	K	L
Puts	M	N	O	P	Q	R	S	T	U	V	W	X

Strike Price Codes

A	B	C	D	E	F	G	H	I	J	K	L	M
5	10	15	20	25	30	35	40	45	50	55	60	65
105	110	115	120	125	130	135	140	145	150	155	160	165
205	210	215	220	225	230	235	240	245	250	255	260	265
305	310	315	320	325	330	335	340	345	350	355	360	365
405	410	415	420	425	430	435	440	445	450	455	460	465
505	510	515	520	525	530	535	540	545	550	555	560	565
605	610	615	620	625	630	635	640	645	650	655	660	665
705	710	715	720	725	730	735	740	745	750	755	760	765

N	O	P	Q	R	S	T	U	V	W	X	Y	Z
70	75	80	85	90	95	100	7½	12½	17½	22½	27½	32½
170	175	180	185	190	195	200	37½	42½	47½	52½	57½	62½
270	275	280	285	290	295	300	67½	72½	77½	82½	87½	92½
370	375	380	385	390	395	400	97½	102½	107½	112½	117½	122½
470	475	480	485	490	495	500	127½	132½	137½	142½	147½	152½
570	575	580	585	590	595	600	157½	162½	167½	172½	177½	182½
670	675	680	685	690	695	700	187½	192½	197½	202½	207½	212½
770	775	780	785	790	795	800	217½	222½	227½	232½	237½	242½

Data source: The Chicago Board of Trade.

appeal to investors who appreciate the leverage offered by options but like the long-term investment horizon afforded to equity holders.

As in the case of alphanumeric codes for different strike prices, expiration months are given codes to facilitate trading. For call options, the letter *A* is used to indicate January, *B* for February, *C* for March, and so on. In the case of put options, the letter *M* is used to indicate January, *N* for February, *O* for March, and so on. Standardized strike price and expiration month codes are combined with company-specific ticker symbols to give option traders unique symbols for call and put options that can be entered quickly and easily during trading hours. The trading symbol for stock options is usually a combination of the stock ticker symbol, plus a letter to indicate the month of the year, plus a final letter to indicate strike price.

Figure 17.4 shows an example of daily trading volume and open interest information for exchange-traded options in Lucent Technologies, Inc., as provided on the CBOE Web site. The most widely held stock in the United States, Lucent manufactures and services systems and software that enable network operators to provide wireline and wireless voice, data, and video services. On April 4, 1996, Lucent was spun off from AT&T and began life as an independent publicly traded company. On the basis of robust growth expectations, Lucent stock soared 1,114% from a split-adjusted $7.56 to an all-time high of $84.19 on December 9, 1999. In January 2000, following the publications of earnings warnings and accounting questions, Lucent's stock price plunged and option trading volume skyrocketed.

Trading volumes and open interest tend to be highest for options with near-term expiration dates and strike prices near the current stock price. For example, on April 27, 2000, Lucent closed at 64⅜ ($64.38), down ⅛. The LUEM option trading symbol in Figure 17.4 refers to a Lucent (ticker symbol LU) call option set to expire in May (call expiration month code E), with a strike price of 65 (strike price code M). The closing bid price was 2½ ($2.50), and the closing ask price for this actively traded call option was 2⅝ ($2.63). Because the minimum contract size for such call options is one contract covering 100 shares, the minimum contract amount for a call buyer was $250, and $262.50 for a call seller. Given a market price for the stock of 64⅜ and a call strike price of 65, these are out-of-the-money calls. Notice that Lucent call options fell in price on a day when the stock price went down fractionally.

LUQM is the option trading symbol for Lucent put options set to expire in May (put expiration month code Q) with a strike price of 50. The put option bid price of 3 is the put option premium received by a seller, expressed as a per-share amount. The ask price of 3⅜ ($3.38) is the option premium per share paid by a

FIGURE 17.4 Detailed Option Quotes Can Be Obtained on the Internet

LU EM-A (2000 May 65 Call) **2 1/2** -1/4 ▼

Price Data Table
Apr 27,2000 @ 21:47 ET(Data 15 Minutes Delayed)

Last Sale	**2 1/2**	Tick	Up
Time of Last Sale	16:01	Exchange	AMEX
Net Change	-1/4	Previous Close	2 3/4
Open	1 15/16	High	2 15/16
Bid	2 1/2	Low	1 15/16
Ask	2 5/8	Volume	336
Open Interest	14801		

Source: <http://www.cboe.com>.

put buyer. Because the minimum contract size for put options is also one contract covering 100 shares, the minimum contract amount received by a put seller is \$300. The minimum amount paid by a put buyer is \$337.50. With a market price for the stock of $64\frac{3}{8}$ and a put strike price of 65, these are in-the-money puts. Daily trading volume in the May65s was 336 calls and 13 puts. Open interest in the May65 calls of 14,801 and 3,379 in the May65 puts indicates the number of options contracts opened but not yet closed as of that trading day. Notice that Lucent put options rose slightly in price on a day when the stock price fell fractionally.

For exchange-traded options, customer market orders and market limit orders for 10 contracts or less will be automatically executed at prevailing market quotes in the most active series. Options generally are traded on U.S. options markets during normal business hours of U.S. securities exchanges and for a period afterward. Normal options market trading hours are from 9:30 AM to 4:02 PM EST. However, option trading may not be confined to these hours. Option trading in the evening and at night occurs for foreign currencies and is becoming more popular for other types of options. During periods of unusual market activity, a given options market may authorize trading to continue substantially longer than under normal conditions. Trading in an expiring option may also close at an earlier time than trading in other options. Closing prices for exchange-traded options are published daily in many newspapers, such as *The Wall Street Journal,* and on the Internet at various Web sites, such as <http://www.cboe.com>.

Options Clearing Corporation

A prime benefit of exchange-traded options is that option buyers are able to look to an established system that guarantees contract fulfillment. Individual option buyers need not depend on the ethical and financial integrity of any other single individual or brokerage firm to live up to the terms of the option contract agreement. A common clearing entity for all exchange traded option transactions severs the link between option buyers and sellers and ensures market integrity.

The **Options Clearing Corporation (OCC)** is the sole issuer of all securities options listed on these five exchanges and the National Association of Securities Dealers, Inc. (NASD). The OCC is the entity through which all option transactions are ultimately cleared. The OCC is a registered clearing agency, and each U.S. options market is subject to regulation by the Securities and Exchange Commission (SEC) under the Securities Exchange Act of 1934. Foreign options markets and their members are not generally subject to regulation by the SEC or to the requirements of the securities or other laws of the United States and may not be subject to the jurisdiction of U.S. courts.

Options Clearing Corporation (OCC)
Issuer of all listed securities options.

As the issuer of all exchange-traded options in the United States, the OCC takes the opposite side of every option traded and allows options traders to buy and sell in a secondary market without having to find the original opposite party. The OCC guarantees contract performance and gives buyers and sellers confidence that the options contracts they enter into will be fulfilled at the agreed-on terms. As such, the OCC substantially reduces the credit risk aspect of trading securities options. To ensure contract fulfillment, the OCC requires buyers and sellers to have a clearing member handle their options transactions and that both sides of every option transaction be exactly matched. The OCC also has the authority to make margin calls on member firms during the trading day.

An option buyer looks to the system created by OCC's rules, rather than to any particular option seller, for performance of the option owned. Similarly, option sellers must perform their obligations under the OCC system and are not obligated to any particular option buyer. Because every option transaction involves both a buyer and a seller, the aggregate rights of option buyers are matched by the aggregate obligations of option sellers. The OCC system is designed so that the performance of all options is between the OCC and a group of clearing member firms that carry the positions of all option buyers and option sellers in their accounts at OCC.

To qualify as a clearing member, a firm must meet OCC's financial requirements, provide the OCC with collateral for the positions of option sellers that they carry, and contribute clearing funds that protect OCC against a clearing member's failure. In this way, the OCC is able to guarantee performance of options sellers' obligations, the financial strength of the options markets.

Market Reform

Increasingly, options on the same equity securities or equity indexes are traded on more than one options market at the same time. Options that are actively traded on more than one exchange are called multiply traded options. Options traded on U.S. options markets may also be traded on foreign options markets. These options are referred to as internationally traded options. Multiply traded and internationally traded options can ordinarily be purchased and sold in any of the options markets in which the options are traded. However, because premiums are affected by market forces, premiums for identical multiply traded or internationally traded options may not be the same in all markets at any given point in time. If an options market decides to discontinue trading in a particular option series for any reason, the options markets may stop introducing new options on that underlying interest or impose restrictions on transactions that open new positions. In such circumstances, trading in the discontinued options series ordinarily continues on at least one options market until the time of expiration.

market makers Dealers.

open-outcry auction Physical auction market.

floor brokers Agents that execute public option orders.

On the CBOE, **market makers** provide liquidity in option trading by risking their own capital for personal trading. They are the backbone of the CBOE's trading system. They take the opposite side of public orders by competing in an **open-outcry auction** market. **Floor brokers,** however, act as agents, executing orders for public or firm accounts. Most option classes listed at the CBOE are traded in an open-outcry system in which certain members of the exchange may trade as market makers. This differs from the trading environment on many other exchanges in which exchange specialists are allowed to accept orders from the public, to manage the public order book, and to deal for their own accounts in the same securities.

In October 1999, the SEC issued an order that directed the five major U.S. options exchanges to develop a linkage plan. The ultimate nature of such a tie-up is not yet certain. AMEX, CBOE, and the International Securities Exchange, a planned electronic exchange, prefer a plan that preserves the right to match the best advertised price for an option contract. The Pacific Exchange and Philadelphia Stock Exchange prefer a price-time priority system that would ensure that orders are executed at the exchange that first posted the best price.

The differences between the two sets of rules may seem insignificant, but it could be a matter of life and death for the exchanges. If larger exchanges can match prices, there may not be an incentive for brokerage firms to take their business to smaller exchanges. Many argue that price-time priority could help the smaller Pacific and Philadelphia exchanges because it would guarantee that they get orders when they post the best price in the market.

In the absence of an industry consensus, the SEC could be forced to decide which rules will govern the coming options market linkage system. In any event, price competition in the options markets is sure to increase, as is the efficiency of the options trading system.

Option Basics

Option Concept

The rapid growth of options markets can be explained by two important underlying causes. First, the option concept is an increasingly useful device for transferring investment risk in an increasingly interconnected and volatile global marketplace. Without this basic economic value, there would be no investor demand for options trading, and options markets would not have developed. Second, the introduction of standardized option contracts provides for orderly, efficient, and liquid options markets. Without the institutional framework provided by the options markets, demand for options would have been stifled.

Exchange-traded options are extremely versatile investment tools. Because of their unique risk/reward characteristics, options can be used in combination with other financial instruments to create **hedged positions** or **speculative positions.** A hedged position is created when an option contract is purchased or sold to offset the risk inherent in some other investment. Hedgers use options to limit risk. A speculative position is created when an option contract is purchased or sold to profit from the inherent riskiness of some underlying asset. Speculators assume risk by taking unhedged positions to profit from anticipated price changes. Options have speculative appeal because they often exhibit significant leverage. This leverage stems from the fact that options can often be purchased for a small fraction of the cost of the underlying asset. Of course, leverage not only magnifies the potential benefits from a favorable change in the price of the underlying asset; it also magnifies the loss potential following an unfavorable change in price.

hedged position Use of options to offset the risk inherent in some other investment.

speculative position Use of options to profit from the inherent riskiness of some underlying asset.

Unlike many other risky investments in which the risks may be unlimited, option buyers are able to precisely control risk exposure. For option buyers, the amount of risk undertaken is no more than the amount paid for the option. Of course, option buyers lose money if the conditions for profitable sale of the contract are not met by a given date. However, even if the option position expires worthlessly, option buyers can lose no more than the amount paid for the option.

Notice that, before commissions and other transaction costs, option contracts represent a **zero sum game** between the buyer and the seller. Before commissions and other transactions costs, when the price of the underlying asset rises unexpectedly, the amount earned by the buyer of a call option is exactly equal to the amount lost by the seller. When the price of the underlying asset

zero sum game Buyer's gain is seller's loss, and vice versa.

WALL STREET WISDOM 17.1

Take a LEAP!

Introduced by the American Stock Exchange in October 1990, equity LEAPS are put and call options on selected underlying stocks that have an expiration period of up to three years. Generally speaking, equity LEAPS with 36 months to expiration are introduced for each January expiration. Initial strike (or exercise) prices are set at approximately the current price of the underlying equity, as well as approximately 25% above and 25% below the current price. This gives investors the opportunity to use the versatility of at-the-money, in-the-money, and out-of-the-money puts and calls. At the present time, equity LEAPS are offered on hundreds of investment-grade equities. LEAPS are seldom offered on low-priced stocks or on equities with thin trading volumes. These long-term options give holders the right to buy (with calls) or sell (with puts) shares of an underlying stock at a specified price on or before a given expiration date that may be up to three years in the future. Except for their longer expiration period, equity LEAPS work in the same manner as all other exchange-listed stock options and may be exercised on any business day prior to expiration. Regular-term options with expiration periods of up to eight months in length are also traded on stocks that underlie LEAPS.

Index LEAPS are long-term options that are generally based on a reduced value of an underlying index. Like equity LEAPS, index LEAPS have expiration periods of up to three years in length. Although LEAPS are listed on indexes on which regular-term options are also traded, LEAPS trade independently of regular-term index options. Like all other broad-market index options, index LEAPs may be exercised only on the last business day prior to expiration. Generally speaking, index LEAPS series with 36 months to expiration are introduced at each December expiration. Two initial strike or exercise prices are listed that bracket the current index value. New LEAPS strike prices are introduced when the index value moves approximately 10–15%. Like all index options, index LEAPS are settled by cash payment based on the difference between the strike price and the final settlement value.

One of the most innovative uses of LEAPS occurs when they are used in conjunction with index shares. Index shares are benchmark securities traded on the American Stock Exchange that reflect the performance of an important market index or market segment. Index shares represent participation in investment trusts that actually hold shares of stock in the underlying components of each respective index or market segment. Index shares are presently available for the DJIA (called DIAMONDS), Nasdaq 100 (QQQs), the S&P 500 (called Standard & Poor's depositary receipts, or SPDRs for short), and for various sectors of the S&P 500 (called Select Sector SPDRs). With index LEAPS based on the Nasdaq 100, for example, investors can leverage their participation in this dynamic market segment. LEAPS on Financial Sector SPDRs allow investors to leverage their participation in the growth of banks, brokerages, and insurance companies.

Like all stock options, LEAPS provide investors with opportunities to control and manage risk. The compelling advantage of LEAPS lies in their ability to help control and manage risk for longer periods of time than are possible using conventional options. With up to three years until expiration, LEAPS hold their time value much longer than conventional stock and index options. Unlike conventional options traders who must precisely time purchase and sale decisions, LEAPS give long-term investors a margin of safety in predicting the timing of market moves. LEAPS are especially appropriate financial instruments for investors who seek long-term protection for a portfolio or for given stock holdings. LEAPS also give speculators the opportunity to use leverage without the risk of a margin call, as might be true if margin debt were used.

Nevertheless, it is important to realize that, like all option traders, LEAPS investors face the possibility of total loss in the value of their investment if market conditions worsen through the end of the expiration period.

See: For more information about LEAPS, see <http://www.cboe.com>.

falls unexpectedly, the amount lost by the buyer of a call option is exactly equal to the amount earned by the seller. The same holds true for put options. Gains and losses for put buyers and sellers are equal in magnitude. A stock option contract is like a side bet between the buyer and the seller about the short-term price action in a stock. No money is earned or lost by the company itself. Only options market participants are affected.

Transaction Type and Option Style

An option holder is said to be long the option position; the writer of an option position is said to be short the position. An **opening transaction** initiates a position in the options market. It is a purchase or sale transaction by which an investor establishes a position as either a holder or writer of an option. In a **closing transaction,** an investor terminates a previously established option position. This is a transaction in which the option holder makes an offsetting sale of an identical option at some point prior to the time of expiration. A closing transaction reduces or completely eliminates the investor's previous position as the holder or the writer of an option.

For example, suppose a given investor buys a single December Ford 50 call at an aggregate contract amount of $500 during the month of August in an opening transaction. By October, assume that the contract amount for the option has increased to $800. To seek to realize a $300 profit, the investor can direct a broker to sell an offsetting December Ford 50 call in a closing transaction. However, if by October the market price of the option has decreased to $300, the investor might decide to sell the option in a closing transaction, thereby limiting the amount of loss to $200.

Although holders of equity options traded in the United States have the right to exercise at any time before expiration, holders frequently elect to realize their profits or losses by making closing transactions in order to take advantage of near-term market volatility. In some instances, the transaction costs of closing transactions may be lower than the transaction costs associated with physical delivery of the underlying asset. The limited exercise period for certain types of specialized options often means that the only feasible means for contract termination is by selling the option in a closing transaction.

Option style refers to the time frame during which an option is exercisable. At the present time, there are three different styles of options that are actively traded on exchanges around the world. An **American-style option** is an option contract that can be exercised at any time between the date of purchase and the expiration date. All stock options traded in the United States are American-style options. The most popular exchange-traded S&P index options are also American-style options. **European-style options** can be exercised only on the **expiration date.** The expiration date is the last day of an American-style option, or the single exercise date of a European-style option. A **capped option** is an option that will be automatically exercised prior to expiration if the options market on which it is trading determines that the value of the underlying asset hits a specified cap price. Capped options may also be exercised, like European-style options, during a designated period before expiration. European-style or capped options having an expiration period that is longer or shorter than their expiration date may be introduced in the future.

opening transaction
Trade that initiates an option position.

closing transaction
Trade that terminates an option position.

American-style option
Option contract that can be exercised at any time between the date of purchase and the expiration date.

European-style options
Options contracts that can only be exercised on the expiration date.

expiration date
Last day of an American-style option, or the single exercise date of a European-style option.

capped option
Option that will be automatically exercised when the underlying asset value hits a specified cap price.

Settlement

physical delivery option
Entails the physical delivery of an asset.

cash-settled option
Entails the promise of a cash payment based on the difference between market and exercise price.

contract size
Trading unit of underlying asset.

When it comes to the point of expiration, there are two different settlement alternatives. Some options require physical delivery, others have cash settlement provisions. A **physical delivery option** gives its owner the right to receive physical delivery of an asset if it is a call, or to make physical delivery of an asset if it is a put, when the option is exercised. In the case of stock options, physical delivery takes the form of stock certificates representing ownership of a specified number of shares. A **cash-settled option** gives the holder the right to receive a cash payment based on the difference between a determined value of the underlying interest at the time the option is exercised and the fixed exercise price of the option. A cash-settled call conveys the right to receive a cash payment if the settlement value exceeds the exercise price. A cash-settled put grants the right to receive a cash payment if the settlement value is less than the exercise price.

The unit of trading or **contract size** of a physical delivery option is the quantity of an underlying asset that is subject to being purchased or sold on the exercise of a single option contract. In the case of common stocks, for example, option contracts are generally for 100 shares of stock unless adjusted for a special event, such as a stock split or a stock dividend. As described previously, Lucent 65 call gives the buyer the right on exercise to purchase 100 shares of Lucent common stock at $65 per share. If the option is trading at a market price of, say, $2.50 per share, then the total price for a single option contract would be $250, plus commissions and other transaction costs. The contract size of a cash-settled option is determined by a multiplier fixed by the options market on which it is traded. This multiplier determines the aggregate value of each point of difference between the exercise price of the option and the exercise settlement value of the underlying asset. For example, a multiplier of 100 means that for each point by which a cash-settled option is in-the-money on exercise, there is a $100 increase in the cash settlement amount. If an option with a multiplier of 100 is trading at a premium of $5, the aggregate premium for a single option contract would be $500.

The cash settlement amount is the amount of cash that the holder of a cash-settled option is entitled to receive on exercise. It is calculated as the difference between the exercise price and the exercise settlement value, times the agreed-on multiplier for the option. For example, assume that a cash-settled call on the Nasdaq 100 Index with a strike price of 125 is exercised when the exercise settlement value of the index is 130. If the multiplier for Nasdaq 100 Index options is 100, the exercising holder would be entitled to receive a cash settlement amount of $500 [= ($130 − $125) × 100].

exercise
Point at which option holder executes his or her right.

assigned
Point at which option writer must fulfill obligation.

Equity option buyers have the right to either buy or sell stock at a predetermined price. When and if they choose to buy or sell at that predetermined price, they are said to **exercise** their right. At that point, the seller, or writer, has the obligation to sell or buy stock. The seller of an option is said to be **assigned** when he or she is asked to fulfill his or her contract obligation. Typically, this occurs when the option is in-the-money at the time of expiration. Individual investors may be automatically assigned or exercised if they hold options that are $\frac{3}{8}$ to $\frac{3}{4}$ of a point or more in-the-money at the time of expiration. If an option is out-of-the-money at the point of expiration, it expires worthlessly. At that point, the buyer or holder loses the premium paid for the option plus whatever commissions and fees were incurred on that transaction. However, it is worth remembering that the writer of an equity option contract in the United States should anticipate being assigned any time the option becomes in-the-money.

As seen in Figure 17.5, the expiration date for stock options is the Saturday immediately following the third Friday of the expiration month. However, brokerage firms typically set an earlier deadline, such as 3:00 PM EST on the third Friday of the month, for notification of an option buyer's intention to exercise. If Friday is a market-closing holiday, the last trading day will be the preceding Thursday. Whereas stock options and stock index options expire on a monthly basis, stock index futures, which are described more fully in Chapter 18, have only four major expiration cycles per year. The expirations of stock index futures coincide with each calendar quarter.

Option market players playfully refer to the last hour of trading on the third Friday of March, June, September, and December as **triple witching** hour because of the tendency of investors to rush to unwind their positions in expiring stock options, index options, and stock index futures. The other eight times per year, when only equity options and equity index options expire, is playfully referred to as **double witching** hour. The expiration of options and futures coincide only four times per year, and triple witching hours are sometimes associated with sharp price swings as investors buy and sell these derivative instruments and the underlying equity securities.

triple witching Expiration of stock and index options and futures on indexes (at calendar quarters).

double witching Expiration of stock and index options and futures on indexes.

FIGURE 17.5 **2001 Options Expiration Calendar**

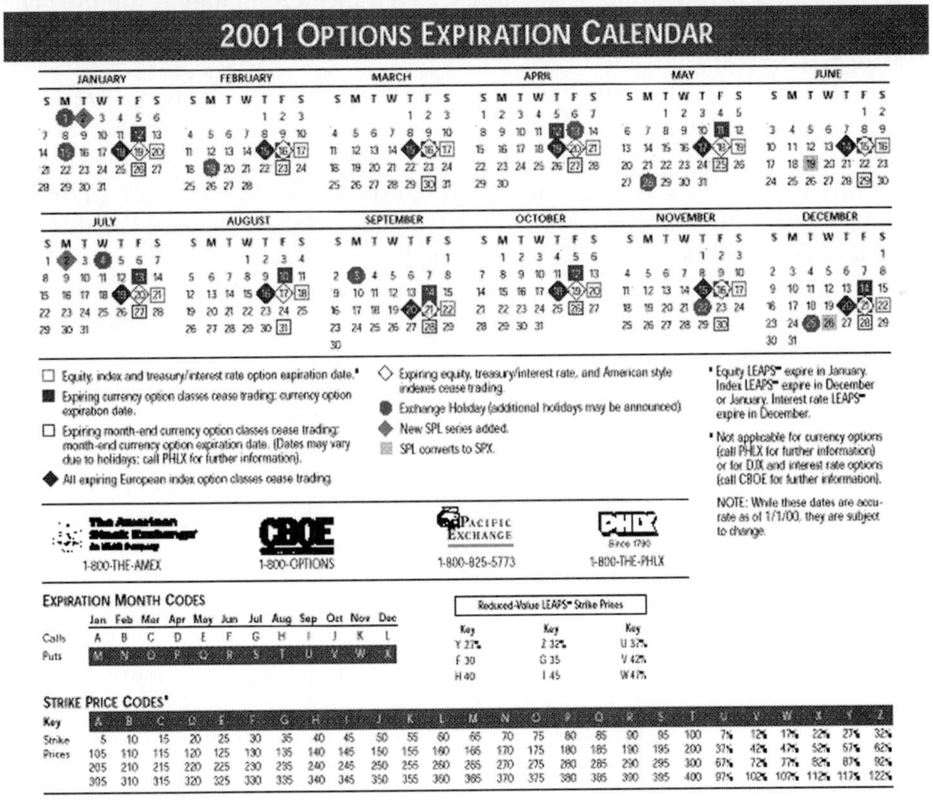

Source: The Options Clearing Corporation.

Option Types

Stock Options

The term *stock option* is used to describe options on common stocks, limited partnership interests, American depositary receipts (ADR), American depositary shares, and preferred stocks. Stock options are available on exchange-traded equities and on unlisted equity securities traded on the Nasdaq stock market. Issuers of underlying equity securities do not participate in the selection of their securities for options trading. Nevertheless, some options markets may determine not to select an underlying security without the consent of the issuer. Issuers of underlying equity securities have no responsibility regarding the issuance, the terms, or the performance of options, and option holders have no rights as security holders.

Options share many similarities with common stocks. Both are listed securities. Orders to buy and sell options are handled through brokers in the same way as orders to buy and sell stocks. Listed option orders are executed on the trading floors of national SEC-regulated exchanges, where all trading is conducted in an open and competitive auction market. Like stocks, options trade with buyers making bids and sellers making offers. In the stock market, those bids and offers are for shares of stock. In the options markets, bids and offers are for the right to buy or sell the underlying stock at a given price per share for a given period of time. Like stock investors, option investors have the ability to follow price movements, trading volume, and other pertinent information day by day or even minute by minute. The buyer or seller of an option can quickly learn the price at which an order has been executed.

Despite these similarities, there are important differences between stock options and common stock. Unlike common stock, an option has a limited life. Common stock can be held indefinitely in the hope that its value may increase, whereas every option has an expiration date. If an option is not closed out or exercised prior to its expiration date, it ceases to exist as a financial instrument. For this reason, an option is often described as a wasting asset. Unlike stock certificates, which provide evidence of ownership, option contracts are entered in book-entry form only. This means that option positions are only indicated on the printed statements issued by a buyer's or seller's brokerage firm. Unlike stock ownership, which conveys proportional ownership, voting rights, and dividends (if any), options owners share only in the potential benefit of stock price movements.

Although stock options generally cover 100 shares of the underlying security, this number of shares may be adjusted as a result of certain events. Adjustments may be made following a variety of material events, including a stock dividend, stock distribution, stock split, rights offering, reorganization, recapitalization, or merger. As a general rule, no adjustment is made for ordinary cash dividends or distributions. A cash dividend or distribution by most issuers is generally considered ordinary unless it exceeds 10% of the aggregate market value of the underlying security. Stock options are not adjusted for ordinary cash dividends and distributions. However, a call holder becomes entitled to the dividend if such an investor exercises the option prior to the exdividend date. Because call holders often seek to capture an impending dividend by exercising call privileges, a call writer's chances of being assigned may increase as the exdate approaches for a dividend on the underlying security.

Stock splits and stock dividends can result in an adjustment in the number of underlying shares, in the exercise price, or both. For example, in January 2000, electronic commerce and transaction processing company Pegasus Systems, Inc., announced a 3:2 stock split. Suppose an individual investor held a Pengus 60 call or put option on the exsplit date. Instead of covering 100 shares of stock with exercise price of $60 per share, each outstanding option was adjusted to cover 150 shares at an exercise price of $40 per share. When a stock distribution results in the issuance of one or more whole shares of stock for each outstanding share, as in a 2:1 stock split, the number of outstanding options is proportionately increased and the exercise price is proportionately decreased. In January 2000, for example, semiconductor chip equipment manufacturer KLA-Tencor Corporation announced a 2:1 stock split. Assume that on the effective date of the stock split, an investor holds an option on 100 shares of KLA-Tencor stock with an exercise price of $70. After adjustment for the split, the investor will hold two KLA-Tencor options, each on 100 shares and with an exercise price of $35. As a general rule, adjustments in exercise prices are rounded to the nearest ⅛ of a dollar, and adjustments in the number of underlying shares are rounded down to eliminate fractional shares. In some cases, the exercise price may be adjusted to compensate for the loss of fractional shares.

Distributions of property other than the underlying security may require different adjustments. Outstanding options might be adjusted to include the distributed property. For example, in December 1999, oil services giant Schlumberger Limited announced the distribution of shares in a subsidiary, Transocean Sedco Forex, Inc., to shareholders. The distribution ratio was 0.1936 shares of common stock in Transocean for each share of common stock of Schlumberger. As a result, outstanding options for Schlumberger were adjusted to require the delivery of 100 shares of Schlumberger, plus 19 shares of Transocean and a specified cash payment in lieu of 0.36 fractional shares of Transocean common. Alternatively, exercise prices for Schlumberger's outstanding options could have been reduced by the value of the distributed property.

Events other than distributions can also result in adjustments. If all the outstanding shares of an underlying security are acquired in a merger or consolidation, outstanding options are usually adjusted to require delivery of the cash, securities, or other property payable to holders of the underlying security as a result of the acquisition. For example, in late 1999, when shareholders of Honeywell Inc. approved the merger between Honeywell and Allied Signal, Inc., each share of Honeywell common stock was converted into the right to receive 1.875 shares of the new combined company, Honeywell International, Inc. Thus, outstanding Honeywell options were adjusted to call for the delivery of 187.5 shares of the new Honeywell instead of 100 shares of stock in the old (premerger) Honeywell. As is usually the case, cash payments were specified in lieu of the delivery of partial shares. When an underlying security is wholly or partially converted into debt or preferred stock, options that have been adjusted to call for delivery of the debt security or preferred stock may be further adjusted to call for payment of appropriate interest or dividends on such debt or preferred stock.

In mergers in which an underlying security is converted into a right to receive a fixed amount of cash, options on that security will generally be adjusted to require the delivery on exercise of that fixed amount of cash. Option trading ordinarily ceases on the date a cash merger becomes effective. After such an adjustment, all out-of-the-money options on that security become worthless. Adjustments are not generally made to reflect changes in the capital structure of the issuer when all the underlying securities outstanding in the hands of the public are not changed into another security, cash, or other property.

All adjustments made in the value of an option become effective on the date established by the primary market for trading in the underlying security. Specific details on adjustments for actively traded equity options can be found on the CBOE Web site at <http://www.cboe.com>.

Index Options

All index options are settled in terms of a fixed cash amount, and cash-settled index options do not relate to a particular number of shares. Premiums for index options are expressed in points and fractions of points, each point representing an amount equal to one U.S. dollar. The size of a cash-settled index option contract is determined by a multiplier and expressed in U.S. dollars. As shown in Figure 17.6, the most actively traded index options in the United States are based on the Standard & Poor's 100 Index (OEX). The OEX is fairly unique among broad-based index options in that American-style OEX options may be exercised on any business day before the expiration date. Almost all other broad-based index options traded in the United States are European-style options, meaning that they can only be exercised at the expiration date. Subject to regulatory approval, trading in index options whose exercise prices or premiums are expressed in a foreign currency may be introduced in the United States in the future.

For example, suppose an investor purchases a July 780 OEX call at 33. The multiplier for OEX index options is $100, meaning that the dollar value of the call premium for a single contract is $3,300 (= 33 × $100). The $100 multiplier is a convenient basis for index option value calculation and is used for many popular index options, such as those tied to the DJIA (DJX) and the Nasdaq 100 Index (NDX).

The exercise settlement values of stock index options are determined in a variety of ways. The exercise settlement values of some index options are based on the reported level of the index derived from the closing (last) prices of the constituent securities on the day of exercise. Exercise settlement values of some other options are based on the reported level of the index derived from the opening (first) prices of the constituent securities on the day of exercise. If a particular constituent security does not open for trading on the day the exercise settlement value is determined, the last reported price of that security is used. Investors must be aware that the exercise settlement value of an index option that is derived from opening prices may not be reported for several hours following the opening of trading in those securities. A number of updated index levels may be reported after the opening before the exercise settlement value is reported, and there could be a substantial discrepancy between those reported index levels and the exercise settlement value. Investors should also be aware that there is no single opening or closing price for securities primarily traded on Nasdaq. The index price used for a Nasdaq security will not necessarily be the price at which a majority of opening or closing trades in that security were made.

FIGURE 17.6 S&P 100 (OEX) Is the Most Popular Basis for Index Options

INDEX OPTIONS TRADING

Wednesday, May 3, 2000

Volume, last, net change and open interest for all contracts. Volume figures are unofficial. Open interest reflects previous trading day. p-Put c-Call

RANGES FOR UNDERLYING INDEXES

Wednesday, May 3, 2000

	High	Low	Close	Net Chg.	From Dec. 31	% Chg.
DJ Indus (DJX)	107.32	104.00	104.80	− 2.51	− 10.17	− 8.8
DJ Trans (DTX)	283.80	278.48	279.65	− 4.60	− 18.07	− 6.1
DJ Util (DUX)	318.16	314.13	316.48	− 1.27	+ 33.12	+ 11.7
S&P 100 (OEX)	779.25	751.54	761.18	−18.07	− 31.65	− 4.0
S&P 500 -A.M.(SPX)	1446.29	1398.36	1415.10	−31.19	− 54.15	− 3.7
CB-Tech (TXX)	1084.02	1025.64	1060.36	−23.69	− 24.26	− 2.2
CB-Mexico (MEX)	108.38	103.07	103.69	− 4.49	− 8.30	− 7.4
CB-Lps Mex (VEX)	10.84	10.31	10.37	− 0.45	− 0.83	− 7.4
MS Multintl (NFT)	872.06	847.45	858.84	−13.30	− 4.96	− 0.6
GSTI Comp (GTC)	469.96	443.81	458.16	−11.83	+ 1.54	+ 0.3
Nasdaq 100 (NDX)	3627.31	3435.30	3562.16	−65.15	−145.67	− 3.9
NYSE (NYA)	645.75	628.04	631.91	−13.84	− 18.39	− 2.8
Russell 2000 (RUT)	505.35	487.33	495.58	− 9.77	− 9.17	− 1.8
Lps S&P 100 (OEX)	155.85	150.31	152.24	− 3.61	− 6.33	− 4.0
Lps S&P 500 (SPX)	144.63	139.84	141.51	+ 1.51	− 5.42	− 3.7
Volatility (VIX)	35.83	32.03	34.51	+ 3.64	+ 7.80	+ 29.2
S&P Midcap (MID)	475.83	460.07	465.76	−10.07	+ 21.09	+ 4.7
Major Mkt (XMI)	1082.25	1049.49	1053.52	−28.73	−112.46	− 9.6
Eurotop 100 (EUR)	390.38	384.06	384.32	− 3.60	+ 16.99	+ 4.6
HK Fltg (HKO)	301.68	301.68	301.68	− 4.69	− 30.32	− 9.1
IW Internet (IIX)	499.94	472.18	488.60	−11.34	− 84.77	− 14.8
AM-Mexico (MXY)	127.35	120.50	121.57	− 5.60	− 7.74	− 6.0
Institut'l -A.M.(XII)	886.67	856.81	868.30	−18.37	− 30.87	− 3.4
Japan (JPN)	...	...	192.79	+ 0.00	− 3.76	− 1.9
MS Cyclical (CYC)	534.88	521.41	523.85	−11.03	− 61.93	− 10.6
MS Consumr (CMR)	517.95	509.38	512.17	− 5.20	− 22.60	− 4.2
MS Hi Tech (MSH)	946.51	890.71	920.71	−25.80	− 0.07	− 0.0
Pharma (DRG)	376.26	369.51	369.65	− 5.81	+ 19.07	+ 5.4
Biotech (BTK)	486.71	460.94	475.10	−11.61	+ 83.66	+ 21.4
Comp Tech (XCI)	1487.64	1412.51	1455.74	−31.90	+ 61.55	+ 4.4
Gold/Silver (XAU)	60.97	58.22	59.80	− 1.22	− 8.17	− 12.0
Utility (UTY)	290.02	287.02	289.20	− 0.60	+ 15.38	+ 5.6
Value Line (VLE)	1063.40	1038.39	1045.40	−18.65	+ 19.60	+ 1.9
Bank (BKX)	788.06	760.88	762.07	−14.78	− 7.88	− 1.0
Semicond (SOX)	1108.75	1027.98	1070.33	−38.42	+365.77	+ 51.9
Street.com (DOT)	883.88	839.20	869.22	− 1.84	−285.23	− 24.7
Oil Service (OSX)	120.47	114.99	115.53	− 5.07	+ 29.57	+ 34.4
PSE Tech (PSE)	1071.86	1007.32	1037.18	−34.68	+ 65.11	+ 6.7

CHICAGO

CB TECHNOLOGY(TXX)

DJ INDUS AVG(DJX)

DJ TRANP AVG(DTX)

GS TECH COMPOSITE(GTC)

NASDAQ-100(NDX)

S & P 100 INDEX(OEX)

RUSSELL 2000(RUT)

S & P 500 INDEX-AM(SPX)

AMERICAN

COMP TECH(XCI)

EURO TOP 100(EUR)

JAPAN INDEX(JPN)

MAJOR MARKET(XMI)

MS CONSUMER(CMR)

MS CYCLICAL(CYC)

MS HITECH 35(MSH)

PHARMACEUTICAL(DRG)

S & P MIDCAP(MID)

PHILADELPHIA

GOLD/SILVER(XAU)

OIL SERVICE(OSX)

PHLX KBW BANK(BKX)

SEMICONDUCTOR(SOX)

STREET.COM(DOT)

UTILITY INDEX(UTY)

LEAPS-LONG TERM

DJ INDUS AVG – CB

S & P 100 INDEX – CB

S & P 500 INDEX – CB

Source: *The Wall Street Journal,* May 4, 2000, C26.

Debt Options

price-based options Rights to purchase or sell a specific debt security.

yield-based options Debt options that are cash-settled based on the difference between the exercise price and the value of an underlying yield.

Two kinds of debt options have been approved for trading. Physical-delivery **price-based options** give holders the right to purchase or sell a specific debt security. Cash-settled price-based options give holders the right to receive a cash payment based on the value of an underlying debt security. **Yield-based options** are debt options that are cash-settled based on the difference between the exercise price and the value of an underlying yield. Although price-based debt options have traded in the past and may be traded in the future, no price-based options are presently traded. Only yield-based options are traded at this time.

To understand debt options, investors must grasp the relationship between the yield-to-maturity and the prices for debt securities. Remember that declining interest rates cause prices of outstanding debt securities to increase. Rising interest rates cause the prices of outstanding debt securities to decline. For example, if a 30-year Treasury bond pays a 7% coupon rate, the only time prior to maturity that investors will pay a price of 100 (or 100% of par value) is when the prevailing yield on such long-term Treasury bonds is exactly 7%. If interest rates move up to 8½%, the price of an outstanding 7% 30-year bond falls to roughly 83⅞ for the bond to yield a competitive 8½%. If rates on such bonds subsequently decline to 6%, the price of a 30-year 7% coupon bond would rise substantially above par to roughly 113¾, at which price it would yield a competitive 6% rate of return.

Price-based call options become more valuable as the prices of underlying debt securities increase. Price-based puts become more valuable as the prices of underlying debt securities decline. This means that as interest rates fall and bond prices rise, price-based call options rise in value. Similarly, as interest rates fall and bond prices rise, price-based put options fall in value. A rise in interest rates causes bond prices to fall, and price-based call options fall in value while price-based put options rise in value.

By contrast, the exercise settlement value of a yield-based option depends on the difference between the value of an underlying yield and the exercise price of the option. Because the underlying yields of yield-based options increase as interest rates rise, yield-based calls become more valuable as interest rates rise. Yield-based puts become more valuable as interest rates decline.

The underlying debt instruments of price-based options and yield-based options are Treasury securities, including short-term Treasury bills, five- and 10-year Treasury notes, and 30-year Treasury bonds. All are direct obligations of the U.S. government. Treasury bills do not pay interest and sell at a discount from par value. The investment return on T-bills consists of the difference between the discounted purchase price and the principal amount payable at maturity. The return on T-bills is commonly expressed as a discount rate that represents an annualized yield-to-maturity based on a 360-day year. T-bills are issued in maturities of 13, 26, or 52 weeks. T-notes are issued for maturities of one to 10 years and are noncallable. T-bonds and notes pay a fixed rate of interest semiannually. T-bonds are issued for maturities of more than 10 years and may be callable prior to maturity.

All yield-based options are European-style options and feature cash settlement. The underlying yield of these options is the annualized yield-to-maturity of the most recently issued Treasury security of a designated term-to-maturity. If the designated debt security is a T-bill, the underlying yield is the annualized discount rate of newly issued Treasury bills. The underlying yield is stated in terms of a yield indicator, which is the annual percentage yield multiplied by 10. For example, if the yield is based on a T-bill having an annualized discount rate of 6.215%, the yield indicator would be 62.15.

The designated maturity of the Treasury security from which the underlying yield is determined is a standardized term of every yield-based option. The underlying yield is derived from the outstanding Treasury security of the designated maturity that has the longest remaining life. Newly auctioned securities having the longest remaining life will replace old issues on the first trading day following their issuance. Therefore, the specific Treasury security from which the underlying yield is derived may change during the life of the yield-based option. Because yield-based options are European-style options, investors ordinarily will know prior to the time of exercise the specific Treasury security from which its exercise settlement value will be determined.

Current bid and asked quotations for recently issued Treasury securities of particular maturities are available from normal market sources. Current yield indicator values based on a sampling of bid and asked quotations from primary dealers are also disseminated at frequent intervals during the trading day by an option reporting source. Exercise settlement values for yield-based options whose underlying yields are derived from Treasury securities are based on the spot yield for the security at a designated time on the last trading day of the option, as announced by the Federal Reserve Bank of New York.

The aggregate cash settlement amount that the assigned writer of a yield-based option is obligated to pay the exercising option holder is the difference between the exercise price of the option and the exercise settlement value multiplied by the multiplier for the option. Different yield-based options may have different multipliers. For example, an exercise price of 63.50 would represent a yield of 6.35%. Each point of premium corresponds to 0.1% of yield. The dollar value of the premium for a single yield-based option equals the quoted premium multiplied by the dollar value of the option multiplier. Thus, a premium of 3½ would equal a premium of \$350 (= \$3½ × 100) for an option having a multiplier of 100, or \$700 (= \$3½ × 200) for an option having a multiplier of 200.

Exercise settlements for yield-based options take place on the business day immediately following the day of exercise. Investors can determine from their brokerage firms when and how settlement amounts will be credited or debited to their brokerage accounts.

dollar-denominated foreign currency options Options to purchase or sell underlying foreign currencies for U.S. dollars.

cross-rate foreign currency options Options to purchase or sell an underlying foreign currency at an exercise price that is denominated in another foreign currency.

Other Specialized Options

Foreign currency options are options to purchase or sell one currency at a price denominated in another currency. The price of one currency in terms of another currency is known as the exchange rate. Therefore, the exercise price of a currency option represents an exchange rate. The trading currency is that in which the premium and exercise price are denominated. The currency to be purchased or sold at the exercise price is the underlying currency.

Dollar-denominated foreign currency options are options to purchase or sell underlying foreign currencies for U.S. dollars. Their exercise prices represent the exchange rates of the underlying foreign currencies and the U.S. dollar. **Cross-rate foreign currency options** are options to purchase or sell an underlying foreign currency at an exercise price that is denominated in another foreign currency. The exercise price of a cross-rate option represents an exchange rate between two foreign currencies. Although most actively traded foreign currency options feature physical delivery, trading has been introduced in cash-settled foreign currency options. In the options market, the term *foreign currency* now includes not only the currencies of individual nations but also the European currency unit (ECU). The ECU, which is composed of specified amounts of various European currencies, is the official medium of exchange of the European Economic Community's European Monetary System and is primarily intended for use in international trade.

For example, assume the exercise price of a cash-settled call option on German marks is 55 (expressed as U.S. cents per mark), the exercise settlement value of the underlying currency is reported as 60, and the unit of trading is 65,000 marks. The cash settlement amount for such an option is \$0.05 (= \$0.60 − \$0.55) multiplied by 65,000, or \$3,250 (= \$0.05 × 65,000). In-the-money cash-settled foreign currency options are automatically exercised on the expiration date.

flex options Flexibly structured options.

Flexibly structured options, or **flex options,** are traded on the U.S. options markets and are issued by the OCC. However, unlike other options, the terms of flex options are not standardized. When a flex option is purchased and sold in an opening transaction, the parties to the transaction have the flexibility, within certain limitations, to fix certain of the option's terms. The terms of a flex option that may be fixed by the parties are called variable terms. The flexibility to fix these variable terms is what makes flex options different from other options. Because many of the terms of flex options are not standardized, it is less likely that there will be an active secondary market.

Flex options may be useful to sophisticated investors seeking to manage particular portfolio and trading risks. However, given large minimum trading sizes and special trading procedures, flex options are generally not suitable for individual investors.

Option Strategies

Call Strategies

Buying call options is a simple and popular option strategy for bullish investors. Buying calls gives the owner the right, but not the obligation, to purchase the underlying stock at a specified strike price for a limited period of time. *The right to buy stock at a fixed price becomes more valuable as the price of the underlying stock increases.* Risk for the call buyer is limited to the call premium, or the amount paid for the call, plus commissions. The call buyer's profit potential is unlimited when the underlying stock price rises above the break-even price. The call buyer's break-even point is reached when the market price of the underlying stock rises during the contract period to a level equal to the strike price plus the premium paid for the call plus commissions.

For example, Figure 17.7A shows the profit or loss earned by a call buyer who is long one strike-price-50 call that was purchased for a call premium of \$2 per share, or \$200 for a single contract covering 100 shares. For simplicity, this example assumes that the call position is maintained until the time of expiration and that commissions are nil. In reality, call buyers often liquidate their positions prior to expiration, and commission charges for options traders can be substantial.

WALL STREET WISDOM 17.2

CEO Stock Options Create Win-Win Situations

Times are good. With business booming, inflationary pressures muted, and the stock market soaring, shareholders and corporate employees have recently experienced the best of times. This is especially true in the case of chief executive officers (CEOs) as the exercise of stock options has led to record-breaking compensation for those skillful enough to find themselves at the top of the corporate ladder.

In a survey of pay practices at 350 large corporations, *The Wall Street Journal* reported that the median salary and bonus earned by top executives during 1999 was $1.6 million, a modest 5.2% rise from prior-year levels. At the same time, the median gain realized by top executives from the exercise of stock options soared to $2.9 million, or 181.3% of base pay. Stock options have long been viewed as an attractive means for giving top executives appropriate incentives to maximize the value of the firm through wise operating and financial decisions. Together with outright share grants, the exercise of executive stock options has resulted in significant share ownership among corporate leaders. At the end of 1999, the median value of stock in their own company owned by the typical CEO rose to $9.9 million.

Among the corporate leaders in total compensation during 1999 were

- L. Dennis Kozlowski, Tyco International, Ltd., with $170 million in total compensation, including a $139.7 million gain from exercising stock options and a restricted-stock grant.
- David S. Pottruck, Charles Schwab Corp., who earned $127.9 million in total compensation, based largely on a $118.9 million gain from option exercises.
- John T. Chambers, Cisco Systems, Inc., took home $121.7 million in total compensation almost exclusively derived from $120.8 million in option gains.
- Stephen M. Case, America Online, Inc., received $117.1 million in total compensation, including $115.5 million from exercising stock options.
- Louis V. Gerstner, Jr., earned $102.2 million in total compensation, boosted by $87.7 million in option gains.

Such eye-popping total compensation for corporate CEOs leaves them open to criticism, but knowledgeable observers of the CEO labor market contend that such pay is fully warranted given the awesome responsibility involved with running a major corporation. Corporate CEOs coordinate the productive effort of tens of thousands of highly skilled employees and are responsible for the productive investment of billions of dollars in corporate resources. A top corporate executive can create literally billions of dollars in additional shareholder value.

To ensure proper motivation for top-flight corporate CEOs, companies have come to rely on performance-based pay plans. At the same time, many boards of directors want to avoid problems involved with measuring corporate performance using accounting data that may be subject to measurement errors, manipulation, or bias. As a result, corporate boards increasingly set incentive pay almost solely on the basis of company stock price performance. The underlying logic is that tying top executive pay to stock price performance gives a direct incentive to maximize the value of the firm.

Critics sometimes argue that corporate pay plans are overly generous and reward top executives for even mediocre performance. Rather than "pay for performance," critics contend that stock option grants should be structured to "pay for outperformance." If salary and bonus compensation fairly rewards top executives for a conventional level of job achievement, stock options should be structured to provide benefits only when stock performance exceeds benchmark norms. At Internet communications infrastructure giant Level 3 Communications, Inc., for example, outperform stock options (OSO) provide a payoff only when company stock price performance exceeds market-wide norms. Truly outstanding performance for Level 3 stock, such as that experienced during 1999, leads to a multiplier effect and outsized gains for CEO James Crowe.

Among others, Level 3 has clearly shown how a properly structured stock options plans can be a "win-win" situation for both CEO and shareholders.

See: Joann Lublin, "Net Envy," *The Wall Street Journal,* April 6, 2000, R1–R3.

FIGURE 17.7 Call Options Are Popular with Bullish Investors

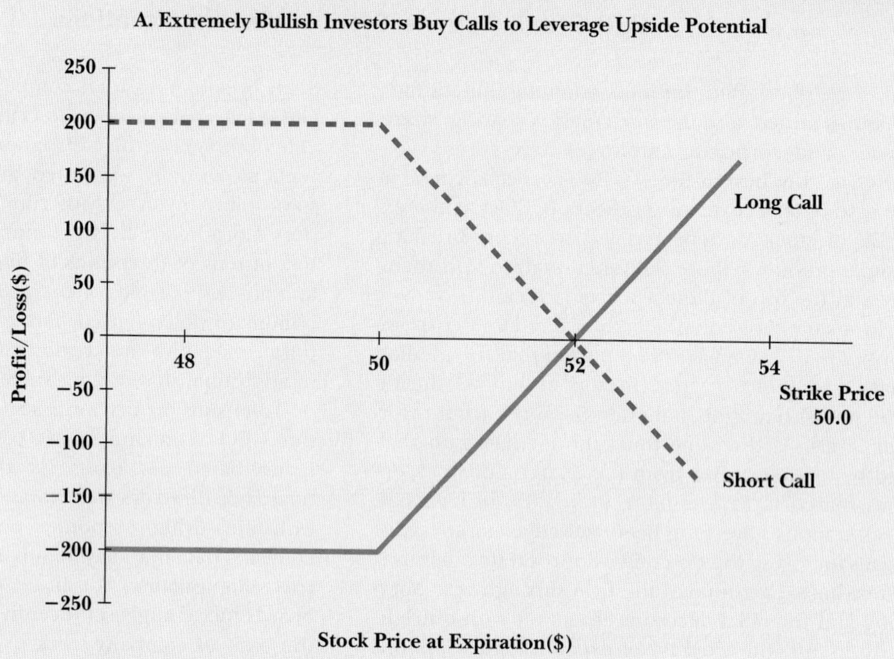

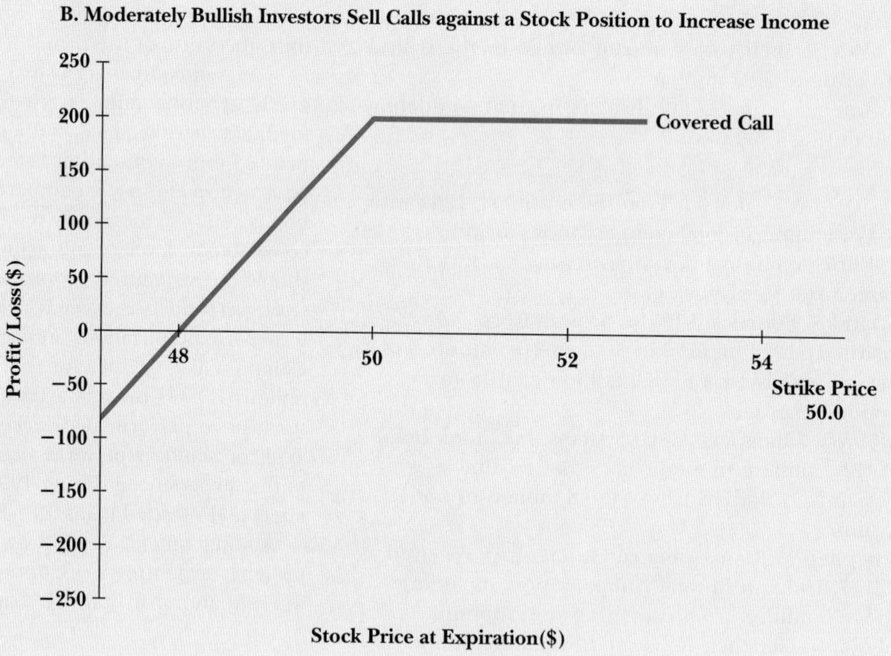

Notice that the call buyer is in a loss position unless the stock price rises to \$52, the strike price of \$50 plus the per-share call premium of \$2. For stock prices greater than \$52, the call buyer's profit per share will rise dollar for dollar with the stock price. If the stock price is less than \$52 at the time of expiration, the call buyer will lose money on the call purchase. However, the amount of the call buyer's loss can be no more than \$2 per share, or \$200 for one call contract. Call buyers have unlimited profit potential with limited loss potential.

Although an investor who expects a quick and sharp rise in the price of a stock might wish to purchase calls, the seller of call options expects to profit from stagnant stock prices. The seller, or writer, of a call option incurs the obligation to sell the underlying stock at a predetermined price if requested by the buyer of the call option, or the call holder. Remember that option transactions are a zero sum game in which the call buyer's profit comes at the expense of the call seller. Similarly, any call seller's profit comes at the expense of the call buyer. As shown in Figure 17.7A, the profit for an investor that sells (or is short) a call option has a payoff pattern that is the mirror image of the payoff pattern for the call buyer. The call seller is in a profit position until the stock price rises to more than \$52, the strike price of \$50 plus the per-share call premium of \$2. For stock prices greater than \$52, the call seller's loss per share will rise dollar for dollar with the stock price. If the stock price is less than \$52 at the time of expiration, the call seller will make money on the call sale. However, the amount of the call seller's profit can be no more than \$2 per share, or \$200 for one call contract. Call sellers have unlimited loss potential with limited profit potential.

Call buying is a popular option strategy because stock prices usually rise, and calls give holders the potential to profit mightily from a steep rise in stock prices. Individual investors also find appealing the fact that calls give the holder the opportunity for large gains with strictly limited losses. However, investors must remember that call buyers profit only when the price of the underlying stock rises far enough and fast enough to exceed the strike price plus the option premium plus commissions prior to the expiration date for the option. Profitable call buying strategies require that the underlying stock price rises faster and by more than the amount expected by savvy call sellers. Call sellers expect to make a profit too, and the amount charged for call premiums has to be large enough to promise call sellers *and* call buyers a profit-making opportunity. Before commissions, the balance of supply and demand suggests that the profit potential for call buyers and call sellers can be no better than a 50-50 proposition. After commissions, which are substantial for option traders, the chance of making a profit from buying or selling calls is less than 50%, especially for small individual investors who bear significant transaction costs.

covered call strategy Simultaneous purchase of a stock and the sale of a call option on that same security.

Figure 17.7B shows the profit potential for a **covered call strategy.** A covered call is the simultaneous purchase of a stock and the sale of a call option on that same security. Generally, one call option is sold for every 100 shares of stock owned. The writer of a covered call receives cash for selling the call but incurs an obligation to sell the stock at the strike price if the call buyer chooses to exercise the option. In other words, the covered call writer receives call premium income in payment for agreeing to sell the underlying stock at the strike price.

naked short seller Uncovered short seller.

Because the covered call writer owns the underlying stock, the investor's option position is hedged against upside volatility in the stock price. Unlike a **naked short seller,** the covered call writer faces limited loss potential from the short call option. Risk is limited for the covered call writer because such an investor can deliver previously purchased shares following an unexpectedly sharp jump in the underlying stock price. This difference between covered and uncovered call writing is important to risk-averse investors. A covered call strategy appeals to investors who are neutral to moderately bullish on a stock or bullish about a given company but wary about the overall market. Covered call writing is a conservative option strategy that is often used by pension and index funds that hold large positions of common stocks. Nevertheless, a disadvantage of the covered call strategy is that it has limited profit potential. High-flying stocks get called away, whereas underperforming or declining stocks get retained by the covered call writer. Moreover, high commissions and other transaction costs can dramatically reduce the call premium income generated.

Put Strategies

Buying put options is a simple and popular option strategy for bearish investors. Buying puts gives the owner the right, but not the obligation, to sell an underlying stock at the specified strike price for a limited period of time. *The right to sell stock at a fixed price becomes more valuable as the price of the underlying stock decreases.* Risk for the put buyer is limited to the put premium, or the amount paid for the put, plus commissions. The put buyer's profit potential is limited only by the fact that the price of the underlying stock can fall no lower than zero. The put buyer's break-even point is reached when the market price of the underlying stock falls during the contract period by an amount more than the strike price plus the premium paid for the put plus commissions.

For example, Figure 17.8A shows the profit or loss earned by a put buyer who is long one strike-price-50 put that was purchased for a put premium of $2 per share, or $200 for a single contract covering 100 shares. For simplicity, this example assumes that the put position is maintained until the time of expiration and that commissions are nil. In reality, put buyers often liquidate their positions prior to expiration, and commission charges for options traders can be substantial.

Notice that the put buyer is in a loss position unless the stock price falls to $48, the strike price of $50 minus the per-share put premium of $2. For stock prices below $48, the put buyer's profit per share will rise dollar for dollar as the underlying stock price falls. If the stock price is greater than $48 at the time of expiration, the put buyer will lose money on the put purchase. However, the amount of the put buyer's loss can be no more than $2 per share, or $200 for one put contract.

Although an investor who expects a quick drop in the price of a stock might wish to purchase puts, the seller of put options expects to profit from stagnant stock prices. The seller, or writer, of a put option incurs the obligation to buy the underlying stock at a predetermined price if requested by the buyer of the put option, or the put holder. As in the case of call options, the put buyer's profit comes at the expense of the put seller. Similarly, any put seller's profit comes at the expense of the put buyer. As shown in Figure 17.8A, the profit for an investor who sells (or is short) a put option has a payoff pattern that is the mirror image of the payoff pattern for the put buyer. The put seller is in a profit position until the stock price drops to less than $48, the strike price of $50 minus the per-share put premium of $2. For stock prices less than $48, the put seller's loss per share will rise dollar for dollar as the underlying share price declines. If the stock price is greater

FIGURE 17.8 **Put Options Are Popular with Bearish Investors**

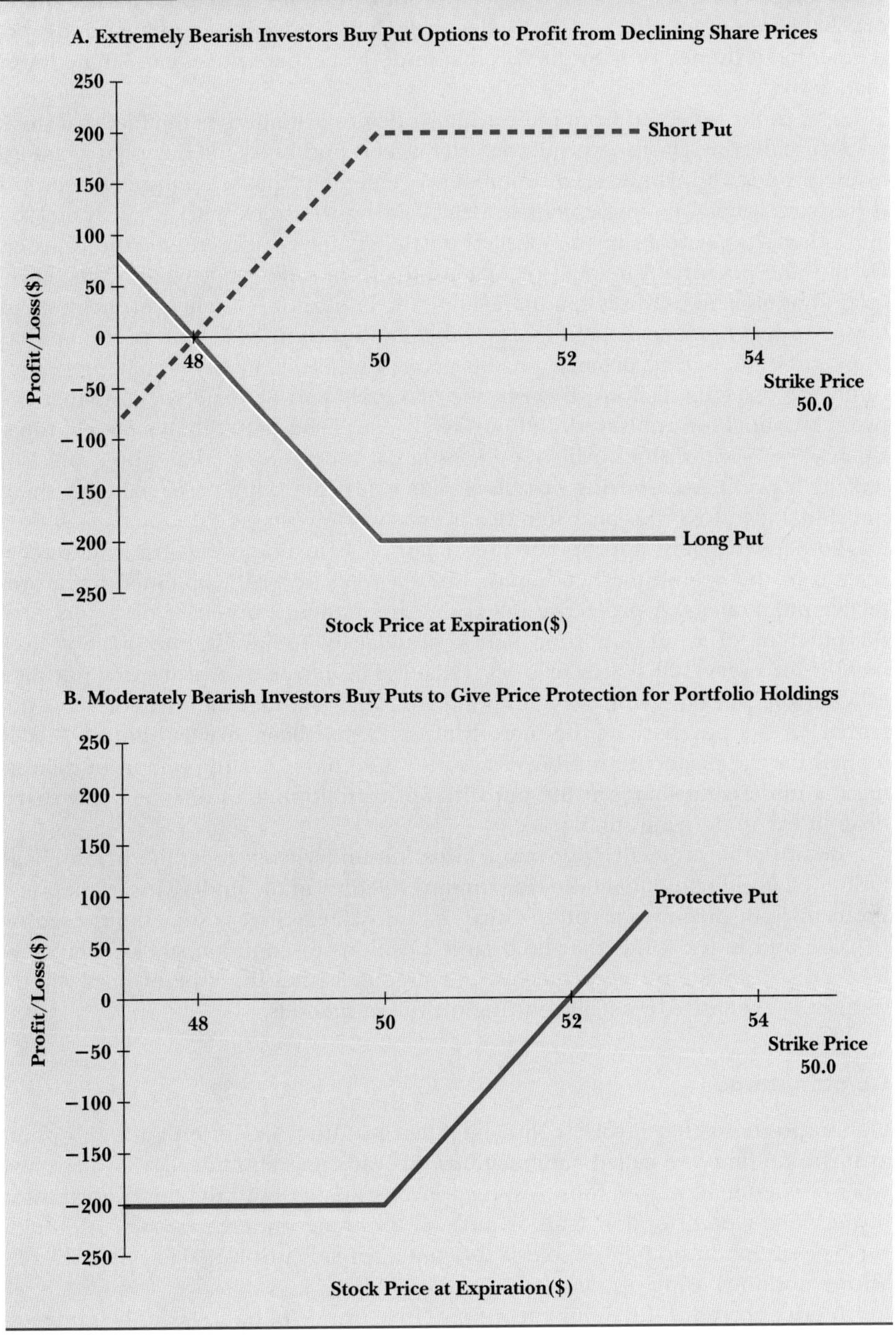

than $48 at the time of expiration, the put seller will make money on the put sale. However, the amount of the put seller's profit can be no more than $2 per share, or $200 for one put contract. Put sellers have limited profit potential and loss potential that is limited only by the fact that underlying share prices can fall no lower than zero.

The profit potential from put buying strategies is limited by the fact that stock prices usually rise. During typically bullish market conditions, put buying is a money-losing proposition. However, investors must remember that selling uncovered puts is far from a risk-free investment strategy. During the stock market crash of 1987 and other sharp breaks in the market, put sellers have suffered enormous losses. Despite the potential for small regular profits from selling uncovered puts, infrequent but enormous losses can undermine the appeal of put selling strategies. Put buyers expect to make a profit too, and the amount charged for put premiums has to be large enough to promise put buyers *and* put sellers a profit-making opportunity. Before commissions, the balance of supply and demand suggests that the profit potential for put buyers and put sellers can be no better than a 50-50 proposition. After commissions, which are substantial for option traders, the chance of making a profit from buying or selling puts is less than 50%, especially for small individual investors who bear significant transaction costs.

protective put strategy Simultaneous purchase of a stock and the purchase of a put option on that same security.

combinations Complementary option positions.

spreads Buying and writing the same type of option (call or put) on the same underlying asset.

straddles Buying a put and call on the same security.

price spread Simultaneous purchase or sale of options on the same underlying stock but with different exercise prices.

time spread Simultaneous purchase or sale of options on the same underlying stock but with different expiration dates.

Perhaps the most appropriate use of puts is as insurance against a sharp correction in the overall market. Figure 17.8B shows the profit potential for a **protective put strategy.** A protective put is the simultaneous purchase of a stock and the purchase of a put option on that same security. Generally, one put option is bought for every 100 shares of stock owned. The buyer of a protective put pays cash for the put but gains peace of mind from the fact that the investor's loss potential on the purchase of the underlying stock has been strictly limited. Risk is limited for the protective put buyer because the holder has the option of delivering the underlying shares at the put strike price following an unexpectedly sharp drop in the underlying stock price.

Because the protective put buyer owns the underlying stock, the investor has unlimited upside potential following upward volatility in the underlying stock price. Protective put buying is a conservative option strategy that is sometimes used by pension and index funds that hold large positions of common stocks. Nevertheless, a disadvantage of the protective put strategy is that this type of portfolio insurance is expensive, especially during turbulent markets.

Combinations

Option positions that involve complementary positions in more than one option at the same time are called **combinations. Spreads** and **straddles** are two specific types of combination positions. A spread involves being both the buyer and writer of the same type of option (call or put) on the same underlying asset. Although the type of option bought or sold is the same, spreads involve taking partially offsetting positions using options.

A **price spread** is the simultaneous purchase or sale of options on the same underlying stock but with different exercise prices. A **time spread** is the simultaneous purchase or sale of options on the same underlying stock but with different expiration dates. Spreads can be used to take a bullish or bearish position with respect to a given security and can incorporate strategies that are complex.

Two popular price-spread strategies are **bull call spreads** and **bull put spreads.** These are considered conservative option strategies because the investor's risk exposure is known and limited. They are most appropriate when the investor's outlook is mildly bullish. A bull call spread is the purchase of a low-strike-price call and the simultaneous sale of another high-strike-price call on the same underlying equity with the same expiration date. A bull call spread is always established as a debit spread. This means that the net effect of the bull call spread transaction is a debit to the customer's account because the amount paid for low-strike-price calls is more than the amount received from the short sale of similar high-strike-price calls. The margin requirement is the amount paid for the bull call spread because that is the defined and limited risk of the spread.

bull call spread Purchase of a low-strike-price call and the simultaneous sale of another high-strike-price call on the same underlying equity with the same expiration date.

A bull put spread is the sale of a high-strike-price put and the simultaneous purchase of another low-strike-price put on the same underlying equity with the same expiration date. A bull put spread is always established as a credit spread. This means that the net effect of the bull put spread transaction is a credit to the customer's account because the amount received from the short sale of high-strike-price puts is more than the amount paid for similar low-strike-price puts. The margin requirement for a bull put spread is the amount by which high-strike-price put sold short exceeds the low-strike-price put purchased, minus the net premium proceeds received on the combined transaction.

bull put spread Sale of a high-strike-price put and the simultaneous purchase of another low-strike-price put on the same underlying equity with the same expiration date.

A straddle consists of both purchasing a call and buying a put on the same underlying asset by using options that have the same exercise price and expiration date. Straddles are used by speculators who anticipate an uptick in volatility but are not clear whether the price move in the underlying stock price will be up or down. For example, suppose a company is about to announce whether it has discovered oil following the completion of a massive drilling program. If oil is discovered, the company's stock can be expected to soar. If no oil is found, the company's stock can be expected to plummet. The purchase of a straddle position might result in a profit in such a case.

Option Pricing

Pricing Concepts

Several factors contribute value to an option contract and thereby influence the option premium or price at which it is traded. Among the most important of these factors are the price of the underlying stock, time remaining until expiration, volatility of the underlying stock price, cash dividends, and prevailing interest rate.

The value of a stock option depends heavily on the price of the underlying stock. In an efficient stock market, near-term changes in stock prices are random and unpredictable. Thus, if a stock last traded at 50 per share, in the absence of new information, it is impossible to know if it will next trade at $50\frac{1}{8}$ or $49\frac{7}{8}$. However, the level of a stock price is not random and reflects the discounted net present value of all future profits. If the last trade was 50, in the absence of new information, an investor can be certain that the next trade price will be in the neighborhood of 50 per share. In the absence of new information, the stock is not apt to trade in the neighborhood of, say, 25 or 75 per share. It is fair to expect that a stock presently trading in the neighborhood of 50 per share is much more likely to trade at 50 per share in the near future than is another stock that presently trades for 25 or 75 per share.

As mentioned previously, if the price of a stock is greater than a call option's strike price, the call option is said to be in-the-money. Likewise, if the stock price is below a put option's strike price, the put option is in-the-money. The difference between an in-the-money option's strike price and the current market price of the underlying security is referred to as the option's **intrinsic value.** Intrinsic value is zero for at-the-money and out-of-the-money options. At the point of expiration, the expiration value of an option equals its intrinsic value. Only in-the-money options have intrinsic value.

intrinsic value Difference between an in-the-money option's strike price and the current market price of the underlying security.

For example, if a call option's strike price is $50 and the underlying shares are trading at $65, the option has intrinsic value of $15 because a holder of that option could exercise the option and buy the shares at $50. The buyer could then immediately sell those shares on the stock market for $65, yielding a profit of $15 per share, or $1,500 per option contract. When an underlying share price is equal to the strike price of $50, the option is at-the-money. An option that is neither in-the-money nor at-the-money is said to be out-of-the-money. Call options with a strike price of $50 are out-of-the-money whenever the current market price of the underlying common stock is less than $50. Put options with a strike price of $50 are out-of-the-money whenever the current market price of the underlying common stock is more than $50. An option expires worthlessly if it is at-the-money or out-of-the-money at the time of expiration.

Prior to expiration, all options are valuable. The fact that at-the-money or out-of-the-money options have no intrinsic value at the present point in time does not mean they are worthless. Unexpired at-the-money and out-of-the-money call and put options are valuable because they *might* someday have intrinsic value. For example, suppose someone offered you a call option on the DJIA with a strike price of 20,000. Given a sufficiently long contract period, say, 10 years or more, the DJIA might indeed rise above 20,000, and such a call option would then have intrinsic value. Despite the lack of intrinsic value, all unexpired options have **time value,** or speculative value, because they might someday have intrinsic value.

time value Speculative value.

Factors that increase the probability of a favorable exercise in the option at some future point in time give rise to the time value of the option. Primary components of time value include the length of time remaining until expiration (the contract period), volatility in the underlying stock price, the amount of cash dividends paid (if any), and prevailing interest rates. In numeric terms, time value is the amount by which the option premium exceeds the option's intrinsic value.

$$\begin{matrix}\text{Call price} \\ \text{(option premium)}\end{matrix} = \begin{matrix}\text{Intrinsic} \\ \text{value}\end{matrix} + \begin{matrix}\text{Time} \\ \text{value}\end{matrix} \qquad \textbf{(17.1)}$$

For in-the-money options, time value is the excess portion of the option premium over its intrinsic value. For at-the-money and out-of-the-money options, time value is the total value of the option premium.

Generally speaking, the longer the time period remaining until an option's expiration date, the higher the option premium because of the greater possibility that the underlying share price might move so as to make the option in-the-money. Time value drops rapidly in the last several weeks of an option's life and reaches zero at the point of expiration.

To illustrate, Figure 17.9 shows a near-the-money option series for retail goliath Wal-Mart on May 4, 2000, or 16 days prior to the expiration of May 2000 call and put options on May 19, 2000. These data from the CBOE Web site show option bid, ask, and related information, including multiple quotes from the various options markets trading Wal-Mart options. Holding all else equal, notice that call option prices fall with an increase in the exercise or strike price. This stems from the fact that the value of a call option's right to buy diminishes as that purchase price rises. For example, Wal-Mart's May55 call option has bid and ask prices of $^{15}/_{16}$ to $1\,^{1}/_{16}$, respectively. At the same time, Wal-Mart's May60 call option has bid and ask prices of $^{3}/_{16}$ to $^{5}/_{16}$, respectively. When Wal-Mart is trading at a market price of $51\,^{3}/_{8}$, the chance of a favorable exercise of a call option that allows the option buyer to purchase the stock at 55 is much greater than the probability of making a profit only if the stock price exceeds 60.

Conversely, put option prices rise with an increase in the strike price. This results from the fact that the value of a put option's right to sell increases as that sale price rises. For example, Wal-Mart's May55 put option has bid and ask prices of $4\,^{3}/_{8}$ to $4\,^{3}/_{4}$, respectively. At the same time, Wal-Mart's May60 put option has bid and ask prices of $8\,^{5}/_{8}$ to 9, respectively. When Wal-Mart is trading at a market price of $51\,^{3}/_{8}$, the chance of a favorable exercise of a put option that allows the option buyer to sell the stock at 60 is much greater than the probability of making a profit only if the stock price falls to less than 55.

Also note from Figure 17.9 that the value of call and put options for a given strike price tend to rise with a lengthening of the expiration period. In the case of both calls and puts, option values rise for a given exercise price as the option period lengthens because of a resulting increase in the probability of a favorable exercise. Options that expire out-of-the-money are worthless, and the shorter the expiration period, the greater is the likelihood that any given out-of-the-money option

FIGURE 17.9 **Option Premiums Are Composed of Intrinsic Value plus Time Value**

WMT (NYSE) **51 3/8**

May 04,2000 @ 11:56 ET (Data 20 Minutes Delayed) **Bid** N/A **Ask** N/A **Size** N/AxN/A **Vol** 10695200

Calls	Last Sale	Net	Bid	Ask	Vol	Open Int	Puts	Last Sale	Net	Bid	Ask	Vol	Open Int
00 May 45 (WMT EI-E)	7 3/8	-1 5/8	6 1/2	6 7/8	4	107	00 May 45 (WMT QI-E)	7/16	+1/8	7/16	1/2	13	1075
00 May 47 1/2 (WMT EW-E)	5 1/4	-5 3/4	4 1/2	4 7/8	23	20	00 May 47 1/2 (WMT QW-E)	7/8	+1/2	3/4	15/16	63	921
00 May 50 (WMT EJ-E)	3 1/8	-1 3/4	2 3/4	3 1/8	314	982	00 May 50 (WMT QJ-E)	1 5/8	+5/8	1 1/2	1 5/8	344	2609
00 May 55 (WMT EK-E)	1	-3/4	15/16	1 1/16	929	2425	00 May 55 (WMT QK-E)	4 5/8	+1 7/8	4 3/8	4 3/4	334	3752
00 May 60 (WMT EL-E)	1/4	-3/16	3/16	5/16	204	11406	00 May 60 (WMT QL-E)	9	+2 1/2	8 5/8	9	15	2170
00 Jun 45 (WMT FI-E)	7 1/2	-1 3/4	7 1/2	7 3/4	40	1224	00 Jun 45 (WMT RI-E)	1 1/8	+1/4	1 1/8	1 1/4	321	2818
00 Jun 47 1/2 (WMT FW-E)	5 5/8	-6 1/8	5 3/4	6 1/8	4	405	00 Jun 47 1/2 (WMT RW-E)	1 7/8	+11/16	1 3/4	1 15/16	163	2783
00 Jun 50 (WMT FJ-E)	4 1/2	-1 1/4	4 1/4	4 5/8	233	2009	00 Jun 50 (WMT RJ-E)	2 3/4	+9/16	2 5/8	3	325	2489
00 Jun 55 (WMT FK-E)	2 3/8	-1 1/8	2 1/4	2 1/2	306	2339	00 Jun 55 (WMT RK-E)	5 5/8	+1 1/8	5 1/2	5 7/8	89	2263
00 Jun 60 (WMT FL-E)	1 1/8	-9/16	1 1/16	1 1/8	205	9075	00 Jun 60 (WMT RL-E)	9 3/4	+2	9 1/4	9 5/8	20	6424

will expire worthless. Figure 17.10 shows how the value of a call option is comprised of time value and intrinsic value. Out-of-the-money and at-the-money call options have no intrinsic value. Their entire value is comprised of time value. In-the-money call options have both time value and intrinsic value. As the stock price rises above the exercise price, intrinsic value rises to constitute the bulk of the value of the call. Similar relationships hold for put options.

The intrinsic value and time value components of option value become clear when May Wal-Mart options are considered. The May50 call options have a bid price of 2¾ and an ask price of 3⅛. With the stock at 51⅜ (or $51.38), the intrinsic value of May50 calls is 1⅜ (or $1.38 = $51.38 − $50). The remainder of this call option's value is time value. The entire premium paid for out-of-the-money May55 and May60 calls, and any higher strike-price calls, is time value and speculative in nature. Similarly, the premium paid for out-of-the money May50 and May45 puts, along with any lower strike-price puts, is time value. Out-of-the-money and at-the-money options have zero intrinsic value.

The probability of a favorable exercise also increases with heightened price volatility in the underlying security. Price volatility is the propensity of the underlying security's market price to fluctuate either up or down. The higher the volatility of the underlying stock, the higher the time value and option premium because of the better possibility that the option will sometime move in-the-money.

Regular cash dividends are paid to the stock owner and are never received by option holders. When cash dividends are high, a substantial portion of the total return earned by shareholders comes in the form of dividend income rather than capital appreciation. Thus, high dividend income is typically associated with stocks that display relatively muted rates of capital appreciation over time. In the short

FIGURE 17.10 **Call Prices Converge toward Intrinsic Value as Option Expiration Draws Near**

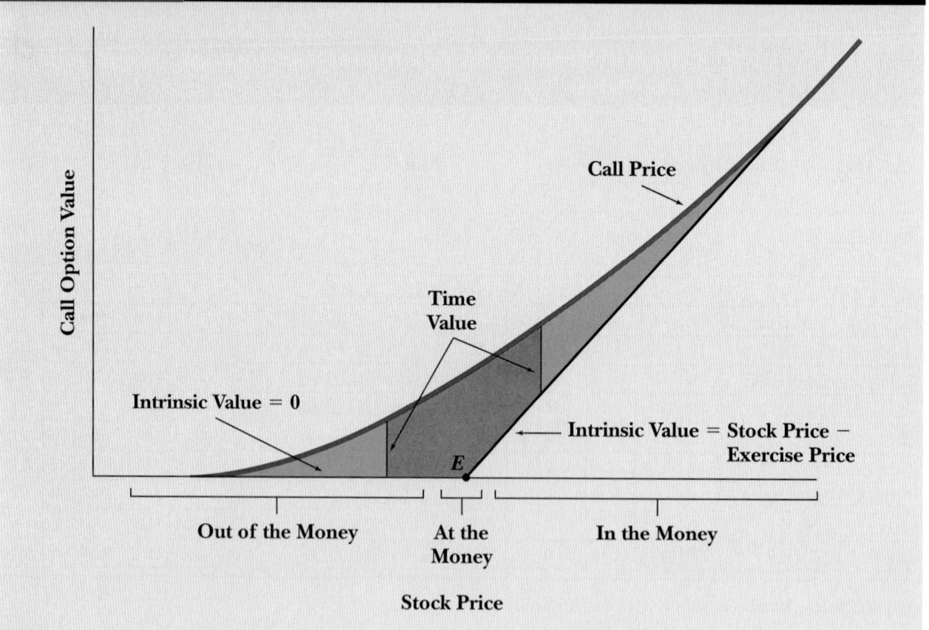

run, cash dividends affect option premiums because stock prices typically fall by the amount of the cash dividend in the period surrounding the exdividend date. Therefore, higher cash dividends typically imply lower call option premiums and higher premiums for put options.

Finally, higher interest rates tend to result in higher call premiums and lower put premiums. Lower interest rates tend to result in lower call premiums and higher put premiums. The reason why is easy to explain. Buying calls can be viewed as a substitute for buying the underlying common stock. When interest rates rise, investors might be tempted to use a portion of their funds to buy calls and invest the remainder in interest-bearing instruments. As interest rates rise, the amount of interest income rises, and the appeal of buying calls rises. This puts upward pressure on call premiums. Conversely, when interest rates fall, interest income falls, and the value of calls tends to decrease. In the case of puts, premiums and interest rates tend to move in the opposite direction. A rise in interest rates causes put prices to fall, and a fall in interest rates causes put prices to rise.

Black-Scholes Option Pricing Model

In related work conducted during the early 1970s, financial economists Fisher Black, Myron Scholes, and Robert Merton developed an option valuation model that is often simply referred to as the **Black-Scholes option pricing model.** The Black-Scholes model includes a formula that is now widely used to calculate economic values for options. Assuming the ability to continuously and instantaneously rebalance portfolios, no transaction costs, and a risk-free asset, the value of a call option is

Black-Scholes option pricing model
Formula used to calculate economic values for options.

$$\text{Call price} = \text{Value of upside potential} - \text{Opportunity cost of invested funds} \tag{17.2}$$

$$CP = CMP\,[N(d_1)] - \frac{EP}{e^{rt}}\,[N(d_2)]$$

where CP is the current price of a call option, CMP is the current market price of the underlying common stock (equity), EP is the exercise price (strike price) for the call option, e is the natural base $e \approx 2.718$, r is the risk-free rate, and t is the time remaining before expiration (in years). $N(d_1)$ and $N(d_2)$ are the cumulative density functions for d_1 and d_2 as defined below:

$$d_1 = \left[\frac{\ln(CMP/EP) + (r + 0.5\sigma^2)t}{\sigma\sqrt{t}}\right] \tag{17.3}$$

$$d_2 = d_1 - \sigma\sqrt{t} \tag{17.4}$$

In these equations, $\ln(CMP/EP)$ is the natural log of (CMP/EP), and σ is the standard deviation of the underlying common stock's annual return. In other words, $N(d)$ is the probability that a random draw from a standard normal distribution will be less than d. This equals the area under the normal curve up to d, as shown by the shaded region of Figure 17.11 and as enumerated in Table 17.3.

Valuing call options by using the Black-Scholes option valuation formula is quick and easy using a simple hand-held calculator. Only five bits of information are required to determine the price of a call, including the current market price of the underlying equity (CMP), exercise price (EP), risk-free rate (r), time to maturity (t),

FIGURE 17.11 **Standard Normal Curve**

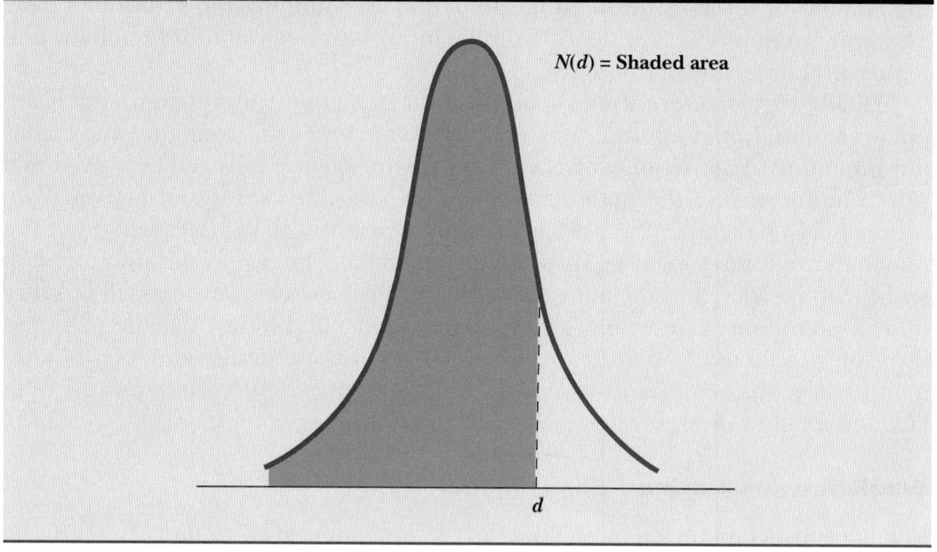

and volatility as captured by the standard deviation of annual returns on the underlying stock (σ). Notice from Equation 17.2 that call prices rise with the stock price, risk-free rate, time-to-maturity, and standard deviation of returns; they fall with a rise in the exercise price.

To illustrate, assume that $CMP = 50$, $EP = 55$, $r = 0.0625$ (or 6.25%), $t = 0.5$ years (or six months), and $\sigma = 0.4$ (or 40%). To solve for d_1, note that

$$d_1 = \left[\frac{\ln(50/55) + [0.0625 + 0.5(0.4^2)](0.5)}{0.4\sqrt{0.5}}\right]$$
$$= \frac{-0.0953 + 0.0713}{0.2828}$$
$$= -0.0851$$

When $d_1 = -0.0851$, $N(d_1) = 0.4661$ from the cumulative probability distribution in Table 17.3. Then, to solve for d_2, note that

$$d_2 = -0.0851 - 0.4\sqrt{0.5}$$
$$= -0.3679$$

When $d_2 = -0.3679$, $N(d_2) = 0.3564$ from the cumulative probability distribution in Table 17.3. Then, the value of this six-month out-of-the-money call can be calculated by using Equation 17.2 as

$$\text{Call price} = CMP\,[N(d_1)] - \frac{EP}{e^{rt}}[N(d_2)]$$
$$= 50[0.4661] - \frac{55}{e^{(0.0625)(0.5)}}[0.3564]$$
$$= \$4.30$$

TABLE 17.3 **Standard Normal Distribution**

d	*N*(*d*)	*d*	*N*(*d*)	*d*	*N*(*d*)
−3.00	0.00013	−1.58	0.0571	−0.76	0.2236
−2.95	0.00016	−1.56	0.0594	−0.74	0.2297
−2.90	0.00019	−1.54	0.0618	−0.72	0.2358
−2.85	0.00022	−1.52	0.0643	−0.70	0.2420
−2.80	0.00026	−1.50	0.0668	−0.68	0.2483
−2.75	0.00030	−1.48	0.0694	−0.66	0.2546
−2.70	0.00035	−1.46	0.0721	−0.64	0.2611
−2.65	0.00040	−1.44	0.0749	−0.62	0.2676
−2.60	0.00047	−1.42	0.0778	−0.60	0.2743
−2.55	0.00054	−1.40	0.0808	−0.58	0.2810
−2.50	0.00062	−1.38	0.0838	−0.56	0.2877
−2.45	0.00071	−1.36	0.0869	−0.54	0.2946
−2.40	0.00082	−1.34	0.0901	−0.52	0.3015
−2.35	0.00094	−1.32	0.0934	−0.50	0.3085
−2.30	0.00107	−1.30	0.0968	−0.48	0.3156
−2.25	0.00122	−1.28	0.1003	−0.46	0.3228
−2.20	0.00139	−1.26	0.1038	−0.44	0.3300
−2.15	0.00158	−1.24	0.1075	−0.42	0.3373
−2.10	0.00179	−1.22	0.1112	−0.40	0.3446
−2.05	0.00202	−1.20	0.1151	−0.38	0.3520
−2.00	0.00228	−1.18	0.1190	−0.36	0.3594
−1.98	0.00239	−1.16	0.1230	−0.34	0.3669
−1.96	0.00250	−1.14	0.1271	−0.32	0.3745
−1.94	0.00262	−1.12	0.1314	−0.30	0.3821
−1.92	0.00274	−1.10	0.1357	−0.28	0.3897
−1.90	0.00287	−1.08	0.1401	−0.26	0.3974
−1.88	0.00301	−1.06	0.1446	−0.24	0.4052
−1.86	0.00314	−1.04	0.1492	−0.22	0.4129
−1.84	0.00329	−1.02	0.1539	−0.20	0.4207
−1.82	0.00344	−1.00	0.1587	−0.18	0.4286
−1.80	0.00359	−0.98	0.1635	−0.16	0.4365
−1.78	0.00375	−0.96	0.1685	−0.14	0.4443
−1.76	0.00392	−0.94	0.1736	−0.12	0.4523
−1.74	0.00409	−0.92	0.1788	−0.10	0.4602
−1.72	0.00427	−0.90	0.1841	−0.08	0.4681
−1.70	0.00446	−0.88	0.1894	−0.06	0.4761
−1.68	0.00465	−0.86	0.1949	−0.04	0.4841
−1.66	0.00485	−0.84	0.2005	−0.02	0.4920
−1.64	0.00505	−0.82	0.2061	0.00	0.5000
−1.62	0.00526	−0.80	0.2119	0.02	0.5080
−1.60	0.00548	−0.78	0.2177	0.04	0.5160
0.06	0.5239	0.86	0.8051	1.66	0.9515
0.08	0.5319	0.88	0.8106	1.68	0.9535
0.10	0.5398	0.90	0.8159	1.70	0.9554
0.12	0.5478	0.92	0.8212	1.72	0.9573
0.14	0.5557	0.94	0.8264	1.74	0.9591
0.16	0.5636	0.96	0.8315	1.76	0.9608
0.18	0.5714	0.98	0.8365	1.78	0.9625
0.20	0.5793	1.00	0.8414	1.80	0.9641
0.22	0.5871	1.02	0.8461	1.82	0.9656
0.24	0.5948	1.04	0.8508	1.84	0.9671
0.26	0.6026	1.06	0.8554	1.86	0.9686
0.28	0.6103	1.08	0.8599	1.88	0.9699
0.30	0.6179	1.10	0.8643	1.90	0.9713
0.32	0.6255	1.12	0.8686	1.92	0.9726
0.34	0.6331	1.14	0.8729	1.94	0.9738
0.36	0.6406	1.16	0.8770	1.96	0.9750
0.38	0.6480	1.18	0.8810	1.98	0.9761
0.40	0.6554	1.20	0.8849	2.00	0.9772

(continued)

TABLE 17.3 ***(continued)***

d	*N*(*d*)	*d*	*N*(*d*)	*d*	*N*(*d*)
0.42	0.6628	1.22	0.8888	2.05	0.9798
0.44	0.6700	1.24	0.8925	2.10	0.9821
0.46	0.6773	1.26	0.8962	2.15	0.9842
0.48	0.6844	1.28	0.8997	2.20	0.9861
0.50	0.6915	1.30	0.9032	2.25	0.9878
0.52	0.6985	1.32	0.9066	2.30	0.9893
0.54	0.7054	1.34	0.9099	2.35	0.9906
0.56	0.7123	1.36	0.9131	2.40	0.9918
0.58	0.7191	1.38	0.9162	2.45	0.9929
0.60	0.7258	1.40	0.9192	2.50	0.9938
0.62	0.7324	1.42	0.9222	2.55	0.9946
0.64	0.7389	1.44	0.9251	2.60	0.9953
0.66	0.7454	1.46	0.9279	2.65	0.9960
0.68	0.7518	1.48	0.9306	2.70	0.9965
0.70	0.7580	1.50	0.9332	2.75	0.9970
0.72	0.7642	1.52	0.9357	2.80	0.9974
0.74	0.7704	1.54	0.9382	2.85	0.9978
0.76	0.7764	1.56	0.9406	2.90	0.9981
0.78	0.7823	1.58	0.9429	2.95	0.9984
0.80	0.7882	1.60	0.9452	3.00	0.9986
0.82	0.7939	1.62	0.9474		
0.84	0.7996	1.64	0.9495		

Thus, the theoretical value of this six-month out-of-the-money call option, according to the Black-Scholes formula, is approximately $4.30. If the current market price of the call option is greater than this theoretical value, the call is overpriced and should not be bought. If the current market price of the call is less than this theoretical value, the call represents a bargain and should be purchased. Of course, this presumes that the underlying assumptions of the model are correct, and the specific assumptions made concerning this call option are accurate.

In practice, it is easy to estimate only some of the information required by the Black-Scholes model. It is relatively easy to estimate the current market price of the underlying equity, exercise price, risk-free rate on T-bills, and the length of time until the option matures. It is impossible to know beforehand the future volatility of the underlying equity, σ. Historical volatility is often a useful guide to future volatility, but changes in volatility occur, especially during turbulent markets. This makes use of the Black-Scholes model difficult. If the current call price is known, then the Black-Scholes model can be used to calculate the level of volatility implicit in this price. Based on the current call price, if the call buyer regards the assumed level of volatility as too high, then the call is overpriced and should be avoided. If the call buyer regards the assumed level of volatility as too low, then the call option is underpriced and should be bought.

Therefore, the Black-Scholes model can be used to estimate the value of a call option, assuming a value for future volatility. Alternatively, the level of assumed future volatility can be calculated for a given option price. However, the usefulness of the Black-Scholes model is limited by the fact that the model cannot be used to tell whether any given assumption regarding future volatility is or is not appropriate.

Finally, the Black-Scholes model can be used to give insight concerning put option prices because of a concept called **put-call parity.** The put-call parity concept expresses the relationship that must hold between the price of a put option and the price of a call option on the same underlying equity. Unless the price of the put and the price of a call bear a certain relationship to each other, options players will have the opportunity to earn riskless arbitrage profits.

put-call parity Relationship that must hold between the price of puts and calls on the same underlying equity.

The put-call parity relationship is

$$\text{Put price} = \frac{EP}{e^{rt}} - CMP + CP \qquad \textbf{(17.5)}$$

where all terms are the same as in Equation 17.2.

For example, using the same numerical values as in the call valuation example above, the theoretical put option price of \$7.61 is consistent with a call option price of \$4.30.

$$\begin{aligned}\text{Put price} &= \frac{EP}{e^{rt}} - CMP + CP \\ &= \frac{55}{e^{(0.0625)(0.5)}} - 50 + 4.30 \\ &= \$7.61\end{aligned}$$

CBOE Option Calculator

In practice, it can become tedious to go through the steps outlined above to value a large number of individual call and put options by using the Black-Scholes formula. In fast-changing markets, it becomes impossible. Thankfully, there is an easy solution. The CBOE offers an option calculator on its Web site, <http://www.cboe.com>, that gives easy access to index and equity option valuations by using the Black-Scholes Option Pricing Model. The CBOE option calculator allows investors to test and understand the dynamic relationships among the value of an option and the factors that affect that value. Once an investor has input all the factors of the option valuation model, the option calculator provides theoretical values for the call and put options. In addition, given a specific call or put price, the option calculator allows investors to use the model to derive an option's implied volatility.

Figure 17.12 shows how the option calculator can be used to value index options. Most index options are European style. However, the most actively traded index option, the OEX, is American style. To calculate the value of a call option on the OEX, each of the factors required by the valuation model must be entered, including the index price, strike price, dividend information, volatility, interest rate, and days to expiration.

The price level for an underlying index or stock can be obtained from either a newspaper (for closing prices) or a variety of quote services on the Internet. The appropriate strike price for a given call or put option can be obtained from the CBOE's Web site. Dividend yields for index options can be easily obtained from financial publications such as the Monday edition of *The Wall Street Journal* or *Barron's*. For stock option evaluation, the quarterly dividend amount should be entered along with the next dividend date in the mm/dd/yy format. Most investors use T-bill rates as a good

FIGURE 17.12 **CBOE Option Calculator Can Be Used to Value Index Options, such as Puts and Calls on the Standard & Poor's 100 (OEX)**

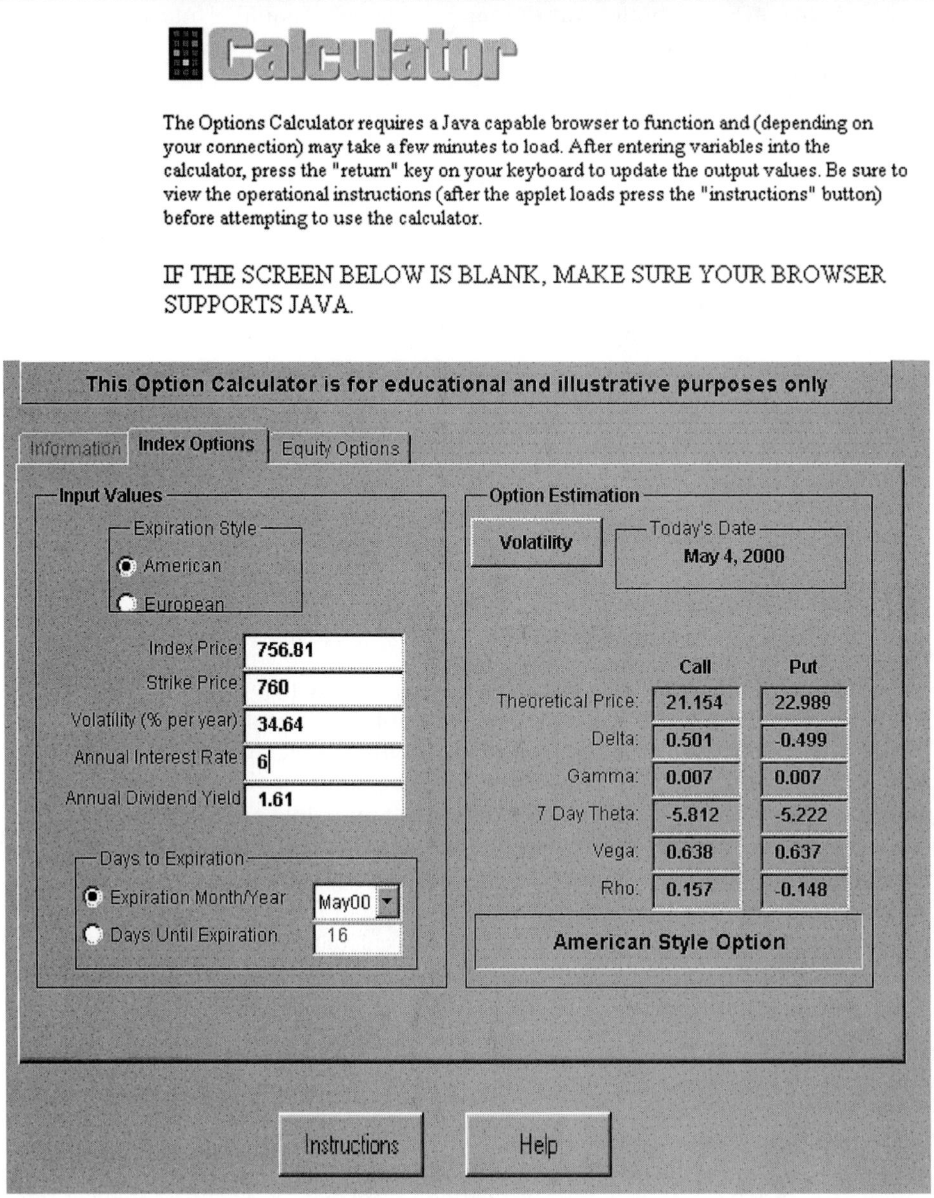

Source: <http://www.cboe.com>.

proxy for the current risk-free interest rate. For a one-month option, use a 30-day rate; for a three-month option, use a 90-day rate, and so on. In calculating the number of days remaining until the option's expiration day, it is important to include all calendar days (seven days to the week, including holidays), not just business days.

Volatility (in percent) must be estimated for the underlying index or common equity. To value at-the-money OEX options, one can use the CBOE's Volatility Index (ticker symbol VIX), which is a rough estimate of the current implied volatility of a hypothetical at-the-money OEX call with 30 calendar days to expiration. Alternatively, one may use an estimate. Remember, it is the implied volatility, or the volatility expected by the marketplace, for the lifetime of the option that is reflected in the option's trading price. If a given call or put price is assumed, the option calculator can be used to derive an estimate of implied volatility. In practice, it is worth emphasizing that volatility estimates greatly affect the calculation of an option's theoretical value. The implied volatility of options on a given underlying index also tend to vary for each expiration and strike price and for calls versus puts. Professional option traders spend a great deal of time and resources in the effort to develop better volatility estimates. In the final analysis, however, this number is very subjective.

In Figure 17.12, the theoretical value of $21.154 is calculated for May strike price 760 OEX call options (symbol OEZEL) as of May 4, 2000. At that time, the underlying index was selling at $756.81, and there were 16 days left until expiration. At this call price, the implied volatility on the index is 34.64% per year. At this same time, and assuming the same level of volatility, the theoretical value is $22.989 for May strike price 760 OEX put options (symbol OEZQL). It is interesting to note that on the trading day in question, the closing bid-ask spread was $20.13 to $22.13 on the calls and $18.63 to $20.13 on the puts. This means that the closing prices on these OEX call options were in line with the theoretical predictions of the Black-Scholes Option Pricing Formula but that the puts were somewhat cheaper than expected. After several down-days, put option players were clearly betting on a rebound in the overall market.

In Figure 17.13, the theoretical value of $1 is calculated for May55 call options on Wal-Mart (symbol WMTEK) when the underlying stock closed at $51.375 and there were 16 days left until expiration. At this call price, the implied volatility on Wal-Mart is 52.53% per year. At this same time, and assuming the same level of volatility, the theoretical value is $4.504 for May55 put options on Wal-Mart (symbol WMTQK). As shown in Figure 17.9, on the trading day in question, the closing bid-ask spread was $^{15}/_{16}$ to $1\,^{1}/_{16}$ on the calls, and $4\,^{3}/_{8}$ to $4\,^{3}/_{4}$ on the puts. This means that the closing prices on these Wal-Mart options were in line with the theoretical predictions of the Black-Scholes option pricing formula.

Option Risks

Option Risk Concepts

The sensitivity of option value to a unit change in the underlying asset's price is called the option's **delta.** Delta indicates a percentage change. For example, in the example of Wal-Mart call options shown in Figure 17.13, a delta of 0.294 indicates that the option's theoretical value will change by 29.4% of the change in the price of the underlying asset, which is Wal-Mart common stock. Be aware, however, that delta is a dynamic concept and its value changes as the price of the underlying asset changes. Therefore, option values can change more or less than the amount indicated by delta. In the options markets, delta is commonly referred to as the **hedge ratio.** In the case of Wal-Mart, a delta of 0.294 means that a $1 increase in

delta
Change in option price following a $1 change in price for the underlying asset (also hedge ratio).

hedge ratio
Shares of stock required to offset the price risk of one option.

FIGURE 17.13 **CBOE Option Calculator Can Be Used to Value Equity Options, such as Calls and Puts on Wal-Mart (here, WMTEK and WMTQK)**

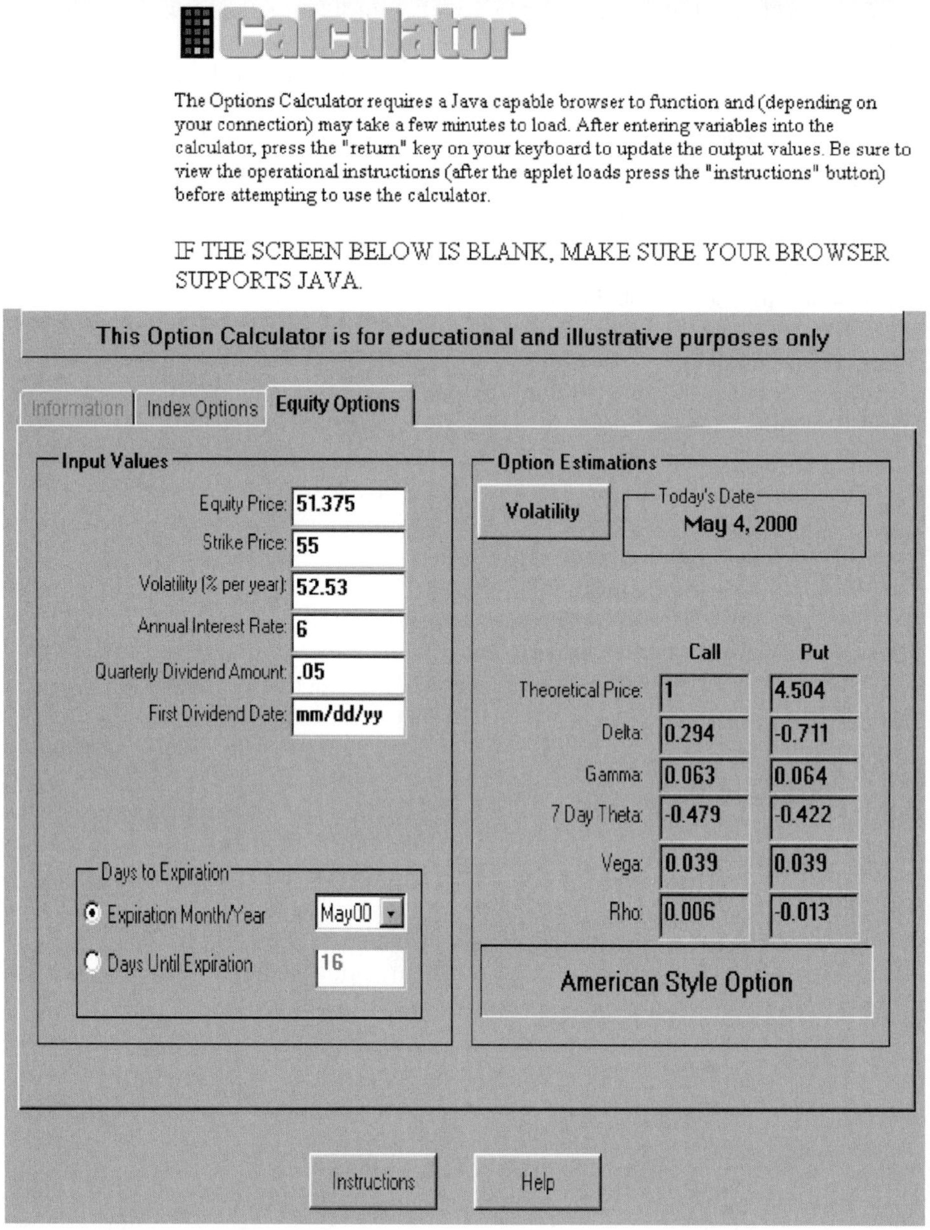

Source: <http://www.cboe.com>.

WALL STREET WISDOM 17.3

Are Options Better than Cash?

Suppose your employer's stock price is presently 40. In a conventional employee stock option plan, key employees are granted the right to buy a fixed number of shares at 40 for a predetermined period. The number of shares granted depends on the employee's level of responsibility. Usually, the number of shares granted under an employee stock option plan is commensurate with total compensation. For example, an employee making $50,000 per year might be granted options that confer the right to buy 1,250 shares at a price of 40 for a period of 10 years, called the exercise period. According to present tax law, the exercise period for employee stock options cannot exceed 10 years but may be less. Because stock prices usually rise by 12–14% per year, on average, from the employee's perspective, the longer the exercise period, the better.

An employee can exercise the right to buy stock covered by a stock option plan once the vesting period has been completed. The vesting period is an employment time frame after which granted options can be exercised. The length of the vesting period is designed by the employer to keep valued employees motivated. It is also designed to keep such employees from bolting to the competition. Structured properly, an employee stock option plan with appropriate vesting requirements can create "golden handcuffs" that benefit both valued employees and their employers.

Once exercised, employee stock options create a taxable event for the employee. The difference between the current market price and the original exercise price, multiplied by the number of shares covered, is used to calculate the amount of employee compensation derived from the option exercise. For example, suppose that the current market price of a company's common stock is 60 and an employee had been granted options that confer the right to buy 1,250 shares of stock at 40. At the time of exercise, the employee would recognize a gain of $25,000 [= ($60 − $40) × 1,250]. Whether the underlying stock is sold immediately or held for further appreciation, this $25,000 gain must be recognized by the employee as income during the current year. A 40% state-plus-federal tax rate on a $25,000 profit would generate a tax liability of $10,000 (= $25,000 × 40%). Because the exercise of employee stock options creates an immediate tax liability, it is common for exercising employees to immediately sell all such shares at the time of exercise.

The long-term success of employee stock option plans has led some employers to supplement traditional plans with special option programs, sometimes called chairman awards programs. Special option programs are flexibly structured to reward valued employees for exceptional performance and to retain exceptional workers who are at risk of leaving. Many such programs are offered in addition to traditional employee stock option programs. Some entail longer vesting periods, or special performance requirements, to entice valued employees to stay. Compensation experts now encourage companies to set aside as much as 5–10% of their stock option pool to cover such special option grants.

One of the most important corporate advantages of employee stock option plans is too little appreciated by investors. By granting employee stock options, employers replace cash compensation that reduces operating income with contingent-based pay that never appears on the income statement. Thus, income statements issued by companies with extensive stock option plans can dramatically understate the total amount of employee compensation. In some instances, this can result in earnings statements that present too rosy a picture of corporate performance. Such problems become especially evident when the company's stock price falters, perhaps due to a general market slowdown, and employees clamor for added cash compensation.

In early 2000, the robust initial public offering (IPO) market even led many landlords to seek rental agreements that substituted stock options for cash lease and rent payments. Especially popular among Internet start-ups, such arrangements allowed cash-starved companies to avoid most major out-of-pocket expenses. Time will tell how enthusiastic investors remain in embracing such "no-profit" companies.

See: Kopin Tan, "Quest Options Benefiting from Speculation Deutsche Telekom Is Seeking U.S. Acquisition," *The Wall Street Journal*, June 20, 2000, C20.

the price of the stock should produce a 29.4¢ change in the price of the option. This implies that a perfectly hedged and riskless position would be established if 0.294 shares of Wal-Mart common stock were purchased for every call option written. Following the sale of a standard 100-share stock call option contract, the purchase of 29.4 shares of Wal-Mart stock would establish a perfect hedge. In that case, a $1 increase in the value of Wal-Mart stock would lead to a stock market profit of $29.40 (= $1 × 29.4 shares) that would exactly offset the $29.40 [= 0.294 × $1 (100 calls)] loss on the call options written. Conversely, a $1 decrease in the value of Wal-Mart stock would lead to a stock-market loss of $29.40 (= $1 × 29.4 shares) that would exactly offset the $29.40 [= 0.294 × $1(100 calls)] gain on the call options written. A perfectly hedged position leaves total wealth unchanged. Notice that because hedge ratios are less than 1.0, a $1 movement in stock prices causes less than a $1 change in option prices. However, because stock options have a lower price basis than the underlying common stock, the percentage change in option prices tends to be larger than the percentage change in stock prices.

gamma
Responsiveness of delta to unit changes in the value of the underlying asset.

The sensitivity of delta to unit changes in the value of the underlying asset is called **gamma.** Gamma indicates an absolute change in delta. For example, in the case of the Wal-Mart call option example, a gamma of 0.063 indicates that delta will increase by 0.063 if the price of Wal-Mart stock were to immediately increase or decrease by $1.

theta
Sensitivity of option value to change in time.

The sensitivity of option value to change in time is called **theta.** Theta indicates an absolute change in option value for a one-unit reduction in time to expiration. The CBOE option calculator assumes one unit of time is seven days. Thus, a theta of −0.479 indicates the option's theoretical value will change by −$0.479 if the number of days to expiration is reduced by seven. When using the CBOE option calculator, this seven-day theta changes to a one-day theta when there are seven or fewer calendar days left until expiration.

vega
Sensitivity of option value to change in volatility.

Vega indicates the sensitivity of option value to change in volatility. Vega depicts an absolute change in option value for a 1% change in volatility. For example, a vega of 0.039 signifies an increase in this specific Wal-Mart call option's theoretical value of $0.039 if the volatility percentage is increased by 1%. Alternatively, a decrease in this option's value of $0.039 will be noted if the volatility percentage is decreased by 1%.

rho
Sensitivity of option value to changes in interest rates.

And finally, the sensitivity of option value to changes in interest rates is captured by **rho.** Rho indicates the absolute change in option value for a 1% change in the market interest rate. In the case of the Wal-Mart call option depicted in Figure 17.13, for example, a rho of 0.006 means that the call option's theoretical value will increase by $0.006 if the interest rate is increased by 1%. Similarly, the call option's theoretical value will decrease by $0.006 if the interest rate is decreased by 1%.

In practice, the numerical values presented for each risk concept in the CBOE option calculator are only approximations. Actual results will vary slightly due to rounding. Perhaps the best way of gaining practical insight about how traders use these important option risk concepts is to log onto the CBOE Web site and experiment by using the CBOE option calculator with some current options market data.

Risk Considerations

Investors must consider option pricing concepts within the context of important underlying risk considerations. At all times, it is of paramount importance that option holders keep in mind the risk of losing the entire amount paid for the option in a relatively short period of time. Options are wasting assets that often become worthless when they expire. Even in-the-money options expire worthlessly unless the option holder sells the option in the secondary market or exercises the option prior to expiration. Options are not buy-and-hold investments. Maintaining option positions requires constant vigilance.

The most popular option contracts tend to have a very short time until expiration, often one month or less. As a result, option holders are short-term speculators who must be right about the direction of an anticipated price change and right about when such a price change will occur. If the price of the underlying asset does not change in the anticipated direction before option expiration, and by an amount sufficient to cover the cost of the option, the investor may lose a significant portion of or all the money invested in the option position. This contrasts with an investor who has the ability and the patience to withstand short-term bumps in the market. Long-term investors have the time to survive temporarily adverse market conditions. Market players in the options markets do not.

Omaha billionaire investor Warren Buffett is famous for remarking that "in the stock market it's easy to tell *what* will happen, but impossible to tell *when* it will happen." Successful long-term investors such as Buffet are prosperous because they have the ability to identify companies with attractive business prospects that are selling at compelling prices. Successful option traders not only have to identify companies with attractive business prospects that are selling at compelling prices, but they must also be able to predict precisely when the share prices of such companies are apt to rise. That is tough. Notice that Buffet says it is *easy* to predict what will happen in the stock market but *impossible* to predict when. In Buffett's opinion, many options market traders are attempting the impossible.

Investors wishing to learn more about the many risks and high transaction costs facing holders and writers of option contracts should carefully read a risk disclosure document prepared by the OCC titled *Characteristics and Risks of Standardized Options.* This highly readable booklet outlines the purposes and risks of option transactions. Despite obvious benefits and their enormous popularity, options are not suitable for all investors. Individual investors should not enter into option transactions until they have read and fully understand this risk disclosure document. Investors can obtain this information online from the CBOE at <http://www.cboe.com> and from the Options Industry Council, an industry trade group, at <www.optionscentral.com>.

Summary

- The **Chicago Board Options Exchange (CBOE)** pioneered the concept of standardized listed options to be traded on a centralized and regulated marketplace. An **option contract** is the right to buy or to sell a given amount or value of a particular asset at a fixed price until a given expiration date. A **call option** gives the right to buy. A **put option** gives the right to sell. Options are **derivative securities** because their economic value is derived or stems from changes in the value of some other asset.
- The number of outstanding options is commonly referred to as **open interest** and depends solely on the number of buyers and sellers interested in receiving and conferring these rights. Activity in stock options tends to be highest for an

exercise price, or **strike price,** that is near the current market price for the underlying common stock. The exercise price, or strike price, of an option is the designated price at which the shares of stock can be bought by the buyer of a call option or sold by the buyer of a put option. When the price of the underlying security is equal to the strike price, the option price is said to be **at-the-money.** A call option is **in-the-money** if the strike price is less than the market price of the underlying security. A put option is in-the-money if the strike price is greater than the market price of the underlying security. A call option is **out-of-the-money** if the strike price is greater than the market price of the underlying security. A put option is out-of-the money if the strike price is less than the market price of the underlying security.

- Options that have the same standardized terms but different strike prices comprise an **option series.** The standardization of terms makes it more likely that there will be a secondary market in which **holders,** or buyers, and **writers,** or sellers, of options can close out their positions by offsetting sales and purchase transactions. The length of time between when an option contract is established and the point of expiration is the **contract period.** The amount paid for the option is the **option premium.** Options can be usually bought with one of four expiration dates into the future from the **front month,** or the time when the option contract is originated. **Long-term equity anticipation securities (LEAPS)** are long-term call and put options.
- The **Options Clearing Corporation (OCC)** is the sole issuer of all listed securities options. To ensure contract fulfillment, the OCC requires buyers and sellers to have a clearing member handle their options transactions and that both sides of every option transaction be exactly matched. On the CBOE, **market makers** provide liquidity in option trading by risking their own capital for personal trading. They take the opposite side of public orders by competing in an **open-outcry auction** market. **Floor brokers** act as agents, executing orders for public or firm accounts.
- A **hedged position** is created when an option contract is purchased or sold to offset the risk inherent in some other investment. Hedgers use options to limit risk. A **speculative position** is created when an option contract is purchased or sold to profit from the inherent riskiness of some underlying asset. Option contracts represent a **zero sum game** between the buyer and the seller. Before commissions and other transactions costs, when the price of the underlying asset rises unexpectedly, the amount earned by the option buyer is exactly equal to the amount lost by the seller, and vice versa.
- An **opening transaction** initiates a position in the options markets. It is a purchase or sale transaction by which an investor establishes a position as either a holder or writer of an option. In a **closing transaction,** an investor terminates a previously established option position.
- An **American-style option** is an option contract that can be exercised at any time between the date of purchase and the expiration date. All stock options are American-style options, and most exchange-traded options are American-style options. **European-style options** are options contracts that can only be exercised on the **expiration date.** The expiration date is the last day of an American-style option or the single exercise date of a European-style option. A **capped option**

is an option that will be automatically exercised prior to expiration if the options market on which it is trading determines that the value of the underlying asset hits a specified cap price.

- A **physical delivery option** gives its owner the right to receive physical delivery of an asset if it is a call or to make physical delivery of an asset if it is a put when the option is exercised. A **cash-settled option** gives the holder the right to receive a cash payment based on the difference between a determined value of the underlying interest at the time the option is exercised and the fixed exercise price of the option. The unit of trading or **contract size** of a physical delivery option is the quantity of an underlying asset that is subject to being purchased or sold on the exercise of a single option contract. When and if they choose to buy or sell at that predetermined price, option holders are said to **exercise** their right. The seller of an option is said to be **assigned** when they are asked to fulfill their contract obligation.

- Options market players playfully refer to the last hour of trading on the third Friday of March, June, September, and December as **triple witching** hour because of the tendency of investors to rush to unwind their positions in expiring stock options, index options, and stock index futures. The other eight times per year, when only equity options and equity index options expire, is playfully referred to as **double witching** hour. The expiration of options and futures coincide only four times per year, and triple witching hours are sometimes associated with sharp price swings as investors buy and sell these derivative instruments and the underlying equity securities.

- Physical-delivery **price-based options** give holders the right to purchase or sell a specific debt security. Cash-settled price-based options give holders the right to receive a cash payment based on the value of an underlying debt security. **Yield-based options** are debt options that are cash-settled based on the difference between the exercise price and the value of an underlying yield.

- **Dollar-denominated foreign currency options** are options to purchase or sell underlying foreign currencies for U.S. dollars. Their exercise prices represent the exchange rates of the underlying foreign currencies and the U.S. dollar. **Cross-rate foreign currency options** are options to purchase or sell an underlying foreign currency at an exercise price that is denominated in another foreign currency. Flexibly structured options, or **flex options,** are traded on the U.S. options markets and are issued by the OCC. However, unlike other options, the terms of flex options are not standardized.

- A **covered call strategy** is the simultaneous purchase of a stock and the sale of a call option on that same security. Unlike a **naked short seller,** the covered call writer faces limited loss potential from the short call option. A **protective put strategy** is the simultaneous purchase of a stock and the purchase of a put option on that same security. Option positions that involve complementary positions in more than one option at the same time are called **combinations. Spreads** and **straddles** are two specific types of combination positions. A spread involves being both the buyer and writer of the same type of option (call or put) on the same underlying asset. A **price spread** is the simultaneous purchase or sale of options on the same underlying stock but with different exercise prices. A **time spread** is the simultaneous purchase or sale of options on the same underlying stock but with different expiration dates. A **bull call spread** is the purchase of a low-strike price call and the simultaneous sale of another high-strike price call on the same underlying equity with the same expiration date. A bull call spread is always established as a debit spread because the net effect of the bull call spread transaction is a debit to the customer's account. A **bull put spread** is the sale of a high-strike price put and the simultaneous purchase of another low-strike price put on the same underlying equity with the same expiration date. A bull put spread is always established as a credit spread. This means that the net effect of the bull put spread transaction is a credit to the customer's account.

- The difference between an in-the-money option's strike price and the current market price of the underlying security is referred to as the option's **intrinsic value.** Intrinsic value is zero for at-the-money and out-of-the-money options. At the point of expiration, the expiration value of an option equals its intrinsic value. Only in-the-money options have intrinsic value. All unexpired options have **time value,** or speculative value, because they might someday have intrinsic value. The **Black-Scholes option pricing model** includes a formula that is now widely used to calculate economic values for options. The Black-Scholes model gives insight concerning put option prices because of a concept called **put-call parity.** The put-call parity concept expresses the relationship that must hold between the price of a put option and the price of a call option on the same underlying equity.
- The sensitivity of option value to a unit change in the underlying asset is called the option's **delta.** In the options markets, delta is commonly referred to as the **hedge ratio.** The responsiveness of delta to unit changes in the value of the underlying asset is called **gamma.** The sensitivity of option value to change in time is called **theta. Vega** indicates the sensitivity of option value to change in volatility. The sensitivity of option value to changes in interest rates is captured by **rho.** The best way for gaining practical insight about how traders use these important option risk concepts is to log onto the CBOE Web site and experiment by using the CBOE option calculator with some current options markets data.

Questions

1. The per-share price at which common stock may be purchased in the case of a call, or sold to a writer in the case of a put, is called the
   a. premium.
   b. strike price.
   c. in-the-money price.
   d. intrinsic value.
2. To protect a profit on an individual stock owned, an investor could
   a. buy a call.
   b. write a put.
   c. buy a stock index option.
   d. buy a put.

3. The writer of a call can terminate that particular contract anytime prior to expiration by
   a. writing a second call.
   b. buying a put.
   c. buying a comparable call.
   d. writing a put.
4. The writer of a naked call faces
   a. a limited potential gain.
   b. an unlimited potential gain.
   c. a specified potential loss.
   d. no chance of loss.
5. The purchase of a straddle
   a. eliminates risk.
   b. generates buyer profits from a stable stock price.
   c. is always more risky than a short sale.
   d. generates writer profits from a stable stock price.
6. A spread is
   a. the purchase and sale of an equivalent option varying in only one respect.
   b. a combination of two puts and a call.
   c. a combination of two calls and a put.
   d. a combination of a put and a call on the same stock with the same exercise date and exercise price.
7. Which of the following statements is true?
   a. The speculative premium reflects the option's immediate value.
   b. If a call is in-the-money, the intrinsic value is zero.
   c. An option's premium almost never declines below its intrinsic value.
   d. If the exercise price exceeds the stock price, a call is said to be in the money.
8. Which of the following statements is false?
   a. An option's premium cannot decline below intrinsic value.
   b. The intrinsic value reflects the option's potential appreciation.
   c. Option prices almost always exceed intrinsic values.
   d. Out-of-the-money for a call means that the stock price is less than the exercising price.
9. Buyers of call options hope to profit from
   a. rising prices.
   b. stagnant prices.
   c. falling prices.
   d. falling interest rates.

10. Writers of put options hope to profit from
    a. rising stock price volatility.
    b. rising stock prices.
    c. falling stock prices.
    d. falling interest rates.
11. The sole issuer of all securities options listed at the Chicago Board Options Exchange is the
    a. CBOE.
    b. NASD.
    c. SEC.
    d. OCC.
12. That party that takes the opposite side of every option created is called the
    a. market maker.
    b. specialist.
    c. issuer.
    d. broker.
13. Parties that provide liquidity in option trading by risking their own capital for personal trading are called
    a. market makers.
    b. floor brokers.
    c. agents.
    d. exchange officials.
14. Parties with an obligation to sell have
    a. bought a call option.
    b. sold a call option.
    c. sold a put option.
    d. bought a put option.
15. The specified price at which shares of stock can be bought or sold by the buyer of an option is the
    a. call price.
    b. put price.
    c. strike price.
    d. straddle price.
16. If the strike price is less than the market price of the underlying security, a call option is
    a. out-of-the-money.
    b. in-the-money.
    c. at-the-money.
    d. none of these.

17. An option contract that can only be exercised on the expiration date is called
    a. American-style.
    b. European-style.
    c. an exchange-traded option.
    d. an over-the-counter option.
18. Open interest refers to the number of option contracts
    a. outstanding.
    b. bought.
    c. sold.
    d. none of the above.
19. Assume that you are long 100 shares of MER and wish to protect against a downturn in the overall market. You could put on a "collar" by simultaneously
    a. selling a put and buying a call.
    b. selling a call and a put.
    c. selling a call and buying a put.
    d. buying a call and a put.
20. To hedge the short sale of AOL, one might
    a. buy a put option.
    b. write a put option.
    c. buy a call option.
    d. write a LEAP put option.

Investment Application

Bull Spreads with LEAPS

LEAPS are long-term stock options that provide the owner the right to purchase or sell shares of a stock at a specified exercise price on or before the expiration date. As with other options, LEAPS are available in two types, calls and puts. Like other exchange-traded stock options, LEAPS are American-style options with an expiration date that falls on the Saturday following the third Friday of the expiration month. However, in the case of equity LEAPS, the expiration month is always January. An initial LEAPS position does not require an investor to manage each position daily because the initial term to maturity can run up to three years in length. LEAPS calls appeal to aggressive investors with a longer-term view of the stock market. Purchase of LEAPS puts provides a hedge for long-term investors against substantial declines in their stocks.

It is their very long time until expiration that distinguishes LEAPS from more traditional call and put options. As seen in Figure 17.3, the most popular options tend to have a very short time remaining until expiration and are at-the-money or out-of-the-money at the time of purchase. Like lottery tickets, the most popular equity call and put options cost only a few dollars apiece and seldom seem to pay off. By contrast, investors who buy LEAPS calls with an extended period of time until expiration obtain an investment position that has many similarities with buying stocks outright. Investors in LEAPS calls have the opportunity to benefit from stock price increases without laying out the full amount required to establish an equity position. In many instances, deep in-the-money LEAPS calls can be purchased for a cash outlay that is no more, and sometimes much less, than the amount required for a stock purchase with 50% margin. Moreover, the investor who takes a position in LEAPS calls need not worry about a margin call. Cash purchases of LEAPS establish a position that can withstand adverse market conditions for extended periods. Of course, as is the case with any option transaction, LEAPS that are out-of-the-money at the end of the contract period expire worthlessly. Thus, LEAPS investors, like all players in the options markets, must not commit an investment amount that they cannot afford to lose.

Given their fairly conservative investment perspective, LEAPS investors are always looking for new ways to invest in the market and at the same time limit their risk exposure. Investors recognize the attractiveness of LEAPS as a tool to limit risk but are sometimes dissuaded from paying the high option premiums common for volatile stocks. For such investors, there is a wide range of option strategies available that can be used to lower those high premiums. Two of the most popular such strategies are bull call spreads and bull put spreads. These are considered conservative LEAPS strategies because the investor's risk exposure is known and limited. They are most appropriate when the investor's outlook is mildly bullish.

A bull call spread is the purchase of a low-strike-price call and the simultaneous sale of another high-strike-price call on the same underlying equity with the same expiration date. A bull call spread is always established as a debit spread. This means that the net effect of the bull call spread transaction is a debit to the customer's account because the amount paid for low-strike-price LEAPS calls is always more than the amount received from the short sale of high-strike-price LEAPS calls. The margin requirement is the amount paid for the bull call spread because that is the defined and limited risk of the spread.

A bull put spread is the sale of a high-strike-price put and the simultaneous purchase of another low-strike-price put on the same underlying equity with the same expiration date. A bull put spread is always established as a credit spread. This means that the net effect of the bull put spread transaction is a credit to the customer's account because the amount received from the short sale of high-strike-price LEAPS puts is always more than the amount paid for low-strike-price LEAPS puts. The margin requirement for a bull put spread is the amount by which high-strike-price put sold short exceeds the low-strike-price put purchased, minus the net premium received on the combined transaction.

To illustrate, Figure 17.14 shows market data for January 2001 and 2002 LEAPS calls and puts for Dell Computer Corp. as of May 4, 2000. At the time these data were obtained, the 2002 LEAPS had 625 days, or about one year and eight months, remaining until expiration.

Suppose an investor established a bull call spread with the purchase of January 2002 strike price 40 LEAPS calls at an ask price of $18.125, and the simultaneous sale of January 2002 strike price 50 LEAPS calls for a bid price of $13.625.

FIGURE 17.14 **Bull Call Spreads and Bull Put Spreads Allow Moderately Bullish Investors to Limit Option Risk Exposure**

JAN 2001 - JAN 2002

						JAN 2001							
Calls	Last Sale	Net Chg.	Bid	Ask	Vol	Open Interest	Puts	Last Sale	Net Chg.	Bid	Ask	Vol	Open Interest
JAN 2001 17.5 ZNAW	$27	0	$27.75	$28	0	7925	JAN 2001 17.5 ZNMW	$0.125	0	$0.0625	$0.125	0	5817
JAN 2001 20 ZNAD	$25	0	$25.5	$25.75	0	2680	JAN 2001 20 ZNMD	$0.25	0	$0.125	$0.1875	0	8068
JAN 2001 22.5 ZDEAX	$21.25	0	$23.125	$23.375	0	1613	JAN 2001 22.5 ZDEMX	$0.375	0	$0.1875	$0.3125	0	4949
JAN 2001 25 ZDEAE	$20.625	0	$21	$21.25	5	4669	JAN 2001 25 ZDEME	$0.4375	0	$0.4375	$0.5	0	8574
JAN 2001 27.5 ZDEAY	$18.5	0	$18.75	$19	0	2551	JAN 2001 27.5 ZDEMY	$0.875	0	$0.6875	$0.75	0	10219
JAN 2001 30 ZDEAF	$16.625	+0.75	$16.875	$17.125	7	10020	JAN 2001 30 ZDEMF	$1.25	0	$1.125	$1.1875	0	21954
JAN 2001 32.5 ZDEAZ	$14.25	0	$15	$15.125	0	7758	JAN 2001 32.5 ZDEMZ	$2	0	$1.6875	$1.6875	0	4290
JAN 2001 35 ZDEAG	$13.125	0	$13.25	$13.375	0	8127	JAN 2001 35 ZDEMG	$2.75	0	$2.25	$2.375	0	6817
JAN 2001 37.5 ZDEAU	$10.375	-1.625	$11.75	$11.75	40	3601	JAN 2001 37.5 ZDEMU	$3.5	0	$3	$3.25	0	7039
JAN 2001 40 ZDEAH	$10.125	+1.25	$10	$10.375	32	18271	JAN 2001 40 ZDEMH	$4.125	-0.75	$4	$4.125	40	20814
JAN 2001 42.5 ZDEAV	$8.125	0	$8.875	$9	0	7223	JAN 2001 42.5 ZDEMV	$5.25	-0.625	$5.25	$5.375	1	3962
JAN 2001 45 ZDEAI	$7.625	+0.75	$7.75	$7.75	2056	17544	JAN 2001 45 ZDEMI	$7	0	$6.25	$6.5	0	17085
JAN 2001 50 ZDEAJ	$5.625	+0.625	$5.625	$5.875	208	36706	JAN 2001 50 ZDEMJ	$9.5	-0.875	$9.25	$9.5	5	15310
JAN 2001 55 ZDEAK	$4	+0.5	$4.125	$4.25	161	20760	JAN 2001 55 ZDEMK	$13	0	$12.75	$13	0	5277
JAN 2001 60 ZDEAL	$3.125	+0.5	$2.9375	$3.125	45	16958	JAN 2001 60 ZDEML	$18.125	+1.125	$16.625	$16.875	10	4317
JAN 2001 65 ZDEAM	$2.125	+0.25	$2.125	$2.25	120	28678	JAN 2001 65 ZDEMM	$21	0	$20.875	$21.125	0	618
JAN 2001 70 ZDEAN	$1.5	+0.25	$1.5	$1.5625	100	16385	JAN 2001 70 ZDEMN	$21	0	$25.375	$25.625	0	1073
JAN 2001 75 ZDEAD	$1.1875	0	$1.0625	$1.125	0	2870	JAN 2001 75 ZDEMD	$30.75	0	$30.25	$30.625	0	105
JAN 2001 80 ZDEAC	$0.75	0	$0.75	$0.8125	0	3168	JAN 2001 80 ZDEMC	$35.875	0	$35.25	$35.5	0	200
JAN 2001 85 ZDEAQ	$0.5625	+0.1875	$0.5	$0.5625	5	11298	JAN 2001 85 ZDEMQ	$41.625	0	$40.25	$40.5	0	495
JAN 2002 25 WDQAE	$26.625	-2.75	$26.75	$27	3	1888	JAN 2002 25 WDQME	$1.8125	0	$1.8125	$1.9375	0	15271
JAN 2002 30 WDQAF	$25.125	0	$23.5	$23.75	0	1500	JAN 2002 30 WDQMF	$2.75	0	$3.125	$3.25	0	1955
JAN 2002 35 WDQAG	$21.625	0	$20.5	$20.75	0	3356	JAN 2002 35 WDQMG	$4.375	0	$4.625	$4.875	0	1666
JAN 2002 40 WDQAH	$17.875	-1.5	$17.875	$18.125	22	10566	JAN 2002 40 WDQMH	$6.25	0	$6.5	$6.75	0	17949
JAN 2002 45 WDQAI	$16.125	-1.5	$15.625	$15.875	40	8067	JAN 2002 45 WDQMI	$8.25	0	$9	$9.25	0	4079
JAN 2002 50 WDQAJ	$14	-0.625	$13.625	$13.875	93	18397	JAN 2002 50 WDQMJ	$11.375	+0.875	$11.625	$11.875	8	7139
JAN 2002 55 WDQAK	$11.625	-0.75	$11.875	$12	38	8177	JAN 2002 55 WDQMK	$13.875	0	$14.5	$14.875	0	1033
JAN 2002 60 WDQAL	$10.375	-0.75	$10.375	$10.5	1237	4129	JAN 2002 60 WDQML	$16.75	0	$18	$18.25	0	421
JAN 2002 65 WDQAM	$9.25	-0.625	$9	$9.125	125	14094	JAN 2002 65 WDQMM	$22.125	0	$21.375	$21.75	0	865
JAN 2002 70 WDQAN	$7.75	-1.25	$7.875	$8	108	1317	JAN 2002 70 WDQMN	$24	0	$25.125	$25.5	0	376

The net effect of such a bull call spread transaction is a debit to the customer's account of \$4.50 (= \$18.125 − \$13.625) plus commissions. In this example, the strike price 40 LEAPS calls that are purchased are in-the-money, whereas the strike price 50 LEAPS calls that are sold short are out-of-the-money. If this spread transaction is held until expiration on the third Friday of January in 2002 (January 18, 2002), the value of the spread will reach a maximum of \$10 if Dell stock is then trading at a price that is greater than or equal to 50. In that event, the investor will have converted an investment of \$4.50 (plus commissions) into \$10 (minus commissions) and earned a 122.2% total return over 625 days, which compounds to an annual 59.4% rate of return (before commissions). At the time of expiration, if Dell trades at a stock price greater than 40 but less than 50, the spread will have an intrinsic value of less than \$10. If Dell trades at a stock price of 40 or less at the time of expiration, the bull call spread will expire worthlessly.

The advantage of a bull spread strategy with LEAPS calls is that, if successful, it gives the moderately bullish option investor a terrific rate of return with only limited risk. Moreover, the risk of loss can be minimized through the purchase of low-strike price LEAPS calls that are deep in-the-money and the simultaneous sale of high-strike price LEAPS calls with significant option premiums. Nevertheless, all LEAPS transactions involve substantial risk, and bull spread strategies still expose the option investor to large losses in the event of adverse market conditions.

A. Suppose an investor established a bull put spread with the sale of January 2002 strike price 60 LEAPS puts and the simultaneous purchase of January 2002 strike price 40 LEAPS puts. Calculate the net credit from such an option transaction and the investor's risk exposure.

B. Calculate the investor's annual rate of return if the bull put spread is held until expiration, and Dell trades at 60, 50, or 40 on January 18, 2002.

Selected References

Attari, Mukarram. "Discontinuous Interest Rate Processes: An Equilibrium Model for Bond Option Prices." *Journal of Financial and Quantitative Analysis* 44 (September 1999): 293–322.

Berk, Jonathan B., Richard C. Green, and Vasant Naik. "Optimal Investment, Growth Options, and Security Returns." *Journal of Finance* 54 (October 1999): 1553–1607.

Bertsimas, Dimitris, Leonid Kogan, and Andrew W. Lo. "When Is Time Continuous?" *Journal of Financial Economics* 55 (February 2000): 173–204.

Bloomfield, Robert, and Maureen O'Hara. "Can Transparent Markets Survive?" *Journal of Financial Economics* 55 (March 2000): 425–459.

Britten-Jones, Mark, and Anthony Neuberger. "Option Prices, Implied Price Processes, and Stochastic Volatility." *Journal of Finance* 55 (April 2000): 839–866.

Brown, David T. "The Determinants of Expected Returns on Mortgage-Backed Securities: An Empirical Analysis of Option-Adjusted Spreads." *Journal of Fixed Income* 9 (September 1999): 8–18.

Christodoulakis, George A., and Stephen E. Satchell. "The Simulation of Option Prices with Application to LIFFE Options on Futures." *European Journal of Operational Research* 14 (April 16, 1999): 249–262.

Deszca, Gene, Hugh Munro, and Hamid Noori. "Developing Breakthrough Products: Challenges and Options for Market Assessment." *Journal of Operations Management* 17 (November 1999): 613–630.

Dunn, Kenneth B., and Chester S. Spatt. "Call Options, Points, and Dominance Restrictions on Debt Contracts." *Journal of Finance* 54 (December 1999): 2317–2237.

Figlewski, Stephen, and Bin Gao. "The Adaptive Mesh Model: A New Approach to Efficient Option Pricing." *Journal of Financial Economics* 53 (September 1999): 313–351.

Graham, John R., and Clifford W. Smith, Jr. "Tax Incentives to Hedge." *Journal of Finance* 54 (December 1999): 2241–2261.

Hui, Cho H. "Modeling Forward Credit Risk—An Options Approach." *Journal of Fixed Income* 9 (September 1999): 54–61.

Ingersoll, Jr., Jonathan E. "Digital Contracts: Simple Tools for Pricing Complex Derivatives." *Journal of Business* 73 (January 2000): 67–88.

Kensinger, John. "International Investment—Value Creation and Appraisal: A Real Options Approach." *Journal of Finance* 54 (December 1999): 2387–2389.

Sorescu, Sorin M. "The Effect of Options on Stock Prices: 1973 to 1995." *Journal of Finance* 55 (February 2000): 487–514.

CHAPTER 18

Futures Markets

It is greasy and it is fattening, but fast-food lovers have a new-found affection for bacon. Bacon is by far and away the most popular pork product found in restaurants. Burger King, McDonald's, and Wendy's all offer at least one sandwich topped with bacon, and they are all enormously well liked by consumers.

The reason behind bacon's new-found popularity is easy to understand. With recent E. coli *scares tied to the consumption of undercooked ground beef, fast-food restaurants have responded to consumer health concerns by literally turning up the heat. As a result, fast-food hamburgers now tend to be drier and less tasty than they were just a few years ago. To liven things up, buyers turned to bacon to add much-needed flavor to overcooked ground beef.*

Surging bacon demand has had a direct influence in the commodities markets. Bacon's resurgence as a fast-food item caused the demand for pork bellies and pork belly futures to skyrocket in 2000. Fresh and frozen pork bellies are among the most actively traded agricultural commodities, and rising demand for bacon caused their May 2000 price to rise toward the all-time high of $1.0525 per pound, first set in 1996.

Of course, pork belly prices depend on both demand and supply. When supply conditions will improve is anybody's guess. This makes speculation in the pork belly futures market hazardous, at best. If industry supply surges to meet or exceed higher demand, pork belly futures prices will crumble. However, so long as supply stays tight, pork belly speculators will continue to benefit from the fast-food customer's new-found mantra: "Make mine a bacon double cheeseburger please!"[1]

Futures Trading

Market Origin

Futures markets have a long and colorful history. The origin of modern futures markets has been traced to the trading of rice futures in 18th-century Osaka, Japan. In the United States, the history of modern futures trading traces from the mid-

[1]See Daniel Rosenberg, "Bacon-Burger Boom," *Barron's,* May 1, 2000, MW17.

19th century and was tied closely to the development of commerce in Chicago and the grain trade in the Midwest. Chicago is strategically located to provide a much-needed commercial hub for agricultural trade. Located on the shores of Lake Michigan, and close to the fertile farmlands of the Midwest, Chicago offers a vital link between the producers of agricultural products and major consumer markets in the east. Chicago's natural geographic advantages led to its emergence as a transportation hub for rail and barge traffic for agricultural products. As the early grain trade in Chicago expanded, however, problems of supply and demand, transportation, and storage led to a chaotic marketing situation.

At harvest time, Midwestern farmers and grain shippers delivered their crops within days of each other, flooding the market with supply and driving down grain prices. At times, downward price swings were so violent that, after deducting shipping and marketing costs, farmers sometimes figured it was cheaper to burn corn for fuel than to send it to market. By midwinter or spring, most of the stored grain was depleted and prices shot up again. Prices often remained high throughout the summer months, only to plunge again in the autumn, when the annual bust-to-boom cycle for grain prices would resume.

By 1848, telegraph communication had progressed to the point at which merchants in Chicago could quickly receive price information from New York, and the **Chicago Board of Trade (CBOT)** was born, as shown in Table 18.1. The CBOT was established by a group of 82 merchants as a centralized marketplace to promote commerce in the city of Chicago by providing a place where buyers and sellers could meet to exchange commodities. In the 1849–50 period, so-called "to arrive" contracts came into use for future delivery of flour, timothy seed, and hay. By 1851, the earliest **forward contract,** for 3,000 bushels of corn, was recorded. A forward contract is an agreement between two parties to buy or sell a stipulated grade and quantity of a commodity at a specific future time for an agreed-on price. In the case of agricultural products, forward contracts are often entered into between producers and merchants. Forward contracts quickly gained popularity among merchants and processors as a means for lending order to sometimes chaotic grain prices.

Chicago Board of Trade (CBOT)
First and largest commodities exchange.

forward contract
Binding agreement to buy or sell a commodity at a future time.

During the 1850s, the importance of Chicago as a commercial link between the nation's breadbasket and eastern markets grew rapidly. In 1853, for example, Chicago's population grew by an astounding 57%. By 1855, European buyers were coming directly to Chicago rather than to New York for wheat and other grains. As Chicago grew in population and economic importance, the CBOT flourished. CBOT membership more than doubled, and the CBOT received a charter from the State of Illinois mandating that it set standards for quality, product uniformity, and routine inspections of grain. The CBOT also became a corporation through special Illinois legislative action.

With the onset of the Civil War, the need for grain storage and pricing dependability grew rapidly. Grain storage capacity in Chicago skyrocketed to the then-astounding amount of 10 million bushels with the completion of new grain elevators. However, a growing incidence of failures to complete forward contracts created great confusion in the grain and agricultural markets. Sometimes, producers proved unable or unwilling to deliver promised grains at agreed-on prices. In other instances, buyers vanished when market prices turned lower that the amounts stipulated in forward contracts. Defaults grew and threatened to undermine the market. To remedy the situation and restore buyer and seller confidence in the grain

TABLE 18.1 Time Line of U.S. Futures Market Development

Date	Event
1848	The Chicago Board of Trade (CBOT) founded by 82 Chicago merchants.
1851	The earliest forward contract for 3,000 bushels of corn recorded. Forward contracts gain popularity among merchants and processors.
1856	A group of merchants organize the Kansas City Board of Trade for the purpose of buying and selling wheat.
1865	Forward contracts create confusion for users and subsequent defaults. CBOT formalizes grain trading by developing standardized futures contracts. CBOT begins requiring margin to be posted by buyers and sellers.
1868	MidAmerica Commodity Exchange founded in Chicago as an open-air market.
1870	New York Cotton Exchange founded by a group of cotton brokers and merchants.
1872	Manhattan dairy merchants form the Butter and Cheese Exchange of New York, later called the Butter, Cheese and Egg Exchange.
1874	Chicago Produce Exchange established to provide a market for butter, eggs, poultry, and other farm products in the city of Chicago.
1881	Twenty-one businessmen form the Minneapolis Chamber of Commerce, an organization designed to encourage and promote trade in corn, oats, and wheat.
1882	The Butter, Cheese and Egg Exchange of New York changes its name to the New York Mercantile Exchange.
1882	Coffee Exchange of the City of New York created by a group of merchants seeking an orderly process for buying and selling coffee.
1898	Chicago Butter and Egg Board formed from a division of the Chicago Produce Exchange.
1916	Coffee Exchange of the City of New York changes its name to the New York Coffee and Sugar Exchange, Inc.
1919	Chicago Butter and Egg Board renamed the Chicago Mercantile Exchange to better reflect its broad purpose.
1922	The federal government establishes the Grain Futures Administration to regulate grain trading.
1925	New York Cocoa Exchange founded.
1947	Minneapolis Chamber of Commerce changes its name to the Minneapolis Grain Exchange.
1966	CBOT introduces the industry's first examination for commodity brokers.
1973	Chicago Board Options Exchange (CBOE) founded by members of the CBOT.
1974	Commodity Futures Trading Commission (CFTC) created by Congress as an independent agency with the mandate to regulate commodity futures and option markets in the United States.
1975	CBOT launches futures on the Government National Mortgage Association (GNMA) mortgaged-backed certificates, the first financial futures instrument.
1979	Coffee and Sugar Exchange merges with the New York Cocoa Exchange to form the Coffee, Sugar & Cocoa Exchange, Inc.
1982	Coffee, Sugar & Cocoa Exchange, Inc., introduces options on sugar futures contracts, creating the first U.S. exchange-traded option on a futures contract. CBOT launches options on U.S. Treasury bond futures. The KCBOT introduces futures contracts based on the Value Line® Index, the first U.S. stock index futures contracts.
1985	MidAmerica Commodity Exchange acquires the Chicago Rice and Cotton Exchange.
1986	MidAmerica Commodity Exchange becomes a wholly owned subsidiary of the CBOT.
1995	CBOT launches MarketPlex, the first futures exchange to open a commercial service on the Internet.
2000	CBOT members become shareholders in two new companies. The first company retains the open-outcry platform of trading and is a closely held, for-profit company. The second company establishes an electronic trading capability.

futures contract
Financially secured binding agreement to buy or sell a commodity at a future time.

markets, the CBOT moved to formalize grain trading by developing a standardized agreement called a **futures contract.** Similar to a forward contract, a futures contract is a standardized agreement between two parties that commits one to buy and the other to sell a stipulated quantity and grade of a commodity at a set price on or before a given date in the future.

Unlike the previously popular but troublesome forward contracts, the CBOT began requiring performance bonds called **margin** to be posted by buyers and sellers of futures. These performance bonds are intended to ensure that both buyers and sellers have the economic incentive and financial wherewithal to complete their futures market transactions. Today, futures **mark-to-market** on a daily basis. This means that there is a daily settlement of gains and losses between buyers and sellers. If the **spot price,** or current price, rises, sellers of futures contracts must place additional funds in their margin account to ensure their ability to deliver now higher-priced commodities. If the spot price falls, buyers of futures contracts must place additional funds in their margin account to ensure their willingness to abide by an earlier agreement to pay higher prices for what are now lower-priced commodities. Unlike the previously popular but increasingly discredited forward contracts, the CBOT moved to broaden market acceptance of futures contracts by standardizing the conditions and terms of futures contract fulfillment. For futures contracts remaining open until trading terminates, the CBOT stipulates mechanisms for either physical delivery or final cash payment (cash settlement).

margin
Performance bond.

mark-to-market
Daily reconciliation of futures contract profits and losses based on spot market prices.

spot price
Current cash price.

Market Development

The development of futures contracts gave farmers and grain merchants a way to lock in predictable prices for agricultural products. An Iowa farmer paying for seed and fertilizer to plant corn in May, for example, can only guess what price will be received for the crop when it is finally harvested and taken to market in November or December. In May, if the farmer sells corn futures contracts for at least a portion of the expected crop, the farmer has the potential to lock in a profit above planting and harvesting costs. The capability to reduce future price risk is an important attraction of the futures market to producers. Similarly, buyers of agricultural products like the ability to lock in future costs. Cereal manufacturers, such as Kellogg's and General Mills, are big players in the grain markets, where they use futures contracts to stabilize their cost of ingredients for ready-to-eat cereals and other products.

Futures markets have a long history of product innovation. Corn, wheat, and cotton trading date from the post–Civil War period in the United States. Metals trading began in the 1920s, and refined agricultural products, such as soybean meal and soybean oil, became available during the 1950s. A new wave of innovation began in the 1960s when futures on livestock, a readily perishable commodity, were introduced. The development of commodity exchanges in New York for coffee, sugar, cocoa, cotton, precious metals, and oil paralleled developments in Chicago's agricultural commodities markets. These futures markets were established and evolved as an efficient means for matching buyers and sellers of standardized commodities with widely fluctuating prices. The obvious economic advantages of agricultural and commodity futures led to widespread business and acceptance, and commodity futures trading activity continued to grow rapidly. However, the most dramatic growth of the industry was not tied to futures based on agricultural products and other commodities but resulted from the development of financial futures tied to a changing world economy following World War II.

Greater global financial interdependence and sharp increases in the amount of government debt fundamentally altered the post–World War II global economy. In the 1970s, the Bretton Woods system of fixed exchange rates between the U.S. dollar and foreign currencies which was established after World War II began to unravel. Suddenly, companies that did business in various parts of the world had to worry about how the changing value of local currencies could affect the profitability of foreign operations. They sought means for locking in U.S. prices for domestic goods sold in foreign markets and U.S. prices for foreign-produced goods that were to be sold in the domestic market. In 1974, currency and interest-rate instability caused global investors to flock to gold, and gold futures began to trade. At the same time, an explosion of government-issued debt and spiraling inflation moved the world economy away from a relatively stable interest rate environment into one that was much more volatile. In 1975, futures exchanges introduced interest-rate futures, beginning with the Ginnie Mae contract based on pools of residential mortgages. The following year saw three-month Treasury bill futures introduced. The highly popular 30-year Treasury bond futures were introduced in 1977. Interest rates became totally unhinged in 1979, when Federal Reserve Board Chairman Paul Volcker announced that interest rates would be allowed to float freely in the marketplace. Futures on petroleum-based products, such as heating oil and gasoline, were another popular introduction in the late 1970s when OPEC's control over oil prices weakened and oil price volatility skyrocketed.

The introduction of financial futures began with foreign currencies and interest-rate futures and led to a huge increase in futures trading volume. In 1972, futures contracts based on foreign currencies were initially dismissed as "pin-stripped pork bellies." However, they gradually built a strong following among leading banks and securities firms in New York, Europe, and Japan. Today, more than one-third of financial futures trading volume originates with foreign banks and other foreign institutions. The CBOT's futures contract on U.S. Treasury bonds is the most actively traded futures contract and accounts for roughly two-thirds of that exchange's trading activity.

Each of these early financial futures contracts adopted the physical delivery mechanism designed for grain and cotton trading in the mid-1800s. That physical delivery mechanism ensured price convergence between expiring futures contracts and the underlying cash market. In 1981, Eurodollar futures became the first futures contract that did not require physical delivery. Instead, the Eurodollar futures contracts call for cash settlement, or a cash payment on the last trading day of the difference between a widely accepted cash price and the futures price. The cash-settlement innovation paved the way for new types of futures contracts for which physical delivery would be impossible or prohibitively expensive. Most notable among these are stock index futures, which began trading in 1982.

The mid- to late 1980s was also a period of tremendous international growth in futures and options markets. As shown in Table 18.2, commodities are actively traded on more than 80 futures exchanges throughout the world. Although most futures exchanges offer a range of contracts, the most successful global products fall into three broad categories: futures for government bonds, futures on short-term interbank interest rates, and stock index futures.

TABLE 18.2 Commodities Are Actively Traded on Futures Exchanges around the World

Country	Exchange
Argentina	Merfox (Mercados de Futuros y Opciones SA)
	Rosario Board of Trade (Bolsa de Comercio de Rosario)
	Rosario Futures Exchange (Mercado a Termino de Rosario)
	Buenos Aires Futures Market (Mercado a Termino de Buenos Aires SA)
	Mercado Abierto Electronico SA
	Buenos Aires Cereal Exchange (Bolsa de Cereales de Buenos Aires)
Australia	Sydney Futures Exchange
Austria	Austrian Futures & Options Exchange (Osterreichische Termin und Optionenborse)
Belgium	Belgian Futures & Options Exchange
Brazil	Brazilian Futures Exchange (Bolsa Brasileira de Futuros)
	The Commodities & Futures Exchange (Bolsa de Mercadoris & Futuros)
Canada	Winnipeg Commodity Exchange
	Toronto Futures Exchange
China	China-Commodity Futures Exchange, Inc., of Hainan
	Shenzhen Mercantile Exchange
	Shanghai Cereals and Oils Exchange
	China Zhengzhou Commodity Exchange
	Guandong United Futures Exchange
	Beijing Commodity Exchange
Finland	Finnish Options Market
	Finnish Options Exchange (Suomen Optioporssi Oy)
France	MONEP (Marche des Options Negociables de Paris)
	MATIF (Marche a Terme International de France)
Germany	Deutsche Terminborse
Hong Kong	Hong Kong Futures Exchange, Ltd.
	Chinese Gold and Silver Exchange Society
Hungary	Budapest Commodity Exchange
Indonesia	Indonesian Commodity Exchange Board (Badan Pelaksana Bursa Komoditi)
Ireland	Irish Futures & Options Exchange
Italy	Italian Derivatives Market
	Italian Financial Futures Market (Mercato Italiano Futures)
Japan	Tokyo Commodity Exchange (Tokyo Kogyoin Torihikijo)
	Osaka Textile Exchange (Osaka Seni Torihikijo)
	Kobe Raw Silk Exchange (Kobe Kiito Torihiksho)
	Kobe Rubber Exchange (Kobe Gomu Torihiksho)
	Nagoya Textile Exchange
	Tokyo Grain Exchange (Tokyo Kokumotsu Shohin Torihikijo)
	Tokyo International Financial Futures Exchange
	Kammon Commodity Exchange (Kammon Shohin Torihikijo)
	Kansai Agricultural Commodities Exchange
	Maebashi Dried Cocoa Exchange (Maebashi Kanken Torihikijo)
	Cubu Commodity Exchange
	Yokohama Raw Silk Exchange (Yokohama Kiito Torihikijo)
Malaysia	Malaysia Monetary Exchange
	Kuala Lumpur Commodity Exchange
	The Kuala Lumpur Options & Financial Futures Exchange
Netherlands	AEX-Agricultural Futures Exchange
	AEX-Options Exchange
New Zealand	New Zealand Futures & Options Exchange, Ltd.
Philippines	Manila International Futures Exchange
Poland	Warsaw Commodity Exchange (Warszawska Gielda Towarowa)
Portugal	Oporto Derivatives Exchange (Bolsa de Derivados do Oporto)
Romania	Romanian Commodities Exchange (Bursa Romana de Marfuri SA)
	Sibiu Monetary-Financial and Commodities Exchange
Russian Federation	Moscow Interbank Currency Exchange
	Russian Exchange
	Moscow Commodity Exchange
	St Petersburg Futures Exchange

(continued)

TABLE 18.2 *(continued)*

Country	Exchange
Saudi Arabia	Saudi Arabian Monetary Authority
Singapore	Singapore Commodity Exchange, Ltd.
	Singapore International Monetary Exchange, Ltd.
Slovenia	Commodity Exchange of Ljubljana
South Africa	South African Futures Exchange SAFEX
Spain	Citrus Fruit and Commodity Market of Valencia (Futuros de Citricos y Mercaderias de Valencia)
	Spanish Options Exchange (MEFF Renta Variable)
	Spanish Financial Futures Market (MEFF Renta Fija)
Sweden	The Swedish Futures and Options Market (OM Stockholm AB)
Switzerland	Swiss Options & Financial Futures Exchange AG
United Kingdom	The London Securities and Derivatives Exchange
	London Metal Exchange
	London Commodity Exchange
	International Petroleum Exchange of London, Ltd.
	Tradepoint Investment Exchange
	London International Futures & Options Exchange
United States	Chicago Board of Trade
	Chicago Mercantile Exchange
	Coffee, Sugar & Cocoa Exchange, Inc.
	Kansas City Board of Trade
	MidAmerica Commodity Exchange
	Minneapolis Grain Exchange
	New York Cotton Exchange
	New York Mercantile Exchange
	Philadelphia Board of Trade

Futures Characteristics

Asset Specification

Wherever a high degree of price volatility is characteristic of the market for any broadly used good or service, there is a potential need for futures contracts. Originally developed for food and fiber crops, active futures markets have grown to encompass dozens of underlying assets from traditional agricultural products, to a wide variety of natural resources, to a growing list of financial assets, products, and services. Figure 18.1 shows a typical daily listing of futures prices and trading volume as described in *Barron's Market Week.* Notice how futures market activity is typically grouped according to seven major underlying asset groups, including grains and oilseeds, livestock and meat, food and fiber, metals and petroleum, interest rates, currencies, and stock indexes. Emerging markets are also developing to trade futures contracts on natural disasters such as hurricanes for catastrophic insurance and weather futures to hedge against temperature extremes.

For any good or service to form a satisfactory basis for futures contracts, four essential ingredients must exist. These are a

- *High Degree of Price Volatility:* The price of the underlying item must change enough to warrant the need for risk shifting. Futures contracts are desirable only so long as they allow those with price risk in the underlying item to shift that risk to other willing market participants.

FIGURE 18.1 ***Barron's* Gives a Weekly Summary of Trading Activity in the Commodities and Financial Futures Markets**

MW76 BARRON'S • MARKET WEEK May 1, 2000

COMMODITIES AND FINANCIAL FUTURES

Commodities, or futures, contracts originally called for delivery of physical items, such as agricultural products and metals, at a specified price at a specified future date. Increasingly, these contracts have come to apply also to Treasury bills, notes and bonds, certificates of deposit, major market indices and major currencies. Our futures options list includes only the week's most actively traded options with a minimum trade volume of 500 contracts.

FOREIGN EXCHANGE

Friday, April 28, 2000

The New York foreign exchange selling rates below apply to trading among banks in amounts of $1 million and more, as quoted at 3 p.m. Eastern time by Dow Jones Markets Inc. and other sources. Retail transactions provide fewer units of foreign currency per dollar.

Country	Foreign Currency in U.S. $ Fri.	Foreign Currency in U.S. $ Last Fri.	U.S. $ in Foreign Currency Fri.	U.S. $ in Foreign Currency Last Fri.
Argentina (Peso)	1.0007	1.0009	.9993	.9991
Australia (Dollar)	.5839	.5927	1.7125	1.6871
Austria (Schilling)	.06624	.06817	15.096	14.669
Bahrain (Dinar)	2.6525	2.6525	.3770	.3770
Belgium (Franc)	.0226	.0233	44.2542	43.0040
Brazil (Real)	.5540	.5626	1.8050	1.7775
Britain (Pound)	1.5534	1.5780	.6437	.6337
1-month forward	1.5537	1.5781	.6436	.6337
3-months forward	1.5548	1.5785	.6432	.6335
6-months forward	1.5572	1.5796	.6422	.6331
Canada (Dollar)	.6756	.6780	1.4802	1.4750
1-month forward	.6761	.6784	1.4791	1.4740
3-months forward	.6771	.6793	1.4769	1.4720
6-months forward	.6787	.6808	1.4735	1.4689
Chile (Peso)	.001941	.001960	515.25	510.25
China (Renminbi)	.1208	.1208	8.2799	8.2785
Colombia (Peso)	.0004979	.0005016	2008.35	1993.50
Czech. Rep. (Koruna)	....	....	....	....
Commercial rate	.02501	.02583	39.982	38.711
Denmark (Krone)	.1221	.1258	8.1903	7.9466
Ecuador (Sucre)	....	....	....	....
Floating rate	.00004000	.00004000	24999.50	24999.50
Finland (Markka)	.1533	.1578	6.5227	6.3384
France (Franc)	.1390	.1430	7.1961	6.9928
1-month forward	.1393	.1433	7.1805	6.9796
3-months forward	.1398	.1438	7.1512	6.9519
6-months forward	.1407	.1447	7.1067	6.9108
Germany (Mark)	.4661	.4796	2.1456	2.0850
1-month forward	.4671	.4805	2.1410	2.0811
3-months forward	.4690	.4824	2.1322	2.0728
6-months forward	.4719	.4853	2.1190	2.0605
Greece (Drachma)	.002706	.002797	369.52	357.55
Hong Kong (Dollar)	.1284	.1284	7.7891	7.7885
Hungary (Forint)	.003528	.003634	283.42	275.20
India (Rupee)	.02291	.02292	43.650	43.625
Indonesia (Rupiah)	.0001262	.0001256	7925.00	7965.00
Ireland (Punt)	1.1574	1.1910	.8640	.8396
Israel (Shekel)	.2476	.2475	4.0394	4.0410
Italy (Lira)	.0004708	.0004845	2124.15	2064.14
Japan (Yen)	.009242	.009448	108.20	105.84
1-month forward	.009292	.009496	107.62	105.31
3-months forward	.009394	.009596	106.45	104.21
6-months forward	.009556	.009755	104.65	102.51
Jordan (Dinar)	1.4085	1.4075	.7100	.7105
Kuwait (Dinar)	3.2468	3.2595	.3080	.3068
Lebanon (Pound)	.0006634	.0006634	1507.50	1507.50
Malaysia (Ringgit)	.2632	.2632	3.8001	3.8000
Malta (Lira)	2.2873	2.3299	.4372	.4292
Mexico (Peso)	....	....	....	....
Floating rate	.1064	.1063	9.3975	9.4050
Netherland (Guilder)	.4137	.4257	2.4175	2.3492
New Zealand (Dollar)	.4859	.4941	2.0580	2.0239
Norway (Krone)	.1118	.1153	8.9412	8.6739
Pakistan (Rupee)	.01925	.01927	51.950	51.900
Peru (new Sol)	.2877	.2882	3.4760	3.4695
Philippines (Peso)	.02422	.02423	41.285	41.275
Poland (Zloty) (d)	.2237	.2330	4.4700	4.2925
Portugal (Escudo)	.004547	.004679	219.94	213.72
Russia (Ruble) (a)	.03516	.03500	28.445	28.575
Saudi Arabia (Riyal)	.2666	.2666	3.7508	3.7506
Singapore (Dollar)	.5860	.5889	1.7065	1.6980
Slovak Rep. (Koruna)	.02192	.02259	45.621	44.263
South Africa (Rand)	.1473	.1484	6.7900	6.7400
South Korea (Won)	.0009011	.0009022	1109.75	1108.45
Spain (Peseta)	.005479	.005638	182.53	177.37
Sweden (Krona)	.1120	.1139	8.9288	8.7821
Switzerland (Franc)	.5817	.5969	1.7190	1.6753
1-month forward	.5835	.5986	1.7139	1.6707
3-months forward	.5866	.6019	1.7046	1.6614
6-months forward	.5916	.6070	1.6902	1.6475
Taiwan (Dollar)	.03269	.03276	30.595	30.525
Thailand (Baht)	.02626	.02636	38.085	37.935
Turkey (Lira)	.00000164	.00000166	611250.00	601130.00
United Arab (Dirham)	.2723	.2723	3.6730	3.6729
Uruguay (New Peso)	....	....	....	....
Financial	.08395	.08426	11.913	11.868
Venezuela (Bolivar)	.001481	.001488	675.26	672.25
SDR	1.3193	1.3349	.7580	.7491
Euro	.9116	.9381	1.0970	1.0660

Special Drawing Rights (SDR) are based on exchange rates for the U.S., German, British, French, and Japanese currencies. Source: International Monetary Fund.

a-Russian Central Bank rate. Trading band lowered on 8/17/98. b-Government rate. d-Floating rate; trading band suspended on 4/11/00.

The 3-month and 6-month forward rates for France, Germany, Japan and Switzerland appearing in the Foreign Exchange column were incorrectly calculated for the period beginning with August 13 and ending with October 7. Corrected data is available from Readers' Reference Service (413) 592-3600.

FUTURES

Fibers

COTTON 2 (NYBT TkrCT)
50,000 lbs.- cents per lb.

Season's High	Season's Low	Month	Week's High	Week's Low	Sett	Net Chg	Open Int.
75.40	50.10	May 00	56.94	55.20	55.71	− .71	301
73.70	51.50	Jul 00	58.48	55.40	55.81	− 2.11	32,110
72.10	53.18	Oct 00	59.50	57.10	57.61	− 1.24	1,365
67.50	53.75	Dec 00	60.10	58.00	58.41	− .92	14,178
65.18	55.10	Mar 01	60.75	59.65	59.80	− .66	1,580
65.63	56.20	May 01	61.35	60.00	60.25	− .75	861
66.40	56.50	Jul 01	62.00	60.98	61.00	− .70	227
63.70	57.10	Dec 01	60.80	60.00	59.98	− .72	193

Fri to Thu sales 29,485 Open int 50,826

Financial & Money

10 YR. TREASURY (CBOT TkrTY)
$100,000 prin-pts & 32nds & a half 32nd

Season's High	Season's Low	Month	Week's High	Week's Low	Sett	Net Chg	Open Int.
99-30	93-11	Jun 00	98-20	96-15	96-305	− 1-09	616,079
99-20	95-105	Sep 00	97-245	96-09	96-23	− 1-11	7,337

Fri to Thu sales 619,367 Open int 623,416

2 YR. TREASURY NOTES (CBOT TkrTU)
$200,000 prin-pts & 32nds & a quarter 32nd

Season's High	Season's Low	Month	Week's High	Week's Low	Sett	Net Chg	Open Int.
99-225	98-075	Jun 00	99-12	98-18	98-197	− 213	47,522
98-17	98-17	Sep 00	98-17	98-17	98-17	...	...

Fri to Thu sales 14,896 Open int 47,522

30 DAY FEDERAL FUNDS (CBOT TkrFF)
$5 million- pts. of 100 pct.

Season's High	Season's Low	Month	Week's High	Week's Low	Sett	Net Chg	Open Int.
94.45	93.91	Apr 00	93.99	93.97	93.98	− .01	16,841
94.20	93.79	May 00	93.87	93.79	93.79	− .08	18,023
94.11	93.55	Jun 00	93.72	93.55	93.57	− .14	11,652
94.06	93.37	Jul 00	93.57	93.37	93.38	− .19	4,783
93.73	93.34	Aug 00	93.53	93.34	93.34	− .21	1,590
93.64	93.26	Sep 00	93.51	93.26	93.27	− .22	1,096
93.52	93.19	Oct 00	93.45	93.19	93.19	− .29	128

Fri to Thu sales 28,071 Spot 6.00 Open int 54,140

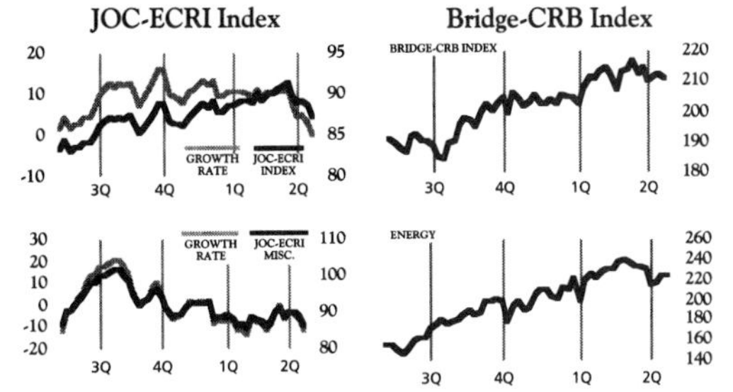

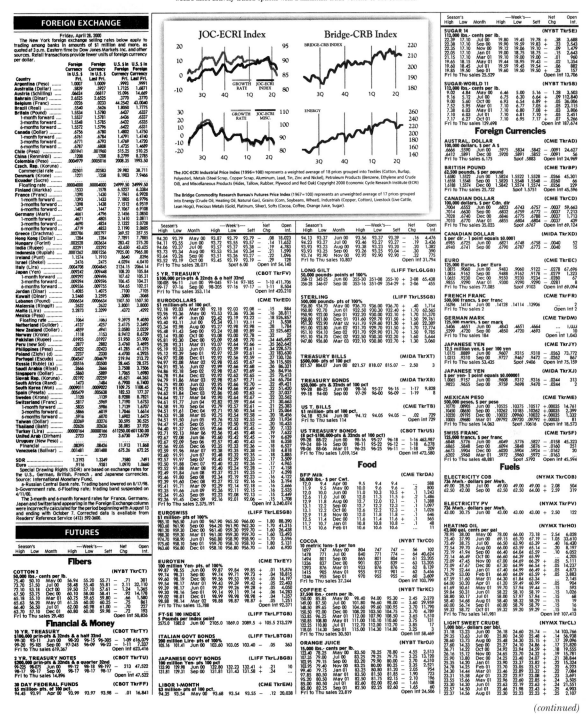

The JOC-ECRI Industrial Price Index (1996=100) represents a weighted average of 18 prices grouped into Textiles (Cotton, Burlap, Polyester), Metals (Steel Scrap, Copper Scrap, Aluminum, Lead, Tin, Zinc and Nickel), Petroleum Products (Benzene, Ethylene and Crude Oil), and Miscellaneous Products (Hides, Tallow, Rubber, Plywood and Red Oak) Copyright 2000 Economic Cycle Research Institute (ECRI)

The Bridge Commodity Research Bureau's Futures Price Index (1967=100) represents an unweighted average of 17 prices grouped into Energy (Crude Oil, Heating Oil, Natural Gas), Grains (Corn, Soybeans, Wheat), Industrials (Copper, Cotton), Livestock (Live Cattle, Lean Hogs), Precious Metals (Gold, Platinum, Silver), Softs (Cocoa, Coffee, Orange Juice, Sugar).

5 YR. TREASURY (CBOT TkrFV)
$100,000 prin-pts & 32nds & a half 32nd

Season's High	Season's Low	Month	Week's High	Week's Low	Sett	Net Chg	Open Int.
100-005	96-11	Jun 00	99-045	97-14	97-185	− 1-10	411,706
99-17	97-16	Sep 00	98-205	97-16	97-17	− 1-11	8,504

Fri to Thu sales 353,114 Open int 420,210

EURODOLLARS (CME TkrED)
$1 million-pts of 100 pct.

Season's High	Season's Low	Month	Week's High	Week's Low	Sett	Net Chg	Open Int.
92.18	92.03	Mar 00	92.18	92.03	92.08	− .15	884
93.96	93.36	May 00	93.53	93.36	93.36	− .16	38,811
95.60	92.49	Jun 00	93.42	93.19	93.22	− .18	526,857
93.40	93.11	Jul 00	93.34	93.11	93.11	− .21	3,538
93.34	92.98	Aug 00	93.27	92.98	92.98	− .28	1,784
95.48	91.43	Sep 00	93.24	92.88	92.89	− .32	525,682
93.14	93.00	Oct 00	93.08	93.00	92.78	− .32	25
95.81	92.30	Dec 00	93.09	92.68	92.70	− .34	445,692
95.28	92.31	Mar 01	93.07	92.64	92.66	− .35	362,642
95.19	92.33	Jun 01	93.01	92.59	92.61	− .34	228,575
95.12	92.39	Sep 01	92.97	92.59	92.61	− .32	183,630
94.97	92.08	Dec 01	92.92	92.56	92.59	− .27	130,126
94.97	92.08	Mar 02	92.98	92.65	92.67	− .26	115,505
94.91	92.16	Jun 02	92.99	92.66	92.68	− .26	86,321
94.86	92.18	Sep 02	92.98	92.67	92.69	− .26	84,916
94.78	91.84	Dec 02	92.92	92.62	92.65	− .25	70,413
94.79	91.86	Mar 03	92.98	92.67	92.71	− .24	65,704
94.75	92.00	Jun 03	92.95	92.66	92.70	− .22	49,421
94.72	91.93	Sep 03	92.94	92.66	92.69	− .22	51,420
94.62	91.84	Dec 03	92.86	92.60	92.63	− .22	37,037
94.64	92.17	Mar 04	92.90	92.64	92.67	− .22	32,562
94.61	91.77	Jun 04	92.82	92.59	92.64	− .21	30,663
94.58	91.70	Sep 04	92.79	92.57	92.61	− .21	25,383
94.51	91.61	Dec 04	92.71	92.50	92.54	− .21	25,064
94.53	91.38	Mar 05	92.75	92.54	92.58	− .20	18,456
94.51	91.50	Jun 05	92.76	92.52	92.55	− .20	11,934
94.47	91.45	Sep 05	92.73	92.50	92.52	− .20	10,433
94.40	91.37	Dec 05	92.66	92.43	92.45	− .20	7,133
92.71	92.13	Mar 06	92.56	92.45	92.48	− .19	7,632
92.67	92.08	Jun 06	92.60	92.42	92.45	− .19	6,639
92.67	92.09	Sep 06	92.57	92.40	92.43	− .18	6,358
92.56	92.05	Dec 06	92.35	92.33	92.36	− .18	6,527
92.59	91.96	Mar 07	92.38	92.35	92.38	− .18	4,818
92.60	91.91	Jun 07	92.48	92.32	92.35	− .18	3,885
92.57	91.97	Sep 07	92.45	92.29	92.33	− .17	3,509
92.50	91.88	Dec 07	92.40	92.32	92.26	− .17	4,965
92.52	91.88	Mar 08	92.40	92.24	92.28	− .17	4,158
92.49	91.84	Jun 08	92.37	92.21	92.25	− .17	4,298
92.46	91.80	Sep 08	92.34	92.19	92.23	− .16	4,122
92.39	91.60	Dec 08	92.27	92.12	92.16	− .16	3,194
92.41	91.71	Mar 09	92.29	92.14	92.18	− .16	2,666
92.35	91.66	Jun 09	92.26	92.11	92.15	− .16	2,535
92.34	91.63	Sep 09	92.23	92.08	92.13	− .15	2,449
92.26	91.45	Dec 09	92.16	92.01	92.06	− .15	1,708

Fri to Thu sales 2,375,191 Open int 3,240,074

EUROSWISS (LIFF TkrLESGB)
$1 million- pts of 100%

Season's High	Season's Low	Month	Week's High	Week's Low	Sett	Net Chg	Open Int.
985.10	965.50	Jun 00	967.90	965.50	966.00	− 1.80	88,390
983.60	961.90	Sep 00	964.20	961.90	962.30	− 1.70	41,315
981.20	959.30	Dec 00	961.40	959.30	959.70	− 1.60	26,438
988.30	959.30	Mar 01	961.00	959.30	959.70	− 1.60	13,493
974.70	958.90	Jun 01	960.80	958.90	958.90	− 1.70	3,596
975.60	958.10	Sep 01	959.70	958.10	958.10	− 1.80	5,131
963.60	956.80	Dec 01	958.10	956.80	956.70	− 1.60	6,920

EUROYEN (CME TkrEY)
100 million Yen- pts. of 100%

Season's High	Season's Low	Month	Week's High	Week's Low	Sett	Net Chg	Open Int.
99.87	98.55	Jun 00	99.87	99.84	99.85	+ .01	15,876
99.74	98.31	Sep 00	99.74	99.71	99.73	+ .04	18,815
99.60	98.19	Dec 00	99.56	99.53	99.55	+ .05	14,197
99.54	98.17	Mar 01	99.43	99.39	99.42	+ .05	22,403
99.39	98.17	Jun 01	99.29	99.26	99.28	+ .05	4,050
99.30	98.16	Sep 01	99.14	99.11	99.14	+ .06	14,283
99.02	98.01	Dec 01	98.99	98.98	98.98	+ .04	1,357
98.88	98.14	Mar 02	98.88	98.87	98.87	+ .05	1,251

Fri to Thu sales 15,788 Open int 92,371

FT-SE 100 INDEX (LIFF TkrLFTGB)
5 Pounds per index point

Season's High	Season's Low	Month	Week's High	Week's Low	Sett	Net Chg	Open Int.
2575.0	1582.0	Jun 00	2105.0	1869.0	2089.5	+ 105.5	213,279

ITALIAN GOVT BONDS (LIFF TkrLBTGB)
200 million Lire- pts of 100%

Season's High	Season's Low	Month	Week's High	Week's Low	Sett	Net Chg	Open Int.
105.16	101.41	Jun 00	103.60	103.05	103.40	− .05	363

JAPANESE GOVT BONDS (LIFF TkrLJBGB)
100 million Yen- pts 100 pct

Season's High	Season's Low	Month	Week's High	Week's Low	Sett	Net Chg	Open Int.
133.90	129.98	Jun 00	132.80	132.23	132.41	+ .21	10
131.81	129.31	Sep 00	131.81	131.43	131.58	+ .24	...

LIBOR 1-MONTH (CME TkrEM)
$3 million- pts of 100 pct.

Season's High	Season's Low	Month	Week's High	Week's Low	Sett	Net Chg	Open Int.
94.35	93.54	May 00	93.68	93.54	93.55	− .12	20,038
94.13	93.37	Jun 00	93.56	93.37	93.39	− .16	4,476
94.23	93.27	Jul 00	93.46	93.27	93.27	− .19	3,436
93.93	93.23	Aug 00	93.38	93.23	93.20	− .20	1,382
93.93	93.25	Sep 00	93.26	93.25	93.04	− .30	390
93.74	92.90	Nov 00	92.92	92.90	92.90	− .32	775

Fri to Thu sales 10,807 Open int 31,794

LONG GILT (LIFF TkrLGLGB)
50,000 pounds- points of 100%

Season's High	Season's Low	Month	Week's High	Week's Low	Sett	Net Chg	Open Int.
358-12	342-25	Jun 00	355-30	351-08	355-10	+ 2-08	65,438
356-28	346-07	Sep 00	353-16	351-09	354-29	+ 2-06	455

STERLING (LIFF TkrLSSGB)
500,000 pounds- pts of 100%

Season's High	Season's Low	Month	Week's High	Week's Low	Sett	Net Chg	Open Int.
936.80	934.70	May 00	936.70	936.00	936.70	+ .40	1,714
950.80	92.70	Jun 01	932.50	930.30	932.40	+ 1.70	62,565
950.90	922.00	Sep 01	932.20	930.00	932.10	+ 1.70	51,370
950.80	921.80	Dec 01	931.60	929.70	931.50	+ 1.50	29,761
951.30	922.90	Mar 02	931.70	929.60	931.50	+ 1.60	22,309
951.00	923.80	Jun 02	931.70	929.70	931.50	+ 1.70	12,774
951.10	924.10	Sep 02	931.70	929.90	931.70	+ 1.50	9,785
951.10	924.70	Dec 02	932.50	930.30	932.20	+ 1.60	5,644
947.80	926.80	Mar 03	932.10	930.80	932.70	+ 1.30	3,060

TREASURY BILLS (MIDA TkrXT)
$500,000- pts of 100 pct

Season's High	Season's Low	Month	Week's High	Week's Low	Sett	Net Chg	Open Int.
821.57	804.07	Jun 00	821.57	818.07	815.07	− 2.50	3

TREASURY BONDS (MIDA TkrXB)
$50,000- pts & 32nds of 100 pct

Season's High	Season's Low	Month	Week's High	Week's Low	Sett	Net Chg	Open Int.
99-28	88-25	Jun 00	98-16	95-27	96-15	− 1-17	9,828
99-18	94-00	Sep 00	97-29	96-00	96-09	− 1-19	8

US T. BILLS (CME TkrTB)
$1 million- pts of 100 pct.

Season's High	Season's Low	Month	Week's High	Week's Low	Sett	Net Chg	Open Int.
94.18	93.94	Jun 00	94.12	94.05	94.05	− .02	729

Fri to Thu sales 114 Open int 729

US TREASURY BONDS (CBOT TkrUS)
(8 pct-$100,000-pts & 32nds of 100 pct)

Season's High	Season's Low	Month	Week's High	Week's Low	Sett	Net Chg	Open Int.
99-28	88-22	Jun 00	98-16	95-27	96-18	− 1-16	463,987
99-24	88-16	Sep 00	98-11	95-22	96-12	− 1-18	6,278
98-06	88-06	Mar 01	96-25	96-25	96-11	− 1-18	209

Fri to Thu sales 1,019,154 Open int 472,580

Food

BFP Milk (CME TkrDA)
50,000 lbs.- $ per Cwt.

Season's High	Season's Low	Month	Week's High	Week's Low	Sett	Net Chg	Open Int.
12.0	9.4	Apr 00	9.5	9.4	9.4	...	588
11.9	9.5	May 00	10.0	9.6	9.6	− .2	800
12.0	10.0	Jun 00	11.0	10.3	10.5	+ .1	1,243
12.6	11.0	Jul 00	12.0	11.3	11.5	+ .2	1,486
12.9	11.8	Aug 00	12.7	12.0	12.1	− .1	1,388
13.1	12.2	Sep 00	12.7	12.2	12.3	− .1	1,097
13.1	12.2	Oct 00	12.6	12.2	12.3	− .1	1,026
12.9	11.8	Nov 00	12.0	11.8	11.8	− .1	646
12.5	11.4	Dec 00	11.6	11.4	11.6	+ .1	565
11.7	10.7	Jan 01	10.8	10.8	10.8	− .1	48
11.5	10.6	Feb 01	10.6	10.6	10.6	...	11

COCOA (NYBT TkrCO)
10 metric tons- $ per ton

Season's High	Season's Low	Month	Week's High	Week's Low	Sett	Net Chg	Open Int.
1697	747	May 00	804	747	747	− 56	102
1478	771	Jul 00	840	771	774	− 64	40,624
1494	801	Sep 00	865	801	804	− 61	23,205
1336	837	Dec 00	901	837	839	− 63	13,205
1393	876	Mar 01	933	876	876	− 62	8,139
1415	905	May 01	955	912	901	− 62	5,456
1246	955	Sep 01	970	955	955	− 60	3,609

Fri to Thu sales 37,244 Open int 103,799

COFFEE C (NYBT TkrKC)
37,500 lbs.- cents per lb.

Season's High	Season's Low	Month	Week's High	Week's Low	Sett	Net Chg	Open Int.
150.00	85.85	May 00	98.40	94.00	95.30	− 2.45	2,270
149.00	87.50	Jul 00	101.80	96.60	98.00	− 3.60	29,959
148.50	89.65	Sep 00	104.60	99.60	100.95	− 3.70	11,790
150.50	92.00	Dec 00	108.20	103.50	104.75	− 3.70	4,789
153.85	96.25	Mar 01	112.00	107.90	108.50	− 3.65	1,510
150.85	108.80	May 01	111.00	110.10	110.60	− 3.75	131
122.25	110.80	Jul 01	112.70	112.00	112.70	− 3.85	17
118.05	114.30	Sep 01	115.00	114.30	114.80	− 3.25	3

Fri to Thu sales 30,501 Open int 58,469

ORANGE JUICE (NYBT TkrOJ)
15,000 lbs.- cents per lb.

Season's High	Season's Low	Month	Week's High	Week's Low	Sett	Net Chg	Open Int.
123.40	78.25	May 00	83.50	78.25	78.80	− 4.55	2,513
107.35	79.00	Jul 00	83.25	79.25	79.75	− 3.25	13,120
102.95	79.15	Sep 00	83.20	79.90	80.00	− 2.70	4,310
103.95	79.40	Nov 00	83.25	80.00	80.25	− 2.35	2,521
99.40	79.75	Jan 01	83.25	80.80	81.20	− 2.05	954
97.85	80.50	Mar 01	83.50	81.50	81.85	− 1.90	723
95.20	80.50	May 01	82.50	81.75	82.15	− 2.10	196
85.00	80.50	Jul 01	82.60	82.00	82.60	− 1.65	108
85.00	82.25	Sep 01	82.50	82.25	82.60	− 1.65	60

Fri to Thu sales 23,819 Open int 24,506

SUGAR 14 (NYBT TkrSE)
112,000 lbs.- cents per lb.

Season's High	Season's Low	Month	Week's High	Week's Low	Sett	Net Chg	Open Int.
22.39	17.10	Jul 00	19.80	19.45	19.78	+ .38	3,688
22.38	17.10	Sep 00	19.90	19.59	19.83	+ .23	2,543
22.35	17.10	Nov 00	19.12	19.06	19.10	− .09	1,479
22.05	17.10	Jan 01	19.00	18.75	18.75	− .15	2,643
21.15	17.10	Mar 01	19.10	19.00	19.00	− .01	960
19.65	18.15	May 01	19.44	18.95	19.43	− .02	1,354
19.60	18.45	Jul 01	19.59	19.45	19.54	− .06	882
19.85	19.50	Sep 01	19.60	19.50	19.50	+ .25	157

Fri to Thu sales 25,529 Open int 13,706

SUGAR-WORLD 11 (NYBT TkrSB)
112,000 lbs.- cents per lb.

Season's High	Season's Low	Month	Week's High	Week's Low	Sett	Net Chg	Open Int.
9.02	4.84	May 00	6.46	5.00	5.16	− 1.28	3,503
9.16	5.12	Jul 00	6.75	6.30	6.64	+ .09	112,840
9.00	5.60	Oct 00	6.93	6.54	6.89	+ .05	36,006
7.52	5.95	Mar 01	7.10	6.77	7.05	+ .05	23,115
7.38	6.03	May 01	7.10	6.80	7.08	+ .03	3,806
7.10	6.03	Jul 01	7.10	6.81	7.10	+ .05	2,451
7.17	6.27	Oct 01	7.10	6.95	7.17	+ .07	5,266

Fri to Thu sales 129,698 Open int 187,674

Foreign Currencies

AUSTRAL. DOLLAR (CME TkrAD)
100,000 dollars, $ per A $

Season's High	Season's Low	Month	Week's High	Week's Low	Sett	Net Chg	Open Int.
.6666	.5590	Jun 00	.5975	.5834	.5842	− .0091	24,627
.6412	.5891	Dec 00	.5920	.5891	.5852	− .0091	56

Fri to Thu sales 6,175 Spot .5883 Open int 24,969

BRITISH POUND (CME TkrBP)
62,500 pounds, $ per pound

Season's High	Season's Low	Month	Week's High	Week's Low	Sett	Net Chg	Open Int.
1.6580	1.5522	Jun 00	1.5824	1.5522	1.5528	− .0266	45,301
1.6558	1.5548	Sep 00	1.5820	1.5548	1.5548	− .0260	66
1.6188	1.5574	Dec 00	1.5842	1.5574	1.5574	− .0256	229

Fri to Thu sales 25,732 Spot 1.5751 Open int 45,596

CANADIAN DOLLAR (CME TkrCD)
100,000 dollars, $ per Cdn. dlr

Season's High	Season's Low	Month	Week's High	Week's Low	Sett	Net Chg	Open Int.
.7004	.6552	Jun 00	.6823	.6743	.6757	− .0037	59,663
.7014	.6630	Sep 00	.6832	.6759	.6772	− .0037	7,213
.7028	.6740	Dec 00	.6846	.6775	.6788	− .0037	1,713
.7010	.6770	Mar 01	.6855	.6804	.6804	− .0037	439

Fri to Thu sales 35,023 Spot .6767 Open int 69,124

CANADIAN DOLLAR (MIDA TkrXD)
$ per dlr.- 1 point equals $0.0001

Season's High	Season's Low	Month	Week's High	Week's Low	Sett	Net Chg	Open Int.
.6985	.6725	Jun 00	.6821	.6748	.6758	− .0040	52
.6940	.6741	Sep 00	.6790	.6787	.6773	− .0040	15

EURO (CME TkrEC)
125,000 Euros, $ per Euro

Season's High	Season's Low	Month	Week's High	Week's Low	Sett	Net Chg	Open Int.
1.0875	.9060	Jun 00	.9483	.9060	.9122	− .0278	67,696
1.0834	.9162	Sep 00	.9488	.9162	.9178	− .0279	1,323
1.0655	.9230	Dec 00	.9550	.9230	.9234	− .0280	67
.9855	.9290	Mar 01	.9300	.9290	.9290	− .0281	8

Fri to Thu sales 77,085 Spot .9103 Open int 69,094

FRENCH FRANC (CME TkrFR)
500,000 francs, $ per franc

Season's High	Season's Low	Month	Week's High	Week's Low	Sett	Net Chg	Open Int.
.16396	.14114	Jun 00	.14128	.14114	.13906	...	2

Fri to Thu sales 2 Open int 2

GERMAN MARK (CME TkrDM)
125,000 marks, $ per mark

Season's High	Season's Low	Month	Week's High	Week's Low	Sett	Net Chg	Open Int.
.5406	.4651	Jun 00	.4843	.4651	.4664	...	1,033
.5299	.4720	Sep 00	.4850	.4720	.4693	...	10

Fri to Thu sales 184 Open int 1,043

JAPANESE YEN (CME TkrJY)
12.5 million yen, $ per 100 yen

Season's High	Season's Low	Month	Week's High	Week's Low	Sett	Net Chg	Open Int.
1.0175	.8889	Jun 00	.9607	.9315	.9318	− .0263	73,772
1.0313	.9310	Sep 00	.9727	.9467	.9472	− .0262	867

Fri to Thu sales 53,435 Spot .9406 Open int 75,159

JAPANESE YEN (MIDA TkrXJ)
$ per yen- 1 point equals $0.000001

Season's High	Season's Low	Month	Week's High	Week's Low	Sett	Net Chg	Open Int.
1.0065	.9157	Jun 00	.9608	.9312	.9316	− .0244	313
.9823	.9655	Sep 00	.9758	.9698	.9470	− .0244	2

MEXICAN PESO (CME TkrME)
500,000 pesos, $ per peso

Season's High	Season's Low	Month	Week's High	Week's Low	Sett	Net Chg	Open Int.
.10770	.08905	Jun 00	.10525	.10375	.10517	+.00035	14,761
.10450	.08650	Sep 00	.10262	.10185	.10262	+.00035	2,399
.10220	.09195	Dec 00	.10032	.09960	.10032	+.00035	1,332
.10005	.09680	Mar 01	.09792	.09720	.09792	+.00035	81

Fri to Thu sales 14,063 Spot .10616 Open int 18,573

SWISS FRANC (CME TkrSF)
125,000 francs, $ per franc

Season's High	Season's Low	Month	Week's High	Week's Low	Sett	Net Chg	Open Int.
.6848	.5776	Jun 00	.6049	.5776	.5827	− .0158	45,323
.6865	.5848	Sep 00	.6094	.5848	.5876	− .0160	251
.6673	.5904	Dec 00	.6020	.5904	.5924	− .0162	20
.6202	.5960	Mar 01	.5972	.5960	.5972	− .0163	...

Fri to Thu sales 48,881 Spot .5792 Open int 45,594

Fuels

ELECTRICITY COB (NYMX TkrCOB)
736 Mwh.- dollars per Mwh.

Season's High	Season's Low	Month	Week's High	Week's Low	Sett	Net Chg	Open Int.
49.00	28.50	Jul 00	49.00	49.00	49.00	+ 2.08	504
62.50	42.00	Sep 00	62.50	62.50	64.00	+ 2.59	319

ELECTRICITY PV (NYMX TkrPV)
736 Mwh.- dollars per Mwh.

Season's High	Season's Low	Month	Week's High	Week's Low	Sett	Net Chg	Open Int.
43.00	30.75	Jun 00	43.00	43.00	43.00	+ 2.50	122

HEATING OIL (NYMX TkrHO)
42,000 gal, cents per gal

Season's High	Season's Low	Month	Week's High	Week's Low	Sett	Net Chg	Open Int.
78.95	38.00	May 00	78.00	66.00	73.18	− 2.54	6,028
75.40	37.90	Jun 00	69.15	65.70	67.19	− 1.05	33,610
73.49	38.75	Jul 00	66.50	63.90	65.39	− .40	16,430
72.54	39.70	Aug 00	66.00	63.59	65.14	− .20	8,197
72.19	41.94	Sep 00	66.40	64.04	65.59	− .10	6,052
72.14	46.49	Oct 00	66.60	64.39	65.99	...	4,205
72.09	47.45	Nov 00	67.00	64.69	66.29	+ .05	5,111
72.09	47.67	Dec 00	67.30	64.99	66.54	+ .05	14,237
71.79	52.44	Jan 01	67.40	64.99	66.49	+ .05	4,873
70.29	53.00	Feb 01	66.60	64.09	65.59	+ .05	3,883
67.59	51.60	Mar 01	64.30	61.84	63.34	...	2,145
64.00	50.20	Apr 01	61.20	59.49	60.99	− .05	904
61.69	50.61	May 01	59.70	57.94	59.44	− .15	593
59.84	50.31	Jun 01	58.22	58.10	58.19	− .15	1,026
58.80	50.17	Jul 01	58.00	57.97	57.94	− .15	68
58.40	54.68	Aug 01	58.40	58.32	58.29	− .15	19
60.00	56.74	Sep 01	60.00	58.79	58.79	− .15	16
59.32	58.72	Oct 01	59.32	59.20	59.29	− .15	16

Fri to Thu sales 141,981 Open int 107,413

LIGHT SWEET CRUDE (NYMX TkrCL)
1,000 bbl.- dollars per bbl.

Season's High	Season's Low	Month	Week's High	Week's Low	Sett	Net Chg	Open Int.
31.18	13.23	Jun 00	26.18	24.60	25.74	− .14	103,766
29.35	13.63	Jul 00	25.80	24.50	25.48	+ .14	56,938
28.60	13.73	Aug 00	25.48	24.30	25.15	+ .17	39,096
27.60	14.33	Sep 00	25.27	24.10	24.86	+ .17	21,820
26.71	14.22	Oct 00	24.92	23.94	24.59	+ .18	19,555
26.16	15.12	Nov 00	24.65	23.70	24.32	+ .19	15,781
25.90	13.80	Dec 00	24.25	23.40	24.07	+ .21	38,844
25.35	14.20	Jan 01	23.90	23.37	23.82	+ .22	15,324
24.78	14.25	Feb 01	23.70	23.05	23.57	+ .22	6,223
24.30	14.44	Mar 01	23.46	22.89	23.32	+ .22	7,084
23.31	15.58	Apr 01	23.22	22.97	23.08	+ .23	3,691
23.55	15.66	May 01	22.96	22.60	22.85	+ .24	3,505
23.30	14.30	Jun 01	22.63	22.19	22.63	+ .24	21,551
22.57	14.50	Jul 01	22.46	21.98	22.43	+ .25	4,903
22.37	14.56	Aug 01	22.30	22.23	22.23	+ .25	2,107

(continued)

COMMODITIES

Season's High	Season's Low	Month	Week's High	Week's Low	Sett	Net Chg	Open Int.
22.01	16.89	Oct 01	21.65	21.28	21.83	+ .25	1,739
21.75	14.70	Dec 01	21.60	20.89	21.44	+ .25	24,872
21.19	12.22	Mar 02	21.00	20.67	20.94	+ .25	2,480
20.86	16.27	Jun 02	20.61	20.45	20.59	+ .25	3,210
23.20	13.80	Dec 02	20.02	20.00	20.00	+ .25	9,523
22.00	15.89	Dec 03	19.40	19.19	19.38	+ .25	8,074
19.58	16.75	Dec 05	19.30	19.16	19.14	+ .25	1,003

Fri to Thu sales 482,657 Open int 422,814

LIQUID PROPANE (NYMX TkrPN)
42,000 gal- cents per gal

Season's High	Season's Low	Month	Week's High	Week's Low	Sett	Net Chg	Open Int.
47.75	34.80	Jun 00	46.50	44.75	46.00	...	375
47.65	35.75	Jul 00	45.65	45.00	46.40	...	133
47.25	36.50	Oct 00	46.50	46.50	47.25	− .25	65

Fri to Thu sales 616 Open int 994

NATURAL GAS (NYMX TkrNG)
10,000 mm btu's, $ per mm btu

Season's High	Season's Low	Month	Week's High	Week's Low	Sett	Net Chg	Open Int.
3.190	2.065	Jun 00	3.175	3.040	3.141	+ .053	65,132
3.195	2.083	Jul 00	3.180	3.045	3.158	+ .056	24,419
3.200	2.090	Aug 00	3.185	3.070	3.166	+ .051	23,018
3.190	2.100	Sep 00	3.180	3.065	3.160	+ .049	23,094
3.200	2.100	Oct 00	3.185	3.085	3.170	+ .051	21,688
3.280	2.048	Nov 00	3.270	3.175	3.255	+ .046	15,867
3.360	2.380	Dec 00	3.360	3.275	3.346	+ .042	21,818
3.375	2.259	Jan 01	3.375	3.290	3.360	+ .041	15,946
3.210	2.305	Feb 01	3.210	3.135	3.200	+ .045	9,568
3.040	2.210	Mar 01	3.040	2.970	3.035	+ .049	9,945
2.885	2.120	Apr 01	2.885	2.830	2.875	+ .039	7,334
2.840	2.114	May 01	2.840	2.791	2.830	+ .035	6,692
2.845	2.095	Jun 01	2.845	2.790	2.830	+ .033	9,083
2.845	2.095	Jul 01	2.845	2.790	2.830	+ .032	6,510
2.845	2.102	Aug 01	2.845	2.800	2.831	+ .033	4,637
2.832	2.132	Sep 01	2.832	2.795	2.829	+ .031	3,535
2.860	2.133	Oct 01	2.860	2.822	2.848	+ .030	4,018
2.961	2.271	Nov 01	2.961	2.930	2.956	+ .029	3,050
3.071	2.410	Dec 01	3.071	3.032	3.058	+ .021	4,711
3.080	2.450	Jan 02	3.080	3.080	3.080	+ .023	4,166
2.961	2.415	Feb 02	2.961	2.930	2.961	+ .023	2,873
2.845	2.347	Mar 02	2.820	2.820	2.818	+ .018	3,246
2.698	2.345	Jun 02	2.698	2.687	2.683	+ .008	4,798
2.695	2.412	Aug 02	2.695	2.690	2.693	+ .015	1,839
2.695	2.423	Sep 02	2.695	2.695	2.691	+ .009	1,529
2.980	2.716	Dec 02	2.975	2.947	2.970	+ .005	1,757
3.010	2.730	Jan 03	3.010	2.995	3.000	+ .005	2,021
2.892	2.685	Feb 03	2.892	2.892	2.887	+ .005	256
2.676	2.610	Apr 03	2.672	2.672	2.672	+ .005	336
2.635	2.629	May 03	2.635	2.629	2.652	...	21

Fri to Thu sales 340,314 Open int 310,104

UNLEADED GASOLINE (NYMX TkrHU)
42,000 gal, cents per gal

Season's High	Season's Low	Month	Week's High	Week's Low	Sett	Net Chg	Open Int.
97.30	51.66	May 00	85.60	79.95	82.59	− 2.93	8,933
92.10	52.08	Jun 00	83.20	79.25	81.45	− 1.25	35,001
88.00	58.20	Jul 00	80.50	77.20	79.50	− .25	16,831
84.80	57.36	Aug 00	77.66	74.70	77.00	+ .10	15,602
81.50	57.65	Sep 00	75.10	72.40	74.50	+ .30	14,108
76.85	60.48	Oct 00	71.11	68.90	70.85	+ .45	7,530
74.65	59.28	Nov 00	69.27	67.30	69.15	+ .50	3,163
73.15	58.58	Dec 00	67.97	67.00	67.80	+ .65	1,839

Fri to Thu sales 194,203 Open int 103,090

Grains and Feed

BARLEY (WCE TkrWA)
20 metric tons- can $ per ton

Season's High	Season's Low	Month	Week's High	Week's Low	Sett	Net Chg	Open Int.
131.50	114.10	May 00	116.90	114.10	114.10	− 1.50	1,264
131.00	116.20	Jul 00	120.70	118.00	118.20	− 1.30	7,662
132.00	119.00	Oct 00	125.30	122.00	122.00	− 1.00	8,238
129.60	121.10	Dec 00	128.60	125.00	125.20	− .70	3,650

CANOLA (WCE TkrRS)
20 metric tons- can $ per ton

Season's High	Season's Low	Month	Week's High	Week's Low	Sett	Net Chg	Open Int.
386.50	252.30	May 00	277.30	268.00	268.00	− 3.10	3,704
390.30	258.00	Jul 00	284.00	274.00	274.20	− 3.30	29,630
377.10	261.50	Aug 00	284.80	277.50	277.50	− 3.00	2,828
298.00	266.50	Sep 00	288.00	285.20	280.00	− 4.00	653
372.00	267.50	Nov 00	294.40	285.00	285.60	− 3.70	19,362
299.40	273.60	Jan 01	299.40	290.50	290.50	− 3.50	3,376
301.00	288.50	Mar 01	294.00	294.00	294.00	− 4.00	134

CORN (CBOT TkrNC)
5,000 bu minimum- cents per bushel

Season's High	Season's Low	Month	Week's High	Week's Low	Sett	Net Chg	Open Int.
261	202½	May 00	231¾	223½	223¾	− 3	26,215
278½	209	Jul 00	241	231½	232	− 3¾	242,813
256½	215¾	Sep 00	250	240	240¼	− 3¼	52,432
260	222½	Nov 00	254½	246	246	− 3¼	920
279½	225¼	Dec 00	258¾	249½	250	− 3¾	117,373
265	234	Jan 01	263	258½	254¼	− 3	91
271	233¾	Mar 01	267¼	258¼	258½	− 4	14,237
275¾	256½	May 01	271¼	263	263¼	− 3¾	2,384
279	241	Jul 01	274½	267	267	− 3¾	3,407
276½	261½	Sep 01	263¾	263	263	− 2¾	203
272½	246	Dec 01	272½	265½	265½	− 2½	4,488
270	260	Dec 02	270	268½	267	− ½	104

Fri to Thu sales 444,550 Open int 464,667

CORN (MIDA TkrXC)
1,000 bu minimum- cents per bushel

Season's High	Season's Low	Month	Week's High	Week's Low	Sett	Net Chg	Open Int.
261	202¼	May 00	231¾	223¼	223¾	− 3	1,241
269½	209¼	Jul 00	241	231½	232	− 3¾	3,735
255¾	217½	Sep 00	248¾	240	240¼	− 3¼	284
282	225¼	Dec 00	258½	249½	250	− 3¾	1,839
270¾	236¼	Mar 01	266¼	260	258½	− 4	419
271¼	263¼	May 01	271¼	263¼	263¼	− 3¾	2
271¼	246	Dec 01	271¼	268¾	265½	− 2½	35

Fri to Thu sales 7,911 Open int 7,587

DURUM WHEAT (MGE TkrDW)
5,000 bu minimum- cents per bushel

Season's High	Season's Low	Month	Week's High	Week's Low	Sett	Net Chg	Open Int.
500	362	May 00	425	425	410	− 15	4
426	400	Sep 00	420	420	415	− 9	60

FLAXSEED (WCE TkrWF)
20 metric tons- can $ per ton

Season's High	Season's Low	Month	Week's High	Week's Low	Sett	Net Chg	Open Int.
333.50	218.00	May 00	243.50	237.40	238.20	+ .20	90
336.00	220.90	Jul 00	247.00	240.00	241.50	− .50	3,135
250.00	236.00	Sep 00	250.00	245.10	244.50	− 1.50	294
323.00	231.00	Nov 00	255.00	248.00	249.00	− .80	1,874

NEW SOYMEAL (MIDA TkrXE)
20 tons- dollars per ton

Season's High	Season's Low	Month	Week's High	Week's Low	Sett	Net Chg	Open Int.
17.62	12.90	May 00	17.62	16.85	17.17	+ .25	86
17.79	13.88	Jul 00	17.79	16.93	17.14	+ .13	217
17.70	14.45	Aug 00	17.70	16.93	17.12	+ .11	37
17.62	14.50	Sep 00	17.53	17.35	17.14	+ .11	9
17.60	14.38	Oct 00	17.60	16.97	17.14	+ .09	12
17.84	13.60	Dec 00	17.84	17.25	17.29	+ .07	15
17.62	14.75	Jan 01	17.32	17.29	17.29	+ .01	2
17.50	17.10	Mar 01	17.41	17.35	17.35	...	1

OATS (CBOT TkrNO)
5,000 bu minimum- cents per bushel

Season's High	Season's Low	Month	Week's High	Week's Low	Sett	Net Chg	Open Int.
150	112¾	May 00	127½	123½	125¾	...	669
126	110½	Jul 00	124¾	121¼	121¾	− 1½	10,902
130	115¾	Sep 00	126½	123¾	123¾	− ¼	2,303
135	123	Dec 00	131¾	128	129	− ½	3,873
135½	130	Mar 01	135½	135	135	+ ½	340

Fri to Thu sales 11,144 Open int 18,008

OATS (MIDA TkrXO)
1,000 bu minimum- cents per bushel

Season's High	Season's Low	Month	Week's High	Week's Low	Sett	Net Chg	Open Int.
146	113½	May 00	126	123	125¾	...	7
125	112	Jul 00	125	121½	121¾	− 1½	62
129¼	117½	Sep 00	126½	123¾	123¾	− ¼	10
130½	123½	Dec 00	130	129	129	− ½	12

Fri to Thu sales 119 Open int 92

ROUGH RICE (CBOT TkrNNR)
2,000 CWT- dollars per CWT

Season's High	Season's Low	Month	Week's High	Week's Low	Sett	Net Chg	Open Int.
6.220	1.240	May 00	5.340	5.140	5.170	− .160	1,347
6.900	5.420	Jul 00	5.640	5.440	5.460	− .170	3,747
6.960	6.160	Sep 00	6.520	6.160	6.180	− .340	727
7.120	6.250	Nov 00	6.660	6.250	6.310	− .330	1,172
7.240	6.430	Jan 01	6.800	6.430	6.450	− .330	261

Fri to Thu sales 7,583 Open int 7,254

SOYBEAN MEAL (CBOT TkrNSM)
100 tons- dollars per ton

Season's High	Season's Low	Month	Week's High	Week's Low	Sett	Net Chg	Open Int.
176.50	127.30	May 00	176.50	168.50	171.70	+ 2.50	15,795
177.70	130.00	Jul 00	177.70	169.50	171.40	+ 1.30	68,087
177.20	131.00	Aug 00	177.20	169.80	171.20	+ 1.10	12,629
177.00	132.00	Sep 00	177.00	169.30	171.40	+ 1.10	7,294
177.20	131.50	Oct 00	177.00	169.50	171.40	+ .90	7,763
180.20	135.50	Dec 00	178.70	171.00	172.90	+ .70	15,678
181.00	148.00	Jan 01	178.50	171.50	172.90	+ .10	1,283
182.50	170.00	Mar 01	179.50	172.50	173.50	...	2,079
185.00	173.00	May 01	179.00	173.00	174.50	− .20	1,534
179.50	174.50	Jul 01	179.50	174.50	175.30	...	42

Fri to Thu sales 188,186 Open int 132,189

SOYBEAN OIL (CBOT TkrNBO)
60,000 lbs- cents per lb

Season's High	Season's Low	Month	Week's High	Week's Low	Sett	Net Chg	Open Int.
23.40	15.60	May 00	18.65	17.47	17.61	− .95	11,341
22.20	15.95	Jul 00	19.02	17.88	18.05	− .89	65,586
21.00	16.12	Aug 00	19.11	18.06	18.23	− .89	13,908
20.65	16.27	Sep 00	19.22	18.25	18.37	− .88	11,072
22.25	16.42	Oct 00	19.40	18.50	18.57	− .86	6,735
20.62	16.75	Dec 00	19.76	18.78	18.92	− .89	20,907
20.10	17.09	Jan 01	20.03	19.25	19.25	− .84	8,189
20.38	17.45	Mar 01	20.28	19.58	19.50	− .83	2,871
20.68	17.70	May 01	20.55	19.70	19.70	− .90	3,520
20.95	18.00	Jul 01	20.85	20.80	19.95	− .90	1,981
20.98	20.10	Aug 01	20.98	20.90	20.10	− .85	16
21.15	20.22	Sep 01	21.15	21.00	20.20	− .85	12

Fri to Thu sales 157,744 Open int 146,328

SOYBEANS (CBOT TkrNS)
5,000 bu minimum- cents per bushel

Season's High	Season's Low	Month	Week's High	Week's Low	Sett	Net Chg	Open Int.
554	432	May 00	547½	522½	526½	− 9¾	12,052
647	440	Jul 00	561½	533	539¼	− 9¾	99,702
569	441	Aug 00	564	537	542	− 10½	10,031
571½	455	Sep 00	566	538½	545	− 10	7,152
633	453	Nov 00	573½	546½	551½	− 10	47,345
586	504	Jan 01	580½	555	559¼	− 10¼	4,079
591½	507	Mar 01	587	563½	566	− 11	3,213
593½	547	May 01	590	566	569	− 11	3,177
598	535	Jul 01	593	568	573½	− 9	2,043
600	501	Nov 01	594	571½	573	− 11	672

Fri to Thu sales 312,650 Open int 189,466

SOYBEANS (MIDA TkrXS)
1,000 bu minimum- cents per bushel

Season's High	Season's Low	Month	Week's High	Week's Low	Sett	Net Chg	Open Int.
555	432	May 00	547	523	526½	− 9¾	780
647	442¼	Jul 00	561	533	539¼	− 9¾	5,429
569	464	Aug 00	563	538½	542	− 10½	146
572	453	Sep 00	566½	540	545	− 10	240
619	454¾	Nov 00	573	547	551½	− 10	1,640
584½	506½	Jan 01	580	556½	559¼	− 10¼	95
589	507½	Mar 01	584	565	566	− 11	40
585	553½	May 01	577	574¾	569	− 11	166
600	537	Nov 01	590½	580	573	− 11	13

Fri to Thu sales 16,374 Open int 8,574

SPRING WHEAT (MGE TkrMW)
5,000 bu minimum- cents per bushel

Season's High	Season's Low	Month	Week's High	Week's Low	Sett	Net Chg	Open Int.
389	314½	May 00	321	314½	320	+ ½	2,270
380	323½	Jul 00	332	323½	325¾	− 5	11,510
385	333	Sep 00	342	333	334¾	− 7¼	5,917
383	344	Dec 00	354½	346	346½	− 9½	2,224
375	355	Mar 01	366	358½	358½	− 7½	246
378	376	Jul 01	378	376	373	...	1

WHEAT (CBOT TkrNW)
5,000 bu minimum- cents per bushel

Season's High	Season's Low	Month	Week's High	Week's Low	Sett	Net Chg	Open Int.
322	240½	May 00	255	240½	242¼	− 8¾	6,864
347	253	Jul 00	268½	253	254¾	− 8¼	83,072
335	265½	Sep 00	282¾	265½	266½	− 8½	14,970
345	280½	Dec 00	295	280¾	282	− 8	18,330
327	294½	Mar 01	307	294½	295½	− 7¼	3,698
353	300	Jul 01	316	305	306½	− 5¾	1,017
343	319	Dec 01	329	319	320½	− 4¾	142

Fri to Thu sales 176,215 Open int 128,143

WHEAT (MIDA TkrXW)
1,000 bu minimum- cents per bushel

Season's High	Season's Low	Month	Week's High	Week's Low	Sett	Net Chg	Open Int.
321	239½	May 00	254½	239½	242¼	− 8¾	253
347	253	Jul 00	268½	253	254¾	− 8¼	1,211
323	266	Sep 00	278½	266	266½	− 8½	104
345	281½	Dec 00	295	281½	282	− 8	115
326	295½	Mar 01	305¼	295½	295½	− 7¼	41

Fri to Thu sales 1,810 Open int 1,727

WHEAT (WCE TkrWW)
20 metric tons- can $ per ton

Season's High	Season's Low	Month	Week's High	Week's Low	Sett	Net Chg	Open Int.
149.00	129.50	May 00	140.50	135.70	135.70	− 2.30	641
151.50	132.80	Jul 00	144.50	141.50	141.60	− .60	3,246
153.00	136.80	Oct 00	148.40	145.00	145.00	− .90	4,229
151.00	139.10	Dec 00	151.00	148.00	148.00	− .40	1,727

WHITE WHEAT (MGE TkrMEW)
5,000 bu minimum- cents per bushel

Season's High	Season's Low	Month	Week's High	Week's Low	Sett	Net Chg	Open Int.
338	288	May 00	296	288	288	− 5	132
314	288	Jul 00	296	288	288	− 10	81
326½	318	Dec 00	318	318	312	− 14½	3

WINTER WHEAT (KCBT TkrKW)
5,000 bu minimum- cents per bushel

Season's High	Season's Low	Month	Week's High	Week's Low	Sett	Net Chg	Open Int.
350	270	May 00	281¼	270	271	− 8½	4,640
366	280¾	Jul 00	293	280¾	281¾	− 8¾	41,399
355½	302	Dec 00	316½	306¼	307¾	− 7¼	8,906
344½	318½	Mar 01	328¼	319½	320	− 7	890
335	327	May 01	334	327	327	− 5	38
353	330	Jul 01	339	330	330	− 7	457

Fri to Thu sales 55,941 Open int 62,991

Indexes

ISDEX INTERNET INDEX (KCBT TkrIS)
100 x index

Season's High	Season's Low	Month	Week's High	Week's Low	Sett	Net Chg	Open Int.
1139.00	595.00	Jun 00	785.00	620.00	781.00	+ 62.00	342

Fri to Thu sales 106 Spot 748.63 Open int 342

MINI VALUE LINE (KCBT TkrMV)
100 x index

Season's High	Season's Low	Month	Week's High	Week's Low	Sett	Net Chg	Open Int.
1087.00	851.00	Jun 00	1076.75	1022.00	1076.75	+ 38.75	139
1083.20	1031.00	Sep 00	1083.20	1060.00	1087.75	+ 38.75	1

Spot 1055.66

NIKKEI 225 AVGS. (CME TkrNK)
$5 x nsa

Season's High	Season's Low	Month	Week's High	Week's Low	Sett	Net Chg	Open Int.
20750	17275	Jun 00	18590	17820	18200	− 920	16,042

Fri to Thu sales 8,136 Open int 16,048

NYSE COMP. INDEX (NYBT TkrYX)
500 x index

Season's High	Season's Low	Month	Week's High	Week's Low	Sett	Net Chg	Open Int.
674.00	585.00	Jun 00	665.25	638.00	649.20	+ 4.80	1,745
676.35	595.50	Sep 00	672.75	670.50	657.30	+ 5.10	250

Fri to Thu sales 2,540 Spot 650.45 Open int 2,988

PSE TECH. INDEX (NYBT TkrTK)
100 x index

Season's High	Season's Low	Month	Week's High	Week's Low	Sett	Net Chg	Open Int.
1299.00	941.00	Jun 00	1106.50	986.00	1095.00	+ 50.00	551

Fri to Thu sales 401 Spot 1073.67 Open int 576

S&P COMP. INDEX (CME TkrSP)
250 x index

Season's High	Season's Low	Month	Week's High	Week's Low	Sett	Net Chg	Open Int.
1574.00	1204.00	Jun 00	1495.00	1417.00	1460.00	+ 12.80	374,466
1592.50	1096.50	Sep 00	1510.00	1443.00	1481.50	+ 14.30	6,150
1597.50	1291.50	Dec 00	1483.30	1460.90	1504.20	+ 16.00	3,346
1593.20	1386.20	Mar 01	1537.00	1495.00	1528.20	+ 17.50	322
1602.00	1394.50	Jun 01	1582.10	1530.30	1552.20	+ 19.00	266
1685.00	1370.00	Sep 01	1590.20	1570.00	1576.20	+ 20.50	113

Fri to Thu sales 351,178 Spot 1464.92 Open int 384,666

S&P MIDCAP 400 (CME TkrMD)
500 x index

Season's High	Season's Low	Month	Week's High	Week's Low	Sett	Net Chg	Open Int.
513.00	425.45	Jun 00	484.40	451.50	482.75	+ 20.65	12,664

Fri to Thu sales 3,148 Spot 475.76 Open int 12,666

S&P Mini INDEX (CME TkrES)
50 x index

Season's High	Season's Low	Month	Week's High	Week's Low	Sett	Net Chg	Open Int.
1574.25	1342.25	Jun 00	1495.25	1417.00	1460.00	+ 12.75	34,645
1560.00	1375.00	Sep 00	1520.00	1445.00	1481.50	+ 14.25	14

Fri to Thu sales 369,572 Open int 34,659

CRB INDEX X 500 (NYBT TkrCR)
500 x index

Season's High	Season's Low	Month	Week's High	Week's Low	Sett	Net Chg	Open Int.
217.40	204.50	Jun 00	213.35	211.00	212.80	− 1.00	1,195
218.50	209.50	Aug 00	214.00	212.20	213.60	− 1.00	1,070
217.25	212.20	Nov 00	215.00	213.00	214.40	− 1.00	527

Fri to Thu sales 533 Spot 210.33 Open int 2,793

DOW JONES INDUSTRIAL (CBOT TkrDJ)
$10 x Dow Jones Industrial Average

Season's High	Season's Low	Month	Week's High	Week's Low	Sett	Net Chg	Open Int.
11977	9810	Jun 00	11260	10760	10810	− 135	17,098
12126	9995	Sep 00	11403	10930	10950	− 132	682
12180	8100	Dec 00	11535	11102	11102	− 124	1,491

Fri to Thu sales 74,199 Spot 10888 Open int 19,277

GSCI (Goldman S. Index) (CME TkrGI)
$250 X Nearby Index

Season's High	Season's Low	Month	Week's High	Week's Low	Sett	Net Chg	Open Int.
206.10	184.60	May 00	205.60	200.50	203.50	− .70	39,044
214.90	184.80	Jun 00	203.40	199.50	202.20	+ .20	51

Fri to Thu sales 427 Spot 202.06 Open int 39,095

MUNICIPAL BONDS (CBOT TkrMB)
$1000x index-pts & 32nds

Season's High	Season's Low	Month	Week's High	Week's Low	Sett	Net Chg	Open Int.
96-19	89-09	Jun 00	94-28	92-23	93-07	− 1-12	23,027
94-05	93-00	Sep 00	93-10	93-00	92-17	− 1-12	2

Fri to Thu sales 6,231 Spot 94-00 Open int 23,029

RUSSELL 2000 INDEX (CME TkrRT)
500 x index

Season's High	Season's Low	Month	Week's High	Week's Low	Sett	Net Chg	Open Int.
624.50	444.00	Jun 00	512.00	463.00	509.00	+ 25.75	13,955
515.25	441.90	Sep 00	515.25	511.00	515.25	+ 25.75	...

Fri to Thu sales 6,560 Spot 494.58 Open int 13,955

US DOLLAR INDEX (NYBT TkrDX)
1000 x index

Season's High	Season's Low	Month	Week's High	Week's Low	Sett	Net Chg	Open Int.
110.15	96.95	Jun 00	110.15	106.62	109.99	+ 2.72	5,921
109.65	95.64	Sep 00	109.65	106.40	109.63	+ 2.71	2,039
109.27	100.90	Dec 00	109.27	108.95	109.27	+ 2.71	...

Fri to Thu sales 6,083 Spot 109.70 Open int 7,960

Livestock & Meat

CATTLE (CME TkrLC)
40,000 lbs.- cents per lb.

Season's High	Season's Low	Month	Week's High	Week's Low	Sett	Net Chg	Open Int.
74.45	67.30	Apr 00	74.45	73.62	74.25	+ .73	2,446
70.87	65.30	Jun 00	70.20	68.95	69.27	+ .20	57,730
71.37	65.70	Aug 00	69.80	69.12	69.65	+ .35	27,738
73.30	68.00	Oct 00	72.55	71.75	72.07	− .08	17,855
74.45	70.50	Dec 00	73.90	73.27	73.57	+ .17	7,204
75.50	73.40	Feb 01	74.85	74.35	74.57	+ .17	3,389
77.30	75.75	Apr 01	76.85	76.40	76.60	+ .18	3,853

Fri to Thu sales 58,294 Open int 120,215

FEEDER CATTLE (CME TkrFC)
50,000 lbs.- cents per lb.

Season's High	Season's Low	Month	Week's High	Week's Low	Sett	Net Chg	Open Int.
87.07	76.30	May 00	84.95	83.85	84.82	+ .80	7,535
88.00	79.25	Aug 00	86.50	85.50	86.32	+ .47	6,032
88.50	85.00	Sep 00	86.40	85.70	86.40	+ .50	1,914
88.60	85.40	Oct 00	87.15	86.40	87.05	+ .53	1,859
89.15	86.25	Nov 00	88.00	87.30	88.00	+ .50	1,282
88.50	86.60	Jan 01	88.35	87.50	88.35	+ .63	571
87.80	87.00	Mar 01	87.70	87.00	87.70	+ .50	45

Fri to Thu sales 7,579 Spot 83.40 Open int 20,038

HOGS-Lean (CME TkrLH)
40,000 lbs.- cents per lb.

Season's High	Season's Low	Month	Week's High	Week's Low	Sett	Net Chg	Open Int.
78.10	52.10	Jun 00	78.10	76.42	76.65	− .05	35,147
74.90	52.05	Jul 00	74.90	73.10	74.25	+ .80	11,136
70.55	52.50	Aug 00	70.55	69.10	70.25	+ .70	10,023
62.35	49.75	Oct 00	62.35	61.15	62.02	+ .65	5,214
59.70	49.70	Dec 00	59.70	58.50	59.25	+ .35	3,703
59.50	53.30	Feb 01	59.50	58.92	59.40	+ .10	941
58.65	54.50	Apr 01	57.35	56.80	57.05	− .27	167
65.30	60.00	Jun 01	65.20	64.60	64.90	...	23

Fri to Thu sales 33,742 Spot 67.68 Open int 66,354

LIVE CATTLE (MIDA TkrXL)
20,000 lbs.- cents per lb.

Season's High	Season's Low	Month	Week's High	Week's Low	Sett	Net Chg	Open Int.
74.50	67.60	Apr 00	74.50	73.60	74.25	+ .73	5
70.75	65.55	Jun 00	70.15	68.95	69.27	+ .20	81
71.07	66.00	Aug 00	69.80	69.07	69.65	+ .35	33
73.10	69.25	Oct 00	72.50	71.82	72.07	− .08	24
74.40	71.00	Dec 00	73.57	73.50	73.57	+ .17	25
75.00	73.60	Feb 01	74.55	74.52	74.57	+ .17	4

LIVE HOGS (MIDA TkrXH)
15,000 lbs.- cents per lb.

Season's High	Season's Low	Month	Week's High	Week's Low	Sett	Net Chg	Open Int.
78.05	52.60	Jun 00	78.05	76.45	76.65	− .05	237
74.85	52.55	Jul 00	74.85	73.20	74.25	+ .80	111
70.50	52.70	Aug 00	70.50	69.25	70.25	+ .70	73
62.17	51.40	Oct 00	62.17	61.32	62.02	+ .65	50
59.55	50.50	Dec 00	59.55	58.52	59.25	+ .35	27
57.10	55.10	Apr 01	57.10	57.00	57.05	− .27	1

PORK BELLIES (CME TkrPB)
40,000 lbs.- cents per lb.

Season's High	Season's Low	Month	Week's High	Week's Low	Sett	Net Chg	Open Int.
101.10	47.50	May 00	101.10	96.25	99.55	+ 1.90	3,505
98.30	56.00	Jul 00	98.30	94.20	96.25	+ .90	2,768
95.30	53.20	Aug 00	95.30	91.10	93.30	+ 1.10	658
80.00	63.50	Feb 01	80.00	75.50	77.75	+ 5.25	37

Fri to Thu sales 9,666 Spot 96.26 Open int 6,970

Lumber

LUMBER (CME TkrLB)
80,000 bd. ft.- $ per 1,000 bd. ft.

Season's High	Season's Low	Month	Week's High	Week's Low	Sett	Net Chg	Open Int.
363.5	292.2	May 00	304.5	292.2	299.5	+ 1.2	1,661
359.9	302.2	Jul 00	311.3	302.2	308.3	+ 2.6	1,235
339.9	304.5	Sep 00	310.7	304.5	307.2	− 1.2	245
331.8	303.0	Nov 00	306.0	303.0	305.2	+ 2.1	89
326.5	308.0	Jan 01	316.0	308.0	305.0	− 6.5	4

Fri to Thu sales 4,601 Open int 3,234

Metals

GOLD-KILO (CBOT TkrKI)
kilo- dollars per oz.

Season's High	Season's Low	Month	Week's High	Week's Low	Sett	Net Chg	Open Int.
334.0	274.0	Jun 00	282.8	274.0	274.8	− 6.7	234
286.0	281.0	Aug 00	285.0	281.0	277.8	− 6.7	27
328.0	287.0	Dec 00	293.0	287.0	285.8	− 6.7	54

Fri to Thu sales 72 Open int 315

GOLD (COMX TkrGC)
100 troy oz.- dollars per troy oz.

Season's High	Season's Low	Month	Week's High	Week's Low	Sett	Net Chg	Open Int.
473.50	257.00	Jun 00	282.90	274.20	274.70	− 6.80	88,885
3160.00	260.40	Aug 00	285.40	276.70	277.40	− 6.70	13,640
329.00	262.10	Oct 00	286.50	282.50	280.10	− 6.70	3,837
474.50	261.70	Dec 00	291.00	282.50	282.90	− 6.60	19,507
333.00	265.40	Feb 01	288.00	287.60	285.30	− 6.50	6,817
308.30	283.50	Apr 01	291.60	289.80	287.90	− 6.50	3,375
447.00	267.10	Jun 01	297.00	290.50	290.50	− 6.50	8,714
429.50	266.80	Dec 01	301.50	298.30	298.30	− 6.30	5,384
359.30	299.40	Dec 03	334.10	334.10	329.90	− 5.70	1,805

Fri to Thu sales 85,626 Open int 150,991

HI GRADE COPPER (COMX TkrHG)
25,000 lbs.- cents per lb.

Season's High	Season's Low	Month	Week's High	Week's Low	Sett	Net Chg	Open Int.
89.50	65.50	May 00	80.10	75.70	79.00	+ 2.40	8,783
89.15	65.90	Jun 00	80.45	76.30	79.30	+ 2.20	3,798
89.85	66.25	Jul 00	80.80	76.60	79.60	+ 2.10	38,939
96.60	67.09	Aug 00	80.30	77.80	79.95	+ 2.05	1,413
96.90	66.95	Sep 00	81.25	77.50	80.15	+ 1.90	6,143
97.10	67.00	Oct 00	80.90	77.70	80.40	+ 1.85	712
90.10	67.35	Nov 00	81.15	80.30	80.65	+ 1.80	710
97.55	67.09	Dec 00	82.10	77.80	80.90	+ 1.75	5,469
89.00	70.20	Mar 01	82.70	79.40	81.55	+ 1.80	1,770
91.60	78.55	Dec 01	80.80	80.80	82.30	+ 1.50	958

Fri to Thu sales 111,393 Open int 62,969

N.Y. GOLD (MIDA TkrXK)
33.2 troy oz.- dollars per troy oz.

Season's High	Season's Low	Month	Week's High	Week's Low	Sett	Net Chg	Open Int.
290.6	0.8	May 00	0.8	0.8	273.1	− 7.2	...
337.0	258.8	Jun 00	282.7	274.2	274.7	− 6.8	242
323.7	280.0	Aug 00	284.7	280.0	277.4	− 6.7	16
341.7	267.9	Dec 00	287.8	282.2	282.9	− 6.6	25

N.Y. SILVER (MIDA TkrXY)
1,000 oz.- cents per oz.

Season's High	Season's Low	Month	Week's High	Week's Low	Sett	Net Chg	Open Int.
560.0	491.5	May 00	502.5	491.5	496.0	− 4.0	259
608.7	498.0	Jul 00	507.5	499.0	501.5	− 2.9	474
537.8	503.5	Sep 00	510.1	503.5	505.8	− 1.9	11
608.6	501.1	Dec 00	517.0	507.2	510.2	− 1.0	415

PALLADIUM (NYMX TkrPA)
100 troy oz- dollars per oz

Season's High	Season's Low	Month	Week's High	Week's Low	Sett	Net Chg	Open Int.
825.00	386.20	Jun 00	625.00	562.50	620.60	+ 58.50	2,300
815.00	575.00	Sep 00	616.60	575.00	616.60	+ 56.50	104

Fri to Thu sales 397 Open int 2,414

PLATINUM (MIDA TkrXU)
25 oz.- dollars per oz.

Season's High	Season's Low	Month	Week's High	Week's Low	Sett	Net Chg	Open Int.
511.5	353.1	Jul 00	498.7	438.1	498.7	+ 35.9	16
438.0	387.0	Oct 00	438.0	425.3	472.1	+ 24.3	1

PLATINUM (NYMX TkrPL)
50 troy oz.- dollars per troy oz.

Season's High	Season's Low	Month	Week's High	Week's Low	Sett	Net Chg	Open Int.
519.00	354.10	Jul 00	502.80	433.10	498.70	+ 35.90	7,003
500.00	394.90	Oct 00	472.10	425.30	472.10	+ 24.30	641
420.00	400.80	Jan 01	420.00	419.00	461.10	+ 24.30	18

Fri to Thu sales 10,063 Open int 7,662

SILVER(1000) (CBOT TkrAG)
1,000 oz.- cents per oz.

Season's High	Season's Low	Month	Week's High	Week's Low	Sett	Net Chg	Open Int.
520.0	490.0	May 00	498.0	490.0	494.0	− 6.0	7
578.0	494.0	Jun 00	505.0	494.0	498.5	− 4.5	629
504.0	500.0	Jul 00	504.0	500.0	504.0	...	5
560.0	503.0	Aug 00	509.0	504.0	506.0	− 2.0	92
578.0	513.0	Dec 00	519.0	513.5	516.0	− 2.0	378
560.0	525.0	Apr 01	525.0	525.0	524.0	− 4.0	10

Fri to Thu sales 397 Open int 1,146

SILVER (COMX TkrSI)
5,000 troy oz.- cents per troy oz.

Season's High	Season's Low	Month	Week's High	Week's Low	Sett	Net Chg	Open Int.
577.0	492.0	May 00	503.5	492.5	496.0	− 4.0	8,227
518.2	496.4	Jun 00	496.4	496.4	498.3	− 3.4	1
590.0	484.5	Jul 00	507.5	497.5	501.5	− 2.9	55,876
580.0	494.0	Sep 00	510.1	503.0	505.8	− 1.9	3,492
685.0	486.3	Dec 00	516.0	507.0	510.2	− 1.0	7,309
531.0	508.4	Jan 01	516.0	508.4	511.4	− .9	57
542.0	507.8	Mar 01	516.0	509.6	512.6	− .8	894
540.5	512.7	May 01	518.0	512.7	514.5	− .4	799
664.1	506.7	Jul 01	516.5	516.5	516.5	− .4	1,131
680.0	486.3	Dec 01	528.0	524.7	521.2	− .4	1,056
613.0	487.0	Dec 02	543.0	525.0	526.8	+ .2	820
542.5	512.0	Jul 04	537.0	537.0	537.0	+ .2	35

Fri to Thu sales 151,644 Open int 77,728

FUTURES OPTIONS

CBOT

10 YR. TREASURY $100,000 prin, pts & 64ths of 100 pct

Month	Strike	Vol	Open Int	Week's High	Week's Low	Sett	Pt Chg	Future Sett
Jun 00 p	91	600	700	...	...	-36	+ -27	96-305
Jun 00 c	92	595	715	...	...	-12	− -48	96-305
Jun 00 p	92	733	1233	-01	-01	1-07	+ 1-06	96-305
Jun 00 p	93	948	17895	-01	-01	-01	...	96-305
Jun 00 c	94	800	10718	4-21	4-20	3-00	− 1-16	96-305
Jun 00 p	94	2565	23465	-05	-03	-03	+ -01	96-305
Jun 00 c	95	1100	15817	3-21	1-44	2-05	− 1-13	96-305
Jun 00 p	95	15255	27866	-12	-05	-08	+ -04	96-305
Jun 00 c	96	1100	17136	1-16	-16	1-16	− 1-07	96-305
Jun 00 p	96	46728	44820	-29	-08	-19	+ -10	96-305
Jun 00 c	97	10587	31359	1-44	-23	-40	− -59	96-305
Jun 00 p	97	61262	34791	-62	-16	-43	+ -23	96-305
Jun 00 c	98	25728	42426	-63	-12	-16	− -40	96-305
Jun 00 p	98	19522	21964	1-38	-34	1-19	+ -42	96-305
Jun 00 c	99	26189	43342	-34	-04	-05	− -22	96-305
Jun 00 p	99	911	7666	2-17	1-32	2-08	+ -60	96-305
Jun 00 c	100	13483	33096	-16	-02	-02	− -10	96-305
Jun 00 c	101	4516	13461	-07	-01	-01	− -04	96-305
Sep 00 p	92	1113	3145	-17	-13	-15	+ -04	96-23
Sep 00 p	94	5300	22361	-40	-37	-34	+ -11	96-23
Sep 00 p	95	609	10248	-43	-32	-51	+ -17	96-23
Sep 00 p	96	7015	7639	1-13	-47	1-09	+ -24	96-23
Sep 00 c	97	1450	1650	1-25	1-21	1-21	− -51	96-23
Sep 00 p	97	4341	4635	1-44	1-21	1-39	+ -34	96-23
Sep 00 c	98	850	3904	1-20	-57	-59	− -40	96-23
Sep 00 c	99	2447	7386	1-11	-38	-39	− -31	96-23
Sep 00 c	100	4885	19206	-54	-25	-25	− -23	96-23
Sep 00 c	102	3129	3531	-24	-11	-11	− -10	96-23
Sep 00 c	104	760	1260	-07	-06	-06	− -03	96-23
Sep 00 c	108	26210	34000	-03	-03	-03	+ -01	96-23

Total Call volume 125,097 **Call Open int** 304,682
Total Put volume 167,462 **Put Open int** 248,942

5 YR. TREASURY $100,000, pts & 64ths of 100 pct

Month	Strike	Vol	Open Int	Week's High	Week's Low	Sett	Pt Chg	Future Sett
Jun 00 p	965	500	8520	-08	-05	-07	+ -04	97-185
Jun 00 p	970	6663	14736	-17	-03	-14	+ -10	97-185
Jun 00 p	975	3132	8626	1-04	-10	-25	+ -19	97-185
Jun 00 p	980	14640	13909	-47	-10	-43	+ -31	97-185
Jun 00 p	985	3325	11479	1-01	-18	1-01	+ -46	97-185
Jun 00 p	990	2456	9305	1-31	-29	1-31	+ -60	97-185
Sep 00 c	980	551	601	-56	-51	-47	...	97-17
Sep 00 c	990	1200	4590	-45	-31	-26	− -32	97-17
Sep 00 p	990	700	4100	2-11	1-56	1-56	+ -53	97-17

Total Call volume 1,968 **Call Open int** 11,628
Total Put volume 32,827 **Put Open int** 130,874

CORN 5,000 bu, cents per bushel

Month	Strike	Vol	Open Int	Week's High	Week's Low	Sett	Pt Chg	Future Sett
Jun 00 p	235	2013	2125	6⅞	3¼	6⅞	+ ⅞	232
Jun 00 c	250	540	527	2½	⅞	⅞	− 1⅜	232
Jun 00 c	280	1000	1000	¼	¼	¼	...	232
Jun 00 c	290	1900	1800	¼	⅛	⅛	...	232
Jun 00 c	300	1880	2000	¼	⅛	⅛	...	232
Jul 00 c	160	569	5	84¾	72	72	− 3¾	232
Jul 00 p	210	962	9686	6	¾	1⅜	+ ⅛	232
Jul 00 p	220	4596	19972	4	2	3⅞	+ ½	232
Jul 00 c	230	1641	13265	16½	10½	10½	− 3	232
Jul 00 p	230	6142	19857	17½	3½	8¾	+ 1⅛	232
Jul 00 c	240	8988	28104	12	7	7	− 2½	232
Jul 00 p	240	2137	8250	15	10¾	15	+ 1⅜	232
Jul 00 c	250	5727	19866	8½	2	4¾	− 1⅞	232
Jul 00 c	260	1589	11371	6	3½	3½	− 1⅜	232
Jul 00 c	270	1358	8196	4¼	2½	2½	− ⅞	232
Jul 00 c	280	1220	4559	3¼	1¾	1⅞	− ⅝	232
Jul 00 c	290	1553	8686	2¼	1⅜	1⅜	− ⅜	232
Jul 00 c	300	1731	13161	1¾	1	1	− ⅜	232
Sep 00 p	220	1542	16048	7	5¼	7	+ ¼	240¼
Sep 00 p	230	3396	9651	18½	8¼	11⅝	+ ½	240¼
Sep 00 p	240	805	4717	17½	13¾	17½	+ 1¼	240¼
Sep 00 c	250	1618	9860	19	14¼	14¼	− 2	240¼
Sep 00 c	260	631	8835	16	11½	11½	− 2	240¼
Sep 00 c	290	1772	4971	9½	6¾	6¾	− 1½	240¼
Sep 00 c	300	3340	13974	8	5½	5⅝	− 1⅜	240¼
Sep 00 c	320	782	5489	5½	3¾	3¾	− 1	240¼
Dec 00 p	230	512	12541	11¼	8¾	10½	+ ½	250
Dec 00 c	250	801	12165	26	21	21	− 2½	250
Dec 00 p	250	1993	13044	21¼	17½	21	+ 1	250
Dec 00 c	270	620	8699	19½	14¾	15	− 2⅛	250
Dec 00 c	280	665	4854	16½	12½	12¾	− 1⅞	250
Dec 00 c	300	826	17095	15	9	9½	− 1¼	250
Dec 00 c	310	598	6647	10	7¾	8	− 1⅛	250
Dec 00 c	320	710	8489	8¾	6½	6¾	− 1⅛	250

Total Call volume 47,142 **Call Open int** 319,107
Total Put volume 27,611 **Put Open int** 176,723

DOW JONES INDUSTRIAL $100 x premium

Month	Strike	Vol	Open Int	Week's High	Week's Low	Sett	Pt Chg	Future Sett
May 00p	10800	523	511	26.00	11.85	25.45	...	10810

Total Call volume 1,721 **Call Open int** 7,165
Total Put volume 2,787 **Put Open int** 8,686

SOYBEAN MEAL 100 tons, dollars per ton

Month	Strike	Vol	Open Int	Week's High	Week's Low	Sett	Pt Chg	Future Sett
Jul 00 p	160	532	1504	2.50	1.00	1.75	−0.75	171.40
Jul 00 p	165	820	1297	4.25	2.00	3.00	−1.50	171.40
Jul 00 p	170	722	1191	6.25	3.50	5.25	−1.50	171.40

Total Call volume 2,646 **Call Open int** 21,936
Total Put volume 4,550 **Put Open int** 15,335

SOYBEAN OIL 60,000 lbs- cents per lb

Month	Strike	Vol	Open Int	Week's High	Week's Low	Sett	Pt Chg	Future Sett
Jun 00 p	1800	750	585	0.60	0.15	0.40	+0.25	18.05
Jun 00 p	1850	1272	800	0.50	0.32	0.71	+0.41	18.05
Jun 00 c	1900	530	1200	0.25	0.15	0.15	−0.35	18.05
Jul 00 p	1600	844	2105	0.11	0.04	0.10	+0.03	18.05
Jul 00 c	1700	534	2432	1.95	1.30	1.35	−0.75	18.05
Jul 00 p	1800	1871	1652	0.94	0.40	0.70	+0.29	18.05
Jul 00 c	1850	514	1609	1.05	0.55	0.55	−0.60	18.05
Jul 00 c	1900	1320	2392	0.76	0.40	0.41	−0.44	18.05

Total Call volume 5,130 **Call Open int** 29,826
Total Put volume 6,397 **Put Open int** 22,121

SOYBEANS 5,000 bu, cents per bushel

Month	Strike	Vol	Open Int	Week's High	Week's Low	Sett	Pt Chg	Future Sett
Jun 00 p	530	928	697	8½	3¼	7½	+ 1¼	539¼

Source: *Barron's Market Week*, May 1, 2000, MW76.

- *Broad Market:* The cash market for the underlying asset must be sufficiently broad to allow for healthy competition. Active trading is needed so that sizable orders can be executed rapidly and inexpensively and to decrease the likelihood of market corners, squeezes, or price manipulation.
- *Standardized Asset:* The commodity, security, index, or item underlying futures contracts must be standardized and/or capable of being graded so as to provide a clear basis for what is being bought and sold.

All futures contracts represent a standardized agreement between two parties that commit one party to sell and the other party to buy a stipulated quantity and grade of a commodity, currency, security, index, or other specified item at a set price on or before a given date in the future. All futures contracts also require the daily settlement of all gains and losses so long as the futures contract remains in force. For futures contracts that remain open until trading terminates, contract specifications provide for physical delivery of the underlying asset or a final cash payment based on the difference between the spot market price and an agreed-on contract price.

The buyer of a futures contract, often referred to as the **long,** agrees to receive delivery of the underlying asset from the seller of the futures contract, or **short,** who agrees to make delivery. Futures contracts are traded on exchanges either by open outcry in specified trading areas, called pits or rings, or electronically via a computerized network. In **open-outcry trading,** exchange members stand in **trading pits** making bids and offers, by voice and with hand signals, to other traders. Customer orders are routed to **floor brokers** or **dual traders** who execute them according to the order's instructions. Brokers and dual traders often assume responsibility for entering complex combinations of buy and sell orders. Hedgers in the futures market typically execute both market orders and various types of stop orders, such as stop-loss or stop-limit orders. All futures contracts are marked-to-market at their end-of-day settlement prices. This means that daily gains and losses are passed through to the gaining and losing accounts. Any futures contracts can be terminated by an **offsetting transaction.** An offsetting trade is a transaction equal but opposite to the one that opened the futures position and is executed at any time prior to the expiration of the futures contract. The overwhelming majority of futures contracts are terminated by offset or a final cash payment rather than by delivery. In practice, only 1–2% of all futures market transactions result in the actual delivery of the underlying asset. The same or similar futures contracts can be traded on more than one exchange in the United States, although exchanges typically specialize in the trading of certain types of futures contracts.

long
Buyer, or to signify ownership.

short
Seller, or to signify sale.

open-outcry trading
Exchange market dependent on physical communication.

trading pit
Futures market trading area.

floor broker
Futures market professional who executes orders for others.

dual trader
Futures market professional who holds positions and executes orders for others.

offsetting transaction
Equal but opposite trade.

Contractual Provisions

Standardized futures contracts specify a common set of five contractual provisions. These include the

- *Underlying Asset:* Commodity, currency, financial instrument index, or other item on which the contract is based must be unambiguously identified.
- *Amount and Quality of the Underlying Asset:* Amount and quality (grade) of the underlying asset covered by the futures contract is precisely identified.
- *Delivery Cycle:* Months for which the futures contracts can be traded must be specified.

- *Expiration Date:* Date by which some particular futures trading month ceases to exist must be clearly laid out. This date identifies when the futures contract terminates.
- *Settlement Mechanism and Delivery Location (if applicable):* Futures contracts lay out how the physical delivery of the underlying item or a terminal cash payment is to be made. The only unspecified item of a futures contract is the price of the underlying unit. This amount is determined in the trading arena.

trading unit
Contract size.

delivery months
Scheduled delivery cycles.

Figure 18.2 shows a typical specification of a futures contract. In this case, the commodity is world sugar traded on the New York Board of Trade's Coffee Sugar & Cocoa Exchange. These sugar futures contracts call for delivery of cane sugar, stowed in bulk, "free on board" (FOB) from any of 28 foreign countries of origin as well as the United States. Each contract represents a **trading unit** of 112,000 pounds, or 50 long tons, of sugar. Prices are quoted in cents, with a minimum price fluctuation of 1/100 cent per pound, equivalent to $11.20 per contract. **Delivery months** for

FIGURE 18.2 **Futures Contact Specifications Are Available on the Internet**

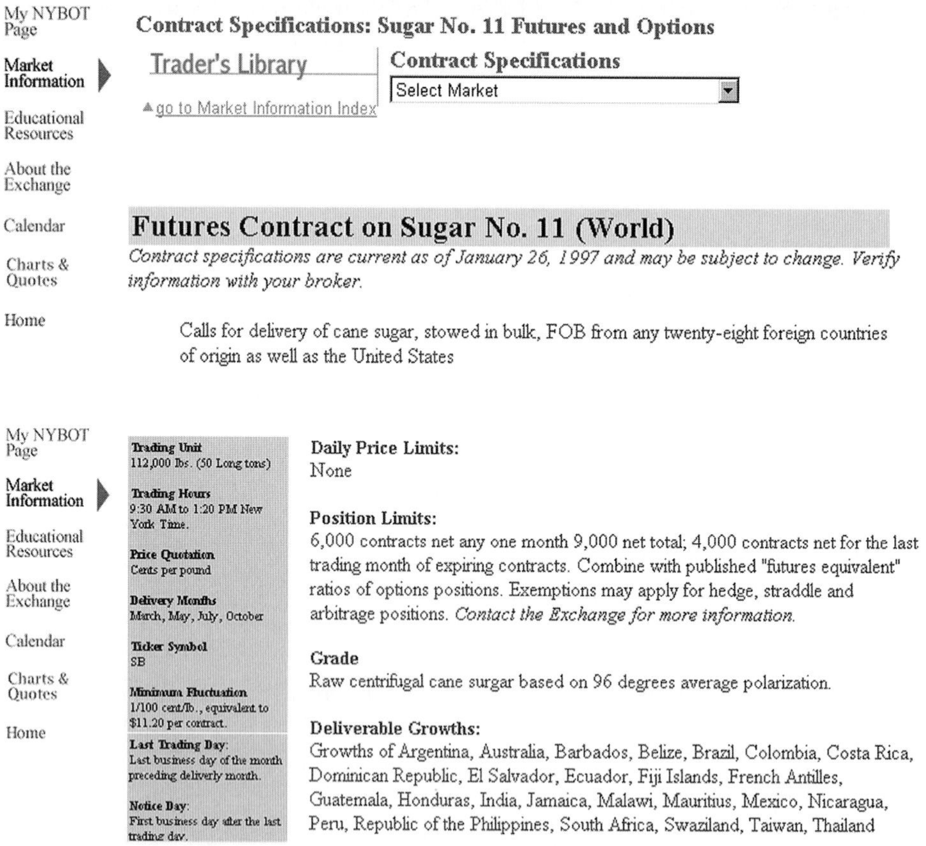

My NYBOT Page
Market Information
Educational Resources
About the Exchange
Calendar
Charts & Quotes
Home
Contract Specifications: Sugar No. 11 Futures and Options
Trader's Library
go to Market Information Index
Contract Specifications
Select Market
Futures Contract on Sugar No. 11 (World)
Contract specifications are current as of January 26, 1997 and may be subject to change. Verify information with your broker.
Calls for delivery of cane sugar, stowed in bulk, FOB from any twenty-eight foreign countries of origin as well as the United States
My NYBOT Page
Market Information
Educational Resources
About the Exchange
Calendar
Charts & Quotes
Home
Trading Unit
112,000 lbs. (50 Long tons)
Trading Hours
9:30 AM to 1:20 PM New York Time.
Price Quotation
Cents per pound
Delivery Months
March, May, July, October
Ticker Symbol
SB
Minimum Fluctuation
1/100 cent/lb., equivalent to $11.20 per contract.
Last Trading Day:
Last business day of the month preceding deliverly month.
Notice Day:
First business day after the last trading day.
Daily Price Limits:
None
Position Limits:
6,000 contracts net any one month 9,000 net total; 4,000 contracts net for the last trading month of expiring contracts. Combine with published "futures equivalent" ratios of options positions. Exemptions may apply for hedge, straddle and arbitrage positions. Contact the Exchange for more information.
Grade
Raw centrifugal cane surgar based on 96 degrees average polarization.
Deliverable Growths:
Growths of Argentina, Australia, Barbados, Belize, Brazil, Colombia, Costa Rica, Dominican Republic, El Salvador, Ecuador, Fiji Islands, French Antilles, Guatemala, Honduras, India, Jamaica, Malawi, Mauritius, Mexico, Nicaragua, Peru, Republic of the Philippines, South Africa, Swaziland, Taiwan, Thailand

Source: <http://www.nybot.com>.

sugar are March, May, July, and October. The **delivery date** is the calendar date by which buyers and sellers of futures contracts are obligated to offset or fulfill their obligations. It occurs on the third Friday of the delivery month. If a given seller wishes to satisfy her or his futures obligation through physical delivery, a written **delivery notice** must be given by the seller to the buyer indicating the seller's intention to make delivery against an open, short futures position on a particular date. **Notice day** is the last date on which written advice of an intent to physically deliver commodities pertaining to a specified delivery month may be issued.

Position limits typically apply to derivative products, such as sugar futures. They identify the maximum allowable market commitment in any single futures or option contract for a given institution. Position limits are measured by the number of contracts bought or sold for which there is no offsetting transaction. For fully hedged positions, there are no position limits. In the case of sugar, no single institution is permitted to take an unhedged or speculative position of more than 9,000 contracts. Position limits are intended to regulate the amount of influence any single buyer or seller might exercise over the market. **Grade** is a precise specification of the quality of the commodity covered by the futures contract. **Deliverable growths** and **delivery points** are acceptable countries of origin and delivery locations for sugar that might be used to satisfy the seller's physical delivery requirements.

The mechanics of futures trading are simple. Both buyers and sellers deposit funds, called margin, with a commodity brokerage firm. Margin can be thought of as a kind of performance bond or good-faith deposit that ensures contract performance. This amount is usually a tiny percentage, often only 5–10%, of the total value of the item underlying the contract. This means that futures contracts typically exhibit tremendous leverage for the buyer and the seller. A move of as little as 1% in the price of the underlying asset can create a profit or loss of as much as 20% for the futures contract buyer or seller. A price move of as little as 5% for the underlying asset can double the buyer or seller's original investment or cause one of them to be wiped out. Of course, because a futures contract represents a legal obligation to buy or sell an agreed-on quantity and quality of the underlying asset at an agreed-on price, the buyer or seller's actual profit or loss is not constrained by the margin amount. During volatile and fast-moving markets, prices for underlying commodities can sometimes move much more than 5% in a single trading day. This means that the minimum required margin can be lost in less than a single trading day and, if not quickly replenished, can result in a margin call and forced liquidation. In the event of forced liquidations under adverse market conditions, futures contract buyers and sellers can remain liable for thousands of dollars of additional losses beyond the amount of foregone margin. Speculation in the futures market is only for players with strong stomachs and big bank accounts.

As indicated in Figure 18.3A, if an investor buys (goes long) a futures contract and the price rises, the investor profits by the amount of the price increase times the contract size. If an investor buys and the price goes down, the investor loses an amount equal to the price decrease times the contract size. Figure 18.3B reflects the profit and loss potential of a short futures position. If an investor sells (goes short) a futures contract and the price goes down, the investor profits by the amount of the price decrease times the contract size. If an investor sells and the price goes up, the investor loses an amount equal to the price increase times the contract size. Just like options contracts, futures contracts represent a zero sum game between the buyer and the seller. Before commissions and other trading costs, the buyer's gain is exactly equal to the seller's loss, and vice versa.

delivery date
Calendar date by which buyers and sellers of futures contracts are obligated to offset or fulfill their obligations.

delivery notice
Written advice of delivery intention.

notice day
Last date on which written advice of an intent to physically deliver commodities may be issued.

position limits
Maximum allowable market commitment in any single futures or option contract for a given institution.

grade
Precise specification of the quality of a commodity covered by the futures contract.

deliverable growths
Acceptable countries of origin.

delivery points
Delivery locations.

FIGURE 18.3 **Futures Contracts Represent a Zero-Sum Game between Buyers and Sellers**

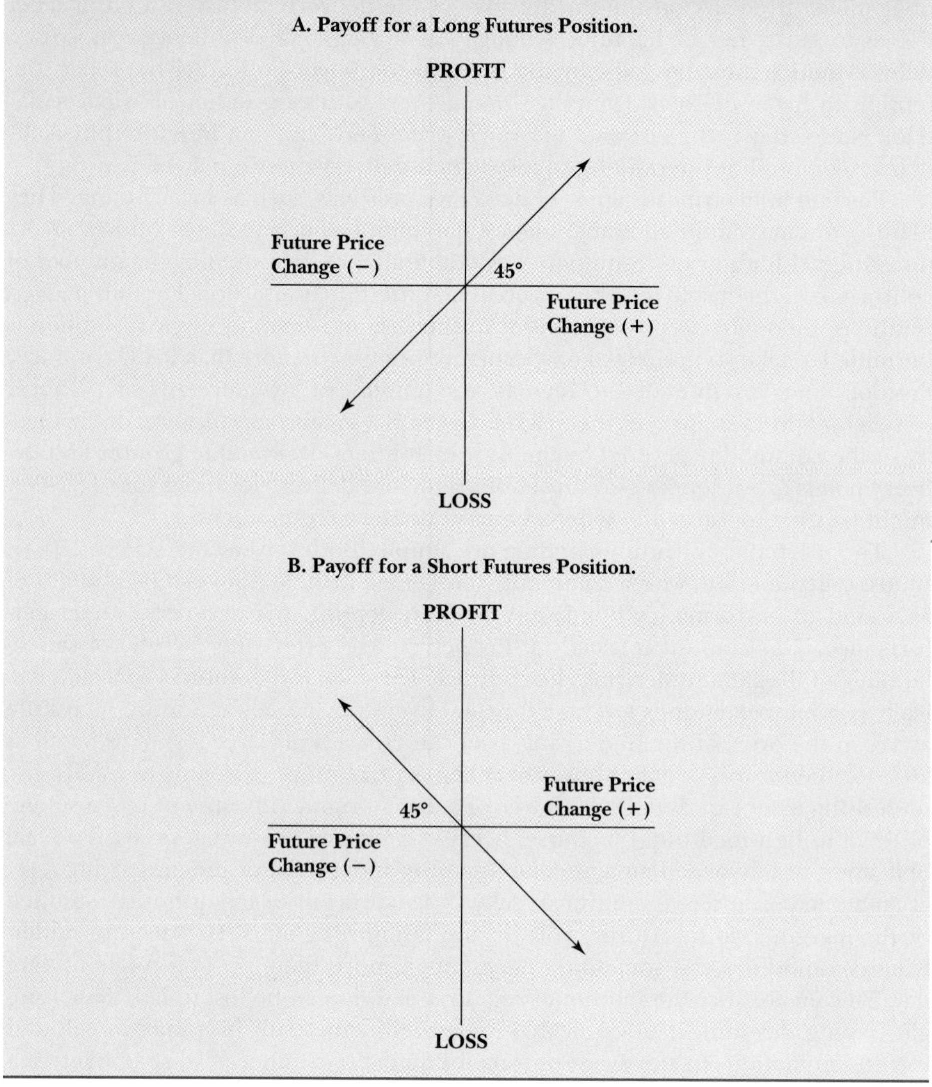

Options on Futures

Before commissions and other transaction costs, futures and option contracts represent a zero sum game between buyers and sellers. For both futures and options, the buyer's gain is exactly equal to the seller's loss. Similarly, the seller's gain is always equal to the buyer's loss. Furthermore, both futures and option contracts represent important types of financial derivatives whose economic value stems from, or is derived from, changes in the price of some underlying asset. As a result, both futures and options represent effective means for risk transfer between buyers and sellers. Despite the fact that futures and options share these important economic characteristics, there is one essential economic difference that gives rise to active financial markets for both futures and options.

A futures contract is a binding legal document that commits the buyer to take delivery, and the seller to make delivery, of an underlying asset in a specified quantity and quality at a specific delivery time and place. Because futures contracts involve *obligations* to buy and sell a specific commodity for a preset price, both buyers and sellers of futures contracts are exposed to the potential for unlimited losses in the event of adverse market conditions.

By contrast, options only represent the *right,* but not the obligation, to buy or sell a specified item, such as stocks, precious metals, or Treasury bonds, for a preset price during a specific period of time. The buyer of a call option has the potential to profit if the price of the underlying asset rises above the option's strike price by more than the amount of the premium paid for the call. Conversely, the buyer of a put option has the potential to profit if the price of the underlying asset falls below the option's strike price by more than the amount of the premium paid for the put. The loss potential for buyers of call options (rights to buy) and put options (rights to sell) is strictly limited to the amount paid for the option. In the case of a call, the worst that can occur for call buyers is that the price of the underlying asset falls to the strike price or below, and the call expires worthlessly. In the case of a put, the worst that can happen to put buyers is that the price of the underlying asset rises to the strike price or above, and the put expires worthlessly. However, sellers of call options and put options incur the obligation to sell or buy the underlying asset and are thereby exposed to the potential for unlimited losses in the event of adverse market conditions. To limit loss potential, sellers of calls and puts typically hedge their risk exposure by using sometimes complex hedging techniques involving the sale or purchase of underlying assets or other financial derivatives. Because sophisticated option hedging techniques are often beyond the expertise of small investors, or prohibitively expensive for them, many small investors shun selling options. For the same reason, many small investors have shunned the futures markets, at least until recently.

Starting in 1982, the various futures markets introduced options on futures to increase the investment appeal of futures contracts among investors who seek financial derivatives with strictly limited loss potential. **Futures options** give the right, but not the obligation, to buy or sell some specific futures contract at a certain price for a limited period of time. As in the case of call and put options on stocks and stock indexes, only the sellers of futures options are obligated to perform according to the terms of the option contract. The loss potential for buyers of futures options, both calls and puts, is strictly limited to the amount of the premium paid for the option. In exchange for the premium received, sellers of futures options are obligated to fulfill the option contract if the buyer so chooses. As in the case of options on stocks and stock indexes, sellers of futures options have unlimited loss potential. As a result, most sellers or writers of futures options tend to be sophisticated institutional investors with hedging expertise and capability.

futures options
Right, but not the obligation, to buy or sell some specific futures contract at a certain price for a limited period of time.

As shown in Figure 18.4, futures options have proved enormously popular with individual and institutional investors since their introduction in 1982. This is especially true with respect to financial futures options. It is now common for futures option activity to rival trading volume in the underlying futures. As shown in Figure 18.1, futures options are now actively traded on all important agricultural, oil, livestock, metals, interest rate, currency, and stock index futures.

FIGURE 18.4 **U.S. Futures and Options Trading Volume**

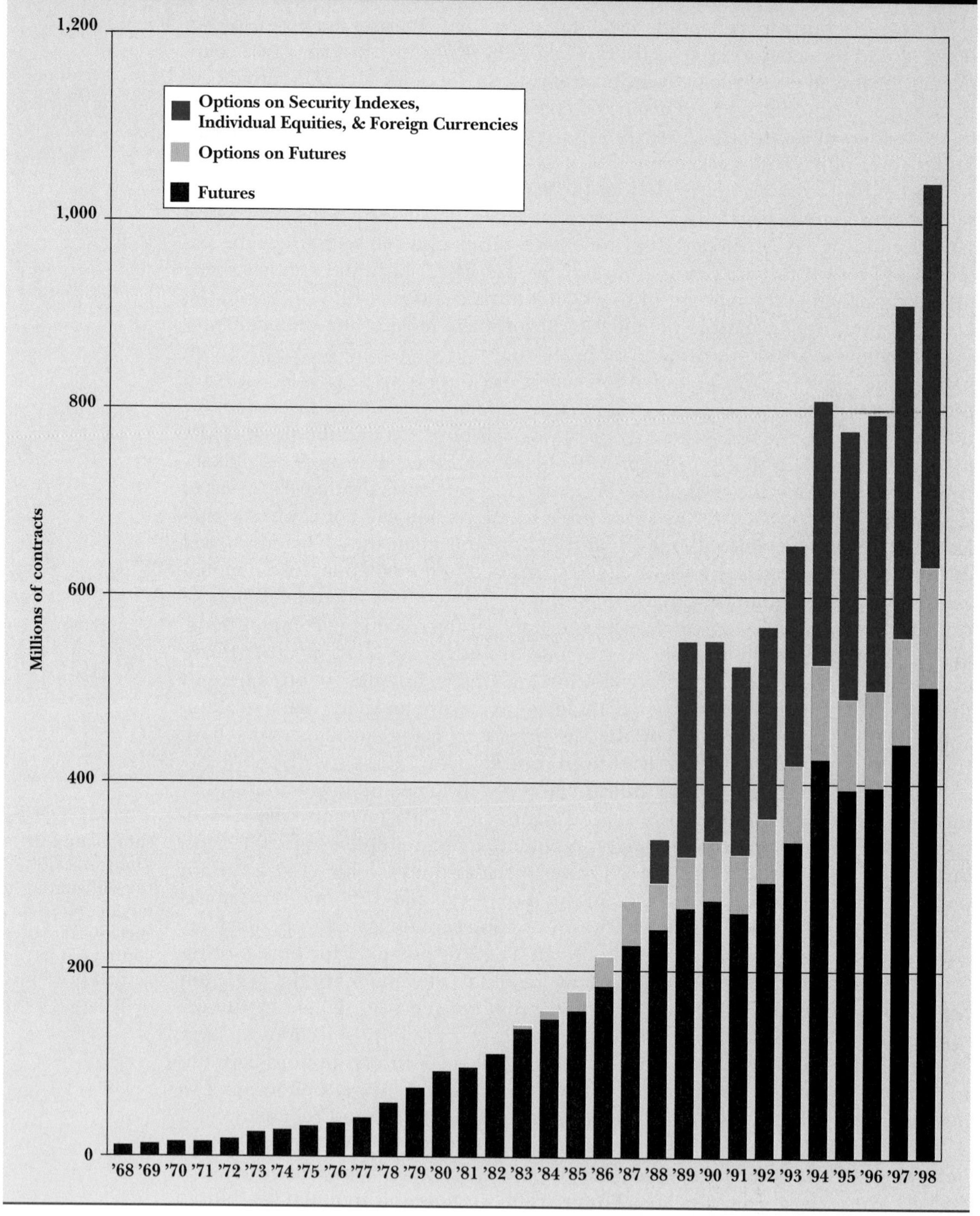

Data source: Futures Industry Association, Inc.

WALL STREET WISDOM 18.1

Do You Have a Future in Futures?

Employment opportunities in the U.S. futures industry revolve around the major exchanges. For example, the Chicago Mercantile Exchange (CME) has a staff of more than 800 professionals in full- and part-time positions. In addition, members and clearing firms who conduct the business of trading on the CME floor employ staffs that handle many key duties. Whether it is working with an exchange, a member of a leading exchange, or a clearing firm, there are many different career paths within the futures industry. Some job opportunities in the futures and option industries are unique; many others are similar to professional jobs found throughout the financial services industry.

Financial economists employed by exchange research departments develop option and futures contracts based on an analysis of the underlying physical cash or spot markets. For example, a Treasury bill futures contract is based on the size and delivery requirements of T-bills that are bought and sold daily through the Federal Reserve banking system. Research staff economists also modify and improve contracts when necessary. The clearinghouses within the various exchanges have many responsibilities. Primary among these is that they must make sure that trade information from buyers and sellers matches at the end of the day. Clearinghouse managers also must see that contract terms are observed, that systems and procedures are in place to facilitate delivery on expired futures contracts, and that the performance bond system functions smoothly.

Working on the exchange floor, market reporters monitor price changes and input appropriate information to ensure fast and accurate transmission of trading information. Programmers and other management information system (MIS) personnel play a vital role in the information transmission process. MIS staff has the responsibility for coding, testing, and documenting new computer programs, as well as responsibility for maintaining existing computer software and hardware facilities. MIS staff also work with trading floor quotation systems, compliance and regulatory tracking, and membership support services. Option and futures exchanges are information-intensive and information-sensitive operations that place a high premium on well-trained and highly motivated MIS personnel.

Often trained as accountants, staff auditors employed by the exchanges play an important role in making sure that those exchange mechanisms function smoothly. They are responsible for monitoring trading systems and ensuring that member firms fall within regulatory guidelines in terms of financial soundness. Exchange auditors are responsible for making sure that member firms comply with capital and other financial requirements. Compliance investigators have the responsibility for monitoring trade practices in exchange markets. They work with arbitration committees appointed by the various exchanges to process and resolve claims between members and customers. When necessary, compliance investigators prepare documentation necessary to bring charges against exchange members for rule violations.

Many key personnel in the options and futures industries are not directly employed by the various exchanges. Instead, they are exchange members or are employed by members or clearing firms. At the center of exchange floor-trading activity is the floor manager. The trading floor is a busy place, and member firms need someone to effectively manage order taking and information processing. These tasks are under the direction of the floor manager. Like floor managers, clerks are employed by member firms. They staff phone work stations around trading pits and communicate trading information from the pits to the phones. Actual trading activity is conducted by option and futures traders, who buy and sell for their own account, and brokers, who execute trading orders for public or business customers. Many member firms employ account executives, responsible for developing and servicing clients. Account executives are registered with the National Futures Association and earn commissions based on the accounts they open and manage. Finally, clearing firms also employ a variety of "back office" personnel to fulfill basic functions such as phone receptionists, margin clerks, wire room clerks, and office managers. Unlike career opportunities with the exchanges or member firms, many clearing firm jobs offer little in the way of pay or advancement opportunities.

See: For further information, contact the exchanges or member firms directly (e.g., <http://www.cme.com>)

Futures Trading Process

U.S. Futures Exchanges

Futures exchanges serve as a forum, or meeting place, for exchange members to buy and sell futures contracts on commodities and financial instruments. Futures exchanges are associations of members organized for a single purpose: to provide competitive markets for the trading of futures and options on futures for commodities, natural resources, and financial instruments. As shown in Figure 18.5, U.S. futures and futures option trading is concentrated on seven major exchanges. Among these seven futures exchanges, the CBOT, Chicago Mercantile Exchange, and the New York Mercantile Exchange are commonly regarded as the "big three" and account for well more than 90% of U.S. futures and futures option trading activity. Although futures and futures options on some popular contracts are listed on more than one U.S. futures exchange, trading on the exchange that first introduced a given product tends to be dominant. As a result, the various U.S. futures exchanges tend to be known by their relative size and by the types of futures contracts with which they are associated.

FIGURE 18.5 **The Seven Major U.S. Futures Exchanges**

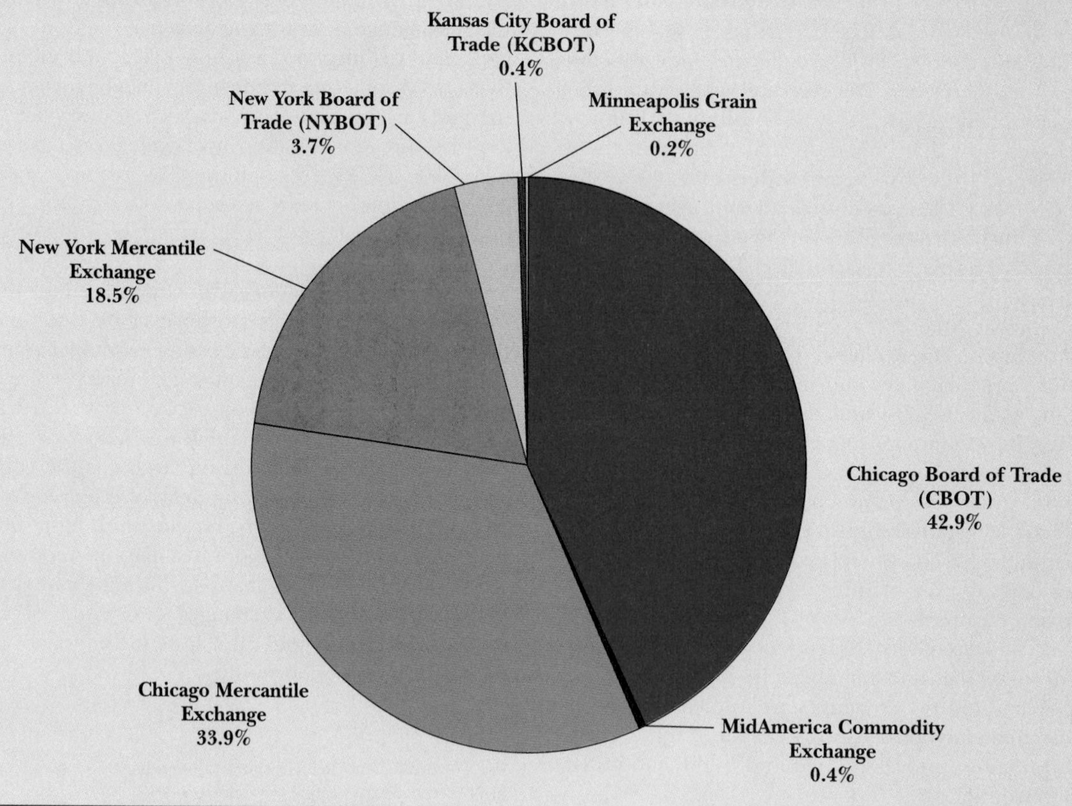

Data sources: Exchange Web sites.

The CBOT, established in 1848, is the world's oldest and largest futures and futures options exchange. More than 3,600 CBOT members trade 61 different futures and options products at the CBOT, accounting for annual trading volume of more than 250 million contracts, or about 42.9% of total futures and futures option trading in the United States. At its inception, the CBOT traded only agricultural futures contracts on wheat, corn, soybeans, and related products. In 1975, the CBOT expanded to include financial futures, including U.S. Treasury bond futures contracts. U.S. Treasury bond futures are now one of the world's most actively traded futures contracts. The CBOT introduced options on futures in 1982. One of the newest CBOT futures contracts is based on the Dow Jones Industrial Average (DJIA). Like more recently founded futures markets, the primary method of trading at the CBOT is an open-outcry system. In the open-outcry system, traders meet face to face in trading pits to buy and sell futures contracts. The CBOT also manages its rapidly growing electronic trading system called Project A®. The Chicago Board Options Exchange (CBOE) was created by the CBOT in 1973 but has always been managed and regulated as an independent entity. The CBOE specializes in options on stocks and stock indexes. The CBOT is on the Internet at <http://www.cbot.com>.

In 1872, a group of Manhattan dairy merchants got together to bring order to the chaotic conditions that were prevalent in the New York commodity markets. At that time, New York had a poorly organized and inefficient system for the storage, pricing, and transfer of agricultural products. Merchants hoped that the newly established Butter and Cheese Exchange of New York would improve market efficiency. Within a few years, the egg trade became an important part of the business conducted on the exchange, and its name was modified to the Butter, Cheese, and Egg Exchange. Efforts were also made to attract traders of groceries, dried fruits, canned goods, and poultry. In 1882, the exchange's name was changed to the **New York Mercantile Exchange** (New York Merc). Today, the New York Merc is the third-largest U.S. futures market and the world's largest physical commodity futures exchange. It accounts for trading activity of more than 100 million futures and futures options contracts per year, or about 18.5% of the overall market. The New York Merc is the preeminent trading forum for crude oil, gasoline, heating oil, natural gas, propane, gold, silver, platinum, palladium, and copper (see <http://www.nymex.com>).

New York Mercantile Exchange Third-largest U.S. futures market, and the world's largest physical commodity futures exchange.

In 1874, the Chicago Produce Exchange was established to provide a systematic market for butter, eggs, poultry, and other farm products in the city of Chicago. In 1898, a division of the produce exchange formed the Chicago Butter and Egg Board. By 1919, the butter and egg board was renamed the **Chicago Mercantile Exchange** (Chicago Merc) to better reflect its broad purpose and to accommodate wider public participation. Today, the Chicago Merc is the second-largest futures exchange in the United States and represents roughly 33.9% of total futures market activity with more than 200 million futures and futures options in annual trading volume. It has a diverse product line that includes futures and futures options on agricultural commodities, foreign currencies (a special expertise), interest rates, and stock indexes. As a truly international marketplace, the Chicago Merc enables institutions and businesses to manage financial risks and efficiently allocate assets. On its trading floors, buyers and sellers meet to trade futures contracts and options on futures through the open-outcry process. In selected contracts, trading continues virtually around the clock on the GLOBEX®2 electronic

Chicago Mercantile Exchange Second-largest futures exchange in the United States.

trading system. Further information about Chicago Merc products can be obtained at <http://www.cme.com>.

New York Board of Trade (NYBOT) Parent company of the New York Cotton Exchange and the Coffee, Sugar & Cocoa Exchange, Inc.

MidAmerica Commodity Exchange Wholly owned subsidiary of the CBOT.

Other important U.S. futures exchanges include the **New York Board of Trade (NYBOT),** parent company of the New York Cotton Exchange, founded in 1870, and the Coffee, Sugar & Cocoa Exchange, Inc., founded in 1880. Through its two exchanges and additional subsidiaries, including the New York Futures Exchange, FINEX, and Citrus Associates, the NYBOT offers a wide variety of agricultural, financial, and index products. The Cantor Exchange is a NYBOT venture with Cantor Fitzgerald designed to provide the first full-time electronic market for U.S. Treasury futures. The NYBOT is responsible for trading volume of more than 20 million futures and futures option contracts per year, or about 3.7% of the U.S. total. NYBOT is on the Internet at <http://nybot.com>. The **MidAmerica Commodity Exchange** (MidAm) was founded in Chicago in 1868 as an open-air market and quickly created a niche for itself by trading smaller-sized contracts. Today, the MidAm is a wholly owned subsidiary of the CBOT and trades more than 2.5 million futures and futures options contracts per year. Virtually all the contracts traded at the MidAm are one-fifth to one-half as large as similar contracts traded at other exchanges. Because of the smaller unit size, these contracts match the special risk management and investment needs of traders who might not have the required capital for futures trading at any other exchange (see <http://midam.com>).

Kansas City Board of Trade Predominant marketplace for hard red winter wheat.

Minneapolis Grain Exchange Smallest major U.S. futures exchange.

Since 1856, the **Kansas City Board of Trade** (KCBOT) has been the world's predominant marketplace for hard red winter wheat, the major ingredient in the world's bread. In 1982, the KCBOT introduced the first U.S. stock index futures contract, based on the Value Line® Index. The KCBOT trades more than 2.5 million futures and futures options contracts per year. Like the MidAm, the KCBOT accounts for less than one-half of 1% of U.S. futures and futures option trading activity (see <http://www.kcbot.com>). Smallest among the major futures exchanges is the **Minneapolis Grain Exchange,** founded in 1881. The grain exchange boasts the only authorized market for hard red spring wheat, white wheat, and durum futures and options, trading an average of 20 million bushels daily. It is also the largest cash exchange market in the world, trading a daily average of one million bushels of grain including wheat, barley, oats, durum, rye, sunflower seeds, flax, corn, soybeans, millet, and milo. The grain exchange trades more than one million futures and futures option contracts per year, or roughly 0.2% of U.S. futures and futures option trading activity. The grain exchange is on the Internet at <http://www.mgex.com>.

clearinghouses Institutions that ensure balance in the number of futures and futures option contracts bought and sold and give fulfillment guarantees.

counterparty risk Chance that counterparty to a futures contract obligation will not fulfill its obligation.

Clearing and Margin Requirements

Each of the various futures exchanges use **clearinghouses** owned by member firms to ensure the financial integrity of futures and options contracts. Clearinghouses ensure balance in the number of futures and futures option contracts bought and sold and give fulfillment guarantees to ensure contract performance. Thus, futures clearinghouses facilitate trade among strangers by eliminating **counterparty risk.** In the United States, each futures exchange has had its own clearinghouse, formed either as a separate entity or as a part of the exchange. Recently, several U.S. futures exchanges have begun exploring the possibility of common clearing, as is typical for options on stocks and stock indexes in which the Options Clearing Corporation (OCC) serves this purpose.

Only clearinghouse members can submit trades to the clearinghouse. Clearinghouse membership involves financial requirements and responsibilities over and above those of exchange membership and includes the maintenance of a guaranty deposit at the clearinghouse. This deposit serves as a reserve fund that can be used, if necessary, to meet the financial obligations of a defaulting clearing member.

It is the clearinghouse's responsibility to collect margin from its members for the futures and options contracts traded on the various exchanges. Margin requirements are generally set at levels sufficient to protect the clearinghouse against one day's maximum price movement in some particular futures or options contract. Minimum margins in futures and options markets are set by the exchanges. For most contracts, there is a difference between **initial margin,** the amount of margin exchanges require to initiate a trade, and **maintenance margin,** the minimum amount of margin the customer must maintain at all times. As part of the daily mark-to-market process, clearing members pay or receive from the clearinghouse funds known as **variation margin.** Variation margin is an additional required deposit to bring an investor's equity account up to the initial margin level when the account balance falls below the maintenance margin requirement. In volatile markets, variation margin may be collected intraday, with clearing members sometimes required to deposit funds within one hour of the margin call.

initial margin Minimum amount required to initiate a trade.

maintenance margin Minimum amount required at all times to sustain a market position.

variation margin Additional required deposit to bring an investor's equity account up to the initial margin level when the account balance falls below the maintenance margin requirement.

The mark-to-market process ensures that the customer account value for each futures buyer and seller is sufficient to guarantee contract fulfillment. If there is a daily profit, this amount can be paid to the customer. If there is a daily loss, the customer must pay this full amount. Importantly, if the loss experienced in any futures trading account is greater than the margin funds on deposit, the customer is required to pay the full amount of this difference.

Market Professionals

Futures brokerage firms, known as **futures commission merchants,** are intermediaries between public customers and the exchanges. They are the only entity outside the futures clearinghouse that can hold customer funds. Brokerage firms provide facilities to execute customer orders on the exchange. They also maintain records of each customer's positions, margin deposits, money balances, and completed transactions. In return for providing these services, a brokerage firm collects commissions.

futures commission merchants Futures brokerage firms.

In the United States, futures brokers must meet a number of regulatory requirements, including the maintenance of a minimum level of net capital. A futures brokerage firm also must be a member of the **National Futures Association (NFA),** an industry-wide self-regulatory organization. Futures brokers may be full-service or discount firms. Some are part of national or regional brokerage companies that also offer securities and other financial services. Others offer only futures or futures options to their customers. Some futures brokers have a company or are related to a commercial bank, agribusiness company, or other commercial enterprise.

National Futures Association (NFA) Futures industry self-regulatory organization.

An **introducing broker** is an individual or firm that has established a relationship with one or more futures brokerage firms. Like futures brokers, introducing brokers are responsible for maintaining customer relationships and servicing customer accounts. However, introducing brokers cannot accept funds from customers and must maintain accounts with a futures broker. Independent introducing brokers who have sufficient capital to meet regulatory requirements may introduce

introducing broker Individual or firm that has established a relationship with one or more futures brokerage firms.

their clients through a number of different futures brokers. A guaranteed introducing broker has a legal and regulatory relationship with the guarantor futures broker through which it introduces its customers.

commodity pool Commingled fund for commodity speculation.

Many large institutions and individual investors include managed futures positions in their investment portfolios. These positions can be in the form of **commodity pools** or individually managed accounts. A private commodity pool or public commodity fund operates much like a stock or bond mutual fund in that they allow investors with limited resources to purchase diversified investments that are professionally managed. As with mutual funds, several commodity pools are sponsored by major brokerage firms. In many cases, commodity pools provide significantly more leverage than stock mutual funds. Commodity pools also provide limited liability to their investors, because the risk of loss is no greater than the amount of capital invested. This contrasts with individual futures accounts, including individually managed accounts, in which the investor can receive margin calls and lose more money than was initially deposited.

commodity trading advisor One who trades for others and/or makes trading recommendations.

A **commodity trading advisor** trades for others and/or makes trading recommendations. Some commodity trading advisors are responsible for trading individually managed accounts. Others are hired to trade on behalf of commodity pools and funds. Trading advisors typically receive two types of compensation. A management fee is often levied whether or not the client makes money. An incentive fee, charged as a percentage of net trading profits in the client's account, is sometimes added.

Futures Trading Example

On Tuesday, January 25, 2000, *The Wall Street Journal*'s regular "Commodities" column ran an extremely bearish article on sugar titled "Sugar Market Is Set on a Bearish Course."[2] In that article, the *Journal* reported that raw-sugar prices slid as heavy selling from producers in Central and South America as well as Australia set the market firmly on a bearish course. On Monday, the March contract on New York's Coffee, Sugar & Cocoa Exchange fell 0.14¢ to 5.29¢ per pound, matching the lowest settlement price in eight months. "Clearly, everyone is selling," said a trader at a New York brokerage firm. The market is "very well entrenched into a downtrend." So bearish was the consensus on sugar prices that the *Journal* quoted a leading analyst as saying, "It sort of flummoxes me why the market hasn't fallen more steeply than it has given the fundamentals."

Suppose an investor read the *Journal*'s assessment of the pricing outlook for sugar and decided to sell (or short) 10 sugar futures contracts in the hope of profiting from the expected fall in sugar prices. As indicated in Figure 18.2, each sugar futures contract represents 112,000 pounds of sugar. At a price of 5.29¢ per pound, the total value of one sugar contract is $5,924.80 (= 112,000 × $0.0529), as shown in Table 18.3. The value of 10 sugar contracts at 5.29¢ per pound is simply $59,248 (= 10 × $5,924.80). According to the New York Board of Trade, parent company of the Coffee, Sugar & Cocoa Exchange, where sugar is traded, the minimum initial margin requirement for sugar is $700 per contract, or $7,000 for 10 contracts.

[2]See Brendan Coffey, "Sugar Market Is Set on a Bearish Course," *The Wall Street Journal,* January 25, 2000, C21.

TABLE 18.3 Sugar Futures Contract Commodity Trading Example

Contract Specifications		
Size of the Contract	112,000 lb	
Minimum Price Change		
Of one ounce	1/100 cents/lb	
Of one contract	$11.20	
Initial Margin Level	$700	
Maintenance Margin Level	$500	
Day 1		
Investor buys 10 sugar futures contract at 5.29¢/lb (Position value = 10 × 112,000 × $0.0529/lb = $59,248)		
Investor deposits initial margin		$7,000
Price rises to close at 5.32¢/lb; investor loss of 0.03¢/lb ($33.60 per contract) paid to clearinghouse		−336
Account balance at end of day 1		$6,664
Day 2		
Opening account balance (from day 1)		$6,664
Price rises further to close at 5.40¢/lb; investor loss of 0.08¢/lb ($89.60 per contract) paid to clearinghouse		−896
Account balance on day 2, after loss is paid to clearinghouse		$5,768
Day 3		
Opening account balance (from day 2)		$5,768
Price jumps to 5.52¢/lb; investor loss of 0.12¢/lb ($134.40 per contract) paid to clearinghouse		−1,344
Intraday account balance on day 3, after loss is paid to clearinghouse		$4,424
Margin call of $2,576 made to restore the account to the initial margin level ($7,000)		2,576
Account balance at end of day 3, after the margin call is met		$7,000
Day 4		
Opening account balance (from day 3)		$7,000
Price falls 0.05¢/lb to 5.47¢/lb; investor gain of $56 per contract		560
Account balance		$7,560
Trader offsets the short futures position at 5.47¢/lb and liquidates the account		7,560
Account balance at the end of day 4		$ 0
Profit/Loss Summary		
Profit/loss = 10 × (Contract selling price − Contract buying price) = 10 × [112,000 lb (5.29¢/lb − $5.47¢/lb)] = −$2,016 (loss)		
Profit/loss = Sum of deposits (−) and receipts (+)		
Day 1 Initial margin deposit	−$7,000	
Day 3 Margin call deposit	−$2,576	
Day 4 Account liquidated receipt	+$7,560	
Net trading loss	−$2,016	

Minimum maintenance margin is $500 per sugar futures contract, or $5,000 for 10 contracts. For simplicity, brokerage commissions and other trading costs will be ignored. In practice, these costs are substantial and greatly diminish trading profits and exacerbate trading losses.

On day 1 (Tuesday), sugar actually closed up 0.03¢ at 5.32¢ per pound. This represents a loss of $336 on a 10-contract short position established at 5.29¢ per pound. This $336 amount has to be paid by the investor to the clearinghouse at the end of the trading day, thereby reducing the investor's account balance from an initial $7,000 to $6,664. On day 2 (Wednesday), sugar closed up another 0.08¢

at 5.40¢ per pound. This represents a further loss of $896 on a 10-contract short position. This $896 amount would have to be paid by the investor to the clearinghouse at the end of the second trading day, thereby reducing the investor's account balance from the day 1 ending balance of $6,664 to $5,768.

On day 3 (Thursday), the price of sugar jumped another 0.12¢ to 5.52¢ per pound, resulting in a trading loss of $1,344 on a 10-contract short position. This loss would also trigger a margin call because it depletes the investor's account value to only $4,424, which is below the $5,000 minimum maintenance margin for a 10-contract short position. Let's assume the affected investor was promptly contacted and able to wire $2,576 in additional funds to the commodity broker. At the end of day 3, the investor's account balance would thus have been restored to its initial margin level of $7,000.

After surging as high as 5.57¢ per pound on day 4 (Friday), sugar settled down to close at 5.47¢ per pound. If the investor involved closed out the 10-contract short position at the closing price, a daily trading profit of 0.05¢ per pound or $560 on a 10-contract short position would have been realized. After closing out the short position, the investor would be left with an account balance of $7,560. This reflects a trading loss of $2,016 over the four-day trading period given the $7,000 in initial margin and $2,576 in additional required margin that was contributed to the account.

This simple illustration shows how an investor could have quickly lost a significant amount of money following reasonable commodity trading advice based on widely publicized sugar market fundamentals. Using actual market prices over a four-day period, a loss of 25–30% of an investor's original capital could have been easily suffered. To be sure, significant trading profits would have been gained if the investor had taken a directly contrarian approach. The problem is, how does a commodity speculator know when to be contrarian or "go with the flow?"

Hedging

Hedgers versus Speculators

hedgers
Investors who seek to reduce risks associated with dealing in the underlying commodity or security.

speculators
Individuals who seek to profit from price changes.

Historically, futures market participants have been divided into two broad categories. **Hedgers** seek to reduce risks associated with dealing in the underlying commodity or security. **Speculators,** including professional floor traders, seek to profit from price changes. For speculators, the attractions of futures markets include the extraordinary amount of leverage that can be used and the ease with which long and short positions can be established. Speculators and market makers assume the risk transferred by hedgers and give futures markets a high degree of liquidity. In contrast to hedgers, many speculators never use commodities in any manufacturing capacity. Most speculators trade strictly for the purpose of acquiring profits. By watching the markets closely, speculators can sometimes take advantage of small fluctuations in futures prices.

Most of the participants in the futures and options markets are commercial or institutional users and hedgers of the commodities traded. The hedger's objective is to lock in a favorable contract price that protects him or her against unforeseen fluctuations in the spot market. Hedgers are often willing to give up the possibility of lower spot prices to avoid the detrimental effects of exorbitantly high spot prices. Farmers, mining companies, and oil drillers are examples of hedgers who use futures contracts as a kind of cost insurance policy for their businesses.

Hedging involves taking a futures position that is opposite to that of a cash market position. A corn farmer would hedge by selling corn futures against the expected crop. An importer of Japanese cars might hedge by buying yen futures against an expected yen liability. A precious metals merchant could hedge by purchasing gold futures against a fixed-price gold sales contract. A pension fund manager can hedge by selling stock index futures against the fund's portfolio of equities in anticipation of a market decline. Risk management objectives that can often be achieved through the use of futures and futures options include stabilizing future cash flows, setting purchase or sale prices for commodities and securities, diversifying holdings, matching balance sheet assets and liabilities, and decreasing storage and inventory costs.

basis
In the futures market, the difference between a commodity's spot price and the futures price.

price risk
Chance of adverse changes in market prices.

basis risk
Chance of adverse change in the futures and spot market price relationship.

Hedging Concepts

In the futures market, the difference between a commodity's cash price, or spot price, and the futures price is known as the **basis,** as illustrated in Figure 18.6. Although hedging strategies with futures can eliminate **price risk,** hedging strategies cannot eliminate **basis risk.** Price risk is the chance that a security or portfolio will decline in value over time. Basis risk is the chance that the underlying basis will change unpredictably and unfavorably during the lifetime of the hedge. Basis risk derives from the hedger's uncertainty about the basis at the time a hedge may be lifted. Hedging techniques substitute basis risk for price risk.

The cash-futures basis is subject to many influences, including seasonal factors, weather conditions, temporary gluts or scarcities of commodities, and the availability of transport facilities. Other factors affecting the relationship between cash and futures prices are costs related to carrying commodities and securities, such as interest rates and warehouse fees. In certain financial markets, basis reflects the

FIGURE 18.6 **Difference between Cash and Futures Prices Is the Cash-Futures Basis**

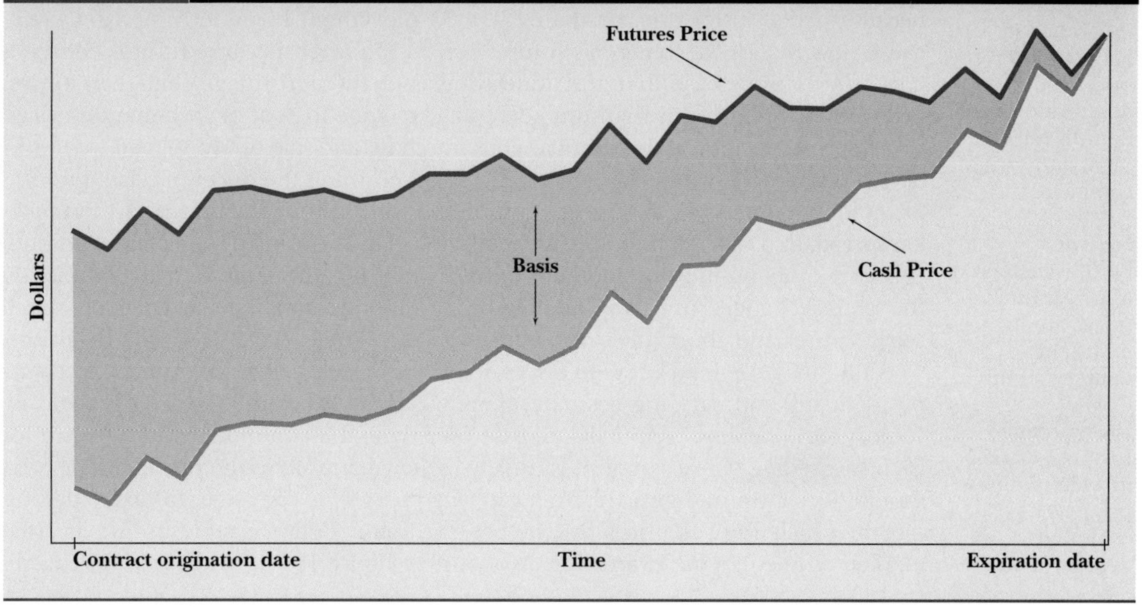

difference between long-term and short-term interest rates. As shown in Figure 18.6, the cash-futures basis, or difference between spot and futures prices, converges toward zero as futures contracts approach the expiration date. However, prior to expiration, the difference between cash and futures prices can widen or narrow for reasons that are hard to predict. Basis risk tends to be prevalent when traders cross-hedge a risk exposure in one commodity by using futures contracts on some different but closely related commodity. For example, a trader might use heating oil futures to hedge jet fuel needs or deutschmarks to hedge Dutch guilder payments. Prices of two related fuels or two related currencies may have moved closely for significant periods of time in the past, but there is no guarantee that historical price relationships will continue into the future.

As in the options market, the futures market delta (or hedge ratio) is the ratio of underlying asset price volatility divided by the price volatility of the hedging instrument. To use futures as a hedge against a long position in an agricultural commodity, natural resource, or financial instrument, hedgers would write a certain number of futures contracts. This number is given by the hedge ratio. For example, suppose a March soybean futures contract representing 5,000 bushels of soybeans has a delta of 0.9. This means that this soybean futures contract's theoretical value should change by 90% of the change in the cash price of soybeans. This implies that a perfectly hedged and riskless position would be established if 4,500 bushels of soybeans (= 0.9 × 5,000 bushels) were purchased for every soybean futures contract written. Following the sale of one standard soybean futures contract covering 5,000 bushels, purchase of 4,500 bushels of soybeans in the spot market would establish a perfect hedge. In that case, a 10¢ per bushel increase in the cash price of soybeans would lead to a cash-market profit of $450 (= 10¢ × 4,500 bushels) that would exactly offset the loss of $450 (= 0.9 × 10¢ × 5,000 bushel futures contract) on the futures contract written. Conversely, a 10¢ per bushel decrease in the cash price of soybeans would lead to a cash-market loss of $450 (= 10¢ × 4,500 bushels) that would exactly offset the gain of $450 (= 0.9 × 10¢ × 5,000 bushel futures contract) on the futures contract written. As in the options market, a perfectly hedged position in the futures market leaves total wealth unchanged. Notice that because hedge ratios are less than 1.0, a $1 movement in underlying asset prices causes less than a $1 change in futures prices. However, because futures contracts have a lower price basis than the underlying asset, the percentage change in futures prices tends to be larger than the percentage change in spot or cash-market prices.

intramarket spread
In the futures market, the difference between futures prices for different delivery months for the same underlying commodity.

contango
Futures market in which futures prices are higher in distant delivery months.

backwardation
Inverted market in which futures prices are lower in distant delivery months.

A spread position is the simultaneous purchase and sale of two related futures or option positions. Investors take on spread positions when the prices of related futures or option contracts are considered out of line with historical patterns. An **intramarket spread,** also called a time spread, combines a long position in one contract month against a short position in another contract month in the same futures contract on the same exchange. An example would be a position that included going long March sugar futures and short July sugar futures on the Coffee, Sugar & Cocoa Exchange. The intramarket spread between prices of various futures delivery months reflects supply, demand, and carrying cost considerations. Because warehouse charges and inventory carrying costs generally increase over time, the commodity futures price for each succeeding delivery month is usually higher than that of the preceding delivery month. As shown in Figure 18.7A, a carrying charge, or **contango,** futures market is one in which futures prices are higher in distant delivery months. An inverted market, or one in a **backwardation,** as shown in Figure 18.7B, features lower futures

FIGURE 18.7 **Intramarket Spreads Reflect Influences of Supply, Demand, and Carrying Costs**

A. With carrying costs, the futures price for each succeeding delivery month is usually higher.

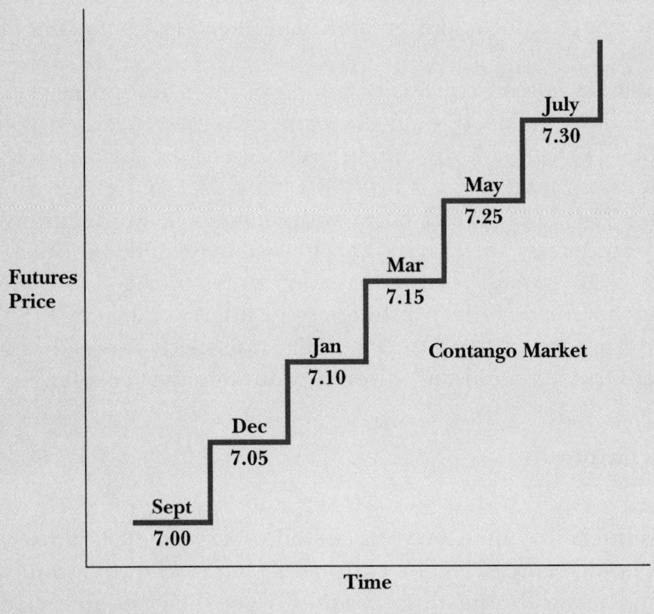

B. In some futures markets, futures prices are inverted with highest prices for the nearby spot month.

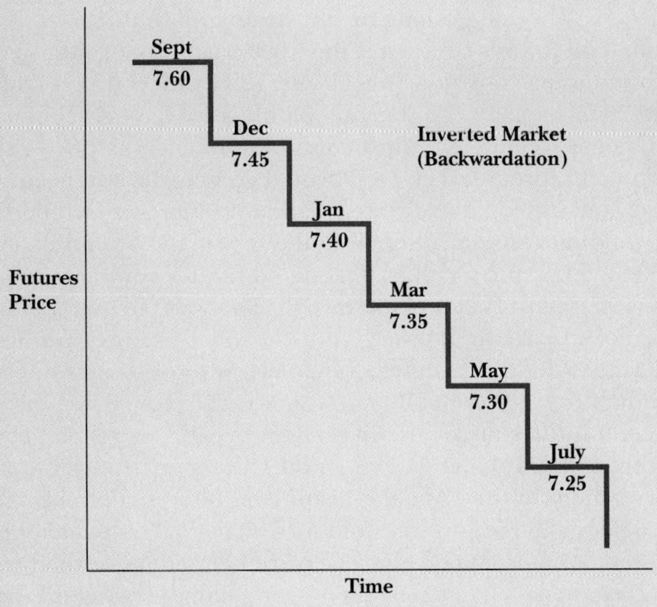

prices in distant delivery months. Inverted markets sometimes occur when demand for the cash commodity is unusually strong relative to current supply. Inverted markets also occur when the income derived from holding a cash position exceeds the costs of carrying the position. For example, a backwardation can occur in U.S. Treasury bond futures when long-term interest rates exceed short-term rates, and therefore, the underlying bond yield is greater than the cost of financing the cash bond portfolio.

intermarket spread Offsetting positions in related commodities.

An **intermarket spread** consists of a long position in one market and a short position in another market trading the same or a closely related commodity. An example is the "TED spread," or the difference between the prices of a U.S. Treasury bill futures contract and a Eurodollar time-deposit futures contract on the Chicago Merc. The TED spread varies with changes in the relationship between short-term interest rates for private and government debt. Another intermarket spread is the "NOB spread," or U.S. Treasury notes over U.S. Treasury bonds on the CBOT. Such spreads reflect differences in interest rates on U.S. Treasury securities of different maturities. Other popular intermarket spreads involve pairs of precious metals, such as gold and silver or platinum and palladium.

Hedging Example

Suppose Heating Oil Transfer, Inc. (HOT), buys heating oil at current wholesale prices from refiners and then markets the oil to large industrial users, school systems, and shopping centers. HOT's customers want to know how much heating oil will cost them during the heating season. To get their business, HOT offers its clients fixed-price contracts. After entering into contracts to deliver heating oil at a fixed price, HOT is exposed to price risk if it doesn't own the oil or have a fixed-price contract to purchase heating oil from a refiner. To hedge its price risk in the futures market, HOT would go long or buy heating oil futures.

Each heating oil futures contract is for 1,000 barrels (42 gallons = 1 barrel) of heating oil. Assume that it is now June 1 and HOT enters into a fixed-price contract to deliver 840,000 gallons of heating oil in early October. Under the circumstances, HOT needs to buy 20 futures contracts to hedge its price risk. To hedge its price risk in the futures market, HOT would go long, or buy, heating oil futures on June 1 and then liquidate its futures market position on October 1. On October 1, HOT would purchase heating oil in the spot market to fulfill its contractual obligations. Remember, the October heating oil futures contract on the New York Merc expires on the third Friday of the month. Thus, HOT could not fulfill its contractual obligations by taking delivery on its October futures contracts. Oil delivered on the October futures contracts would arrive too late for HOT's customers.

Consider the three different oil price scenarios illustrated in Table 18.4. In scenario A, cash and futures prices rise in tandem by 10¢ per gallon. The cash price for oil rises from 65¢ to 75¢ per gallon, and the October 1 futures price rises from 60¢ to 70¢ per gallon. In this case, the heating oil futures contracts that were purchased for 60¢ per gallon in June are sold for 70¢ per gallon in October, for a gain of 10¢ per gallon. What is HOT's effective price per gallon for the heating oil it is delivering to customers? The answer is 65¢ per gallon. Heating oil for delivery in October is purchased on the spot market on October 1 for 75¢ per gallon. HOT's gain on the long futures position of 10¢ per gallon is subtracted from the spot cost of 75¢ per gallon for a net cost of 65¢ per gallon. Under this scenario, HOT's June

TABLE 18.4 Hypothetical Hedging Example for the Heating Oil Market

Prices per gallon on June 1:		
	Cash Price (Spot Price)	**(Oct) Futures**
	65¢	**60¢**
A. Cash and futures prices rise (in tandem), such that		
Prices (per gal)	**Local Cash**	**(Oct) Futures**
on Oct. 1	75¢	70¢
B. Cash and futures prices fall (in tandem), such that		
Prices (per gal)	**Local Cash**	**(Oct) Futures**
On Oct 1	60¢	55¢
C. Cash and futures prices remain the same, such that		
Prices (per gal)	**Local Cash**	**(Oct) Futures**
On Oct 1	65¢	60¢

decision to lock in the June 1 cash price of 65¢ per gallon by using the futures market saved the company from having to pay higher heating oil prices that emerged the following October.

In scenario B, cash and futures prices fall in tandem by 5¢ per gallon. The cash price for oil falls from 65¢ to 60¢ per gallon, and the October 1 futures price falls from 60¢ to 55¢ per gallon. In this case, the heating oil futures contracts that were purchased for 60¢ per gallon in June are sold for 55¢ per gallon in October, for a loss of 5¢ per gallon. HOT's effective price per gallon for the heating oil it is delivering is again 65¢ per gallon. Heating oil for delivery in October is purchased on the spot market on October 1 for 60¢ per gallon. HOT's loss on the long futures position of 5¢ per gallon is added to the spot cost of 60¢ per gallon for a net cost of 65¢ per gallon. Under this scenario, HOT's June decision to lock in the June 1 cash price of 65¢ per gallon by using the futures market made it impossible for the company to enjoy the benefits from lower heating oil prices that materialized the following October. By locking in prices in the futures market, HOT avoids the risk of higher prices but loses the potential for cost savings from lower prices.

Finally, in scenario C, cash and futures prices remain constant at 65¢ per gallon (cash price) and 60¢ per gallon (futures price). In this case, the heating oil futures contracts locked in the June cash price of 65¢ per gallon, which is exactly the same as the October cash market price of 65¢ per gallon. No gain or loss results from HOT's futures market transactions, and the effective price per gallon is 65¢ per gallon, the October spot price, with no futures gain or loss introduced into the calculation.

portfolio insurance Trading strategy of using a mix of index futures, leveraged stock portfolios, and stock options to create the right to sell stock portfolios at a fixed price in the event of a decline in prices.

Program Trading

One of the most popular examples of hedging activity relates to the stock market and the use of stock index futures and options on stock index futures. The development of stock index futures introduced a whole new group of investors to the futures markets. As opposed to buying or selling just a handful of stocks, stock index futures give investors the ability to offset security risk through a host of complicated investment strategies, referred to as **portfolio insurance** or **index arbitrage.**

index arbitrage Trading strategy that exploits divergences between actual and theoretical futures prices.

FIGURE 18.8 **Program Trading Data Are Published Weekly in *The Wall Street Journal***

PROGRAM TRADING

NEW YORK—Program trading in the week ended April 28 accounted for 19.2%, or an average 193 million daily shares, of New York Stock Exchange volume.

Brokerage firms executed an additional 89.1 million daily shares of program trading away from the NYSE, mostly on foreign markets. Program trading is the simultaneous purchase or sale of at least 15 different stocks with a total value of $1 million or more.

Of the program total on the NYSE, 13.6% involved stock-index arbitrage, down from 17.7% the prior week. In this strategy, traders dart between stocks and stock-index options and futures to capture fleeting price differences.

Some 71.9% of program trading was executed by firms for their customers, while 25.1% was done for their own accounts, or principal trading. An additional 3% was designated as customer facilitation, in which firms use principal positions to facilitate customer trades.

The report includes a special profile of trading whenever the Dow Jones Industrial Average rises or falls more than 200 points from its previous close during any one-hour period. There were no such periods during the week.

Of the five most-active firms, Deutsche Bank Securities, Bear Stearns, BNP Securities and Goldman Sachs executed all or most of their program trading activity for customers as agents. Morgan Stanley executed its program activity as principal for its own accounts.

NYSE PROGRAM TRADING

Volume (in millions of shares) for the week ended April 28, 2000

Top 15 Firms	Index Arbitrage	Derivative-Related*	Other Strategies	Total
Deutsche Bank Securities	17.5	.....	91.2	108.7
Bear Stearns	.....	.....	96.0	96.0
Morgan Stanley Dn Wttr	31.5	.....	60.7	92.2
BNP Securities	.....	.....	87.1	87.1
Goldman, Sachs & Co.	.....	.....	66.6	66.6
CS First Boston	6.2	.....	58.2	64.4
TLW Securities LLC	11.9	0.8	45.8	58.5
RBC Dominion	25.3	.....	25.2	50.5
W&D Securities	.....	.....	45.1	45.1
Salomon Smith Barney	.....	.....	42.5	42.5
Interactive Brokers	.....	.....	37.4	37.4
CIBC World Markets	12.5	.....	22.7	35.2
Susquehanna Bkrg. Srvs.	3.0	.....	31.3	34.3
Merrill Lynch	2.1	.....	23.1	25.2
Nomura Securities	13.0	.....	8.7	21.7
OVERALL TOTAL	130.9	8.9	825.1	964.9

*Other derivative-related strategies besides index arbitrage

Source: New York Stock Exchange

Source: *The Wall Street Journal,* May 5, 2000, C3.

Portfolio insurance is an investment strategy of using a mix of index futures, leveraged stock portfolios, and stock options in such a manner as to create the right to sell stock portfolios at a fixed price in the event of a decline in prices. The strategy's goal is to ensure that the value of the portfolio does not fall below some critical level, say, 3–5% below current prices. Index arbitrage is a similar trading strategy that exploits divergences between actual and theoretical futures prices. For example, buying stock index futures while selling baskets of stocks that underlie the index is a sometimes effective means for capturing elusive trading profits. Stock index futures also allow traders to make bets on the direction of stock prices as measured by broad market benchmarks.

However, the popularity of portfolio insurance and index arbitrage have declined precipitously since the stock market crash of 1987, when the DJIA dropped 508 points (or 22.6%) in a single day. Portfolio insurance and index arbitrage have been blamed for worsening the crash of 1987 and minicrashes such as that experienced on August 31, 1998, when the DJIA plunged 512.6 points (or 6.3%). Individual and institutional investors were burned badly in both instances, and many have sworn off what they now regard as treacherous investment strategies.

Program trading of bundles of stocks tied to expiring options is a type of arbitrage used by institutional investors to exploit price differences between financial derivatives and the underlying securities. Although program trading is sometimes criticized for creating market turmoil, others say it makes for more liquid and efficient markets. In any event, program trading can represent a significant portion of trading activity, especially during weeks tied to the expiration of options on stocks and stock indexes. For example, as shown in Figure 18.8, program trading for the week ended April 28, 2000, accounted for 19.2%, or an average 193 million daily shares, of New York Stock Exchange volume. Brokerage firms executed an additional 89.1 million daily shares of program trading away from the Big Board, mostly on foreign markets. In these data, program trading is defined as the simultaneous purchase or sale of at least 15 different stocks with a total value of at least $1 million.

Of the program trading total on the Big Board, *The Wall Street Journal* reported that 13.6% involved stock index arbitrage, down from 17.7% the prior week. In this strategy, traders dart between stocks and stock index options and futures to capture fleeting price differences. Some 71.9% of program trading was executed by firms for their customers, whereas 25.1% was done for their own accounts, or principal trading. An additional 3% was designated as customer facilitation, in which firms use principal positions to facilitate customer trades. Of the five most active firms, *The Wall Street Journal* reported that Deutsche Bank Securities, Bear Stearns, BNP Securities, and Goldman Sachs executed all or almost all program activity for customers. Morgan Stanley Dean Witter executed most of its activity as principal for its own accounts.

Futures Pricing

Economic Features

Futures share a number of significant economic features with equities (common stock), forward contracts, options, and over-the-counter financial derivatives. Futures also have a number of meaningful distinguishing characteristics. A brief consideration of the economic features of futures contracts and other common financial instruments can be helpful in understanding the function and pricing of futures contracts.

Important economic factors differentiate futures from common stocks. As seen in Table 18.5A, futures markets exist to facilitate risk shifting and price discovery

WALL STREET WISDOM 18.2

Tips for Futures Traders

Futures trading is a risky proposition at best and extremely hazardous for the unsophisticated nonprofessional. To help novice speculators get started and to avoid some of the many pitfalls associated with futures trading, the Chicago Mercantile Exchange (Merc) offers a wealth of investor education. At the Merc's Web site, for example, novice speculators can develop their trading skills by using *On-Line Simulated Trading,* including *Currency Trading Simulation,* software. A variety of Web instant lessons are also offered, as is the *CME Commodity Trading How-To Kit and Video.*

When getting started in the risky business of futures trading, novice speculators need to be aware of a few simple, time-tested rules used by successful traders:

- *Start small.* Funds put into a speculative trading account should be completely discretionary. Be able to afford to lose whatever amount you place in a trading account. Savings for college, retirement, or emergencies should not be included. Do not confuse speculating with investing.
- *Set definite risk parameters.* Before entering into a trade, determine how much of a loss you are willing to accept. This can be a dollar figure or a percentage of a trading account. Always keep something in reserve. Do not let emotions dictate trading decisions when the market turns against you.
- *Diversify.* Never expose an entire trading account to a single dominant position in one futures contract. It is always more prudent to take smaller positions in several contracts. At the same time, do not trade too many markets. It is difficult to track positions and follow market fundamentals in a large number of markets.
- *Choose your instruments and trading strategy carefully.* Futures contracts that experience extremely wide daily trading ranges are especially risky. Larger contracts often carry greater risk, although risk also depends on contract tick size and the average trading range. Be careful about the excessive use of margin. Being right does you no good if you get stopped out just prior to a big move up in price.
- *Have a workable trading strategy, and stick to it.* Before entering into a futures position, develop a workable trading plan based on the economic fundamentals. Specify a reasonable price target, and decide to sell if your goal is met. How will you know when you are wrong? When is it time to sell?

Successful futures market traders know that their success depends on having a superior grasp of the economic fundamentals of the market and maintaining a strict trading discipline. Successful trading strategies can be easily ruined when traders let rumors or offhand remarks undercut their confidence. At the same time, successful traders are able to recognize when conditions have changed and are able to quickly adapt to the new situation.

Finally, it is important to recognize that successful trading typically depends on capitalizing on a few big moves during a given year. Every trade in the futures markets comes with a hefty price tag in the form of bid-ask spreads and commission charges. Successful traders avoid trading strategies that have them constantly jumping in and out of the market. Frenetic trading is often good for brokers and tax collectors but seldom profitable for traders themselves. Frequently trading in and out of the market only tends to be appropriate for scalpers on the floor of the exchange where their exchange membership entitles them to much lower trading fees. It is vital that off-the-floor traders focus their efforts on making a few well-timed trades. Day trading never works for long. Most successful traders enter and exit their positions no more than four or five times per year.

For investor education and trading tips, see the Chicago Mercantile Exchange Web site at <http://www.cme.com>.

TABLE 18.5 Futures Compared with Common Stocks, Forwards, and Options

Characteristic		
A. Common Stock and Futures Contract Differences		
	Common Stock	**Futures Contract**
Economic purpose	Capital formation	Price discovery, risk shifting
Investment requirement	Ownership stake	Performance bond (margin)
Income potential	Dividends	None
Leverage potential	Initial 2:1	Initial 10:1 to 20:1
Investor risk	Low to high	Huge
Price and position limits	None	Both
Ownership evidence	Stock certificate	Brokerage statement
Trading mechanism	Market-maker system	Open-outcry auction method
B. Forwards and Futures Contract Differences		
	Forwards	**Futures**
Contract specifications	Unstandardized	Standardized
Contract guarantee	No clearinghouse backing	Clearinghouse backing
Counterparty risk	Variable	None
Investor types	Institutional investors	Institutional and individual investors
Market development	Small private market	Large public market
Settlement	Delivery date	Mark-to-market daily
Trading location	Over-the-counter market	Organized exchanges
Liquidity	Illiquid market	Active, liquid market
C. Options and Futures Contract Differences		
	Options	**Futures**
Basic nature	Buyer right/seller obligation	Obligation for buyers and sellers
Buyer payment	Up-front	Mark-to-market daily
Buyer risk	Limited to premium	Unlimited
Seller risk	Unlimited	Unlimited
Hedging flexibility	Ability to separate upside/downside	Cannot separate upside/downside
Writer income	Yes	No
Termination	Reverse trade	Reverse trade
Delivery (rare)	Anytime prior to expiration	During delivery period

for an underlying asset that might be an agricultural commodity, natural resource, or financial instrument. By contrast, the principal purpose of equity markets is to foster capital formation. In futures trading, there is a short for every long. In the stock market, short positions are normally a minor factor. Customer funds deposited to carry futures positions constitute a performance bond or good-faith deposit to secure the investor's promise to fulfill contractual obligations. Futures positions are marked-to-market on a daily basis, and no interest is earned on customer account balances. Futures market investors always run the risk of a margin call following modest changes in market prices. When investors use margin debt to help finance stock purchases, investor funds act as a down payment and the balance of the purchase price is borrowed with interest charged. There is no daily marking-to-market in the equities markets, but maintenance margin calls are possible following adverse market moves. Of course, although futures trading is typically marked by the use of enormous 10:1 or 20:1 leverage, initial positions in common stocks are limited to no more than 2:1 leverage. Most common stock investors shun the use of leverage. The lives of futures contracts are limited to stipulated expiration dates. However, equities are issued without a termination date.

Futures and equity trading practices are also starkly different. Many futures markets have price and/or position limits. Equities typically do not. Price limits on futures contracts establish the maximum range for trading prices during a given day. Futures position limits establish the maximum exposure a market participant may assume in a particular market. Although the outstanding number of equities is fixed at a given moment, there is no theoretical limit on the number of futures or futures options that may exist at a particular time in a specific market. The number of futures and futures option contracts are set by the forces of supply and demand. Unlike equities, in which customers obtain certificates that provide evidence of ownership, there are no comparable certificates for futures or futures options. In the futures and futures options markets, a brokerage trade confirmation is the customer's only written record. And finally, open-outcry futures markets typically operate with a multiple market-maker system, involving floor traders and floor brokers competing on equal footing in an auction-style market. Exchange-traded equities use a specialist system, in which the designated specialist has specific privileges and responsibilities. Equities traded on Nasdaq or the over-the-counter markets use a multiple market-maker system that is similar to futures markets.

In contrast with many obvious dissimilarities between futures and equities, there are notable similarities between futures and forward contracts. A forward contract can be regarded as some customized futures contract involving delivery of an underlying commodity or financial instrument. A forward is an agreement between two parties to buy or sell a commodity or asset at a specific future time for an agreed-on price. Forward contracts represent an obligatory agreement to transact in the *future* based on future price expectations. Futures contracts are an obligatory agreement to transact *today* based on future price expectations. (In the world of romance, getting engaged is a forward contract to marry at some future date. Getting married is a futures contract. Both are based on blissful expectations.)

Both futures and forwards represent contracts specifying the price, quantity, and future delivery date for a given agricultural commodity, natural resource, or financial instrument. However, important differences in cash settlement properties give futures and forward contracts different cash-flow patterns, even for an identical underlying asset. As seen in Table 18.5B, important distinctions between forward and futures contracts start with differences in counterparty risk. Performance of exchange-traded futures and futures option contracts are guaranteed by the clearinghouse of the exchange on which the contracts are executed. Because no such clearinghouse exists for forward contracts, forward market participants must pay particular attention to counterparty creditworthiness. Thus, although Florida orange growers may be willing to enter into forward contracts with highly reputable parties such as Coca-Cola's Minute Maid division, they would be most reluctant to enter into forward contracts with unknown market speculators. This explains why futures markets have grown tremendously in popularity, while smaller forward markets are only available to large, well-known, and financially strong institutional investors.

Exchange-traded futures contracts involve daily payments of profits and losses through the mark-to-market margin system, whereas forward contracts generally do not involve periodic payments of accumulated gains or losses. As a result, the investor's cash-flow pattern can be sharply different for buyers and sellers of futures and forward contracts on the same underlying asset. Large paper losses and gains can accumulate with forward contracts and thereby increase the likelihood and cost of default. Exchange-traded futures contracts are standardized, whereas customized forward contracts often vary with respect to terms such as the grade of the underlying commodity or asset, delivery location and date, credit arrangements, and default provisions. In the absence of standardized contract provisions, forward contracts often lack the liquidity and low transaction costs characteristic of futures markets.

Differences between options and futures begin with the fact that buyers of options enjoy the right, but not the obligation, to transact (see Table 18.5C). Sellers of options incur the obligation to transact if the buyer chooses to exercise the option. Both buyers and sellers of futures contracts incur the obligation to transact in the future. Both options and futures represent a zero sum game because buyer losses are exactly equal to seller profits. Similarly, buyer profits are exactly equal to seller losses. Option buyer risk is limited to the option premium, or the price paid for the option. Risk is potentially unlimited for option sellers and both buyers and sellers of futures.

synthetic financial instruments Hybrid financial instruments created by blending an underlying price on a cash instrument with the price of some financial derivative.

Law of One Price

Different economic characteristics for common stocks, forwards, options, and futures give rise to predictable relationships between the prices of these and related financial derivatives. Indeed, using complex combinations of long and short positions, it is often possible to create **synthetic financial instruments** that have risk and return characteristics identical to some other underlying asset or financial derivative. Synthetics are customized or hybrid financial instruments created by blending an underlying price on a cash instrument with the price of some financial derivative. Alternatively, synthetic financial instruments represent a combination of security holdings that mimic price movements of another security. For example, a synthetic call option on a stock can be created with a long position in the stock combined with the purchase of a put option on that same security. A synthetic put option can be created with a short position in the stock combined with the purchase of a call option on that same security.

swap Arrangement whereby two companies agree to lend to each other on different terms.

swaptions Options to engage in a specific interest rate swap on or before a specific date.

Financial derivative markets encompass a plethora of tailored financial instruments, such as **swaps, swaptions, caps,** and **collars,** that are traded by the world's leading financial institutions. Swaps are arrangements whereby two companies agree to lend to each other on different terms, such as in different currencies or at different interest rates. For example, financial institutions sometimes conduct swaps to trade fixed interest-rate obligations for floating interest-rate obligations. Swaptions are simply options to engage in a specific interest-rate swap on or before a specific date. Caps are upper limits on the interest rate paid on floating-rate notes or adjustable-rate mortgages. Collars are upper and lower limits on the interest rate paid on floating-rate notes or adjustable-rate mortgages. The fact that financial futures and other financial derivatives are actively traded by savvy financial institutions in active and liquid financial markets ensures that prices are effectively and efficiently linked among various financial derivatives.

caps Upper limits on the interest rate paid on floating-rate notes or adjustable-rate mortgages.

collars Upper and lower limits on the interest rate paid on floating-rate notes or adjustable-rate mortgages.

In perfectly competitive financial markets, the **law of one price** states that identical assets have identical prices. When equilibrium prices are efficiently determined by supply and demand, a strict relationship holds between the expected rate of return and risk. Higher expected rates of return are only possible at the cost of greater return variability. If risk-free T-bills yield 6% in the credit market, the law of one price implies that any asset yielding more than 6% cannot be risk free. Financial assets with an expected rate of return higher than the riskfree rate are risky, by

law of one price Concept that identical assets have identical prices.

definition. Similarly, the law of one price implies that strict relations exist between the prices for underlying assets and related financial derivatives. This means that the futures price for any agricultural commodity or natural resource equals the spot (or cash market) price plus the cost of carry including interest and storage costs:

$$\text{Commodity futures price} = \text{Spot price} + \text{Cost of carry} \tag{18.1}$$
$$= \text{Spot price}\left(1 + \text{Risk-free interest rate} + \text{Percentage storage cost}\right)$$

Equation 18.1 simply means that the commodity futures price can be viewed as a composite of the spot market price plus the costs necessary to hold such agricultural commodities or natural resources until the expiration of the futures contract.

For example, suppose the spot market price for gold is \$300 per ounce, and the risk-free interest rate is 6% per year. If the gold market anticipated sufficient additional production during the next 12 months, there would be no additional gold storage costs necessary to meet gold futures contract commitments. In such circumstances, the one-year gold futures price would simply be \$318 = (\$300 × 1.06). If the gold spot market price was \$300 and the futures price was above \$318, the firm could buy gold in the spot market and sell gold futures and earn risk-free arbitrage profits. If the gold spot market price was \$300 per ounce and the futures price was less than \$318, the firm could buy gold futures and sell gold in the spot market and earn risk-free arbitrage profits. Similarly, if the gold spot market price was greater than \$300 and gold futures were \$318, the firm could sell gold in the spot market and buy gold futures and earn risk-free arbitrage profits. If the gold spot market price was less than \$300 and gold futures were \$318, the firm could buy gold in the spot market and sell gold futures and earn risk-free arbitrage profits.

In this example, if there was insufficient anticipated production during the next 12 months to meet futures contract commitments, carrying costs would have to be adjusted upward to account for storage costs. This would have the effect of raising futures prices. Simply put, every spot market price translates into a specific futures price given interest and storage costs.

In the case of financial futures, pension funds and other institutional investors use sophisticated hedging strategies to ensure conformance between spot market prices for financial instruments and futures prices. As in the case of futures for agricultural commodities and natural resources, arbitrage between the spot and futures market ensures efficiency in the pricing of financial futures:

$$\text{Financial futures price} = \text{Spot price for financial instrument} + \text{Borrowing costs of carry} - \text{Dividend yield or interest income} \tag{18.2}$$
$$= \text{Spot price}\left(1 + \text{Risk-free interest rate} - \text{Percentage income on financial instrument}\right)$$

Equation 18.2 signifies that the financial futures price is a mixture of the spot market price and the borrowing costs necessary to hold instruments until the expiration of the futures contract minus the amount of dividend or interest income that would be generated by the underlying financial instrument.

For example, if the risk-free interest rate is 6% per year and the dividend yield on an underlying stock index is 2% per year, the net cost of carry is only 4% (= 6% − 2%) per year. If the spot market price for the underlying index is $1,500, a one-year futures contract would have a price of $1,560 (= $1,500 × 1.04). If the index spot price was $1,500 and the futures price was greater than $1,560, investors could buy in the spot market and sell in the futures market and earn risk-free arbitrage profits. If the index spot price was $1,500 and the futures price was less than $1,560, investors could sell in the spot market and buy in the futures market and earn risk-free arbitrage profits. Similarly, if the index spot price was less than $1,500 and the futures price was $1,560, investors could buy in the spot market and sell in the futures market and earn risk-free arbitrage profits. If the index spot price was greater than $1,500 and the futures price was $1,560, investors could sell in the spot market and buy in the futures market and earn risk-free arbitrage profits.

Investor Risk Considerations

The primary social benefits of futures markets lie in their price discovery and risk-shifting roles. Financial institutions and individual investors both look to the futures markets to help determine the best current market prices. That is because futures markets provide a forum that is somewhat independent from cash markets for buyers and sellers who want to trade. Futures markets give buyers and sellers an alternative means for collecting bids and offers and bringing them together in an open-outcry auction market. Another major function of futures markets is to transfer risk. If you were a cattle rancher, your objective might be to raise and sell cattle at a price that would give the most profit. A major risk would stem from declining cattle prices. You could transfer this risk by selling cattle futures. If cattle prices plunge, you could buy back the futures contracts at a lower price and offset your cash loss. Hence, the risk of lower prices is transferred to a buyer who may be a speculator or commercial user, such as a beef processor. Those who accept a transfer of risk through futures markets hope to generate profits.

However, it is worth keeping in mind that prosaic examples such as the cattle rancher and the beef processor described above account for little of the actual trading activity in futures markets. In practice, only 1–2% of futures contracts ever result in the delivery of an actual commodity. Futures markets are not intended as an alternative to gambling casinos, but that is what they are for many individual speculators. For most individual speculators, futures represent a high-risk gamble and a losing proposition. In the best of times, individual futures market speculators have less than an even chance of making money because of high trading costs and informational disadvantages. Individuals often find themselves trading against huge grain-trading companies or financial institutions. Not only do the pros have nearly instant access to market-moving information, their own multimillion-dollar trades can send futures prices soaring or skidding in seconds. Before speculating on the trend in oil prices, ask yourself a simple question: What is the chance of your beating Exxon on oil? In the grain markets, what is the chance that you know more than the Archer-Daniels-Midland Co. knows about soybeans?

It does not get any better when the individual speculator is betting against the pros on the trading floor of the CBOT and other major exchanges. All applicants for futures exchange membership must attend seminars and pass qualifying examinations covering the basics of the commodity industry and futures contracts.

The pros know their stuff before they start trading. Experience adds to their advantage. Professional futures-pit speculators can make split-second trading decisions before any individual is able to trade through a broker. Why else would professional speculators pay roughly $500,000 for membership at the CBOT, for example, and a front-row "seat" in a trading pit?

Given brokerage commissions and other trading costs, making a single bet on the direction of futures prices should only be a little worse than a 50-50 proposition for the experienced and savvy commodities trader. However, commodity traders are prone to make multiple bets, and the odds favor the house when more bets are placed. Individuals who put up no more than the 5% required margin enjoy tremendous leverage when they bet correctly but often get wiped out in seconds by a sudden swing in futures prices. *The Wall Street Journal* estimates that no more than 5% of all commodity traders end a single trading year without losing money. The National Futures Association, an industry trade group, estimates that 60–90% of all individual speculators lose money in the futures markets. Academic studies corroborate the suggestion that an overwhelming majority of individual speculators and many professional speculators lose money trading futures.

For most individuals, the best futures market trading advice is simple: Don't.

Futures Market Regulation

Commodity Futures Trading Commission

Although federal and state regulation has governed the futures industry since 1924, the scope of oversight increased dramatically during the early 1970s when a series of economic events brought dramatic change to the U.S. futures industry. Global demand for agricultural products grew while supplies dwindled. Wild price fluctuations on agricultural futures contracts and the emergence of new futures contracts on metals, lumber, and currencies attracted new, and largely unregulated, participants to the industry. Customer losses due to firm insolvencies and unethical business practices increased, and the industry's reputation was threatened.

Recognizing a need for additional regulation, Congress enacted The Commodity Exchange Act in 1974 and established the **Commodity Futures Trading Commission (CFTC),** an independent federal regulatory agency with jurisdiction over futures trading. The CFTC strives to protect market participants against manipulation, abusive trade practices, and fraud. Through effective oversight and regulation, the CFTC enables the markets to better serve their important functions in the nation's economy—providing a mechanism for price discovery and a means of offsetting price risk. Other governmental bodies with an important interest in futures market regulation include the House Committee on Agriculture; Securities and Exchange Commission; Senate Committee on Agriculture, Nutrition and Forestry; U.S. Department of Agriculture; and the Federal Trade Commission.

Commodity Futures Trading Commission (CFTC) Independent federal regulatory agency with jurisdiction over futures trading.

To ensure the financial soundness and market integrity of the futures markets, the CFTC reviews the terms and conditions of proposed futures and option contracts. Before an exchange is permitted to trade a futures and option contract in a specific commodity, it must demonstrate that the contract reflects the normal market flow and commercial trading practices in the actual commodity. The CFTC also conducts daily market surveillance and can, in an emergency, order an exchange to take specific action or to restore orderliness in any futures contract that

WALL STREET WISDOM 18.3

Regulatory Reform for Financial Derivatives

At the start of the new millennium, regulators in Washington, D.C., the Futures Industry Association, and other industry representatives are working to derive new regulations to fit the rapidly evolving marketplace for financial derivatives. All such parties seek regulations that protect the public's right to fair and complete price and risk disclosure. At the same time, it is necessary to promote industry innovation and efficiency. High on the list of desired outcomes for both regulators and the industry is the establishment of means for giving legal certainty to arrangements involving swaps and equity derivatives. Another priority is the need to design appropriate regulations for financial derivatives delivered through new electronic media. Given the rapid pace of innovation in the financial derivatives market, both the speed and clarity of regulatory reform are of utmost importance. Without timely and insightful changes to historical methods of regulation, the global competitiveness of U.S. financial markets can be undermined.

On a global level, the U.S. futures industry is in danger of falling behind European and other offshore competitors. Important changes in market structure are being driven by fundamental differences in regulatory oversight and by the quickening pace of innovation. Innovation is rapidly reshaping the types of financial derivatives offered and methods for the dissemination of financial markets information.

Perhaps the primary reason comprehensive regulation was developed for U.S. exchange-traded futures markets was that the price discovery role played by the open-outcry market system conferred significant economic benefits on the exchanges and various market participants. In an open-outcry market, physical location confers pivotal advantages to certain market participants. Pit traders are literally at the center of trading activity and have, by virtue of their location, access to valuable market-moving information. In such a setting, trading activity must be regulated and information must be quickly disseminated to ensure the public's interest in fair and complete disclosure. In an open-outcry market, the exchange also plays a vital role in the information dissemination process. Users of the Internet auction Web site ebay.com realize the advantage of having regular access to a large number of active buyers and sellers. Similarly, futures exchanges such as the Chicago Merc enjoy a fundamental advantage over competitors due to the fact that they create enormously valuable pricing information by virtue of their role as a centralized marketplace for commodities and financial instruments.

Barriers to entry in the futures market used to be very high, and these markets became oligopolistic. Historically, few organizations were prepared to spend the millions of dollars necessary to build an open-outcry infrastructure, attract the necessary players, set up a clearinghouse operation, and meet self-regulatory requirements. In the beginning, the cost of developing a proprietary electronic trading system was also relatively high. However, all this has changed with new computer software and the Internet. With new technology and the Internet, the cost of establishing the trade execution function has gone down precipitously. It is now possible to establish a viable exchange for niche financial derivatives by using the Internet at minimal cost. Further reducing the cost of establishing exchanges for financial derivatives is the possibility of unbundling clearing and self-regulatory functions from the execution function.

With a lighter regulatory burden for electronic markets, new financial derivatives markets could grow up rather quickly. Financial markets that are dominated by professionals and sophisticated institutions may even be allowed to function efficiently with little or no regulation. Although such an innovation might at first appear startling, various electronic community networks (ECN) that allow institutions to trade stocks and bonds effectively have already applied to the Securities and Exchange Commission for permission to act as exchanges.

As we start the new century, it is clear that the dismantling of sometimes burdensome financial regulation is only beginning. Impetus for change clearly comes from customers with a global view who seek state-of-the-art financial services. Ultimately, customers benefit when they can monitor positions on a real-time basis across a wide variety of markets and use a minimum amount of capital to support their trading needs.

See: Glen R. Simpson and Michelle Schroeder, "Federal Agencies Reach 14 Settlements over Claims Made about Day Trading," *The Wall Street Journal,* May 2, 2000, C20.

is being traded. The CFTC monitors futures and options markets from its headquarters office in Washington, D.C., and at offices in cities that have futures exchanges—New York, Chicago, Kansas City, and Minneapolis. The CFTC also maintains an enforcement office in Los Angeles.

The CFTC has five major operating units, including the Division of Economic Analysis, Division of Trading and Markets, Division of Enforcement, Office of the General Counsel, and the Office of the Executive Director. The purpose of the Division of Economic Analysis (DEA) is to ensure that markets remain competitive and responsive to underlying supply and demand factors by protecting against price manipulation. DEA conducts daily market surveillance to detect actual or potential price manipulation. DEA also reviews applications for new futures and option contracts and changes to existing contracts to ensure that the terms and conditions conform to cash market practices. The Division of Trading and Markets (T&M) oversees the compliance activities of the commodity exchanges, conducts trade practice surveillance, and performs financial and sales practice audits of selected registrants. The Division of Enforcement investigates and prosecutes alleged violations of the Commodity Exchange Act and CFTC regulations. Violations may involve commodity futures or option trading on domestic commodity exchanges or the improper marketing of commodity investments. The division may, at the direction of the commission, file complaints before the agency's administrative law judges or in the U.S. district courts. Criminal violations of the Commodity Exchange Act or violations of other federal laws that involve commodity futures trading may be referred to the Justice Department for prosecution. The Office of the General Counsel is the commission's legal advisor. General counsel staff represent the CFTC in litigation and reviews all substantive regulatory, legislative, and administrative matters. The Office of the Executive Director formulates and implements the management and administrative policies and functions of the agency.

The CFTC consists of five commissioners appointed by the president with the advice and consent of the Senate to serve staggered five-year terms. The commission develops and implements agency policy and direction. One of the commissioners is designated by the president to serve as chairperson. The chairperson's staff has direct responsibility for providing information about the CFTC to the public and interacting with other governmental agencies and Congress. The chairperson's staff also ensures that the CFTC is responsive to requests filed under the Freedom of Information Act. The chairperson's staff also includes the Office of the Inspector General, which conducts audits of CFTC programs and operations, and the Office of International Affairs, which is the focal point for the commission's global regulatory coordination efforts.

Major policy decisions and CFTC actions, such as approval of exchange designations, adoption of agency rules and regulations, and the authorization of enforcement actions, must be approved by a majority vote of the commissioners. Although most CFTC meetings are open to the public, information about such meetings and CFTC rules and regulations can be obtained from the commission's office of public affairs or the CFTC's home page on the Internet at <http://www.cftc.gov>.

National Futures Association

The Commodity Exchange Act authorized the creation of registered futures associations to give the industry an opportunity to develop self-regulatory organizations that might work in conjunction with government oversight. As a result, the National Futures Association (NFA) was created and officially began operations on October 1, 1982. Today, any company or individual who handles customer funds or gives trading advice in the futures market must apply for registration through the NFA. Like the National Association of Securities Dealers (NASD), whose actions are approved by the Securities and Exchange Commission, the NFA is a self-regulatory organization. In the case of the NFA, its actions must be approved by the CFTC. Together with the NFA, the CFTC seeks to protect customers by requiring brokers and dealers to disclose market risks and past performance information to prospective customers. To guard against customer loss from trading firm insolvency, customer funds must also be kept in separate accounts from those maintained by futures trading firms. To guard against trading firm losses from customer insolvency, the CFTC requires that customer accounts be adjusted to reflect current market value at the close of trading each day. In addition, the CFTC monitors registrant supervision systems, internal controls, and sales practice compliance programs.

Rule-making actions of the NFA and the various futures and option exchanges complement federal regulation. Such rules cover the clearance of trades, trade records, position limits, price limits, disciplinary actions, floor-trading practices, and standards of business conduct. Any new or amended exchange rule may be implemented only on approval by the CFTC. On its own, the CFTC may direct the exchanges to change their rules or practices.

As shown in Figure 18.9, the NFA provides an additional layer of self-regulation over the futures markets. The NFA is an industry-wide, industry-supported, self-regulatory organization for the futures and options-on-futures markets. NFA's

FIGURE 18.9 **Commodity Futures Trading Commission (CFTC) Provides Federal Regulatory Oversight for the Futures Industry**

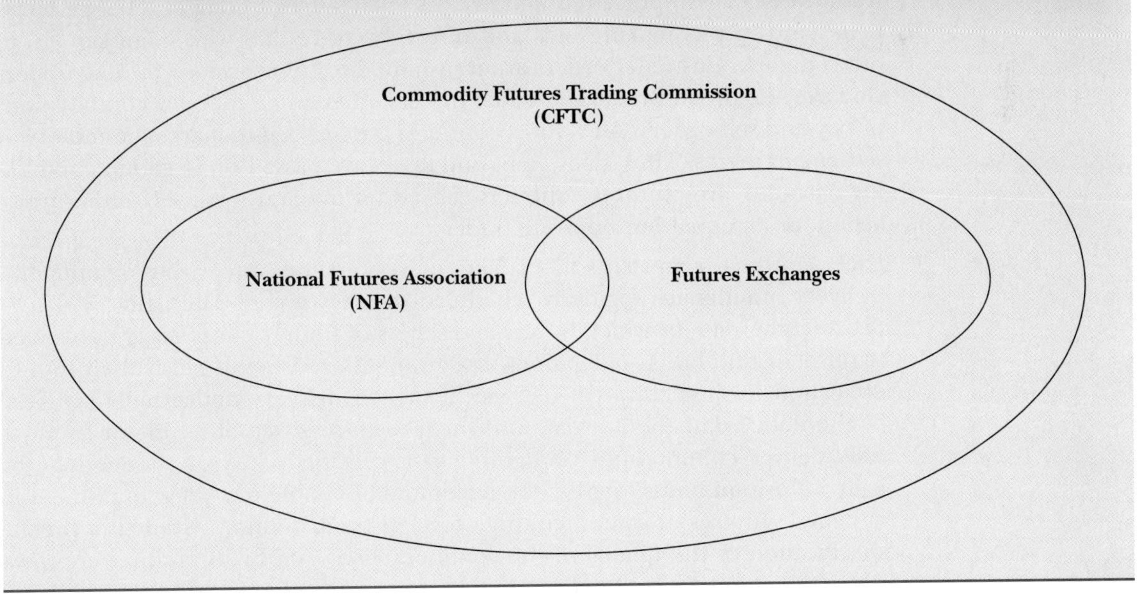

mandate is to adopt and implement a comprehensive self-regulatory program for the futures industry. It is through the actions of the individual exchanges, NFA, and the government regulators that the financial interest of all market participants is protected. NFA is on the Internet at <http://www.nfa.futures.org>. Other trade groups with an important interest in the futures industry include the Futures Industry Association, International Organization of Securities Commissioners (IOSCO), National Association of Securities Dealers Regulation (NASD Regulation), and North American Securities Administrators Association (NASAA).

Summary

- The **Chicago Board of Trade (CBOT)** is the first and largest commodities exchange. Like a **forward contract,** a **futures contract** is an agreement between two parties to buy or sell a stipulated grade and quantity of a commodity at a specific future time for an agreed-on price. Unfortunately, forward contracts can be difficult to enforce. As a result, futures require a performance bond called **margin** to be posted by buyers and sellers. Margin ensures that buyers and sellers have the economic incentive and financial wherewithal to complete their contractual agreement. Futures also **mark-to-market** on a daily basis. This means that there is a daily settlement of gains and losses between buyers and sellers. If the **spot price,** or current price, rises, sellers of futures contracts must place additional funds in their margin account to ensure their ability to deliver now higher-priced commodities. If the spot price falls, buyers of futures contracts must place additional funds in their margin account to ensure their willingness to abide by an earlier agreement to pay higher prices for what are now lower-priced commodities.
- The buyer of a futures contract, often referred to as the **long,** agrees to receive delivery of the underlying asset from the seller of the futures contract, or **short,** who agrees to make delivery. Futures contracts are traded on exchanges either by open outcry in specified trading areas, called **trading pits** or rings, or electronically via a computerized network. In **open-outcry trading,** exchange members stand in pits making bids and offers, by voice and with hand signals, to other traders. Customer orders are transmitted to **floor brokers** or **dual traders** who execute them. Brokers and dual traders often enter complex combinations of buy and sell orders. All futures contracts are marked-to-market at end-of-day settlement prices. Thus, daily gains and losses are passed on to gaining and losing accounts. Any futures contracts can be terminated by an **offsetting transaction,** or an equal but opposite trade.
- Each contract represents a **trading unit** of some underlying commodity. **Delivery months** are regularly scheduled delivery cycles. The **delivery date** is the calendar date by which buyers and sellers of futures contracts are obligated to offset or fulfill their obligations. If a given seller wishes to satisfy their futures obligation through physical delivery, a written **delivery notice** must be given by the **notice day,** the last date on which written advice of an intent to physically deliver commodities pertaining to a specified delivery month may be issued. **Position limits** identify the maximum allowable market commitment in any single futures or option contract for a given institution. **Grade** is a precise specification of the quality of the commodity covered by the futures contract. **Deliverable growths** and **delivery points** are acceptable countries of origin and

delivery locations. **Futures options** give the right, but not the obligation, to buy or sell some specific futures contract at a certain price for a limited period of time.

- The CBOT is the world's oldest and largest futures and futures option exchange and responsible for about 42.9% of total futures and futures option trading in the United States. The **New York Mercantile Exchange** is the third-largest U.S. futures market and the world's largest physical commodity futures exchange. It accounts for about 18.5% of the overall market. The **Chicago Mercantile Exchange** is the second-largest futures exchange in the United States and represents roughly 33.9% of total futures market activity. The **New York Board of Trade (NYBOT)** is parent company of the New York Cotton Exchange and the Coffee, Sugar & Cocoa Exchange, Inc., and responsible for about 3.7% of U.S. futures market activity. The **MidAmerica Commodity Exchange** is a wholly owned subsidiary of the CBOT, and the **Kansas City Board of Trade** is the world's predominant marketplace for hard red winter wheat. Like the MidAm, the KCBOT accounts for less than one-half of 1% of U.S. futures and futures option trading activity. The smallest major futures exchange is the **Minneapolis Grain Exchange,** which trades roughly 0.2% of U.S. futures and futures option trading activity.
- Each of the various futures exchanges use **clearinghouses** to ensure balance in the number of futures and futures option contracts bought and sold and give fulfillment guarantees to ensure contract performance. Clearinghouses facilitate trade among strangers by eliminating **counterparty risk.** For most futures contracts, there is a difference between **initial margin,** the amount of margin that exchanges require to initiate a trade, and **maintenance margin,** the minimum amount of margin that the customer must maintain at all times. As part of the daily mark-to-market process, clearing members pay or receive from the clearinghouse funds known as **variation margin.** Variation margin is an additional required deposit to bring an investor's equity account up to the initial margin level when the account balance falls below the maintenance margin requirement.
- Futures brokerage firms, known as **futures commission merchants,** are intermediaries between public customers and the exchanges. A futures brokerage firm also must be a member of the **National Futures Association** (NFA), an industry-wide self-regulatory organization. An **introducing broker** is an individual or firm that has established a relationship with one or more futures brokerage firms. Many large institutions and individual investors include managed futures positions in their investment portfolios. These positions can be in the form of **commodity pools** or individually managed accounts. A **commodity trading advisor** trades for others and/or makes trading recommendations.
- **Hedgers** seek to reduce risks associated with dealing in the underlying commodity or security. **Speculators,** including professional floor traders, seek to profit from price changes. In the futures market, the difference between a commodity's spot price and the futures price is known as the **basis.** Although hedging strategies with futures can eliminate **price risk,** hedging strategies cannot eliminate **basis risk.** An **intramarket spread** combines a long position in one contract month against a short position in another contract month in the same futures contract on the same exchange. A carrying-charge, or **contango,** futures

market is one in which futures prices are higher in distant delivery months. An inverted market, or one in a **backwardation,** features lower futures prices in distant delivery months. Inverted markets sometimes occur when demand for the cash commodity is unusually strong relative to current supply. Inverted markets also occur when the income derived from holding a cash position exceeds the costs of carrying the position. An **intermarket spread** consists of a long position in one market and a short position in another market trading the same or a closely related commodity.

- Stock index futures give investors the ability to offset security risk through a host of complicated investment strategies, referred to as **portfolio insurance** or **index arbitrage.** Portfolio insurance is an investment strategy of using a mix of index futures, leveraged stock portfolios, and stock options in such a manner as to create the right to sell stock portfolios at a fixed price in the event of a decline in prices.
- Using complex combinations of long and short positions, it is often possible to create **synthetic financial instruments** that have risk and return characteristics identical to some other underlying asset or financial derivative. Synthetics are customized or hybrid financial instruments created by blending an underlying price on a cash instrument with the price of some financial derivative. Financial derivative markets encompass a plethora of tailored financial instruments, such as **swaps, swaptions, caps,** and **collars,** that are traded by the world's leading financial institutions. Swaps are an arrangement whereby two companies agree to lend to each other on different terms, such as in different currencies or at different interest rates. Swaptions are simply options to engage in a specific interest-rate swap on or before a specific date. Caps are upper limits on the interest rate paid on floating-rate notes or adjustable-rate mortgages. Collars are upper and lower limits on the interest rate paid on floating-rate notes or adjustable-rate mortgages. In perfectly competitive financial markets, the **law of one price** states that identical assets have identical prices.
- Recognizing a need for additional regulation, Congress enacted the Commodity Exchange Act in 1974 and established the **Commodity Futures Trading Commission (CFTC),** an independent federal regulatory agency with jurisdiction over futures trading.

Questions

1. Futures contracts can be settled only by
   a. delivery.
   b. offset.
   c. delivery or offset.
   d. none of the above.
2. Unique characteristics of futures contracts include:
   a. short selling can be done only on an uptick.
   b. margin is not allowed.
   c. positions can remain open indefinitely.
   d. a lack of specialist buying and selling.

3. Which of the following securities is not available as an interest-rate futures contract?
   a. corporate bonds
   b. Treasury notes
   c. Ginnie Mae securities
   d. certificates of deposit
4. To protect the value of a bond portfolio against a rise in interest rates by using interest-rate futures, the portfolio owner could execute a
   a. long hedge.
   b. weighted long hedge.
   c. short hedge.
   d. none of the above.
5. Which one of the following statements is true about the basis?
   a. Basis risk can be eliminated completely.
   b. Although the basis fluctuates over time, it can be predicted precisely.
   c. Changes in the basis cannot affect the final results while a hedge is in effect.
   d. A hedge will reduce risk as long as basis fluctuations are usually less volatile than price fluctuations.
6. A futures contract is
   a. a nonnegotiable, nonmarketable instrument.
   b. a security, such as stocks and bonds.
   c. a firm agreement by two parties to make or take delivery of an item sometime in the future.
   d. not a legal contract, and therefore its terms can be changed during the life of the contract.
7. With financial futures, margin
   a. is seldom used.
   b. constitutes a performance bond.
   c. is limited to 50% at the time of purchase.
   d. must be maintained at 25% of account value.
8. An obligatory agreement to transact in the future based on future price expectations is a
   a. futures contract.
   b. forward contract.
   c. call option.
   d. spread contract.
9. An obligatory agreement to transact today based on future price expectations is a
   a. futures contract.
   b. forward contract.

c. call option.

d. spread contract.

10. The maintenance margin requirement for most commodities is

a. 5–10% margin.

b. 5–50% margin.

c. 50% margin.

d. 100% margin.

11. Actively traded futures markets are *not* available for

a. heating oil.

b. pork bellies.

c. stock indexes.

d. water.

12. At a futures exchange, contracts are not standardized with respect to

a. quality and quantity.

b. delivery time.

c. price.

d. location.

13. A binding legal obligation is incurred by the

a. buyer of a financial futures option.

b. buyer of a commodity futures call option.

c. buyer of a commodity futures put option.

d. seller of any futures option.

14. Selling futures contracts to offset a long futures position results in a

a. long position.

b. hedged position.

c. short position.

d. none of these.

15. In the futures market, a local trades for

a. himself or herself.

b. the general public.

c. financial institutions.

d. the exchange.

16. Hedgers differ from speculators in that they only

a. expect to profit.

b. take offsetting positions.

c. buy futures.

d. sell futures.

17. A forward contract

a. is an obligatory agreement to transact in the *future* based on current price expectations.

b. is an obligatory agreement to transact *today* based on future price expectations.

c. is an obligatory agreement.

d. has the same cash settlement as a futures contract on an *identical* commodity.

18. Futures markets require

a. limited demand for the underlying commodity or financial instrument.

b. thin primary markets.

c. standardized commodities or financial instruments.

d. low variance price patterns on the underlying commodity or financial instrument.

19. The economic risk of commodity futures trading is reduced by

a. low maintenance margin requirements.

b. trading halts during volatile markets.

c. price limits during stable markets.

d. regulatory oversight of the CFTC.

20. Commodity futures trading

a. contract availability and liquidity depends only partially on supply and demand conditions.

b. specialists issue contract fulfillment guarantees.

c. specialists record changes in open interest.

d. is an auction process that occurs in a "pit" *without* a specialist.

Investment Application

Weather Futures

Estimates suggest that nearly 20% of the U.S. economy is directly affected by the weather. Business profits can be adversely affected by summers that are hotter than normal or winters that are colder than anticipated. Utility profits can suffer from temperate summers with less need for air conditioning and mild winters with less residential heating demand.

On the Chicago Mercantile Exchange and other futures markets such as the Minneapolis Grain Exchange, weather derivatives have been created to enable businesses that could be adversely affected by unanticipated temperature swings to transfer this risk. Just as professionals regularly use futures and options to hedge their risk in interest rates, equities, and foreign exchange, now there are tools available for the management of risk from extreme temperatures. This sector of hedging and risk management products represents one of today's fastest growing derivative markets.

The Chicago Merc Heating Degree-Day (HDD) and Cooling Degree-Day (CDD) futures and options on futures were the first exchange-traded, temperature-related weather derivatives. These contracts are designed to help businesses protect their revenues during times of depressed demand or excessive costs because of unexpected weather conditions. The Chicago Merc offers HDD and CDD futures and options on futures for selected population centers and energy hubs with significant weather-related risks throughout the United States. Cities are chosen based on population, the variability in their seasonal temperatures, and the activity seen in over-the-counter trade in HDD/CDD derivatives.

In the weather derivatives market, an important concept is a degree-day. A degree-day is the measure of how much a day's average temperature deviates from 65° Fahrenheit. Years ago, the utility industry adopted 65° Fahrenheit as a temperature baseline because that was the temperature at which furnaces tend to be switched on. It is used with the assumption that for each degree below 65°, consumers will use more energy to heat their homes. For each degree above 65°, more energy will be consumed to run air conditioners. An HDD measures the coldness of the daily temperature compared with the 65° Fahrenheit standard. An average daily temperature of 40° Fahrenheit gives a daily HDD of 25. If the average temperature is 67° Fahrenheit, it is assumed that no energy would be used to heat homes, and the daily HDD would be zero. The Chicago Merc HDD index is an accumulation of daily HDDs over a calendar month, with $100 attached to each HDD for final cash settlement.

For example, assume the average daily HDDs for a city in the month of November is 25 (= 65° Fahrenheit − 40° Fahrenheit). With 30 days in the month of November, the HDD index would be 750 (= 25 daily HDDs × 30 days). With an HDD index of 750 for November, the nominal value of a futures contract on that city would be $75,000 (= 750 HDD index × $100). To illustrate, suppose a trader was to go short, or sell, the November 2001 HDD futures on the city of Chicago at a price of 750 on January 10, 2001. If, on October 11, 2001, the trader bought the futures contract back at a price of 625, closing out the position, the trader would show a gain of $12,500 (= $100 × 125 HDD index points) on the position taken in January.

CDDs work in a similar manner. A CDD measures the warmth of the daily temperature compared with a standard of 65° Fahrenheit. An average daily temperature of 75° Fahrenheit gives a daily CDD of 10. If the average temperature is 58° Fahrenheit, it is assumed that no energy would be used to cool homes, and the daily CDD would be zero. Like the HDD index, the Chicago Merc CDD index is an accumulation of daily CDDs over a calendar month, with $100 attached to each CDD for final cash settlement. For example, assume the average daily CDDs for a city in the month of June is 10 (= 75° Fahrenheit − 65° Fahrenheit). With 30 days in the month of June, the CDD index could be 300 (= 10 daily CDDs × 30 days). With a CDD index of 300 for June, the nominal value of a futures contract on that city would be $30,000 (= 300 CDD index × $100).

These weather futures contracts can be used to hedge the risk a utility or a power provider may face as the result of a warmer than expected winter or a summer that does not get too hot. Utilities have long used derivative instruments to hedge the price of fossil fuels or electricity. They can now use weather derivatives to hedge against revenue losses when HDDs and CDDs are unseasonably low. If a power company's revenue stream is vulnerable to a summer in which there is less need for air conditioning, that company could choose to sell Chicago Merc CDD futures or to purchase CDD put options. If historical data on CDDs for a city implied a summer with temperatures in the 80s, but forecasts called for one month with temperatures closer to 100° Fahrenheit, the company might decide to hedge with a purchase of an out-of-the-money CDD call. Although utilities normally benefit from hot summer weather, a sustained upward spike in temperatures might require a more costly, less efficient method of electricity generation during peak usage periods. A long position in CDD calls could help compensate for these unexpected costs.

HDD index futures began Chicago Merc trading on September 22, 1999. Starting January 30, 2000, the Chicago Merc expanded hedging and trading opportunities in weather futures to six new cities. This brought to 10 the number of cities covered by HDD contracts, including Chicago, Cincinnati, New York, Atlanta, Philadelphia, Dallas, Des Moines, Las Vegas, Tucson, and Portland. Also, on January 30, 2000, CDD futures began trading for the first time on the Chicago Merc for these same 10 cities. The minimum tick size is 1.00 HDD or CDD index point, with each having a value of $100 dollars. At any point in time, 12 consecutive contract months of HDD and CDD futures and options are listed.

The practical usefulness of these weather futures instruments is shown by the strong relation that exists between power usage and temperature. Figure 18.10 depicts power usage in megawatts at different temperatures Fahrenheit for the city of Baltimore over a period from January 1993 to December 1995. Although all U.S. cities might not have as dramatic an energy demand profile as seen in this graph, this is a clear example of how consumer demand for power rises and falls around the 65° Fahrenheit baseline. The surge in power usage demand when temperatures stray from the 65° Fahrenheit level is clear.

To further illustrate the practical usefulness of weather futures, suppose that the Windy City Power Co. (WCP) sells electricity in the Chicago area. Assume that the retail price charged in the winter months is locked in at $0.08/kilowatt-hour

FIGURE 18.10 **Maximum Power Load versus Average Daily Temperature in Baltimore**

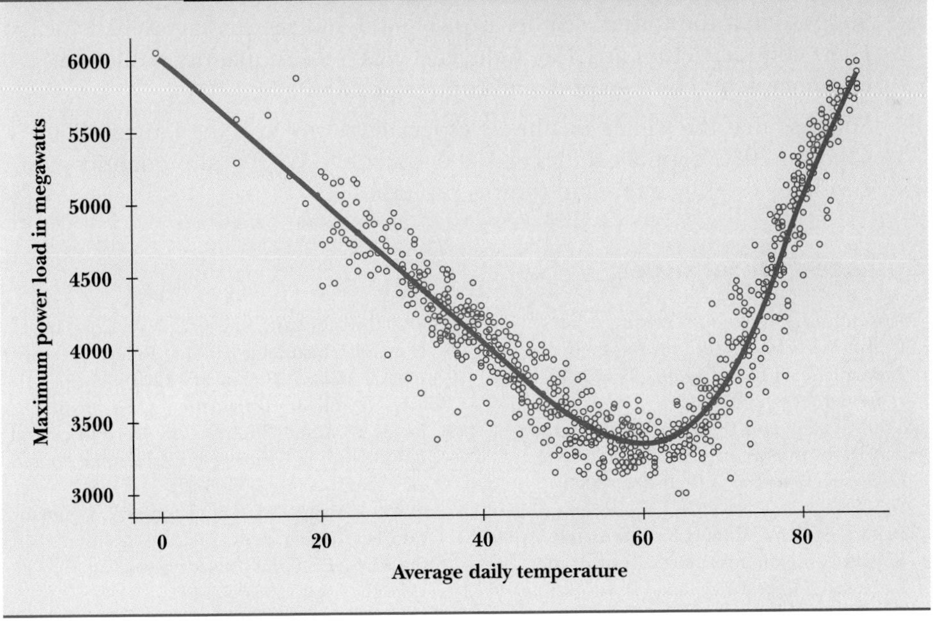

Source: Chicago Mercantile Exchange.

(kwh). With a normal winter, the power sales quantity is forecasted as 1 billion kwh. Thus, projected revenue for a normal winter is \$80 million (= 1 billion kwh × \$0.08/kwh). However, WCP worries that the coming winter could be relatively mild and the sales quantity would be reduced. The research department at WCP finds that power sales are positively correlated with the Chicago Merc Chicago HDD index with a weather risk sensitivity of 0.9. This means that a 1% decrease in the Chicago Merc HDD index results in a 0.9% (= 0.9 × 1%) reduction in sales quantities. Thus, Chicago HDD index futures can be used as a cross-hedge for WCP's revenue fluctuations.

To stabilize its winter revenue, WCP considers selling the Chicago HDD index January 2001 futures that are valued at 1,250. It is important to note that a seasonal hedge would typically involve the sale of a series of HDD contracts, for example, October 2000 through March 2001. For the sake of keeping this illustration simple, however, assume the entire hedge is placed in the January contract, which is typically the coldest month of the year in Chicago. To discover the number of HDD contracts to sell, or what is referred to as the hedge ratio, WCP reviews statistical research. They know that a 1% decline in the HDD index corresponds to a 0.9% fall in revenue. At current price levels, a 1% decline in the HDD index would be worth \$1,250 (= 0.01 × 1,250 HDD price × \$100 per HDD tick). A 0.9% decline in revenue is worth \$720,000 (= 0.009 × \$80,000,000 projected revenue). Thus, to fully protect against weather-related fluctuations in its winter revenues, WCP would have to sell 576 weather futures contracts, since:

$$\begin{aligned}\text{Hedge ratio} &= \text{Change in revenue/Change in contract value} \\ \text{576 contracts} &= \$720{,}000/\$1{,}250\end{aligned}$$

Assume that on October 1, 2000, WCP shorts 576 of the January 2001 HDD futures at a price of 1,250.

A. Suppose that the winter weather is truly mild and the January 2001 Chicago HDD contract settles at 1,150. Calculate WCP's sales quantity reduction, customer revenue reduction, and futures position gain.

B. Suppose that the winter weather is especially severe and the January 2001 Chicago HDD contract settles at 1,400. Calculate WCP's sales quantity gain, customer revenue gain, and futures position loss.

Selected References

Angus, John E. "A Note on Pricing Asian Derivatives with Continuous Geometric Averaging." *Journal of Futures Markets* 19 (October 1999): 845–858.

Bakshi, Gurdip, and Dilip Madan. "Spanning and Derivative-Security Valuation." *Journal of Financial Economics* 55 (February 2000): 205–238.

Barnhart, Scott W., Robert McNown, and Myles S. Wallace. "Non-informative Tests of the Unbiased Forward Exchange Rate." *Journal of Financial and Quantitative Analysis* 34 (June 1999): 265–291.

Bookstaber, Richard, and Joseph A. Langsam. "Portfolio Insurance Trading Rules." *Journal of Futures Markets* 20 (January 2000): 41–57.

Brewer III, Elijah, Bernadette A. Minton, and James T. Moser. "Interest-Rate Derivatives and Bank Lending." *Journal of Banking and Finance* 24 (March 2000): 353–379.

Copeland, Maggie M., and Thomas E. Copeland. "Market Timing: Style and Size Rotation Using the VIX." *Financial Analysts Journal* 55 (March/April 1999): 73–81.

Daigler, Robert T., and Marilyn K. Wiley. "The Impact of Trader Type on the Futures

Volatility-Volume Relation." *Journal of Finance* 54 (December 1999): 2297–2315.
De Jong, Frank, and Pedro Santa-Clara. "The Dynamics of the Forward Interest Rate Curve: A Formulation with State Variables." *Journal of Financial and Quantitative Analysis* 34 (March 1999): 131–157.
Haushalter, G. David. "Financing Policy, Basis Risk, and Corporate Hedging: Evidence from Oil and Gas Producers." *Journal of Finance* 55 (February 2000): 107–152.
Hong, Harrison. "A Model of Returns and Trading in Futures Markets." *Journal of Finance* 55 (April 2000): 959–988.
Mayhew, Stewart. "Options, Futures and Exotic Derivatives: Theory, Application and Practice." *Journal of Finance* 54 (April 1999): 817–820.
Stutzer, Michael, and Muinul Chowdhury. "A Simple Non-parametric Approach to Bond Futures Option Pricing." *Journal of Fixed Income* 8 (March 1999): 67–76.
Tian, Yisong. "A Flexible Binomial Option Pricing Model." *Journal of Futures Markets* 19 (October 1999): 817–843.
Tse, Yiuman. "Market Microstructure of FT-SE 100 Index Futures: An Intraday Empirical Analysis." *Journal of Futures Markets* 19 (February 1999): 31–58.
Tse, Yiuman. "Price Discovery and Volatility Spillovers in the DJIA Index and Futures Markets." *Journal of Futures Markets* 19 (December 1999): 911–930.

APPENDIX A

Compounding and the Time Value of Money

The concepts of compound growth and the time value of money are widely used in all areas of finance. This is especially true of investments. Compounding is the principle that underlies growth, whether it is growth in market value, growth in sales, or growth in assets. The time value of money—the fact that a dollar received in the future is worth less than a dollar in hand today—also plays an important role in investments. In business valuation, cash flows occurring in different periods must be adjusted to their value at a common point in time to be analyzed and compared. Because of the importance of these concepts in investments, a brief review of compounding and the time value of money is appropriate.

Future Value (or Compound Value)

Suppose that you deposit \$100 in a bank savings account that pays 5% interest compounded annually. How much will you have at the end of one year? To begin, define the following terms as follows:

PV = Present value of your account, or the beginning amount, \$100

i = Interest rate the bank pays you = 5% per year, or, expressed in decimal terms, 0.05

I = Dollars of interest earned during the year

FV_N = Future value, or ending amount, of your account at the end of N years. Whereas PV is the value now, at the present time, FV_N is the value N years into the future, after compound interest has been earned. Note also that FV_0 is the future value zero years into the future, which is the present, so $FV_0 = PV$

In our example, $N = 1$, so $FV_N = FV_1$, and it is calculated as follows:

$$\begin{aligned} FV_1 &= PV + I \\ &= PV + PV \times i \\ &= PV(1 + i) \end{aligned} \quad \textbf{(A.1)}$$

TABLE A.1 Compound Interest Calculations

Year	Beginning Amount, PV	× $(1 + i)$	= Ending Amount, FV_N
1	\$100.00	1.05	\$105.00
2	105.00	1.05	110.25
3	110.25	1.05	115.76
4	115.76	1.05	121.55
5	121.55	1.05	127.63

We can now use Equation A.1 to find how much the account is worth at the end of one year:

$$FV_1 = \$100(1 + 0.05) = \$100(1.05) = \$105$$

Your account earned \$5 of interest ($I = \$5$), so you have \$105 at the end of the year.

Now suppose that you leave your funds on deposit for five years; how much will you have at the end of the fifth year? The answer is \$127.63; this value is worked out in Table A.1.

Notice that the Table A.1 value for FV_2, the value of the account at the end of year 2, is equal to

$$FV_2 = FV_1(1 + i) = PV(1 + i)(1 + i) = PV(1 + i)^2$$

FV_3, the balance after three years, is

$$FV_3 = FV_2(1 + i) = PV(1 + i)^3$$

In general, FV_N, the future value at the end of N years, is found as

$$FV_N = PV(1 + i)^N \qquad \textbf{(A.2)}$$

Applying Equation A.2 in the case of a five-year account that earns 5% per year gives

$$\begin{aligned} PV_5 &= \$100(1.05)^5 \\ &= \$100(1.2763) \\ &= \$127.63 \end{aligned}$$

which is the same as the value in Table A.1.

If an electronic calculator is handy, it is easy enough to calculate $(1 + i)^N$ directly.[1] However, tables have been constructed for values of $(1 + i)^N$ for wide

[1]For example, to calculate $(1 + i)^N$ for $i = 5\% = 0.05$ and $N = 5$ years, simply multiply $(1 + i) = (1.05)$ times (1.05); multiple this product by (1.05); and so on:

$$(1 + i)^N = (1.05)(1.05)(1.05)(1.05)(1.05) = (1.05)^5 = 1.2763$$

TABLE A.2 Future Value of $1 at the End of N Periods: $FVIF_{i,N} = (1 + i)^N$

Period (*N*)	1%	2%	3%	4%	5%	6%	7%	8%	9%	10%
0	1.0000	1.0000	1.0000	1.0000	1.0000	1.0000	1.0000	1.0000	1.0000	1.0000
1	1.0100	1.0200	1.0300	1.0400	1.0500	1.0600	1.0700	1.0800	1.0900	1.1000
2	1.0201	1.0404	1.0609	1.0816	1.1025	1.1236	1.1449	1.1664	1.1881	1.2100
3	1.0303	1.0612	1.0927	1.1249	1.1576	1.1910	1.2250	1.2597	1.2950	1.3310
4	1.0406	1.0824	1.1255	1.1699	1.2155	1.2625	1.3108	1.3605	1.4116	1.4641
5	1.0510	1.1041	1.1593	1.2167	1.2763	1.3382	1.4026	1.4693	1.5386	1.6105
6	1.0615	1.1262	1.1941	1.2653	1.3401	1.4185	1.5007	1.5869	1.6771	1.7716
7	1.0721	1.1487	1.2299	1.3159	1.4071	1.5036	1.6058	1.7138	1.8280	1.9487
8	1.0829	1.1717	1.2668	1.3686	1.4775	1.5938	1.7182	1.8509	1.9926	2.1436
9	1.0937	1.1951	1.3048	1.4233	1.5513	1.6895	1.8385	1.9990	2.1719	2.3579
10	1.1046	1.2190	1.3439	1.4802	1.6289	1.7908	1.9672	2.1589	2.3674	2.5937
11	1.1157	1.2434	1.3842	1.5395	1.7103	1.8983	2.1049	2.3316	2.5804	2.8531
12	1.1268	1.2682	1.4258	1.6010	1.7959	2.0122	2.2522	2.5182	2.8127	3.1384
13	1.1381	1.2936	1.4685	1.6651	1.8856	2.1329	2.4098	2.7196	3.0658	3.4523
14	1.1495	1.3195	1.5126	1.7317	1.9799	2.2609	2.5785	2.9372	3.3417	3.7975
15	1.1610	1.3459	1.5580	1.8009	2.0789	2.3966	2.7590	3.1722	3.6425	4.1772

ranges of i and N, as Table A.2 illustrates. Table B.1 in Appendix B contains a more complete set of compound value interest factors. Interest compounding can occur over periods of time different from one year. Thus, although compounding is often on an annual basis, it can be quarterly, semiannual, monthly, or for any other period.

The term *future value interest factor* ($FVIF_{i,N}$) equals $(1 + i)^N$. Therefore, Equation A.2 may be written as $FV_N = PV(FVIF_{i,N})$. One need only go to an appropriate interest table to find the proper interest factor. For example, the correct interest factor for our five-year, 5% illustration can be found in Table A.2. Simply look down the Period column to 5, then across this row to the 5% column to find the interest factor, 1.2763. Then, using this interest factor, we find the value of $100 after five years as $FV_N = PV(FVIF_{i,N}) = \$100(1.2763) = \$127.63$, which is identical to the value obtained by the long method in Table A.1.

Graphic View of the Compounding Process: Growth

Figure A.1 shows how $1 (or any other initial quantity) grows over time at various rates of interest. The higher the rate of interest, the faster the rate of growth. The interest rate is, in fact, the growth rate: If a sum is deposited and earns 5%, then the funds on deposit grow at the rate of 5% per period. Similarly, the sales of a firm or the gross domestic product (GDP) of a country might be expected to grow at a constant rate. Projections of future sales or GDP could be obtained by using the compound value method.

Future value curves could be drawn for any interest rate, including fractional rates. In Figure A.1, we have plotted curves for 0%, 5%, and 10%, using the data from Table A.2.

FIGURE A.1 **Relations among Future Value Interest Factors, Interest Rates, and Time**

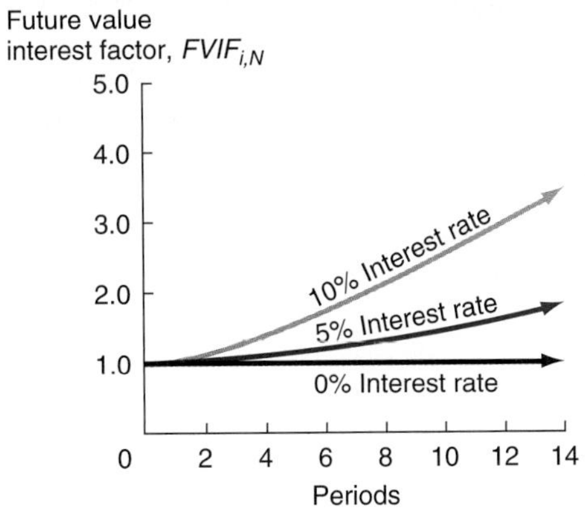

The future value interest factor rises with increases in the interest rate and in the number of periods for interest compounding.

Present Value

Suppose that you are offered the alternative of receiving either \$127.63 at the end of five years or *X* dollars today. There is no question that the \$127.63 will be paid in full (perhaps the payer is the U.S. government). Having no current need for the money, you would deposit it in a bank account that pays 5% interest. (Five percent is your *opportunity cost,* or the rate of interest you could earn on alternative investments of equal risk.) What value of *X* will make you indifferent between *X* dollars today or the promise of \$127.63 five years hence?

Table A.1 shows that the initial amount of \$100 growing at 5% a year yields \$127.63 at the end of five years. Thus, you should be indifferent in your choice between \$100 today and \$127.63 at the end of five years. The \$100 is the present value, or *PV,* of \$127.63 due in five years when the applicable interest rate is 5%. Therefore, if *X* is anything less than \$100, you would prefer the promise of \$127.63 in five years to *X* dollars today.

In general, the present value of a sum due *N* years in the future is the amount that, if it were invested today, would grow to equal the future sum over a period of *N* years. Since \$100 would grow to \$127.63 in five years at a 5% interest rate, \$100 is the present value of \$127.63 due five years in the future when the appropriate interest rate is 5%.

Finding present values (or *discounting,* as it is commonly called) is simply the reverse of compounding, and Equation A.2 can readily be transformed into a present-value formula:

$$FV_N = PV(1 + i)^N$$

which, when solved for *PV*, gives

$$PV = \frac{FV_N}{(1+i)^N} = FV_N\left[\frac{1}{(1+i)^N}\right] \tag{A.3}$$

Tables have been constructed for the term in brackets for various values of i and N; Table A.3 is an example. For a more complete table, see Table B.2 in Appendix B. For the case being considered, look down the 5% column in Table A.3 to the fifth row. The figure shown there, 0.7835, is the *present-value interest factor* ($PVIF_{i,N}$) used to determine the present value of $127.63 payable in five years, discounted at 5%:

$$\begin{aligned} PV &= FV_5(PVIF_{i,N}) \\ &= \$127.63(0.7835) \\ &= \$100 \end{aligned}$$

Graphic View of the Discounting Process

Figure A.2 shows how the interest factors for discounting decrease as the discounting period increases. The curves in the figure were plotted with data taken from Table A.3; they show that the present value of a sum to be received at some future date decreases (1) as the payment date is extended further into the future and (2) as the discount rate increases. If relatively high discount rates apply, funds due in the future are worth very little today. Even at relatively low discount rates, the present values of funds due in the distant future are small. For example, $1 due in 10 years is worth about 61¢ today if the discount rate is 5%. It is worth only 25¢ today at a 15% discount rate. Similarly, $1 due in five years at 10% is worth 62¢ today, but at the same discount rate, $1 due in 10 years is worth only 39¢ today.

FIGURE A.2 Relations among Present Value Interest Factors, Interest Rates, and Time

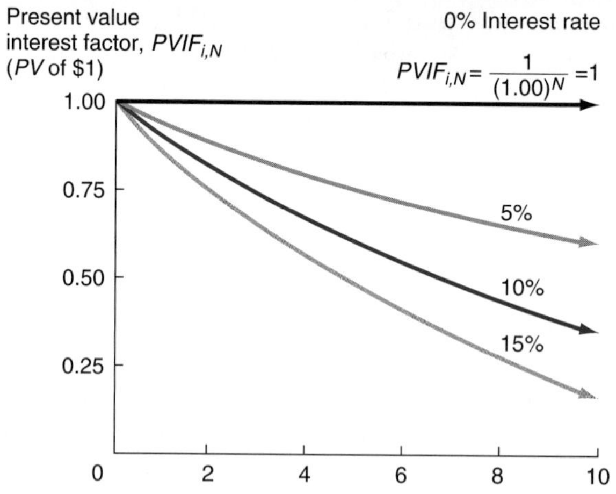

The present value interest factor falls with increases in the interest rate and in the number of periods prior to payment.

TABLE A.3 **Present Values of $1 Due at the End of *N* Periods**

$$PVIF_{i,N} = \frac{1}{(1+i)^N} = \left[\frac{1}{(1+i)}\right]^N$$

Period (*N*)	1%	2%	3%	4%	5%	6%	7%	8%	9%	10%	12%	14%	15%
1	.9901	.9804	.9709	.9615	.9524	.9434	.9346	.9259	.9174	.9091	.8929	.8772	.8696
2	.9803	.9612	.9426	.9246	.9070	.8900	.8734	.8573	.8417	.8264	.7972	.7695	.7561
3	.9706	.9423	.9151	.8890	.8638	.8396	.8163	.7938	.7722	.7513	.7118	.6750	.6575
4	.9610	.9238	.8885	.8548	.8227	.7921	.7629	.7350	.7084	.6830	.6355	.5921	.5718
5	.9515	.9057	.8626	.8219	.7835	.7473	.7130	.6806	.6499	.6209	.5674	.5194	.4972
6	.9420	.8880	.8375	.7903	.7462	.7050	.6663	.6302	.5963	.5645	.5066	.4556	.4323
7	.9327	.8706	.8131	.7599	.7107	.6651	.6227	.5835	.5470	.5132	.4523	.3996	.3759
8	.9235	.8535	.7894	.7307	.6768	.6274	.5820	.5403	.5019	.4665	.4039	.3506	.3269
9	.9143	.8368	.7664	.7026	.6446	.5919	.5439	.5002	.4604	.4241	.3606	.3075	.2843
10	.9053	.8203	.7441	.6756	.6139	.5584	.5083	.4632	.4224	.3855	.3220	.2697	.2472

Future Value versus Present Value

Notice that Equation A.2, the basic equation for compounding, was developed from the logical sequence set forth in Table A.1; the equation merely presents in mathematical form the steps outlined in the table. The present value interest factor ($PVIF_{i,N}$) in Equation A.3, the basic equation for discounting or finding present values, was found as the *reciprocal* of the future value interest factor ($FVIF_{i,N}$) for the same *i,N* combination:

$$PVIF_{i,N} = \frac{1}{FVIF_{i,N}}$$

For example, the *future value interest factor* for 5% over five years is seen in Table A.2 to be 1.2763. The *present-value interest factor* for 5% over five years must be the reciprocal of 1.2763:

$$PVIF_{5\%,\ 5\ \text{years}} = \frac{1}{1.2763} = 0.7835$$

The $PVIF_{i,N}$ found in this manner does, of course, correspond with the $PVIF_{i,N}$ shown in Table A.3.

The reciprocal relation between present value and future value permits us to find present values in two ways—by multiplying or by dividing. Thus, the present value of $1,000 due in five years and discounted at 5% may be found as

$$PV = FV_N\left[\frac{1}{1+i}\right]^N = FV_N(PVIF_{i,N}) = \$1{,}000(0.7835) = \$783.50$$

or as

$$PV = \frac{FV_N}{(1+i)^N} = \frac{FV_N}{FVIF_{i,N}} = \frac{\$1{,}000}{1.2763} = \$783.50$$

To conclude this comparison of present and future values, compare Figures A.1 and A.2.[2]

Future Value of an Annuity

An annuity is defined as a series of payments of a fixed amount for a specified number of periods. Each payment occurs at the end of the period.[3] For example, a promise to pay $1,000 a year for three years is a three-year annuity. If you were to receive such an annuity and were to deposit each annual payment in a savings account paying 4% interest, how much would you have at the end of three years? The answer is shown graphically as a *time line* in Figure A.3. The first payment is made at the end of year 1, the second at the end of year 2, and the third at the end of year 3. The last payment is not compounded at all, the second payment is compounded for one year, and the first is compounded for two years. When the future values of each of the payments are added, their total is the sum of the annuity. In the example, this total is $3,121.60.

Expressed algebraically, with S_N defined as the future value, R as the periodic receipt, N as the length of the annuity, and $FVIFA_{i,N}$ as the future value interest factor for an annuity, the formula for S_N is

$$\begin{aligned} S_N &= R(1+i)^{N-1} + R(1+i)^{N-2} + \cdots + R(1+i)^1 + R(1+i)^0 \qquad \textbf{(A.4)} \\ &= R[(1+i)^{N-1} + (1+i)^{N-2} + \cdots + (1+i)^1 + (1+i)^0] \\ &= R\sum_{t=1}^{N}(1+i)^{N-t} \\ &= R\sum_{t=1}^{N}(1+i)^{t-1} \\ &= R(FVIFA_{i,N}) \end{aligned}$$

The expression in parentheses, $FVIFA_{i,N}$, has been calculated for various combinations of i and N.[4] An illustrative set of these annuity interest factors is given in Table A.4.[5] To find the answer to the three-year, $1,000 annuity problem, simply refer to Table A.4, look down the 4% column to the row of the third period, and multiply the factor 3.1216 by $1,000. The answer is the same as the one derived by the long

---

[2]Notice that Figure A.2 is not a mirror image of Figure A.1. The curves in Figure A.1 approach ∞ as N increases; in Figure A.2 the curves approach zero, not $-\infty$.

[3]Had the payment been made at the beginning of the period, each receipt would simply have been shifted back one year. The annuity would have been called an *annuity due;* the one in the present discussion, with payments made at the end of each period, is called a *regular annuity* or, sometimes, a *deferred annuity.*

[4]The third equation is simply a shorthand expression in which sigma (Σ) signifies "sum up" or "add the values of N factors." The symbol $\sum_{t=1}^{N}$ simply says, "Go through the following process: Let $t = 1$ and find the first factor. Then let $t = 2$ and find the second factor. Continue until each individual factor has been found, and then add these individual factors to find the value of the annuity."

[5]The equation given in Table A.4 recognizes that the *FVIFA* factor is the sum of a geometric progression. The proof of this equation is given in most algebra texts. Notice that it is easy to use the equation to develop annuity factors. This is especially useful if you need the *FVIFA* for some interest rate not given in the tables (for example, 6.5%).

FIGURE A.3 **Time Line for an Annuity: Future Value ($i = 4\%$)**

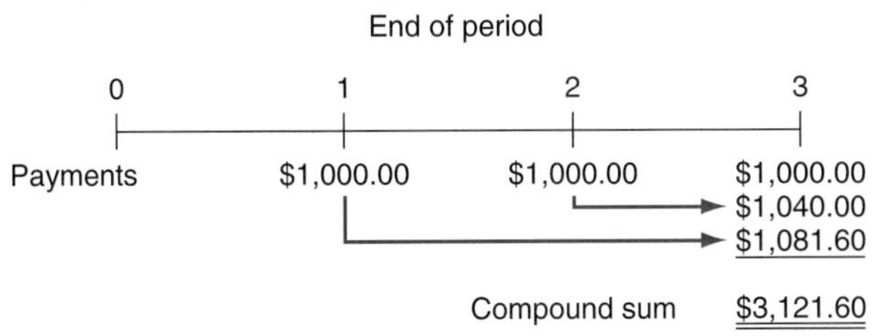

When the interest rate is 4%, the future value of a $1,000 annuity to be paid over 3 years is $3,121.60.

method illustrated in Figure A.3:

$$S_N = R(FVIFA_{i,N})$$
$$S_3 = \$1{,}000(3.1216) = \$3{,}121.60$$

Notice that for all positive interest rates, the $FVIFA_{i,N}$ for the sum of an annuity is always equal to or greater than the number of periods the annuity runs.[6]

TABLE A.4 **Future Value of an Annuity of $1 per Period for *N* Periods**

$$FVIFA_{i,N} = \sum_{t=1}^{N}(1+i)^{t-1} = \frac{(1+i)^N - 1}{i}$$

Number of Periods	1%	2%	3%	4%	5%	6%	7%	8%
1	1.0000	1.0000	1.0000	1.0000	1.0000	1.0000	1.0000	1.0000
2	2.0100	2.0200	2.0300	2.0400	2.0500	2.0600	2.0700	2.0800
3	3.0301	3.0604	3.0909	3.1216	3.1525	3.1836	3.2149	3.2464
4	4.0604	4.1216	4.1836	4.2465	4.3101	4.3746	4.4399	4.5061
5	5.1010	5.2040	5.3091	5.4163	5.5256	5.6371	5.7507	5.8666
6	6.1520	6.3081	6.4684	6.6330	6.8019	6.9753	7.1533	7.3359
7	7.2135	7.4343	7.6625	7.8983	8.1420	8.3938	8.6540	8.9228
8	8.2857	8.5830	8.8923	9.2142	9.5491	9.8975	10.2598	10.6366
9	9.3685	9.7546	10.1591	10.5828	11.0266	11.4913	11.9780	12.4876
10	10.4622	10.9497	11.4639	12.0061	12.5779	13.1808	13.8164	14.4866

[6]It is worth noting that the entry for each period t in Table A.4 equals the sum of the entries in Table A.2 up to the period $N - 1$. For example, the entry for period 3 under the 4% column in Table A.4 is equal to $1.000 + 1.0400 + 1.0816 = 3.1216$.

Also, had the annuity been an *annuity due,* with payments received at the beginning rather than at the end of each period, the three payments would have occurred at $t = 0$, $t = 1$, and $t = 2$. To find the future value of an annuity due, look up the $FVIFA_{i,N}$ for $N + 1$ years, then subtract 1.0 from the amount to get the $FVIFA_{i,N}$ for the annuity due. In the example, the annuity due $FVIFA_{i,N}$ is $4.2465 - 1.0 = 3.2465$, versus 3.1216 for a regular annuity. Because payments on an annuity due come earlier, it is a little more valuable than a regular annuity.

Present Value of an Annuity

Suppose that you were offered the following alternatives: a three-year annuity of \$1,000 per year or a lump-sum payment today. You have no need for the money during the next three years, so if you accept the annuity, you would simply deposit the receipts in a savings account paying 4% interest. How large must the lump-sum payment be to make it equivalent to the annuity? The time line shown in Figure A.4 will help explain the problem.

The present value of the first receipt is $R[1/(1+i)]$, the second is $R[1/(1+i)]^2$, and so on. Designating the present value of an annuity of N years as A_N and the present value interest factor for an annuity as $PVIFA_{i,N}$, we may write the following equation:

$$\begin{aligned} A_N &= R\left(\frac{1}{1+i}\right)^1 + R\left(\frac{1}{1+i}\right)^2 + \cdots + R\left(\frac{1}{1+i}\right)^N \\ &= R\left(\frac{1}{(1+i)^1} + \frac{1}{(1+i)^2} + \cdots + \frac{1}{(1+i)^N}\right) \\ &= R\sum_{t=1}^{N}\frac{1}{(1+i)^t} \\ &= R(PVIFA_{i,N}) \end{aligned} \quad \textbf{(A.5)}$$

Again, tables have been worked out for $PVIFA_{i,N}$, the term in parentheses in Equation A.5, as Table A.5 illustrates; a more complete listing is found in Table B.4 in Appendix B. From Table A.5, the $PVIFA_{i,N}$ for a three-year, 4% annuity is found to be 2.7751. Multiplying this factor by the \$1,000 annual receipt gives \$2,775.10, the present value of the annuity. This figure is identical to the long-method answer shown in Figure A.4:

$$\begin{aligned} A_N &= R(PVIFA_{i,N}) \\ A_3 &= \$1{,}000(2.7751) \\ &= \$2{,}775.10 \end{aligned}$$

FIGURE A.4 Time Line for an Annuity: Present Value ($i = 4\%$)

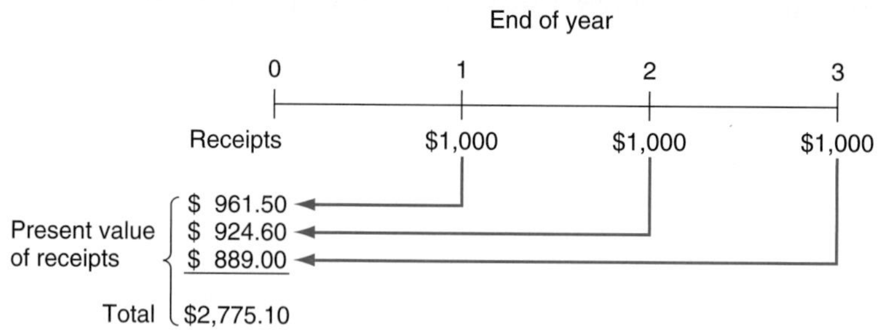

When the interest rate is 4%, the present value of a \$1,000 annuity to be paid over 3 years is \$2,775.10.

TABLE A.5 Present Value of an Annuity of $1 per Period for *N* Periods

$$PVIFA_{i,N} = \sum_{t=1}^{N} \frac{1}{(1+i)^t} = \frac{1 - \dfrac{1}{(1+i)^N}}{i}$$

Period	1%	2%	3%	4%	5%	6%	7%	8%	9%	10%
1	0.9901	0.9804	0.9709	0.9615	0.9524	0.9434	0.9346	0.9259	0.9174	0.9091
2	1.9704	1.9416	1.9135	1.8861	1.8594	1.8334	1.8080	1.7833	1.7591	1.7355
3	2.9410	2.8839	2.8286	2.7751	2.7232	2.6730	2.6243	2.5771	2.5313	2.4869
4	3.9020	3.8077	3.7171	3.6299	3.5460	3.4651	3.3872	3.3121	3.2397	3.1699
5	4.8534	4.7135	4.5797	4.4518	4.3295	4.2124	4.1002	3.9927	3.8897	3.7908
6	5.7955	5.6014	5.4172	5.2421	5.0757	4.9173	4.7665	4.6229	4.4859	4.3553
7	6.7282	6.4720	6.2303	6.0021	5.7864	5.5824	5.3893	5.2064	5.0330	4.8684
8	7.6517	7.3255	7.0197	6.7327	6.4632	6.2098	5.9713	5.7466	5.5348	5.3349
9	8.5660	8.1622	7.7861	7.4353	7.1078	6.8017	6.5152	6.2469	5.9952	5.7590
10	9.4713	8.9826	8.5302	8.1109	7.7217	7.3601	7.0236	6.7101	6.4177	6.1446

Notice that the entry for each period *N* in Table A.5 is equal to the sum of the entries in Table A.3 up to and including period *N*. For example, the *PVIFA* for 4%, three periods as shown in Table A.5, could have been calculated by summing values from Table A.3:

$$0.9615 + 0.9246 + 0.8890 = 2.7751$$

Notice also that for all positive interest rates, $PVIFA_{i,N}$ for the *present value* of an annuity is always less than the number of periods.[7]

Present Value of an Uneven Series of Receipts

The definition of an annuity includes the words *fixed amount*—in other words, annuities involve situations in which cash flows are *identical* in every period. Although many managerial decisions involve constant cash flows, some important decisions are concerned with uneven cash flows. Consequently, it is necessary to deal with varying payment streams.

The *PV* of an uneven stream of future income is found as the sum of the *PVs* of the individual components of the stream. For example, suppose that we are trying to find the *PV* of the stream of receipts shown in Table A.6, discounted at 6%. As shown in the table, we multiply each receipt by the appropriate $PVIF_{i,N}$, then sum these products to obtain the *PV* of the stream, $1,413.24. Figure A.5 gives a graphic view of the cash-flow stream.

[7] To find the $PVIFA_{i,N}$ for an *annuity due,* look up the $PVIFA_{i,N}$ for $n - 1$ periods, then add 1.0 to this amount to obtain the $PVIFA_{i,N}$ for the annuity due. In the example, the $PVIFA_{i,N}$ for a 4%, three-year annuity due is 1.8861 + 1.0 = 2.8861.

The *PV* of the receipts shown in Table A.6 and Figure A.5 can also be found by using the annuity equation; the steps in this alternative solution process are as follows:

- *Step 1:* Find *PV* of \$100 due in one year:

$$\$100(0.9434) = \$94.34$$

- *Step 2:* Recognize that a \$200 annuity will be received during years 2 through 5. Thus, we can determine the value of a five-year annuity, subtract from it the value of a one-year annuity, and have remaining the value of a four-year annuity whose first payment is due in two years. This result is achieved by subtracting the *PVIFA* for a one-year, 6% annuity from the *PVIFA* for a five-year annuity and then multiplying the difference by \$200:

$$\begin{aligned} PV \text{ of the annuity} &= (PVIFA_{6\%,\,5\text{ yr}} - PVIFA_{6\%,\,1\text{ yr}})(\$200) \\ &= (4.2124 - 0.9434)(\$200) \\ &= \$653.80 \end{aligned}$$

Thus, the present value of the annuity component of the uneven stream is \$653.80.

- *Step 3:* Find the *PV* of the \$1,000 due in year 7:

$$\$1{,}000(0.6651) = \$665.10$$

- *Step 4:* Sum the components:

$$\$94.34 + \$653.80 + \$665.10 = \$1{,}413.24$$

Either of the two methods can be used to solve problems of this type. However, the alternative (annuity) solution is easier if the annuity component runs for many years. For example, the alternative solution would be clearly superior for finding the *PV* of a stream consisting of \$100 in year 1, \$200 in years 2 through 29, and \$1,000 in year 30.

TABLE A.6 Present Value of an Uneven Stream of Receipts (i = 6%)

Year	Stream of Receipts	×	$PVIF_{i,N}$	=	*PV* of Individual Receipts
1	\$100		0.9434		\$ 94.34
2	200		0.8900		178.00
3	200		0.8396		167.92
4	200		0.7921		158.42
5	200		0.7473		149.46
6	0		0.7050		0
7	1,000		0.6651		665.10
				PV = Sum =	\$1,413.24

FIGURE A.5 Time Line for an Uneven Cash Flow Stream

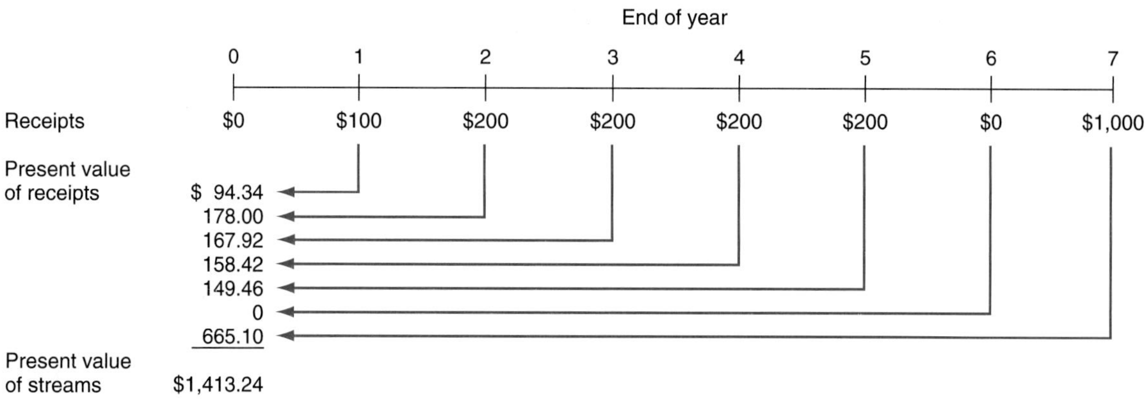

When the interest rate is 4%, the present value of a $1,000 annuity to be paid over 3 years is $2,775.10.

Annual Payments for Accumulation of a Future Sum

Suppose that you want to know the amount of money that must be deposited at 5% for each of the next five years to have $10,000 available to pay off a debt at the end of the fifth year. Dividing both sides of Equation A.4 by *FVIFA* obtains

$$R = \frac{S_N}{FVIFA_{i,N}} \quad \textbf{(A.6)}$$

Looking up the future value of an annuity interest factor for five years at 5% in Table A.4 and dividing this figure into $10,000 gives

$$R = \frac{\$10{,}000}{5.5256} = \$1{,}810$$

Thus, if $1,810 is deposited each year in an account paying 5% interest, at the end of five years the account will have accumulated to $10,000.

Annual Receipts from an Annuity

Suppose that on September 1, 2000, you received an inheritance of $7,500. The money is to be used for your education and is to be spent during the academic years beginning September 2001, 2002, and 2003. If you place the money in a bank account paying 6% annual interest and make three equal withdrawals at each of the specified dates, how large can each withdrawal be so as to leave you with exactly a zero balance after the last one has been made?

The solution requires application of the present value of an annuity formula, Equation A.5. Here, however, we know that the present value of the annuity is

$7,500, and the problem is to find the three equal annual payments when the interest rate is 6%. This calls for dividing both sides of Equation A.5 by $PVIFA_{i,N}$ to derive Equation A.7:

$$R = \frac{A_N}{PVIFA_{i,N}} \quad \textbf{(A.7)}$$

The interest factor is found in Table A.5 to be 2.6730, and substituting this value into Equation A.7, the three annual withdrawals are calculated to be $2,806:

$$R = \frac{\$7{,}500}{2.6730} = \$2{,}806$$

This particular calculation is used frequently to set up insurance and pension-plan benefit schedules and to find the periodic payments necessary to retire a loan within a specified period. For example, if you want to retire in three equal annual payments a $7,500 bank loan accruing interest at 6% on the unpaid balance, each payment would be $2,806. In this case, the bank is acquiring an annuity with a present value of $7,500.

Determining Interest Rates

We can use the basic equations developed earlier to determine the interest rates implicit in financial contracts.

Example 1. A bank offers to lend you $1,000 if you sign a note to repay $1,610.50 at the end of five years. What rate of interest are you paying? To solve the problem, recognize that $1,000 is the *PV* of $1,610.50 due in five years, and solve Equation A.3 for the present value interest factor ($PVIF_{i,N}$).

$$PV = FV_N\left[\frac{1}{(1+i)^N}\right] = FV_N(PVIF_{i,N}) \quad \textbf{(A.3)}$$

$$\begin{aligned} \$1{,}000 &= \$1{,}610.50(PVIF_{i,N} \text{ for 5 years}) \\ \$1{,}000/\$1{,}610.50 &= 0.6209 = PVIF_{i,5 \text{ yr}} \end{aligned}$$

Now, go to Table A.3 and look across the row for year 5 until you find 0.6209. It is in the 10% column, so you would be paying a 10% rate of interest.

Example 2. A bank offers to lend you $100,000 to buy a house. You must sign a mortgage calling for payments of $8,882.73 at the end of each of the next 30 years, equivalent to roughly $740.23 per month. What interest rate is the bank charging you?

1. Recognize that $100,000 is the *PV* of a 30-year, $8,882.73 annuity:

$$\$100{,}000 = PV = \sum_{t=1}^{30} \$8{,}882.73\left[\frac{1}{(1+i)^t}\right] = \$8{,}882.73(PVIFA_{i,30 \text{ yrs}})$$

2. Solve for $PVIFA_{i,30 \text{ yr}}$:

$$PVIFA_{i,30 \text{ yr}} = \$100{,}000/\$8{,}882.73 = 11.2578$$

3. Turn to Table B.4 in Appendix B, because Table A.5 does not cover a 30-year period. Looking across the row for 30 periods, find 11.2578 under the column for 8%. Therefore, the rate of interest on this mortgage is 8%.

Semiannual and Other Compounding Periods

All the examples thus far have assumed that returns were received once a year, or annually. Suppose, however, that you put your $1,000 in a bank that offers to pay 6% interest compounded *semiannually*. How much will you have at the end of one year? Semiannual compounding means that interest is actually paid every six months, a fact taken into account in the tabular calculations in Table A.7. Here, the annual interest rate is divided by 2, but twice as many compounding periods are used because interest is paid twice a year. Comparing the amount on hand at the end of the second six-month period, $1,060.90, with what would have been on hand under annual compounding, $1,060, shows that semiannual compounding is better from the standpoint of the saver. This result occurs because you earn interest on interest more frequently.

Throughout the economy, different types of investments use different compounding periods. For example, bank and savings and loan accounts generally pay interest quarterly, some bonds pay interest semiannually, and other bonds pay interest annually. Thus, if we are to compare securities with different compounding periods, we need to put them on a common basis. This need has led to the development of the terms *nominal,* or *stated, interest rate* and *effective annual,* or *annual percentage rate* (*APR*). The stated, or nominal, rate is the quoted rate; thus, in our example the nominal rate is 6%. The annual percentage rate is the rate that would have produced the final compound value, $1,060.90, under annual rather than semiannual compounding. In this case, the effective annual rate is 6.09%:

$$\$1{,}000(1 + i) = \$1{,}060.90$$
$$i = \frac{\$1{,}060.90}{\$1{,}000} - 1 = 0.0609 = 6.09\%$$

Thus, if one bank offered 6% with semiannual compounding, whereas another offered 6.09% with annual compounding, they would both be paying the same effective rate of interest. In general, we can determine the effective annual rate of interest, given the nominal rate, as follows:

- *Step 1:* Find the *FV* of $1 at the end of one year, using the equation

$$FV = 1\left(1 + \frac{i_n}{M}\right)^M$$

TABLE A.7 Compound Interest Calculations with Semiannual Compounding

	Beginning Amount (*PV*)	×	(1 + *i*/2)	=	Ending Amount, FV_N
Period 1	$1,000.00		(1.03)		$1,030.00
Period 2	1,030.00		(1.03)		1,060.90

Here, i_n is the nominal rate, and M is the number of compounding periods per year.

- *Step 2:* Subtract 1.0 from the result in step 1; then multiply by 100. The final result is the effective annual rate.

Example. Find the effective annual rate if the nominal rate is 6%, compounded semiannually:

$$\begin{aligned}\text{Effective annual rate} &= \left(1 + \frac{0.06}{2}\right)^2 - 1.0\\ &= (1.03)^2 - 1.0\\ &= 1.0609 - 1.0\\ &= 0.0609\\ &= 6.09\%\end{aligned}$$

The points made about semiannual compounding can be generalized as follows. When compounding periods are more frequent than once a year, use a modified version of Equation A.2:

$$FV_N = PV(1 + i)^N \quad \textbf{(A.2)}$$

$$FV_N = PV\left(1 + \frac{i}{M}\right)^{MN} \quad \textbf{(A.2a)}$$

Here, M is the number of times per year compounding occurs. When banks compute daily interest, the value of M is set at 365, and Equation A.2a is applied.

The interest tables can be used when compounding occurs more than once a year. Simply divide the nominal, or stated, interest rate by the number of times compounding occurs, and multiply the years by the number of compounding periods per year. For example, to find the amount to which $1,000 will grow after six years with semiannual compounding and a stated 8% interest rate, divide 8% by 2 and multiply the six years by 2. Then look in Table A.2 under the 4% column and in the row for period 12. You will find an interest factor of 1.6010. Multiplying this by the initial $1,000 gives a value of $1,601, the amount to which $1,000 will grow in six years at 8% compounded semiannually. This compares with $1,586.90 for annual compounding.

The same procedure applies in all of the cases covered—compounding, discounting, single payments, and annuities. To illustrate semiannual discounting in finding the present value of an annuity, consider the case described in the section "Present Value of an Annuity"—$1,000 a year for three years, discounted at 4%. With annual discounting, the interest factor is 2.7751, and the present value of the annuity is $2,775.10. For semiannual discounting, look under the 2% column and in the period 6 row of Table A.5 to find an interest factor of 5.6014. This is now multiplied by half of $1,000, or the $500 received each six months, to get the present value of the annuity, $2,800.70. The payments come a little more rapidly—the first $500 is paid after only six months (similarly with other payments)—so the annuity is a little more valuable if payments are received semiannually rather than annually.

Summary

Investment decisions often require determining the future value of various investment alternatives, such as stocks, bonds, or financial derivatives. Investors and finance professionals alike must know how to calculate the future amount of financial obligations and the predictable investment return from fixed-rate instruments. Similarly, investors and finance professionals must have facility with the present-value concept because business valuation often requires determining the present value of future cash flows. The examples described in this appendix will help develop the understanding necessary to effectively use the key investment concepts of compounding and the time value of money.

The key procedures covered in this appendix are summarized below:

- *Future Value:* $FV_N = PV(1 + i)^N$, where FV_N is the future value of an initial amount, PV, compounded at the rate of i percent for N periods. The term $(1 + i)^N$ is the future value interest factor, $FVIF_{i,N}$. Values for $FVIF$ are contained in tables.
- *Present Value:* $PV = FV_N[1/(1 + i)]^N$. This equation is simply a transformation of the future value equation. The term $[1/(1 + i)]^N$ is the present-value interest factor, $PVIF_{i,N}$.
- *Future Value of an Annuity:* An annuity is defined as a series of constant or equal payments of R dollars per period. The sum, or future value of an annuity, is given the symbol S_N, and is found as follows:

$$S_N = R\left[\sum_{t=1}^{N}(1 + i)^{t-1}\right].$$

  The term

$$\left[\sum_{t=1}^{N}(1 + i)^{t-1}\right]$$

  is the future value interest factor for an annuity, $FVIFA_{i,N}$.
- *Present Value of an Annuity:* The present value of an annuity is identified by the symbol A_N, and is found as follows:

$$A_N = R\left[\sum_{t=1}^{N}(1/1 + i)^{t}\right].$$

  The term

$$\left[\sum_{t=1}^{N}(1/1 + i)^{t}\right] = \text{PVIFA}_{i,N}$$

  is the present-value interest factor for an annuity.

APPENDIX B

Interest Factor Tables

TABLE B.1 Future Value of \$1: $FVIF_{I,N} = (1 + I)^N$

Period	1%	2%	3%	4%	5%	6%	7%	8%	9%	10%
1	1.0100	1.0200	1.0300	1.0400	1.0500	1.0600	1.0700	1.0800	1.0900	1.1000
2	1.0201	1.0404	1.0609	1.0816	1.1025	1.1236	1.1449	1.1664	1.1881	1.2100
3	1.0303	1.0612	1.0927	1.1249	1.1576	1.1910	1.2250	1.2597	1.2950	1.3310
4	1.0406	1.0824	1.1255	1.1699	1.2155	1.2625	1.3108	1.3605	1.4116	1.4641
5	1.0510	1.1041	1.1593	1.2167	1.2763	1.3382	1.4026	1.4693	1.5386	1.6105
6	1.0615	1.1262	1.1941	1.2653	1.3401	1.4185	1.5007	1.5869	1.6771	1.7716
7	1.0721	1.1487	1.2299	1.3159	1.4071	1.5036	1.6058	1.7138	1.8280	1.9487
8	1.0829	1.1717	1.2668	1.3686	1.4775	1.5938	1.7182	1.8509	1.9926	2.1436
9	1.0937	1.1951	1.3048	1.4233	1.5513	1.6895	1.8385	1.9990	2.1719	2.3579
10	1.1046	1.2190	1.3439	1.4802	1.6289	1.7908	1.9672	2.1589	2.3674	2.5937
11	1.1157	1.2434	1.3842	1.5395	1.7103	1.8983	2.1049	2.3316	2.5804	2.8531
12	1.1268	1.2682	1.4258	1.6010	1.7959	2.1022	2.2522	2.5182	2.8127	3.1384
13	1.1381	1.2936	1.4685	1.6651	1.8856	2.1329	2.4098	2.7196	3.0658	3.4523
14	1.1495	1.3195	1.5126	1.7317	1.9799	2.2609	2.5785	2.9372	3.3417	3.7975
15	1.1610	1.3459	1.5580	1.8009	2.0789	2.3966	2.7590	3.1722	3.6425	4.1772
16	1.1726	1.3728	1.6047	1.8730	2.1829	2.5404	2.9522	3.4259	3.9703	4.5950
17	1.1843	1.4002	1.6528	1.9479	2.2920	2.6928	3.1588	3.7000	4.3276	5.0545
18	1.1961	1.4282	1.7024	2.0258	2.4066	2.8543	3.3799	3.9960	4.7171	5.5599
19	1.2081	1.4568	1.7535	2.1068	2.5270	3.0256	3.6165	4.3157	5.1417	6.1159
20	1.2202	1.4859	1.8061	2.1911	2.6533	3.2071	3.8697	4.6610	5.6044	6.7275
21	1.2324	1.5157	1.8603	2.2788	2.7860	3.3996	4.1406	5.0338	6.1088	7.4002
22	1.2447	1.5460	1.9161	2.3699	2.9253	3.6035	4.4304	5.4365	6.6586	8.1403
23	1.2572	1.5769	1.9736	2.4647	3.0715	3.8197	4.7405	5.8715	7.2579	8.9543
24	1.2697	1.6084	2.0328	2.5633	3.2251	4.0489	5.0724	6.3412	7.9111	9.8497
25	1.2824	1.6406	2.0938	2.6658	3.3864	4.2919	5.4274	6.8485	8.6231	10.834
26	1.2953	1.6734	2.1566	2.7725	3.5557	4.5494	5.8074	7.3964	9.3992	11.918
27	1.3082	1.7069	2.2213	2.8834	3.7335	4.8223	6.2139	7.9881	10.245	13.110
28	1.3213	1.7410	2.2879	2.9987	3.9201	5.1117	6.6488	8.6271	11.167	14.421
29	1.3345	1.7758	2.3566	3.1187	4.1161	5.4184	7.1143	9.3173	12.172	15.863
30	1.3478	1.8114	2.4273	3.2434	4.3219	5.7435	7.6123	10.062	13.267	17.449
40	1.4889	2.2080	3.2620	4.8010	7.0400	10.285	14.974	21.724	31.409	45.259
50	1.6446	2.6916	4.3839	7.1067	11.467	18.420	29.457	46.901	74.357	117.39
60	1.8167	3.2810	5.8916	10.519	18.679	32.987	57.946	101.25	176.03	304.48

TABLE B.1 *(continued)*

Period	12%	14%	15%	16%	18%	20%	24%	28%	32%	36%
1	1.1200	1.1400	1.1500	1.1600	1.1800	1.2000	1.2400	1.2800	1.3200	1.3600
2	1.2544	1.2996	1.3225	1.3456	1.3924	1.4400	1.5376	1.6384	1.7424	1.8496
3	1.4049	1.4815	1.5209	1.5609	1.6430	1.7280	1.9066	2.0972	2.3000	2.5155
4	1.5735	1.6890	1.7490	1.8106	1.9388	2.0736	2.3642	2.6844	3.0360	3.4210
5	1.7623	1.9254	2.0114	2.1003	2.2878	2.4883	2.9316	3.4360	4.0075	4.6526
6	1.9738	2.1950	2.3131	2.4364	2.6996	2.9860	3.6352	4.3980	5.2899	6.3275
7	2.2107	2.5023	2.6600	2.8262	3.1855	3.5832	4.5077	5.6295	6.9826	8.6054
8	2.4760	2.8526	3.0590	3.2784	3.7589	4.2998	5.5895	7.2058	9.2170	11.703
9	2.7731	3.2519	3.5179	3.8030	4.4355	5.1598	6.9310	9.2234	12.166	15.916
10	3.1058	3.7072	4.0456	4.4114	5.2338	6.1917	8.5944	11.805	16.059	21.646
11	3.4785	4.2262	4.6524	5.1173	6.1759	7.4301	10.657	15.111	21.198	29.439
12	3.8960	4.8179	5.3502	5.9360	7.2876	8.9161	13.214	19.342	27.982	40.037
13	4.3635	5.4924	6.1528	6.8858	8.5994	10.699	16.386	24.758	36.937	54.451
14	4.8871	6.2613	7.0757	7.9875	10.147	12.839	20.319	31.691	48.756	74.053
15	5.4736	7.1379	8.1371	9.2655	11.973	15.407	25.195	40.564	64.358	100.71
16	6.1304	8.1372	9.3576	10.748	14.129	18.488	31.242	51.923	84.953	136.96
17	6.8660	9.2765	10.761	12.467	16.672	22.186	38.740	66.461	112.13	186.27
18	7.6900	10.575	12.375	14.462	19.673	26.623	48.038	85.070	148.02	253.33
19	8.6128	12.055	14.231	16.776	23.214	31.948	59.567	108.89	195.39	344.53
20	9.6463	13.743	16.366	19.460	27.393	38.337	73.864	139.37	257.91	468.57
21	10.803	15.667	18.821	22.574	32.323	46.005	91.591	178.40	340.44	637.26
22	12.100	17.861	21.644	26.186	38.142	55.206	113.57	228.35	449.39	866.67
23	13.552	20.361	24.891	30.376	45.007	66.247	140.83	292.30	593.19	1178.6
24	15.178	23.212	28.625	35.236	53.108	79.496	174.63	374.14	783.02	1602.9
25	17.000	26.461	32.918	40.874	62.668	95.396	216.54	478.90	1033.5	2180.0
26	19.040	30.166	37.856	47.414	73.948	114.47	268.51	612.99	1364.3	2964.9
27	21.324	34.389	43.535	55.000	87.259	137.37	332.95	784.63	1800.9	4032.2
28	23.883	39.204	50.065	63.800	102.96	164.84	412.86	1004.3	2377.2	5483.8
29	26.749	44.693	57.575	74.008	121.50	197.81	511.95	1285.5	3137.9	7458.0
30	29.959	50.950	66.211	85.849	143.37	237.37	634.81	1645.5	4142.0	10143.
40	93.050	188.88	267.86	378.72	750.37	1469.7	5455.9	19426.	66520.	*
50	289.00	700.23	1083.6	1670.7	3927.3	9100.4	46890.	*	*	*
60	897.59	2595.9	4383.9	7370.1	20555.	56347.	*	*	*	*

*FVIF > 99,999.

TABLE B.2 Present Value of $1: $PVIF_{i,N} = 1/(1 + i)^N = 1/FVIF_{i,N}$

Period	1%	2%	3%	4%	5%	6%	7%	8%	9%	10%
1	.9901	.9804	.9709	.9615	.9524	.9434	.9346	.9259	.9174	.9091
2	.9803	.9612	.9426	.9246	.9070	.8900	.8734	.8573	.8417	.8264
3	.9706	.9423	.9151	.8890	.8638	.8396	.8163	.7938	.7722	.7513
4	.9610	.9238	.8885	.8548	.8227	.7921	.7629	.7350	.7084	.6830
5	.9515	.9057	.8626	.8219	.7835	.7473	.7130	.6806	.6499	.6209
6	.9420	.8880	.8375	.7903	.7462	.7050	.6663	.6302	.5963	.5645
7	.9327	.8706	.8131	.7599	.7107	.6651	.6227	.5835	.5470	.5132
8	.9235	.8535	.7894	.7307	.6768	.6274	.5820	.5403	.5019	.4665
9	.9143	.8368	.7664	.7026	.6446	.5919	.5439	.5002	.4604	.4241
10	.9053	.8203	.7441	.6756	.6139	.5584	.5083	.4632	.4224	.3855
11	.8963	.8043	.7224	.6496	.5847	.5268	.4751	.4289	.3875	.3505
12	.8874	.7885	.7014	.6246	.5568	.4970	.4440	.3971	.3555	.3186
13	.8787	.7730	.6810	.6006	.5303	.4688	.4150	.3677	.3262	.2897
14	.8700	.7579	.6611	.5775	.5051	.4423	.3878	.3405	.2992	.2633
15	.8613	.7430	.6419	.5553	.4810	.4173	.3624	.3152	.2745	.2394
16	.8528	.7284	.6232	.5339	.4581	.3936	.3387	.2919	.2519	.2176
17	.8444	.7142	.6050	.5134	.4363	.3714	.3166	.2703	.2311	.1978
18	.8360	.7002	.5874	.4936	.4155	.3503	.2959	.2502	.2120	.1799
19	.8277	.6854	.5703	.4746	.3957	.3305	.2765	.2317	.1945	.1635
20	.8195	.6730	.5537	.4564	.3769	.3118	.2584	.2145	.1784	.1486
21	.8114	.6598	.5375	.4388	.3589	.2942	.2415	.1987	.1637	.1351
22	.8034	.6468	.5219	.4220	.3418	.2775	.2257	.1839	.1502	.1228
23	.7954	.6342	.5067	.4057	.3256	.2618	.2109	.1703	.1378	.1117
24	.7876	.6217	.4919	.3901	.3101	.2470	.1971	.1577	.1264	.1015
25	.7798	.6095	.4776	.3751	.2953	.2330	.1842	.1460	.1160	.0923
26	.7720	.5976	.4637	.3607	.2812	.2198	.1722	.1352	.1064	.0839
27	.7644	.5859	.4502	.3468	.2678	.2074	.1609	.1252	.0976	.0763
28	.7568	.5744	.4371	.3335	.2551	.1956	.1504	.1159	.0895	.0693
29	.7493	.5631	.4243	.3207	.2429	.1846	.1406	.1073	.0822	.0630
30	.7419	.5521	.4120	.3083	.2314	.1741	.1314	.0994	.0754	.0573
35	.7059	.5000	.3554	.2534	.1813	.1301	.0937	.0676	.0490	.0356
40	.6717	.4529	.3066	.2083	.1420	.0972	.0668	.0460	.0318	.0221
45	.6391	.4102	.2644	.1712	.1113	.0727	.0476	.0313	.0207	.0137
50	.6080	.3715	.2281	.1407	.0872	.0543	.0339	.0213	.0134	.0085
55	.5785	.3365	.1968	.1157	.0683	.0406	.0242	.0145	.0087	.0053

TABLE B.2 *(continued)*

Period	12%	14%	15%	16%	18%	20%	24%	28%	32%	36%
1	.8929	.8772	.8696	.8621	.8475	.8333	.8065	.7813	.7576	.7353
2	.7972	.7695	.7561	.7432	.7182	.6944	.6504	.6104	.5739	.5407
3	.7118	.6750	.6575	.6407	.6086	.5787	.5245	.4768	.4348	.3975
4	.6355	.5921	.5718	.5523	.5158	.4823	.4230	.3725	.3294	.2923
5	.5674	.5194	.4972	.4761	.4371	.4019	.3411	.2910	.2495	.2149
6	.5066	.4556	.4323	.4104	.3704	.3349	.2751	.2274	.1890	.1580
7	.4523	.3996	.3759	.3538	.3139	.2791	.2218	.1776	.1432	.1162
8	.4039	.3506	.3269	.3050	.2660	.2326	.1789	.1388	.1085	.0854
9	.3606	.3075	.2843	.2630	.2255	.1938	.1443	.1084	.0822	.0628
10	.3220	.2697	.2472	.2267	.1911	.1615	.1164	.0847	.0623	.0462
11	.2875	.2366	.2149	.1954	.1619	.1346	.0938	.0662	.0472	.0340
12	.2567	.2076	.1869	.1685	.1372	.1122	.0757	.0517	.0357	.0250
13	.2292	.1821	.1625	.1452	.1163	.0935	.0610	.0404	.0271	.0184
14	.2046	.1597	.1413	.1252	.0985	.0779	.0492	.0316	.0205	.0135
15	.1827	.1401	.1229	.1079	.0835	.0649	.0397	.0247	.0155	.0099
16	.1631	.1229	.1069	.0930	.0708	.0541	.0320	.0193	.0118	.0073
17	.1456	.1078	.0929	.0802	.0600	.0451	.0258	.0150	.0089	.0054
18	.1300	.0946	.0808	.0691	.0508	.0376	.0208	.0118	.0068	.0039
19	.1161	.0829	.0703	.0596	.0431	.0313	.0168	.0092	.0051	.0029
20	.1037	.0728	.0611	.0514	.0365	.0261	.0135	.0072	.0039	.0021
21	.0926	.0638	.0531	.0443	.0309	.0217	.0109	.0056	.0029	.0016
22	.0826	.0560	.0462	.0382	.0262	.0181	.0088	.0044	.0022	.0012
23	.0738	.0491	.0402	.0329	.0222	.0151	.0071	.0034	.0017	.0008
24	.0659	.0431	.0349	.0284	.0188	.0126	.0057	.0027	.0013	.0006
25	.0588	.0378	.0304	.0245	.0160	.0105	.0046	.0021	.0010	.0005
26	.0525	.0331	.0264	.0211	.0135	.0087	.0037	.0016	.0007	.0003
27	.0469	.0291	.0230	.0182	.0115	.0073	.0030	.0013	.0006	.0002
28	.0419	.0255	.0200	.0157	.0097	.0061	.0024	.0010	.0004	.0002
29	.0374	.0224	.0174	.0135	.0082	.0051	.0020	.0008	.0003	.0001
30	.0334	.0196	.0151	.0116	.0070	.0042	.0016	.0006	.0002	.0001
35	.0189	.0102	.0075	.0055	.0030	.0017	.0005	.0002	.0001	*
40	.0107	.0053	.0037	.0026	.0013	.0007	.0002	.0001	*	*
45	.0061	.0027	.0019	.0013	.0006	.0003	.0001	*	*	*
50	.0035	.0014	.0009	.0006	.0003	.0001	*	*	*	*
55	.0020	.0007	.0005	.0003	.0001	*	*	*	*	*

*The factor is zero to four decimal places.

TABLE B.3 Future Value of an Annuity of $1 for *N* Periods

$$FVIFA_{i,N} = \sum_{t=1}^{N} (1+i)^{t-1} = \frac{(1+i)^N - 1}{i}$$

Number of Periods	1%	2%	3%	4%	5%	6%	7%	8%	9%	10%
1	1.0000	1.0000	1.0000	1.0000	1.0000	1.0000	1.0000	1.0000	1.0000	1.0000
2	2.0100	2.0200	2.0300	2.0400	2.0500	2.0600	2.0700	2.0800	2.0900	2.1000
3	3.0301	3.0604	3.0909	3.1216	3.1525	3.1836	3.2149	3.2464	3.2781	3.3100
4	4.0604	4.1216	4.1836	4.2465	4.3101	4.3746	4.4399	4.5061	4.5731	4.6410
5	5.1010	5.2040	5.3091	5.4163	5.5256	5.6371	5.7507	5.8666	5.9847	6.1051
6	6.1520	6.3081	6.4684	6.6330	6.8019	6.9753	7.1533	7.3359	7.5233	7.7156
7	7.2135	7.4343	7.6625	7.8983	8.1420	8.3938	8.6540	8.9228	9.2004	9.4872
8	8.2857	8.5830	8.8923	9.2142	9.5491	9.8975	10.259	10.636	11.028	11.435
9	9.3685	9.7546	10.159	10.582	11.026	11.491	11.978	12.487	13.021	13.579
10	10.462	10.949	11.463	12.006	12.577	13.180	13.816	14.486	15.192	15.937
11	11.566	12.168	12.807	13.486	14.206	14.971	15.783	16.645	17.560	18.531
12	12.682	13.412	14.192	15.025	15.917	16.869	17.888	18.977	20.140	21.384
13	13.809	14.680	15.617	16.626	17.713	18.882	20.140	21.495	22.953	24.522
14	14.947	15.973	17.086	18.291	19.598	21.015	22.550	24.214	26.019	27.975
15	16.096	17.293	18.598	20.023	21.578	23.276	25.129	27.152	29.360	31.772
16	17.257	18.639	20.156	21.824	23.657	25.672	27.888	30.324	33.003	35.949
17	18.430	20.012	21.761	23.697	25.840	28.212	30.840	33.750	36.973	40.544
18	19.614	21.412	23.414	25.645	28.132	30.905	33.999	37.450	41.301	45.599
19	20.810	22.840	25.116	27.671	30.539	33.760	37.379	41.446	46.018	51.159
20	22.019	24.297	26.870	29.778	33.066	36.785	40.995	45.762	51.160	57.275
21	23.239	25.783	28.676	31.969	35.719	39.992	44.865	50.422	56.764	64.002
22	24.471	27.299	30.536	34.248	38.505	43.392	49.005	55.456	62.873	71.402
23	25.716	28.845	32.452	36.617	41.430	46.995	53.436	60.893	69.531	79.543
24	26.973	30.421	34.426	39.082	44.502	50.815	58.176	66.764	76.789	88.497
25	28.243	32.030	36.459	41.645	47.727	54.864	63.249	73.105	84.700	98.347
26	29.525	33.670	38.553	44.311	51.113	59.156	68.676	79.954	93.323	109.18
27	30.820	35.344	40.709	47.084	54.669	63.705	74.483	87.350	102.72	121.09
28	32.129	37.051	42.930	49.967	58.402	68.528	80.697	95.338	112.96	134.20
29	33.450	38.792	45.218	52.966	62.322	73.639	87.346	103.96	124.13	148.63
30	34.784	40.568	47.575	56.084	66.438	79.058	94.460	113.28	136.30	164.49
40	48.886	60.402	75.401	95.025	120.79	154.76	199.63	259.05	337.88	442.59
50	64.463	84.579	112.79	152.66	209.34	290.33	406.52	573.76	815.08	1163.9
60	81.669	114.05	163.05	237.99	353.58	533.12	813.52	1253.2	1944.7	3034.8

TABLE B.3 *(continued)*

Number of Periods	12%	14%	15%	16%	18%	20%	24%	28%	32%	36%
1	1.0000	1.0000	1.0000	1.0000	1.0000	1.0000	1.0000	1.0000	1.0000	1.0000
2	2.1200	2.1400	2.1500	2.1600	2.1800	2.2000	2.2400	2.2800	2.3200	2.3600
3	3.3744	3.4396	3.4725	3.5056	3.5724	3.6400	3.7776	3.9184	4.0624	4.2096
4	4.7793	4.9211	4.9934	5.0665	5.2154	5.3680	5.6842	6.0156	6.3624	6.7251
5	6.3528	6.6101	6.7424	6.8771	7.1542	7.4416	8.0484	8.6999	9.3983	10.146
6	8.1152	8.5355	8.7537	8.9775	9.4420	9.9299	10.980	12.135	13.405	14.798
7	10.089	10.730	11.066	11.413	12.141	12.915	14.615	16.533	18.695	21.126
8	12.299	13.232	13.726	14.240	15.327	16.499	19.122	22.163	25.678	29.731
9	14.775	16.085	16.785	17.518	19.085	20.798	24.712	29.369	34.895	41.435
10	17.548	19.337	20.303	21.321	23.521	25.958	31.643	38.592	47.061	57.351
11	20.654	23.044	24.349	25.732	28.755	32.150	40.237	50.398	63.121	78.998
12	24.133	27.270	29.001	30.850	34.931	39.580	50.894	65.510	84.320	108.43
13	28.029	32.088	34.351	36.786	42.218	48.496	64.109	84.852	112.30	148.47
14	32.392	37.581	40.504	43.672	50.818	59.195	80.496	109.61	149.23	202.92
15	37.279	43.842	47.580	51.659	60.965	72.035	100.81	141.30	197.99	276.97
16	42.753	50.980	55.717	60.925	72.939	87.442	126.01	181.86	262.35	377.69
17	48.883	59.117	65.075	71.673	87.068	105.93	157.25	233.79	347.30	514.66
18	55.749	68.394	75.836	84.140	103.74	128.11	195.99	300.25	459.44	700.93
19	63.439	78.969	88.211	98.603	123.41	154.74	244.03	385.32	607.47	954.27
20	72.052	91.024	102.44	115.37	146.62	186.68	303.60	494.21	802.86	1298.8
21	81.698	104.76	118.81	134.84	174.02	225.02	377.46	633.59	1060.7	1767.3
22	92.502	120.43	137.63	157.41	206.34	271.03	469.05	811.99	1401.2	2404.6
23	104.60	138.29	159.27	183.60	244.48	326.23	582.62	1040.3	1850.6	3271.3
24	118.15	158.65	184.16	213.97	289.49	392.48	723.46	1332.6	2443.8	4449.9
25	133.33	181.87	212.79	249.21	342.60	471.98	898.09	1706.8	3226.8	6052.9
26	150.33	208.33	245.71	290.08	405.27	567.37	1114.6	2185.7	4260.4	8233.0
27	169.37	238.49	283.56	337.50	479.22	681.85	1383.1	2798.7	5624.7	11197.9
28	190.69	272.88	327.10	392.50	566.48	819.22	1716.0	3583.3	7425.6	15230.2
29	214.58	312.09	377.16	456.30	669.44	984.06	2128.9	4587.6	9802.9	20714.1
30	241.33	356.78	434.74	530.31	790.94	1181.8	2640.9	5873.2	12940.	28172.2
40	767.09	1342.0	1779.0	2360.7	4163.2	7343.8	22728.	69377.	*	*
50	2400.0	4994.5	7217.7	10435.	21813.	45497.	*	*	*	*
60	7471.6	18535.	29219.	46057.	*	*	*	*	*	*

*$FVIFA > 99{,}999$.

TABLE B.4 Present Value of an Annuity of $1 for *N* Periods

$$PVIFA_{i,N} = \sum_{t=1}^{N} \frac{1}{(1+i)^t} = \frac{1 - \frac{1}{(1+i)^N}}{i}$$

Number of Payments	1%	2%	3%	4%	5%	6%	7%	8%	9%
1	0.9901	0.9804	0.9709	0.9615	0.9524	0.9434	0.9346	0.9259	0.9174
2	1.9704	1.9416	1.9135	1.8861	1.8594	1.8334	1.8080	1.7833	1.7591
3	2.9410	2.8839	2.8286	2.7751	2.7232	2.6730	2.6243	2.5771	2.5313
4	3.9020	3.8077	3.7171	3.6299	3.5460	3.4651	3.3872	3.3121	3.2397
5	4.8534	4.7135	4.5797	4.4518	4.3295	4.2124	4.1002	3.9927	3.8897
6	5.7955	5.6014	5.4172	5.2421	5.0757	4.9173	4.7665	4.6229	4.4859
7	6.7282	6.4720	6.2303	6.0021	5.7864	5.5824	5.3893	5.2064	5.0330
8	7.6517	7.3255	7.0197	6.7327	6.4632	6.2098	5.9713	5.7466	5.5348
9	8.5660	8.1622	7.7861	7.4353	7.1078	6.8017	6.5152	6.2469	5.9952
10	9.4713	8.9826	8.5302	8.1109	7.7217	7.3601	7.0236	6.7101	6.4177
11	10.3676	9.7868	9.2526	8.7605	8.3064	7.8869	7.4987	7.1390	6.8052
12	11.2551	10.5753	9.9540	9.3851	8.8633	8.3838	7.9427	7.5361	7.1607
13	12.1337	11.3484	10.6350	9.9856	9.3936	8.8527	8.3577	7.9038	7.4869
14	13.0037	12.1062	11.2961	10.5631	9.8986	9.2950	8.7455	8.2442	7.7862
15	13.8651	12.8493	11.9379	11.1184	10.3797	9.7122	9.1079	8.5595	8.0607
16	14.7179	13.5777	12.5611	11.6523	10.8378	10.1059	9.4466	8.8514	8.3126
17	15.5623	14.2919	13.1661	12.1657	11.2741	10.4773	9.7632	9.1216	8.5436
18	16.3983	14.9920	13.7535	12.6593	11.6896	10.8276	10.0591	9.3719	8.7556
19	17.2260	15.6785	14.3238	13.1339	12.0853	11.1581	10.3356	9.6036	8.9501
20	18.0456	16.3514	14.8775	13.5903	12.4622	11.4699	10.5940	9.8181	9.1285
21	18.8570	17.0112	15.4150	14.0292	12.8212	11.7641	10.8355	10.0168	9.2922
22	19.6604	17.6580	15.9369	14.4511	13.1630	12.0416	11.0612	10.2007	9.4424
23	20.4558	18.2922	16.4436	14.8568	13.4886	12.3034	11.2722	10.3711	9.5802
24	21.2434	18.9139	16.9355	15.2470	13.7986	12.5504	11.4693	10.5288	9.7066
25	22.0232	19.5235	17.4131	15.6221	14.0939	12.7834	11.6536	10.6748	9.8226
26	22.7952	20.1210	17.8768	15.9828	14.3752	13.0032	11.8258	10.8100	9.9290
27	23.5596	20.7069	18.3270	16.3296	14.6430	13.2105	11.9867	10.9352	10.0266
28	24.3164	21.2813	18.7641	16.6631	14.8981	13.4062	12.1371	11.0511	10.1161
29	25.0658	21.8444	19.1885	16.9837	15.1411	13.5907	12.2777	11.1584	10.1983
30	25.8077	22.3965	19.6004	17.2920	15.3725	13.7648	12.4090	11.2578	10.2737
35	29.4086	24.9986	21.4872	18.6646	16.3742	14.4982	12.9477	11.6546	10.5668
40	32.8347	27.3555	23.1148	19.7928	17.1591	15.0463	13.3317	11.9246	10.7574
45	36.0945	29.4902	24.5187	20.7200	17.7741	15.4558	13.6055	12.1084	10.8812
50	39.1961	31.4236	25.7298	21.4822	18.2559	15.7619	13.8007	12.2335	10.9617
55	42.1472	33.1748	26.7744	22.1086	18.6335	15.9905	13.9399	12.3186	11.0140

TABLE B.4 *(continued)*

Number of Payments	10%	12%	14%	15%	16%	18%	20%	24%	28%	32%
1	0.9091	0.8929	0.8772	0.8696	0.8621	0.8475	0.8333	0.8065	0.7813	0.7576
2	1.7355	1.6901	1.6467	1.6257	1.6052	1.5656	1.5278	1.4568	1.3916	1.3315
3	2.4869	2.4018	2.3216	2.2832	2.2459	2.1743	2.1065	1.9813	1.8684	1.7663
4	3.1699	3.0373	2.9137	2.8550	2.7982	2.6901	2.5887	2.4043	2.2410	2.0957
5	3.7908	3.6048	3.4331	3.3522	3.2743	3.1272	2.9906	2.7454	2.5320	2.3452
6	4.3553	4.1114	3.8887	3.7845	3.6847	3.4976	3.3255	3.0205	2.7594	2.5342
7	4.8684	4.5638	4.2883	4.1604	4.0386	3.8115	3.6046	3.2423	2.9370	2.6775
8	5.3349	4.9676	4.6389	4.4873	4.3436	4.0776	3.8372	3.4212	3.0758	2.7860
9	5.7590	5.3282	4.9464	4.7716	4.6065	4.3030	4.0310	3.5655	3.1842	2.8681
10	6.1446	5.6502	5.2161	5.0188	4.8332	4.4941	4.1925	3.6819	3.2689	2.9304
11	6.4951	5.9377	5.4527	5.2337	5.0286	4.6560	4.3271	3.7757	3.3351	2.9776
12	6.8137	6.1944	5.6603	5.4206	5.1971	4.7932	4.4392	3.8514	3.3868	3.0133
13	7.1034	6.4235	5.8424	5.5831	5.3423	4.9095	4.5327	3.9124	3.4272	3.0404
14	7.3667	6.6282	6.0021	5.7245	5.4675	5.0081	4.6106	3.9616	3.4587	3.0609
15	7.6061	6.8109	6.1422	5.8474	5.5755	5.0916	4.6755	4.0013	3.4834	3.0764
16	7.8237	6.9740	6.2651	5.9542	5.6685	5.1624	4.7296	4.0333	3.5026	3.0882
17	8.0216	7.1196	6.3729	6.0472	5.7487	5.2223	4.7746	4.0591	3.5177	3.0971
18	8.2014	7.2497	6.4674	6.1280	5.8178	5.2732	4.8122	4.0799	3.5294	3.1039
19	8.3649	7.3658	6.5504	6.1982	5.8775	5.3162	4.8435	4.0967	3.5386	3.1090
20	8.5136	7.4694	6.6231	6.2593	5.9288	5.3527	4.8696	4.1103	3.5458	3.1129
21	8.6487	7.5620	6.6870	6.3125	5.9731	5.3837	4.8913	4.1212	3.5514	3.1158
22	8.7715	7.6446	6.7429	6.3587	6.0113	5.4099	4.9094	4.1300	3.5558	3.1180
23	8.8832	7.7184	6.7921	6.3988	6.0442	5.4321	4.9245	4.1371	3.5592	3.1197
24	8.9847	7.7843	6.8351	6.4338	6.0726	5.4510	4.9371	4.1428	3.5619	3.1210
25	9.0770	7.8431	6.8729	6.4642	6.0971	5.4669	4.9476	4.1474	3.5640	3.1220
26	9.1609	7.8957	6.9061	6.4906	6.1182	5.4804	4.9563	4.1511	3.5656	3.1227
27	9.2372	7.9426	6.9352	6.5135	6.1364	5.4919	4.9636	4.1542	3.5669	3.1233
28	9.3066	7.9844	6.9607	6.5335	6.1520	5.5016	4.9697	4.1566	3.5679	3.1237
29	9.3696	8.0218	6.9830	6.5509	6.1656	5.5098	4.9747	4.1585	3.5687	3.1240
30	9.4269	8.0552	7.0027	6.5660	6.1772	5.5168	4.9789	4.1601	3.5693	3.1242
35	9.6442	8.1755	7.0700	6.6166	6.2153	5.5386	4.9915	4.1644	3.5708	3.1248
40	9.7791	8.2438	7.1050	6.6418	6.2335	5.5482	4.9966	4.1659	3.5712	3.1250
45	9.8628	8.2825	7.1232	6.6543	6.2421	5.5523	4.9986	4.1664	3.5714	3.1250
50	9.9148	8.3045	7.1327	6.6605	6.2463	5.5541	4.9995	4.1666	3.5714	3.1250
55	9.9471	8.3170	7.1376	6.6636	6.2482	5.5549	4.9998	4.1666	3.5714	3.1250

Credits

Figure 2.1	Courtesy of DailyStocks.com.
Figure 2.2	Reprinted by permission of *Barron's*, January 24, 2000, p. MW11. Copyright © 2000 by Dow Jones & Company, Inc. All rights reserved worldwide.
Figure 2.3	Reprinted by permission of *Barron's*, January 24, 2000, p. MW71. Copyright © 2000 by Dow Jones & Company, Inc. All rights reserved worldwide.
Figure 2.4	From <www.yahoo.com>. Reprinted by permission of Yahoo!.
Figure 2.5	Reprinted by permission of *The Wall Street Journal*, Interactive Edition screenshot, February 12, 2000. Copyright © 2000 by Dow Jones & Company, Inc. All rights reserved worldwide.
Figure 2.7	Data from <www.askmerrill.com>.
Figure 2.8	Data from <www.askmerrill.com>.
Table 2.4	Data from <www.askmerrill.com>.
Figure 3.2	Reprinted by permission of *The Wall Street Journal*, February 14, 2000, p. C3. Copyright © 2000 by Dow Jones & Company, Inc. All rights reserved worldwide.
Table 3.1	Used with permission of NYSE.
Table 3.2	Used with permission of NYSE.
Table 3.3	Used with permission of NYSE.
Figure 3.1	Used with permission of NYSE.
Figure 3.5	From <www.bloomberg.com>.
Figure 3.6	From <www.dripcentral.com>. Reprinted by permission of Investorama.
Table 3.5	From <www.bloomberg.com>.
Table 3.6	From <www.spglobal.com>. Reprinted by permission of Standard & Poor's, a division of the McGraw-Hill Companies.
Table 3.7	From <www.wilshire.com>.
Table 3.8	From <www.nasdaq.com>. Copyright © 2000, The Nasdaq Stock Market, Inc. All rights reserved. Reprinted with permission.
Figure 4.1	Reprinted by permission of *The Wall Street Journal*, February 15, 2000, p. C2, C3. Copyright © 2000 by Dow Jones & Company, Inc. All rights reserved worldwide.
Figure 4.2	Reprinted by permission of *Barron's*, January 24, 2000, p. MW53. Copyright © 2000 by Dow Jones & Company, Inc. All rights reserved worldwide.
P. 134	Reprinted by permission of *The Wall Street Journal*, January 27, 2000, p. C1. Copyright © 2000 by Dow Jones & Company, Inc. All rights reserved worldwide.
Table 4.1	From <www.freerealtime.com>.
Table 4.2	From <www.freerealtime.com>.
Table 4.5	Reprinted by permission of *The Wall Street Journal*, January 3, 2000, p. R24. Copyright © 2000 by Dow Jones & Company, Inc. All rights reserved worldwide.
Table 4.6	From <www.nasdaq.com>. Copyright © 2000, The Nasdaq Stock Market, Inc. All rights reserved. Reprinted with permission.
Table 4.7	Reprinted by permission of *Barron's*, December 13, 1999, p. 38. Copyright © 1999 by Dow Jones & Company, Inc. All rights reserved worldwide.
Table 4.11	Reprinted by permission of *Barron's*, March 15, 1999, p. 32. Copyright © 1999 by Dow Jones & Company, Inc. All rights reserved worldwide.
Table 5.7	Courtesy of DailyStocks.com.
Figure 6.2	Reprinted by permission of *The Wall Street Journal*, February 25, 2000, p. C20. Copyright © 2000 by Dow Jones & Company, Inc. All rights reserved worldwide.
Figure 6.3	Reprinted by permission of *The Wall Street Journal*, February 25, 2000, p. C1. Copyright © 2000 by Dow Jones & Company, Inc. All rights reserved worldwide.
Figure 6.6	Reprinted by permission of *The Wall Street Journal*, February 25, 2000, p. C15. Copyright © 2000 by Dow Jones & Company, Inc. All rights reserved worldwide.
Figure 6.7	Reprinted by permission of *The Wall Street Journal*, February 25, 2000, p. C15. Copyright © 2000 by Dow Jones & Company, Inc. All rights reserved worldwide.
Figure 6.8	Reprinted by permission of *The Wall Street Journal*, February 25, 2000, p. C15. Copyright © 2000 by Dow Jones & Company, Inc. All rights reserved worldwide.
Figure 7.2	Reprinted by permission of *Barron's*, February 21, 2000, p. MW13. Copyright © 2000 by Dow Jones & Company, Inc. All rights reserved worldwide.
Figure 7.3	Data courtesy of Vanguard.
Figure 7.5	Reprinted by permission of *The Wall Street Journal*, February 22, 2000, p. C33. Copyright © 2000 by Dow Jones & Company, Inc. All rights reserved worldwide.

Figure 7.6	Reprinted by permission of *The Wall Street Journal*, February 22, 2000, p. C33. Copyright © 2000 by Dow Jones & Company, Inc. All rights reserved worldwide.
Figure 7.8	Reprinted by permission of *The Wall Street Journal*, February 17, 2000, p. C1. Copyright © 2000 by Dow Jones & Company, Inc. All rights reserved worldwide.
Figure 8.1	Reprinted with the permission of Value Line.
Figure 8.2	Reprinted with the permission of Value Line.
Figure 8.3	Reprinted with the permission of Value Line.
Figure 8.5	Reprinted with the permission of Value Line.
Table 9.1	From <www.conference-board.org>.
Table 9.2	From <www.conference-board.org>.
Figure 9.3	Reprinted by permission of *Barron's*, March 6, 2000, p. MW73. Copyright © 2000 by Dow Jones & Company, Inc. All rights reserved worldwide.
Figure 9.4	Reprinted by permission of *Barron's*, September 6, 1999, p. 28. Copyright © 1999 by Dow Jones & Company, Inc. All rights reserved worldwide.
Figure 9.6	Reprinted by permission of *Barron's*, February 21, 2000, p. MW70, MW71. Copyright © 2000 by Dow Jones & Company, Inc. All rights reserved worldwide.
Figure 10.1	Reprinted with the permission of Value Line.
Figure 10.2	Reprinted with the permission of Value Line.
Figure 10.3	Copyright © 2000 Janus Distributors, Inc. Reprinted with permission of Janus Distributors, Inc. All rights reserved.
Figure 10.4	Copyright © 2000 Janus Distributors, Inc. Reprinted with permission of Janus Distributors, Inc. All rights reserved.
Figure 10.5	Reprinted with the permission of Value Line.
Figure 10.6	Reprinted by permission of *The Wall Street Journal*, March 10, 2000, p. C4. Copyright © 2000 by Dow Jones & Company, Inc. All rights reserved worldwide.
Figure 10.7	Reprinted by permission of Harry Aloof, Editor and Publisher. <http:\\wstraders.com>.
Figure 10.8	Reprinted with the permission of Value Line.
Figure 10.9	Reprinted with the permission of Value Line.
Table 10.9	Reprinted by permission of *Barron's*, March 15, 1999, pp. 21–22. Copyright © 1999 by Dow Jones & Company, Inc. All rights reserved worldwide.
Table 11.1	From <www.barra.com>. Reprinted by permission of Barra, Berkeley, CA.
Figure 11.3	Reprinted with the permission of Value Line.
Figure 11.4	Reprinted with the permission of Value Line.
Figure 11.5	Reprinted with the permission of Value Line.
Figure 11.6	Reprinted with the permission of Value Line.
P. 449	Reprinted by permission of *The Wall Street Journal*, March 13, 2000, p. C1. Copyright © 2000 by Dow Jones & Company, Inc. All rights reserved worldwide.
Figure 11.7	From <www.barra.com>. Reprinted by permission of Barra, Berkeley, CA.
Figure 11.8	From <www.barra.com>. Reprinted by permission of Barra, Berkeley, CA.
Figure 11.9	Reprinted with the permission of Value Line.
Figure 11.11	Reprinted with the permission of Value Line.
Figure 12.1	This print advertisement is the property of Ameritrade Holding Corporation and is being displayed with the permission of Ameritrade Holding Corporation. All rights in the copyrightable contents and trademarks are owned and reserved by Ameritrade and Ameritrade is a registered trademark of Ameritrade Holding Corporation.
Figure 12.5	Reprinted by permission of Harry Aloof, Editor and Publisher. <http:\\wstraders.com>.
Table 12.6	Data from <www.vanguard.com>.
P. 548	Reprinted by permission of *Barron's*, January 24, 2000, p. 22. Copyright © 2000 by Dow Jones & Company, Inc. All rights reserved worldwide.
Table 14.1	Data from <www.vanguard.com>.
Figure 14.1	Used with permission of NYSE.
Table 14.2	From <www.nasdaq.com>. Copyright © 2000, The Nasdaq Stock Market, Inc. All rights reserved. Reprinted with permission.
Figure 14.3	Used with permission of NYSE.
Figure 14.4	Used with permission of NYSE.
Figure 14.5	Used with permission of NYSE.
Table 14.4	Reprinted by permission of *The Wall Street Journal* Interactive edition, <interactive.wsj.com>. Copyright © 2000 by Dow Jones & Company, Inc. All rights reserved worldwide.
Table 14.5	From <www.rightline.net>. Reprinted by permission.
Table 14.6	Reprinted by permission of *The Wall Street Journal*, February 9, 1998, p. C1. Copyright © 1998 by Dow Jones & Company, Inc. All rights reserved worldwide.

Table 14.7	From <www.spglobal.com>. Reprinted by permission of Standard & Poor's, a division of the McGraw-Hill Companies.
Figure 15.2	Reprinted by permission of *Barron's*, July 10, 2000. Copyright © 2000 by Dow Jones & Company, Inc. All rights reserved worldwide.
Figure 15.3	Reprinted by permission of Morningstar, Inc. Chicago-based Morningstar, Inc. is a leading provider of investment information, research, and analysis.
Table 15.2	Reprinted by permission of *Barron's*, April 10, 2000, p. F127. Copyright © 2000 by Dow Jones & Company, Inc. All rights reserved worldwide.
Figure 15.4	Reprinted by permission of *The Wall Street Journal*, August 14, 1998, p. C1. Copyright © 1998 by Dow Jones & Company, Inc. All rights reserved worldwide.
Table 15.4	Data from <www.vanguard.com>.
Figure 15.5	Data from <www.vanguard.com>.
Figure 15.6	Data courtesy of Legg Mason.
Figure 15.7	Data courtesy of Legg Mason.
Figure 15.8	Data courtesy of Legg Mason.
Figure 15.10	From <www.nasdaq.com>. Copyright © 2000, The Nasdaq Stock Market, Inc. All rights reserved. Reprinted with permission.
Figure 15.11	Reprinted by permission of *Barron's*, April 10, 2000, p. F126. Copyright © 2000 by Dow Jones & Company, Inc. All rights reserved worldwide.
Table 15.6	Data from <www.vanguard.com>.
Table 15.7	Data source: Investment Company Institute.
Table 15.8	Courtesy of Berkshire Hathaway. <www.berkshirehathaway.com>.
Figure 16.1	Data from <www.msci.com>.
Table 16.1	From <www.bloomberg.com>.
Table 16.2	Data from <www.msci.com>.
Table 16.3	Data from <www.msci.com>.
Figure 16.2	Data from <www.msci.com>.
Table 16.4	Data from <www.msci.com>.
Table 16.5	Data from <www.msci.com>.
Figure 16.4	Data from <www.msci.com>.
Figure 16.5	Data from <www.msci.com>.
P. 679	Reprinted by permission of *The Wall Street Journal*, March 24, 2000, p. C1. Copyright © 2000 by Dow Jones & Company, Inc. All rights reserved worldwide.
Table 16.7	Data from <www.msci.com>.
Figure 16.6	Data from <www.msci.com>.
Table 16.8	Data from <www.msci.com>.
Figure 16.8	Data from <www.vanguard.com>.
Table 16.9	Data from <www.msci.com>.
Figure 16.9	Data from <www.adr.com>.
Table 16.10	Data from <www.adr.com>.
Table 16.11	From "US Multinational Companies," *Forbes*, July 26, 1999, pp. 202–204. Reprinted by permission of Forbes Magazine. © 2000 Forbes
Figure 16.10	From <www.templeton.com>.
Figure 17.3	Reprinted by permission of *The Wall Street Journal*, May 4, 2000, C26. Copyright © 2000 by Dow Jones & Company, Inc. All rights reserved worldwide.
Figure 17.4	From <www.cboe.com>.
Figure 17.5	"2001 Options Expiration Calendar," from <www.optionscentral.com>. or <www.optionsclearing.com>. Reprinted by permission of The Options Clearing Corporation.
Figure 17.6	Reprinted by permission of *The Wall Street Journal*, May 4, 2000, C26. Copyright © 2000 by Dow Jones & Company, Inc. All rights reserved worldwide.
Figure 17.9	© 2000 Chicago Board Options Exchange. All rights reserved.
Figure 17.12	From <www.cboe.com>.
Figure 17.13	From <www.cboe.com>.
Figure 18.1	Reprinted by permission of *Barron's*, May 1, 2000, pp. MW76-MW77. Copyright © 2000 by Dow Jones & Company, Inc. All rights reserved worldwide.
Figure 18.2	From <www.nybot.com>.
Figure 18.4	Reprinted by permission of the Futures Industry Association, Inc., Washington, DC
Figure 18.8	Reprinted by permission of *The Wall Street Journal*, May 5, 2000, C3. Copyright © 2000 by Dow Jones & Company, Inc. All rights reserved worldwide.

Index